Geological Society of America
Memoir 191

The Nature of Magmatism in the Appalachian Orogen

Edited by

A. Krishna Sinha
Department of Geological Sciences
Virginia Polytechnic Institute and State University
Blacksburg, Virginia 24061-0420

Joseph B. Whalen
Geological Survey of Canada
601 Booth Street
Ottawa, Ontario K1A 0E8, Canada

and

John P. Hogan
School of Geology and Geophysics
University of Oklahoma
810 Sarkeys Energy Center
100 East Boyd Street
Norman, Oklahoma 73019-0628

1997

Published by The Geological Society of America, Inc.
3300 Penrose Place, P.O. Box 9140, Boulder, Colorado 80301

Printed in U.S.A.

GSA Books Science Editor Abhijit Basu

Library of Congress Cataloging-in-Publication Data
The nature of magmatism in the Appalachian orogen / edited by A.
  Krishna Sinha, Joseph B. Whalen, and John P. Hogan.
      p.   cm. -- (Memoir / Geological Society of America ; 191)
    Includes bibliographical references and index.
    ISBN 0-8137-1191-6
    1. Magmatism--Appalachian Region.   2. Rocks, Igneous--Appalachian
Region. I. Sinha, A. Krishna, 1941- . II. Whalen, Joseph Bruce.
III. Hogan, John P., 1959- . IV. Series: Memoir (Geological
Society of America) ; 191.
QE461.N3664   1997
551.1'3--dc21
                                          97-7591
                                          CIP

10 9 8 7 6 5 4 3 2 1

Contents

iv   *Contents*

Preface

The thermal and mechanical evolution of the crust is strongly influenced by the extent and duration of magmatism. Addition of large volumes of magmas and accompanying changes in the thermal response of the preexisting rocks must play a significant role in subsequent deformation and tectonism of large regions of the crust. Therefore, the characterization of the nature, duration, and location of magmatic pulses is a key in understanding the evolution of the crust and mantle.

In this volume, dedicated to earth scientists with a keen affinity to igneous rocks, we have assembled a series of papers that reflects the current thinking on the relationship of magmatism to the evolution of the Appalachian orogen. Contributors of 20 manuscripts share their data and interpretations that cover the wide spectrum of geologic questions addressed by investigations of magmatic rocks.

Although the chapters are organized alphabetically by senior author's surname, the overall emphasis of the contributions clearly falls into two distinct categories that are the current focus of igneous petrologists.

COMPOSITIONAL VARIATIONS AND FINGERPRINTING OF TECTONIC SETTINGS AND SOURCE REGIONS

As the need for developing tools for assessing past tectonic settings for igneous rocks has increased, due to the complexities highlighted by geodynamic models, Arth and Ayuso present a three-dimensional image of the crust and mantle as recorded in magmas representing the Northeast Kingdom batholith, whereas Barr and Kerr utilize petrologic and geochronologic criteria for recognizing terranes. Bédard and Wilson demonstrate the importance of recognizing the petrochemical differences between intra-suite and inter-suite geochemical variations to discriminate between AFC processes and mantle heterogeneity. On a similar theme, Clarke, MacDonald, and Tate relate the development of two spatial-chemical-genetic types of granites as the result of derivation from crustal melting and mixing of mantle and crust melts. Coish, in his studies of greenstones from Vermont, elaborates on the geochemical signatures that reveal in some detail the progressive development of a rift valley to an ocean basin. Drummond, Neilson, Allison, and Tull have been able to trace regional sequence of tectonic events and variations in source regions in the southern Appalachians through chemical signatures of granitic rocks, and Fullagar, Goldberg, and Butler use Nd and Sr isotopes to identify non-Laurentian terranes and their relationship to granitoid complexes located within them. Miller, Fullagar, Sando, Kish, Solomon, Russell, and Wood Steltenpohl use geochemical and isotopic data to demonstrate the relationship between crustal thickening and melting of mafic lithologies to generate "pseudo-adakite" magmas. Higgins, Arth, Wooden, Crawford, Stern, and Crawford use the age and geochemical signature of the Austell pluton to place constraints on the age of thrusting that records a time of slope reversal in the Valley and Ridge Province of the southern Appalachians. Kerr presents a spatial and temporal correlation among plutonic suites in Newfoundland to delineate tectonic zones. McSween and Harvey illustrate the limitations of applying trace element patterns and mineral compositions as tectonic discriminants. Murphy, Hynes, and Cousens utilize field, geochemical, and isotopic data to demonstrate that apparent differentiation trends can be formed through mixing and mingling of mafic and felsic magmas. Sinha, Hanan, and Wayne elaborate on the metamorphic paragenesis of zircons in mafic rocks, and utilize U-Pb ages of zircons in plagiogranites to draw together both the metamorphic and crystallization age of the Baltimore mafic complex. Swinden, Jenner, and Szybinski show that significant correlations exist between changing magma sources and episodes of volcanism over a time span of ~18 m.y. On a similar theme, Whalen, Jenner, Longstaffe, Gariépy, and Fryer describe the geochemical processes related to modification of slab and mantle-derived magmas in the lower crust through AFC processes.

PROCESSES THAT MODIFY IGNEOUS SIGNATURES

In an attempt to identify the magnitude of chemical, isotopic, and petrologic changes recorded in igneous rocks, Ayuso and Arth demonstrate the occurrence of a unique class of composite plutons in coastal Maine that preserves a record of underplating of mafic magmas and mixing of magmas formed by crustal melting following collision. Beard highlights the significant constraints on tonalite genesis through the application of data derived from experimental petrology, and the importance of fluids in melt compositions. Srogi and Lutz present a quantitative appraisal of the mechanism of melt migration that can produce large ranges in observed chemistries and linear correlation among elements. Speer and Hoff present a geochemical database for Alleghanian magmatic rocks in the southern Appalachians to suggest that compositional variations result from crystal-melt segregation, mixing with disaggregated enclaves, and the compositional differences of the source rocks. Wiebe, Holden, Coombs, Wobus, Schuh, and Plummer argue for intrusion of basaltic liquids within a granitic magma chamber to transform a resident granitic magma from I-type to A-type.

In summary, the contributions in this volume provide the most recent data available for significant portions of the Appalachian Mountains system. However, it is more important that they provide a unique opportunity to assess the current thinking about Appalachian magmatism by the researchers studying this mountain belt. Future direction of research will be greatly influenced by this volume, and the editors thank all the participants and reviewers for their contributions.

A. K. Sinha

Acknowledgments

This memoir has benefited greatly from thoughtful and careful reviews by the following individuals:

R. Ayuso	R. Kistler
R. Badger	M. Malo
F. Barker	J. McLelland
S. Barr	C. A. Miller
J. Beard	E. Moll-Stalcup
J. Bédard	J. B. Murphy
D. B. Clarke	R. D. Nance
R. A. Coish	D. Pyle
K. L. Currie	N. Ratcliffe
W. Davis	G. Russell
M. Dorais	K. Schulz
M. S. Drummond	S. J. Seaman
G. N. Eby	A. K. Sinha
C. Frost	J. A. Speer
P. Fullagar	L. Srogi
H. Gaudette	R. Stern
N. Green	B. L. Weaver
D. Hermes	J. B. Whalen
J. Hogan	R. Wiebe
M. Horan	J. Winchester
A. Kerr	M. B. Wolf

Geological Society of America
Memoir 191
1997

The Northeast Kingdom batholith, Vermont: Geochronology and Nd, O, Pb, and Sr isotopic constraints on the origin of Acadian granitic rocks

Joseph G. Arth
548 Riverwood Lane, Oakland, Oregon 97462
Robert A. Ayuso
U.S. Geological Survey, National Center, MS 954, Reston, Virginia 20192

ABSTRACT

The Northeast Kingdom batholith is a suite of gabbro to granite composite plutons, part of the New Hampshire plutonic suite, that intrudes Silurian to Early Devonian supracrustal rocks of the Waits River and Gile Mountain formations in northeastern Vermont. The Nulhegan, Willoughby, and Derby plutons have Rb-Sr whole-rock isochron ages, respectively, of 390 ± 14 Ma, 376 ± 9 Ma, and 370 ± 17 Ma. Granite at Derby quarry has an Rb-Sr muscovite–whole rock isochron age of 372 ± 6 Ma. Echo Pond pluton has three petrographic and isotopic zones that have limited ranges of Rb/Sr, and weakly defined Devonian isochrons.

Initial Sr isotopic ratios (SIR), initial Nd isotopic ratios (NIR), oxygen isotopic ratios ($\delta^{18}O$), and initial $^{206}Pb/^{204}Pb$ (PIR6) for the plutons and zones within plutons fall into three groups:

Group	SIR	NIR	$\delta^{18}O$	PIR6
1)	0.7040–0.7055	0.5120–0.5122	6–9	18.2–18.3
2)	0.7068–0.7071	0.5118–0.5120	8–14	18.1–18.5
3)	0.7125	0.51177	9.9	18.22

Group 1 consists primarily of gabbro, diorite, and granodiorite from the West Charleston and Echo Pond plutons that are generally of magmatic arc composition. The magma sources were probably dominated by either a Grenville ultramafic to mafic assemblage, or an Acadian subduction zone. Some crustal contamination occurred. Granodiorite magma of this group mixed with granite magma of Group 2 to produce the silicic part of the Echo Pond pluton.

Group 2 constitutes the most voluminous part of the batholith and consists primarily of quartz monzodiorite, granodiorite, and granite of the Nulhegan, Derby, and Willoughby plutons. The magmas that formed the Nulhegan pluton probably originated as a hybrid of melts from a diverse Grenville mantle and crustal assemblage of ultramafic to silicic gneiss. The Derby pluton magmas probably originated as a hybrid of melts from Grenville mafic and silicic gneisses in the deep crust. The Willoughby pluton magmas probably received a large contribution of magma from melting of Grenville paragneisses or Paleozoic metasedimentary rocks.

Arth, J. G., and Ayuso, R. A., 1997, The Northeast Kingdom batholith, Vermont: Geochronology and Nd, O, Pb, and Sr isotopic constraints on the origin of Acadian granitic rocks, *in* Sinha, A. K., Whalen, J. B., and Hogan, J. P., eds., The Nature of Magmatism in the Appalachian Orogen: Boulder, Colorado, Geological Society of America Memoir 191.

Group 3 consists of a small volume of two-mica granite found in and near the Derby quarry. Magma for this body probably originated by melting of Grenville paragneiss, country rock metasedimentary strata, or both.

Viewed collectively, the plutons preserve a record of melting in a significant vertical section extending from the upper mantle through the lower crust to the middle crust. The largest volume, perhaps 80%, of magma was generated in Grenville gneiss, and these were largely orthogneiss. Mafic to ultramafic mantle and deepest crust contributed most of the remainder. Only a very small percentage resulted from simple melting of metasedimentary rocks.

INTRODUCTION

The Northeast Kingdom batholith is a suite of intrusive gabbro to granite plutons in northeastern Vermont (Ayuso and Arth, 1992) that crops out over about half the area known as the Northeast Kingdom (Fig. 1). The plutons are part of the New Hampshire plutonic suite, originally described by Billings (1934) in central New Hampshire to "consist of diorite, quartz diorite, granodiorite, trondhjemite, and granite" that "are younger than the Lower Devonian and essentially contemporaneous with the great period of folding." Silurian and Devonian plutons are the most voluminous in New England (Sinha, 1988), and are commonly associated with the Acadian orogeny (Osberg et al., 1989). Plutons of the Northeast Kingdom not only display the broad range of compositions found in Acadian plutons, but also were emplaced in a part of the Appalachians that has been little affected by post-Acadian regional metamorphism (Morgan, 1972). They are thus suitable candidates for detailed study.

Study of the batholith is part of a larger investigation by us of plutons along a traverse that crosses the strike of many major structural features of New England from northern Vermont to coastal Maine (Fig. 1, inset). The goals of this and the larger study are to characterize the petrology and chemistry of the plutons, to refine their geochronology, to measure their isotopic compositions, to model the evolution of the magmas, and to infer the composition and age of their source rocks. The studies will provide a better understanding of the generation of Acadian magmas, and of the composition and age of the unseen deeper parts of the continental crust beneath the Appalachians during the Silurian and Devonian.

Five plutons in the Northeast Kingdom were selected for examination, and were petrologically and chemically characterized by Ayuso and Arth (1992). In this paper we report new Rb-Sr isotopic data to complement an earlier geochronologic study by Naylor (1971). We also report new isotopic analyses of neodymium, lead, and oxygen. These analyses indicate that each pluton had its own distinctive magmatic evolution, that magma mixing and fractionation were major mechanisms, and that there were at least three sources at depth that contributed magma to the batholith.

GEOLOGIC SETTING

The area of study was mapped on a scale of 1:62,500 by Doll (1951), Dennis (1956), Goodwin (1963), Johansson (1963), Myers (1964), and Woodland (1965). The country rocks consist of two northeast-trending metamorphosed and strongly deformed supracrustal assemblages. The Waits River Formation is principally quartzose and micaceous crystalline limestone interbedded with quartz muscovite phyllite or schist. The Gile Mountain Formation is dominantly quartz muscovite phyllite or schist interbedded with micaceous quartzite or graywacke, and calcareous mica schist. Metamorphism in these rocks ranges from biotite zone, through garnet zone, to staurolite-andalusite zone and sillimanite zone at the contacts of the plutons (Doll et al., 1961).

The Waits River and Gile Mountain formations and their stratigraphic equivalents extend about 1,200 km along the Connecticut River valley of New England, through southern Quebec and northern Maine, and along the Gaspé Peninsula. These rocks vary in degree of deformation and metamorphic grade. Their stratigraphic relationship and age have been reinterpreted repeatedly over the past hundred years, as summarized and discussed by Hueber et al. (1990). Current interpretations suggest that the two formations are stratigraphically continuous (Fisher and Karabinos, 1980), that the Waits River underlies the Gile Mountain (Hatch, 1988), and that the sequence is of Silurian to Early Devonian age (Hueber et al., 1990). Fossil evidence that the formations in the Northeast Kingdom are Silurian and Devonian was summarized by Doll (1984).

NORTHEAST KINGDOM BATHOLITH

The five bodies studied include the West Charleston pluton, consisting of gabbro, diorite, and minor granodiorite; the Echo Pond pluton, consisting of gabbro, quartz diorite, granodiorite, and granite; the Nulhegan pluton, consisting largely of quartz monzodiorite; the Derby pluton, consisting of granodiorite and minor tonalite; and the Willoughby pluton, consisting of leucogranite. The plutons collectively range in SiO_2 content from 48 to 77 wt%, and display generally calc-alkalic trends on major-element variation diagrams (Ayuso and Arth, 1992). In view of this chemical coherence,

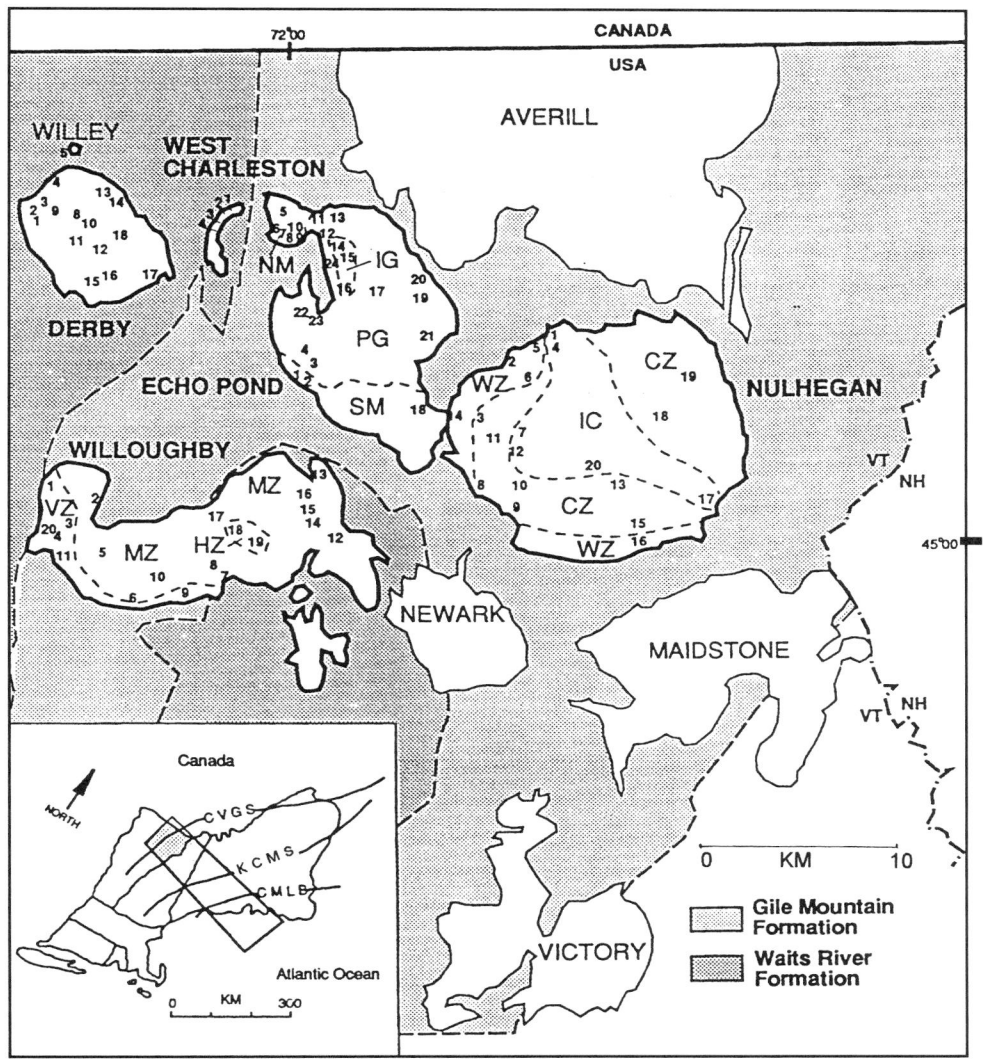

Figure 1. Geologic map of the Northeast Kingdom, Vermont, simplified from Doll et al. (1961), showing numbered locations of samples from the Derby, Echo Pond, Nulhegan, West Charleston, and Willoughby plutons. Petrographic zones within plutons are shown by dashed lines. Echo Pond: IG—interior granodiorite to granite; NM—northwestern mafic rim; PG—predominant granodiorite; SM—southern mafic rim. Nulhegan: CZ—central zone; IC—inner core of central zone; WZ—western rim. Willoughby: HZ—hydrothermally-altered zone; MZ—main zone; VZ—variant of main zone. Inset map of New England shows the Northeast Kingdom of Vermont (shaded) and the path (polygon) of our larger study of plutons that intrude several major structural features of northern New England, including the Connecticut Valley–Gaspe synclinorium (CVGS), the Kearsage–Central Maine synclinorium (KCMS), and the coastal Maine lithotectonic block (CMLB).

and because the plutons are geographically grouped and are thought to be similar in age, we regard them as a "batholith" in the same sense that the term is used in western North America (e.g., Boulder, Coast, Idaho, Sierra Nevada batholiths). Other nearby plutons, including Averill, Newark, Maidstone, and Victory (Fig. 1), may also be part of this igneous suite.

In spite of their general chemical coherence on some variation diagrams, the plutons collectively exhibit incoherent trends for some major and trace elements. For example, the Derby pluton is more sodic, and the Nulhegan pluton more magnesian and potassic, than other intermediate rocks in the batholith. The batholith did not have a single magma source, and no simple melting, fractionation, or assimilation scheme can explain all the chemical variations from gabbro to granite (Ayuso and Arth, 1992).

PREVIOUS GEOCHRONOLOGY

The earliest isotopic age on a pluton of northeastern Vermont was a K-Ar age of 349 Ma reported by Faul et al. (1963) on biotite from granite of the Adamant quarry north of Barre (44°20.37′N, 72°30.05′W). Faul et al. considered K-Ar ages in igneous samples to reflect not the time of crystallization of the mica, but rather the time of cooling to lower temperature, which was perhaps significantly later than the time of intrusion. However, their analytical data on the granite of Adamant quarry do not support the reported age, making the age questionable.

Naylor (1971) reported Rb-Sr analyses on a whole-rock sample and mica separates from four plutons in eastern Vermont. Muscovites yielded ages of 375 to 329 Ma (adjusted to the decay constant of ^{87}Rb currently in use of 1.42×10^{-11} yr^{-1}). Biotites yielded younger ages of 355 to 309 Ma. Naylor regarded ages of 372 Ma obtained on coarse muscovite from both the Derby pluton of northern Vermont and the Black Mountain pluton of southern Vermont as reliable minimum ages for the plutons. Naylor (1971) noted that the plutons cut Silurian and Devonian or Lower Devonian supracrustal rocks after they were folded and regionally metamorphosed. Thus folding and metamorphism were constrained to a period of 30 m.y. or less within the Early and Middle Devonian.

ANALYTICAL METHODS

Chemical procedures for the Rb-Sr analyses (Tables 1 and 2) are those outlined by Arth et al. (1980). Strontium content and ^{87}Sr/^{86}Sr were determined by isotope dilution using a fully automated MAT 261 mass spectrometer. Rb content was measured by isotope dilution using a partly automated, 6 in, 60° sector, National Bureau of Standards (NBS)-type mass spectrometer. Strontium isotope ratios were corrected for fractionation on the basis of an ^{86}Sr/^{88}Sr ratio of 0.11940 for natural Sr. Blank determinations were less than 2 ng for Sr and 0.2 ng for Rb. The accuracy of the Sr isotope measurements is based on 11 analyses of NBS SRM 987, which gave a mean ^{87}Sr/^{86}Sr value of 0.710235 ± 0.000005 (95% confidence level). The precision of individual rock determinations, based on complete replicate whole-rock determinations, is 0.01% for ^{87}Sr/^{86}Sr, 0.6% for Rb, and 1.0% for Sr at the 67% confidence level.

Neodymium was extracted from completely dissolved whole-rock samples by elution of rare earths on a cation-exchange column using AG 50W-X8 resin and HCl, followed by Nd elution on an ammoniated cation-exchange column using AG 50W-X4 resin and 2-methyllactic acid. Isotopic

TABLE 1. Rb-Sr ISOCHRON DATA FOR PLUTONS OF THE NORTHEAST KINGDOM BATHOLITH, VERMONT

Sample	Rb (ppm)	Sr (ppm)	^{87}Rb/^{86}Sr	^{87}Sr/^{86}Sr
DERBY PLUTON				
MED04	68.7	642.6	0.3094	0.70899
MED10	67.6	578.7	0.3380	0.70875
MED02L	76.5	593.5	0.3732	0.70951
MED17	84.1	544.1	0.4470	0.70877
MED03	109.3	420.7	0.7519	0.71106
MED03A	123.5	45.1	7.963	0.74911
GRANITE AT DERBY QUARRY				
MED05	181.0	200.0	2.624	0.72660
ECHO POND PLUTON				
MEEP07	100.3	682.8	0.4248	0.70902
IPEP15	91.1	506.5	0.5200	0.70685
IPEP14	97.2	458.5	0.6135	0.70777
IPEP09	114.7	479.8	0.6921	0.70957
IPEP16	113.0	424.4	0.7700	0.70835
IPEP20	111.1	406.6	0.7905	0.70915
IPEP19	119.1	397.1	0.8674	0.70958
IPEP12	127.4	394.5	0.9344	0.70988
IPEP17	130.1	379.2	0.9927	0.71001
IPEP13	131.0	379.7	0.9990	0.71011
IPEP24	133.4	361.1	1.070	0.71036
IPEP21	136.5	339.3	1.164	0.71153
IPEP22	137.2	338.9	1.172	0.71149
IPEP04	150.6	351.6	1.240	0.71215
IPEP03	142.4	280.3	1.471	0.71271
NULHEGAN PLUTON				
IPNU07	149.6	609.8	0.7098	0.71100
IPNU20	164.7	648.0	0.7357	0.71076
IPNU04	154.9	586.7	0.7641	0.71131
AVNU17	174.2	505.7	0.9968	0.71203
IPNU05	220.6	166.6	3.837	0.72826
WILLOUGHBY PLUTON				
MEWI01	129.8	717.7	0.5232	0.70969
LYWI08	246.6	222.5	3.211	0.72341
MEWI03	269.2	133.5	5.850	0.73981
LYWI07	279.6	75.7	10.753	0.76284
LYWI05	262.8	50.9	15.052	0.78751

TABLE 2. Rb-Sr ISOTOPIC DATA FOR WEST CHARLESTON PLUTON AND WAITS RIVER FORMATION, VERMONT

Sample	Rb (ppm)	Sr (ppm)	Rb/Sr	^{87}Sr/^{86}Sr measured	^{87}Sr/^{86}Sr at 376 Ma
NORTHEAST KINGDOM BATHOLITH					
WEST CHARLESTON PLUTON					
MEWC01	123	364	0.338	0.71213	0.7069
MEWC02	22	330	0.067	0.70621	0.7052
MEWC04	23	547	0.042	0.70539	0.7047
WAITS RIVER FORMATION					
ME01	142	107	1.327	0.73276	0.7122
ME04	110	200	0.550	0.72089	0.7124

TABLE 3. Sm-Nd ISOTOPIC DATA FOR PLUTONS OF THE NORTHEAST KINGDOM BATHOLITH AND WAITS RIVER FORMATION, VERMONT

Sample	Sm (ppm)	Nd (ppm)	$^{147}Sm/^{144}Nd$	$^{143}Nd/^{144}Nd$*	Age (m.y.)	Initial $^{143}Nd/^{144}Nd$
NORTHEAST KINGDOM BATHOLITH						
DERBY PLUTON						
MED17	1.96	9.0	0.1317	0.51219	370	0.51187
GRANITE AT DERTY QUARRY						
MED05	3.56	18.0	0.1196	0.51206	372	0.51177
ECHO POND PLUTON						
IPEP03	4.62	22.6	0.1236	0.51230	376	0.51200
IPEP14	3.33	20.5	0.0982	0.51234	376	0.51210
IPEP19	4.15	27.0	0.0929	0.51223	376	0.51200
Nulhegan Pluton						
AVNU17	6.37	31.0	0.1242	0.51230	376	0.51199
IPNU05	3.46	19.0	0.1101	0.51219	376	0.51192
WEST CHARLESTON PLUTON						
MEWC01	2.76	11.4	0.1464	0.51229	376	0.51193
MEWC02	4.71	19	0.1499	0.51250	376	0.51213
MEWC04	6.83	24	0.1721	0.51255	376	0.51213
WILLOUGHBY PLUTON						
LYWI08	3.65	23.0	0.0959	0.51226	376	0.51202
MEWI01	4.17	18.0	0.1401	0.51227	376	0.51193

Sample	Sm (ppm)	Nd (ppm)	$^{147}Sm/^{144}Nd$	$^{143}Nd/^{144}Nd$*	$^{143}Nd/^{144}Nd$ at 376 Ma
WAITS RIVER FORMATION					
ME-1	5.84	28.0	0.1261	0.51198	0.51167
ME-4	5.21	27.0	0.1167	0.51200	0.51171

*$^{143}Nd/^{144}Nd$ normalized to $^{146}Nd/^{144}Nd$ = 0.72190.

TABLE 4. Pb ISOTOPIC DATA FOR FELDSPARS FROM THE NORTHEAST KINGDOM BATHOLITH AND FOR WHOLE ROCKS FROM THE WAITS RIVER FORMATION, VERMONT

Sample	$^{206}Pb/^{204}Pb$	$^{207}Pb/^{204}Pb$	$^{208}Pb/^{204}Pb$
NORTHEAST KINGDOM BATHOLITH (FELDSPARS)			
DERBY PLUTON			
MED02	18.293	15.609	38.179
MED04	18.289	15.608	38.203
MED15	18.317	15.602	38.161
MED17	18.286	15.592	38.107
MAFIC ENCLAVES WITHIN DERBY PLUTON			
MED02I	18.275	15.566	38.056
MED03I	18.311	15.577	38.079
GRANITE AT DERBY QUARRY			
MED05	18.199	15.574	38.083
ECHO POND PLUTON			
IPEP03	18.208	15.559	37.988
IPEP04	18.269	15.608	38.196
IPEP14	18.239	15.549	37.961
IPEP19	18.291	15.588	38.071
IPEP20	18.219	15.544	37.975
IPEP22	18.235	15.558	38.012
IPEP24	18.247	15.562	38.058
NULHEGAN PLUTON			
AVNU17	18.156	15.572	38.039
AVNU18	18.111	15.541	37.943
IPNU06	18.141	15.579	38.069
IPNU07	18.151	15.585	38.097
IPNU09	18.116	15.535	37.958
IPNU12	18.121	15.564	38.017
WEST CHARLESTON PLUTON			
MEWC01	18.382	15.603	38.184
MEWC03	18.326	15.611	38.217
WILLOUGHBY PLUTON			
LYWI05	18.369	15.651	38.423
LYWI06	18.445	15.611	38.217
LYWI07	18.228	15.635	38.157
LYWI08	18.303	15.551	38.054
MEWI01	18.427	15.634	38.275
MEWI03	18.302	15.641	38.264
WAITS RIVER FORMATION (WHOLE ROCKS)			
ME01	19.021	15.711	38.763
ME02	18.676	15.663	38.001
ME04	18.795	15.676	38.608
ME05	18.799	15.703	38.793

ratios of Nd (Table 3) were measured on a MAT 261 mass spectrometer to a precision of less than ±0.00002 and corrected for fractionation to a $^{146}Nd/^{144}Nd$ of 0.72190. Analyses of U.S. Geological Survey rock standard BCR-1 gave a value of 0.51263. Initial ratios were calculated using Sm and Nd concentrations measured by neutron activation at a precision of about 5%. Uncertainties in the calculated initial ratios, propagated to include uncertainties for Sm and Nd concentrations, measured isotopic ratios, and age measurements, are less than ±0.00005 at the 95% confidence level.

Chemical procedures for the lead isotopic analyses of feldspars (Table 4) are those outlined by Ayuso et al. (1988). Isotopic ratios of lead were measured on a partially-automated 12 in, 90° sector, NBS-type mass spectrometer, and on a fully automated MAT 261 mass spectrometer. They were corrected for fractionation by comparison with runs on NBS SRM-982. Total lead blanks are less than 0.1 ng. The precision of the Pb isotopic measurements, based on replicate determinations, is about 0.15% at the 95% confidence level.

Oxygen was extracted from whole-rock powders by reaction with ClF_3 at 550 °C and converted to CO_2 for isotopic analysis on an automated MAT 251 mass spectrometer. The data (Table 5) are reported in the delta (δ) notation relative to standard mean ocean water (SMOW). Replicate extractions had a precision of about 0.10‰, and quartz standard NBS-28 gave a value of +9.60‰.

**TABLE 5. OXYGEN ISOTOPE DATA ON WHOLE-ROCK SAMPLES
OF NORTHEAST KINGDOM BATHOLITH AND
WAITS RIVER FORMATION, VERMONT**

Sample	$\delta^{18}O$	Sample	$\delta^{18}O$
DERBY PLUTON		NULHEGAN PLUTON	
MED02D	+8.86	AVNU17	+8.60
MED02L	+8.77	AVNU18	+8.38
MED03	+9.91	IPNU04	+8.28
MED03A	+10.21	IPNU05	+8.98
MED04	+8.57	IPNU06	+9.77
MED10	+9.71	IPNU07	+8.61
MED15	+10.99	IPNU09	+8.96
MED17	+8.99	IPNU12	+8.36
Averages:		Averages:	
This chapter (8)	+9.5	This chapter (8)	+8.7
Beaulieu et al. (14)	+9.4	Beaulieu et al. (10)	+8.9
GRANITE AT DERBY QUARRY		WEST CHARLESTON PLUTON	
MED05	+9.92	MEWC01	+10.57
		MEWC02	+11.85
ECHO POND PLUTON		MEWC03	+9.25
IPEP03	+7.94	MEWC04	+8.60
IPEP12	+7.29		
IPEP13	+7.38	WILLOUGHBY PLUTON	
IPEP14	+5.97	LYWI05	+5.57
IPEP15	+9.50	LYWI06	+10.09
IPEP16	+6.18	LYWI07	+10.76
IPEP17	+7.20	LYWI08	+12.15
IPEP18	+8.59	MEWI01	+13.45
IPEP19	+7.26	MEWI03	+10.02
IPEP20	+7.44	Averages:	
IPEP22	+7.66	This chapter (6)	+10.3
IPEP24	+7.09	Beaulieu et al. (13)	+10.6
Averages:			
This chapter (9)	+7.5	WAITS RIVER FORMATION	
Beaulieu et al. (4)	+7.5	ME01	+19.0
		ME02	+18.1
		ME04	+20.2
		ME05	+19.0

RB-SR ISOCHRONS

New Rb-Sr isotopic analyses for 32 whole-rock samples from 4 plutons of the batholith are listed in Table 1 and plotted on isochron diagrams in Figure 1. Isochrons were fit by the regression method of York (1966) and uncertainties are quoted at the 67% confidence level. The decay constant of ^{87}Rb used for age determinations is 1.42×10^{-11} yr^{-1}. Rb-Sr ages quoted from the literature are adjusted to this constant.

Derby pluton

Samples from the Derby area (Fig. 2A) may be divided into two groups of differing petrologic and isotopic composition. A small mass of muscovite, biotite granite at Willey quarry to the north of the pluton is physically separated and distinct from the biotite granodiorites of the principal mass of the pluton. A whole-rock sample from the quarry, VND-2, and a coarse-muscovite separate from it were analyzed by Naylor (1971), who reported an age of 372 Ma. A whole-rock sample, MED05, from the quarry collected for this study has an isotopic composition similar to VND-2. A regression of muscovite from VND-2 and the two whole-rock samples (upper line in Fig. 2A) yields an age of 372 ± 6 Ma and an initial $^{87}Sr/^{86}Sr$ of 0.7125 ± 0.0003. The high initial ratio for the quarry granite distinguishes it from not only the granodiorites of Derby pluton, but from all of the plutons in the batholith.

Five samples of granodiorite from the principal mass of Derby pluton have $^{87}Rb/^{86}Sr$ ratios of less than 1 (Table 1), and isotopic ratios that do not fall on the trend of the quarry samples (Fig. 2A). If plotted with an aplite sample from the principal mass, they form a separate line (lower line of Fig. 2A) giving an age of 370 ± 17 Ma. The age has a large uncertainty because of its dependence on the single aplite sample, but is similar to that of the quarry rocks. The initial $^{87}Sr/^{86}Sr$ ratio (SIR) of 0.70708 ± 0.00023 is well determined because most of the samples are close to the intercept. The SIR of the granodiorites and aplite is distinctly lower than the SIR of the quarry granite.

Willoughby pluton

The Willoughby pluton is subdivided into a main zone and a hydrothermally altered zone (Ayuso and Arth, 1992). Five whole-rock samples from the main zone have a large range of $^{87}Rb/^{86}Sr$ ratios (Table 1). They fit a single regression line (Fig. 2B) within analytical uncertainty, and provide an isochron age of 376 ± 9 Ma. The intercept indicates an SIR of 0.70683 ± 0.00039, a value that is similar (within 1 standard deviation) to the SIR for granodiorites and aplite of the Derby pluton.

Nulhegan pluton

The Nulhegan pluton is petrographically divided into a central zone, a core zone, and a western rim zone (Ayuso and Arth, 1992). Four samples of the core zone have $^{87}Rb/^{86}Sr$ ratios of less than 1.0 (Table 1). A sample of aplite (IPNU05) from the western rim zone has a higher ratio. An isochron formed by the core-zone quartz monzodiorites and the aplite (Fig. 2C) yields an age of 390 ± 14 Ma. The age has a large uncertainty because it depends strongly on the aplite sample. The SIR of 0.70684 ± 0.00024 is nearly identical to that of the Willoughby pluton and similar to that of the Derby pluton.

Echo Pond pluton

The Echo Pond pluton is a composite body having a predominant granodiorite zone, an interior granodiorite to granite zone, and rim zones to the south and west that range from gab-

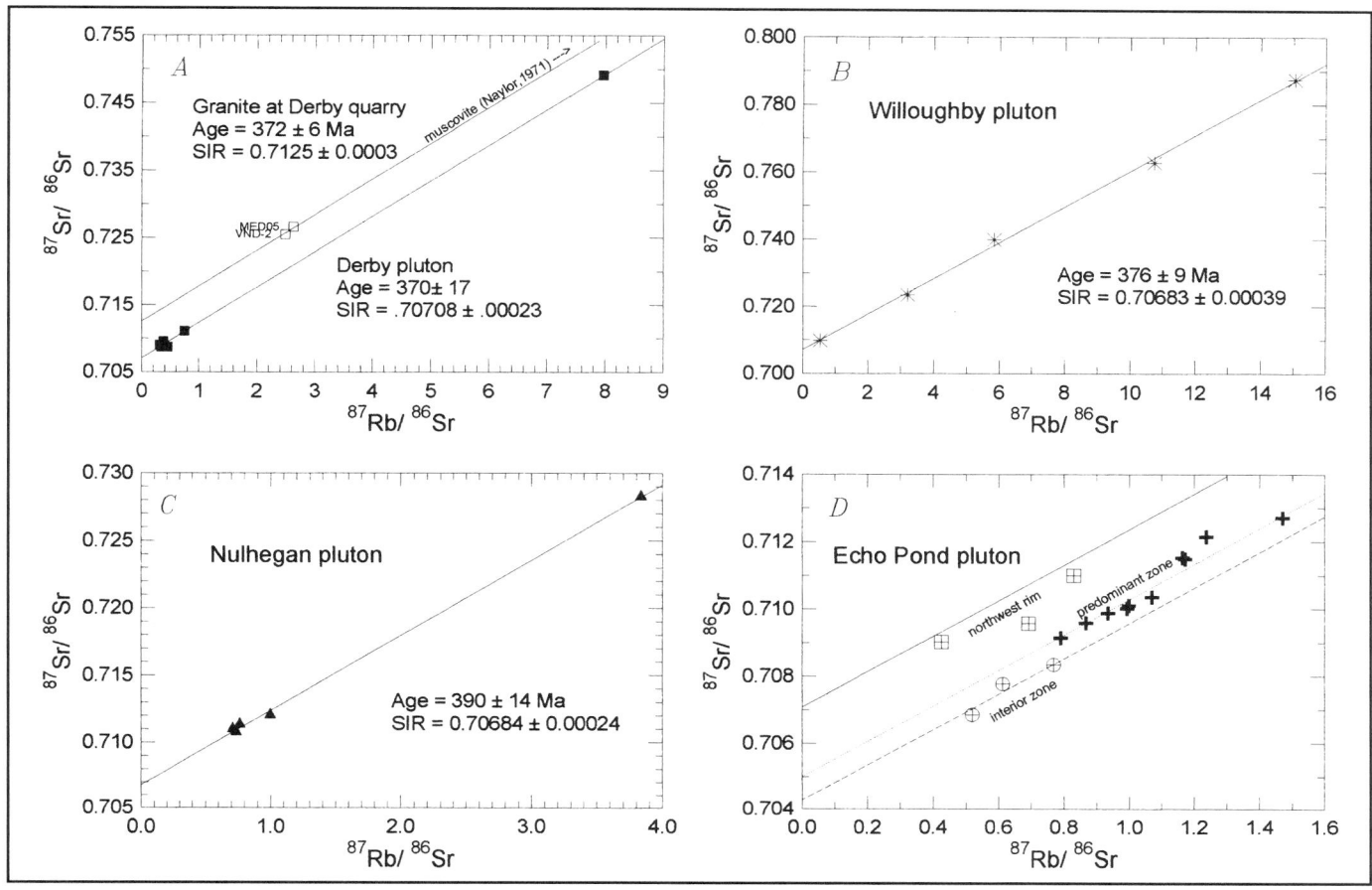

Figure 2. Rb-Sr isochron diagrams for the Northeast Kingdom batholith: A: Derby pluton. Whole-rock samples from the Derby pluton define the lower line. The upper line for granite at Derby quarry is defined by whole-rock sample MED05, and whole rock and muscovite samples VND-2 of Naylor (1971). B: Rb-Sr isochron diagram for whole-rock samples from Willoughby granite. C: Rb-Sr isochron diagram for whole-rock samples from the Nulhegan pluton. Upper point is from a distinct petrographic zone. D: Rb-Sr isochron diagram for whole-rock samples from three petrographic zones of the Echo Pond pluton. All zones show a limited range of Rb-Sr and some scatter of data points. Three samples from the northwest rim zone (crosses enclosed by squares, including sample VEP-1 of Naylor [1971]), fall close to the upper solid line—the isochron from the neighboring Derby pluton. The two lower dashed lines are drawn parrallel to the Derby isochron, and pass close to samples from the predominant zone (crosses) and the interior zone (crosses enclosed by circles), suggesting that these zones have similar ages of about 370–380 Ma, but distinct initial ^{87}Sr/^{86}Sr.

bro to granite (Ayuso and Arth, 1992). Whole-rock sample VEP-1 of Naylor (1971) and two samples from this study (MEEP07 and IPEP09) are from the northwestern rim zone. These samples fall above the trend of samples from the predominant zone (Fig. 2D), but have a limited range of ^{87}Rb/^{86}Sr and do not define an isochron. They do, however, fall close to the isochrons of nearby Willoughby and Derby plutons, and may have been related to those plutons.

Three samples from the interior zone (IPEP14, IPEP15, and IPEP16) fall below the trend of the predominant zone, have a limited range of ^{87}Rb/^{86}Sr, and do not define an isochron. They do, however, fall close to a line drawn parallel to the Derby and Willoughby isochrons, perhaps indicating a similar age, but a lower SIR of about 0.7045.

Ten samples from the predominant zone have higher ^{87}Rb/^{86}Sr than those of the rim or interior zones, but are also of limited range and display too much scatter to define an isochron. A line drawn through these points and parallel to the Willoughby isochron, or assuming an age of about 375 Ma, suggests an initial ratio for these samples of about 0.705.

West Charleston pluton

No isochron was attempted on the West Charleston pluton due to limited and heterogeneous outcrops, and low Rb/Sr values (<0.4). Three samples were isotopically analyzed (Table 2) to ascertain initial isotopic ratios, based on an assumed age of about 375 Ma.

Summary of ages

Most of the plutons have Rb-Sr ages in the range 380 to 370 Ma. The somewhat older age of 390 Ma for the Nulhegan pluton has a large uncertainty that overlaps the range for the other bodies. The most definitive age is provided by the whole-rock isochron for Willoughby pluton of 376 ± 9 Ma. The Rb-Sr data indicate that the plutons in the Northeast Kingdom batholith of Vermont are Middle and Late Devonian. This is consistent with the Silurian to Early Devonian ages assigned to their country rocks, and consistent with the earlier age interpretations of Naylor (1971).

ISOTOPIC TRACERS

In addition to initial Sr determinations (Tables 1 and 2), the isotopic compositions of Nd, Pb, and O were measured (Tables 3, 4, and 5, respectively) in order to develop a better understanding of the consanguinity of the magmas from zone to zone within each of the plutons, and the relationship between plutons of the batholith. We also wished to constrain the composition and age of the rocks that melted or interacted to supply magma to the plutons. In order to simplify the text and diagrams that follow, a set of acronyms used by us in several other reports is adopted here:

Initial $^{87}Sr/^{86}Sr$ ratio(s) = SIR
Initial $^{143}Nd/^{144}Nd$ ratio(s) = NIR
Initial $^{206}Pb/^{204}Pb$ ratio(s) = PIR6
Initial $^{207}Pb/^{204}Pb$ ratio(s) = PIR7
Initial $^{208}Pb/^{204}Pb$ ratio(s) = PIR8

Strontium initial ratios (SIR)

Initial Sr ratios are available for several plutons from the whole-rock isochrons of Figure 2 (A, B, and C). Initial ratios for Echo Pond pluton, which does not yield a single isochron, can be calculated for each sample by assuming an age of 375 Ma. There is a large range of initial Sr ratios, from about 0.704 to about 0.713, for the rocks that formed the Northeast Kingdom batholith. Within this range there appear to be three groupings, as illustrated on a plot of SIR versus SiO_2 content (Fig. 3A). Rocks having the lowest SIR of 0.704 to 0.706, from the mafic West Charleston (Table 2) and Echo Pond plutons, also have the broadest span of SiO_2, 47 to 74 wt%. Rocks having intermediate SIR of 0.7068 to 0.7071, from the Derby, Nulhegan, and Willoughby plutons, are the most voluminous in the batholith and have intermediate to high SiO_2 contents of 58 to

77 wt%. Rocks having high SIR are restricted to a small volume of two-mica granite at Derby quarry, which has an SiO_2 content of 72%.

The composite Echo Pond pluton was not isotopically homogeneous. If it is assumed to be about the same age as the other plutons, then its magmas had SIR that were different in each of three petrographic zones. The northwest rim zone (NM of Fig. 1) had SIR of 0.7059 to 0.7067. The predominant granodiorite zone within Echo Pond pluton (PZ of Fig. 1) had SIR of 0.7046 to 0.7055, and the small interior granodiorite zone (IG of Fig. 1) had the lowest SIR of 0.7041 to 0.7045.

The West Charleston pluton also has heterogeneous SIR. A silicic sample (MEWC01, Table 2) had a ratio of 0.7069 at 375 Ma, a value that is indistinguishable from those of the Willoughby and Nulhegan plutons. Two mafic samples (MEWC02 and MEWC04) had ratios close to 0.705 at 375 Ma and resemble those of the Echo Pond pluton.

Neodymium initial ratios (NIR)

The initial $^{143}Nd/^{144}Nd$ ratios (NIR) for each of the plutons has been calculated from the data reported in Table 3. NIR for all of the plutons are in the range 0.51177 to 0.51213. This range far exceeds the uncertainty in the calculated initial ratios of individual samples (about 0.00005 at the 95% confidence level, if uncertainties in Sm, Nd, $^{143}Nd/^{144}Nd$, and age are propagated).

The highest NIR, 0.51213, is found in the mafic rocks of West Charleston pluton. Echo Pond samples also have high NIR of 0.51210–0.51200. The NIR in the Derby, Nulhegan, and Willoughby plutons are intermediate, 0.51202 to 0.51187. The lowest NIR, 0.51177, is found in the very small granite body of Derby quarry. Thus the groupings having high, intermediate, and low NIR correspond, respectively, to those having low, intermediate, and high SIR.

Lead initial ratios (PIR)

Lead isotopic ratios were measured in potassium feldspar separates from several samples of each pluton, and in four whole-rock samples from the Waits River Formation (Table 4). The feldspar values are taken to be initial ratios because potassium feldspar contains negligible amounts of uranium and thorium. Whole-rock values for the supracrustal rocks were adjusted to their approximate Devonian values by assuming that $^{238}U/^{204}Pb = 9$ and Th/U = 3.5.

PIR6 values for the plutons are within a limited range, 18.11 to 18.45. However, within this range both the Nulhegan and the Willoughby plutons can be distinguished from the other plutons (Fig. 3B). Only the Nulhegan pluton has a PIR6 lower than 18.2 (18.11 to 18.16). Only the Willoughby pluton contains rocks having a PIR6 greater than 18.4. Thus the PIR6 ratios do not correspond to the SIR and NIR groupings, in that two plutons having intermediate SIR and NIR have extremes of PIR6.

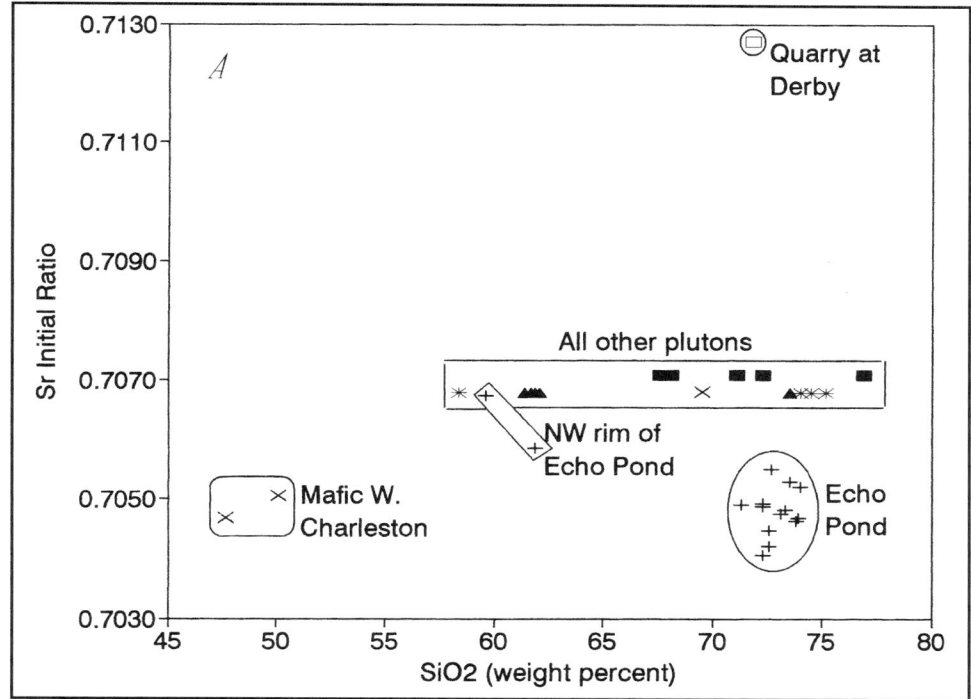

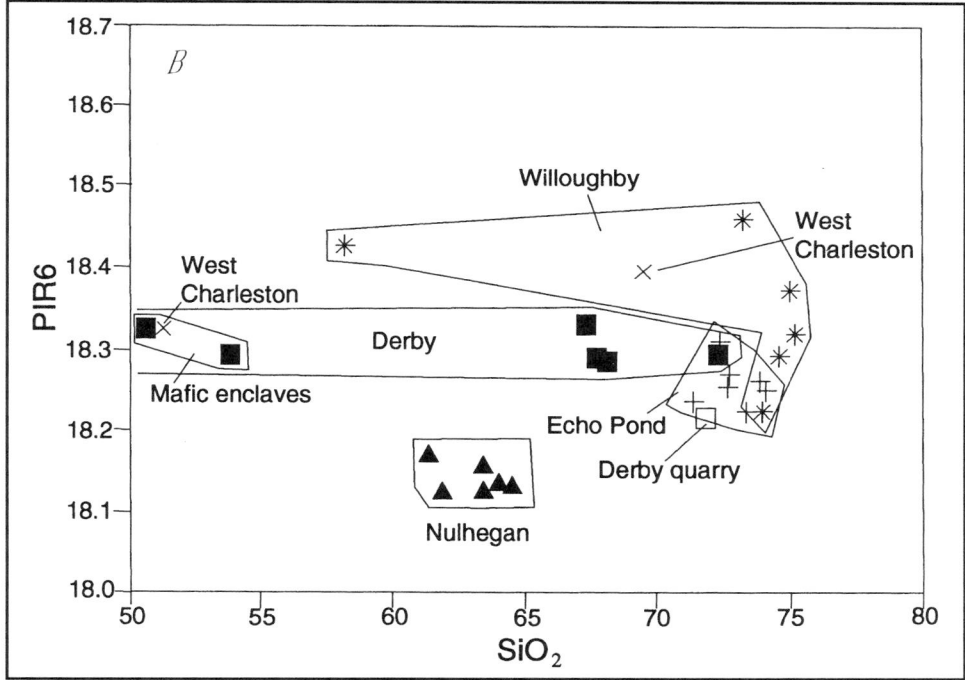

Figure 3 A: Plot of initial $^{87}Sr/^{86}Sr$ (SIR) versus SiO_2 for whole-rock samples from the Northeast Kingdom batholith. The rocks form three distinct groups. (1) high SIR, high SiO_2, represented only by a small volume of two-mica granite in the quarry at Derby. (2) Moderate SIR, moderate to high SiO_2, represented by a large volume of quartz monzodiorites, granodiorites, and granites. (3) Low SIR, low to high SiO_2, represented by dioritic to granitic rocks of the West Charleston and Echo Pond plutons. B: Plot of initial $^{206}Pb/^{204}Pb$ versus SiO_2 for plutons of the Northeast Kingdom batholith.

PIR7 values for all plutons are similar to each other and are within a small range of 15.54 to 15.65. Only the Willoughby pluton has values greater than 15.61.

PIR8 values for the plutons fall in a limited range from 37.9 to 38.4. Values for most of the plutons overlap, but the Willoughby is the only pluton that has values above 38.22. Thus the Willoughby pluton can be distinguished from the other plutons in having the highest PIR6, PIR7, and PIR8.

Country-rock samples from the Waits River Formation have uranogenic lead ratios, after age adjustment, that overlap and exceed the higher PIR6 and PIR7 of the plutons. Age-adjusted thorogenic lead ratios of 38.0 to 38.4 also overlap the highest PIR8 of the plutons.

Oxygen isotopic compositions

Beaulieu et al. (1981) reported average $\delta^{18}O$ of +7.5‰ to +14.5‰ for several plutons in Vermont. For this study, we measured $\delta^{18}O$ in duplicate on samples from five plutons, and in the Waits River Formation (Table 5). The pluton samples have $\delta^{18}O$ values of +5.6‰ to +13.5‰. A more limited range is characteristic of each pluton. The lowest values are found in Echo Pond pluton (+6‰ to +9.5‰). Although one sample from Willoughby pluton has the lowest of all values (+5.6‰), most samples from this pluton have the highest values in the batholith (+10.0‰ to +13.5‰). The Derby, Nulhegan, and West Charleston plutons are between these extremes. The Nulhegan pluton has a small range of values (+8.3‰ to +9.8‰). The Derby pluton and West Charleston plutons overlap in a larger range (+8.6‰ to +11.9‰).

IMPLICATIONS FOR DIFFERENTIATION OF MAGMAS

Fractional crystallization

On the basis of petrologic and chemical variations, Ayuso and Arth (1992) suggested that fractional crystallization may have operated within several plutons. Some of the plutons exhibit SIR, PIR, and NIR that do not vary significantly over a range of SiO_2 contents, and these include the Derby, Nulhegan, and Willoughby plutons (included in "all other plutons" in Fig. 3A). This isotopic uniformity suggests that these plutons may have differentiated internally by a process, such as fractional crystallization, that does not produce changes in the isotopic composition of the magma.

Because the Derby, Nulhegan, and Willoughby plutons have SIR that are similar to each other (0.7068 to 0.7070), one might suspect that they were all related to a single fractionating magma body at depth. However, this is highly unlikely because they are different from each other in PIR6 (Fig. 3B) and PIR7, and display different chemical trends (Ayuso and Arth, 1992). At a given content of SiO_2, the Nulhegan pluton has signifi-

cantly higher MgO, Cr, and Th contents than the other plutons. The Derby pluton is more sodic than the Willoughby pluton, and has more fractionated rare earth patterns.

Magma mixing

The Echo Pond and West Charleston plutons exhibit heterogeneous initial Sr isotopic ratios. These cannot be the product of simple closed system fractionation, but may have originated by processes such as magma mixing, or fractionation accompanied by assimilation. The West Charleston pluton appears to be composite on a fine scale. It contains, in closely spaced outcrops, mafic magma isotopically similar to that of the Echo Pond pluton, and silicic magma isotopically like that of the Willoughby or Derby plutons. Because the West Charleston pluton is located between the Echo Pond, Derby, and Willoughby plutons, it probably contains magma intruded from the source for one or more of the surrounding magma bodies, and thus represents a physical mixture of magmas.

In the Echo Pond pluton the situation is more complex, as illustrated in Figure 4, which is a plot of SIR versus 1/Sr. On this plot, rock samples from isotopically uniform plutons, such as the Willoughby and Nulhegan, plot along a horizontal line. Rocks that fall along a line of finite slope, as do the interior and predominant zones of Echo Pond pluton, may be the result of mixing of two isotopically distinct magmas. To test this possibility, 13 granodiorite and granite samples from the interior and predominant zones that have little variation in SiO_2 content (72% to 74%), are compared for their contents of various major and trace elements. Figure 5 shows the results for three parameters that show a large variation: SIR, the ratio of Na_2O/K_2O, and the concentration of Th. There are well-defined trends for these parameters that extend from granodiorites having SIR of 0.7041, Na_2O/K_2O of 1.5, and Th of 9 ppm, to granites having SIR of 0.7055, Na_2O/K_2O of 0.9, and Th of 22 ppm. This systematic variation suggests that much of the Echo Pond pluton represents the product of magma mixing of granodiorite and granite magmas of distinct isotopic composition. Unlike the West Charleston pluton, mixing in Echo Pond pluton was sufficient to produce homogeneous and similar looking rocks throughout most of the pluton. The Echo Pond pluton can thus be considered largely a chemical mixture, because mixing of magma took place at least to the scale of individual crystals in the magma. It is probable that magmas in the rim zones of this pluton were not as well mixed, because they are heterogeneous in outcrop and appear more like the physical mixtures of West Charleston pluton.

Assimilation

Ayuso and Arth (1992) suggested, due to distinct chemical trends among plutons, that the variation from gabbroic

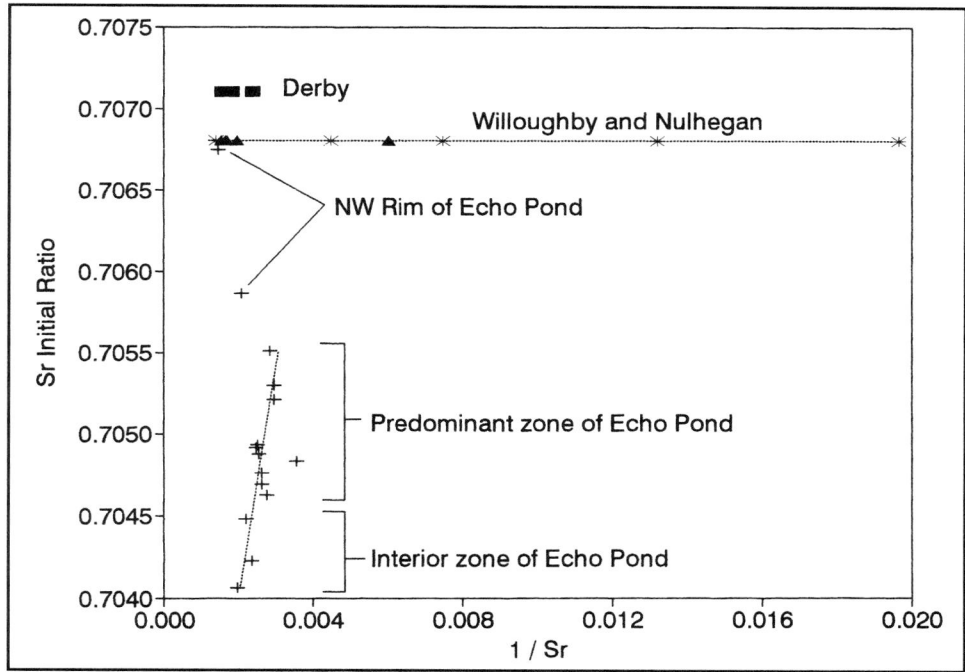

Figure 4. Plot of initial $^{87}Sr/^{86}Sr$ (SIR) versus 1/Sr for Northeast Kingdom batholith except West Charleston pluton. The Willoughby, Derby, and Nulhegan plutons form linear trends of zero slope on this plot, suggesting that fractionation or mixing of isotopically uniform magmas may have produced their compositional diversity. Samples from the interior and predominant zones of Echo Pond form a nearly linear trend of finite slope, suggesting that mixing of two isotopically distinct magmas may have occurred in this pluton.

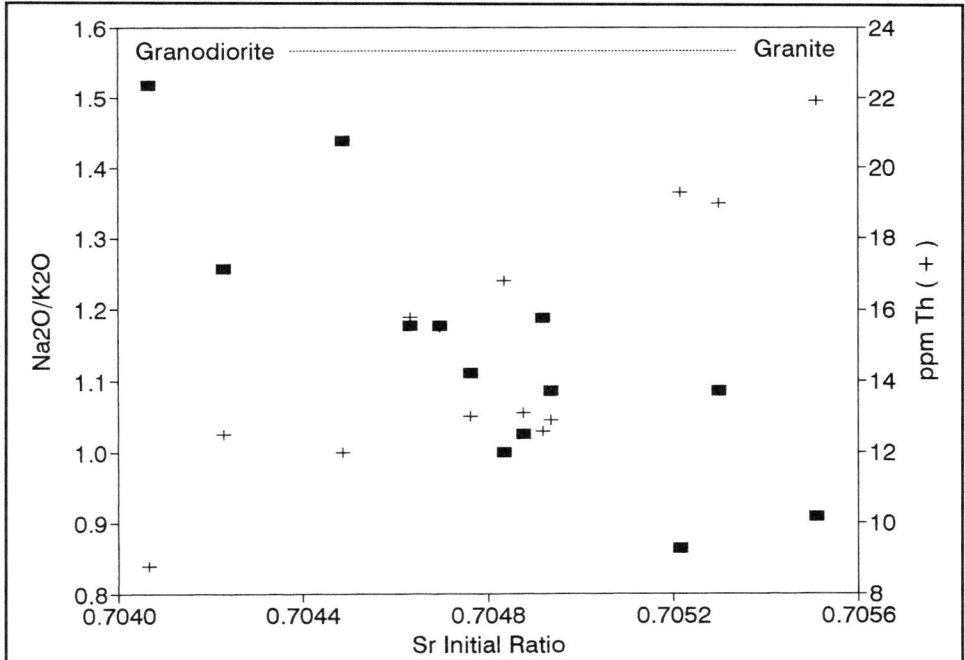

Figure 5. Plots of Na_2O/K_2O (filled squares) and Th (crosses) versus initial $^{87}Sr/^{86}Sr$ (SIR) for samples from the interior and predominant zones of the Echo Pond pluton. The trends of decreasing Na_2O contents and increasing Th contents as SIR increases support the hypothesis that the pluton formed by mixing of granodiorite magma (SIR ~0.7040) and granite magma (SIR ~0.7055).

to granitic magma in the Northeast Kingdom batholith could not be explained by a single fractionation or assimilation scheme, but that individual plutons may have evolved their unique chemical features by processes that included assimilation of country rock. Specifically, they suggested that assimilation of some Gile Mountain Formation rocks by gabbroic magma, accompanied by fractional crystallization, might explain the enrichment in Th in the granites of Echo Pond. However, as discussed in the previous section, a large Th increase within Echo Pond silicic rocks is probably related to mixing of granodiorite magma having about 9 ppm Th, and granite magma having about 22 ppm. In addition, there is little change in the $\delta^{18}O$ from the dioritic to granitic parts of this pluton. One sample of diorite (IPEP15) has $\delta^{18}O$ of +8.6‰, three samples of granodiorite of the inner core have an average value of +7.2‰, and four samples of granite containing more than 15 ppm Th have an average of +7.5‰. These values contrast with four measurements of $\delta^{18}O$ in the country rock (Waits River Formation of Table 5) that range from 18.1‰ to 20.2‰. If assimilation of country rock was significant to the evolution of Echo Pond magmas, the Echo Pond rocks should have higher $\delta^{18}O$ values than those observed.

CONSTRAINTS ON THE SOURCES OF MAGMA

The initial isotopic ratios of the plutonic rocks can be used as "fingerprints" or tracers of the source material from which magma was generated. They place constraints on both the composition and age of the rocks that melted to provide magma to the Northeast Kingdom batholith. There are two alternate approaches to interpreting the isotopic ratios. One involves comparisons of data from a variety of geologic terranes worldwide and utilizes global averages and evolution models. The second involves comparisons with data on potential source rocks in the region of the batholith. Because the regional rocks have not been fully characterized, a combination of both approaches is used here.

Potential sources

There are several rock units that may have been present beneath the area occupied by the batholith that may have locally melted and contributed magma to the batholith. Magmas from the mantle may also have been present. The potential sources include the following.

1. Supracrustal rocks of Cambrian to Devonian age. These include Cambrian and Ordovician rocks that crop out to the west and east of the batholith, and the Silurian and Devonian formations intruded by the batholith. Sr, Nd, and O isotopic data on the Waits River and Gile Mountain formations near Mt.

Ascutney, Vermont, were reported by Foland et al. (1985, 1988). New Sr, Nd, Pb, and O isotopic data on the Barton River Member of Waits River Formation in the vicinity of the Derby pluton are reported, respectively, in Tables 2, 3, 4, and 5.

2. Crystalline rocks of Grenville age. These rocks unconformably underlie the Paleozoic supracrustal rocks to the west in the Adirondack Mountains of New York, and to the southwest in the Green Mountain massif and Chester dome of Vermont. They range from supracrustal assemblages at high metamorphic grade to orthogneiss that may represent the lower crust and upper mantle. Combined Sr, Nd, and O isotopic data were reported on tonalitic gneisses of the Chester dome of Vermont by Foland et al. (1985, 1988), and on granitic intrusions and paragneisses in the Frontenac arc, adjacent to the Adirondacks on the northwest in Canada, by Marcantonio et al. (1990). Combined Sr and Nd data on ultramafic, mafic, and anorthositic rocks of the Marcy Anorthosite in the Adirondacks, were reported by Ashwal and Wooden (1983), and on charnockites, mafic to anorthositic gneisses, and pegmatites of the Pedlar and Lovingston massifs of central Virginia by Pettengill et al. (1984). Nd isotopic data on granitic gneisses and metapelite of the Adirondack highlands were reported by Daly and McLelland (1991), and on granitic gneisses of the Adirondack lowlands by McLelland et al. (1993). Pb isotopic data were reported by Zartman (1969), but these may not be compatible with modern data due to changes in measurement techniques. We utilize a set of modern analyses of tonalitic gneisses from the Green Mountain massif (Ayuso and Ratcliffe, unpublished data). Oxygen isotope data from granitic rocks in Ontario were reported by Shieh and Schwartz (1974).

3. Early Paleozoic rocks of the Chain Lakes massif. These rocks are to the northeast of the batholith, in western Maine, and constitute a potential exposed basement assemblage. Lead and oxygen data on these rocks were reported by Ayuso et al. (1988).

4. Proterozoic and possibly older basement rocks in Avalonian terranes. These rocks are to the east of the area in coastal Maine, and constitute a basement that may have underthrust the area during the Paleozoic. No isotopic data are available for these rocks.

5. Magmatic-arc basalt or andesite. Arc-type magmas may have been present as the result of subduction during the Acadian event. Arc-type rocks may be present at depth due to thrusting of parts of an Ordovician island-arc assemblage now found to the east of the area as the Ammonoosuc volcanics (Leo, 1991). Measured values for oxygen isotopes on arc rocks were given by Taylor (1968). Model Pb isotopic values for orogenic arcs were given by Zartman and Doe (1981). As an approximation to arc values for Sr and Nd, we use "bulk-earth" values at 375 Ma (DePaolo and Wasserburg, 1976; O'Nions et al., 1979). Although modern arcs show a range of Sr and Nd isotopic ratios, their average is approximately that of bulk earth values (e.g., Hawkesworth, 1982).

6. Mid-ocean-ridge basalt (MORB). MORB is considered

because there are still proponents of MORB as the ultimate source of all magmas, and because rocks of oceanic affinity are thought to constitute some Appalachian mafic-ultramafic complexes. For example, an oceanic origin was suggested on the basis of Nd and Sr isotopic composition for the Hazen's Notch Formation of the Belvidere Mountain area, Vermont (~24 km west of the Willoughby pluton) by Shaw and Wasserburg (1984). Oxygen isotope data for MORB were reported by Taylor (1968). As an approximation for Pb, we use the "mantle" values of Zartman and Doe (1981), which are based on MORB.

Although most potential sources have been partially characterized isotopically, additional data are needed to rigorously characterize them. The constraints developed in the following discussions utilize what is currently available, and are subject to revision as new data on potential sources become available.

Isotopic comparison of plutons and sources

Three isotopic plots (Figs. 6, 7, and 8) illustrate the possible relationship between the batholith magmas and their potential sources. Figure 6 shows plots of the measured PIR6, PIR7, and PIR8 for the plutons, and for five potential sources of magma adjusted to their likely values at 375 Ma. As a group, the plutons of the Northeast Kingdom batholith are in and between the fields for Grenville gneiss, magmatic arcs, and local metasedimentary country rock. Samples of the Nulhegan pluton, having the lowest PIR6, fall closest to the fields of Grenville and magmatic-arc rocks. Samples of the Willoughby pluton, having the highest PIR6, fall closest to the fields of Grenville and metasedimentary country rocks. None of the samples fall close to the values for MORB. Rocks of the Chain Lakes massif (not shown) plot to the left of MORB at PIR6 of 17.2 to 17.6, and are not likely sources of lead in the batholith.

Figure 7 is a plot of $\delta^{18}O$ versus PIR6. Fields for plutons are shown by solid lines; those for potential sources by dashed lines. None of the plutons fall near oceanic mantle (MORB). Values for Grenville and magmatic arcs overlap in both $\delta^{18}O$ and PIR6. The Echo Pond pluton falls largely within the field for Grenville rocks, whereas the Derby and Willoughby plutons are between the fields of Grenville and country rocks. Nulhegan samples are between the same fields, and also on a line between arc magmas and country rocks. None of the plutons plot near MORB or the Chain Lakes massif.

Figure 8 is a plot of the initial Sr versus the initial Nd isotopic ratios for the batholith, and the fields for potential sources adjusted to 375 Ma. In the upper left of the diagram, rocks equivalent to Paleozoic MORB are represented by mafic rocks of Belvidere Mountain. Magmatic-arc rocks are represented approximately by the value for "bulk earth" at 375 Ma.

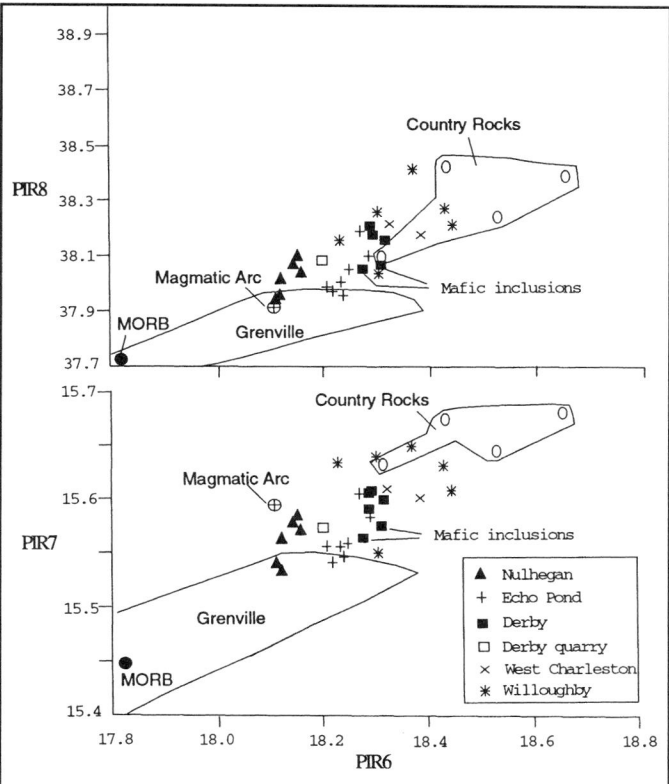

Figure 6. Plots of PIR7 (initial $^{207}Pb/^{204}Pb$) versus PIR6 (initial $^{206}Pb/^{204}Pb$), and PIR8 (initial $^{208}Pb/^{204}Pb$) versus PIR6 for feldspar samples from the Northeast Kingdom batholith. Potential source rocks, adjusted to their values at 375 Ma, are shown by enclosed fields, and include whole rocks of the Gile Mountain Formation (field labeled country rocks; samples indicated by ovals). Values for oceanic mantle (mid-ocean-ridge basalt, MORB) and orogenic magmatic arcs are from Zartman and Doe (1981); Grenville field represents modern analyses from the Green Mountain massif (Ayuso and Ratcliffe, unpublished data). Most plutons fall between the fields for Grenville basement rocks and country rocks of the Gile Mountain Formation.

Supracrustal metasedimentary rocks are represented by local "country rocks." Grenville rocks occupy a very large field, reflecting a diversity of rock compositions that include mafic, anorthositic, granitic, and metasedimentary rocks. The Grenville rocks tend to differ in isotopic composition according to rock type, as illustrated in Figure 9. At 375 Ma, mafic Grenville rocks occupy the upper left side of the field having low $^{87}Sr/^{86}Sr$ and high $^{143}Nd/^{144}Nd$ values. Grenville anorthosites and tonalites are relatively low in both $^{87}Sr/^{86}Sr$ and $^{143}Nd/^{144}Nd$ values. Granitic Grenville rocks tend to have moderate to high $^{87}Sr/^{86}Sr$, and moderate $^{143}Nd/^{144}Nd$. Metasedimentary Grenville rocks had a large range of high $^{87}Sr/^{86}Sr$ and relatively low $^{143}Nd/^{144}Nd$.

Sr and Nd data for the Northeast Kingdom batholith fall into

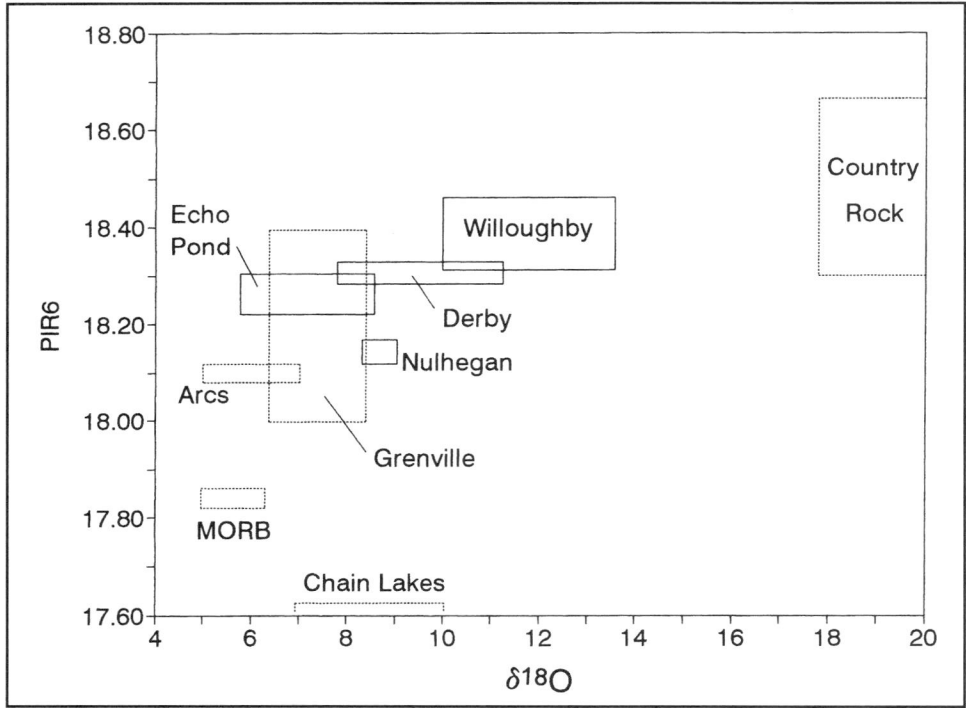

Figure 7. Plot showing fields (solid lines) for initial $^{206}Pb/^{204}Pb$ (PIR6) from K-feldspars versus $\delta^{18}O$ of whole rocks in plutons of the Northeast Kingdom batholith. A few atypical $\delta^{18}O$ values have been excluded in defining these fields. Also shown are fields for potential sources of magma (dashed lines) adjusted to 375 Ma, including upper crustal rocks of Gile Mountain Formation (data from Tables 4 and 5), lower crustal rocks of Grenville province (Ayuso et al., 1988), and orogenic arc magmas (Zartman and Doe, 1981; Taylor, 1968). Data for most samples fall between Grenville basement and country-rock values.

three groups in Figure 8. Samples from the West Charleston and Echo Pond plutons fall in the field for mafic Grenville rocks, and close to the values of magmatic-arc rocks. It has been suggested on the basis of Nd isotopic composition that some Grenville rocks in the Adirondacks are themselves of arc affinity (Daly and McLelland, 1991; McLelland et al., 1993). It is likely that mafic magmas of island-arc affinity of any age, including those of the Ordovician arc rocks underlying the area, or perhaps Late Proterozoic Avalonian mafic volcanic rocks, would have similar average Sr and Nd isotopic compositions, because all of these would evolve along a path close to that of "bulk earth."

The granite from the quarry at Derby has an SIR that is higher or more evolved than that of oceanic igneous rocks, most igneous rocks of convergent continental margins, and Grenville mafic to tonalitic rocks. In Figure 8, the quarry data fall close to the fields for both Grenville paragneiss and for country-rock samples from the nearby Waits River Formation. It is likely that the quarry granite had a source of magma dominated by metasedimentary rocks.

The SIR and NIR for the other plutons (Derby, Nulhegan, and Willoughby) fall in a separate and restricted cluster between those of the Echo Pond and Derby quarry rocks. They are in the middle of the large field for Grenville basement rocks, and it is likely that melts from Grenville silicic orthogneisses contributed strongly to the magma for these plutons.

Probable sources of magma

Taken collectively, the isotopic plots provide evidence that the magmas of the batholith received contributions from at least two, and probably three, sources. Of the sources considered, there is no evidence of significant contributions from MORB-like assemblages, or from rocks like those of Chain Lakes massif.

The dominant magmas in the batholith, represented by the Derby, Nulhegan, and Willoughby plutons, probably formed by melting in the deep crust of sections that included diverse rock types. Each of these plutons probably originated by the melting of somewhat different lithologies, or the same lithologies in dif-

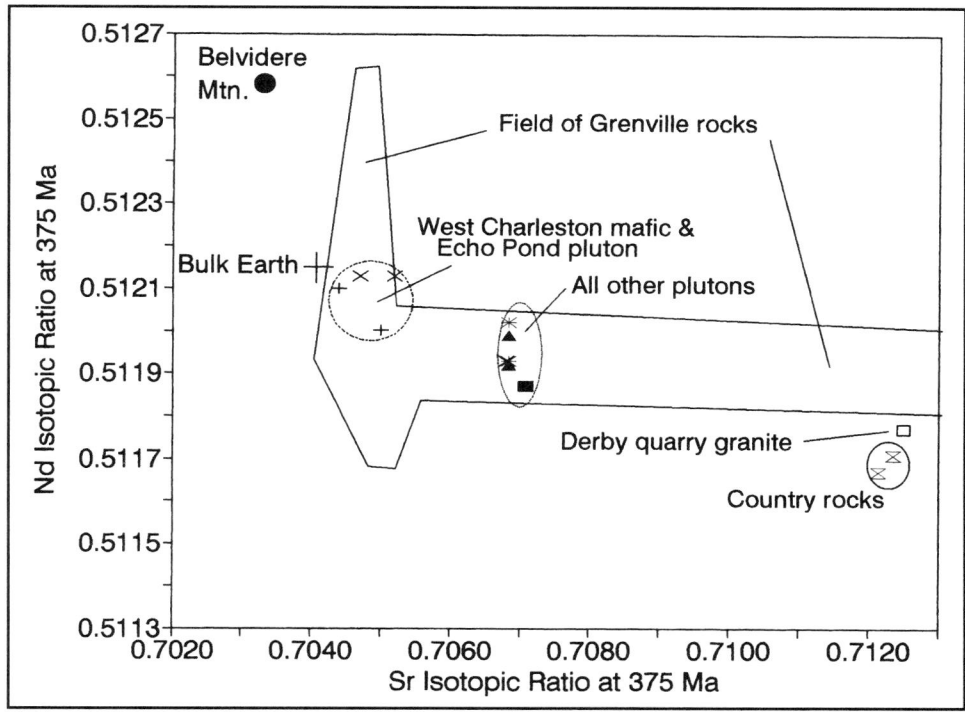

Figure 8. Plot of ^{143}Nd/^{144}Nd versus ^{87}Sr/^{86}Sr at 375 Ma for plutons of the Northeast Kingdom batholith, Vermont (symbols as in Figs. 3 and 6), and for potential source rocks, including part of the large field for Grenville gneiss, country rocks from Waits River Formation, and rocks having mid-ocean-ridge basalt–like ratios from the Belvidere Mountain area, Vermont. The bulk earth values for 375 Ma approximate those of magmatic-arc rocks. Samples from the Northeast Kingdom batholith form three groups: one near mafic Grenville rocks and arc magmas, one in the middle of Grenville field near orthogneiss, and one near local country rock and Grenville paragneiss.

ferent proportions. For example, the potassic and mafic character of Nulhegan is suggestive of a source that includes continental mantle. The sodic character and the presence of tonalites within Derby suggest a high proportion of metamafic rocks in the source. The siliceous character of the Willoughby pluton, and its high pegmatite content suggest a strong contribution from a metasedimentary source.

A moderate volume of gabbroic to dioritic magma, represented by mafic West Charleston and mafic Echo Pond rocks, may have originated either by melting in a mafic to ultramafic section of Grenville basement, or by melting of a mafic to ultramafic section of magmatic-arc rocks, or by melting in the mantle, perhaps related to a subduction regime. Some granodiorite to granite magma, represented by the silicic Echo Pond pluton, probably originated by mixing of granodiorite evolved from mafic rocks with the more abundant granites that originated in the deep crust.

A small volume of two-mica granite magma, represented by the Derby quarry pluton, was probably formed by melting of

metasedimentary rocks like those of the local country rock, or by melting of Grenville paragneiss, or some combination of these.

A summary of the representative isotopic data and the dominant sources inferred for each pluton is given in Table 6, and is based on the petrologic and chemical data of Ayuso and Arth (1992), and the isotopic data of this report. On the basis of the data and inferred source of the magmas, the rocks can be subdivided into three groups: Group 1 includes rocks having a mafic to ultramafic source in the mantle or lower crust; Group 2 includes rocks having a source composed largely of deep crustal orthogneiss; and Group 3 includes rocks having a source in crustal paragneiss.

The proportion of magma contributed by each source can be estimated in a rough way by comparing the map area occupied by rocks from each group. Group 1 constitutes about 20%, Group 2 about 80%, and Group 3 less than 1%. If this crude estimate reflects magma volumes, then we can conclude that about 80% of the Acadian magmas in this area were contributed by melting of Grenville age deep crustal rocks, and that about 20%

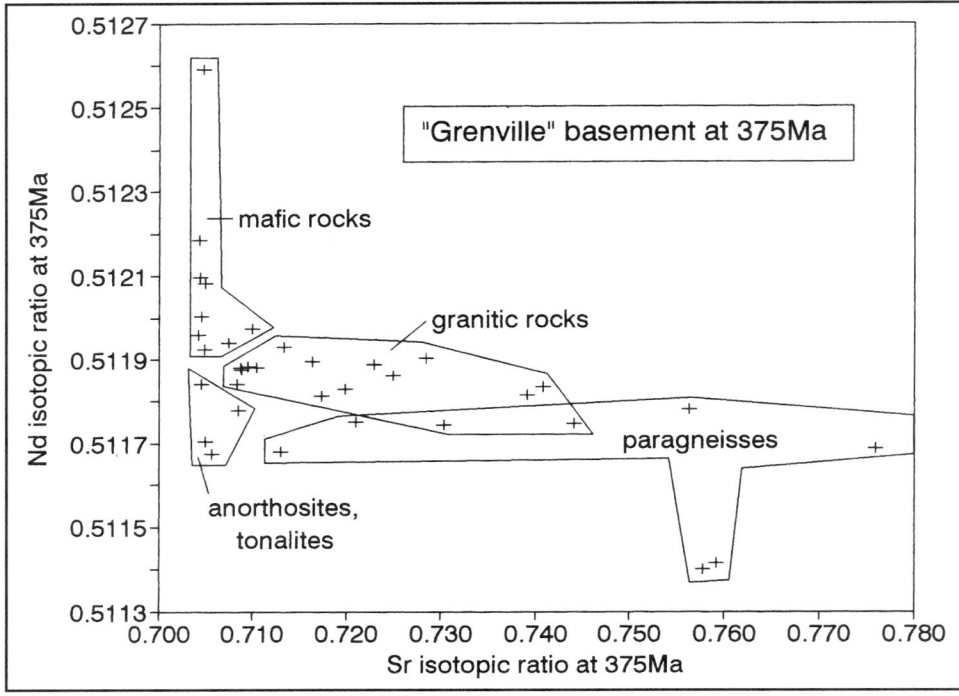

Figure 9. Plot of $^{143}Nd/^{144}Nd$ versus $^{87}Sr/^{86}Sr$ at 375 Ma for potential source rocks of Grenville age (see text for references).

TABLE 6. REPRESENTATIVE VALUES AND PROBABLE SOURCES FOR NORTHEAST KINGDOM BATHOLITH

Pluton	SiO_2	SIR	NIR	$\delta^{18}O$	PIR6	DOMINANT SOURCE and dominant process
GROUP 1						MANTLE ROCKS
W. Charleston-mafic	47.7–51.1	0.7047–0.7052	0.51213	8.6–11.9	18.33	Contamination of mantle melts.
Echo Pond-interior (IG)	72.3–72.6	0.7041–0.7045	0.51210	6.0–6.2	18.26	Fractionation of mantle melt.
Echo Pond-predominant (PG)	71.3–74.0	0.7046–0.7055	0.51200	7.1–7.9	18.22–18.31	Mixing of IG and granite of Group 2
GROUP 2						CRUSTAL ORTHOGNEISS
Nulhegen	57.3–64.5	0.7068	0.51199	8.3–9.8	18.11–18.16	Melting of Grenville ultramafic to silicic gneiss
Derby	62.8–76.9	0.7071	0.51187	8.9–11.0	18.29–18.32	Melting of Grenville mafic and silicic gneiss
Willoughby	73.2–76.4	0.7068	0.51202	10.1–12.2	18.23–18.45	Melting of Grenville silicic gneiss.
GROUP 3						CRUSTAL PARAGNEISS
Derby quarry	71.8	0.7125	0.51177	9.9	18.20	Melting of Grenville or Paleozoic paragneiss

came from the mantle or mafic-ultramafic deep crust. Less than 1% represents melting of pure metasedimentary rocks in the crust, although melts from metasedimentary rocks contributed in varying proportions to the more dominant magma groups.

CONCLUSIONS

The plutons that intruded the Connecticut Valley–Gaspe synclinorium in northeastern Vermont are of Middle and Late Devonian age, the largest proportion being 380 to 370 Ma. The petrographic zones within plutons correspond to magmas having distinct chemical and isotopic features that reflect distinct origins. Gabbroic and dioritic zones in the West Charleston pluton and the rim of the Echo Pond pluton had mafic to ultramafic sources in the mantle and deep crust. Some of the mafic magma fractionated to a granodiorite that now constitutes the interior zone of the Echo Pond pluton. The granodiorite magma was mixed with granite magma like that of the Derby or Willoughby plutons, and the gradational mixtures are preserved in the predominant zone of the Echo Pond pluton. The Willoughby pluton was largely the product of melting siliceous Grenville gneiss, followed by fractionation to volatile-rich compositions. The Derby pluton probably resulted by melting of Grenville gneiss that contained substantial mafic assemblages. The Nulhegan pluton is likely the product of melting of continental mantle and mafic to silicic Grenville gneiss. Two-mica granite of the Derby quarry represents a small volume of melt from Grenville or Paleozoic paragneiss.

The plutons of the Northeast Kingdom batholith thus preserve a record of melting through a significant vertical section from the upper mantle to the middle crust. The largest volume of magma was generated in the deep Grenville crust.

ACKNOWLEDGMENTS

We are grateful to E-an Zen for stimulating our interest in the area. Mary Horan and Lanford Adami made the oxygen isotopic analyses. Marcia Newell maintained the mass spectrometer laboratory and assisted in the lead isotopic analyses. Jodi Carlson and Clara Zmuda-Stader assisted in the Rb-Sr and Nd isotopic analyses. Michael Cabell prepared the whole-rock samples. Helpful reviews of the manuscript were provided by Ronald Kistler, Nicholas Ratcliffe, James McLelland, and Andrew Kerr.

REFERENCES CITED

Arth, J. G., Barker, F., and Stern, T. W., 1980, Geochronology of Archean gneisses in the Lake Helen area, southwestern Big Horn Mountains, Wyoming: Precambrian Research, v. 11, p. 11–22.

Ashwal, L. D., and Wooden, J. L., 1983, Sr and Nd isotope geochronology, geologic history, and the origin of Adirondack anorthosite: Geochimica et Cosmochimica Acta, v. 47, p. 1875–1885.

Ayuso, R. A., and Arth, J. G., 1992, The Northeast Kingdom Batholith, Vermont, Part I: Geochemistry and metallogeny: Contributions to Mineralogy and Petrology, v. 111, p. 1–23.

Ayuso, R. A., Horan, M. A., and Criss, R. E., 1988, Pb and O isotopic geochemistry of granitic plutons in northern Maine, in Sinha, A. K., Hewitt, D. A., and Tracy, R. J., eds., Frontiers in petrology: American Journal of Science, v. 288A, p. 421–460.

Beaulieu, G. M., Wenner, D. B., and Whitney, J. A., 1981, δO^{18}, geochemistry, and petrography of a portion of the Devonian New Hampshire Magma Series of Vermont: Eos (Transactions, American Geophysical Union), v. 62, p. 437.

Billings, M. P., 1934, Paleozoic age of the rocks of central New Hampshire: Science, v. 79, p. 55–56.

Daly, J. S., and McLelland, J. M., 1991, Juvenile Middle Proterozoic crust in the Adirondack Highlands, Grenville province, northeastern North America: Geology, v. 19, p. 119–122.

Dennis, J. D., 1956, The geology of the Lyndonville area, Vermont: Vermont Geological Survey Bulletin no. 8, 98 p.

DePaolo, D. J., and Wasserburg, G. J., 1976, Nd isotopic variations and petrogenetic models: Geophysical Research Letters, v. 3, p. 743–746.

Doll, C. G., 1951, The Memphremagog quadrangle and the southeastern portion of the Irasburg quadrangle, Vermont: Vermont Geological Survey Bulletin no. 3, 113 p., scale 1:62,500.

Doll, C. G., 1984, Fossils from the metamorphic rocks of the Silurian-Devonian Magog belt in northern Vermont: Vermont Geology, v. 3, p. 1–16.

Doll, C. G., Cady, W. M., Thompson, J. B., and Billings, M. P., 1961, The centennial geologic map of Vermont: Montpelier, Vermont Geological Survey, scale 1:250,000.

Faul, H., Stern, T. W., Thomas, H. H., and Elmore, P. L. D., 1963, Ages of intrusion and metamorphism in the northern Appalachians: American Journal of Science, v. 261, p. 1–19.

Fisher, G. W., and Karabinos, P., 1980, Stratigraphic sequence of the Gile Mountain and Waits River Formations near Royalton, Vermont: Geological Society of America Bulletin, v. 91, p. 282–286.

Foland, K. A., Henderson, C. M. B., and Gleason, J., 1985, Petrogenesis of the magmatic complex at Mount Ascutney, Vermont, USA. I. Assimilation of crust by mafic magmas based on Sr and O isotopic and major element relationships: Contributions to Mineralogy and Petrology, v. 90, p. 331–345.

Foland, K. A., Raczek, I., Henderson, C. M. B., and Hofman, A. W., 1988, Petrogenesis of the magmatic complex at Mount Ascutney, Vermont, USA. II. Contamination of mafic magmas and country rock model ages based upon Nd isotopes: Contributions to Mineralogy and Petrology, v. 98, p. 408–416.

Goodwin, B. K., 1963, Geology of the Island Pond Area, Vermont: Vermont Geological Survey Bulletin no. 20, 111 p., scale 1:62,500.

Hatch, N. L., Jr., 1988, Some revisions to the stratigraphy and structure of the Connecticut Valley trough, eastern Vermont: American Journal of Science, v. 288, p. 1041–1059.

Hawkesworth, C. J., 1982, Isotopic characteristics of magmas erupted along destructive plate margins, in Thorpe, R. S., ed., Andesites: New York, John Wiley & Sons, p. 549–574.

Hueber, F. M., Bothner, W. A., Hatch, N. L., Jr., Finney, S. C., and Aleinikoff, J. N., 1990, Devonian plants from southern Quebec and northern New Hampshire and the age of the Connecticut Valley trough: American Journal of Science, v. 290, p. 360–395.

Johansson, W. I., 1963, Geology of the Lunenburg-Brunswick-Guildhall area, Vermont: Vermont Geological Survey Bulletin no. 22, 86 p.

Leo, G. W., 1991, Oliverian domes, related plutonic rocks, and mantling Ammonoosuc Volcanics of the Bronson Hill anticlinorium, New England Appalachians: U.S. Geological Survey Professional Paper 1516, 92 p.

Marcantonio, F., McNutt, R. H., Dickin, A. P., and Heaman, L. M., 1990, Isotopic evidence for the crustal evolution of the Frontenac Arch in the Grenville Province of Ontario, Canada: Chemical Geology, v. 83, p. 297–314.

McLelland, J. M., Daly, J. S., and Chiarenzelli, J., 1993, Sm-Nd and U-Pb isotopic evidence of juvenile crust in the Adirondack lowlands and implications for the evolution of the Adirondack Mts.: Journal of Geology, v. 101, p. 97–105.

Morgan, B. A., 1972, Metamorphic map of the Appalachians: U.S. Geological Survey Miscellaneous Geologic Investigations Map I-274, scale 1:2,500,000.

Myers, P. B., Jr., 1964, Geology of the Vermont portion of the Averill quadrangle, Vermont: Vermont Geological Survey Bulletin no. 27, 69 p., scale 1:62,500.

Naylor, R. S., 1971, Acadian orogeny: An abrupt and brief event: Science, v. 172, p. 558–559.

O'Nions, R. K., Evenson, N. M., and Hamilton, P. J., 1979, Geochemical modelling of mantle differentiation and crustal growth: Journal of Geophysical Research, v. 84, p. 6091–6101.

Osberg, P. H., Tull, J. F., Robinson, P., Hon, R., and Butler, J. R., 1989, The Acadian orogen, in Hatcher, R. D., Jr., Thomas, W. A., and Viele, G. W., eds., The Appalachian-Ouachita Orogen in the United States: Boulder, Colorado, Geological Society of America, The Geology of North America, v. F-2, p. 179–232.

Pettingill, H. S., Sinha, A. K., and Tatsumoto, M., 1984, Age and origin of anorthosites, charnockites, and granulites in the Central Virginia Blue

J. G. Arth and R. A. Ayuso

Ridge: Nd and Sr isotopic evidence: Contributions to Mineralogy and Petrology, v. 85, p. 279–291.

Shaw, H. F., and Wasserburg, G. J., 1984, Isotopic constraints on the origin of Appalachian mafic complexes: American Journal of Science, v. 284, p. 319–349.

Shieh, Y. N., and Schwartz, H. P., 1974, Oxygen isotope studies of granite and migmatite, Grenville province of Ontario, Canada: Geochimica et Cosmochimica Acta, v. 38, p. 21–45.

Sinha, A. K., 1988, Plutonism in the Appalachians, *in* Sinha, A. K., Hewitt, D. A., and Tracy, R. J., eds., Frontiers in petrology: American Journal of Science, v. 288A, p. viii–xii.

Taylor, H. P., 1968, The oxygen isotope geochemistry of igneous rocks: Contributions to Mineralogy and Petrology, v. 19, p. 1–71.

Woodland, B. G., 1965, The geology of the Burke quadrangle, Vermont: Vermont Geological Survey Bulletin no. 28, 151 p., scale 1:62,500.

York, D., 1966, Least squares fitting of a straight line: Canadian Journal of Physics, v. 44, p. 1079–1086.

Zartman, R. E., 1969, Lead isotopes in igneous rocks of the Grenville Province as a possible clue to the presence of older crust, *in* Age relations in high-grade metamorphic terraines: Geological Association of Canada Special Paper 5, p. 193–205.

Zartman, R. E., and Doe, B. R., 1981, Plumbotectonics—The model: Tectonophysics, v. 75, p. 135–162.

MANUSCRIPT ACCEPTED BY THE SOCIETY JULY 2, 1996

Geological Society of America
Memoir 191
1997

The Spruce Head composite pluton: An example of mafic to silicic Salinian magmatism in coastal Maine, northern Appalachians

Robert A. Ayuso
U. S. Geological Survey, National Center, MS 954, Reston, Virginia 20192
Joseph G. Arth*
U. S. Geological Survey, 345 Middlefield Road, MS 937, Menlo Park, California 94025

ABSTRACT

The Spruce Head pluton is among the best examples of the predominantly calc-alkaline Silurian igneous activity in coastal Maine generated during Salinian (Late Ordovician to Early Silurian) orogenic events. This pluton is composite and consists of distinct petrographic groups: quartz gabbro, quartz diorite, and tonalite (group I); hornblende-biotite granodiorite and granite (group II); sheared, medium-grained biotite-muscovite (garnet) granodiorite and granite (group III); and aplitic biotite-muscovite-garnet granodiorite and granite (group IV). Samples from each petrographic group also define distinct chemical groups having related chemical characteristics. Quartz gabbro, diorite, and tonalite are metaluminous and have SiO_2 from ~47–56 wt.%; they are separated by a gap of ~8 wt.% SiO_2 from the bulk of the granodiorites and granites. The majority of the granodiorites and granites are weakly peraluminous (A/CNK < 1.1) and have SiO_2 from ~64–76%; some of the silicic, muscovite- and garnet-rich rocks are strongly peraluminous (A/CNK = 1.1–1.2). Systematic major- and trace-element variations distinguish the quartz gabbro, quartz diorite, and tonalite group (group I), from the hornblende-biotite granodiorite to granite (group II), and from the aplitic biotite-muscovite-garnet granodiorite to granite (group IV). The granodiorites and granites from group III overlap all other groups. Rare earth element (REE) contents span a wide range, broadly decreasing with increasing SiO_2 in the granodiorites and granites (~350–110 ppm). Variations in the abundance of CaO, Fe_2O_3, TiO_2, K_2O, P_2O_5, Rb, total REE, Ta, and Th, among others, illustrate the unique ranges and trends of groups I, II, and IV, and indicate that the pluton formed from at least three distinct pulses of magma. The ranges in initial isotopic ratios for Nd ($^{143}Nd/^{144}Nd$ = 0.51224–0.51172), Sr ($^{87}Sr/^{86}Sr$ = 0.7035–0.7158), and Pb ($^{206}Pb/^{204}Pb$ = 18.319–18.461; $^{207}Pb/^{204}Pb$ = 15.640–15.732; $^{208}Pb/^{204}Pb$ = 38.146–38.465) are consistent with a general origin by mixing of mantle-derived magmas (best represented by quartz gabbro and quartz diorite) and crustal magmas. Fractional crystallization could account for the majority of the chemical variations in the quartz gabbro and quartz diorite. Granodiorites and granites from groups II, III, and IV cannot be related by simple fractional crys-

*Present address: 548 Riverwood Lane, Oakland, Oregon 97462.

Ayuso, R. A., and Arth, J. G., 1997, The Spruce Head composite pluton: An example of mafic to silicic Salinian magmatism in coastal Maine, northern Appalachians, *in* Sinha, A. K., Whalen, J. B., and Hogan, J. P., eds., The Nature of Magmatism in the Appalachian Orogen: Boulder, Colorado, Geological Society of America Memoir 191.

tallization because they show major compositional gaps and offsets between trends, despite otherwise systematic internal trends. The Spruce Head pluton belongs to a unique class of composite plutons in coastal Maine that owes its genesis to intrusion and underplating of mafic magmas and mixing of magmas formed by crustal melting following collisions of peri-Gondwanan rocks during the Salinian orogeny.

INTRODUCTION

The Spruce Head pluton is one of the best-studied examples of a distinctive group of Silurian igneous complexes found along the coast of Maine (Hogan and Sinha, 1989). These complexes typically contain gabbroic, intermediate, and granitic rocks in close temporal and spatial relation. They were emplaced into the more easterly terranes of the Appalachians during the earlier parts of what has traditionally been called the Acadian orogeny. The complexes are now of particular interest because their origin is a petrologic challenge, and because they are related in some way to the amalgamation of terranes that were either native or exotic to North America prior to Acadian events. This chapter summarizes results of our detailed geochemical study of the quartz gabbro to granite zones of the Spruce Head complex, and delimits the evolution of each magmatic component. Because the magmas originated in deeper parts of the lithosphere, their chemical and isotopic signatures provide evidence of the identity of sources at depth, and help to delimit the spatial extent of native and exotic terranes.

This study of the Spruce Head pluton is part of a larger study by us of granitoid plutons along a transect across the Appalachian terranes at about lat 44°N, from northeastern Vermont to coastal Maine (see inset of Fig. 1). The transect study focuses on the magmatic history of Acadian plutons, the character of their source lithologies at depth, and any implications for the distribution of lithospheric blocks during the Silurian and Devonian. Results from the western part of the transect in Vermont were reported by Ayuso and Arth (1992) and by Arth and Ayuso (this volume).

RELATION OF COASTAL MAINE PLUTONISM TO APPALACHIAN TERRANES

The stratified rocks of coastal Maine are intruded, metamorphosed, and displaced by plutons of largely Silurian and Devonian granitoid rocks. These include gabbroic, granitic, and composite gabbroic through granitoid bodies (Hogan and Sinha, 1989) that intruded the Ellsworth-Mascarene and St. Croix terranes (Ludman, 1987; Stewart et al., 1993), as summarized by Rankin (1994), and the Merrimack-Mascarene composite terrane (hereafter referred to as the Merrimack-Mascarene collage) in what used to be known as the Coastal Maine lithotectonic block of Osberg et al. (1985) (Fig. 1).

Recent work has suggested that the Appalachian orogen resulted from many of the same tectonic processes that operate in the Pacific Ocean margins, including amalgamation and long-distance translation of island-arcs, back-arc basins, and continental blocks (Zen, 1983; van Staal and Williams, 1992; van Staal,

1994; Stewart et al., 1995, 1996). More important, basement rocks in coastal Maine are distinctive because they show no evidence for effects associated with the Middle to Late Ordovician Taconian orogeny commonly evident throughout the Appalachians; instead, basement rocks in coastal Maine were affected by tectonism in the Late Ordovician and Early Silurian (Salinian) prior to their accretion to Laurentia during the Acadian orogeny (West et al., 1992; Stewart et al., 1995). This orogenic belt is now known to extend from coastal Maine into the Canadian Maritime Provinces (central New Brunswick, van Staal and Fyffe, 1991; Nova Scotia, Dunning et al., 1990; Newfoundland, O'Brien et al., 1991), and into Scotland and Scandinavia (Dunning et al., 1990).

Regional geochemical surveys indicate that this part of coastal Maine consisted of numerous mafic and felsic Silurian to Early Carboniferous plutons that were used to define the Coastal Maine magmatic province (Hogan and Sinha, 1989) within the Ellsworth-Mascarene and St. Croix terranes in the Merrimack-Mascarene collage. The Ellsworth-Mascarene terrane, bounded on the northwest by the right-lateral strike-slip Turtle Head fault zone, contains many but not all of these composite mafic-silicic plutons. The St. Croix terrane, northwest of the Ellsworth-Mascarene terrane (Fig. 1), is bounded by the Sennebec Pond thrust fault, and constitutes the westernmost terrane containing the characteristic Silurian and Devonian Baltic faunal assemblage (Brookins et al., 1973) included within Avalonian rocks (Williams, 1978), which are collectively better referred to as peri-Gondwanan terranes. Silurian magmatism in this part of the Merrimack-Mascarene collage may be characterized by coeval, composite mafic-silicic intrusions (Wones, 1980; Hogan and Sinha, 1989) such as the Spruce Head pluton. In the Penobscot Bay region, for example, at least four additional Silurian mafic-silicic composite plutons have been described: the South Penobscot intrusive suite (Stewart et al., 1988), the Pleasant Bay mafic-silicic complex (Wiebe, 1993), and the Isle au Haute and Cadillac Mountain intrusive complexes (Wiebe and Chapman, 1993). Farther north, two additional examples of intrusions into the Ellsworth-Mascarene and the St. Croix terranes in the Coastal Maine lithotectonic block are the Moosehorn igneous complex (Jurinski and Sinha, 1989; Hill, 1991) and the Pocomoonshine pluton (Westerman, 1991).

ANALYTICAL METHODS

Samples were collected from all rock types and from all exposed parts of the pluton on the basis of mapped relations (Guidotti, 1979, and this study). We analyzed 50 alteration-free representative samples for major and trace elements. Nd, Sr, and Pb isotopic compositions were also determined on several of these samples. Analytical techniques (X-ray fluorescence, instru-

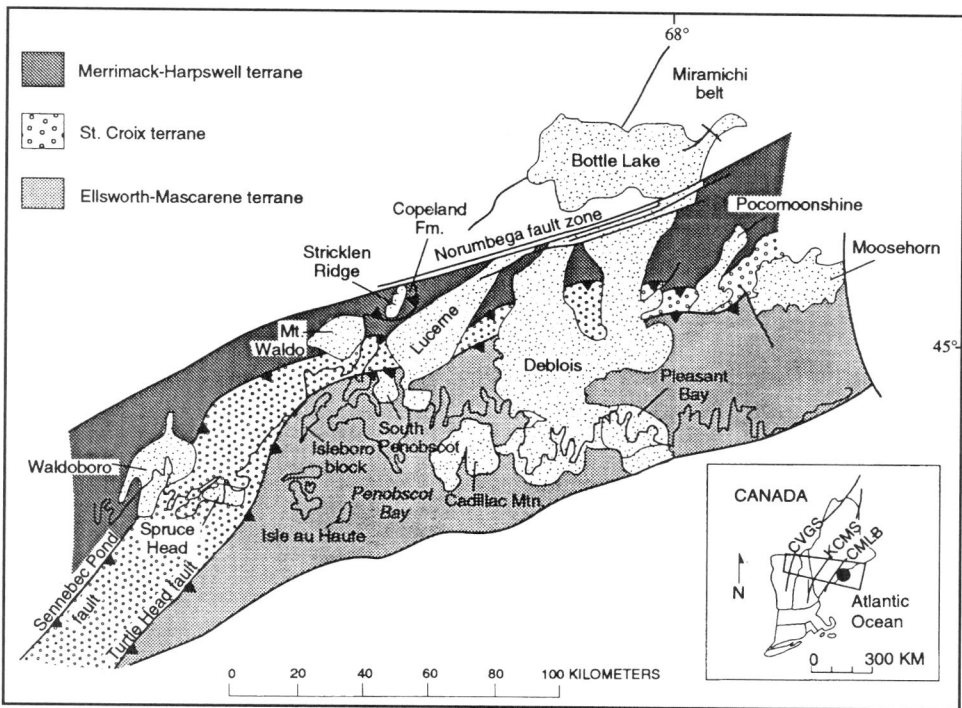

Figure 1. Generalized map showing terranes, major faults, location of the Spruce Head pluton, and selected Paleozoic plutonic rocks in south-central coastal Maine. The Isleboro block in the Ellsworth-Mascarene terrane contains the Seven Hundred Acre Island Formation; the Copeland Formation is in the Merrimack-Harpswell terrane. The St. Croix terrane and the Ellworth-Mascarene terrane are parts of the Merrimack-Mascarene composite terrane or collage, and were originally part of proto-Gondwana (after Rankin, 1994). The inset map of New England shows trends of the Connecticut Valley–Gaspe synclinorium (CVGS), Kearsarge–Central Maine synclinorium (KCMS), and Coastal Maine lithotectonic block (CMLB) (Osberg et al., 1985). The trend of our ongoing plutonic transect across New England is shown as a polygon on the inset map. The Spruce Head pluton is in the St. Croix terrane in the dark circle of inset map. The Coastal Maine lithotectonic belt contains the St. Croix and the Ellsworth-Mascarene terranes; all of which are part of the Merrimack-Mascarene composite terrane (Rankin, 1994).

mental neutron activation, inductively coupled plasma-atomic emission spectrometry, and classical wet-chemistry methods) and uncertainties in the determinations during the course of this study were summarized by Baedecker (1987). Isotopic techniques are summarized in Arth and Ayuso (this volume) for Nd, Arth et al. (1980) for Sr, and in Ayuso et al. (this volume) for Pb.

GEOLOGIC SETTING

The composite Spruce Head pluton is exposed along the Maine coast in a fault-bounded block on the western side of Penobscot Bay and on numerous nearby islands, including Clark, Sprucehead, and the Muscle Ridge Islands to the east (Figs. 1 and 2). The Turtle Head fault zone, a major tectonic boundary, juxtaposed low- and middle-amphibolite facies rocks in the St. Croix terrane containing the Spruce Head pluton against chlorite-grade, Late Proterozoic Avalonian basement rocks in the Isleboro block of the Ellsworth-Mascarene terrane (Stewart et al., 1993). Much of the pluton is under water or poorly exposed, and consequently internal relations between its constituent parts can rarely

be examined directly. Isolated small exposures and stocks of gabbroic, dioritic, and granodioritic rocks are also found along the coast to the south of the pluton boundary shown on the generalized geologic map. Such rocks may be connected at depth and also may be part of the pluton.

The Spruce Head pluton is probably ovoid shaped (<140 km²) and has been divided into four zones on the basis of the petrography of sampled rocks and limited field relations (Fig. 2). Zone I contains quartz gabbro, quartz diorite, and tonalite; zone II consists of hornblende-biotite granodiorite; zone III is biotite-muscovite (minor garnet) granodiorite and granite; and zone IV consists of aplitic, muscovite-biotite-garnet granodiorite and granite (Figs. 2 and 3, and Tables 1 and 2). Reconnaissance petrographic studies recognized wide variations within the plutonic rocks (Chayes, 1952), as well as complex intermixing of country rocks and magmatic rocks, especially near the western and southern boundaries of the pluton (Guidotti, 1979).

Exposures along the coast indicate a relatively large volume of gabbroic and dioritic rocks compared to more felsic rocks (up to a ratio of 1:4 of the total volume). However, consideration of

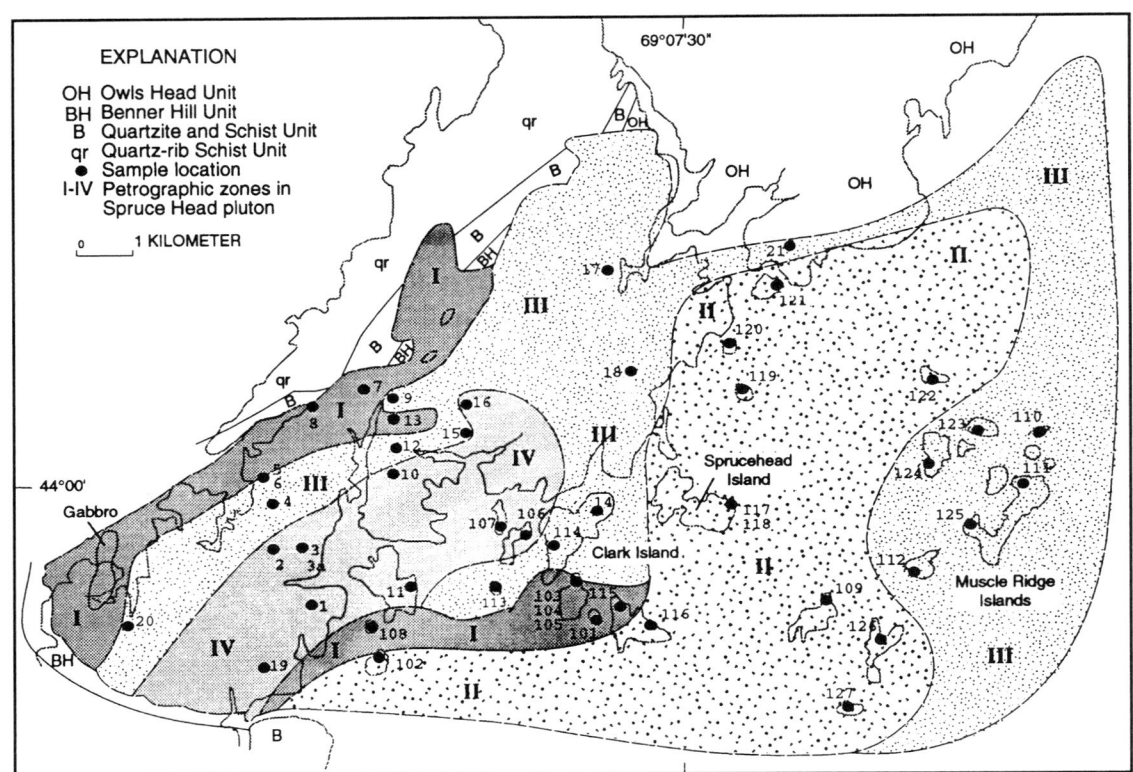

Figure 2. Geologic map of the composite Spruce Head pluton (after Guidotti, 1979; and this study) showing sample locations. Roman numerals refer to the petrographic zones: zone I (quartz gabbros, quartz diorites, and tonalites), zone II (hornblende-bearing granodiorites), zone III (biotite-bearing granodiorites and granites), and zone IV (garnet-muscovite granodiorites and granites).

the inferred volumes of unexposed felsic rock suggests a predominance of granodiorite and granite over gabbro and diorite (6:1), as depicted in the generalized geologic map (Fig. 2). The zones are not arranged concentrically, in the manner of normally or reversely zoned intrusions. Zone I is found at the western contact as a border unit, but also as an interior unit surrounded by granite and granodiorite. If, as we speculate, isolated exposures of mafic rocks to the south are also part of zone I, then this would result in a more regular and extensive border of mafic rocks around the southern part of the pluton.

PETROGRAPHY, FIELD, AND AGE RELATIONS

Contacts between gabbros, diorites, and tonalites in zone I and granodiorites in zone II are generally concealed and a rigorous field determination of age relations between them cannot be done. However, outcrops of granodiorites from zone II often contain pods and partially dismembered, sheared, plastically deformed mafic enclaves (up to 1 m), as well as biotite streaks and glomerocrysts (up to 7.5 cm) of hornblende and biotite (pyroxene in trace amounts). Areas containing numerous mafic enclaves are concentrated near the contacts between zones I and II; thus they provide compelling evidence for mingling of gabbroic and dioritic rocks with granodiorites and result in high

contents of mafic minerals in the host rocks (up to 20%). Gabbros and diorites of zone I are predominantly hornblende and biotite rich (with trace amounts of pyroxene as remnants and relics) and typically enriched in plagioclase. Consequently, rocks from zone I plot mostly near the quartz-plagioclase side of the modal ternary (from quartz gabbro and diorite to tonalite). Mafic enclaves span from diorites and tonalites to granodiorites. Zone II rocks consist of hornblende, biotite, K-feldspar, plagioclase, and quartz, and accessory minerals (apatite, titanite, zircon,

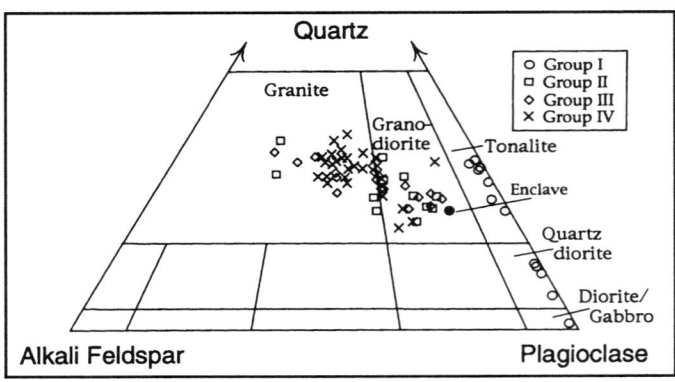

Figure 3. Modes of granitic rocks (this study, and Chayes, 1952) from the Spruce Head pluton (after Streckeisen, 1976).

and allanite); the rocks are coarse, seriate to equigranular and porphyritic, and locally are miarolitic. Traces of pyroxene are also found in granodiorites from zone II. Rocks from zones II and III plot on a trend away from the plagioclase-quartz sideline in a modal ternary diagram (Fig. 3), and lie for the most part in the granodiorite field. Mild hydrothermal alteration and minor amounts of sulfides (pyrite and molybdenite) are mostly concen-trated along joint and fracture surfaces in some of these grano-diorites. Muscovite and garnet are absent in zone II and horn-blende is absent from zone III. Aplitic granodiorites and granites of zone IV are distinctive because of their texture and abundance of muscovite and garnet. Pink pegmatites, aplites, and feldspathic pods are irregularly distributed throughout both types of grano-diorites.

TABLE 1. PETROGRAPHIC SUMMARY OF THE SPRUCE HEAD PLUTON, MAINE

	Zone I	Zone II	Zone III	Zone IV
Rock Type	Quartz gabbro to quartz diorite and tonalite.	Granodiorite to granite.	Granodiorite to granite.	Granodiorite to granite.
Texture	Medium to coarse, hypid-iomorphic.	Coarse, hypidiomorphic, prominent quartz granules.	Coarse, hypidiomorphic, some quartz granules. Ghost layers of mafic and felsic minerals. Subporphyritic.	Fine to medium, aplitic, myrmekitic. Highly jointed in places.
	Medium grained, massive, ophitic. Spotted appearance.	Massive, coarse, seriate to porphyritic. Prominent and rounded quartz.	Massive to foliated (N55°E, vertical?). Some quartz granules.	Fine grained, aplitic. Poi-kilitic K-feldspar.
Mafic Minerals	Ophitic hornblende in gab-bros. Hornblende>/=biotite. Pyroxene trace (relics, rem-nants).	Biotite>hornblende. Pyrox-ene trace (remnants).	Biotite>/=muscovite. Sub-hedral epidote. Hexagonal biotite.	Biotite>/=muscovite. Subhe-dral epidote.
Aluminous Minerals	Trace of secondary mus-covite.	Trace of secondary mus-covite.	Subhedral muscovite; poikilitic, subhedral, locally abundant garnet.	Subhedral muscovite, sub-hedral to rounded garnet.
Mafic Enclaves	Clots of hornblende, biotite, and subhedral epidote surrounded by plagioclase and K-feldspar (as much as 15 cm)	Elongated, sheared, and plastically deformed abun-dant quartz diorite; biotite streaks. Gabbro and diorite pillows (about 1 m diameter).	Biotite-rich, ellipsoidal (as much as 0.5 m).	Biotite-rich (and epidote), zoned enclaves as much as 1 m.
Aplites, Pegmatites	Plagioclase-rich pods, peg-matitic streaks; late-stage aplites.	Poikilitic, abundant tourma-line. Abundant garnet in numerous leucogranites and pegmatites; miarolitic aplites.	Pegmatitic dikes and pods. Abundant garnet (as much as 1 cm).	Pegmatitic dikes and pods. Abundant garnet (as much as 1 cm).
Secondary Minerals	Chlorite, epidote, sericite; tourmaline in leucogranites, aplites.	Chlorite, epidote, sericite; tourmaline, pyrite, molyb-denite, arsenopyrite?	Epidote, chlorite, sericite pyrite.	Epidote, chlorite, sericite, tourmaline.
Accessory Minerals	Titanite, apatite, zircon, pyrite, ilmenite/magnetite ~1.	Apatite, allanite, zircon, titan-ite, ilmenite/magnetite <1?	Titanite, apatite, zircon, ilmenite/magnetite <1.	Titanite, apatite, zircon, ilmenite/magnetite <1.
Remarks	Gabbros contain pods, streaks, and layers of dior-ites/granodiorites of Groups II, III. Cut by late-stage leucogranites resembling Group IV rocks. Contains country-rock screens.	Mixed crops of gabbro, dior-ite, and granodiorite. Cut by leucogranites of group IV. Cut by mylonitic veins. Local hydrothermal alteration con-taining disseminated quartz and sulfides. Highly fractured in places (15 to 20 cm apart).	Associated with shearing. Myrmekitic. Complex mixing near boundary with Group I.	Associated with shearing. Found as dikes in other rocks. Late, fine, dense, dia-base dikes.
Samples	38 (mafic enclave, 6, 7, 8, 13, 101, 104, 105, 108, 115.	102, 109, 116, 117, 118 (aplitic), 119, 120, 121, 122, 126, 127.	4, 5, 9, 12, 14, 15, 17, 18, 20, 21, 103, 110, 111, 112, 113, 114, 118, 123, 124, 125.	1, 2, 3, 10, 11, 16, 19, 106, 107.

TABLE 2. MODAL ANALYSES OF REPRESENTATIVE SAMPLES FROM THE SPRUCE HEAD PLUTON, MAINE

Sample	I THSH-105 Gabbro (wt%)	I TTSH-13 Diorite (wt%)	I TTSH-7 Tonalite (wt%)	I TTSH-8 Tonalite (wt%)	I THSH-108 Tonalite (wt%)	II THSH-102 Granodiorite (wt%)	II ROSH-119 Granodiorite (wt%)	II ROSH-120 Granodiorite (wt%)	II ROSH-121 Granodiorite (wt%)
Quartz	7.3	9.2	31.8	32.9	29.7	23.5	20.6	22.5	21.8
Plagioclase	50.6	50.1	56.2	60.7	58	45.9	50.2	52.2	48.6
Alkali Feldspar	tr.	tr.	tr.	tr.	tr.	15.9	18.4	13.8	14.3
Biotite	28.3	36.5	10.6	4.6	11.2	11.9	9.6	9.2	13.5
Hornblende	13.8	4.2	1.4	1.8	1.1	1.8	1.2	1.3	1.8
Muscovite	tr.	tr.	tr.	tr.	tr.	tr.	tr.	tr.	tr.
Pyroxene	tr.	tr.	tr.	tr.	tr.	tr.	tr.	tr.	0
Garnet	0	0	0	0	0	0	0	0	0
Titanite	<1	<1	<1	<1	<1	<1	<0.1	<0.1	<0.1
Apatite	<1	<1	<1	<1	<1	<1	<0.1	<0.1	<0.1
Zircon	<1	<1	<1	<1	<1	<1	<0.1	<0.1	<0.1
Allanite	tr.	tr.	tr.	tr.	tr.	tr.	tr.	tr.	tr.
Magnetite/ilmenite	<1	<1	<1	<1	<1	<1	<0.1	<0.1	<0.1
Epidote	<1	<1	<1	<1	<1	<1	<0.1	<0.1	<0.1
Tourmaline	tr.	tr.	tr.	tr.	tr.	tr.	tr.	tr.	tr.
Pyrite	tr.	tr.	tr.	tr.	tr.	tr.	tr.	tr.	tr.

Sample	II ROSH-122 Granite (wt%)	II HISH-126 Granite (wt%)	III THSH-4 Granodiorite (wt%)	III THSH-20 Granodiorite (wt%)	III TTSH-12 Granodiorite (wt%)	III TTSH-9 Granodiorite (wt%)	III TTSH-15 Granodiorite (wt%)	III THSH-14 Granodiorite (wt%)	III ROSH-123 Granite (wt%)
Quartz	23	25.3	24.7	27.1	23.8	29.2	30.9	32.8	34.5
Plagioclase	43.4	41.5	52.1	40.3	50.6	39.4	39.2	39.7	22.6
Alkali Feldspar	24	23.5	20.9	19.6	11.4	20.4	21.3	19.7	37.6
Biotite	8.6	7.6	2.3	13	14.2	11	8.6	6.8	5.3
Hornblende	1	2.1	0	0	0	0	0	0	0
Muscovite	tr.	tr.	tr.	tr.	tr.	tr.	tr.	1	tr.
Pyroxene	0	0	0	0	0	0	0	0	0
Garnet	0	0	tr.	tr.	tr.	tr.	tr.	tr.	tr.
Titanite	<0.1	<0.1	<0.1	<0.1	<0.1	<0.1	<0.1	<0.1	<0.1
Apatite	<0.1	<0.1	<0.1	<0.1	<0.1	<0.1	<0.1	<0.1	<0.1
Zircon	<0.1	<0.1	<0.1	<0.1	<0.1	<0.1	<0.1	<0.1	<0.1
Allanite	tr.	tr.	tr.	tr.	tr.	tr.	tr.	tr.	<1
Magnetite/ilmenite	<0.1	<0.1	<0.1	<0.1	<0.1	<0.1	<0.1	<0.1	<0.1
Epidote	<0.1	<0.1	<0.1	<0.1	<0.1	<0.1	<0.1	<0.1	<0.1
Tourmaline	tr.	tr.	tr.	tr.	tr.	tr.	tr.	tr.	tr.
Pyrite	tr.	tr.	0	0	0	0	0	0	0

Sample	IV TTSH-16 Granodiorite (wt%)	IV TTSH-10 Granodiorite (wt%)	IV THSH-2 Granodiorite (wt%)	IV THSH-3 Granodiorite (wt%)	IV THSH-5 Granodiorite (wt%)	IV THSH-1 Granodiorite (wt%)	IV THSH-11 Granite (wt%)
Quartz	33.5	28.7	20.1	24.1	21.9	26.8	33.7
Plagioclase	36.3	39	49.2	47.6	53.1	44.1	25.7
Alkali Feldspar	19.6	19.2	23.3	22.1	22.2	22.6	32.6
Biotite	10.5	10.1	4.3	6.2	2.8	6.4	6
Hornblende	0	0	0	0	0	0	0
Muscovite	tr.	3	3.1	tr.	tr.	tr.	2
Pyroxene	0	0	0	0	0	0	0
Garnet	tr.	tr.	tr.	tr.	tr.	tr.	tr.
Titanite	<0.1	<0.1	<0.1	<0.1	<0.1	<0.1	<0.1
Apatite	<0.1	<0.1	<0.1	<0.1	<0.1	<0.1	<0.1
Zircon	<0.1	<0.1	<0.1	<0.1	<0.1	<0.1	<0.1
Allanite	<1	<1	<1	<0.1	<0.1	<0.1	<0.1
Magnetite/ilmenite	<0.1	<0.1	<0.1	<0.1	<0.1	<0.1	<0.1
Epidote	<0.1	<0.1	<0.1	<0.1	<0.1	<0.1	<0.1
Tourmaline	<0.1	<0.1	<0.1	<0.1	<0.1	<0.1	<0.1
Pyrite	0	0	0	0	0	0	0

Field relations suggest that zone IV granodiorites and granites found in the interior of the intrusion are the youngest felsic rocks—they are found as dikes cutting zones I and II. Here, contacts between the main mass of zone IV and the rest of the intrusion are not well exposed. Mafic enclaves are rare in zone IV granodiorites and aplitic granites, in contrast to the granodiorites of zone II, where such enclaves are numerous. Rapakivi texture occurs locally. Zone III granodiorites and granites are locally foliated and sheared in thin section; a few prominent quartz granules typical of zone II are also found in these granites.

Country rocks adjacent to the pluton are at lower than sillimanite grade except in nearby rocks to the west and southwest, where migmatized schist and small stocks of diorite and granodiorite are abundant and the grade is much higher (Guidotti, 1979). Country rocks intruded by the pluton include the Cambrian(?) to Ordovician(?) Owls Head unit (OH, Fig. 2; thick-bedded quartzites, schists, and granulites), the Ordovician Benner Hill unit (B, Fig. 2; thinly interbedded quartz-mica schist and quartzite), which contains fossils of Caradocian age (as old as 443 Ma; Harland et al., 1989), and both a biotite quartzite and schist unit (B, Fig. 2) and an informally named quartz-rib schist unit (QR, Fig. 2) of unknown ages (Ordovician?); the two latter units have been described as progressively flooded by granitic magma (bedding is disrupted and finally obliterated by increasing amounts of granitic magma) where the metamorphic grade is higher (Guidotti, 1979). Middle Silurian $^{40}Ar/^{39}Ar$ cooling ages were obtained on hornblende from rocks that host the Spruce Head pluton (West et al., 1992).

Field relations summarized above indicate that although contacts between the mafic and felsic rocks are not well exposed, the majority of field observations suggest that the gabbros, diorites, and tonalites of zone I are somewhat older than granodiorites from zones II and III. Moreover, rocks from zone I intruded country rocks that contain Caradocian fossils in their basal units (C. V. Guidotti, 1994, personal commun.), thus constraining the age of zone I to be younger than the upper boundary of the Caradocian at 443 Ma (Harland et al., 1989). U-Pb determinations on zircon from a granodiorite of zone II were discordant and indicated a $^{207}Pb/^{206}Pb$ age of 440 ± 5 Ma (R. E. Zartman, 1991, written commun., 1991). An Ar plateau age of 426.6 ± 0.4 Ma was obtained for hornblende from a similar granodiorite from zone II, and an Ar plateau age of 369.4 ± 3.3 Ma on muscovite was obtained for a sample from zone IV (D. West, 1994, written commun.). The discrepancy in the ages measured by the U-Pb and Ar systems often indicates the presence of an older inherited component in the zircon, that the Ar system has been reset, or both. The zircon age of 440 Ma for granodiorites of zone II closely resembles the Rb-Sr whole-rock age of 436 Ma for a similar sequence of rocks in the nearby South Penobscot intrusive suite (Stewart et al., 1988). Our ongoing efforts, however, using the whole-rock Rb-Sr and Sm-Nd techniques, yield preliminary ages of from 406–425 Ma, and these results together with alternate interpretations of the zircon age (R. E. Zartman, 1991, written commun.) suggest that an age of about 440 Ma

may be too old and 369 Ma too young. In the following discussion we assume that the age of crystallization of the entire pluton is about 415 ± 15 Ma.

That the pods of gabbros and diorites in the granodiorites were plastically deformed and partially dismembered in the host granodiorites is evidence, however, that the mafic rocks were not much older than the felsic rocks of zone II. Thus, significant field evidence exists for contemporaneity between zones I, II, and III. Some of the nearby small stocks of gabbros and diorites have been described as folded and metamorphosed prior to intrusion of a binary granite (Osberg and Guidotti, 1974). It is unclear, however, how these gabbros are related to gabbros and diorites of zone I within the bulk of the Spruce Head pluton that are only mildly altered and that behaved plastically relative to the granodioritic rocks. Contacts between rocks in zone II and IV (zone IV is probably equivalent to the binary granites of Osberg and Guidotti, 1974) were not observed, but dikes resembling granites from zone IV cut granodiorites from zone II as well as gabbros and diorites from zone I.

In the main part of the pluton, metasedimentary inclusions are found near the borders; in addition, screens of the Benner Hill unit occur within the mafic rocks. The majority of these inclusions lack mineral banding, prominent color changes, or wide grain-size variations. Moreover, the inclusions have parallel attitudes regardless of abundance and the extent of dispersion, thus implying that the aggregate of crystalline magmas and inclusions flowed (or were deformed) together. In contrast, metamorphic rocks from west and southwest of the intrusion contain migmatites and small stocks of granite (Guidotti, 1979), and show evidence for intermixing of mafic and felsic magmas.

GEOCHEMISTRY

Major and minor elements

Representative samples from throughout the Spruce Head pluton were analyzed for major and trace elements (Table 3). The samples are subdivided into numbered groups, each corresponding to the petrographic zone from which the samples were taken. The Spruce Head pluton contains a wide compositional spectrum of predominantly calc-alkaline granodiorites and granites (groups II, III, and IV), and predominantly calc-alkaline quartz gabbros, diorites, and tonalites (group I). Mafic rocks in group I have values of SiO_2 ranging from ~47–56 wt%, and granodiorites and granites from groups II, III, and IV have SiO_2 from ~64–77% (Table 3, Fig. 4). Variation diagrams illustrate inverse correlations with abundances of several oxides (Fe_2O_3, MgO, CaO, TiO_2, and MnO) with increasing SiO_2 (Fig. 4 shows examples; Fig. 5 shows chondrite-normalized diagrams). Notable differences in overall composition and trends of major and many trace elements within the petrographic groups are evident. For example, trends in the abundances of major and minor elements for granodorites from group II are subtly offset relative to group IV, so that at a given value of silica the groups can be distinguished (e.g., higher Fe_2O_3,

TABLE 3. MAJOR AND TRACE ELEMENT COMPOSITIONS OF REPRESENTATIVE SAMPLES FROM THE SPRUCE HEAD PLUTON AND COPELAND SCHIST, MAINE (Page 1)

Sample	I THSH-105 Gabbro	I TTSH-13 Diorite	I TTSH-7 Diorite	I TTSH-8 Tonalite	I THSH-108 Tonalite	II THSH-102 Granodiorite	II ROSH-119 Granodiorite	II ROSH-120 Granodiorite	II ROSH-121 Granodiorite	II ROSH-122 Granite
(wt%)										
SiO_2	46.90	48.70	53.70	55.40	56.10	65.00	65.60	71.90	67.80	70.70
Al_2O_3	16.50	18.10	15.10	18.10	17.70	16.80	15.90	14.10	15.50	14.70
Fe_2O_3	15.10	7.81	10.10	8.46	8.84	4.46	5.23	2.32	3.81	2.76
MgO	5.00	9.60	4.86	2.81	2.95	1.27	1.39	0.57	0.99	0.71
CaO	10.50	10.60	7.93	7.87	6.89	3.94	4.07	2.09	3.33	2.30
Na_2O	2.24	2.09	2.45	2.83	3.14	3.75	3.60	3.01	3.46	3.34
K_2O	0.56	0.59	2.16	1.62	1.64	2.84	2.35	4.35	3.26	3.99
TiO_2	2.13	0.58	1.67	1.03	1.28	0.56	0.66	0.25	0.45	0.32
P_2O_5	0.24	0.06	0.31	0.15	0.29	0.16	0.18	0.06	0.12	0.10
MnO	0.25	0.12	0.19	0.13	0.17	0.08	0.09	0.04	0.07	0.06
CO_2	0.12	0.02	0.47	0.08	0.02	0.01	0.02	0.01	0.02	0.01
S	0.26	0.05	0.10	0.12	0.04	0.07	0.06	0.04	0.05	0.03
Cl	0.03	0.01	0.03	0.02	0.02	0.01	0.02	0.02	0.01	0.01
F	0.03	0.01	0.04	0.02	0.05	0.05	0.07	0.04	0.06	0.06
H_2O^+	1.00	2.49	1.46	1.47	1.20	0.72	0.75	0.66	0.85	0.78
H_2O^-	0.10	0.19	0.21	0.17	0.10	0.16	0.13	0.16	0.15	0.11
Subtotal	100.96	101.02	100.78	100.28	100.43	99.88	100.12	99.62	99.93	99.98
Less O	0.02	0.01	0.02	0.01	0.03	0.02	0.03	0.02	0.03	0.03
Total	100.94	101.01	100.76	100.27	100.40	99.86	100.09	99.60	99.90	99.95
Na_2O-K_2O	2.80	2.68	4.61	4.45	4.78	6.59	5.95	7.36	6.72	7.33
A/CNK mol	0.71	0.78	0.73	0.87	0.91	1.02	1.00	1.05	1.02	1.05
K_2O/Na_2O mol	0.16	0.19	0.58	0.38	0.34	0.50	0.43	0.95	0.62	0.79
(ppm)										
Large cations										
Rb	28	27	86	56	75	94	93	122	105	138
Cs	0.87	2.16	2.51	2.41	5.57	4.63	3.7	2.97	3.02	4.83
Sr	379	150	268	355	340	288	274	280	232	188
Ba	194	76	336	348	406	1,040	591	539	853	647
Pb	5.4	10	16	10	8.2	11	11	15	14	16
Rb/Sr	0.07	0.18	0.32	0.16	0.22	0.33	0.34	0.68	0.45	0.73
Rb/Cs	32.2	12.5	34.3	23.2	13.5	20.3	25.1	41.1	34.8	28.6
Rare earth elements and Y										
La	13.5	5.16	26.8	24.6	23	30.1	49.6	12.7	38.9	26.6
Ce	29.5	10.5	59.2	48.8	47.2	79	107	41.6	82.2	59.6
Nd	17.8	<19	36	20.5	25.1	25.1	39.6	14.1	32.9	25.5
Sm	4.56	2.16	8.88	5.85	5.7	5.67	8.45	2.86	6.9	5.86
Eu	1.38	0.7	1.88	1.37	1.59	1.55	1.72	1.05	1.48	1.23
Tb	0.74	0.43	1.21	0.8	0.87	0.76	1.11	0.38	0.85	0.82
Yb	2.23	1.5	3.91	2.97	2.75	1.91	2.85	1.26	2.37	2.85
Lu	0.317	0.215	0.528	0.407	0.418	0.296	0.44	0.163	0.359	0.418
Y	27	18	49	27	33	29	32	17	29	36
Eu/Eu*	0.93	0.93	0.70	0.77	0.88	0.88	0.67	1.16	0.74	0.69
Ce/Yb	13.2	7.0	15.1	16.4	17.2	41.4	37.5	33.0	34.7	20.9
Total REE	101.8	51.7	201.5	157.1	156.6	225.3	320.6	117.0	250.5	185.3

P_2O_5, and TiO_2, among others, for group IV; higher CaO for group II) (Fig. 3 shows examples). Granodiorites from group III, in contrast, show more scatter, but follow the same general trends for most elements. Only K_2O, among the major oxides, increases with increasing silica (Fig. 4).

Alkali oxide contents change systematically in the Spruce Head pluton, increasing with silica—the lowest values of $Na_2O +$

K_2O are in the mafic rocks (~2.7–4.8%) and the highest are in the silicic rocks (~5.4–8.6%) (Fig. 6). Values of K_2O/Na_2O (mol) have unique ranges and broadly increase from the sodic mafic rocks of group I (~0.16–0.58), to the sodic granodiorites from group II (~0.43–0.95), and to the potassic granodiorites and granites from group IV (~1.1–1.5). The total alkali contents of the majority of granodiorites and granites from group III are similar

TABLE 3. MAJOR AND TRACE ELEMENT COMPOSITIONS OF REPRESENTATIVE SAMPLES FROM THE SPRUCE HEAD PLUTON AND COPELAND SCHIST, MAINE (Page 2)

Sample	I THSH-105 Gabbro	I TTSH-13 Diorite	I TTSH-7 Diorite	I TTSH-8 Tonalite	I THSH-108 Tonalite	II THSH-102 Granodiorite	II ROSH-119 Granodiorite	II ROSH-120 Granodiorite	II ROSH-121 Granodiorite	II ROSH-122 Granite
High valence cations										
Zr	82	58	152	128	151	207	253	117	188	153
Hf	1.8	1.5	3.7	3.8	4.1	5.8	7.6	3.4	5.9	5.2
Nb	14	1.8	14	8.4	13	11	13	11	10	13
Ta	0.48	0.17	0.94	0.56	0.71	0.47	0.86	0.45	0.70	1.01
Th	2.14	1.38	4.41	6.36	2.65	6.65	13.5	5.18	10.17	10.14
U	0.41	0.5	1.22	1.81	1.27	0.89	2.66	1.22	1.87	2.23
Zr/Hf	44.6	37.9	41.5	33.6	36.7	35.6	33.4	34.1	32.1	29.5
Nb/Ta	29.2	10.9	14.9	15.0	18.3	23.2	15.1	24.2		12.9
Th/U	5.2		3.6	3.5	2.1	7.5	5.1	4.3	5.4	4.6
Ferromagnesian elements										
Sc	41.9	22.8	29.5	23.9	23.6	11.12	14.52	5.87	9.69	7.03
Cr	8.1	278	90	19.5	8.7	13	16	12	13	15
Co	38.8	44.8	29.1	21.9	18.3	6.99	8.45	2.8	5.7	3.9
Ni	6.6	220	37	13	6	5.9	7.2	7	6.7	5.3
Cu	11	65	28	4	6	2	6	2	3	5
Zn	135	58	99	78	101	61.5	66	35.9	51	40.9
Li	18	22	27	20	96	54	39	31	37	55
Be	1.2	0.5	1.5	1.1	1.1	1.5	1.7	1.1	1.6	1.8
B	3.2	3	4	3	13	9.9	8.4	6.7	8.9	11
Sn	<1	1.2	1.9	1.3	2.3	1.6	3	1.2	1.9	2.7
W	<1	<1	<1	<1	<1	<1	<1	<1	<1	<1
Mo	<1	<1	<1	<1	<1	<1	<1	<1	<1	<1
Sb	<0.4	<0.4	<0.4	0.19	<0.09	0.15	0.23	0.21	0.24	0.18
K/Rb	1.7	1.8	2.1	2.4	1.8	2.5	2.1	3.0	2.6	2.4
Rb/Zr	0.3	0.5	0.6	0.4	0.5	0.5	0.4	1.0	0.6	0.9
Ba/Ta	404.2	460.6	357.5	621.4	571.8	2,194.1	687.2	1,187.2	1,218.6	640.6
Nb/U	34.2	3.6	11.5	4.6	10.2	12.4	4.9	9.0	5.4	5.8
La/Th	6.3	3.7	6.1	3.9	8.7	4.5	3.7	2.5	3.8	2.6
Hf/Th	0.9	1.1	0.8	0.6	1.6	0.9	0.6	0.7	0.6	0.5
Hf/Ta	3.8	9.3	3.9	6.8	5.8	12.3	8.8	7.6	8.4	5.1
Th/Ta	4.5	8.4	4.7	11.4	3.7	14.0	15.7	11.4	14.5	10.0
Th/Sm	0.5	0.6	0.5	1.1	0.5	1.2	1.6	1.8	1.5	1.7
Ca/Pb	5.5	1.1	3.7	4.9	5.8	7.2	9.7	2.8	5.9	3.7

to those of group II; a few, however, are as potassic as the aplitic granites from group IV.

Another important feature is that trends for the mafic and silicic rocks do not coincide. Plots of total alkalis (Na$_2$O + K$_2$O) relative to SiO$_2$ (Fig. 6) and AFM (Na$_2$O + K$_2$O-Fe$_2$O$_3$-MgO) (plot not shown) again emphasize the subalkaline (calc-alkalic) nature of the granodiorites and granites. A few silicic samples from groups III and IV have high contents of Na$_2$O + K$_2$O (>8 wt% at SiO$_2$ >72 wt%) and show alkalic tendencies on a Na$_2$O + K$_2$O versus SiO$_2$ plot. The majority of the samples in the pluton, however, are subalkaline. The AFM plot shows that granodiorites from group II are more magnesian than granites from group IV (Table 2), and that the mafic rocks from group I straddle the boundary between the calc-alkaline and tholeiitic series. Again, a compositional gap separates the mafic from the silicic rocks.

Relatively low values of the alumina saturation index (molar Al$_2$O$_3$/CaO + Na$_2$O + K$_2$O) or A/CNK are characteristic of the pluton as a whole. For example, A/CNK values in the mafic rocks of group I increase with silica (~0.7–0.9, metaluminous) and are slightly lower than granodiorites from group II (~1.0– 1.07, subaluminous), and granodiorites and granites from groups III and IV (A/CNK = ~1.01–1.16, subaluminous-peraluminous). Moreover, minor and trace element variations discussed below show that the silicic rocks from groups II, III, and IV have separate trends, suggesting different sources and/or processes of evolution. We contend that the absence of a continuum of rock compositions between all the groups indicates that the pluton formed from several magmas, and that these were not related to one another by a simple process such as in situ crystal fractionation, mixing, or assimilation-fractional crystallization, all of which would require coherent elemental trends.

**TABLE 3. MAJOR AND TRACE ELEMENT COMPOSITIONS OF REPRESENTATIVE SAMPLES FROM
THE SPRUCE HEAD PLUTON AND COPELAND SCHIST, MAINE** (Page 3)

Sample	II HISH-126 Granite	III THSH-4 Granodiorite	III THSH-20 Granodiorite	III TTSH-12 Granodiorite	III TTSH-9 Granodiorite	III TTSH-15 Granodiorite	III THSH-14 Granodiorite	III ROSH-123 Granite	IV TTSH-16 Granodiorite	IV TTSH-10 Granodiorite	IV THSH-2 Granodiorite
(wt%)											
SiO_2	72.10	64.00	66.40	68.00	68.50	70.20	72.80	74.00	68.10	68.30	71.10
Al_2O_3	14.30	16.80	16.30	15.80	15.30	14.40	14.00	13.60	14.20	14.30	13.80
Fe_2O_3	2.57	5.24	4.54	3.44	3.74	3.10	1.68	1.54	5.16	5.04	2.97
MgO	0.66	1.50	1.32	0.88	0.99	0.88	0.37	0.35	0.95	0.91	0.54
CaO	2.19	4.43	4.41	3.00	3.23	2.35	1.03	1.28	2.06	1.97	1.62
Na_2O	3.29	3.73	3.65	3.68	3.20	3.09	2.90	3.29	2.22	2.38	2.65
K_2O	3.70	2.19	1.80	3.47	3.41	4.21	5.34	4.64	4.62	4.68	5.16
TiO_2	0.32	0.69	0.59	0.39	0.45	0.39	0.19	0.15	0.65	0.62	0.38
P_2O_5	0.09	0.19	0.16	0.12	0.12	0.14	0.16	0.06	0.30	0.31	0.17
MnO	0.06	0.09	0.07	0.08	0.07	0.07	0.05	0.08	0.14	0.14	0.06
CO_2	0.02	0.01	0.07	0.03	0.02	0.08	0.07	0.01	0.05	0.07	0.23
S	0.04	0.05	0.05	0.05	0.05	0.05	0.05	0.06	0.05	0.05	0.05
Cl	0.01	0.02	0.02	0.01	0.01	0.01	0.01	0.02	0.01	0.01	0.01
F	0.05	0.04	0.03	0.03	0.03	0.02	0.05	0.07	0.07	0.05	0.05
H_2O^+	0.57	0.86	0.82	0.77	0.70	0.73	0.73	0.48	1.15	1.02	0.76
H_2O^-	0.18	0.19	0.20	0.12	0.16	0.10	0.13	0.13	0.19	0.11	0.14
Subtotal	100.15	100.03	100.43	99.87	99.98	99.82	99.56	99.76	99.92	99.96	99.69
Less O	0.02	0.02	0.02	0.01	0.01	0.01	0.02	0.03	0.03	0.02	0.02
Total	100.13	100.01	100.41	99.86	99.97	99.81	99.54	99.73	99.89	99.94	99.67
Na_2O+K_2O	6.99	5.92	5.45	7.15	6.61	7.30	8.24	7.93	6.84	7.06	7.81
A/CNK mol	1.07	1.01	1.02	1.04	1.03	1.04	1.13	1.07	1.15	1.14	1.07
K_2O/Na_2O mol	0.74	0.39	0.32	0.62	0.70	0.90	1.21	0.93	1.37	1.29	1.28
(ppm)											
Large cations											
Rb	131	92	79	128	115	161	260	192	173	196	211
Cs	4.31	3.47	2.91	6.57	3.65	6.61	14.2	7.87	5.77	8.14	8.28
Sr	169	307	359	190	219	177	55	90	106	98	87
Ba	647	765	632	399	824	774	346	343	669	514	544
Pb	16	11	10	19	14	20	28	23	29	34	39
Rb/Sr	0.78	0.30	0.22	0.67	0.53	0.91	4.73	2.13	1.63	2.00	2.43
Rb/Cs	30.4	26.5	27.2	19.5	31.5	24.4	18.3	24.4	30.0	25.5	21.9
Rare earth elements and Y											
La	26.7	48.1	20.4	37.3	51.1	40.3	24.8	18.5	56	41.5	38.7
Ce	56.9	89	33.6	61	96.8	75.5	51.9	39.8	113	85	82.2
Nd	22	33	16.7	34.9	38	27.2	21.9	16.3	46	36	37
Sm	5.09	7.7	2.79	7.19	8.13	6.81	5.74	5.25	12.3	9.59	8.95
Eu	1.07	1.77	1.56	1.37	1.46	1.15	0.75	0.65	1.94	1.64	1.23
Tb	0.7	0.88	0.33	0.84	0.85	0.8	0.74	1.04	1.44	1.34	1.18
Yb	2.42	2.34	1.1	1.76	2.08	2.14	2.15	4.29	4.03	3.94	3.49
Lu	0.343	0.337	0.177	0.258	0.298	0.374	0.304	0.568	0.556	0.552	0.499
Y	30	28	16	27	20	30	22	47	41	51	46
Eu/Eu*	0.69	0.81	2.00	0.68	0.66	0.60	0.44	0.35	0.56	0.56	0.46
Ce/Yb	23.5	38.0	30.6	34.7	46.5	31.3	24.1	9.3	28.0	21.6	23.6
Total REE	174.5	274.5	111.4	207.4	297.6	232.5	162.3	130.5	352.3	268.5	258.9

Trace elements

Normalized diagrams (Fig. 5) illustrating a range of compatible-incompatible trace elements (elements normalized to chondritic abundances except for Rb, K, and P; Thompson, 1982) show troughs at Ba, Nb, Sr, and P, and smaller troughs for Th and Ta for the pluton as a whole. We thus accept that it is possible that

a mechanism such as fractional crystallization operated within individual groups because troughs in the normalized diagrams and changes in the major element compositions discussed above are consistent with the effects of fractionation (e.g., plagioclase to deplete Sr, and titanomagnetite, titanite, and apatite to deplete Ti, Nb, and P). However, similar depletions could well have formed if the appropriate minerals with high crystal/liquid distribution coef-

TABLE 3. MAJOR AND TRACE ELEMENT COMPOSITIONS OF REPRESENTATIVE SAMPLES FROM THE SPRUCE HEAD PLUTON AND COPELAND SCHIST, MAINE (Page 4)

Sample	II HISH-126 Granite	III THSH-4 Granodiorite	III THSH-20 Granodiorite	III TTSH-12 Granodiorite	III TTSH-9 Granodiorite	III TTSH-15 Granodiorite	III THSH-14 Granodiorite	III ROSH-123 Granite	IV TTSH-16 Granodiorite	IV TTSH-10 Granodiorite	IV THSH-2 Granodiorite
High valence cations											
Zr	146	254	224	164	177	173	119	97	330	243	208
Hf	4.5	7.0	6.0	5.4	6.1	5.4	3.8	3.3	9.2	7.2	5.9
Nb	14	10	6.8	12	9.7	11	14	14	19	21	15
Ta	0.87	0.53	0.38	0.96	0.69	1.02	2.16	1.33	1.50	1.72	1.64
Th	13.5	7.63	3.05	10.06	11.9	12.62	11.32	11	16.3	12.2	14.95
U	2.18	1.36	0.98	1.75	1.54	2.98	5.62	3.19	2.71	2.85	4.14
Zr/Hf	32.4	36.3	37.3	30.4	29.2	32.3	31.2	29.3	35.9	33.6	35.1
Nb/Ta	16.1	18.9	17.7	12.5	14.1	10.8	6.5	10.5	12.7	12.2	9.2
Th/U	6.2	5.6	3.1	5.8	7.7	4.2	2.0	3.5	6.0	4.3	3.6
Ferromagnesian elements											
Sc	6.24	14.36	5.34	9.76	11.56	7.93	4.33	5.64	10.54	11	7.35
Cr	8.9	12	15.1	11.3	14.6	12	12.4	14	17.4	18.8	13.1
Co	3.57	8.58	6.91	4.74	5.75	4.64	2.03	1.81	6.93	7.05	3.55
Ni	5.4	9	6	8	9	6	8	3.6	11	11	7
Cu	4	2	2	2	2	2	3	4	7	2	2
Zn	37.1	71	59.9	50	56	45.6	40.8	31.1	70.5	68	48.6
Li	60	42	35	35	29	39	84	97	40	57	50
Be	1.7	1.8	1.5	2.3	1.8	1.8	2.4	2	1.9	2.7	2.2
B	7.3	2	2	3	2	2	53	8.7	3	4	2
Sn	2.4	3.6	1.6	2.1	0.7	2.5	7.6	4.6	4.3	5.4	5.9
W	<1	<1	<1	<1	<1	<1	<1	<1	<1	<1	<1
Mo	2.3	<1	<1	<1	<1	<1	1.5	<1	1.5	1.6	1.8
Sb	0.16	<0.3	0.16	0.16	<0.4	0.22	0.18	<0.3	<0.3	0.17	0.1
K/Rb	2.4	2.0	1.9	2.3	2.5	2.2	1.7	2.0	2.2	2.0	2.0
Rb/Zr	0.9	0.4	0.4	0.8	0.7	0.9	2.2	2.0	0.5	0.8	1.0
Ba/Ta	743.7	1,443.4	1,645.8	415.6	1,194.2	761.1	160.2	257.9	446.0	298.8	331.7
Nb/U	6.4	7.4	6.9	6.9	6.3	3.7	2.5	4.4	7.0	7.4	3.6
La/Th	2.0	6.3	6.7	3.7	4.3	3.2	2.2	1.7	3.4	3.4	2.6
Hf/Th	0.3	0.9	2.0	0.5	0.5	0.4	0.3	0.3	0.6	0.6	0.4
Hf/Ta	5.2	13.2	15.6	5.6	8.8	5.3	1.8	2.5	6.1	4.2	3.6
Th/Ta	15.5	14.4	7.9	10.5	17.3	12.4	5.2	8.3	10.9	7.1	9.1
Th/Sm	2.7	1.0	1.1	1.4	1.5	1.9	2.0	2.1	1.3	1.3	1.7
Ce/Pb	3.6	8.1	3.4	3.2	6.9	3.8	1.9	1.7	3.9	2.5	2.1

ficients remained as residues after partial melting of the source rocks, or if the rocks represent accumulations of crystals rather than liquids. Moreover, groups II, III, and IV show unique features in these normalized plots (Fig. 5). The most homogeneous patterns and deepest troughs for Ti, for example, are in the most silicic granodiorites and granites from group III and in the granodiorites and granites from group IV. The most heterogeneous patterns are in the quartz gabbros, diorites, and tonalites of group I. The presence of significant troughs at Nb and Ta eliminates granite sources associated with within-plate granitic rocks, as exemplified by intracontinental ring complexes, or in granitic rocks generated in areas with attenuated crust, or granitic rocks that are part of igneous complexes in oceanic island environments, all of which commonly are enriched in Nb and Ta (e.g., Oslo rift, Mull and Ascension islands; Pearce et al., 1984).

Abundances of Sr (~380–30 ppm) and Ba (~1100–100 ppm) systematically decrease with increasing SiO_2 (Fig. 4). Offsets in the Sr trends for groups I, II, and IV are also evident and gaps separate granodiorites from group II (Sr ~288–169 ppm) from those in group IV (~106–54 ppm) (Fig. 7, A–E); quartz gabbros and diorites have higher abundances (~379–259 ppm; except for sample TTSH-13 at 150 ppm) than the silicic rocks (Table 3). Similar gaps are evident for Rb (Fig. 4) and Pb, which increase with silica, and Cs and Ba, which decrease with silica (Table 3). The granodiorites have up to 379 ppm Sr and 1040 ppm Ba (Fig. 7B), a range of values that distinguishes the Spruce Head pluton from granodiorites of northern Maine, where higher abundances are prevalent (Sr up to 800 ppm and Ba up to 1300 ppm; Ayuso, 1989; Ayuso and Loferski, 1992). Lower abundances of Sr and Ba in the Spruce Head pluton resemble those in granitic rocks from the St. Croix and Ellsworth-Mascarene terranes (Sr up to ~400 ppm and Ba ~1000 ppm; Loiselle and Ayuso, 1980; Carl et al., 1984; Stewart et al., 1988; Hogan and Sinha, 1989; Wones and Ayuso, 1993). Variations in Rb and Cs contents do

TABLE 3. MAJOR AND TRACE ELEMENT COMPOSITIONS OF REPRESENTATIVE SAMPLES FROM THE SPRUCE HEAD PLUTON AND COPELAND SCHIST, MAINE (Page 5)

Sample	IV THSH-3 Granodiorite	IV THSH-5 Granodiorite	IV THSH-1 Granodiorite	IV THSH-11 Granite	Country Rock SR-8-84 Copeland Schist	Sample	IV THSH-3 Granodiorite	IV THSH-5 Granodiorite	IV THSH-1 Granodiorite	IV THSH-11 Granite	Country Rock SR-8-84 Copeland Schist
(wt%)						High valence cations					
SiO_2	71.10	71.50	71.50	72.60	76.10	Zr	198	228	191	173	371
Al_2O_3	13.90	13.70	14.00	13.70	10.80	Hf	6.2	6.6	5.7	5.2	9.9
Fe_2O_3	3.01	2.84	2.90	2.33	5.01	Nb	15	14	14	14	20
MgO	0.50	0.64	0.49	0.41	1.11	Ta	1.86	1.05	2.25	1.94	1.15
CaO	1.73	1.14	1.63	1.24	0.56	Th	15.4	19.9	13.03	14.25	11.39
Na_2O	2.89	2.46	2.95	2.84	0.51	U	5.91	2.2	4.14	5.24	2.59
K_2O	4.83	5.70	4.82	5.11	2.74	Zr/Hf	32.0	34.7	33.5	33.5	37.6
TiO_2	0.36	0.44	0.35	0.27	0.93	Nb/Ta	8.1	13.3	6.2	7.2	17.4
P_2O_5	0.16	0.21	0.16	0.15	0.09	Th/U	2.6	9.1	3.2	2.7	4.4
MnO	0.07	0.03	0.06	0.05	0.12	Ferromagnesian elements					
CO_2	0.13	0.02	0.08	0.08	0.01	Sc	7.75	6.31	7.34	6.1	10.45
S	0.05	0.05	0.05	0.05	0.12	Cr	8	13.2	8	9.5	51.3
Cl	0.01	0.01	0.01	0.01	0.01	Co	3.14	3.95	3.03	2.39	12.01
F	0.06	0.03	0.06	0.04	0.09	Ni	4	7	4	7	31
H_2O^+	0.74	0.82	0.72	0.68	1.80	Cu	2	2	2	2	<2
H_2O^-	0.18	0.20	0.18	0.10	0.58	Zn	50.4	47.9	48.8	43.4	62
Subtotal	99.72	99.79	99.96	99.66	100.58	Li	54	32	67	76	110
Less O	0.03	0.01	0.03	0.02	0.04	Be	3.2	1.3	3.2	2.9	1.7
Total	99.69	99.78	99.93	99.64	100.54	B	2	3	3	2	330
Na_2O+K_2O	7.72	8.16	7.77	7.95	3.25	Sn	6.2	2.4	6.5	7.3	3.1
A/CNK mol	1.06	1.12	1.07	1.10	2.24	W	<1	<1	<1	<1	1.5
K_2O/Na_2O mol	1.10	1.52	1.08	1.18	3.54	Mo	1.1	<1	<1	1	<1
(ppm)						Sb	0.17	0.11	0.17	<0.2	0.15
Large cations						K/Rb	2.0	2.4	1.8	1.8	1.9
Rb	203	201	221	241	118	Rb/Zr	1.0	0.9	1.2	1.4	0.3
Cs	9.29	5.13	9.83	13.3	23	Ba/Ta	251.1	587.6	216.0	256.7	594.8
Sr	86	91	95	81	85	Nb/U	2.5	6.4	3.4	2.7	7.7
Ba	467	617	486	498	684	La/Th	2.4	2.4	2.7	2.5	3.2
Pb	36	36	36	25	9	Hf/Th	0.4	0.3	0.4	0.4	0.9
Rb/Sr	2.36	2.21	2.33	2.98	1.39	Hf/Ta	3.3	6.3	2.5	2.7	8.6
Rb/Cs	39.2	22.5	26.1	20.9	5.1	Th/Ta	8.3	19.0	5.8	7.4	9.9
Rare earth elements and Y						Th/Sm	1.8	2.0	1.7	1.8	1.6
La	37	48	35.3	36.1	36.6	Ce/Pb	2.2	2.7	2.1	2.9	8.4
Ce	78.2	97.6	74.1	73.5	75.8						
Nd	37	37.2	33	33.9	32.6						
Sm	8.82	9.9	7.88	7.78	7.13						
Eu	1.28	1.23	1.21	1.07	1.26						
Tb	1.2	1.01	1.04	1.03	0.93						
Yb	3.81	2.1	3.38	2.97	3.1						
Lu	0.524	0.287	0.469	0.446	0.458						
Y	38	28	40	41	38						
Eu/Eu*	0.48	0.46	0.51	0.46	0.60						
Ce/Yb	20.5	46.5	21.9	24.8	24.5						
Total REE	249.8	297.0	233.9	233.3	157.9						

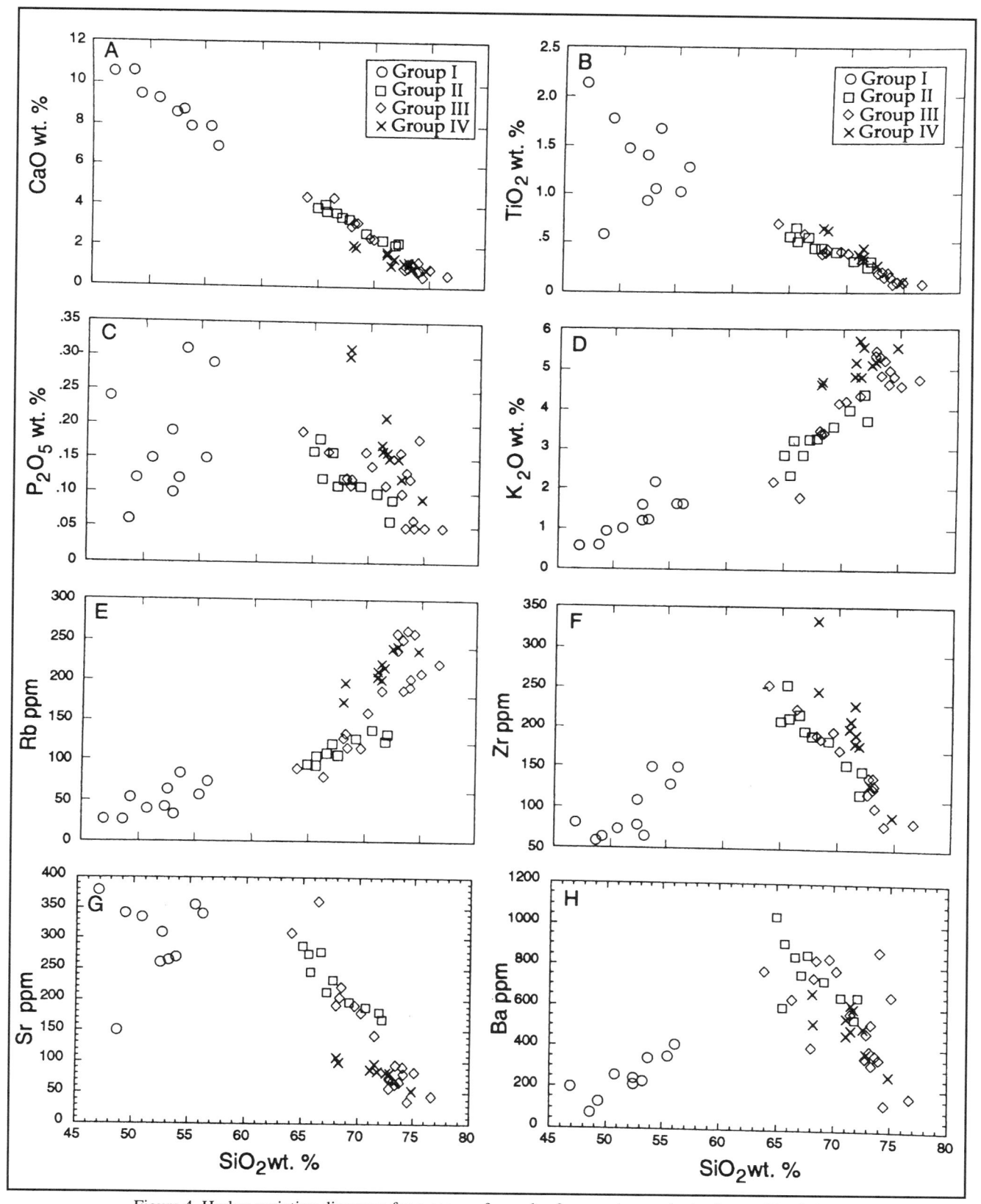

Figure 4. Harker variation diagrams for a group of samples from each zone in the Spruce Head pluton. A: CaO. B: TiO₂. C: P₂O₅. D: K₂O. E: Rb. F: Zr. G: Sr. H: Ba.

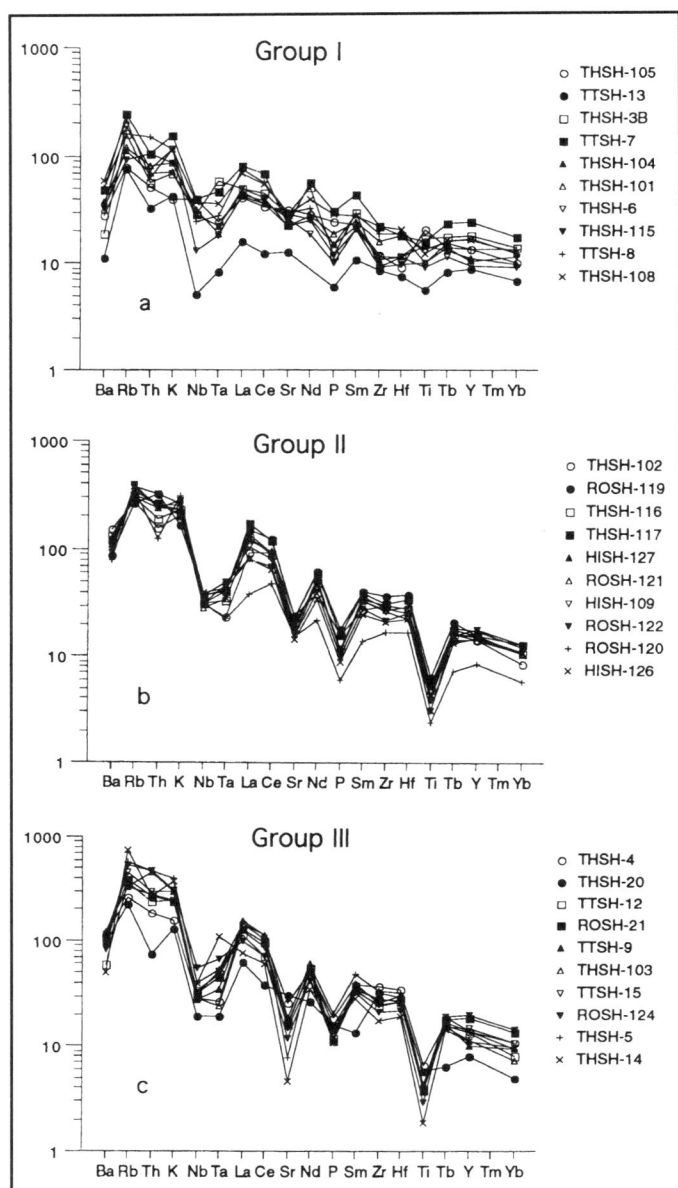
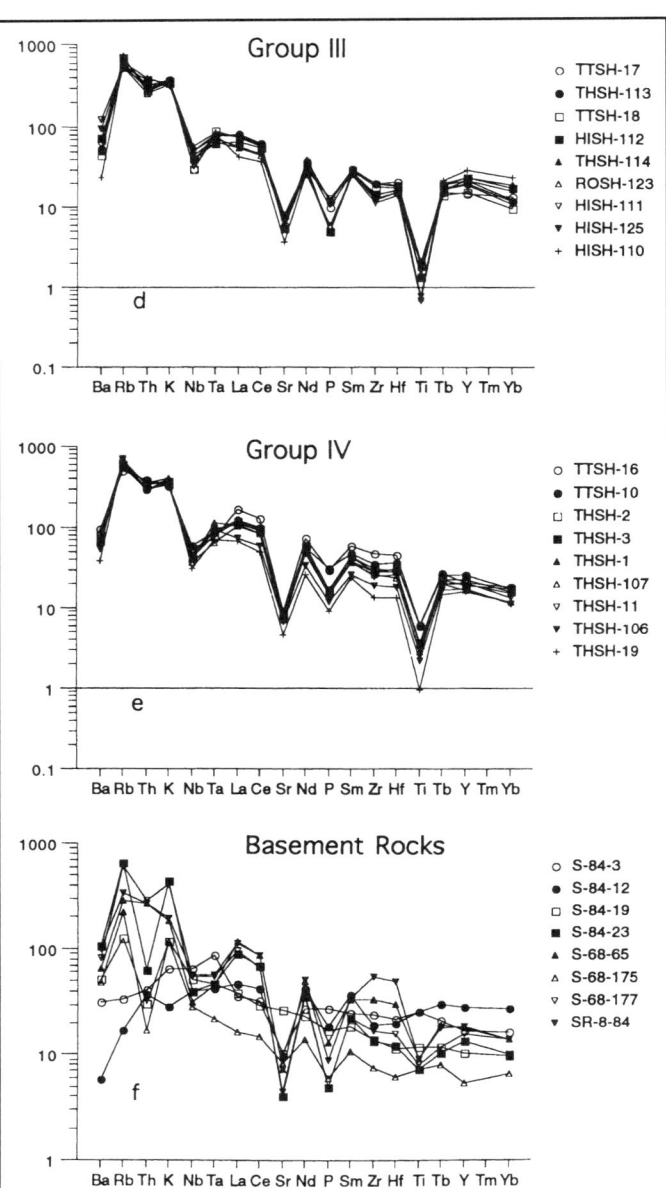

Figure 5. Chondrite-normalized element diagrams for the Spruce Head pluton. Chondritic values except for Rb, K, and P, which are normalized to primitive terrestrial mantle abundances (Thompson, 1982). a: Quartz gabbros, quartz diorites, tonalites, and mafic enclave (THSH-3B) from group I. b: Granodiorites and granites from group II. c and d: Granodiorites and granites from group III. e: Granodiorites and granites from group IV. f: Late Proterozoic basement rocks (amphibolites, schists) from Seven Hundred Acre Island in the Isleboro block in west Penobscot Bay, Maine; and migmatitic Copeland Formation from the Merrimack-Harpswell terrane on the mainland (sample SR-8–84). groups are arranged from top to bottom in order of increasing SiO₂.

not link the mafic and silicic rocks, and the highest concentrations in Rb (up to ~263 ppm) and Cs (up to ~14.2 ppm) are generally found among the most evolved granitic rocks in group III and IV (Table 3). Variations in Rb/Sr for mafic rocks in group I, granodiorites in group II (<1), and granitic rocks from group IV (1.6–4.4) (Table 3) result in separate fields and trends (Fig. 7C). groups I and II covary or have a parallel trend as a function of

increasing Rb/Sr and silica, but the aplitic granites from group IV are offset and do not intersect this trend. Group III overlaps the fields of groups II and IV.

Rare earth element (REE) contents in the Spruce Head pluton span a wide range. Silicic rocks generally have higher total REE contents (110–350 ppm) than the mafic rocks (~52–202 ppm; Table 2; Fig. 8). Total REE abundances generally increase in the

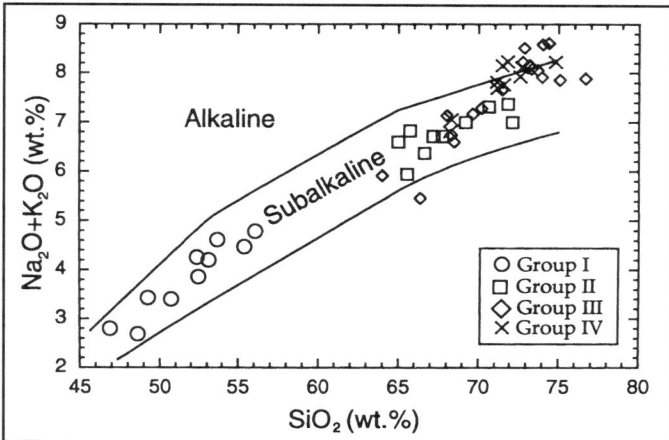

Figure 6. Total alkalis versus silica diagram showing the subdivision of alkaline and subalkaline (tholeiitic) (Kuno, 1966) for rocks from the Spruce Head pluton.

mafic rocks with increasing silica and predictably decrease in virtually every granitic group as silica increases. Moreover, granodiorites from group II (total REE ~321–117 ppm) and aplitic granodiorites and granites from group IV (352–138 ppm) have generally parallel trends, although they differ in that group IV samples tend to have deeper negative Eu anomalies. In the gabbros, diorites, and tonalites the REE chondrite-normalized patterns are somewhat flatter (Ce/Yb <18) than in the granitic rocks from groups II and IV (Ce/Yb = 17–46). Systematic REE variations in the gabbros and diorites from group I result in similar trends (Fig. 8) and a general increase in Ce/Yb with silica. Sample TTSH-13 (SiO_2 = 48.70%) probably represents one of the most primitive samples—it also has the flattest REE pattern (Ce/Yb = 7), the lowest abundances (all REE ~10–20× chondrites), and lacks a significant Eu anomaly (Eu/Eu* ~0.93). REE patterns in group II are generally coincident with each other, light-REE enriched, lack pronounced Eu anomalies (Eu/Eu* ~0.6–0.9, except for sample ROSH-120 at 1.2, which may be cumulate), and remain constant as a function of silica (Fig. 8). The most distinctive patterns are in the granodiorites and granites from group III and aplitic granites of group IV, which have large negative Eu anomalies (Eu/Eu* ~0.2–0.7) that deepen with increasing silica. One exception is sample TTSH-20 at Eu/Eu* = 2 (Fig. 8, Table 3) from the contact between group II and group I, which may represent a hybrid rock or one containing cumulate feldspar. In addition to the large negative Eu anomalies in these samples, a positive correlation of Eu/Eu* with Sr is consistent with both changes being the effects of plagioclase fractionation.

Variations in the abundances of Nb, Ta, Zr, and Hf (HFS, high field strength elements), and in Th and U, further illustrate the unique trends and ranges characteristic of the constituent groups within the pluton. Normalized plots show pronounced troughs for Nb and Ta (typical of calc-alkaline rocks) and spiked spidergram patterns (Fig. 5). In all these plots, we notice the remarkable homogeneity of the silicic rocks as a group, especially the grano-

diorites and granites of group IV, and particularly for Ba, Rb, Th, and K. In the silicic rocks, Nb (~7–21 ppm), Ta (~0.4–2.3 ppm), Th (~3–20 ppm), and U abundance ranges are wide and tend to increase with increasing SiO_2 (Table 3). More important, virtually all granodiorites of group II have Ta <1 ppm and Th <14 ppm, in contrast to the higher contents in group IV; Nb and Ta abundances do not show systematic trends in the granodiorites of group III. Zr contents in the pluton define compositional gaps between the mafic rocks and granodiorites. In Figure 4, one can see that granitic rocks from group IV are higher in Zr (Zr ~330–130 ppm; except for sample TTSH-19 at 91 ppm) at a given silica content than granodiorites from group II, and that the groups have subparallel decreasing trends with increasing silica. Zr and Hf generally behave as incompatible elements in the mafic rocks.

The ferromagnesian elements (Sc, Cr, Co, Ni, and Zn) decrease in abundance relative to SiO_2, consistent with compatible-element behavior during evolution of the pluton (Table 3). Zn abundances are especially notable, distinguishing between the granodiorites and granites of group IV, with higher abundances (27–72 ppm) than granodiorites from groups II and III (8–62 ppm) at a given value of SiO_2 (Table 3). In fact, plots comparing K_2O and Rb to Co and Sc (compatible) (Fig. 9) illustrate the major offsets and gaps distinguishing the mafic rocks from the bulk of the pluton, and among the granodiorites and granites. Plots of Co versus K_2O and Sc versus Rb (Fig. 9) also show that the trends diverge among the Groups. We interpret such diverging trends among the silicic rocks as proof that the pluton did not evolve by simple fractional crystallization of mafic rocks (a common parent)—instead, the trends may indicate that the granitic magmas had distinct origins or that the magmas fractionated differently due to contrasting mineral assemblages at distinct pressures, temperatures, and f_{O2}; these ideas are explored more completely in the following.

Base metal (Cu, Mo, Sn, and W) abundances in outcrop samples of the Spruce Head pluton are not enhanced relative to average values in granitic rocks (Nockolds, 1954), even though some of the samples have small amounts of sulfide minerals (Table 3). For example, most samples contain low abundances of Cu (up to 65 pm) Mo (up to 4.4 ppm), Sn (up to 7.9 ppm), and W (up to 2 ppm). The pluton, moreover, is not enriched in Li, Be, B, and P, elements that are known to be enhanced in rocks associated with mineralization (Table 3).

Internal evolution of the Spruce Head pluton

In order to test whether internal evolution of individual groups within the pluton could be explained by fractional crystallization, appropriate minerals were used in quantitative trace-element models. We assumed that the starting compositions were represented by rocks having the lowest SiO_2 in each group. We used a Rayleigh fractionation or crystal surface-liquid equilibrium model (e.g., Hanson, 1978) and bulk distribution coefficients taken from compilations (Arth, 1976; Henderson, 1986; monazite from Yurimoto et al., 1990). For group I, we assumed that sample

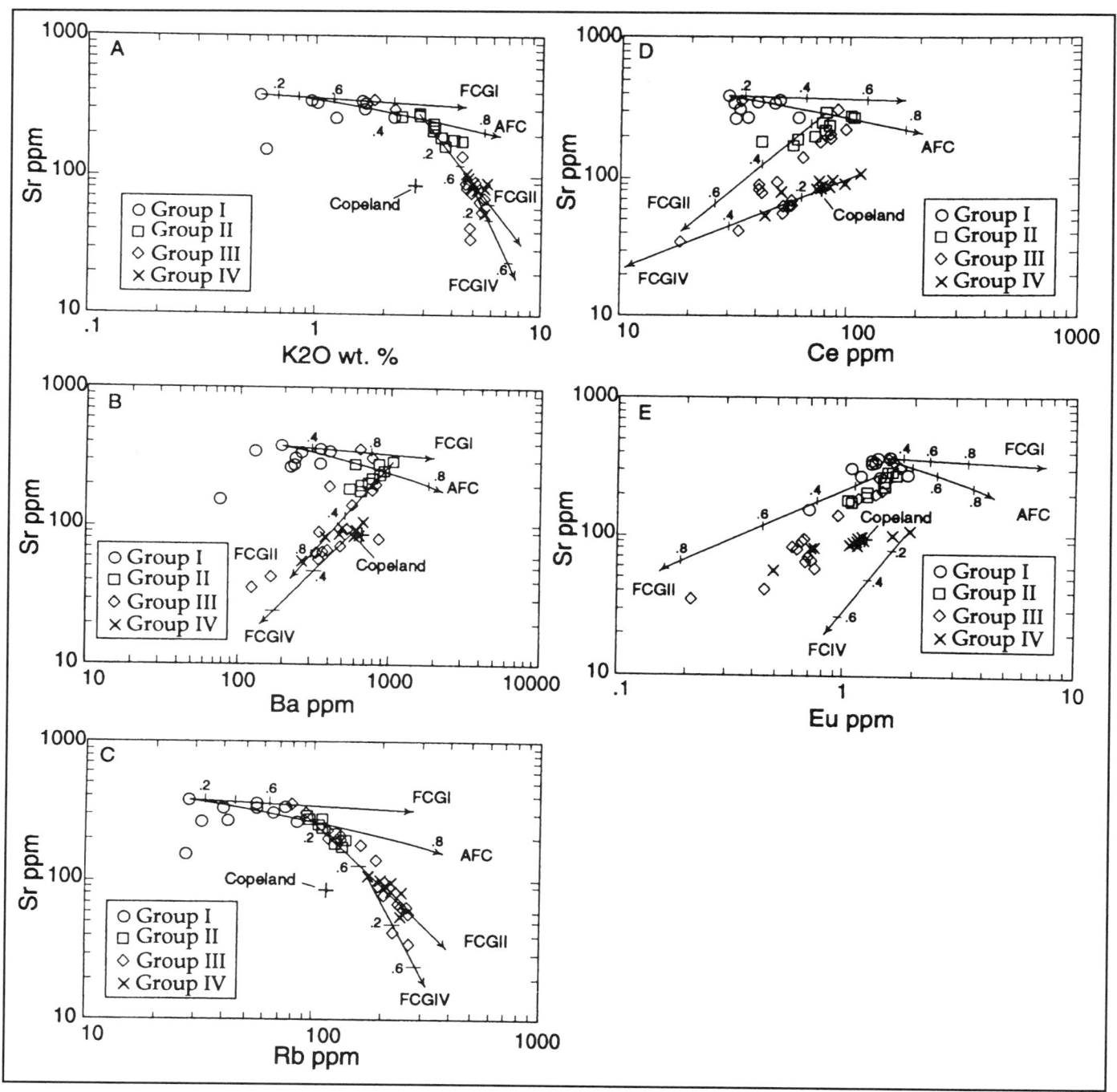

Figure 7. Log-log variation diagrams illustrating trends of models for fractional crystallization and assimilation-fractional crystallization (AFC) superposed on data points for the Spruce Head pluton. A: Sr-K$_2$O. B: Sr-Ba. C: Sr-Rb. D: Sr-Ce. E: Sr-Eu. Abbreviations are as follows: FCGI, path of fractional crystallization of quartz gabbro and diorite from group I; FCGII, fractional crystallization of granodiorite and granite from group II; FCGIV, fractional crystallization of granodiorite and granite from group IV; AFC, path of assimilation-fractional crystallization of group I (r = 0.3, assimilant is Copeland Formation). Trends show the evolution of the liquid. Bulk distribution coefficients for basaltic systems (group I) and for dacitic systems (groups II and IV), respectively, are as follows: Sr (group I = 1.08; group II = 1.95; group IV = 2.64), K$_2$O (0.16; 0.52; 0.52), Ba (0.16; 1.74; 2.49), Rb (0.07; 0.42; 0.51), Ce (0.14; 1.67; 3.6), Eu (0.42; 2.35; 1.84) (from Arth, 1976; Henderson, 1986). For group I we assumed that sample TTSH-105 was the parent (mode: quartz, 7%; plagioclase, 51%; total mafic minerals: 42%; Table 2); our calculations suggested an assemblage dominated by plagioclase (55%), clinopyroxene (40%), and hornblende (5%). For group II, sample TTSH-102 was the parent (mode: Table 2); the estimated assemblage is composed of plagioclase (45.3%), K-feldspar (15.1%), hornblende (30.0%), biotite (9.2%), allanite (0.2%), zircon 0.1%), and titanite (0.1%). For group IV, sample TTSH-16 was the parent (mode: Table 2) and the assemblage consists of plagioclase (59.0%), K-feldspar (24.5%), biotite (12.2%), garnet (4.0%), zircon (0.1%), titanite (0.1%), and monazite (0.1%). See text for additional explanation.

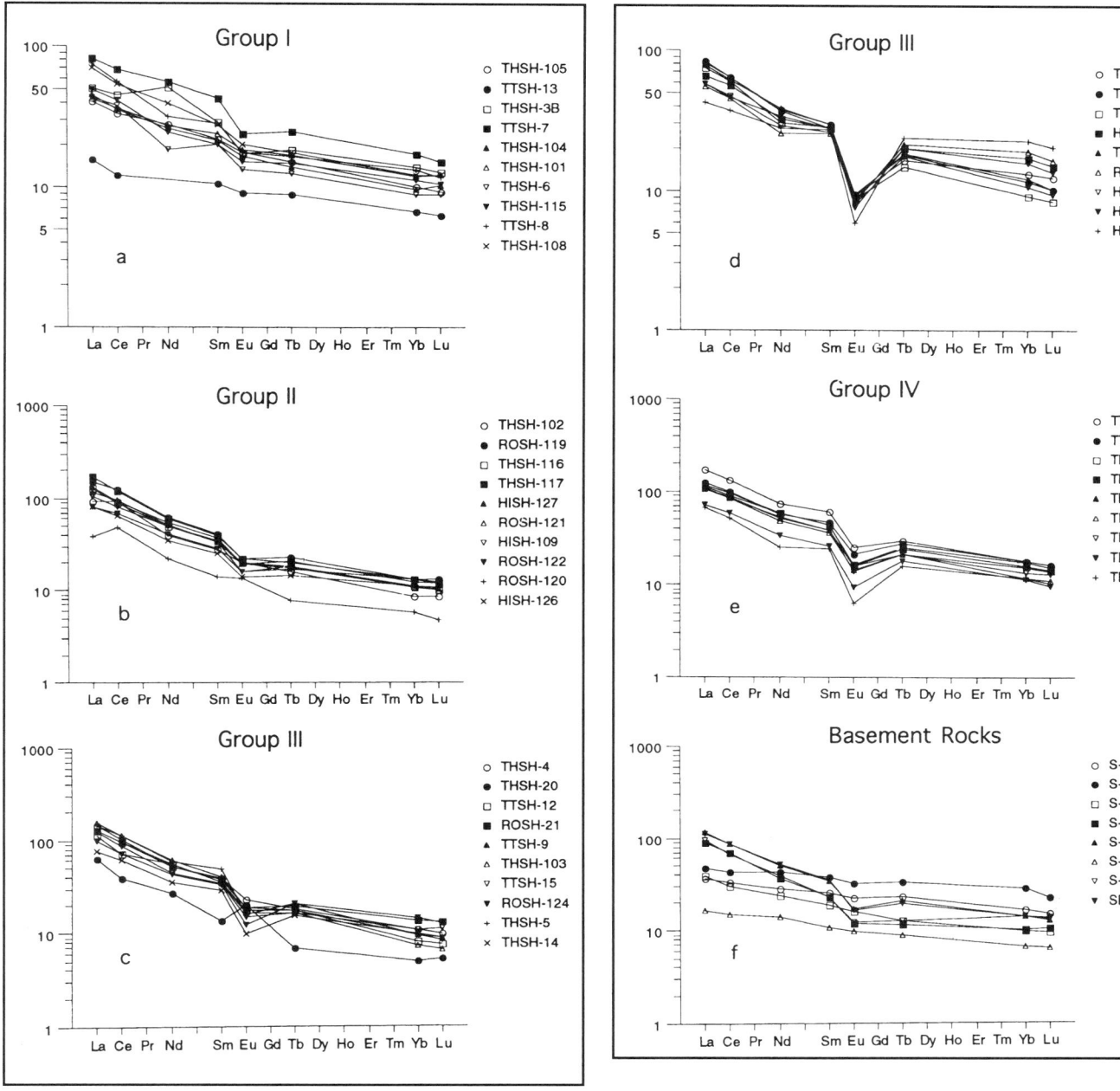

Figure 8. Chondrite-normalized rare earth element patterns for (a) group I; (b) group II; (c and d) group III; (e) group IV; (f) basement rocks. Within groups, samples are arranged in order of increasing SiO$_2$ (also see Table 3).

TTSH-105 was the parent; our calculations suggested a crystallizing assemblage dominated by plagioclase (55%) and clinopyroxene (40%) along with some hornblende (5%). The estimated crystallization path, summarized in Figures 7 and 9, is the most likely way to fractionate from gabbros to quartz diorites and tonalites in group I. The mafic enclave (sample TTSH-3B) does not appear to be a residue because its composition does not exactly match the required abundances for Sr (too low) and Rb (too high), among others. Perhaps this is because mafic enclaves

represent mixtures of mafic and granite magma and of their fractionated crystallizing residues.

In contrast to group I, granodiorites and granites from group II (starting from sample TTSH-102) have trends that are best explained by an assemblage composed of plagioclase (45.3%), K-feldspar (15.1%), hornblende (30.0%), biotite (9.2%), allanite (0.2%), zircon (0.1%), and titanite (0.1%). This assemblage is capable of linking the internal variations in the group from 65% through 72% SiO$_2$ in less than 60% crystallization by

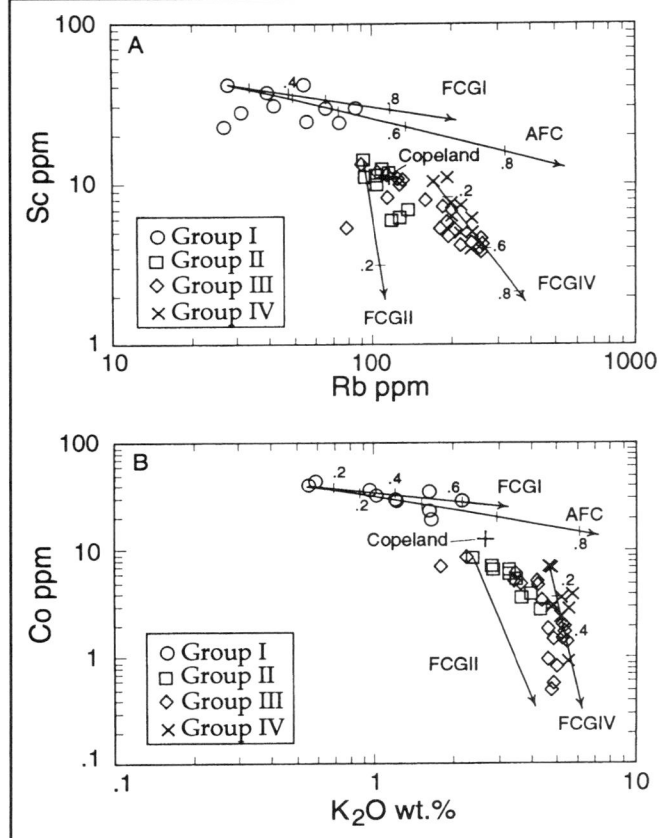

Figure 9. Log-log variation diagrams for compatible-incompatible elements. A: Sc versus Rb. B: Co versus K₂O. Bulk distribution coefficients for groups I, II, and IV, respectively, are as follows: Sc (1.29; 7.07; 2.06), Co (1.21; 16.2; 3.73), and as in Figure 7. Crystallization and assimilation paths as in Figure 7.

weight (Figs. 7 and 9). Modeling of trace elements in granodiorites and granites from group IV (from sample TTSH-16) suggests that an assemblage consisting of plagioclase (59.0%), K-feldspar (24.5%), biotite (12.2%), garnet (4.0%), zircon (0.1%), titanite (0.1%), and monazite (0.1%) could have controlled the internal evolution of this group from 68–75% SiO₂, within reasonable extents of crystallization (<80%) (Figs. 7 and 9).

Our results do not identify a mineral assemblage capable of linking all the granodiorites and granites (groups II, III, and IV) within the whole pluton. Could the differences between the groups, for example, be the result of combined effects of assimilation-fractional crystallization (AFC; DePaolo, 1981) of middle to upper crustal rocks? The impact of such AFC reactions can be illustrated by assuming that selected samples represent compositions of end-member components. In order to test this possibility, we assumed that the parent magma of the Spruce Head pluton was the least evolved, quartz gabbro (sample TTSH-105), as in the fractional crystallization model, and that the main contaminant had the composition of migmatitic schists from the nearby Copeland Formation (sample SR-8-84; Table 3). The residual assemblage used in

the calculation was as estimated in our fractional crystallization model; AFC paths are illustrated in Figures 7 and 9. Results show that at a low ratio of mass assimilated to mass fractionated, as expected from the high level of intrusion of the composite pluton, the offsets and diverging trends of the mafic rocks and granodiorites cannot be the result of AFC reactions involving this type of crustal contaminant or assemblage. For ratios of mass assimilated to mass fractionated (r) between 0.1 and 0.3, however, it is feasible to evolve the mafic rocks and intersect the compositions of the most primitive rocks in group II, generally between 60 and 80% of assimilation and fractional crystallization. Thus, an AFC mechanism could genetically link groups I and II, although it fails to connect group I and group IV. We concede in this case that it is possible that other rocks deeper in the crust could have been the most important contaminants, and that these rocks have compositions that would make the AFC curves link data for all the groups within the Spruce Head pluton. We think, however, that the extent and effects of reactions between the magmas and country rocks were limited (r <0.3) and that these AFC reactions did not produce significant changes in composition of the host granitic magmas. Moreover, there is no obvious AFC scheme that would relate the evolution of groups II and IV using the migmatitic Copeland Formation or any other basement rock in Penobscot Bay as contaminants, including the Late Proterozoic amphibolites and schists from the Seven Hundred Acre Island Formation (Stewart et al., 1995). We note that it is possible that the compositions of granodiorites and granites from group IV lie along the crystallization paths of group II in some diagrams (Fig. 7; for Sr, K₂O, Rb); this feature permits a close genetic association between some of the least-evolved rocks in group IV and the main evolution trend for group II. We conclude that no obvious AFC schemes can be devised involving upper crustal rocks as exemplified by the Copeland Formation and various basement rocks from Penobscot Bay to link the gabbros and all the granodiorites and granites in the pluton.

Isotopic results

There are 14 samples from the Spruce Head pluton that show a large range in Rb/Sr (0.16–4.7) (Table 4). Mafic rocks of group I and granodiorites of group II have initial ⁸⁷Sr/⁸⁶Sr isotopic values at 415 Ma (assumed age of the pluton) of less than 0.7060. Granodiorites from group III and group IV yield a range of initial ⁸⁷Sr/⁸⁶Sr ratios from about 0.7053 to 0.7172. Initial ⁸⁷Sr/⁸⁶Sr values plotted versus 1/Sr show no clear evidence for mixing and are not correlated to SiO₂ or K₂O for the pluton as a whole. The granodiorites and granites vary greatly in initial ⁸⁷Sr/⁸⁶Sr, a feature that is inconsistent with a simple evolution of the felsic rocks by fractional crystallization from mafic rocks of group I, which have relatively low Sr initial ratios.

Initial ¹⁴³Nd/¹⁴⁴Nd isotopic compositions at 415 Ma (Table 4) range from about 0.5120 in the mafic rocks of group I down to 0.5117 in the granodiorites and granites of group IV. A plot combining initial ¹⁴³Nd/¹⁴⁴Nd and initial ⁸⁷Sr/⁸⁶Sr isotopic compositions generally distinguishes between the ranges of indi-

TABLE 4. Sm-Nd AND Rb-Sr ISOTOPIC DATA FOR WHOLE-ROCK SAMPLES AND Pb DATA ON FELDSPARS FROM THE SPRUCE HEAD PLUTON, MAINE

Sample	Group	Sm* (ppm)	Nd* (ppm)	Sm/Nd	$\frac{^{143}Nd}{^{144}Nd}$	$\left(\frac{^{143}Nd}{^{144}Nd}\right)i'$	Rb† (ppm)	Sr† (ppm)	Rb/Sr	$\frac{^{87}Sr}{^{86}Sr}$	$\left(\frac{^{87}Sr}{^{86}Sr}\right)i\S$	$\frac{^{206}Pb}{^{204}Pb}$	$\frac{^{207}Pb}{^{204}Pb}$	$\frac{^{208}Pb}{^{204}Pb}$	$\frac{^{238}U}{^{204}Pb}$
THSH-7	I	8.88	36.0	0.247	0.512460	0.51205 (7)	86	268	0.321	0.71058	0.70509 (47)	18.399	15.673	38.237	10.00
THSH-8	I	5.85	20.5	0.285	0.512444	0.51198 (7)	56	355	0.158	0.70712	0.70442 (23)	18.408	15.657	38.259	9.93
THSH-13	I	N.A.	N.A.	N.A.	N.A.	N.A.	27	150	0.180	0.70680	0.70372 (38)	18.614	15.662	38.395	10.10
THSH-102	II	5.67	25.1	0.226	0.512326	0.51195 (6)	94	288	0.326	0.71167	0.70609 (46)	N.A.	N.A.	N.A.	N.A.
ROSH-119	II	N.A.	N.A.	N.A.	N.A.	N.A.	N.A.	N.A.	N.A.	N.A.	N.A.	18.382	15.708	38.371	10.16
ROSH-121	II	N.A.	N.A.	N.A.	N.A.	N.A.	N.A.	N.A.	N.A.	N.A.	N.A.	18.319	15.640	38.146	9.88
ROSH-122	II	N.A.	N.A.	N.A.	N.A.	N.A.	N.A.	N.A.	N.A.	N.A.	N.A.	18.354	15.643	38.186	10.10
HISH-126	II	5.09	22.0	0.231	0.512351	0.51197 (6)	131	169	0.775	0.71918	0.7059 (12)	18.333	15.643	38.186	9.89
THSH-9	II	8.13	38.0	0.214	0.512265	0.51191 (6)	115	219	0.525	0.71570	0.70672 (76)	18.329	15.655	38.196	9.94
THSH-12	III	N.A.	N.A.	N.A.	N.A.	N.A.	N.A.	N.A.	N.A.	N.A.	N.A.	18.349	15.663	38.235	9.97
THSH-14	III	5.74	21.9	0.262	0.512201	0.51177 (8)	260	55	4.727	0.7879	0.7063 (93)	18.331	15.681	38.249	10.06
THSH-15	III	6.81	27.2	0.250	0.512276	0.31186 (6)	161	177	0.910	0.72242	0.7068 (14)	18.354	15.662	28.230	9.96
ROSH-123	III	N.A.	N.A.	N.A.	N.A.	N.A.	N.A.	N.A.	N.A.	N.A.	N.A.	18.330	15.660	38.211	9.96
THSH-1	IV	7.88	33.0	0.239	0.512140	0.51175 (7)	221	95	2.362	0.75718	0.7172 (34)	15.423	15.692	38.337	10.08
THSH-2	IV	8.95	37.0	0.242	0.512143	0.51175 (6)	211	87	2.425	0.75795	0.7163 (36)	18.397	18.675	38.277	10.01
THSH-3	IV	8.82	37.0	0.238	0.512181	0.51179 (6)	203	86	2.361	0.75506	0.7145 (35)	18.438	15.722	38.424	10.21
THSH-5	IV	N.A.	N.A.	N.A.	N.A.	N.A.	N.A.	N.A.	N.A.	N.A.	N.A.	18.382	15.664	38.268	9.97
THSH-10	IV	9.59	36.0	0.266	0.512214	0.51178 (7)	196	98	2.000	0.73960	0.7053 (29)	18.369	15.716	38.359	10.21
THSH-11	IV	7.78	33.9	0.230	0.512125	0.51175 (6)	241	81	2.975	0.76279	0.7117 (44)	18.403	15.691	38.324	10.08
THSH-16	IV	12.3	46.0	0.267	0.512180	0.51174 (7)	173	106	1.632	0.74395	0.7159 (24)	18.345	15.692	38.274	10.10
THSH-36	Mafic enclave	N.A.	N.A.	N.A.	N.A.	N.A.	N.A.	N.A.	N.A.	N.A.	N.A.	18.461	15.732	38.465	10.25

*Determined by neutron activation analysis.
†Determined by X-ray fluorescence analysis.
§Initial ratios at 415 Ma; propagated errors shown in parenthesis reflect 15 Ma uncertainty in age.
N.A. = not analyzed.

vidual groups in the pluton (Fig. 10). The widest range in initial $^{87}Sr/^{86}Sr$ as well as most of the lowest initial $^{143}Nd/^{144}Nd$ isotopic values are in the granodiorites and granites of group IV; in contrast, group I generally has low initial Sr and high initial Nd isotopic values (Fig. 10). Granodiorites from groups II and III are intermediate. AFC evolution paths calculated at various values of r (mass assimilated/mass fractionated) between the isotopic compositions of gabbros and granites from group I (sample THSH-7) and group IV (sample THSH-1, assumed to represent a crustal melt), and between group II (sample ROSH-126) and group IV (sample THSH-1) fail, as in the case of the major and trace element variations, to link all of the data within the pluton (e.g., Fig. 10). The distinct isotopic fields support a unique origin for each group.

Initial Pb isotopic analyses obtained on K-feldspar and plagioclase from the Spruce Head pluton (Table 4) plot above the Stacey and Kramers (1975) crustal evolution model curve for uranogenic Pb (Fig. 11a); the samples straddle but also mostly plot above the thorogenic Pb curve (Fig. 11b). The range of initial Pb isotopic ratios is relatively narrow ($^{206}Pb/^{204}Pb$ = 18.319–18.461; $^{207}Pb/^{204}Pb$ = 15.640–15.732; $^{208}Pb/^{204}Pb$ = 38.146–38.465). Moreover, the major- and trace-element contents and Pb isotopic values are uncorrelated. Calculated ($^{238}U/^{204}Pb$ = μ) values of the mafic and silicic rocks are generally higher (μ = 9.89–10.21; mafic enclave = 10.25) than the average Pb evolution curve (μ = 9.74). They are thus consistent with the range commonly associated with high values of μ in rocks derived predominantly from the upper crust (e.g., Doe and Zartman, 1979). The majority of the analyzed samples lie along a broad, steep band of high $^{207}Pb/^{204}Pb$ values at nearly constant $^{206}Pb/^{204}Pb$ values. Only sample TTSH-13 from group I plots to the right of this broad band. The mafic enclave (THSH-3b) has the highest $^{207}Pb/^{204}Pb$ and $^{208}Pb/^{204}Pb$ values yet found in the pluton. No samples plot

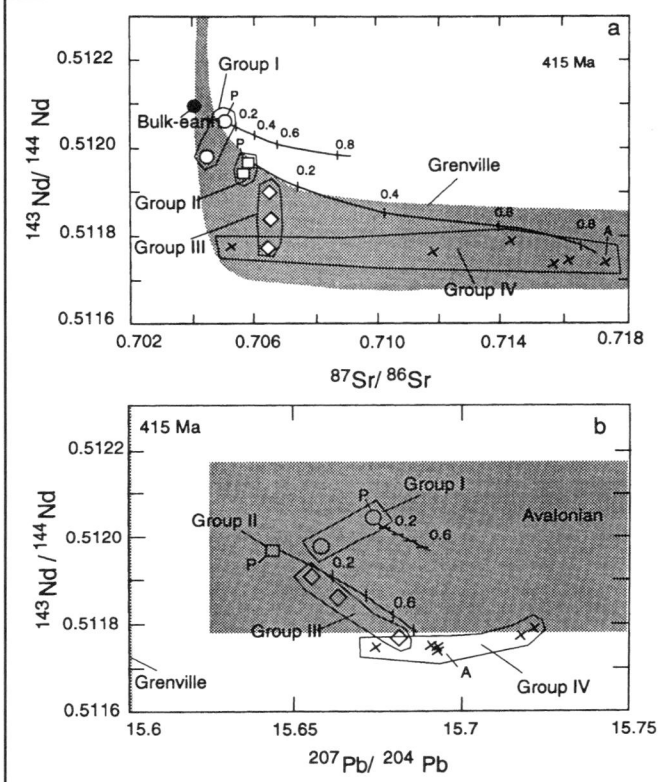

Figure 10. a: Plot of $^{143}Nd/^{144}Nd$ versus $^{87}Sr/^{86}Sr$ at 415 Ma for the Spruce Head pluton. Estimated value for island-arc basalts (bulk earth) in the Silurian plots near field of group I. Field of Grenville basement rocks (compilation by Arth and Ayuso, this volume) closely overlaps the compositions of the Spruce Head pluton. Model AFC paths for group I (TTSH-7) and group IV (sample THSH-1) for r = 0.3, and for group II (ROSH-126) and group IV (THSH-1) for r = 0.5. Bulk distribution coefficients are as determined for fractional crystallization (TTSH-7, Nd = 0.19, Sr = 1.08, Pb = 0.85; ROSH-126, Nd = 0.94; Sr = 1.95; Pb = 0.85). Symbols are as in previous figures; P = parent, A = assimilant. b: Plot of $^{143}Nd/^{144}Nd$ versus $^{207}Pb/^{204}Pb$ showing model AFC paths as above. Fields for the Grenville basement (compilation by Arth and Ayuso, this volume) and Avalonian basement from New Brunswick (Whalen et al., 1994; Ayuso and Bevier, 1991) show the wide difference in $^{207}Pb/^{204}Pb$ values between the Grenville and Avalonian basements. An estimate of $^{207}Pb/^{204}Pb$ values in island-arc or orogenic environments at 415 Ma plots off the diagram ($^{207}Pb/^{204}Pb$ <15.6; Doe and Zartman, 1979).

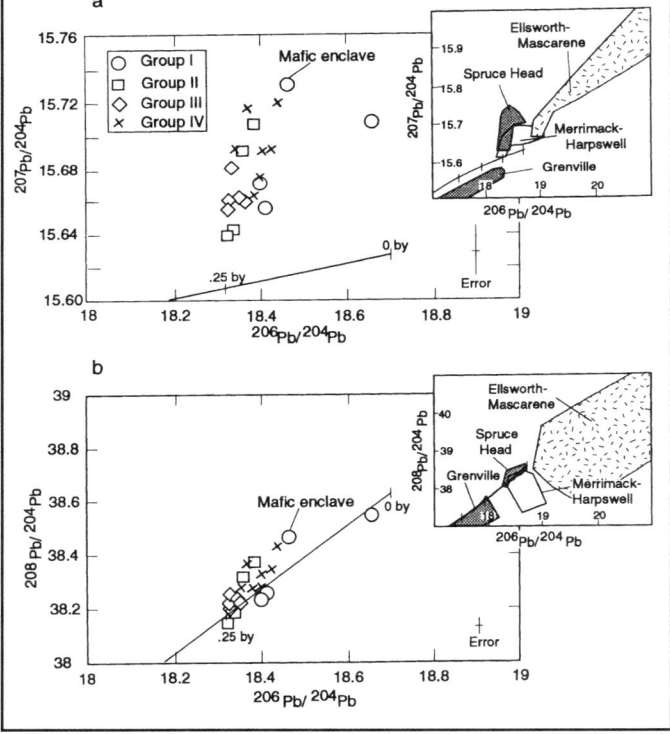

Figure 11. (a) $^{207}Pb/^{204}Pb$ versus $^{206}Pb/^{204}Pb$ and (b) $^{208}Pb/^{204}Pb$ versus $^{206}Pb/^{204}Pb$ diagrams showing the Spruce Head pluton and the crustal Pb evolution curve (Stacey and Kramers, 1975). Sources of data: Ellsworth-Mascarene (Seven Hundred Acre Island Formation) and the Merrimack-Harpswell (Copeland Formation) terranes; Grenville basement (orthogneiss and paragneiss in the Green Mountains massif, Vermont) shown as shaded field.

below the evolution curve, which would be evidence for a component of mantle-derived Pb in the source region of the granitic rocks. As in the Nd and Sr variations, a combined plot of initial values for $^{143}Nd/^{144}Nd$ and $^{207}Pb/^{204}Pb$ shows that the fields for group III are intermediate between groups I and II and group IV (Fig. 10b). On a regional basis, the initial Pb isotopic values plot within the field for granitic rocks from the Coastal Maine lithotectonic block, represented by the Southern group of granitic rocks of Ayuso and Bevier (1991). Such granitic rocks are thought to have been derived from Avalonian basement. The Pb isotopic compositions, however, do not exactly match the fields for age-corrected basement rocks from nearby representative Avalonian basement rocks—for example, the Ellsworth-Mascarene (Seven Hundred Acre Island Formation) terrane or the Merrimack-Harpswell (Copeland Formation) terrane (Fig. 11, a and b).

SUMMARY AND DISCUSSION

General statement

The importance of granitic rocks during continental growth and crustal recycling has long been known, and the processes by which mafic-felsic magmatic associations could represent new additions of mantle-derived material into the crust have been summarized (Clarke, 1992, Pitcher, 1993). Ongoing debate regarding the origin of such magmatic associations centers on the merits of general models (e.g., Barbarin, 1990) whereby large volumes of felsic magmas coexisted with mafic magmas while both were still partly liquid. Among the most important alternatives that could account for composite plutons, such as at Spruce Head, are (1) fractional crystallization of basaltic magmas in situ to produce the entire spectrum of granitic rocks; (2) progressive melting of heterogeneous (mafic to felsic) crustal rocks and successive intrusion; and (3) combinations of the above. In the following section we contend that the foregoing geochemical data support a model for the genesis of the Spruce Head magma from at least three distinct sources which provided crustal melts and mantle-derived magmas, some of which mixed to produce hybrid rocks.

Mantle-derived and crustal contributions

That mantle-derived rocks were involved in the genesis of the Spruce Head pluton is supported by a common feature throughout the St. Croix, Ellsworth-Mascarene, and Merrimack-Harpswell terranes—ubiquitous Silurian mafic rocks found with or without closely associated granitic units (e.g., Wones, 1980; Stewart et al., 1988; Hogan and Sinha, 1989; Wiebe, 1993). Plutons dominated by mafic rocks include, for example, the Union diorite, the Winterport quartz diorite, the Parks Pond quartz monzonite (Eriksson and Hogan, 1989), and the Pocomoonshine gabbro-diorite (Westerman, 1991), and constitute evidence for substantial mantle-derived mafic magmatism and its transport through the crust during orogeny (e.g., Wones, 1980; Stewart et al., 1988; Hogan

and Sinha, 1989; Wiebe, 1993). Similarly, in the model advocated here for the Spruce Head pluton, such mafic magmas may have contributed heat that produced crustal melting.

The occurrence of pillow-like blobs of gabbro and diorite commingled with granitic rocks in the Spruce Head pluton is consistent with contributions from mantle-derived magmas; these mafic blobs resemble the gabbros and diorites of group I which have relatively high contents of Co (up to 44.8 ppm), Cr (up to 278 ppm), and Ni (up to 220 ppm), among others (Table 3). Furthermore, a general resemblance to mafic orogenic rocks (Nb/U = 1–7, Ba/Ta >450, La/Th = 2–7; Gill, 1981; Hawkesworth et al., 1991) is indicated by gabbros and diorites having the lowest silica contents (Nb/U ~5–34, Ba/Ta = 110–645, and La/Th ~4–9; Table 3). The majority of the gabbros and diorites, in addition, have pronounced negative Nb and Ta anomalies in normalized plots (Fig. 5), low La/Yb values (~3–8), and elevated Th contents relative to Hf and Ta (Hf/Th = 0.60–1.1), again akin to those from orogenic basaltic rocks. Many mafic intrusives in the St. Croix, Ellsworth-Mascarene, and Merrimack-Harpswell terranes are quartz bearing, and at Spruce Head they have elevated K_2O contents (up to 2.16%)—features that may suggest crustal contamination (e.g., see the compilation for the Coastal Maine magmatic province by Hogan and Sinha, 1989). In addition, a crustal contribution into the mafic magmas is evident because of the general enrichments in large ion lithophile elements such as Sr, K, Rb, Ba, Th, and light REEs, and incompatible element ratios unlike those from mantle-derived rocks (e.g., Hf/Ta >2–4 representative of average upper crust; Taylor and McLennan, 1985). This means that the mafic rocks may represent mantle-derived magmas that evolved and were contaminated.

Initial Nd isotopic ratios in group I are close to the estimated value for bulk earth (characteristic of island-arc environments) in the Silurian (Fig. 10). Pb isotopic data, however, fail to match the equivalent values for orogenic rocks (Doe and Zartman, 1979), particularly because of the radiogenic $^{207}Pb/^{204}Pb$ and high μ values in the pluton (all have $^{207}Pb/^{204}Pb$ >15.62) (Fig. 11). The Pb data indicate that the pluton evolved from source rocks having a time-integrated, high U/Pb environment, higher than represented by average crustal and orogenic Pb model curves (Doe and Zartman, 1979; Stacey and Kramers, 1975). The Pb data are thus consistent with a major crustal contribution to the source of the granitic magmas.

Our results show that the petrographic groups within the Spruce Head pluton cannot be linked genetically by in situ fractional crystallization of mafic rocks (alternative 1), as suggested by the gap in SiO_2 contents, the major offsets in the trace-element variations within the pluton, and by the unique ranges of initial Nd and Sr isotopic values in each group. The resulting granitic magmas may even represent melts from different levels in the crust (e.g., see Hogan and Sinha, 1989), as suggested by the inference that garnet was in the residue of granitic rocks in group IV.

In order to explain commingling and hybridization at the Spruce Head pluton we invoke the process whereby repeated pulses of basalt invaded the silicic magma chamber, as documented in various composite mafic-granitic complexes in general (Reid et al., 1983), and particularly in Maine (Wiebe, 1993). Features that commonly are associated with the formation of hybrid granitic rocks (Frost and Mahood, 1987; Zorpi et al., 1991) also support the suggestion that hybrid granodioritic rocks of group II were produced in the Spruce Head pluton, where high volumes of mafic rocks of group I mixed with crustally derived magmas. That the granodioritic magmas intruded as several pulses is indicated by trace element differences between the granodiorites from groups II, III, and IV, and as documented by the general grouping of these rocks in many diagrams. Such granitic magmas probably intruded along east-dipping to vertical faults (e.g., Hogan and Sinha, 1989; Wones, 1980; Stewart et al., 1995). A paucity of mafic enclaves and the uniformly evolved compositions in the aplitic granites of group IV indicates that mixing with mantle-derived magmas was less important in their genesis.

Tectonic setting

Geophysical and geologic data indicate that the bulk of the Spruce Head pluton was generated during Late Ordovician–Early Silurian terrane amalgamation events that were part of a Salinian orogenic belt (Stewart et al., 1995, 1996). That the mafic rocks in the Spruce Head pluton resemble orogenic basaltic rocks is important because magmatic rocks in the Merrimack-Mascarene collage were thought to have been generated in a transtensional setting characterized by a bimodal magmatic association with alkalic tendencies (Hogan and Sinha, 1989). We advocate, instead, that the Spruce Head pluton was generated in a setting involving the closing stages of crustal collision to account for the calc-alkaline nature and overall magmatic-arc character, especially in group II. In our scenario, because voluminous andesitic volcanism that would have resulted from closing a large ocean during the Silurian is absent, we invoke the idea that a small ocean was developed and consumed prior to Devonian amalgamation of the collage containing the Spruce Head pluton (St. Croix and Ellsworth-Mascarene terranes) to preexisting composite peri-Gondwanan terranes to the west. We contend that as a result of this collision, crustal blocks having distinct pre-Devonian metamorphic histories were juxtaposed (Guidotti, 1989), and that intrusion and underplating of mafic magmas (Clemens and Vielzuf, 1987) from the mantle wedge above the subduction zone ultimately resulted in crustal melting and mixing with crustal melts.

In a crustal region affected by progressive anatexis (as in alternative 2) the first generation of magmas would be granitic, followed by granodioritic magmas, and then by even more mafic magmas (e.g., Wyllie, 1977). This is, however, inconsistent with field observations pointing principally to coexistence of the mafic rocks of group I and granodiorites of group II. We have noted, in addition, that there is evidence that at least some of the gabbros and diorites are somewhat older than the granodiorites of groups II and III (Guidotti, 1979). More important, field relations show that aplitic granodiorites and granites of group IV appear to

be the youngest phase of granitic magmatism, making a simple melting model inappropriate, because mafic, higher temperature rocks would have preceded intrusion of more felsic, lower temperature magmas.

In the mixing scenario in a collision zone (England and Thompson, 1986; Harris et al., 1986) that we advocate here, we suggest that melting of hydrous mid- to lower crustal rocks (20 km or deeper?) can produce granodioritic and granitic magmas (Wyllie, 1977). Simple binary mixing between mantle-derived mafic and homogeneous granitic magmas of crustal origin, however, cannot account for the diversity of granitic rocks in the Spruce Head pluton because no coherent, systematic mixing trends (Langmuir et al., 1978) exist for all the rocks. Thus, we think that rocks underlying the deeper parts of the region could well have provided fertile sources for melting, producing magmas that were partially mixed during the orogeny (alternative 2). Regional studies indicate that crustal thickening from thrusting during collision of the terranes within the Merrimack-Mascarene collage (including the St. Croix, Ellsworth-Mascarene, and Isleboro crustal blocks) during a complex, long-lived orogeny would enhance the effects of underplating hot, mantle-derived magmas, and thus produce crustal melting.

That groups III and IV significantly overlap and have trace element and isotopic variations (high Sr initial ratios, low Nd initial ratios) resembling syncollisional granitic rocks (Harris et al., 1986) that are in contrast with granodiorites from group II again suggests that different sources were involved during the generation of the pluton. Tectonic reconstructions indicate that potential representatives of the middle to lower crust are exposed nearby as the Late Proterozoic middle amphibolite andalusite-garnet grade (~4 kbar) schists and amphibolites in the Seven Hundred Acre Island Formation (Isleboro block in the Ellsworth-Mascarene terrane) in Penobscot Bay, as well as in the Copeland Formation on the mainland (in the Merrimack-Harpswell terrane) (Stewart, 1989; Stewart et al., 1995). Furthermore, we note that the Copeland Formation shows evidence for migmatization ca. 420 ± 10 Ma (Wones, 1991; R. E. Zartman, 1974, personal commun.), a time generally consistent with the age of the Spruce Head pluton. These potential sources, in fact, represent older orogenic rocks (amphibolites and tonalites) available for anatexis. Melting of such protoliths would imprint some trace-element features on the resulting granitic magmas akin to those of rocks from volcanic arc settings (e.g., Ayuso and Arth, 1992; Barker et al., 1992; Atherton, 1993). There is a general resemblance in Pb isotopic and trace element compositions between the Spruce Head pluton and representative samples of these potential crustal sources, particularly the Copeland Formation and various schists in the Seven Hundred Acre Island Formation (Fig. 5).

Regional comparison

Most petrographic and geochemical features of the Silurian Spruce Head pluton have direct counterparts in the New England Appalachians, and particularly in coastal Maine (e.g., see compilation by Hogan and Sinha, 1989). All such composite plutons occur in an area thought to be underlain by peri-Gondwanan basement in the St. Croix and Ellsworth-Mascarene terranes, in contrast to granitic batholiths from the Central Maine synclinorium, and especially from northern Maine and Vermont, which are thought to be underlain by Grenville basement (Ayuso and Bevier, 1991; Ayuso and Arth, 1992; Arth and Ayuso, this volume). Thus, a fundamental difference in source regions may exist between coastal Maine and more inboard lithotectonic blocks, as indicated by previous studies summarizing trace element variations in the Merrimack-Mascarene collage (Loiselle and Ayuso, 1980; Carl et al., 1984; Stewart et al., 1988; Hogan and Sinha, 1989; Wones and Ayuso, 1993).

CONCLUSIONS

1. The composite Spruce Head pluton consists of four distinct petrographic zones of quartz gabbro, quartz diorite, and tonalite (zone I), hornblende-biotite granodiorite (zone II), medium-grained biotite-muscovite (garnet) granodiorite to granite (zone III), and aplitic biotite-muscovite-garnet granodiorite to granite (zone IV).

2. Samples from each petrographic zone define distinct chemical groups. The suite is tholeiitic to calc-alkaline, and a compositional gap between 56% and 64% SiO_2 separates group I from groups II, III, and IV. Variations in the abundances of CaO, Fe_2O_3, TiO_2, K_2O, P_2O_5, Rb, total REE, Ta, and Th, among others, document distinct ranges and trends of groups I, II, and IV.

3. Fractional crystallization might account for most of the chemical variations within group I and within group II. Granodiorites and granites from groups II, III, and IV cannot be related to each other by simple fractional crystallization, because these groups show major compositional gaps and offsets between trends.

4. Trace-element and isotopic data indicate that the pluton formed from at least three distinct pulses of magma.

5. The ranges in initial isotopic ratios for Nd ($^{143}Nd/^{144}Nd = 0.51224$–$0.51172$), Sr ($^{87}Sr/^{86}Sr = 0.7035$–$0.7158$), and Pb ($^{206}Pb/^{204}Pb = 18.319$–$18.461$; $^{207}Pb/^{204}Pb = 15.640$–$15.732$; $^{208}Pb/^{204}Pb = 38.146$–$38.465$) are consistent with a general origin by melting mantle rocks (group I), upper crustal rocks (group IV), and potentially lower crustal rocks or mixed sources (groups II and III).

6. The Spruce Head pluton represents a unique group of mafic-felsic composite Silurian plutons in coastal Maine produced by intrusion and underplating of mafic magmas and mixing of magmas formed by crustal melting following Silurian collisions of peri-Gondwanan (Avalonian) rocks.

ACKNOWLEDGMENTS

We have benefited from detailed constructive reviews by M. Horan, E. Moll-Stalcup, and K. Schulz that have improved the presentation and content of our ideas. We thank D. B. Stewart for greatly enhancing our understanding of the crustal evolution of New England through discussions and comments on an earlier version of the paper. Constructive and helpful reviews by M. Dorais, R. Wiebe, and J. Hogan are appreciated. We also thank C. Guidotti and D. West for providing summaries of their recent work on the stratigraphic and age relations of the country rocks hosting the Spruce Head pluton. Whole-rock samples were prepared by M. Cabell; C. Holdsworth assisted in the Nd and Sr analyses and N. Rait assisted in the Pb analyses.

REFERENCES CITED

Arth, J. G., 1976, Behavior of trace elements during magmatic processes—A summary of theoretical models and their applications: U.S. Geological Survey Journal of Research, v. 4, p. 41–47.

Arth, J. G., Barker, F., and Stern, T. W., 1980, Geochronology of Archean gneisses in the Lake Helen area, southwestern Big Horn Mountains, Wyoming: Precambrian Research, v. 11, p. 11–22.

Atherton, M. P., 1993, Granite magmatism: Geological Society of London Journal: v. 150, p. 1009–1023.

Ayuso, R. A., 1989, Geochemistry of the Catheart Mountain porphyry copper deposit, Maine, *in* Tucker, R. D., and Marvinney, R. G., eds., Studies in Maine geology, Volume 4: Augusta, Maine Geological Survey Special Geological Studies Series, p. 139–162.

Ayuso, R. A., and Arth, J. G., 1992, The Northeast Kingdom batholith, Vermont: Magmatic evolution, and geochemical constraints on the origin of Acadian rocks: Contributions to Mineralogy and Petrology, v. 111, p. 1–23.

Ayuso, R. A., and Bevier, M. L., 1991, Regional differences in Pb isotopic compositions of feldspars in plutonic rocks of the northern Appalachian Mountains, USA and Canada: a geochemical method of terrane correlation: Tectonics, v. 10, p. 191–212.

Ayuso, R. A., and Loferski, P. J., 1992, Trace element geochemistry of syenite and granodiorite in the Deboullie pluton, northern Maine: Geological Association of Canada/Mineralogical Association of Canada, Abstracts, v. 17, p. A-5.

Ayuso, R. A., Barr, S. M., and Longstaffe, F. J., 1996, Pb and O isotopic constraints on the source of granitic rocks from Cape Breton Island, Nova Scotia: American Journal of Science, v. 296, p. 789–817.

Baedecker, P. A., 1987, Methods for geochemical analysis: U. S. Geological Survey Bulletin 1770, 140 p.

Barbarin, B., 1990, Granitoids: Main petrogenetic classification in relation to origin and tectonic setting: Geological Journal, v. 25, p. 227–238.

Barker, F., Farmer, G. L., Ayuso, R. A., Plafker, G., and Lull, J. S., 1992, 50-Ma granodiorite of the eastern Gulf of Alaska: Melting in an accretionary prism in the forearc: Journal of Geophysical Research, v. 97, p. 6757–6778.

Brookins, D., Berdan, J. M., and Stewart, D. B., 1973, Isotopic and paleontologic evidence for correlating three volcanic sequences in the Maine Coastal Volcanic Belt: Geological Society of America Bulletin, v. 84, p. 1619–1628.

Carl, J. D., Liptak, A. R., Savitz, S. L., Schmidt, D. T., Shay, S. G., Tom, V. J., and Wink, J. T., 1984, Geochemical characteristics of granitoid plutons in the Penobscot Bay area, Maine: Northeastern Geology, v. 6, p. 12–24.

Chayes, F., 1952, The finer-grained calc-alkaline granites of New England: Journal of Geology, v. 60, p. 207.

Clarke, D. B., 1992, Granitoid rocks: New York, Chapman and Hall, Topics in the Earth Sciences, Volume 7, 283 p.

Clemens, J. D., and Vielzuf, D. , 1987, Constraints on melting and magma production in the crust: Earth and Planetary Science Letters, v. 86, p. 287–306.

DePaolo, D. J., 1981, Trace element and isotopic effects of combined wall-rock assimilation and fractional crystallization: Earth and Planetary Science Letters, v. 53, p. 189–202.

Doe, B. R., and Zartman, R. E., 1979, Plumbotectonics I: The Phanerozoic, *in* Barnes, H., ed., Geochemistry of hydrothermal ore deposits: New York, John Wiley, p. 22–70.

Dunning, G. R., Barr, S. M., Raeside, R. P., and Jamieson, R. A., 1990, U-Pb zircon, titanite, and monazite ages in the Bras d'Or and Aspy terranes of Cape Breton Island, Nova Scotia: Implications for magmatic and metamorphic history: Geological Society of America Bulletin, v. 102, p. 322–330.

England, P. C., and Thompson, R., 1986, Some thermal and tectonic models for crustal melting in continental collision zones, in Coward, M. P., and Ries, A. C., eds., Collision tectonics: Geological Society of London Special Publication 19, p. 83–84.

Eriksson, S. C., and Hogan, J. P., 1989, Ion microprobe resolution of age details in heterogeneous sources of plutonic rocks from a comagmatic province: Geological Society of America Abstracts with Programs, v. 21, no. 2, p. 361.

Frost, T. P., and Mahood, G. A., 1987, Field, chemical, and physical constraints on felsic-mafic magma interaction in the Lamarck granodiorite, Sierra Nevada, California: Geological Society of America Bulletin, v. 99, p. 272–291.

Gill, J., 1981, Orogenic andesites and plate tectonics: New York, Springer, 385 p.

Guidotti, C. V., 1979, Preliminary report on the bedrock geology of the Tenants Harbor 7 $\frac{1}{2}'$ quadrangle and a portion of the Friendship 7 $\frac{1}{2}'$ quadrangle, Maine: Maine Geological Survey Open-File no. 79-16.

Guidotti, C. V., 1989, Metamorphism in Maine: An overview, in Tucker, R. D., and Marvinney, R. G., eds., Studies in Maine geology, Volume 3: Augusta, Maine Geological Survey, p. 1–17.

Hanson, G. N., 1978, The application of trace elements to the petrogenesis of igneous rocks of granitic composition: Earth and Planetary Science Letters, v. 38, p. 26–43.

Harland, W. B., Armstrong, R. L., Cox, A. V., Craig, L. E., Smith, A. G., and Smith, D. G., 1989, A geologic time scale 1989: Cambridge, United Kingdom, Cambridge University Press, 263 p.

Harris, N. B. W., Pearce, J. A., and Tindle, A. G., 1986, Geochemical characteristics of collision zone magmatism, in Coward, M. P., and Ries, A. C., eds., Collision tectonics: Geological Society of London Special Publication 19, p. 67–81.

Hawkesworth, C. J., Hergt, J. M., McDermott, F., and Ellam, R. M., 1991, Destructive margin magmatism and the contributions from the mantle wedge and subducted crust: Australian Journal of Earth Sciences, v. 38, p. 577–594.

Henderson, P., 1986, Inorganic geochemistry: Oxford, England, Pergamon Press, 356 p.

Hill, M., 1991, Petrology of the Moosehorn igneous complex, Calais, Maine, in Ludman, A., ed., Geology of the Coastal Lithotectonic belt and neighboring terranes, eastern Maine and southern New Brunswick: New England Intercollegiate Geological Conference Guidebook, p. 55–63.

Hogan, J. P., and Sinha, A. K., 1989, Compositional variation of plutonism in the coastal Maine magmatic province: Mode of origin and tectonic setting, in Tucker, R. D., and Marvinney, R. G., eds., Studies in Maine Geology, Volume 4: Augusta, Maine Geological Survey, p. 1–34.

Jurinski, J. B., and Sinha, A. K., 1989, Igneous complexes within the Coastal Maine Magmatic Province: Evidence for a Silurian tensional event: Geological Society of America Abstracts with Programs, v. 21, no. 2, p. 25.

Kuno, H., 1966, Lateral variation of basalt magma types across continental margins and island arcs: Bulletin of Volcanology, v. 29, p. 195–222.

Langmuir, C. H., Vocke, R. D., Hanson, G. N., and Hart, S. R., 1978, A general mixing equation with applications to Icelandic basalts: Earth and Planetary Science Letters, v. 37, p. 380–392.

Loiselle, M. C., and Ayuso, R. A., 1980, Geochemical characteristics of granitoids across the Merrimack synclinorium eastern and central Maine, in Wones, D. R., ed., The Caledonides in the USA: Blacksburg, Virginia Polytechnic Institute and State University, Department of Geological Sciences, p. 123–130.

Ludman, A., 1987, Pre-Silurian stratigraphy and tectonic significance of the St. Croix Belt, southeastern Maine: Canadian Journal of Earth Sciences, v. 24, p. 2459–2469.

Nockolds, S. R., 1954, Average chemical compositions of some igneous rocks:

Geological Society of America Bulletin, v. 65, p. 1007–1032.

O'Brien, B. H., O'Brien, S. J., and Dunning, G. R., 1991, Silurian cover, late Precambrian–Early Ordovician basement, and the chronology of Silurian orogenesis in the Hermitage (Newfoundland Appalachians): American Journal of Science, v. 291, p. 760–799.

Osberg, P. H., and Guidotti, C. V., 1974, The geology of the Camden-Rockland area: New England Intercollegiate Geological Conference Guidebook, p. 48–60.

Osberg, P. H., Hussey, A. M., and Boone, G. M., 1985, Bedrock geologic map of Maine: Augusta, Maine Geological Survey, scale 1:500,000.

Pearce, J. A., Harris, N. B.W., and Tindle, A. G., 1984, Trace element discrimination diagrams for the tectonic interpretation of granitic rocks: Journal of Petrology, v. 25, p. 956–983.

Pitcher, W. S., 1993, The nature and origin of granite: London, Blackie Academic and Professional, 321 p.

Rankin, D. W., 1994, Continental margin of the eastern United States: Past and present: Boulder, Colorado, Geological Society of America, Decade of North American Geology Continent-Ocean Transect, Phanerozoic Evolution of North American Continent-Ocean Transitions, p. 129–218.

Reid, J. B., Evans, O. C., and Fates, D. G., 1983, Magma mixing in granitic rocks of the central Sierra Nevada, California: Earth and Planetary Science Letters, v. 66, p. 243–261.

Stacey, J. D., and Kramers, J. N., 1975, Approximation of terrestrial lead isotope evolution by a two-stage model: Earth and Planetary Science Letters, v. 36, p. 207–222.

Stewart, D. B., 1989, Crustal processes in Maine: American Mineralogist, v. 74, p. 698–714.

Stewart, D. B., Arth, J. G., and Flohr, M. J.K., 1988, Petrogenesis of the South Penobscot Intrusive Suite, Maine: American Journal of Science, v. 288-A, p. 74–114.

Stewart, D. B., Wright, B. E., Unger, J. D., Phillips, J. D., and Hutchinson, D. R., 1993, Global geoscience transect 8, Quebec–Maine–Gulf of Maine transect, southeastern Canada, northeastern United States of America: U.S. Geological Survey Miscellaneous Investigations Series Map I-2329 and pamphlet, 17 p., scale 1:1,000,000.

Stewart, D. B., Tucker, R. D., and West, D. P., 1995, Genesis of Silurian composite terrane in northern Penobscot Bay: New England Intercollegiate Geologic Conference, p. A3-1–A3-21.

Stewart, D. B., Unger, J. D., and Hutchinson, D. R., 1995, Silurian tectonic history of Penobscot Bay region, Maine: Atlantic Geology, v. 31, p. 67–79.

Streckeisen, A., 1976, To each plutonic rocks its proper name: Earth Science Reviews, v. 12, p. 1–13.

Taylor, S. R., and McLennan, S. M., 1985, The continental crust: its composition and evolution: Oxford, England, Blackwell Scientific, 312 p.

Thompson, R. N., 1982, Magmatism of the British Tertiary volcanic province: Scottish Journal of Geology, v. 18, p. 49–107.

van Staal, C. R., 1994, Brunswick subduction complex in the Canadian Appalachians: Record of the Late Ordovician to Late Silurian collision between Laurentia and the Gander margin of Avalon: Tectonics, v. 13, p. 946–962.

van Staal, C. R., and Fyffe, L. R., 1991, Dunnage and Gander zones, New Brunswick: Canadian Appalachian region: New Brunswick Department of Natural Resources and Energy, Mineral Resources, Geoscience Report 91-2, p. 1–39.

van Staal, C. R., and Williams, H., 1992, Dunnage-Gander relations in the Appalachian orogen: Evidence for an Early Ordovician arc-continent collision: Geological Association of Canada/Mineralogical Association of Canada, Abstracts, v. 17, p. A112–A113.

West, D. P., Guidotti, C. V., and Lux, D. R., 1992, [40]Ar/[39]Ar mineral ages from southwestern Penobscot Bay, Maine: Evidence for Silurian metamorphism: Geological Society of America Abstract with Programs, v. 24, no. 7, p. A289.

Westerman, D. S., 1991, Mafic and ultramafic rocks of the Pocomoonshine gabbro-diorite in southeastern Maine, in Ludman, A., ed., Geology of the Coastal Lithotectonic block and neighboring terranes, eastern Maine and southern New Brunswick: New England Intercollegiate Geological Conference Guidebook, p. 265–285.

Whalen, J. B., Jenner, G. A., Currie, K. L., Barr, S. M., Longstaffe, F. J., and Hegner, E., 1994, Geochemical and isotopic characteristics of granitoids of the Avalon zone, southern New Brunswick: Possible evidence for repeated delamination events: Journal of Geology, v. 102, p. 269–282.

Wiebe, R. A., 1993, The Pleasant Bay layered gabbro-diorite, coastal Maine: Ponding and crystallization of basaltic injections into a silicic magma chamber: Journal of Petrology, v. 34, p. 461–489.

Wiebe, R. A., and Chapman, M., 1993, Layered-gabbro-diorite intrusions of coastal Maine: Basaltic infusions into floored silicic magma chambers, *in* Cheney, J. T. and others, eds., Field trip guidebook for the northeastern United States: Boston, Geological Society of America meeting v. 1, p. A-1–A-29.

Williams, H., 1978, Tectonic lithofacies map of the Appalachian orogen: St. John's, Memorial University of Newfoundland, Map no. 1, scale 1:1,000,000.

Wones, D. R., 1980, A comparison between granitic plutons from New England, USA, and the Sierra Nevada batholith, California, *in* Wones, D. R., ed., The Caledonides in the USA: Blacksburg, Virginia Polytechnic Institute and State University Department of Geological Sciences, p. 123–130.

Wones, D. R., 1991, Bedrock geologic map of the Bucksport quadrangle, Waldo, Hancock, and Penobscot counties, Maine: U.S. Geological Survey Map GQ-1692, scale 1:62,500.

Wones, D. R., and Ayuso, R. A., 1993, Geologic map of the Lucerne granite, Hancock and Penobscot counties, Maine: U.S. Geological Survey Miscellaneous Investigations Series Map I-2360, scale 1:125,000.

Wyllie, P. J., 1977, Crustal anatexis: An experimental review: Tectonophysics, v. 43, p. 41–71.

Yurimoto, H., Duke, E. F., Papike, J. J., and Shearer, C. K., 1990, Are discontinuous chondrite-normalized REE patterns in pegmatitic granite systems the results of monazite fractionation?: Geochimica et Cosmochimica Acta, v. 54, p. 2141–2145.

Zen, E-an, 1983, Exotic terranes in the New England Appalachians—Limits, candidates, and ages: A speculative essay: Geological Society of America Memoir 158, p. 55–81.

Zorpi, M. J., Coulon, C., and Orsini, J. B., 1991, Hybridization between felsic and mafic magmas in calc-alkaline granitoids—A case study in northern Sardinia, Italy: Chemical Geology, v. 92, p. 45–86.

MANUSCRIPT ACCEPTED BY THE SOCIETY JULY 2, 1996

Geological Society of America
Memoir 191
1997

Late Precambrian plutons in the Avalon terrane of New Brunswick, Nova Scotia, and Newfoundland

Sandra M. Barr
Department of Geology, Acadia University, Wolfville, Nova Scotia B0P 1X0, Canada
Andrew Kerr
Geological Survey of Newfoundland and Labrador, Department of Natural Resources, P. O. Box 8700, St. John's, Newfoundland A1B 4J6, Canada

ABSTRACT

Comparison of late Precambrian plutonic rocks in three parts of the Avalon terrane of the northern Appalachian orogen (the Caledonia terrane in southern New Brunswick, the Mira terrane of southeastern Cape Breton Island, and the type area of the Avalon terrane in eastern Newfoundland) shows that ca. 620 Ma plutonic rocks and voluminous coeval volcanic rocks occur in all three areas. The ca. 620 Ma plutonic rocks range from gabbro and diorite to granite, and have petrochemical features indicative of origin in continental margin volcanic arcs. Remnants of older, ca. 680 Ma, arc complexes occur in the western part of the Newfoundland Avalon terrane and in the Mira terrane, although granitoid plutonic rocks of that age are preserved only in the former area. Younger, ca. 580–550 Ma, plutonic rocks occur in all three areas but differ in petrological features and apparent tectonic setting: (1) in the Caledonia terrane, ca. 560–550 Ma bimodal granitic-dioritic and/or gabbroic plutons are a major component, and apparently formed during major extension within the former ca. 620 Ma arc; (2) in the Mira terrane granitic plutons have ages of ca. 575 Ma, and formed in association with a ca. 575–560(?) Ma volcanic arc; (3) in the central part of the Newfoundland Avalon terrane, arc-related plutonic and volcanic rocks of ca. 580–560 Ma age may also be widespread, but their ages are poorly constrained. Bimodal, dominantly alkaline to peralkaline ca. 570 Ma and ca. 550 Ma plutonic suites are also present in Newfoundland, but do not appear to be present in either the Mira or Caledonia terranes.

INTRODUCTION

Plutonic rocks of late Precambrian age are a major component of the Avalon zone or terrane of the northern Appalachian orogen (e.g., Williams, 1978, 1979; O'Brien et al., 1983, 1990; Nance, 1986). Recent U-Pb dating of the plutonic rocks and their host volcanic-sedimentary sequences has shown that they may record several discrete late Precambrian magmatic events, even within one geographic area of the terrane (e.g., Barr et al., 1994; Bevier et al., 1993; Hepburn et al., 1993; O'Brien et al., 1992a, 1992b, 1994). In addition, a still-growing petrochemical data base now enables a more detailed interpretation of the varied tec-

tonic settings in which the rocks were formed (e.g., Barr and White, 1988, 1996a; Barr, 1993; Kerr et al., 1995).

This chapter focuses on Late Precambrian plutonic rocks in three parts of the Avalon terrane: southern New Brunswick, southeastern Cape Breton Island, and eastern Newfoundland (Fig. 1). Although some aspects of plutonism in each of these areas have been described previously, this paper is the first overview and comparative analysis of the plutonic rocks in terms of age, petrochemistry, and tectonic setting. The analysis corroborates some of the long-assumed similarities among these classic Avalonian areas (e.g., Williams, 1978, 1979), but also demonstrates previously unemphasized differences. It forms a basis for further compar-

Barr, S. M., and Kerr, A., 1997, Late Precambrian plutons in the Avalon terrane of New Brunswick, Nova Scotia, and Newfoundland, *in* Sinha, A. K., Whalen, J. B., and Hogan, J. P., eds., The Nature of Magmatism in the Appalachian Orogen: Boulder, Colorado, Geological Society of America Memoir 191.

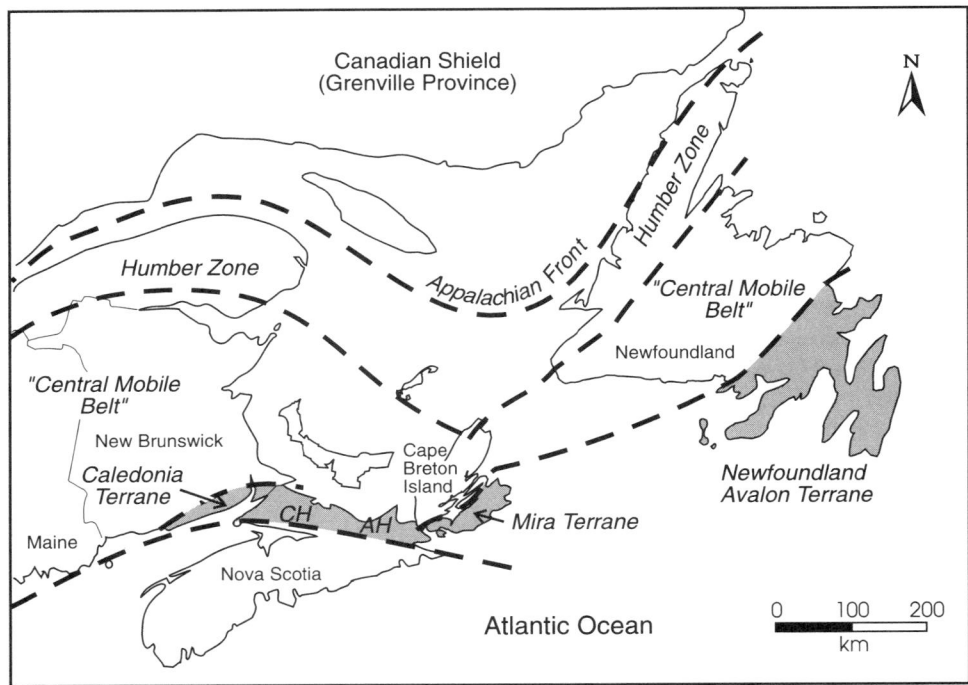

Figure 1. Distribution of the Avalon terrane sensu stricto (stippled pattern) in the Atlantic provinces of Canada. CH, Cobequid Highlands; AH, Antigonish Highlands. Maps of the Caledonia, Mira, and Newfoundland Avalon terranes are shown in Figures 2, 3, and 4, respectively. The "Central mobile belt" includes Gander, Dunnage, Bras d'Or, and equivalent terranes.

isons with other parts of the Avalon terrane, and with adjacent terranes of less certain affinity.

The extent of the Avalon terrane is controversial because rocks of Avalonian (late Precambrian) age have been widely recognized within parts of the Appalachian central mobile belt (e.g., Dunning and O'Brien, 1989; O'Brien et al., 1991), and because some areas traditionally assigned to Avalon have been reinterpreted as either separate terranes (e.g., Barr and Raeside, 1989; Barr et al., 1990; Barr and White, 1996b, White and Barr, 1996), or as part of an Avalon composite terrane (e.g., Keppie, 1989; Keppie et al., 1992; Nance and Dallmeyer, 1994) or superterrane (Gibbons, 1990). In this chapter we confine our comparisons to late Precambrian plutons in three areas within the Avalon terrane: the Caledonia terrane in New Brunswick (Barr and White, 1989a, 1996), the Mira terrane in Cape Breton Island (Barr and Raeside, 1989; Barr et al., 1990, 1994b), and the part of Newfoundland east of the Dover-Hermitage Bay fault (O'Brien et al., 1983, 1990, 1992b, 1994), here termed the Newfoundland Avalon terrane. Although these three areas have been given different names to emphasize their present geographic separation, we emphasize that we do not consider them to be separate terranes; they are all part of the Avalon terrane. Plutons in the Antigonish and Cobequid highlands of northern mainland Nova Scotia, although also part of Avalon terrane, have been described by others (Doig et al., 1991; Murphy et al., 1991; Pe-Piper and Piper, 1989) and are not included here.

CALEDONIA TERRANE, SOUTHERN NEW BRUNSWICK

Geologic setting

Recent mapping and geochronological studies in the Caledonian Highlands of southern New Brunswick (Barr and White, 1988, 1989b, 1991, 1993; Barr et al., 1994; Bevier and Barr, 1990) have resulted in subdivision of late Precambrian volcanic and sedimentary rocks, which were previously assigned or considered equivalent to the Coldbrook Group (e.g., Ruitenberg et al., 1979; Dostal and McCutcheon, 1990), into two groups. The Broad River Group forms most of the eastern Caledonian Highlands (Fig. 2), and has yielded ages ranging from 600 Ma to 635 Ma, but mainly ca. 620 Ma, whereas the redefined Coldbrook Group forms most of the western Caledonian Highlands and has yielded ages between ca. 560 and 550 Ma (Bevier and Barr, 1990; Barr et al., 1994).

The Broad River Group consists mainly of well-cleaved, greenschist-facies intermediate and felsic crystal and lithic-crystal tuffs and tuffaceous sedimentary rocks, interpreted to have formed in a continental margin subduction zone (Barr and White, 1996a). The Coldbrook Group includes intermediate to felsic tuffs, basaltic, dacitic, and rhyolitic flows and plugs, and volcaniclastic sedimentary rocks. The basaltic and rhyolitic flows, which are interpreted to form the upper part of the group, extend into the

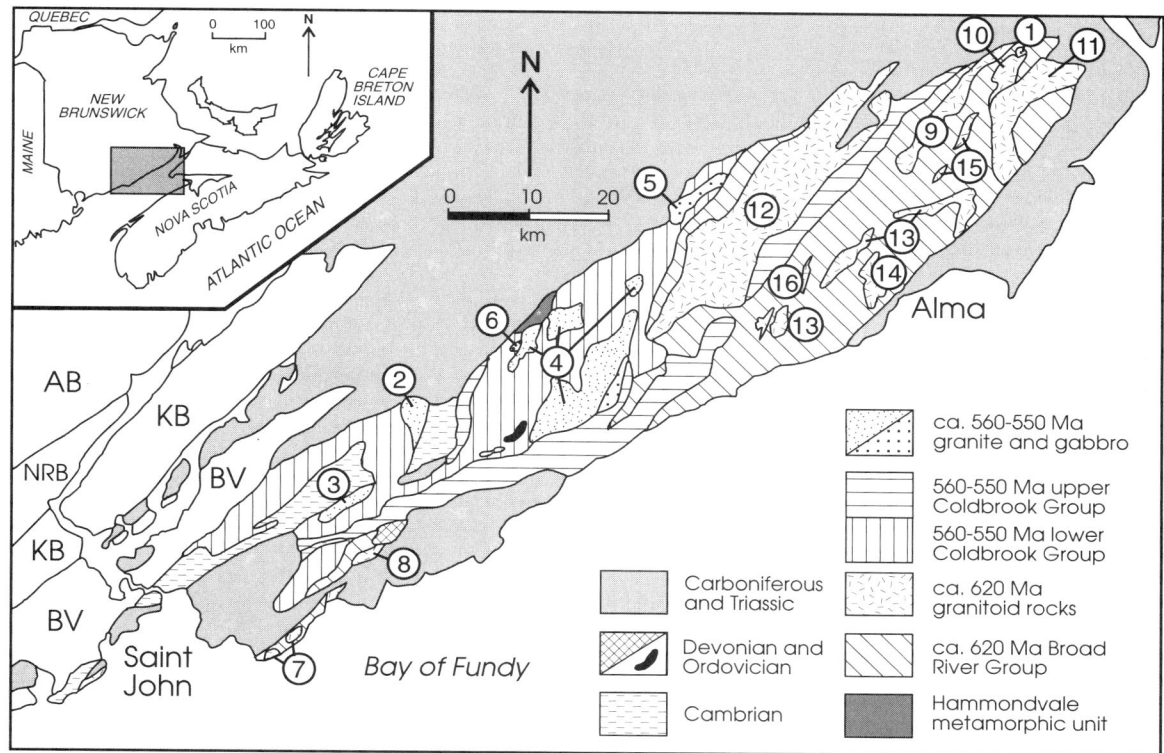

Figure 2. Simplified geologic map of the Caledonia terrane, New Brunswick, after Barr and White (1989b, 1991, 1993). Key to plutons: 1, Caledonia Mountain; 2, Upham Mountain; 3, Baxters Mountain; 4, Bonnell Brook; 5, Mechanic Settlement; 6, Devine Corner; 7, Millican Lake; 8, Emerson Creek; 9, Kent Hills; 10, Caledonia Brook; 11, Caledonia Road; 12, Point Wolfe River; 13, Fortyfive River; 14, Alma; 15, Rat-tail Brook; 16, Goose Creek. Pluton characteristics are summarized in Table 1.

southern and eastern highlands where they unconformably overlie or are in faulted contact with the Broad River Group (Fig. 2). These rocks are generally less deformed than those of the Broad River Group, and show no evidence of regional metamorphism. On the basis of petrochemistry, Currie and Eby (1990) interpreted the Coldbrook Group to have formed in a subduction-related ensialic arc, but Barr and White (1988, 1996a) suggested that it formed during extension within the older volcanic arc represented by the Broad River Group.

Plutonic rocks

Plutonic suites in the Caledonia terrane are divided into two types that correspond in age to the two volcanic-sedimentary sequences, i.e., ca. 620 Ma and ca. 560–550 Ma (Table 1). The ca. 620 Ma plutonic rocks are abundant in the eastern Caledonian Highlands in association with the Broad River Group, whereas plutons in the ca. 560–550 Ma group are widespread throughout the central and western parts of the Caledonian Highlands (Fig. 2).

Ca. 620 Ma plutons. Ca. 620 Ma plutonic rocks range in composition from gabbro and diorite to tonalite, granodiorite, and granite, but hornblende-biotite granodiorite and monzogranite are dominant (Table 1). The largest pluton is Point Wolfe River (Fig. 2,

no. 12), which extends for a distance of nearly 50 km through the central and eastern highlands. It intruded the Broad River Group on its northwestern margin, whereas the southern margin is faulted against younger rhyolite and basalt of the Coldbrook Group. The Point Wolfe River pluton has been subdivided into six lithologic units, ranging from diorite to granite, hornblende-biotite granodiorite being the dominant rock type (Barr and White, 1988). Granitic and granodioritic units have yielded U-Pb (zircon) ages of 616 ± 3 Ma and 625 ± 5 Ma, respectively (Bevier and Barr, 1990). The Kent Hills granodiorite (Fig. 2, no. 9) has a similar U-Pb age (Table 1) and is also composed mainly of hornblende-biotite granodiorite; strongly sheared and mylonitic granite along its northern margin is similar in composition to mylonitic granite that occurs along the southeastern margin of the Point Wolfe River pluton. Other compositionally similar plutons are Fortyfive River (Fig. 2, no. 13), Caledonia Brook (Fig. 2, no. 10), and the Caledonia Road granitoid suite (Fig. 2, no. 11). Other plutons of inferred ca. 620 Ma age in the eastern highlands include the Alma pluton (Fig. 2, no. 14), composed mainly of diorite and quartz diorite, and less abundant tonalite and granodiorite, the Rat Tail Brook tonalite (Fig. 2, no. 15), and the Goose Creek leucotonalite (Fig. 2, no. 16). The latter two units, as well as numerous smaller unnamed bodies of similar compositions, tend to be strongly deformed (protomy-

TABLE 1. PRECAMBRIAN PLUTONS IN THE CALEDONIA TERRANE, NEW BRUNSWICK

	Name and reference	Principle rock types	Contact relations	Geochronological data	Isotopic data	Additional comments
1	Caledonia Mountain gabbro (Ruitenberg et al., 1979; Barr and White, 1993).	Gabbro, locally with ultramafic and anorthositic layers.	Intruded Coldbrook Group; well-developed contact aureole.	None. Age of ca. 550 Ma inferred by comparison with Mechanic Settlement pluton.	None.	Also known as Weldon Creek stock.
2	Upham Mountain pluton (Ruitenberg et al., 1979; Barr and White, 1991).	Syenogranite, minor diorite, and gabbro.	Chilled margins against dacitic tuff of Coldbrook Group; faulted against Cambrian rocks on east, and Carboniferous rocks to north.	554 ± 5 Ma (U-Pb zircon) (Barr et al., 1994).	ε_{Nd} = +0.3 at 554 Ma (Whalen et al., 1994).	Petrologically similar to Bonnell Brook pluton.
3	Baxters Mountain pluton (Ruitenberg et al., 1979; Barr and White, 1991).	Diorite, gabbro, syenogranite; porphyritic dikes.	Forms dikes in adjacent Coldbrook Group.	None. Age of ca. 550 Ma inferred by comparison with Upham Mountain and Bonnell Brook plutons.	None.	Poorly exposed.
4	Bonnell Brook pluton (Ruitenberg et al., 1979; Barr and White, 1988).	Fine-grained to medium-grained syenogranite, fine-grained granophyric syenogranite (grades to spherulitic rhyolite), diorite, minor gabbro.	Intruded Coldbrook Group and Point Wolfe River pluton.	550 ± 1 Ma (U-Pb zircon) (Bevier and Barr, 1990).	ε_{Nd} = +2.8 in diorite and +0.4 and +1.5 in syenogranite at 550 Ma (Whalen et al., 1994).	Deeper parts exposed in south, grades to granophyric granite and spherulitic rhyolite to north.
5	Mechanic Settlement pluton (Ruitenberg et al., 1979; Barr and White, 1988; Grammatikopoulos, 1992; Grammatikopoulos et al., 1995).	Gabbro, gabbronorite, olivine gabbronorite, troctolite, anorthosite, pyroxenite, quartz diorite.	Intruded Coldbrook Group. Well-developed contact metamorphic aureole.	557 ± 3 Ma (U-Pb zircon); ca. 545 Ma (Ar/Ar phlogopite) (Barr et al., 1994).	None.	Layered intrusion with Ni and platinum-group elements mineralization.
6	Devine Corner gabbro (Grammatikopoulos, 1992).	Gabbro.	Intruded Coldbrook Group.	None. Ca. 550 Ma inferred from proximity to Bonnell Brook pluton.	None.	Similar to dioritic/gabbroic parts of Bonnell Brook pluton.
7	Millican Lake plutons (Ruitenberg et al., 1979; Watters, 1993).	Sheared granite and granodiorite.	Faulted against slivers of Broad River Group(?) and Carboniferous sedimentary rocks.	623 ± 2 Ma (Watters, 1993).	ε_{Nd} = +0.1 at 625 Ma (Whalen et al., 1994).	Fragmented by faulting. Protomylonitic.
8	Emerson Creek pluton (Ruitenberg et al., 1979; Barr and White, 1991).	Sheared granite and granodiorite.	Faulted against Broad River Group(?) and varied Carboniferous rocks.	None. Ca. 620 Ma inferred from similarity to Millican Lake plutons.	ε_{Nd} = +0.5 at 625 Ma (Whalen et al., 1994).	Similar to Millican Lake plutons. Formerly called Black River pluton.
9	Kent Hills granodiorite (Barr and White, 1993).	Hornblende-biotite granodiorite.	Intruded and sheared against Broad River Group.	615 + 1/2 Ma (U-Pb zircon) (Barr et al., 1994).	None.	Poorly exposed but large. Sheared.

TABLE 1. PRECAMBRIAN PLUTONS IN THE CALEDONIA TERRANE, NEW BRUNSWICK (Continued - page 2)

	Name and reference	Principle rock type	Contact relations	Geochronological data	Isotopic data	Additional comments
10	Caledonia Brook pluton (Ruitenberg et al., 1979; Barr and White, 1993)	Biotite-hornblende granodiorite.	Intruded Broad River Group. Intruded by gabbroic dikes from Caledonia Mountain gabbro.	None. Ca. 620 Ma inferred by similarity to Kent Hills granodiorite.	None.	More mafic than Kent Hills granodiorite.
11	Caledonia Road granitoid suite (Ruitenberg et al., 1979; Barr and White, 1993).	Granodiorite, granite, diorite.	Intruded Broad River Group.	None. Ca 620 inferred from similarity to other plutons in Broad River Group.	None.	Includes former Caledonia Road, Crooked Creek, and Memel Creek sills. Complex mix of lithologies cannot be subdivided into mappable units.
12	Point Wolfe River pluton (Ruitenberg et al., 1979; Barr and White, 1988).	Large composite pluton; main units (in order of inferred increasing age): Blueberry Hill granite, Old Shepody Road granite and granodiorite, Pollett River granodiorite, quartz monzodiorite-tonalite, quartz diorite-tonalite.	Contacts with Broad River Group along northern margin appear intrusive but southern contacts with the Coldbrook Group are sheared and faulted.	Pollett River granodiorite: 625 ± 5 Ma; Old Shepody Road granite: 616 ± 3 Ma (U-Pb zircon; Bevier and Barr, 1990).	ε_{Nd} = +0.9 (Pollett River granodiorite) and + 1.7 (Old Shepody Road granite) at 625 and 616 Ma, respectively (Whalen et al., 1994).	A large and complex pluton (really a batholith). In places protomylonitic, especially southern margin of Old Shepody Road granite and the Blueberry Hill granite (Barr and White, 1988).
13	Fortyfive River granodiorite (Ruitenberg et al., 1979; Barr and White, 1988).	Granodiorite gradational to granite.	Intruded ca. 620 Ma Broad River Group.	597 ± 18 Ma (Rb-Sr wholerock, Barr and White, 1988). Ca 620 Ma inferred age.	ε_{Nd} = +2.5 at 600 Ma (Whalen et al., 1994).	Three separate bodies with similar petrology.
14.	Alma diorite (Ruitenberg et al., 1979; Barr and White, 1988).	Mainly diorite and quartz diorite; varied grain size.	Intruded ca. 620 Ma Broad River Group.	598 ± 27 Ma (K-Ar hornblende; Barr and White, 1988). Ca. 620 Ma inferred age.	None.	Generally less altered and deformed than the Goose Creek and Rat-tail Brook plutons.
15	Rat-tail Brook tonalite (Barr and White, 1993).	Tonalite.	Intruded ca. 620 Ma Broad River Group.	None. Ca. 620 Ma inferred based on similarity to other plutons in the Broad River Group.	None.	Includes three small sheared and altered plutons. Appears more mafic than the Goose Creek leucotonalite but no primary mafic minerals are preserved.
16	Goose Creek leucotonalite (Ruitenberg et al., 1979; Barr and White, 1988).	Mainly granophyric, leucocratic tonalite.	Intruded ca. 620 Ma Broad River Group.	None. Ca. 620 Ma inferred, based on close association with Broad River Group.	None.	Includes several small, sheared and altered plutons. No primary mafic minerals are preserved.

lonitic) and intensely altered; mafic minerals are mainly replaced by epidote and chlorite.

In the western part of the Caledonian Highlands, plutons of ca. 620 Ma age occur only near the Bay of Fundy coast south of the city of Saint John (the Millican Lake and Emerson Creek plutons; Fig. 2, nos. 7, 8). They have tonalitic to granodioritic compositions, similar to units in the eastern part of the terrane, and are sheared and altered as a result of Carboniferous and probably also older deformation (Watters, 1993).

Ca. 560–550 Ma plutons. Ca. 560–550 Ma plutons are dominantly of either granitic or dioritic to gabbroic composition, or both (Table 1). Like their host rocks, they are generally less deformed and altered than the ca. 620 Ma plutons, and original igneous features are well preserved.

The largest pluton is Bonnell Brook (Fig. 2, no. 4), which consists mostly of granite containing less than 3% biotite, amphibole, titanite, and allanite (Barr and White, 1988). Granophyric granite occurs mainly along the northern margins of the pluton, and in places can be mapped as a separate unit (Barr and White, 1988, 1991). Areas of diorite to quartz diorite are present on the southeastern margin of the pluton, and are cut by dikes of the granite. The Bonnell Brook pluton is interpreted to be a high-level intrusion; shallower parts are exposed toward the northern part of the map area where it appears to grade to rhyolite (Barr and White, 1988).

The Upham Mountain pluton (Fig. 2, no. 2) consists mainly of granite, together with minor diorite and gabbro. The granite is everywhere granophyric, and similar to the granophyric parts of the Bonnell Brook pluton. The Baxters Mountain pluton (Fig. 2, no. 3) consists mainly of quartz diorite and gabbro in the southwest, with granite in the central and northeastern parts.

The Mechanic Settlement pluton (Fig. 2, no. 5) is mainly gabbroic but grades to ultramafic compositions (plagioclase-bearing lherzolite and pyroxenite) and to diorite, quartz diorite, and quartz monzodiorite (Grammatikopoulos, 1992; Grammatikopoulos et al., 1995). Smaller gabbroic plutons such as Caledonia Mountain (Weldon Creek stock of Ruitenberg et al., 1979) (Fig. 2, no. 1) and Devine Corner (Fig. 2, no. 6) are probably of similar age. U-Pb and ^{40}Ar/^{39}Ar dates have confirmed a 560–550 Ma age for the Mechanic Settlement pluton (Grammatikopoulos et al., 1995), essentially the same as the ages of the Bonnell Brook and Upham Mountain granites and the volcanic rocks of the Coldbrook Group. Hence, the 560–550 Ma igneous rocks represent a major event during which more than half of the rocks now exposed in the Caledonia terrane were formed.

MIRA TERRANE, CAPE BRETON ISLAND

Geologic setting

Late Precambrian volcanic and sedimentary rocks in the Mira terrane of southeastern Cape Breton Island, formerly assigned to the Fourchu Group (e.g., Keppie, 1979), have now been divided into six groups on the basis of age, geographic distribution, and lithology (Bevier et al., 1993; Barr et al., 1996).

The ca. 680 Ma Stirling Group forms much of the area known as the Stirling belt (Fig. 3), and consists mainly of andesitic to basaltic lapilli tuff, tuffaceous litharenite, and laminated siltstone, together with less abundant basaltic flows and breccias, rhyolitic crystal-rich lapilli tuff, and rhyolitic quartz-feldspar porphyry. The volcanic rocks show wide scatter and inconsistencies on the standard discrimination diagrams (Barr, 1993; Macdonald and Barr, 1993), but overall appear to have chemical features indicative of a volcanic arc setting.

The East Bay Hills, Coxheath Hills, and Pringle Mountain groups form the northwestern parts of the Mira terrane (Fig. 3). All three areas consist of rocks with ages of ca. 620 Ma (Bevier et al., 1993), mainly lapilli tuffs with abundant crystal and lithic fragments, and less abundant flows ranging from basaltic to rhyolitic in composition (Barr et al., 1988, 1996). They have petrochemical features similar to high-K calc-alkalic suites formed at continental margin subduction zones (Barr, 1993).

The redefined ca. 575 Ma Fourchu Group forms most of the Coastal belt south of Louisbourg Harbour (Fig. 3), and consists dominantly of varied lapilli tuff and coarse ash tuff and rare flows of dacitic composition, and subordinate amounts of basaltic to andesitic lapilli tuff and flows, rhyolitic tuffs and flows, and very minor tuffaceous sedimentary rocks. The Main-à-Dieu Group occurs northeast of Louisbourg Harbour, on Scatarie Island, and along the faulted western margin of the Coastal belt (Fig. 3). It consists dominantly of tuffaceous sedimentary or epiclastic rocks, and subordinate basaltic and rhyolitic flows. On the basis of field relations (Barr et al., 1994), the Main-à-Dieu sequence is interpreted to be younger than the Fourchu sequence, although the two sequences may be in part facies equivalents, the Main-à-Dieu Group having been deposited in intra-arc basins developed adjacent to the stratovolcanoes represented by the Fourchu Group. The volcanic rocks of the Coastal belt have chemical features transitional between calc-alkalic and tholeiitic, and may represent magmas derived early in the development of a ca. 575 Ma subduction zone (Barr, 1993).

The Coxheath Hills, Sporting Mountain, and East Bay Hills belts have been interpreted to represent different parts of a ca. 620 Ma volcanic arc complex, formed by subduction to the present southeast, under an older arc complex built on continental crust, now represented only by the Stirling belt (Macdonald and Barr, 1993). In this model, the Coastal belt was interpreted to have formed significantly later at ca. 575–550 Ma, by subduction toward the present northwest, beneath the much older volcanic arc complex represented by the Stirling belt. However, these interpretations are complicated by the presence of major faults within and between the belts with unknown amounts of Paleozoic lateral offset; hence, it is not known with certainty where these belts of rocks originated relative to one another.

Plutonic rocks

The most abundant and widespread plutons in the Mira terrane have yielded ages of ca. 620 Ma (Table 2), and occur in association with volcanic rocks of similar age in the East Bay

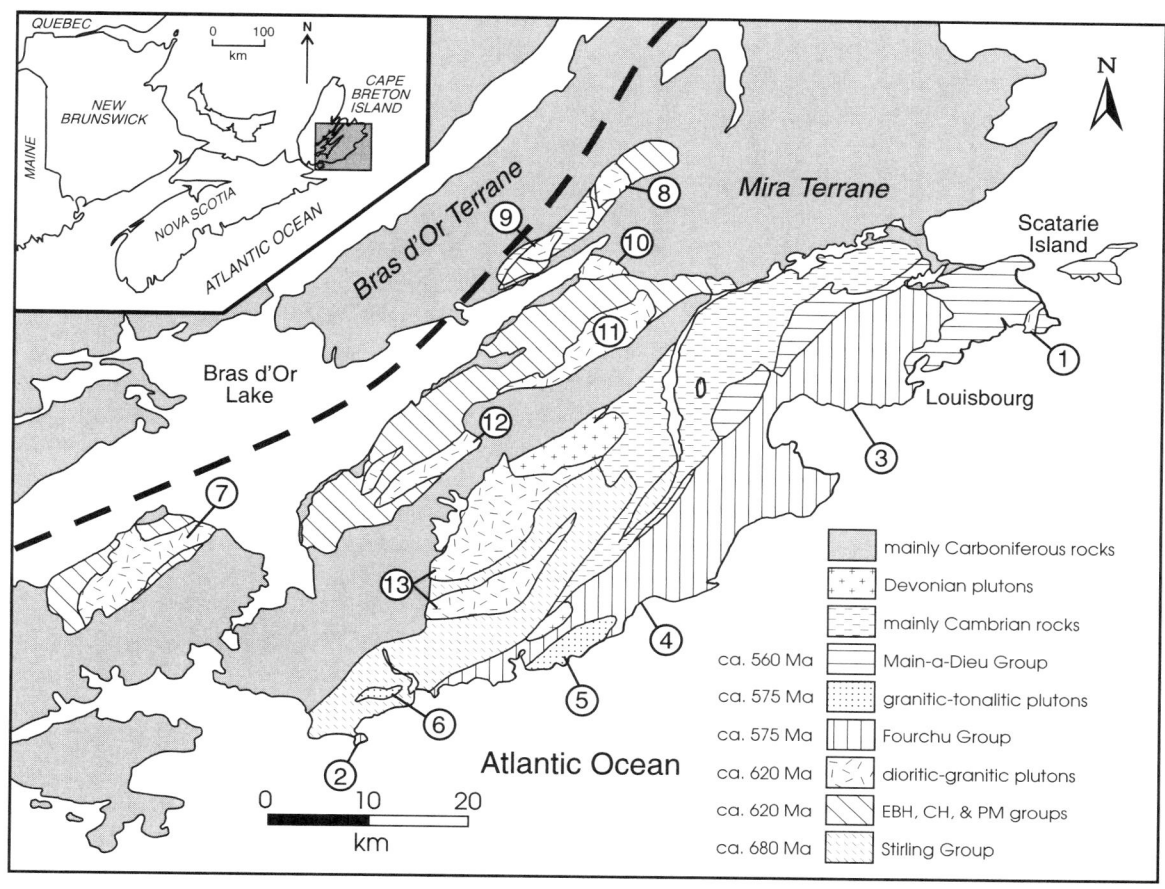

Figure 3. Simplified geologic map of the Mira terrane, Cape Breton Island, after Barr et al. (1988, 1989, 1996). Key to plutons: 1, Baleine; 2, Point Michaud; 3, Kennington Cove; 4, Belfrey Gut; 5, Capelin Cove; 6, Grand River; 7, Sporting Mountain; 8, Coxheath Hills; 9, Spruce Brook; 10, MacEachern Lake; 11, Huntington Mountain; 12, Irish Cove; 13, Chisholm Brook. Pluton characteristics are summarized in Table 2.

Hills, Coxheath Hills, and Sporting Mountain belts, and also with ca. 680 Ma rocks in the Stirling belt (Fig. 3). Gabbroic dikes, sills, and small plutons in the ca. 680 Ma Stirling Group are interpreted to be similar in age to the host volcanic rocks (Macdonald and Barr, 1993), and no granitoid rocks of that age have been recognized. Small granitic plutons dated at ca. 575 Ma occur in the Fourchu Group and possibly in the adjacent Stirling Group, and both the Fourchu and Main-à-Dieu groups are intruded by numerous small gabbroic plutons of uncertain, but probable latest Precambrian, age.

Ca. 620 Ma plutons. As in the Caledonia terrane, the ca. 620 Ma plutons range from diorite to granite, biotite-hornblende granodiorite and granite being the most abundant rock types in most plutons except Huntington Mountain. The Huntington Mountain pluton (Fig. 3, no. 11) underlies much of the northeastern part of the East Bay Hills, and consists mainly of heterogeneous dioritic rocks and two varieties of granite: medium- to coarse-grained leucocratic monzogranite and fine- to medium-grained syenogranite, and dikes and small granitoid bodies of varied mafic to felsic composition (Barr et al., 1982, 1988). The Irish

Cove pluton (Fig. 3, no. 12) in the southern and central part of the East Bay Hills is a high-level pluton that contains numerous inclusions and roof pendants of the host volcanic rocks (Barr et al., 1996). It consists mainly of relatively homogeneous medium-grained monzogranite, which does not closely resemble any of the units of Huntington Mountain pluton. However, it is similar in texture and mineralogy to granodiorite of the Chisholm Brook suite (Fig. 3, no. 13) in the adjacent Stirling belt, although the latter contains less K-feldspar and more mafic minerals. Unlike Irish Cove, the Chisholm Brook Suite also includes large bodies of dioritic rocks and quartz monzodiorite, and has been interpreted to represent a deeper level of exposure of a single plutonic suite (McMullin, 1984). The MacEachern Lake, Coxheath Hills, and Spruce Brook plutons (Fig. 3, nos. 10, 8, 9) are all small composite plutons that consist mainly of granodiorite, monzogranite, and dioritic rocks (Thicke, 1987). The Sporting Mountain pluton (Fig. 3, no. 7) consists mainly of granodiorite grading to monzogranite and tonalite (Sexton, 1988). Subporphyritic texture and abundance of granophyre suggest that the pluton was emplaced at a relatively high crustal level (Sexton, 1988).

TABLE 2. PRECAMBRIAN PLUTONS IN THE MIRA TERRANE, CAPE BRETON ISLAND, NOVA SCOTIA

	Pluton name and reference	Principle rock types	Contact relationships	Age constraints	Isotopic data	Additional comments
1	Baleine gabbro (Murphy, 1977; Grammatikopoulos, 1992; Barr et al., 1996).	Gabbro.	Intruded ca. 560 Ma Main-à-Dieu Group.	None. Ca. 560 Ma inferred from close association with Main-à-Dieu Group.	None.	Similar small gabbroic plutons occur through the northern part of the Coastal belt. Their absence in Cambrian units and petrochemical similarity to Main-à-Dieu Group basalts indicates that they are late Precambrian in age.
2	Point Michaud leucogranite (Barr et al., 1996).	Leucogranite.	Sheets in Fourchu Group.	None. Ca. 575 Ma inferred from similarity and proximity to Capelin Cove Pluton.	None.	Similar to both Capelin Cove pluton and Grand River pluton.
3	Kennington Cove pluton (Donohoe, 1981; Barr et al., 1996).	Tonalite.	Intruded ca. 575 Ma Kennington Cove tuff member of Fourchu Group.	None. Ca. 575 Ma inferred from close association with Kennington Cove tuff.	None.	Locally sheared.
4	Belfrey Gut pluton (Barr et al., 1996).	Monzogranite; leucocratic.	Intruded tuff of ca. 575 Ma Fourchu Group.	None. Ca. 575 Ma inferred from similarity and proximity to Capelin Cove Pluton.	None.	Similar to parts of Capelin Cove pluton.
5	Capelin Cove pluton (Cormier, 1972; O'Reilly, 1977; Barr et al., 1988, 1989, 1996).	Monzogranite, leucogranite, granodiorite.	Intruded ca. 575 Ma Fourchu Group.	574 ± 3 Ma (U-Pb zircon, Bevier et al., 1993). Rb-Sr by Cormier (1972) considered unreliable.	$\varepsilon_{Nd} = +5.0$ at 574 Ma (Barr and Hegner, 1992).	Cogenetic with Fourchu Group, pervasively sheared and locally protomylonitic.
6	Grand River pluton (Barr et al., 1988, 1989).	Leucogranite.	Poorly exposed; surrounded by volcanic and sedimentary rocks of ca. 680 Ma Stirling Group.	None. Inferred ca. 575 Ma based on petrological similarity to Capelin Cove pluton.	None.	Pervasively altered and deformed albite has replaced K-spar in granophyre. No primary mafic minerals.
7	Sporting Mountain pluton (Weeks, 1954; Sexton, 1988; Barr et al., 1996).	Granodiorite transitional to monzogranite; tonalite; sheared with volcanic host rocks on southern margin.	Intruded undated Pringle Mountain Group.	Rb-Sr and K-Ar dates (Sexton, 1988) of ca. 577 and 587 Ma are unreliable. Ca. 620 Ma inferred from similarity to plutons in Coxheath and East Bay Hills.	None.	Based on similarity to Spruce Brook and Coxheath Hills plutons, ca. 620 Ma age is assumed. Some Cu-Mo-Au.
8	Coxheath Hills pluton (Barr and Setter, 1986; Thicke, 1987; Barr et al., 1996).	Largest unit is granodiorite grading to monzogranite; also units of diorite to quartz diorite, quartz monzodiorite, and gabbronorite, and abundant granitic dikes.	Intruded ca. 620 Ma Coxheath Group.	Ca. 621 Ma (Ar-Ar hb; Keppie et al., 1990). Various Rb-Sr and K-Ar dates in older literature are considered unreliable.	None.	Cogenetic with volcanic rocks of Coxheath Group. Significant porphyry-type Cu-Mo-Au.

TABLE 2. PRECAMBRIAN PLUTONS IN THE MIRA TERRANE, CAPE BRETON ISLAND, NOVA SCOTIA (Continued - page 2)

	Pluton name and reference	Principle rock types	Contact relationships	Age constraints	Isotopic data	Additional comments
9	Spruce Brook pluton (Barr and Setter, 1986; Thicke, 1987; Barr et al., 1996).	Mainly granodiorite with minor bodies of monzo-granite and dioritic rocks.	Intruded ca. 620 Ma Coxheath Group. Nonconformably overlain by Cambrian sedimentary rocks.	None. Ca. 620 Ma inferred from similarity to Coxheath Hills and plutons in East Bay Hills.	None.	Similar to Coxheath Hills pluton.
10	MacEachern Lake pluton (Thicke, 1987; Barr et al., 1996).	Mainly granodiorite with smaller areas of monzo-granite and quartz diorite.	Intruded ca. 620 Ma East Bay Hills Group.	None. Ca. 620 Ma inferred from similarity to Coxheath Hills and East Bay Hills plutons.	None.	Most similar to Coxheath Hills pluton.
11	Huntington Mountain pluton (Barr et al., 1982, 1996).	Mainly dioritic rocks of varied grain size and texture intruded by medium- to coarse-grained leucogranite and fine- to medium-grained syenogranite; minor bodies of monzogranite and granodiorite; abundant varied mafic to felsic dikes.	Intruded ca. 620 Ma East Bay Hills Group. Contact aureole in adjacent metavolcanic rocks.	619 ± 4 Ma (U-Pb zircon; leucogranite unit; Barr et al., 1996); ca. 631 and 618 Ma (Ar-Ar hb, dioritic unit).	ε_{Nd} = +2.9 at 620 Ma (Barr and Hegner, 1992).	No units identical to Irish Cove pluton, but age similar. Cogenetic with volcanic rocks of East Bay Hills Group.
12	Irish Cove pluton (Weeks, 1954; O'Reilly, 1977; McMullin, 1984; Barr et al., 1996).	Monzogranite, with fine-grained porphyritic felsite and mafic dikes.	Intruded ca. 620 Ma East Bay Hills Group. Abundant xenoliths and roof pendants of host rocks.	None, but assumed ca. 620 Ma based on petrological similarity to Chisholm Brook suite.	None.	Interpreted to represent more evolved correlative of Chisholm Brook suite.
13	Chisholm Brook suite (McMullin, 1984; Barr et al., 1996).	Mainly granodiorite with areas of quartz monzodiorite and diorite grading to quartz diorite.	Intruded ca. 680 Ma Stirling Group and intruded by Salmon River rhyolite porphyry and many mafic dikes.	620 +3/-2 Ma (U-Pb zircon, granodiorite unit; Dunning et al., 1990); ca. 628 and 608 Ma (Ar-Ar hb, dioritic unit; Keppie et al., 1990).	ε_{Nd} = +1.5 at 620 Ma (Barr and Hegner, 1992).	Well-exposed contact metamorphic aureole in Stirling Group. Dioritic to granodioritic rocks genetically related (McMullin, 1984).

Ca. 575 Ma plutons. The Capelin Cove pluton (Fig. 3, no. 5) consists mainly of coarse-grained leucocratic monzogranite. Shearing and cataclasis are widespread over its entire width, as a result of which the rock in most places consists of porphyroclasts of feldspar in a foliated matrix of granulated quartz, feldspar, and minor chlorite and epidote. In rare enclaves of less intense shearing, the granite is coarse grained, with about equal proportions of quartz, plagioclase, and microcline, and minor chloritized biotite. Other similar plutons in the Fourchu Group include the Kennington Cove pluton (Fig. 3, no. 3) and Belfrey Gut granite (Fig. 3, no. 4). In addition, small sheets and bodies of granite, diorite, and granodiorite are numerous.

The Grand River pluton (Fig. 3, no. 6) in the adjacent Stirling belt is composed of leucogranite similar to the sheets at Point Michaud, and parts of the Capelin Cove pluton. Although undated, it is inferred to be of similar age on the basis of lithological similarity, and thus provides an important link between the Coastal and Stirling belts (Macdonald and Barr, 1993).

Ca. 550 Ma(?) plutons. Gabbroic plutons in the Main-à-Dieu Group and northern part of the Fourchu Group are undated, but are inferred to have an age of ca. 550 Ma, based on their presence in the Main-à-Dieu sequence, but apparent absence in overlying Cambrian units (Barr et al., 1996). The largest of these plutons is the Baleine gabbro (Fig. 3, no. 1). All are relatively homogeneous gabbroic plutons, composed mostly of plagioclase and clinopyroxene. They differ from ca. 560–550 Ma gabbroic plutons in the Caledonia terrane in that they do not show pronounced effects of fractional crystallization (Grammatikopoulos, 1992; Grammatikopoulos et al., 1995), and are not associated with coeval granitic plutons.

NEWFOUNDLAND AVALON TERRANE, EASTERN NEWFOUNDLAND

Geologic setting

Recent mapping and geochronology (Krogh et al., 1988; Swinden and Hunt, 1991; O'Brien et al., 1992a, 1992b, 1994; Rabu et al., 1993) indicate that late Precambrian rocks in eastern Newfoundland, like those in the Mira and Caledonia terranes, can be divided into units of distinctly different ages (Fig. 4). However, the Newfoundland Avalon terrane is larger and more complex, and the distribution of these units is not yet well constrained.

The oldest known rocks are sedimentary and mafic volcanic rocks and gabbros exposed in the fault-bounded Burin Group, for which a gabbro sill dated at 763 ± 2 Ma provides a minimum age (Krogh et al., 1988). On the basis of lithology and petrochemistry, as well as correlations with other Pan-African terranes, the Burin Group has been viewed as ophiolitic (e.g., Strong, 1979), but the volcanic rocks have compositions transitional to those of primitive arc rocks (Strong and Dostal, 1980). The Burin Group may represent a sample of basement to the Avalon terrane or, alternatively, a completely exotic terrane (Gibbons, 1990).

Felsic volcanic rocks of the Tickle Point Formation in the Hermitage Peninsula area (Fig. 4) have been dated at 682 ± 3 Ma, and

are intruded by granites dated at 673 ± 3 Ma (O'Brien et al., 1992a, 1992b). The full extent of these 680–670 Ma rocks in the southwestern Avalon terrane of Newfoundland is presently unknown.

Volcanic rocks dated at ca. 630 Ma to ca. 600 Ma (Dallmeyer et al., 1981; Krogh et al., 1988; O'Brien et al., 1992b) are a major component of the Avalon terrane in Newfoundland. West of the Paradise Sound fault, they include the Marystown, Love Cove, and Connaigre Bay groups (O'Brien et al., 1983, 1990, 1992a) (Fig. 4), and east of the fault, the Harbour Main Group. All four groups consist of mafic to felsic volcanic rocks of both submarine and subaerial setting, but those west of the fault have tholeiitic to calc-alkaline affinities, whereas the Harbour Main Group has mildly alkaline affinities (Nixon and Papezik, 1979). Hence, although the units west and east of the Paradise Sound fault overlap in age, they might not have been spatially associated at the time of their formation.

Recent work on the French islands of St. Pierre et Miquelon indicates slightly younger felsic volcanism with an age of ca. 580 Ma (Rabu et al., 1993). Volcanic rocks of this age are not yet known in adjacent parts of Newfoundland, although rhyolitic dikes in the Harbour Main Group have yielded a similar age (Krogh et al., 1988).

The ca. 620 Ma volcanic piles are overlain by sedimentary sequences on both sides of the Paradise Sound fault (Fig. 4), but sedimentary sequences are more extensive in the east, where they are represented by turbidites of the Connecting Point and Conception groups (e.g., King, 1986; Knight and O'Brien, 1988). The Conception Group is conformably to disconformably overlain by shale and sandstone of the St. John's Group, and by shallow marine to alluvial rocks of the Signal Hill Group; the Connecting Point Group is unconformably overlain by the Musgravetown Group, which is lithologically similar, and presumed to be equivalent, to the St. John's and Signal Hill groups (King, 1986; O'Brien et al., 1990). Bimodal alkalic volcanic rocks of the Bull Arm Formation are associated with the Musgravetown Group. West of the Paradise Sound fault, the Long Harbour Group includes similar alkalic volcanic rocks, and dated units now indicate that the group represents a time interval from 568 ± 5 Ma to 552 ± 3 Ma (O'Brien et al., 1994).

Plutonic rocks

Late Precambrian plutonic rocks in the Newfoundland Avalon terrane are much more abundant west than east of the Paradise Sound fault (Fig. 4). Reliably dated plutons are of four ages (excluding the ca. 763 Ma gabbroic sill in the Burin Group): ca. 673 Ma, 620 Ma, 570 Ma, and 550 Ma (Table 3). These ages generally correspond within error limits to the ages of volcanic rocks noted above. However, numerous plutons are undated, or have imprecise ages, such as the Swift Current granite described below.

Ca. 673 Ma plutons. The 673 ± 3 Ma Furbys Cove intrusive suite in the westernmost part of the terrane (Fig. 4, no. 1) is the only plutonic suite known to be of this age in Newfoundland.

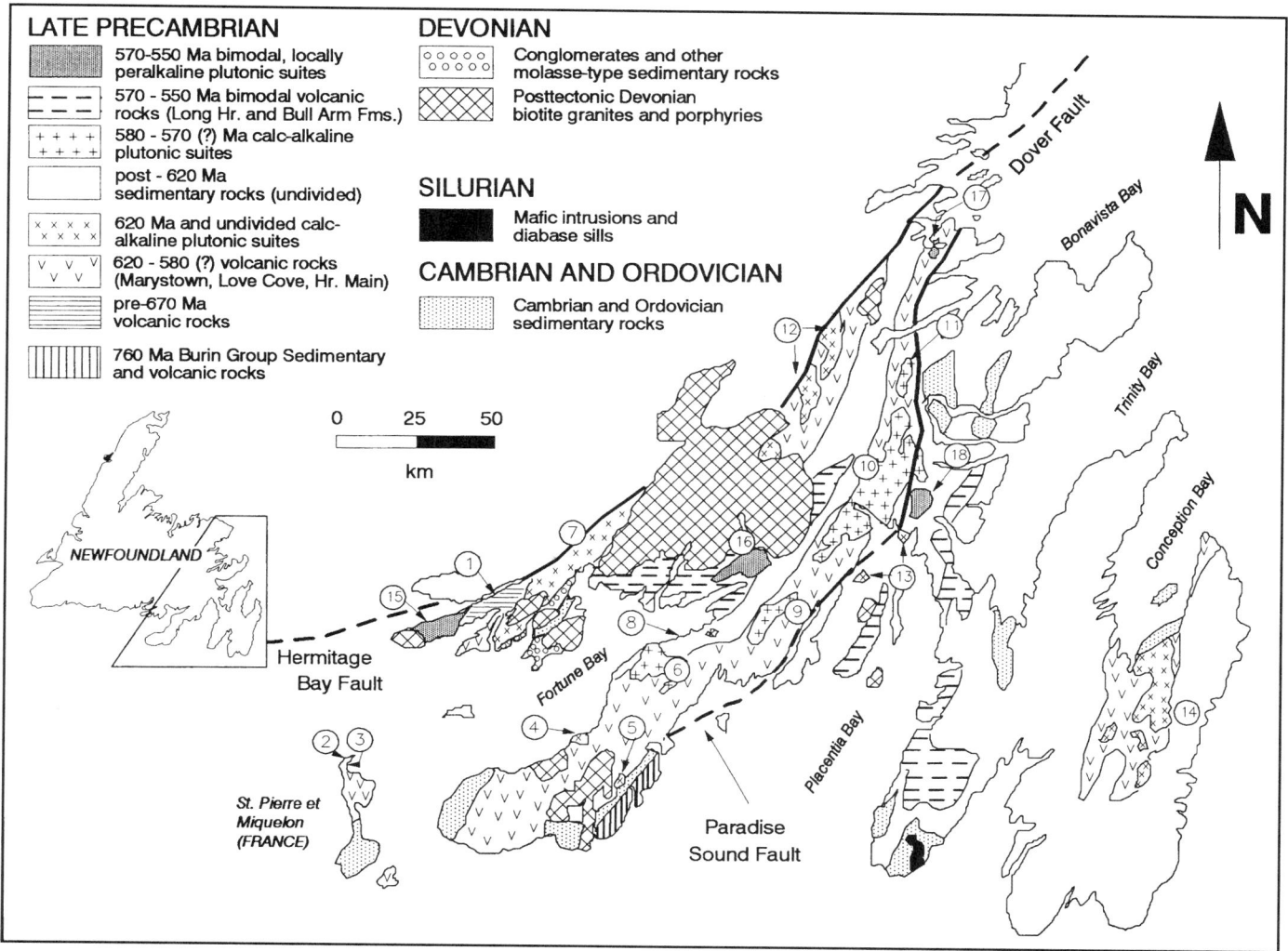

Figure 4. Simplified geologic map of the Avalon terrane in Newfoundland. Geology after Colman-Sadd et al. (1990) with modifications after O'Brien et al. (1992a). Key to plutons: 1, Furby's Cove; 2, Cap Blanc (Miquelon); 3, Anse à la Vierge (Miquelon); 4, Seal Cove; 5, Anchor Drogue; 6, the "Knee Granites"; 7, Simmons Brook; 8, Deepwater Point; 9, Cape Roger Mountain; 10, Swift Current; 11, Georges Pond; 12, Salmon Pond; 13, Sall the Maid and Placentia Bay; 14, Holyrood; 15, Grole; 16, Cross Hills; 17, Louil Hills; 18, Powderhorn. Pluton characteristics are summarized in Table 3.

O'Brien et al. (1992a) divided the suite into three components: altered mafic intrusive rocks, equigranular granite, and a bimodal dike swarm. The entire suite covers only a few square kilometers, and is currently represented by only a single chemical analysis. O'Brien et al. (1992b) described the Furbys Cove intrusive suite and its ca. 680 Ma host rocks as arc-like, on the basis of their general lithological features. Due to the few data available, we do not discuss these rocks further.

Ca. 620 Ma plutons. West of the Paradise Sound fault, reliably dated plutons with ages of ca. 620 Ma include the Simmons Brook intrusive suite (Fig. 4, no. 7) (Greene and O'Driscoll, 1976; O'Driscoll and Strong, 1979; O'Brien et al., 1994), which is dominated by variably foliated hornblende (± biotite) granodiorite, the Cap Blanc hornblende granodiorite on the French island of

Miquelon (Fig. 4, no. 2) (Rabu et al., 1993), and a quartz-feldspar porphyry boulder in conglomerate of the Rock Harbour Group of the Burin Peninsula (Krogh et al., 1988). These results suggest that the 620 Ma plutonism may have been of regional significance in the area west of the Paradise Sound fault, consistent with the abundance of volcanic rocks of similar age in that area.

East of the Paradise Sound fault, ca. 620 Ma plutonic rocks are represented mainly by the Holyrood intrusive suite (Fig. 4, no. 14) (Rose, 1952; Strong and Minatidas, 1975; Krogh et al., 1988). The suite is dominated by hornblende-biotite quartz diorite, granodiorite, and monzogranite. Mafic rocks are subordinate, and dioritic phases present in granitic outcrops display complex relationships suggestive of mingling, mixing, and hybridization. Miarolitic, equigranular granites with accessory tourmaline and

TABLE 3. LATE PRECAMBRIAN PLUTONS IN THE AVALON TERRANE OF NEWFOUNDLAND

	Name and reference	Principal rock types	Contact relations	Geochronological data	Isotopic data	Additional comments
1	Fruby's Cove intrusive suite (O'Brien et al., 1992a) including Furby's Cove Granite of Greene and O'Driscoll (1976).	Variably altered gabbro to quartz diorite, equigranular granite with blue quartz mafic and felsic dikes.	Intruded recently recognized ~680 Ma volcanic rocks, but overlain by Connaigre Bay Group (redefined).	673 ± 2 Ma (U-Pb zircon) O'Brien et al. (1992b).	None.	Of limited areal extent, but important in defining early volcanic rocks of the Hermitage Peninsula.
2	Cap Blanc granodiorite, Ile de Miquelon (Rabu et al., 1993).	Hb-Bi granodiorite with poorly developed magmatic banding.	Intruded pelitic schists, metavolcanic rocks and tuffs of the Cap de Miquelon area, which are in faulted contact with ~580 Ma St. Pierre Group.	615 ± 14 Ma (U-Pb zircon); thermal evaporation; 614 + 11/-6 (U-Pb, discordia method (Rabu et al., 1993).	None.	Very small body confined to the northern tip of Ile de Miquelon.
3	Anse à la Vierge granodiorite, Ile de Miquelon (Rabu et al., 1993).	Melanocratic Hb-Bi granodiorite.	Intruded Cap Blanc granodiorite.	None.	None.	Very small body confined to the northern tip of Ile de Miquelon.
4	Seal Cove pluton (Strong et al., 1977).	Described as gabbroic by Strong et al. (1977), but roadcut outcrops are granodioritic.	Presumed to intrude Marystown Group.	None.	ε_{Nd} of -4 at 600 Ma (Kerr et al., 1995).	Very small, poorly exposed body. Contains minor disseminated chalcopyrite.
5	Anchor Drogue pluton (Strong et al., 1977).	Equigranular, leucocratic granodiorite and granite, variably chlonitized. Many internal "screens" resemble country rocks.	Intruded felsic volcanic rocks of the Marystown Group; cut by fluorite vein related to St. Lawrence granite.	None.	None.	Suggested by Strong et al. (1977), to be a subvolcanic intrusion related to the Marystown Group.
6	The "Knee" Granites (named by Hayes et al., 1987, on the basis of location at the "knee" of the Burin Peninsula). Described by O'Brien and Taylor (1983).	Hb-Bi granodiorite, monzogranite, and granite, with subordinate diorite, gabbro, and porphyry. Internal anatomy and intrusive relationships are poorly known.	Intruded felsic volcanic rocks of the Marystown Group. Foliated, sheared, and epidotized around margins of the pluton.	None.	None.	Inaccessible, rugged area of the peninsula, but mountainous and well exposed. Descriptions suggest similarities to Swift Current granite.
7	Simmons Brook intrusive suite (O'Brien et al., 1992a); Simmons Brook "batholith" of Greene and O'Driscoll (1976).	Foliated Hb (± Bi) granodiorite, locally tonalite to quartz diorite, lesser granite. Minor altered diorite and gabbro; enclaves of these (locally cumulate) are common in the granodiorites. Sheared and epidotized.	Intruded volcanic rocks of (redefined) Connaigre Bay Group; cut by diabase dikes which are foliated and altered; cut by pink posttectonic granites probably related to nearby Devonian granites.	621 ± 3 Ma (U-Pb zircon) described as coeval with redefined Connaigre Bay Group, dated at 626 ± 3 Ma (O'Brien et al., 1992b, 1994).	ε_{Nd} of -6 to -8 at 620 Ma (Fryer et al., 1992; Kerr et al., 1995).	Northwest margin of suite defined by Hermitage Bay fault.

TABLE 3. LATE PRECAMBRIAN PLUTONS IN THE AVALON TERRANE OF NEWFOUNDLAND (Continued - page 2)

	Name and references	Principal rock types	Contact relations	Geochronological data	Isotopic data	Additional comments
8	Deepwater Point Granodiorite (O'Brien et al., 1984).	Equigranular Hb-granodiorite, locally gradational to leucocratic granite.	Intruded sedimentary rocks of the Love Cove Group.	None.	None.	Small body.
9	Cape Roger Mountain Granite (O'Brien et al., 1984). Cape Roger Mountain "batholith" of Bradley, (1962).	Six descrete units, but areally dominated by equigranular Hb-Bi granodiorite, monzogranite, and granite, with subordinate leucocratic granite and gabbro.	Intruded volcanic rocks of the Love Cove Group, and is in places "overlain" by them, suggesting that the roof of the body is close to erosion surface.	None.	None.	Assemblage of rock types is closely similar to that of the Swift Current granite, and the two are considered to be related.
10	Swift Current granite (Jenness, 1963; O'Driscoll, 1977).	Dominated by equigranular Hb-Bi granodiorite, monzogranite, and granite, with subordinate siliceous granite, Hb-rich cumulate facies, and subvolcanic porphyry. Mafic enclaves common in granitoid rocks.	Intruded volcanic rocks of the Love Cove Group, and suggested to be comagmatic with them by Dallmeyer et al. (1981).	580 ± 20 Ma (U-Pb zircon), 548 ± 11 Ma (Rb-Sr whole-rock), 566-560 Ma (Ar-Ar) (Dallmeyer et al., 1981).	Initial Sr ratio = 0.70326 ± 37 (Dallmeyer et al., 1981). ε_{Nd} of +1.4 at 600 Ma (Kerr et al., 1995).	Largest Precambrian plutonic complex in the Avalon zone. ~580 Ma U-Pb is imprecise and may be unreliable (Krogh et al., 1988).
11	George's Pond granite (Jenness, 1963).	Equigranular Hb-Bi granodiorite with numerous dioritic enclaves, associated with very coarse Hb-plagioclase rocks, possibly of cumulate origin.	Presumed to intrude volcanic rocks of the Love Cove Group; cut by schistose diabase dikes.	None.	None.	Granodiorite phase has a strong resemblance to parts of Swift Current granite.
12	Salmon Pond plutons (Reusch and O'Driscoll, 1987).	Granodiorite and granite, with minor gabbro and quartz-feldspar porphyry.	Intruded volcanic rocks of the Love Cove Group, and intruded by Ackley granite.	None.	None.	Poorly exposed, and poorly known. Reusch and O'Driscoll (1987) suggested affinities to Swift Current granite.
13	Placentia Bay Precambrian granites, including parts of the Sall the Maid Granite (O'Driscoll, 1977) and granitoid rocks of Bar Haven Island.	Melanocratic, equigranular, Hb and Hb-biotite granodiorites, variably foliated, and strongly deformed adjacent to Paradise Sound fault.	Fault-bounded, with schistose mafic dikes. Cut by red, undeformed granite of probable Devonian age.	None.	ε_{Nd} of +4.8 at 600 Ma (Kerr et al., 1995).	Note that "Sall the Maid" granite of O'Driscoll also includes red granites of probable Devonian age.

TABLE 3. LATE PRECAMBRIAN PLUTONS IN THE AVALON TERRANE OF NEWFOUNDLAND (Continued - page 3)

	Name and references	Principal rock types	Contact relations	Geochronological data	Isotopic data	Additional comments
14	Holyrood intrusive suite. Holyrood granite of Rose, 1952; Holyrood plutonic series (Strong and Minatidis, 1975).	Polyphase, but dominated by equigranular Hb-Bi granodiorite, monzogranite, and granite, lesser tonalite and gabbro. Evidence for mingling and mixing of mafic and felsic magmas, and for high-level emplacement.	Intruded volcanic rocks of the Harbour Main Group, but suggested by Strong and Minatidis (1975), to be unrelated. Overlain unconformably by Cambrian sedimentary rocks.	590 ± 11 Ma (Rb-Sr WR) McCartney et al. (1966); 620 ± 2 Ma (U-Pb zircon) Krogh et al. (1988).	Initial Sr ratio = 0.704. ε_{Nd} from +0.7 to +2.9 at 600 Ma (Kerr et al., 1995).	Hosts disseminated and fracture-style Cu (± Mo) mineralization; associated with large-scale hydrothermal alteration of Harbour Main volcanics.
15	Grole intrusive suite (O'Brien et al., 1992a). Grole diorite of Greene and O'Driscoll (1976).	Dominated by altered, polyphase gabbro and diorite, generally heterogeneous, cut by later pink granite and felsite veins.	Intruded ~680 Ma volcanic rocks, and also redefined Connaigre Bay Group (O'Brien et al., 1992a). Cut by Pass Island granite.	567 ± 3 Ma (U-Pb zircon) (O'Brien et al., 1994).	None.	Similar in many respects to mafic rocks of Cross Hills intrusive suite, and to Powderhorn diorite.
16	Cross Hills intrusive suite (O'Brien et al., 1984; Tuach, 1991).	Four main units, but granodiorite unit of Tuach (1991) is considered unrelated here. Dominated by variably altered gabbro and diorite, with subordinate peralkaline granite and biotite-granite.	Intruded various units of the Long Harbour Group, and is intruded by granites linked to nearby Ackley granite.	515 ± 43, 515 ± 10 Ma (Rb-Sr WR) (Tuach, 1991); 547 +3/-6 (U-Pb zircon) (Dunning, in Tuach, 1991).	Initial Sr ratio = 0.70495 ± 26. ε_{Nd} from +4.0 to +5.4 at 570 Ma (Kerr et al., 1995).	Hosts minor disseminated and aplite-related Zr-Y-Nb-Th-REE mineralization (Tuach, 1991).
17	Louil Hills intrusive suite (O'Brien, 1987). Louil Hills granite (Jenness, 1958; Strong et al., 1974).	Dominated by heterogeneous, locally pegmatitic gabbro to diorite, intruded by diabase, with subordinate equigranular peralkaline granite.	Intruded volcanic rocks of the Love Cove Group.	573 ± 3 Ma (U-Pb zircon) (Dunning, in O'Brien et al., 1990).	ε_{Nd} from +5.3 to +6.8 at 570 Ma (Kerr et al., 1995).	General assemblage of rock types is closely similar to Cross Hills, but no mineralization reported.
18	Powderhorn diorite (O'Driscoll, 1977).	Dominated by very hetrogeneous, polyphase gabbro and diorite, dissected by lesser granite and quartz-feldspar porphyry, and abundant diabase.	Intruded volcanic rocks of the Love Cove Group, but contacts rarely exposed.	None.	ε_{Nd} of +4.2 at 570 Ma (Kerr et al., 1995).	Has been viewed as Devonian (O'Driscoll, 1977), but has a deformational overprint, and resembles Cross Hills suite.

comb-quartz layering, and hydrothermal brecciation textures, suggest locally high emplacement levels (Hughes, 1971), and some massive feldspar and quartz-feldspar porphyries may be related to the granite. High-level emplacement is also indicated by disseminated and fracture-hosted Cu (±Mo) mineralization (Strong et al., 1974; B. Dalton, 1994, personal commun.), and the genetic and spatial relationship between the granite and the Fox-trap pyrophyllite deposit, hosted by severely altered felsic volcanic rocks adjacent to the granite contact (Papezik et al., 1978).

The only other plutonic rocks of possible ca. 620 Ma age east of the Paradise Sound fault include parts of the Sall the Maid granite (O'Driscoll, 1977) and small fault-bounded granitoid units in the Woody Island–Bar Haven Island area in western Placentia Bay (Fig. 4, no. 13). They were previously considered to be Devonian, but include foliated, melanocratic, hornblende-rich granodiorites, cut by schistose diabase dikes (Kerr et al., 1993). On the basis of these field relationships they are now viewed as Precambrian, but their specific age is unknown.

Ca. 570 Ma plutons. The Louil Hills and Grole intrusive suites (Fig. 4, no. 17, 15; Table 3) have yielded reliable ages of ca. 570 Ma (O'Brien et al., 1990, 1994). Although these plutons occur in widely separated areas, their similar ages and rock types suggest a possible relationship. The Louil Hills intrusive suite is dominated by gabbro and diorite, associated with a subordinate grey to buff granophyric granite, which contains sodic amphibole and has peralkaline composition (Strong et al., 1974). The Grole Intrusive Suite is similarly dominated by heterogeneous, locally pegmatitic, gabbro and diorite, cut by lesser pink granite and felsite veins.

The Powderhorn complex, located just east of the Paradise Sound fault (Fig. 4, no. 18), may also be of this age, on the basis of a similar association of rock types. It is dominated by green-gray, equigranular, leucocratic gabbro and diorite, containing enclaves of older melanocratic gabbro, and is dissected extensively by pink to white granitic veins and numerous diabase dikes. Granite and quartz-feldspar porphyry veins are younger than the dominant gabbro, but are cut by most (but not all) diabase dikes. The contacts between large enclaves of psammitic (hornfelsed) metasedimentary rock and the fine-grained gabbro are folded, indicating a deformational overprint that is consistent with (but not diagnostic of) a Precambrian age; a penetrative fabric is also locally visible.

Ca. 550 Ma plutons. The Cross Hills intrusive suite (Fig. 4, no. 16) was divided into four principal units by Tuach (1991), but one of these (the Route 211 granodiorite) is here included, with the Swift Current pluton, as subsequently described. With this modification, about 75% of the Cross Hills intrusive suite consists of gray to green altered gabbro, in which the primary mafic mineralogy is extensively transformed to chlorite and actinolite. The gabbro is ubiquitously net-veined by pink to brick-red granite and pegmatite. The most distinctive granitic phase of the suite is a maroon to purple alkali-feldspar granite with interstitial sodic amphibole, and a variably peralkaline composition. Minor non-peralkaline granite and syenite are also present. Tuach (1991) sug-

gested that peralkaline and nonperalkaline magmas coexisted as immiscible liquids. The peralkaline granite has given a U-Pb zircon age of 547 +3/–6 Ma (G. R. Dunning, *in* Tuach, 1991). However, the general association of rock types in the Cross Hills suite resembles that seen in the ca. 570 Ma plutonic suites.

Plutons of uncertain age. The Swift Current granite (Fig. 4, no. 10) (Jenness, 1963; O'Driscoll, 1977), Georges Pond granite (Fig. 4, no. 11), Cape Roger Mountain granite (Fig. 4, no. 9), and the Knee granites (Fig. 4, no. 6) are lithologically similar and form a belt, 120 km long, extending from the central Burin Peninsula toward Bonavista Bay (Fig. 4). The Swift Current granite is dominated by biotite-hornblende granodiorite and monzogranite. Small, rounded enclaves of broadly dioritic composition are common, but no mappable mafic units have been recognized. Subordinate lithologies include leucocratic granite that is locally transitional to quartz-feldspar porphyry. The granites range from massive to weakly foliated to strongly mylonitized, and are strongly deformed on the projected course of the Paradise Sound fault. The easternmost lobe of the pluton is located east of the fault, and could be a separate pluton. The other plutons in this association contain similar rock types, and minor gabbroic and dioritic components.

The age of the Swift Current granite and lithologically similar plutons is not well constrained. A U-Pb (zircon) age of 580 ± 20 Ma was viewed by Dallmeyer et al. (1981) as a minimum age, due to probable Pb loss. However, Krogh et al. (1988) subsequently pointed out that these data are not colinear, and advised caution in their interpretation. At face value, the U-Pb data suggest that these plutons may be younger than the ca. 620 Ma association described above, and $^{40}Ar/^{39}Ar$ (hornblende) ages of ca. 570–560 Ma also support this view (Dallmeyer et al., 1981). However, a final resolution requires more U-Pb dating.

Other plutons of uncertain age include (1) the Deepwater Point granodiorite (Fig. 4, no. 8) (O'Brien et al., 1984); (2) the Anchor Drogue pluton (Fig. 4, no. 5), described by Strong et al. (1977) as a high-level, subvolcanic sheeted complex associated with felsic volcanic rocks of the Marystown Group; (3) the Seal Cove pluton (Fig. 4, no. 4), described as gabbro by Strong et al. (1977), although granodiorite was found during recent sampling; (4) the Salmon Pond granites (Fig. 4, no. 12), three small plutons adjacent to the Dover fault that include granite, granodiorite, and minor gabbro and quartz-feldspar porphyry correlated with the Swift Current granite by Reusch and O'Driscoll (1987); and (5) the Route 211 granodiorite, a hornblende-biotite granodiorite with mafic enclaves that was included in the Cross Hills suite by Tuach (1991), but that more closely resembles rock types of the Swift Current granite and associated plutons. It yielded an imprecise Rb-Sr whole-rock age much older than the ages obtained from other members of the Cross Hills suite (Tuach, 1991).

In the geochemical diagrams discussed below, we have included the Route 211 granodiorite with the Swift Current and associated suites for comparative purposes. The remaining plutons of uncertain age for which chemical data are available (Placentia Bay, Deepwater Point, and Seal Cove) are also plotted together.

PETROCHEMICAL CHARACTERISTICS
OF THE PLUTONIC ROCKS

Ca. 620 Ma plutons

Chemical data from ca. 620 Ma plutons in the Caledonia, Mira, and Newfoundland Avalon terranes reflect the wide range of rock types present; SiO_2 contents vary more or less continuously from about 45% to 78% (e.g., Fig. 5, a, b, c). Although

there are some differences between specific suites within each terrane in terms of compositional ranges (e.g., samples from the more mafic parts of plutons in the Caledonia and Mira terranes extend to lower SiO_2 contents than those in Newfoundland), the combined patterns for plutons of ca. 620 Ma age in all three terranes are very similar. Major element oxides show strong negative or positive correlations with SiO_2, as exemplified by Al_2O_3, CaO, and K_2O (Figs. 5, a–c, 6, a–c, 7 a–c), such as are typical of

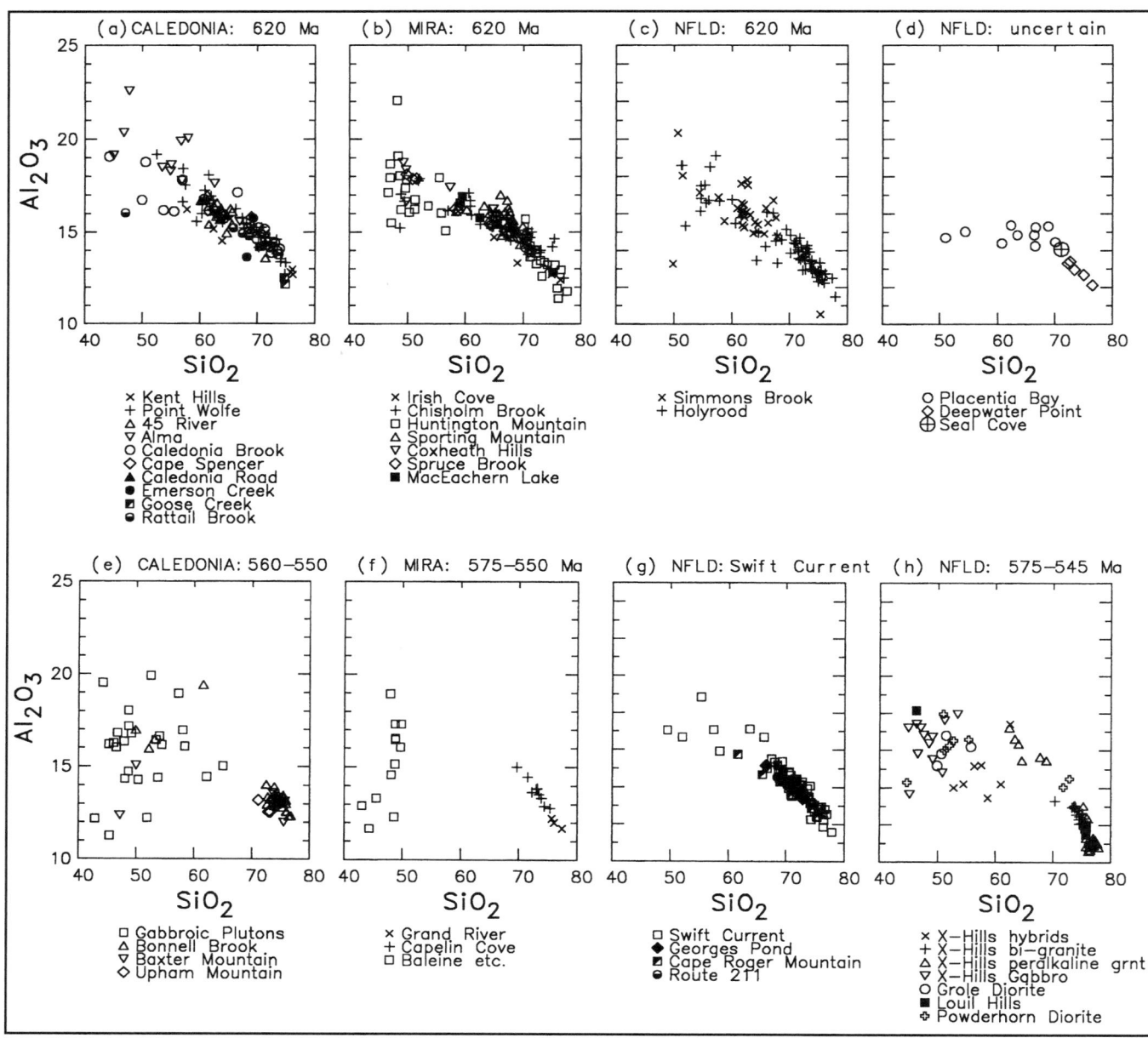

Figure 5. Plots of Al_2O_3 against SiO_2 for analyzed samples from plutons in the Caledonia, Mira, and Newfoundland Avalon terranes grouped according to age divisions as described in the text. (a) ca. 620 Ma plutons in the Caledonia terrane, (b) ca. 620 Ma plutons in the Mira terrane, (c) ca. 620 Ma plutons in the Newfoundland Avalon terrane, (d) plutons of uncertain age in the Newfoundland Avalon terrane, (e) ca. 560–550 Ma plutons in the Caledonia terrane, (f) ca. 575 Ma plutons (Grand River, Capelin Cove, and similar plutons) and ca. 550(?) Ma plutons (Baleine and similar gabbros) in the Mira terrane, (g) Swift Current and similar plutons of uncertain age in the Newfoundland Avalon terrane, and (h) ca. 575–565 Ma plutons (Grole, Louil Hills, and Powderhorn), and ca. 547 Ma Cross Hills suite in the Newfoundland Avalon terrane. Data sources for this and subsequent diagrams are discussed in Appendix 1. Abbreviations: X-Hills, Cross Hills; bi, biotite; grnt, granite.

calc-alkalic suites (e.g., Gribble, 1969). The plot of K_2O against SiO_2 shows the relatively steep trends typical of high-K calc-alkalic suites (Fig. 7 a–c). The AFM diagrams reveal essentially identical calc-alkalic trends (Fig. 8 a–c); although the more mafic samples tend to show a spread in FeO/MgO ratio, they do not show a tholeiitic (iron-enrichment) trend.

In terms of alkali-alumina relationships, the samples have ratios of KN/A less than 1, except for a few syenogranite samples from the Huntington Mountain and Chisholm Brook suites that are marginally peralkaline (Fig. 9, a–c). The majority of samples are metaluminous to peraluminous (Shand, 1950); most plutons in Newfoundland and the Mira terrane have A/CNK ratios between 1 and 1.1, but the Caledonia terrane suites are more pera-

luminous; many samples have A/CNK more than 1.2 (Fig. 9). The value of 1.1 was used as the dividing line between I-type and S-type granites (Chappell and White, 1974), and by this definition, most of these suites qualify as I-type granites. None, including those with A/CNK more than 1.1, have other petrologic characteristics typical of S-type suites (Chappell and White, 1974). The increased A/CNK in the Caledonia samples may be the result of redistribution of these elements during low-grade metamorphism and alteration (Barr and White, 1996a).

Trace-element patterns also show marked similarity among the various ca. 620 Ma suites in the three terranes. High-field strength elements (e.g., Nb, Zr) and large-ion lithophile elements (e.g., Rb, Th) show no significant enrichment in these rocks. Nb

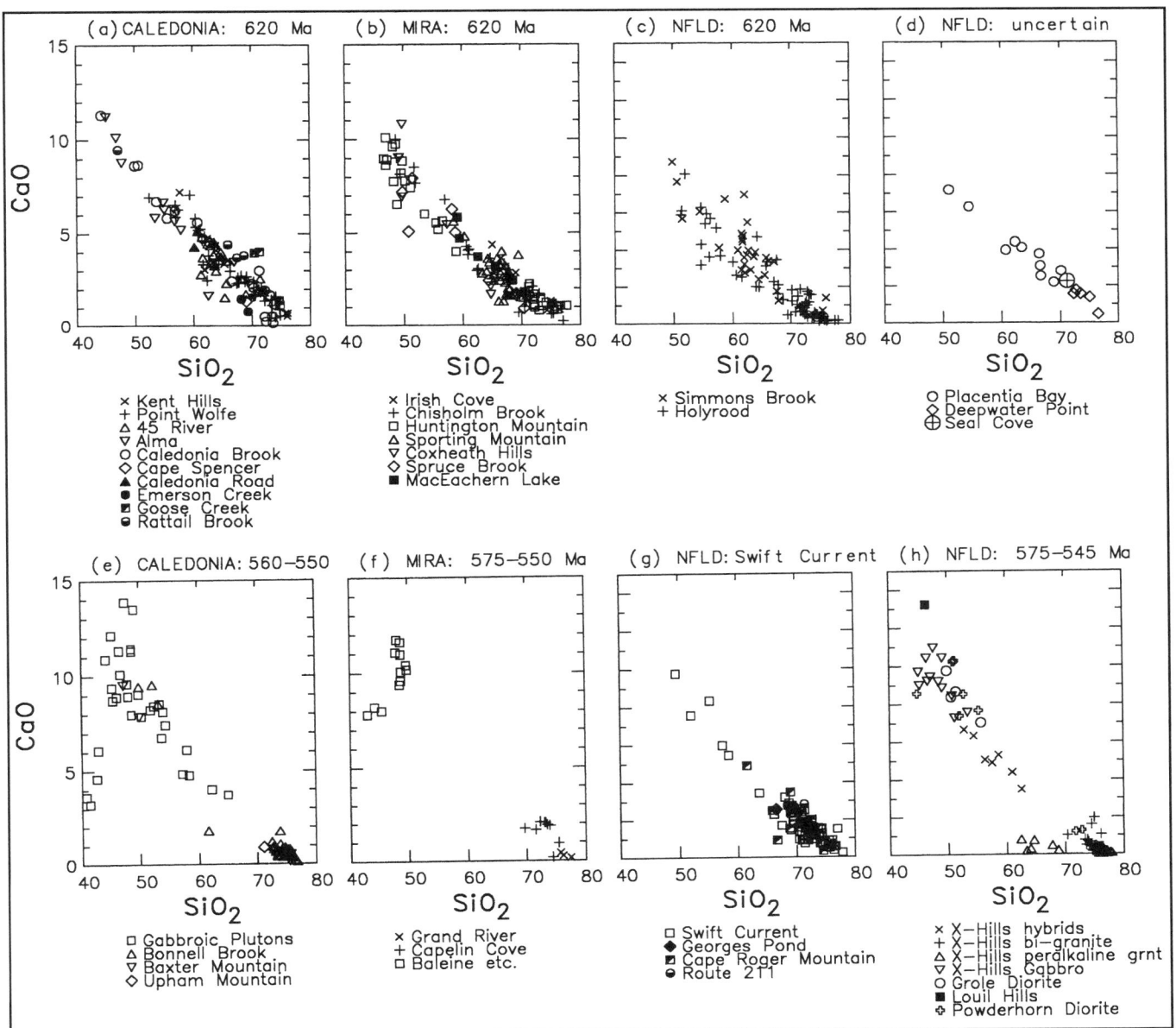

Figure 6. Plots of CaO against SiO_2 for analyzed samples from plutons in the Caledonia, Mira, and Newfoundland Avalon terranes grouped according to age divisions as in Figure 5.

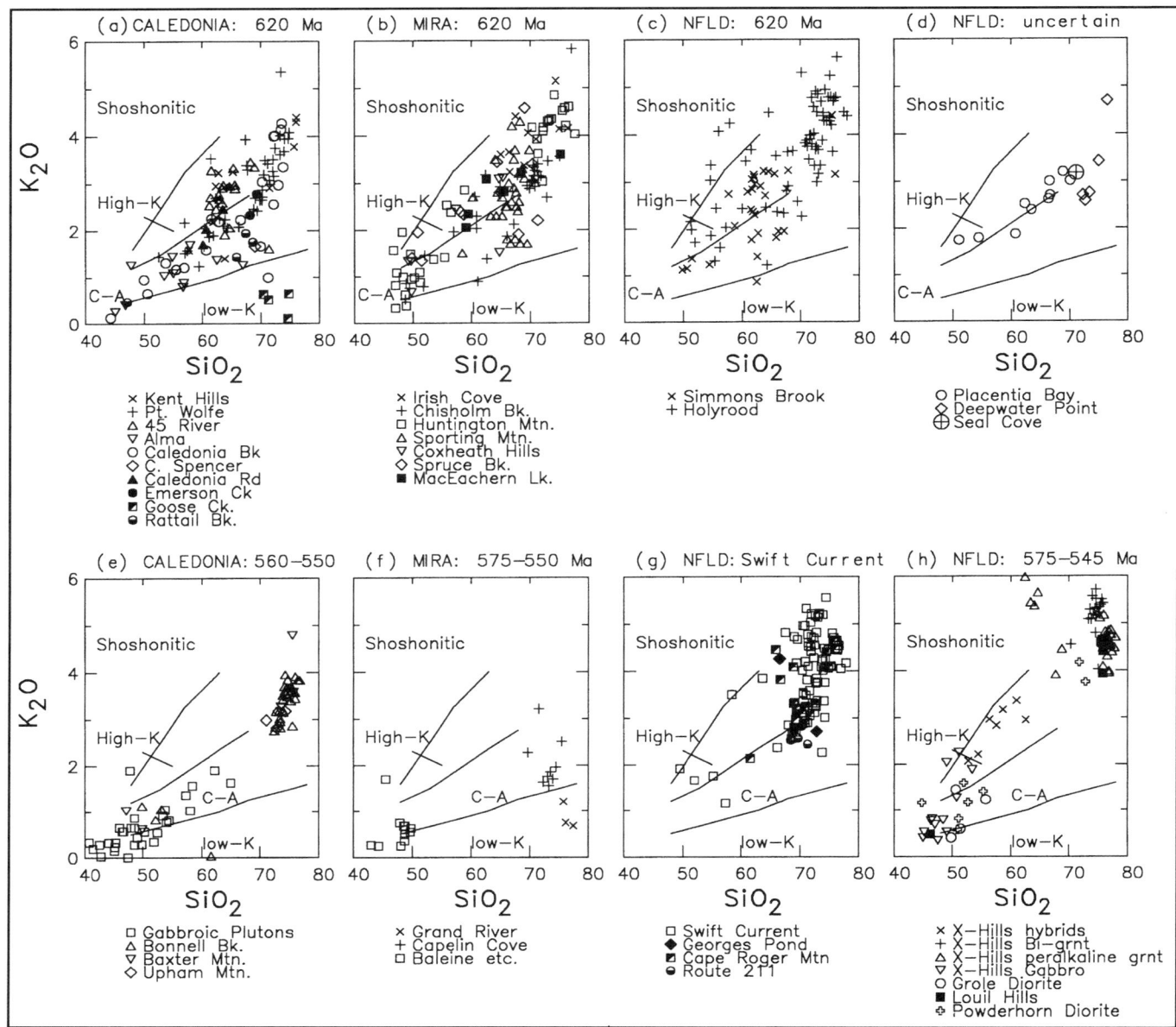

Figure 7. Plots of K_2O against SiO_2 for analyzed samples from plutons in the Caledonia, Mira, and Newfoundland Avalon terranes grouped according to age divisions as in Figure 5. Field boundaries are from Middlemost (1975).

contents of 5–12 ppm are low compared to typical granite values of ca. 20 ppm. Although zirconium shows some scatter, it exhibits a consistent pattern, increasing to about 65% SiO_2 and then decreasing (Fig. 10, a–c), presumably reflecting the onset of zircon fractionation. On the ternary plot of Rb-Ba-Sr, all of the suites show a trend of increasing Ba and relatively smaller increase in Rb with decreasing Sr, resulting in a linear array of data at a small angle to the Sr-Ba join (Fig. 11, a–c); only a few samples (principally from Huntington Mountain) show elevated Rb indicative of highly evolved granites (El Bouseily and El Sokkary, 1979). This general pattern, combined with major element oxide variations (e.g.,

Figs. 5–7), suggests that fractionation of plagioclase and mafic minerals (hornblende, pyroxene) largely controlled the chemical evolution of the magmas.

On the Rb-(Y+Nb) diagram of Pearce et al. (1984), the ca. 620 Ma suites from all three terranes plot almost exclusively in the volcanic-arc granite field (Fig. 12, a–c). On the Zr-(Ga/Al) diagram of Whalen et al. (1987), these suites mostly fall in the field of I-type granites, and very few samples have compositions that correspond to those of A-type suites (Fig. 13, a–c).

With the exception of the Simmons Brook suite, the ca. 620 Ma plutons have positive ε_{Nd} values, ranging from +0.1 to

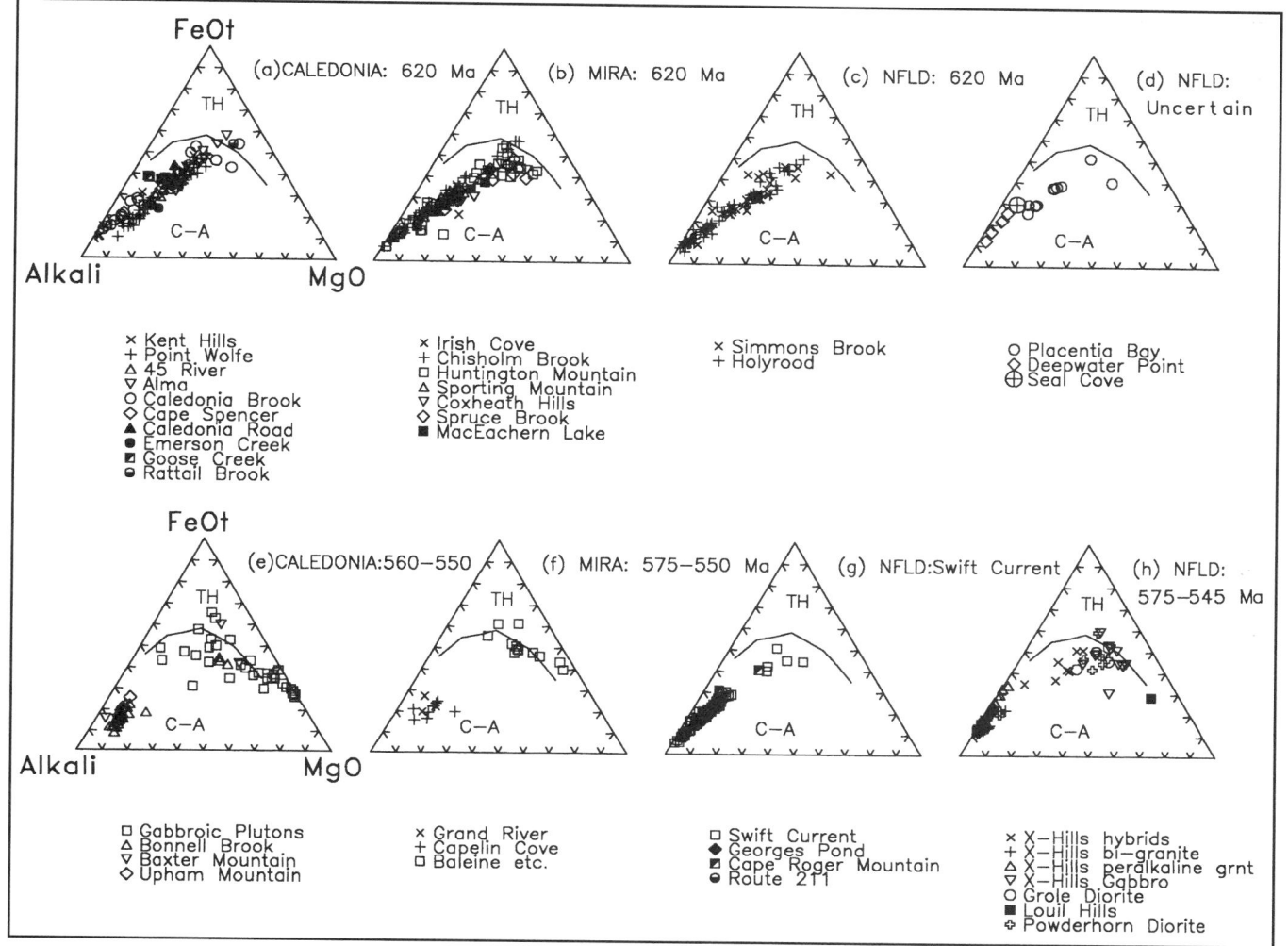

Figure 8. AFM diagrams for analyzed samples from plutons in the Caledonia, Mira, and Newfoundland Avalon terranes, grouped according to age divisions as in Figure 5. Tholeiitic (TH)/calc-alkalic (CA) dividing line from Irvine and Baragar (1971).

+5.9 (Tables 1, 2, and 3). These results suggest dominantly juvenile sources for these suites, which is consistent with their proposed development in an arc-type environment (Barr and Hegner, 1992; Barr, 1993; Barr and White, 1996a; Kerr et al., 1995; Whalen et al., 1994). Small amounts of ancient crust can be introduced in such environments by sediment subduction, perhaps producing the observed range in values.

The negative ε_{Nd} value in the Simmons Brook suite is enigmatic, because it suggests that ancient crust of at least Early Proterozoic age made a significant contribution to the magma, which is inconsistent with the primitive, unevolved geochemistry of this suite. Melting of a mafic precursor with a long crustal residence period is a possibility or, alternatively, the contamination of a mantle-derived magma by small amounts of Early Proterozoic (or even Archean) crust. The presence of ancient crust in the Simmons Brook intrusive suite has also been confirmed by Hf isotope studies of zircons (O'Brien et al., 1994).

Ca. 575–565 Ma plutons

Ca. 575 Ma plutons in the Mira terrane (Grand River, Capelin Cove, and related plutons) are dominantly granitic, whereas those in Newfoundland (Louil Hills, Grole, and Powderhorn suites) are dominated by dioritic and gabbroic rocks and subordinate granite. Samples from the ca. 575 Ma plutons in the Mira terrane have SiO_2 contents between about 70% and 77%, which is similar to SiO_2 in granites from the Louil Hills and Powderhorn suites (e.g., Fig. 5, f and h). However, the latter granites have higher K_2O contents (Fig. 7, f and h). They also have lower MgO, and hence cluster along the FeOt-alkalies join on the AFM diagram (Fig. 8, f and h). The Mira terrane granites have lower KN/A ratios (less than 0.85) and higher A/CNK (more than 1.2), whereas the Louil Hills granites have KN/A and A/CNK close to 1 (Fig. 9, f and h). The Louil Hills granites are enriched in Rb and Y + Nb, and plot in the within-plate granite field in Figure 12,

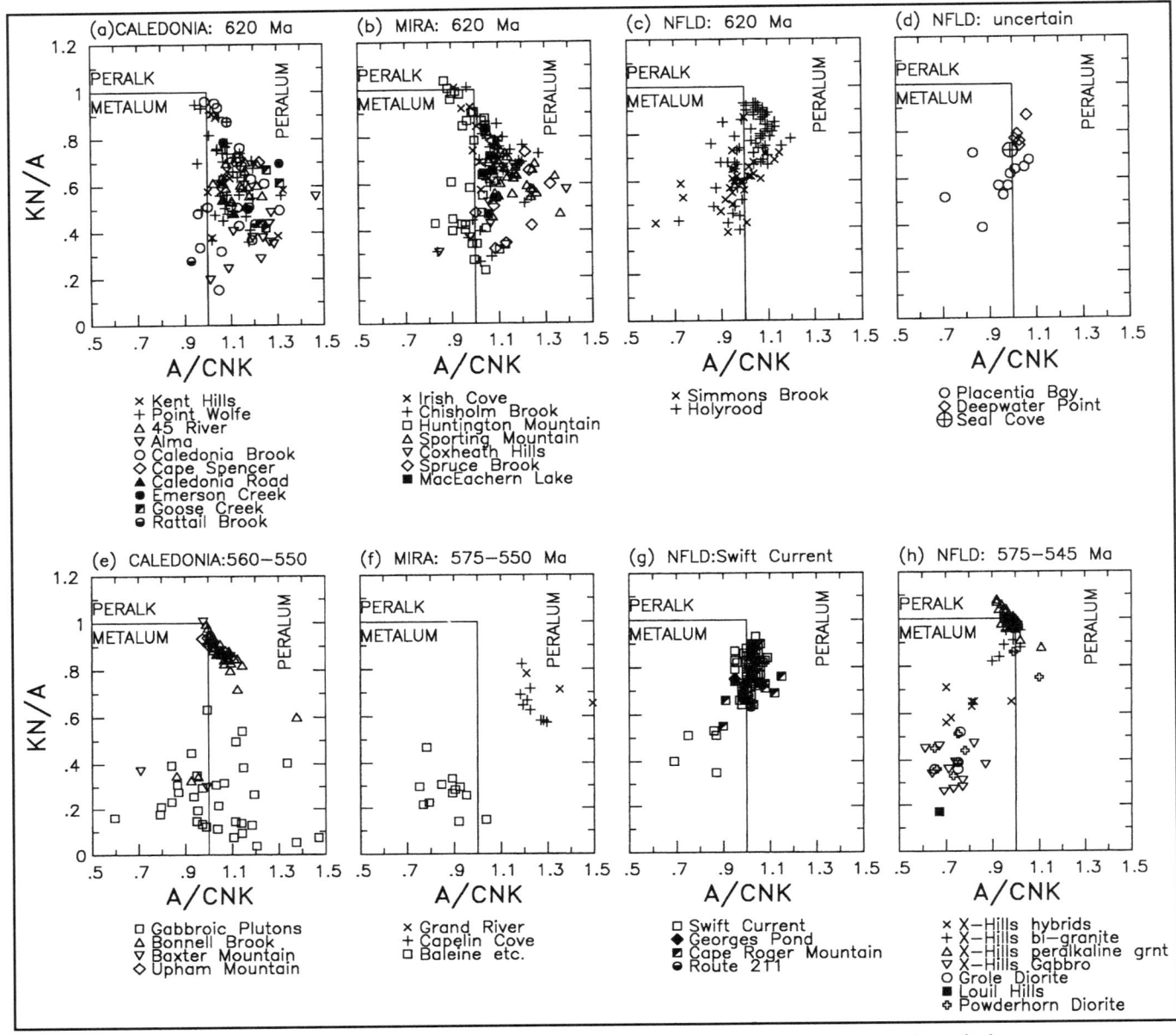

Figure 9. Plots of molecular proportions of K+Na/Al against Ca+Na+K/Al for samples from plutons in the Caledonia, Mira, and Newfoundland Avalon terranes, grouped according to age divisions as in Figure 5.

whereas the Mira granites fall in the volcanic-arc granite field. The two Powderhorn granite samples are more similar to the Mira terrane granites than to the Louil Hills granites on most of these plots, but the small number of samples and uncertain age of these granites makes it difficult to draw firm conclusions from this. The mafic rocks of the Louil Hills, Grole, and Powderhorn suites show scatter, but no clear systematic differences among the suites (Figs. 5h–12h), although all the Powderhorn samples have low Zr compared to others of similar SiO_2 content (Fig. 9h). Nd isotopic data from both the Capelin Cove (Table 2) and Louil Hills granites (Table 3) are strongly positive (+5 to +6.8), indicative of a juvenile (mantle?) source region. Samples from the Powderhorn

diorite also have positive ε_{Nd}. Although no Nd isotopic data are yet available from the Grole intrusive suite, results from studies of zircon (O'Brien et al., 1994) suggest that it has positive ε_{Hf}, also suggesting juvenile sources.

Ca. 560–550 Ma plutons

Samples from the 560–550 Ma gabbroic plutons in the Caledonia terrane show a wide range in silica, from less than 40% to about 65%, but their average composition is mafic, with average SiO_2 of about 51% (e.g., Fig. 5e). Mira terrane gabbros of similar inferred age show less range in SiO_2, and a slightly lower average value of 47.7%. Cross Hills gabbros have an intermediate mean

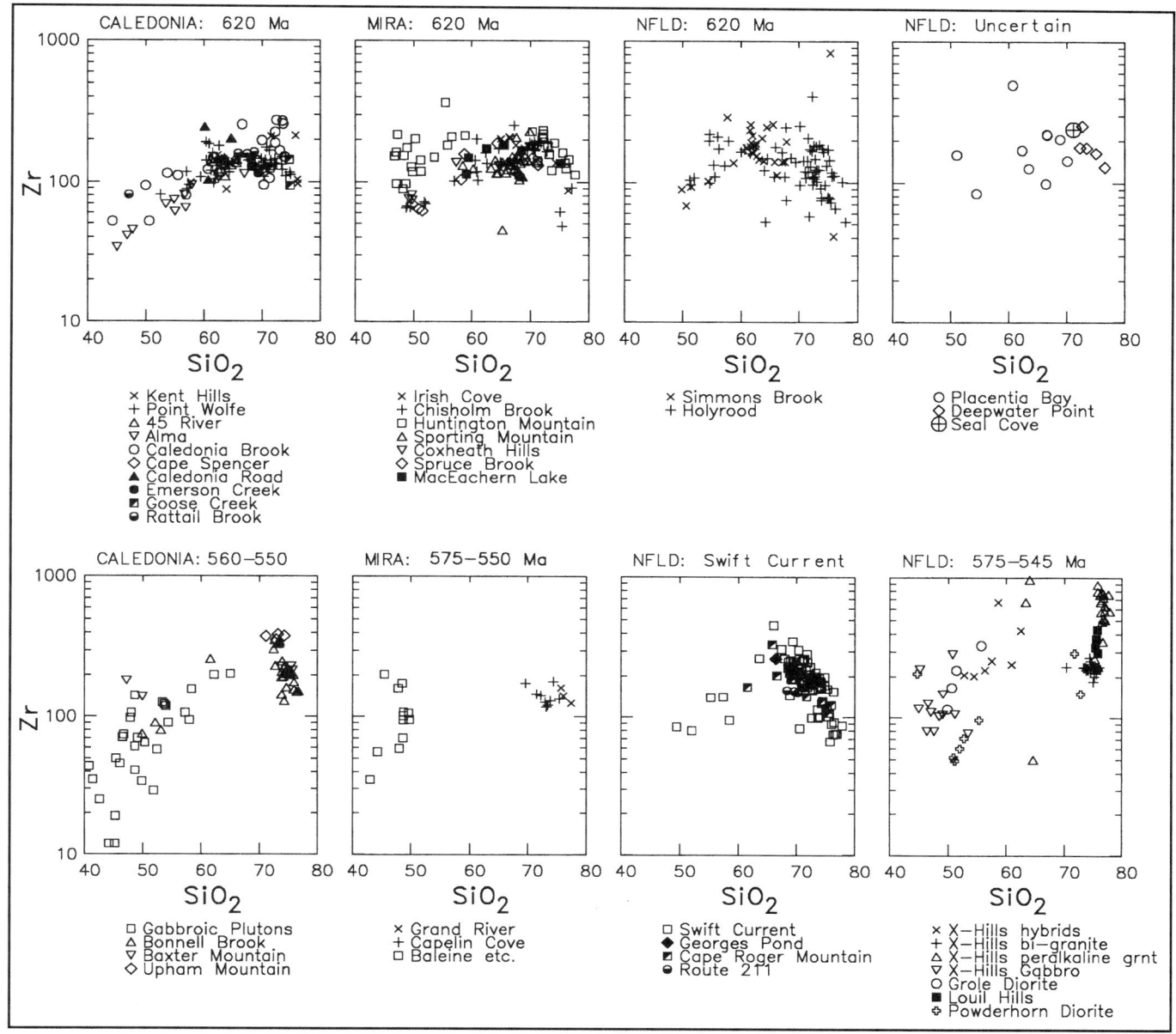

Figure 10. Plots of Zr against SiO$_2$ for analyzed samples from plutons in the Caledonia, Mira, and New-foundland Avalon terranes grouped according to age divisions as in Figure 5.

SiO$_2$ of 48.25%. All of the gabbros show scatter in chemical data, but in general have high Al$_2$O$_3$ (15%–16%) and CaO (~9%), and low K$_2$O (<1%). The Caledonia and Mira terrane samples show a tholeiitic (iron enrichment) trend on the AFM diagram (Fig. 8, e and f), but this trend is less clear for the Cross Hills gabbroic samples (Fig. 8h).

The granitic rocks from the Caledonia terrane contain high SiO$_2$ contents of 72% to 77%, similar to the biotite granite samples from the Cross Hills suite (e.g., Fig. 5, e and h). However, granites in the Cross Hills suite are potassic (K$_2$O>Na$_2$O), whereas granites from the Caledonia terrane are sodic, with <4%

K$_2$O. The peralkaline granites from the Cross Hills suite have similar SiO$_2$ and higher Na$_2$O and lower K$_2$O compared to the biotite granites, but K$_2$O is still higher than in Caledonia granites, and CaO is much lower (Figs. 6 and 7). Differences in granites between the two areas are also prominent in trace element patterns. On the Rb versus (Y+Nb) diagram, Cross Hills granites are clearly in the within-plate granite field (Fig. 12h). On the Zr versus Ga/Al diagram (Fig. 13), the Caledonia terrane samples plot near the boundary of or outside the A-type granite field, whereas the Cross Hills biotite granite and especially the peralkaline granite are clearly A-type (Fig. 13, e and h). Only two

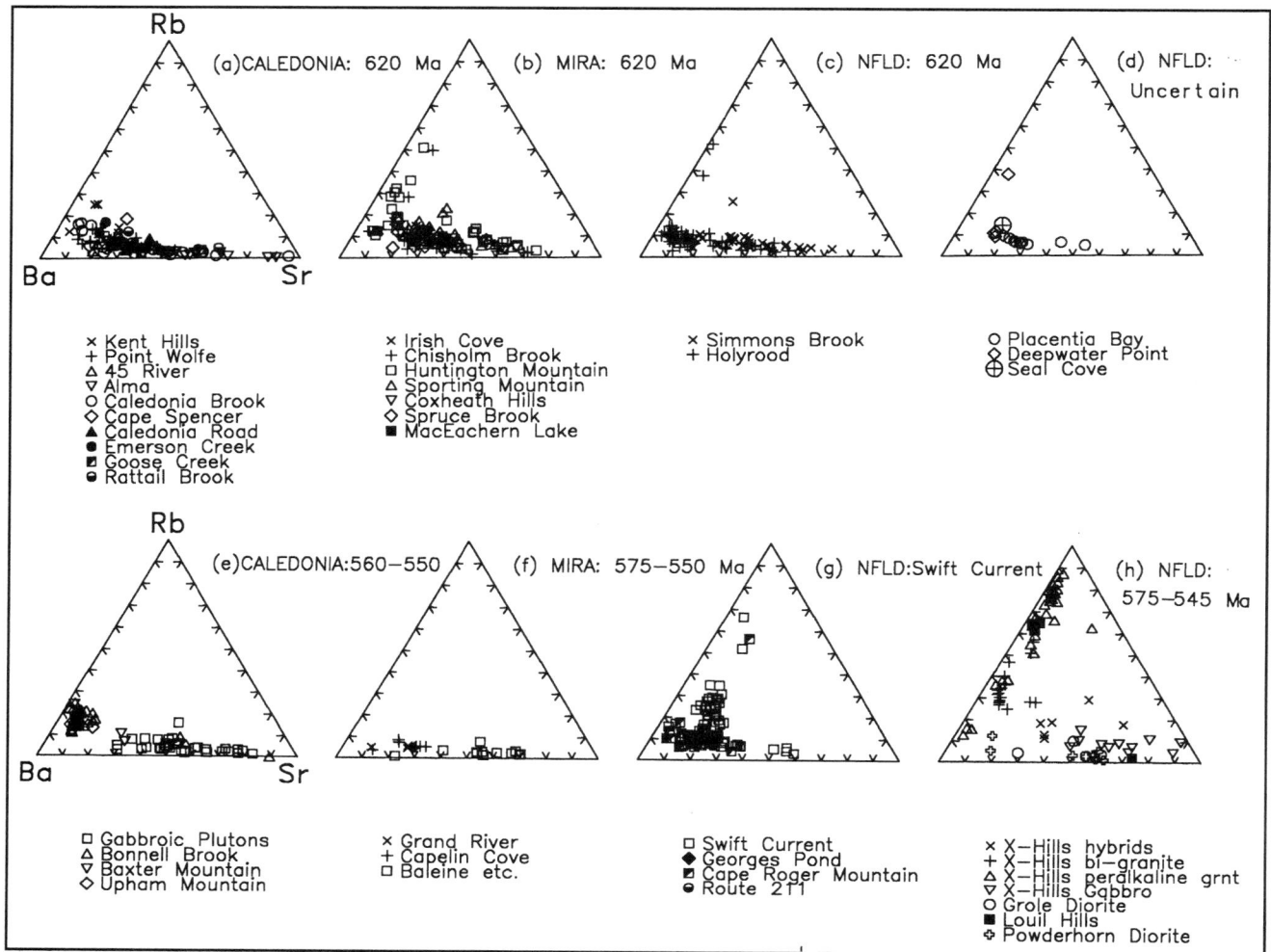

Figure 11. Ternary Rb-Ba-Sr plots for samples from plutons in the Caledonia, Mira, and Newfoundland Avalon terranes, grouped according to age divisions as in Figure 5.

Caledonia terrane samples are marginally peralkalic (agpaitic index about 1), and most are peraluminous (Fig. 9e). In contrast, the Cross Hills peralkaline granites mainly have KN/A of more than one, and the associated biotite granites are metaluminous, not peraluminous (Fig. 9h). The suites show similar patterns in Ba-Rb-Sr, but the low Ba trend of peralkaline rocks is not apparent in the Caledonia suite (Fig. 11, e and h). On the AFM diagrams (Fig. 8, e and h), relatively higher MgO is evident in the Caledonia terrane granites; the Cross Hills granites cluster near the alkalies-FeO join, like the Louil Hills samples.

Limited initial Sr and Nd isotopic data from the Cross Hills suite (Tuach, 1991; Fryer et al., 1992; Kerr et al., 1995) reveal that most of these rocks are derived from primitive, probably mantle-like sources, and that the mafic and felsic components likely had common modes of origin. In contrast, the Upham Mountain and Bonnell Brook plutons in the Caledonia terrane have only slightly positive ε_{Nd} values (Table 1).

Plutons of uncertain age in the Newfoundland Avalon terrane

Samples from the Swift Current granite and similar plutons (Georges Pond, Cape Roger Mountain, and Route 211) range in SiO$_2$ from about 50% to 77% (e.g., Fig. 5g). The samples from the Placentia Bay, Deepwater Point, and Seal Cove plutons (e.g., Fig. 5d) show a similar range in SiO$_2$ (e.g., Fig. 5d). The wide range in composition in these suites most resembles that in the ca. 620 Ma suites, and they are chemically indistinguishable from them in most major element (e.g., Figs. 5, 6, 7, and 8) and trace element (e.g., Fig. 10) patterns. However, the Swift Current samples and the Cape Roger Mountain granite have high Rb contents (Fig. 11), and some samples from the Swift Current granite are transitional toward the syncollisional granite field (Fig. 12g). Other samples with lower Rb and higher Y+Nb plot near or in the within-plate granite field (Fig. 12g). Some samples from Deepwater Point and Georges Pond also show this tendency (Fig. 12, d and g).

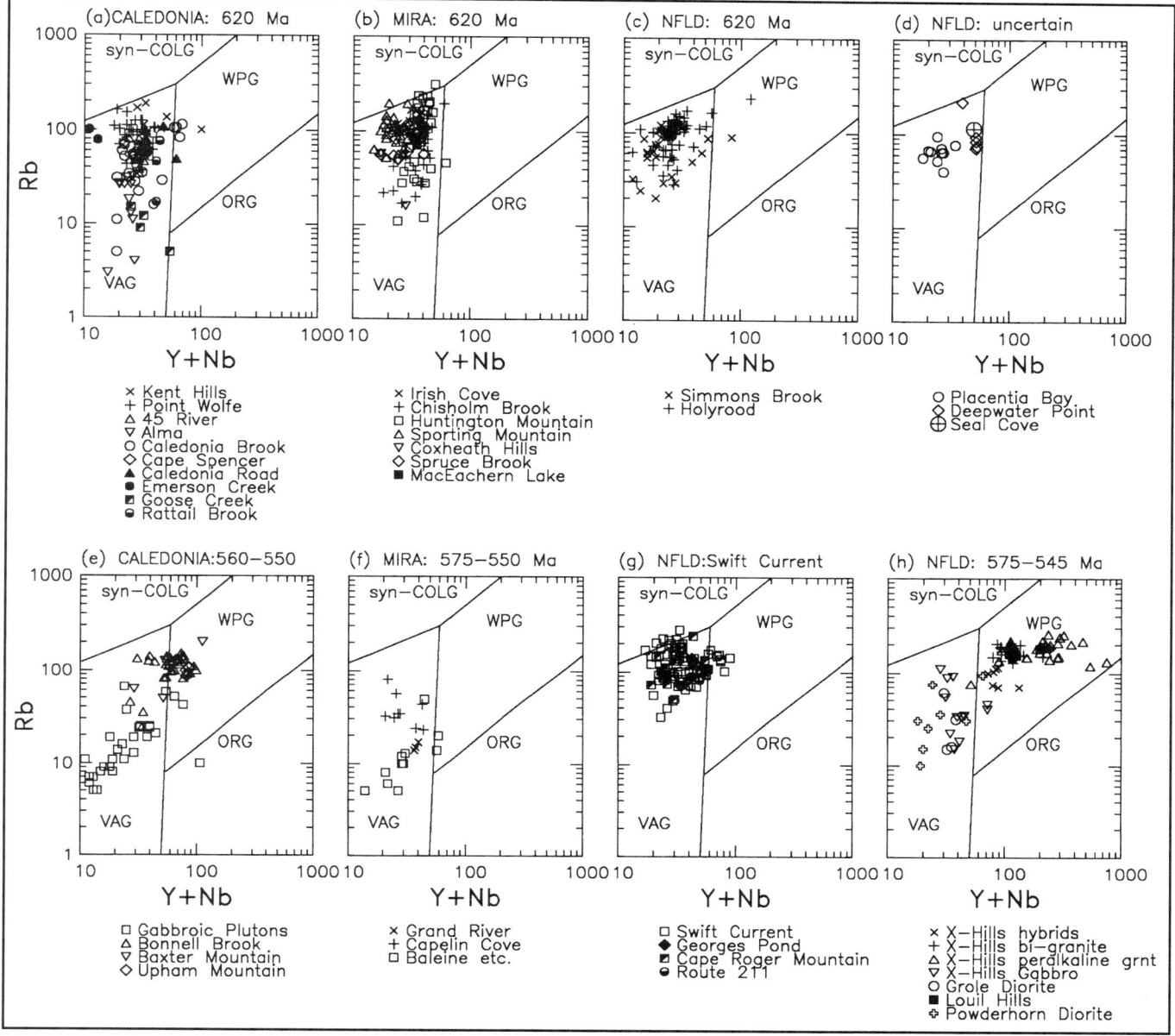

Figure 12. Plots of Rb against Y + Nb for samples from plutons in the Caledonia, Mira, and Newfoundland Avalon terranes, grouped according to age divisions as in Figure 5. Fields from Pearce et al. (1984).

Samples from the Swift Current granite have positive ε_{Nd}, indicating a juvenile source. However, the Seal Cove pluton has negative ε_{Nd}, like the Simmons Brook suite—the rarity of negative ε_{Nd} values in Avalonian plutons is a strong indication that the Seal Cove and Simmons Brook suites may be linked.

In summary, there are similarities between the Swift Current and associated suites and the ca. 620 Ma plutonic suites of the Newfoundland Avalon terrane, but there are also subtle differences. In particular, the Swift Current and similar suites appear to be more compositionally evolved, with higher SiO_2 and K_2O, and higher abundances of elements such as Rb. The Swift Current and other suites are different from the ca. 575 Ma plutons of the Mira terrane, which are dominantly granitic and not compositionally evolved. They are also distinct from the Louil Hills, Grole, and Powderhorn suites, which are bimodal and alkaline to peralkaline in major and trace element chemistry.

DISCUSSION

The stratigraphy and plutonic history of the Caledonia, Mira, and Newfoundland Avalon terranes are summarized in Figure 14, which illustrates both the similarities and differences among these areas.

Ca. 620 Ma granitoid suites are a major component in all three areas (Fig. 14); they are distributed throughout the Newfoundland Avalon terrane but are concentrated only in parts of the Caledonia and Mira terranes (Figs. 2, 3, 4). Overall, these suites range more or less continuously in composition from gabbro and diorite through to granite, and are dominated by hornblende-biotite granodiorite and granite. Other features characteristic of ca. 620 Ma plutons in all three areas include relatively high level emplacement and their clearly cogenetic and probably comagmatic association with volcanic rocks of similar age. Although

ages of ca. 630 to 600 Ma are commonly cited for the volcanic rocks, the most reliable ages from the plutons in all three areas are ca. 620 Ma.

The major element chemistry of the ca. 620 Ma plutonic suites is clearly calc-alkaline, and they remain relatively enriched in CaO, MgO, and FeO, even at high SiO_2 contents. This and their wide compositional ranges, unevolved trace element compositions, and metaluminous to peraluminous character suggest that they have affinities to arc-type plutonic suites developed in convergent margin settings, i.e., so-called volcanic-arc granites (Pearce et al., 1984) or Cordilleran I-type granites (Pitcher, 1983). This interpretation is supported by tectonic discrimination

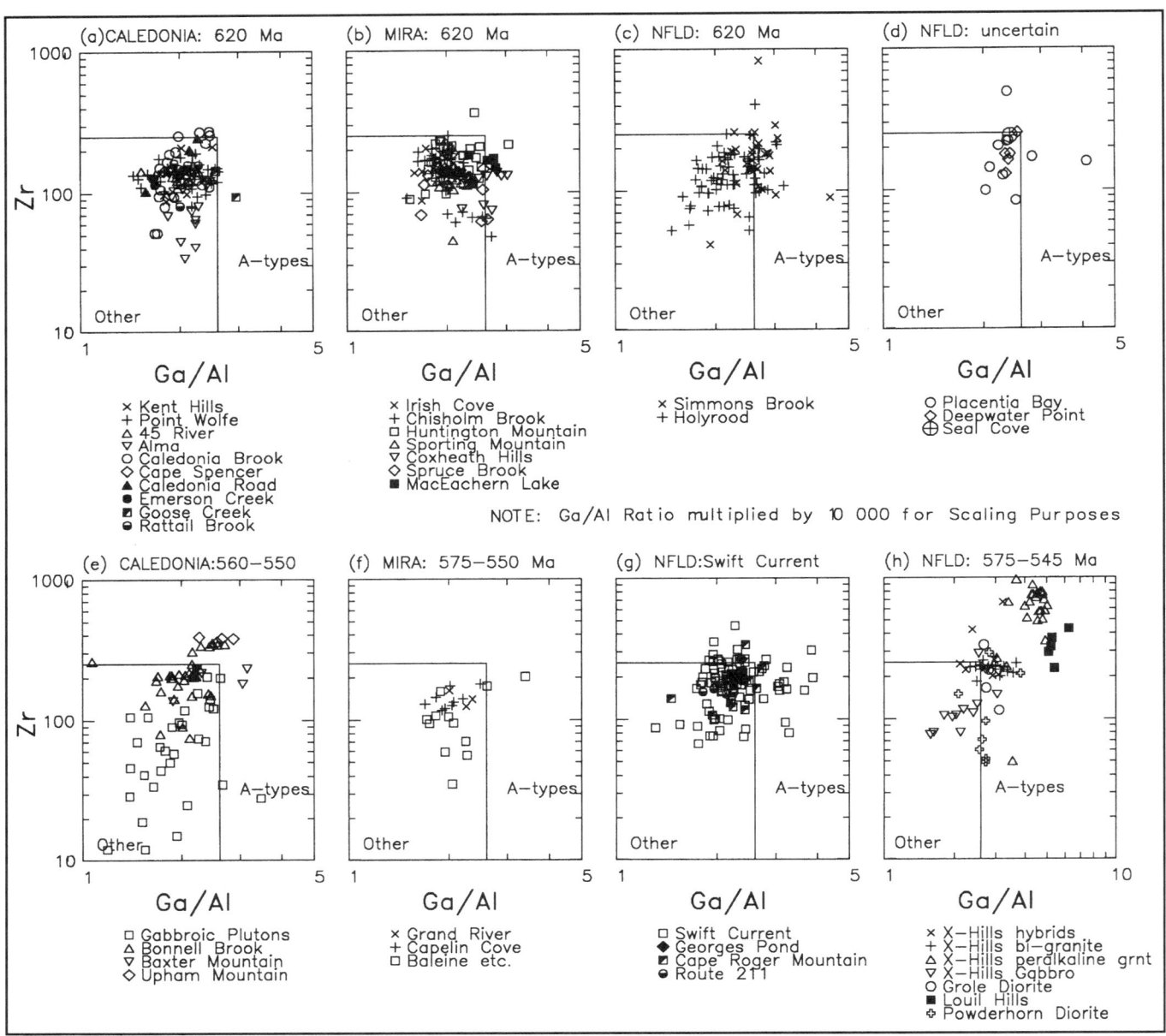

Figure 13. Plots of Zr against Ga/Al for samples from plutons in the Caledonia, Mira, and Newfoundland Avalon terranes, grouped according to age divisions as in Figure 5. Fields from Whalen et al. (1987).

diagrams using trace elements, and also by other features such as late Ba depletion and Nb depletion, all of which are recognized as features of arc-type magmas.

Ca. 575–565 Ma volcanic and plutonic rocks are represented in the Coastal belt of the Mira terrane, and in the Newfoundland Avalon west of the Paradise Sound fault. If the Bull Arm Formation is included, then volcanic rocks of this age are also present east of the fault. In the Mira terrane the plutons are mostly associated with arc-type stratovolcanic rocks of the redefined Fourchu Group, with which they are interpreted to be cogenetic (Barr, 1993). In Newfoundland, plutons known (Grole and Louil Hills intrusive suites) or inferred (Powderhorn Complex) to be of ca. 570 Ma age are not known to be spatially associated with abundant volcanic rocks of similar age, although some volcanic rocks of this age occur in the lower part of the Long Harbour Group (O'Brien et al., 1992b, 1994) and on the island of Miquelon (Rabu et al., 1993). By analogy with the Mira terrane, volcanic (and plutonic) rocks of this age may be more widespread in the central part of the Newfoundland Avalon terrane than currently recognized. Plutonic candidates are the Swift Current granite and associated similar plutons in the area west of the Paradise Sound fault. Although broadly similar to the 620 Ma suites, the Swift Current and related suites are more compositionally evolved, which suggests the possibility that they formed in a younger, more mature, arc-type setting. If so, this differs from the ca. 575 Ma arc-related suites of the Mira terrane, which appear to represent a less evolved subduction complex (Dostal et al., 1990; Barr, 1993, this study).

Plutonic rocks of ca. 560–550 Ma age, together with cogenetic volcanic rocks, are a major component of the Caledonia terrane, but apparently not of the Mira or Newfoundland Avalon terranes. In the Caledonia terrane, these rocks represent a major magmatic event during which large volumes of melt were produced. In the Mira terrane, they consist of only a few small tholeiitic gabbro bodies that may be comagmatic with limited basalts in the Main-à-Dieu Group. In Newfoundland, the Cross Hills intrusive suite is close to this age, as well as bimodal alkalic volcanic rocks in the upper part of the Long Harbour Group. These alkalic and peralkalic rocks suggest a more localized and limited melting event.

Because both have peralkaline affinities, the ca. 570 Ma Louil Hills suite and the ca. 550 Ma Cross Hills suite generally have been regarded as a continuum, especially in combination with the ca. 569 and 552 Ma ages reported from the Long Harbour Group (O'Brien et al., 1994; Kerr et al., 1995). As shown above, granites in the Louil Hills and Cross Hills suites display geochemical characteristics that are very different from those of the ca. 620 Ma granites, and also from the Swift Current and similar granites of uncertain age. Both the Louil Hills and Cross Hills intrusive suites are dominated by mafic rocks, and in the Grole intrusive suite and Powderhorn complex, granitic rocks are present only as minor crosscutting veins. The mafic rocks of these suites have transitional to alkaline compositions, and the granites of the Louil Hills and Cross Hills intrusive suites are in

part strongly peralkaline; the latter are associated with Zr-Nb-rare earth element mineralization, and have been compared to late Precambrian A-type granites in the Arabian Shield (Tuach, 1991). However, minor granites associated with the Powderhorn complex are nonperalkaline, and similar to the nonperalkaline biotite granites associated with the Cross Hills intrusive suite.

The timing of ca. 570–550 Ma extension indicated by alkaline to peralkaline magmatism in the Avalon terrane in Newfoundland has been linked to the opening of the Iapetus ocean recorded in western Newfoundland (e.g., Williams et al., 1989); however, late Precambrian global reconstructions (e.g., Murphy and Nance, 1989) suggest that a direct relationship is unlikely.

Traditionally, the Avalon zone has been viewed in terms of a late Precambrian (Avalonian) orogeny that affected the entire region. However, the differences in plutonic history documented here, the complimentary differences in volcanic history (Fig. 14), and the variations in intensity of deformation and metamorphism in the various parts of the terrane show that this traditional view is an oversimplification, and there is no compelling evidence for a single Avalonian orogeny.

TERRANE CORRELATIONS

The Mira and Caledonia terranes show most similarity to the part of the Newfoundland Avalon terrane west of the Paradise Sound fault, although the ca. 760 Ma rocks of the Newfoundland Burin Group are apparently not preserved, or at least not exposed, in either the Mira or Caledonia terranes. All three areas contain widespread ca. 620 Ma volcanic sequences, representing arc magmatism on a continental margin, accompanied by ca. 620 Ma compositionally expanded (dioritic and/or gabbroic through to granitic) suites dominated by granodiorite. Both the Mira terrane and the western part of the Newfoundland Avalon terrane preserve vestiges of older arc rocks (ca. 680 Ma; Stirling Group and Tickle Point Formation), although the associated ca. 673 Ma granites (Furbys Cove intrusive suite) appear to be absent from the Mira terrane. The volcanic rocks in both areas have volcanic arc affinities (Macdonald and Barr, 1993; O'Brien et al., 1994), and may be a link between these two parts of the. Avalon terrane. However, more detailed comparisons of the volcanic rocks are required to assess this possibility.

Ca. 570 Ma rocks like those of the Coastal belt of the Mira terrane appear to be minor in Newfoundland. The Long Harbour Group may be temporally equivalent to the Fourchu and Main-à-Dieu groups, although the bimodal magmatism in Newfoundland suggests a different environment of formation. Voluminous volcanism and plutonism at 560–550 Ma in the Caledonia terrane is apparently not represented in either the Mira or Newfoundland Avalon terranes.

The area east of Paradise Sound fault in Newfoundland does not show as much similarity to the Mira and Caledonia terranes as does the area west of the fault. The thick turbidite sequences of the Connecting Point and Conception groups are not represented in the Mira or Caledonia terranes, nor are the

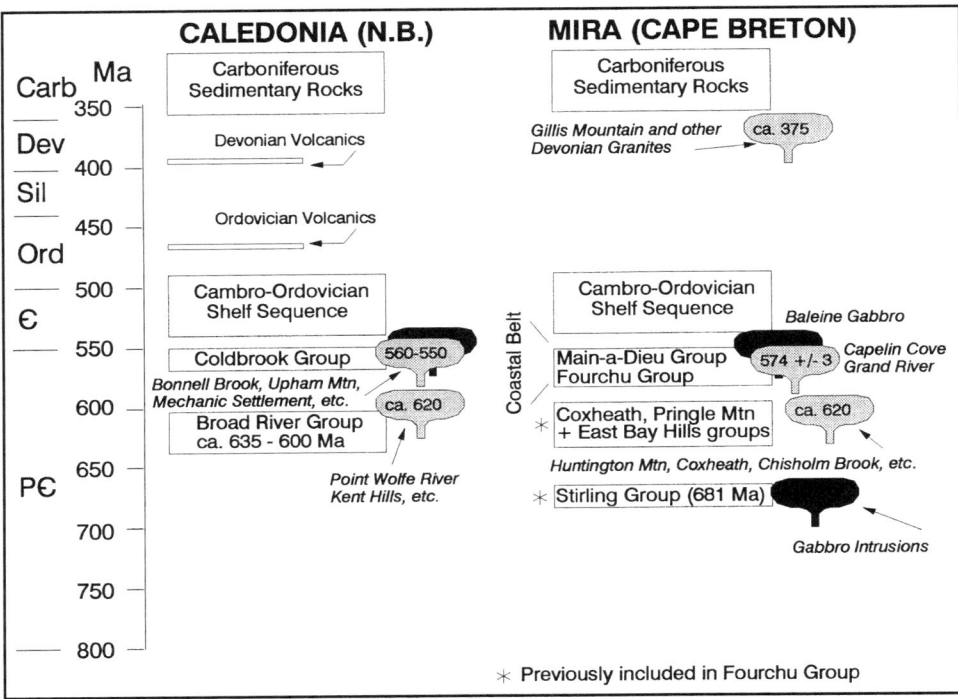

Figure 14 (on this and facing page). Comparative stratigraphic and intrusive relationships of major units in the Avalon terrane sensu stricto of New Brunswick (Caledonia terrane), Cape Breton Island (Mira terrane), and the Newfoundland Avalon terrane, after Barr et al. (1994, 1996) and O'Brien et al. (1990, 1992a, 1992b). Note that the vertical (time) extent of some units has been exaggerated in order to represent them at this scale.

shales and sandstones of the St. John's Group (Fig. 14). Similarities in the evolution of these areas do not appear until the shallow marine to alluvial Signal Hill Group, which has lithologically equivalent units in the Musgravetown Group west of the Paradise Sound fault and in the Main-à-Dieu and upper Coldbrook groups in the Mira and Caledonia terranes, respectively (Fig. 14). However, even at that time, the bimodal alkalic volcanic rocks of the Bull Arm Formation are not represented in the Mira and Caledonia terranes. The models of Barr and Raeside (1989) imply that the Antigonish and Cobequid highlands of northern mainland Nova Scotia are more likely correlatives of the Newfoundland Avalon east of the Paradise Sound fault, consistent with the thick turbiditic sequences of the Georgeville and Jeffers groups in those areas (Murphy et al., 1992).

CONCLUSIONS

Most descriptions of the Avalon terrane have emphasized its similarities to the type area in eastern Newfoundland. However, comparison of plutonic rocks in the Newfoundland Avalon terrane with other parts of the terrane in southern New Brunswick (Caledonia terrane) and southeastern Cape Breton Island (Mira terrane) shows that only ca. 620 Ma plutons are similar, and hence indicate a similar tectonic setting in all three areas. Older units are recognized so far only in Newfoundland and the Mira terrane, and data are too limited to make detailed comparisons.

Younger plutonic (and volcanic) units are present in all three areas, but show significant differences. More detailed geochronology is required, particularly from units of unknown age in the central part of the Newfoundland Avalon terrane, before we can assemble a more detailed tectonic model for all three areas and speculate more on the original position of these various components of the Avalon terrane relative to one another.

ACKNOWLEDGMENTS

We are grateful to the many geologists, cited in this chapter, who have worked in the areas described, and contributed to the database. Work in the Caledonia and Mira terrane by S. Barr and her colleagues has been funded by the Geological Survey of Canada through various contracts under the Canada–New Brunswick and Canada–Nova Scotia mineral development and mineral cooperation agreements, and by research grants to Barr from the Natural Sciences and Engineering Research Council of Canada. Field work and geochemical studies of plutonic suites in Newfoundland, including those of the Avalon zone, were funded by the Canada–Newfoundland Mineral Development Agreement. We thank the reviewers, J. B. Murphy and R. D. Nance, for their helpful comments, which led to improvements in the manuscript. We are grateful to Colin Macdonald for his assistance with production of Figures 1, 2, and 3.

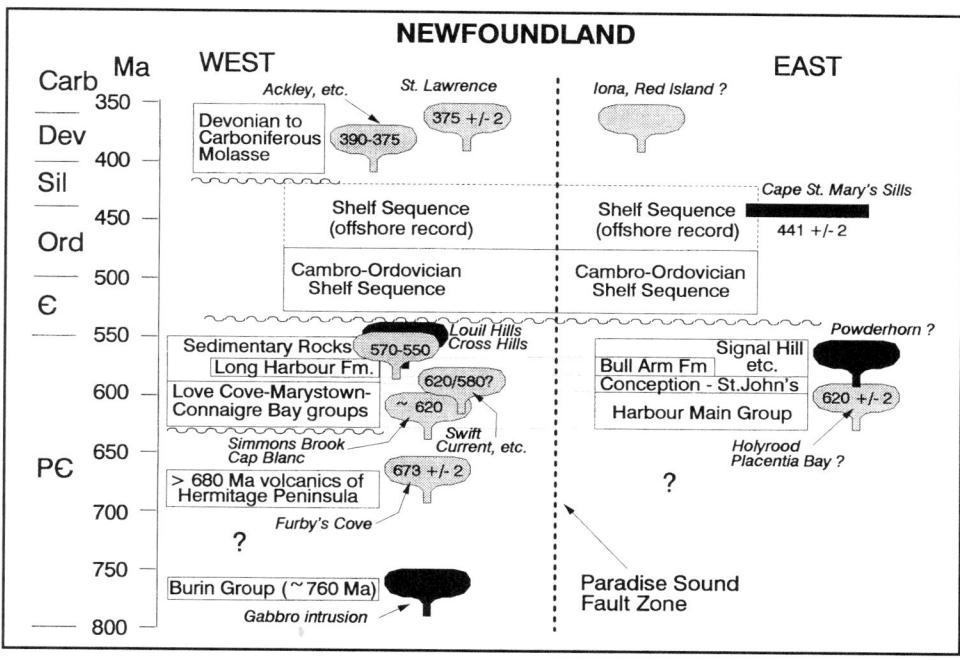

APPENDIX 1. GEOCHEMICAL DATA SOURCES AND REPRESENTATION

Geochemical data for plutons from the Caledonia and Mira terranes were obtained by X-ray fluorescence analysis at the Nova Scotia Regional Geochemical Centre, St. Marys University, Halifax. Data for the Caledonia terrane are from Barr (1987), Barr and White (1988, 1996a), Grammatikopoulos et al. (1995), and Whalen et al. (1994); a compilation of these data together with a small amount of previously unpublished data will in the future be published in a report of the Geological Survey of Canada. The total number of analyses depicted on the diagrams is 200. Data for the Mira terrane are from McMullin (1984), Sexton (1988), Thicke (1987), and Barr et al. (1996). The total number of analyses depicted on the diagrams is 165.

The Precambrian plutonic suites of the Avalon terrane in Newfoundland are represented by ~300 major and trace element analyses, which form part of a recent open-file release by the Geological Survey Branch (Kerr et al., 1994). These data are from a variety of original sources, but all are recent (post-1988) analyses of consistent quality. A portion of the database comes from a suite of samples collected during an early geochemical survey of granites in eastern Newfoundland (Strong et al., 1974), which were also utilized in some earlier discussions of the Precambrian granites (e.g., Strong and Minatidis, 1975; O'Driscoll and Strong, 1979). The original powders were completely reanalyzed for major elements and a wide trace element suite. In addition, the database includes samples collected since 1989, as part of a regional project to compile and collect data from granitoid plutonic suites throughout Newfoundland (Kerr et al., 1991). Data from the Cross Hills intrusive suite are from Tuach (1991); some mineralized and/or altered samples have been excluded, along with minor rock types such as aplite.

REFERENCES CITED

Barr, S. M., 1987, Field relations, petrology, and age of plutonic and associated metavolcanic and metasedimentary rocks, Fundy National Park area, New Brunswick, *in* Current research, part A: Geological Survey of Canada Paper 87–1A, p. 263–280.

Barr, S. M., 1993, Geochemistry and tectonic setting of Late Precambrian volcanic and plutonic rocks in southeastern Cape Breton Island, Nova Scotia: Canadian Journal of Earth Sciences, v. 30, p. 1147–1154.

Barr, S. M., and Hegner, E., 1992, Nd isotopic compositions of felsic igneous rocks in Cape Breton Island, Nova Scotia: Canadian Journal of Earth Sciences, v. 29, p. 650–657.

Barr, S. M., and Raeside, R. P., 1989, Tectono-stratigraphic terranes in Cape Breton Island, Nova Scotia: Implications for the configuration of the northern Appalachian orogen: Geology, v. 17, p. 822–825.

Barr, S. M., and Setter, J. R. D., 1986, Petrology of granitoid rocks of the Boisdale Hills, central Cape Breton Island, Nova Scotia: Nova Scotia Department of Mines and Energy Paper 84–1, 75 p.

Barr, S. M., and White, C. E., 1988, Petrochemistry of contrasting Late Precambrian volcanic and plutonic associations, Caledonian Highlands, southern New Brunswick: Maritime Sediments and Atlantic Geology, v. 24, p. 353–372.

Barr, S. M., and White, C. E., 1989a, Re-interpretation of Precambrian stratigraphy in southern New Brunswick, *in* Abbot, S. A., ed., Project summaries for 1989 and fourteenth annual review of activities: New Brunswick Department of Natural Resources and Energy, Minerals and Energy Division, Information Circular 89-2, p. 182–189.

Barr, S. M., and White, C. E., 1989b, Revised geological map of the central Caledonian Highlands, southern New Brunswick (parts of 21H5, 6, 10, 11, 12, 14, 15): Geological Survey of Canada Open File 2071, scale 1:50,000.

Barr, S. M., and White, C. E., 1991, Late Precambrian–Early Cambrian geology, Saint John–St. Martins area, southern New Brunswick: Geological Survey of Canada Open-File 2353, scale 1:50,000.

Barr, S. M., and White, C. E., 1993, Geological mapping of the eastern Caledonia Highlands, southern New Brunswick: Geological Survey of Canada Open-File 2600, scale 1:50,000.

Barr, S. M., and White, C. E., 1996a, Tectonic setting of Avalonian volcanic and plutonic rocks in the Caledonian Highlands, southern New Brunswick, Canada: Canadian Journal of Earth Sciences, v. 33, p. 156–168.

Barr, S. M., and White, C. E., 1996b, Contrasts in late Precambrian–early Paleozoic tectonothermal history between Avalon composite terrane sensu stricto and other possible peri-Gondwanan terranes in southern New Brunswick and Cape Breton Island, Canada, *in* Nance, R. D., and Thompson, M. D., eds., Avalonian and related peri-Gondwanan terranes of the Circum-North Atlantic: Geological Society of America Special Paper 304, p. 95–108.

Barr, S. M., O'Reilly, G. A., and O'Beirne, A. M., 1982, Geology and geochemistry of selected granitoid plutons of Cape Breton Island: Nova Scotia Department of Mines and Energy Paper 82-1, 176 p.

Barr, S. M., Macdonald, A. S., and White, C. E., 1988, The Fourchu Group and associated granitoid rocks, Coxheath Hills, East Bay Hills, and southwestern Stirling and Coastal belts, southeastern Cape Breton Island, Nova Scotia: Geological Survey of Canada Open-File 1759, scale 1:50,000.

Barr, S. M., Macdonald, A. S., and White, C. E., 1989, The Fourchu Group and associated granitoid rocks, Stirling and Coastal belts, southeastern Cape Breton Island: Geological Survey of Canada Open-File 1988, scale 1:50,000.

Barr, S. M., Dunning, G. R., Raeside, R. P., and Jamieson, R. A., 1990, Contrasting U-Pb ages from plutons in the Bras d'Or and Mira terranes of Cape Breton Island, Nova Scotia: Canadian Journal of Earth Sciences, v. 27, p. 1200–1208.

Barr, S. M., Bevier, M. L., White, C. E., and Doig, R., 1994, Magmatic history of the Avalon terrane of southern New Brunswick, Canada, based on U-Pb (zircon) geochronology: Journal of Geology, v. 102, p. 399–409.

Barr, S. M., White, C. E., and Macdonald, A. S., 1996, Late Precambrian and Early Cambrian rocks of southeastern Cape Breton Island, Nova Scotia: Geological Survey of Canada Bulletin 468, 84 p.

Bevier, M. L., and Barr, S. M., 1990, U-Pb age constraints on the stratigraphy and tectonic history of the Avalon terrane, New Brunswick, Canada: Journal of Geology, v. 98, p. 53–63.

Bevier, M. L., Barr, S. M., White, C. E., and Macdonald, A. S., 1993, U-Pb geochronologic constraints on the volcanic evolution of the Mira (Avalon) terrane, southeastern Cape Breton Island, Nova Scotia: Canadian Journal of Earth Sciences, v. 30, p. 1–10.

Bradley, D. A., 1962, Gisborne Lake and Terrenceville map areas, Newfoundland: Geological Survey of Canada Memoir 321, 56 p.

Chappell, B. W., and White, A. J. R., 1974, Two contrasting granite types: Pacific Geology, v. 8, p. 173–174.

Colman-Sadd, S. P., Hayes, J. P., and Knight, I., 1990, Geology of the Island of Newfoundland: Newfoundland Department of Mines and Energy, Geological Survey Branch, Map 90-1, scale 1:1,000,000.

Cormier, R. F., 1972, Radiometric ages of granitic rocks, Cape Breton Island, Nova Scotia: Canadian Journal of Earth Sciences, v. 9, p. 1074–1086.

Currie, K. L., and Eby, G. N., 1990, Geology and geochemistry of late Precambrian Coldbrook Group near Saint John, New Brunswick: Canadian Journal of Earth Sciences, v. 27, p. 1418–1430.

Dallmeyer, R. D., Odom, A. L., O'Driscoll, C. F., and Hussey, E. M., 1981, Geochronology of the Swift Current Granite, and host volcanic rocks of the Love Cove Group, southwestern Avalon Zone, Newfoundland: Evidence of a Late Proterozoic volcanic-subvolcanic association: Canadian Journal of Earth Sciences, v. 18, p. 699–707.

Doig, R., Murphy, J. B., and Nance, R. D., 1991, U-Pb geochronology of Late Proterozoic rocks of the eastern Cobequid Highlands, Nova Scotia: Canadian Journal of Earth Sciences, v. 28, p. 504–511.

Donohoe, H. V. Jr., 1981, Geological studies in southeastern Cape Breton Island: Nova Scotia Department of Mines and Energy Report 81–1, p. 107–122.

Dostal, J., and McCutcheon, S. R., 1990, Geochemistry of Late Proterozoic basaltic rocks from southeastern New Brunswick, Canada: Precambrian Research, v. 47, p. 83–98.

Dostal, J., Keppie, J. D., and Murphy, J. B., 1990, Geochemistry of Late Proterozoic basaltic rocks from southeastern Cape Breton Island, Nova Scotia: Canadian Journal of Earth Sciences, v. 27, p. 619–631.

Dunning, G. R., and O'Brien, S. J., 1989, Late Proterozoic–early Paleozoic crust in the Hermitage flexure, Newfoundland Appalachians: U-Pb ages and tectonic significance: Geology, v. 17, p. 548–551.

Dunning, G. R., Barr, S. M., Raeside, R. P., and Jamieson, R. A., 1990, U-Pb zircon, titanite, and monazite ages in the Bras d'Or and Aspy terranes of

Cape Breton Island, Nova Scotia: Implications for igneous and metamorphic history: Geological Society of America Bulletin, v. 102, p. 322–330.

El Bouseily, A. M., and El Sokkary, A. A., 1979, The relation between Rb, Ba, and Sr in granitic rocks: Chemical Geology, v. 16, p. 207–219.

Fryer, B. J., Kerr, A., Jenner, G. A., and Longstaffe, F. J., 1992, Probing the crust with plutons: Regional isotopic geochemistry of granitoid intrusions across insular Newfoundland: Newfoundland Geological Surveys Branch Report 92-1, p. 119–140.

Gibbons, W., 1990, Transcurrent ductile shear zones and the dispersal of the Avalon superterrane, *in* D'Lemos, R. S., Strachen, R. A., and Topley, C. G., eds., The Cadomian orogeny: Geological Society of London Special Publication 51, p. 407–423.

Grammatikopoulos, A. L., 1992, Petrogenesis, age, and economic potential of gabbroic plutons in the Avalon terrane in southern New Brunswick and southeastern Cape Breton Island [M.S. thesis]: Wolfville, Nova Scotia, Acadia University, 378 p.

Grammatikopoulos, A. L., Barr, S. M., Reynolds, P., and Doig, R., 1995, Petrology and age of the Mechanic Settlement Pluton, Avalon terrane, southern New Brunswick: Canadian Journal of Earth Sciences, v. 32, p. 2147–2158.

Greene, B. A., and O'Driscoll, C. F., 1976, Gaultois map area: Newfoundland Department of Mines and Energy. Mineral Development Division Report of Activities for 1975, p. 56–63.

Gribble, C. D., 1969, Distribution of elements in igneous rocks of the normal calc-alkaline sequence: Scottish Journal of Geology, v. 5, p. 322–327.

Hayes, J. P., Dickson, W. L., and Tuach, J., 1987, Newfoundland granitoid rocks: Newfoundland Department of Mines and Energy, Mineral Development Division, Open-File Map 87-85, scale 1:500,000.

Hepburn, J. C., Hon, R., Dunning, G. R., Bailey, R., and Galli, K., 1993, The Avalon and Nashoba terranes (eastern margin of the Appalachian orogen in southeastern New England), *in* Cheney, J. T., and Hepburn, J. C., eds., Field trip guidebook for the northeastern United States: Boulder, Colorado, Geological Society of America, Centennial Field Guide, v. 2, p. X1–X31.

Hughes, C. J., 1971, Anatomy of a granophyre intrusion: Lithos, v. 4, p. 403–415.

Irvine, T. N., and Baragar, W. R.A., 1971, A guide to the chemical classification of the common volcanic rocks: Canadian Journal of Earth Sciences, v. 8, p. 523–548.

Jenness, S. E., 1958, Geology of the Newman Sound map area, northeast Newfoundland: Geological Survey of Newfoundland Report 12, 36 p.

Jenness, S. E., 1963, Terra Nova and Bonavista map area, Newfoundland: Geological Survey of Canada Memoir 327, 184 p.

Keppie, J. D., 1979, Geological map of the Province of Nova Scotia: Nova Scotia Department of Mines and Energy, scale 1:500,000.

Keppie, J. D., 1989, Northern Appalachian terranes and their accretionary history, *in* Dallmeyer, R. D., ed., Terranes in the Circum-Atlantic Paleozoic orogens: Geological Society of America Special Paper 20, p. 159–192.

Keppie, J. D., Dallmeyer, R. D., and Murphy, J. B., 1990, Tectonic implications of $^{40}Ar/^{39}Ar$ hornblende ages from Late Proterozoic–Cambrian plutons in the Avalon composite terrane, Nova Scotia, Canada: Geological Society of America Bulletin, v. 102, p. 516–528.

Keppie, J. D., Dallmeyer, R. D., and Krogh, T. E., 1992, U-Pb and $^{40}Ar/^{39}Ar$ mineral ages from Cape North, northern Cape Breton Island: Implications for accretion of the Avalon composite terrane: Canadian Journal of Earth Sciences, v. 29, p. 277–295.

Kerr, A., Hayes, J. P., Dickson, W. L., and Butler, A. J., 1991, Toward an integrated database for Newfoundland granitoid suites: A project outline and progress report: Newfoundland Department of Mines and Energy, Geological Survey Branch, Report 91-1, p. 127–140.

Kerr, A., Dickson, W. L., Hayes, J. P., and Fryer, B. J., 1993, Devonian postorogenic granites on the southeastern margin of the Newfoundland Appalachians: A review of geology, geochemistry, petrogenesis and mineral potential: Newfoundland Department of Mines and Energy, Geological Survey Branch Report 93-1, p. 239–278.

Kerr, A., Hayes, J. P. Colman-Sadd, S. P., Dickson, W. L., and Butler, A. J., 1994, An integrated lithogeochemical database for the granitoid plutonic suites of Newfoundland: Newfoundland Department of Mines and Energy, Geological Survey Branch, Open-File Report NFLD/2377, 44 p.

Kerr, A., Jenner, G. A., and Fryer, B. J., 1995, Sm-Nd isotopic geochemistry of Precambrian to Paleozoic granitoid suites and the deep-crustal structure of the southeast margin of the Newfoundland Appalachians: Canadian Journal of Earth Sciences, v. 32, p. 224–245.

King, A. F., 1986, Geology of the St. John's area, Newfoundland: Newfoundland Department of Mines and Energy, Geological Survey Branch, Report 86–1, p. 209–218.

Knight, I., and O'Brien, S. J., 1988, Stratigraphic and sedimentological studies of the Connecting Point Group, portions of the Eastport (2C/12) and St. Brendan's (2C/13) map areas, Bonavista Bay, Newfoundland: Newfoundland Department of Mines and Energy, Geological Survey Branch, Report 88-1, p. 207–228.

Krogh, T. E., Strong, D. F., O'Brien, S. J., and Papezik, V. S., 1988, Precise U-Pb zircon dates from the Avalon Terrane in Newfoundland: Canadian Journal of Earth Sciences, v. 25, p. 442–453.

Macdonald, A. S., and Barr, S. M., 1993, Geological setting and depositional environment of the Stirling Group of southeastern Cape Breton Island, Nova Scotia: Atlantic Geology, v. 29, p. 137–147.

McCartney, W. D., Poole, W. H., Wanless, R. K., Williams, H., and Loveridge, W. D., 1966, Rb/Sr age and geological setting of the Holyrood granite, southeast Newfoundland. Canadian Journal of Earth Sciences, v. 3, p. 947–957.

McMullin, D. W., 1984, The Loch Lomond plutonic complex, Cape Breton Island, Nova Scotia [M.S. thesis]: Wolfville, Nova Scotia, Acadia University, 239 p.

Middlemost, E. A. K., 1975, The basalt clan. Earth Science Reviews, v. 11, p. 337–364.

Murphy, J. B., 1977, The stratigraphy and geological history of the Fourchu Group, southeastern Cape Breton, Nova Scotia. [M.S. thesis]: Wolfville, Nova Scotia, Acadia University, 183 p.

Murphy, J. B., and Nance, R. D., 1989, Model for the evolution of the Avalonian-Cadomian belt: Geology, v. 17, p. 735–738.

Murphy, J. B., Keppie, J. D., and Hynes, A. J., 1991, Geology of the northern Antigonish Highlands, Nova Scotia. Geological Survey of Canada Paper 89-10, 114 p.

Murphy, J. B., Pe-Piper, G., Keppie, J. D., and Piper, D. J.W., 1992, Correlation of Neoproterozoic III sequences in the Avalon composite terrane of mainland Nova Scotia: Tectonic implications: Atlantic Geology, v. 28, p. 143–151.

Nance, R. D., 1986, Precambrian evolution of the Avalon terrane in the northern Appalachians: A review: Maritime Sediments and Atlantic Geology, v. 22, p. 214–238.

Nance, R. D., and Dallmeyer, R. D., 1994, Structural and ^{40}Ar/^{39}Ar mineral age constraints for the tectonothermal evolution of the Green Head Group and Brookville Gneiss, southern New Brunswick, Canada: Implications for the configuration of the Avalon composite terrane: Geological Journal, v. 29, p. 293–322.

Nixon, G. T., and Papezik, V. S., 1979, Late Precambrian ash-flow tuffs and associated rocks of the Harbour Main Group near Colliers, eastern Newfoundland: Chemistry and magmatic affinities: Canadian Journal of Earth Sciences, v. 16, p. 167–171.

O'Brien, S. J., 1987, Geology of the Eastport (west half) map area, Bonavista Bay, Newfoundland: Newfoundland Department of Mines and Energy, Mineral Development Division Report 87–1, p. 257–270.

O'Brien, S. J., and Taylor, S. W., 1983, Geology of the Baine Harbour and Point Enragee map areas: Newfoundland Department of Mines and Energy, Mineral Development Division Report 83-5, 70 p.

O'Brien, S. J., Wardle, R. J., and King, A. F., 1983, The Avalon Zone: A Pan-African terrane in the Appalachian orogen of Canada: Geological Journal, v. 18, p. 195–222.

O'Brien, S. J., Nunn, G. A., Dickson, W. L., and Tuach, J., 1984, Geology of the Terrenceville (1M/10) and Gisborne Lake (1M/15) map areas, southeast Newfoundland: Newfoundland Department of Mines and Energy. Min-

eral Development Division Report 84-4, 54 p.

O'Brien, S. J., Strong, D. F., and King, A., 1990, The Avalon Zone type area: Southeastern Newfoundland Appalachians, *in* Strachan, R. A., and Taylor, G. K., eds., Avalonian and Cadomian geology of the North Atlantic: Glasgow, Blackies and Sons, p. 166–194.

O'Brien, B. H., O'Brien, S. J., and Dunning, G. R., 1991, Silurian cover, Late Precambrian–Early Ordovician basement, and the chronology of Silurian orogenesis in the Hermitage Flexure (Newfoundland Appalachians): American Journal of Science, v. 291, p. 760–799.

O'Brien, S. J., O'Driscoll, C. F., and Tucker, R. D., 1992a, A reinterpretation of the geology of parts of the Hermitage Peninsula, southwestern Avalon Zone, Newfoundland: Newfoundland Department of Mines and Energy, Geological Survey Branch Report 92-1, p. 185–194.

O'Brien, S. J., O'Driscoll, C. F., Tucker, R. D., and Dunning, G. R., 1992b, Four-fold subdivision of the late Precambrian magmatic record of the Avalon type area (east Newfoundland): Nature and significance: Geological Association of Canada–Mineralogical Association of Canada Program with Abstracts, v. 17, p. A85.

O'Brien, S. J., Tucker, R. D., and O'Driscoll, C. F., 1994, Neoproterozoic basement-cover relationships and the tectonomagmatic record of the Avalon Zone on the Hermitage peninsula and environs, Newfoundland: Geological Association of Canada NUNA Conference, Abstract Volume, p. 21.

O'Driscoll, C. F., 1977, Geology of the Sound Island map area (east half): Newfoundland Department of Mines and Energy, Mineral Development Division, Report of Activities for 1976, p. 43–47.

O'Driscoll, C. F., and Strong, D. F., 1979, Geology and geochemistry of Late Precambrian volcanic and intrusive rocks of the southwestern Avalon Zone, Newfoundland: Precambrian Research, v. 8, p. 19–48.

O'Reilly, G. A., 1977, Field relations and mineral potential of the granitoid rocks of southeast Cape Breton Island: Nova Scotia Department of Mines and Energy Report 77-1, p. 81–87.

Papezik, V. S., Keats, H. F., and Vahtra, J., 1978, Geology of the Foxtrap pyrophyllite deposit, Avalon Peninsula, Newfoundland: Montreal, Canadian Institute of Mining and Metallurgy, p. 1–9.

Pearce, J. A., Harris, N. B. W., and Tindle, A. G., 1984, Trace element discrimination diagrams for the tectonic interpretation of granitic rocks: Journal of Petrology, v. 25, p. 856–983.

Pe-Piper, G., and Piper, D. J. W., 1989, The upper Hadrynian Jeffers Group, Cobequid Highlands, Avalon Zone of Nova Scotia: A back-arc volcanic complex: Geological Society of America Bulletin, v. 101, p. 364–376.

Pitcher, W. S., 1983, Granite type and tectonic environment, *in* Hsü, K., ed., Mountain building processes: London, Academic Press, p. 19–40.

Rabu, D., Guerrot, C., Doig, R., Tegyey, M., Murphy, J. B., and Keppie, J. D., 1993, Premieres donnees geochronologiques sur Saint-Pierre et Miquelon: Paris, Académie des Sciences Comptes Rendus, ser. II, v. 314, p. 639–646.

Reusch, D. N., and O'Driscoll, C. F., 1987, Geological and metallogenic investigations in the western belt of the Love Cove Group (NTS 2D/1,2,8), Avalon Zone, Newfoundland: Newfoundland Department of Mines and Energy, Mineral Development Division, Report 87–1, p. 93–103.

Rose, E. R., 1952, Torbay map-area, Newfoundland: Geological Survey of Canada Memoir 265, 65 p.

Ruitenberg, A. A., Giles, P. S., Venugopal, D. V., Buttimer, S. M., McCutcheon, S. R., and Chandra, J., 1979, Geology and mineral deposits, Caledonia area: New Brunswick Department of Natural Resources, Mineral Resources Branch Memoir 1, 213 p.

Sexton, A. S., 1988, Geology of the Sporting Mountain area, southeastern Cape Breton Island, Nova Scotia [M.S. thesis]: Wolfville, Nova Scotia, Acadia University, 215 p.

Shand, S. J., 1950, Eruptive rocks (fourth edition): London, Thomas Murby, 488 p.

Strong, D. F., 1979, Proterozoic tectonics of northwestern Gondwanaland: New evidence from eastern Newfoundland: Tectonophysics, v. 54, p. 81–101.

Strong, D. F., and Dostal, J., 1980, Dynamic melting of Proterozoic upper mantle: Evidence from rare earth elements in oceanic crust of Eastern Newfoundland: Contributions to Mineralogy and Petrology, v. 72, p. 165–173.

Strong, D. F., and Minatidas, D. G., 1975, Geochemistry and tectonic setting of the Late Precambrian Holyrood plutonic series of eastern Newfoundland: Lithos, v. 8, p. 283–295.

Strong, D. F., Dickson, W. L., O'Driscoll, C. F., and Kean, B. F., 1974, Geochemistry of eastern Newfoundland granitoid rocks: Newfoundland Department of Mines and Energy, Mineral Development Division Report 74-3, 140 p.

Strong, D. F., O'Brien, S. J., Taylor, S. W., Strong, P. G., and Wilton, D., 1977, Geology of the Marystown (1M/3) and St. Lawrence (1L/14) map areas Newfoundland: Newfoundland Department of Mines and Energy, Mineral Development Division Report 77-8, 81 p.

Swinden, S., and Hunt, P. A., 1991, A U-Pb age from the Connaigre Bay Group, southwestern Avalon Zone, Newfoundland: Implications for regional correlations and metallogenesis, *in* Radiometric age and isotopic studies, Report 4: Geological Survey of Canada Paper 90-2, p. 3–10.

Thicke, M. J., 1987, Geology of Late Hadrynian metavolcanic and granitoid rocks of the Coxheath Hills and northeastern East Bay Hills areas, Cape Breton Island, Nova Scotia [M.S. thesis]: Wolfville, Nova Scotia, Acadia University, 300 p.

Tuach, J., 1991, The geology and geochemistry of the Cross Hills Plutonic Suite, Fortune Bay, Newfoundland (1M/10): Newfoundland Department of Mines and Energy, Geological Survey Branch Report 91-2, 73 p.

Watters, S. E., 1993, Structure and alteration related to Hercynian gold deposition, Cape Spencer, New Brunswick, Canada [Ph.D. thesis]: London, University of Western Ontario, 351 p.

Weeks, F. J., 1954, Southeast Cape Breton Island, Nova Scotia: Geological Survey of Canada Memoir 277, 112 p.

Whalen, J. B., Currie, K. L., and Chappell, B. W., 1987, A-type granites: Geochemical characteristics, discrimination, and petrogenesis: Contributions to Mineralogy and Petrology, v. 95, p. 407–419.

Whalen, J. B., Jenner, G. A., Currie, K. L., Barr, S. M., Longstaffe, F. J., and Hegner, E., 1994, Geochemical and isotopic characteristics of granitoids of the Avalon Zone, southern New Brunswick: Possible evidence of repeated delamination events: Journal of Geology, v. 102, p. 269–282.

White, C. E., and Barr, S. M., 1996, Geology of the Brookville terrane, southern New Brunswick, Canada, *in* Nance, R. D., and Thompson, M. D., eds., Avalonian and related peri-Gondwanan terranes of the Circum-North Atlantic: Geological Society of America Special Paper 304, p. 133–147.

Williams, H., 1978, Tectonic lithofacies map of the Appalachians: St. John's, Newfoundland, Canada, Memorial University Map No. 1, scale 1:1,000,000.

Williams, H., 1979, The Appalachian orogen in Canada: Canadian Journal of Earth Sciences, v. 16, p. 792–807.

Williams, H., Dickson, W. L., Currie, K. L., Hayes, J. P., and Tuach, J., 1989, Preliminary report on classification of Newfoundland granitic rocks and their relations to tectonostratigraphic zones and lower crustal blocks, *in* Current research, Part B: Geological Survey of Canada Paper 89-1B, p. 47–53.

MANUSCRIPT ACCEPTED BY THE SOCIETY JULY 2, 1996

Geological Society of America
Memoir 191
1997

Geochemistry and petrogenesis of tonalite dikes in the Smith River allochthon, south-central Virginia

James S. Beard

Virginia Museum of Natural History, 1001 Douglas Avenue, Martinsville, Virginia 24112

ABSTRACT

Tonalite dikes within the Smith River allochthon (SRA) in south-central Virginia intrude gabbro and granite of the Martinsville igneous complex (MIC), migmatites in the contact aureole surrounding the MIC, and schist and gneiss of the Fork Mountain Formation. The tonalites are chemically distinct from migmatitic leucosomes and muscovite granite dikes in the gneiss and from the gabbro and granite of the MIC, and appear to be unrelated to any of these rock types by either fractionation or mixing. The tonalites have high Sr (average 710 ppm), positive Eu anomalies, and are depleted in heavy rare earth elements and Y (La_{ch}/Yb_{ch} average 25, Y average 7.4 ppm). They are, in addition, aluminous (Al_2O_3 = 17% at 70% SiO_2), peraluminous, and Fe-poor (most <2% FeO (total) at 70% SiO_2). The chemistry of the tonalites is consistent with their formation by water-excess melting of basalt or amphibolite in the garnet stability field and above plagioclase stability at total pressure (P_{total}) >8–10 kbar and P_{H_2O} >2–3 kbar. In particular, the tonalites appear to be too aluminous and Fe-poor to have formed by dehydration melting, even at pressures >30 kbar. Trace element modeling suggests that the tonalites can be generated by partial melting of either a local crustal source (Bassett amphibolite) or by melting of a subducted slab of enriched mid-ocean ridge basalt (MORB) composition. Normal MORB is not an appropriate source. Bassett amphibolite models require a higher proportion of restitic amphibole and a higher degree of partial melting than enriched MORB models, consistent with melting under relatively wet conditions. The elevated $^{87}Sr/^{86}Sr$ (average at 500 Ma = 0.70496) of the tonalites also favors crustal input. The Sr isotopic characteristics of modern slab melts (adakites) as well as their Al and Fe contents all favor an origin by dehydration-melting of relatively uncontaminated normal MORB. On balance, the evidence seems to favor a crustal melting origin for the tonalites. Melting may have been induced by influx of water from the cool, upper portion of the lower plate into the hot, lower portion of the SRA during or after emplacement of the thrust sheet.

INTRODUCTION

The chemistry of low-K silicic magmas (tonalites and dacites) can be an important aid in reconstructing the geologic history of a region. Experimental studies have shown that the compositions of tonalitic melts formed by partial melting of amphibolites and crystallization of basalts are functions of water content and total pressure (Helz, 1976; Spulber and Rutherford, 1983; Luhr, 1990;

Beard and Lofgren, 1989, 1991; Rapp et al., 1991; Rushmer, 1991; Wolf and Wyllie, 1991, 1994; Patino Douce and Beard, 1995). Most tonalites found in modern and ancient magmatic arcs have chemical characteristics consistent with their derivation by dehydration melting of amphibolite or crystal fractionation of relatively dry basalt at pressure (P) <8–12 kbar and P_{H_2O} <2 kbar. Drummond and Defant (1990) recognized that some tonalites (adakites) have chemical characteristics (high Sr, low Y, heavy rare earth ele-

Beard, J. S., 1997, Geochemistry and petrogenesis of tonalite dikes in the Smith River allochthon, south-central Virginia, *in* Sinha, A. K., Whalen, J. B., and Hogan, J. P., eds., The Nature of Magmatism in the Appalachian Orogen: Boulder, Colorado, Geological Society of America Memoir 191.

ments [REE]) consistent with a petrogenesis by high-pressure melting of amphibolite in the garnet stability field. Such melting requires total pressures of at least 8–12 kbar (Rapp et al., 1991; Wolf and Wyllie, 1991; Patino Douce and Beard, 1995) and can reflect melting of hot oceanic crust in a subduction zone at or around the time of ridge subduction (Drummond and Defant, 1990; Peacock et al., 1994). High P_{H_2O} ($\geq$ 2 kbar) during partial melting of amphibolite produces strongly peraluminous, iron-poor tonalites (Beard and Lofgren, 1989; Luhr, 1990). Under some circumstances, partial melting of pelites at high P_{H_2O} can produce tonalitic melts (Whitney and Irving, 1994).

The Smith River allochthon (SRA; Conley and Henika, 1973; Conley, 1985) of south-central Virginia is a rootless, Paleozoic thrust sheet (Fig. 1). Tonalite dikes intrude the Paleozoic and late Precambrian(?) igneous and metamorphic rocks of the allochthon. These tonalites, informally termed the tonalites of the Martinsville igneous complex (MIC), may have formed by melting of a subducted slab. However, it appears more likely that the MIC tonalites formed by hydrous melting of amphibolite in the lower crust of the SRA.

DESCRIPTION AND AGE

The MIC tonalites dikes are tabular, 2 cm to 2 m in width, and most are undeformed except for local foliations parallel to dike margins. Larger dikes are commonly zoned, and both mafic and felsic margins are observed. Most dikes are fine grained, but biotite-bearing tonalite pegmatites are also common. Dike orientations are variable and both conjugate and parallel dike sets are seen in large quarry exposures. Folding is not apparent from orientation patterns, but open folding of these variably oriented dikes would be difficult to detect.

Sr isotope analyses of variably mafic samples from a single zoned dike did not yield an isochron. The dikes cut metamorphic foliations in the strongly deformed gneisses and schists of the late Precambrian(?) Fork Mountain Formation and intrude relatively undeformed gabbros and granites of the 516 Ma (Sinha et al., 1989) MIC (Fig. 1; Ragland, 1974; Conley, 1985). The contacts between tonalite and gabbroic and granitic rocks of the MIC range from sharp to diffuse; the latter suggests that dike intrusion was penecontemporaneous with later stages of MIC cooling. However, no clear liquid-liquid contacts or chilled mafic xenoliths have been found. The ages of the allochthon-bounding faults are unclear. A K-Ar age of 321 Ma (Deuser and Herzog, 1962) on pegmatite that cuts the eastern bounding fault (Ridgeway fault, Conley and Henika, 1973; Fig. 1) must be interpreted cautiously. Both the Ridgeway fault and the western bounding fault (Bowen's Creek fault; Conley and Henika, 1970) appear to merge into the Brevard zone to the south (Conley, 1985) and may share that structure's long history of Paleozoic activity (e.g., Sinha et al., 1988). The age of the tonalite relative to the faults is unclear. It is not known whether the dikes intrude the faults, and most felsite and alaskite intrusives mapped just outside the boundaries of the SRA (Conley and Henika 1970, 1973) do not resemble the MIC tonalite dikes.

However, a deeply weathered, but apparently undeformed, biotite-muscovite tonalite of unknown form and affinity intrudes Grenville-age gneiss 3 km southwest of the Ridgeway fault.

PETROGRAPHY

The tonalites consist largely of normally zoned oligoclase-andesine, 20%–35% quartz, and 5%–20% biotite. Coarse-bladed and apparently primary muscovite occurs in all dikes. Its abundance ranges from trace amounts in the most mafic tonalites to around 5% in some felsic tonalites. In samples where it is abundant, muscovite may be overgrown by biotite. Presumably secondary muscovite occurs as oriented crystals in plagioclase in several samples. Epidote is present in most dikes. Many epidote crystals are euhedral to subhedral, and contacts against biotite and muscovite are generally euhedral. Some epidote crystals are zoned or have allanite cores, many of which are metamict. Epidote rarely (one sample) occurs as crystallographically oriented inclusions in plagioclase. Given these petrographic features and the minimal low-temperature alteration in these rocks, it appears that most epidote is a primary igneous phase (e.g., Zen and Hammarstrom, 1984). Common accessory minerals are apatite, sphene, monazite, zircon, and allanite. Sphene rarely occurs as euhedral to subhedral crystals, but is most common as reaction rims around ilmenite and may be largely secondary. Some apatite (having cores filled with dusty inclusions) and zircon (relatively large, rounded crystals) appear to be xenocrystic. Ilmenite, pyrrhotite, and very small amounts of chalcopyrite have been identified in polished section. Magnetite is absent. Biotite, epidote, ore minerals, and accessory phases commonly occur together in clots or stringers and are concentrated in the mafic portions of zoned dikes. Potassium feldspar is generally absent, except for pink microcline found in the cores of some tonalitic pegmatites.

GEOCHEMISTRY

The MIC tonalites are peraluminous, high-Al tonalites to trondhjemites (Barker, 1979) (Table 1; Fig. 2). Felsic dikes and the felsic portions of zoned dikes are enriched in the major- and trace-element constituents of quartz and feldspar (Si, Al, Na, Ca, Sr). All other elements, compatible and incompatible, are enriched in the mafic dikes and mafic portions of zoned dikes (Table 1; examples given in Fig. 3). The tonalites are depleted in heavy REE (average normalized La/Yb = 24) and all have a positive Eu anomaly (Fig. 4). There is a negative correlation between the magnitude of the Eu anomaly and total REE content of the sample (Fig. 4). The tonalites are depleted in Y relative to Sr (Fig. 5). High Sr/Y and heavy REE depletion in tonalites are

Figure 1. Map of part of the southeastern edge of the Smith River allochthon (modified after Conley, 1985) showing the location of the main body of the Martinsville igneous complex and the sample localities. MSQ indicates location of all samples having the MSQ prefix. US220BYP indicates the route 220 bypass.

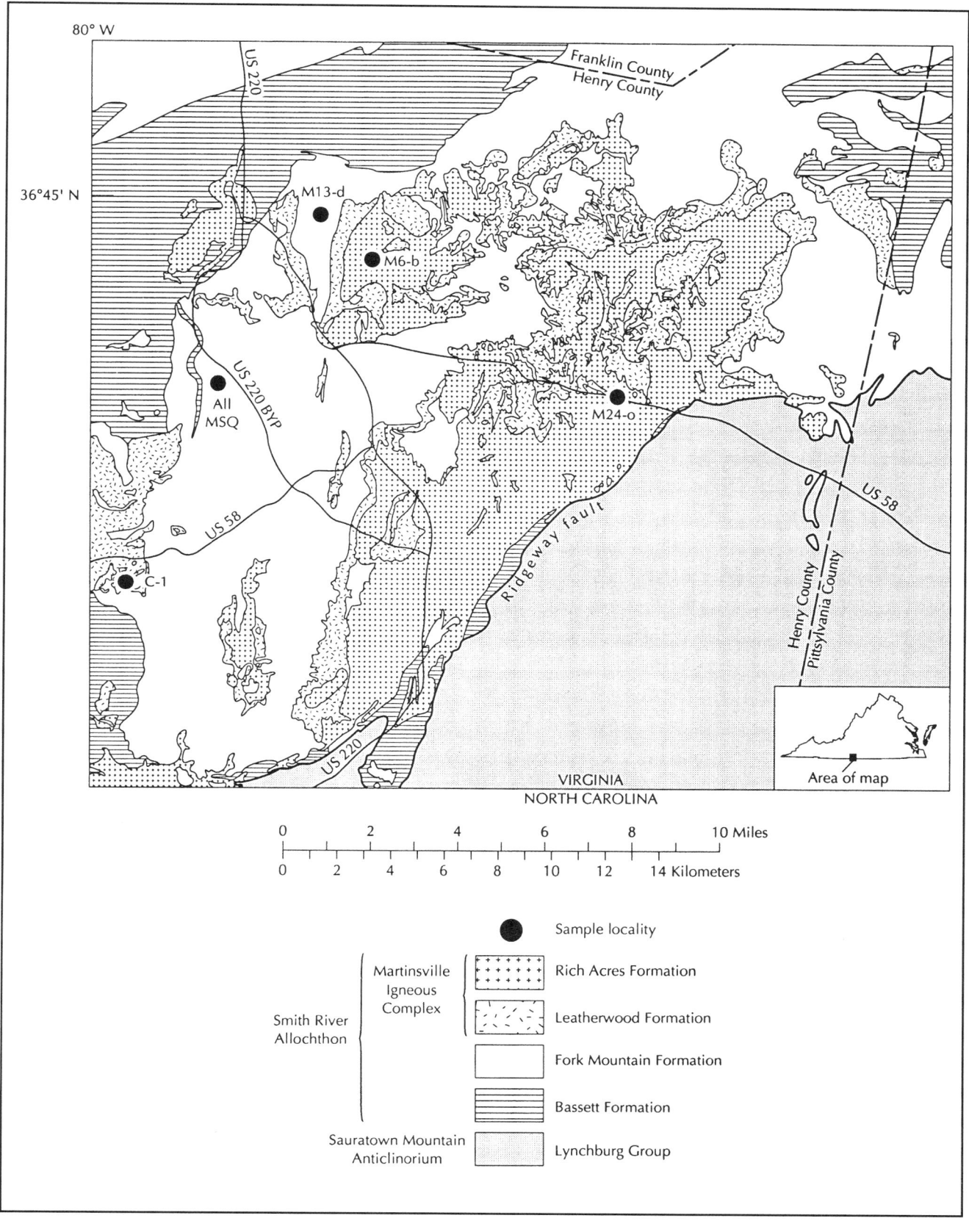

0   2   4   6   8   10 Miles

0   2   4   6   8   10   12   14 Kilometers

●   Sample locality

Smith River Allochthon {
  Martinsville Igneous Complex {
    [+] Rich Acres Formation
    [∴] Leatherwood Formation
  }
  Fork Mountain Formation
  [≡] Bassett Formation
}
Sauratown Mountain Anticlinorium {
  Lynchburg Group
}

J. S. Beard

TABLE 1. MAJOR- AND TRACE-ELEMENT GEOCHEMISTRY*

	C1	MSQ-9d	Zoned dike MSQ-9e Dark	MSQ-9e Ave.	MSQ-9e Light	MSQ-1	Zoned dike MSQ-2b Dark	MSQ-2b Ave.	MSQ-2b Light	MSQ-2c	MSQ-8b	MSQ-2a	M13-d	M6-b	Ave. Bassett M24-o Pegmatite	amphibolite N=12
(wt %)																
SiO_2	63.58	62.52	67.95	68.09	69.06	69.21	69.21	71.45	72.28	69.7	71.33	72.37	72.84	69.02	73.64	47.7
TiO_2	0.65	0.65	0.48	0.34	0.17	0.04	0.42	0.42	0.16	0.34	0.28	0.14	0.26	0.39	0.22	2.51
Al_2O_3	18.27	19.32	17.54	18.24	18.54	16.88	17.09	15.53	16.57	17.46	15.89	16.67	16.22	16.56	14.73	13.94
Fe_2O_3	1.07	0.81	0.42	0.33	0.26	0.49	0.36	0.76	0.02	0.17	0.32	0.17	0.46	0.86	0.41	14.93
FeO	2.56	3.19	2.16	1.42	0.65	1.7	1.79	1.56	0.69	1.5	1.7	0.38	1.18	1.65	0.9	
MnO	0.06	0.03	0.03	0.02	0.01	0.04	0.03	0.04	0.02	0.03	0.02	0.01	0.03	0.05	0.02	0.21
MgO	1.15	1.13	0.94	0.77	0.4	0.84	0.84	0.7	0.31	0.63	0.68	0.23	0.41	0.85	0.44	5.89
CaO	4.07	4.78	4.35	4.59	4.92	3.11	3.31	3.42	3.58	3.55	3.27	3.42	2.51	3.23	2.41	10.06
Na_2O	5.76	4.87	4.36	4.72	5.13	4.49	4.99	4.44	5.44	5.24	4.57	5.19	4.01	4.54	4.08	1.82
K_2O	1.5	1.66	1.18	0.86	0.52	1.68	1.41	1.01	0.62	1.15	0.99	0.85	1.41	1.42	2.03	0.43
P_2O_5	0.18	0.24	0.1	0.09	0.05	0.06	0.07	0.06	0.05	0.09	0.03	0	0.02	0.08	0.08	0.22
LOI	0.71	1.12	0.8	0.67	0.6	1.07	0.79	0.69	0.44	0.57	1.19	0.89	0.9	0.82	0.48	1.21
Total	99.56	100.32	100.31	100.14	100.31	99.97	100.31	100.08	100.18	100.43	100.27	100.32	100.25	99.47	99.44	98.92
Mg#	24.6	22.4	27.1	30.9	31.3	28.2	28.5	23.8	30.4	27.6	25.5	30.3	20.5	26.0	25.7	43.9
A/CNK	0.99	1.04	1.07	1.07	1.03	1.14	1.08	1.06	1.03	1.07	1.09	1.06	1.28	1.11	1.11	
(ppm)																
Rb	54	42	22	14	6	34	25	20	10	19	24	9	30	31	21	9
Sr	352	725	667	706	756	846	864	731	870	880	596	860	529	556	555	271
Ba	308	488	342	266	172	461	382	267	205	310	357	245	471	493	1,982	242
Y	4	15	7	6	4	7	9	12	5	8	8	4	7	8	7	32
Zr	282	312	223	185	117	183	213	238	98	171	135	82	114	166	45	140
V	51	69	41	28	13	33	33	28	12	27	24	10	18	30	12	
Ni	4	2	2	1	0	1	2	1	1	1	2	0	3	0	1	19
Cr	21	20	21	17	11	7	11	9	9	7	11	17	19	12	11	134
Be	1.8	0.9	0.9	0.9	0.8	1.6	1.2	1.1	1.1	1.2	1	1.2	1.4	1.2	0.7	
Co	20	18	19	22	34	13	17	14	22	10	36	31	13	20	19	
Sc	7.2	5.6	3.2	2.3	1.4	3	3.4	3.5	1.5	2.9	4	1.6	3	3.1	3.1	41
Th	4.4	1.5	4.4	4.6	2.8	7	8	6.7	1.6	4.2	5	0.6	6.1	6.9		1.5
U	0	0.3	1	0.8	0.3	1.4	0.8	1	0.4	0.5	0.6	0.4	1.2	0.9		
La	42.1	12.4	28.6	28.8	19.1	32	41.6	30.9	10.5	23.1	24.9	6.3	23.7	26.7	65	18
Ce	71	24	49	55	32	54	70	54	18	42	44	11	42	48	98	
Nd	23	11	17	18	11	18	23	20	6	14	16	3	15	16		
Sm	2.9	2.11	2.83	2.72	1.63	2.69	3.33	3.07	0.98	2.05	2.62	0.52	2.25	2.47		
Eu	1.06	1.33	1.25	0.92	0.95	1.32	1.54	1.44	1.45	1.49	1.67	1.27	1.19	1.03		
Tb	0.2	0.2	0.2	0.3	0.2	0.3	0.3	0.3	0.1	0.2	0.3	0	0.2	0.3		
Yb	0.6	1.37	0.66	0.5	0.33	0.94	0.98	1.23	0.64	0.83	0.65	0.43	0.54	0.7	0.5	3.7
Lu	0.09	0.22	0.1	0.1	0.04	0.13	0.14	0.18	0.1	0.13	0.09	0.07	0.07	0.1		
$(La/Yb)_n$	47.27	6.10	29.19	38.81	38.90	22.94	28.60	16.93	11.05	18.75	25.81	9.87	29.57	25.70		
Sr/Y	88.0	48.3	95.3	117.7	189.0	120.9	96.0	60.9	174.0	110.0	74.5	215.0	75.6	69.5	79.3	
REE	140.95	52.63	99.64	106.34	65.25	109.38	140.89	111.12	134.79	83.8	90.23	22.59	84.95	95.3		
$(Eu/Eu^*)_n$	1.27	2.10	1.54	1.10	1.85	1.59	1.55	1.06	4.86	2.41	2.05	6.94	1.78	1.33		

*Th, U, and REE by INAA. Others by XRF and ICP at Franklin and Marshall College. Bassett amphibolite is the average of 12 analyses from Achaibar (1983).

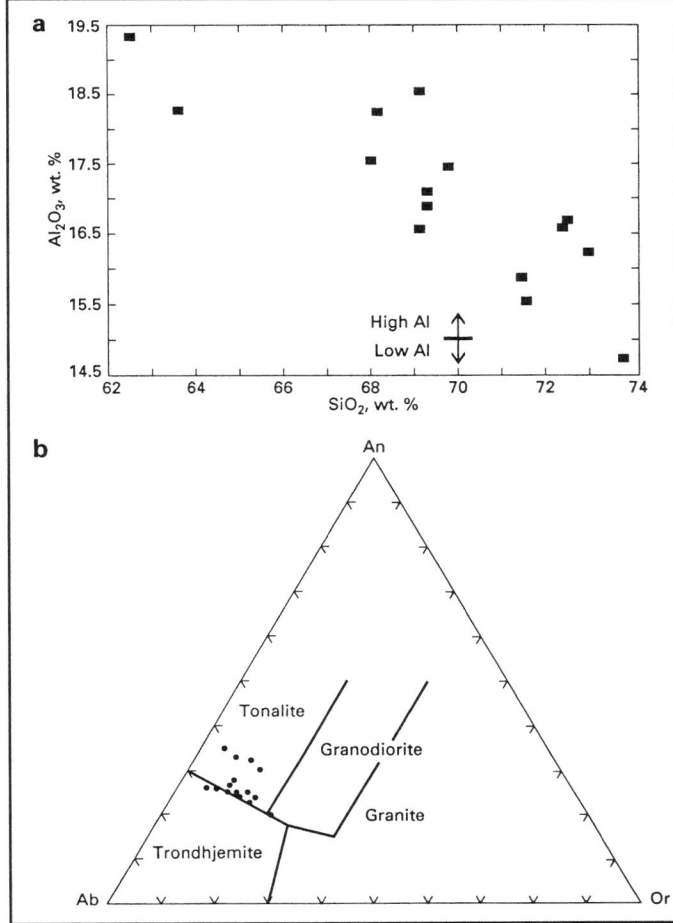

Figure 2. a: Al₂O₃ vs. SiO₂ showing the high Al vs. low Al discriminant of Barker (1979). b: Plot of normative feldspar showing fields of Barker (1979).

characteristic of derivation from a basaltic source under conditions where garnet is stable but plagioclase is not (e.g., Rapp et al., 1991; Drummond and Defant, 1990).

Sr isotopes were determined for three samples of different composition from a single zoned dike (Table 2). Present day $^{87}Sr/^{86}Sr$ is 0.70515–0.70568 and initial $^{87}Sr/^{86}Sr$ calculated at 500 Ma (probably a maximum age, given contact relationships with the MIC) ranges from 0.70447 to 0.70553 and averages 0.70496.

PETROGENETIC MODELS

Basalt and/or amphibolite melting models

Three basaltic sources were chosen to model a partial melting origin for the MIC tonalites (Table 3). The two subcrustal sources are normal and enriched mid-ocean ridge basalt (MORB)

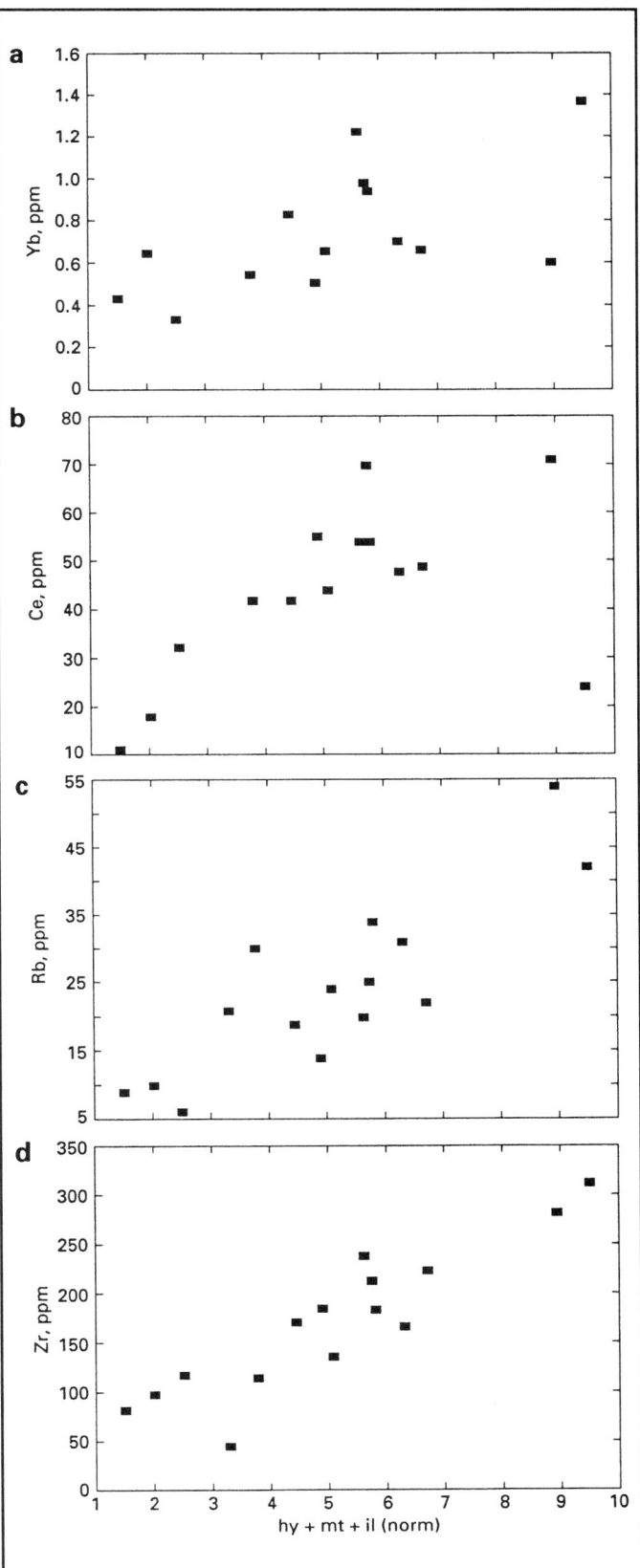

Figure 3. Yb, Ce, Rb, and Zr versus normative mafic constituents. Note that all of these elements behave in a more or less compatible fashion.

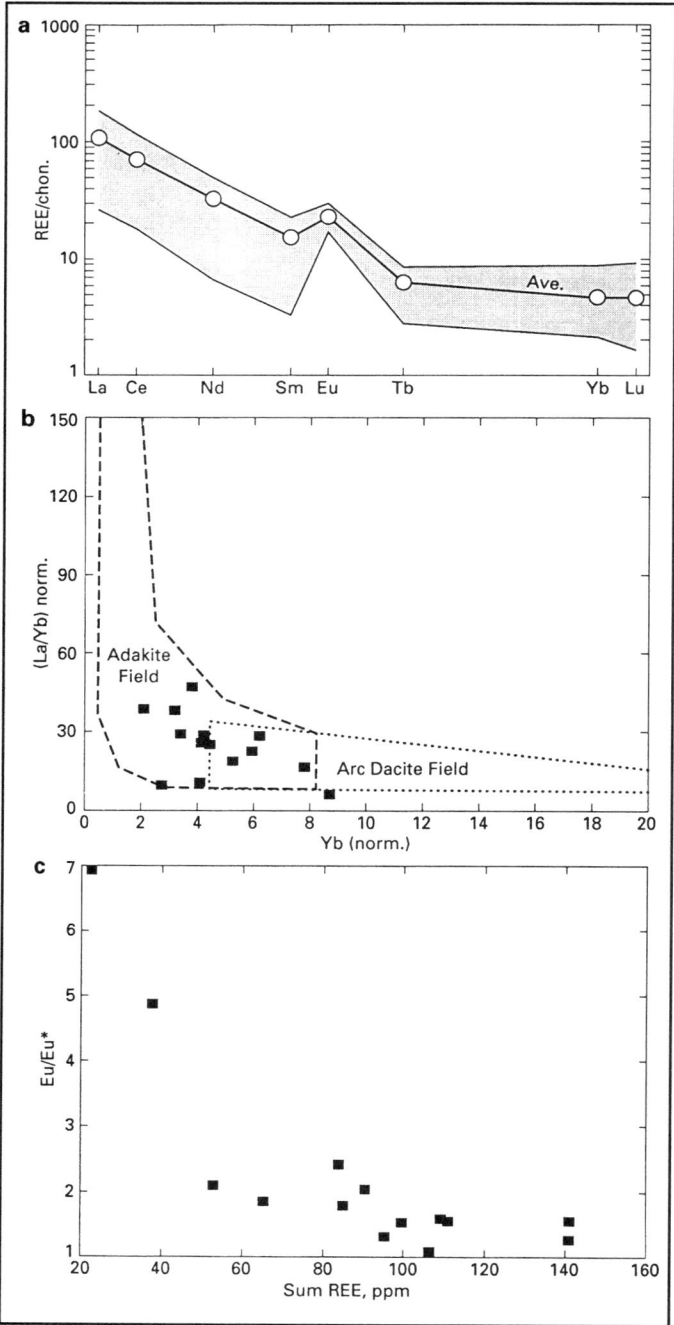

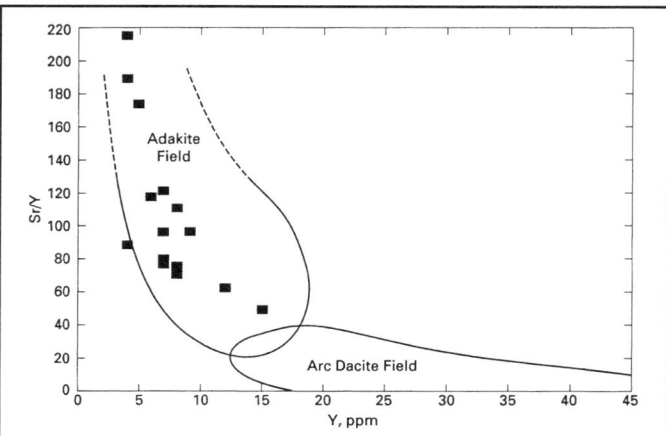

Figure 5. Sr/Y vs. Y. Adakite and arc dacite fields after Defant et al. (1991).

TABLE 2. Sr ISOTOPE DATA OF WHOLE-ROCK SAMPLES TAKEN FROM SINGLE ZONED DIKE

Sample	Rb* (ppm)	Sr* (ppm)	$^{87}Rb/^{86}Sr$	$^{87}Rb/^{86}Sr$†	$^{87}Sr/^{86}Sr(i)$
9e light	6	756	0.02296	0.70568(6)	0.70552
9e medium	14	706	0.0574	0.70530(8)	0.70489
9e dark	22	667	0.0954	0.70515(6)	0.70447

*Rb and Sr determined by ICP. Sr isotopes analysed by A. K. Sinha at Virginia Polytechnic Institute and State University. See Essex, 1992, for methods.
†Number in parentheses is error in last decimal place. Initial $^{87}Sr/^{86}Sr$ calculated at 500 Ma.

Figure 4. a: Average and range of rare earth element (REE) concentration in the tonalites. All samples have a positive Eu anomaly. b: La/Yb vs. Yb, both chondrite normalized. Adakite and Arc dacite fields after Drummond and Defant (1990). c: Magnitude of the Eu anomaly versus total REE.

averages taken from Wood (1979). The crustal source is the Bassett amphibolite, part of the Bassett Formation of the SRA. The Bassett amphibolite is an amphibolite facies metabasalt with chemical affinities to continental tholeiite (Achaibar, 1983). Distribution coefficients used in the models are given in Table 3. Par-

tition coefficients determined or extrapolated from experiments were used for amphibole and pyroxene whenever possible (Green and Pearson, 1985; Gallahan and Neilsen, 1992). The values used for garnet were estimated from published values for garnet in granitic rocks (Henderson, 1982). The behaviors of Y and Yb in the modeled system require the presence of garnet in the restite. Sr is highly compatible in plagioclase coexisting with silicic melts (the plagioclase-melt partition coefficient is around 3; e.g., Hanson, 1989; Nash and Crecraft, 1985). However, the high concentration of Sr in the tonalites requires that it behave incompatibly. Hence, the presence of all but a minute fraction of plagioclase in the restite assemblage is prohibited. All models presented here have a garnet-bearing, plagioclase-free restite.

Normal MORB does not appear to be an acceptable sole source for the MIC tonalites (Fig. 6). However, 15%–30% partial melting of enriched MORB and 20%–40% melting of Bassett amphibolite leaving residua with 15% garnet and the rest a mixture of pyroxene and amphibole can reproduce the observed tonalite Sr, Y, and REE chemistry (Fig. 6). Enriched MORB models favor a residuum somewhat richer in pyroxene than Bassett amphibolite models. Note that extreme values of MIC tonalite composition are not well reproduced by these models. This probably reflects modification of the tonalite melts during and after emplacement (e.g., Fig. 3; see discussion below).

TABLE 3. ROCK COMPOSITIONS AND PARTITION COEFFICIENTS USED IN MODELING

	NMORB*	EMORB*	Bassett†	Average Tonalite§
a. Source and daughter compositions for partial melting models (ppm)				
Ba	12	68	242	341
Rb	1	4	9	25
K	1,060	1,920	3,570	9,628
Sr	120	200	271	710
La	2	13	18	25
Y	23	33	32	7.4
Yb	2	3	3.7	0.74
Th	0.2	0.55	1.5†	4.6
Ti	9,300	8,060	15,047	2,186
P	393	872	960	349
Cr	400	324	134	14
Sc	38	38	41	3.3
Ni	173	124	19	1.4
Co	45	51		21

	Garnet**	Amph.**	CPX**
b. Mineral/melt partition coefficients			
Sr	0.01 (1)	0.43 (3)	0.08 (1)
La	0.4 (2)	0.46 (3)	0.15 (4)
Y	28 (2)	2.66 (3)	0.57 (4)
Yb	42 (2)	2.18 (3)	0.55 (4)
Cr	22 (1)	30 (1)	30 (1)
Sc	4-16 (2)	3.2-20 (2)	3.3 (4)
Ni	0.6 (1)	10 (1)	6 (1)
Co	2-2.6 (1, 2)	13 (1)	1.2-8 (2)

*Data from Schilling et al. (1983) and Wood (1979) tabulated in Wilson (1989) and Hess (1989).
†Data from Archaibar (1983), average of 12 analyses. Average for Th excludes one value of 20.5 ppm. The average including this value is 3.1.
§Average excludes the evolved tonalite pegmatite M24-o, which contains 1,982 ppm Ba and for which INAA analyses of Th, Yb, and La are not available. Th and REE by INAA. Others by ICP and XRF at Franklin and Marshall College.
**Numbers in parentheses indicate data sources. 1 = Gill, 1981; 2 = Henderson, 1982; 3 = Green and Pearson, 1985; 4 = Gallahan and Neilsen, 1992.
Some REE data interpolated. Where multiple values are given, the lower value generally reflects a basaltic Kd to upper value, a rhyolitic Kd. The actual value for fractionation will lie between the two. Values given by Gill are for andesites.

All models require that Ti and P behave compatibly during melting (Tables 1 and 3). This behavior is consistent with experimental results at low degrees of partial melting (e.g., Beard and Lofgren, 1991; Rapp et al., 1991) and with the experimental observation that apatite (e.g., Beard et al., 1994) and Fe-Ti oxides are common restite phases (Beard and Lofgren, 1991; Sisson and Grove, 1993). The presence of xenocrystic apatite in the MIC tonalites also suggests that it is stable in the restite. Within the large range permitted by available distribution coefficients, the concentrations of the more standard incompatible elements (Cr, Co, Ni, Sc) are consistent with the MORB and Bassett amphibolite melting models.

Rb, K, and Th behave incompatibly in the systems modeled here. For the enriched MORB models, a bulk partition coefficient of near zero is required for these elements (and for Ba) for 12% (Th) to 20% (K, Rb, Ba) melting; 30% melting of the enriched MORB composition modeled here cannot yield the observed abundances of these elements in the MIC tonalites. Higher degrees of melting are acceptable for a Bassett amphibolite source, with calculated bulk distribution coefficients (D) ranging from near zero at 32%–38% melting to 0.16–0.2 at 20% melting. Ba is only mildly incompatible in the Bassett amphibolite models, with a calculated bulk D of 0.63–0.52 for 20%–40% melting. Even given a bulk D of zero, the normal MORB models will produce acceptable quantities of Rb, Th, K, and Ba only if the melt fraction is less than 5%–11%.

Gneiss melting

Partial melting of pelitic gneiss at high P_{H_2O} has been shown to yield low-K silicic melts that coexist with a biotite and garnet-rich restite (Whitney and Irving, 1994). Quantitative modeling of this system is largely precluded by the lack of information concerning biotite/melt partition coefficients. However, qualitative modeling is possible if samples of the restite and partial melt are available. A garnet-biotite rock collected from the hanging wall of a tonalitic pegmatite was chosen as an example of a restite generated by high P_{H_2O} partial melting of Fork Mountain gneiss. The composition of the Fork Mountain gneiss is estimated from an analyses of splits of two 25 kg lots of quarry run gravel from a quarry in the gneiss (Table 4).

A model assuming 50% melting of the gneiss to yield tonalite plus restite gives varying results. The model successfully predicts many observed trace element abundances (i.e., within 20% of their actual values), but fails badly for Sr and less badly for Y and Yb (Fig. 7). This is troubling considering the important roles that these elements play in constraining the character of melt-forming reactions in hydrous systems. Element mobility (e.g., caused by fluid flux from the crystallizing pegmatite), modal heterogeneity within the restite, and other factors may explain some of these discrepancies. However, in the absence of other putative examples of the restite, this model must be considered equivocal at best.

DISCUSSION

Major and trace element covariation and comparison to MIC igneous rocks

Element variation in the MIC tonalites reflects modal variation. Quartz, feldspar, and their constituent elements are concentrated in felsic dikes, and accessory phases and biotite, and hence most compatible and incompatible elements, are concentrated in the more mafic tonalites (Table 1). The negative correlation of the magnitude of the Eu anomaly with total REE content (Fig. 4) also reflects modal variations, increasing amounts of accessory phases relative to plagioclase resulting in increased total REE, but lower Eu relative to other REE. The origin of modal variation in the MIC tonalites dikes is problematic, especially given that mafic

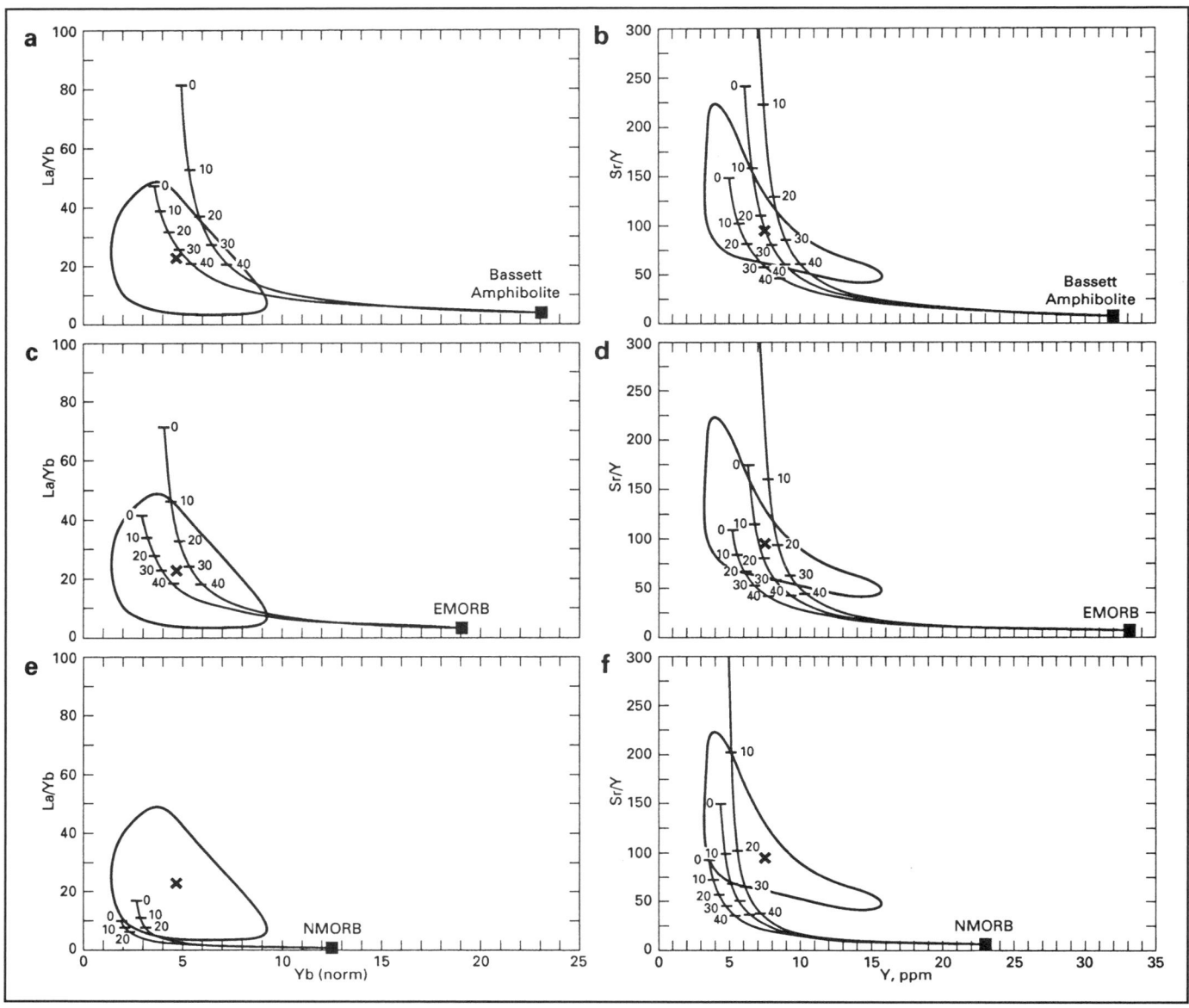

Figure 6. Melting models, basalt sources. Pertinent data are in Table 3. Tick marks on curves are melt fraction. Rare earth element models shown have a restite containing 15% garnet and the remainder either amphibole or pyroxene. Sr and Y models have, in addition, an intermediate restite composition of Gar15, Amph30, Px55. In all cases, the amphibole-bearing models are displaced to the left of the clinopyroxene models. N is normal, EMORB is enriched mid-ocean ridge basalt.

rocks may be concentrated in either the margins or cores of individual dikes. Flow differentiation, chilled margins, and tapping of zoned or heterogeneous magma reservoirs are several possibilities. The heterogeneous initial $^{87}Sr/^{86}Sr$ seen within one zoned dike appears to favor the latter possibility.

The MIC tonalites are apparently unrelated to other igneous rock types in the MIC. By inspection of Figure 8, for example, it is clear that: (1) the tonalites are chemically distinct from MIC granites and gabbros; (2) the tonalites are unlikely to be related to either of these rock types along a liquid line of

descent; and (3) the tonalites cannot be a major end member in a petrogenetic mixing scheme relating MIC gabbro and MIC granite. The tonalites are more similar to migmatitic muscovite granites found within the contact aureole of the pluton. Nevertheless, there are important chemical differences between the tonalites and the migmatitic granites. In particular, the muscovite granites contain less Sr (125–351 ppm) and have lower Sr/Y (6–15) than the tonalites. The tonalites do not lie along an a mixing line (or within a mixing field) that would relate the migmatitic granites and the gabbros or granites of the MIC.

TABLE 4. COMPOSITION OF RESTITE, FORK MOUNTAIN GNEISS,
AND AVERAGE TONALITE*

	MSQ-6b Restite	Fork Mt. Gneiss (n = 2)	Average MICT†
(wt %)			
SiO_2	41.53	62.39	69.19
TiO_2	2.08	1.35	0.36
Al_2O_3	22.68	16.45	17.20
Fe_2O_3	8.87	1.89	0.46
FeO	9.28	5.68	1.58
MnO	0.25	0.13	0.03
MgO	3.71	2.15	0.71
CaO	2.10	2.73	3.72
Na_2O	1.60	2.12	4.84
K_2O	4.63	3.11	1.16
P_2O_5	0.40	0.20	0.08
LOI	2.44	2.07	0.80
Total	99.57	100.20	100.14
(ppm)			
Rb	159	90	25
Sr	253	262	710
Ba	706	811	341
Y	126	51	7.4
Zr	575	478	180
Th	26	14	4.6
U	4.6	2.3	0.7
La	112	59.5	25
Nd	98	55	15
Sm	19.2	10.7	2.3
Eu	3.06	2.10	1.3
Yb	11.7	4.72	0.74

*Major elements, Rb, Sr, Ba, Y, and Zr by XRF and ICP at Franklin and Marshall College. Others by INAA.
†Average does not include evolved, pegmatitic tonalite with 1,982 ppm Ba.

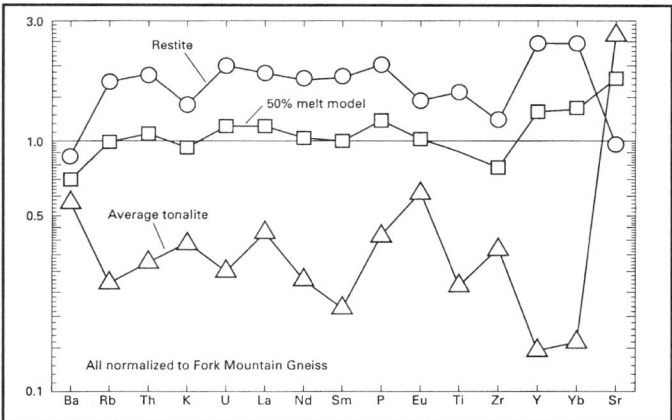

Figure 7. Melting model, Fork Mountain gneiss source. Pertinent data are in Table 4. Both restite and average Martinsville igneous complex tonalite compositions are normalized to the composition of the Fork Mountain gneiss (see text). The intermediate line represents the estimated source composition if the tonalite represents a 50% melt of the gneiss. There are serious deviations from the actual gneiss composition for Sr, Y, and Yb. See text for discussion.

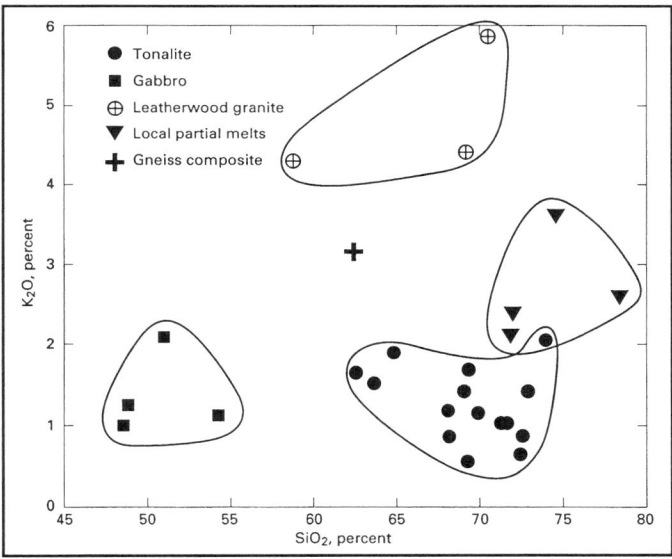

Figure 8. K_2O vs. SiO_2 for the various rock types of the Martinsville igneous complex.

Geochemical constraints on MIC tonalite formation

Taken together, high Sr and low Y and heavy REE in the MIC tonalite suggest that garnet was stable and plagioclase was unstable during their formation. In a basaltic system, garnet stability during partial melting requires pressures of at least 8–12 kbar and could reflect subcrustal melting of a warm subducted slab at pressures of 20–30 kbar (Drummond and Defant, 1990; Peacock et al., 1994; Rapp et al., 1991; Wolf and Wyllie, 1994; Patino Douce and Beard, 1995). Plagioclase becomes unstable during dehydration-melting at pressures above 15 kbar (Rapp et al., 1991; Patino Douce and Beard, 1995). During water-saturated melting, however, a plagioclase-free restite coexisting with a tonalitic melt can form at pressures as low as 2–3 kbar (Luhr, 1990; Beard and Lofgren, 1991).

Although Sr isotopes are heterogeneous, they appear to be more radiogenic than would be expected in either a slab melt (<0.7038; Defant et al., 1992) or in a differentiate of typical basalt derived from a nonenriched mantle source (e.g., Faure, 1986, p. 166). Alkaline and calc-alkaline basalts whose initial $^{87}Sr/^{86}Sr$ exceed 0.705 are typically strongly enriched in Rb and other incompatible elements (e.g., Wilson, 1989) and are unlikely parents for silicic, peraluminous tonalites with 25 ppm Rb, 25 ppm La, and 1.2% K_2O (Table 1). It is clear that the isotopic data do not rule out a mantle or slab component in the MIC tonalites: however, it is suggestive and permissive of a role for crustal melting in MIC tonalite petrogenesis.

Although high total pressure leading to garnet stability is required to explain the Sr, Y, and REE chemistry of the tonalites, high total pressure alone is insufficient to explain aspects of their mineralogy, petrography, and major element chemistry. First, the presence of igneous epidote and muscovite in the tonalites and the relative abundance of pegmatitic tonalite dikes require high P_{H_2O} at some stage of tonalite crystallization (Naney, 1983; Zen and Hammarstrom, 1984). Second, it appears that P_{H_2O} on the order of 2 kbar (as well as total pressure of at least 8 kbar) is required to produce the MIC tonalite compositions from a basaltic source (Fig. 9). The major element composition of tonalitic partial melts of amphibolite is a strong function of P_{H_2O} (Spulber and Rutherford, 1983; Beard and Lofgren, 1989, 1991). Specifically, the stabilization of mafic silicates and oxides at the expense of plagioclase with increasing P_{H_2O} leads to the formation of melts that are increasingly enriched in Al and depleted in Fe. The MIC tonalites, even those enriched in mafic phases and depleted in plagioclase, have the high Al and low Fe of tonalitic partial melts produced under conditions of elevated P_{H_2O} (Fig. 9). Increasing total pressure during melting of basaltic and andesitic amphibolite also produces elevated Al and decreased Fe in tonalitic partial melts (Rapp et al., 1991; Patino Douce and Beard, 1995), but the effect is generally smaller than the effects of increased water content. In fact, most MIC tonalite compositions are not reproduced by the dehydration-melting experiments of Rapp et al. (1991), Wolf and Wyllie (1994), or Patino Douce and Beard (1995) (Fig. 9).

High P_{H_2O} permits substantial amphibolite melting to commence at temperatures well below the amphibolite dehydration melting solidus. In the presence of excess H_2O, the amphibolite solidus is probably around 700 °C (e.g., Helz, 1976), compared to the dehydration-melting solidus of 825 °C or above (Beard and Lofgren, 1991; Rapp et al., 1991; Rushmer, 1991; Wolf and Wyllie, 1991). Even at 2 kbar P_{H_2O}, a basalt may yield more than 30% melt by 800 °C (Luhr, 1990).

The relatively high compatible trace-element content of the tonalites (Tables 1 and 3) suggests that they did not form by crystal fractionation of basalt. For example, even given a relatively low bulk D of 5 for Sc (e.g., Table 3), 65% Raleigh fractionation of a primitive basalt with a typical Sc content (40 ppm) would yield a melt with less than one-fourth the Sc content of the MIC tonalites. However, batch melting of the same source with a more realistic bulk D of 10 for Sc (calculated using partition coefficients [Kd] for rhyolite/dacite from Henderson (1982) and a restite with garnet, clinopyroxene, and amphibole in the proportions 15:55:30) will yield a melt with a minimum of 4 ppm Sc, more in line with the observed values for the MIC tonalites. Similar arguments can be developed for the other compatible trace elements.

Constraints from modeling

Normal MORB is not an appropriate source for the MIC tonalites (Fig. 6). The models for pelite melting cannot be dismissed out of hand, but fail to reproduce some key chemical characteristics of the MIC tonalites (Fig. 7).

The high melt fractions and high amphibole-pyroxene ratio

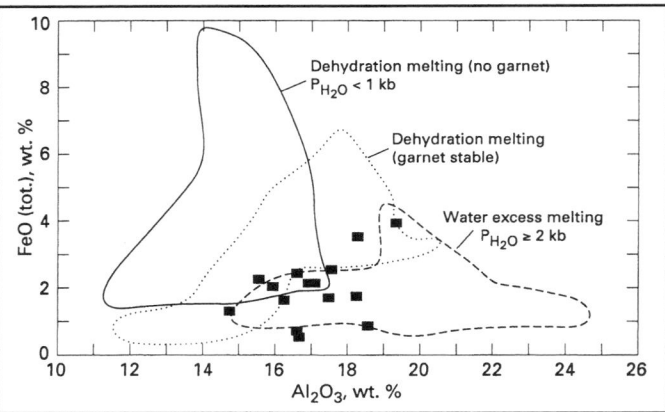

Figure 9. FeO (total) vs. Al_2O_3 comparing Martinsville igneous complex (MIC) tonalite compositions with experimentally produced tonalitic melts. Field for low-pressure (P) dehydration melting (garnet not stable; P_{total} = 1–7 kbar) from Beard and Lofgren (1991). Melt compositions for dehydration melting in the garnet stability field (P_{total} = 10–32 kbar) from Rapp et al. (1991), Wolf and Wyllie (1994), and Patino Douce and Beard (1995). Water-saturated melting data (P_{H_2O} = 2–7 kbar) from Helz (1976), Luhr (1990), and Beard and Lofgren (1991). Most MIC tonalites plot in the water-saturated melting field, implying the presence of excess water (e.g., in excess of that provided by dehydration-melting reactions) during melting.

required of the Bassett amphibolite models are suggestive of high P_{H_2O} during melting. Because a Bassett amphibolite source implies crustal melting at relatively low pressures, the absence of plagioclase from its model restite is also suggestive of high P_{H_2O}. However, the low melt fractions and high proportion of restitic clinopyroxene in the enriched MORB models suggest a drier environment of melting. The enriched MORB models are more consistent, as would be expected, with a slab melting origin for the MIC tonalites, the absence of plagioclase from the restite being due to pressures of >15 kbar at the time of partial melting (Rapp et al., 1991; Patino Douce and Beard, 1995).

Petrogenesis and geologic setting of the MIC tonalites

Two models for the petrogenesis of the MIC tonalites are defensible on the basis of the data, models, and discussion presented above. They are (1) melting of enriched MORB in a subducted slab (with a contribution from the crust or subducted sediment to account for the Sr isotopes) and (2) water-excess melting of Bassett amphibolite or similar rock in the middle or deep crust.

Trace-element models for MIC tonalite genesis by enriched MORB melting predict a relatively dry, pyroxene-rich restite coexisting with relatively small melt fraction. This model is suggestive of dehydration melting rather than the water excess melting required by MIC tonalite chemistry (e.g., see Beard and Lofgren, 1991). The slab melting model requires the subducted crust to be enriched MORB, a source not commonly cited for modern adakites (e.g., Drummond and Defant, 1990). Enriched

MORB is generally associated with plateaus and other oceanic highs and may, in fact, be difficult to subduct. Most modern slab melts, while aluminous, are not as aluminous as the MIC tonalites (e.g., Defant et al., 1992) and are best explained as dehydration melts (not water excess melts) of metamorphosed ocean crust.

I tentatively favor the Bassett amphibolite or a similar source for the MIC tonalites for the following reasons. (1) Melting models for the Bassett amphibolite predict large degrees of melting and an amphibole-rich restite, both of which favor water-excess melting. (2) The Bassett is a convenient, proximal source for the tonalites and lies structurally beneath much of the area where the tonalite dikes are found (Conley, 1985). (3) The Bassett amphibolite is locally migmatitic and occurs within a high-grade metamorphic terrane where partial melting of pelitic rocks has been documented.

A potential problem with the Bassett as a source for the tonalites is the scarcity of garnet and the presence of plagioclase in the exposed portions of the amphibolite. Thus, any zone of extensive melting in which the MIC tonalites might have been generated is either not currently exposed or, at least, not currently recognized.

The most plausible and best documented geologic environment for water-excess melting in the crust is the upper plate in a collision-related overthrust, a situation analogous to that of a subduction zone, where a relatively cool, hydrous, lower plate releases water into a hotter upper plate (e.g., LeFort et al., 1987). There are many cases where metamorphic petrology suggests that melting and migmatization related to regional metamorphism occurred at temperatures of 650–800 °C. Experimental and other studies suggest that little melt can be produced by dehydration melting alone at temperatures below 800 °C (e.g., Thompson, 1982; Patino Douce and Johnston, 1991). This paradox is leading to a new appreciation of the role of water-excess melting during overthrusting related to collision and regional metamorphism (Whitney and Irving, 1994).

If the MIC tonalite suite formed in this fashion, its age will give a minimum age for the emplacement thrust of the SRA. The MIC tonalites are likely to postdate the onset of overthrusting, with the delay reflecting the time required for the lower plate to heat up to the temperatures required for metamorphic dewatering reactions. Thus, one prediction of this model is that the MIC tonalites are younger than the age of thrusting. A key test of the model will be a study of the biotite tonalites that intrude the Grenville-age rock southeast of the Ridgeway fault.

CONCLUSIONS

Although a slab melting origin cannot be definitively ruled out, the petrology of the MIC tonalites is consistent with their formation by water-excess melting of the Bassett amphibolite or a similar rock type within the crust. The occurrence of the tonalites in the upper plate of a thrust system is consistent with this interpretation, the excess water being provided by prograde metamorphic reactions in the cooler, lower grade lower plate. Such a scenario predicts that the tonalites will postdate the thrust faults that bound the SRA. This prediction appears to be testable.

The difference in age between the MIC tonalites and the faults will help to define the thermal history of the region and should help constrain the temperature-time, uplift, and denudation history of the area.

ACKNOWLEDGMENTS

I thank Krishna Sinha of the Virginia Polytechnic Institute and State University for providing the Sr isotopic analyses and Ellen Compton-Gooding for drafting the figures. I also thank Mike Wolf and LeeAnn Srogi for careful and thoughtful reviews. This work was supported by the Virginia Museum of Natural History.

REFERENCES CITED

Achaibar, J., 1983, A petrologic and geochemical study of some amphibolite bodies in the Smith River allochthon, Virginia [M.S. thesis]: Knoxville, University of Tennessee, 93 p.

Barker, F., 1979, Trondhjemite: Definition, environment and hypotheses of origin, *in* Barker, F., ed., Trondhjemites, dacites and related rocks: New York, Elsevier, p. 1–12.

Beard, J. S., and Lofgren, G. E., 1989, Effect of water on the composition of partial melts of greenstone and amphibolite: Science, v. 244, p. 195–197.

Beard, J. S., and Lofgren, G. E., 1991, Dehydration melting and water-saturated melting of basaltic and andesitic greenstones and amphibolites at 1, 3, and 6.9 kb: Journal of Petrology, v. 32, p. 365–401.

Beard, J. S., Lofgren, G. E., Sinha, A. K., and Tollo, R. P., 1994, Partial melting of apatite-bearing charnockite, granulite, and diorite: Melt compositions, restite mineralogy, and petrologic implications: Journal of Geophysical Research, v. 99, p. 21591–21604.

Conley, J. F., 1985, Geology of the southwestern Virginia Piedmont: Virginia Division of Mineral Resources Publication 59, 33 p.

Conley, J. F., and Henika, W. S., 1970, Geology of the Philpott Reservoir quadrangle, Virginia: Virginia Division of Mineral Resources Report of Investigations 22, 46 p.

Conley, J. F., and Henika, W. S., 1973, Geology of the Snow Creek, Martinsville East, Price and Spray quadrangles, Virginia: Virginia Division of Mineral Resources Report of Investigations 33, 77 p.

Defant, M. J., and 8 others, 1991, Dacite genesis via both slab melting and differentiation: Petrogenesis of La Yeguada Volcanic Complex, Panama: Journal of Petrology, v. 32, p. 1101–1142.

Defant, M. J., Jackson, T. E., Drummond, M. S., De Boer, J. Z., Bellon, H., Feigenson, M. D., Maury, R. C., and Stewart, R. H., 1992, The geochemistry of young volcanism throughout western Panama and southeastern Costa Rica: An overview: Geological Society of London Journal, v. 149, p. 569–579.

Deuser, W. G., and Herzog, L. F., 1962, Rubidium-strontium age determinations of muscovites and biotites from pegmatites of the Blue Ridge and Piedmont: Journal of Geophysical Research, v. 67, p. 1997–2004.

Drummond, M. S., and Defant, M. J., 1990, A model for trondhjemite-tonalite-dacite genesis and crustal growth during slab melting: Archaean to modern comparison: Journal of Geophysical Research, v. 95, p. 21503–21521.

Essex, R. M., 1992, Age and petrogenesis of the Striped Rock Granite Pluton: Blue Ridge province, southwestern Virginia [M.S. thesis]: Blacksburg, Virginia Polytechnic Institute and State University, 98 p.

Faure, G., 1986, Principles of isotope geology: New York, John Wiley and Sons, 589 p.

Gallahan, W. E., and Neilsen, R. L., 1992, The partitioning of Sc, Y, and the rare earth elements between high-Ca pyroxene and natural mafic to intermediate lavas at 1 atmosphere: Geochimica et Cosmochimica Acta, v. 56, p. 2387–2404.

Gill, J. B., 1981, Orogenic andesites and plate tectonics: New York, Springer-Verlag, 390 p.

Green, T. H., and Pearson, N. J., 1985, Experimental determination of REE partition coefficients between amphibole and basaltic to andesitic liquids at high pressure: Geochimica et Cosmochimica Acta, v. 49, p. 1465–1468.

Hanson, G. N., 1989, An approach to trace-element modeling using a simple igneous system as a model, *in* Lipin, B. R., and McKay, G. A., eds., Geochemistry and mineralogy of rare-earth elements: Mineralogical Society of America Reviews in Mineralogy, v. 21, p. 79–97.

Helz, R. T., 1976, Phase relations of basalts in their melting ranges at P_{H_2O} = 5 kb. Part II. Melt compositions: Journal of Petrology, v. 17, p. 139–193.

Henderson, P., 1982, Inorganic geochemistry: New York, Pergamon Press, 353 p.

Hess, P. C., 1989, Origins of igneous rocks: Cambridge, Massachusetts, Harvard University Press, 336 p.

Le Fort, P., Cuney, M., Deniel, C., France-Lanord, C., Sheppard, S. M. F., Upreti, B. N., and Vidal, P., 1987, Crustal generation of Himalayan leucogranites: Tectonophysics, v. 134, p. 39–57.

Luhr, J. F., 1990, Experimental phase relations of water- and sulfur-saturated arc magmas and the 1982 eruptions of El Chichon Volcano: Journal of Petrology, v. 31, p. 1071–1114.

Naney, M. T., 1983, Phase equilibria of rock-forming ferromagnesian silicates in granitic systems: American Journal of Science, v. 283, p. 993–1033.

Nash, W. P., and Crecraft, H. R., 1985, Partition coefficients for trace elements in silicic magmas: Geochimica et Cosmochimica Acta, v. 49, p. 2309–2322.

Patino-Douce, A. E., and Beard, J. S., 1995, Dehydration melting of biotite gneiss and quartz amphibolite from 3 to 15 kbars: Journal of Petrology, v. 36, p. 707–738.

Patino-Douce, A. E., and Johnston, A. D., 1991, Phase equilibria and melt productivity in the pelitic system: Implications for the origin of peraluminous granitoids and aluminous granulites: Contributions to Mineralogy and Petrology, v. 107, p. 202–218.

Peacock, S. M., Rushmer, T., and Thompson, A. B., 1994, Partial melting of subducting oceanic crust: Earth and Planetary Science Letters, v. 121, p. 227–244.

Ragland, P. C., 1974, Geochemical evidence for the existence of two igneous rock series, Martinsville igneous complex: Geological Society of America Abstracts with Programs, v. 6, p. 390.

Rapp, R. P., Watson, E. B., and Miller, C. F., 1991, Partial melting of amphibolite/eclogite and the origin of Archean trondhjemites and tonalites: Precambrian Research, v. 51, p. 1–25.

Rushmer, T., 1991, Partial melting of two amphibolites: Contrasting experimental results under fluid-absent conditions: Contributions to Mineralogy and Petrology, v. 107, p. 41–57.

Schilling, J.-G, Zajac, M., Evans, R., Johnston, T., White, W., Devine, J. D., and Kingsley, R., 1983, Petrologic and geochemical variations along the Mid-Atlantic Ridge from 27°N to 73°N: American Journal of Science, v. 283, p. 510–586.

Sinha, A. K., Hewitt, D. A., and Rimstidt, J. D., 1988, Metamorphic petrology and strontium isotope geochemistry associated with the development of mylonites: An example from the Brevard fault, North Carolina: American Journal of Science, v. 288a, p. 115–147.

Sinha, A. K., Hund, E. A., and Hogan, J. P., 1989, Paleozoic accretionary history of the North American plate margin (central and southern Appalachians): Constraints from the age, origin, and distribution of granitic rocks: Washington, D.C., International Union of Geology and Geophysics and American Geophysical Union Joint Publication, p. 219–238.

Sisson, T. W., and Grove, T. L., 1993, Experimental investigations of the role of H_2O in calc-alkaline differentiation and subduction zone magmatism: Contributions to Mineralogy and Petrology, v. 113, p. 143–166.

Spulber, S. D., and Rutherford, M. J., 1983, The origin of rhyolite and plagiogranite in oceanic crust: An experimental study: Journal of Petrology, v. 24, p. 1–25.

Thompson, A. B., 1982, Dehydration melting of pelitic rocks and the generation of H_2O-undersaturated granitic liquids: American Journal of Science, v. 282, p. 1567–1595.

Whitney, D. L., and Irving, A. J., 1994, Origin of K-poor leucosomes in a metasedimentary migmatite complex by ultrametamorphism, syn-metamorphic magmatism and subsolidus processes: Lithos, v. 32, p. 173–192.

Wilson, M., 1989, Igneous petrogenesis: New York, Chapman and Hall, 466 p.

Wolf, M. B., and Wyllie, P. J., 1991, Dehydration-melting of solid amphibolite at 10 kbar: Textural development, liquid interconnectivity and applications to the segregation of magmas: Mineralogy and Petrology, v. 44, p. 151–179.

Wolf, M. B., and Wyllie, P. J., 1994, Dehydration-melting of amphibolite at 10 kbar: The effects of temperature and time: Contributions to Mineralogy and Petrology, v. 115, p. 369–383.

Wood, D. A., 1979, A variably veined suboceanic upper mantle: Genetic significance for mid-ocean ridge basalts from geochemical evidence: Geology, v. 7, p. 499–503.

Zen, E-an, and Hammarstrom, J. M., 1984, Magmatic epidote and its petrologic significance: Geology, v. 12, p. 515–518.

Manuscript Accepted by the Society July 2, 1996

Geological Society of America
Memoir 191
1997

Fractionation and contamination of Maquereau Group lavas, southern Gaspé, Québec Appalachians

Jean H. Bédard
Geological Survey of Canada, Centre Géoscientifique de Québec, 2535 Boulevard Laurier, C. P. 7500, Ste-Foy, Québec G1V 4C7, Canada
Caroline Wilson*
Ministère des Ressources Naturelles du Québec, 5700 4e Avenue Ouest, Charlesbourg, Québec G1H 6R1, Canada

ABSTRACT

Most Maquereau Group lavas are tholeiitic basalts that exhibit an Fe-Ti–enrichment trend. The tholeiites are divisible into incompatible-element–enriched and depleted types. Enriched tholeiites have chondrite-normalized La/Yb > 1 and higher incompatible element contents than do depleted, normal mid-ocean ridge basalt–like tholeiites. Subordinate transitional-alkaline basalts are even more enriched in TiO_2, P_2O_5, Nb, and light rare-earth elements (REE). Intrasuite geochemical variations are consistent with coupled fractional crystallization and assimilation of Grenvillean continental crust or sediments derived therefrom. Assimilation leads to the development of characteristic enrichment in Ba, Th, Zr, and light REE. Intersuite variations cannot be accounted for through crystal fractionation or crustal contamination, and must reflect either source-mantle heterogeneity or mantle melting processes. Most major- and trace-element paleotectonic discriminants do not favor an arc-related environment for these lavas. An intracontinental rift or an incipient spreading ridge environment are most consistent with the geochemical data and field relationships.

INTRODUCTION

There is an ongoing debate about which processes control the chemistry of continental basalts, and considerable uncertainty regarding the relative roles of mantle source chemistry, crustal contamination, mantle melting, and fractionation (e.g., Dupuy and Dostal, 1984; Thompson et al., 1984; Huppert and Sparks, 1985; Sparks, 1986; Marsh, 1987; Carlson, 1991; Gallagher and Hawkesworth, 1992; Arndt and Christensen, 1992; Hooper and Hawkesworth 1993; Legault et al., 1994; Bernstein, 1994). In this chapter we attempt to evaluate the relative contributions of fractionation, crustal contamination, and source chemistry in the generation of the Maquereau Group basalts. These lavas are associated with the opening of Iapetus ocean in late Precambrian

time, and we argue that they are fairly typical representatives of the continental or flood-basalt association. We begin by characterizing the lavas of the Maquereau Group with regard to their petrology and geochemistry. We then test various petrogenetic hypotheses using these data. Melting and source models will be presented elsewhere.

GEOLOGIC SETTING

Continental rifting of paleo-North America and the opening of Iapetus ocean in the Late Proterozoic and Cambrian was accompanied by clastic sedimentation and the eruption of tholeiitic and alkaline magmas (Williams, 1979; Coish et al., 1985; Vermette et al., 1993; LaFlèche et al., 1993; Camiré et al., 1995). The Iapetus rift-margin sequence is assigned to the Humber zone (Williams,

*Present address: B. P. 198, 56 Cité du Niger, Mali.

Bédard, J. H., and Wilson, C., 1997, Fractionation and contamination of Maquereau Group lavas, southern Gaspé, Québec Appalachians, *in* Sinha, A. K., Whalen, J. B., and Hogan, J. P., eds., The Nature of Magmatism in the Appalachian Orogen: Boulder, Colorado, Geological Society of America Memoir 191.

1979; Malo et al., 1992) and has been disrupted by Ordovician deformation and metamorphism related to the docking against North America of the oceanic and arc terranes of the Dunnage zone (e.g., St. Julien and Hubert, 1975; Tremblay and Pinet, 1994). The relationships between the different segments of the rift-margin sequence are further obscured by the thick Silurian-Devonian cover, and by subsequent Acadian deformation, metamorphism, and plutonism (Kirkwood and Malo, 1993).

The Maquereau Group of southern Gaspé, Québec (Fig. 1), occurs as a small inlier that is in fault contact with Ordovician rocks of the Dunnage zone, and is unconformably overlain by Silurian cover rocks. The group comprises a sequence of pre-Early Ordovician lavas and quartzo-feldspathic clastic rocks that are as thick as 10 km. On the basis of sedimentological similarities, the Maquereau Group has previously been correlated with other Iapetus rift margin rocks from southern Québec (Caldwell Group) and northern Gaspé (Shickshock Group) (St. Julien and Hubert, 1975; Williams and St. Julien, 1982; DeBroucker, 1987; Cousineau, 1990; Schwab, 1994); but their petrology and geochemistry have never been systematically investigated.

FIELD RELATIONS

The Maquereau Group is separated from the Ordovician flysch deposits of the Mictaw Group to the west by a mélange (the Port-Daniel Complex) (DeBroucker, 1987). The Port Daniel Complex is composed of igneous and sedimentary blocks in a sedimentary matrix (DeBroucker, 1987). Both the Port Daniel mélange and Mictaw Group belong to the Dunnage zone (Williams and St. Julien, 1982). Maquereau Group rocks are unconformably overlain by Silurian sedimentary rocks of the Chaleurs Group to the south, and by Carboniferous redbeds to the northeast (Logan, 1846). The Maquereau Group is separated from Chaleurs Group rocks to the north by a major shear zone, which also contains slivers of Grenvillean age gneiss (DeBroucker, 1987). These gneissic slivers were interpreted to signify that the Maquereau lavas were deposited upon continental crust (DeBroucker, 1987). The Maquereau Group has been affected by up to five phases of ductile deformation (Ringele, 1982), and is cut by several important reverse faults (Caron, 1984; DeBroucker, 1987). Rocks of the Maquereau Group and the adjoining Mictaw Group have been metamorphosed to greenschist grade, in contrast to the prehnite-pumpelleite grade of surrounding Silurian and Carboniferous rocks (Bédard, 1986).

The poor exposure, penetrative deformation and pervasive metamorphism of Maquereau Group rocks commonly obscure contact relations between lavas and sediments. Although there are local intrusive contacts, the broad parallelism of volcanic and sedimentary lithologies (see map in Caron, 1984) is more consistent with a volcanic setting. Massive flows appear to dominate, but pillow lavas can be recognized locally. The most common sedimentary rocks are quartzo-feldspathic sandstones, with subordinate conglomerates and metapelites (DeBroucker, 1987). These sediments were interpreted to have a dominantly Grenvillean source, although they also contain clasts of mafic volcanic rocks that imply local recycling of Maquereau lavas (DeBroucker, 1987).

PETROGRAPHY, MINERALOGY, AND ALTERATION

Most Maquereau Group lavas are phenocryst poor (<15%), very fine grained, microdiabasic rocks. Pseudomorphs after plagioclase, pyroxene, and/or olivine phenocrysts were recognized. Fe-Ti–oxide microphenocrysts are common groundmass phases. (For descriptions of representative samples, see Bédard and Wilson, 1994.) Pillow lavas 93MQ54, 92MQ125, 83JB45, and 83JB46 contain 5%–10% mafic phenocrysts in microspinifex textured groundmass. One volcanic band (92MQ122) is composed of medium- to coarse-grained ferro-gabbroic rocks and may represent a slowly cooled sill. Some metavolcanic samples (92MQ127) contain abundant quartz and feldspar grains and could represent sandy siltstones with a large volcanogenic fraction, xenocryst-laden lavas, or tuffaceous deposits of a hybrid eruption. They do not form a coherent group with the sedimentary rocks, having tholeiitic basalt chemical signatures. We refer to them as tuffs in the figure captions, but will not discuss them in detail. Two Fe-andesitic samples (92MQ114B and 93MQ58) were collected from the same volcanic band.

Greenschist facies metamorphism and deformation has almost completely destroyed the original textures and mineralogy of these rocks. Relict clinopyroxene was analyzed on a Cameca Camebax in the Geological Survey Labs in Ottawa. Many probe analyses gave low totals, suggesting incipient hydration. All analyzed clinopyroxenes are augites with Mg/Mg + Fe between 0.62 and 0.78. The Ca-depletion trend of these pyroxenes is shallower than that of the Skaergaard intrusion, and resembles the magnesian end of the Palisades sill trend (Walker et al., 1973). The chemistry of the pyroxenes in the tholeiitic lavas does not differ systematically from that of pyroxenes in the transitional alkaline lavas. Localized enrichment of Ti and Al in the pyroxenes probably represents a crystallization-kinetics effect (Hall et al., 1985), rather than being a function of lava chemistry (Kushiro, 1960).

Plagioclase is completely replaced by assemblages of albite (Ab_{92-99}, one analysis at Ab_{85}), epidote, quartz, and hematite. Mafic minerals are replaced by chlorite, titanite, iddingsite, pumpelleite(?) talc, hematite, magnetite, and goethite(?). There are abundant prekinematic and postkinematic veins filled with combinations of epidote > calcite > quartz > chlorite > pyrite > chalcopyrite > hematite > magnetite > zoisite(?) > talc or actinolite(?). Intense silicification is observed locally. Sulfides are almost ubiquitous, generally as disseminations and clots up to 1.5 cm in length, locally in veins. Sulfide clots form elongated, lineation-parallel ovoids. Incipiently brecciated pyrite cubes are commonly rimmed by chalcopyrite and a third, purplish sulfide containing both Cu and Fe (qualitative analysis).

GEOCHEMISTRY

Major and trace elements were analysed by X-ray fluorescence on fused glass and pressed powder pellets, and by instru-

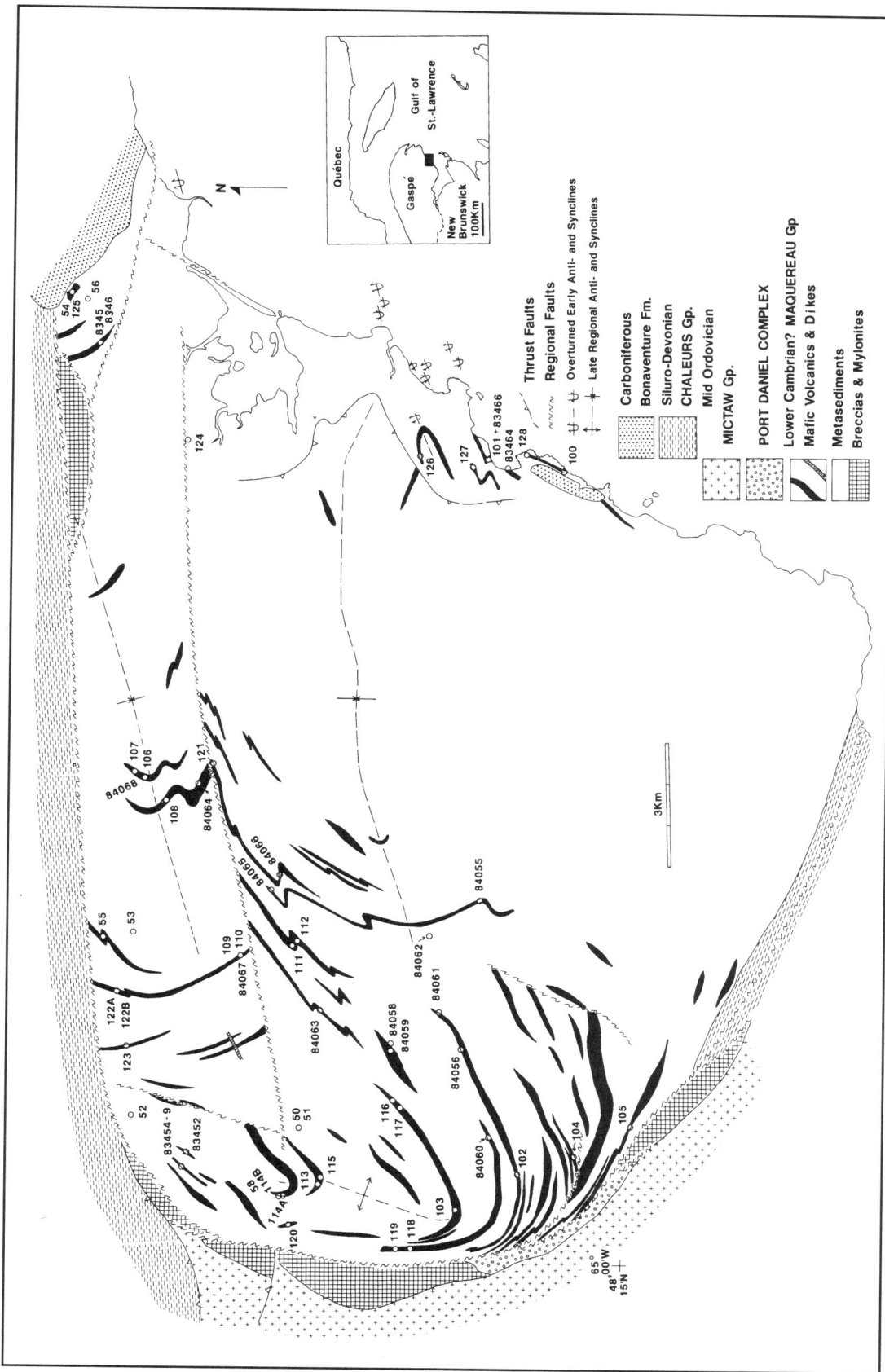

Figure 1. Map of the Maquereau inlier, adapted from Caron (1984) and De Broucker (1987). Samples with 83 and 84 prefixes were collected in 1983–1984 by Bédard or Wilson. Samples without prefixes are from the 1992–1993 field seasons.

mental neutron activation analysis (INAA) at the Institut National de la Recherche Scientifique (INRS) labs in Québec and at the Université de Montréal. The two datasets overlap almost perfectly. Detection limits and estimated precisions are presented in Table 1.

Because of the ubiquitous veining and metamorphism, CaO, MgO, FeO*, SiO$_2$, Na$_2$O, K$_2$O, Rb, Sr, and perhaps Ba are only partly reliable indicators of the original lava chemistry. Some samples have been very seriously perturbed by gain or loss of Na$_2$O, gain of K$_2$O, and near-total loss of CaO. Even the least-altered samples have been affected by metamorphic effects to some extent, and this produces considerable scatter in some of the variation diagrams. Nonetheless, we can still recognize trends to which we attribute a primary magmatic origin. Recognizing the pitfalls created by elemental mobility during metamorphism, we have used the less-easily remobilized elements like Ti, P, Y, Nb, Zr, and the rare earth elements (REE) (see Jenner and Swinden, 1993, p. 438) to subdivide lavas into suites, test petrogenetic hypotheses, and determine paleotectonic affinities. The lavas are plotted against FeO*/MgO in Figure 2, against MgO in Figures 3 and 4, and in Figure 5 they are plotted on mid-ocean ridge basalt (MORB) normalized spidergrams. Trace element ratio diagrams are shown in Figure 6. The data are presented in Table 1; averages are presented in Table 2.

When plotted on variation diagrams and normalized plots, the data from Maquereau Group lavas form consistent and distinct subgroups despite the metamorphic overprint. We divide the Maquereau lavas into four suites on the basis of these natural groupings, which we refer to as high Zr/Y and low Zr/Y transitional-alkaline, and enriched and depleted tholeiitic. This is a purely empirical subdivision with no a priori assumptions, and we point out that the lavas actually form a geochemical continuum that probably represents a spectrum of primary magmas. Nevertheless, examination of Figures 3 and 4 clearly shows that as MgO decreases, each suite shows a trend of decreasing Ni and Sc (also Cr, not shown), and increasing Zr, FeO*, TiO$_2$, P$_2$O$_5$, and REE (also Y, not shown). These geochemical signatures are consistent with an interpretation whereby each suite represents a fractionation series (or a cluster of similar fractionation series). Variability in differentiation and crustal contamination processes (in addition to some amount of metamorphic redistribution) account for scatter in the trends. Some of these petrogenetic hypotheses are quantified and weighed in the discussion.

Lavas with the lowest contents of incompatible elements show an FeO-enrichment trend similar to that of the Skærgaard intrusion (Fig. 2), but at lower TiO$_2$, and higher SiO$_2$ contents. In all respects they closely resemble typical continental tholeiites (see also Fig. 7A). We subdivide the Maquereau tholeiites into enriched and depleted on the basis of their relative abundances of incompatible trace elements. This division is arbitrary, and there is in fact a complete gradation between the two subtypes. The enriched tholeiites have higher concentrations of Zr, Nb, TiO$_2$, and P$_2$O$_5$ (Figs. 3 and 4), and higher La/Yb, Zr/Y, Nb/Y, and Ti/Y ratios (Fig. 6) in comparison to the depleted tholeiites.

Enriched tholeiites have La/Yb > 1 (chondrite-normalized), depleted tholeiites have La/Yb < 1 or only slightly higher than 1. The tholeiites have flat MORB-normalized profiles for elements more compatible than La (Fig. 5), suggesting that garnet was not involved in their petrogenesis. However, the Ba-Th-Nb-Ta segments of the two tholeiitic suites are nearly indistinguishable (Fig. 5), suggesting that the process that controls the concentration of these elements may be decoupled from that which controls the less incompatible elements. The profiles appear to show weak negative Nb anomalies, but the significance of these anomalies is uncertain, because our Nb and Ta analyses are close to the limit of detection in most of the tholeiitic basalts. Ongoing induced coupled plasma mass spectromerty (ICPMS) analytical work may resolve this problem.

Many Maquereau lavas have significantly higher concentrations of Nb, Y, Zr, TiO$_2$, and P$_2$O$_5$ (Table 1, Figs. 3 and 4), and higher La/Yb, Zr/Y, Nb/Y, and Ti/Y ratios (Fig. 6) than do the tholeiitic lavas. On the basis of their high absolute concentrations of incompatible elements, we infer a transitional-alkaline affinity for these lavas. We subdivide the Maquereau transitional-alkaline lavas into a low Zr/Y and a high Zr/Y suite. The low Zr/Y transitional-alkaline lavas are very similar to the enriched tholeiites in many ways (Fig. 5C) although incompatible element concentrations are generally higher at a given MgO content, particularly Zr, Nb, TiO$_2$ and P$_2$O$_5$ (Figs. 3 and 4). The enrichment patterns are not uniform, however, only some elements showing enrichment relative to the tholeiitic lavas. The low Zr/Y suite may be intermediate between the enriched tholeiites and the high Zr/Y transitional-alkaline lavas. The high Zr/Y transitional-alkaline lavas show more uniform trace-element enrichment, prominent positive Ti-P spikes (Fig. 5C), and the highest La/Yb, Nb/Y, Ti/Y, and Zr/Y ratios (Fig. 6). The heavy REE show significant slope variations in the transitional-alkaline lavas, which may imply the involvement of garnet in their petrogenesis.

Two lavas have high FeO* and TiO$_2$, and low MgO contents (Fig. 2), and appear to be ferro-andesites. They have high abundances of incompatible trace elements (Figs. 3, 4 and 6), with profiles that mimic those of the tholeiitic basalts (Fig. 5), though at higher abundances. Their geochemical signatures are consistent with an origin by fractionation from more primitive magmas similar to the enriched tholeiites.

The sedimentary rocks interbedded with the Maquereau lavas and Grenvillean basement gneisses are plotted and compared in Figure 5, D and E; and are compared to published syntheses (Condie, 1993) of Proterozoic rocks from the Canadian shield in Figure 5F. DeBroucker (1987) analyzed the Grenvillean-age slivers of gneiss that are caught up in the strike-slip fault that bounds the Maquereau Group to the north. His data were complemented by using the compilations of Condie (1993), who gave average values for Proterozoic rocks in the Canadian shield, in order to generate a model felsic Grenvillean contaminant (Fig. 5E) that will be used in the modeling calculations. The Maquereau sediment data are from this study and DeBroucker (1987). Note that the Maquereau sedimentary rocks, Grenvillean gneiss, and Proterozoic granitoids and sedimentary rocks have very similar profiles, consistent with the interpretation that the Maquereau sandstones are derived from erosion of the Grenvillean craton.

DISCUSSION

Field relations imply that the Maquereau lavas erupted on a continental shelf where active clastic sedimentation was occurring, and that they may have erupted through Proterozoic continental crust. There is little consensus about what controls the chemistry of continental basaltic suites (e.g., Thompson et al., 1984; Sparks, 1986; Marsh, 1987; Carlson, 1991; Gallagher and Hawkesworth, 1992; Arndt and Christensen, 1992; Hooper and Hawkesworth, 1993). Some favor shallow or high-pressure assimilation-fractionation processes, and others think that the mantle source chemistry and melting processes are paramount. It seems evident that the potential consequences of intracrustal fractional crystallization and crustal contamination must be constrained before any attempt can be made to evaluate the degree to which source chemistry or melting processes control the lava chemistry. In the following sections, we develop a series of fractionation and coupled assimilation-fractionation (AFC) models in order to determine the extent to which these processes can explain the observed geochemical variations in the Maquereau lavas. Quantitative mantle melting models will be presented elsewhere.

Differentiation models

Choice of parent. Model parents were derived graphically from the examination of variation diagrams, and are reported in Table 2, although to simplify the figures, only the depleted tholeiite model parent is shown. This model parent is used in the fractionation models we report herein, and will be used in the melting models that we will present elsewhere. Concentrations of elements were chosen so that the model parent composition for each suite would plot within the data cluster at the high-MgO end of the range for each suite. CaO, which is particularly mobile, was fixed at about 10 wt%. Incompatible and compatible elements were fixed at the lower and upper ends (respectively) of the data clusters, and the data were adjusted to yield fairly smooth profiles on the MORB-normalized diagrams.

Closed System Models. Fractional crystallization calculations of different mixtures of Cr-spinel + olivine + clinopyroxene + plagioclase were explored. Major elements were modeled by extracting troctolitic or olivine gabbro assemblages (olivine: plagioclase:clinopyroxene = 40:60:0 and 14:43:43, respectively) from the model parents. Mineral compositions used were those from probe analyses (clinopyroxene), or were estimated by applying the Nielsen (1988, 1991) CHAOS.FRACT program. Mineral/ liquid partition coefficient data used are from the compilation of Bédard (1994). Representative results of these calculations are plotted in Figures 3, 4, 6, and 7.

Modeling results show that fractionation of common basaltic phenocryst assemblages cannot generate the enriched tholeiites

from a depleted tholeiitic parent, nor can the transitional alkaline suite be derived from the enriched tholeiitic parent by this mechanism (results not shown). However, about 30% closed-system fractionation of troctolitic or olivine gabbro assemblages can account for most of the internal geochemical range for each suite. Separation of minor Cr-spinel is necessary to explain the rapid decrease in Cr, but this phase was not included in the calculations. Olivine fractionation is required by the rapid decrease in Ni. Fractionation of plagioclase is required to inhibit enrichment in Al_2O_3. Significant clinopyroxene fractionation is required by the rapid decrease in Sc (Fig. 4C), implying that the olivine gabbro assemblage is more applicable to the Maquereau lavas. This conclusion is also supported by the steep trends of Zr-TiO_2-P_2O_5 vs. MgO shown by the data (Fig. 4); the trends are steeper than would be expected from troctolitic fractionation.

Experimental data on basaltic lavas suggest that shallow fractionation favors fractionation of olivine + plagioclase assemblages, whereas higher confining pressures cause the liquidus phase volume of clinopyroxene to increase in basaltic systems (e.g., Cohen et al., 1967; Thompson, 1972; Bender et al., 1978; Stolper, 1980; Takahashi and Kushiro, 1983), and so favor fractionation of olivine gabbro assemblages. Numerical experiments on the model parents for the Maquereau lavas executed using the Nielsen (1988, 1991) CHAOS.FRACT program suggest that 1 atm crystallization of the Maquereau lavas would be dominated by olivine and plagioclase. However, the geochemical evidence appears to require a high proportion of clinopyroxene in the fractionating assemblage. This could signify that Maquereau magmas fractionated at higher pressures. Models invoking infracrustal magmatic underplating during continental rifting (Cox, 1980; White, 1992; Bernstein, 1994) are gaining wider acceptance, and may also be applicable to the Maquereau basalts.

Closed-system fractionation can explain many of the observed geochemical variations seen in the Maquereau lavas. However, it was not possible to generate the average enriched tholeiite from a depleted tholeiitic parent by a closed-system fractionation mechanism (Figs. 3, 4, and 7B). The implausibility of this type of fractionation scheme should be evident from the examination of Figure 3 (B and C), because the two tholeiitic suites exhibit parallel trends on TiO_2 or P_2O_5 vs. MgO plots.

Open System Models. All of the Maquereau suites include rocks with unusually high concentrations of large-ion lithophile elements (LILE) (Ba and Th), Zr, and the light REE, enrichments that are not correlated to enrichment in other incompatible elements like Nb, Y, P, and Ti, but that show rough correlations with increasing SiO_2. Crustal contamination is one mechanism by which these geochemical characteristics may develop. Coupled assimilation-fractional crystallization (AFC) models were explored to see if some of the intrasuite and intersuite variations can be attributed to crustal contamination effects.

The major-element concentrations of the contaminated residual melts were estimated using the CHAOS-FRACT (Nielsen, 1988, 1991) program. The program yielded liquid residua with major element compositions very similar to those of the

J. H. Bédard and C. Wilson

TABLE 1. WHOLE-ROCK ANALYSES OF MAQUEREAU GROUP LAVAS AND SEDIMENTARY ROCKS*

Sample	SiO_2	TiO_2	Al_2O_3	Fe_2O_3*	FeO*	MgO	MnO	CaO	Na_2O	K_2O	P_2O_5	S	LOI	Total
Enriched														
92MQ100	48.9	1.92	12.1	13.9		4.31	0.23	6.18	2.98	0.15	0.20	0.00	8.70	99.67
92MQ101	47.6	1.77	12.2	17.6		6.57	0.21	5.96	2.16	0.05	0.19	0.00	7.41	101.77
92MQ101V	46.8	1.90	12.8	18.9		6.95	0.22	4.73	2.38	0.05	0.18	0.00	6.15	101.33
92MQ107	43.4	1.54	13.0	16.2		6.41	0.22	6.80	1.94	0.14	0.21	0.00	12.07	102.00
92MQ108	44.6	1.07	14.0	11.3		6.88	0.19	9.88	1.93	0.04	0.11	0.00	9.77	99.95
92MQ111	48.8	1.65	12.6	15.0		7.21	0.23	7.74	3.45	0.35	0.17	0.13	3.36	100.76
92MQ112B	48.2	1.67	12.6	14.6		7.06	0.24	6.81	3.25	0.37	0.19	0.05	3.77	98.85
92MQ119	47.9	1.56	13.0	15.0		6.27	0.19	7.95	1.62	0.07	0.20	0.00	4.85	98.85
92MQ121A	46.5	1.43	13.9	12.9		7.13	0.17	9.97	1.44	0.06	0.16	0.00	6.60	100.49
92MQ121B	45.2	1.39	13.3	12.8		6.63	0.18	10.8	1.46	0.05	0.16	0.00	6.09	98.18
83JB045	47.4	1.12	14.9		10.4	7.77	0.19	8.13	2.68	1.42	0.06	0.05	3.04	97.16
83CW456	50.7	1.36	14.2		13.5	8.02	0.20	7.24	1.28	3.36	0.17			100 (N)
83CW457	49.7	1.60	15.2		14.8	9.70	0.17	4.66	1.87	2.17	0.17			100 (N)
83CW459	50.0	1.41	14.7		13.1	8.07	0.20	8.94	1.75	1.71	0.16			100 (N)
83CW466	53.0	1.93	13.5		15.6	6.25	0.22	7.32	1.88	0.11	0.19			100 (N)
84CW059	48.8	1.13	16.2		11.9	8.99	0.17	10.1	2.56	0.03	0.13			100 (N)
84CW060	51.0	1.60	13.5		14.9	7.19	0.19	6.97	4.12	0.34	0.20			100 (N)
84CW062	48.2	1.74	13.6		15.9	6.62	0.23	10.2	2.77	0.44	0.20			100 (N)
84CW063	49.5	1.15	15.6		12.3	9.40	0.25	7.41	4.12	0.21	0.12			100 (N)
84CW064	48.1	1.43	12.8		15.8	9.64	0.21	9.95	1.87	0.10	0.17			100 (N)
84CW066	48.6	1.34	14.8		13.5	7.89	0.24	8.91	4.05	0.35	0.21			100 (N)
Depleted														
92MQ102	47.1	0.75	13.6	14.4		7.72	0.22	9.00	2.25	0.07	0.04	0.00	4.02	99.33
92MQ103	50.2	1.31	13.8	14.7		7.08	0.21	5.59	3.24	0.08	0.12	0.12	5.67	102.18
92MQ104	49.9	1.01	12.8	14.8		6.16	0.29	8.00	3.23	0.29	0.09	0.00	4.13	100.84
92MQ105	48.8	1.17	12.7	14.2		6.78	0.22	8.94	1.81	0.16	0.12	0.00	4.12	99.17
92MQ106	51.0	1.22	13.2	14.0		6.99	0.19	7.21	3.20	0.08	0.12	0.00	3.60	100.98
92MQ113A	51.3	0.86	11.7	12.9		6.62	0.17	5.54	3.27	0.05	0.07	0.00	8.51	101.07
92MQ113B	52.4	1.01	15.5	13.9		8.68	0.10	0.22	3.94	0.04	0.09	0.00	5.47	101.47
92MQ115	49.6	0.71	11.4	10.4		8.66	0.21	6.17	2.42	0.05	0.07	0.00	11.14	100.99
92MQ116A	47.2	1.11	14.7	11.6		7.58	0.17	11.3	1.70	0.05	0.12	0.12	3.90	99.63
92MQ116B	47.5	1.11	14.3	12.0		6.76	0.19	11.6	0.52	0.19	0.11	0.00	7.85	102.27
92MQ117A	45.8	1.14	15.1	13.0		6.95	0.18	12.0	1.68	0.20	0.13	0.00	3.83	100.36
92MQ117B	46.1	0.82	14.7	13.5		8.45	0.21	7.76	2.37	0.08	0.07	0.00	5.44	99.62
92MQ118A	49.8	1.00	12.9	14.3		7.47	0.20	8.51	2.45	0.07	0.08	0.10	3.89	100.82
92MQ118B	48.3	1.04	12.9	14.5		7.08	0.21	9.36	2.08	0.07	0.08	0.16	4.71	100.47
92MQ120	50.3	1.16	12.9	13.8		7.30	0.22	8.02	2.10	0.40	0.11	0.09	4.14	100.65
92MQ125A	49.8	0.67	14.0	9.9		9.00	0.15	8.19	2.88	0.06	0.08	0.00	6.12	100.98
92MQ125B	50.6	0.66	13.3	9.4		7.98	0.19	9.03	2.95	0.13	0.07	0.00	4.87	99.33
92MQ128	49.5	0.67	11.2	10.2		4.31	0.15	10.1	0.30	0.66	0.05	0.00	13.61	100.80
93MQ54	46.5	0.86	15.4	10.0		9.27	0.19	9.51	2.70	0.19	0.10	0.00	6.10	100.87
93MQ55	47.6	1.13	15.7	11.9		6.35	0.19	10.8	2.96	0.06	0.11	0.00	3.57	100.39
83CW464	48.8	1.11	17.5		11.4	9.30	0.16	8.04	3.50	0.07	0.05			100 (N)
84CW055	51.3	1.13	13.1		14.7	5.84	0.28	11.0	2.32	0.22	0.08			100 (N)

TABLE 1. WHOLE-ROCK ANALYSES OF MAQUEREAU GROUP LAVAS AND SEDIMENTARY ROCKS* (continued - page 2)

Sample	SiO₂	TiO₂	Al₂O₃	Fe₂O₃*	FeO*	MgO	MnO	CaO	Na₂O	K₂O	P₂O₅	S	LOI	Total
Depleted (continued)														
84CW056	53.0	1.01	13.8		12.1	7.68		9.27	3.11	0.03	0.05			100 (N)
84CW061	52.1	1.08	13.6		13.2	6.44	0.20	10.1	2.98	0.20	0.12			100 (N)
84CW065	49.6	1.05	15.4		11.2	7.22	0.22	12.0	3.13	0.01	0.10			100 (N)
84CW068	51.8	1.10	13.5		13.3	7.09	0.23	9.51	3.29	0.05	0.09			100 (N)
Trans-Alk Low Zr/Y														
92MQ109A	45.9	1.73	16.5	13.4		8.74	0.38	2.78	4.30	0.05	0.22	0.00	7.10	101.30
92MQ110	41.5	1.56	14.9	12.9		6.88	0.43	8.28	4.11	0.04	0.30	0.00	9.98	101.06
92MQ114A	48.4	1.17	13.1	14.7		7.24	0.25	4.90	4.13	0.16	0.12	0.00	5.24	99.59
83CW452	50.7	1.51	15.6		12.9	9.23	0.17	5.85	2.17	1.73	0.15			100 (N)
83CW454	49.1	3.35	18.2		14.4	5.02	0.12	3.14	5.31	0.61	0.76			100 (N)
83CW455	49.9	1.66	14.2		14.3	7.35	0.21	7.53	1.18	3.46	0.21			100 (N)
83CW458	49.6	3.27	16.3		14.8	4.21	0.18	5.17	5.49	0.44	0.59			100 (N)
High Zr/Y														
92MQ109B	43.6	1.77	16.0	12.6		7.55	0.40	5.52	4.44	0.04	0.24	0.00	7.99	100.21
92MQ122A	48.3	4.49	12.1	17.1		4.88	0.51	6.52	4.61	0.06	0.46	0.00	2.83	101.98
92MQ122B	47.4	3.03	13.3	13.9		6.68	0.25	8.02	3.53	0.76	0.29	0.15	3.44	100.92
83JB46	48.8	2.00	13.8		11.0	8.57	0.16	6.94	3.80	0.82	0.24	0.04	4.65	100.80
Andesite														
92MQ114B	51.5	2.11	11.2	18.6		3.11	0.20	5.24	3.46	1.29	0.27	0.21	4.17	101.17
93MQ58	49.1	2.20	14.1	18.7		4.92	0.22	3.39	4.58	0.09	0.35	0.00	4.19	101.98
Tuffs?														
92MQ127A	48.0	1.98	11.5	16.4		5.75	0.20	6.85	1.62	0.04	0.20	0.00	9.68	102.31
92MQ127B	49.7	2.22	13.0	17.7		5.90	0.17	2.42	2.72	0.05	0.21	0.00	6.67	100.97
Sedimentary Rocks														
92MQ109C	72.9	0.49	13.2	1.8		0.50	0.02	0.91	5.97	0.70	0.13	0.00	1.43	98.08
92MQ123	54.2	1.03	19.4	9.7		2.30	0.14	0.99	2.90	3.17	0.22	0.15	4.34	98.62
92MQ124	90.4	0.36	5.3	1.4		0.43	0.01	0.28	0.50	0.90	0.05	0.00	1.47	101.07
92MQ126	56.1	1.02	15.6	9.2		7.96	0.05	0.54	4.34	0.04	0.13	0.00	4.95	100.02
93MQ50	52.5	1.24	19.4	11.4		5.03	0.11	0.37	2.02	3.03	0.23	0.00	5.13	100.60
93MQ51	56.3	1.39	16.5	6.7		2.93	0.08	4.55	4.84	1.22	0.23	0.00	5.86	100.76
93MQ52	64.9	0.87	16.9	4.2		2.36	0.07	1.57	5.06	1.83	0.10	0.00	2.55	100.56
93MQ53	57.3	1.02	20.3	8.5		2.16	0.09	0.46	2.65	3.43	0.18	0.00	3.75	99.93
93MQ56	77.7	0.68	10.8	3.1		0.84	0.04	0.55	1.80	2.51	0.09	0.00	1.95	100.15

J. H. Bédard and C. Wilson

TABLE 1. WHOLE-ROCK ANALYSES OF MAQUEREAU GROUP LAVAS AND SEDIMENTARY ROCKS* (continued - page 3)

Sample	As	Cs	Ba	Rb	Sr	Cr	Ni	Cu	Zn	Pb	V	Nb	Y	Zr	Ga
Enriched															
92MQ100			<50	7	67	157	58	44	119	16	868	5	24	101	14
92MQ101	3.06	<0.5	<50	3	300	196	80	103	120	14	982	4	37	98	14
92MQ101V	2.53	<0.5	<50	3	301	212	71	109	132	14	1,098	4	39	98	18
92MQ107			<50	<3	190	397	101	87	81	6	470	<3	23	59	5
92MQ108			<50	<3	92	479	131	108	111	9	668	7	30	102	9
92MQ111	2.38	<0.5	131	7	295	263	101	114	115	10	749	5	30	88	15
92MQ112B			<50	3	69	145	80	66	80	5	473	<3	22	43	10
92MQ119			<50	<3	145	371	97	108	107	11	805	3	38	98	13
92MQ121A			337	5	192	400	119	102	87	11	565	6	24	76	11
92MQ121B			<50	4	205	393	105	96	87	13	565	7	27	77	9
83JB045			610	41	210	293	100	160	110		330	5	23	54	
83CW456			<20	58	66	117	73		113			10	34	74	
83CW457			<20	34	104	119	69		134			8	34	81	
83CW459			<20	24	198	138	75		111			9	32	78	
83CW466			<20	<3	533	96	44		145			4.6	41	110	
84CW059			41	<3	121	343	112		100			4	25	63	
84CW060			499	5	511	172	74		143			7	34	91	
84CW062			197	<3	158	134	61		142			6	31	73	
84CW063			24	3	232	320	97		91			5.5	24	70	
84CW064			55	<3	152	275	185		130				24	77	
84CW066			132	11	324	302	126		113			9	29	87	
Depleted															
92MQ102	2.77	<0.5	158	3	230	289	99	135	109	12	726	<3	30	70	10
92MQ103			174	10	218	205	92	120	97	8	667	<3	23	48	8
92MQ104			<50	6	216	219	100	110	98	13	677	<3	31	66	17
92MQ105	4.17	1.03	<50	3	254	237	86	118	108	8	669	<3	27	65	14
92MQ106			<50	7	54	381	106	41	104	10	814	3	34	95	12
92MQ113A	1.23	<0.5	<50	<3	16	172	74	110	97.6	7	545	<3	21	45	10
92MQ113B	<1	<0.5	<50	5	87	275	88	131	123	10	737	5	31	66	11
92MQ115	<1	<0.5	<50	3	148	424	99	89	82.6		493	<3	24	59	15
92MQ116A	1.08	<0.5	<50	11	293	433	103	87	88.5	10	518	3	23	64	11
92MQ116B			<50	9	198	457	106	91	80	5	519	<3	24	65	10
92MQ117A	2.05	<0.5	<100	11.1	193	307	<100	99		11	575	<3	29	45	13
92MQ117B			61	4	210	208	96	107	90	12	668	<3	31	48	13
92MQ118A			<50	6	77	236	90	124	90	11	769	<3	31	49	10
92MQ118B			<50	3	106	221	83	139	99	14	656	<3	28	62	11
92MQ120			59	10	207	240	89	135	91	10	459	<3	26	38	6
92MQ125A	5.12	<0.5	80		154	483	101	82	88.4	10	388	<3	18	40	5
92MQ125B			230	4	378	464	102	74	79	13	402	<3	16	33	11
92MQ128	4.93	<0.5	<50	19	121	111	53	33	61	10	216	<3	20	57	13
93MQ54			164	6	163	334	117	122	109	<5	274	<3	23	65	19
93MQ55			<50	3	250	265	111	130	85			5	31	49	
83CW464			611	4	378	93	61		90						
84CW055			376	<3	286	60	70		116			4.3	33	65	

TABLE 1. WHOLE-ROCK ANALYSES OF MAQUEREAU GROUP LAVAS AND SEDIMENTARY ROCKS* (continued - page 4)

Sample	As	Cs	Ba	Rb	Sr	Cr	Ni	Cu	Zn	Pb	V	Nb	Y	Zr	Ga
Depleted (continued)															
84CW056			41	<3	<30	118	92		231						
84CW061			184	6	234	139	61		101				25	65	
84CW065			21	<3	231	333	105		92			4	25	63	
84CW068			57	<3	322	146	69		99			4	30	66	
Trans-Alk Low Zr/Y															
92MQ109A	2.32	<0.5	<50	4	99	461	118	124	97	5	577	9	36	107	15
92MQ110	1.41	<0.5	207	7	355	283	101	122	113	5	747	3	29	81	14
92MQ114A			234	31	122	109	44	55	141	13	788	20	62	158	10
83CW452			200	<3	206	440	140		134			13.5	22	65	
83CW454			140	<3	76	145	67		150			15.5	28	104	
83CW455			<20	64	81	113	66		133			14	36	94	
83CW458			267	29	59	181	88		121			12	31	83	
High Zr/Y															
92MQ109B			191	19	93	51	17	16	35	10	35	8	18	237	3
92MQ122A	5.05	<0.5	<50	4	143	93	38	31	133	17	654	26	36	198	18
92MQ122B			878	13	238	192	78	76	115	11	575	15	29	161	11
83JB46			220	12	390	330	110	110	100		280	14	23	140	
Andesite															
92MQ114B	1.22	1.09	251	3	56	119	71	59	119	9	336	<3			
93MQ58	2.36	<0.5	497	5	51	81	45	165	166	17	595	24	68	149	25
Tuffs?															
92MQ127A	3.08	<0.5	171	<3	144	167	67	76	122	10	948	4	40	96	13
92MQ127B			<50	5	90	188	67	29	119	16	1,178	7	44	106	17
Sedimentary Rocks															
92MQ109C	1.04	<0.5	188	3	140	416	92	79	63	9	509	6	37	115	12
92MQ123	11.3	0.88	1,260	63.95	97	129	50	78	115	25	209	15	28	221	22
92MQ124	2.38	<0.5	177	30.9	<30	n.d.	n.d.	n.d.	23	n.d.	n.d.	n.d.	n.d.	n.d.	n.d.
92MQ126			594	3	53	278	52	25	68	6	358	<3	16	54	8
93MQ50	1.07		880	85	30	92	45	62	122	13	204	19	19	172	28
93MQ51	<1	1.02	741	32	109	84	29	15	79	13	98	16	52	418	18
93MQ52		0.78	364	36	267	84	23	4	49	6	51	10	26	190	12
93MQ53	1.55	1.75	482	93	62	71	40	39	115	11	117	19	44	190	21
93MQ56	3.1	0.91	728	78	72	122	24	15	48	14	47	13	18	339	10

J. H. Bédard and C. Wilson

TABLE 1. WHOLE-ROCK ANALYSES OF MAQUEREAU GROUP LAVAS AND SEDIMENTARY ROCKS* (continued - page 5)

Sample	La	Ce	Nd	Sm	Eu	Yb	Lu	Sc	Hf	Ta	Th
Enriched											
92MQ101	5.91	14.7	14.2	3.81	1.21	4.51	0.672	48.9	2.82	0.483	0.537
92MQ101V	5.94	14.6	12.4	4.04	1.32	4.9	0.749	53.9	2.89	0.414	0.701
92MQ111	6.75	15.4	9.42	3.41	1.2	3.35	0.544	48.7	2.33		0.454
84CW060	7.1	18	11	3.36	1.19	3.5	0.6	48.4	2.6	0.6	1
Depleted											
92MQ102	1.43	3.31		1.58	0.623	2.8	0.49	50.9	0.987		
92MQ105	4.37	9.95	8.44	2.85	1.04	3.65	0.578	48.2	1.93	0.355	0.539
92MQ113A	3.42	9.19	7.23	1.82	0.711	2.41	0.392	41.4	1.23		0.437
92MQ113B	2.29	5.56	<5	1.57	0.644	2.15	0.399	42.4	1.45	<0.3	<0.2
92MQ115	3.53	8.24	6.7	1.74	0.675	2.09	0.339	35	1.13		0.409
92MQ116A	4.13	10.3	7.21	2.72	0.935	2.7	0.387	48.5	1.73		0.238
92Mq117A	4.07	10.7	7.7	2.7	0.941	2.64	0.449	48.5	1.74	0.33	<0.2
92MQ125A	2.09	4.61		1.57	0.68	3.17	0.448	44.6	0.907		
93MQ54	3.25	7.871	5.289	1.832	0.671	1.99	0.3237	38.6	1.184	0.397	0.317
83CW464	2.5	7	7	2.29	0.95	3.6	0.6	60.7	1.7	0.3	0.5
84CW061	4	10	8	2.6	0.95	3.5	0.62	49	2.1	0.7	0.5
Trans-Alk Low Zr/Y											
92MQ109A	7.77	19.6	12.5	4.07	1.43	3.55	0.552	52.1	3.13	0.51	0.305
92MQ110	9.34	21.1	17.6	4.18	1.14	3.38	0.508	47	3.07	0.465	0.557
83CW458	7.9	16	13	3.08	0.94	3.3	0.51	50.5	2.4	1	1
High Zr/Y											
92MQ122A	18	46.4	32.6	7.84	2.4	3.07	0.5	32.9	5.62	1.49	1.41
83JB46	12.4	30	19.4	5.47	1.47	2.3	0.3		3.7	0.9	0.8
Andesite											
92MQ114B	16.6	35	20.3	5.9	1.72	7.18	1.17	43.7	4.63	1.36	2.61
93MQ58	16.2	33.95	21.41	5.655	1.68	6.81	1.073	42.3	4.078	1.79	2.43
Tuffs?											
92MQ127A	5.93	14.8	10.8	4.03	1.37	4.72	0.744	46	2.97	0.393	0.778
Sedimentary Rocks											
92MQ109C	20	39.6	20.6	4.07	1.36	1.37	0.243	4.92	6.15	0.427	2.67
92MQ123	35.7	83.6	41.9	7.2	1.6	3.18	0.584	18.3	6.42	1.13	10.1
92MQ124	15	32.1	14.2	2.35	0.512	0.849	0.153	2.92	8.07	1.09	4.05
93MQ51	58	69.05	64.44	11.23	2.73	3.89	0.6008	11.7	11.98		7.11
93MQ52	21.4	34.14	29.92	5.696	1.58	2.58	0.3787	6.38	4.71	0.853	4.03
93MQ53	46.8	91.86	51.47	9.495	1.89	3.64	0.5854	17.5	5.185	1.31	9.9
93MQ56	27.2	58.83	26.69	4.11	1.02	1.59	0.2536	5.78	10.02	0.904	9.31

TABLE 1. WHOLE-ROCK ANALYSES OF MAQUEREAU GROUP LAVAS AND SEDIMENTARY ROCKS* (continued - page 6)

*The 83CW- and 84CW-series were analyzed at the Université de Montréal using techniques and with accuracies described in Bédard (1986, 1994). The CW-series analyses are all normalized to 100%. Other analyses were executed at the INRS labs at the Québec Geoscience Center. The major elements were analyzed by conventional X-ray fluorescence techniques on glass disks. The trace elements were analyzed on pressed powder pellets. Methods and accuracies are similar to those described in Bédard (1986, 1994). Rare-earth elements and Sc, Hf, Ta, Th, and Co were analyzed by instrumental neutron activation. About 2 cm³ of powder were irradiated 20 min at the nuclear reactor at McMaster University, Ontario. The first count (1 hr) was done at 2.2 cm from the detector, the second (2 hr) at 0.3 cm from GEN series and EG and G germanium detectors. Detection limits are 0.5 ppm for La and Ho, 0.05 ppm for Sm and Lu, 2 ppm for Ce, 5 ppm for Nd and Cr, 1 ppm for As and Co, 0.3 ppm for Ta, 0.2 ppm for Hf, Tm, Th, and Yb, 0.1 ppm for Eu, Sc, and Tb, and 10 ppm for Zn. Precision is estimated to be 5% or better for most elements. For Ta and Th: analysis of international standard BHVO-1 gave abundances of 1.245 and 1.08 ppm (respectively), compared to certified abundances of 1.23 and 1.17 ppm. Repeat analyses (26) of an internal standard (PJL) yielded an error of 12% on Ta (0.7 ppm) and 6% on Th (1.5 ppm). For Nb: repeat analyses (11) of standard GSR 4 (certified abundance of 6 ppm) gave an average of 5.6 ppm Nb with a range from 3 to 8 ppm. Repeat analyses (11) of SARM1 (certified abundance of 53 ppm) gave an average of 53.4 ppm Nb with a range from 50 to 58.

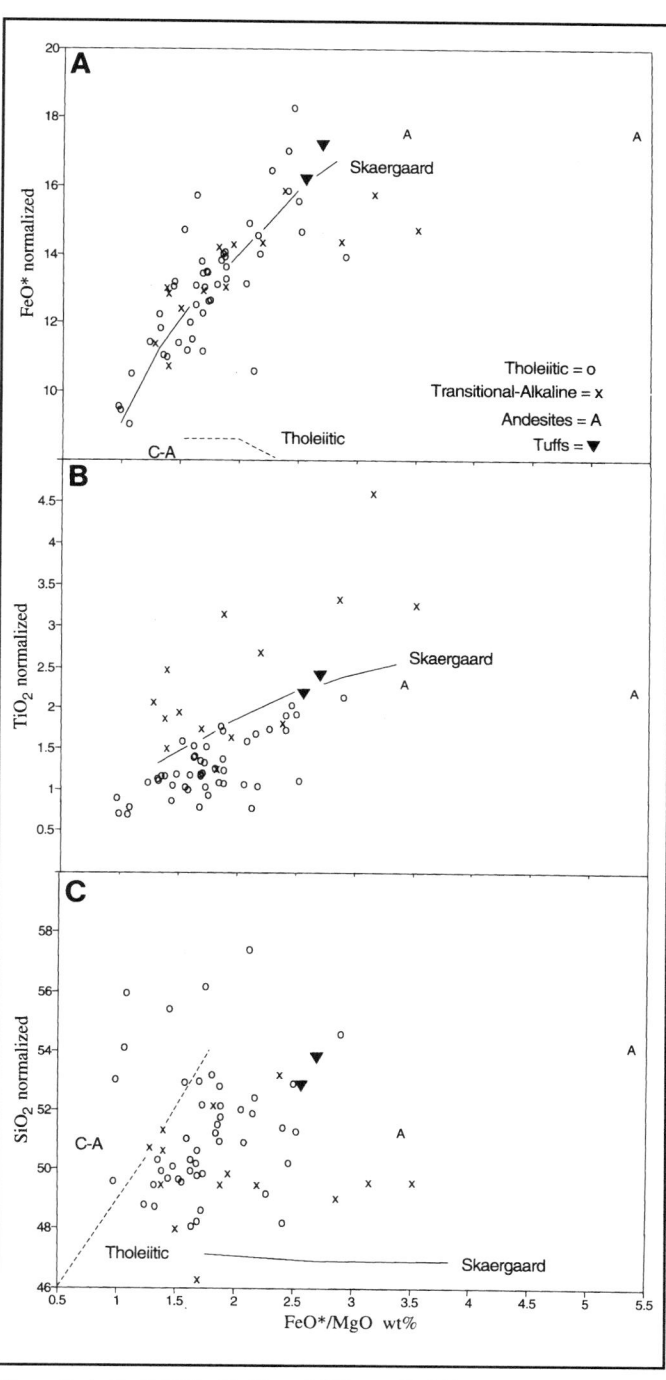

Figure 2. A, B, C: TiO₂, FeO*, and SiO₂ vs. FeO*/MgO discriminant diagrams of Miyashiro (1973). C-A = calc-alkaline. Data from this paper and DeBroucker (1987).

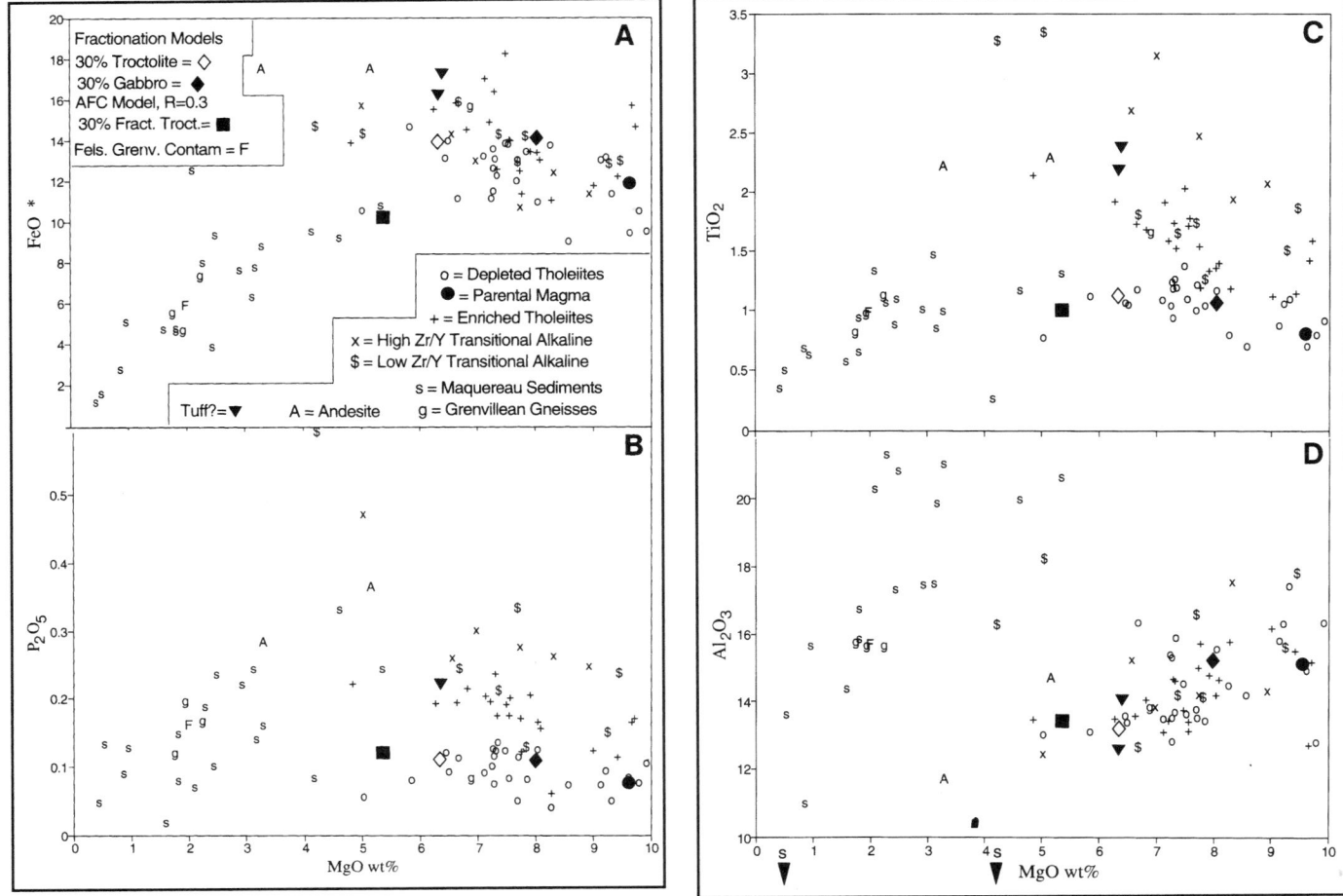

Figure 3. Variation diagrams for Maquereau lavas. All elements normalized volatile free, all iron as FeO. A: wt% FeO*, B: P$_2$O$_5$, C: TiO$_2$, and D: Al$_2$O$_3$, all vs. wt% MgO. Fractionation model results show calculated liquid compositions for 30% fractionation of olivine gabbro or troctolite from the depleted tholeiite model parent. The AFC model residua were calculated using the CHAOS.FRACT program of Nielsen (1988, 1991) for the major elements, the equations of DePaolo (1981) for the trace elements, and a model Grenvillean felsic gneiss contaminant F. Grenvillean gneisses, g, are from DeBroucker (1987), as are some of the sediment analyses.

troctolitic fractionation model described above (e.g., Fig. 3). However, the concentration of incompatible elements in the residual melt is not sensitive to the relative proportions of plagioclase, olivine, and clinopyroxene in the fractionating assemblage; the most significant variables are the fraction crystallized, the concentration of the element in the contaminant vs. the fractionating magma, and the ratio of mass assimilated/mass crystallized, or R-factor. The trace-element concentrations of the residual melts were calculated using the equations of DePaolo (1981) with crystallization increments of 1%, and using the same troctolitic crystallization assemblage as the closed-system models.

Two contaminants were investigated, an average sediment (Table 2), and a felsic Grenvillean gneiss constructed from the analyses of DeBroucker (1987), complemented by felsic Proterozoic rock using the synthesis of Condie (1993). Both of the contaminants gave similar results, though the Grenvillean contaminant was more effective at causing deviations from the closed-system fractionation path, because it has higher abundances of Zr and LILE. The R-factor was fixed at 0.3 during the calculation.

The results of the modeling illustrate the great potential of crustal contamination (as well as its limitations) for gener-

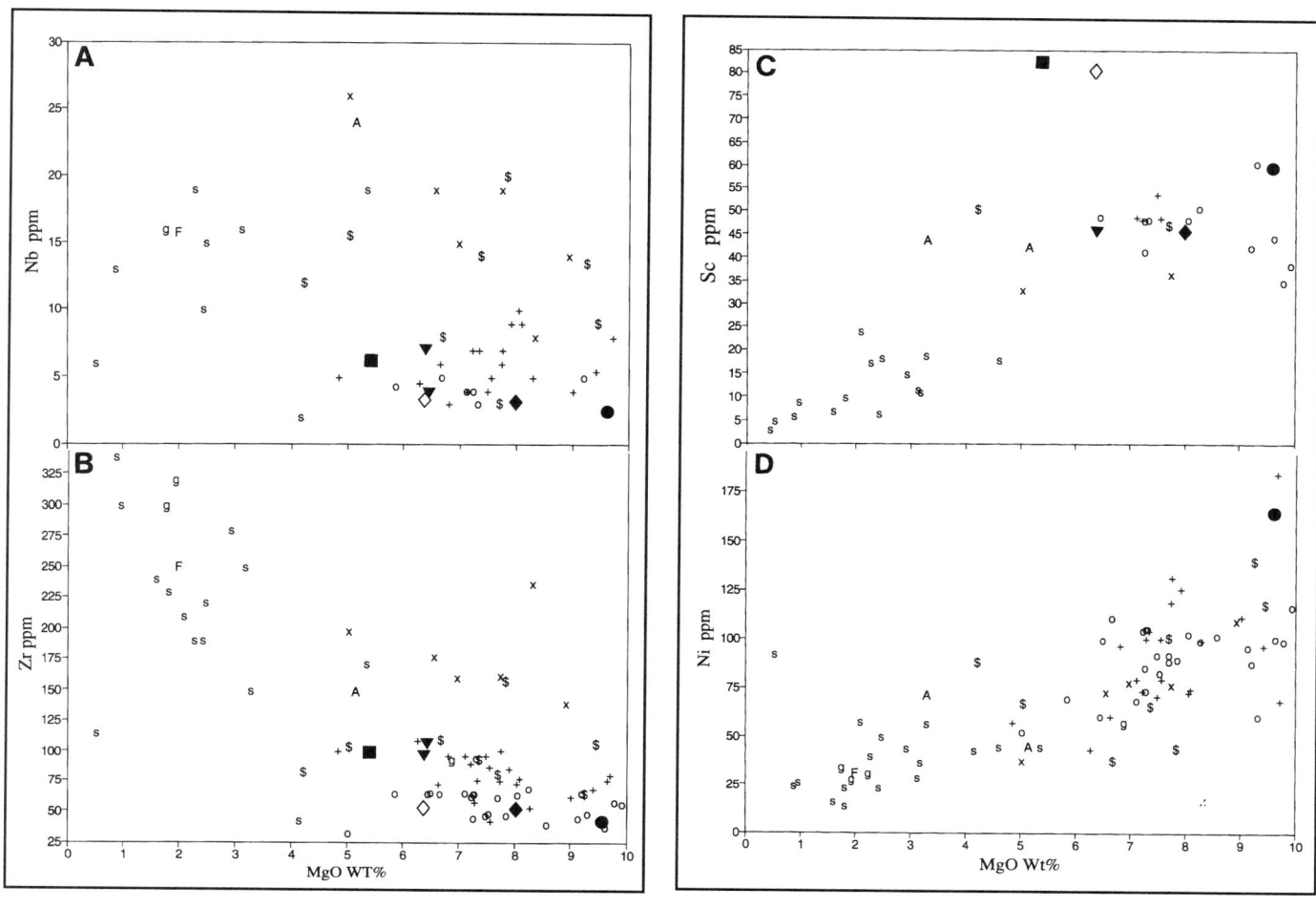

Figure 4. Same legend as Figure 3. Trace elements not normalized. A: Nb (ppm), B: Zr, C: Sc, and D: Ni, all vs. MgO wt%. Some of the sediment analyses plot offscale on the Zr vs. MgO diagram.

ating certain types of geochemical anomalies. The modeling confirms that crustal contamination has a significant effect on the LILE (Ba and Th), Zr, the light REE, and SiO_2, but little or no effect on other high field strength cations (HFSC) like Nb, Y, Ti, and P. This is illustrated in the ratio plots (Fig. 6) and on the spidergrams (Fig. 7B), and is a straightforward consequence of the fact that crustal contaminants have low abundances of HFSC and high abundances of LILE, Zr, light REE, and SiO_2.

The modeling suggests that 20%–30% AFC can reproduce most of the spread in Th/P, La/Yb, Zr/Y, and Ba/P seen in the Maquereau lavas (Figs. 6 and 7). Although these models are nonunique, we consider this to be an adequate degree of accuracy in view of the uncertainties involved, recognizing that the actual values of the degree of fractionation and R-factor may dif-

fer somewhat or fluctuate locally. For example, some of the Maquereau lavas have very high Ba/P ratios, in excess of the model results. This could be interpreted in many ways: it could signify locally higher R-ratios, a contaminant with a higher Ba/P, a parental magma with lower Ba abundances, diffusive transfers of LILE into the magma, and so on. It is not possible to choose among these hypotheses for the Maquereau lavas because of the uncertainties associated with their poor degree of preservation.

Generally speaking, closed-system fractionation cannot efficiently fractionate ratios like La/Yb or Zr/Y, so fractionation series have subhorizontal arrays when these ratios are plotted against an incompatible element (Fig. 6, A to C), or plot as points on ratio/ratio diagrams (Fig. 6, D and E). As can be seen from these figures, addition of a Zr-La–rich contaminant can cause increases in La/Yb and Zr/Y that mimic the geochemical

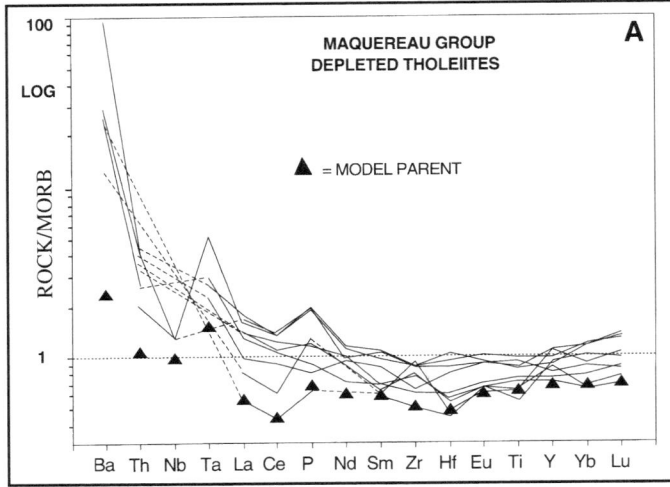

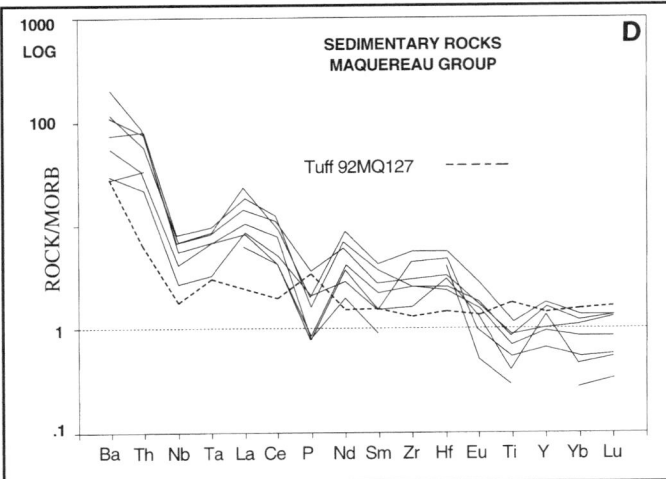

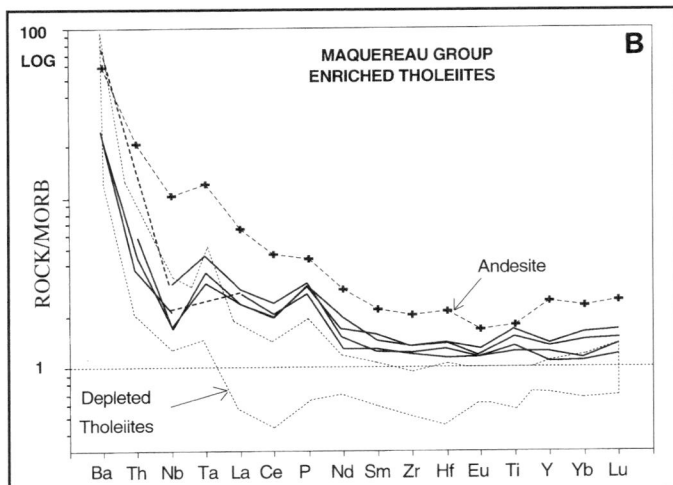

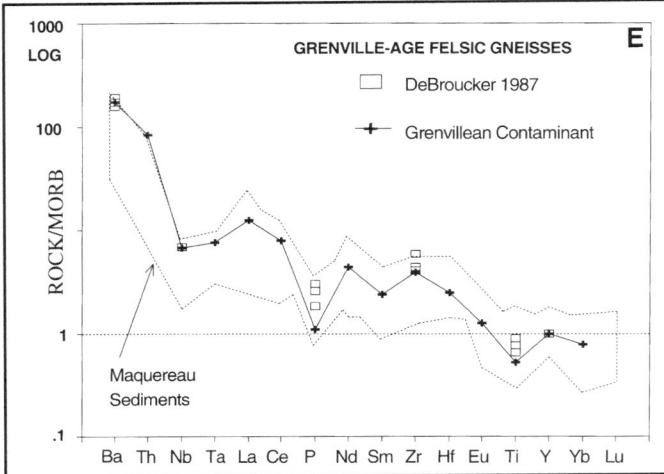

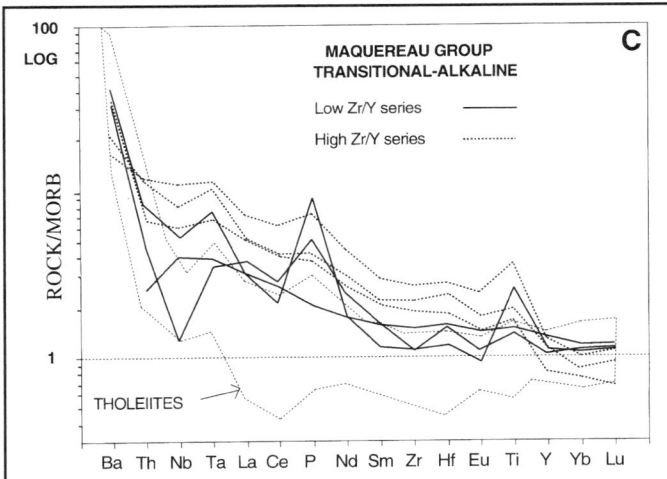

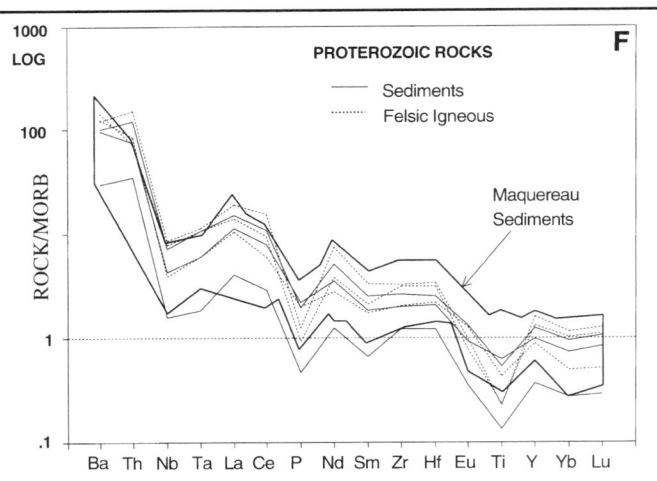

Figure 5. Mid-ocean ridge basalt–normalized extended trace element plots (normalizing factors from Sun and McDonough, 1989) for (A) depleted tholeiites, (B) enriched tholeiites and ferro-andesites, (C) low Zr/Y and High Zr/Y transitional alkaline lavas, and (D) Maquereau Group sedimentary rocks. Tuff is sample 92MQ127A. E: Felsic gneisses from the gneissic sliver exposed along the fault that bounds the Maquereau Group, data from DeBroucker (1987). F: Proterozoic sedimentary rocks and felsic igneous averages of Grenvillean sandstone, shale, graywacke, trondjhemite, rhyolite, and granitoids from Condie (1993).

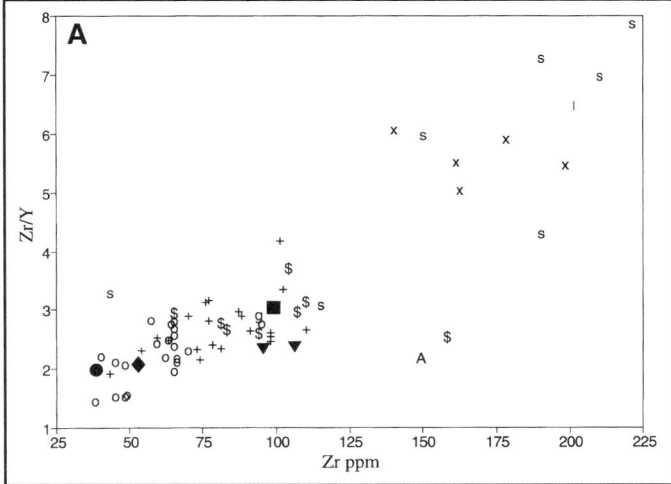

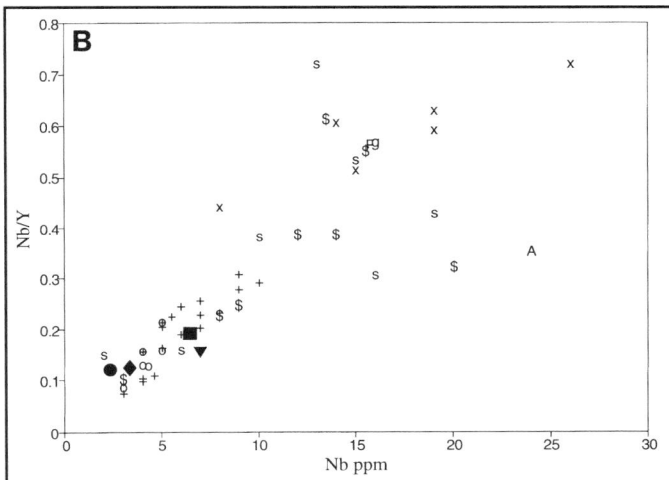

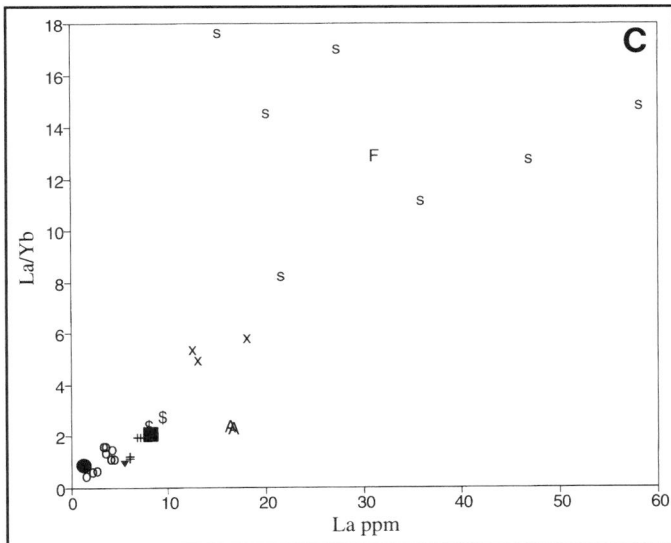

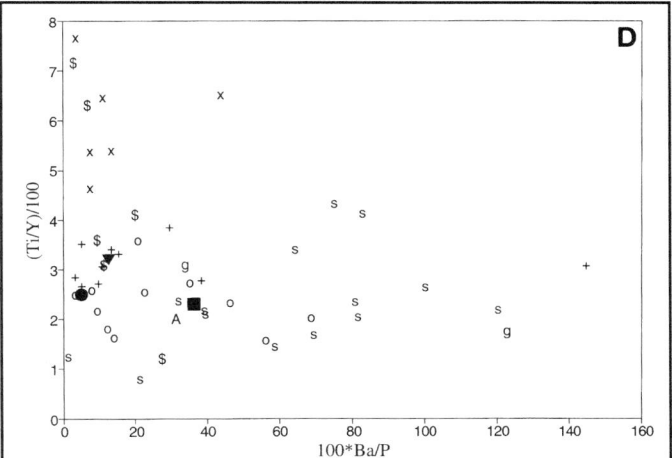

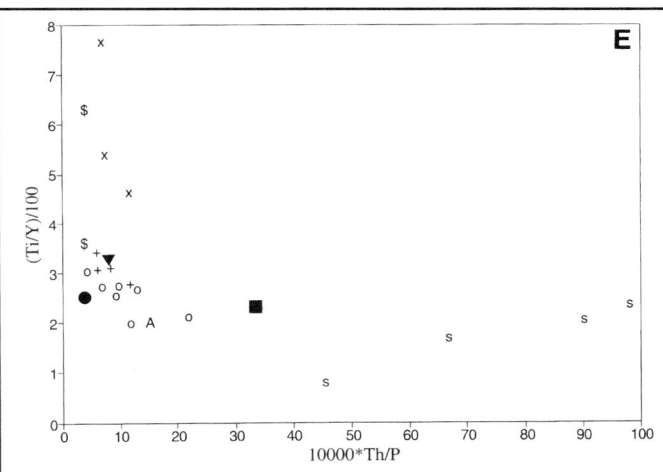

Figure 6. Same legend as in Figure 3. On the scale of A and B, troctolitic and gabbroic closed-system residua are indistinguishable. On the scale of C to E, the closed-system residual melts are indistinguishable from the parent compositions. Analyses of sediments and gneisses plot offscale to the right in A and E. A: Zr/Y vs. Zr. B: Nb/Y vs. Nb. C: La/Yb vs. La. D: (Ti/Y)/100 vs. 100 Ba/P. E: (Ti/Y)/100 vs. 10000(Th/P).

TABLE 2. AVERAGES OF DIFFERENT ROCK TYPES OF MAQUEREAU GROUP AND MODEL PARENTS*

Sample	THOL ENR	N	THOL DEP	N	ALK LoZrY	N	ALK HiZrY	N	AND	N	ALL SEDS	N
(wt%)												
SiO$_2$	50.4	21	52.1	26	50.1	8	49.8	6	52.7	2	64.4	21
TiO$_2$	1.58	21	1.05	26	2.06	8	2.83	6	2.26	2	1.03	21
Al$_2$O$_3$	14.4	21	14.5	26	15.7	8	14.6	6	13.2	2	16.2	21
FeO*	14.2	21	12.3	26	14.1	8	13.0	6	17.6	2	7.70	21
MnO	0.22	21	0.21	25	0.27	8	0.30	6	0.22	2	0.10	21
MgO	7.68	21	7.73	26	7.18	8	7.25	6	4.21	2	3.09	21
CaO	8.31	21	9.18	26	5.62	8	6.87	6	4.53	2	2.01	21
Na$_2$O	2.56	21	2.68	26	3.88	8	4.58	6	4.21	2	3.29	21
K$_2$O	0.56	21	0.15	26	0.84	8	0.46	6	0.73	2	2.09	21
P$_2$O$_5$	0.18	21	0.09	26	0.33	8	0.30	6	0.32	2	0.16	21
(ppm)												
Ba	219	10	158	13	205	6	277	6	374	2	563	20
Rb	14	15	7	20	25	6	10	6	4	2	43	10
Sr	213	21	201	25	149	8	198	6	54	2	112	20
Cr	253	21	263	26	218	8	187	6	100	2	139	12
Ni	93	21	90	25	83	8	66	6	58	2	43	20
Cu	91	11	104	19	140	4	58	4	112	2	35	20
Zn	113	21	100	26	127	7	104	6	140	2	95	19
Pb	10	10	10	15	8	3	13	3	13	2	12	10
V	631	11	567	19	658	4	386	4	466	2	256	18
Nb	6	18	4	6	12	8	17	6	24	1	11	10
Y	30	21	26	24	35	8	28	6	68	1	26	19
Zr	81	21	58	24	100	8	179	6	149	1	209	19
La	6.43	4	3.19	11	8.34	3	14.5	3	16.4	2	28.8	8
Ce	15.7	4	7.88	11	18.9	3	35.8	3	34.5	2	53.0	8
Nd	11.8	4	7.20	9	14.4	3	24.7	3	20.9	2	32.5	8
Sm	3.66	4	2.12	11	3.78	3	6.34	3	5.78	2	6.02	8
Eu	1.23	4	0.80	11	1.17	3	1.87	3	1.70	2	1.51	8
Yb	4.07	4	2.79	11	3.41	3	2.66	3	7.00	2	2.73	8
Lu	0.64	4	0.46	11	0.52	3	0.41	3	1.12	2	0.44	8
Sc	50.0	4	42.3	11	49.9	3	34.8	2	43.0	2	14.2	17
Hf	2.66	4	1.34	11	2.87	3	4.71	3	4.35	2	6.94	8
Ta	0.50	3	0.42	5	0.66	3	1.26	3	1.58	2	0.87	7
Th	0.67	4	0.42	7	0.62	3	1.20	3	2.52	2	5.99	8

variation (depleted to enriched) of Maquereau tholeiites. However, coupled fractionation–crustal contamination cannot be responsible for generation of the enriched tholeiites from depleted tholeiite parents, because the enriched tholeiites have much higher concentrations of Ti and P than do the depleted tholeiites (Fig. 3, C and D). Because potential crustal contaminants are impoverished in Ti and P, crustal contamination cannot lead to large increases in the concentrations of these elements. Similarly, the transitional-alkaline lavas cannot just be a crustally contaminated facies of the tholeiitic lavas, and must therefore represent a distinct mantle melt.

Because the Maquereau sandstones and Grenvillean felsic gneisses have low Nb-Ta-contents, and high Ba-Th-La-contents (Fig. 5, C and D), AFC processes will result in progressively deeper negative Nb-Ta anomalies (Fig. 7C). Thus it is possible that the Maquereau tholeiites developed

their negative Nb anomalies as a consequence of crustal contamination (cf. Dupuy and Dostal, 1984; Thompson et al., 1984; Arndt and Christensen, 1992; Legault et al., 1994). The implication is that this signature would not indicate an arc environment for these lavas.

We conclude that the intrasuite variations among the Maquereau lavas are due to a combination of intermediate-pressure (lower crustal) fractional crystallization of an olivine gabbro assemblage, coupled with assimilation of crustal rocks. Intrasuite chemical variablity can be explained satisfactorily by about 20%–30% fractionation coupled with moderate assimilation of Grenvillean felsic gneiss or Maquereau Group sandstones derived from such gneiss. The intersuite variations cannot be explained in this way, however, and must either be inherited from the source, or be a function of mantle melting processes.

TABLE 2. AVERAGES OF DIFFERENT ROCK TYPES OF MAQUEREAU GROUP AND MODEL PARENTS* (continued - page 2)

Sample	MAF SEDS	N	FELS SEDS	N	FELS GREN	N	AV PROT	DEP PARENT	ENR PARENT	ALK PARENT
(wt%)										
SiO_2	59.1	9	68.4	12	68.2	3	73.7	49.2	49.0	48.0
TiO_2	1.31	9	0.82	12	0.98	3	0.46	0.80	1.40	2.10
Al_2O_3	16.6	9	15.8	12	15.7	3	13.4	15.1	14.5	14.1
FeO*	10.5	9	5.56	12	5.89	3	3.74	11.8	11.9	12.0
MnO	0.13	9	0.08	12	0.05	3		0.16	0.24	0.18
MgO	4.98	9	1.68	12	1.96	3	1.26	9.60	9.50	9.40
CaO	2.73	9	1.48	12	0.73	3	1.59	10.0	9.94	9.00
Na_2O	3.28	9	3.31	12	2.72	3	2.48	3.03	3.00	4.00
K_2O	1.21	9	2.75	12	3.56	3	3.26	0.06	0.20	0.83
P_2O_5	0.20	9	0.12	12	0.16	3	0.10	0.08	0.16	0.24
(ppm)										
Ba	524	8	589	12	1,096	3	644	15	25	106
Rb	31	4	51	6	63	1	112	3	3	4
Sr	105	9	118	11	153	3	185	77	200	76
Cr	137	6	141	6	24	1	47	483	479	460
Ni	49	9	37	11	31	3	24	163	185	118
Cu	45	8	28	11	35	3				
Zn	111	8	84	11						
Pb	12	5	13	5						
V	401	8	141	10	79	3	65			
Nb	10	5	13	5	16	1	13	2.3	4	13
Y	28	9	24	10	28	1	30	19	28	25
Zr	183	9	232	10	238	3	176	38	74	140
La	32.0	2	27.7	6			30.9	1.43	5.00	7.90
Ce	41.9	2	56.7	6			65.7	3.31	13.5	16.0
Nd	37.6	2	30.8	6			29.1	4.50	9.42	13.0
Sm	7.63	2	5.49	6			5.36	1.57	2.63	3.08
Eu	2.05	2	1.33	5			0.95	0.62	1.02	0.94
Yb	4.31	2	2.20	6			2.33	2.09	3.05	2.30
Lu	0.67	2	0.37	6			0.38	0.32	0.51	0.30
Sc	21.1	5	11.0	11			11.7	60.0	49.0	37.0
Hf	7.48	2	6.76	6			4.98	1.20	2.05	3.70
Ta	0.74	2	0.92	5			1.02	0.30	0.30	0.90
Th	3.94	2	6.68	6			10.7	0.13	0.26	0.80

*N = number of analyses per average. Analyses below the detection limit were not included, so that some of the averages are slightly biased toward higher abundances. Averages include data from DeBroucker (1987). THOL ENR = enriched tholeiite, THOL DEP = depleted tholeiite, ALK LoZrY and Hi ZrY = transitional alkaline low Zr/Y and high Zr/Y suites, respectively. AND = andesite. All SEDS = average of all Maquereau sedimentary rocks, while MAF and FELS are the average mafic and felsic sedimentary rocks (separated at 3% MgO). FELS GREN = average of three felsic gneisses from DeBroucker (1987), AV PROT = average sediment, felsic lava, and felsic plutonic rocks from the Proterozoic rocks of the Grenville Province in Condie (1993). PARENTS are the three different parental magmas derived graphically from the variation diagrams.

Tectonic environment

The FeO-TiO_2 enrichment trend shown by Maquereau lavas implies a tholeiitic affinity (Fig. 2). Although tholeiitic lavas occur in arc environments, associations of tholeiitic and alkaline lavas and ferro-andesites are most common in continental flood-basalt or rifted margin environments. Continental basalts are notoriously difficult to classify using paleotectonic environment diagrams (e.g., Duncan, 1987; Marsh, 1987; Wang and Glover, 1992). The trace-element discriminants of Pearce and Cann (1973), Pearce and Norry (1979), Meschede (1986), and Wood (1980) (shown in Bédard and Wilson, 1994) classify rocks of the alkaline suites as "within-plate" or "alkaline," and rocks of the tholeiitic suites as ocean floor basalt.

CONCLUSIONS

Maquereau Group lavas are dominantly subalkaline tholeiitic basalts, and subordinate transitional-alkaline basalts and ferro-

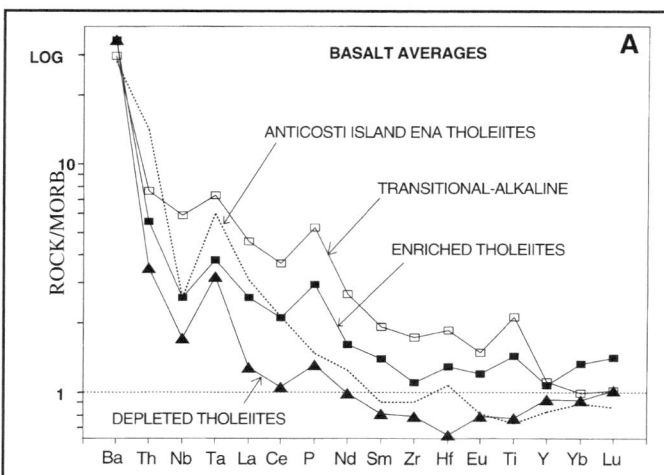

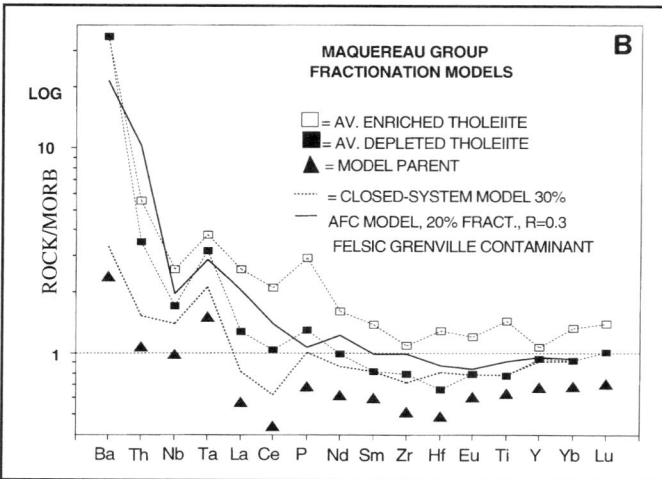

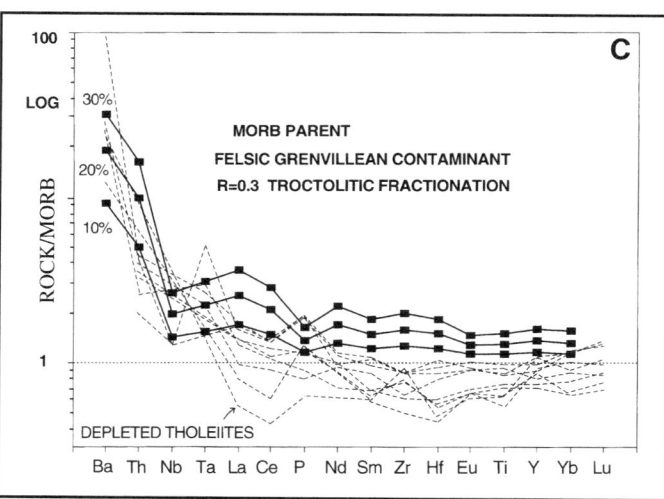

Figure 7. Mid-ocean ridge basalt (MORB) normalized averages and fractionation models (conventions as in Fig. 5). A: Average values for the different Maquereau lava suites. Anticosti is a Mesozoic East North American quartz-normative continental tholeiite from Bédard (1992). B: Modeling results from the CHAOS-FRACT program of Nielsen (1988, 1991) and equations of DePaolo (1981), using the Grenvillean contaminant with R = 0.3, and the partition coefficients in Bédard (1994). Note that a closed-system fractionation model using the depleted tholeiite model parent successfully reproduces the average depleted tholeiite for elements more compatible than Sm, but that the deviations are serious for the more incompatible elements. 20% AFC yields a reasonable fit for the entire profile. C: Theoretical model showing predicted consequences of fractionating a MORB parent with simultaneous contamination by Grenvillean felsic gneiss. Same conventions as Figure 7B. Note the progressive development of a negative Nb-Ta anomaly in the fractionated basalt.

andesites. The tholeiites exhibit a classic Fe-Ti–enrichment trend. Trace- and major-element discriminants imply a normal MORB-like chemistry for the most depleted tholeiites. Tholeiitic lavas are variably affected by coupled fractionation-crustal contamination, and resemble continental flood basalts. Intrasuite geochemical variations are adequately modeled by 20%–30% fractionation coupled with assimilation of Maquereau sedimentary rocks or Grenvillean felsic gneiss. Intersuite variations are not the result of fractional crystallization or crustal contamination, and reflect either variations in mantle source chemistry or melting processes. The geochemical data and geologic associations suggest that the Maquereau Group is not of arc affinity, but represents a transition from rifted continental margin to sea-floor–spreading environments.

ACKNOWLEDGMENTS

Field work in 1983 and 1984, and analyses by C. Wilson, were financed by the Ministère des Ressources du Québec (MRQ), and by National Science and Engineering Research Council (N.S.E.R.C.) grants to J. Ludden (Université de Montréal). Samples 92MQ100–128 were collected by G. Camiré, who also provided comments. K. Oravec helped to collect samples 93MQ50–58. M. Laflèche provided invaluable assistance with the modeling programs and comments. M. Malo and two anonymous reviewers provided many useful suggestions. Rocks and standards were analyzed by J.-P. Ricqbourg, J. Ludden, R. Gosselin, M. Greendale, A. Hébert, and G. Gauthier. Y. Houde assisted with drafting. Some figures were produced with NEW-PET by Daryl Keen (Memorial University of Newfoundland). This is MRQ contribution number 95–5110–01 and Geological Survey of Canada contribution number 55994.

REFERENCES CITED

Arndt, N. T., and Christensen, U., 1992, The role of lithospheric mantle in continental flood volcanism: Thermal and geochemical constraints: Journal of Geophysical Research, v. 97, p. 10967–10981.

Bédard, J. H., 1986, Les suites magmatiques Paléozoïques de la Gaspésie: Ministère de L'Énergie et des Ressources du Québec, ET84-09, 111 p.

Bédard, J. H., 1992, Jurassic quartz-normative tholeiite dikes from Anticosti Island, Québec, *in* Puffer, J. H., and Ragland, P. C., eds, Eastern North American Mesozoic magmatism: Geological Society of America Special Paper 268, p. 161–167.

Bédard, J. H., 1994, A procedure for calculating the equilibrium distribution of trace elements among the minerals of cumulate rocks, and the concentration of trace elements in the coexisting liquids: Chemical Geology, v. 118, p. 143–153.

Bédard, J. H., and Wilson, C., 1994, Maquereau Group lavas, southern Gaspésie, Quebec Appalachians, *in* Current research: Geological Survey of Canada Paper 1994-D, p. 143–154.

Bender, J. F., Hodges, F. N., and Bence, A. E., 1978, Petrogenesis of basalts from the project FAMOUS area: Experimental study from 0 to 15 kbars: Earth and Planetary Science Letters, v. 41, p. 277–302.

Bernstein, S., 1994, High-pressure fractionation in rift-related basaltic magmatism: Faeroe plateau basalts: Geology, v. 22, p. 815–818.

Camiré, G. E., LaFlèche, M. R., and Jenner, G. A., 1995, Geochemistry of pre-Taconian mafic volcanism in the Humber Zone of the northern Appalachians: Chemical Geology, v. 119, p. 55–77.

Carlson, R. W., 1991, Physical and chemical evidence on the cause and source characteristics of flood basalt volcanism: Australian Journal of Earth Sciences, v. 38, p. 525–544.

Caron, A., 1984, Géologie de la région de Chandler, Gaspésie: Ministère de L'Énergie et des Ressources du Québec, DP86–07, 25 p., scale 1:20,000.

Cohen, L. H., Ito, K., and Kennedy, G. C., 1967, Melting and phase relations in an anhydrous basalt to 40 kilobars: American Journal of Science, v. 265, p. 475–518.

Coish, R. A., Fleming, F. S., Larsen, M., Poyner, R., and Seiberg, J., 1985, Early rift history of the proto-Atlantic ocean: Geochemical evidence from metavolcanic rocks in Vermont: American Journal of Science, v. 285, p. 351–378.

Condie, K. C., 1993, Chemical composition and evolution of the upper continental crust: Contrasting results from surface samples and shales: Chemical Geology, v. 104, p. 1–37.

Cousineau, P., 1990, Le Groupe de Caldwell et le domaine océanique entre Saint-Joseph-de-Beauce et Sainte-Sabine: Ministère de L'Énergie et des Ressources du Québec, MM87–02, 165 p.

Cox, K. G., 1980, A model for flood basalt vulcanism: Journal of Petrology, v. 21, p. 629–650.

DeBroucker, G., 1987, Stratigraphie, pétrographie et structure de la boutonnière de Maquereau-Mictaw (Région de Port Daniel, Gaspésie): Ministère de L'Énergie et des Ressources du Québec, MM86-03, 160 p.

DePaolo, D. J., 1981, Trace element and isotopic effects of combined wall rock assimilation and fractional crystallization: Earth and Planetary Science Letters, v. 53, p. 189–202.

Duncan, A. R., 1987, The Karoo Igneous Province—A problem area for inferring tectonic setting from basalt geochemistry: Journal of Volcanology and Geothermal Research, v. 32, p. 13–34.

Dupuy, C., and Dostal, J., 1984, Trace element geochemistry of some continental tholeiites: Earth and Planetary Science Letters, v. 67, p. 61–69.

Gallagher, K., and Hawkesworth, C., 1992, Dehydration melting and the generation of continental flood basalts: Nature, v. 358, p. 57–59.

Hall, R. P., Hughes, D. J., and Friend, C. R. L., 1985, Geochemical evolution and unusual pyroxene chemistry of the MD tholeiite dyke swarm from the Archaean Craton of southern west Greenland: Journal of Petrology, v. 26, p. 253–282.

Hooper, P. R., and Hawkesworth, C. J., 1993, Isotopic and geochemical constraints on the origin and evolution of the Columbia River basalt: Journal of Petrology, v. 34, p. 1203–1246.

Huppert, H. E., and Sparks, R. S. J., 1985, Cooling and contamination of mafic and ultramafic magmas during ascent through continental crust: Earth and Planetary Science Letters, v. 74, p. 371–386.

Jenner, G. A., and Swinden, H. S., 1993, The Pipestone Pond Complex, central Newfoundland: Complex magmatism in an eastern Dunnage Zone ophiolite: Canadian Journal of Earth Sciences, v. 30, p. 434–448.

Kirkwood, D., and Malo, M., 1993, Across-strike geometry of the Grand Pabos Fault Zone: Evidence for Devonian dextral transpression in the Quebec Appalachians: Canadian Journal of Earth Sciences, v. 30, p. 1363–1373.

Kushiro, I., 1960, Si-Al relation in clinopyroxenes from igneous rocks: American Journal of Sciences, v. 258, p. 548–554.

LaFlèche, M. R., Schrijver, K., and Tremblay, A., 1993, Geochemistry, origin, and provenance of Upper Proterozoic to Upper Cambrian alkaline to transitional basaltic rocks in and contiguous to a sector of the Appalachian Humber Zone, Canada: American Journal of Science, v. 293, p. 980–1009.

Legault, F., Francis, D., Hynes, A., and Budkewitsch, P., 1994, Proterozoic continental volcanism in the Belcher Islands: Implications for the evolution of the Circum Ungava Fold Belt: Canadian Journal of Earth Sciences, v. 31, p. 1536–1549.

Logan, W. E., 1846, Sections on Chaleur Bay and coast of Gaspe, *in* Progress report for 1844: Ottawa, Geological Survey of Canada, p. 78–110.

Malo, M., Kirkwood, D., DeBroucker, G., and St. Julien, P., 1992, A reevaluation of the position of the Baie Verte–Brompton Line in the Quebec Appalachians: The influence of Middle Devonian strike-slip faulting in Gaspé Peninsula: Canadian Journal of Earth Sciences, v. 29, p. 1265–1273.

Marsh, J. S., 1987, Basalt geochemistry and tectonic discrimination within continental flood basalt provinces: Journal of Volcanology and Geothermal Research, v. 32, p. 35–49.

Meschede, M., 1986, A method of discriminating between different types of mid-ocean ridge basalts and continental tholeiites with the Nb-Zr-Y diagram: Chemical Geology, v. 56, p. 207–218.

Miyashiro, A., 1973, The Troodos ophiolitic complex was probably formed in an island arc: Earth and Planetary Science Letters, v. 19, p. 218–224.

Nielsen, R. L., 1988, A model for the simulation of combined major and trace element liquid lines of descent: Geochimica et Cosmochimica Acta, v. 52, p. 27–38.

Nielsen, R. L., 1991, CHAOS 5 (FORTRAN) program to model petrologic processes: Corvallis, Oregon State University, College of Oceanography.

Pearce, J. A., and Cann, J. R., 1973, Tectonic setting of basic volcanic rocks determined using trace element analyses: Earth and Planetary Science letters, v. 19, p. 290–300.

Pearce, J. A., and Norry, M. J., 1979, Petrogenetic implications of Ti, Zr, Y, and Nb variations in volcanic rocks: Contributions to Mineralogy and Petrology, v. 69, p. 33–47.

Ringele, H., 1982, La déformation taconienne en Gaspésie du Sud: Le Groupe de Maquereau et son encaissant [M.S. thesis]: Montréal, Québec, Université de Montréal, 68 p.

Schwab, F. L., 1994, Provenance and plate tectonic indexing of lower Paleozoic sandstones, Quebec and Maine: American Journal of Science, v. 294, p. 401–427.

Sparks, R. S. J., 1986, The role of crustal contamination in magma evolution through geologic time: Earth and Planetary Science Letters, v. 78, p. 211–223.

St. Julien, P., and Hubert, C., 1975, Evolution of the Taconic Orogen in the Québec Appalachians: American Journal of Science, v. 275A, p. 337–362.

Stolper, E., 1980, A phase diagram for mid-ocean ridge basalt: Preliminary results and implications for petrogenesis: Contributions to Mineralogy and Petrology, v. 74, p. 13–27.

Sun, S.-S., and McDonough, W. F., 1989, Chemical and isotopic systematics of oceanic basalts: Implications for mantle compositions and processes, *in* Saunders, A. D., and Norry, M. J., eds., Magmatism in the ocean basins: Geological Society of London Special Publication no. 42, p. 313–345.

Takahashi, E., and Kushiro, I., 1983, Melting of a dry peridotite at high pressures and basalt magma genesis: American Mineralogist, v. 68, p. 859–879.

Thompson, R. N., 1972, Primary basalts and magma genesis. I. Skye, north-west Scotland: Contributions to Mineralogy and Petrology, v. 45, p. 317–341.

Thompson, R. N., Morrison, M. A., Hendry, G. L., and Parry, S. A., 1984, An assessment of the relative roles of crust and mantle in magma genesis: An elemental approach: Royal Society of London Philosophical Transactions, ser. A, v. 310, p. 549–590.

Tremblay, A., and Pinet, N., 1994, Distribution and characteristics of Taconian and Acadian deformation, southern Quebec Appalachians: Geological

Society of America Bulletin, v. 106, p. 1172–1181.

Vermette, D. R., Hébert, R., and Bergeron, M., 1993, Petrological and geochemical characteristics related to early rifting of Iapetus Ocean, Quebec Appalachians: American Journal of Science, v. 293, p. 81–110.

Walker, K. R., Ware, N. G., and Lovering, J. F., 1973, Compositional variations in the pyroxenes of the differentiated palisades sill, New Jersey: Geological Society of America Bulletin, v. 84, p. 89–110.

Wang, P., and Glover, L., III., 1992, A tectonics test of the most commonly used geochemical discriminant diagrams and patterns: Earth Science Reviews, v. 33, p. 111–131.

White, R. S., 1992, Crustal structure and magmatism of North Atlantic continental margins: Geological Society of London Journal, v. 149, p. 841–854.

Williams, H., 1979, The Appalachian orogen in Canada: Canadian Journal of Earth Sciences, v. 16, p. 792–807.

Williams, H., and St-Julien, P., 1982, The Baie-Verte–Brompton Line: Early Paleozoic continent ocean interface in the Canadian Appalachians, *in* St-Julien, P., and Béland, J., eds., Major structural zones and faults of the northern Appalachians: Geological Association of Canada Special Paper 24, p. 177–208.

Wood, D. A., 1980, The application of a Th-Hf-Ta diagram to problems of tectonomagmatic classification, and to establishing the nature of crustal contamination of basaltic lavas of the British Tertiary volcanic province: Earth and Planetary Science Letters, v. 50, p. 11–30.

MANUSCRIPT ACCEPTED BY THE SOCIETY JULY 2, 1996

Geological Society of America
Memoir 191
1997

Late Devonian mafic-felsic magmatism in the Meguma Zone, Nova Scotia

D. Barrie Clarke
Department of Earth Sciences, Dalhousie University, Halifax, Nova Scotia B3H 3J5, Canada
Michael A. MacDonald
Nova Scotia Department of Natural Resources, P.O. Box 698, Halifax, Nova Scotia B3J 2T9, Canada
Marcus C. Tate*
Department of Earth Sciences, Dalhousie University, Halifax, Nova Scotia B3H 3J5, Canada

ABSTRACT

The Meguma Zone of southern Nova Scotia docked with North America in the mid-Late Devonian. Associated magmatic activity involved small calc-alkaline lamprophyric mafic bodies and large peraluminous granitoid plutons.

The mafic bodies include ten dikes and one sheet cutting the Meguma Group metasedimentary rocks, two plugs in the Liscomb Complex, and four synplutonic bodies in some of the smaller granitoid plutons. They are generally coarse-grained hornblende-biotite gabbronorites, diorites, and spessartites, and all have highly fractionated rare earth element patterns and negligible Eu/Eu* anomalies.

The granitoid plutons fall into two spatial-chemical-genetic types:

1. The central plutons, including the South Mountain Batholith, are ca. 372 Ma, late-tectonic to posttectonic, predominantly unfoliated, emplaced into low-grade metamorphic host rocks, generally not spatially associated with mafic intrusions, and exclusively peraluminous with Sn-W-Mo-U greisen- and vein-dominated mineral deposits;

2. The peripheral plutons, at the northeastern and southwestern extremities of the Meguma Zone, may be slightly older (376 Ma); they are late-tectonic, moderately foliated, emplaced into higher grade metamorphic host rocks, invariably spatially associated with Late Devonian mafic intrusions, and mostly peraluminous with only limited Be-pegmatite mineralization. The central plutons are apparently entirely crustally derived (sub-Meguma Group source rocks and Meguma Group contamination), and probably owe their origin to crustal thickening associated with the collision of the Meguma terrane against the Avalon terrane. The peripheral plutons are of mixed derivation (sub-Meguma Group source rocks and mantle-derived mafic magmas), and probably owe their origin to the lower to mid-crustal intrusion of subduction-related mafic magmas prior to the final emplacement of the Meguma terrane.

INTRODUCTION

The Meguma Zone of Nova Scotia (Keppie, 1985; Williams and Hatcher, 1983) is the most outboard of the northern Appalachian terranes, and hosts a large number of Late Devonian, late syntectonic to posttectonic, peraluminous granitoid intrusions. This chapter is the first comprehensive review of the significant advances in understanding these granitoids since the compilation of Clarke and Muecke (1985), and it synthesizes all relevant information into a comprehensive model for their origin, evolution, and tectonic setting. This new model proposes thermal and material involvement of mantle-derived magmas to generate at least some of the predominantly crustally derived peraluminous granitoids.

*Present address: School of Earth Sciences, Macquarie University, Sydney, N. S.W. 2109, Australia.

Clarke, D. B., MacDonald, M. A., and Tate, M. C., 1997, Late Devonian mafic-felsic magmatism in the Meguma Zone, Nova Scotia, *in* Sinha, A. K., Whalen, J. B., and Hogan, J. P., eds., The Nature of Magmatism in the Appalachian Orogen: Boulder, Colorado, Geological Society of America Memoir 191.

In this chapter, we consider only the subaerially exposed part of the Meguma Zone (not the submarine part) and its vertical extension into the lower crust and upper mantle. We also consider essentially those tectonic and magmatic events that occurred ca. 375 ± 10 Ma. Of necessity, this review draws heavily on our understanding of the South Mountain Batholith (SMB) because it is the largest, most diverse, and most economically important of the intrusions; however, critical components of the new petrogenetic and tectonic model come from smaller granitic plutons and the contemporary small-volume mafic intrusions (plugs, sills, dikes). This chapter first describes the mafic and felsic rocks separately, following a classical development from field-based observations, to geochronology, petrology, geochemistry, and economic geology. Each topic focuses mainly on data relevant to developing the petrogenetic and tectonic synthesis in the discussion.

GENERAL REGIONAL GEOLOGY OF THE MEGUMA ZONE

The Cobequid-Chedabucto fault defines the northern boundary of the Meguma Zone (Fig. 1), and separates it from the adjacent Avalon Zone. The continental shelf margin defines its extent to the southwest, south, and east. Two distinct packages of rock dominate the onshore bedrock geology of the Meguma Zone: metawackes and metapelites of the Cambrian-Ordovician Meguma Group, and peraluminous granitoid rocks of Late Devonian age. Relatively minor volcanic and sedimentary units lie temporally between and over these two main packages. The Meguma Group represents a turbidite fan deposited on the continental margin of Gondwana (Schenk, 1991). The entire sequence, including the overlying Silurian and Early Devonian volcanic and sedimentary rocks (White Rock to Torbrook formations), was deformed and metamorphosed in the Acadian orogeny (Keppie and Dallmeyer, 1987; Muecke et al., 1988).

The youngest rocks cut by plutons of peraluminous granite belong to the Torbrook Formation of Emsian age (Boucot, 1960). The oldest sedimentary rocks disconformably overlying the granites belong to the Horton Group of late Famennian age (Martel et al., 1993). Thus, emplacement and unroofing are geologically constrained between about 386 and 363 Ma (absolute ages after Harland et al., 1990). The estimated depth of emplacement of the granites of 10–12 km, and the implied rate of uplift in the Meguma Zone is comparable to that occurring today for some exposed peraluminous granites in the High Himalayas (France-Lanord and LeFort, 1988).

The granitoid plutons range in composition from tonalite to leucogranite, although most small bodies show little internal variation. Most of the central plutons (Fig. 1) are massive and undeformed; however, many show locally well developed magmatic foliation, and some of the peripheral plutons in southwestern and eastern Nova Scotia appear to preserve evidence of syntectonic deformation. The small mafic igneous bodies (Fig. 1) are massive and undeformed.

GEOCHRONOLOGY

Over the past three decades or so, geochronological studies have focused on the Meguma Group host rocks, the granitoid rocks, and the granite-related mineral deposits (both intra-batholithic and peribatholithic). Recent Nd model ages from the Liscomb gneisses (Clarke et al., 1993a) and granulite xenoliths from the Tangier dike (Eberz et al., 1991) have demanded a new interpretation for the stratigraphy of the Meguma Zone, and new geochronological data from the mafic intrusions now require a new consideration of a genetic relationship between felsic and mafic magmatism in the Meguma Zone. In this section we focus on the ages of the main lithological groups in the Meguma Zone.

Table 1 presents key radiometric age determinations for host rocks, mafic intrusions, and felsic intrusions in the Meguma Zone. In summary, it shows the following.

1. The Meguma Group has a depositional age of ca. 500 Ma, metamorphic age of 405–390 Ma, and a T_{CHUR} Nd model age of 1358 ± 104 Ma (Clarke and Halliday, 1985).

2. The deeper-seated rocks (Liscomb gneisses and Tangier xenoliths) have T_{CHUR} Nd model ages considerably younger than those of the Meguma Group, and similar to those in the Avalon Zone (Eberz et al., 1991; Clarke et al., 1993a).

3. The field relations in the Port Mouton pluton and Shelburne pluton demand synplutonic coexistence of mafic and felsic magmatism, and geochronological data from the Barrington Passage pluton, Mersey Point picrite, Liscomb Complex, and Weekend dikes show that mafic magmas are at least temporal, if not precisely spatial, equivalents of the main felsic magmatism.

4. The best estimates for the mafic intrusion age are 376 Ma (U-Pb) or 385–370 Ma ($^{40}Ar/^{39}Ar$).

5. The best estimates for the granite intrusion ages are 372 ± 3 Ma for the central plutons and 378 ± 3 Ma for the peripheral plutons.

6. The agreement, within analytical error, between the age determinations from several isotopic systems suggests rapid cooling through the respective blocking temperatures, and probably means rapid uplift and unroofing of the granites as indicated by the overlying Late Devonian–Early Carboniferous sediments.

7. The large number of radiometric ages <370 Ma (ca. 360–250 Ma; Kontak and Cormier, 1991) involves partial to complete resetting of Rb-Sr isochrons (SMB, East Kemptville, Long Lake) and resetting of the Ar-Ar geochronometer, but how many episodes and at what times is currently unclear (with the intrusion age for the granitoids now reasonably well known, attention can now turn to understanding these postintrusion thermal events).

Thus, radiometric ages for intrusion are tightly constrained and agree with the geological constraints, the younger ages (<370 Ma) appear to be the result of partial to complete resetting, and the demonstrated coexistence of mafic and felsic magmas in the Meguma Zone crust creates opportunities for mechanical and chemical interaction between them.

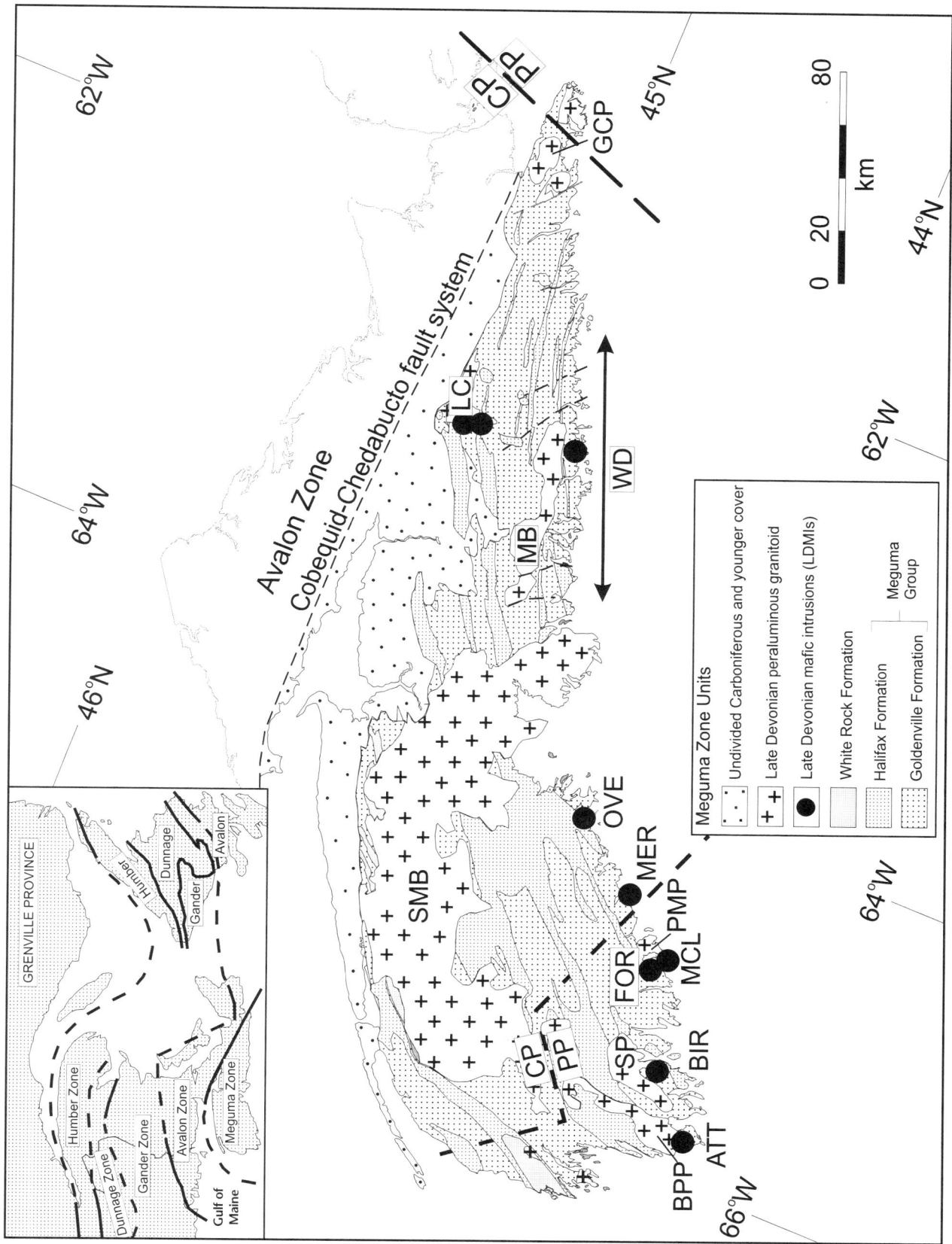

Figure 1. Geologic map of the Meguma Zone of southern Nova Scotia showing the major intrusions of peraluminous granitoid rocks and calc-alkaline mafic rocks. Inset map shows location of the Meguma Zone with respect to other lithotectonic zones in eastern North America (ATT—Attwoods; BIR—Birchtown; BPP—Barrington Passage pluton; CP—central plutons; FOR—Forbes Point; GCP—Guysborough County plutons; LC—Liscomb Complex; MB—Musquodoboit batholith; MCL—Mcleods Cove; MER—Mersey Point; OVE—Ovens; PMP—Port Mouton pluton; PP—peripheral plutons; SMB—South Mountain Batholith; SP—Shelburne pluton; WD—Weekend dykes).

TABLE 1. SUMMARY OF RADIOMETRIC AGE DETERMINATIONS IN THE MEGUMA ZONE

Time	Host rocks	Mafic intrusions	Felsic intrusions
Post-365 Ma			Many determinations, especially on altered granites and granite-related mineral deposits, probably representing resetting of isotopic systems by fluids (Kontak and Cormier, 1991).
370–365 Ma		Weekend dykes 370 ± 2, 367 ± 2 (Ar-Ar hornblende) (Kempster et al., 1989).	East Kemptville tin deposit 366 ± 4 (Pb-Pb whole rocks and mineral separates) (Kontak and Chatterjee, 1992). Liscomb granites 368–373 Ma (Ar-Ar micas) (Clarke et al., 1993b).
375–370 Ma	Liscomb gneisses 368–373 Ma (Ar-Ar micas and amphiboles) (Clarke et al., 1993b).	Weekend dykes ca. 370 Ma (Ar-Ar biotite and hornblende) (Kempster et al., 1989; Tate, 1995). Ten Mile Lake gabbro-diorite 368–373 Ma (Ar-Ar) (Clarke et al., 1993b).	Granodiorite 372 ± 2 (Rb-Sr whole rock and mineral separates) (Clarke and Halliday, 1980) monzogranite-leucomonzogranite 374 ± 2, 373 ± 2 (U-Pb monazite) (Harper, 1988) leucomonzogranite-leucogranite 372 ± 2 (Ar-Ar micas) (Clarke et al., 1993a) biotite granodiorite 373 ± 4 (Pb-Pb whole-rock and mineral separates) (Chatterjee and Ham, 1991).
380–375 Ma		Bog Island Lake gabbro-diorite 377 Ma (Ar-Ar biotite) (Clarke et al., 1993b) Birchtown diorite 376 ± 2 Ma (U-Pb zircon) (Tate, 1995).	
Pre–380 Ma	Meguma Group regional metamorphism 405–390 Ma (Ar-Ar) (Muecke et al., 1988). Meguma Group depositional age 500 Ma. Meguma Group T_{CHUR} Nd whole-rock model age 1358 ± 104 Ma (Clarke and Halliday, 1985). Tangier basement T_{CHUR} whole-rock model age 500–700 Ma (Eberz et al., 1991).		

MAFIC IGNEOUS ROCKS

Field relations and emplacement mechanisms

Late Devonian mafic intrusions in the Meguma Zone crop out as small (10–100 m) dikes, sheets, and plugs with gabbroic, dioritic, or lamprophyric compositions (Tate and Clarke, 1993; Tate, 1995). These intrusions either crop out proximal to the Liscomb Complex and Musquodoboit Batholith, or represent synplutonic intrusions into the small granitoid plutons of the southwestern shore of Nova Scotia (Fig. 1). The contacts of the mafic bodies intruding peraluminous granitoids are either pillowed or gradational, and reflect mafic-granitoid magmatic interaction (considered further below). In contrast, contacts between other mafic bodies and the Meguma Group are rarely exposed. In general, elongation of these bodies oblique to regional fold trends indicates their discordant nature, and the few exposed contacts of the Weekend dikes are sharp, steeply dipping, and discordant. The Weekend dikes intrude Acadian fractures, and the other bodies

may also have similar magma conduits. The lack of tectonic strain in these rocks, and the discordant intrusive relationships of some bodies with regional fold trends in the Meguma Group, indicate a late- to post-Acadian intrusive age. Furthermore, their spatial associations with the Late Devonian granitoids confirm the contemporaneity of mafic-felsic magmatism. The apparent occurrence of these small bodies solely in coastal localities and inland quarries strongly suggests that the poor exposure in southwestern Nova Scotia obscures other mafic intrusions. No known mafic body has a significant gravity anomaly, and some bodies have only a weak magmatic contrast with the Meguma Group, so discovery of additional bodies will be difficult.

Mineralogy and petrology

Table 2 summarizes the modal characteristics of the Late Devonian mafic intrusions, all of which have coarse grain sizes and variably hydrous mineral assemblages containing olivine and/or pyroxene and/or titanian hornblende, a ferromagnesian mica, and feldspar. Their lithological classification follows Streckeisen

TABLE 2. AVERAGE CHEMICAL COMPOSITIONS FOR THE LATE DEVONIAN MAFIC INTRUSIONS*

Intrusion	ATT	BIR	FOR	LC	MCL	MER	OVE	WD
N	7	6	2	4	1	6	8	14
(wt%)								
SiO_2	52.94	57.41	51.06	53.98	53.13	46.13	64.28	54.80
TiO_2	0.82	0.86	1.12	1.55	1.25	0.52	0.72	0.74
Al_2O_3	17.49	12.32	11.81	18.70	12.34	9.75	17.60	16.09
Fe_2O_3T	6.87	8.31	9.02	9.33	7.89	11.53	4.92	8.41
FeOT	6.33	7.70	8.45	8.60	7.26	10.62	4.71	7.81
MnO	0.12	0.14	0.19	0.25	0.12	0.18	0.07	0.17
MgO	9.09	9.80	13.38	6.00	13.27	23.99	3.06	10.02
CaO	9.81	7.38	9.08	6.57	6.05	6.96	2.96	6.45
Na_2O	2.50	1.77	1.76	2.82	1.32	0.91	4.33	2.14
K_2O	0.59	2.27	2.45	1.33	4.39	0.82	2.09	1.66
P_2O_5	0.30	0.36	0.73	0.20	0.86	0.13	0.24	0.12
Total	100.00	100.00	100.00	100.00	100.00	100.00	100.00	100.00
LOI	1.40	1.53	2.00	1.76	1.29	1.10	3.96	3.77
(ppm)								
Ba	211	619	605	349	1,920	471	512	602
Rb	16	95	93	44	132	25	45	44
Sr	781	221	509	323	2,567	285	730	401
Y	17	22	25	23	19	12	18	19
Zr	81	143	192	103	421	63	100	114
Nb	8	9	15	11	36	5	9	7
Th	1	5	4	4		3	10	4
Pb	10	10	5	13		11	11	12
Ga	13	12	16	23	19	9	20	16
Zn	67	70	100		105	76	59	86
Cu	24	10	27		41	27	5	30
Ni	40	15	51	27	194	293	9	181
V	134	206	211	185	144	140	96	195
Cr	189	724	1,002	105	551	1,586	25	744
Hf	1	4	4	3	9	2	4	3
Cg								6
Sc	29	41		27		25		26
Ta	1	2	1	1		1	1	1
Co	57	94		30		116		62
Li				38				
U	1	1	0	1		1		1
La	14.51	17.80		16.62	79.12	14.51	32.68	18.21
Ce	35.74	40.50	60.79	39.51	167.60	32.53	68.49	38.66
Pr					19.29		8.04	5.14
Nd	17.33	22.95	33.52	23.81	73.15	13.53	31.35	19.58
Sm	3.49	4.52	6.52	4.74	11.55	2.48	5.89	3.95
Eu	1.22	1.14	1.82	1.62	3.15	0.76	1.57	1.21
Gd			5.01		7.52		4.71	3.98
Tb			0.70	0.65	0.80		0.57	0.58
Dy					4.33		3.33	3.56
Ho					0.75		0.62	0.97
Er					1.92		1.63	2.20
Tm					0.25		0.22	0.28
Yb	1.44	2.14	1.68	2.08	1.59	1.13	1.43	2.07
Lu	0.16	0.27	0.24	0.33	0.34	0.13	0.21	0.31
Sum_7REE	73.89	89.32	>104.57	88.71	336.50	65.06	141.63	83.99
$^{87}Sr/^{86}Sr_i$	0.7043	0.70509	0.70397	0.70439	0.70369	0.70514		0.70487
$^{143}Nd/^{144}Nd_i$	0.512594	0.512599	0.512414	0.512512	0.512566	0.512449		0.512536
εNd_i	2.51	3.69	-0.96	-2.78	3.47	0.20		1.44

*Tate, 1995.

(1976). Of the most primitive gabbroic rocks, the Mersey Point picrite contains magnesian olivine (Fo_{80}), and both the picrite and the Attwoods Brook gabbronorite have augite (Wo_{48-23} En_{44-60} Fs_{3-17}), hypersthene (En_{69}), magnesio-hornblende, phlogopite, and variably calcic plagioclase (An_{80-50}), with cumulate textures. Lamprophyres have hornblende > biotite, and plagioclase > K-feldspar, and so represent heteromorphic spessartites and kersantites (Rock, 1990). They contain compositionally variable seriate hornblende (magnesio-hornblende, tschermakite, actinolite) and groundmass plagioclase (An_{70-50}); diorites and gabbrodiorites of the Liscomb Complex have similar mineral compositions and mineral assemblages to the lamprophyres, although they lack lamprophyric textures and primary magmatic carbonates. In all intrusions, hydrous minerals occur as magmatic phenocrysts and late-magmatic overgrowths on clinopyroxene, and the accessory minerals include chromite, chalcopyrite, zircon, sphene, and perovskite. Epidote and chlorite formed predominantly under deuteric conditions in all intrusions, except in the hydrothermally altered Ovens dikes.

Geochemistry

The mafic intrusions collectively show a wide range of all major oxides (e.g., SiO_2 46–64 wt%, Al_2O_3 10–19 wt%, MgO 3–24 wt%, and CaO 3–10 wt%) that reflects their lithological diversity (Tables 2 and 3). On an AFM diagram (Fig. 2a) they plot within the calc-alkaline field and define a weak evolutionary trend with moderate enrichment of total iron relative to MgO and alkalies. All intrusions have calc-alkaline or high-K calc-alkaline characteristics (K_2O 0.6–2.0 wt%), except for the synplutonic lamprophyres in the Port Mouton pluton (Table 1), both of which are shoshonitic (K_2O < 4 wt%) (Fig. 2b). No strong evolutionary trends exist for major oxides. All bodies contain variable but generally high concentrations of large-ion lithophile elements (e.g., Ba 211–1920 ppm, Sr 221–2567 ppm) relative to high field strength elements (e.g., Y 12–25 ppm, Zr 63–421 ppm).

The intrusions contain highly variable total rare-earth concentrations (Σ_7REE 72–142 ppm), but the chondrite-normalized spider diagrams are all similar in shape (Fig. 2c). Light REEs show ten times enrichment relative to heavy REEs, and only the Liscomb Complex intrusions have a small positive Eu anomaly. Mafic bodies intruding the Meguma Group show a wide variation of $^{87}Sr/^{86}Sr$ (total = 370) ratios (0.7043–0.7079), and $^{143}Nd/^{144}Nd$ (total = 370) (0.51222–0.512654) isotopic values (Table 3).

Economic geology

No known metallic mineral occurrences are directly associated with the Late Devonian mafic intrusions; however, Greenough et al. (1993) proposed a possible link between vein-type gold mineralization and spatially associated Weekend lamprophyre dikes in the eastern Meguma Zone. Mafic igneous rocks have only been the focus of very limited mineral exploration, and their metallogenic significance remains unclear.

FELSIC IGNEOUS ROCKS

Field relations and emplacement mechanisms

Late Devonian felsic rocks constitute ~30% of the exposed portion of the Meguma Zone and occur as about 40 bodies ranging in size from ~2–7500 km². Volumetrically insignificant felsic dikes

TABLE 3. DESCRIPTION OF LATE DEVONIAN MAFIC INTRUSIONS IN THE MEGUMA ZONE

Intrusion	Location	Lithology	Morphology	Length (m)	Width (m)	Mode (n)	Reference
ATT	Attwoods Brook	Gabbro-Norite	Plug (?)	~750	~250	Pl 63 Cpx19 Opx6 Hbl6Bt1 Qtz0.1 Opq0.4 Ch15 (5)	Rogers and White (1984)
BIR	Birchtown	Diorite	Sheet (?)	>250	>250	Pl19 Kfs0.6 Hbl45 Bt23 Qtz11 Opq0.6 Chl1 (4)	de Albuquerque (1979)
FOR	Forbes Point	Spessartite	Dike		5	Pl18 Kfs2 Hbl40 Bt37 Qtz3 Opq0.1 (1)	Douma (1988); Tate (1995)
LC	Liscomb Complex	Gabbro-Diorite	Plug	2500–5000	2500–7000	Pl Cpx Hbl Bt Opq	Clarke et al. (1993b)
MCL	Mcleods Cove	Kersantite-Spessartite	Sheet	>80	0.1–1	Pl11 Kfs3 Hbl34 Bt46 Qtz5 Opq0.5 (3)	Douma (1988); Tate (1995)
MER	Mersey Point	Picrite	Plug	~200	~300	Ol31 Pl23 Cpx8 Opx3 Hbl27 Bt6 Qtz0.2 Opq0.8 Chl1 (4)	de Albuquerque (1979)
OVE	Ovens	Diorite (altered)	Dike	>1000	0.75–3.2	Pl8 Kfs9 Qtz<1 Cal14 (3)	Hall (1979); Tate (1995)
WD	Eastern Shore	Spessarite	Dikes	....	0.1–15.1	Pl34 Cpx2 Kfs4 Hbl45 Bt3 Qtz4 Cal2 Ep2 Opq2 Chl2 (6)	Kempster et al. (1989) Tate and Clarke (1993) Greenough et al. (1993)

Figure 2. Geochemical variation in 44 samples of mafic intrusions from the Meguma Zone. A: AFM plot showing variation in the individual occurrences. B: SiO$_2$-K$_2$O chemical classification diagram. C: Rare earth element (REE) diagram showing strongly fractionated REE patterns with insignificant Eu/Eu* anomalies. (This figure is after Tate and Clarke, 1995.)

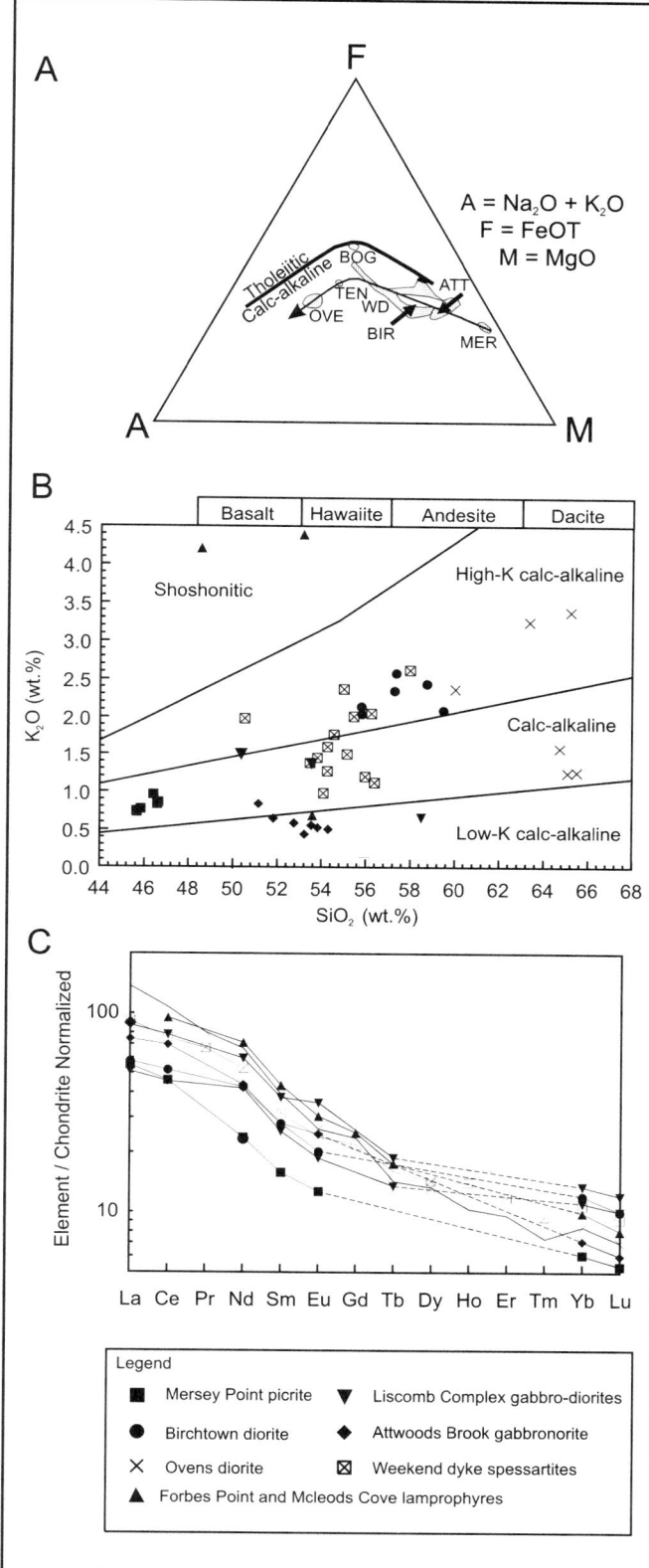

and plugs (~10–100 m^2) also occur. Contacts between felsic igneous bodies and their respective Cambrian-Devonian metasedimentary and metavolcanic country rocks are mostly sharp and intrusive. Granitic bodies generally are devoid of contact-related features; however, some bodies show locally developed primary flow(?) features along their margins, including schlieren banding and concentrations of feldspar megacrysts and small xenoliths (Clarke and Muecke, 1980; Abbott, 1989; Tate, 1995). Some bodies also have large concentrations of country rock enclaves along small portions of their borders (e.g., SMB northwest of Halifax; Jamieson, 1974). Contact-related features in the country rocks mostly consist of narrow contact-metamorphic aureoles (~100 m– 2 km) that have porphyroblastic growth of andalusite and cordierite; and, in southwestern and northeastern regions, narrow migmatite zones have developed around several plutons (Douma, 1988; Raeside et al., 1988). Country rocks were largely undeformed by the emplacement of the granites; however, several roof zones in the central SMB contain highly contorted, metasedimentary rocks with abundant granite dikes (MacDonald and Ham, 1992). Similarly, a northwest-trending anticlinal-synclinal structure along the margin of the SMB near Halifax (Faribault, 1908) is normal to regional structural trends and may indicate forceful emplacement (Horne et al., 1992).

Central plutons. These intrusions are mostly circular or elliptical in shape, intrude greenschist facies country rocks, and crosscut the regional Acadian structural trends. Most plutons are massive, and are either late tectonic or posttectonic with respect to the regional Acadian deformation. Many of the early granodiorite and biotite monzogranite plutons in the SMB have weakly defined, northeast-trending alignment of feldspar megacrysts that Horne et al. (1992) interpreted as reflecting residual Acadian stress during emplacement and crystallization. Shear and fault zones with brittle or ductile features crosscut, and hence postdate, many granite bodies, most notably the SMB.

Internal contacts between granite phases are either sharp and intrusive or gradational. Contact-related features, including the development of chilled margins, are rare or absent in most intrusions. MacDonald et al. (1992) used crosscutting relationships, including dikes and the presence of granite xenoliths, to work out the following general sequence of intrusion for the SMB: (1) emplacement of early granodiorite and biotite monzogranite (stage I plutons); (2) intrusion by coarse-grained leucocratic monzogranite (stage II plutons); and (3) intrusion of fine-grained leucocratic monzogranite and leucogranite bodies into stage I and stage II plutons (Fig. 3).

These field relations for the SMB are consistent with those

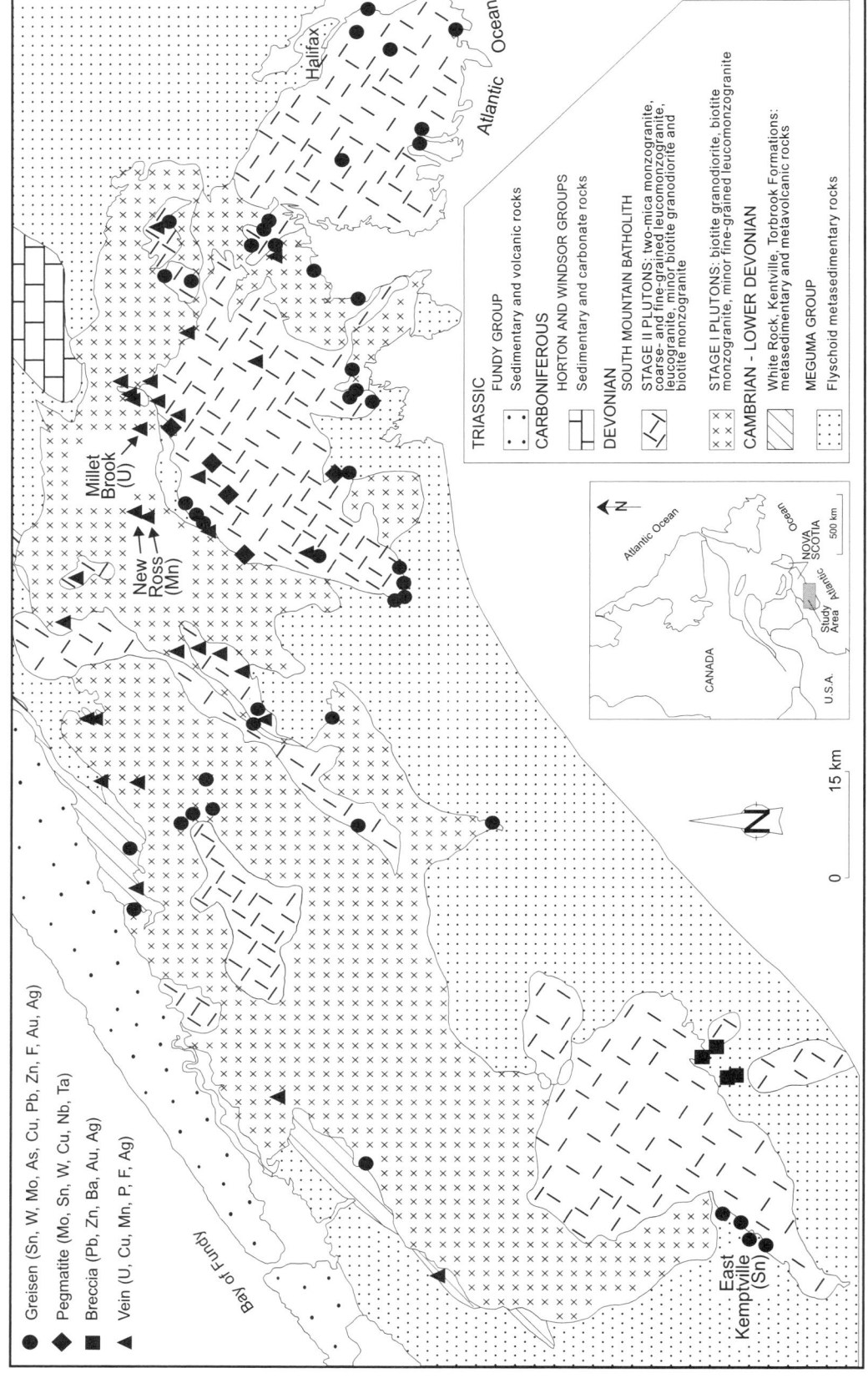

Figure 3. Geologic map of the South Mountain Batholith showing the composite plutons and principal mineral deposits.

for several other central plutons, including the Musquodoboit Batholith (MacDonald and Clarke, 1985).

Peripheral plutons. The peripheral plutons (Fig. 1) are generally small, intrude amphibolite facies country rocks, and are normally homogeneous, but the Port Mouton pluton (Douma, 1988) and the Canso plutons (Hill, 1988) have complex sequences of intrusion involving multiple injection of tonalite (not present in the central plutons), granodiorite, monzogranite, and leucogranite units. Several tonalite-monzogranite bodies in the southwestern and eastern parts of the Meguma Zone have penetrative fabrics that lie parallel to regional fold trends in the country rocks, manifested as planar alignment of biotite and, to a lesser extent, by deformed metasedimentary enclaves (Rogers, 1988; Hill, 1988, 1991). In addition, some of the small felsic bodies (Barrington Passage pluton, Shelburne pluton, Port Mouton pluton) show synplutonic relationships with mafic intrusive rocks.

In summary, the central plutons are large to small, tend to intrude country rocks of lower grades of metamorphism, show foliation that is for the most part magmatic, and have no synplutonic mafic intrusions. The peripheral plutons however, are small, tend to intrude country rocks of higher grades of metamorphism, show foliation that is for the most part tectonic, and contain synplutonic mafic intrusions.

Mineralogy and petrology

Figure 4 shows modal compositions for the main mappable lithological units of the South Mountain Batholith. In addition, all central plutons in the Meguma Zone contain a wide range of primary magmatic minerals characteristic of their peraluminous bulk compositions. From granodiorite, through monzogranite and leucomonzogranite, to leucogranite, the assemblages of characteristic alumina-rich minerals are generally biotite, biotite + cordierite, biotite + cordierite + andalusite, biotite + andalusite, biotite + andalusite + muscovite, biotite + muscovite, biotite + muscovite + garnet, muscovite + garnet, and muscovite + topaz (Clarke et al., 1976; Clarke, 1981; Allan and Clarke, 1981; Maillet and Clarke, 1985; MacDonald et al., 1992; Clarke, 1994; Ding, 1995). All these characteristic minerals have xenocrystic and metasomatic, as well as demonstrated magmatic, origins. Accessory minerals may include one or more of ilmenite, rutile, tapiolite, apatite, monazite, xenotime, and zircon. Late-stage, chemically evolved rocks show effects of hydrothermal alteration, predominantly chloritization, sericitization, albitization, K-feldspathization, and hematization. Table 4 summarizes some of the mineral assemblage, mineral composition, and textural data for the principal granitoid rock types of the SMB.

The peripheral plutons (among them, Port Mouton, Shelburne, Barrington Passage, and Canso) are less peraluminous, and mainly contain biotite as the principal alumina-rich mineral. Compositions range from tonalite, through granodiorite, to monzogranite. The tonalites, in particular, may contain hornblende as an apparent primary phase, and its presence keeps the A/CNK ratio close to one in these rocks. Late aplite-pegmatite dikes in the Port Mouton and Shelburne plutons contain abundant magmatic garnet in association with primary muscovite and biotite.

Geochemistry

The geochemical data base for granitic rocks from the Meguma Zone now contains more than 1000 analyses (Ham et al., 1990; Tate and Merrett, 1994). Chemical compositions range from tonalite (mean SiO_2 66.09 ± 3.62, $n = 59$) to leucogranite (mean SiO_2 73.62 ± 0.89, $n = 34$), and they are exclusively peraluminous (mol $Al_2O_3/(CaO + Na_2O + K_2O) > 1$) in the central plutons and predominantly peraluminous in the peripheral plutons (Table 5; Fig. 5A). Clarke and Muecke (1985), Clarke and Chatterjee (1988), Kontak et al. (1988), and MacDonald and Clarke (1991) reviewed the extent and causes of chemical variation in the South Mountain Batholith. The already established causes of variation are fractional crystallization, contamination, and hydrothermal alteration. These processes, combined with potential differences in source regions, should account for all the compositional variation within the suite of granitoid rocks.

Evidence for fractional crystallization comes from strong correlations between pairs of elements, indicating the addition to, or removal from, the granitoid magma of one or more crystalline phases. Figure 5B shows a strong positive correlation between TiO_2 and Zr, reflecting the fractionation of accessory ilmenite and rutile plus major biotite (Ti) with inclusions of zircon (Zr) from the early tonalitic and granodioritic magmas. Collectively, these types of correlations on variation diagrams indicate that fractional crystallization of plagioclase + K-feldspar + biotite + zircon + apatite + monazite accounts for a significant amount of the variation in the granitic rocks.

Given the uniformly siliceous and peraluminous nature of the Meguma Group host rocks, wall-rock contamination is not easy to detect, except isotopically. More evolved members of the SMB contain little physical evidence of the incorporation of Meguma Group material in terms of partially digested xenoliths, but they show distinct chemical evidence (higher $^{87}Sr/^{86}Sr$ and lower Nd than the more primitive members) (Clarke and Halliday, 1980; Clarke et al., 1988). Similarly, sulfur isotope data (Kubilius, 1983; Poulson et al., 1991) show that later monzogranitic rocks are chemically more like the Meguma host rocks than the early granodiorite, again suggesting incorporation of Meguma Group material in the more evolved magmas. Together, the combination of assimilation-contamination and fractional crystallization (AFC) accounts for most of the primary chemical variation in the peraluminous granites of the Meguma Zone.

Hydrothermal interaction, whether involving magmatic, metamorphic, or meteoric waters, has had three principal effects on the final compositions of the granitic rocks. (1) At mild degrees of interaction, whether at temperatures above or below the solidus, it causes departures from compositions controlled solely by the fluid-absent part of the magmatic processes, and partially obscures the record of the igneous processes. (2) At

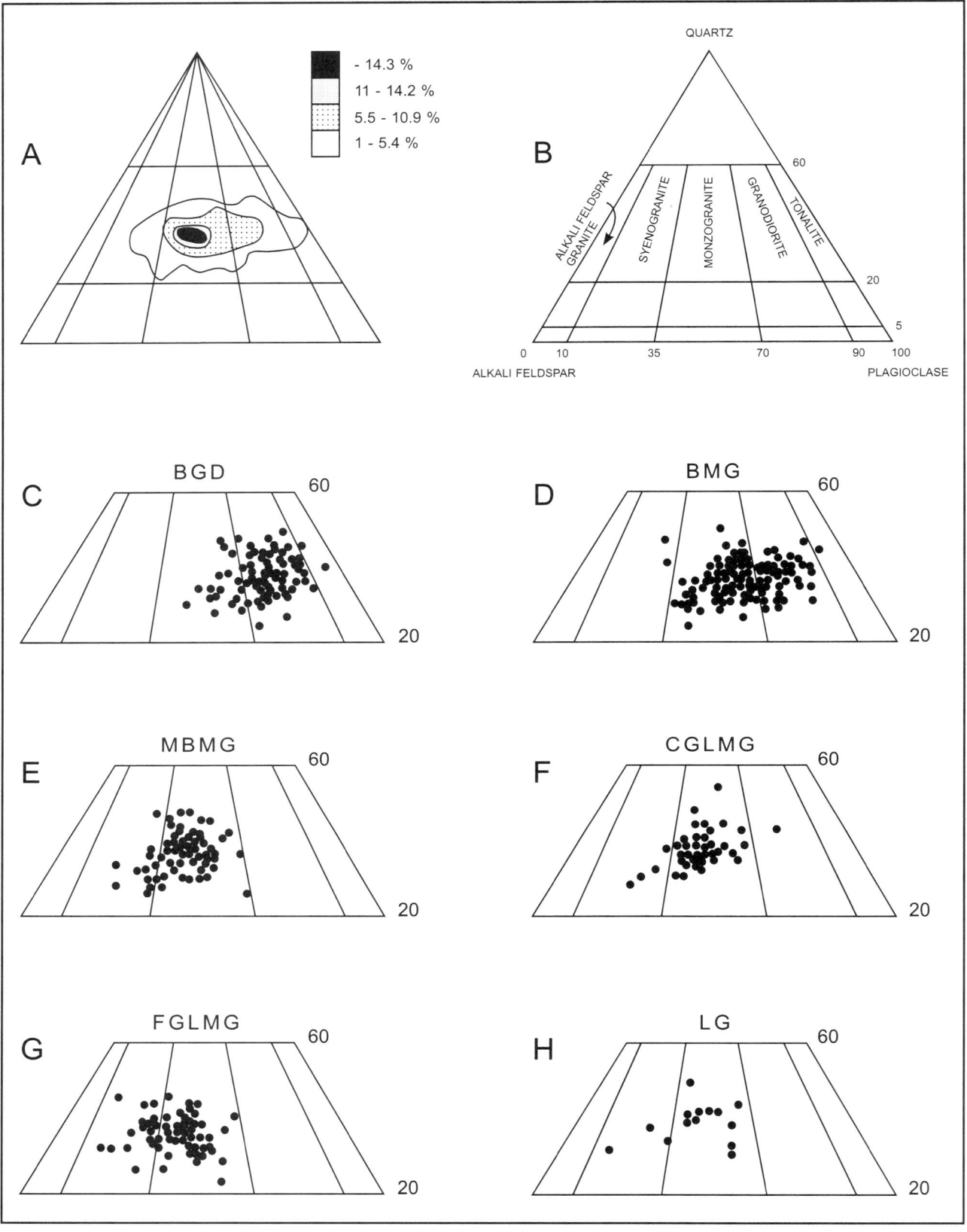

Figure 4. Quartz–alkali feldspar–plagioclase (QAP) plots for the South Mountain Batholith according to mappable rock type (BGD—biotite granodiorite; BMG—biotite muscovite granite; MBMG—muscovite biotite monzogranite; CGLMG—coarse-grained leucomonzogranite; FGLMG—fine-grained leucomonzogranite; LG—leucogranite). Individual units designated as BGD and BMG in the field commonly contain samples that plot in adjoining fields on the QAP diagram. This feature is probably the result of textural and compositional heterogeneities within these units. Variations in FGLMG and LG may be the result of late-magmatic or postmagmatic albitization or K-feldspathization.

moderate degrees of interaction, it produces geochemical trends completely different from those created by silicate melt–silicate solid equilibria (Fig. 5C), or exaggerates the trend of REE depletion caused by fractional crystallization (Fig. 5D). (3) At strong degrees of interaction, it generates greisens and mineral deposits, all of which are clearly related to magma-fluid or solid-fluid reactions (see following section on mineral deposits). MacDonald and Clarke (1991) used Spearman rank correlation coefficients to distinguish between the various processes of fractional crystallization and hydrothermal fluid interaction.

The Meguma Zone represents a large geographical area of granite production, and thus it probably involves some variation in the bulk chemical compositions of the source rocks as a function of space, and perhaps even time. With our current data, we know that some plutons within the SMB have small, but statistically significant, compositional differences that may be related to source compositions (Horne et al., 1990). In addition, differences in the Pb isotope compositions between granites of the Liscomb Complex and the SMB (A. K. Chatterjee, 1993, personal commun.) suggest different sources for the granitic magmas. Thus, although evidence shows that source rocks exert some control on the compositional variation in the granites, this control does not appear to be the main cause of their geochemical diversity.

Economic geology

Granitoid bodies of the Meguma Zone host numerous metallic mineral deposits and occurrences. MacDonald (1994) devised a four-fold classification scheme for the SMB based upon modes of occurrence and elemental assemblages. An evaluation of published information indicates that this scheme can be applied to the entire Meguma Zone. The four types of mineral occurrences in the SMB (Fig. 3) are as follows.

1. The greisen type (Sn, W, Mo, As, Cu, Pb, Zn, F, Au, Ag) includes the East Kemptville Sn-Zn-Cu-Ag deposit in the southwestern part of the SMB (Kontak, 1990). Greisens occur as (1) massive zones (generally 1–100 m²); (2) northwest-trending greisen-bordered quartz veins (generally 1 cm–1 m wide); and (3) sheeted quartz-greisen vein systems (up to 500 m long). Associated host-rock alteration includes muscovitization, albitization, K-feldspathization, or silicification. The largest deposits occur at pluton margins, particularly where contacts are sinuous and shallow dipping. Some deposits are associated with major

fault or shear zones; however, the genetic relationship between structure and mineralization largely remains unclear.

2. The vein type (U, Cu, Mn, P, F, Ag) includes the Millet Brook (U-Cu-Ag) and the New Ross (Mn-Fe-P) deposits of the South Mountain Batholith (Chatterjee et al., 1985; O'Reilly et al., 1992). Mineralized zones occur in intensely hematized (± desilicified ± albitized ± clay alteration) northeast-trending, steeply dipping fracture (shear?) zones. Vein-type deposits are distributed throughout the granitoid bodies with no apparent affinity to pluton margins.

3. The breccia type (Pb, Zn, Ba, Au, Ag) includes mineralized zones that occur along major fault zones and are characterized by complex, superimposed brecciation, alteration (silicification ± kaolinization), and mineralization. Breccia-type quartz veins with cockade, colloform, and crustiform textures are indicative of epithermal conditions of formation.

4. The pegmatite type (Be, Li, Mo, Sn, W, Cu, Nb, Ta) includes two subtypes: (1) predominantly Be ± Li pegmatites hosted by granitoid or metasedimentary rocks in the southwest; and (2) polymetallic (Mo, Sn, W, Cu, Nb, Ta) pegmatites in granitoid bodies throughout the Meguma Zone, the largest dikes occurring in the central SMB (O'Reilly et al., 1982). Mineralized pegmatites mostly occur as randomly oriented pods, lenses, and dikes, except for some beryl-bearing dikes that form subhorizontal sheet-like bodies in the Port Mouton pluton (see Fig. 1 for its location).

Most granite-related mineral occurrences are spatially associated with muscovite-rich leucomonzogranites and leucogranites with specialized trace-element compositions (i.e., extreme enrichment of Li, Cs, Sn, F, U, and Rb compared with lesser evolved biotite granodiorite). For example, greisen- and pegmatite-type occurrences are mostly hosted by leucomonzogranites and leucogranites (e.g., East Kemptville). Similarly, small fine-grained leucomonzogranite plugs were noted near some breccia-type occurrences. Vein-type mineral occurrences are mostly hosted by biotite monzogranite or biotite granodiorite; however, leucogranite dikes or plugs occur at several deposits (e.g., Millet Brook; Chatterjee et al., 1985).

Chatterjee (1983) proposed a series of metallogenic domains for the Meguma Zone, and MacDonald et al. (1992) noted that several of these domain boundaries within the SMB correspond with the margins of plutons. They suggested that variations in polymetallic character between domains probably reflected differences in bulk magma composition, physico-chemical conditions during emplacement and crystallization, and possibly varying amounts of contamination from country rocks.

SYNTHESIS OF LATE DEVONIAN MAGMATISM IN THE MEGUMA ZONE

Tectonic setting

Well-established tectono-magmatic discriminators, based on immobile elements, provide equivocal results concerning the tectonic setting for the mafic intrusions, but generally support a con-

TABLE 4. DESCRIPTION OF MAJOR ROCK TYPES IN THE SOUTH MOUNTAIN BATHOLITH*

Rock type	SMB (%)	Grain size†	Dominant textures§	Biotite** (%)	Muscovite** (%)	Muscovite type‡	Plagioclase anorthite§§	Plagioclase zoning	K-Spar exsol***	Cordierite** (%)	Andalusite** (%)	Topaz** (%)	Xenoliths‡‡
Leucogranite	0.7	f-m(c)	porp, equi, pegm	0-2	3-28	euh>repl	<5	unzoned	non-exsolved	tr.	0-2	0-8	None
Fine-grained leucomonzogranite	6.8	f-m(c)	porp, equi	2-7	3-13	←	←	←	←	tr.	0-tr.	0	Rare
Coarse-grained leucomonzogranite	21.8	m-c(f)	mega, seri	2-7	4-8	repl>euh	←	zoned> unzoned	patch> rod and bead	tr.-5	0-tr.	0	Rare
Muscovite-biotite monzogranite	8.9	m-c(f)	mega, seri, equi	7-12	1-3	←	←	←	←	tr.-5	0	0	Common
Biotite monzogranite	52.2	m-c(f)	mega, seri	10-17	tr.-1	←	←	←	←	tr.-1	0	0	Common-Abundant
Biotite granodiorite	9.6	m-c(f)	mega, seri	15->25	tr.	repl	<5-35	zoned	rod and bead	tr.	0	0	Abundant

*After MacDonald et al. (1992).
†Grain sizes: f = fine (<0.1 cm); m = medium (0.1–0.5 cm); c = coarse (>0.5 cm); letter in parentheses denotes minor occurrence.
§Dominant texture: equi = equigranular; porp = porphyritic; pegm = pegmatitic; mega = megacrystic; seri = seriate, listed in descending order of importance.
**Modal determinations from point counting (500–1000 points) of stained rock slabs and thin sections.
‡Muscovite type: euh = euhedral (primary?); repl = replacement (secondary).
§§Anorthite content (from microprobe analysis).
***K-spar exsol = alkali feldspar exsolution textures.
‡‡Xenoliths: abundance of metasedimentary xenoliths: abundant = several in all outcrops; common = a few in most outcrops; rare = minor occurrence in some outcrops.

TABLE 5. AVERAGE CHEMICAL COMPOSITIONS FOR MAJOR GRANITOID ROCK TYPES FROM THE MEGUMA ZONE

Rock N	Central granitoids*						Peripheral granitoids*			
	GDIO 65	BMZ 113	MBMZ 62	CLMZ 96	FLMZ 105	LUGR 34	TONA 59	GDIO 50	MONZ 42	FLMZ 5
(wt%)										
SiO_2	67.12	69.39	71.74	73.07	73.90	73.62	66.09	71.77	73.30	73.98
TiO_2	0.68	0.49	0.32	0.20	0.13	0.07	0.62	0.31	0.22	0.12
Al_2O_3	15.46	14.84	14.51	14.25	14.26	14.57	16.66	14.97	14.45	14.48
Fe_2O_3	4.57	3.62	2.45	1.91	1.45	1.34	4.00	1.85	1.44	0.75
MnO	0.09	0.08	0.06	0.05	0.05	0.04	0.08	0.05	0.04	0.02
MgO	1.83	1.48	1.16	0.93	0.85	0.76	1.75	0.77	0.40	0.28
CaO	1.94	1.38	0.83	0.64	0.41	0.39	3.10	1.53	0.86	0.91
Na_2O	3.45	3.36	3.43	3.45	3.50	3.69	3.92	3.83	3.53	3.52
K_2O	3.70	4.22	4.65	4.64	4.48	4.10	2.57	3.64	4.70	4.91
P_2O_5	0.21	0.20	0.23	0.23	0.26	0.41	0.22	0.22	0.22	0.20
LOI	0.65	0.58	0.63	0.54	0.64	0.82	0.68			
A/CNK†	1.18	1.18	1.19	1.20	1.26	1.31	1.12	1.14	1.07	1.05
(ppm)										
Ba	667	513	348	217	146	56	491	561	527	580
Rb	149	179	270	310	343	641	114	138	190	165
Sr	168	120	76	51	31	19	314	157	103	99
Zr	196	165	119	89	59	39	163	133	126	63
Nb	12	12	13	12	12	23	11	9	15	6
V	56	37	20	9	4	2	64	30	14	4
Y	32	33	26	30	22	32	17	16	17	15
Ga	21	19	20	19	21	27	20	18	19	16
Cu	7	4	3	1	3	22	7.5			
Pb	14	17	17	11	19	16	17.2	20	22	23
Zn	78	65	57	48	45	68	89	55	46	28
Hf	6	5	4	3	2	1	6			
Ta	1.2	1.4	1.9	2.3	2.6	5.0				
Sc	11.0	8.5	4.7	3.1	3.1	2.5				
La	36	29	23	16	9	4	37.9			
Th	12.9	11.6	13.5	11.3	6.3	5.3	5.1	10.3	6.4	3.8
U	3.0	3.7	5.8	7.4	7.9	7.4	5.3			
Li	64	75	91	106	108	236	62			
F	666	604	924	1,105	1,002	2,550	500			
As	4.6	4.5	9.3	2.6	6.2	2.5				
Sn	5	6	9	15	18	23	9.5			
W	1	1	4	3	7	36				

*Rock types: TONA = tonalite; GDIO = granodiorite; BMZ = biotite monzogranite; MBMZ = muscovite-biotite monzogranite; CLMZ = coarse grained leucomonzogranite; FLMZ = fine grained leucomonzogranite; LUGR = leucogranite.
†A/CNK = Molecular Al_2O_3 / (CaO + Na_2O + K_2O).
Tonalite analysis is from the peripheral plutons; all other analyses are from the South Mountain Batholith.

tinental margin arc environment. For example, the Ta/Yb-Th/Yb diagram (Fig. 6A) (Pearce, 1983) identifies the mafic intrusions as continental margin arc rocks derived from depleted mantle sources that had been subsequently enriched in large-ion lithophile elements by metasomatism(?) in the source region, although they may contain variable levels of subduction contamination. Spider diagrams normalized to mid-ocean ridge basalt (MORB) have similar shapes for all of the bodies, and show particularly obvious peaks at Rb, K, Sr, and P, with pronounced troughs at Nb and in many cases also at Ti (Fig. 6B). The mafic intrusions appear to have the combined geochemical characteristics of island-arc and within-plate tectonic settings.

Geochemical means of distinguishing among tectonic set-tings for granitoid rocks are problematic, particularly as a result of the compositional continuum between primary igneous and secondary metasedimentary sources. Nevertheless, Figure 7 presents two discriminant diagrams that show a tendency for the peripheral plutons to be less peraluminous and more like volcanic arc intrusions than the central plutons. Otherwise the compositions of all Meguma Zone granitoids fall close to a boundary between syncollisional and volcanic arc granitoids.

Petrogenesis—processes and sources

The similar ages and internally consistent mineral assemblages, mineral compositions, and geochemical characteristics of the mafic intrusions support the concept of a related calc-alkaline

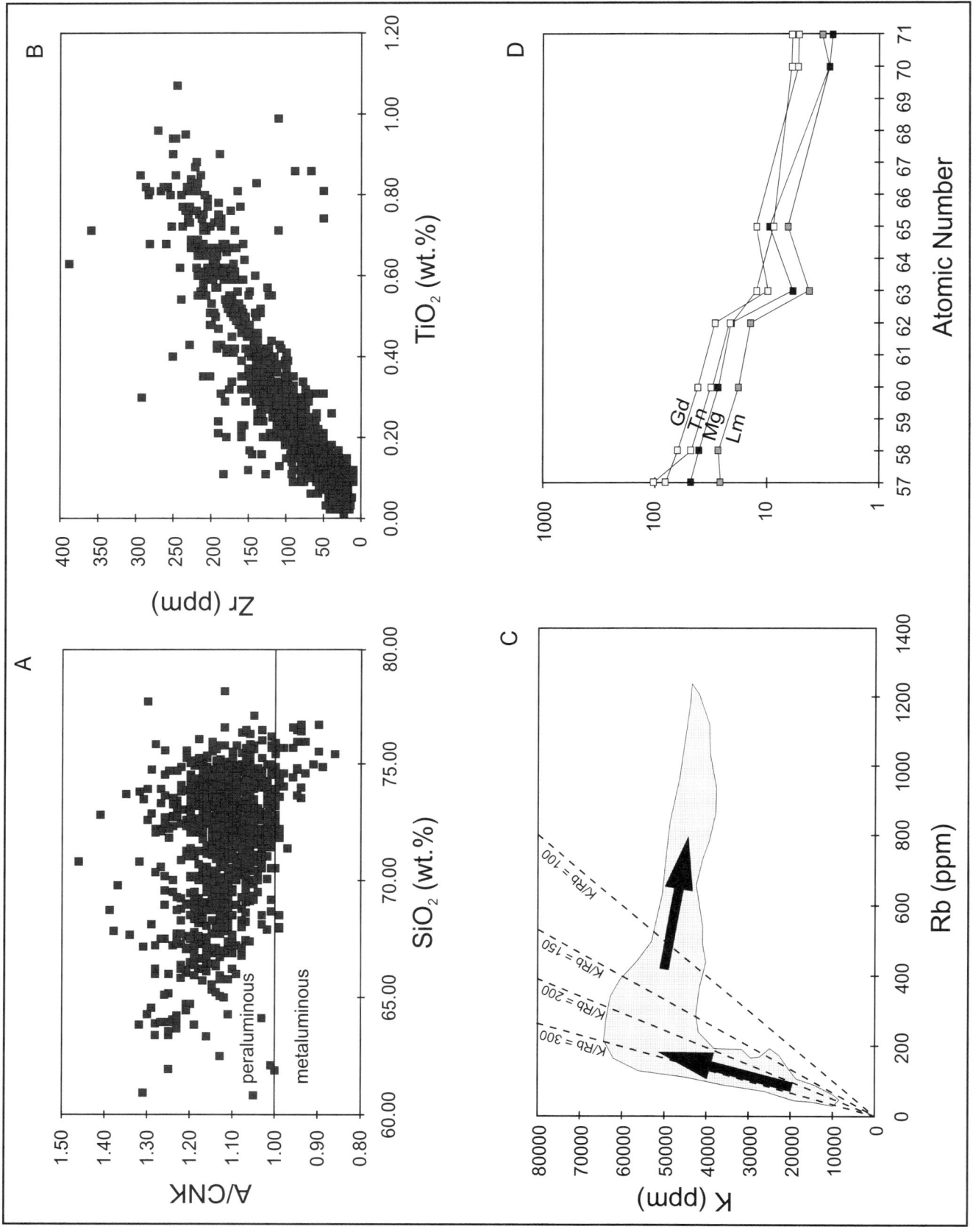

Figure 5. Geochemical variation in 1149 samples of granitoid rocks from the Meguma Zone. A: SiO_2-A/CNK plot demonstrating that, except for a few samples from the Port Mouton pluton, all granitoid rocks are peraluminous. B: Strong positive Ti-Zr correlation controlled primarily by fractional crystallization. C: K-Rb plot showing two strong trends, one at high and nearly constant K/Rb that is the product of fractional crystallization, and the other at increasing K/Rb that is the product of hydrothermal alteration. D: Average rare-earth element patterns for major lithologies—only the tonalites (exclusively from the peripheral plutons) lack significant Eu/Eu* anomalies.

⟵ ▬▬▬▬▬▬▬▬▬▬▬▬▬▬▬▬▬▬▬▬▬▬

suite in the Late Devonian. Major oxide scatter for the collective suite probably reflects their cumulate characteristics and/or deuteric alteration, but similar spider diagram patterns suggest that they represent a series of fractionated products derived from similar parent magma compositions by the fractionation of all their major modal phases (Tate, 1995). The Liscomb Complex gabbro-diorites contain Sr-Nd isotopic evidence for contamination by Meguma Group or sub-Meguma basement lithologies. High concentrations of the first transition series metals (e.g., Ti, Sc, V, Co) (Table 3) similar to those of MORB, in conjunction with the general absence of Eu anomalies and heavy REEs at $7–10_{CN}$ (Fig. 2c) suggest a peridotite source lacking abundant garnet.

High concentrations of large-ion lithophile and light rare-earth elements in even the most primitive intrusions suggest that these characteristics probably originate in the mantle source. Nd values less depleted than MORB, coupled with high and variable initial $^{87}Sr/^{86}Sr$ ratios up to 0.7079, are typical features of island-arc rocks derived from variably enriched mantle sources (e.g., Wyman and Kerrich, 1989). Negative Ta, Nb, and Ti anomalies suggest a subduction origin for the enrichment (Beard and Day, 1988), and erratically fractionated high field strength elements similar to those of within-plate basalt suggest a subcontinental lithospheric source (Salters and Hart, 1991; Hawkesworth et al., 1993).

Chemical differentiation within the Meguma Zone granitoids includes two different types of mechanisms: (1) closed-system processes, which include fractional crystallization (achieved by gravitational and flowage separation of crystals and liquid), and deuteric alteration (at temperatures both above the solidus and below the solidus) (MacDonald and Clarke, 1991); and (2) open-system processes, which include wall-rock contamination (e.g., rounded xenoliths), influxes of metamorphic and meteoric water (Clarke et al., 1993a), and mafic-felsic hybridization (Tate, 1995). No systematic or extensive investigations of oxygen isotope systematics yet exist for the Meguma Zone granitoids; however, the data currently available (Longstaffe et al., 1980; Chatterjee and Strong, 1985; Kontak et al., 1988, 1991; Clarke et al., 1993a) show that the peripheral plutons ($\delta^{18}O_{SMOW}$ = 8‰– 10‰) are lower than the South Mountain Batholith ($\delta^{18}O_{SMOW}$ = 10.8‰). These data are certainly consistent with a mafic-felsic hybridization model for the peripheral plutons, although other processes such as interaction with meteoric water could be partly responsible.

Eberz et al. (1991) and Clarke et al. (1993b) used Sr-Nd systematics to show that granulite facies xenoliths from the Tangier mafic dike and amphibolite-facies gneisses exposed in the Liscomb Complex are suitable sources for the more primitive members of the SMB and Liscomb granitoids, respectively.

Petrogenetic-tectonic model for Late Devonian magmatism in the Meguma Zone

Spatially and temporally related mafic and felsic magmatism in the peripheral plutons demands consideration of hybridization as another process to produce chemical variation in some of the granitoid rocks. Figure 8 shows a possible connection between the Late Devonian mafic intrusions and the peripheral plutons through known hybrids from the Shelburne pluton. The central plutons show chemical variation trends that are not colinear with the hybridization trends, suggesting that mantle-derived material is not an important component in their compositions.

Figure 9 is a compilation of all Sr-Nd isotopic data for the Meguma Zone. It separates all possible sources (mantle, lower crust, upper crust) from the granitoid rocks. Figure 10 is a schematic representation of the current petrogenetic model. Neither of the closed-system processes (fractional crystallization and deuteric alteration) should have any vector on this Sr-Nd diagram, whereas all open-system processes (wall-rock contamination, hydrothermal alteration, and mafic-felsic hybridization) should show strong trends between the discrete compositional reservoirs. Open-system hydrothermal alteration is difficult to assess, but it probably only causes variation in initial $^{87}Sr/^{86}Sr$. The remainder of the variation in Sr-Nd space must be related to a combination of source compositions and mixing. On one hand, the primitive granodiorites of the central plutons have Tangier-Liscomb sources, and more evolved monzogranites and leucogranites in these plutons show variation trends toward Meguma Group compositions as a result of wall-rock contamination by Meguma Group lithologies at the level of emplacement. On the other hand, the peripheral plutons show some compositions that are consistent with derivation from Tangier-Liscomb sources, and other compositions that show variation trends toward Late Devonian mafic intrusions (LDMI) compositions as a result of hybridization of mafic and felsic magmas. More precisely, the central plutons show Meguma Group contamination much greater than LDMI hybridization (or possibly Liscomb sources more important than Tangier sources), whereas the peripheral plutons show LDMI hybridization greater than Meguma Group contamination.

As for the tectonic setting, Keen et al. (1991) interpreted northerly dipping mantle reflectors in deep seismic reflection studies across the Gulf of Maine as remnants of subducted ocean lithosphere, and Keppie and Dostal (1991) interpreted the offshore Collector anomaly as a potential mafic and ultramafic ophiolite preserved along the Cobequid-Chedabucto fault. The characteristic subduction fingerprint preserved in the mafic bodies apparently provides additional evidence for subduction. We assume, but cannot prove, that the subduction occurred immediately prior to the main collisional phase of the Acadian orogeny.

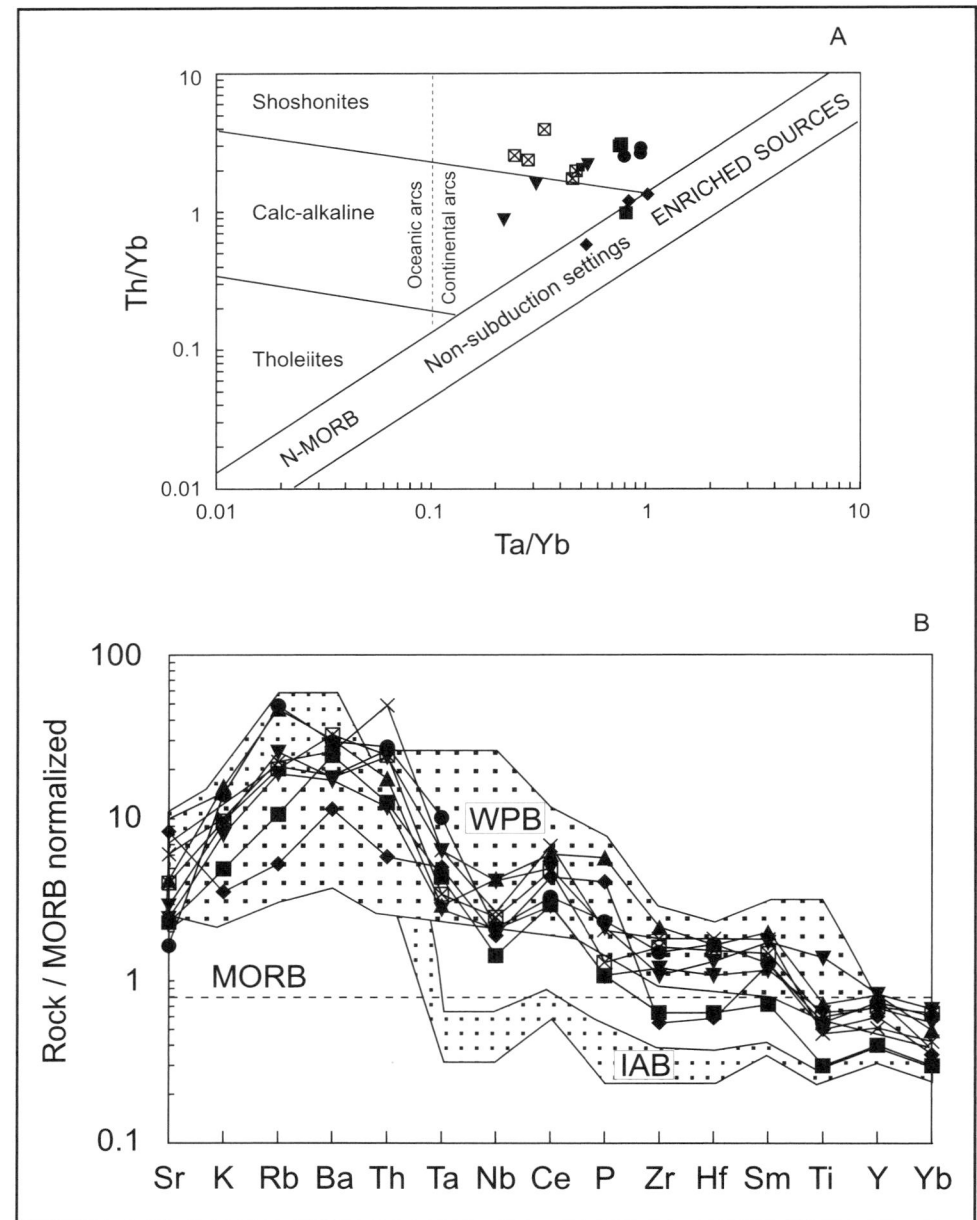

Figure 6. Tectonic discriminator diagrams for selected samples of the mafic intrusions. A: Ta/Yb-Th/Yb plot showing continental arc affinities. B: Mid-ocean ridge basalt (MORB)-normalized spider diagram showing within-plate tectonic setting (symbols as in Fig. 2). IAB is island arc basalt; WPB is within-plate basalt.

Throughout the Late Silurian and Early Devonian, the Meguma Group lay outboard of the North American continental margin, and approached a subduction zone (Fig. 11). Final closure of the Theic ocean obducted Meguma sedimentary rocks onto Avalon basement, deforming and metamorphosing them in the process. Subduction-type mafic magmas intruded after the collision. The variable model ages for these intrusions probably reflect various mixtures between mantle-derived and subduction-derived components, so they do not reliably indicate the timing

of magmatism. In addition, the subcontinental mantle may have represented an isolated repository for miscellaneous mantle signatures generated during enrichment events throughout geologic time (e.g., Johnson, 1987; Hart, 1988), so the subduction may be much older than the mid-Late Devonian and may correspond to the accretion of some other inboard Appalachian terrane. Nevertheless, the combination of subduction and collision culminated in a major Late Devonian mafic-felsic magmatic event in the Meguma Zone. The central plutons, which have little or no phys-

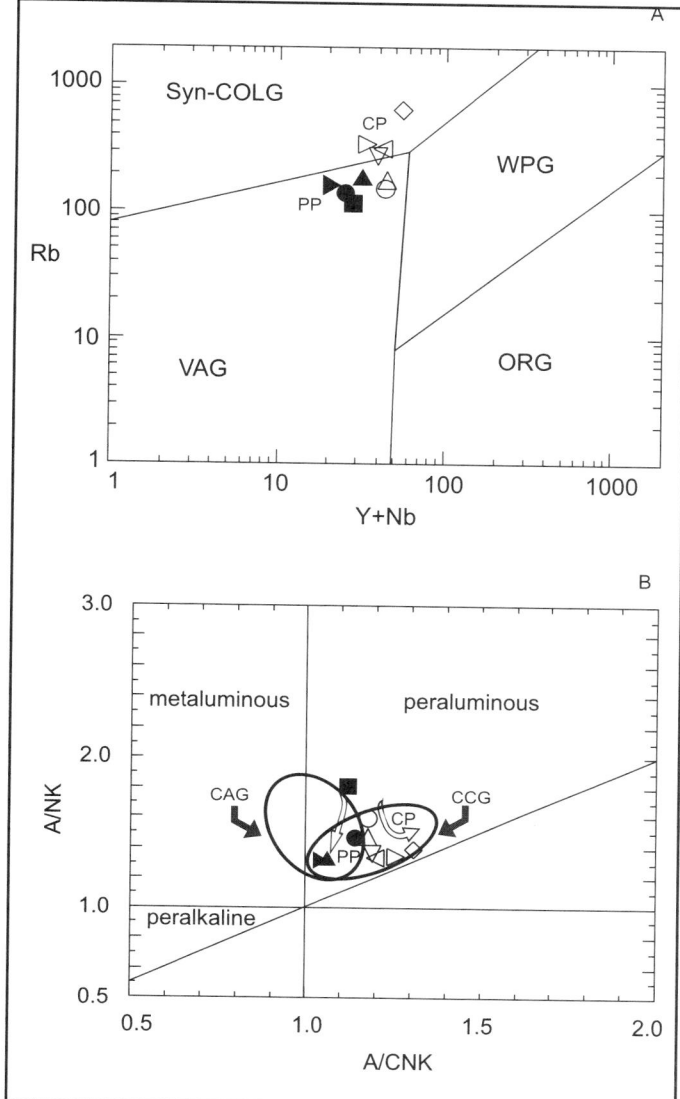

Figure 7. Tectonic discriminator diagrams for averages of granitoid types. Peripheral granites (closed symbols) are less peraluminous and show a tendency toward more volcanic arc characteristics than a syn-collisional geochemical signature. COLG, collisional granites; WPG, within-plate granites; ORG, ocean ridge granites; VAG, volcanic arc granites; CCG, continental collision granites; CAG, continental arc granites; PP, peripheral plutons; CP, central plutons.

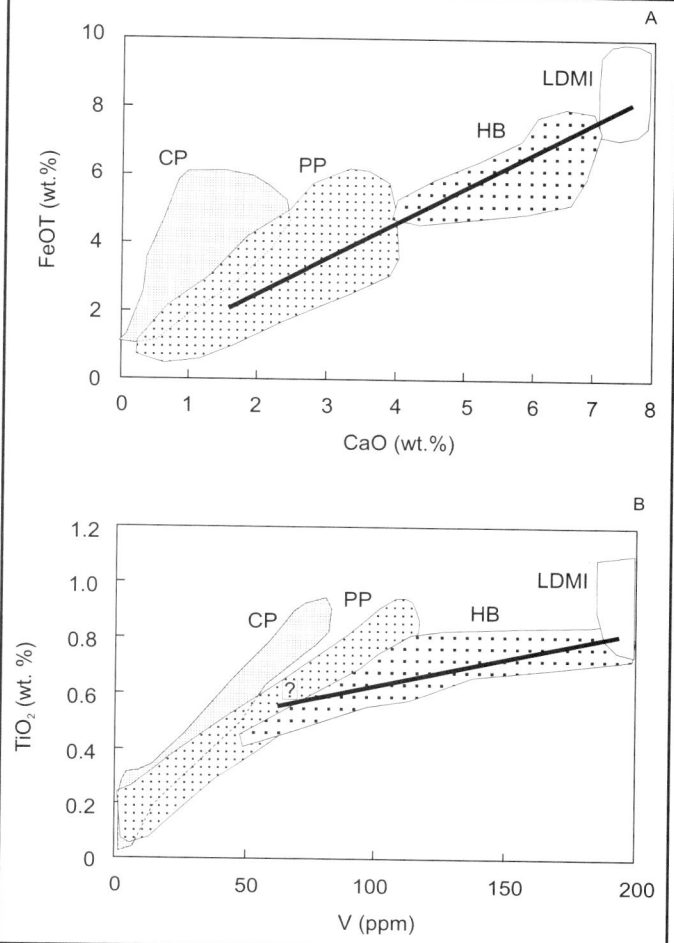

Figure 8. Major- and trace-element geochemical relationship between mafic and felsic rocks in the Meguma Zone. Known hybrids (HB) from the Shelburne pluton provide a link between the Late Devonian mafic intrusions (LDMIs) and the chemical variation trends in the peripheral plutons (PP). Chemical variation in the central plutons (CP) is less obviously connected with the Late Devonian mafic intrusion–hybrid–peripheral pluton trend.

ical or chemical evidence of interaction with mafic magmas, may be the products of crustal melting caused by crustal thickening. The peripheral plutons, which have significant physical and chemical evidence of interaction with mafic magmas, are probably the combined products of crustal melting and hybridization with the mafic magmas that supplied the heat for melting.

SUMMARY AND CONCLUSIONS

The Meguma Zone of southern Nova Scotia is the most outboard lithotectonic terrane in the northern Appalachians, and it is now well known for its many peraluminous granitoid plutons, particularly the South Mountain Batholith and its numerous mineral deposits. Recognition of mafic magmatism, roughly coeval with granitoid emplacement, requires an examination of its potential role as thermal and material input to the granitoids of the Meguma Zone.

In this light, detailed inspection shows that two distinctly different types of granitoid plutons occur in the Meguma Zone.

1. The central plutons, including the South Mountain Batholith, are ca. 372 Ma, late-tectonic to posttectonic, predominantly unfoliated, emplaced into low-grade metamorphic host rocks, generally not spatially associated with mafic intrusions, exclusively peraluminous with polymetallic Sn-W-Mo-U greisen- and vein-dominated mineral deposits, and entirely crustally-derived (sub-Meguma Group source rocks and Meguma Group contami-

D. B. Clarke and Others

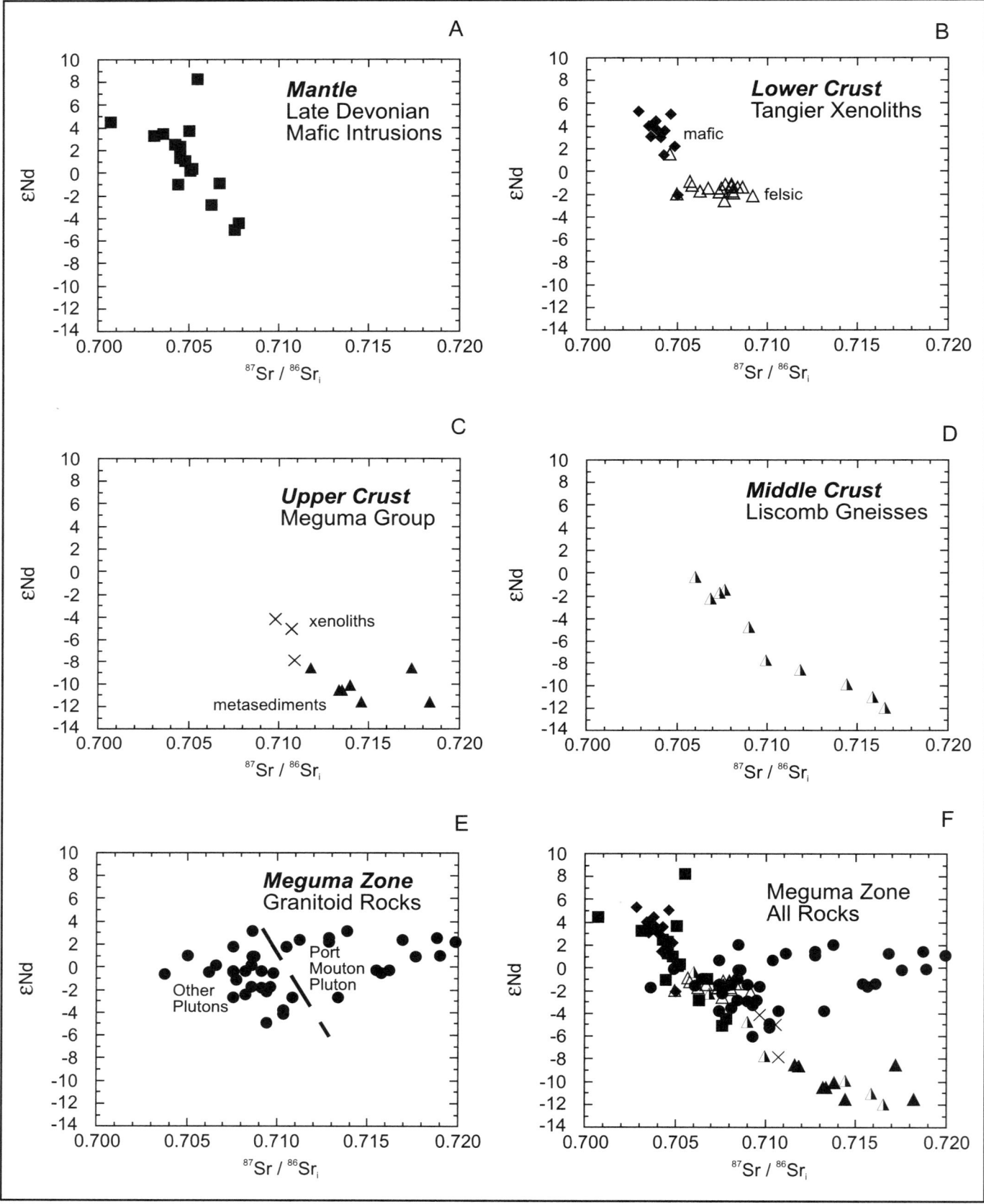

Figure 9. Summary of Sr-Nd isotopic data for all granitoid rocks in the Meguma Zone, including all potential source rocks (see text for details). Granitoid rocks of the Port Mouton pluton have anomalously high radiogenic strontium.

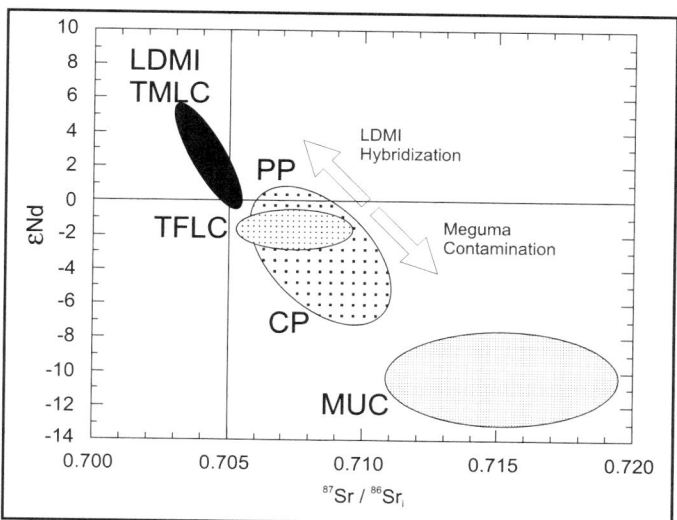

Figure 10. Schematic strontium-neodymium isotopic relationships between granitoid rocks and source rocks in the Meguma Zone. Dominant source materials for both the central plutons (CP) and peripheral plutons (PP) are the felsic rocks of the Tangier felsic lower crust (TFLC). Other possible material inputs include the Tangier mafic lower crust (TMLC) during partial melting, Late Devonian mafic intrusions (LDMI) as hybrids with partial melts of TFLC, and the Meguma upper crust (MUC) metasedimentary rocks as contaminants with partial melts of TFLC. In general, the central plutons are the entirely crustal products of Tangier felsic sources and Meguma Group contamination, whereas the peripheral plutons are the hybridized products of crustal Tangier felsic sources and mantle-derived Tangier mafic sources and Late Devonian mafic intrusion magmas.

nation), and probably owe their origin to crustal thickening associated with the collision of the Meguma terrane against the Avalon terrane.

2. The peripheral plutons, at the northeastern and southwestern extremities of the Meguma Zone, are probably slightly older (≥376 Ma), late-tectonic, moderately foliated, emplaced into higher-grade metamorphic host rocks, invariably spatially associated with mafic intrusions (the spatial association of mafic intrusions and high-grade metamorphism may not be accidental), mostly peraluminous with only limited Be-pegmatite mineralization, and of mixed derivation (sub-Meguma Group source rocks and mantle-derived mafic magmas), and probably owe their origin to the lower to mid-crustal emplacement of subduction-related mafic magmas intruded prior to the final emplacement of the Meguma terrane.

We believe that our integration of felsic and mafic magmatism represents a new and significant petrogenetic and tectonic paradigm for the Meguma Zone in the Late Devonian.

ACKNOWLEDGMENTS

This paper is the result of work done by many university and government colleagues and a generation of students, all of whom contributed directly or indirectly to the model presented here. Many of their names appear in the references cited. The National Sciences and Engineering Research Council of Canada funded the research of Clarke and his students. We thank L. Heaman for his collaboration in the U-Pb analysis of one of the mafic intrusions; P. H. Reynolds for his ongoing career dedicated to unravelling the geochronology of the Meguma Zone; A. K. Chatterjee for his critical petrographic and isotopic work on the Liscomb Complex and the Tangier lower crustal xenoliths; and Andrew Henry for giving the heterogeneous figures from three authors some stylistic integrity. We also appreciate the constructive criticism of S. Barr and an anonymous reviewer.

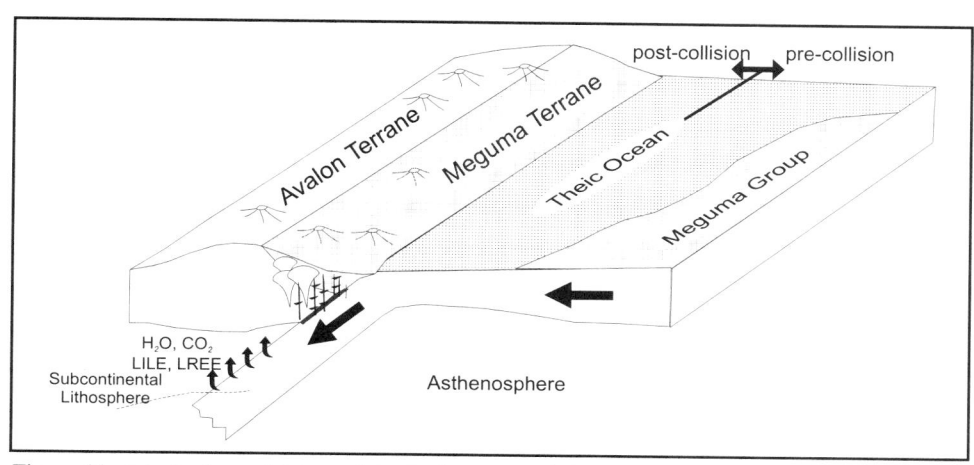

Figure 11. A tectonic model to explain the known spatial and temporal relationships between the Meguma Zone and the Avalon Zone, and between mafic and felsic magmatism in the Meguma Zone in the Late Devonian. See text for details. LILE = large-ion lithophile elements, LREE = light rare earth elements.

REFERENCES CITED

Abbott, R. N., 1989, Internal structures in part of the South Mountain batholith, Nova Scotia, Canada: Geological Society of America Bulletin, v. 101, p. 1493–1506.

Allan, B. D, and Clarke, D. B., 1981, Occurrence and origin of garnets in the South Mountain Batholith, Nova Scotia: Canadian Mineralogist, v. 19, p. 19–24.

Beard, J. S., and Day, H. W., 1988, Petrology and emplacement of the Smartville Complex, northern California: Journal of Petrology, v. 29, p. 965–995.

Boucot, A. J., 1960, Implications of Rhenish Lower Devonian brachiopods from Nova Scotia: International Geological Congress, Report of the Twenty-First Session, v. 12, p. 129–137.

Chatterjee, A. K., 1983, Metallogenic map of Nova Scotia: Nova Scotia Department of Mines and Energy Map, scale 1:500,000.

Chatterjee, A. K., and Ham, L. J., 1991, U-Th-Pb systematics of the South Mountain Batholith, Nova Scotia: Sackville, New Brunswick, Atlantic Geoscience Society Annual Colloquium, Proceedings with Abstracts.

Chatterjee, A. K., and Strong, D. F., 1985, Geochemical characteristics of the polymetallic tin domain southwestern Nova Scotia, Canada [extended abs.], in Taylor, R. P., and Strong, D. F., eds., Granite-related mineral deposits—Geology, petrogenesis and tectonic setting: Montreal, Canadian Institute of Mining, p. 41–52.

Chatterjee, A. K., Strong, D. F., Clarke, D. B., Robertson, J., Pollock, D., and Muecke, G. K., 1985, Geochemistry of the granodiorite hosting uranium mineralization at Millet Brook, in Chatterjee, A. K., and Clarke, D. B., eds., Guide to the granites and mineral deposits of southwestern Nova Scotia: Nova Scotia Department of Mines and Energy Paper 85-3, p. 63–114.

Clarke, D. B., 1981, The mineralogy of peraluminous granites: A review: Canadian Mineralogist, v. 19, p. 3–19.

Clarke, D. B., 1994, Cordierite in felsic igneous rocks: A synthesis: Mineralogical Magazine, v. 59, p. 311–325.

Clarke, D. B., and Chatterjee, A. K., 1988, Physical and chemical processes in the South Mountain Batholith, in Taylor, R. P., and Strong, D. F., eds., Recent advances in the geology of granite-related mineral deposits: Canadian Institute of Mining and Metallurgy Special Volume 39, p. 223–233.

Clarke, D. B., and Halliday, A. N., 1980, Strontium isotope geology of the South Mountain Batholith, Nova Scotia: Geochimica et Cosmochimica Acta, v. 44, p. 1045–1058.

Clarke, D. B., and Halliday, A. N., 1985, Sm/Nd isotopic investigation of the age and origin of the Meguma Zone metasedimentary rocks: Canadian Journal of Earth Sciences, v. 22, p. 102–107.

Clarke, D. B., and Muecke, G. K., 1980, Igneous and metamorphic geology of Nova Scotia: Geological Association of Canada–Mineralogical Association of Canada, Field Trip Guidebook, v. 21, 101 p.

Clarke, D. B., and Muecke, G. K., 1985, Review of the petrochemistry and origin of the South Mountain Batholith and associated plutons, Nova Scotia, Canada, in High heat production (HHP) granites, hydrothermal circulation and ore genesis: London, England, Institution of Mining and Metallurgy, p. 41–54.

Clarke, D. B., McKenzie, C. B., Muecke, G. K., and Richardson, S. W., 1976, Magmatic andalusite from the South Mountain Batholith, Nova Scotia: Contributions to Mineralogy and Petrology, v. 56, p. 279–287.

Clarke, D. B., Halliday, A. N., and Hamilton, P. J., 1988, Neodymium and strontium isotopic constraints on the origin of peraluminous granitoids of the South Mountain Batholith, Nova Scotia, Canada: Chemical Geology (Isotope Geoscience Section), v. 73, p. 15–24.

Clarke, D. B., Chatterjee, A. K., and Giles, P. S., 1993a, Petrochemistry, tectonic history, and Sr-Nd systematics of the Liscomb Complex, Meguma Lithotectonic Zone, Nova Scotia: Canadian Journal of Earth Sciences, v. 30, p. 449–464.

Clarke, D. B., MacDonald, M. A., Reynolds, P. H., and Longstaffe, F. J., 1993b, Leucogranites from the eastern part of the South Mountain Batholith, Nova Scotia: Journal of Petrology, v. 34, p. 653–679.

de Albuquerque, C. A. R., 1979, Origin of the plutonic mafic rocks of southern Nova Scotia: Geological Society of America Bulletin, v. 90, p. 719–731.

Ding, Y., 1995, AFM Minerals in the Halifax Pluton [M.S. thesis]: Halifax, Nova Scotia, Dalhousie University, 191 p.

Douma, S., 1988, The mineralogy, petrology and geochemistry of the Port Mouton Pluton, Nova Scotia, Canada [M.S. thesis]: Halifax, Nova Scotia, Dalhousie University, 324 p.

Eberz, G. W., Clarke, D. B., Chatterjee, A. K., and Giles, P. S., 1991, Chemical and isotopic composition of the lower crust beneath the Meguma lithotectonic zone, Nova Scotia: Evidence from granulite facies xenoliths: Contributions to Mineralogy and Petrology, v. 109, p. 69–88.

Faribault, E. R., 1908, City of Halifax Sheet, Map No. 68: Geological Survey of Canada Publication no. 1019, scale 1:63,360.

France-Lanord, C., and Le Fort, P., 1988, Crustal melting and granite genesis during the Himalayan collision orogenesis: Royal Society of Edinburgh Transactions, Earth Sciences, v. 79, p. 183–195.

Greenough, J. D., Owen, V. J., and Ruffman, A., 1993, Noble metal concentrations in shoshonitic lamprophyres: Analysis of the Weekend dykes, Eastern Shore, Nova Scotia, Canada: Journal of Petrology, v. 34, p. 1247–1269.

Hall, L. R., 1979, Geology of the LaHave River area, Lunenburg County, Nova Scotia [M.S. thesis]: Wolfville, Nova Scotia, Acadia University, 174 p.

Ham, L. J., Corey, M. C., Horne, R. J., and MacDonald, M. A., 1990, Lithogeochemistry of the western portion of the South Mountain Batholith, Nova Scotia: Nova Scotia Department of Mines and Energy Open File Report 90-007, 31 p.

Harland, W. B., Armstrong, R. L., Cox, A. V., Craig, L. E., Smith, A. G., and Smith, D. G., 1990, A geologic time scale 1989: Cambridge, England, Cambridge University Press, 263 p.

Harper, C. L., 1988, On the nature of time in the cosmological perspective [Ph.D. thesis]: Oxford, England, Oxford University, 508 p.

Hart, S. R., 1988, Heterogeneous mantle domains: Signatures, genesis, and mixing chronologies: Earth and Planetary Science Letters, v. 90, p. 273–296.

Hawkesworth, C. J., Gallagher, K., Hergt, J. M., and McDermott, F., 1993, Mantle and slab contributions in arc magmas: Annual Review of Earth and Planetary Sciences, v. 21, p. 175–204.

Hill, J. D., 1988, Late Devonian peraluminous granitic plutons in the Canso area, eastern Meguma Terrane, Nova Scotia: Maritime Sediments and Atlantic Geology, v. 24, p. 11–19.

Hill, J. D., 1991, Petrology, tectonic setting, and economic potential of Devonian peraluminous granitoid plutons in the Canso and Forest Hills areas, Eastern Meguma Terrane, Nova Scotia: Geological Survey of Canada Bulletin, v. 383, 96 p.

Horne, R. J., Corey, M. C., Ham, L. J., and MacDonald, M. A., 1990, Lithogeochemical variation within the biotite-rich envelope rocks of the eastern South Mountain Batholith: Implications for its intrusive and post-intrusive history, in Brown, Y., and MacDonald, D. R., eds., Report of activities 1988: Nova Scotia Department of Mines and Energy, Mines and Minerals Branch, Report 89-1, Part B, p. 37–50.

Horne, R. J., Corey, M. C., Ham, L. J., and MacDonald, M. A., 1992, Structure and emplacement of the South Mountain Batholith, southwestern Nova Scotia: Atlantic Geology, v. 29, p. 29–50.

Jamieson, R. A., 1974, The contact of the South Mountain Batholith near Mount Uniacke, Nova Scotia [B.S. thesis]: Halifax, Nova Scotia, Dalhousie University, 52 p.

Johnson, R. W., 1987, Delayed partial melting of subduction-modified magma sources in Western Melanesia; new results from the late Cainozoic, in Pacific Rim congress 87; an international congress on the geology, structure, mineralisation, and economics of the Pacific Rim: Parkville, Australia, Australasian Institute of Mining and Metallurgy, p. 211–214.

Keen, C. E., Kay, W. A., Keppie, J. D., Marillier, F., Pe-Piper, G., and Waldron, J. W. F., 1991, Deep seismic reflection data from the Bay of Fundy and

Gulf of Maine: Tectonic implications for the northern Appalachians: Canadian Journal of Earth Sciences, v. 28, p. 1096–1111.

Kempster, R. M. F., Clarke, D. B., Reynolds, P. H., and Chatterjee, A. K., 1989, Late Devonian lamprophyric dykes in the Meguma Zone of Nova Scotia: Canadian Journal of Earth Sciences, v. 26, p. 611–613.

Keppie, J. D., 1985, The Appalachian collage, *in* Gee, D. G., and Sturt, B. A., eds., The Caledonide Orogen—Scandinavia and related areas: New York, John Wiley and Sons, p. 1217–1226.

Keppie, J. D., and Dallmeyer, R. D., 1987, Dating transcurrent terrane accretion; an example from the Meguma and Avalon composite terranes in the northern Appalachians: Tectonics, v. 6, p. 831–847.

Keppie, J. D., and Dostal, J., 1991, Late Proterozoic tectonic model for the Avalon terrane in Maritime Canada: Tectonics, v. 10, p. 842–850.

Kontak, D. J., 1990, The East Kemptville muscovite-topaz leucogranite. I. Geological setting and whole rock geochemistry: Canadian Mineralogist, v. 28, p. 787–825.

Kontak, D. J., and Chatterjee, A. K., 1992, The East Kemptville tin deposit, Yarmouth County, Nova Scotia III. A Pb isotope study of the leucogranite and mineralized greisen: Evidence for a 366 Ma metallogenic event: Canadian Journal of Earth Sciences, v. 29, p. 1180–1196.

Kontak, D. J., and Cormier, R. F., 1991, A Rb/Sr geochronological study of the East Kemptville leucogranite, East Kemptville tin deposit, Yarmouth County, Nova Scotia: Evidence for multiple tectonothermal overprinting events: Canadian Journal of Earth Sciences, v. 28, p. 209–224.

Kontak, D. J., Strong, D. F., and Kerrich, R., 1988, Crystal-melt ± fluid phase equilibria versus late-stage fluid-rock interaction in granitic rocks of the South Mountain Batholith, Nova Scotia: Whole rock geochemistry and oxygen isotope evidence: Maritime Sediments and Atlantic Geology, v. 24, p. 97–110.

Kontak, D. J., Kerrich, R., and Strong, D. F., 1991, The role of fluids in the late-stage evolution of the South Mountain Batholith, Nova Scotia: Further geochemical and oxygen isotopic studies: Atlantic Geology, v. 27, p. 29–47.

Kubilius, W. P., 1983, Sulphur isotopic evidence for country rock contamination of granitoids in southwestern Nova Scotia [M.S. thesis]: University Park, Pennsylvania State University, 103 p.

Longstaffe, F. J., Smith, T. E., and Muehlenbachs, K., 1980, Oxygen isotope evidence for the genesis of Upper Paleozoic granitoids from southwestern Nova Scotia: Canadian Journal of Earth Sciences, v. 17, p. 132–141.

MacDonald, M. A., 1994, A review of the exploration history and mineral deposit types in the South Mountain batholith, *in* MacDonald, D. R., ed., Report of activities: Nova Scotia Department of Natural Resources, Mines and Energy Branch, Report 94-1, p. 43–64.

MacDonald, M. A., and Clarke, D. B., 1985, The petrology, geochemistry and economic potential of the Musquodoboit Batholith, Nova Scotia: Canadian Journal of Earth Sciences, v. 22, p. 1633–1642.

MacDonald, M. A., and Clarke, D. B., 1991, Use of nonparametric ranking statistics to characterize magmatic and post-magmatic processes in the eastern South Mountain Batholith, Nova Scotia, Canada: Chemical Geology, v. 92, p. 1–20.

MacDonald, M. A., and Ham, L. J., 1992, Geological map of Gaspereau Lake (N.T.S. sheets 21A/15 and part of 21H/02): Nova Scotia Department of Natural Resources Map 92-1, scale 1:50,000.

MacDonald, M. A., Corey, M. C., Ham, L. J., and Horne, R. J., 1992, An overview of recent bedrock mapping and follow-up petrological studies of the South Mountain Batholith, southwestern Nova Scotia, Canada: Atlantic Geology, v. 28, p. 7–28.

Maillet, L. A., and Clarke, D. B., 1985, Cordierite in the peraluminous granites of the Meguma Zone, Nova Scotia, Canada: Mineralogical Magazine, v. 49, p. 695–702.

Martel, T. A., McGregor, C. D., and Utting, J., 1993, Stratigraphic significance of Upper Devonian and Lower Carboniferous miospores from the type area

of the Horton Group, Nova Scotia: Canadian Journal of Earth Sciences, v. 30, p. 1091–1098.

Muecke, G. K., Elias, P., and Reynolds, P. H., 1988, Hercynian/Alleghanian overprinting of an Acadian terrane: ^{40}Ar/^{39}Ar studies in the Meguma Zone, Nova Scotia, Canada: Chemical Geology, v. 73, p. 153–167.

O'Reilly, G. A., Farley, E. J., and Charest, M. H., 1982, Metasomatic-hydrothermal mineral deposits of the New Ross–Mahone Bay area, Nova Scotia: Nova Scotia Department of Mines and Energy Paper 82-2, 96 p.

O'Reilly, G. A., MacDonald, M. A., Kontak, D. J., and Corey, M. C., 1992, Granite- and metasediment-hosted mineral deposits of southwest Nova Scotia: Geological Association of Canada, Mineralogical Association of Canada, Joint Annual meeting, Field Trip C-3, Guidebook, 91 p.

Pearce, J. A., 1983, Role of the subcontinental lithosphere in magma genesis at active continental margins, *in* Hawkesworth, C. J., and Norry, M. J., eds., Continental basalts and mantle xenoliths: Nantwich, Shiva Publishing, p. 230–249.

Poulson, S., Kubilius, W. P., and Ohmoto, H., 1991, Geochemical behaviour of sulfur in granitoids during intrusion of the South Mountain Batholith, Nova Scotia, Canada: Geochimica et Cosmochimica Acta, v. 55, p. 3809–3830.

Raeside, R. P., Hill, J. D., and Eddy, B. G., 1988, Metamorphism of Meguma Group metasedimentary rocks, Whitehead Harbour area, Guysborough County, Nova Scotia: Maritime Sediments and Atlantic Geology, v. 24, p. 1–9.

Rock, N. M. S., 1990, Lamprophyres: Glasgow, Blackie and Son, Ltd., 285 p.

Rogers, H. D., 1988, Field relations, petrography, and geochemistry of granitoid plutons in the Shelburne area, southern Nova Scotia: Geological Survey of Canada Open File Report 1835, 128 p.

Rogers, H. D., and White, C. E., 1984, Geology of the igneous-metamorphic complex of the Shelburne and eastern Yarmouth counties, Nova Scotia: Geological Survey of Canada Paper 84-1A, p. 463–465.

Salters, V. J. M., and Hart, S. R., 1991, The mantle sources of ocean ridges, islands, and arcs: The Hf-isotope connection: Earth and Planetary Science Letters, v. 104, p. 364–380.

Schenk, P. E., 1991, Events and sea-level changes on Gondwana's margin: The Meguma Zone (Cambrian to Devonian) of Nova Scotia, Canada: Geological Society of America Bulletin, v. 103, p. 512–521.

Streckeisen, A., 1976, To each plutonic rock its proper name: Earth Science Reviews, v. 12, p. 1–33.

Tate, M. C., 1995, The relationship between Late Devonian mafic intrusions and peraluminous granitoid generation in the Meguma Lithotectonic Zone, Nova Scotia, Canada [Ph.D thesis]: Halifax, Nova Scotia, Dalhousie University, 528 p.

Tate, M. C., and Clarke, D. B., 1993, Origin of the Late Devonian Weekend lamprophyre dykes, Meguma Zone, Nova Scotia: Canadian Journal of Earth Sciences, v. 30, p. 2295–2304.

Tate, M. C., and Clarke, D. B., 1995, Petrogenesis and regional tectonic significance of Late Devonian mafic intrusions in the Meguma Zone, Nova Scotia: Canadian Journal of Earth Sciences, v. 32, p. 1883–1898.

Tate, M. C., and Merrett, D., 1994, Compilation of major oxide, trace element and rare-earth element analyses for Late Devonian peraluminous granitoids in the Meguma Zone, Nova Scotia: Nova Scotia Department of Natural Resources Open File Report 94-14, 71 p.

Williams, H., and Hatcher, R. D., Jr., 1983, Appalachian suspect terranes, *in* Hatcher, R. D., ed., Contributions to the tectonics and geophysics of mountain chains: Geological Society of America Memoir 158, p. 33–53.

Wyman, D. A., and Kerrich, R., 1989, Archean lamprophyre dykes of the Superior Province, Canada: Distribution, petrology, and geochemical characteristics: Journal of Geophysical Research, v. 94, p. 4667–4696.

MANUSCRIPT ACCEPTED BY THE SOCIETY JULY 2, 1996

Geological Society of America
Memoir 191
1997

Rift and ocean floor volcanism from the Late Proterozoic and early Paleozoic of the Vermont Appalachians

R. A. Coish

Geology Department, Middlebury College, Middlebury, Vermont 05753

ABSTRACT

Greenstone bodies from the western Vermont Appalachians and dikes intruding the Adirondack massif comprise metavolcanic rocks that originated as basalt formed during break-up of the Laurentian continent and formation of the Iapetus ocean in the Late Proterozoic to Early Cambrian. In spite of metamorphism, the chemistry of the metavolcanic rocks reveals some detail on the progressive development of the rift valley and ocean basin. Basaltic rocks in the western part of the area (zones 1 and 2) formed in early stages of a continental rift. Basaltic rocks in central Vermont (zone 4) formed in oceanic stages, presumably early Iapetus ocean. Basaltic rocks found in between (zone 3) probably formed at a transitional (proto-oceanic) stage of the rift evolution. The rocks were then emplaced along thrusts and metamorphosed to greenstones during subsequent closure of the Iapetus ocean in the Early Ordovician. The greenstone bodies thus are now in discrete tectonic slices that probably all originated on or close to the edge of the ancient Laurentian continent.

INTRODUCTION

This chapter presents new data and a comprehensive review of old data on metamorphosed volcanic rocks from the Vermont Appalachians. Data were collected over about a 15 year period by me and undergraduates at Middlebury College, Vermont. The geochemistry of the rocks is emphasized, although in most cases detailed field and structural work have also been done on the areas by students and faculty at Middlebury College and the University of Vermont (principally Rolfe Stanley). Geochemical data are used primarily to interpret possible tectonic environments of formation of the metavolcanic rocks; these tectonic environments are integrated into an overall model for the early Paleozoic tectonic evolution of Vermont (Stanley and Ratcliffe, 1985). In addition, there is some discussion of magmatic evolution of the rocks, including potential sources, and partial melting and crystallization effects.

The metavolcanic rocks show a change in chemistry from west to east across western Vermont that is consistent with their formation in an evolving continental rift–oceanic basin environment (Coish, 1989; Coish et al., 1991). Coish et al. (1991) distin-guished four geochemical zones labeled 1, 2, 3, and 4—zone 1 represents metavolcanic rocks farthest west and zone 4 represents metavolcanic rocks farthest east in central Vermont (Fig. 1). For the most part, early rift volcanic rocks are found in the west and later ocean-ridge volcanic rocks crop out farther east. In between, volcanic compositions are varied and some formations may contain volcanic rocks with chemical characteristics of several stages of rifting. Thus, a spatial and temporal distribution of rift volcanic rocks appears to be preserved.

In this chapter, I first briefly present a regional geologic and tectonic framework for western Vermont and adjacent New York. I then provide a general background in the application of geochemistry to tectonic problems. Finally, the geochemistry and interpretation of the metavolcanic rocks are described in the order (1) early stages of Iapetan rifting (zones 1 and 2), which includes dikes from the Adirondack massif and greenstone bodies from the Pinnacle and Underhill formations, (2) intermediate stages of rifting (zone 3), which includes greenstone bodies from the Hazens Notch and Pinney Hollow formations, and (3) late stages of Iapetan rifting (zone 4), which includes greenstone bodies from the Ottauquechee and Stowe formations.

Coish, R. A., 1997, Rift and ocean floor volcanism from the Late Proterozoic and early Paleozoic of the Vermont Appalachians, *in* Sinha, A. K., Whalen, J. B., and Hogan, J. P., eds., The Nature of Magmatism in the Appalachian Orogen: Boulder, Colorado, Geological Society of America Memoir 191.

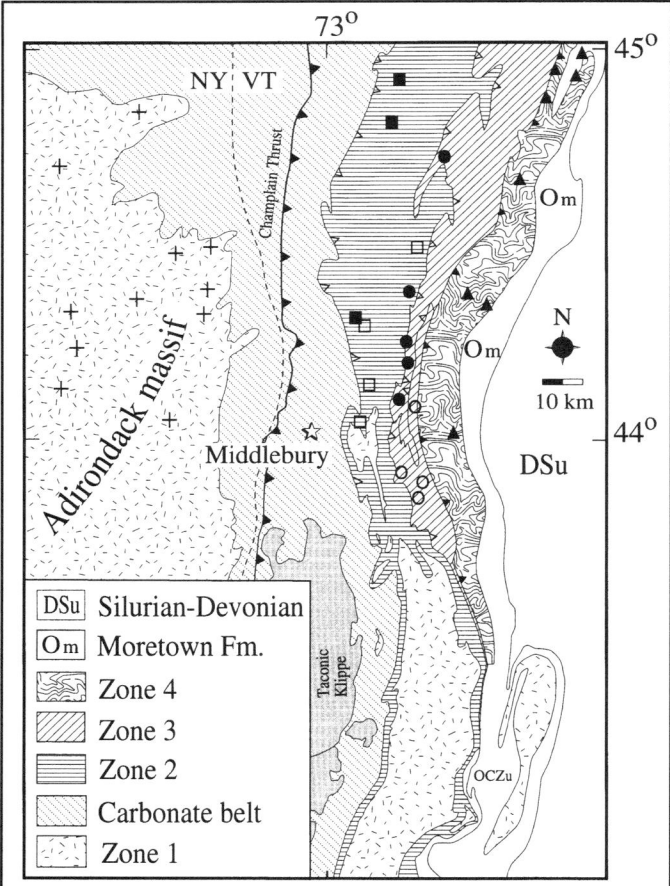

Figure 1. Simplified geologic map of Vermont and adjacent eastern New York (Doll et al., 1961; Stanley and Ratcliffe, 1985) showing locations of metamorphosed volcanic rocks. Zone 1 is a region where dikes intrude the Adirondack massif. Zone 2 includes the Pinnacle and Underhill formations (Hinesburg and Underhill tectonic slices). Zone 3 includes the Hazens Notch and Pinney Hollow formations (also tectonic slices). Zone 4 includes the Ottauquechee and Stowe formations (Rowe tectonic slice).

REGIONAL GEOLOGY AND TECTONIC SETTING

The study area is in the western Vermont Appalachians and adjacent Adirondack massif (Fig. 1); in tectonic terms, it includes part of the ancient Laurentian continent and western Appalachian terranes that were attached to Laurentia in the early Paleozoic (Rankin, 1994). The Adirondack massif includes anorthosite suites, charnockite, and granitic and sedimentary gneiss formed in collision and rifting processes between 1.3 and 1.1 Ga (McLelland and Chiarenzelli, 1990; McLelland, 1991; McLelland et al., 1993). Mafic dikes of Proterozoic and Mesozoic ages cut through these granulite facies metamorphic rocks. The Proterozoic magmatic event was probably related to early stages of continental rifting that eventually led to formation of the Iapetus ocean (Rankin, 1976; Coish and Sinton, 1992; Kumarapeli, 1993; Rankin, 1994).

Western and central Vermont is a classic example of a fore-land thrust belt in which a passive margin sequence was deformed by collision of a volcanic arc with the ancient Laurentian continent. Eastward-directed subduction led to the collision (Taconic orogeny) in which parts of the passive margin sequence, Laurentian basement, early rift facies rocks, and more exotic oceanic terranes were thrust westward over autochthonous passive margin sedimentary rocks. Thus, most of central Vermont is now a series of tectonic slices (Stanley and Ratcliffe, 1985; Rankin, 1994). Western Vermont is dominated by rocks of the early Paleozoic carbonate platform, which comprises a thick sequence of Cambrian to Ordovician quartzite, dolostone, and limestone (Fig. 1). Immediately east of the carbonate sequence is the core of the Green Mountains, which includes slivers of 1.2 Ga basement overlain by deformed cover sequences interpreted as terranes thrust onto the Laurentian continent during the Taconic orogeny. The rocks in central Vermont are part of the Brompton Cameron terrane (Rankin, 1994), and include, from west to east, the Hinesburg, Underhill, Hazens Notch, Pinney Hollow, and Rowe-Hawley slices (Stanley and Ratcliffe, 1985). For this chapter, zone 2 rocks are from the Hinesburg and Under-hill slices, which include the Pinnacle and Underhill formations (Doll et al., 1961); zone 3 rocks are in the Hazens Notch and Pinney Hollow slices; and zone 4 rocks are in the Rowe tectonic slice, which includes the Ottauquechee and Stowe formations. The Hinesburg and Underhill slices are interpreted as slivers of terranes that were part of an early rift facies sequence, whereas the Hazens Notch and Pinney Hollow slices have been interpreted as oceanic facies (Rankin, 1994). The Rowe slice is interpreted as a tectonic melange assembled in an accretionary wedge west of an early Paleozoic volcanic arc now represented by the Hawley volcanic belt (Stanley and Ratcliffe, 1985). Greenstone occurs within the central Vermont slices as slivers, pods, and lenses surrounded by dominantly metasedimentary assemblages. Most of the greenstone bodies were volcanic or intrusive mafic rocks; in rare cases, pillow structures are seen, but most commonly, deformation has obliterated original textures and structures to such a degree that it is not possible to tell whether the igneous rock was a flow, a fragmental deposit, or a high-level intrusive rock. Greenstone bodies are the main focus of this chapter: however, before describing details of their origin, I provide some background on general principles of using geochemistry to interpret the origin of igneous rocks.

APPLICATION OF GEOCHEMISTRY TO IGNEOUS ROCKS

Major and trace elements are very useful in deciphering the magmatic evolution of igneous rocks, which can be influenced by processes such as varying degrees of partial melting, fractional crystallization, contamination, and variable compositions of source rocks that melt to form the magmas. Inasmuch as some of those processes change with tectonic environment, then geochemistry can also be used to help fingerprint the environment of formation of igneous rocks. I briefly discuss some ways in which the above processes affect the chemistry of basaltic magmas in particular; this knowledge then can be used to work backward to discuss the origin of any particular suite of volcanic rocks.

Basalt magmas originate as partial melts of mantle material, so clearly the detailed geochemistry of a basalt is greatly influenced by the composition of the mantle that melts. Even though the mantle might seem to be a rather uniform peridotite composition on a grand scale, it is in detail heterogeneous, especially in minor- and trace-element geochemistry. There is general agreement that the upper parts of the mantle have zones that include mantle lithosphere, depleted mantle asthenosphere, and primary (or enriched) deep upper mantle. Immediately below the crust is mantle lithosphere, which in continental areas may extend down to 200 or 300 km (Hawkesworth et al., 1988, 1990; Lightfoot et al., 1993). The mantle lithosphere is believed to be peridotite that is enriched in incompatible elements such as K, Rb, Ba, light rare-earth elements (REE), and probably also high-field strength elements such as Ti. The physical nature of this enrichment is not understood, but may be in veins formed as partial melts crystallize on trying to escape the mantle. The importance here is that the mantle lithosphere can be either a direct source rock for basalt magma or act as contaminant of basaltic magmas that originate from deeper levels. The mantle lithosphere is implicated, particularly in the origin of continental flood basalt and early rift basalt (Leeman and Fitton, 1989; White and McKenzie, 1989; Altherr et al., 1990). Below the mantle lithosphere is depleted mantle asthenosphere. This is depleted in incompatible elements, including K, Ba, Rb, and the light REE. It is the source for mid-ocean ridge basalt magmas, but may also contribute to the origin of rift and ocean-island basalt magmas. Below depleted asthenosphere is probably primary or enriched asthenosphere and mesosphere. This and deeper regions may give rise to mantle plumes that are thought to be the major source rock for ocean-island and perhaps some rift basalt magmas. Thus, in contemplating the origin of basalt, one has to consider which of these mantle types was the source rock.

Apart from variations in the source composition, three other important processes can affect the composition of an igneous rock. First, different amounts of partial melting of any one source can also give variable basalt magma chemistry. Low degree partial melts have higher incompatible elements concentrations than do high degree melts. Second, crystal fractionation can change the composition of succeeding eruptions if magmas accumulate in magma chambers before being erupted onto the surface. In basaltic magmas, crystallization of early formed olivine, pyroxene, and plagioclase leads to depletion in MgO, Ni, Cr, and enrichment in elements such as K, Ba, Rb, REE, Zr, and Y. Titanium increases in melts until titanomagnetite becomes a fractionating phase. Third, contamination by country rock can change the composition of magmas on ascent. The main contaminants in basaltic magmas are lithospheric mantle and continental crust.

Because the composition of mantle sources, possible contaminants, partial melting, and fractionation processes are not the same for all tectonic environments, then the geochemistry of resulting basalt magmas may vary with tectonic environment.

This principle has enabled many workers to attempt to use geochemistry to fingerprint ancient tectonic environments (Pearce and Cann, 1973; Pearce, 1975; Pearce and Norry, 1979; Wood, 1980; Pearce, 1983). It has worked reasonably well for basaltic rocks, although it clear that there is often overlap in chemistry among environments, and thus geochemical fingerprinting should be accompanied by other evidence for a particular tectonic environment. Finally, a word of caution in the application of these tectonic discriminants is in order. Most ancient basaltic rocks have undergone low-grade metamorphism, which mobilizes some major and trace elements, and hence can change the composition of the original rock. Therefore, when dealing with metamorphosed volcanic rocks, one should use diagrams that employ the relatively immobile elements. In this chapter, I have chosen only a few classic tectonic discriminant diagrams to discuss the origin of metavolcanic rocks in the Vermont Appalachians; other diagrams, in general, support the proposed interpretations.

EARLY STAGES OF IAPETAN RIFTING

Zone 1: Adirondack dikes

Abundant Proterozoic dikes of basaltic composition cut anorthosite, granitic gneiss, and charnockite of the Adirondack massif (Buddington, 1939; Isachsen, 1985; Coish and Sinton, 1992; Badger, 1994). A separate swarm of Mesozoic dikes also cuts the massif and can sometimes be confused with the Proterozoic dikes. In this chapter, only Proterozoic dikes are considered; the petrography and geochemistry of the Mesozoic dikes have been documented elsewhere (McHone and Butler, 1984). Recognition of dikes as Proterozoic age is based partly on K/Ar dating and on the evidence that these dikes do not cut lower Paleozoic carbonate sedimentary rocks (Isachsen, 1985; Isachsen et al., 1988). In fact, at Trembleau Point, a swarm of dikes is overlain unconformably by the cover sequence (McHone and Butler, 1984). Furthermore, Mesozoic dikes that cut Paleozoic carbonates have a petrography and geochemistry distinct from the Proterozoic dikes.

The Proterozoic dikes range from a few centimeters to 2 m in width, and extend along strike for kilometers in directions between N20E and N75E (Sinton, 1988). Most dikes are dark, fine-grained mafic rocks that often exhibit chilled margins against country rock. They are sometimes amygdaloidal and rarely contain inclusions of country rock. The dikes are often porphyritic, and have phenocrysts of olivine, clinopyroxene, and plagioclase in a matrix of plagioclase, magnetite, chlorite, calcite, and serpentine. Dendritic textures may be present. The rocks are altered; notably most olivine phenocrysts are pseudomorphed by serpentine, calcite, and chlorite, and plagioclase is clouded by a fine-grained epidote-calcite-chlorite-muscovite mass. The degree of alteration is greatest near hydrothermal veins or along dike contacts.

The geochemistry of these dikes indicates that they are mostly alkalic to transitional basaltic rocks with moderate to high TiO_2 contents (Fig. 2 A and B; Table 1). The alkalinity of the basaltic rocks is based on the immobile element plot, TiO_2 versus

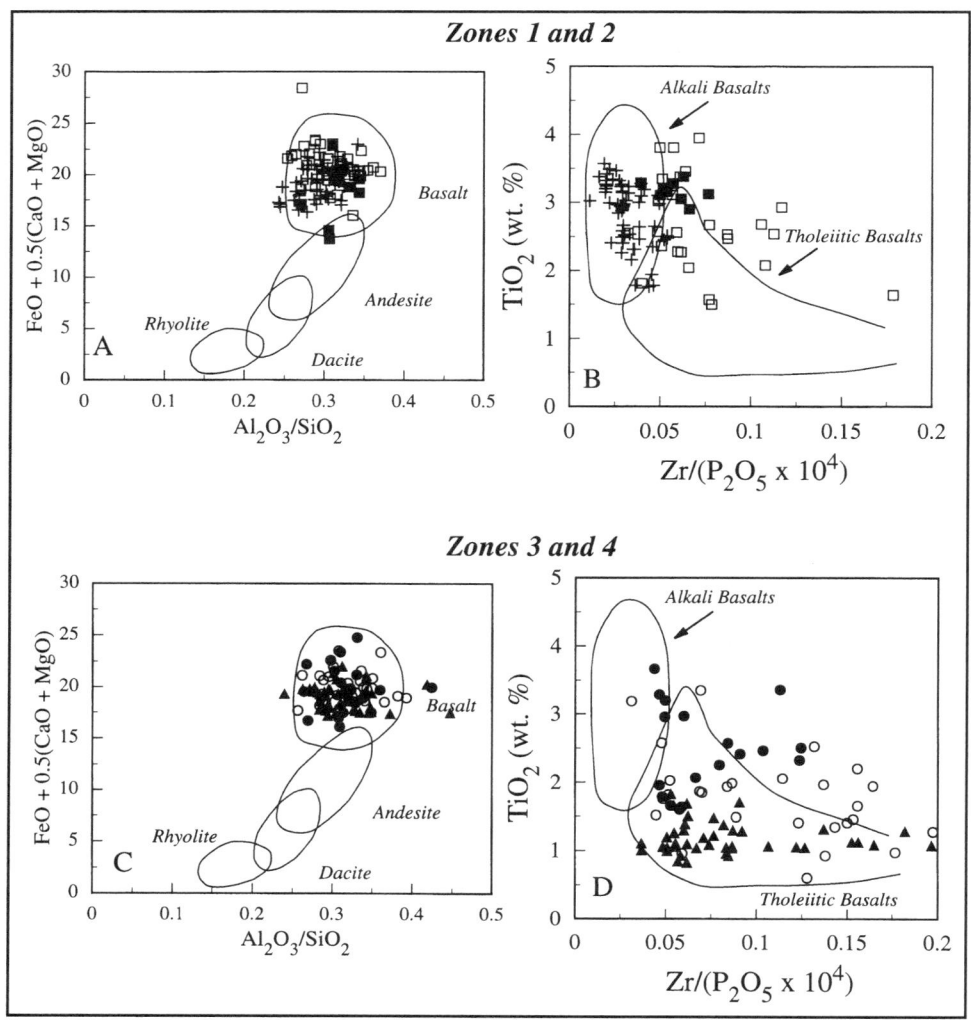

Figure 2. Classification of dikes and greenstone bodies from the Vermont Appalachians. Note that samples from all zones are classified as basaltic in Al/Si versus Fe + Ca + Mg diagrams (Church, 1975). On a Zr/P versus Ti diagram (Floyd and Winchester, 1975), zone 1 samples are dominantly alkaline to transitional and zone 2 samples are transitional to tholeiitic (A). Samples from zones 3 and 4 are dominantly tholeiitic (D). Plus signs are Adirondack dikes, black squares are the Pinnacle Formation, white squares are the Underhill Formation, black circles are the Hazens Notch Formation, white circles are the Pinney Hollow Formation, and black triangles are the Stowe Formation.

P_2O_5, but an alkalis versus silica plot is consistent with this assignment. The dikes are all evolved with Mg numbers[1] between 64 and 45 (Coish and Sinton, 1992). In an extended rare earth diagram, where elements are arranged in order of decreasing incompatibility and increasing field strength from left to right, basaltic rocks from zone 1 show an overall enrichment relative to mantle with a characteristic humpback-shaped pattern (Fig. 3). The low field strength elements are significantly enriched with a peak at La and then a gradual decrease to Yb (Figs. 3 and 4A). It is significant that Nb and Ti are not depleted

relative to adjacent elements. This is important because negative Nb (and to a lesser extent Ti) anomalies are used to indicate a subduction component in mantle sources, including subcontinental lithosphere (Fitton et al., 1988; Leat et al., 1988; Thompson and Morrison, 1988). Negative Sr anomalies reflect the influence of plagioclase in fractionation processes involved in the origin of these basaltic magmas. The mantle source for the alkaline to transitional basaltic magmas was probably a garnet peridotite from the deeper mantle: there is no obvious geochemical evidence for involvement of either the mantle lithosphere or the continental crust in their origin (Coish and Sinton, 1992). Moreover, the geochemistry is consistent with the origin of the basaltic magmas as partial melts of a mantle plume.

---

[1] Magnesium numbers calculated as moles of MgO/ (MgO + FeO[t]).

What is the tectonic environment for the production of these basaltic magmas from a mantle plume? All geochemical discriminant diagrams clearly show that the basaltic magmas are in the within-plate fields (e.g., Fig. 5, A and B). Note that there are some dikes which extend into the field of plume-type mid-ocean ridge basalt, clearly seen in the Nb-Zr-Y diagram. These same dikes are lower in TiO_2 and have tholeiitic affinity. The within-plate environment is postulated to be the early stages of a continental rift initiated by a large mantle plume northeast of the Adirondacks (Kumarapeli et al., 1990; Coish and Sinton, 1992; Kumarapeli, 1993; St. Seymour and Kumarapeli, 1995). In this scenario, the dikes with tholeiitic affinity that plot as plume-type mid-ocean ridge basalt (MORB) simply represent later stages of rifting than the majority of dikes. The strikes of Proterozoic dikes in the Adirondacks and in Ontario and Quebec indicate that the center of the plume may coincide with the location of the Tibbit Hill volcanic rocks in southern Quebec (Kumarapeli, 1993). According to this hypothesis, the emergence of the plume produced a rift with a failed arm in an east-west direction now represented by the Ottawa-Bonnéchere graben, and two arms in northeasterly and southeasterly directions that eventually spread to form the Iapetus ocean. The chemistry of the Adirondack dikes is similar to early rift basalt from the 30 Ma Gregory rift of the East African rift system (Coish et al., 1991), a region in which a mantle plume is also postulated to be the source of the basaltic magmas (Latin et al., 1993).

ZONE 2: GREENSTONE FROM THE PINNACLE AND UNDERHILL FORMATIONS

Zone 2 comprises rocks from the Pinnacle and Underhill formations (Doll et al., 1961), corresponding to the Hinesburg and Underhill tectonic slices (Stanley and Ratcliffe, 1985). In the Hinesburg slice, rocks include greenish-gray to gray-blue quartzose graywacke, minor beds of greenish quartz-sericite-chlorite phyllite, boulder and pebble conglomerate, and interbedded basaltic volcanic rocks of the Tibbit Hill volcanic member. In addition, schistose greenstone, feldspathic greenstone, actinolite greenstone, and calcareous greenstone occur in northern Vermont. These were igneous mafic rocks; clearly some were extrusive flows, as evidenced by pillow structures, but others may have been shallow-level intrusives or even pyroclastic flows. In the Underhill slice, rocks vary from sericite-chlorite schist, to amphibolite, to greenstone, to carbonaceous schist, to albitic schist, and finally to small amounts of graywacke (Stanley and Ratcliffe, 1985). Greenstone samples from zone 2 of this study come from the Tibbit Hill member in northern Vermont, and several small bodies in the general area of Lincoln to Huntington in central Vermont. In central Vermont, little trace of igneous mineralogy or texture is preserved—the greenstone bodies are greenschist facies metamorphic rocks. The age of the Tibbit Hill volcanic rocks is 554 Ma, on the basis of U-Pb systematics from felsic rocks found in southern Quebec (Kumarapeli et al., 1989).

The geochemistry of zone 2 greenstone bodies indicates that they are all basaltic rocks (Fig. 2, A and B; Table 1). Samples from zone 2 have low Ni (145 to 10 ppm) and Cr contents, indicating that they are evolved. The range of Ni, Cr, Sr, Ti, Zr, and Y values is consistent with fractionation of olivine, plagioclase, clinopyroxene, and titanomagnetite (Coish et al., 1985). However, a close look at the data shows that there are small differences between the Pinnacle Formation and the Underhill Formation that may suggest some slight differences in the formation of their basalt units. Pinnacle Formation greenstones are mostly alkalic to transitional basaltic rocks much like dikes from zone 1, whereas the Underhill Formation rocks tend to be more tholeiitic in character (Fig. 2B). Furthermore, on average, Pinnacle Formation greenstones are higher in Ti, Zr, Y, and the REEs than Underhill Formation rocks. The REEs in Pinnacle Formation rocks have more restricted range of La/Yb ratios; for example, Pinnacle Formation samples have $(La/Yb)_N$ from 3.5 to 6.5, whereas Underhill Formation samples range from La/Yb of 1.5 to 8.8 (Table 1; Fig. 4, B and C). There also appears to be a difference in isotopic composition of the two formations. Nd isotopes in the Pinnacle Formation samples consistently have ε_{Nd} (550 Ma) of +3.1 to +3.2, whereas samples from the Underhill Formation range from +2.5 to +5.4 (Table 2). The Nd-isotopic data indicate that the source for *both* units was mantle relatively enriched compared to MORB-type mantle ($\varepsilon_{Nd} \sim$ +6 to +9). Coish et al. (1985) suggested, on the basis of trace element modeling, that the mantle source consisted of peridotite with about 65% olivine, 20% orthopyroxene, 13% clinopyroxene, and 2% garnet. However, the variation in Nd isotopes within zone 2 suggests that the enriched mantle source was not entirely homogeneous. More discussion on the nature of the enriched mantle follows later.

The tectonic environment in which the precursors of zone 2 greenstone bodies erupted is shown consistently on many discriminant diagrams to be within plate (Fig. 5, C and D). On both Ti-Zr-Y and Nb-Zr-Y diagrams, the Pinnacle Formation samples plot in slightly different locations from the Underhill Formation rocks. In the Ti-Zr-Y diagram, the Pinnacle Formation rocks are clearly within the within-plate field, whereas the Underhill Formation rocks range toward the MORB field. In the Nb-Zr-Y field, there is a clear trend with the Pinnacle Formation rocks in the within-plate field and the Underhill Formation rocks in mostly the plume-type MORB field. I think that this trend is significant, and may represent an evolving environment through time. The chemistry is consistent with either a within-plate oceanic or continental environment, but the field evidence of conglomeratic and graywacke metasedimentary rocks overlying Precambrian basement clearly suggests that the environment is within a continental plate (Coish et al., 1985). In particular, the protolith of zone 2 greenstone could have formed in the early stages of the development of a continental rift. Furthermore, the variations seen in the Underhill Formation rocks might be due to their eruption in a slightly more advanced (but still early) stage of the rifting than the Pinnacle Formation rocks. In this context, Nd isotopes are consistent with the source of the Pinnacle Formation rocks being plume-type mantle, whereas the source for some

R. A. Coish

TABLE 1. REPRESENTATIVE MAJOR AND TRACE ELEMENT ANALYSES OF BASALTIC ROCKS FROM THE VERMONT APPALACHIANS*

Sample	Zone 1 Adirondack Dikes					Zone 2 Pinnacle Formation						Zone 2 Underhill Formation			
	6159	6198	6265	87-90	6266	4373	4383	4384	4390	4402	5428	5842	5853	6549	6554
(wt%)															
SiO_2	46.55	50.16	47.99	47.50	49.08	53.12	48.95	47.88	54.09	53.15	50.04	44.41	47.41	43.81	49.32
TiO_2	3.32	2.64	2.84	3.00	1.76	3.21	3.16	3.28	2.90	3.12	2.27	2.93	2.37	3.49	3.47
Al_2O_3	13.88	13.75	13.77	14.62	14.66	16.23	15.55	16.45	16.57	14.38	15.25	12.79	15.00	16.69	15.92
Fe_2O_3	12.62	11.75	14.91	13.44	14.51	11.60	12.68	12.62	10.75	11.51	13.63	16.52	12.98	12.98	13.44
MnO	0.18	0.15	0.17	0.17	0.12	0.07	0.09	0.09	0.01	0.07	0.27	0.18	0.13	0.17	0.18
MgO	6.80	7.67	5.65	7.37	6.77	3.06	5.96	4.41	3.05	4.97	8.21	3.83	6.95	5.82	5.44
CaO	10.89	7.87	9.12	8.47	7.00	4.95	9.61	9.00	4.81	8.24	5.76	12.88	10.69	10.37	8.40
Na_2O	2.97	3.43	3.89	3.16	3.87	6.76	3.50	5.20	7.67	4.15	4.26	4.77	3.03	3.43	4.71
K_2O	0.35	1.55	1.02	0.56	0.35	0.28	0.69	0.30	0.07	0.27	0.00	0.04	0.46	1.66	0.46
P_2O_5	0.87	0.49	0.73	0.43	0.21	0.46	0.39	0.37	0.33	0.38	0.11	0.53	0.29	0.34	0.28
Total	98.43	99.46	100.09	98.72	98.33	99.74	100.58	99.60	100.25	100.24	99.80	98.88	99.31	98.76	101.62
(ppm)															
Sc	21	21	20	20	23	23	26	22	28	24	38	39	41	32	30
V	228	206	207	224	236	......	......	......	......	......	......	271	295	364	343
Cr	220	233	156	164	133	95	110	74	125	111	111	42	114	63	48
Ni	139	173	63	140	95	56	60	63	93	74	88	15	33	77	57
Sr	755	488	416	596	251	102	......	22	57	332	162	180	332	277	290
Y	31	27	31	25	27	35	30	30	23	39	32	55	27	28	37
Zr	237	188	196	164	92	237	209	211	218	291	124	257	160	148	234
Nb	40	28	30	25	8	33	26	28	34	35	16	19	17	......	......
Ba	129	429	339	284	119	96	152	128	71	91	70	46	188	863	71
Th	1.7	2.0	1.4	1.5	......	2.0	1.9	2.8	1.9	4.2	......	2.5	1.5	4.7	2.6
Ta	2.0	2.2	1.6	1.8	......	5.6	1.6	1.6	4.5	3.1	......	1.3	1.1	3.3	2.5
Hf	5.3	4.8	6.0	4.8	......	5.1	5.4	4.9	4.4	7.4	......	6.8	4.8	5.1	2.5
La	37.8	26.9	30.8	22.4	......	21.1	26.7	14.9	18.8	30.3	9.8	24.3	16.5	36.4	26.1
Ce	93.0	55.0	75.0	55.0	......	53.8	64.1	38.4	48.7	71.6	24.6	56.0	42.0	70.0	52.0
Nd	49.0	29.0	44.0	27.0	......	33.4	37.0	24.8	26.7	37.0	16.4	34.0	24.0	37.0	31.0
Sm	9.3	7.0	9.2	6.2	......	7.8	8.1	6.3	6.6	8.7	4.5	8.5	5.6	7.4	6.3
Eu	3.1	1.8	2.8	2.1	......	2.2	2.7	1.8	2.0	2.6	1.7	2.5	2.0	2.5	2.3
Tb	0.8	0.7	1.1	0.8	......	1.5	1.4	0.9	1.2	1.8	0.7	1.5	0.9	1.1	0.9
Yb	2.1	1.9	2.3	1.6	......	2.9	3.3	2.8	2.6	3.8	2.7	5.5	2.6	3.1	2.2
Lu	0.3	0.3	0.3	0.3	......	0.5	0.5	0.4	0.4	0.6	0.4	0.8	0.4	0.4	0.3

TABLE 1. REPRESENTATIVE MAJOR AND TRACE ELEMENT ANALYSES OF BASALTIC ROCKS FROM THE VERMONT APPALACHIANS* (continued - page 2)

Sample	Zone 3 Hazens Notch Formation				Zone 3 Pinney Hollow Formation						Zone 4 Stowe Formation					
	5802	5804	6537	6545	4495	4497	5809	5817	4645	5212	5334	5351	92-41	6116	6118	6119
(wt%)																
SiO$_2$	48.65	46.39	51.77	55.02	48.76	49.73	47.00	53.61	47.05	49.96	48.98	47.08	51.84	50.69	48.90	49.31
TiO$_2$	1.66	1.96	2.51	2.32	1.95	1.41	3.19	0.61	1.07	1.29	1.11	1.29	0.90	1.31	1.35	1.58
Al$_2$O$_3$	13.00	19.68	16.01	14.81	18.62	16.94	15.74	13.76	21.04	14.85	16.05	16.13	14.14	14.08	15.93	14.78
Fe$_2$O$_3$	13.57	13.74	11.68	11.72	12.68	10.51	12.78	8.59	9.54	10.94	9.77	12.29	9.63	10.33	10.94	11.68
MnO	0.22	0.21	0.17	0.21	0.14	0.13	0.13	0.18	0.09	0.19	0.20	0.25	0.19	0.19	0.18	0.22
MgO	5.45	5.84	4.89	6.53	7.27	8.64	5.43	8.61	7.91	5.95	7.62	8.23	6.52	8.14	7.79	8.61
CaO	14.22	9.04	6.05	5.51	7.85	9.45	12.46	11.11	9.68	13.52	13.00	11.56	15.10	12.06	10.81	10.83
Na$_2$O	1.66	3.26	5.18	4.90	2.65	2.91	2.86	4.00	3.69	3.27	3.15	1.92	2.13	2.68	3.15	2.40
K$_2$O	0.93	0.20	0.52	0.61	0.10	0.10	0.37	0.00	0.17	0.01	0.24	1.18	0.09	0.01	0.01	0.01
P$_2$O$_5$	0.18	0.23	0.15	0.01	0.07	0.06	0.55	0.05	0.03	0.05	0.12	0.09	0.09	0.11	0.11	0.14
Total	99.54	100.55	98.93	101.64	100.09	99.88	100.51	100.52	100.27	100.03	100.24	100.02	100.63	99.60	99.17	99.56
(ppm)																
Sc	51	47	28	24	42	38	39	53	40	39	39	52	41	......	......	......
V	405	284	261	283	241	370	286	202	......	222	......	......	260	244	281	304
Cr	51	44	147	217	......	......	213	390	674	......	324	511	......	451	319	286
Ni	51	20	81	132	110	139	84	83	......	94	98	146	104	103	109	236
Sr	282	301	185	133	326	230	187	257	94	126	119	104	139	118	147	161
Y	35	26	41	31	25	26	36	13	20	33	29	31	24	30	29	34
Zr	95	107	187	168	115	90	171	64	32	91	76	83	45	92	92	103
Nb	11	14	......	......	19	10	28	......	......	......	......	......	10	30	......	......
Ba	121	38	141	356	79	87	89	......	......	9	46	13	......	......	10	10
Th	0.3	0.5	1.6	1.5	1.1	0.3	1.5	0.3	......	......	0.3	0.6	0.6	0.3	0.6	0.1
Ta	0.5	0.5	1.3	1.4	0.7	2.0	1.4	0.2	......	......	0.8	0.7	0.7	0.2	......	......
Hf	2.1	2.3	4.0	3.5	2.1	2.1	4.2	0.9	......	......	1.7	1.8	1.8	2.6	2.2	0.4
La	5.7	9.6	18.9	15.4	8.2	8.7	29.2	2.0	1.5	2.9	2.5	3.6	4.3	2.6	5.0	1.0
Ce	15.0	25.0	39.0	35.0	21.3	20.0	62.0	5.0	5.2	9.4	8.2	10.9	11.6	5.6	11.6	0.9
Nd	10.0	15.0	22.0	20.0	13.5	12.1	32.0	3.0	4.0	7.5	5.8	7.2	7.7	2.6	8.0	2.3
Sm	2.9	3.6	6.0	5.2	3.9	3.3	7.6	1.3	1.5	2.7	2.3	2.6	2.7	0.7	3.0	0.4
Eu	1.2	1.4	1.9	1.5	1.5	1.2	2.6	0.5	0.7	1.0	0.9	1.0	1.0	0.2	1.3	0.3
Tb	0.8	0.8	1.1	0.9	0.6	0.7	1.4	0.3	0.7	0.6	0.7	0.6	0.7	0.2	0.8	0.2
Yb	4.3	3.0	2.9	2.2	2.4	2.1	3.7	1.5	2.3	3.1	2.7	2.9	3.0	0.6	3.6	0.7
Lu	0.7	0.4	0.4	0.3	0.4	0.3	0.5	0.3	0.3	0.5	0.4	0.4	0.5	0.1	0.5	0.1

*Complete set of analyses available from the author upon request.

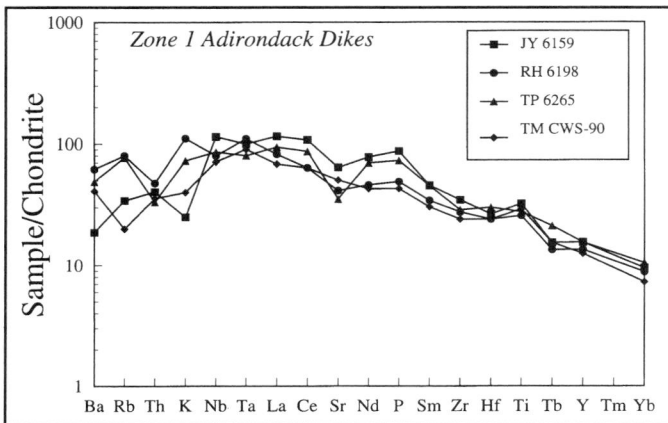

Figure 3. Extended rare-earth element diagram (Thompson et al., 1984) for selected dikes from zone 1.

Underhill Formation rocks may have had a small component of depleted MORB-type mantle added.

INTERMEDIATE STAGES OF IAPETAN RIFTING

Zone 3: Greenstone from Hazens Notch and Pinney Hollow formations

Greenstone bodies in zone 3 are from the Hazens Notch and Pinney Hollow slices (Stanley and Ratcliffe, 1985). These slices are separated from each other, and from the Underhill slice to the west and the Rowe slice to the east, by thrust faults. Serpentinized ultramafic bodies occur in the Hazens Notch, Pinney Hollow, and Rowe slices, prompting workers to suggest that these slices are part of a Taconian accretionary wedge (Stanley and Ratcliffe, 1985) and thus of "oceanic" affinity (Rankin, 1994). Metasedimentary rocks are abundant in both slices, whereas metavolcanic rocks (greenstones) are sparse, occurring as small pods and lenses. The Hazens Notch slice has a heterogeneous array of metasedimentary rocks: rusty-weathering, chlorite-biotite-muscovite albitic schist, carbonaceous chlorite-muscovite biotite schist, dolomitic pods, and discontinuous quartzite layers (O'Loughlin and Stanley, 1986; Thompson and Thompson, 1991). Discontinuous greenstone layers are common; they have variable mineralogy ranging from chlorite-albite-carbonate-epidote to Ca-amphibole-albite-chlorite assemblages. The more amphibole-rich rocks commonly are coarse grained. For this study, most of the greenstone bodies from the Hazens Notch slice were sampled in central Vermont in the area of Lincoln Gap. In general, zone 3 greenstone bodies in the field show a wider array of mineralogy than in either zone 2 to the west or zone 4 to the east.

Geochemically, all greenstone bodies from zone 3 are basaltic (Fig. 2, C and D; Table 1). However, they show the great-

est variation in chemistry of any zone (Table 1). For example, TiO_2 values range from 0.61 to 3.67 wt%, Zr from 64 to more than 200 ppm, Y from 13 to more than 50 ppm, and $(La/Yb)_N$ from 0.75 to about 5.0. The variability is reflected in the scatter of data in the TiO_2-Zr/P_2O_5 plot (Fig. 2D) and in the REE patterns (Fig. 4, D and E). Most REE patterns have moderate light REE enrichment; greenstone samples from the Hazens Notch Formation are slightly more enriched than those from the Pinney Hollow Formation. REE patterns similar to these are seen in some continental tholeiites; for example, Coppermine River, Canada (Dostal et al., 1983), and also in basaltic rocks from the Manda Harraro, Afar region of the East African rift (Treuil and Joron, 1976; Barrat et al., 1990). These "normal" patterns from zone 3 have light REE enrichments that are intermediate between those seen in zone 2 greenstone samples and those in zone 4. However, there are examples in zone 3 greenstone bodies of light REE-enriched patterns similar to those in zone 2, and light REE-depleted or flat patterns similar to those seen in zone 4 (Fig. 4, D and E). Although island-arc volcanics can show REE patterns similar to those of zone 3, Ti contents are higher and also Y values are higher at a given Cr content in zone 3 greenstone samples. As discussed later, other elements in zone 3 greenstone samples show similar overlap with greenstone bodies to the west and east of zone 3. This variation in chemistry is among individual greenstone bodies in most cases, but in one remarkable area considerable chemical variation is seen within what is apparently a single body (Kafka et al., 1993). Zone 3 greenstone bodies were interpreted as 10% partial melts of a spinel peridotite mantle that then underwent shallow-level fractional crystallization (Coish et al., 1985). It appears now that the processes were not that simple. Instead, it is likely that the mantle source for the dominant or "normal" type of greenstone in zone 3 was a mixture of enriched (plume-type?) mantle and depleted MORB-type mantle. In addition, there are examples in zone 3 of greenstone bodies that formed by melting of enriched mantle alone, and other examples of bodies that formed by melting depleted (MORB-like) spinel peridotite mantle alone. For lack of evidence to the contrary, I assume that these chemically diverse types of volcanic rocks were all formed in the same general area, although not necessarily at the same time.

Tectonic discriminant diagrams show very interesting information about zone 3 greenstone samples (Fig. 5, E and F). In Ti-Zr-Y space, the greenstone samples plot in an area ranging from the within-plate field to the MORB–island-arc tholeiite field, and in Nb-Zr-Y space, they plot in the plume-type MORB (plume or enriched MORB) field. Although there is some overlap with zone 2 greenstone samples at the high Ti and Zr end of the trend, zone 3 greenstone samples extend to much lower Ti and Nb contents. Information from the tectonic discriminant diagrams is consistent with the precursors of zone 3 greenstone bodies forming in the intermediate stages of a continental rift environment, possibly similar to the transitional oceanic–continental environment (or proto-oceanic) in the Afar triangle of the East African rift.

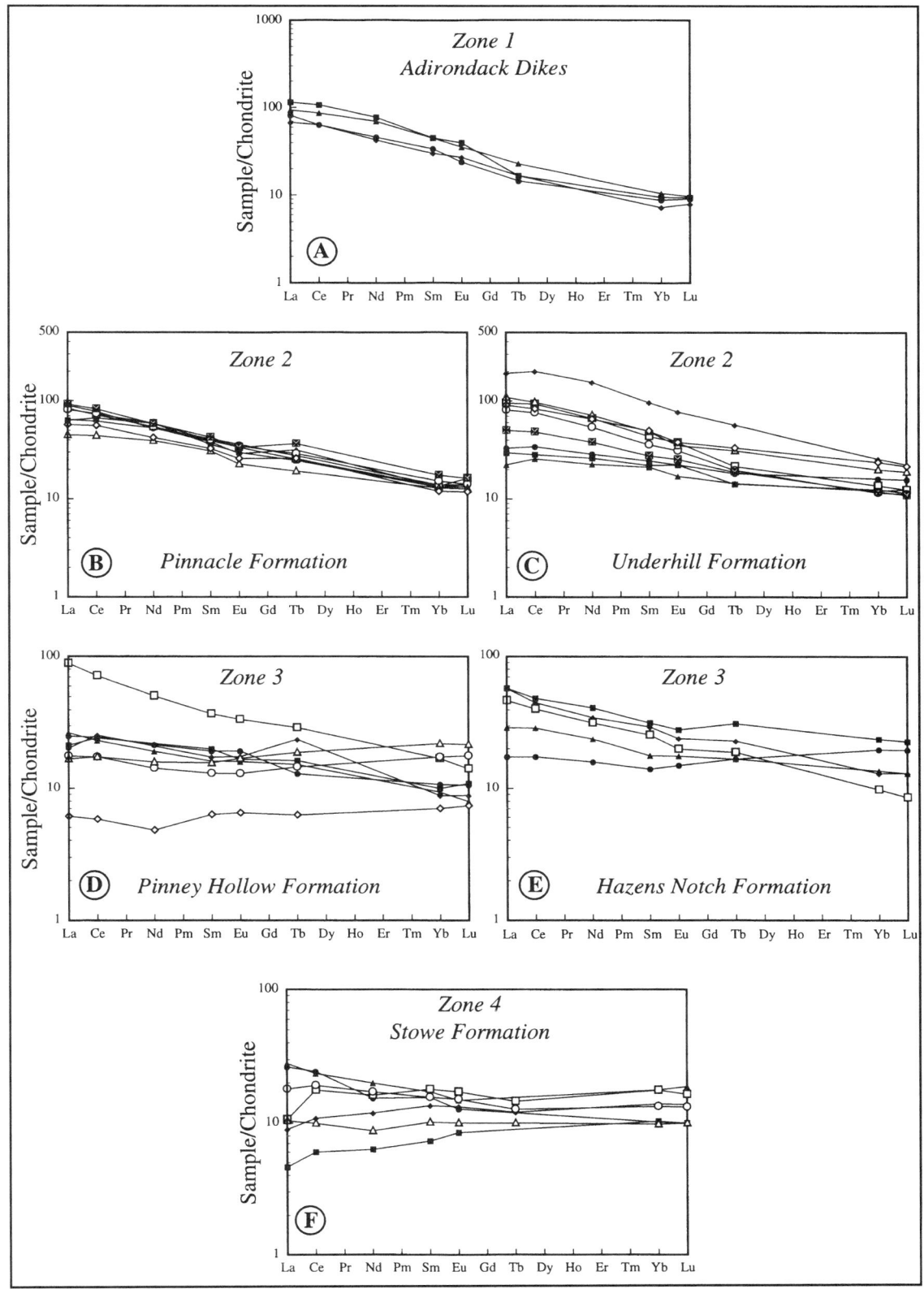

Figure 4. Rare-earth element normalized diagrams (Nakamura, 1974) for basaltic rocks from zone 1 (A), zone 2 (B, C), zone 3 (D, E), and zone 4 (F). Note the overall decrease in light rare-earth enrichment from zone 1 through to zone 4.

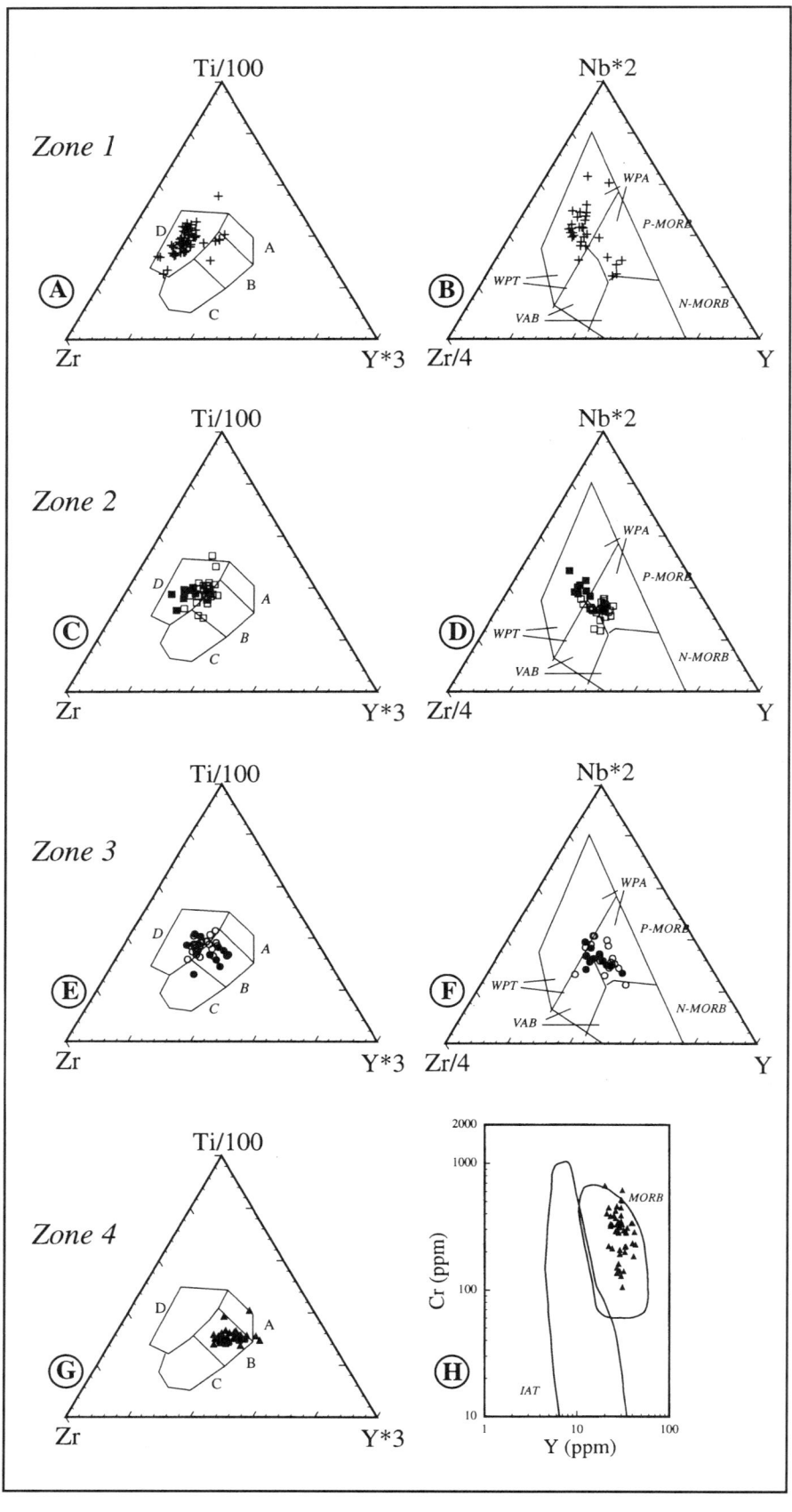

TABLE 2. Nd ISOTOPES FOR GREENSTONES FROM ZONES 2 AND 4 IN THE VERMONT APPALACHIANS*

Sample	$^{147}Sm/^{144}Nd$	$^{143}Nd/^{144}Nd$	$\varepsilon_{Nd}(0)$	I(t)CHUR	143Nd/^{144}Nd(t)	$\varepsilon_{Nd}(t)$
Zone 2[†]						
P4384	0.1564	0.512655	0.3	0.51193	0.512091	3.2
P4402	0.145	0.512611	-0.5	0.51193	0.512088	3.1
U5430	0.1826	0.512866	4.4	0.51193	0.512208	5.4
U5470	0.1408	0.512562	-1.5	0.51193	0.512055	2.5
U5475	0.1364	0.512580	-1.1	0.51193	0.512088	3.1
Zone 4[§]						
4677	0.248	0.513270	12.3	0.51196	0.512409	8.9
5212	0.218	0.513170	10.4	0.51196	0.512413	8.9
5216**	0.144	0.512810	3.4	0.51196	0.512310	6.9
5351	0.205	0.513140	9.8	0.51196	0.512428	9.2

*Nd isotope analyses for zone 2 samples done by Patrick Jenks at Virginia Polytechnic Institute and for zone 4 done by Mike Hingston at Dartmouth College. Note that for zone 2 rocks, the age(t) for calculation of ε_{Nd} values is 550 Ma based on the age of Tibbit Hill volcanic rocks in Quebec (Kumarapeli et al., 1989), whereas the age of zone 4 rocks is an estimate of 530 Ma.
[†]Samples with a P prefix are from the Pinnacle Formation and U prefix are from the Underhill Formation.
[§]All samples are from the Stowe Formation.
**This sample is from the uncommon Type II greenstones of the Stowe Formation (Coish et al., 1986).

LATE STAGES OF IAPETAN RIFTING

Zone 4: Greenstone from the Ottauquechee and Stowe formations

Greenstone bodies from the Ottauquechee and Stowe formations are in the Rowe tectonic slice, east of zone 3 and west of the Hawley terrane (Stanley and Ratcliffe, 1985). The Rowe tectonic slice is thought to be the remnants of an accretionary wedge assembled during early Paleozoic eastward-directed subduction. As such, it is interpreted as an exotic oceanic terrane. It comprises metasedimentary rocks, greenstone, and serpentinite. The serpentinite occurs as elongate bodies from 1 m to several kilometers in length. Their contacts with surrounding metasedimentary rocks are sheared. The serpentinite bodies were interpreted by Stanley and Ratcliffe (1985) as fault slivers of ancient oceanic crust imbricated with continental margin sedimentary rocks in an accre-

Figure 5. Tectonic discriminant diagrams, Ti-Zr-Y (Pearce and Cann, 1973), Nb-Zr-Y (Meschede, 1986), and Cr-Y (Pearce, 1982), for basaltic rocks from geochemical zones 1, 2, 3, and 4 in the Vermont Appalachians. There is an overall change from a within-plate to an ocean-floor tectonic field from zone 1 through zone 4. Rocks from zone 3 plot in both tectonic fields. See text for discussion. Symbols as in Figure 2. For the Ti-Zr-Y diagram, A is island-arc tholeiite, B is ocean-ridge–island-arc tholeiite, C is calc-alkaline arc basalt, D is within-plate basalt. For the Nb-Zr-Y diagram, WPA is within-plate alkalic, WPT is within-plate tholeiitic, VAB is volcanic arc basalt, P-MORB is plume-type mid-ocean ridge basalt, N-MORB is normal mid-ocean ridge basalt. For the Cr-Y diagram, IAT is island-arc tholeiite, MORB is mid-ocean ridge basalt.

tionary wedge. Greenstone also occurs as pods and lenses from several meters to several kilometers long. Contacts with metasedimentary rocks are often marked by a zone where greenstone and metasedimentary rocks are interfingered over a distance of several meters. In a few places, black phyllite occurs between greenstone and metasedimentary rocks. It is clear that some contacts are faulted, but in many cases, contacts are not exposed. Greenstone bodies in zone 4 are all light green, reflecting the abundance of epidote along with albite, chlorite, actinolite, and carbonate. Two mineral assemblages are noted: (1) albite, epidote, chlorite, and calcite, and (2) epidote, actinolite, and chlorite. A small number of samples has a high abundance (~15%) of sphene, usually also with high amounts of calcite. Some greenstone is massive, but most has a well-developed foliation parallel to the dominant regional fabric, usually in an approximately north-south direction. No relict minerals or igneous textures are preserved. For this study, greenstone bodies were sampled from central and northern Vermont within the Rowe tectonic slice (Fig. 1), including the Braintree, Mad River, and Waterbury bodies of Coish et al. (1986). Not included in the dataset, but discussed at the end of this section, is a group of small greenstone bodies in northern Vermont near the Canadian border. These rocks will be described in detail in a separate publication.

As with all other zones, greenstone from zone 4 is basaltic in composition (Fig. 2, C D; Table 1). Moreover, the compositions clearly have tholeiitic affinity (Fig. 2D). In general, they are lower in TiO_2, Zr, Y, and total REE than greenstone samples from zones to the west. REE patterns are around 10 times chondrite, and either depleted in the light REE or flat with no systematic Eu anomaly (Fig. 4F). There is a range of compositions within the greenstone bodies shown by increasing FeO/MgO with TiO_2 and by variation in the total REE content. These variations can be accounted for by crystal fractionation of typical basaltic minerals, olivine and minor clinopyroxene (Coish et al., 1986). Plagioclase fractionation, if it occurred, is not revealed by the chemistry. Nd isotopes of zone 4 greenstone samples have values of around +7 to +9 ε_{Nd}, calculated for an age of 530 Ma (Table 2). These values indicate that the source rock for zone 4 greenstone bodies was depleted mantle, because undepleted mantle melt would have an ε_{Nd} value of 0. The Nd isotopes of zone 4 rocks are distinct from the lower values shown for zone 2 samples, indicating there is a fundamental difference in the mantle source materials for the two magma types.

The tectonic environment as indicated by the geochemistry of zone 4 greenstone samples appears to be oceanic spreading. This is determined only after analysis of several geochemical diagrams. Most diagrams show expected equivocal evidence pointing to either ocean ridge or island-arc environments, but the Cr-Y diagram seems to be successful at distinguishing these two environments. Four pieces of geochemical evidence are important. First, the depleted or flat REE patterns are very similar to patterns from MORB and some island-arc tholeiites (Coish et al., 1986). Second, the Ti-Zr-Y tectonic discriminant diagram indicates that the greenstone samples are not within-plate basaltic rocks, because they fall in the MORB–island-arc field (Fig. 5G). Third, the high Nd-isotopes are consistent with an oceanic ridge environment. Fourth, and most convincing, on the Cr-Y diagram the zone 4 greenstone samples plot exclusively within the ocean-ridge field and separate from the island-arc tholeiite field (Fig. 5H). Using the above evidence, I conclude that the precursors to zone 4 greenstone bodies were formed at an oceanic spreading center. The tectonic environment could have been an ocean ridge in a wide, open ocean or, as is more consistent with geological considerations, a spreading center in a small ocean basin formed at the end stages of continental break-up. Unfortunately, there are no geochemical constraints to help specify the size of the ocean basin.

In northern Vermont, near the town of Jay next to the Canadian border, the Stowe Formation and the Moretown Formation (Fig. 1) are intimately associated with each other (Stanley et al., 1984). In most other places in Vermont, the Moretown Formation lies immediately east of the Stowe Formation. The Moretown Formation is interpreted as part of the fore-arc region of an island-arc system (Stanley and Ratcliffe, 1985). Thus, the northern Vermont area was mapped in detail to search for remnants of ancient arc volcanic rocks. Three students from Middlebury College sampled and analyzed greenstone samples across the Stowe and Moretown formations (Dick, 1989; Pugin, 1989; Evans, 1994). The results of these studies will be presented elsewhere, but in short, all greenstone samples appear to be like those from the Stowe Formation and their geochemistry is consistent with formation at an oceanic spreading center. Thus, it seems that in this area either the Moretown Formation simply formed in the same environment as the Stowe Formation rocks, or that rocks previously mapped as Moretown actually belong to the Stowe Formation.

REGIONAL TRENDS AND TECTONIC IMPLICATIONS

From the previous section, it is clear that there are variations in geochemistry of greenstone bodies from zone 1 through zone 4 in the Vermont Appalachians. In this section I present more detail on the geochemical variations, compare the changes to variations seen in an active rift area, and apply a rift tectonic model to explain the geochemistry of the Vermont greenstone bodies.

In general, greenstone bodies from the western zones 1 and 2 consist of transitional to alkali basaltic rocks, whereas greenstone bodies from the eastern zones 3 and 4 comprise tholeiitic basaltic rocks. Detailed elemental variations with location can best be seen when averages for each formation are plotted (Fig. 6). For example, TiO_2, $(La/Yb)_N$, and Zr/Y decrease, whereas Sc and Al_2O_3/TiO_2 increase from west to east. Within each formation and zone, there is considerable variation, as noted by the standard deviation. This is particularly true for samples within zone 3, as discussed earlier. Note that zones 1 and 2 are distinct from zone 4, but zone 3 samples show overlap with both zones 1 and 2 and zone 4. Even though the data are too few for detailed comparisons, Nd isotopes for zone 4 are higher than for zone 2 rocks, consistent with the trends in the other elements. The variation in Nd isotopes (and Zr/Y, Al_2O_3/TiO_2) is particularly important because these differences between the western and eastern zones cannot be explained by simple igneous processes such as partial melting or fractional crystallization, but must be related to fundamental differences in the source regions of the magmas.

The change from an enriched mantle source for zones 1 and 2 greenstone samples to a depleted source for zone 4 greenstone samples may represent a progressive evolution of a continental to oceanic rift system. The East African rift system is a modern example of continental rifting (Martinez and Cochran, 1988). All stages from early continental rifting to ocean floor spreading are represented. The southern part of the Eastern African rift, the Main Ethiopian rift, and the Gregory rift of Kenya is underlain by distended but still thick continental crust and is at an early stage of continental rifting. In the northern part of the rift valley, in the Afar triangle, continental crust is much thinner and the region is apparently at a transitional stage between continental and oceanic conditions, the so-called "proto-oceanic" stage. The northern part of the Red Sea may be at a similar or slightly more advanced stage. The central axial deeps of the Red Sea, however, represent true oceanic spreading conditions. In all of these areas, basaltic magmas have been produced and record the change in volcanism during splitting of a continent. In general, early rift basaltic magmas are alkaline with high Ti, Zr, La/Yb, and low Nd isotopes compared with Red Sea basaltic magmas, which are tholeiitic with lower Ti, R, La/Yb, and higher Nd isotopes (Hart et al., 1989; Altherr et al., 1990; Barrat et al., 1990; Coish et al., 1991). Basaltic

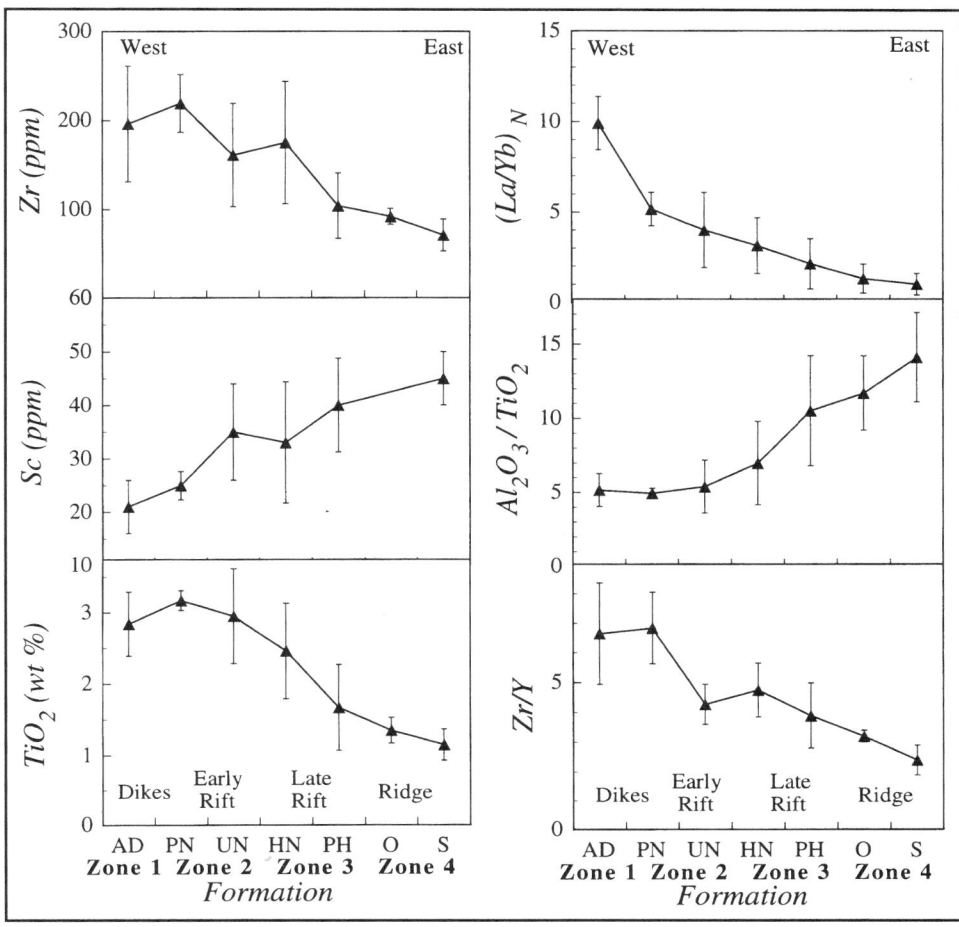

Figure 6. Systematic variation in TiO_2, Sc, Zr, Zr/Y, Al_2O_3/TiO_2, and $(La/Yb)_N$ ratio in greenstones from west to east across the western Vermont Appalachians. AD—Adirondack dikes, PN—Pinnacle Formation, UN—Underhill Formation, HN—Hazens Notch Formation, PH—Pinney Hollow Formation, O—Ottauquechee, S—Stowe Formation.

magmas erupted at the transitional tectonic stage seem to have transitional chemical characteristics. Workers generally agree that the different basaltic magmas from the different regions are generated from different mantle sources. Early rift basaltic magmas are partial melts of enriched mantle, either plume-type or mantle lithosphere or both (Hart et al., 1989; Chazot and Bertrand, 1993); late oceanic basaltic magmas from the Red Sea are partial melts of depleted asthenospheric mantle (Altherr et al., 1988, 1990; Brueckner et al., 1988; Coleman and McGuire, 1988; Barrat et al., 1990); and basaltic magmas produced at transitional stages have components of both enriched and depleted mantle (Barberi et al., 1980; Betton and Civetta, 1984; Vidal et al., 1991). There is remarkable similarity between the chemical changes shown in basaltic magmas from different parts of the East African rift system and those across the geochemical zones in Vermont (Coish et al., 1991). This similarity strongly supports the interpretation of the greenstone bodies from Vermont as products of basaltic eruptions in an evolving rift environment.

Whereas greenstone bodies from zones 1 and 2 and zone 4

unambiguously are early rift and oceanic spreading center respectively, greenstone bodies from zone 3 have a variety of compositions. Some greenstone bodies do have chemistries intermediate between those of zone 4 and zone 2; however, there are also discrete bodies similar to zone 2 and others similar to zone 4. Mixing of basalt types within zone 3 can be explained by either (1) tectonic shuffling of basaltic rocks from different environments or (2) generation of distinct magmas from heterogeneous mantle sources. Although there is ample evidence for numerous thrust faults in zone 3, and movement along those faults may contribute to mixing of greenstone bodies, large chemical variations within a single greenstone (Kafka et al., 1993) and the occurrence of a modern analog in the Afar region make the magmatic alternative more attractive. Under this scheme, mantle sources beneath zone 3 included enriched plume mantle as well as depleted asthenospheric mantle. Magmas produced thus could be from melting the plume, melting the depleted asthenosphere, or melting some mixture. Thus, basaltic rocks with characteristics of zones 1 and 2 (plume-type), basaltic rocks with characteristics of zone 4 (MORB-type), and basaltic rocks with mixed chemistry would occur in the same geographic region. This could also explain why, within a single formation in some areas of Vermont, there is a range of chemistry from "early rift" to "ocean ridge" (Ratcliffe, 1993).

The variation in chemistry of greenstone bodies across Vermont reveals the tectonic history of the development of the Iapetus ocean in the Vermont Appalachians (Fig. 7). Initial magmatism through the Laurentian continent produced dikes seen today as part of zone 1 in the Adirondack massif. The age of this event is not well defined, but on the basis of Ar ages, the dikes are probably older than 585 Ma (Isachsen et al., 1988). The age of the Grenville dike swarm to the northwest is 590 Ma (Kamo et al., 1995) and dikes cutting Grenville basement in Newfoundland are about 615 Ma (Kamo et al., 1989). Thus, a minimum age of 585 Ma for dike intrusion in the Adirondack massif is consistent with these other regions (Fig. 7A). The intrusion of dikes preceded and accompanied the rise of a mantle plume beneath the northern Vermont–southern Quebec area to form the Sutton Mountain triple junction (Kumarapeli, 1993; Rankin et al., 1993; St. Seymour and Kumarapeli, 1995). One arm of the triple junction, the Ottawa-Bonnechére graben, became a failed arm. The other two arms developed into a rift valley that evolved into the Iapetus ocean. The formation of the rift valley was accompanied by extrusion of zone 2 volcanics and the deposition of conglomeratic sedimentary rocks in the early stages. The volcanics formed by partial melting of enriched mantle probably dominated by a mantle plume. The Tibbit Hill volcanic rocks, part of zone 2 volcanism, provide the best age constraint on this stage. The youngest part of this sequence is 554 Ma (Kumarapeli et al., 1989); thus, I have chosen 560 Ma to represent this early rift stage (Fig. 7B). Then, as the plume beneath the triple junction spread out and possibly began to break apart, asthenospheric mantle convected upward and became available as a source for basalt magma. Thus, with both mantle sources available, mixed basalt types erupted in the evolving rift valley to form zone 3 volcanic rocks (Fig. 7C). There is no radiometric evidence for the age of this event, other than it was probably later than zone 2 samples and earlier than zone 4. The rift valley eventually evolved into an ocean basin, by which time the mantle plume had nearly completely dispersed and the asthenospheric mantle became the dominant source rock (Fig. 7D). Eruptions during this time produced oceanic basaltic rocks now preserved as greenstone bodies in zone 4.

Exactly when ocean crust began to form (rift-drift transition) is not well known. I have suggested that oceanic crust was forming at 530 Ma, implying that it started earlier. The limits on this age are based on both radiometric ages and the first occurrence of marine sediments. The radiometric age constraints are broad. Continental rift volcanics in the Pinnacle Formation were forming at 554 Ma (Kumarapeli et al., 1989) and subduction of oceanic crust was probably occurring by 500 Ma, based on ages of metamorphic minerals from zone 3 rocks (Sutter et al., 1985; Rankin, 1994). Thus, the first oceanic crust must have formed between 550 and 500 Ma, and to allow time for the ocean to grow and then begin subducting, it seems likely that the first crust

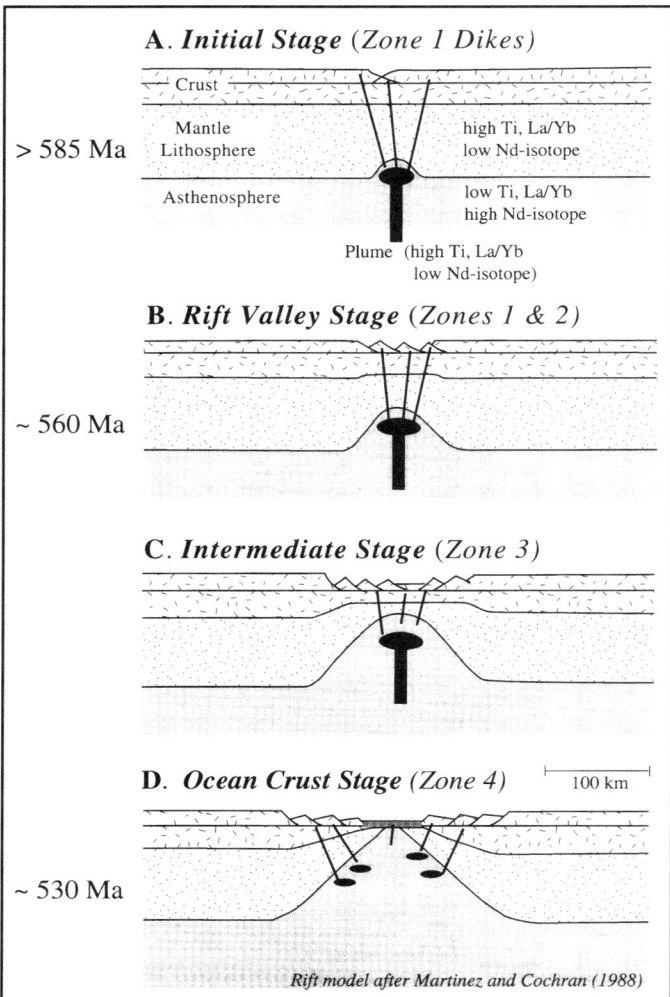

Figure 7. Model to illustrate the progressive development of a rift valley in the Laurentian continent and its evolution to the Iapetus ocean. Possible mantle sources and timing of eruptions in the various zones in Vermont are shown. See text for discussion.

must have formed a considerable time before 500 Ma. If it can be assumed that the first occurrence of marine sediments corresponds to the rift-drift transition and to the first appearance of oceanic crust, then ages of sedimentary rocks in western Vermont have bearing on resolving when ocean crust began to form. Conclusions based on stratigraphy are somewhat controversial: arguments were summarized in Rankin et al. (1993), but the essence is that workers in the Taconic sequence suggest a Late Proterozoic age (Ratcliffe, 1987) and workers in the Green Mountains suggest a later, Early to Middle Cambrian age. The sedimentary record of the rift-drift transition is sometimes taken as the appearance of the earliest quartzite unit, the Cheshire Quartzite found just west of zone 2 (Fig. 1). The unit is dated as Early Cambrian by the presence of the trilobite *Olenellus* (Walcott, 1888; Osberg, 1952) . The base of the Cheshire Quartzite is then close to the Cambrian-Precambrian boundary, 560–570 Ma on most time scales. However, the radiometric age of rift volcanics in the Pinnacle Formation stratigraphically below the Cheshire Quartzite is 554 Ma. This apparent paradox can be reconciled by recent work suggesting that the age of the Precambrian-Cambrian boundary may be as young as 544 Ma (Bowring et al., 1993). Using this time scale, the Cheshire Quartzite has a younger absolute age than the Pinnacle Formation, consistent with the stratigraphy. Moreover, the rift-drift transition is then about 540 Ma or slightly younger, but still in the earliest Cambrian. Therefore, it seems reasonable to assume that by 530 Ma, oceanic crust was forming and a small ocean basin could have been established (Fig. 7D).

The interpretations presented above for zones 2 through 4 have some implications for terrane analysis in the western Appalachians. The Hinesburg slice (zone 2), Hazens Notch and Pinney Hollow slices (zone 3), and Rowe slice (zone 4) all have tectonic boundaries. How much movement has occurred along those boundaries, or in other words, how exotic is each slice? On the basis of the interpretation that the greenstone samples represent progressive evolution of a rift valley, I suggest that all the slices are either on the ancient Laurentian continent or very nearby. Thus, none are really "exotic." Rocks from the Hinesburg slice clearly formed in a continental rift underlain by Laurentian continent. The only true oceanic conditions are represented by the Rowe slice; I suspect that greenstone bodies preserved in this slice formed as part of oceanic crust very close to the ancient continent. Furthermore, preliminary indications are that the western parts of the Hawley slice are the same as the Stowe slice. Between zones 2 and 4, the Hazens Notch and Pinney Hollow slices appear to have formed on transitional crust before true oceanic magmatic conditions were reached. This, however, could correspond to a time of "oceanic" sedimentation, for example, as for the northern part of the Red Sea today.

CONCLUSIONS

Greenstone bodies from the Vermont Appalachians have chemistries indicating that they formed in an evolving continental rift in Late Proterozoic to Early Cambrian time. The greenstone bodies were all basaltic rocks before metamorphism. In western zones (1 and 2), dikes cutting Laurentian basement and greenstone bodies in the Hinesburg slice have high Ti, Zr, REE, and low Nd isotopes consistent with their formation in the earliest stages of development of a continental rift. These basaltic rocks were intruded and extruded between 585 and 554 Ma. In eastern zones (4), greenstone bodies from the Rowe tectonic slice have lower Ti, Zr, REE, and high Nd isotopes consistent with their formation at an oceanic spreading ridge. These basaltic rocks probably formed in the early stages of development of this ocean basin at around 530 to 540 Ma. Between zone 2 and zone 4, greenstone bodies from the Hazens Notch and Pinney Hollow slices have variable chemistries; some are similar to zone 2, others are similar to zone 4, and some have intermediate compositions. These could have been erupted at an intermediate

stage of rift development at the transition from continental to oceanic crust. The change in chemistry of basaltic rocks is consistent with a change in mantle source rock beneath the evolving rift. The rift may been initiated by a mantle plume, which provided the bulk of magmatism to early stages (zones 1 and 2). As the influence of the plume lessened with progressive rifting, depleted asthenosphere convected upward and partially melted. At this intermediate stage, a variety of basalt compositions could have been formed from plume, depleted asthenosphere, and mixtures of the two. When the rift developed into an oceanic spreading center, only depleted asthenosphere partially melted to form basaltic rocks of zone 4.

The next steps toward a more complete understanding of early Paleozoic volcanism in Vermont are to look in more detail at small-scale variations in chemistry, especially in zone 3, to investigate more closely volcanic rocks in the Hawley slice and formations farther east, and to obtain igneous age dates on the metavolcanic rocks.

ACKNOWLEDGMENTS

I thank the scores of undergraduate geology majors who have contributed, helped, and inspired much of this work, in particular, S. Fleming, R. Poyner, D. Bailey, D. Perry, C. Anderson, T. Gavigan, R. Masinter, G. Dick, P. Pugin, A. Bramley, C. Clark, T. Kafka, B. Welch, C. Sinton, M. Evans, J. Doolittle, M. Larsen, and J. Seibert. Rolfe Stanley and students at the University of Vermont provided help in the field and valuable discussion of problems in Vermont geology. Financial support for the work was provided by National Science Foundation (NSF) grants EAR-9017873, NSF-EPSCoR R11–8610679, DUE-9351213, and a Keck Foundation equipment grant. Reviews by R. Badger and B. L. Weaver were very helpful.

REFERENCES CITED

Altherr, R., Henjes-Kunst, F., Puchelt, H., and Baumann, A., 1988, Volcanic activity in the Red Sea axial trough—Evidence for a large mantle diapir?: Tectonophysics, v. 150, p. 121–133.

Altherr, R., Henjes-Kunst, F., and Baumann, A., 1990, Asthenosphere versus lithosphere as possible sources for basaltic magmas erupted during formation of the Red Sea: Constraints from Sr, Pb and Nd isotopes: Earth and Planetary Science Letters, v. 96, p. 269–286.

Badger, R. L., 1994, Mantle composition and lithospheric thickness beneath the NW Adirondack region during late Proterozoic Iapetus extension: Geological Society of America Abstracts with Programs, v. 26, no. 3, p. 4.

Barberi, F., Ciretta, F. L., and Varet, J., 1980, Sr isotopic composition of Afar volcanics and its implication for mantle evolution: Earth and Planetary Science Letters, v. 50, p. 247–259.

Barrat, J.-A., Jahn, B. M., Joron, J.-L., Auvray, B., and Hamdi, H., 1990, Mantle heterogeneity in northeastern Africa: Evidence from Nd isotopic compositions and hygromagmaphile element geochemistry of basaltic rocks from the Gulf of Tadjoura and southern Red Sea regions: Earth and Planetary Science Letters, v. 101, p. 233–247.

Betton, P. J., and Civetta, L., 1984, Strontium and neodymium isotopic evidence for the heterogeneous nature and development of the mantle beneath Afar

(Ethiopia): Earth and Planetary Science Letters, v. 71, p. 59–70.

Bowring, S. A., Grotzinger, J. P., Isachsen, C. E., Knoll, A. H., Pelechaty, S. M., and Kolosov, P., 1993, Calibrating rates of Early Cambrian evolution: Science, v. 261, p. 1293.

Brueckner, H. K., Zindler, A., Seyler, M., and Bonatti, E., 1988, Zabargad and the isotopic evolution of the sub-Red Sea mantle and crust: Tectonophysics, v. 150, p. 163–176.

Buddington, A. F., 1939, Adirondack igneous rocks and their metamorphism: Geological Society of America Memoir 7, 354 p.

Chazot, G., and Bertrand, H., 1993, Mantle sources and magma-continental crust interactions during early Red Sea–Gulf of Aden rifting in southern Yemen—elemental and Sr, Nd, Pb isotope evidence: Journal of Geophysical Research, v. 98, p. 1819–1835.

Church, B. N., 1975, Quantitative classification and chemical comparison of common volcanic rocks: Geological Society of America Bulletin, v. 86, p. 257–263.

Coish, R. A., 1989, The significance of geochemical trends in Vermont greenstones, in Colpron, M., and Doolan, B., eds., Proceedings of the Quebec-Vermont Appalachian Workshop: Burlington, Vermont Geological Society, p. 82–85.

Coish, R. A., and Sinton, C. W., 1992, Geochemistry of mafic dikes in the Adirondack mountains: Implications for the constitution of Late Proterozoic mantle: Contributions to Mineralogy and Petrology, v. 110, p. 500–514.

Coish, R. A., Fleming, F. S., Larsen, M., Poyner, R., and Seibert, J., 1985, Early rift history of the proto-Atlantic ocean: Geochemical evidence from metavolcanic rocks in Vermont: American Journal of Science, v. 285, p. 351–378.

Coish, R. A., Perry, D. A., Anderson, C. D., and Bailey, D., 1986, Metavolcanic rocks from the Stowe Formation, Vermont: Remnants of ridge and intraplate volcanism in the Iapetus ocean: American Journal of Science, v. 286, p. 1–28.

Coish, R. A., Bramley, A., Gavigan, T., and Masinter, R., 1991, Progressive changes in volcanism during Iapetan rifting: Comparisons with the East African Rift–Red Sea system: Geology, v. 19, p. 1021–1024.

Coleman, R. G., and McGuire, V., 1988, Magma systems related to the Red Sea opening: Tectonophysics, v. 150, p. 77–100.

Dick, G., 1989, Geochemistry of diabasic dikes and metavolcanic rocks from the Jay area, northern Vermont [B.A. thesis]: Middlebury, Vermont, Middlebury College, 50 p.

Doll, C. G., Cady, W. M., Thompson, J. B., and Billings, M. P., Jr., 1961, Centennial geologic map of Vermont: Montpelier, Vermont Geological Survey, scale 1:250,000.

Dostal, J., Dupuy, C., and Baragar, H., 1983, Geochemistry and petrogenesis of basaltic rocks from Coppermine River area, Northwest Territory, Canada: Canadian Journal of Earth Sciences, v. 20, p. 684–698.

Evans, M. J., 1994, Geochemistry of metadiabasic dikes and metavolcanic rocks from north-central Vermont [B.A. thesis]: Middlebury, Vermont, Middlebury College, 60 p.

Fitton, J. G., James, D., Kempton, P. D., Ormerod, D. S., and Leeman, W. P., 1988, The role of lithospheric mantle in the generation of late Cenozoic basic magmas in the western United States, in Cox, K. G., and Menzies, M. A., eds., Special Lithosphere Issue: Journal of Petrology Special Volume, p. 331–349.

Floyd, P. A., and Winchester, J. A., 1975, Magma type and tectonic setting discrimination using immobile elements: Earth and Planetary Science Letters, v. 27, p. 211–218.

Hart, W. K., WoldeGabriel, G., Walter, R. C., and Mertzman, S. A., 1989, Basaltic volcanism in Ethiopia: Constraints on continental rifting and mantle interactions: Journal of Geophysical Research, v. 94, p. 7731–7748.

Hawkesworth, C., Mantovani, M., and Peate, D., 1988, Lithosphere remobilization during Paraná CFB magmatism, in Cox, K. G., and Menzies, M. A., eds., Special Lithosphere Issue: Journal of Petrology Special Volume, p. 205–223.

Hawkesworth, C. J., Kempton, P. D., Rogers, N. W., Ellam, R. M., and van Cal-

steren, P. W., 1990, Continental mantle lithosphere, and shallow level enrichment processes in the Earth's mantle: Earth and Planetary Science Letters, v. 96, p. 256–268.

Isachsen, Y. W., 1985, Structural and tectonic studies in New York State: U.S. Nuclear Regulatory Commission Report CR-3178, 72 p.

Isachsen, Y. W., Coish, R., Sinton, C., Heisler, M., and Kelley, B., 1988, Dikes of the northeast Adirondack region: Their distribution, orientation, mineralogy, chronology, chemistry and mystery, in Olmsted, J. F., ed., Field trip guidebook: New York State Geological Association, p. 215–243.

Kafka, T. K., Elbert, D. C., and Coish, R. A., 1993, Geochemistry of a sheared greenstone in the Pinney Hollow Formation: Small scale igneous variations: Geological Society of America Abstracts with Programs, v. 25, no. 2, p. 27.

Kamo, S. L., Gower, C. F., and Krogh, T. E., 1989, Birthdate for the Iapetus Ocean? A precise U-Pb zircon and baddeleyite age for the Long Range dikes, southeast Labrador: Geology, v. 17, p. 602–605.

Kamo, S. L., Krogh, T. E., and Kumarapeli, P. S., 1995, Age of the Grenville dyke swarm, Ontario-Quebec: Implications for the timing of Iapetan rifting: Canadian Journal of Earth Sciences, v. 32, p. 273–280.

Kumarapeli, P. S., 1993, A plume-generated segment of the rifted margin of Laurentia, southern Canadian appalachians, seen through a completed Wilson Cycle: Tectonophysics, v. 219, p. 47–55.

Kumarapeli, P. S., Dunning, G. R., Pinston, H., and Shaver, J., 1989, Geochemistry and U-Pb zircon age of comenditic metafelsites of the Tibbit Hill Formation, Quebec Appalachians: Canadian Journal of Earth Sciences, v. 26, p. 1374–1383.

Kumarapeli, S., St. Seymour, K., Pinston, H., and Hasselgren, E., 1990, Volcanism on the passive margin of Laurentia: An early Paleozoic analogue of Cretaceous volcanism on the northeastern American margin: Reply: Canadian Journal of Earth Sciences, v. 27, p. 1552–1554.

Latin, D., Norry, M. J., and Tarzey, R. J. E., 1993, Magmatism in the Gregory Rift, East Africa—Evidence for melt generation by a plume: Journal of Petrology, v. 34, p. 1007–1027.

Leat, P. T., Thompson, R. N., Morrison, M. A., Hendry, G. L., and Dickin, A. P., 1988, Compositionally diverse Miocene-recent rift-related magmatism in northwest Colorado: Partial melting, and mixing of mafic magmas from 3 different asthenospheric and lithospheric mantle sources, in Cox, K. G., and Menzies, M. A., eds., Special Lithosphere Issue: Journal of Petrology Special Volume, p. 351–377.

Leeman, W. P., and Fitton, J. G., 1989, Magmatism associated with lithospheric extension: Introduction: Journal of Geophysical Research, v. 94, p. 7682–7684.

Lightfoot, P. C., Hawkesworth, C. J., Hergt, J., Naldrett, A. J., Gorbachev, N. S., Fedorenko, V. A., and Doherty, W., 1993, Remobilisation of the continental lithosphere by a mantle plume—Major-element, trace-element, and Sr-isotope, Nd-isotope, and Pb-isotope evidence from picritic and tholeiitic lavas of the Norilsk district, Siberian trap, Russia: Contributions to Mineralogy and Petrology, v. 114, p. 171–188.

Martinez, F., and Cochran, J. R., 1988, Structure and tectonics of the northern Red Sea: Catching a continental margin between rifting and drifting: Tectonophysics, v. 150, p. 1–32.

McHone, J. G., and Butler, R. J., 1984, Mesozoic igneous provinces of New England and the opening of the North Atlantic ocean: Geological Society of America Bulletin, v. 95, p. 757–765.

McLelland, J. M., 1991, The early history of the Adirondacks as an anorogenic magmatic complex, in Perchul, L. L., ed., Progress in metamorphic and magmatic petrology: London, Cambridge University Press, p. 287–321.

McLelland, J. M., and Chiarenzelli, J. R., 1990, Geochronological studies in the Adirondack Mountains and the implications of a middle Proterozoic tonalitic suite, in Gower, C. F., Rivers, T., and Ryan, B., eds., Mid-Proterozoic geology of the southern margins of Proto Laurentia-Baltica, p. 175–194.

McLelland, J. M., Isachsen, Y., Whitney, P., Chiarenzelli, J., and Hall, L., 1993, Geology of the Adirondack Massif, New York, in Reed, J. C., Jr., et al., eds., Precambrian: Conterminous United States: Boulder, Colorado, Geological Society of America, The Geology of North America, v. C-2, p. 338–353.

Meschede, M., 1986, A method of discriminating between different types of mid-ocean ridge basalts and continental tholeiites with the Nb-Zr-Y diagram: Chemical Geology, v. 56, p. 207–218.

Nakamura, N., 1974, Determination of REE, Ba, Fe, Mg, Na and K in carbonaceous and ordinary chondrites: Geochimica et Cosmochimica Acta, v. 38, p. 757–775.

O'Loughlin, S. B., and Stanley, R. S., 1986, Bedrock geology of the Mt. Abraham—Lincoln Gap area, central Vermont: Vermont Geological Survey Special Bulletin 6, 29 p.

Osberg, P. H., 1952, The Green Mountain Anticlinorium in the vicinity of Rochester and East Middlebury, VT: Vermont Geological Survey Bulletin no. 5, 127 p.

Pearce, J. A., 1975, Basalt geochemistry used to investigate past tectonic environments on Cyprus: Tectonophysics, v. 25, p. 41–67.

Pearce, J. A., 1982, Trace element characteristics of lavas from destructive plate boundaries, *in* Thorpe, R. S., ed., Andesites: Chichester, United Kingdom, Wiley, p. 525–548.

Pearce, J. A., 1983, Role of sub-continental lithosphere in magma genesis at active continental margins, *in* Hawkesworth, C. J., and Norry, M. J., eds., Continental basalts and mantle xenoliths: Cheshire, United Kingdom, Shiva Publishing, p. 230–249.

Pearce, J. A., and Cann, J. R., 1973, Tectonic setting of basic volcanic rocks determined using trace element analysis: Earth and Planetary Science Letters, v. 19, p. 290–300.

Pearce, J. A., and Norry, M. J., 1979, Petrogenetic implications of Ti, Zr, Y and Nb variations in volcanic rocks: Contributions to Mineralogy and Petrology, v. 69, p. 33–47.

Pugin, P. A., 1989, Geochemistry of the Belvidere Mountain amphibolite, Troy, Vermont [B.A. thesis]: Middlebury, Vermont, Middlebury College, 48 p.

Rankin, D. W., 1976, Appalachian salients and recesses: Late Precambrian continental breakup and opening of the Iapetus ocean: Journal of Geophysical Research, v. 81, p. 5605–5619.

Rankin, D. W., 1994, Continental margin of the eastern United States: past and present, *in* Speed, R. C., ed., Phanerozoic evolution of North American continent-ocean transitions: Boulder, Colorado, Geological Society of America, Continent-Ocean Transect Volume, p. 129–218.

Rankin, D. W., Drake, A. A., Jr., and Ratcliffe, N. M., 1993, Proterozoic North America (Laurentian) rocks of the Appalachian orogen, *in* Reed, J. C., Jr., et al., eds., Precambrian: Conterminous United States: Boulder, Colorado, Geological Society of America, The geology of North America, v. C-2, p. 378–422.

Ratcliffe, N. M., 1987, High TiO$_2$ metadiabase dikes of the Hudson Highlands, New York and New Jersey: Possible late Proterozoic rift rocks in the New York recess: American Journal of Science, v. 287, p. 817–850.

Ratcliffe, N. M., 1993, Searching for the root zone(s) of the Taconic allocthon: Leaving no stones unturned: Geological Society of America Abstracts

with Programs, v. 25, no. 2, p. 72.

Sinton, C. W., 1988, Geochemistry and tectonic setting of eastern Adirondack dikes [B.A. thesis]: Middlebury, Vermont, Middlebury College, 58 p.

Stanley, R. S., and Ratcliffe, N. M., 1985, Tectonic synthesis of the Taconian orogeny in western New England: Geological Society of America Bulletin, v. 96, p. 1227–1250.

Stanley, R. S., Roy, D. L., Hatch, N. L., and Knapp, D. A., 1984, Evidence for tectonic emplacement of ultramafic and associated rocks in the Pre-Silurian belt of western New England: American Journal of Science, v. 284, p. 559–595.

St. Seymour, K., and Kumarapeli, P. S., 1995, Geochemistry of the Grenville dyke swarm: Role of plume-source mantle in magma genesis: Contributions to Mineralogy and Petrology, v. 120, p. 29–41.

Sutter, J. F., Ratcliffe, N. M., and Mukasa, S. B., 1985, ^{40}Ar/^{39}Ar and K-Ar data bearing on the metamorphic and tectonic history of western New England: Geological Society of America Bulletin, v. 96, p. 123–136.

Thompson, P. J., and Thompson, T. B., 1991, Bedrock geology of the Camels Hump–Bolton Mountain area, north-central Vermont: Vermont Geological Survey Special Bulletin 12, 32 p.

Thompson, R. N., and Morrison, M. A., 1988, Asthenospheric and lower-lithospheric mantle contributions to continental extension magmatism: An example from the British Tertiary Province: Chemical Geology, v. 68, p. 1–15.

Thompson, R. N., Morrison, M. A., Hendry, G. L., and Parry, S. J., 1984, An assessment of the relative roles of crust and mantle in magma genesis: An elemental approach: Royal Society of London Philosophical Transactions, v. 310, p. 549–590.

Treuil, M., and Joron, J. L., 1976, Etude geochemique des elements en traces dans le magmatisme de l'Afar: Implications petrogenetiques et comparison avec le magmatisme de l'Islande et de dorsale medio-atlantique, *in* Pilger, A., and Rosler, A., eds., Afar between continental and oceanic rifting: Stuggart, E. Schweizerbart'sche Verlagsbuchhandlung, p. 26–79.

Vidal, P., Deniel, C., Vellutini, P. J., Piguet, P., Coulon, C., Vincent, J., and Audin, J., 1991, Changes of mantle sources in the course of a rift evolution: Geophysical Research Letters, v. 18, p. 1913–1916.

Walcott, C. D., 1888, The Taconic system of Emmons, and the name in geologic nomenclature: American Journal of Science, v. 35, p. 229–242, 307–327, 394–401.

White, R., and McKenzie, D., 1989, Magmatism at rift zones: The generation of volcanic continental margins and flood basalts: Journal of Geophysical Research, v. 94, p. 7685–7729.

Wood, D. A., 1980, The application of a Th-Hf-Ta diagram to problems of tectonomagmatic classification and to establishing the nature of crustal contamination of basaltic lavas of the British Tertiary volcanic province: Earth and Planetary Science Letters, v. 50, p. 11–30.

MANUSCRIPT ACCEPTED BY THE SOCIETY JULY 2, 1996

Geological Society of America
Memoir 191
1997

Igneous petrogenesis and tectonic setting of granitic rocks from the eastern Blue Ridge and Inner Piedmont, Alabama Appalachians

Mark S. Drummond and Michael J. Neilson
Department of Geology, University of Alabama at Birmingham, Birmingham, Alabama 35294
David T. Allison
Department of Geology and Geography, University of South Alabama, Mobile, Alabama 36688
James F. Tull
Department of Geology, Florida State University, Tallahassee, Florida 32306

ABSTRACT

The eastern Blue Ridge (EBR) and Inner Piedmont (IP) are the two major host terranes for granitic rocks in the Alabama Appalachians. Four discrete episodes of granitic magmatism over an ~150 m.y. time span are recorded by the EBR and IP granitic rocks: the Late Cambrian–Early Ordovician Penobscotian stage, the Middle Ordovician Taconic stage, the Middle to Late Devonian Acadian stage, and an Early Mississippian late to post-Acadian stage. The Penobscotian Elkahatchee quartz diorite batholith of the EBR is interpreted to represent continental margin magmatism associated with incipient subduction and melting of an oceanic slab beneath Laurentia. Generation of the I-type granites and granodiorites of the Kowaliga and Zana gneisses of the EBR may result from intracrustal melting during the Taconic orogen. S-type plutonism accompanied Acadian prograde regional dynamothermal metamorphism in the EBR (Bluff Spring and Rockford granites) and Opelika Complex (Farmville metagranite) of the IP. A tectonic model that calls upon collision between the EBR and IP supports the observed magmatic and metamorphic responses to Acadian orogenesis in the Alabama Appalachians. The Hog Mountain and Blakes Ferry plutons are small, I-type plutons that impart a contact-metamorphic aureole on the host metasedimentary rocks. These late to post-Acadian plutons may have been generated and/or emplaced into thickened continental crust following collisional tectonics. Granitic magmatism plays a pivotal role in evaluating the growth and tectonic evolution of the Alabama Appalachians through time.

INTRODUCTION

Granitic rocks can provide important information on the evolving tectonic character of the host terrane over time. Specific granitic rock types, their petrogenesis, and geochemical characteristics can commonly be restricted to specific tectonic regimes. Geochronologic and geothermobarometric studies of granitic rocks and host metamorphic rocks measure pressure-temperature (*P-T*) adjustments in an orogenic terrane through time in response to kinematic and thermal events.

Granitic rocks of the Alabama Appalachians occur in polydeformed, amphibolite facies, regionally metamorphosed terranes. Evaluation of these bodies is imperative to the understanding of the tectonic evolution of this region. A span of ~150 m.y. of magmatic activity is recorded by the Alabama granites. This study provides an overview of the major granitic bodies in the eastern Blue Ridge (EBR, Fig. 1A) and Inner Piedmont (IP, Fig. 1B) of Alabama, which are the two major terranes hosting granitic rocks in the Alabama Appalachians. We will present the current state of knowledge about the major granitic bodies in

Drummond, M. S., Neilson, M. J., Allison, D. T., and Tull, J. F., 1997, Igneous petrogenesis and tectonic setting of granitic rocks from the eastern Blue Ridge and Inner Piedmont, Alabama Appalachians, *in* Sinha, A. K., Whalen, J. B., and Hogan, J. P., eds., The Nature of Magmatism in the Appalachian Orogen: Boulder, Colorado, Geological Society of America Memoir 191.

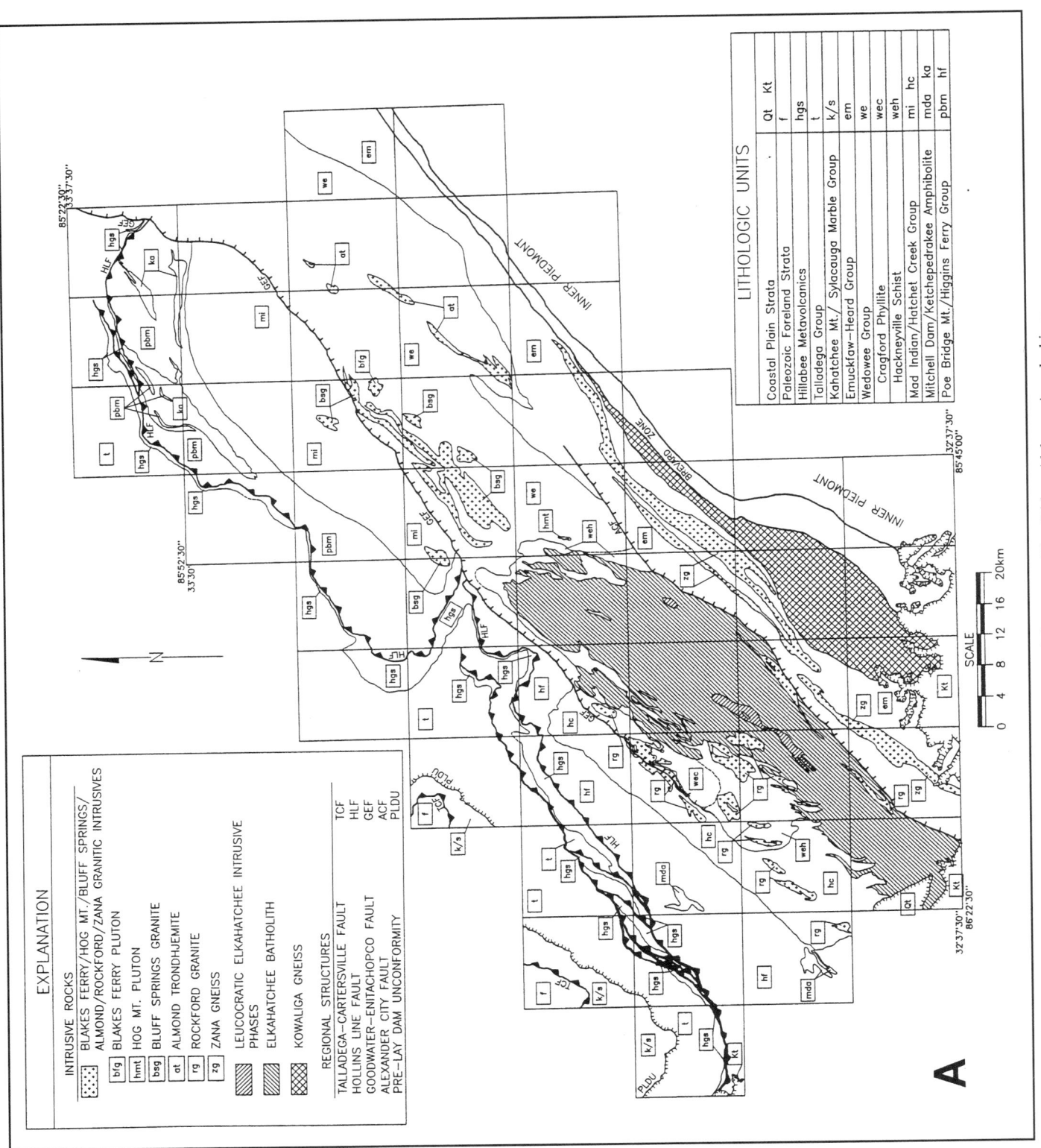

Figure 1A: Geologic map of the eastern Blue Ridge, Alabama Appalachians.

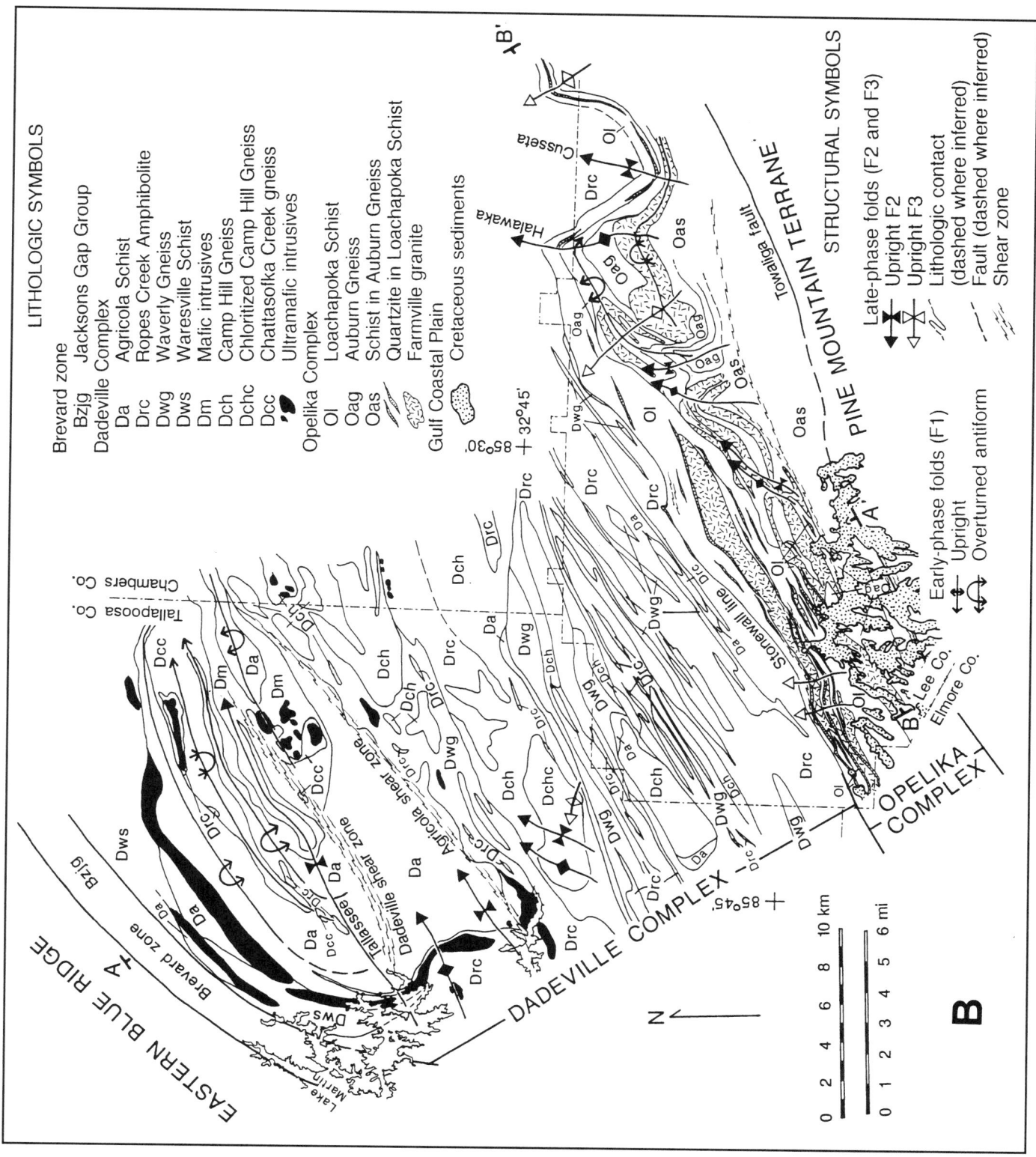

Figure 1B: Geologic map of the Inner Piedmont, Alabama Appalachians (taken from Steltenpohl et al., 1990, Plate 1).

this region, relate this information to a working tectonic model for the EBR and IP of the Alabama Appalachians, and discuss avenues for future research. New geochemical data and quantitative metamorphic *P-T* estimates on IP granitic rocks and host metamorphic rocks are presented in this study.

GEOLOGIC SETTING

The Alabama Appalachians represent the southwesternmost exposures of the Appalachian orogen and comprise part of the postulated Alabama promontory of the Laurentian-Iapetus margin (Thomas, 1977) plus terranes that have accreted to this margin during the growth of the Appalachians. Lithotectonic block subdivisions have been made in the Alabama Appalachians on the basis of major fault zones and/or lithological contrast between adjacent blocks. The focus of this study is on the granitic rocks of the Coosa and Tallapoosa blocks of the EBR (Tull, 1978) and Dadeville complex of the IP (Bentley and Neathery, 1970). The EBR and IP are polydeformed regionally metamorphosed terranes that are composed of a variety of metasedimentary rocks, amphibolites, and granitic rocks. Prograde regional metamorphism (D_1–M_1) in both the EBR and IP is interpreted to be an Acadian event (380–340 Ma; Glover et al., 1983), on the basis of Rb-Sr whole-rock dates from synmetamorphic S-type granites in both belts (refer to later discussion for details). Acadian isotopic ages have also been determined for metasedimentary rocks and amphibolites in the EBR (Wampler et al., 1970; Russell, 1978). The D_1 episode was responsible for generating the prograde regional dynamothermal metamorphism (M_1) and dominant metamorphic foliation (S_1) in the region (Tull, 1978).

This chapter reviews the field and metamorphic relationships and geochemical character of the granitic rocks of the EBR and IP of the Alabama Appalachians. The granitic rocks are utilized to compare and contrast the EBR and IP, and to provide tectonic implications concerning the growth and evolution of this segment of the Appalachians. The study area lies in a key tectonic location; the northwest border (Hollins Line fault) is the Talladega belt, which has been shown to represent Laurentian margin material (Tull, 1982; Tull et al., 1988). Studies of the EBR and IP granitic rocks could potentially shed light on the exotic terrane status of these two lithotectonic belts, and could indicate whether these two belts should be considered together as one terrane (e.g., Piedmont terrane; Hatcher and Odom, 1980) or separate terranes (Jefferson terrane and Piedmont terrane; Horton et al., 1989).

LITHOLOGIC AND GEOLOGIC DESCRIPTION OF THE GRANITIC ROCKS

The granitic rocks of the EBR and IP form discontinuous belts of northeast-trending intrusions (Fig. 1, A and B) on a variety of scales. Most of the granitic bodies occur as tabular concordant bodies that are interpreted as sills, and range in size

from centimeter-scale leucocratic layers in stromatic migmatites to intrusions several kilometers thick. Approximately 25%–30% of the surface area of the EBR is granitic rocks (Table 1); although direct measurements of granitic surface area have not been made in the IP, geologic maps (Osborne et al., 1988; Steltenpohl et al., 1990) indicate a percentage similar to that of the EBR. The following discussion provides a brief description of the granitic rocks and their host rocks, structural setting and timing of the intrusions, and mode of emplacement for some of the intrusions.

Eastern Blue Ridge granitic rocks

The eastern Blue Ridge (EBR) of Alabama is a composite terrane containing probable elements of Laurentian distal margin rocks (late Precambrian slope-rise sediments) and possibly younger accretionary sequences tectonically interleaved with the Laurentian sequences or sutured against them. There is no direct stratigraphic evidence, however, that links the EBR to Laurentia during the time of its deposition. Classically, these rocks constitute the Northern Alabama Piedmont and have been referred to as the Ashland-Wedowee belt (Tull, 1978). Field studies have shown that the lithostratigraphic units of the EBR (Fig. 1A) are internally bounded by stratigraphic contacts (Muangnoicharoen, 1975; Neathery, 1975; Tull, 1978, 1987; Drummond, 1986; Beiler and Deininger, 1987; Allison, 1992). The EBR contains at least two significant internal faults, the Goodwater-Enitachopco fault on the northwest and the Alexander City fault on the southeast (Fig. 1A). Both faults are linear, occurred very late in the kinematic sequence, and display dominantly normal displacement (Drummond, 1986; Allison, 1992; Drummond et al., 1994). The current geologic mapping in the region suggests that the EBR granitic bodies are contained in a single lithotectonic terrane.

The Elkahatchee quartz diorite (EQD) is a premetamorphic (M_1) gneiss of batholithic dimensions (Table 1) and represents the largest intrusive complex exposed in the Blue Ridge province of the southern Appalachians. The areal size of the EQD is a minimum; its eastern termination is the Alexander City dextral normal fault, there is a nonconformable overlap of coastal plain sediments along the southern border, and northeast-plunging folds along the northeastern border project the EQD into the subsurface (Fig. 1A). The EQD represents the oldest granitic body in the EBR (490–500 Ma; Russell et al., 1987) and has undergone all of the deformational phases recognized in the region. Wedowee Group and Hatchet Creek Group metasedimentary rocks are the host rocks to the EQD. Conformable, knife-sharp contacts occur between the EQD and Wedowee Group host rocks, whereas at lower structural levels (southwest) the EQD crosscuts at least 6 km of Hatchet Creek Group stratigraphy (Fig. 1A). These structural relationships suggest an upper mushroom-shaped (laccolithic) form that merges into a structurally lower discordant feeder dike portion. Structurally, the

TABLE 1. FOUR STAGES OF GRANITIC MAGMATISM, EASTERN BLUE RIDGE (EBR), ALABAMA APPALACHIANS

	Size (km²)	Lithology	Enclave type	SiO₂ Range (%)	Geochemical characterization	δ¹⁸O (per mil)	(⁸⁷Sr/⁸⁶Sr)ᵢ
Penobscotian							
EQD (495 Ma)*	880	Gabbro-granite	Cumulate gabbro/diorite	47-74	I-type, metaluminous-weakly peraluminous	9.7 ± 0.4	0.7036
Taconic							
Kowaliga augen gneiss	379	Granodiorite-granite	Mafic schlieren	67-76	I-type (K) with potential meta-sediment contamination (Z), metaluminous-peraluminous		0.7044 (K)
Zana granite gneiss (460 Ma)	131 / 510						0.7061 (Z)
Acadian							
Rockford granite	94	Granite-trondhjemite	Metasediment	65-76	S-type, strongly peraluminous	11.2 ± 1.8	~0.706
Bluff Springs (366 Ma)	75	Granite-trondhjemite	Metasediment	67-75	S-type, strongly peraluminous	8.8	0.7059
Almond trondhjemite	36 / 205	Trondhjemite	Metasediment + tonalite	68-76	I-type, peraluminous	8.0	~0.705
Late to Post Acadian							
Blakes Ferry pluton	6.0	Trondhjemite	Bt schlieren	68-77	I-type, peraluminous	7.9	~0.7045
Hog Mt. pluton	0.6	Tonalite-granodiorite	Metasediment	66-75	Contaminated I-type, peraluminous	9.6-11.4	

Σ = 1,606 km² or ~27 percent of EBR of the Alabama Appalachians.
*EQD = Elkahatchee quartz diorite.

EQD lies in the core of a large synform; Wedowee Group stratigraphy has been mapped around the northeastern F₃-fold closure of the EQD (Tull, 1987; Drummond et al., 1994). This synformal structural relationship indicates that Wedowee Group rocks to the southeast of the EQD represent the overturned limb of a regional northwest-verging synform.

Slightly peraluminous to metaluminous (I-type) biotite tonalite-granodiorite is the principal lithology of the EQD batholithic complex (Tables 1 and 2, Fig. 2); there are subordinate cumulate hornblende-biotite gabbro-diorite and biotite-epidote schistose enclaves, quartz-biotite metadacite porphyry, and felsic granitoids (granite, trondhjemite, and quartz monzonite; Fig. 2). A slight normal zonation of these lithologies is displayed with accumulation of rare gabbro-diorite enclaves around the outer margin, followed by the dominant tonalite-granodiorite, and a concentration of felsic granitoids in the batholithic core. Hornblende barometry and hornblende-plagioclase thermometry of the EQD gabbro-diorite enclaves provide crystallization estimates of 1 to 4 kbar at 710–850 °C (Drummond et al., 1994). The lower 1 kbar end of the pressure range and the presence of cogenetic metadacites suggest that the EQD may have undergone final epizonal emplacement into its own volcanic ejecta.

The EQD contains magmatic Fe-epidote that exhibits petrographic relationships (Zen and Hammarstrom, 1984) indicative of early crystallization from the EQD magmatic system (Drummond et al., 1994). Geochemical modeling of the EQD petrogenesis (discussed later) indicates that Fe-epidote crystallized out during the initial 23% of the crystallization history. Experimental evidence indicates that Fe-epidote is stable in granitic magmas at

pressure greater than 6 kbar (Naney, 1983; Schmidt, 1992, 1993). Field studies of magmatic epidote-bearing plutons have supported the high-pressure origin for these plutons (Zen and Hammarstrom, 1984; Barth, 1990). Hornblende was also an early crystallizing phase in the EQD, but hornblende barometry records pressures of 1–4 kbar, which are interpreted as compositional equilibration of hornblende during crystallization of the critical barometric assemblage of hornblende–biotite–quartz–plagioclase–K-feldspar–sphene–Fe-Ti oxide.

Two potential explanations for the appearance of Fe-epidote in a magmatic system, the final emplacement pressures of which are estimated to as low as 1 kbar in a subvolcanic regime, are: (1) the possibility that magmatic epidote may be stable in granitic systems at pressures as low as ~3 kbar, as suggested by Vyhnal et al. (1991) for Alleghanian-age plutons in the southern Appalachians; or (2) rapid ascent and emplacement of the EQD magma(s) allowed Fe-epidote to persist metastably. Explanation 1 ignores current experimental evidence for the high-pressure origin of magmatic epidote (Naney, 1983; Schmidt, 1992, 1993). Petrologic studies of dacitic dikes from the Colorado Front Range (Dawes and Evans, 1991) and the White Creek batholith, British Columbia (Brandon and Lambert, 1994; Brandon et al., 1994) are confronted with the same apparent dilemma of magmatic epidote presence in granites that undergo final solidification at 2–4 kbar. These studies also call upon process 2 to preserve the Fe-epidote metastably. The sole mechanism to allow rapid magma ascent rates through the crust is by fracture-controlled (dike or shear zone) transport (Clemens and Mawer, 1992; Petford et al., 1994). Method 2 is consistent with the Drummond

M. S. Drummond and Others

TABLE 2. MEAN (STANDARD DEVIATION) OF WHOLE-ROCK COMPOSITIONAL DATA OF ALABAMA APPALACHIAN GRANITIC ROCKS*

	EQD	Kowaliga Zana	Rockford Granite	Bluff Springs	Almond	Blakes Ferry	Hog Mountain	Camp Hill	CCG
N =	79	20	23	12	19	28	33	12	10
SiO_2	66.13(0.13)	71.51(3.05)	71.74(1.41)	71.23(2.03)	71.50(1.85)	73.63(1.63)	69.74(1.65)	74.34(1.40)	74.72(1.63)
TiO_2	0.54(0.17)	0.33(0.21)	0.24(0.12)	0.23(0.14)	0.21(0.07)	0.21(0.04)	0.43(0.10)	0.26(0.05)	0.18(0.09)
Al_2O_3	16.62(0.69)	14.45(0.88)	15.05(0.95)	16.01(0.88)	15.92(1.01)	15.47(0.92)	16.52(0.92)	13.54(0.80)	14.44(0.70)
Fe_2O_3	1.45(0.41)					0.84(0.39)		2.97(0.79)	1.31(0.61)
FeO	2.17(0.68)	2.11(1.06)	1.59(0.75)	1.60(0.82)	1.43(0.63)		3.08(0.58)		
MnO	0.06(0.01)	0.10(0.15)	0.03(0.02)	0.04(0.02)	0.03(0.01)	0.01(0.01)	0.05(0.02)	0.08(0.04)	0.03(0.01)
MgO	1.52(0.55)	0.96(0.79)	0.51(0.35)	0.48(0.36)	0.43(0.21)	0.28(0.13)	1.31(0.19)	0.84(0.31)	0.31(0.30)
CaO	3.60(0.66)	2.29(1.14)	1.36(0.64)	1.83(0.79)	1.96(0.49)	1.84(0.39)	2.85(0.31)	2.60(0.58)	0.69(0.29)
Na_2O	4.19(0.46)	3.64(0.77)	3.33(0.68)	4.25(0.30)	5.34(0.64)	5.26(0.34)	3.95(0.33)	3.90(0.41)	2.06(0.35)
K_2O	2.35(0.64)	3.67(1.27)	3.97(1.29)	2.85(0.58)	1.96(0.64)	1.79(0.52)	1.79(0.27)	1.05(0.25)	5.25(0.67)
P_2O_5	0.19(0.07)	0.15(0.11)	0.18(0.10)	0.13(0.09)	0.06(0.01)	0.05(0.01)	0.19(0.05)	0.05(0.05)	0.07(0.05)
LOI	0.99(0.43)		1.67(1.00)	1.59(0.90)	0.91(0.48)	0.50(0.17)		0.73(0.39)	2.07(0.42)
Total	99.74(0.55)	99.11(1.52)	99.57(0.64)	100.23(0.75)	99.69(1.34)	99.65(0.48)	99.91(0.10)	100.36(0.88)	101.13(0.59)
Mg#	44.0 (3.0)	37.4(15.2)	34.6 (7.5)	33.7(10.0)	35.5 (7.0)	37.4 (4.6)	43.2 (2.7)	35.5 (7.3)	27.9(12.5)
ASI	1.06(0.03)	1.04(0.16)	1.25(0.17)	1.20(0.10)	1.11(0.07)	1.11(0.05)	1.22(0.09)	1.11(0.07)	1.40(0.11)
Na/K	1.70(0.46)	1.04(0.51)	0.83(0.32)	1.39(0.30)	2.48(0.92)	2.79(0.63)	2.04(0.46)	3.54(0.99)	0.36(0.10)
Rb	108 (29)		186 (52)	80 (14)	44 (15)	28 (4)	60 (11)	35 (10)	162 (41)
Sr	628 (115)		234 (118)	556 (175)	430 (104)	782 (22)	597 (189)	99 (17)	105 (42)
Ba	633 (343)		562 (424)	804 (277)	521 (106)	540 (24)	760 (73)	267 (100)	643 (436)
Sc	7.4 (2.1)			3.5			7.7 (0.9)		
Zr	147 (42)		92 (49)	74 (52)	27 (60)	35 (2)	176 (35)	108 (14)	125 (56)
Y	10.4 (4.3)			11			22 (11)	28 (18)	15
V	51 (18)			33 (22)	19 (7)	16 (3)			
Nb	7.5 (2.3)			5.3				9.3 (5.1)	12.4 (6.3)
Cr	30 (9)		103 (40)	81 (100)	63 (50)	6 (2)	10 (1)		
Co	40 (5)		6 (1)	38	51 (23)	44 (8)	6 (1)		
Ni	25 (11)		7 (2)	27 (6)	8 (2)	10 (1)	26 (30)		
Cu	6 (4)		13 (10)	11 (15)	13 (9)	4 (1)			
Zn	66 (15)		57 (20)	47 (23)	44 (15)	35 (18)	96 (17)		
Li	48 (14)		100 (5)	41		20 (9)			
U	1.7 (0.5)		3.5 (2.3)	4.0	0.9 (0.4)	0.6 (0.1)	1.5 (0.3)	1.0 (0.5)	2.6 (0.8)
Th	7.1 (1.7)		6.0 (1.3)	5.7	2.8 (1.4)	1.6 (0.4)	5.1 (0.5)	7.7 (3.1)	19.7 (7.4)
La	31.0 (5.3)		20.8(13.3)	24.0	9.4 (0.9)	7.1 (1.1)	21.3 (2.3)	12.3 (8.2)	8.1(10.2)
Ce	61.1(11.6)		50.6(31.9)	48.0	20.0 (0.0)	14.0 (2.8)	46.8 (5.2)	27.4(14.8)	25.6(20.1)
Pr	6.8 (1.4)								
Nd	28.0 (5.2)		18.3 (8.2)	25.0	10.0 (1.4)	7.5 (3.5)	21.3 (3.3)	13.8 (6.6)	12.0(12.1)
Sm	5.1 (0.6)		4.8 (2.5)	4.6	2.2 (0.2)	1.4 (0.3)	4.4 (0.5)	2.9 (1.0)	1.4 (2.0)
Eu	1.23(0.19)		0.92(0.36)	1.7	0.50(0.14)	0.70(0.00)	1.13(0.14)	0.73(0.18)	0.38(0.31)
Gd	3.7 (0.4)								
Tb	0.50(0.07)		0.24 (0.13)	0.8	0.35(0.07)	0.20(0.00)	0.50(0.08)	0.67(0.10)	0.50(0.00)
Dy	2.5 (0.4)			3.8	1.50(0.28)	0.65(0.21)			
Ho	0.42(0.10)								
Er	1.0 (0.4)								
Yb	0.70(0.28)		0.78(0.36)	2.1	0.70(0.00)	0.30(0.00)	1.68(0.22)	3.06(1.08)	0.55(0.34)
Lu	0.09(0.04)		0.30(0.08)	0.28	0.08(0.01)	0.04(0.00)	0.26(0.03)	0.46(0.18)	0.10(0.06)

*Data sources: EQD (Elkahatchee quartz diorite) = Drummond, 1986; Drummond et al., 1994. Kowaliga-Zana = Deninger, 1975; Beiler and Deininger, 1987. Rockford granite = Drummond, 1986, 1987; Drummond et al., 1986, 1988; Allison, 1992. Bluff Springs granite = Deninger et al., 1973; Size and Dean, 1987; Drummond et al., 1994. Almond trondhjemite = Deninger et al., 1973; Size and Dean, 1987. Blakes Ferry pluton = Defant et al., 1987; Size and Dean, 1987. Hog Mt. pluton = Green and Lesher, 1988. Camp Hill and Chattasofka Creek (CCG) gneisses = Neilson et al., 1996. N = total number of major element analyses.

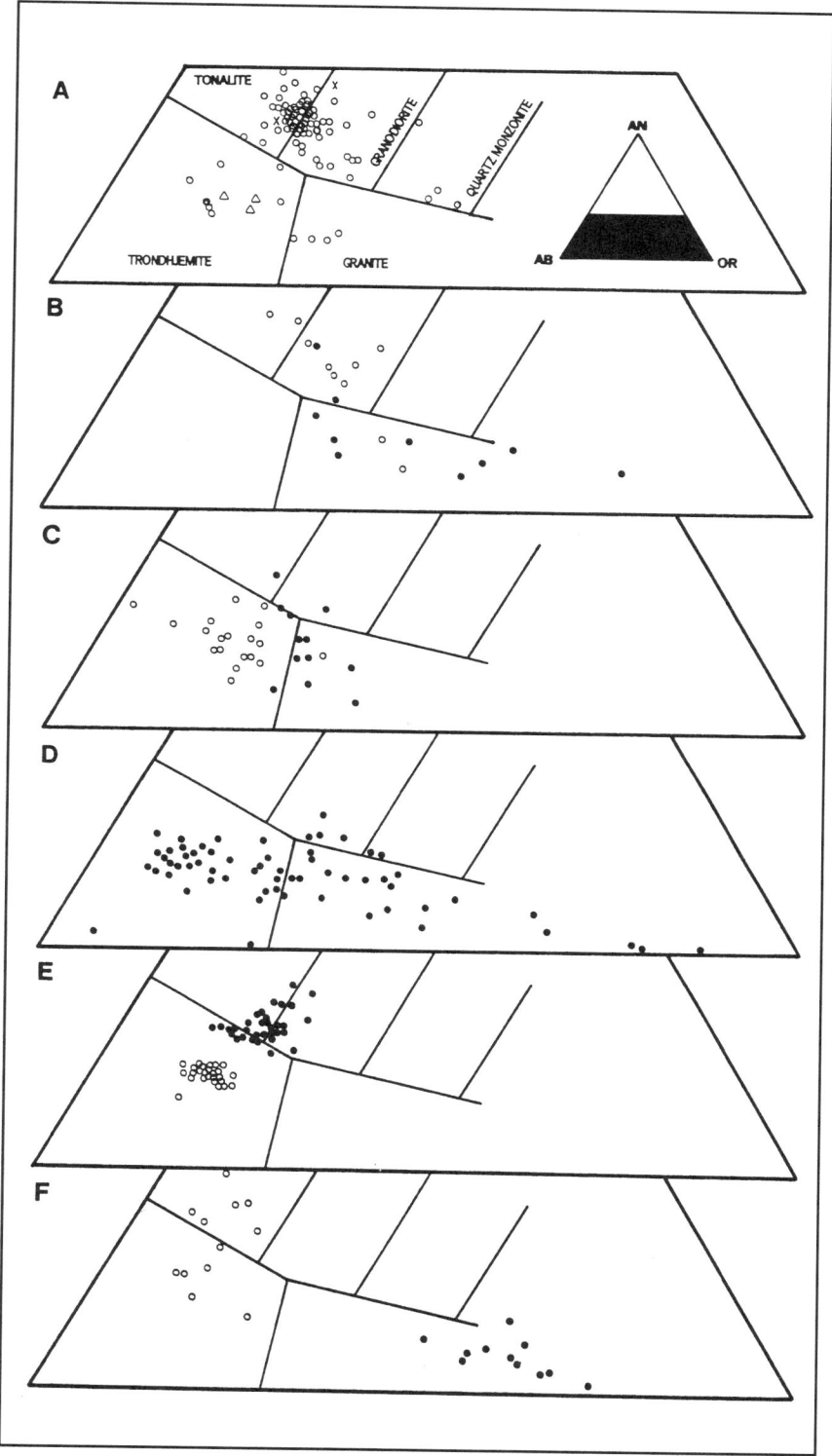

Figure 2. CIPW normative Ab-An-Or (albite, anorthite, orthoclase) granite classification ternary after Barker (1979). A: Elkahatchee quartz diorite. B: Kowaliga gneiss (white circles) and Zana gneiss (black circles). C: Almond trondhjemite (white circles) and Bluff Springs Granite (black circles). D: Rockford granite. E: Blakes Ferry pluton (white circles) and Hog Mountain pluton (black circles). F: Camp Hill gneiss (white circles) and Chattasofka Creek gneiss (black circles). Sources of geochemical data for all geochemical plots are provided in Table 2.

et al. (1994) model of initial dike emplacement and laccolith formation of the EQD batholith in an intra-arc extensional setting. A study by Speer et al. (1994) on southern Appalachian plutons (studied by Vyhnal et al., 1991) has shown that these individual plutons underwent fracture-controlled ascent and were emplaced and crystallized very rapidly in the upper crust. Thus, the apparently incongruent behavior of high-pressure Fe-epidote in granitic systems that were finally emplaced at low pressures can be explained by rapid ascent via dike transport.

The Zana and Kowaliga gneisses are the easternmost granitic bodies of the EBR (Fig. 1A). The host rock of the Zana-Kowaliga gneisses is the Emuckfaw Group metasedimentary rocks (Fig. 1A). The Kowaliga gneiss contains a conspicuous feldspar augen structure, pervasive foliation (S_1), and a strong mineral lineation. Tonalite, granodiorite, and granite represent the lithologic range of the Kowaliga (Fig. 2). The Zana gneiss is a strongly lineated and foliated granite to granodiorite (Fig. 2). Beiler and Deininger (1987) showed that what has been mapped as the Zana gneiss consists of several lithologic types that may not be coeval or cogenetic. The age of the Kowaliga gneiss and one of the Zana lithologic types were determined by Russell (1978) and Russell et al. (1987) by U-Pb zircon and Rb-Sr whole-rock methods to be 460 Ma.

The Bluff Springs granite is a peraluminous, S-type, muscovite-biotite granite with minor granodiorite, trondhjemite, and tonalite (Tables 1 and 2, Fig. 2). We interpret the Bluff Springs granite to represent the along strike continuum of the well-studied Rockford granite, on the basis of similar geochemical traits (discussed later), structural setting (Fig. 1A), and relative timing (foliated, synmetamorphic plutons). Russell (1978) and Russell et al. (1987) reported a 366 Ma Rb-Sr whole-rock age for the Bluff Spring granite, which is taken to closely approximate the age of the Rockford granite and prograde regional metamorphism. The host rock of the Bluff Springs granite is the Wedowee Group.

The Rockford Granite is a plutonic suite of synmetamorphic (D_1–M_1), muscovite-biotite granitoids which intrude graphite-bearing Wedowee and Hatchet Creek Group metasedimentary rocks (Fig. 1A). About 50 small plutons make up the Rockford granite, and range in size from <1–15 km². Superposed kinematic events have produced irregularly shaped plutonic outlines, but the majority of plutons are elongated along strike to the northeast. The geochemical classification indicates strongly peraluminous granite and trondhjemite with subordinate granodiorite (Tables 1 and 2, Fig. 2).

The Rockford trondhjemites are products of pervasive, infiltrative Na metasomatism of an original granite (Drummond et al., 1986; Drummond, 1986, 1987), and represent ~25% (22 km²) of the estimated Rockford granite outcrop area (Table 1). The metasomatic trondhjemites are predominantly concentrated in the northeastern and structurally uppermost portion of the Rockford Granite distribution. The granite to trondhjemite transformation was accomplished by infiltration of an Na- and $\delta^{18}O$-rich metamorphic fluid. Observed metasomatic

replacement reactions include: sodic oligoclase after K-feldspar, Al-epidote + paragonitic muscovite replacing biotite, Al-epidote alteration of apatite, and secondary metasomatic zircon crystallization. These mineralogic alterations resulted in a net loss in K_2O, FeO, MgO, TiO_2, P_2O_5, Th, Rb, U, rare earth elements, V, Pb, Sn, F, and Li, and a net gain in CaO, Na_2O, Zr, Sr, and $\delta^{18}O$ (Drummond et al., 1986; Drummond, 1986, 1987).

The Rockford Granite is associated with Sn and Ta mineralization found within complex pegmatites and greisens (Cook et al., 1987; Foord and Cook, 1989). Wesolowski and Drummond (1990) interpreted the genesis of these Sn-Ta ore deposits to be the result of Na metasomatism of the Rockford granite via biotite decomposition and liberation of biotite Sn content into the migrating metasomatic fluid. The spatial restriction of the tin deposits to the trondhjemitic regions of the Rockford granite and the linearity of these deposits along strike may be the result of focused fluid flow during Na metasomatism. Granites and granodiorites of the Rockford granite retain primary igneous geochemistry suitable for detailed petrogenetic modeling, as discussed below.

The Almond trondhjemite is a high-Al (>15% Al_2O_3 at 70% SiO_2 level; Barker, 1979) trondhjemite (Tables 1 and 2, Fig. 2) that is found as several separate plutons southeast of the Bluff Springs granite (Fig. 1A). These plutons occur as thin sheets and isolated elongate lenses, the gneissosity of which is conformable with schistosity (S_1) in the host Wedowee Group rocks. Tull (1987) has interpreted the Almond to be a premetamorphic to synmetamorphic (D_1–M_1) intrusion on the basis of structural and field criteria.

The Hog Mountain pluton is a fine- to medium-grained equigranular muscovite-biotite tonalite-granodiorite (Fig. 2) pluton (Green and Lesher, 1988). This post-D_1–M_1 pluton is a small elongate sill that intrudes and imposes a contact-metamorphic aureole on the host graphite phyllonite of the Wedowee Group (Green and Lesher, 1988; Stowell et al., 1989). The pluton is noteworthy because of its spatial relationship to the Hog Mountain gold deposits. Gold veins are associated with retrograde shear zones that crosscut the pluton and S_1–S_2 fabric in the host Wedowee Group metasedimentary rock (Green and Lesher, 1988). A 333 ± 11 Ma Rb-Sr whole-rock age of gold veining and hydrothermal alteration of the pluton and host Wedowee Group rocks (Green et al., 1988) provides a minimum age for the pluton.

The Blakes Ferry pluton is a heterogeneous stock composed of leucocratic trondhjemite (Fig. 2) with a biotite schlieren component that is randomly mixed throughout the pluton. The curved, bifurcated, and truncated nature of the biotite schlieren is considered to be the result of magmatic flow (Defant et al., 1987, 1988). The lack of metamorphic foliation, preservation of igneous structures, subcircular map outline (Fig. 1A), and presence of a contact aureole (Gibson and Speer, 1986) indicate a post-D_1–M_1 age for the Blakes Ferry pluton. The composition of biotite dispersed in the Blakes Ferry coincides with the biotite in the schlieren and biotite in the host Wedowee Group metasedimentary rocks (Defant et al., 1987, 1988). As the result of contact metamorphism, biotite-rich selvages are generated from the Wedowee host rocks, which are incorporated within the stock as the biotite schlieren. Garnets in the Wedowee contact aureole exhibit petrographic zonation; an outer zone helicitically overgrows the Wedowee graphite phyllonite S_2 fabric. Thus, the Blakes Ferry pluton is interpreted to postdate both prograde D_1–M_1 and retrograde D_2–M_2 metamorphism in the EBR. The timing of intrusion of the Blakes Ferry pluton and the D_2–M_2 event can be bracketed between the 366 Ma date of the syn-metamorphic Bluff Springs granite and the 324 ± 11 Ma K-Ar muscovite age (Cambell, 1973) of the Blakes Ferry pluton.

Inner Piedmont granitic rocks

The Inner Piedmont is separated from the Blue Ridge by the Brevard zone and consists of two lithologic belts that are separated by the Stonewall line: the Dadeville complex and the Opelika complex (Fig. 1B). The only detailed study of the granitic rocks of the Dadeville complex has centered on the Tallassee synform (Neilson, 1987; Neilson et al., 1996). Two distinct gneissic units have been differentiated in the Tallassee synform area, and include the Camp Hill gneiss and Chattasofka Creek gneiss (Fig. 1B). Neilson (1987) suggested that this two-fold gneissic subdivision may be applicable throughout the Dadeville complex. The predominant granitic unit in the Opelika complex is the Farmville metagranite (Goldberg and Burnell, 1987; Goldberg and Steltenpohl, 1990).

The Camp Hill gneiss is a biotite tonalite-trondhjemite (Fig. 2) containing minor hornblende and sphene. Highly peraluminous (Table 2) biotite muscovite granite (Fig. 2) defines the lithologic character of the Chattasofka Creek gneiss. These gneisses form a major portion of the dominantly metaigneous Dadeville complex and are hosted by the Ropes Creek amphibolite and Agricola schist. Both the Camp Hill and Chattasofka Creek gneisses contain xenoliths of amphibolite and schist indicating that they are intrusive into the hosts rocks of the Dadeville complex (Neilson, 1987). On the basis of reequilibration of mica chemistry and geothermobarometric estimates on the gneisses, we (Drummond and Neilson, unpublished data, 1996) interpret the Camp Hill gneiss to be premetamorphic and the Chattasofka Creek gneiss to be late metamorphic.

The Farmville metagranite is not considered in the following geochemical discussion; however, this body is an integral part of our understanding of the IP, given the well-constrained isotopic age. The Opelika complex is composed dominantly of metasedimentary rocks (Auburn gneiss and Loachapoka schist) that are intruded by the Farmville metagranite (Fig. 1B). A 369 ± 5 Ma Rb-Sr whole-rock age (initial Sr isotopic ratio = 0.7098) has been determined on the synmetamorphic Farmville metagranite (Goldberg and Burnell, 1987). This granite is considered an S-type granite on the basis of the elevated initial Sr ratio and peraluminous character (Goldberg and Burnell, 1987). Steltenpohl et al. (1990) suggested, on the basis of structural evidence, that the Farmville metagranite was emplaced within a shear zone.

GEOCHEMICAL CHARACTER AND PETROGENESIS

Geochemical characterization and detailed modeling and evaluation of the data on all the granites of the EBR and IP are incomplete. However, some of the granitic bodies have undergone rigorous geochemical and tectonic evaluation and can provide cornerstones to comprehensive tectonic interpretations of the EBR and IP. Major element comparison is possible for all granitic rocks in this study and trace element data are available for all except the Kowaliga-Zana gneisses (Table 2). New geochemical data from the Dadeville complex granitic rocks are included in this evaluation. In the following discussion, we compare and contrast geochemical data between and within the EBR and IP granitic rocks in order to test whether any compositional correlations exist among the granitic rocks and to constrain their petrogenesis.

With the exception of the EQD, all of the granitic rocks studied are within a restricted, high SiO_2 range (Tables 1 and 2), and each suite is either dominantly trondhjemitic-tonalitic or granitic-granodioritic (Fig. 2) in composition. Each of the granitic suites from this study can be categorized as I-type or S-type (Chappell and White, 1974) or displays a mixed I-type and S-type character. Thus, the EBR and IP granitic rocks are interpreted to be crustally derived from either an igneous (I-type) or sedimentary (S-type) source in an orogenic setting. Figure 3 demonstrates a fundamental geochemical distinction between the low-K_2O trondhjemites-tonalites and the high-K_2O granites-granodiorites. The following discussion deals with the granites

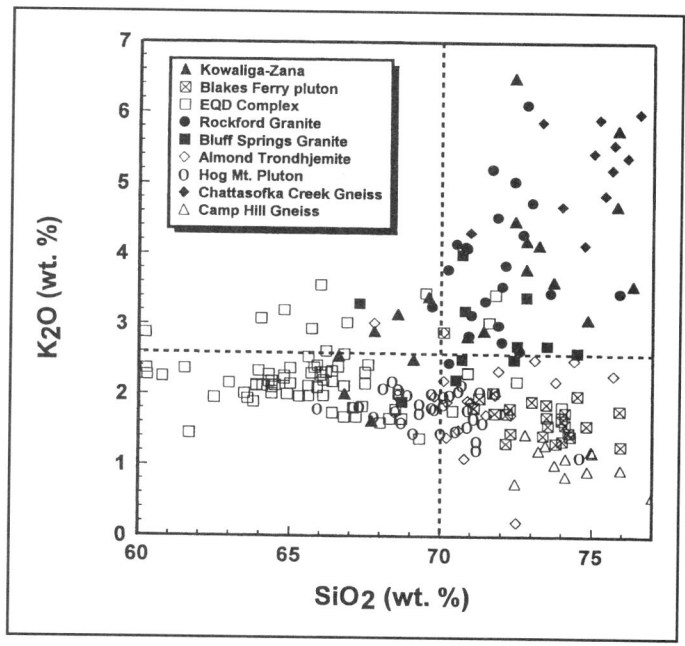

Figure 3. SiO_2 versus K_2O plot of granitic rocks from the eastern Blue Ridge (EBR) and Inner Piedmont (IP), Alabama Appalachians. EQD is Elkahatchee quartz diorite.

and granodiorites separately from the trondhjemites and tonalites, and presents petrogenetic schemes within each group.

Granite-granodiorite group

Most of the granites and granodiorites fall within a restricted field in Figure 3; SiO_2 and K_2O are limited to >70% and >2.6%, respectively. A plot of CaO versus ASI (aluminum saturation index) discriminates the three basic petrogenetic types of granites-granodiorites from the EBR and IP (Fig. 4). The ASI is one of the key discriminate factors between S-type (ASI > 1.1) and I-type (ASI < 1.1) granite chemistry (Chappell and White, 1974; White and Chappell, 1988).

The Kowaliga-Zana gneisses show a wide range in CaO at a low ASI (<1.1) (Fig. 4), which may be a function of plagioclase differentiation in a parental I-type magma. The initial Sr isotopic ratio for the Kowaliga gneiss is 0.7041 (Russell et al., 1987), and is consistent with an I-type origin. The lack of mafic or intermediate rocks associated with the Kowaliga gneiss and the high-K_2O character argue against a mafic or ultramafic source, and for an intermediate to felsic igneous crustal source. An initial Sr ratio of 0.7061 for the Zana gneiss suggests that the relatively elevated initial Sr isotopic ratio may be an artifact of metasediment contamination from a Kowaliga-like parental magma (Russell et al., 1987). One Zana gneiss sample has an extremely high ASI (1.54) at low CaO (0.95%), providing an outlier from the typical Zana-Kowaliga samples (Fig. 4). This highly peraluminous Zana sample also has abnormally high SiO_2 (76%) and P_2O_5 (0.28%), which is a geochemical signature of an extremely fractionated S-type granite (Chappell and White, 1992; Bea et al., 1992). Thus, as suggested by Beiler and Deininger (1987), there are many lithologic types that make up what has been called Zana gneiss; some of these lithotypes are potentially unrelated genetically or temporally. Due to the lack of trace-element data on the Kowaliga and Zana gneisses, detailed petrogenetic modeling is unwarranted.

The synmetamorphic S-type Bluff Springs and Rockford granites have moderately high ASI values (average 1.20–1.25; Table 2) over a range in CaO values (Fig. 4). These two S-type granite suites are comparable geochemically, with the exception of the Bluff Springs granite, which has higher average Na/K, Sr, and middle rare earth element (REE) contents (Table 2, Fig. 5). Major- and trace-element and stable isotopic (O and C isotopes) studies (Drummond et al., 1988) indicate that the Rockford granite was generated from 40% equilibrium partial melting of a metagraywacke source, leaving a restite assemblage of 49% oligoclase, 31% quartz, 14% biotite, 5.5% apatite, and 0.5% zircon. Allison (1992) showed that garnet (restite assemblage = 48% garnet, 16% biotite, and 36% oligoclase) also played a role in the Rockford granite petrogenesis by modeling of melanosome-leucosome-granite geochemical relationships. Linear major- and trace-element trends support a restite-melt unmixing model (White and Chappell, 1977; Chappell et al., 1987) for the Rockford granite petrogenesis. Muscovite dehydration melting produces migmatitic paragneisses in the Rockford granite region that are most common in the structurally lowermost (southwestern) part of the study area and grade structurally upward (northeast) into 5–15 km² muscovite-biotite granites (Drummond, 1986; Drummond and Allison, 1987; Drummond et al., 1988; Allison, 1992). Thus, a combination of regional structural plunge and erosional level provides a rare glimpse of the source region of S-type granite production, melt accumulation, and para-autochthonous emplacement of the small plutonic masses.

The Chattasofka Creek gneiss of the Dadeville complex is a highly differentiated (SiO₂ range of 71.0%–76.5%), strongly peraluminous (average ASI = 1.4), S-type granite. Low CaO values (Fig. 4) and high Rb/Sr and K_2O (average 1.54 and 5.25, respectively) suggest that the Chattasofka Creek gneiss was derived from a metapelitic source. Comparison between the metagraywacke-derived Rockford granite and the Chattasofka Creek gneiss indicates higher CaO and lower ASI and Rb-Sr (average 0.80) for the Rockford granite relative to the Chattasofka Creek gneiss.

Trondhjemite-tonalite group

The tonalite-trondhjemite group exhibits a wide SiO_2 range at K_2O < 2.6%, but there are some intergroup distinctions (Fig. 3). For example, (1) granitic rocks of the EQD display a wide SiO₂ range at generally low K₂O; (2) most of the Hog Mountain pluton and Almond trondhjemite samples have intermediate SiO₂ (67%–71%) values at low K₂O; and (3) high SiO₂ (>71%) and low K₂O categorize the highly differentiated trondhjemites of the Blakes Ferry pluton and Camp Hill gneiss. Each of these low-K₂O granitic rocks has a distinct petrogenetic history. Detailed petrogenetic studies have been completed on the EQD (Drummond et al., 1994), Blakes Ferry pluton (Defant et al., 1987 and 1988), and Hog Mountain pluton (Green and Lesher, 1988), and are summarized below.

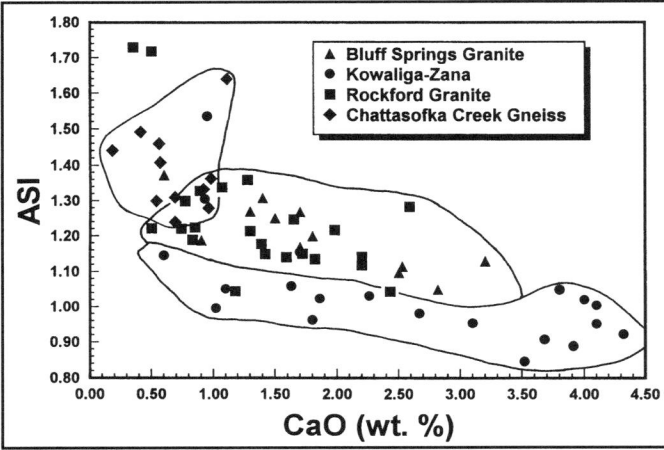

Figure 4. CaO versus aluminum saturation index (ASI) (mol Al_2O_3/[mol CaO + Na_2O + K_2O]) for the granite-granodiorite group.

The EQD has a wide compositional range represented by mafic-intermediate enclaves (<60% SiO_2) and host granitic rocks (>60% SiO_2). Rare hornblende gabbro-diorite enclaves are found around the outer margin of the EQD, whereas schistose (biotite-epidote-plagioclase) enclaves are scattered throughout the EQD as meter- to centimeter-sized elliptical bodies. The enclaves are interpreted to represent disrupted fragments of cumulate material that formed as near-liquidus sidewall crystallization products. Active convection in the EQD magma chamber segmented the gabbro-diorite cumulates into discrete meter-size enclaves along the batholith's outer margin. Convective transport of gabbro-diorite enclaves into the interior of the evolving granitic magma chamber led to mechanical disaggregation, solid-melt reaction, and schistose enclave generation (Drummond et al., 1994).

Petrogenetic modeling of the EQD by least squares mixing calculations of major- and minor-element covariation indicates a dominant crystal fractionation process for EQD compositional diversification (Drummond et al., 1994). A two-stage crystallization process is invoked to represent the changing proportions of crystalline phases with magma evolution. The first stage of crystallization explains the compositional variation in the 60%–67% SiO_2 range and involves 23% crystallization of an assemblage composed of 61% andesine, 13% hornblende, 13% biotite, 12% Fe-epidote, and 1% apatite. The proportion of minerals associated with crystallization stage 1 is similar to the mineral content in the gabbro-diorite enclaves. Geochemical variation between 67%–74% SiO_2 can be explained by 77% crystallization of the assemblage 51% andesine, 26% quartz, 18% biotite, 4% K-feldspar, and 1% hornblende.

Modeling of REEs (Fig. 5), Sr and O isotopes, and other trace-element parameters indicates that the parental EQD magma was derived from partial melting of a source consisting of altered mid-ocean ridge basalt (MORB) plus minor deep-sea sediment (Drummond et al., 1994). Mafic tonalite-granodiorite parental magmas would exist in equilibrium with a restite assemblage of 30% hornblende, 30% garnet, 40% clinopyroxene. A combination of cogenetic hornblende gabbro-diorite, low initial Sr isotopic ratio (0.7036; Russell et al., 1987), and metaluminous to weakly peraluminous composition confirms an I-type heritage for the EQD. The EQD was probably generated from a subducting slab during Penobscotian orogenesis, underwent dynamic sidewall crystallization upon ascent through middle- to upper-crustal levels, and was finally emplaced in a subvolcanic regime.

The heterogeneity in color index displayed by the Blakes Ferry pluton due to mixing biotite schlieren with leucocratic trondhjemitic melt is expressed geochemically by two separate trends on major element Harker diagrams (Defant et al., 1987, 1988). One group of geochemical trends is related to the leucocratic Blakes Ferry pluton samples and is controlled by fractional crystallization of 41% oligoclase. Another group of geochemical trends associated with the biotite-rich trondhjemitic samples and biotite schlieren represents mixing lines between leucocratic trondhjemite and biotite schlieren end members. Assimilation-

fractional crystallization (AFC) modeling supports plagioclase fractionation contemporaneously with assimilation of the biotite schlieren to explain the petrogenesis of the Blakes Ferry pluton. Modeling of the REE patterns of the leucocratic trondhjemite (Fig. 5) suggests that the Blakes Ferry pluton's parental trondhjemitic melt was generated by 10%–30% partial melting of a MORB source, leaving behind a hornblende eclogite residue (15% hornblende, 25% garnet, 50% clinopyroxene, and 10% quartz). The Blakes Ferry pluton is interpreted to represent a trondhjemitic magma derived from partial melting of a subducting slab.

Green and Lesher (1988) showed that the Hog Mountain pluton was derived from partial melting of a hydrous amphibolite source at mid-crustal conditions (750–825 °C, ≥6.4 kbar = maximum barometric estimate on surrounding contact metamorphic aureole). The Hog Mountain REE patterns (Fig. 5) exhibit a gentle light REE/heavy REE slope, small negative Eu anomaly, and moderate Yb_N value, all of which are consistent with melting of an amphibolite source, leaving a plagioclase-hornblende-pyroxene restite assemblage. Least squares mixing calculations have shown that parental mafic tonalite can fractionate varying proportions of plagioclase, biotite, quartz, ilmenite, and apatite to generate the more differentiated Hog Mountain samples.

The petrogenesis of the Almond trondhjemite is currently not known. Previous workers (Deininger et al., 1973; Deininger, 1975) have grouped the Blakes Ferry pluton as one of several intrusive bodies of the Almond trondhjemite in spite of the distinct textural differences (foliated Almond and nonfoliated Blakes Ferry) between these two bodies. Comparison of the average geochemistry (Table 2) and chondrite-normalized REE patterns (Fig. 5) indicates that the Almond and Blakes Ferry trondhjemites closely coincide. Exceptions to this compositional match include the negative Eu anomaly and lower Sr content of the Almond trondhjemite that may be a function of plagioclase fractionation. If the Blakes Ferry and Almond trondhjemites are cogenetic, then this magmatic stage would be required to outlast the kinematic effects associated with the D_1–M_1 event. More work is required on the Almond trondhjemite to determine its potential cogenesis with the Blakes Ferry pluton.

The Camp Hill gneiss of the Dadeville complex is a highly differentiated (average SiO_2 of 74.3, Table 2) trondhjemite-tonalite (Fig. 2). Chondrite-normalized REE patterns of the Camp Hill gneiss (Fig. 5) display slight light REE enrichment, high heavy REE ($Yb_N \geq 10$), and negative Eu anomaly, which are distinct from the EBR trondhjemites-tonalites. The Camp Hill REE patterns are consistent with derivation of the trondhjemites by low- to moderate-pressure partial melting (≤8 kbar) of a basaltic source leaving a plagioclase-rich residuum (Beard and Lofgren, 1991; Rapp et al., 1991; Rushmer et al., 1994).

A plot of Zr/Sm versus Sr/Yb (Fig. 6) subdivides the EBR-IP trondhjemites-tonalites. The Zr/Sm axis is sensitive to the proportion of hornblende in either the restite or fractionation assemblage (Pearce et al., 1992), because hornblende displays incompatible and compatible behavior for Zr and Sm, respec-

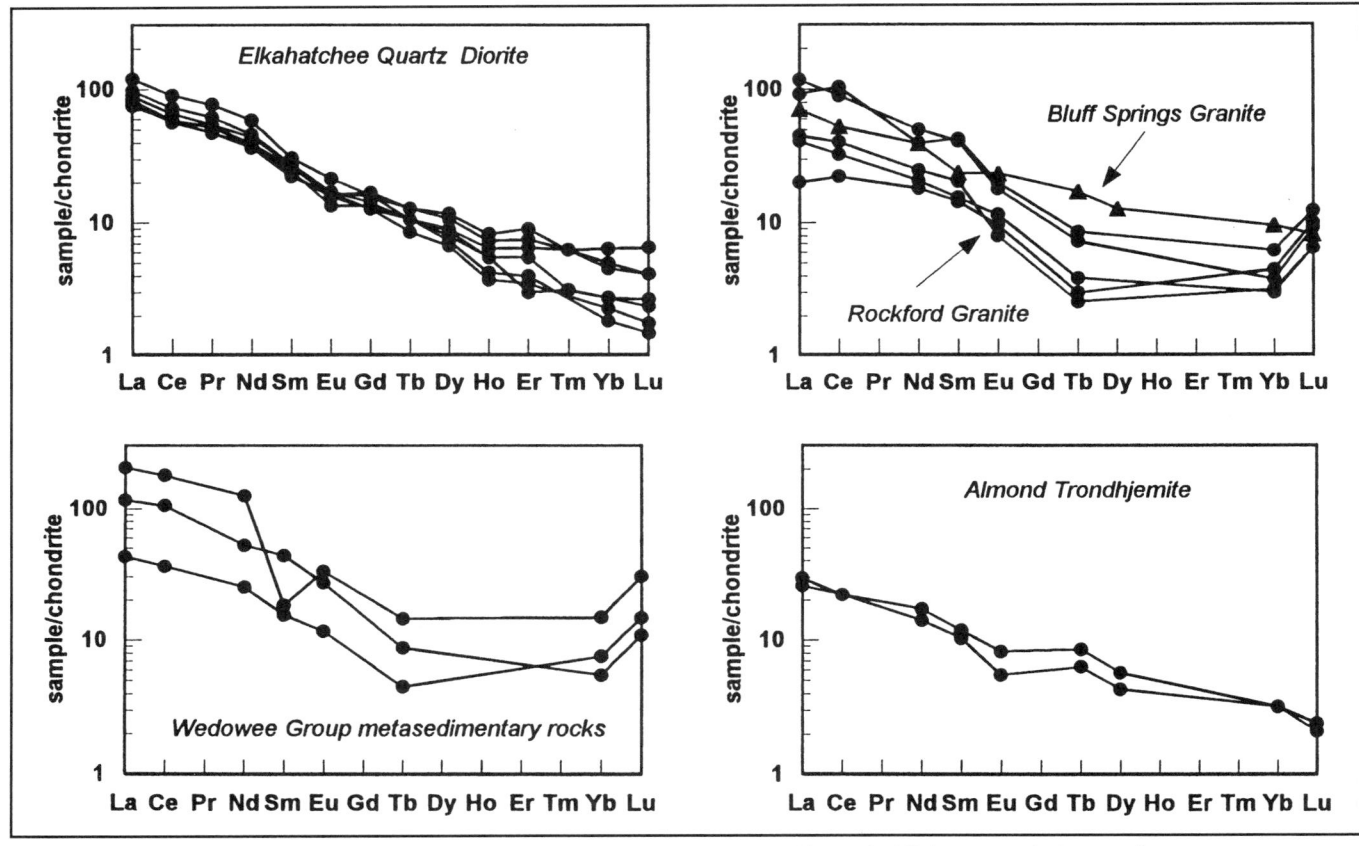

Figure 5 (on this and facing page). Chondrite-normalized (Wakita et al., 1971) rare earth element diagrams of the Alabama granitic rocks.

tively (i.e., high Zr/Sm suggests high proportion of hornblende
in the extract assemblage). In addition, a decrease of Zr/Sm at
approximately constant Sr/Yb within a specific granitic suite
may also result from zircon removal (Fig. 6). Drummond and
Defant (1990) and Defant and Drummond (1990) have shown
that partial melts of basalt leaving a garnet amphibolite to eclogite restite will generate trondhjemitic melts with high Sr/Y due
to the efficient removal of Y in residual garnet and entry of Sr
into the melt due to selective fusion of the source's plagioclase
component at high pressure. Most of the EBR-IP data lack Y
analyses, but Yb and Y are basically synonymous relative to their
role as garnet indicators. Numerous experimental studies have
documented the barometric sensitivity of garnet presence or
absence in restite associated with melting metabasalt (Beard and
Lofgren, 1991; Rapp et al., 1991; Rushmer, 1991; Rushmer et al.,
1994; Thompson and Ellis, 1994; Wolf and Wyllie, 1993, 1994).
We suggest that the Sr/Yb ratio in trondhjemite-tonalite magmas
closely monitors the garnet/plagioclase ratio in the restite and
acts as a crude geobarometer for the site of partial melting.

The two bodies postulated as slab melts, the EQD and the
Blakes Ferry pluton, exhibit high Sr/Yb as a function of plagioclase instability and the garnet-rich nature of the eclogitic melting conditions (Fig. 6). A slightly higher Zr/Sm for the EQD

relative to the Blakes Ferry pluton is consistent with a higher
proportion of residual hornblende in the EQD (30% hornblende;
Drummond et al., 1994) versus the Blakes Ferry (15% hornblende; Defant et al., 1988). The Camp Hill Gneiss records
extremely low Sr/Yb and variable Zr/Sm (Fig. 6), suggesting
partial melting conditions of a basaltic source that was garnet
free, and dominated by a plagioclase-rich restite with variable
hornblende content. High average Y content (28 ppm, Table 2)
for the Camp Hill supports the lack of garnet at the site of partial
melting. Middle- to upper-crustal melting conditions are implied
by the inferred melting conditions for the Camp Hill gneiss. Hog
Mountain pluton Zr/Sm-Sr/Yb data (Fig. 6) plot between garnet-
free amphibolite and eclogitic melting conditions of the Camp
Hill gneiss and the EQD-Blakes Ferry pluton, respectively. An
amphibolitic source at middle- to lower-crustal conditions is
inferred for the Hog Mountain pluton, supporting the petrogenetic model of Green and Lesher (1988).

METAMORPHISM AND GRANITE GENESIS

Orogenic belts can be classified as "fertile" and capable of
prodigenous granite production or "sterile" and granite poor.
The fertility or sterility of a specific crustal section is reliant on

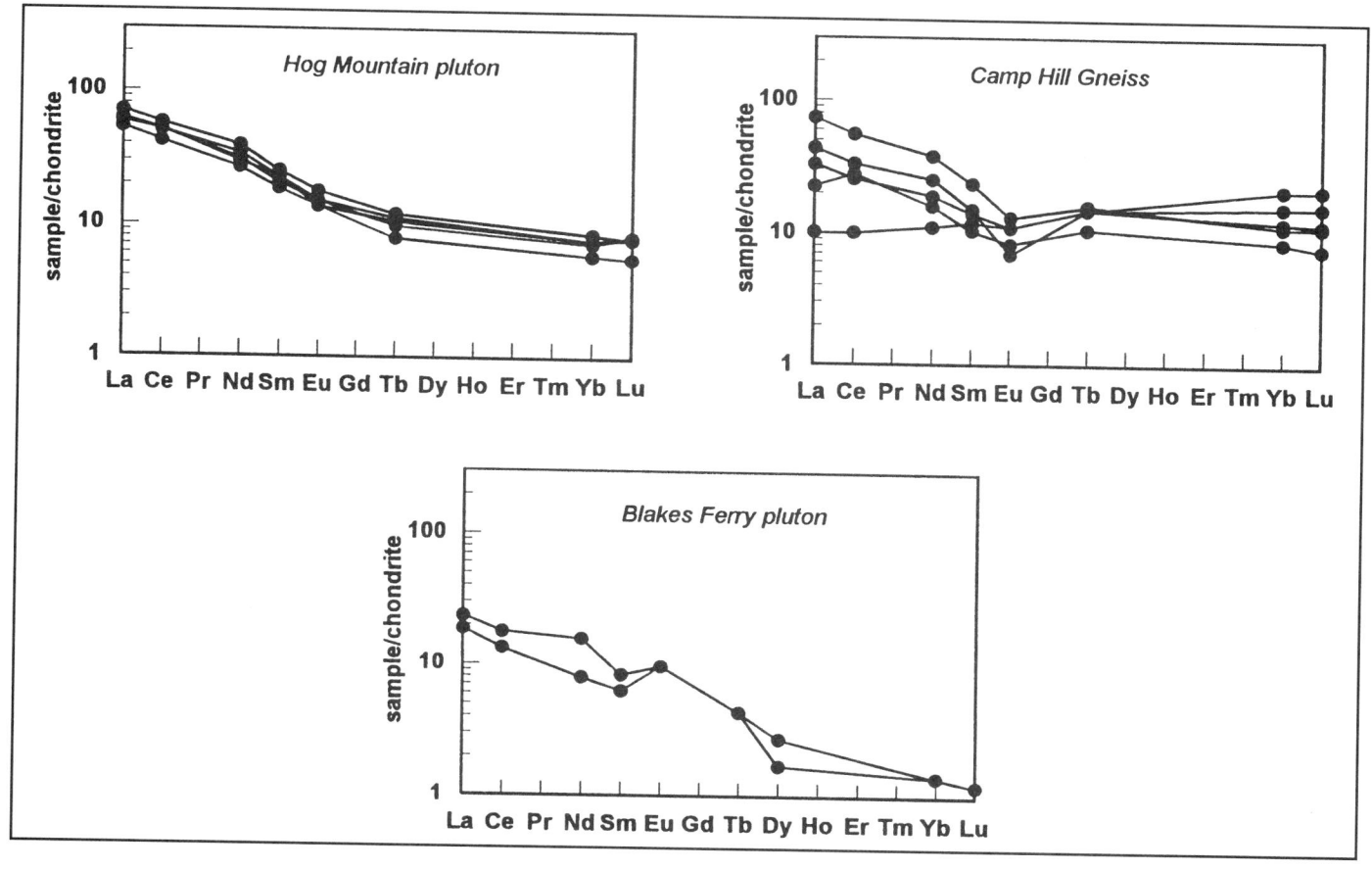

the major rock types and degree of previous melt extraction (Vielzeuf et al., 1990). The EBR and IP Opelika complex are lithologically fertile, having a preponderance of metagray-wackes and metapelites. If pre-Acadian metamorphism affected either the EBR or Opelika complex, then metamorphic grade did not exceed crustal melting conditions due to the lack of S-type granite older than the Acadian-age Bluff Springs granite, Rockford granite, and Farmville metagranite. Thus, the peak prograde regional metamorphic event (D_1–M_1) in the EBR and IP is inter-preted to be contemporaneous with synmetamorphic S-type granite production.

S-type Rockford, Bluff Springs, and Farmville granites are heat sinks and not heat producers, because crustal melting is an endothermic process and is typically the ultimate byproduct of the metamorphic thermal peak. The Rockford and Bluff Springs granites contain a well-developed foliation along the country-rock interface and are weakly foliated within the pluton interi-ors, suggesting a timing of emplacement during the waning stages of prograde metamorphic kinematic effects. The Farm-ville metagranite exhibits strong metamorphic fabric develop-ment and is spatially associated with shear zones (Steltenpohl et al., 1990), which suggests that kinematic events occurred dur-ing and after its emplacement.

Quantitative geothermobarometric estimates for the Rock-ford granite and surrounding metasedimentary rocks indicate kyanite-sillimanite facies regional metamorphism (Drummond et al., 1988). The positively sloped portion of the Rockford *P-T* path (Fig. 7) records geothermobarometric estimates of peak metamorphic conditions for the Wedowee, Hatchet Creek, and Higgins Ferry groups. Those samples residing in a relatively low *P* (4–5 kbar)–high *T* (630–680 °C) zone (Fig. 7) represent highly migmatitic metamorphic rocks and Rockford granite samples. This low-*P*–high-*T* regime exceeds muscovite dehydration and minimum melting conditions, but not biotite dehydration melt-ing conditions. Experimental data indicate that muscovite dehy-dration melting occurs at 665 °C at 5 kbar (Clemens and Vielzeuf, 1987), which corresponds well with the *P-T* range of the Rockford granite and attendant migmatites. The prograde *P-T* path recorded by the nonmigmatitic metamorphic rocks of the Rockford region (Fig. 7) is abruptly terminated by nearly isother-mal decompression, which is interpreted to be due to muscovite dehydration melting of the metasediments, diapiric ascent, and associated thermal doming.

The late- to post-Acadian Blakes Ferry and Hog Mountain plutons of the EBR impose contact-metamorphic effects on the host Wedowee Group metasedimentary rocks. Contact-meta-morphic geothermobarometric estimates in the Blakes Ferry contact-metamorphic aureole yield 470–540 °C and 5–7 kbar (Gibson and Speer, 1986). Metasedimentary xenoliths, contact-metamorphosed rocks, and gold vein material associated with

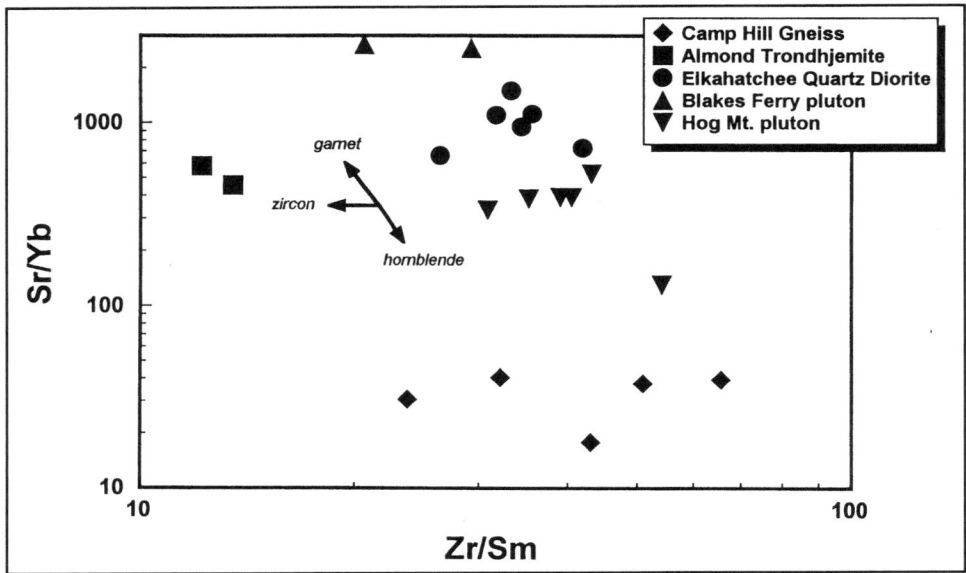

Figure 6. Zr/Sm versus Sr/Yb plot of trondhjemite-tonalite group.

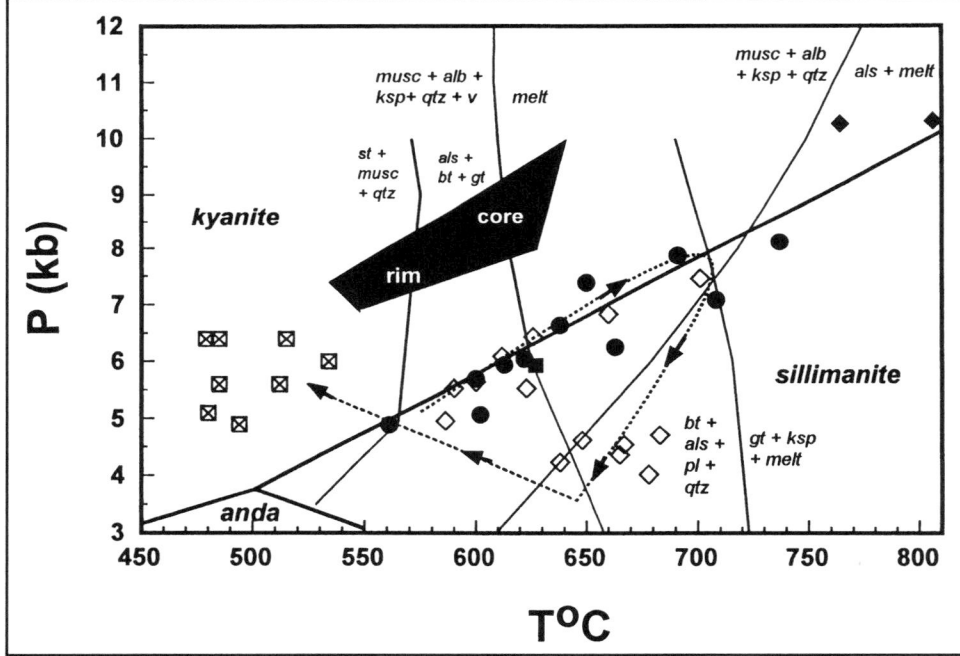

Figure 7. Temperature-pressure (*T-P*) diagram of the quantitative estimates of metamorphism from the eastern Blue Ridge (EBR) and Inner Piedmont (IP). Sources for phase equilibria curves: Al_2SiO_5 stability fields (Holdaway, 1971), staurolite breakdown (Carmichael, 1978), pelite minimum (wet) melting and muscovite dehydration melting curves (Thompson and Tracy, 1979), biotite (Mg# = 0.4) dehydration melting curves (Le Breton and Thompson, 1988). Dadeville complex symbol explanation: black circles = Agricola Schist, black square = Camp Hill gneiss, and black diamonds = Ropes Creek amphibolite (our data [Drummond and Neilson]). Black region = *P-T* field of garnet core-rim calculations from the Opelika complex (Goldberg and Steltenpohl, 1990), white diamonds = eastern Blue Ridge (Drummond, 1986; Drummond et al., 1988), squares with x = contact metamorphic *P-T* estimates from Hog Mountain (Green and Lesher, 1988; Stowell et al., 1989) and Bluff Springs (Gibson and Speer, 1986) plutons, and dashed curve = postulated Acadian *P-T* path for the EBR of the Alabama Appalachians.

the Hog Mountain pluton indicate that temperatures and pressures of contact metamorphism were 465–500 °C and 5.1–6.4 kbar (Green and Lesher, 1988; Stowell et al., 1989). Figure 7 illustrates the contact-metamorphic *P-T* data relative to the EBR prograde metamorphic path measured for the Rockford region. The arrows on the *P-T* path are indicative of the polychronic nature of prograde regional metamorphism followed by localized contact metamorphism, and circumscribe an overall clockwise *P-T* path. Brown (1994) showed that orogens characterized by clockwise *P-T*-time paths are typically associated with crustally derived granites in collisional settings.

Two of us (Drummond and Neilson) have completed a quantitative survey of metamorphic conditions in the Dadeville complex. Kyanite-sillimanite zone metamorphic conditions were calculated from the Agricola schist, Camp Hill gneiss, and Ropes Creek amphibolite (Fig. 7). The Dadeville complex and EBR (Rockford granite region) *P-T* data closely coincide with the exception of the extremely high *P-T* of the Ropes Creek amphibolite. The measured thermal maximum for the Agricola schist of the Dadeville complex was constrained by the thermal buffering capacity of anatexis, as evidenced by localized migmatization of this unit. The Ropes Creek amphibolite, however, was not thermally constrained by anatexis, because hornblende dehydration melting at 8–10 kbar exceeds 800 °C (Hacker, 1990; Rapp et al., 1991; Rushmer, 1991). Isobaric comparison of thermal data from the Dadeville complex and Opelika complex (Goldberg and Steltenpohl, 1990) indicates that the Dadeville complex is elevated ~100 °C over the Opelika complex. An inverted metamorphic gradient, structurally underlying kyanite-staurolite–grade Opelika complex rocks passing up-section into sillimanite-grade Dadeville complex rocks, is recognized for the IP.

TECTONIC IMPLICATIONS AND CONCLUSIONS

The granitic rocks of the EBR can be temporally linked to three orogenic phases: (1) the Penobscotian orogeny (~490–500 Ma), (2) the Taconic orogeny (~460 Ma), and (3) the Acadian orogeny (~360–370 Ma). The chronology given does not imply the age range for each orogenic episode, but simply provides the timing of plutonism associated with each orogenic phase. The fourth stage of granitic magmatism in the EBR, the late- to post-Acadian stage (Table 1), is not interpreted to correspond temporally with the peak thermal or kinematic conditions of the Acadian orogen, and is discussed separately.

Drummond et al.'s (1994) petrogenetic survey of the EQD reveals that this intrusive complex was derived from partial melting a MORB source under eclogitic conditions. They further suggested that the EQD represents continental margin magmatism associated with incipient subduction of an oceanic slab beneath Laurentia. Numerous Penobscot age (520–485 Ma) plutonic, tectonic (ophiolite emplacement), and metamorphic events distributed throughout the Appalachians (Drummond et al., 1994) closely coincide spatially to previously proposed positions of the

Laurentian margin (e.g., Blue-Green-Long axis; Rankin, 1975; eastern North American gravity high; Cook and Oliver, 1981). We suggest that the Penobscotian age orogeny may have spanned the length of the Appalachians and is, in part, represented by initial continental margin magmatism, such as the EQD. There is no known Penobscotian magmatism in the IP of Alabama.

Erickson and Arkani-Hamed (1993) showed that the initiation of subduction is best accomplished if the following conditions exist: (1) extensional or strike-slip setting rather than compressive; (2) failure is within the continental rather than oceanic lithosphere; and (3) oceanic lithosphere is heated by some mechanism. Drummond et al. (1994) suggested that during EQD genesis subduction of young, hot oceanic crust beneath Laurentia was accompanied by extensional deformation in the overriding continental plate. These observations are consistent with the derivation of the EQD from young, hot oceanic crust, incipient subduction, and fracture-controlled emplacement of the EQD as a laccolith in an extensional setting.

The lack of detailed geochemical and petrogenetic information on the Taconic-age Kowaliga and Zana gneisses prohibits any attempt of providing tectonic discrimination of these units. The existing data suggest that these bodies are I-type granitoids potentially derived from a crustal felsic to intermediate igneous source. IP granitoids do not correspond compositionally to the Zana-Kowaliga gneisses. However, the granite-granodiorite suite of the Taconic Franklin gneiss (462 ± 4 Ma; Seal and Kish, 1989, 1990) of the western Georgia Inner Piedmont is compositionally similar to the Zana-Kowaliga gneisses. Sinha et al. (1989) found that most of the Middle to Late Ordovician (460–440 Ma) plutons of the central and southern Appalachians are dominantly quartz monzonite–granodiorite–granite hosted by the EBR and IP, and rarely occur in the Carolina slate belt. Thus, both the EBR and IP underwent crustal melting episode(s) during the Taconic orogeny.

The absolute timing of Camp Hill gneiss generation is not known, but relative timing information suggests that this body is premetamorphic (pre-Acadian). Neilson et al. (1996) have determined that the Camp Hill gneiss consistently falls into the volcanic-arc granitoid field in numerous major- and trace-element tectonic discriminate diagrams. A volcanic-arc setting also coincides with the arc geochemical signatures of the premetamorphic mafic (Slaughters suite) and mafic-ultramafic (Doss Mountain suite) bodies in the Dadeville complex (Stow et al., 1984; Neilson and Stow, 1986). These mafic and felsic arc plutonic rocks intrude into Dadeville complex lithologies that are interpreted as ocean-floor volcanics (Ropes Creek amphibolite) and sediments formed in a back-arc basin (Stow et al., 1984).

The Acadian plutons of the EBR and IP are dominated by synmetamorphic to late-metamorphic S-type granites that formed in response to peak metamorphic temperatures and crustal anatexis. Trace-element discriminate diagrams (Pearce et al., 1984) and the muscovite-biotite, S-type granite lithology (Harris et al., 1986) for the Rockford granite (Drummond et al., 1988) and Chattasofka Creek gneiss (Neilson et al., 1996) sug-

gest a syncollisional setting for the EBR and IP. The presence of
an inverted metamorphic gradient in the IP, where sillimanite-
grade Dadeville complex structurally overlies the kyanite-staurolite–grade Opelika complex, is attributed to a collisional
tectonic setting. The following evidence supports a collisional
tectonic setting for the EBR and IP during the Acadian orogeny:
(1) there is collision-related S-type granite formation by muscovite dehydration melting in thickened crust, as observed in the
high Himalayas (Inger and Harris, 1993; Harris and Massey,
1994); (2) the clockwise *P-T* path for the EBR is indicative of
collisional tectonics (Brown, 1994); and (3) the IP displays an
inverted metamorphic gradient like that found in the collisional
tectonic regime of the high Himalayas (see Barnicoat and Treloar, 1989, for review).

A tectonic model that calls upon Acadian collision between
the EBR and IP is not without ambiguity, but is the most consistent with currently available geochemical information on the
Acadian granites and quantitative metamorphic information for
both lithotectonic belts. Closure of a marginal basin (Ropes
Creek amphibolite equivalent) between the Laurentian EBR
(Drummond et al., 1994) and an IP volcanic arc (Stow et al.,
1984; Neilson and Stow, 1986) could represent the collisional
components. This model implies that the axis of collision
between the EBR and IP would spatially coincide with the Brevard zone (Fig. 1). The Brevard zone has been referred to as a
variety of structures by a number of researchers, including a
transported suture separating dissimilar terranes (Odom and Fullagar, 1973; Rankin, 1975).

The late- to post-Acadian Blakes Ferry and Hog Mountain
plutons may have been generated and/or emplaced into thickened continental crust following Acadian collisional tectonics.
The Hog Mountain tonalitic parental melt may have resulted
from thermal relaxation in the lower crust and subsequent mid-
crustal melting after collision. The eclogitic MORB-derived
Blakes Ferry pluton (Defant et al., 1988) may represent partial
melting of remnant slab material following closure of the postulated marginal basin separating the EBR and IP. The petrogene-
ses interpreted for the Blakes Ferry and Hog Mountain plutons
closely follow the characteristics of post-late collisional granitic
magmatism presented by Harris et al. (1986). The geochemical
and lithologic character of the Blakes Ferry pluton is similar to
the postmetamorphic trondhjemite dikes of the North Carolina
EBR studied by Miller et al. (this volume). A minimum age for
the North Carolina dikes can be approximated by a whole-rock
plus mineral Rb-Sr isotopic date of 335 ± 3 Ma (Kish, 1989),
which coincides with the 333 Ma minimum age for the Hog
Mountain pluton, discussed previously. This late- to post-Acadian stage of plutonism can be assigned an Early Mississippian
range (333–360 Ma; Palmer, 1983), and is considered to predate
Alleghanian (330–245 Ma; Hatcher, 1987) orogenic effects,
which culminated in the Gondwanan collisional events.

REFERENCES CITED

Allison, D. T., 1992, Structural development and petrogenesis of a granite-metasediment complex, Coosa County, Alabama [Ph.D. thesis]: Tallahassee, Florida State University, 444 p.

Barker, F., 1979, Trondhjemite: definition, environment and hypotheses of origin, *in* Barker, F., ed., Trondhjemites, dacites, and related rocks: New York, Elsevier, p. 1–12.

Barnicoat, A. C., and Treloar, P. J., 1989, Himalayan metamorphism (special issue): Journal of Metamorphic Geology, v. 7, p. 1–150.

Barth, A. P., 1990, Mid-crustal emplacement of Mesozoic plutons, San Gabriel Mountains, California, and implications for the geologic history of the San Gabriel terrane, *in* Anderson, J. L., ed., The nature and origin of Cordilleran magmatism: Geological Society of America Memoir 174, p. 33–45.

Bea, F., Fershtater, G., and Corretge, L. G., 1992, The geochemistry of phosphorus in granitic rocks and the effects of aluminum: Lithos, v. 29, p. 43–56.

Beard, J. S., and Lofgren, G. E., 1991, Dehydration melting and water-saturated melting of basaltic and andesitic greenstones and amphibolites at 1, 3, and 6.9 kb: Journal of Petrology, v. 32, p. 365–401.

Beiler, D. B., and Deininger, R. W., 1987, Geologic setting of Kowaliga Augen Gneiss and the Zana Granite, northern Alabama Piedmont, *in* Drummond, M. S., and Green, N. L., eds., Granites of Alabama: Tuscaloosa, Geological Survey of Alabama, Special Publication, p. 57–72.

Bentley, R. D., and Neathery, T. L., 1970, Geology of the Brevard fault zone and related rocks of the Inner Piedmont of Alabama, *in* Bentley, R. D., and Neathery, T. L., eds., Geology of the Brevard fault zone and related rocks of the Inner Piedmont of Alabama: Tuscaloosa, Alabama Geological Society, 8th Annual Field Trip Guidebook, p. 1–79.

Brandon, A. D., and Lambert, R. St., 1994, Crustal melting in the Cordilleran interior: The mid-Cretaceous White Creek batholith in the southern Canadian Cordillera: Journal of Petrology, v. 35, p. 239–269.

Brandon, A. D., Creaser, R. A., and Chacko, T., 1994, Rapid ascent of granitoid magmas from the lower crust: Mineralogical Magazine, v. 58A, p. 115–116.

Brown, M., 1994, The generation, segregation, ascent and emplacement of granite magma: The migmatite-to-crustally-derived granite connection in thickened orogens: Earth Science Reviews, v. 36, p. 83–130.

Cambell, D. G., 1973, Site investigation: Preliminary report for the Alabama Power Company: Alabama Geological Survey Open-File Report, 67 p.

Carmichael, D. M., 1978, Metamorphic bathozones and bathograds: A measure of the depth of post-metamorphic uplift and erosion on the regional scale: American Journal of Science, v. 278, p. 769–797.

Chappell, B. W., and White, A. J. R., 1974, Two contrasting granite types: Pacific Geology, v. 8, p. 173–174.

Chappell, B. W., and White, A. J. R., 1992, I- and S-type granites in the Lachlan Fold Belt: Royal Society of Edinburgh Transactions, v. 83, p. 1–26.

Chappell, B. W., White, A. J. R., and Wyborn, D., 1987, The importance of residual source material (restite) in granite petrogenesis: Journal of Petrology, v. 28, p. 1111–1138.

Clemens, J. D., and Mawer, C. K., 1992, Granite magma transport by fracture propagation: Tectonophysics, v. 204, p. 339–360.

Clemens, J. D., and Vielzeuf, D., 1987, Constraints on melting and magma production in the crust: Earth and Planetary Science Letters, v. 86, p. 287–306.

Cook, F. A., and Oliver, J. E., 1981, The late Precambrian–early Paleozoic continental edge in the Appalachian orogen: American Journal of Science, v. 281, p. 993–1008.

Cook, R. B., Jr., Dean, L. S., and Foord, E. E., 1987, Tin-tantalum mineralization with the Rockford Granites, Coosa County, Alabama, *in* Drummond, M. S., and Green, N. L., eds., Granites of Alabama: Tuscaloosa, Geological Survey of Alabama, Special Publication, p. 209–220.

Dawes, R. L., and Evans, B. W., 1991, Mineralogy and geothermobarometry of magmatic epidote-bearing dikes, Front Range, Colorado: Geological Society of America Bulletin, v. 103, p. 1017–1031.

Defant, M. J., and Drummond, M. S., 1990, Derivation of some modern arc magmas by melting of young subducted lithosphere: Nature, v. 347, p. 662–665.

Defant, M. J., Drummond, M. S., Arthur, J. D., and Ragland, P. C., 1987, The petrogenesis of the Blakes Ferry pluton, Randolph County, Alabama, *in* Drummond, M. S., and Green, N. L., eds., Granites of Alabama: Tuscaloosa, Geological Survey of Alabama, Special Publication, p. 97–116.

Defant, M. J., Drummond, M. S., Arthur, J. D., and Ragland, P. C., 1988, An example of trondhjemite petrogenesis: The Blakes Ferry pluton, Alabama, U.S.A.: Lithos, v. 21, p. 161–181.

Deininger, R. W., 1975, Granitic rocks in the northern Alabama Piedmont, *in* Neathery, T. L., and Tull, J. F., eds., Geologic profiles of the northern Alabama Piedmont: Tuscaloosa, Alabama Geological Society, 13th Annual Field Trip Guidebook, p. 49–62.

Deininger, R. W., Neathery, T. L., and Bentley, R. D., 1973, Genetic relationships among granitic rocks in the northern Alabama Piedmont: Alabama Geological Survey Open File Report, 23 p.

Drummond, M. S., 1986, Igneous, metamorphic and structural history of the Alabama Tin Belt, Coosa County, Alabama [Ph.D. thesis]: Tallahassee, Florida State University, 411 p.

Drummond, M. S., 1987, Rockford Granite, Coosa County, Alabama: I. Geologic setting, occurrence, petrography and mineral chemistry, *in* Drummond, M. S., and Green, N. L., eds., Granites of Alabama: Tuscaloosa, Geological Survey of Alabama, Special Publication, p. 117–130.

Drummond, M. S., and Allison, D. T., 1987, Rockford Granite, Coosa County, Alabama: III. Igneous petrogenesis and tectonic setting, *in* Drummond, M. S., and Green, N. L., eds., Granites of Alabama: Tuscaloosa, Alabama, Geological Survey of Alabama, Special Publication, p. 155–182.

Drummond, M. S., and Defant, M. J., 1990, A model for trondhjemite-tonalite-dacite genesis and crustal growth via slab melting: Journal of Geophysical Research, v. 95, p. 21,503–21,521.

Drummond, M. S., Ragland, P. C., and Wesolowski, D., 1986, An example of trondhjemite genesis by means of alkali metasomatism, Rockford Granite, Alabama Appalachians: Contributions to Mineralogy and Petrology, v. 93, p. 98–113.

Drummond, M. S., Wesolowski, D., and Allison, D. T., 1988, Generation, diversification, and emplacement of the Rockford Granite, Alabama Appalachians: Mineralogic, petrologic, isotopic (C & O), and P-T constraints: Journal of Petrology, v. 29, p. 869–897.

Drummond, M. S., Allison, D. T., and Wesolowski, D. J., 1994, Igneous petrogenesis and tectonic setting of the Elkahatchee Quartz Diorite, Alabama Appalachians: Implications for Penobscotian magmatism in the eastern Blue Ridge: American Journal of Science, v. 294, p. 173–236.

Erickson, S. G., and Arkani-Hamed, J., 1993, Subduction initiation at passive margins: The Scotian Basin, eastern Canada as a potential example: Tectonics, v. 12, p. 678–687.

Foord, E. E., and Cook, R. B., 1989, Mineralogy and paragenesis of the McAllister Sn-Ta–bearing pegmatite, Coosa County, Alabama: Canadian Mineralogist, v. 27, p. 93–105.

Gibson, R. G., and Speer, J. A., 1986, Contact aureoles as constraints on regional P-T trajectories: An example from the northern Alabama Piedmont, USA: Journal of Metamorphic Geology, v. 4, p. 285–308.

Glover, L., Speer, J. A., Russell, G. S., and Farrar, S. S., 1983, Ages of regional metamorphism and ductile deformation in the central and southern Appalachians: Lithos, v. 16, p. 223–245.

Goldberg, S. A., and Burnell, J. R., 1987, Rubidium-strontium geochronology of the Farmville granite, Alabama Inner Piedmont, *in* Drummond, M. S., and Green, N. L., eds., Granites of Alabama: Tuscaloosa, Geological Survey of Alabama, Special Publication, p. 251–257.

Goldberg, S. A., and Steltenpohl, M. G., 1990, Timing and characteristics of Paleozoic deformation and metamorphism in the Alabama Inner Piedmont: American Journal of Science, v. 290, p. 1169–1200.

Green, N. L., and Lesher, C. M., 1988, Geology of the Hog Mountain tonalite and associated lode gold deposits, northern Alabama Piedmont: Tuscaloosa, University of Alabama, School of Mines and Energy Development Faculty Research Report 88, 42 p.

Green, N. L., Sinha, A. K., and Lesher, C. M., 1988, Gold associated with retrograde shear zones: An Alleghanian episode of mineralization in the southern Appalachians: Geological Society of America Abstracts with Programs, v. 20, no. 7, p. 277.

Hacker, B. R., 1990, Amphibolite-facies-to-granulite-facies reactions in experimentally deformed, unpowdered amphibolite: American Mineralogist, v. 75, p. 1349–1361.

Harris, N. B. W., and Massey, J., 1994, Decompression and anatexis of Himalayan metapelites: Tectonics, v. 13, p. 1537–1546.

Harris, N. B. W., Pearce, J. A., and Tindle, A. G., 1986, Geochemical characteristics of collision-zone magmatism, *in* Coward, M. P., and Ries, A. C., eds., Collision tectonics: Oxford, United Kingdom, Blackwell Scientific, p. 67–81.

Hatcher, R. D., Jr., 1987, Tectonics of the southern and central Appalachian internides: Annual Review of Earth and Planetary Sciences, v. 15, p. 337–362.

Hatcher, R. D., and Odom, A. L., 1980, Timing of thrusting in the southern Appalachians, USA: Model for orogeny?: Geological Society of London Journal, v. 137, p. 321–327.

Holdaway, M. J., 1971, Stability of andalusite on the aluminum silicate phase diagram: American Journal of Science, v. 271, p. 97–131.

Horton, J. W., Drake, A. A., and Rankin, D. W., 1989, Tectonostratigraphic terranes and their Paleozoic boundaries in the central and southern Appalachians, *in* Dallmeyer, R. D., ed., Terranes in the circum-Atlantic Paleozoic orogens: Geological Society of America Special Paper 230, p. 213–245.

Inger, S., and Harris, N., 1993, Geochemical constraints on leucogranite magmatism in the Langtang Valley, Nepal Himalaya: Journal of Petrology, v. 34, p. 345–368.

Kish, S. A., 1989, Igneous and metamorphic history of the eastern Blue Ridge, southwestern North Carolina: K-Ar and Rb-Sr studies, *in* Fritz, W. J., Hatcher, R. D., Jr., and Hopson, J. L., eds., Geology of the eastern Blue Ridge of northeast Georgia and adjacent Carolinas: Georgia Geological Society Guidebook, v. 9, p. 1–40.

Le Breton, N., and Thompson, A. B., 1988, Fluid-absent (dehydration) melting of biotite in metapelites in the early stages of crustal anatexis: Contributions to Mineralogy and Petrology, v. 99, p. 226–237.

Muangnoicharoen, N., 1975, The geology and structure of a portion of the northern Piedmont, east-central Alabama [M.S. thesis]: Tuscaloosa, University of Alabama, 74 p.

Naney, M. T., 1983, Phase equilibria of rock-forming ferromagnesian silicates in granitic systems: American Journal of Science, v. 283, p. 993–1033.

Neathery, T. L., 1975, Geology of the Lineville East, Ofelia, Wadley North and Mellow Valley quadrangles, Alabama: Geological Survey of Alabama Bulletin 109, 120 p.

Neilson, M. J., 1987, The felsic gneisses of the Inner Piedmont, *in* Drummond, M. S., and Green, N. L., eds., Granites of Alabama, Tuscaloosa, Geological Survey of Alabama, Special Publication, p. 9–16.

Neilson, M. J., and Stow, S. H., 1986, Geology and geochemistry of the mafic and ultramafic intrusive rocks, Dadeville belt, Alabama: Geological Society of America Bulletin, v. 97, p. 354–368.

Neilson, M. J., Seal, T. L., and Kish, S. A., 1996, Two high-silica gneisses from the Dadeville Complex of Alabama's Inner Piedmont: Southeastern Geology, v. 36, p. 123–132.

Odom, A. L., and Fullagar, P. D., 1973, Geochronologic and tectonic relationships between the Inner Piedmont, Brevard zone, and Blue Ridge belts, North Carolina: American Journal of Science, v. 273-A, p. 133–149.

Osborne, W. E., Szabo, M. W., Neathery, T. L., and Copeland, C. W., 1988, Geologic map of Alabama: Alabama Geological Survey Special Map 220, scale 1:250 000, 4 sheets.

Palmer, A. R., 1983, The Decade of North American Geology 1983 geologic time scale: Geology, v. 11, p. 503–504.

Pearce, J. A., Harris, N. B. W., and Tindle, A. G., 1984, Trace element discrimination diagrams for the tectonic interpretation of granitic rocks: Journal of Petrology, v. 25, p. 956–983.

Pearce, J. A., van der Laan, S. R., Arculus, R. J., Morton, B. J., and Ishii, T., 1992, Boninite and harzburgite from ODP Leg 125 (Bonin-Mariana forearc): A case study of magma genesis during the initial stages of subduction, *in* Fryer, P., Pearce, J. A., and Stokking, L. B., Proceedings of the Ocean Drilling Program Scientific results, Leg 125: College Station, Texas, Ocean Drilling Program, p. 623–659.

Petford, N., Lister, J. R., and Kerr, R. C., 1994, The ascent of felsic magmas in dykes: Lithos, v. 32, p. 161–168.

Rankin, D. W., 1975, The continental margin of eastern North America in the southern Appalachians: The opening and closing of the proto-Atlantic Ocean: American Journal of Science, v. 275-A, p. 298–336.

Rapp, R. P., Watson, E. B., and Miller, C. F., 1991, Partial melting of amphibolite/eclogite and the origin of Archean trondhjemites and tonalites: Precambrian Research, v. 51, p. 1–25.

Rushmer, T., 1991, Partial melting of two amphibolites: Contrasting experimental results under fluid-absent conditions: Contributions to Mineralogy and Petrology, v. 107, p. 41–59.

Rushmer, T., Pearce, J. A., Ottolini, L., Bottazzi, P., 1994, Trace element behavior during slab melting: Experimental evidence [abs.]: Eos (Transactions, American Geophysical Union), v. 75, p. 746.

Russell, G. S., 1978, U-Pb, Rb-Sr, and K-Ar isotopic studies bearing on the tectonic development of the southernmost Appalachian orogen, Alabama [Ph.D.]: Tallahassee, Florida State University, 196 p.

Russell, G. S., Odom, A. L., and Russell, C. W., 1987, Uranium-lead and rubidium-strontium isotopic evidence for the age and origin of granitic rocks in the Northern Alabama Piedmont, *in* Drummond, M. S., and Green, N. L., eds., Granites of Alabama: Tuscaloosa, Geological Survey of Alabama, Special Publication, p. 239–249.

Schmidt, M. W., 1992, Amphibole composition in tonalite as a function of pressure: An experimental calibration of the Al-in-hornblende barometer: Contributions to Mineralogy and Petrology, v. 110, p. 304–310.

Schmidt, M. W., 1993, Phase relations and compositions in tonalite as a function of pressure: an experimental study at 650 °C: American Journal of Science, v. 293, p. 1011–1060.

Seal, T. L., and Kish, S. A., 1989, The Franklin gneiss: An Ordovician batholith within the western Georgia Inner Piedmont: Geological Society of America Abstracts with Programs, v. 21, no. 3, p. 58.

Seal, T. L., and Kish, S. A., 1990, The geology of the Dadeville Complex of the western Georgia and eastern Alabama Inner Piedmont: Initial petrographic, geochemical, and geochronological results, *in* Steltenpohl, M. J., Kish, S. A., and Neilson, M. J., eds., Geology of the southern Inner Piedmont, Alabama and southwest Georgia (field trip VII guidebook): Tuscaloosa, Alabama, Southeastern Section Geological Society of America, p. 65–78.

Sinha, A. K., Hund, E. A., and Hogan, J. P., 1989, Paleozoic accretionary history of the North American plate margin (central and southern Appalachians): Constraints from the age, origin, and distribution of granitic rocks, *in* Hillhouse, J. W., ed., Deep structure and past kinematics of accreted terranes: Washington, D.C., American Geophysical Union Geophysical Monograph 50, p. 219–238.

Size, W. B., and Dean, L. S., 1987, Structural petrology and petrogenesis of trondhjemite, northern Alabama Piedmont, *in* Drummond, M. S., and Green, N. L., eds., Granites of Alabama: Tuscaloosa, Geological Survey of Alabama, Special Publication, p. 73–96.

Speer, J. A., McSween, H. Y., Jr., and Gates, A. E., 1994, Generation, segregation, ascent, and emplacement of Alleghanian plutons in the southern Appalachians: Journal of Geology, v. 102, p. 249–267.

Steltenpohl, M. G., Neilson, M. J., Bittner, E. I., Colberg, M. R., and Cook, R. B., 1990, Geology of the Alabama Inner Piedmont terrane: Geological Survey of Alabama Bulletin 139, 80 p.

Stow, S. H., Neilson, M. J., and Neathery, T. L., 1984, Petrography, geochemistry, and tectonic significance of the amphibolites of the Alabama Piedmont: American Journal of Science, v. 284, p. 416–436.

Stowell, H. H., Guthrie, G. M., and Lesher, C. M., 1989, Metamorphism and gold mineralization in the Wedowee Group, Goldville district, northern Piedmont, Alabama, *in* Lesher, C. M., Cook, R. B., and Dean, L. S., eds., Gold deposits of Alabama: Tuscaloosa, Geological Survey of Alabama, Bulletin 136, p. 133–158.

Thomas, W. A., 1977, Evolution of Appalachian-Ouachita salients and recesses from reentrants and promontories in the continental margin: American Journal of Science, v. 277, p. 1233–1278.

Thompson, A. B., and Ellis, D. J., 1994, CaO + MgO + Al_2O_3 + SiO_2 + H_2O to 35 kb: Amphibole, talc, and zoisite dehydration and melting reactions in the silica-excess part of the system and their possible significance in subduction zones, amphibolite melting, and magma fractionation: American Journal of Science, v. 294, p. 1229–1289.

Thompson, A. B., and Tracy, R. J., 1979, Model systems for anatexis of pelitic rocks. II. Facies series melting and reactions in the system CaO-$KAlO_2$-$NaAlO_2$-Al_2O_3-SiO_2-H_2O: Contributions to Mineralogy and Petrology, v. 70, p. 429–438.

Tull, J. F., 1978, Structural development of the Alabama Piedmont northwest of the Brevard Zone: American Journal of Science, v. 278, p. 442–460.

Tull, J. F., 1982, Stratigraphic framework of the Talladega slate belt, Alabama Appalachians, *in* Bearce, D. N., Black, W. W., Kish, S., and Tull, J. F., eds., Tectonic studies in the Talladega and Carolina slate belts, southern Appalachian orogen: Geological Society of America Special Paper 191, p. 3–18.

Tull, J. F., 1987, Structural setting of granitic plutonism in the northern Piedmont, Alabama Appalachians, *in* Drummond, M. S., and Green, N. L., eds., Granites of Alabama: Tuscaloosa, Geological Survey of Alabama, Special Publication, p. 17–31.

Tull, J. F., Harris, A. G., Repetski, J. E., McKinney, F. K., Garrett, C. B., and Bearce, D. N., 1988, New paleontologic evidence constraining the age and paleotectonic setting of the Talladega slate belt, southern Appalachians: Geological Society of America Bulletin, v. 100, p. 1291–1299.

Vielzeuf, D., Clemens, J. D., Pin, C., and Moinet, E., 1990, Granites, granulites and crustal differentiation, *in* Vielzeuf, D., and Vidal, P., eds., Granulites and crustal evolution: Dordrecht, The Netherlands, Kluwer, p. 59–85.

Vyhnal, C., McSween, H. Y., Jr., and Speer, J. A., 1991, Hornblende chemistry in southern Appalachian granitoids: Implications for aluminum hornblende thermobarometry and magmatic epidote stability: American Mineralogist, v. 76, p. 176–188.

Wakita, H., Rey, P., and Schmitt, R. A., 1971, Abundances of the 14 rare-earth elements and 12 other trace elements in Apollo 12 samples: Five igneous and one breccia rocks and four soils, *in* Proceedings, the Lunar Science Conference, 2nd: Houston, Texas, Lunar and Planetary Institute, p. 1319–1329.

Wampler, J. M., Neathery, T. L., and Bentley, R. D., 1970, Age relations in the Alabama Piedmont, *in* Bentley, R. D., and Neathery, T. L., eds., Geology of the Brevard Fault Zone: Tuscaloosa, Alabama Geological Society, 8th Annual Field Trip Guidebook, p. 81–90.

Wesolowski, D. J., and Drummond, M. S., 1990, The Rockford Tin District, Alabama Piedmont: A result of Na-metasomatism associated with trondhjemitic alteration of the Rockford Granite?, *in* Cook, R. B., ed., Economic mineral deposits of the southeast: Metallic ore deposits: Atlanta, Georgia Geological Survey Bulletin 117, p. 208–228.

White, A. J. R., and Chappell, B. W., 1977, Ultrametamorphism and granitoid genesis: Tectonophysics, v. 112, p. 7–22.

White, A. J. R., and Chappell, B. W., 1988, Some supracrustal (S-type) granites of the Lachlan Fold Belt: Royal Society of Edinburgh, Transactions, v. 79, p. 169–181.

Wolf, M. B., and Wyllie, P. J., 1993, Garnet growth during amphibolite anatexis: implications of a garnetiferous restite: Journal of Geology, v. 101, p. 357–373.

Wolf, M. B., and Wyllie, P. J., 1994, Dehydration-melting of amphibolite at 10 kbar: The effects of temperature and time: Contributions to Mineralogy and Petrology, v. 115, p. 369–383.

Zen, E-An, and Hammarstrom, J. M., 1984, Magmatic epidote and its petrologic significance: Geology, v. 12, p. 515–518.

MANUSCRIPT ACCEPTED BY THE SOCIETY JULY 2, 1996

Geological Society of America
Memoir 191
1997

Nd and Sr isotopic characterization of crystalline rocks from the southern Appalachian Piedmont and Blue Ridge, North and South Carolina

Paul D. Fullagar, Steven A. Goldberg, and J. Robert Butler
Department of Geology, University of North Carolina, Chapel Hill, North Carolina 27599–3315

ABSTRACT

Nd and Sr isotopic data are presented for 88 samples collected along a transect across the structural trend of the southern Appalachian orogen. The samples are primarily granites and granitic gneisses from the Blue Ridge, Inner Piedmont, and belts of the central and eastern Piedmont of North and South Carolina. Initial ε_{Nd} values for the western Blue Ridge gneisses range from –3.3 to 1.8, reflecting limited contribution of a depleted mantle component, and extensive recycling of Laurentian crust. Depleted mantle model ages (T_{DM}) ranging from 1.8 to 1.4 Ga are similar to model ages obtained from Precambrian exposures of Laurentia elsewhere in North America. The eastern Blue Ridge appears to be distinguished by a juvenile Late Proterozoic source component not recognized in the western Blue Ridge. On the basis of a limited number of analyses, T_{DM} ages for Inner Piedmont rocks define two groups at ca. 1.8 to 1.6 and 1.3 to 0.8 Ga. Samples with T_{DM} ages between 1.6 and 1.3 Ga, which are recognized in the western Blue Ridge and in the Grenville Province, are absent from the Inner Piedmont dataset. Inner Piedmont samples are isotopically intermediate between those of the Blue Ridge and more easterly Piedmont belts. The central and eastern Piedmont contains a significant volume of magmatic rocks derived largely from juvenile Late Proterozoic crust. T_{DM} ages for central and eastern Piedmont samples are mainly between 1.0 and 0.6 Ga, regarded as a Pan-African or Avalonian signature, but there is also a minor contribution of a Grenville component in the range of ~1.2 to 1.0 Ga. Piedmont granites show a relationship of decreasing initial ε_{Nd} and increasing initial $^{87}Sr/^{86}Sr$ as their crystallization age decreases. This suggests a proportionally greater contribution of an older enriched crustal component to the source of the granites as a function of time. All lithotectonic belts east of the western Blue Ridge contain one or more crustal components apparently derived from a non-Laurentian terrane.

INTRODUCTION

One of the major problems in deciphering the evolution of the Appalachian orogen is our limited knowledge of the origin and tectonic provenance of individual lithotectonic belts. In the southern Appalachian orogen (Figs. 1 and 2) several of these belts were apparently accreted to the eastern margin of Laurentia during one of several Paleozoic collisional events. By resolving the chronology of events that generated continental crust in these belts and by defining the isotopic signatures of the crust, it becomes possible to distinguish various lithotectonic domains which may have evolved in different tectonic settings.

Nd isotopic data are used in this study to test for the presence of juvenile, mantle-derived crust versus ancient recycled

Fullagar, P. D., Goldberg, S. A., and Butler, J. R., 1997, Nd and Sr isotopic characterization of crystalline rocks from the southern Appalachian Piedmont and Blue Ridge, North and South Carolina, *in* Sinha, A. K., Whalen, J. B., and Hogan, J. P., eds., The Nature of Magmatism in the Appalachian Orogen: Boulder, Colorado, Geological Society of America Memoir 191.

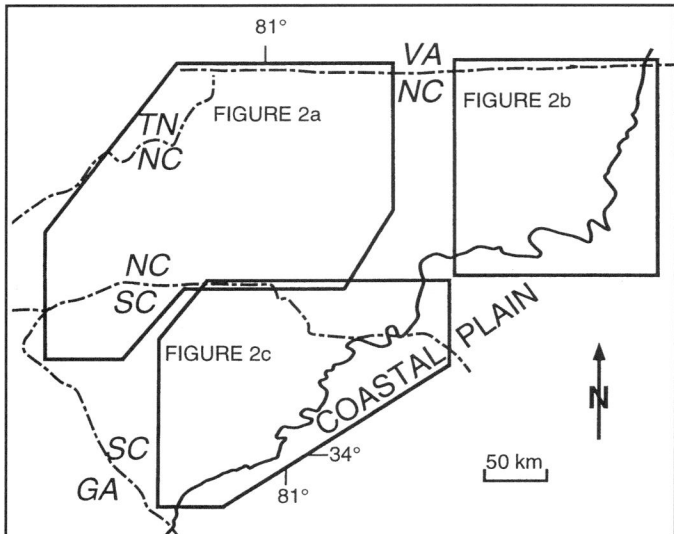

Figure 1. Generalized map showing geologic belts of the southern Appalachians (modified from Horton and Zullo, 1991), and the map areas shown in more detail in Figure 2.

1987). The Nd model age calculation requires knowledge of the Nd isotopic composition of the mantle source of continental crust as a function of time. If the source is depleted mantle, as is conventionally inferred (e.g., DePaolo, 1981), then the model age is designated T_{DM}. A T_{DM} age is the time when a sample and a mantle source had identical isotopic compositions, and can be displayed graphically in Nd evolution diagrams. In practice, Nd isotopic data and Nd model ages are used as chemical fingerprints to distinguish between crustal provinces or terranes within an orogen (e.g., Patchett and Ruiz, 1989; Samson et al., 1991; Bennett and DePaolo, 1987).

In this study we present Nd and Sr isotopic data obtained primarily on granites, granitic gneisses, and felsic volcanic rocks to provide a sampling of crustal source regions in the Blue Ridge, Inner Piedmont, and central and eastern Piedmont of North and South Carolina (Figs. 1 and 2). Granitic rocks are voluminous and among the best-known lithologies in the southern Appalachians, traditionally providing constraints on the timing of Paleozoic tectonothermal events (Sinha et al., 1989; McSween et al., 1991, and references therein). The samples were obtained from a 400 km transect across the structural trend of the southern Appalachian orogen, and yield isotopic evidence for contrasts in crustal composition that provide additional tests of regional tectonic models.

GEOLOGIC SETTING

crust in each of the belts. Nd and Sm may undergo appreciable fractionation during extraction of crustal material from the mantle, but are typically not fractionated during processes such as erosion and metamorphism. Sm-Nd isotopic data for a rock can be used to calculate a model age, representing either a crustal extraction or average crustal residence age. The meaning of the model age depends on the proportion of juvenile versus ancient sources contributing to the rock (e.g., Arndt and Goldstein,

Crystalline rocks in the southern Appalachians of North and South Carolina are divided into lithotectonic belts; from west to east these are the Blue Ridge, Inner Piedmont, Kings Mountain

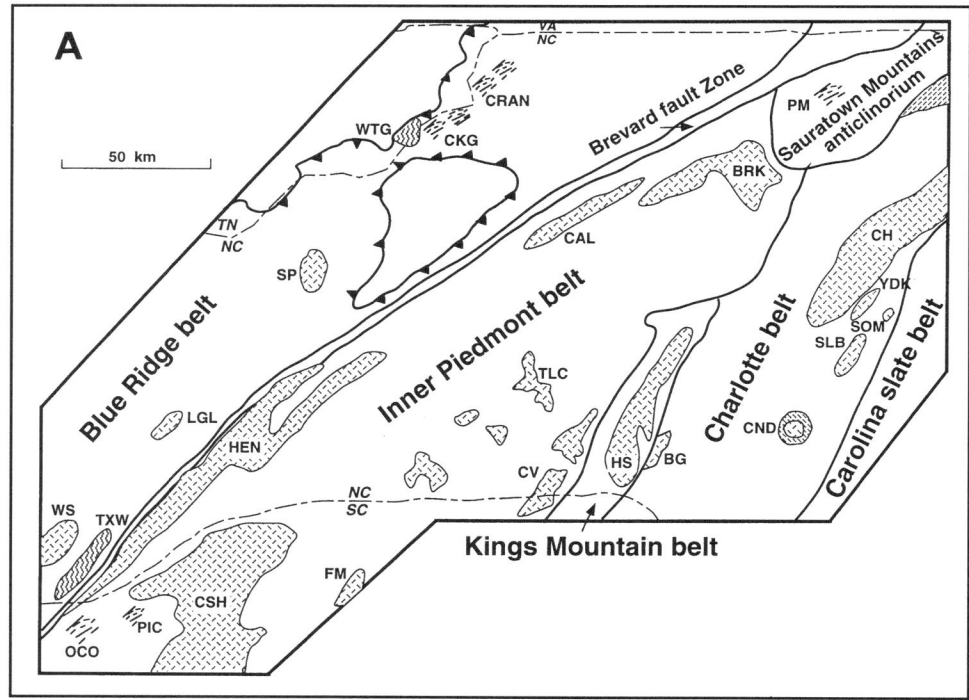

belt, Charlotte belt, Carolina slate belt, Raleigh-Kiokee belts, and the Eastern slate belt (Figs. 1 and 2). A brief summary of these belts is presented here. Additional references can be found in Hatcher (1987) and Horton and Zullo (1991).

The Blue Ridge province (or belt) in the western portion of the Appalachian orogen lies between the Valley and Ridge province to the west and the Piedmont province to the east (Fig. 2A). The Blue Ridge is divided into a western segment consisting of a rift-facies sequence of clastic sedimentary rocks deposited on Laurentian basement, and an eastern segment characterized by the presence of oceanic crust derived from the Iapetus ocean or an exotic terrane (Williams and Hatcher, 1983). The western Blue Ridge belt contains Middle Proterozoic (1.6 to 1.0 Ga; Plumb, 1990) quartzofeldspathic basement gneisses, Late Proterozoic (1.0 Ga to base of Cambrian; Plumb, 1990) plutons, Late Proterozoic metasedimentary and metavolcanic rift sequences, and early Paleozoic continental margin deposits. These rocks were thrust northwestward over Paleozoic sedimentary rocks of the Valley and Ridge province. Older rocks of the Blue Ridge record the Grenville orogeny, a ca. 1.1 Ga collisional event involved in the assembly of a large Proterozoic supercontinent (Moore, 1986). Late Proterozoic rifting and supercontinent break-up resulted in the separation of the North American paleocontinent, Laurentia. This was followed by formation of passive margin sedimentary strata at the edge of Laurentia and Iapetus ocean. The Middle Ordovician Taconic orogeny led to initial closure of Iapetus and destruction of the continental margin by island arc or continental collision. Evidence for the Aca-

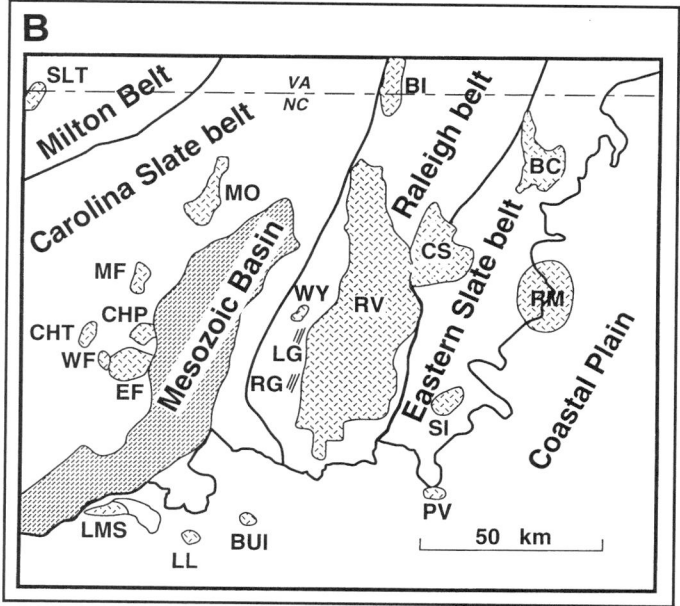

Figure 2 (on this and facing page). A: Sample location map for the Blue Ridge and western Piedmont of North and South Carolina. B: Sample location map for the central and eastern Piedmont of North Carolina. C: Sample location map for the central and eastern Piedmont of South Carolina and adjacent North Carolina. For each unit shown with a symbol, one or more samples have been analyzed for Sm-Nd isotopic composition. Analytical data and explanation of symbols are in Table 1.

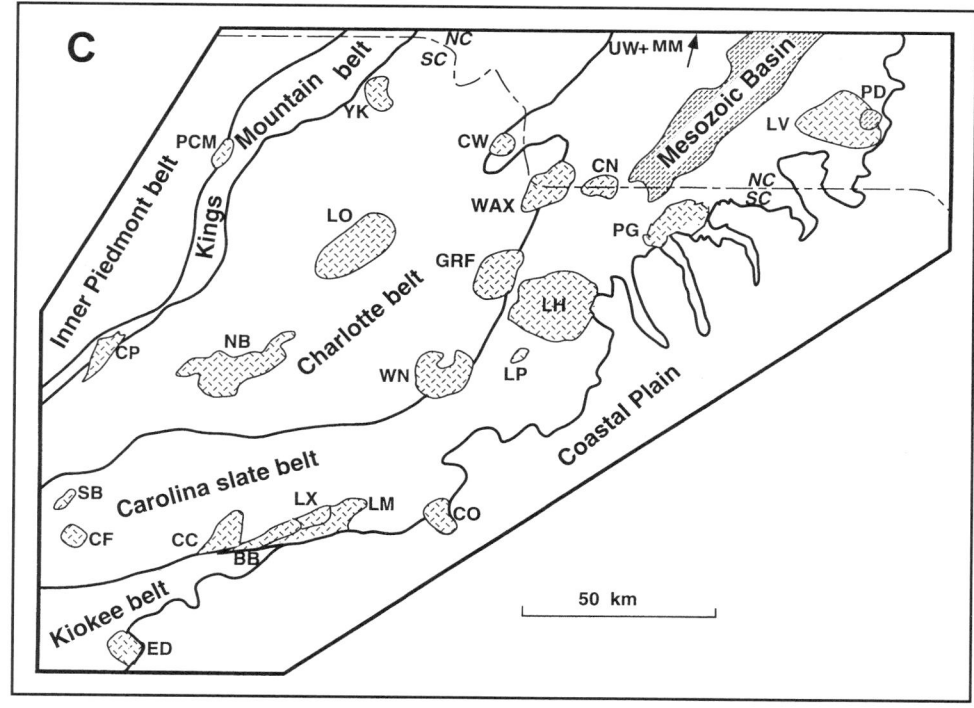

dian orogeny in the Blue Ridge is limited, but the Alleghanian orogeny resulted in Late Carboniferous–Permian deformation and metamorphism, including thrusting and strike-slip motion, related to the collision of Laurentia and Gondwana. The eastern boundary of the Blue Ridge is marked by the Brevard fault zone that separates the Blue Ridge from the Inner Piedmont (including the Chauga belt).

The Inner Piedmont was deformed and metamorphosed during the Taconic orogeny, as was the Blue Ridge Laurentian basement and its cover rocks. Unless this Ordovician metamorphism of the Inner Piedmont occurred when it was separate from Laurentia (e.g., Dalziel et al., 1994), the Inner Piedmont must have been part of North America by this time. The Inner Piedmont is a composite stack of thrust sheets, consisting mainly of gneisses, schists, amphibolites, and granitoids, with a complex history of plutonism, deformation, and metamorphism. Relatively little is known about the timing of major geologic events in the Inner Piedmont, and about the relationship of this block to adjacent parts of the southern Appalachians. A limited number of isotopic dates suggests that the rocks are Late Proterozoic to early Paleozoic in age. The Kings Mountain and Lowndesville shear zones mark the eastern boundary of the Inner Piedmont.

The Kings Mountain belt, which is in the western part of the central Piedmont (Fig. 2A), consists mainly of quartzite, metaconglomerate, and marble, plus mica schist. Metavolcanic rocks in the Kings Mountain belt have lithologic and chemical affinities to the belts farther east, but not to the Inner Piedmont. To the east of the Kings Mountain belt, the Charlotte belt consists largely of Paleozoic intrusive rocks ranging in composition from gabbro to granite. Both the Kings Mountain belt and Charlotte belt have undergone amphibolite facies regional metamorphism. Farther east, the Carolina slate belt is composed of lower greenschist facies metavolcanic and metasedimentary rocks intruded by a variety of plutons, and some of the metavolcanic and metasedimentary rocks are correlated with higher-grade rocks in the Charlotte belt. The oldest metaigneous rocks (~700 to 500 Ma) in the Kings Mountain belt, Charlotte belt, and Carolina slate belt are similar in composition.

East of the Carolina slate belt, the Raleigh and Kiokee belts have high-grade gneisses in their cores, and were regionally metamorphosed during the Alleghanian. Alleghanian granites underlie or intrude large parts of the Raleigh belt and Kiokee belts. In the easternmost part of the Piedmont, the Eastern slate belt consists mainly of greenschist facies metavolcanic rocks, metamorphosed plutons, and postmetamorphic intrusions, units similar to those in the Carolina slate belt.

Secor et al. (1983) suggested that the Charlotte and Carolina slate belts are part of an exotic (Carolina) terrane that did not join North America until after the Cambrian. The suture between North America and the Carolina terrane may be at or near the Inner Piedmont–Kings Mountain belt boundary (e.g., Hatcher, 1987). An Alleghanian suture with Africa is probably located beneath the Coastal Plain (Secor et al., 1989).

SAMPLING AND ANALYTICAL TECHNIQUES

Lithologic units analyzed in this isotopic study were selected on the basis of existing field, isotopic, and geochemical data (see references in Horton and Zullo, 1991). Of the samples, 83 are from plutonic and volcanic rocks of granitic composition, and 5 are from dioritic to gabbroic plutons (Table 1). Samples were chosen to avoid weathering and alteration, and to obtain representative examples of each lithology.

Powdered whole-rock samples chosen for Sm-Nd isotopic analyses were dissolved in Parr Teflon bombs using a 10:1 mixture of 2× distilled $HF:HNO_3$. Isotopic tracer solutions prepared from enriched (>97%) ^{150}Nd and ^{147}Sm spikes were added to the samples and dried prior to dissolution. Samples and isotopic tracers were weighed on a calibrated Mettler semimicro balance (s.d. = ±0.01 mg). Mixed Sm/Nd tracer solutions are calibrated against normal solutions of high-purity mixed Sm and Nd metals obtained from Ames Laboratory, and checked against U.S. Geological Survey BCR-1 and Sm/Nd solutions supplied by the California Institute of Technology (Wasserburg et al., 1981). Based on replicate analyses of BCR-1 and mixed normal solutions, 2σ uncertainties in the Sm/Nd ratio are known to better than ± 0.2%.

Sm and Nd are separated first as a bulk rare earth element (REE) fraction eluted in 6M HCl on AG50W×8 resin. The bulk REE fraction is adsorbed onto AG50W×4 (200–400 mesh) resin equilibrated with α-HIBA, and Nd and Sm are selectively eluted with 0.15 and 0.225M α-HIBA. Nd is measured as the metal species using a triple Ta-Re-Ta filament assembly, or as the oxide on a single Re filament using silica gel/H_3PO_4. Sm aliquots are loaded with H_3PO_4 onto single degassed Ta filaments. Blanks are measured regularly on Teflon bombs and vials to test for memory effects between sample digestions and cleaning. Total procedural blanks using new clean lab facilities are below 60 pg Nd. Neodymium ratios are measured using a VG Sector 54 mass spectrometer in quintuple dynamic multicollector mode, typically with ^{144}Nd = 1V. Internal precision for sample analyses is typically less than 0.000012 (2σ). External precision is typically 0.3 ε_{Nd} units for rocks similar to those analyzed in this study. Samarium is analyzed in static multicollector mode with ^{147}Sm = 200–500 mV. Mass fractionation is corrected using $^{146}Nd/^{144}Nd$ = 0.7219 and $^{149}Sm/^{152}Sm$ = 0.51685. Recent analyses of the La Jolla Nd standard yield a $^{143}Nd/^{144}Nd$ value of 0.511854 ± 0.000014 (2σ; n = 30). Analyses of the Ames Nd metal (n = 17) yield a $^{143}Nd/^{144}Nd$ ratio of 0.512136 ± 0.000016 (2σ). Three analyses of BCR-1 yield $^{143}Nd/^{144}Nd$ = 0.512633 ± 0.000014 (2σ).

Rb-Sr ages and Sr isotopic data are summarized in Table 1 as are the references to these data. Rb and Sr analytical procedures are summarized in Fullagar and Butler (1979) and Kish (1983).

Sm-Nd ISOTOPIC DATA

Blue Ridge

Figure 3 summarizes isotopic data from Blue Ridge samples (Table 1), and data for Late Proterozoic Crossnore complex plu-

TABLE 1. Sm-Nd ISOTOPIC DATA AND Sr ISOTOPIC RATIOS AND AGES

Sample	Unit		Type*	Symbol	Sm (ppm)	Nd (ppm)	^{147}Sm/^{144}Nd	^{143}Nd/^{144}Nd (±2σ)†	εNd(1)	TDM (Ma)§	^{87}Sr/^{86}Sr (i) (±2σ)**	Age, Ma (±2σ)**	Reference**
Blue Ridge													
1859	Cranberry	(CRAN)	GN		7.89	64.73	0.07547	0.511707 (06)	-2.37	1472	0.7080 (6)	1018 (38)	A
1934	Cranberry	(CRAN)	GN		4.59	25.23	0.11268	0.511960 (10)	-2.29	1631	0.7080 (6)	1018 (38)	A
1946	Cranberry	(CRAN)	GN		3.36	16.42	0.12722	0.512024 (06)	-2.92	1791	0.7080 (6)	1018 (38)	A
1953	Cranberry	(CRAN)	GN		16.03	99.44	0.09976	0.511902 (07)	-1.73	1524	0.7080 (6)	1018 (38)	A
1970	Cranberry Mine	(CRAN)	GN		4.41	27.04	0.10096	0.511853 (07)	-2.82	1610	0.7080 (6)	1018 (38)	A
1848	Crossing Knob	(CKG)	GN		2.28	11.78	0.11993	0.511990 (06)	-3.34	1707	0.7128 (34)	947 (114)	A
LG-17	Looking Glass	(LGL)	GR		1.30	5.54	0.14548	0.512441 (07)	-1.32	1340	0.7051 (8)	386 (74)	B
GG-PT-5	Toxaway	(TXW)	GN		3.81	24.12	0.09779	0.511926 (08)	1.82	1467	0.7020	1240	B
GQ-1	Toxaway	(TXW)	GN		9.57	54.31	0.10905	0.511950 (11)	0.56	1588	0.7021 (14)	1244 (91)	A
1960	Watauga River	(WTG)	GN		9.69	56.69	0.10582	0.511942 (06)	0.11	1553	0.7035 (14)	1177 (58)	B
WS-14	Whiteside	(WS)	GR		1.52	7.36	0.12749	0.512319 (07)	-2.69	1280	0.7080	400	B
1265	Spruce Pine	(SP)	GR		1.93	3.70	0.32304	0.512573 (07)	-7.64	......	0.7072 (38)	394 (34)	A
Sauratown Mountains													
IA-3	Pilot Mountain	(PM)	GN		8.98	66.34	0.13532	0.511835 (05)	2.60	1415	0.7010 (4)	1262 (98)	A
Inner Piedmont													
1398	Brooks Crossroads	(BRK)	GR		3.65	19.62	0.11517	0.512413 (05)	0.06	978	0.7041 (4)	427 (18)	A
1490	Brooks Crossroads	(BRK)	GR		4.10	25.39	0.09997	0.512251 (08)	-2.28	1064	0.7041 (4)	427 (18)	A
1495	Brooks Crossroads	(BRK)	GR		2.88	18.47	0.09637	0.512263 (07)	-1.85	1016	0.7041 (4)	427 (18)	A
1630	Brooks Crossroads	(BRK)	GR		4.80	24.11	0.12319	0.512357 (08)	-1.47	1155	0.7041 (4)	427 (18)	A
2037	Caesars Head	(CSH)	GR		5.10	29.41	0.10740	0.512446 (05)	0.93	862	0.7057 (24)	409 (40)	A
1502	Call	(CAL)	GR		8.53	47.08	0.11208	0.512229 (07)	-3.00	1220	0.7044 (6)	460 (18)	A
1636	Call	(CAL)	GR		6.01	30.97	0.12005	0.512021 (10)	-7.53	1658	0.7044 (6)	460 (18)	A
790	Cherryville	(CV)	GR		5.38	23.56	0.14122	0.512226 (09)	-5.56	1713	0.7121 (14)	351 (8)	A
2074	Fairmont Mills	(FM)	GR		16.43	80.06	0.12695	0.512316 (06)	-2.56	1275	0.7073 (14)	418 (26)	B
2076	Fairmont Mills	(FM)	GR		6.25	33.13	0.11676	0.512291 (06)	-2.49	1181	0.7073 (14)	418 (26)	B
1616	Pickens Co.	(PIC)	GN		8.19	48.98	0.10352	0.512342 (09)	-0.74	974	0.7069 (10)	423 (12)	H
1675	Pickens Co.	(PIC)	GN		9.59	52.55	0.11301	0.512382 (12)	-0.47	1003	0.7069 (10)	423 (12)	A
1690	Oconee Co.	(OCO)	GN		4.55	25.44	0.11020	0.512438 (06)	0.77	897	0.7069 (10)	423 (12)	A
1696	Oconee Co.	(OCO)	GN		2.55	12.26	0.12856	0.512368 (07)	-1.59	1208	0.7069 (10)	423 (12)	A
NC-203	Henderson (NC)	(HEN)	GN		6.85	33.94	0.12493	0.512328 (08)	-1.34	1226	0.7042 (12)	513 (34)	A
2193	Henderson (SC)	(HEN)	GN		7.45	27.43	0.16813	0.512549 (07)	-0.11	1640	......	445 (20)	B
NC-183	Toluca	(TLC)	GN		5.83	25.64	0.14080	0.512265 (06)	-3.71	1620	......	500	I, J
Kings Mountain Belt													
CC-294	High Shoals	(HS)	GR		8.61	56.32	0.09457	0.512292 (09)	-2.59	965	......	320	A
2155	Pacolet Mills	(PCM)	GR		8.04	61.55	0.08082	0.512256 (6)	-1.78	907	0.7046 (4)	383 (10)	A
Charlotte Belt													
GS-62A	Boogertown	(BG)	GR		2.27	11.37	0.12359	0.512623 (09)	4.88	722	0.7033 (2)	552 (30)	B
1343	Churchland	(CH)	GR		9.89	67.54	0.14647	0.512355 (09)	-1.71	859	0.7048	282	B
2136	Cold Point	(CP)	GR		14.67	90.00	0.10086	0.512385 (08)	-1.29	895	0.7049 (2)	299 (18)	A
NC-16	Concord	(CND)	SY		2.07	10.35	0.12392	0.512517 (08)	1.37	899	0.7040 (12)	401 (60)	A
SC-148	Great Falls	(CND)	GR		2.27	12.58	0.11177	0.512426 (06)	1.99	928	0.7032 (52)	565 (114)	A
SC-118	Lowrys	(LO)	GR		1.46	8.25	0.10954	0.512487 (09)	1.51	821	0.7023 (6)	399 (8)	B, G

TABLE 1. Sm-Nd ISOTOPIC DATA AND Sr ISOTOPIC RATIOS AND AGES (Continued - page 2)

Sample	Unit	Symbol	Type*	Sm (ppm)	Nd (ppm)	$^{147}Sm/^{144}Nd$	$^{143}Nd/^{144}Nd$ (± 2σ)†	εNd(1)	TDM (Ma)§	$^{87}Sr/^{86}Sr$ (i) (± 2σ)**	Age, Ma (± 2σ)**	Reference**
Charlotte Belt (continued)												
2000	Newberry	(NB)	GR	5.28	34.55	0.09460	0.512406 (05)	0.89	822	0.7023 (6)	415 (18)	A
522	Salisbury	(SLB)	GR	6.62	15.71	0.26056	0.513013 (06)	4.03	......	0.7036 (8)	403 (6)	A
554	Salisbury	(SLB)	GR	6.08	19.26	0.19527	0.512842 (07)	4.06	1627	0.7036 (8)	403 (6)	A
743	Southmont-A	(SOM)	GR	5.93	18.79	0.19539	0.512858 (05)	4.36	1509	0.7056 (14)	393 (10)	A
744	Southmont-B	(SOM)	GR	5.92	18.08	0.20280	0.512884 (07)	4.50	2225	0.7036 (12)	386 (8)	A
SC-19	Winnsboro	(WN)	GR	15.15	91.56	0.10241	0.512404 (10)	-1.01	881	0.7046 (4)	295 (4)	A
747	Yadkin	(YDK)	GR	4.60	12.26	0.23202	0.512872 (05)	2.86	......	......	378 (12)	A
1369	York	(YK)	GR	2.66	16.69	0.09869	0.512350 (09)	-1.59	923	0.7044 (6)	321 (24)	A
Milton Belt												
K-78-50	Shelton	(SLT)	GN	13.71	70.55	0.12025	0.512496 (06)	1.38	898	0.7066 (12)	424 (6)	A
Carolina Slate Belt												
2170	Cane Creek	(CN)	FL	3.48	17.81	0.12102	0.512484 (07)	1.65	924	0.7048 (4)	480 (16)	B, C
767	Catawba	(CW)	GR	3.23	13.25	0.15089	0.512584 (10)	0.84	1114	0.7036 (6)	322 (18)	A
NC-151	Chapel Hill	(CHP)	GR	2.49	13.09	0.11779	0.512577 (09)	5.78	752	0.7031 (4)	690 (40)	A
SW-144C	Chatham	(CHT)	GR	2.40	11.67	0.12713	0.512641 (06)	4.87	720	0.7039 (6)	539 (38)	A
1001	Clouds Creek	(CC)	GR	7.13	34.67	0.12732	0.512379 (07)	-2.26	1171	0.7099 (22)	315 (58)	A
1984	Clouds Creek	(CC)	DIO	4.09	15.63	0.16177	0.512699 (06)	2.60	1034	......	315	A
1773	Columbia	(CO)	GR	6.53	45.39	0.08908	0.512515 (07)	1.53	657	0.7050 (4)	286 (6)	A
1593	Cuffeytown Creek	(CF)	GR	5.60	25.35	0.13661	0.512494 (12)	-0.55	1086	......	294 (60)	A
NC-476	E. Farrington	(EF)	GR	9.35	42.61	0.13575	0.512709 (08)	5.43	669	0.7030 (12)	517 (76)	A
LRD-1-211	Lamar Prospect	(LP)	FL	3.59	20.45	0.10875	0.512543 (06)	3.59	737	0.7082 (12)	424 (14)	A
B-LS-3	Lemon Springs	(LMS)	GR	10.41	46.93	0.13725	0.512594 (06)	2.41	902	0.7115 (16)	430 (30)	B
736	Liberty Hill	(LH)	GR	9.57	72.60	0.08153	0.512481 (08)	-1.10	796	0.7044 (22)	295 (32)	F
1288	Lilesville	(LV)	GR	6.92	38.29	0.11186	0.512481 (15)	0.46	848	0.7048 (14)	324 (54)	A
NC-236A	Meadow Flats	(MF)	GB	1.48	5.17	0.17750	0.512808 (07)	4.85	997	0.7031 (4)	625 (70)	A
NC-238	Meadow Flats	(MF)	DIO	6.38	28.51	0.13858	0.512662 (08)	5.12	786	0.7025 (12)	625 (70)	A
SC16-71	Moriah-Oxford	(MO)	GR	4.56	22.07	0.12827	0.512662 (07)	5.09	694	0.7033 (4)	527 (30)	B
HD-20	Morrow Mt.	(MM)	FL	5.91	25.41	0.14378	0.512537 (05)	1.51	1104	0.7040 (2)	514 (30)	F
1293	Pageland	(PG)	GR	8.60	50.81	0.10469	0.512450 (07)	-0.18	837	0.7038 (8)	297 (18)	A
NC-106	Pee Dee	(PD)	GB	7.59	35.86	0.13103	0.512564 (06)	1.19	890	0.7041 (4)	314 (10)	E
19A	Spring Branch	(SB)	FL	2.30	13.60	0.10457	0.512332 (08)	-0.38	997	0.7084 (18)	475 (16)	B, C
2209	Uwharrie	(UW)	FL	6.47	31.20	0.12836	0.512447 (10)	0.54	1066	0.7067 (10)	488 (14)	B
1724	Waxhaw	(WAX)	GR	5.54	25.19	0.23603	0.512496 (08)	1.07	1075	0.7037 (14)	495 (42)	A
NC-477	W. Farrington	(WF)	GR	4.70	24.34	0.11957	0.512591 (06)	4.43	743	0.7026 (4)	541 (84)	A
Raleigh Belt												
K-78-21	Buggs Island	(BI)	GR	2.31	11.86	0.12025	0.512420 (06)	-1.19	1022	0.7047 (10)	314 (32)	A
K-77-74	Lake Gresham	(LG)	GN	13.46	60.68	0.13722	0.512325 (08)	-4.05	1426	0.7071 (6)	272 (14)	E
2249	Raleigh	(RG)	GN	3.16	14.56	0.13403	0.512636 (07)	3.65	789	0.7031 (16)	459 (120)	B
2223	Rolesville	(RV)	GR	3.79	29.97	0.07827	0.512468 (06)	1.82	658	0.7034 (4)	340 (24)	B
WY-1	Wyatt	(WY)	GR	2.53	10.96	0.14275	0.512533 (06)	0.07	1102	0.7044 (4)	307 (6)	A
Kiokee Belt												
K-77-3	Batesburg (augen)	(BB)	GN	6.74	40.92	0.10185	0.512436 (07)	-0.42	834	0.7045 (4)	291 (8)	A

TABLE 1. Sm-Nd ISOTOPIC DATA AND Sr ISOTOPIC RATIOS AND AGES (Continued - page 3)

Sample	Unit	Symbol	Type*	Sm (ppm)	Nd (ppm)	$^{147}Sm/^{144}Nd$	$^{143}Nd/^{144}Nd$ (± 2σ)†	$\varepsilon Nd^{(t)}$	TDM (Ma)§	$^{87}Sr/^{86}Sr$ (i) (± 2σ)**	Age, Ma (± 2σ)**	Reference**
Kiokee Belt (continued)												
K-77-5	Batesburg (lineated)	(BB)	GN	9.94	55.84	0.11008	0.512130 (08)	-6.77	1341	0.7045 (12)	285 (34)	A
K-77-36	Edgefield	(ED)	GN	4.17	19.53	0.13219	0.512413 (06)	-1.18	1120	0.7107 (14)	317 (8)	A
K-77-83	Lake Murray	(LM)	GN	5.78	27.49	0.13010	0.512418 (07)	-1.64	1139	0.7121 (12)	311 (22)	A
1741	Lewxington	(LX)	GR	4.39	27.41	0.09915	0.512440 (07)	-0.22	810	0.7047 (12)	293 (40)	A
Eastern Slate Belt												
2182	Buies Creek	(BUI)	GR	10.52	40.94	0.15903	0.512767 (05)	4.92	786	0.7147 (12)	497 (6)	A
BW-1	Butterwood Creek South	(BC)	GR	2.76	8.93	0.19110	0.512497 (07)	-2.55	4236	0.7081 (8)	282 (6)	A
1141	Castalia	(CS)	GR	2.28	8.91	0.15798	0.512676 (07)	2.29	1009	0.7138 (74)	314 (22)	A
A-38-72	Lillington	(LL)	GR	2.19	8.72	0.15528	0.512606 (07)	0.95	1139	0.7038 (10)	297 (10)	A
2176	Princeton	(PV)	FL	4.84	20.23	0.14810	0.512588 (09)	1.29	1060	0.7182 (8)	365 (8)	B, C
RM-3	Rocky Mount	(RM)	GR	21.98	85.71	0.15871	0.512633 (16)	1.59	1135	0.7044 (2)	345 (2)	B, D
RM-52	Rocky Mount	(RM)	GR	5.38	25.08	0.13269	0.512595 (07)	1.98	858	0.7044 (2)	345 (2)	B, D
NC-119	Sims	(SI)	GR	4.94	29.28	0.10441	0.512500 (10)	0.69	767	0.7045 (6)	287 (18)	A

*Type of unit: DIO, diorite; FL, felsic volcanics; GB, gabbro; GN, gneiss; GR, granite; SY, syenite.

†2σ errors on $^{143}Nd/^{144}Nd$ ratios reported as last two significant digits.

§TDM ages calculated as in DePaolo (1981).

**Initial $^{87}Sr/^{86}Sr$ ratios were obtained mainly from isochron plots; errors are 2σ, and represent the last significant digits of $^{87}Sr/^{86}Sr$ ratios and reported ages. References for crystallization ages used to calculate initial ε_{Nd} values: A—McSween et al. (1991); B—new data reported in this chapter; C—Fullagar et al. (1987); D—Fullagar and Spruill (1989); E—Kish (1983); F—Hills and Butler (1969); G—Fullagar (1983); H—Harper and Fullagar (1981); I—Davis et al. (1962); J—Odom and Fullagar (1973). Crystallization ages were estimated for two samples. For the Clouds Creek diorite, we assumed that the crystallization age is the same as that for the Clouds Creek granite (315 Ma; Fullagar and Butler, 1979). The Toluca Granite has a $^{207}Pb/^{206}Pb$ zircon age of 480 Ma (Davis et al., 1962), but because the U-Pb results are quite discordant, it is possible that the actual time of crystallization is older than 480 Ma, and thus we assume an age of 500 Ma. Initial $^{87}Sr/^{86}Sr$ ratios for several plutons either have not been obtained or are equivocal, and these include the Clouds Creek diorite, and the Cuffeytown, Henderson (SC), High Shoals, Toluca, and Yadkin granites. Sr analytical procedures for these data were summarized in Fullagar and Butler (1979), and Kish (1983).

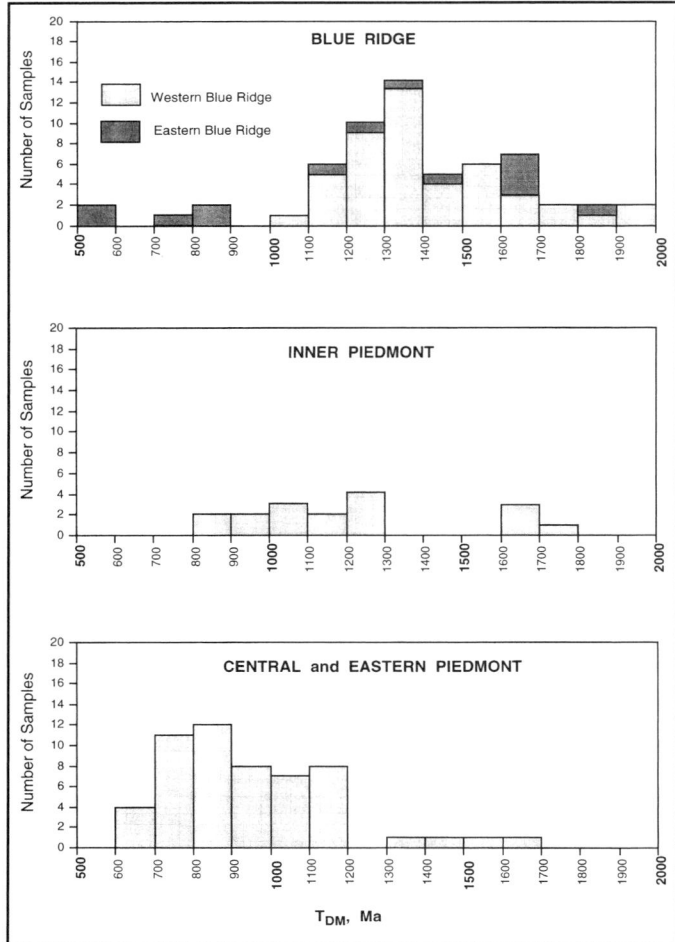

Figure 3. Histograms of Sm-Nd T_{DM} ages for Blue Ridge, Inner Piedmont, and central and eastern Piedmont samples. In addition to data from this study (Table 1), the histogram for the Blue Ridge includes data from the Crossnore complex in the western Blue Ridge of North Carolina (Su and Fullagar, 1995; Fetter and Goldberg, 1995, plus results from the eastern Blue Ridge (Goldberg et al., 1994b; Goldberg and Dallmeyer, 1996). All data in the histograms for the Inner Piedmont and for the central and eastern Piedmont are from this study.

tons that intrude rocks of the western Blue Ridge (Su and Fullagar, 1995; Fetter and Goldberg, 1995). One sample of quartzofeldspathic gneiss from the Sauratown Mountains, considered to be an outlier of Grenville crust, is included with the western Blue Ridge data. These results are compared to data for pelitic schists and amphibolites from the eastern Blue Ridge (Goldberg and Dallmeyer, 1996; Goldberg et al., 1994b), and indicate that younger crustal sources are absent in the western Blue Ridge, although they are present in the eastern Blue Ridge.

On the basis of the data in Figure 3, the Blue Ridge contains the oldest T_{DM} ages of any belt in the southern Appalachians, reflecting the large contribution of one or more Proterozoic sources. Quartzofeldspathic gneisses of the western Blue Ridge

and Sauratown Mountains generally exhibit a range in T_{DM} ages from 1.8 to 1.4 Ga (Table 1). Plutonic and volcanic rocks of the Crossnore complex represent crustal additions to the western Blue Ridge during the Late Proterozoic, although these rocks generally exhibit T_{DM} ages of 1.5 to 1.2 Ga and are interpreted to be derived from a combination of Laurentian crust and mantle (Fetter and Goldberg, 1995). T_{DM} ages younger than 1.0 Ga are not observed in the western Blue Ridge. In contrast, five samples of amphibolite from the eastern Blue Ridge, which were metamorphosed during the Ordovician Taconic orogeny, have T_{DM} ages of 0.9 to 0.6 Ga (Fig. 3) and appear to represent juvenile additions to the crust. The Late Proterozoic T_{DM} ages are similar to ages for juvenile crust recognized in Pan-African or Avalonian terranes. The term "Pan-African" refers to events largely centered about but not restricted to the period from ca. 0.75 to 0.55 Ga (e.g., Black and Liegeois, 1993). Amphibolites, schists, and granitic gneisses from the eastern Blue Ridge exhibit a considerable range in T_{DM} ages from 1.9 to 0.5 Ga; approximately one-fourth of the samples plot between 1.7 and 1.6 Ga (Fig. 3). Middle Proterozoic model ages of 1.7 and 1.6 Ga also are observed in the western Blue Ridge. On the basis of available data (Goldberg and Dallmeyer, 1996; Goldberg et al., 1994b), the eastern Blue Ridge appears to be distinguished by a Late Proterozoic source component not recognized in the western Blue Ridge.

Inner Piedmont

Initial ε_{Nd} values for granitic plutons and orthogneisses range from 0.9 to –7.3 (Table 1), corresponding to a range in T_{DM} ages from 1.8 to 0.8 Ga. This variation suggests the presence of heterogeneous crust, with only some similarities to the Blue Ridge. The histogram for 17 Inner Piedmont rocks in Figure 3 shows two groups of T_{DM} ages: 1.8 to 1.6, and 1.3 to 0.8 Ga. Absent from Inner Piedmont rocks are T_{DM} ages between 1.6 and 1.3 Ga, which are common in the western Blue Ridge and the Grenville province. Also absent are T_{DM} ages of <0.8 Ga (i.e., younger Pan-African–Avalonian ages). Because the number of T_{DM} ages is limited, additional data may alter the age patterns that now are observed. In addition, the somewhat uncertain effect of high-grade metamorphism on Sm-Nd fractionation could mean that the apparent distribution of Inner Piedmont T_{DM} ages is less significant than is the case for samples from belts of lower metamorphic grade.

Central and eastern Piedmont

The central and eastern Piedmont is characterized by the predominance of Late Proterozoic T_{DM} ages and the lack of a significant contribution from components older than 1.2 Ga (Fig. 3). T_{DM} ages range mainly from 1.0 to 0.6 Ga for each of the various belts in the Piedmont (Table 1). The distribution of ages between 1.0 and 0.6 Ga is regarded as a Pan-African or Avalonian signature; a minor contribution of a Grenville component is in the range of ca. 1.2 to 1.0 Ga. These model ages suggest a tectonic link to cratons composing Gondwana that contain significant volumes of juvenile crust formed between ca. 900 and 650 Ma (Rogers et al., 1994).

The Charlotte belt in the central Piedmont exhibits a fairly narrow range of relatively young T_{DM} ages of 0.9 to 0.7 Ga, excluding the apparently anomalous T_{DM} ages for members of the Salisbury plutonic suite. In general, Nd data from the Charlotte belt indicate an absence of crust older than 1.0 Ga. The Salisbury plutonic suite plutons (Salisbury, Southmont, Yadkin) have very high $^{147}Sm/^{144}Nd$ ratios (0.20 to 0.26, Table 1), and two samples have indeterminate T_{DM} ages (Table 1). These samples may reflect alteration or derivation from unusual garnet-rich sources, and they are not discussed further.

In the eastern Piedmont, the Lake Gresham gneiss in the Raleigh belt and the Batesburg lineated gneiss in the Kiokee belt have Nd isotopic signatures reflecting an older enriched crustal component (T_{DM} age of 1.4 and 1.3 Ga, respectively). This contrasts to results for the majority of eastern Piedmont samples (Table 1) that reflect the importance of a Late Proterozoic juvenile source. A sample from the Butterwood Creek South pluton in the Eastern slate belt of the easternmost Piedmont has an anomalous T_{DM} age (4.2 Ga), but we note that this sample is highly sheared, and it is not discussed further.

COMPARATIVE Nd AND Sr ISOTOPIC DATA

Crystallization ages used to calculate initial isotopic ratios (Table 1) are based mainly on the Rb-Sr whole-rock method. This method may result in dates that are younger than the time of igneous crystallization, for example, in cases where fluids have interacted with the rock, or where there has been considerable deformation and recrystallization (e.g., Hanson et al., 1969; Page and Bell, 1986; Schleicher et al., 1983; Su and Fullagar, 1995). Other studies have shown that resetting of Rb-Sr isotopic systems did not occur even during deformation at amphibolite facies conditions (e.g., Black et al., 1979; Welin et al., 1980). For the purpose of contrasting crustal domains across an orogen, the use of Rb-Sr dates, which sometimes may underestimate crystallization ages, should not significantly change the relative pattern of initial ε_{Nd} values, and will not affect Nd model ages, because the model ages are calculated using $^{147}Sm/^{144}Nd$ and present-day $^{143}Nd/^{144}Nd$ ratios.

Initial Nd and Sr isotopic compositions for western Blue Ridge and some Inner Piedmont plutonic rocks indicate recycled Middle Proterozoic crust as the principal source from which the magmas originated. This is based on the presence of low initial $^{143}Nd/^{144}Nd$ and high initial $^{87}Sr/^{86}Sr$ ratios and Middle Proterozoic T_{DM} ages (Table 1 and Fig. 3). These data (Fig. 4) are consistent with a source region consisting of mixtures of depleted mantle and 1.8 to 1.6 Ga crust. The central and eastern Piedmont contain a significant volume of magmatic rocks derived from juvenile crust that retains much of its depleted mantle character. The older Late Proterozoic rocks of the central and eastern Piedmont are the most common rocks to reflect the presence of juvenile crust.

For purposes of comparison, the plutons in the central and eastern Piedmont are subdivided below into three groups based on isotopic and age criteria: Late Proterozoic–Cambrian juvenile plutons, mid-late Paleozoic plutons, and Easternmost Alleghanian plutons. The majority of granitic plutons in these three groups are characterized by initial ε_{Nd} values generally greater than –2 and initial $^{87}Sr/^{86}Sr$ ≤0.7050 (Fig. 5). These values indicate a significant contribution from a source with a time-integrated history of Rb/Sr and light REE depletion. T_{DM} ages for all groups generally range from ca. 0.9 to 0.7 Ga. The plutons have either Late Proterozoic–Cambrian or middle to late Paleozoic (Late Silurian to Early Permian) crystallization ages.

Late Proterozoic–Cambrian juvenile plutons exhibit the highest initial ε_{Nd} values (+4 to +6), lowest initial $^{87}Sr/^{86}Sr$ ratios (0.7025 to 0.7039), and oldest crystallization ages (~650 to 500 Ma) (Fig. 5). Their T_{DM} ages of ~800 to 700 Ma are only about 200 m.y. older than their crystallization ages. These plutons include the Chatham, Chapel Hill, East Farrington, Meadow Flats, Moriah-Oxford, and West Farrington plutons, located in the northeastern part of the Carolina slate belt of North Carolina, and the Raleigh gneiss, which is in the adjacent Raleigh belt (Fig. 2B). All are granitic in composition except the Meadow Flats pluton, which is dioritic-gabbroic.

Mid-late Paleozoic plutons exhibit initial ε_{Nd} values of –2 to +4 and initial $^{87}Sr/^{86}Sr$ ratios of 0.702 to 0.705, and have middle to late Paleozoic crystallization ages (Fig. 5). These plutons also have T_{DM} ages that range from ca. 1.1 to 0.7 Ga (not including the older dates for the Salisbury plutonic suite); most are between 0.9 and 0.8 Ga. Compared to Late Proterozoic–Cambrian juvenile plutons, the slightly higher initial $^{87}Sr/^{86}Sr$ ratios and lower initial ε_{Nd} values for mid-late Paleozoic plutons indicate a source containing a more evolved crustal component. Two Late Proterozoic plutons, the Great Falls granite from the Charlotte belt and the Waxhaw granite from the Carolina slate belt, plot within the mid-late Paleozoic plutons field. These granites exhibit low initial $^{87}Sr/^{86}Sr$ ratios similar to Late Proterozoic–Cambrian juvenile granites, but exhibit lower initial ε_{Nd} values of +2.0 and +1.1, respectively.

Easternmost Alleghanian plutons occur in a contiguous area which includes the Eastern slate belt, Raleigh belt, Kiokee belt, and eastern part of the Carolina slate belt (Fig. 2, B and C). They have crystallization ages of ca. 300 Ma (Fig. 6, Table 1), and are characterized by initial $^{87}Sr/^{86}Sr$ ratios generally >0.705 and initial ε_{Nd} values between –7 and +3 (Fig. 5), plus relatively old T_{DM} ages (1.4 to 1.0 Ga). Isotopic data for this group reflect a source(s) with a significant contribution of recycled older crust.

Felsic volcanic rocks from the eastern Piedmont (Fig. 5) have initial ε_{Nd} values between –0.5 and +3, which are comparable to those exhibited by mid-late Paleozoic plutons (–2 to +6). The volcanic rocks, however, have initial $^{87}Sr/^{86}Sr$ ratios of 0.704 to 0.718, values significantly higher than those shown by mid-late Paleozoic plutons (0.702 to 0.705). Apparent crystallization ages for these volcanic rocks generally decrease as the initial $^{87}Sr/^{86}Sr$ ratios increase (Table 1). Large dispersion in initial $^{87}Sr/^{86}Sr$ ratios at relatively constant initial ε_{Nd} is interpreted to reflect modified Sr isotopic compositions, possibly the result of interaction with seawater (e.g., Jacobsen and Wasserburg, 1979).

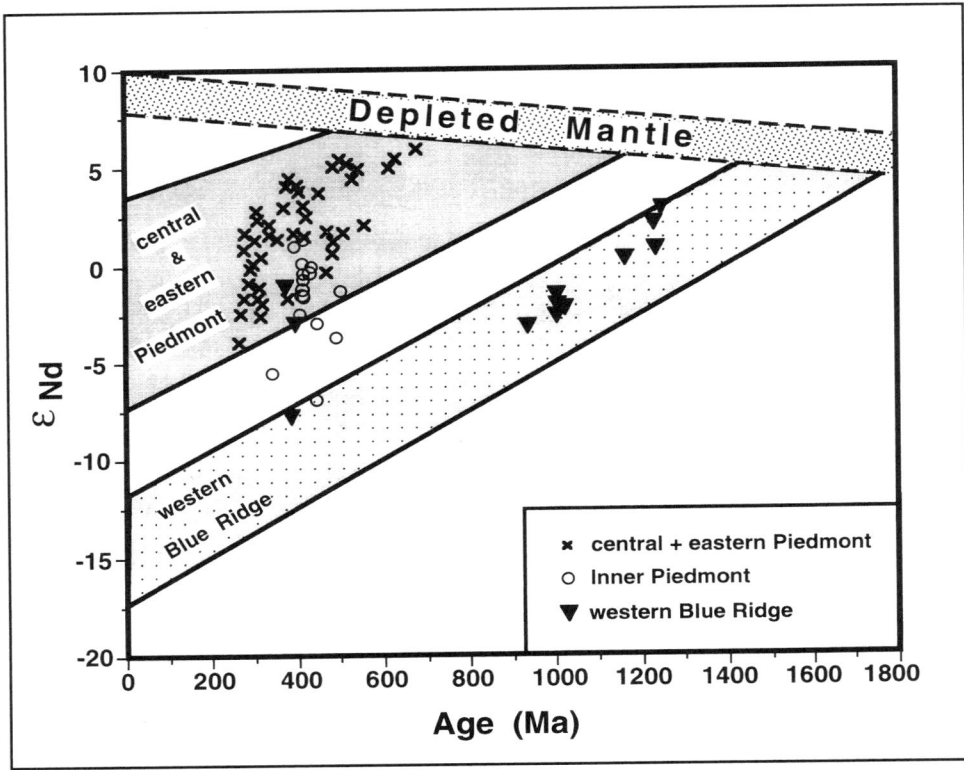

Figure 4. Nd evolution diagram showing crystallization age (Ma) versus initial ε_{Nd} for North and South Carolina Blue Ridge, Inner Piedmont, and central and eastern Piedmont samples analyzed in this study (Table 1). Fields for the western Blue Ridge and central and eastern Piedmont represent the range of essentially parallel Nd evolution lines (lines not shown) for samples listed in Table 1. The western Blue Ridge field is defined by North and South Carolina basement gneisses with ages ≥1.0 Ga. Inner Piedmont data points are mainly intermediate between those for central and eastern Piedmont samples and those for western Blue Ridge samples.

Central and eastern Piedmont granitic samples from the Buies Creek, Lemon Springs, Southmont, and Castalia plutons exhibit relatively high initial $^{87}Sr/^{86}Sr$ ratios with a considerable range from 0.706 to 0.715, but a narrow range in initial ε_{Nd} of 2.4 to 4.9, similar to other plutons from the central and eastern Piedmont. These values may also reflect preferential mobility of Sr.

A comparison of samples from central and eastern Piedmont granites (i.e., subgroups Late Proterozoic–Cambrian juvenile plutons, mid-late Paleozoic plutons, and Easternmost Alleghanian plutons) with Inner Piedmont samples indicates that the latter generally have overlapping to lower initial ε_{Nd} values and higher initial $^{87}Sr/^{86}Sr$ ratios than do the samples of the Late Proterozoic–Cambrian juvenile plutons and the mid-late Paleozoic plutons (Fig. 5). These values suggest the presence of a significant evolved crustal component in some Inner Piedmont samples (Fig. 5). The Cherryville granite is an example that apparently records a significant amount of an older, evolved component based on the highest initial $^{87}Sr/^{86}Sr$ ratio (0.7121) and low initial ε_{Nd} value (–5.6). Inner Piedmont samples have T_{DM} model ages similar to easternmost Alleghanian plutons, but the Inner Piedmont samples have significantly older crystallization ages (Fig. 6, Table 1).

DISCUSSION

Quartzofeldspathic gneisses of the western Blue Ridge with crystallization ages greater than 1.0 Ga have T_{DM} model ages of 1.8 to 1.4 Ga (Table 1). These T_{DM} ages are broadly similar to model ages obtained from Precambrian exposures of Laurentia elsewhere within North America: e.g., Texas (Patchett and Ruiz, 1989), Virginia (Pettingill et al., 1984), New York (Daly and McLelland, 1991; McLelland et al., 1993), and Ontario (Dickin and McNutt, 1990). Rocks having age and isotopic characteristics similar to those of the Grenville province (sensu strictu) appear to be present along much of the eastern and southern margin of Laurentia.

A histogram of T_{DM} ages for western Blue Ridge basement gneisses (Fig. 3) exhibits a frequency maximum between 1.7 and 1.1 Ga. Characteristic crystallization ages of plutonic igneous activity in the Grenville province are centered about 1.6, 1.4, and 1.1 Ga (Emslie and Hunt, 1989). Existing U-Pb zircon dates for the Blue Ridge indicate the presence of rocks with pre-Grenville orogenic ages of 1.9 to 1.3 Ga (e.g., Davis, 1974; Herz and Force, 1984; Sinha and Bartholomew, 1984; Su et al., 1994). Middle

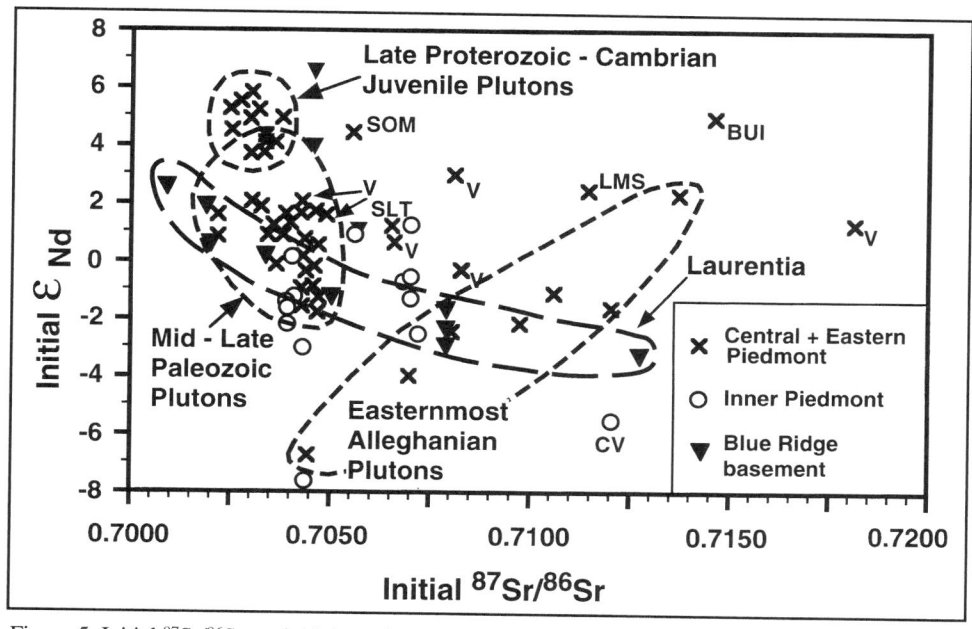

Figure 5. Initial $^{87}Sr/^{86}Sr$ vs. initial ε_{Nd} for western Blue Ridge, Inner Piedmont, and central and eastern Piedmont samples analyzed in this study (Table 1). Sample subgroups or fields are defined in the text, and they include the following numbers of samples: Laurentia (western Blue Ridge) field, 12 samples; Late Proterozoic-Cambrian juvenile plutons field, 8 samples; mid-late Paleozoic plutons field, 30 samples; easternmost Alleghanian plutons field, 7 samples. Many Inner Piedmont samples plot in the area of the Laurentian field, but others differ with respect to either Nd and/or Sr isotopic compositions. Labeled samples are either discussed in the text (i.e., CV, Cherryville granite; SOM, Southmont granite), and/or they do not plot with other samples of their sub-group (i.e., BUI, Buies Creek granitic gneiss; LMS, Lemon Springs granite). Shelton granitic gneiss (SLT) is the only sample we analyzed from the Milton belt; it may correlate with Inner Piedmont samples. V represents felsic volcanic rocks.

Proterozic depleted mantle is estimated to have had ε_{Nd} values of ~+5 at 1.6 Ga, indicating that western Blue Ridge rocks that crystallized at 1.3 to 1.2 Ga (initial ε_{Nd} values of 0 to +3; T_{DM} ages of 1.6 to 1.4 Ga) could not have been derived exclusively by melting of juvenile depleted mantle. Nd isotopic data for these rocks suggest that they could have been derived from a mixture of predominantly older crustal material and a juvenile depleted component ($\leq$30%). We note that the Blue Ridge exhibits a few T_{DM} ages between 2.0 and 1.7 Ga, ages that are also recognized within the Grenville province (Dickin and McNutt, 1990), possibly reflecting the influence of an older Early Proterozoic (2.5 to 1.6 Ga; Plumb, 1990) component in the Blue Ridge.

Grenville and post-Grenville orogenic granites with crystallization ages of ca. 1.1 to 0.9 Ga in the western Blue Ridge have relatively low initial ε_{Nd} values (–1.5 to –3.5) and high initial $^{87}Sr/^{86}Sr$ (0.708 to 0.713). Fullagar and Odom (1973) suggested, on the basis of crystallization ages and Sr isotopic data, that older Blue Ridge crust was recycled during the Grenville orogeny, with little or no addition of new material at that time. Our Nd data support this suggestion that the Grenville-age rocks were derived mainly by reworking of older Laurentian crust (Fig. 4). Felsic magmatism intruding the Blue Ridge during the period 0.8 to 0.7 Ga exhibits initial ε_{Nd} values of ~ –3 to 0 and also appears to be derived mainly from Middle Proterozoic crust (Fetter and

Goldberg, 1995; Su and Fullagar, 1995). In contrast, mafic magmatism of Late Proterozoic age (ε_{Nd} values of ~0 to +4) shows a greater quantity of a depleted mantle source component (Goldberg et al., 1994b; Fetter and Goldberg, 1995). Figure 5 shows a negative trend (see field labeled Laurentia) for initial ε_{Nd} values versus initial $^{87}Sr/^{86}Sr$ ratios for western Blue Ridge gneisses with crystallization ages of ~1.3 to 1.0 Ga. The most isotopically enriched samples exhibit the youngest crystallization ages, reflecting either time-dependent isotopic evolution of Laurentian basement, or variable contributions of evolved and depleted source components.

Nd isotopic data for five western Blue Ridge samples from Virginia (Pettingill et al., 1984) are generally similar to those of this study, although the Virginia Blue Ridge data extend to slightly higher initial ε_{Nd} values (T_{DM} ages between 1.9 and 1.3 Ga). There appear to be observable differences in Pb and Nd isotopic compositions in different segments of the Blue Ridge (Parks et al., 1992; Sinha, 1994). These isotopic variations in Laurentian crust and the limited amount of Nd data for much of the southern Appalachians may simply limit our ability to recognize Laurentian crust outside of the Blue Ridge province.

Although Blue Ridge crust has isotopic affinities to other segments of Laurentia, typical western Blue Ridge crust is not clearly recognized in lithotectonic belts of the Piedmont. In these

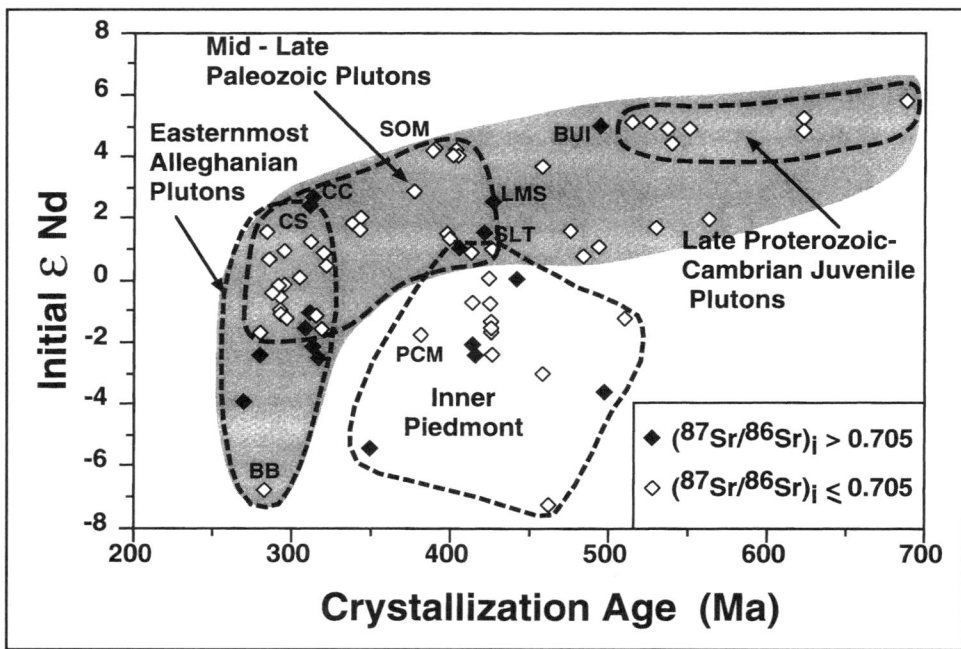

Figure 6. Crystallization age versus initial ε_{Nd} for Piedmont plutons only (Inner Piedmont, central and eastern Piedmont). This figure is an enlargement of a portion of Figure 4, with the addition of sample subgroups. All central and eastern Piedmont samples plot within the shaded area except the Pacolet monzogranite (PCM); this pluton straddles the Inner Piedmont–Kings Mountain belt boundary and plots with Inner Piedmont samples. The central and eastern Piedmont subgroups (Late Proterozoic–Cambrian juvenile plutons; mid-late Paleozoic plutons; easternmost Alleghanian plutons) are defined in the text. Symbols are used to distinguish samples with initial $^{87}Sr/^{86}Sr > 0.7050$, and initial $^{87}Sr/^{86}Sr \le$ 0.7050. Fields and pluton symbols are the same as in Figure 5. BB represents the Batesburg lineated gneiss; CS, Castalia granite; CC, Clouds Creek granite.

regions, Laurentian crust has either been modified by influx of Paleozoic depleted mantle components, or the belts have originated outside of Laurentia and Laurentian crust is absent. When Nd data for the central and eastern Piedmont are compared to the Blue Ridge (Fig. 4), it is shown that central and eastern Piedmont rocks follow different evolutionary paths and cannot be produced by simple melting of Blue Ridge gneisses. Melts produced from typical western Blue Ridge basement gneiss, for example at 300 Ma, would have ε_{Nd} values of about –12, significantly lower than obtained for any Piedmont pluton of that age.

The oldest T_{DM} ages for Inner Piedmont samples (1.8 to 1.6 Ga) correspond to those for Blue Ridge samples, but there are no Inner Piedmont rocks with T_{DM} ages of 1.6 to 1.3 Ga. In general, Inner Piedmont T_{DM} ages are younger than those for samples from the western Blue Ridge, and older than those for samples from the central and eastern Piedmont (Fig. 3). This intermediate relationship for Inner Piedmont samples is also shown in Figure 4. Nd isotopic evolution lines (not shown) define distinct fields for western Blue Ridge and for central plus eastern Piedmont samples; the Inner Piedmont samples overlap both fields. The Inner Piedmont rocks thus cannot be derived exclusively from Blue Ridge basement, although the Inner Piedmont contains comparable 1.8 to 1.6 Ga and Grenville-age source components.

U-Pb data now provide evidence of Middle Proterozoic crust in the Inner Piedmont of South Carolina. U-Pb analyses of zircon from two granitoid gneisses of the Table Rock plutonic suite indicate the presence of magmatic zircon with a minimum crystallization age of ca. 400 Ma and older zircon components of ca. 1.1 and 1.0 Ga (Fullagar and Su, 1995). The older dates may represent the ages of the granitic protoliths. Other isotopic studies have suggested the presence of Middle Proterozoic crust in the Inner Piedmont: initial $^{87}Sr/^{86}Sr$ ratios as high as 0.712 for Inner Piedmont rocks indicated the possibility of older crust in this area (Kish, 1977, 1983). Wenner (1981) concluded, on the basis of $\delta^{18}O$ values and initial $^{87}Sr/^{86}Sr$ ratios (e.g., Fullagar, 1971; Fullagar and Butler, 1979), that an old crustal component was present in some areas of the Inner Piedmont, mainly in Georgia and South Carolina. Stuckless et al. (1986) obtained a whole-rock Pb-Pb secondary isochron date of ca. 1.7 Ga on the Elberton granite in the Inner Piedmont of Georgia, and interpreted the date as the age of the granite protolith. On the basis of a limited number of Pb isotopic analyses, LeHuray (1986) suggested that Inner Piedmont rocks were derived in part from old continental crust; plutons in the adjacent Kings Mountain belt, plus the Charlotte belt and Carolina slate belt, had Pb values very similar to one another, but distinctly different from Inner Piedmont plutons. These Pb isotopic data are consistent with the view that the Inner Piedmont–Kings Mountain belt boundary separates two terranes (e.g., Hatcher and Zietz, 1980). Based in part on Sm-Nd isotopic analyses of four Inner Piedmont samples from Georgia, Samson et al. (1995a) suggested that at least the southern part of the Inner Piedmont is composed of more evolved crust than are belts to the east.

Nd and Sr isotopic data for most central and eastern Piedmont plutons indicate either the absence of an evolved crustal source older than 1.0 Ga, or only minimal contribution of such crust to the formation of these Phanerozoic plutons. This suggestion is not new; the low initial $^{87}Sr/^{86}Sr$ ratios (0.702 to 0.705) of most central and eastern Piedmont plutons have been interpreted as indicating the absence of 1.0 Ga or older evolved crust in this region (e.g., Fullagar, 1971; Fullagar and Butler, 1979).

Plutons with similar crystallization ages from the Charlotte belt of the central Piedmont and the Carolina slate belt of the eastern Piedmont generally have similar Nd isotopic values, and there are recognized similarities in Sr isotopic compositions and field relationships. Charlotte belt samples have a somewhat narrower range of T_{DM} ages (0.9 to 0.7 Ga) than Carolina slate belt samples (1.2 to 0.7 Ga). Results of other recent isotopic studies in the central and eastern Piedmont (Faggart and Basu, 1987; Samson and Speer, 1993; Kozuch et al., 1993; Wortman et al., 1994; Coler et al., 1994; Samson et al., 1995a, 1995b) are consistent with our results. Existing isotopic data suggest that much of the central and eastern Piedmont can be grouped as a single Carolina terrane (Secor et al., 1983).

Late Proterozoic–Cambrian juvenile plutons, mainly in the northern part of the Carolina slate belt in the North Carolina eastern Piedmont, have isotopic characteristics consistent with a juvenile, depleted mantle source (Fig. 5). Samson et al. (1995b) reported similar initial ε_{Nd} values and crystallization ages for a different set of plutons, plus volcanic and metamorphic rocks from the same general area. Initial ε_{Nd} values from both datasets indicate that these rocks could not contain a significant amount of old continental crust. Our data support the suggestion by Samson et al. (1995b) that this terrane may have formed on oceanic crust and that it evolved in a juvenile intraoceanic arc environment for an extended period. If the magmas intruded a craton, they did so without significant crustal assimilation. We suggest that the Late Proterozoic–Cambrian juvenile plutons (this study) and related rocks (e.g., Samson et al., 1995b) compose part of the earliest juvenile crust in the Carolina terrane.

Central and eastern Piedmont granites show a relationship of decreasing initial ε_{Nd} with decreasing crystallization age (Fig. 6). The highest initial ε_{Nd} values are correlated with the lowest initial $^{87}Sr/^{86}Sr$ ratios (Table 1; Fig. 5). With decreasing age, Piedmont plutons generally exhibit higher initial $^{87}Sr/^{86}Sr$ ratios (Fig. 6). These relationships suggest that the middle and late Paleozoic plutons could have formed by melting of juvenile depleted crust (isotopically similar to the Late Proterozoic–Cambrian juvenile plutons) with small but variable contributions from a more evolved, perhaps Grenville-age source. Samson et al. (1995a) recognized a similar petrogenesis. The steepest decrease in initial ε_{Nd} versus

crystallization age occurs at about 300 Ma (Fig. 6), as indicated by some plutons with initial ε_{Nd} values as low as –7 and initial $^{87}Sr/^{86}Sr$ ratios as high as 0.714 (easternmost Alleghanian plutons of Figs. 5 and 6). These isotopic signatures may reflect significant influx of evolved crustal component during Alleghanian overthrusting resulting from collision of North America and Gondwana.

Seismic reflection profiles have also been used to infer the presence of Grenville basement beneath the eastern Piedmont (Cook et al., 1983). Grenville $^{207}Pb/^{206}Pb$ ages from detrital zircon are recognized in the Falls Lake melange (Goldberg, 1994), which occurs structurally between juvenile eastern Piedmont terranes. The Falls Lake melange appears to contain detritus from a continental fragment affected by the Grenville orogeny, and may represent the source of the isotopically evolved component in some Piedmont plutons.

CONCLUSIONS

1. Low initial $^{143}Nd/^{144}Nd$ ratios, high initial $^{87}Sr/^{86}Sr$ ratios, and Middle Proterozoic T_{DM} ages for western Blue Ridge plutonic rocks indicate recycled Laurentian Middle Proterozoic crust as the principal source from which the rocks originated. Some Inner Piedmont plutons could have formed from the same source.

2. Rocks of the western Blue Ridge exhibit a range in T_{DM} ages from 1.8 to 1.4 Ga. No evidence of a juvenile Late Proterozoic source component has been discovered in the western Blue Ridge, but a juvenile Late Proterozoic (non-Laurentian? Avalonian?) source component appears to be present in the eastern Blue Ridge. On the basis of Nd isotopic data, the eastern Blue Ridge does not appear to have been amalgamated to Laurentia (western Blue Ridge) prior to the Late Proterozoic.

3. Inner Piedmont plutons have T_{DM} ages ranging from 1.8 to 1.6, and from 1.3 to 0.8 Ga. Both the Inner Piedmont and Blue Ridge exhibit T_{DM} ages of 1.8 to 1.6 Ga, and 1.3 to 1.1 Ga. On the basis of available data, Inner Piedmont rocks with T_{DM} ages between 1.6 and 1.3 Ga are absent, although these ages are common in the western Blue Ridge and in the Grenville province; T_{DM} ages of late Pan-African–Avalonian age are also absent in the Inner Piedmont. Inner Piedmont samples are isotopically intermediate between samples from the western Blue Ridge and more easterly Piedmont belts. This may indicate variable contributions of source components from Laurentian evolved crust and central and eastern Piedmont (Carolina terrane) volcanogenic materials.

4. The central and eastern Piedmont is characterized by the predominance of Late Proterozoic T_{DM} ages and the presence of a minor source component older than 1.0 Ga. The older Late Proterozoic magmatic rocks of the central and eastern Piedmont are derived largely from a juvenile source with an isotopic composition similar to or approaching that of depleted mantle.

5. Central and eastern Piedmont granites show a relationship of decreasing initial ε_{Nd} with decreasing crystallization age; initial $^{87}Sr/^{86}Sr$ ratios commonly increase with decreasing crystallization age. These relationships suggest an increasing contribution of an

older enriched crustal component to the source of the granites as a function of time.

6. All lithotectonic belts east of the western Blue Ridge appear to contain one or more crustal components derived from a non-Laurentian terrane.

ACKNOWLEDGMENTS

We thank H. Bauert and Q. Su for preparation of some of the figures, and J. Cargill and Q. Su for assistance with sample preparation and analysis. Reviews by R. Ayuso and C. Frost significantly improved the manuscript.

REFERENCES CITED

Arndt, N. T., and Goldstein, S. L., 1987, Use and abuse of crust-formation ages: Geology, v. 15, p. 893–895.

Bennett, V. C., and DePaolo, D. J., 1987, Proterozoic crustal history of the western United States as determined by neodymium isotopic mapping: Geological Society of America Bulletin, v. 99, p. 674–685.

Black, L. P., Bell, T. H., Rubenach, M. J., and Withnall, I. W., 1979, Geochronology of discrete structural-metamorphic events in a multiply deformed Precambrian terrain: Tectonophysics, v. 54, p. 103–137.

Black, R., and Liegeois, J. P., 1993, Cratons, mobile belts, alkaline rocks and continental lithospheric mantle: The Pan-African testimony: Geological Society of London Journal, v. 150, p. 89–98.

Coler, D. G., Samson, S. D., and Speer, J. A., 1994, Detailed Sm-Nd isotopic study of the Rolesville batholith, NC: Evidence for variable source compositions of an Alleghanian granite: Geological Society of America Abstracts with Programs, v. 26, no. 4, p. 8.

Cook, F. A., Brown, L. D., Kaufman, S., and Oliver, J. E., 1983, The COCORP seismic reflection traverse across the southern Appalachians: American Association of Petroleum Geologists Studies in Geology no. 14, 61 p.

Daly, J. S., and McLelland, J., 1991, Juvenile Middle Proterozoic crust in the Adirondack highlands, Grenville Province, northeastern North America: Geology, v. 19, p. 119–122.

Dalziel, I. W. D., Dalla Salda, L. H., and Gahagan, L. M., 1994, Paleozoic Laurentia-Gondwana interaction and the origin of the Appalachian-Andean mountain system: Geological Society of America Bulletin, v. 106, p. 243–252.

Davis, G. L., Tilton, G. R., and Wetherill, G. W., 1962, Mineral ages from the Appalachian province in North Carolina and Tennessee: Journal of Geophysical Research, v. 67, p. 1987–1996.

Davis, R. G., 1974, Pre-Grenville ages of basement rocks in central Virginia: A model for the interpretation of zircon ages [M. S. thesis]: Blacksburg, Virginia Polytechnic Institute and State University, 46 p.

DePaolo, D. J., 1981, Nd isotopes in the Colorado Front Range and implications for crust formation and mantle evolution in the Proterozoic: Nature, v. 291, p. 193–196.

Dickin, A. P., and McNutt, R. H., 1990, Nd model-age mapping of Grenville lithotectonic domains: Mid-Proterozoic crustal evolution in Ontario, in Gower, C. F., Rivers, T., and Ryan, B., eds., Mid-Proterozoic Laurentia-Baltica: Geological Association of Canada Special Paper 38, p. 79–94.

Emslie, R. F., and Hunt, P. A., 1989, The Grenville event: Magmatism and high grade metamorphism, in Current research, Part C: Geological Survey of Canada Paper 89–1C, p. 11–17.

Faggart, B. E., Jr., and Basu, A. R., 1987, Evolution of the Kings Mountain belt of the Carolinas: Implications from Sm-Nd systematics: Geological Society of America Abstracts with Programs, v. 19, p. 658.

Fetter, A. H., and Goldberg, S. A., 1995, Age and geochemical characteristics of bimodal magmatism in the Neoproterozoic Grandfather Mountain Rift basin: Journal of Geology, v. 103, p. 311–323.

Fullagar, P. D., 1971, Age and origin of plutonic intrusions in the Piedmont of the southeastern Appalachians: Geological Society of America Bulletin, v. 82, p. 2845–2862.

Fullagar, P. D., 1983, Post-metamorphic Siluro-Devonian granitic plutons in the Charlotte belt of South Carolina: Geological Society of America Abstracts with Programs, v. 15, p. 64.

Fullagar, P. D., and Butler, J. R., 1979, 325 to 265 m. y.-old granitic plutons in the Piedmont of the southeastern Appalachians: American Journal of Science, v. 279, p. 161–185.

Fullagar, P. D., and Odom, A. L., 1973, Geochronology of Precambrian gneisses in the Blue Ridge province of northwestern North Carolina and adjacent parts of Virginia and Tennessee: Geological Society of America Bulletin, v. 84, p. 3065–3080.

Fullagar, P. D., and Spruill, R. K., 1989, Geochronological studies of the Rocky Mount igneous complex, Eastern slate belt of North Carolina: Geological Society of America Abstracts with Programs, v. 21, no. 3, p. 16.

Fullagar, P. D., and Su, Q., 1995, Evidence for Grenville-age or older crust in the southern Appalachian Inner Piedmont of North and South Carolina: Geological Society of America Abstracts with Programs, v. 27, no. 6, p. 397.

Fullagar, P. D., Goldberg, S. A., and Butler, J. R., 1987, Rb-Sr ages of felsic metavolcanic rocks from the Carolina and Eastern slate belts of North and South Carolina: Geological Society of America Abstracts with Programs, v. 19, p. 84.

Goldberg, S. A., 1994, U-Pb geochronology of volcanogenic terranes of the eastern North Carolina Piedmont: preliminary results, in Stoddard, E. F., and Blake, D. E., eds., Geology and field trip guide, western flank of the Raleigh metamorphic belt, North Carolina: Raleigh, Carolina Geological Society and North Carolina Geological Survey, p. 13–18.

Goldberg, S. A., and Dallmeyer, R. D., 1996, Chronology of Paleozoic metamorphism and deformation in the Blue Ridge thrust complex, North Carolina and Tennessee: American Journal of Science (in press).

Goldberg, S. A., Adams, M. G., Trupe, C. H., Stewart, K. G., and Butler, J. R., 1994a, Sm-Nd isotopic constraints on a Blue Ridge eclogite, northwestern North Carolina: Geological Society of America Abstracts with Programs, v. 26, no. 7, p. 196.

Goldberg, S. A., Su, Q., and Fetter, A. H., 1994b, Isotopic constraints on the source and petrogenesis of Late Proterozoic plutonic and volcanic rocks of the Blue Ridge: Geological Society of America Abstracts with Programs, v. 26, no. 4, p. 16.

Hanson, G. N., Grünenfelder, M., and Soptrayanova, G., 1969, The geochronology of a recrystallized tectonite in Switzerland—The Rofna gneiss: Earth and Planetary Science Letters, v. 5, p. 413–422.

Harper, S. B., and Fullagar, P. D., 1981, Rb-Sr ages of granitic gneisses of the Inner Piedmont belt of northwestern North Carolina and southwestern South Carolina: Geological Society of America Bulletin, v. 92, p. 864–872.

Hatcher, R. D., Jr., 1987, Tectonics of the central and southern Appalachian internides: Annual Review of Earth and Planetary Sciences, v. 15, p. 337–362.

Hatcher, R. D., Jr., and Zietz, I., 1980, Tectonic implications of regional aeromagnetic and gravity data from the southern Appalachians, in Wones, D. R., ed., Proceedings, The Caledonides in the USA, IGCP Project 27—Calidonide Orogen, 1979 Meeting: Blacksburg, Virginia Polytechnic Institute and State University, Department of Geological Sciences Memoir 2, p. 235–244.

Herz, N., and Force, E. R., 1984, Rock suites in Grenvillian terranes of the Roseland district, Virginia, part 1: Lithologic relations, in Bartholomew, M. J., et al., eds., The Grenville event in the Appalachians and related topics: Geological Society of America Special Paper 194, p. 187–200.

Hills, F. A., and Butler, J. R., 1969, Rubidium-strontium dates for some rhyolites from the Carolina slate belt of the North Carolina Piedmont, in Abstracts for 1968: Geological Society of America Special Paper 121, p. 445.

Horton, J. W., Jr., and Zullo, V. A., eds., 1991, The geology of the Carolinas: Carolina Geological Society 50th anniversary volume: Knoxville, University of Tennessee Press, 406 p.

Jacobsen, S. B., and Wasserburg, G. J., 1979, Nd and Sr isotopic study of the Bay of Islands ophiolite complex and the evolution of the source of midocean ridge basalts: Journal of Geophysical Research, v. 84, p. 7429–7445.

Kish, S. A., 1977, Geochronology of plutonic activity in the Inner Piedmont and Kings Mountain belt of North Carolina, *in* Burt, E. R., ed., Field guides for Geological Society of America, Southeastern Section Meeting, Winston-Salem, North Carolina: Raleigh, North Carolina Geological Survey, p. 144–149.

Kish, S. A., 1983, A geochronological study of deformation and metamorphism in the Blue Ridge and Piedmont of the Carolinas [Ph.D. thesis]: Chapel Hill, University of North Carolina, 220 p.

Kozuch, M., Mueller, P., Heatherington, A., Wooden, J., Koeppen, R., and Klein, T., 1993, Isotopic evidence in the Carolina slate and Charlotte belts (North Carolina) for reactivated Grenvillian and older sources: Geological Society of America Abstracts with Programs, v. 25, no. 6, p. A-35.

LeHuray, A. P., 1986, Isotopic evidence for a tectonic boundary between the Kings Mountain and Inner Piedmont belts, southern Appalachians: Geology, v. 14, p. 784–787.

McLelland, J. M., Daly, J. S., and Chiarenzelli, J., 1993, Sm-Nd isotopic and U-Pb evidence of juvenile crust in the Adirondack Lowlands and implications for the evolution of the Adirondack Mountains: Journal of Geology, v. 101, p. 97–105.

McSween, H. Y., Jr., Speer, J. A., and Fullagar, P. D., 1991, Plutonic rocks, *in* Horton, J. W., Jr., and Zullo, V. A., eds., The geology of the Carolinas: Carolina Geological Society 50th anniversary volume: Knoxville, University of Tennessee Press, p. 109–126.

Moore, J. M., 1986, Introduction: The "Grenville problem" then and now, *in* Moore, J. M., Davidson, A., and Baer, A. J., eds., The Grenville Province: Geological Association of Canada Special Paper 31, p. 1–11.

Odom, A. L., and Fullagar, P. D., 1973, Geochronologic and tectonic relationships between the Inner Piedmont, Brevard Zone, and Blue Ridge belts, North Carolina: American Journal of Science, v. 273-A, p. 133–149.

Page, R. W., and Bell, T. H., 1986, Isotopic and structural responses of granite to successive deformation and metamorphism: Journal of Geology, v. 94, p. 365–379.

Parks, J. E., Jenks, P. J., and Sinha, A. K., 1992, Crustal evolution of Grenville terranes in the central and southern Appalachians: The Pb isotope perspective for Grenville tectonics: Geological Society of America Abstracts with Programs, v. 24, no. 7, p. A-187.

Patchett, P. J., and Ruiz, J., 1989, Nd isotopes and the origin of Grenville-age rocks in Texas: Implications for Proterozoic evolution of the United States mid-continent region: Journal of Geology, v. 97, p. 685–695.

Pettingill, H. S., Sinha, A. K., and Tatsumoto, M., 1984, Age and origin of anorthosites, charnockites, and granulites in the Central Virginia Blue Ridge: Nd and Sr isotopic evidence: Contributions to Mineralogy and Petrology, v. 85, p. 279–291.

Plumb, K. A., 1990, New Precambrian time scale: Episodes, v. 14, p. 139–140.

Rogers, J. J. W., Unrug, R., and Sultan, M., 1994, Tectonic assembly of Gondwana: Journal of Geodynamics, v. 19, p. 1–34.

Samson, S. D., and Speer, J. A., 1993, Nd isotopic geochemistry of Alleghanian granitoid plutons in the southern Appalachians: Eos (Transactions, American Geophysical Union), v. 74, p. 335.

Samson, S. D., Patchett, P. J., McLelland, W. C., and Gehrels, G. E., 1991, Nd isotopic characterization of metamorphic rocks in the Coast Mountains, Alaska and Canadian Cordillera; ancient crust bounded by juvenile terranes: Tectonics, v. 10, p. 770–780.

Samson, S. D., Coler, D. G., and Speer, J. A., 1995a, Geochemical and Nd-Sr-Pb isotopic composition of Alleghanian granites of the southern Appalachians: Origin, tectonic setting, and source characterization: Earth and Plan-

etary Science Letters, v. 134, p. 359–376.

Samson, S. D., Hibbard, J. P., Wortman, G. L., 1995b, Nd isotopic evidence for juvenile crust in the Carolina terrane, southern Appalachians: Contributions to Mineralogy and Petrology, v. 121, p. 171–184.

Schleicher, H., Lippolt, H. J., and Raczek, I., 1983, Rb-Sr systematics of Permian volcanites in the Schwarzwald (SW-Germany): Contributions to Mineralogy and Petrology, v. 84, p. 281–291.

Secor, D. T., Jr., Samson, S. L., Snoke, A. W., and Paler, A. R., 1983, Confirmation of the Carolina slate belt as an exotic terrane: Science, v. 221, p. 649–651.

Secor, D. T., Jr., Murray, D. P., and Glover, L., III, 1989, Geology of the Avalonian rocks, *in* Hatcher, R. D., Jr., Viele, G. W., and Thomas, W. A., eds., The Appalachian-Ouachita orogen in the United States: Boulder, Colorado, Geological Society of America, The geology of North America, v. F-2, p. 57–85.

Sinha, A. K., 1994, Magmatic axes, crustal reservoirs and terranes: Geological Society of America Abstracts with Programs, v. 26, p. 62.

Sinha, A. K., and Bartholomew, M. J., 1984, Evolution of the Grenville terrane in the central Virginia Appalachians, *in* Bartholomew, M. J., et al., eds., The Grenville event in the Appalachians and related topics: Geological Society of America Special Paper 194, p. 175–186.

Sinha, A. K., Hund, E. A., and Hogan, J. P., 1989, Paleozoic accretionary history of the North American plate margin (central and southern Appalachians): Constraints from the age, origin, and distributions of granitic rocks, *in* Hillhouse, H. W., ed., Deep structure and post kinematics of accreted terranes: American Geophysical Union Geophysical Monograph 50, and International Union of Geodesy and Geophysics Volume 5, p. 219–238.

Stuckless, J. S., Wenner, D. B., and Nkomo, L. T., 1986, Lead-isotope evidence for a pre-Grenville crust beneath the Piedmont of Georgia, *in* Peterman, Z. E., ed., Shorter contributions to isotope research: U.S. Geological Survey Bulletin 1622, p. 181–200.

Su, Q., and Fullagar, P. D., 1995, Rb-Sr and Sm-Nd isotopic systematics during greenschist facies metamorphism and deformation: Examples from the southern Appalachian Blue Ridge: Journal of Geology, v. 103, p. 423–436.

Su, Q., Goldberg, S. A., and Fullagar, P. D., 1994, Precise U-Pb ages of Late Proterozoic plutons in the southern Appalachian Blue Ridge and their implications for the initial rifting of Laurentia: Precambrian Research, v. 68, p. 81–96.

Wasserburg, G. J., Jacobsen, S. B., DePaolo, D. J., McCulloch, M. T., and Wen, T., 1981, Precise determination of Sm/Nd ratios, Sm and Nd isotopic abundances in standard solutions: Geochimica et Cosmochimica Acta, v. 45, p. 2311–2323.

Welin, E., Kähr, A. -M., and Lundegårdh, P. H., 1980, Rb-Sr isotope systematics at amphibolite facies conditions, Uppsala region, eastern Sweden: Precambrian Research, v. 13, p. 87–101.

Wenner, D. B., 1981, Oxygen isotopic compositions of the late orogenic granites in the southern Piedmont of the Appalachian Mountains, U. S. A., and their relationship to subcrustal structures and lithologies: Earth and Planetary Science Letters, v. 54, p. 186–199.

Williams, H., and Hatcher, R. D., Jr., 1983, Appalachian suspect terranes, *in* Hatcher, R. D., Jr., Williams, H., and Zietz, I., eds., Contributions to the tectonics and geophysics of mountain chains: Geological Society of America Memoir 158, p. 33–53.

Wortman, G. L., Samson, S. D., and Hibbard, J. P., 1994, Nd isotopic character of the northern Carolina slate and Milton belts, north-central North Carolina and south-central Virginia: Geological Society of America Abstracts with Programs, v. 26, p. 71.

MANUSCRIPT ACCEPTED BY THE SOCIETY JULY 2, 1996

Geological Society of America
Memoir 191
1997

Age and origin of the Austell Gneiss, western Georgia Piedmont–Blue Ridge, and its bearing on the ages of orogenic events in the southern Appalachians

Michael W. Higgins
U.S. Geological Survey, Suite 130 Peachtree Business Center, 3039 Amwiler Road, Atlanta, Georgia 30360-2824
Joseph G. Arth* and Joseph L. Wooden
U.S. Geological Survey, 345 Middlefield Road, MS 937, Menlo Park, California 94025
Thomas J. Crawford
Department of Geology, State University of West Georgia, Carrollton, Georgia 30117
Thomas W. Stern
U.S. Geological Survey, National Center, MS 981, Reston, Virginia 22092
Ralph F. Crawford
IDS, 1297 Briardale Lane, N.E., Atlanta, Georgia 30306

ABSTRACT

The Austell Gneiss is a metamorphosed biotite granite in the northeastern closure of the Austell-Frolona anticlinorium, a major northeast-trending early fold on the northwestern side of the Brevard fault zone. The anticlinorium is a structural window that exposes rocks of a parautochthonous continental-margin assemblage beneath rocks of an allochthonous oceanic assemblage. The Austell Gneiss and the Austell-Frolona anticlinorium were deformed by younger en echelon folds during dextral wrench faulting along the Brevard and Olley Creek fault zones. The Austell Gneiss has intruded the Bill Arp Formation and the Gothards Creek Gneiss, but is in fault contact with other units.

The Austell Gneiss has yielded Pb-U ages on older zircon fractions and a six point Rb-Sr whole-rock isochron that are interpreted to indicate a crystallization age as a granite of about 430 Ma (Early Silurian). A still older zircon fraction is interpreted to be inherited from ~1.1 Ga basement. Younger zircon fractions yield ages interpreted to indicate synmetamorphic deformation during strike-slip and thrust faulting throughout the Silurian and Early Devonian. The Early Silurian crystallization age of the Austell indicates (1) that the thrusting that placed the allochthonous assemblage upon the parautochthonous assemblage took place prior to Early Silurian; we postulate that it took place during the Middle Ordovician, the time of slope reversal in the Valley and Ridge province. All rocks involved in that thrusting must be older than Early Silurian. (2) The early folding that produced the Austell-Frolona anticlinorium and folded the Austell Gneiss took place during and/or after the Early Silurian. (3) Most of the dextral wrench and strike-slip faulting and wrench folding along the Brevard and Olley

*Present address: 548 Riverwood Lane, Oakland, Oregon 97462.

Higgins, M. W., Arth, J. G., Wooden, J. L., Crawford, T. J., Stern, T. W., and Crawford, R. F., 1997, Age and origin of the Austell Gneiss, western Georgia Piedmont–Blue Ridge, and its bearing on the ages of orogenic events in the southern Appalachians, *in* Sinha, A. K., Whalen, J. B., and Hogan, J. P., eds., The Nature of Magmatism in the Appalachian Orogen: Boulder, Colorado, Geological Society of America Memoir 191.

Creek fault zones in western Georgia took place after the Early Silurian, and the same timing probably applies to the Dahlonega fault zone. (4) Repetition of the Austell Gneiss in the antiformal stack in the northeastern closure of the Austell-Frolona anticlinorium took place during ductile, synmetamorphic thrust faulting accompanying dextral wrench faulting along the Brevard fault zone and concomitant strike-slip faulting along the Olley Creek fault zone during and after the Early Silurian.

INTRODUCTION

The Austell Gneiss is a metamorphosed biotite granite in the northeastern closure of the Austell-Frolona anticlinorium, a major structural window along the northwestern side of the Brevard fault zone in the Piedmont–Blue Ridge of Georgia (Fig. 1). The Austell Gneiss intruded the Bill Arp Formation and Gothards Creek Gneiss and the fault(s) that carried an assemblage of allochthonous oceanic rocks over the Bill Arp Formation, which belongs to an assemblage of parautochthonous continental-margin rocks. The Austell has been folded along with the Bill Arp and the structurally overlying allochthonous assemblage and then truncated

along its southeastern side by strike-slip faults of the Brevard fault zone, along its northeastern side by faults of the Olley Creek fault zone, and along its northwestern side by faults of the Oak Mountain fault zone. Folding that accompanied the high-angle strike-slip faulting along the Brevard fault zone is interpreted to be en echelon folding, and the Brevard fault zone is interpreted to be a wrench-fault zone bounded by high-angle faults.

The purpose of this chapter is to report and interpret radiometric age dates by both the whole-rock Rb-Sr isochron method and by the Pb-U-Th method on zircons from the Austell Gneiss. The interpreted age of ~430 Ma of the Austell Gneiss bears on the age of the parautochthonous and allochthonous assemblages;

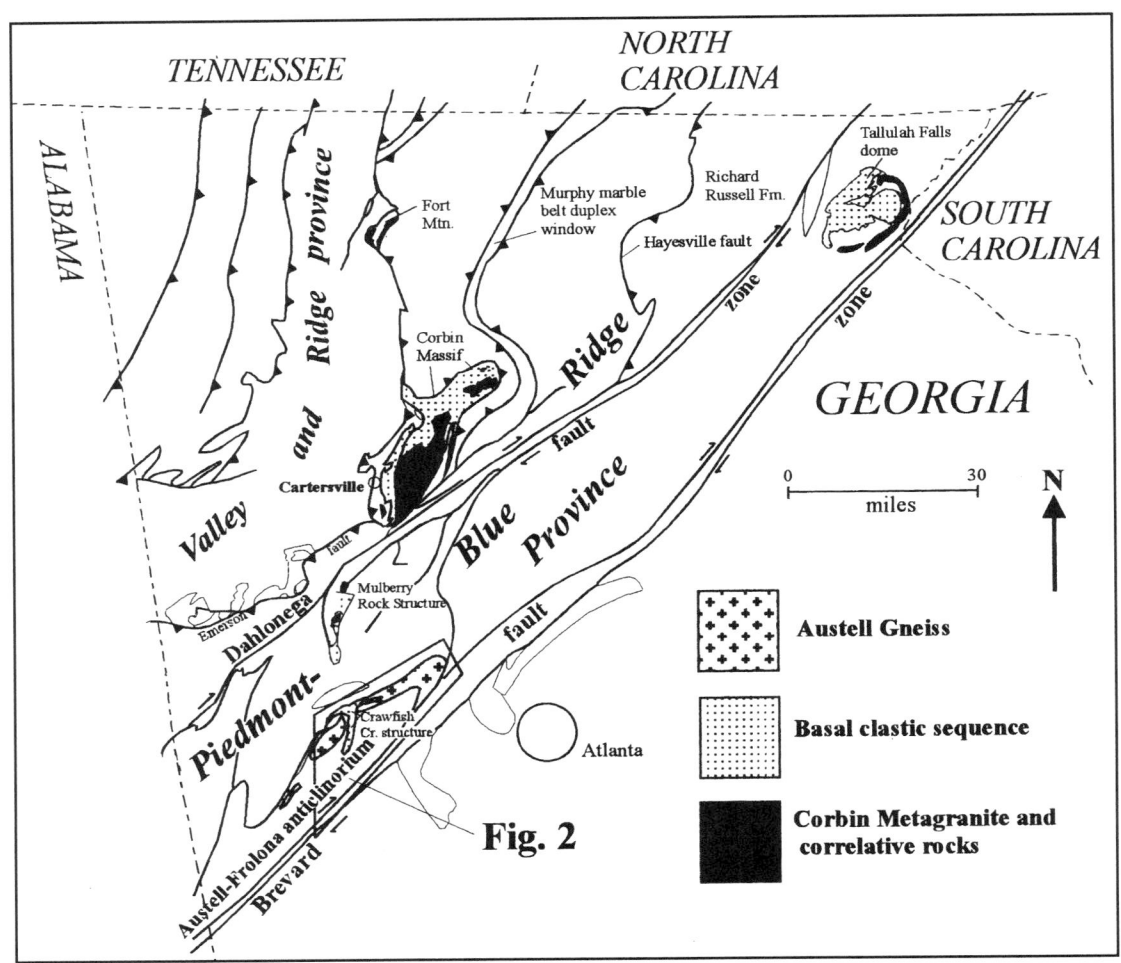

Figure 1. Generalized tectonic map of northern Georgia showing location and geologic setting of the Austell-Frolona anticlinorium, Middle(?) to Late Proterozoic Corbin Metagranite, and the Austell Gneiss (modified from Higgins et al., 1996, Fig. 8a).

the age of the faults that placed the allochthonous assemblage upon the parautochthonous assemblage; the age of the early folding that produced the Austell-Frolona anticlinorium and folded the Austell Gneiss; the age of strike-slip and wrench faulting along the Brevard, Olley Creek, and Oak Mountain fault zones, and the age of the en echelon folding that accompanied the wrench faulting.

GEOLOGIC SETTING

By the mid 1970s geologic mapping had shown that the Brevard fault zone in western Georgia is a zone of major dextral strike-slip (oblique-slip) faults (Higgins, 1966, 1968) and that a major feature of the northwestern side of the Brevard fault zone in western Georgia is the Austell-Frolona anticlinorium (Crawford and Medlin, 1973, 1974; Medlin and Crawford, 1973). Crawford and Medlin (1974, p. 2) also recognized that the Piedmont–Blue Ridge in western Georgia is made up of two assemblages of rocks that Higgins et al. (1997) called the parautochthonous continental margin *assemblage*, genetically linked to Grenville basement, and the allochthonous oceanic *assemblage* (Fig. 1), made up of rocks formed in an ancient ocean that probably lay offshore from the continental margin of the parautochthonous assemblage.

The allochthonous assemblage is interpreted to have been obducted onto the parautochthonous assemblage, probably in Middle Ordovician through Late Ordovician time, on the basis of the time of slope reversal in the Valley and Ridge province (Higgins et al., 1997), shown by deposition of dark pelites (Rockmart Slate, Athens Shale) on a subsiding shelf. The folded thrusts were in turn displaced in a dextral wrench-fault system similar to the San Andreas system in California (Crowell, 1962, 1974; Dibblee, 1977) and other wrench-fault systems (e.g., Wilcox et al., 1973).

The northeastern end of Austell-Frolona anticlinorium is occupied by the Austell Gneiss, a folded sill-like body in which antiformal foliation is defined by preferred orientation of biotite and megacrysts of microcline. The gneiss overlies the Bill Arp Formation, which occupies the core of the antiform; to the southwest the Bill Arp Formation is stratigraphically underlain by the schist of Hulett and below it the Illinois Creek, Sweetwater Creek, and Nantahala Formations (Fig. 2). Different rocks are structurally above the Austell Gneiss in different places on the northwestern flank of the anticlinorium (Fig. 2). The Gothards Creek Gneiss, thought to belong to the basement (parautochthonous assemblage), structurally overlies the Austell north and northeast of the City of Austell and for several kilometers to the southwest; farther southwest different units of the allochthonous assemblage overlie the gneiss, and still farther to the southwest rocks of the Nantahala Formation overlie the gneiss.

The southeastern side of the Austell Gneiss and the Austell-Frolona anticlinorium are truncated by the Chattahoochee fault (Medlin and Crawford, 1973; Hurst, 1973), a dextral-oblique fault that has placed rocks of the allochthonous assemblage against the Austell Gneiss and the Bill Arp Formation. On the

basis of the antiformal structure of the northeastern end of the Austell-Frolona anticlinorium, Crawford and Medlin (1974) interpreted the Frolona Formation to stratigraphically underlie the Bill Arp Formation, and the Austell Gneiss to be stratigraphically above the Bill Arp. They mapped a narrow belt of schist and metagraywacke, which they showed as the same lithology as the Bill Arp, dividing the Austell, and showed the allochthonous assemblage of this chapter (their sequence III) extending along the axis of the Crawfish Creek structure near Hulett (Fig. 2). More detailed mapping by M. W. Higgins and T. J. Crawford has shown that the narrow belt of Bill Arp Formation within the Austell Gneiss northeast of Douglasville also contains a small thin slice of Nantahala Formation. Four reasonable interpretations are (1) that the thin belt of Bill Arp and Nantahala Formation rocks crop out along the axial trace of an early fold that has been folded by the later nearly upright Austell-Nantahala antiform; (2) that the thin belt of Bill Arp and Nantahala Formation rocks are a folded xenolith within the Austell Gneiss; (3) that the thin belt of Bill Arp and Nantahala Formation rocks is a fault slice along a thrust fault that repeats the section as a two-horse antiformal stack in the sense of Boyer and Elliott (1982, p. 1211–1215); and (4) that the Austell Gneiss intruded the Bill Arp Formation as a thin sill that was later duplicated along with part of the Bill Arp Formation by faulting and subsequently folded. Each event could be separated by tens of millions of years and be within the framework of the age restrictions.

Despite the importance of the northeastern end of the Austell-Frolona anticlinorium and the Austell Gneiss to interpretations of the stratigraphy, structure, chronology, and geologic history of the Piedmont–Blue Ridge in Georgia, and along strike in Alabama and North Carolina, questions remained because critical parts of the anticlinorium had not been mapped in enough detail by 1992. Detailed mapping by M. W. Higgins and T. J. Crawford shows that the narrow belt of Bill Arp Formation that divides the Austell Gneiss joins the main body of the Bill Arp to the southwest on the southeastern side of the anticlinorium (Figs. 1 and 2) at Coursey Lake on the Campbellton, Georgia 7.5′ quadrangle. On the northwestern side of the anticlinorium the narrow belt either truncates against the southernmost fault in the Oak Mountain fault zone or wedges out along the faults that have placed fault slices of Nantahala Formation against fault slices of the Austell Gneiss a few kilometers to the southwest; the point of juncture is not exposed at present in creeks, road cuts, or outcrops. The distance between the last observed section of schist and metagraywacke and the southeasternmost fault in the Oak Mountain fault zone is about 300 m (~1000 ft). The Bill Arp schists and metagraywackes in the narrow belt within the Austell Gneiss are locally sheared to button schists and phyllonites in the terminology of Higgins (1971) or S-C mylonites in the terminology of Berthé et al. (1979) and Lister and Snoke (1984). Along with geologic map evidence, the mylonitic textures are interpreted as indicating the presence of faulting along the belt. Faulting along the margins of the narrow belt of the Bill Arp

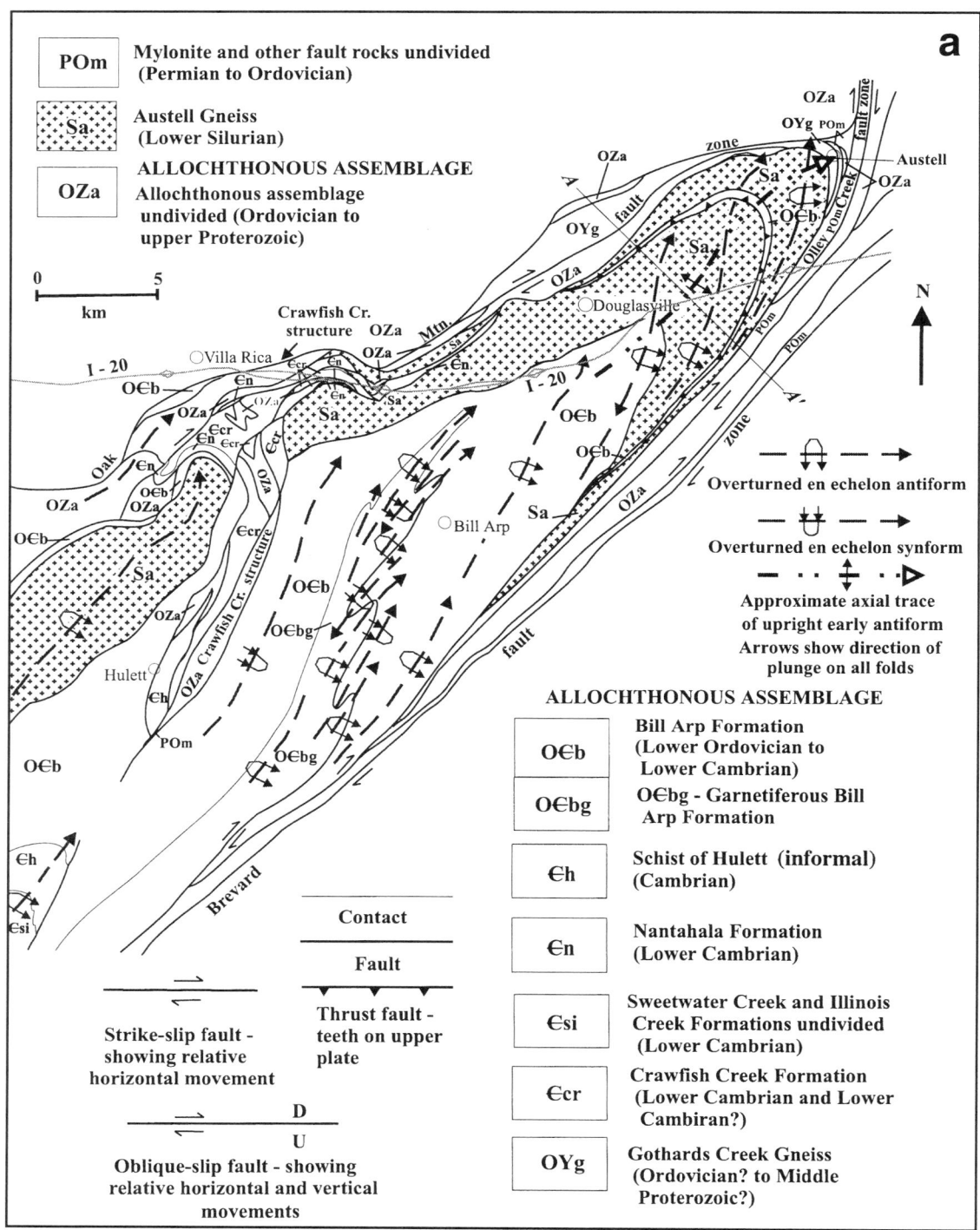

Figure 2 (on this and facing page). a: Generalized geologic map of the northeastern end of the Austell-Frolona anticlinorium (from M. W. Higgins, T. J. Crawford, and R. F. Crawford, III, unpublished geologic maps of the Austell, Campbellton, Nebo, and Winston, Georgia 7.5′ quadrangles). b: Cross section a-a′; Note that cross-section is enlarged and therefore not at same scale as map in (a).

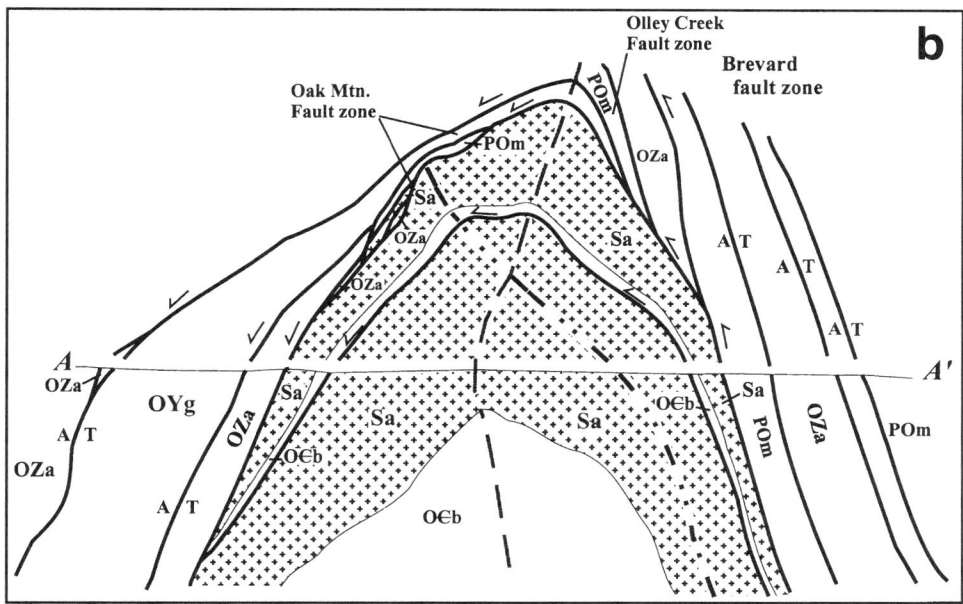

Formation is also indicated by the presence of mylonitized Austell Gneiss cropping out along the edge of the belt in several places; one of the better exposures of this mylonite gneiss is in the pavement outcrops southeast of Vulcan road where it curves westward a few hundred meters north of Interstate 20 to parallel that highway (Fig. 3). Because of the mylonitization and the field relations described above, we currently favor the interpretation that the repetition of the Austell Gneiss on the northwest (down-plunge) side of the narrow outcrop belt of Bill Arp Formation is due to thrust faulting, and that the northeastern end of the Austell-Frolona structure is an antiformal stack (Fig. 2b) in the sense of Boyer and Elliott (1982, p. 1211–1215). In addition, the Bill Arp and Nantahala formations are interpreted to be exposed in a window through the allochthonous assemblage.

The northeastern end of the Austell-Frolona anticlinorium is not a simple antiformal structure but is an older northeast-trending antiform (folded antiformal stack) that has been refolded by en echelon folds, the axes of which trend at an angle of about 30° from the northwestern edge of the Brevard fault zone and then trend northward (Figs. 1, 2, and 4). Lineations, consisting of minor fold axes, crinkle axes, and mineral alignments, in rocks of the Bill Arp Formation in the northeastern end of the Austell-Frolona anticlinorium trend with the fold axes and fall into two sets (Fig. 4). One set arcs northeastward to northward with the en echelon folds from the Brevard fault zone and the other trends northeastward parallel to the older antiform. Most outcrops of Bill Arp Formation rocks in the northeastern end of the Austell-Frolona anticlinorium contain lineations belonging to both sets as shown in Figure 4 (a and b), where the areas identified as B are interpreted to represent the lineations associated with en echelon folding caused by dextral wrench faulting along the Brevard and Olley Creek fault zones, and the areas identified as A are interpreted to represent the lineations associated with the earlier folding that resulted in the Austell-Frolona anticlinorium.

AUSTELL GNEISS

The Austell Gneiss is a light gray, medium- to coarse-grained, strongly foliated, biotite-oligoclase-microcline-quartz gneiss that commonly contains microcline megacrysts 5 mm to 3 cm long (Coleman et al., 1973; Crawford and Medlin, 1974) that make up 20%–50%, but most commonly 25%–30% of the rock. Accessory minerals in the gneiss include euhedral to sub-

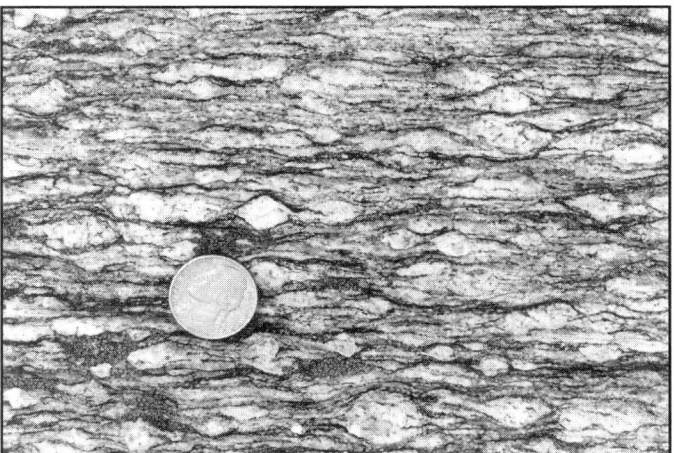

Figure 3. Photograph of outcrop of Austell Gneiss showing mylonitic texture. Large pavement outcrop is located along Vulcan Road where it curves westward a few hundred meters north of Interstate 20 to parallel that highway in the Austell, Georgia, 7.5′ quadrangle. Photograph looks northwest and down on pavement outcrop. Porphyroclasts are interpreted as indicating a dextral sense of shear (Hanmer and Passchier, 1991); however, the rock has probably had a complex deformation history (Simpson, 1986, p. 252). Diameter of coin is ~21 mm.

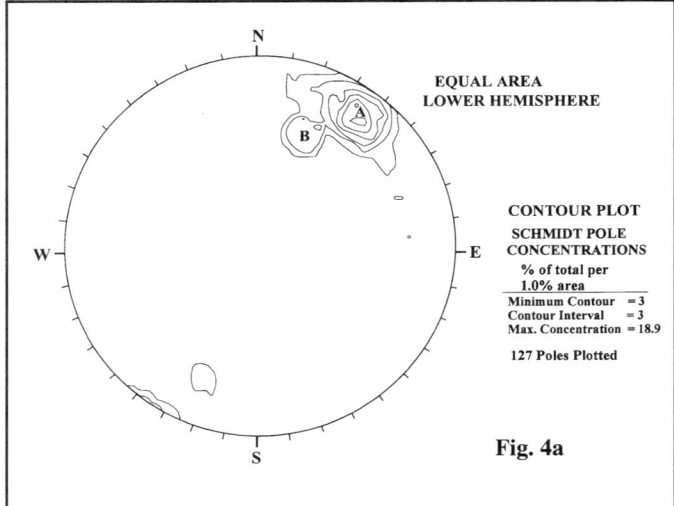

Fig. 4a

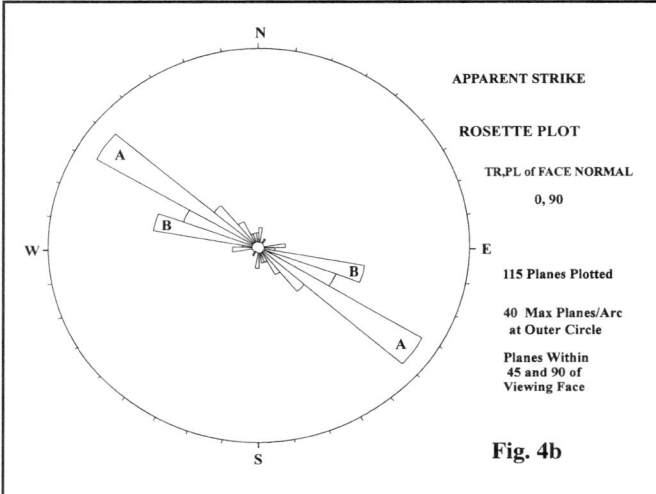

Fig. 4b

Figure 4. Lower hemisphere equal-area plot and rosette plot of planes to poles of lineations in Austell Gneiss, Bill Arp Formation, Gothards Creek Gneiss, and rocks of the allochthonous assemblage in the northeastern end of the Austell-Frolona anticlinorium in the Austell, Campbellton, Nebo, and Winston, Georgia, 7.5′ quadrangles as in Figure 2. a: Contour plot of 127 Schmidt pole concentrations. b: Rosette plot of planes to poles of 118 lineations plotted in (a).

hedral grains of sphene and allanite as well as muscovite, garnet, zircon, and opaques. Minerals of probable secondary origin include epidote, chlorite, and sericite.

The structural position of the Austell Gneiss is so dominated by faults that in many outcrops it is a mylonite or mylonite gneiss (Fig. 3). Locally, away from the faults, the gneiss contains undeformed megacrysts of K-feldspar. In addition to occupying the same structural position as the Middle(?) to Late Proterozoic Corbin Metagranite basement (Higgins et al., 1997; Fig. 1) in the Mulberry Rock structure, the Austell Gneiss occupies the same structural position as the thrust fault that brought the allochthonous assemblage over the parautochthonous assemblage (Figs. 1 and 2).

The chemical composition of the Austell Gneiss (Table 1) is close to that of a "minimum-melt" (Tuttle and Bowen, 1958), and rare-earth elements, other trace elements, and isotopic ratios can be interpreted as indicating that the Austell Gneiss was produced by anatectic melting of older quartz-feldspar gneiss.

The Austell Gneiss has intruded the Bill Arp Formation and the Gothards Creek Gneiss. The Austell Gneiss can be seen intruding Bill Arp schist and metagraywacke in lit-par-lit fashion at their contact along the northern fork of Little Bear Creek, in the Campbellton, Georgia, 7.5′ quadrangle. Xenoliths of Bill Arp schist in Austell Gneiss can be seen in the road cut along the left side of the east-bound lanes of Interstate 20 ~3.5 km west of the juncture of Interstate 20 with Georgia Highway 5. Features interpreted to be contact effects produced by intrusion of the Austell into the Bill Arp can be seen along Mason Creek Road near its juncture with Johnson Road in the Winston, Georgia, 7.5′ quadrangle, where graded metagraywacke and schist of the Bill Arp Formation that crop out within a few meters of Austell Gneiss have grown coarse cross-muscovite. Features interpreted to be contact effects produced by intrusion of the Austell gneiss into the Bill Arp Formation can also be seen in the road cut along Interstate 20 (described above). They consist of "spots" of white mica growing in xenoliths of Bill Arp schist and metagraywacke located a few meters from the contact of the gneiss with its Bill Arp Formation country rocks.

West and northwest of Austell, Georgia (Fig. 2), the contact between the Austell Gneiss and the Gothards Creek Gneiss is a fault zone. In this fault zone strongly deformed Gothards Creek Gneiss is locally intruded in a lit-par-lit fashion by Austell Gneiss; this lit-par-lit intrusion can be seen in a pavement outcrop on the south bank of Sweetwater Creek about 60 m west of U.S. Highway 278 (Camp Creek Parkway) in the Austell, Georgia, 7.5′ quadrangle. On the basis of the above evidence, we interpret the Bill Arp Formation and Gothards Creek Gneiss to be older than the Austell Gneiss. The fault(s) that emplaced the allochthonous assemblage upon the parautochthonous assemblage has been cut and displaced by the faults that have sliced up the Austell Gneiss west of Douglasville, so it must be as old as, or more likely older than, the Early Silurian Austell Gneiss, an age that fits well with the time of slope reversal in the Valley and Ridge province nearby (Higgins et al., 1997). Because the contact of the Gothards Creek Gneiss with the allochthonous assemblage is everywhere a fault contact and the Gothards Creek is also in fault contact with rocks of the parautochthonous assemblage, it is unknown whether it belongs to the allochthonous or parautochthonous assemblage. One interpretation permitted by present evidence is that the Gothards Creek is sheared and recrystallized basement gneiss. Geochemical data presented by Sanders (1990) show that the Gothards Creek Gneiss has about the same chemical composition as Corbin Metagranite basement.

The Austell Gneiss has been truncated along its southeastern side by the Chattahoochee fault of Medlin and Crawford (1973) and Hurst (1973) at the northwestern edge of the Brevard fault zone, along its northeastern side by the Olley Creek fault zone,

TABLE 1. MAJOR-OXIDE AND TRACE-ELEMENT ABUNDANCES IN THE AUSTELL GNEISS*

Sample†	A.1	A.3	A.5	A.7	A.8	A.11	A.13	A.14
(wt. %)								
SiO_2	68.6	68.6	71.0	72.6	73.1	76.2	77.1	77.1
Al_2O_3	14.2	14.1	13.2	13.4	13.7	12.3	12.1	12.2
Fe_2O_3	1.2	1.0	0.96	0.45	0.44	0.78	0.22	0.20
FeO	2.0	2.1	1.4	1.6	1.4	0.72	0.76	0.64
MgO	1.1	0.96	0.81	0.68	0.64	0.65	0.35	0.42
CaO	2.9	2.2	1.9	1.5	1.2	1.1	1.2	0.93
Na_2O	3.8	3.3	3.8	3.2	3.2	3.4	3.4	3.5
K_2O	3.5	4.6	5.0	4.4	4.7	4.9	4.8	4.6
H_2O^+	0.73	0.66	0.75	0.70	0.83	0.91	0.13	0.50
H_2O^-	0.12	0.13	0.11	0.01	0.09	0.12	0.18	0.05
TiO_2	0.54	0.65	0.36	0.36	0.31	0.24	0.23	0.14
P_2O_5	0.19	0.28	0.09	0.24	0.23	0.07	0.05	0.04
MnO	0.07	0.07	0.09	0.05	0.06	0.06	0.06	0.04
CO_2	0.03	0.05	0.33	0.05	0.01	0.01	0.03	0.03
Total	99.0	98.9	99.8	99.2	99.9	101.5	100.6	100.4
(ppm)								
Rb	180	210	180	240	230	190	240	330
Ba	450	160	270	260	270	150	110	88
Sr	100	37	55	81	81	52	39	36
Cs	1.8	2.2	2.3	7.15	7.65	3.8	2.3	3.3
Th	16.7	21.7	21.8	9.3	9.4	17.17	20.1	21.5
U	4.2	4.0	5.75	9.35	8.55	6.6	5.9	8.2
Zr	190	170	235	120	100	95	120	78
Hf	4.2	4.35	5.0	3.3	3.25	3.5	3.8	3.8
Ta	1.38	1.69	1.69	2.80	2.83	1.77	2.15	3.34
Co	3.1	1.85	2.0	2.9	3.15	1.4	1.1	0.9
Li	37	46	42	59	76	73	78	100
Ni	2	<1	<1	1	2	1	<1	<1
Cr	16	13	12	18	20	8	7	5
Sc	5.5	6.23	4.63	5.32	5.56	4.95	5.08	4.95
Cu	1	<1	1	14	16	3	<1	1
Zn	35	25	32	32	110	78	36	18
La	38.5	39.5	98.5	22.5	23	30	33	
Ce	73	77	103	48	49	63	71	42
Nd	28.5	31.5	73	23	24	25	28	
Sm	5.5	6.55	15.2	5.15	5.5	5.8	6.4	2.0
Eu	0.66	0.44	1.36	0.60	0.63	0.33	0.40	0.11
Gd	5.15	6.21	3.25	4.95	4.6	6.1	6.2	2.9
Tb	0.77	1.05	1.94	0.68	0.64	1.08	1.04	0.45
Ho	0.9	0.9	1.9	0.6	0.8	1.0	1.2	0.7
Tm	0.39	0.49	0.72	0.28	0.31	0.65	0.59	0.57
Yb	2.85	3.65	5.8	2.35	2.3	4.8	4.2	4.4
Lu	0.42	0.51	0.77	0.32	0.35	0.66	0.61	0.66
Y	28	33	74	36	32	23	49	40

*Major-oxide composition analyses by H. Smith and J. Reid. Trace elements analyses by J. Fletcher and L. J. Schwartz.

†Sample localities, latitude and longitude: A.1 = N33°39′58″ x W84°55′27″; A.3 = N33°46′22″ x W84°40′13″; A.5 = 33°45′31″ x W84°41′16″; A.7 = N33°45′55″ x W84°39′49″; A.8 = N33°44′07″ x W84°47′08″; A.11 = N33°43′05″ x W84°49′03″; A.13 = N33°43′34″ x W84°47′40″; A.14 = N33°43′29″ x W84°47′15″.

and along its northern side by the Oak Mountain fault zone (Higgins et al., 1997). Kinematic indicators, although sparse (outcrops are also sparse in the highly urbanized area of the Olley Creek fault zone), indicate that the Olley Creek fault zone is a dextral strike-slip fault zone. Because the strike-slip faults cut the Early Silurian Austell Gneiss, some of the strike-slip faulting must be younger than the gneiss, but earlier strike-slip faulting is not precluded, and the early thrusting may have accompanied early strike-slip faulting.

FOLDING

We separate the folds in western Georgia (Fig. 1) into (1) a set of early minor isoclinal folds (f_{ei}) within the foliation that range in amplitude from a few centimeters to several meters and have axial planes that dip with the foliation and axes that plunge down the dip of the foliation and are therefore nearly vertical in places. Similar vertical-axes folds have been observed in other major strike-slip fault zones, such as along the King fault in the Early Proterozoic Nonacho basin in Canada (Aspler and Donaldson, 1985, p. 205, Fig. 9F). (2) A second set of major early folds (f_e) that formed after the isoclinal (f_{ei}) folds because they fold the foliation and the isoclinal folds (Figs. 1 and 2). The first two fold sets (f_{ei} and f_e) are folded by (3) a set of folds interpreted to be en enchelon folds (f_{en}) that formed in the dextral wrench fault system that includes the Brevard and Dahlonega fault zones. En echelon folds are folds that occur along strike-slip faults and have an angle of $30°–45°$ to the principal deformation zone of the strike-slip fault. Wilcox et al. (1973) called these folds en echelon folds and illustrated their development along many major wrench fault systems. They have been well documented along the San Andreas wrench fault system in California by Dibblee (1977). En echelon folds in the Bill Arp Formation in the northeastern end of the Austell-Frolona anticlinorium are documented by (1) bedding and/or foliation reversals, (2) lineations, and (3) folded contacts. All of the early folds including the en echelon folds are deformed by gentle open folds.

In addition to the en echelon folds in the Bill Arp Formation in the northeastern end of the Austell-Frolona anticlinorium, there are garnet-rich zones in the Bill Arp Formation in the northeastern part of the anticlinorium that trend north-northeast from the southeastern margin of the anticlinorium nearly to the Austell Gneiss along the northwestern margin (Fig. 2). One set of lineations, which includes mineral elongations, rodding, and minor folds in rocks of the Bill Arp Formation in the Austell-Frolona window, also trends northward and is interpreted to be the result of en echelon folding. The trends of the lineations and of the garnet-rich zones are interpreted to be the result of Middle Silurian (Austell Gneiss age) and younger dextral movement along the Brevard fault zone.

We have hypothesized elsewhere (Higgins et al., 1997) that the early layer and/or schistosity-parallel isoclinal folds (f_{ei}) formed during the thrusting that emplaced the allochthonous assemblage upon the parautochthonous assemblage, because they are fairly common in allochthonous assemblage rocks, but have

not been observed in the Austell Gneiss or in parautochthonous cover-sequence rocks (including Sweetwater Creek, Illinois Creek, Nantahala, and Bill Arp formations) in the northeastern end of the Austell-Frolona anticlinorium. These early isoclinal (f_{ei}) folds may be older than the Austell Gneiss, but there is only negative evidence for this at present and there is the added complication that the isoclinal folds are most commonly seen in amphibolite, whereas the cover sequence rocks are mostly metamorphosed pelitic clastic rocks.

The second set of early folds (f_e) have folded the Austell Gneiss and its foliation, and therefore must be younger than the Early Silurian Austell Gneiss. The en echelon folds (f_{en}) are younger than the second set of early folds (f_e).

In the Atlanta $30' \times 60'$ quadrangle (Higgins et al., 1997b) the axial-traces of wrench folds trend south-southeast from the Rivertown fault at the southeastern edge of the Brevard fault zone with an orientation appropriate for folds formed during dextral movement on that fault (e.g., Moody and Hill, 1956; Wilcox et al., 1973; Harding, 1976; Sylvester and Smith, 1976; Dibblee, 1977).

FOLIATION

The foliation in the Austell Gneiss is defined by aligned K-feldspar megacrysts, biotite laths, and elongate quartz domains, and is the same foliation as that in the parautochthonous assemblage country rocks. This foliation and the early (f_e) folds and en echelon folds (f_{en}), which have folded the Austell Gneiss foliation, are younger than the Austell Gneiss. This foliation is probably the same as the isocline-bearing foliation in the allochthonous assemblage.

GEOCHEMISTRY

Major- and trace-element analyses (Table 1) show that the Austell Gneiss is siliceous, with a range in SiO_2 of 68.6 to 77.1 wt%. Al_2O_3 content is 12.1% to 14.2% and three samples have normative corundum, so the pluton is metaluminous to mildly peraluminous. K_2O exceeds Na_2O by 1% or more in most samples, so the rocks are mildly potassic. In the scheme of Streckeisen (1974) the Austell Gneiss is a biotite granite. The Peacock index, determined by extrapolation on a $Na_2O + (K_2O + CaO)$ versus SiO_2 plot, is ~50, so the pluton is alkali-calcic. The normative composition of the gneiss is dominated by quartz, albite, and orthoclase (Q, Ab, Or); on a Q-Ab-Or normative diagram; the samples fall in the field of a large number of rhyolites and granites and close to the experimentally determined "minimum melt" granite composition of Tuttle and Bowen (1958) for pressures <3 kbar.

Among the trace elements, alkali-element contents (Rb, Cs, Li) are moderate and alkaline earth contents (Ba, Sr) are low. Ferromagnesian elements (Co, Ni, Cr, Sc, Cu, Zn) and high-valence cations (Th, U, Zr, Hf, Ta) are at low levels commonly found in unmineralized granitic rocks. On a plot of chondrite-normalized rare earth element abundances (Fig. 5), all samples have similarly fractionated patterns with higher light than heavy rare earth contents (normalized Ce/Yb of 2.5 to 6.7). Light rare

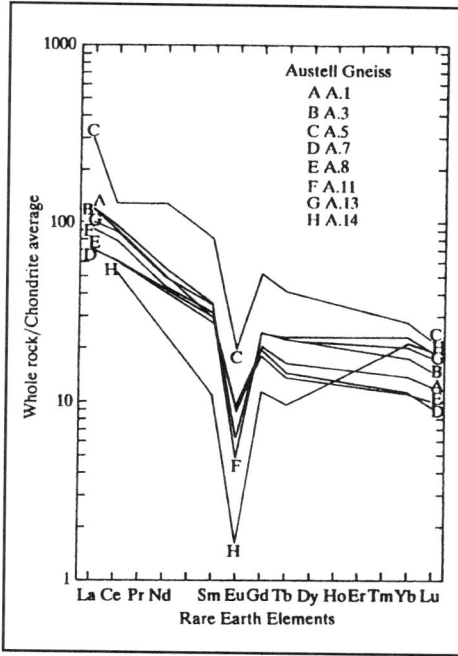

Figure 5. Plot of chondrite-normalized rare-earth element abundances from the Austell Gneiss.

TABLE 2. Rb-Sr ANALYTICAL DATA FOR WHOLE-ROCK SAMPLES OF THE AUSTELL GNEISS*

Sample[†]	Concentration		Atomic Ratios		
	Rb (ppm)	Sr (ppm)	Rb/Sr	^{87}Rb/^{86}Sr	^{87}Sr/^{86}Sr
Aus-1	235.9	35.7	6.61	19.33	0.82587
Aus-2	157.0	153.6	1.02	2.963	0.72624
Aus-3	191.0	42.2	4.53	13.19	0.79046
Aus-4	127.2	167.1	0.76	2.206	0.72055
Aus-6	241.8	59.4	4.07	11.86	0.77955
Aus-7	183.9	75.5	2.44	7.076	0.74962

*Whole-rock splits and zircon separates prepared by Michael Cabell and John Mangum; chemical separations by Marcia Newell, Charles Scozzie, and Clara Zmuda. Sr-isotope ratios were corrected for fractionation to an ^{86}Sr/^{88}Sr ratio of 0.11940. Blank determinations were <2 ng for Sr and <0.2 ng for Rb. Eleven analyses of NBS SRM 987 gave a mean ^{87}Sr/^{86}Sr value of 0.710235 ± 0.000005 (2s). Precision of replicate whole-rock determinations is 0.001% for ^{87}Sr/^{86}Sr, 0.6% for Rb, and 1.0% for Sr (1s). In the U-Th-Pb analyses, fractionation resulting in depletion of heavy isotopes by <0.05% was measured by using NBS SRM 982; no correction is applied. Accuracy of the concentration determinations is estimated at 1.0% (1s). Isotopic and decay constants are those of Steiger and Jaeger (1977).
[†]Sample localities, latitude, longitude: Aus-1 = N33°44′07″ x W84°47′08″; Aus-2 = N33°43′05″ x W84°49′03″; Aus-3 = N33°46′22″ x W84°40′13″; Aus-4 = N33°45′31″ x W84°41′16″; Aus-6 = 33°48′48″ x W84°39′20″.

earth contents (La and Ce) in most samples are 60 to 120 times chondritic values, and heavy rare earth contents (Yb and Lu) are 10 to 20 times chondritic values. All patterns show large negative Eu anomalies (Eu/Eu* of 0.14 to 0.38). Two samples differ from the others in having higher (sample A.5) and lower (sample A.14) rare earth contents.

GEOCHRONOLOGY

Samples from the Austell Gneiss were dated at the U.S. Geological Survey by both the Rb-Sr isochron method on whole rocks (Table 2), and the U-Pb method on zircons (Table 3). The Rb-Sr analyses were done in Reston, Virginia. The U-Pb analyses were done in two laboratories; in Reston on a nonmagnetic fraction from sample Aus-3, and in Menlo Park, California, on fractions of differing size and magnetic character from sample Aus-102. Isotopic and decay constants for both methods are those recommended by the IUGS Subcommission on Geochronology (Steiger and Jaeger, 1977).

Rb and Sr were extracted by ion-exchange chromatography after dissolution of a 300–500 mg split of each sample. Sr isotopic ratios were measured on a fully automated MAT 261 mass spectrometer and corrected for fractionation on the basis of an ^{86}Sr/^{88}Sr of 0.11940. Blank determinations were <2 ng for Sr and 0.2 ng for Rb. Accuracy of the Sr-isotope measurements is based on 11 analyses of NBS SRM 987, which gave a mean ^{87}Sr/^{86}Sr of 0.710235 ± 0.000005 (95% confidence level). The precision of individual rock determinations, based on complete replicate analyses, is 0.001% for ^{87}Sr/^{86}Sr, 0.6% for Rb, and 1.0% for Sr at the 67% confidence level.

U, Th, and Pb were extracted from zircon separates that were washed in hot HNO_3 and HCl (Reston), or in dilute cold HNO_3 (Menlo Park) to remove surface contamination.

Rb-Sr Results

An Rb-Sr whole-rock isochron for the Austell Gneiss is shown in Figure 6. The sizes of the individual data points reflect the analytical uncertainty for each whole-rock determination at the 95% confidence level. The regression line, determined by the method of York (1969), fits all data points within analytical uncertainty. The calculated isochron age of 432 Ma has an uncertainty of 8 Ma at the 67 percent confidence level.

The range of ^{87}Rb/^{86}Sr, from 2.2 to 19.3, is very large in this body. This suggests that any metamorphic events that led to the current fabric of the gneiss did not chemically or isotopically homogenize the body, at least not sufficiently to produce an isochron reflecting the time of metamorphism. More likely, the linear isochron reflects the time of crystallization of the Austell body from a granite magma.

The initial ^{87}Sr/^{86}Sr is 0.70729 ± 0.00052. This moderately high value suggests that the source of Austell magmas involved a significant fraction of crustal rocks. The origin of the orthogneiss is discussed further below.

U-Pb RESULTS

Ten fractions of zircon from two different samples of the Austell Gneiss have been analyzed. Sample Aus-3 represents the original sample from which a single fraction of nonmagnetic zir-

TABLE 3. U-Th-Pb ANALYTICAL DATA ON ZIRCONS FROM THE AUSTELL GNEISS, GEORGIA*

Sample	Fraction	Concentrations Pb (ppm)	U (ppm)	Th (ppm)	Measured Ratios 206Pb/204Pb	208Pb/206Pb	Corrected Atomic Ratios 206Pb/238U	± %	207Pb/235U	± %	207Pb/206Pb	± %	Ages 206Pb/238U (Ma)	207Pb/235U (Ma)	207Pb/206Pb (Ma)	208Pb/232Th (Ma)
Aus-3	NM<120mh	95.1	1,463	491	12,500	0.1259	0.06385	1.00	0.48840	1.00	0.05664	0.26	399.0	403.6	430.1	451.7
Aus-102	M<100	55.2	834		1,285	0.1743	0.06111	0.09	0.46744	0.29	0.05547	0.35	382.4	389.4	431.4	
	M100-130	57.5	831		1,537	0.1627	0.06468	0.05	0.49890	0.38	0.05595	0.26	404.0	411.0	450.2	
	NM<100	44.6	631		1,315	0.1752	0.06529	0.08	0.49745	0.28	0.05526	0.56	407.7	410.0	422.7	
	NM100-130	46.6	620		550	0.2090	0.06529	0.17	0.50842	0.62	0.05647		407.7	417.4	471.0	
Aus-102R	M<80	79.4	1,179		1,098	0.1797	0.06170	0.07	0.47095	0.29	0.05536	0.26	386.0	391.8	426.7	
	M80-100	67.6	986		1,464	0.1681	0.06379	0.11	0.48831	0.41	0.05552	0.37	398.6	403.8	433.1	
	M>163	58.1	826		1,270	0.1617	0.06562	0.12	0.50582	0.91	0.05591	0.85	409.7	415.6	448.8	
	NM<100	47.3	682		2,618	0.1597	0.06565	0.36	0.51120	0.76	0.05647	0.63	409.9	419.2	470.9	
	NM130	51.9	623		314	0.2523	0.06726	0.11	0.52710	0.53	0.05684	0.49	419.6	429.9	485.2	

*Zircon fractions are designated as magnetic (M) or nonmagnetic (NM) by their behavior on a Frantz isodynamic separator at maximum current, 1° side tilt, and 15° forward tilt. Size ranges of fractions are in microns except for Aus-3, which is mesh.

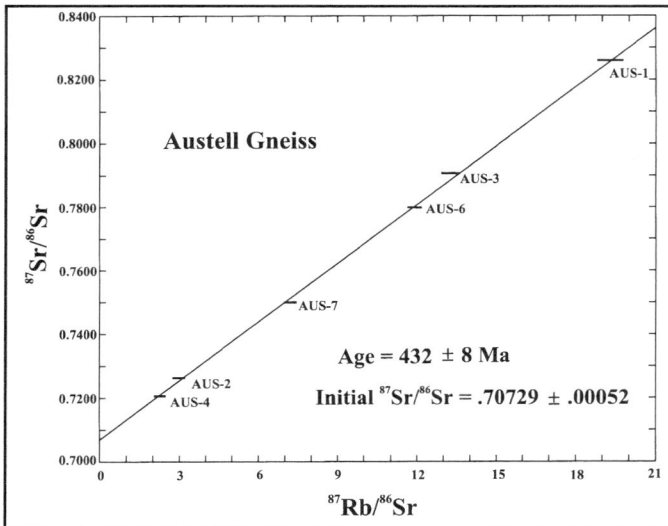

Figure 6. Whole-rock Rb-Sr isochron plot for six samples of Austell Gneiss.

con was analyzed. The data for this fraction are discordant, but the two Pb-U ages indicate a minimum age of about 400 Ma. Given this discordance the $^{207}Pb/^{206}Pb$ age of 430 Ma is considered a better estimate of the minimum crystallization age of the sample.

Zircons were separated from a second sample (Aus-102) in order to provide more detailed knowledge of the U-Pb systematics of different fractions of zircon. The data from the first four zircon fractions analyzed from this sample were discordant and did not define a single discordia line (Table 3, Fig. 7), but the smallest size fractions had the lowest $^{207}Pb/^{206}Pb$ ages (423 and 431 Ma), and these are similar to that from sample Aus-3. The two larger size fractions had $^{207}Pb/^{206}Pb$ ages of 450 and 471 Ma suggesting an older crystallization age, or inheritance of an older zircon component.

To better understand these complicated U-Pb systematics, five additional fractions of zircon were analyzed from this sample (Aus-102R in Table 3). The <100 μm magnetic fraction was split into two fractions at 80 μm. The data from these five fractions followed the same pattern as the original four fractions. The two smallest magnetic fractions have $^{207}Pb/^{206}Pb$ ages of 427 and 433 Ma; the larger magnetic fraction and the nonmagnetic fractions have ages of 449 to 485 Ma. These five fractions also show a strong inverse correlation between U concentration and Pb-U and Pb-Pb age (Table 3).

The patterns of all the data on a concordia diagram (Fig. 7) suggest the following interpretation. The smaller zircon fractions (2, 6, 7, 4), which will normally have the least amount of inherited zircon, define a limiting line between 0 and about 430 Ma. $^{207}Pb/^{206}Pb$ ages for these four fractions range from 423 to 433 Ma. The bulk zircon fraction also falls along this line. The best estimate from the zircon data of the crystallization age of the Austell Gneiss is the average $^{207}Pb/^{206}Pb$ age of 429 ± 4(15) Ma of these five fractions. An actual fit of these data, forced through a

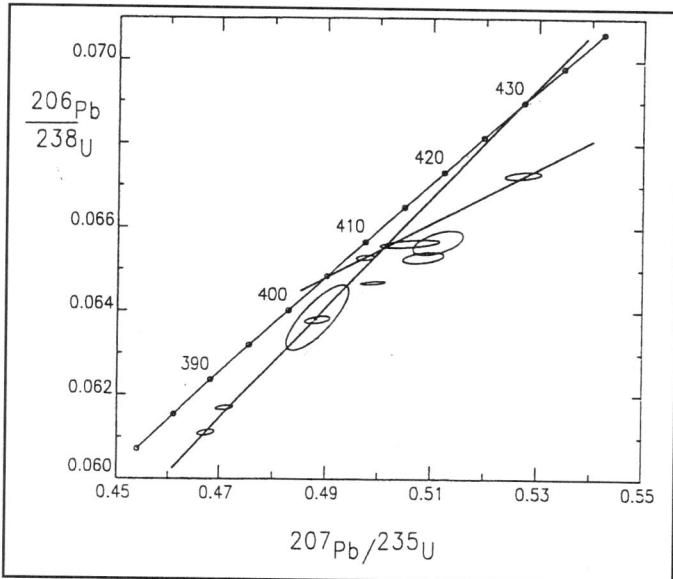

Figure 7. Concordia plots of zircon U-Pb analyses from the Austell Gneiss.

0 Ma lower intercept, gives an upper intercept of 429 ± 7 Ma (95% confidence level).

The larger zircon fractions (3, 5, 8, 10) and one smaller (9) nonmagnetic fraction scatter away from this line, and have ^{207}Pb/^{206}Pb ages from 449 to 485 Ma. These fractions do not define a discordia line, but a limiting discordia line can be drawn for reference from about 405 Ma to 1500 Ma. The smaller and more U-rich zircon fractions (2, 6, 7) have clearly lost a small amount of Pb recently, and some Pb loss from all fractions must be considered. The chord between 405 Ma and 1500 Ma, therefore, probably provides only an estimate of the minimum crystallization age and a maximum average inheritance age. Inherited components typically have a range of ages, and for this sample, mixtures among zircon populations ranging from about 600 Ma to 1.5 Ga are feasible. Single zircon or ion-microprobe analyses are required to adequately identify the ages of inheritance.

ORIGIN OF THE AUSTELL GNEISS AND IMPLICATIONS OF ITS AGE

The rare-earth patterns of the Austell Gneiss are similar in shape to those of "minimum melt" granites and rhyolites. The large negative Eu anomaly suggests that feldspar was an abundant residual mineral or a fractionating phase. The moderate slope and negative Eu anomaly suggest garnet and amphibole were not abundant in the residue. The low Ba content of the gneiss may indicate the presence of biotite in the residue. A residue that included feldspar and biotite, but not much amphibole or garnet, may indicate that the magma was dominantly derived by melting of mica-feldspar-quartz gneiss.

The mode of generation of a "minimum melt" granite such as the Austell Gneiss is partly delimited by the geochemical data

given above. Granites of "minimum-melt" composition such as the Austell Gneiss can originate in many ways, the more likely being partial melting of crustal rocks, or fractionation of granodioritic or more mafic magma. The rare-earth content of the Austell Gneiss is generally higher than that of rhyolites from oceanic island arcs (e.g., Arth, 1981), but lower than that of highly evolved granites in a continental setting (e.g., Hudson and Arth, 1983). Concentration levels are similar to those of granites in continental margin settings (e.g., Barker et al., 1986).

The initial ^{87}Sr/^{86}Sr ratio (0.7073) is higher than would be expected from a subduction related magma in a purely oceanic setting, but not unlike those of volcanic and plutonic rocks erupted or intruded in a continental margin magmatic arc in which some continental crust is present at depth and provides part or all of the granitic melt (e.g., Hawkesworth, 1982, p. 553). We thus conjecture that the Austell Gneiss magma was produced by partial melting of mica-feldspar-quartz gneiss in a continental margin setting.

Therefore, field relations, mineralogy, geochemistry, and isotope ratios indicate that the Austell Gneiss originated by anatexis of crustal rocks. All evidence is compatible with the hypothesis that the Austell Gneiss originated through anatectic melting of basement.

CONCLUSIONS

The age of the Austell Gneiss places constraints on the age(s) of metamorphism, thrust faulting, folding, foliation, and wrench faulting in the Piedmont–Blue Ridge of Georgia that are also important to the ages of these features and/or events in the rest of the Appalachian orogen. Geochemical and geological evidence indicate that the Austell Gneiss originated by anatectic melting of older rocks. Therefore, the age of the Austell Gneiss probably roughly dates the age of one metamorphic peak in the southern Appalachians as approximately Early Silurian, and evidence from zircon analyses indicates disturbance from the Early Silurian to the Early Devonian. Because the Austell Gneiss intruded the early thrust faults that are interpreted to have placed the allochthonous assemblage upon the parautochthonous assemblage, these faults must be older than about 430 Ma (Early Silurian). Because the foliation of the Austell Gneiss is the same foliation as that in the parautochthonous assemblage rocks that underlie it in the Austell-Frolona anticlinorium (Fig. 1), the foliation must date and/or postdate the Early Silurian, implying that the foliation in the parautochthonous assemblage rocks elsewhere is younger than Early Silurian. Moreover, with some reservations, the foliation in the allochthonous assemblage rocks is probably the same age as the foliation in the parautochthonous assemblage rocks and in the Austell Gneiss. This implies that the foliation in the rocks of the Piedmont–Blue Ridge throughout the Southern Appalachians is younger than Early Silurian. Because the Austell Gneiss has been cut and deformed by strike-slip faults belonging to major wrench fault systems, displacements on faults in these systems must have taken place during and/or after the

Early Silurian, although earlier displacement is not precluded. The en echelon folds (f_{en}) that fold the Austell Gneiss must also be younger than about 430 Ma.

ACKNOWLEDGMENTS

We thank Marcia F. Newell, Charles Scozzie, and Clara Zmuda for chemical separations of isotopically analyzed elements. Michael Cabell and John Mangum prepared the whole-rock splits and zircon separates for isotopic analysis. Willis G. Hester helped with drafting. We thank James DeCinque of Vulcan Materials for access to the large quarry in Austell Gneiss near Lithia Springs. The manuscript was greatly improved because of constructive reviews by John P. Hogan and Henri B. Gaudette.

REFERENCES CITED

Arth, J. G., 1981, Rare-earth element geochemistry of the island-arc volcanic rocks of Rabaul and Talasea, New Britain: Geological Society of America Bulletin, v. 92, p. 858–863.

Aspler, L. B., and Donaldson, J. A., 1985, The Nonacho basin (Early Proterozoic), Northwest Territories, Canada: Sedimentation and deformation in a strike-slip setting, *in* Biddle, K. T., and Christie-Blick, N., ed., Strike-slip deformation, basin formation, and sedimentation: Society of Economic Paleontologists and Mineralogists Special Publication 37, p. 193–209.

Barker, F., Arth, J. G., and Stern, T. W., 1986, Evolution of the Coast batholith along the Skagway Traverse, Alaska and British Columbia: American Mineralogist, v. 71, p. 632–643.

Berthé, D., Choukroune, P., and Jegouzo, P., 1979, Orthogneiss, mylonite and non-coaxial deformation of granites: the example of the South Armorican shear zone: Journal of Structural Geology, v. 1, p. 31–42.

Boyer, S. E., and Elliott, D., 1982, Thrust systems: American Association of Petroleum Geologists Bulletin, v. 66, p. 1196–1230.

Coleman, S. L., Medlin, J. H., and Crawford, T. J., 1973, Petrology and geochemistry of the Austell gneiss in the western Georgia Piedmont: Geological Society of America Abstracts with Programs, v. 5, p. 338.

Crawford, T. J., and Medlin, J. H., 1973, The western Georgia Piedmont between the Cartersville and Brevard fault zones: American Journal of Science, v. 273, p. 712–722.

Crawford, T. J., and Medlin, J. H., 1974, Brevard fault zone in western Georgia and eastern Alabama: Georgia Geological Survey Guidebook 12, p. 1-1–1-67.

Crowell, J. C., 1962, Displacement along the San Andreas fault, California: Geological Society of America Special Paper 71, 61 p.

Crowell, J. C., 1974, Origin of late Cenozoic basins in southern California, *in* Dickinson, W. R., ed., Tectonics and sedimentation: Society of Economic Paleontologists and Mineralogists Special Paper 22, p. 190–204.

Dibblee, T. W., Jr., 1977, Strike-slip tectonics of the San Andreas fault and its role in Cenozoic basin evolvement, *in* Nilsen, T. H., ed., Late Mesozoic and Cenozoic sedimentation and tectonics in California: Bakersfield,

California, San Joaquin Geological Society, p. 26–38.

Hanmer, S., and Passchier, C., 1991, Shear-sense indicators: A review: Geological Survey of Canada Paper 90-17, 72 p.

Harding, T. P., 1976, Tectonic significance and hydrocarbon trapping consequences of sequential folding synchronous with San Andreas faulting, San Joaquin Valley, California: American Association of Petroleum Geologists Bulletin, v. 60, p. 356–378.

Hawkesworth, C. J., 1982, Isotope characteristics of magmas erupted along destructive plate margins, *in* Thorpe, R. S., ed., Andesites: New York, John Wiley and Sons, p. 549–571.

Higgins, M. W., 1966, The geology of the Brevard lineament near Atlanta, Georgia: Georgia Geological Survey Bulletin 77, 49 p.

Higgins, M. W., 1968, Geologic map of the Brevard fault zone near Atlanta, Georgia: U.S. Geological Survey Miscellaneous Geologic Investigations Map I-511, scale 1:50,000.

Higgins, M. W., 1971, Cataclastic rocks: U.S. Geological Survey Professional Paper 687, 97 p.

Higgins, M. W., Crawford, T. J., Atkins, R. L., and Crawford, R. F., 1997, Geologic map of the Atlanta, Georgia, 30′ × 60′ quadrangle: U.S. Geological Survey, scale 1:100,000 (in press).

Hudson, T., and Arth, J. G., 1983, Tin granites of Seward Peninsula, Alaska: Geological Society of America Bulletin, v. 94, p. 768–790.

Hurst, V. J., 1973, Geology of the southern Blue Ridge belt: American Journal of Science, v. 273, p. 643–670.

Lister, G. S., and Snoke, A. W., 1984, S-C mylonites: Journal of Structural Geology, v. 6, p. 617–638.

Medlin, J. H., and Crawford, T. J., 1973, Stratigraphy and structure along the Brevard Fault Zone in western Georgia and Alabama: American Journal of Science, v. 273-A, p. 89–104.

Moody, J. D., and Hill, M. J., 1956, Wrench-fault tectonics: Geological Society of America Bulletin, v. 67, p. 1207–1246.

Sanders, R., 1990, Geochemistry and origin of the Villa Rica trondhjemite gneiss, west Georgia Piedmont: Geological Society of America Abstracts with Programs, v. 22, no. 4, p. 61.

Simpson, C., 1986, Determination of movement sense in mylonites: Journal of Geological Education, v. 34, p. 246–261.

Steiger, R. H., and Jaeger, E., 1977, Subcommission on Geochronology: Convention on the use of decay constants in geochronology and cosmochronology: Earth and Planetary Science Letters, v. 36, p. 359–362.

Streckeisen, A., 1974, Classification and nomenclature of plutonic rocks: Geologische Rundschau, v. 63, p. 773–786.

Sylvester, A. G., and Smith, R. R., 1976, Tectonic transpression and basement-controlled deformation in San Andreas fault zone, Salton trough, California: American Association of Petroleum Geologists Bulletin, v. 60, p. 2081–2102.

Tuttle, O. F., and Bowen, N. L., 1958, Origin of granite in light of experimental studies in the system $NaAlSi_3O_8$-$KAlSi_3O_8$-SiO_2-H_2O: Geological Society of America Memoir 74, 153 p.

Wilcox, R. E., Harding, T. P., and Seely, D. R., 1973, Basic wrench tectonics: American Association of Petroleum Geologists Bulletin, v. 57, p. 74–96.

York, D., 1969, Least squares fitting of a straight line with correlated errors: Earth and Planetary Science Letters, v. 5, p. 320–324.

MANUSCRIPT ACCEPTED BY THE SOCIETY JULY 2, 1996

Geological Society of America
Memoir 191
1997

Space-time composition relationships among Appalachian-cycle plutonic suites in Newfoundland

Andrew Kerr
Geological Survey of Newfoundland and Labrador, Department of Natural Resources, P. O. Box 8700, St. John's, Newfoundland A1B 4J6, Canada, and Department of Earth Sciences, Memorial University of Newfoundland, St. John's, Newfoundland A1B 3X5, Canada

ABSTRACT

Spatial and temporal geochemical trends among Appalachian-cycle plutonic suites in Newfoundland demonstrate that each tectonic zone contains distinct plutonic assemblages. Within tectonic zones, there is a generalized trend toward more evolved, restricted compositions, but the details of plutonic evolution are subtly different across the orogenic belt. The majority of Appalachian-cycle plutonic suites in Newfoundland postdate closure of the Iapetus ocean, and may have a broad relationship to postcollisional lithospheric delamination processes.

Cambrian-Ordovician plutonism is largely restricted to the Dunnage zone. In the west, these suites generally resemble arc-related batholiths, but include both trondhjemites (intraoceanic arcs?), and calc-alkaline suites (mature or continental arcs?). In contrast, Ordovician suites of the eastern Dunnage zone record anatexis of the underlying Gander zone following Dunnage-Gander juxtaposition. On an orogen-wide scale, the paucity of preserved early-orogenic arc-related plutonic rocks is significant, and deeper erosion would completely destroy this record of subduction processes, as it apparently has in many Precambrian mobile belts.

Silurian plutonism has the widest distribution, affecting all areas except the Avalon zone. The onset of plutonism in the Humber and Gander zones is a significant development, and most likely indicates the closure of the main Iapetus ocean. Within the Dunnage zone, Silurian plutonic suites are bimodal, and have an alkali-calcic, A-type geochemistry, in sharp contrast to Ordovician suites. This temporal shift likely records the transition from compressional to extensional tectonic environments, and the commonality of Silurian plutonism across the Dunnage zone does not support wide separation of its western and eastern parts. Silurian suites of the Humber and Gander zones, on opposite sides of the orogen, are dominated by peraluminous, I-type granite suites, commonly K-feldspar megacrystic granites, and subordinate muscovite-biotite granites of broadly S-type affinity. In the Gander zone, these form a continuum, and reflect at least three source components of supracrustal, infracrustal, and subcrustal origin. Gander zone Silurian suites could be distal arc-related magmas, linked to subduction of oceanic crust located between the Gander and Avalon zones. The absence of Silurian granites in the Avalon zone, and the eastward shift of the locus of magmatism, are consistent with this model, but the absence of more primitive arc-type suites is not. An alternative model, preferred here, interprets Silurian suites across the entire orogen as a lateorogenic, postclosure assemblage unrelated to subduction, within which internal compositional contrasts largely reflect the nature of the host terranes and their lower crustal blocks.

Kerr, A., 1997, Space-time composition relationships among Appalachian-cycle plutonic suites in Newfoundland, *in* Sinha, A. K., Whalen, J. B., and Hogan, J. P., eds., The Nature of Magmatism in the Appalachian Orogen: Boulder, Colorado, Geological Society of America Memoir 191.

In post-Silurian times the locus of magmatism shifted eastward again, because Devonian plutonic suites are most abundant in the Gander and Avalon zones, where they intrude the Gander-Avalon boundary, and postdate juxtaposition of the zones. The restricted, evolved compositions of Devonian suites are inconsistent with subduction zone magmatism, and these granites are interpreted to be entirely postcollisional in setting.

INTRODUCTION

Newfoundland is a key area in understanding the evolution of the Appalachian orogen and contains one of the most complete records of plutonism over the span of the Appalachian "Wilson Cycle." This record provides constraints on evolutionary models for the Appalachian-Caledonian belt, and is also an important reference database for other ancient orogenic belts, particularly those of Precambrian age, which commonly lack upper-crustal hallmarks of plate tectonic processes such as ophiolite suites and preserved arc volcanic sequences. This chapter evaluates compositional groupings among Ordovician to Devonian plutonic suites across Newfoundland and their relationships to spatial subdivisions of the orogen and to temporal sequences within discrete tectonostratigraphic zones. This regional analysis is facilitated by compilation and acquisition of geochemical data from granites by the Geological Survey of Newfoundland and Labrador (e.g., Kerr et al., 1991, 1993a, 1994), and by studies conducted under the LITHOPROBE project (e.g., Fryer et al., 1992; Kerr et al., 1995). The geochemical database upon which it is based is available in digital form (Kerr et al., 1994). This paper continues work initiated in the 1970s that first summarized the broad association of plutonic groupings with tectonic zones (e.g., Strong, 1980). Although more recent studies have altered our views on plutonic groupings and evolution, some threads of this initial classification remain unbroken.

GEOLOGICAL FRAMEWORK

The Newfoundland Appalachians (Fig. 1A) comprise four main tectonostratigraphic zones (Williams, 1979; Williams et al., 1988). From west to east, these are the Humber zone (the ancient North American continental margin), the Dunnage zone (various remnants of the early Paleozoic Iapetus ocean, mostly comprising island arcs and back-arc basins), the Gander zone (a largely metasedimentary belt possibly representing an opposing, Gondwanan, continental margin) and the Avalon zone (a Late Proterozoic orogenic province with a thin Paleozoic cover sequence, probably a fragment of Gondwana). The Dunnage zone is subdivided into the Notre Dame subzone and Exploits subzone, which each have distinct lithological, faunal, and evolutionary characteristics (Williams et al., 1988). Dunnage zone rocks also occur in the higher (ophiolitic) slices of Taconic allochthons in western Newfoundland. Zonal affinities are less clear on the south coast of Newfoundland, where the presence of late Precambrian rocks has led to suggestions that it be included as part of the Avalon zone (Dunning and O'Brien, 1989). In this paper, the south coast region is discussed in conjunction with the Gander zone, largely

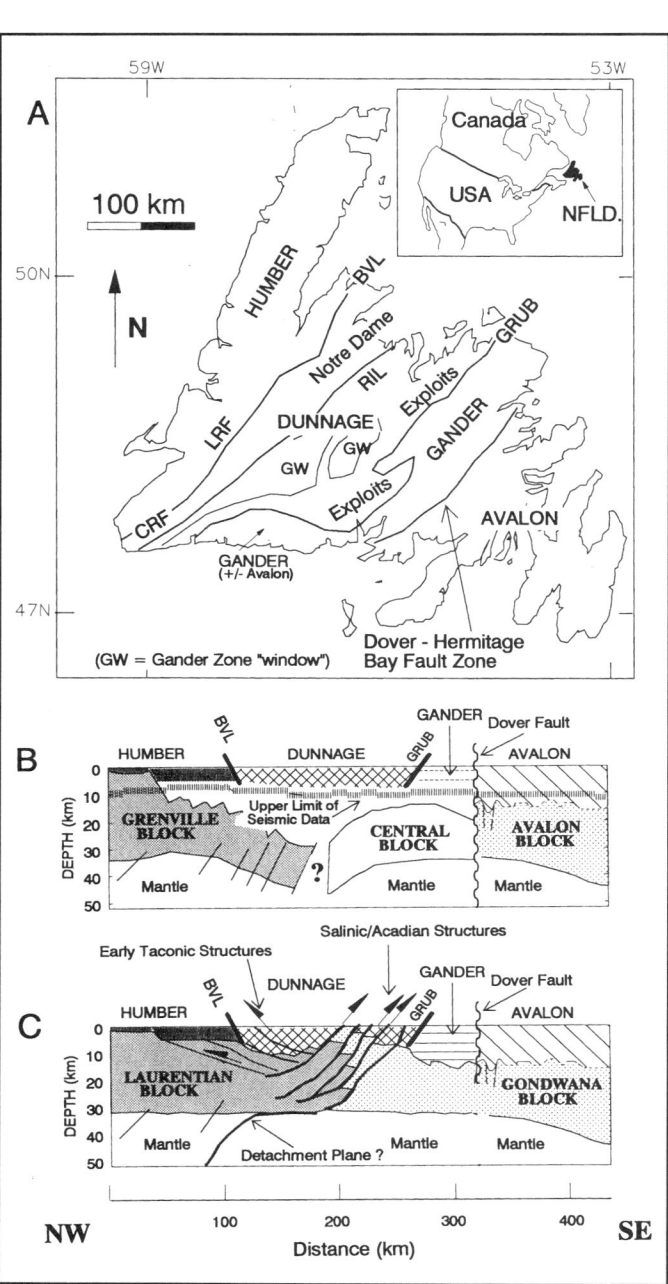

Figure 1. Major subdivisions of the Newfoundland (NFLD) Appalachians and interpretations of crustal structure. A: Distribution of surface tectonostratigraphic zones (after Williams et al., 1988). B: Schematic illustration of interpretation of Marillier et al. (1989) showing proposed Grenville, Central, and Avalon blocks, and crustal-scale Dover fault structure. C: Schematic illustration of interpretation of Quinlan et al. (1992) showing proposed Laurentian and Gondwana blocks. BVL = Baie Verte Line. GRUB = Gander River ultramafic belt.

because its Paleozoic plutonic evolution is similar. Colman-Sadd and Swinden (1984) proposed that the eastern Dunnage zone (Exploits subzone) was allochthonous, and that metasedimentary rocks of the Gander zone formed tectonic "windows" within it, a concept supported by gravity data (Karlstrom, 1983).

In western Newfoundland, the Humber and Dunnage zones are separated by the Baie Verte line, associated with dismembered ophiolites, and by the Long Range fault zone. In the east, the Dunnage and Gander zones are separated by the Gander River ultramafic belt, and by ring-like ophiolites, which surround Gander zone structural windows (e.g., the Mount Cormack subzone). The Gander and Avalon zones are separated by an obvious boundary, defined by a dextral mylonite zone (Dover fault) in the northeast, and a largely brittle structure (Hermitage Bay fault) in the southwest (Dallmeyer et al., 1981; Holdsworth, 1991). Williams et al. (1988) proposed that a major boundary termed the Red Indian line separates the Notre Dame and Exploits subzones in central Newfoundland.

Marine seismic-reflection profiles (Keen et al., 1986; Marillier et al., 1989) indicate that there are three lower crustal blocks beneath Newfoundland, termed the Grenville, Central, and Avalon blocks (Fig. 1B). Interpretations of onland seismic-reflection profiles envisage only two such blocks, termed the Laurentian and Gondwanan blocks (Fig. 1C; after Quinlan et al., 1992). In the latter model, the Central block of the marine profiles is partly interpreted as a region where Laurentian and Gondwanan crust is tectonically interleaved, and the Dover–Hermitage Bay fault system is viewed as an intraplate structure within the Gondwanan block, rather than a major lower crustal boundary.

From the perspective of Appalachian-cycle plutonism, the most important portion of the orogen is the Central mobile belt, that is, the Dunnage and Gander zones combined (Fig. 2). Devonian plutons occur in the Avalon zone, but there are virtually no Appalachian-cycle plutonic suites in the Humber zone, except at its easternmost edge. Proterozoic granitoid rocks are, however, important components of both the Humber and Avalon zones (Fig. 2), where they are largely manifestations of earlier Grenvillian and Pan-African cycles, respectively, although some may record the initial Iapetus rifting episode (Williams et al., 1989). Various classifications of plutonic suites in Newfoundland (e.g., Strong, 1980; Hayes et al., 1987, Williams et al., 1989) have been based on combinations of age, petrological features, and relationships to tectonic zones. In this chapter, age is used as the primary discussion framework, and plutonic suites are divided into Proterozoic-Eocambrian (>540 Ma), Cambrian-Ordovician (540–440 Ma), Silurian (440–410 Ma), and Devonian (410–360 Ma) categories (Fig. 2; time scale after Palmer, 1984). The geographic distribution of these broad age categories is significant (Fig. 2). Proterozoic-Eocambrian suites are mostly restricted to the bounding Laurentian and Avalon continental blocks, although important examples are present on the south coast and in central Newfoundland. Cambrian-Ordovician suites are mostly restricted to the Dunnage zone, whereas Silurian suites are abundant throughout the Central mobile belt, and also occur in the Humber zone. Devonian suites have the widest distribution, intrud-

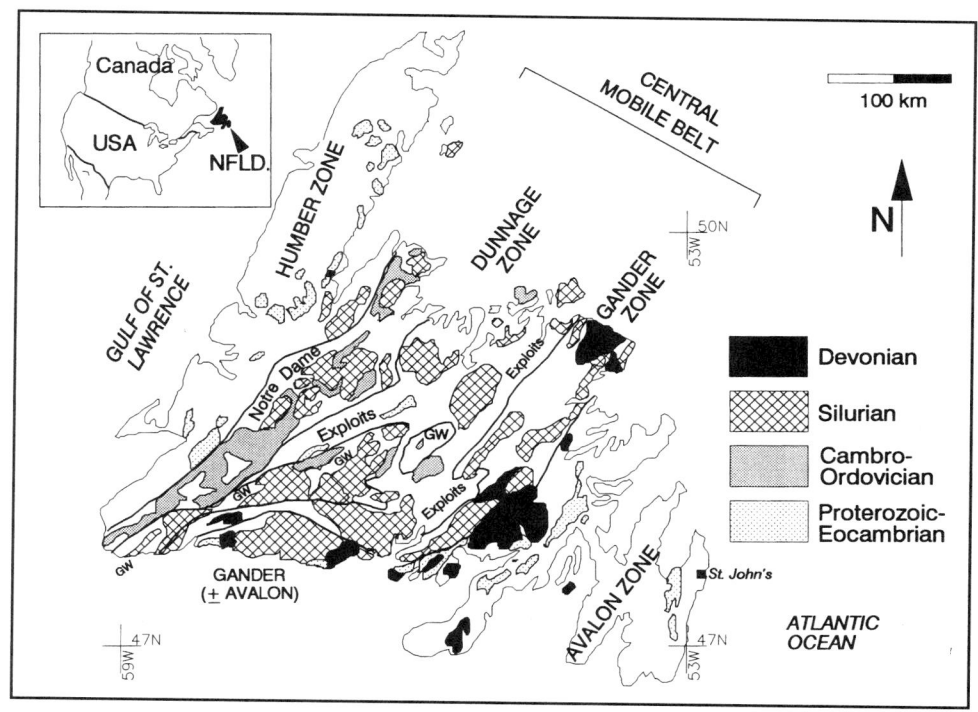

Figure 2. Distribution of Proterozoic-Eocambrian, Cambrian-Ordovician, Silurian, and Devonian plutonic suites across the Newfoundland (NFLD) Appalachians.

bution, intruding all zones, but are most abundant in the Gander and Avalon zones, suggesting that the locus of magmatism shifted eastward (relatively) with time. In terms of their relationship to the protracted and/or episodic tectonism that accompanied and followed the destruction of the Iapetus ocean and collision of Laurentia and Gondwana, these age groupings can be thought of loosely as preorogenic, early orogenic, late orogenic, and postorogenic (Kerr et al., 1992), because they likely reflect discrete stages in Appalachian evolution.

APPALACHIAN-CYCLE PLUTONIC SUITES IN NEWFOUNDLAND

Cambrian-Ordovician plutonic suites

Ordovician plutonic suites, and a few examples of Late Cambrian age, are largely restricted to the Dunnage zone of central Newfoundland, and to Dunnage zone klippen represented by the Bay of Islands and Hare Bay allochthons (Fig. 3).

Dunnage zone (Notre Dame subzone). Within the Notre Dame subzone, Cambrian-Ordovician plutonic suites are of variable age and affinity (Fig. 3). The best-known example is the 507 +3/–2 Ma Twillingate pluton (Williams and Payne, 1975; Payne and Strong, 1979; Elliot et al., 1991). This is variably deformed, but the best-preserved examples are massive, coarse-grained, gray rocks dominated by quartz and plagioclase, with

5%–10% amphibole ± biotite. Blue quartz patches (or augen) are particularly distinctive, and amphibolitic pods and layers include both preintrusion enclaves and later dikes (Williams and Payne, 1975). Distinctive blue-quartz–bearing granitoid rocks similar to the Twillingate pluton occur elsewhere in the Notre Dame subzone, and include the 479 ± 3 Ma Mansfield Cove pluton (Dunning et al., 1987), parts of the undated South Lake igneous complex (O'Brien, 1992), and some rocks in southwestern Newfoundland (see below). Other small plutonic bodies in the Notre Dame Bay area (Fig. 3) are associated with Ordovician volcanic sequences and are likely comagmatic with them. These plutons are more varied in petrology, but are for the most part granodiorites, and lesser gabbro, diorite, and tonalite.

The most extensive belt of Ordovician plutonic suites is in central and southwestern Newfoundland (Fig. 3). The Hungry Mountain complex (467 ± 8 Ma; Whalen et al., 1987a) includes gabbro, diorite, and tonalite, and lesser granodiorite and metamorphic rocks, and is a composite terrane. The Hinds Lake granodiorite has a similar age of 460 ± 10 Ma (Whalen et al., 1987a). To the southwest, extensive tonalitic and granodioritic plutonic rocks (Van Berkel, 1987; Van Berkel and Currie, 1988), were dated as 456 ± 3 Ma in one location, where they include an inherited Middle Proterozoic component (Dunning et al., 1989). It is significant that these intrude paragneisses interpreted to be high-grade equivalents of the Fleur-de-Lys Supergroup, a component of the Humber zone. In the southwestern corner of Newfoundland, variably foliated to gneissic, gray, tonalitic to

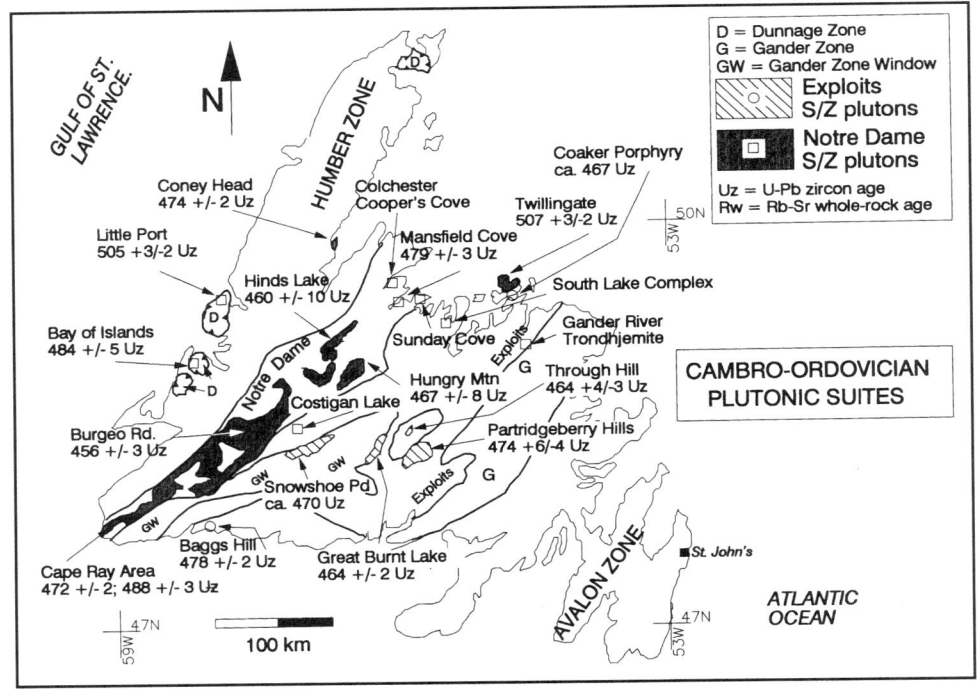

Figure 3. Principal Cambrian-Ordovician plutonic suites of the Dunnage zone in Newfoundland. Note that examples that cannot adequately be represented at the scale of the map are denoted by symbols. For sources of geochronological data, see text.

rocks closely resemble trondhjemitic and tonalitic plutonic rocks in Notre Dame Bay (see above). The tonalites have been dated as 472 ± 2 Ma, and spatially associated granodiorites have been dated as 488 ± 3 Ma (Dubé et al., 1993; 1994). These extensive tonalitic and granodioritic rocks include remnants of older mafic

intrusive rocks, but are also intruded by Silurian mafic and granitic rocks (Fig. 4; see following).

West Coast allochthons (transported Notre Dame subzone?). Granitoid plutonic suites are a minor but significant component of the Taconic allochthons of western Newfoundland

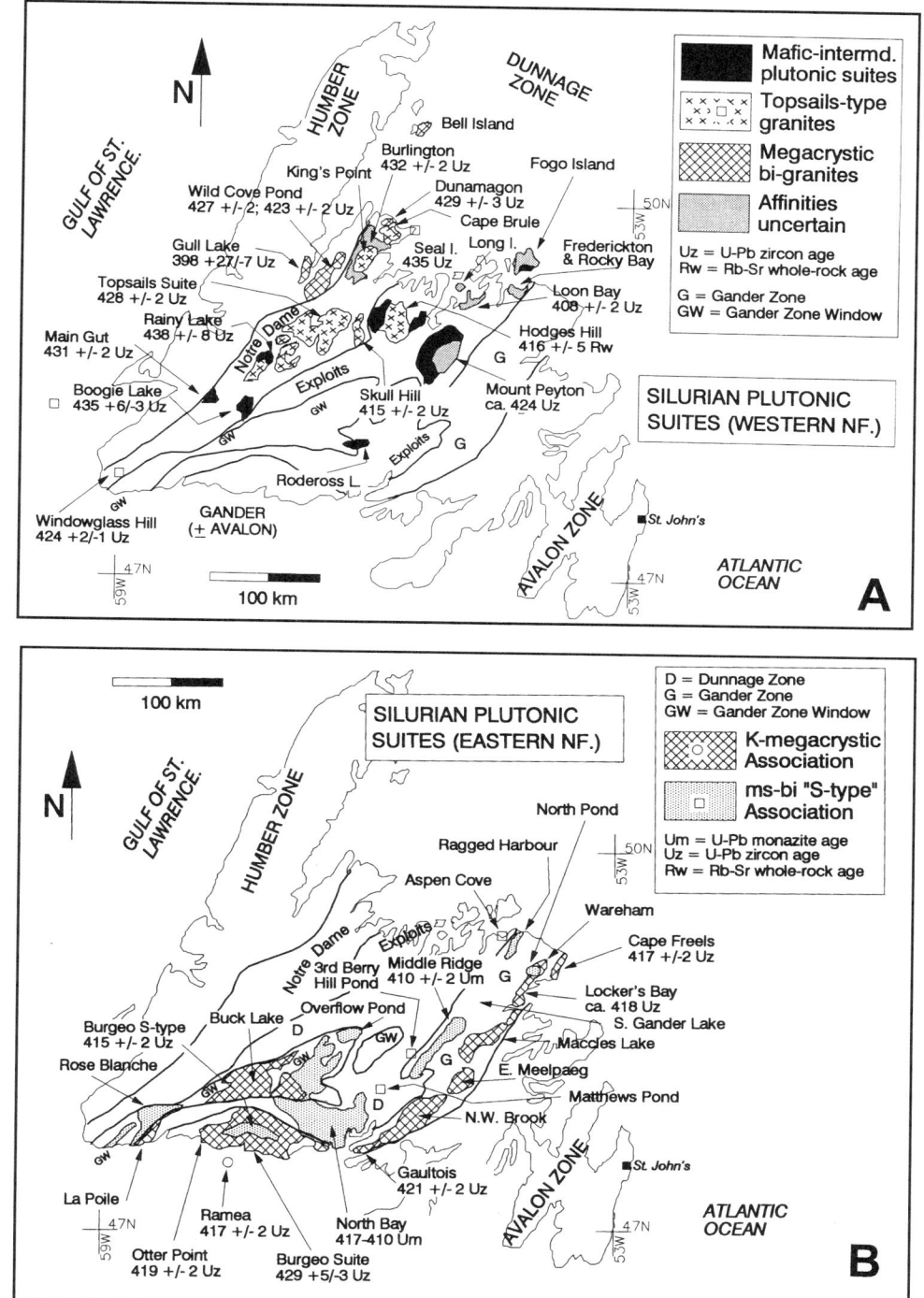

Figure 4. A: Principal Silurian plutonic suites of the Humber and Dunnage zones in Newfoundland (NF). B: Principal Silurian plutonic suites of the Gander zone and south coast region in Newfoundland. Note that examples that cannot adequately be represented at the scale of the map are denoted by symbols. For sources of geochronological data, see text.

(Fig. 3). The 505 +3/–2 Ma Little Port complex consists of gabbro, amphibolite, and trondhjemite (Malpas, 1979; Jenner et al., 1991), and is probably a transported equivalent of Notre Dame Bay plutonic suites such as Twillingate. Minor plagioclase-rich granitoid rocks in the Bay of Islands complex have somewhat different character (Malpas, 1979) and are younger (484 ± 5 Ma; Jenner et al., 1991). Diorite, tonalite, and granite are known from the Coney Head allochthon of White Bay, where they have been dated at 474 ± 2 Ma (Dunning, 1987).

Dunnage zone (Exploits subzone). Cambrian-Ordovician tonalitic and trondhjemitic plutonic rocks akin to those of the Notre Dame subzone are rare in the Exploits subzone. However, minor quartz-rich plagiogranite is associated with ophiolites of the Gander River ultramafic belt (Fig. 3), and the ca. 475 Ma Costigan Lake pluton in central Newfoundland includes trondhjemites that closely resemble Notre Dame subzone examples. Ordovician plutonic suites elsewhere in the Exploits subzone are of radically different character. The best-known examples, around the Mount Cormack window (Fig. 3), intrude Gander zone rocks within the window, and also the surrounding Dunnage zone ophiolitic and volcanic rocks, constraining Dunnage-Gander interaction (Colman-Sadd et al., 1992). The 474 +6/–4 Ma Partridgeberry Hills granite includes biotite-chlorite (± muscovite) granite, containing minor cordierite, andalusite, and garnet (Colman-Sadd, 1985). Associated rocks include the pegmatitic Through Hill granite (464 +4/–3 Ma) and the 464 ± 2 Ma Great Burnt Lake granite (Colman-Sadd, 1985; Colman-Sadd et al., 1992), and the Snowshoe Pond and Ebbegunbaeg granites (Fig. 3). Muscovite is not present in all examples. Potential correlatives elsewhere include the hypabyssal plutonic rocks of the ca. 467 Ma Coaker porphyry in Notre Dame Bay (Dunning, *in* Elliot et al., 1991), and the 478 ± 2 Ma Baggs Hill granite (Tucker et al., 1994), on the south coast (Fig. 3). The 453 ± 3 Ma Port-aux-Basques granite in southwestern Newfoundland (van Staal et al., 1994) may also belong to this group.

Silurian plutonic suites

Silurian plutonic suites occur throughout the Central mobile belt and (locally) intrude the adjacent Humber zone (Fig. 4). These plutonic suites display significant variation in petrology and geochemistry across the Central mobile belt, and several discrete compositional associations are recognized.

Humber zone. The only Appalachian-cycle plutonic suites in the Humber zone of Newfoundland occur in the White Bay area (Fig. 4A). The largest is the Wild Cove Pond intrusive suite (Hibbard, 1983), which intrudes metasedimentary rocks of the Fleur-de-Lys Supergroup. The Wild Cove Pond suite is dominated by coarse-grained, K-feldspar megacrystic, biotite granites, but also includes subordinate muscovite-biotite granites, and older gabbro and diorite. Metasedimentary xenoliths are common, and some granites have a banded appearance, suggesting large-scale assimilation (Hibbard, 1983). The dominant granite has been dated as 423 ± 2 Ma, but muscovite-bearing phases are 427 ± 2 Ma, similar in age to migmatitic sweats in the country rocks (Cawood and

Dunning, 1993). The 429 ± 3 Ma (Cawood and Dunning, 1993) Dunamagon granite (Hibbard, 1983) partly intrudes Fleur-de-Lys equivalents, and also intrudes the Humber-Dunnage boundary (Baie Verte line). The muscovite-bearing Bell Island granite (Williams and Smyth, 1983) intrudes Fleur-de-Lys equivalents on the Grey Islands (Fig. 4), and is probably analogous to the Wild Cove Pond suite. The Gull Lake intrusive suite (Smyth and Schillereff, 1982) includes similar K-feldspar megacrystic granites, and lesser tonalitic rocks. A Silurian age is permitted by an imprecise U-Pb age of 398 +27/–7 Ma (Erdmer, 1986). Williams et al. (1989) grouped these Humber zone intrusions with the Topsails association of the adjacent Notre Dame subzone (see following), but this link was questioned by Kerr et al. (1990). Their closest equivalents, in terms of petrology, are the Silurian suites of the Gander zone, hosted by compositionally similar metasedimentary terranes on the opposite side of the orogen (see below).

Dunnage zone (Notre Dame subzone). Silurian plutonic suites in the Notre Dame subzone (Fig. 4A) are dominated by alkali-calcic to alkaline granites, with subordinate mafic to intermediate plutonic suites. All of these intrude Cambrian-Ordovician volcanic sequences and associated Cambrian-Ordovician plutonic suites (see above). On the Baie Verte Peninsula, alkali-calcic granites intrude the Burlington granodiorite, previously dated as Ordovician (461 ± 15 Ma; Dallmeyer, *in* Hibbard, 1983), but now dated as 432 ± 2 Ma (Cawood and Dunning, 1993). The Burlington granodiorite has a closer resemblance to nearby Ordovician suites (e.g., Hinds Lake) than to other Silurian plutons. The best-known Silurian complex in the Notre Dame subzone is the Topsails intrusive suite (Taylor et al., 1980; Whalen et al., 1987a; Whalen, 1989), which is dominated by massive granodiorite, syenite, and granite of variably peralkaline composition, dated as 429 ± 3 Ma, and 427 ± 3 Ma (Whalen et al., 1987a). The spatially associated 415 ± 2 Ma Skull Hill syenite (Kean and Jayasinghe, 1982) is probably related to the Topsails intrusive suite. The 429 ± 4 Ma caldera-type volcanic rocks of the Springdale Group are considered to be extrusive equivalents of the Topsails intrusive suite (Coyle and Strong, 1987; Whalen, 1989). On the Baie Verte Peninsula, similar rocks include the largely subvolcanic King's Point complex, (Hibbard, 1983; Mercer et al., 1985), the Cape Brule porphyry (Hibbard, 1983), the 435 ± 15 Ma Seal Island Bight syenite (DeGrace et al., 1976), and the 430–425 Ma volcanic rocks of the Cape St. John Group (DeGrace et al., 1976; Cawood and Dunning, 1993). Caldera-type structures are important features of all the volcanic and subvolcanic examples (Neale et al., 1960; Coyle and Strong, 1987).

Mafic and intermediate plutonic rocks of Silurian age occur throughout the Notre Dame subzone, and some are spatially associated with the Topsails association granites, although the mafic plutonic rocks are slightly older (Fig. 4). The Rainy Lake complex consists of altered gabbro and diorite, and lesser tonalite and granodiorite, dated as 438 ± 8 Ma (Whalen et al., 1987a). Other examples include the Main Gut and Boogie Lake intrusions, dated as 431 ± 2 Ma and 435 +6/–3 Ma, respectively (Dunning et al., 1990). Several other undeformed mafic to intermediate plutons in southwestern Newfoundland (Van Berkel, 1987; Van Berkel and Currie, 1988) probably also belong to this group, as do minor mafic rocks within the Topsails intrusive suite and related plutons.

Dunnage zone (Exploits subzone). Silurian plutonic rocks are less abundant at surface in the Exploits subzone than in the Notre Dame subzone (Fig. 4A), and are partly of bimodal type. The Mount Peyton intrusive suite (Strong and Dupuy, 1982; Dickson, 1992, 1993) is dominated by homogeneous hornblende-gabbro and diorite, intruded by equigranular biotite granite. The gabbro has been dated as ca. 424 Ma in two locations, and the granite has given a similar preliminary age (Dickson, 1993). Mafic rocks are also present in the Rodeross Lake intrusion (Colman-Sadd, 1985) and on Fogo Island, where they include complex cumulate-layered zones (Cawthorn, 1978). However, Fogo Island is areally dominated by biotite granites, and subordinate high-silica granites (Sandeman and Malpas, 1993). Other granitic intrusions of similar character, but lacking associated mafic phases, include the 408 ± 2 Ma Loon Bay granodiorite (Elliot et al., 1991), the Long Island intrusion, and the small Rocky Bay and Frederickton plutons (Strong and Dickson, 1978). Close to the boundary between Exploits and Notre Dame subzones, the 416 ± 5 Ma (Rb-Sr; Moore, 1984) Hodges Hill granite includes peralkaline, hypersolvus granites that are similar to those of the Topsails intrusive suite (Kerr, 1995).

Gander zone and south coast region. Silurian plutonic suites in the Gander zone and along the south coast (Fig. 4B) are very different from those of the Dunnage zone. In contrast to the Dunnage zone plutons, which are largely posttectonic, Gander zone examples have a broadly syntectonic relationship to major Silurian deformation throughout this region (e.g., Dunning et al., 1990). Strong (1980) and Williams et al. (1989) distinguished two compositional groups within this region, which are here termed the K-feldspar megacrystic and muscovite-biotite associations.

K-feldspar megacrystic biotite-granites form a semicontinuous belt localized in the eastern, higher-grade, portion of the area, adjacent to its boundary with the Avalon zone (Fig. 4A). The Burgeo intrusive suite (O'Brien et al., 1986; Dickson et al., 1989), the largest plutonic complex on the south coast, is dominated by variably foliated, K-feldspar megacrystic biotite granodiorite and granite, but includes a wide range of compositions from gabbro to granite. Younger muscovite-bearing phases are here grouped with the muscovite-biotite association (see below). Enclaves of migmatitic gneiss, of metasedimentary or possibly igneous origin, are widespread, and various mafic and intermediate enclaves also commonly occur. Variably sheared, equigranular, pink granites intrude the dominant megacrystic granites. The megacrystic biotite granite has a U-Pb age of 429 +5/–3 Ma (Dunning et al., 1990). Closely similar, coarse-grained, K-feldspar megacrystic, biotite (± hornblende) granites are recognized throughout the Gander zone and south coast region. On the south coast, these include the 421 +/–2 Ma Gaultois granite (Colman-Sadd et al., 1979; Dunning et al., 1990), the McCallum granite (Dickson et al., 1989), the 419 ± 2 Ma Otter Point granite (O'Brien et al.,

1991), and the La Poile granite (Chorlton, 1978). All are variably deformed, and are interpreted as broadly syntectonic, suggesting major Silurian orogenesis (Dunning et al., 1990). They include enclaves of metasedimentary aspect, and also cognate melanocratic inclusions. In northeastern Newfoundland, equivalent rocks include the 417 ± 2 Ma (R. D. Tucker, 1990, personal commun.) Cape Freels granite, the ca. 418 Ma (Dunning et al., 1993) Locker's Bay granite, and the undated Wareham granite, all described by Blackwood (1977) and Jayasinghe (1978). These are variably affected by early sinistral and later dextral shearing associated with the Gander-Avalon boundary, and are interpreted to have been emplaced synchronously with Silurian deformation (Holdsworth, 1991). Metasedimentary enclaves are common in these suites, and are particularly abundant in the Wareham and Locker's Bay granites. Much of the adjacent Maccles Lake granite also belongs to this association (O'Brien and Holdsworth, 1992; Kerr et al., 1993a). From the south coast to Bonavista Bay, the K-feldspar megacrystic granites are cut by biotite-muscovite granites, and also by posttectonic Devonian granites (see following). The Northwest Brook and Eastern Meelpaeg complexes (Fig. 4B) are composite units that also include abundant biotite-muscovite granites.

The muscovite-biotite association is more abundant in interior, lower-grade, portions of the region, and locally intrudes nearby portions of the Exploits subzone (Fig. 4B). The best-known example is the Middle Ridge granite, dominated by medium- to coarse-grained, white to pink, variably porphyritic, locally garnetiferous, biotite-muscovite monzogranite to granite. Associated pegmatites contain garnet, tourmaline, and beryl. The pluton is weakly foliated, but foliations are subparallel to outer contacts, possibly indicating a relationship to emplacement, rather than pervasive deformation (Blackwood, 1983). The granite has been dated at 410 ± 2 Ma using monazite, and zircon populations suggest Early to Middle Proterozoic inheritance (R. D. Tucker, 1990, personal commun.). In northeastern Newfoundland, similar biotite-muscovite granites in the Gander zone include the North Pond and Business Cove granites (Jayasinghe, 1978), and numerous small, unnamed bodies that cut Burgeo Association plutons. The muscovite-rich Ragged Harbour pluton (Currie and Pajari, 1977) is of similar type, as are parts of the Aspen Cove pluton, located in the adjacent Exploits subzone. Geochronological constraints are lacking for most of these plutons, but they are clearly older than nearby Devonian granites, and contain fabrics interpreted as Silurian (Holdsworth, 1991). In southern Newfoundland, large parts of the "North Bay Granite Suite" of Dickson (1990) comprise medium-grained, equigranular, biotite-muscovite (± garnet) granites, and coarse-grained, K-feldspar porphyritic biotite-muscovite granites. Monazite ages are imprecise, but suggest emplacement ca. 417–410 Ma, similar to the Middle Ridge granite. Note that undeformed granites included with the North Bay granite suite by Dickson (1990) are Devonian, and discussed separately. On the south coast, 415 ± 2 Ma (Dunning et al., 1990) biotite-muscovite granites that intrude Burgeo association granites (O'Brien et al., 1986; Dickson et al., 1989), and the 418 ± 2 Ma

Rose Blanche granite (Brown, 1977; van Staal et al., 1994), are also assigned to this group.

Devonian plutonic suites

Devonian plutonic suites of largely posttectonic character are mostly concentrated in the Gander zone (including the south coast region) and the Avalon zone (Fig. 5). Minor examples occur in the Dunnage zone and in the Humber zone.

Humber zone. The Devil's Room granite (Smyth and Schillereff, 1982) intrudes Grenvillian basement rocks, and is a K-feldspar porphyritic biotite granite, dated as 400 ± 2 Ma (Erdmer, 1986).

Dunnage zone (Notre Dame subzone). Most plutons in this region that previously gave Devonian Rb-Sr and K-Ar ages are now known to be Silurian (see previous discussion). However, the Strawberry granite, a coarse-grained, K-feldspar megacrystic biotite-granite adjacent to the Cape Ray fault zone, has been precisely dated as 384 ± 2 Ma (Dubé et al., 1993). Other small bodies of similar, but undated, potassic, posttectonic granite in southwestern Newfoundland may be of similar age.

Dunnage zone (Exploits subzone). Devonian plutonism is also rare in the Exploits subzone; however, some granites currently grouped as Silurian (e.g., Fogo Island) have yet to be dated precisely. Undated posttectonic granites in parts of the south coast tentatively linked to the Exploits subzone (e.g., the Ironbound pluton of Chorlton, 1978) may also be Devonian.

Gander zone and south coast region. Devonian plutonic suites are a major component of the Gander zone and south coast region (Fig. 5) and the adjacent Avalon zone (see following). These granites were reviewed in detail by Kerr et al. (1993a). A well-known example is the Ackley granite (Strong et al., 1974; Dickson, 1983; Tuach et al., 1986; Kontak et al., 1988), which intrudes the Gander-Avalon boundary. The Ackley granite is dominated by coarse-grained, variably porphyritic, K-feldspar megacrystic biotite (± hornblende), granodiorite, and granite on the northwest (Gander) side, and by quartz-rich, leucocratic, biotite granites on the southeast (Avalon) side. Minor Mo and Sn-W mineralization is associated with the southern contact. Tuach et al. (1986) interpreted petrological and geochemical variations to indicate liquid-state fractionation processes (e.g., Hildreth, 1981), and suggested that the Ackley represented a "frozen" zoned magma chamber. The most recent and comprehensive geochronological study (Kontak et al., 1988) suggested Ar-Ar ages of 378–374 Ma for the main phases of the pluton, and 373–371 Ma for hydrothermal mineralization, and indicated that the pluton consists of several discrete phases or lobes.

Other Devonian plutons in the Gander zone include the ca. 400 Ma (Ar-Ar; O'Neill and Lux, 1989) Deadman's Bay granite, the Newport granite, and the Middle Brook granite (Blackwood, 1977; Jayasinghe, 1978; Kerr et al., 1993a). These are similar K-feldspar megacrystic, biotite granites, which locally contain metasedimentary enclaves. The Deadman's Bay and Middle Brook granites are locally foliated at their margins, and are prob-

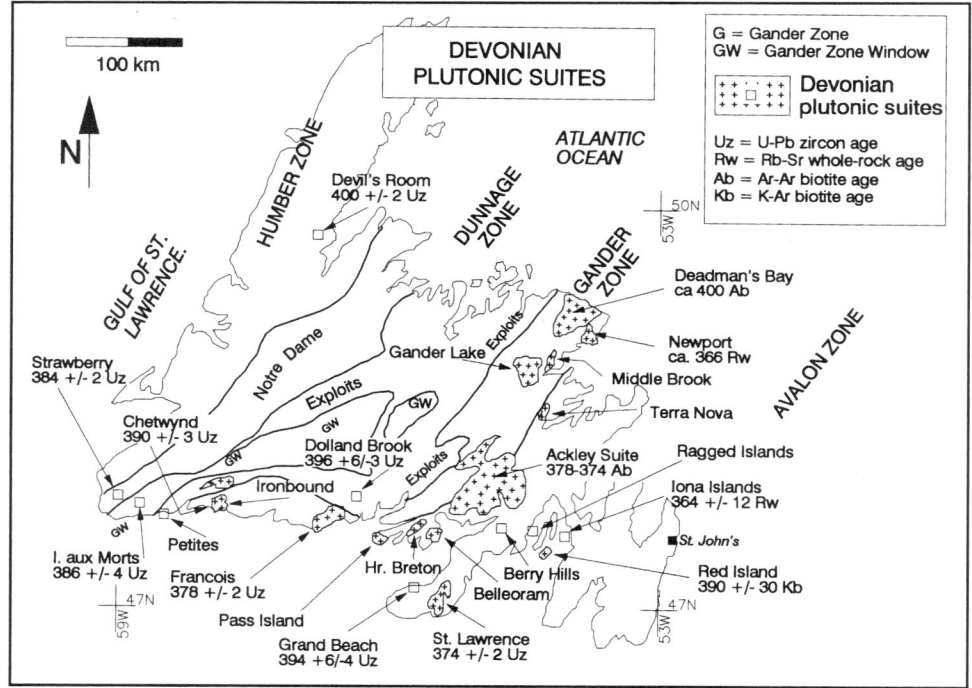

Figure 5. Principal Devonian plutonic suites of the Newfoundland Appalachians, mostly in the Gander and Avalon zones. Note that examples that cannot adequately be represented at the scale of the map are denoted by symbols. For sources of geochronological data, see text.

ably older than the Newport granite. The Gander Lake granite includes massive megacrystic biotite granite with metasedimentary enclaves, and also equigranular siliceous granites, with minor muscovite. All of these plutons intrude metasedimentary rocks of the Gander Group and its presumed equivalents, and also the variably foliated Silurian K-feldspar megacrystic and muscovite-biotite granites. Their ages are constrained by Rb-Sr and K-Ar ages (reviewed by Kerr et al., 1993a), many of which may underestimate their true emplacement ages. On the south coast, prominent Devonian plutons include the 378 ± 2 Ma (Kerr et al., 1993b) François granite, the 396 +6/–3 Ma (Dunning et al., 1990) Dolland Brook granite (part of the North Bay granite suite of Dickson, 1990), and the 390 ± 3 Ma (O'Brien et al., 1991) Chetwynd granite. These locally include K-feldspar megacrystic granites that resemble those of the northeast Gander zone, but are dominated by equigranular, high-silica, biotite granites. The François granite contains well-preserved ring-complex structures indicative of high-level emplacement (Poole et al., 1985). In southwestern Newfoundland, the undated Petites granite and the 386 ± 4 Ma (Dubé et al., 1993) Isle aux Morts Brook granite (Brown, 1977; Kerr et al., 1993a) also form part of this group.

Avalon zone. Devonian plutonic suites of the Avalon zone (Fig. 5) were reviewed in detail by Kerr et al. (1993a). In general, Avalon zone Devonian plutonic suites are more variable in lithology and setting than their counterparts in the Gander zone, and locally include associated intermediate and mafic rocks.

The Terra Nova granite is a K-feldspar megacrystic, biotite granite that resembles adjacent Devonian plutons in the northeast Gander zone, and locally intrudes the Dover fault (O'Brien and Holdsworth, 1992). Other examples in the western Avalon zone (Fig. 5) include the Berry Hills granite (O'Brien et al., 1984), the Belleoram granite (Furey, 1985), the Harbour Breton granite (Greene and O'Driscoll, 1976; Furey and Strong, 1986) and the Pass Island granite (Greene and O'Driscoll, 1976). These are petrologically varied, but (excluding Belleoram) all are evolved, leucocratic, high-silica granites. The Pass Island granite closely resembles parts of the François granite, in the adjacent south coast region. Age constraints on these suites are mostly provided by field relations and by early Rb-Sr and K-Ar ages (reviewed by Kerr et al., 1993a). In the Placentia Bay area, the Ragged Islands intrusions (O'Driscoll and Muggridge, 1979) are dominated by homogeneous, pink granites, but also include gray granodiorites. The Iona Islands intrusions (McCartney, 1967; Peckham, 1992) consist mostly of gabbro and diorite, intruded by minor fine-grained, leucocratic, granite, dated as 364 ± 12 Ma (Rb-Sr; Peckham, 1992). The 390 ± 30 Ma (K-Ar) Red Island granite (Strong et al., 1974; O'Driscoll and Muggridge, 1979) consists of red, quartz-rich, leucocratic, biotite granite, and minor associated mafic rocks. A large positive magnetic anomaly exists beneath Placentia Bay, suggesting an extensive Devonian batholith at depth in this area (Kerr et al., 1993a). On the southern Burin Peninsula, the St. Lawrence granite (Teng and Strong, 1976; Strong et al., 1977, 1984; Collins and Strong, 1988) is dominated by equigranular, orange to brick-red, leucocratic alkali-feldspar

granite, containing reibeckite-arfvedsonite and aegirine. Fine-grained quartz-feldspar porphyry dikes, and volcanic rocks of similar aspect, are associated with the pluton. Early Rb-Sr ages indicated a ca. 315 Ma (Carboniferous) age, but the pluton has now been dated as 374 ± 2 Ma (Kerr et al., 1993b). The nearby Grand Beach porphyry gave a tentative U-Pb age of 394 +6/–4 Ma (Krogh et al., 1988).

GEOCHEMICAL PATTERNS IN SPACE AND TIME

Sources and representation of geochemical data

A database of almost 5000 major- and trace-element analyses (Kerr et al., 1994) forms the basis for discussions below. Some additional data from the Topsails intrusive suite were compiled from Whalen et al. (1987b). Graphical representation of such large amounts of data is difficult, because conventional scattergrams become ineffective at high point densities. Certain areas (notably southern Newfoundland) are represented by disproportionately large amounts of data, due to high-density grid sampling during mapping (e.g., Dickson, 1983; Dickson et al., 1989). To reduce this bias, and render diagrams legible, some suites are represented by a randomly selected subset (~10% of data) for production of diagrams. Univariate statistics for random subsets are essentially identical those for the original datasets, indicating that this procedure is statistically valid. The full datasets were retained for other procedures such as frequency calculations, and analysis of evolutionary trends.

Spatial geochemical trends

Cambrian-Ordovician plutonic suites. SiO_2-CaO relationships (Fig. 6A) and normative classification (Fig. 6B) indicate a wide range of major element compositions in the Notre Dame subzone, particularly in southwestern Newfoundland. Notre Dame subzone suites range in composition from calcic tonalite to granite (sensu stricto), in contrast to the Exploits subzone suites, which are tightly clustered in the monzogranite and granite (sensu stricto) fields. Suites in both subzones are dominantly peraluminous (A/CNK > 1), but those of the Exploits subzone are strongly peraluminous, with A/CNK > 1.1 (Fig. 6C). Notre Dame subzone suites are dominantly sodic, whereas those from the Exploits subzone have potassic affinities (Fig. 6D). There are plutonic suites of contrasting composition within the Notre Dame subzone, as illustrated by the Na_2O-K_2O-CaO ternary plot (Fig. 6E), which shows contrasting trondhjemitic and calc-alkaline evolutionary tendencies. Trondhjemitic tendencies are shown by data from the Twillingate pluton and the Mansfield Cove complex, whereas most of the southwestern Newfoundland examples show a different calc-alkaline pattern. In view of the wide age range among these suites, such disparity is not surprising.

Notre Dame subzone suites have low Rb and (Y + Nb) contents that place them in the field of volcanic-arc granites (Fig. 7, A and B), although a few are transitional to within-plate

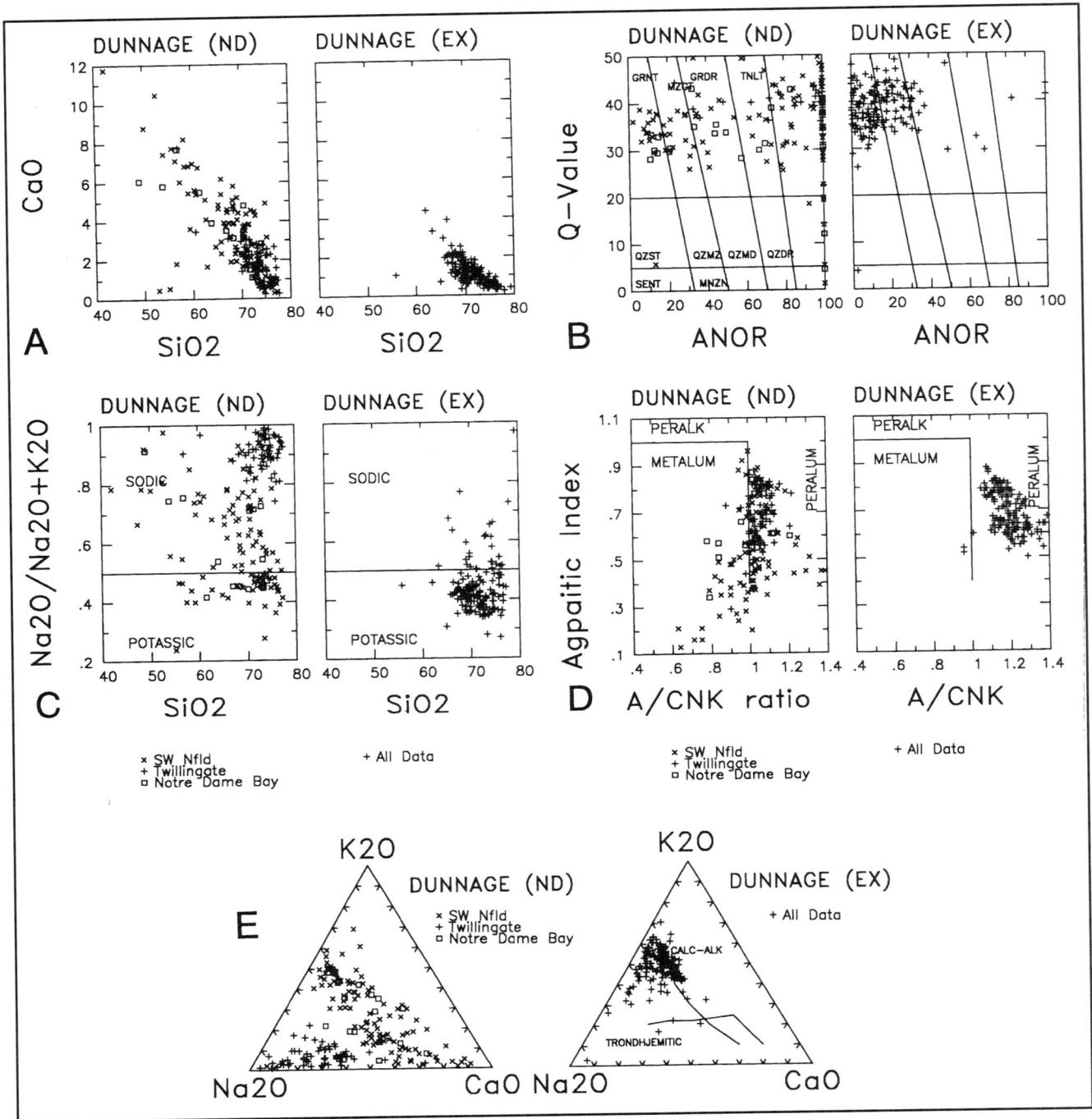

Figure 6. Major element compositional traits of Cambrian-Ordovician plutonic suites in the Dunnage zone of Newfoundland. A: CaO-SiO$_2$ plot. B: Normative equivalent to International Union of Geological Sciences rock classification (after Streckeisen and LeMaitre, 1979); ANOR = An (An + Or) ×100, Q-value = Q/(Q + Ab + Or + An) ×100. Rock type abbreviations: GRNT (granite), QZST (quartz syenite) SENT (syenite), MZGT (monzogranite), QZMZ (quartz monzonite), MNZN (monzonite), GRDR (granodiorite), QZMD (quartz monzodiorite), TNLT (tonalite), and QZDR (quartz diorite). C: Na:K-SiO$_2$ plot; N/N + K = Na$_2$O/(Na$_2$O + K$_2$O). D: Alkali:alumina plot; A/CNK = molecular Al/(Ca + Na + K), Agpaitic index = molecular (K + Na)/Al. E: Na$_2$O-K$_2$O-CaO ternary plot.

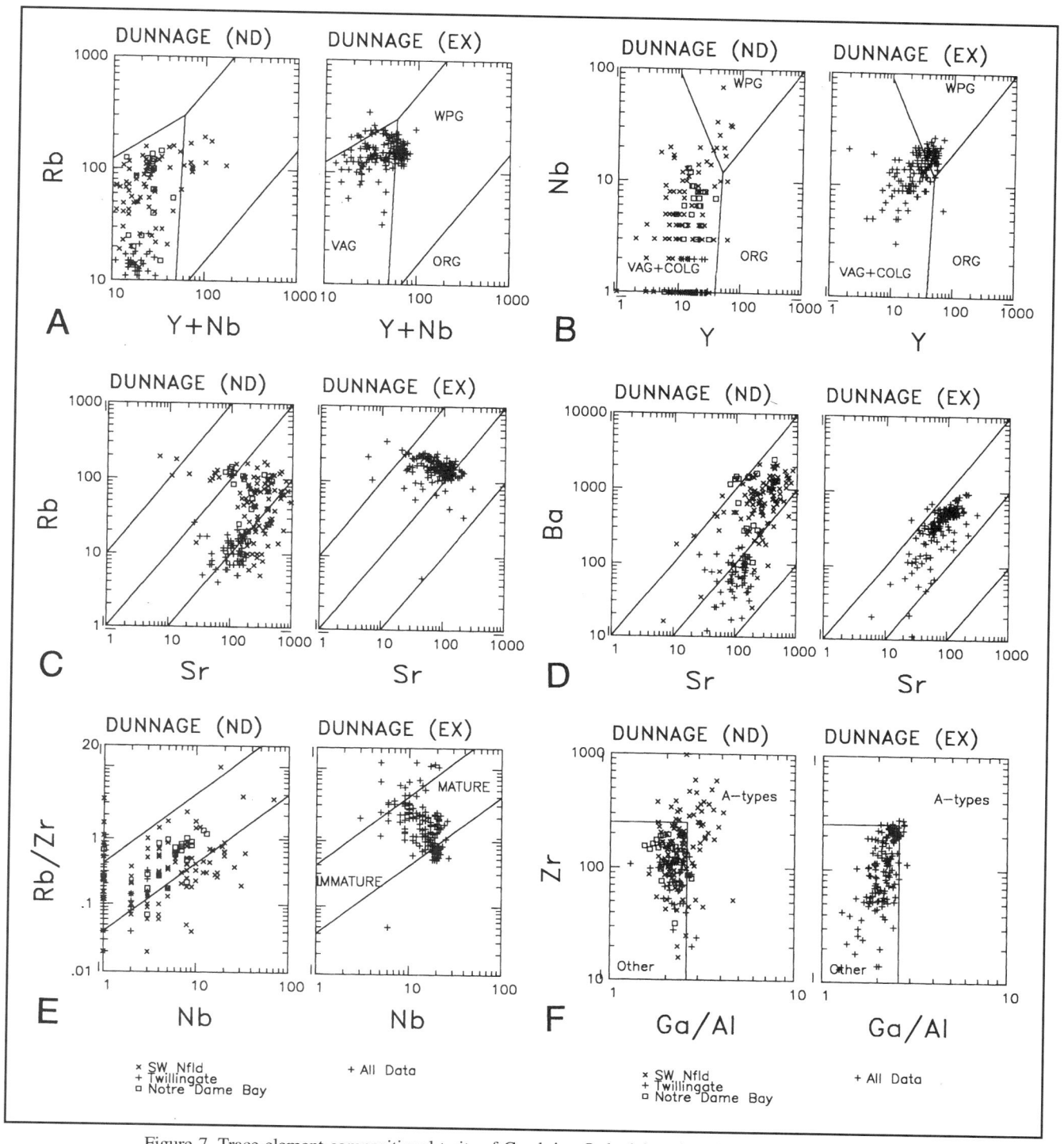

Figure 7. Trace element compositional traits of Cambrian-Ordovician plutonic suites in the Dunnage zone of Newfoundland. A: Rb-(Y + Nb) plot, after Pearce et al. (1984). B: Nb-Y plot, after Pearce et al. (1984). C: Rb-Sr plot. D: Ba-Sr plot; E: Rb/Zr-Nb plot, after Brown et al. (1984). F: Zr-(Ga/Al × 10^4) plot, after Whalen et al. (1987b).

granites. Exploits subzone examples are tightly clustered, reflecting their lesser compositional range, but have higher average Nb and Y. Ba-Rb-Sr relationships (Fig. 7, C and D) show that Exploits subzone suites are relatively evolved, with Rb/Sr mostly >1, in contrast to unevolved, Sr-rich suites of the Notre Dame subzone. The two groups overlap in Ba/Sr ratios, but Exploits subzone examples have more consistent Ba/Sr of 5–10, and contain no rocks with Ba/Sr <1. They are also distinguished by higher Rb/Zr ratios and Nb (Fig. 7E), but there is relatively little contrast between the two subzones in the Zr-(Ga/Al) discrimination diagram (Fig. 7F).

Silurian plutonic suites. There are contrasts between Silurian plutonic suites emplaced into bounding metasedimentary terranes (Humber zone and Gander zone), and those within the Dunnage zone (Figs. 8 and 9). CaO-SiO_2 relationships (Fig. 8A) show that Humber and Gander zone examples are dominated by samples with >60% SiO_2, whereas both the Notre Dame and Exploits subzones have a wider (possibly bimodal) SiO_2 distribution. Humber zone suites have the smallest range of compositions, as shown in the normative equivalent to the International Union of Geological Sciences (IUGS) classification (Fig. 8B). The bimodality of Dunnage zone suites is shown well by this diagram, as is the separation between the Burlington granodiorite and other Silurian granitoid rocks of the Notre Dame subzone. The predominantly tonalitic-granodioritic affinity of this suite is similar to spatially associated Ordovician plutonic suites, with which it was previously grouped (Williams et al., 1989; Fig. 6). In the Gander zone, mafic rocks are virtually absent, and both the K-feldspar megacrystic and muscovite-biotite associations include a similar range of IUGS rock types; however, the latter has a particularly dense concentration in the granite (sensu stricto) field. Differences across the orogen are also evident in alkali: alumina ratios (Fig. 8C). Humber and Gander zone examples are dominantly peraluminous in composition, as opposed to the dominantly metaluminous to peralkaline granitoid rocks of the Dunnage zone. The highest A/CNK (>1.1) is shown by the muscovite-biotite association of the Gander zone, whereas K-feldspar megacrystic suites are in part metaluminous, with A/CNK mostly <1.1. The Topsails intrusive suite and similar suites of the Notre Dame subzone show variable peralkalinity, but the Hodges Hill granite and some granites from Fogo Island also have high KN/A. Hodges Hill is locally peralkaline. Na_2O:K_2O relationships (Fig. 8D) show that Humber zone and Gander zone examples tend to be dominantly potassic, whereas Dunnage zone suites (particularly in the Exploits subzone) are dominantly sodic. Gander zone suites, particularly those of muscovite-biotite affinity, show wide variations in $Na_2O/(Na_2O + K_2O)$.

In the Rb-(Y + Nb) diagram (Fig. 9A), Notre Dame subzone suites show a clear affinity to within-plate granites, as do many suites from the Exploits subzone. Other Silurian granitoid rocks of the Dunnage zone, including the Burlington granodiorite, correspond mostly to volcanic-arc granites. Gander zone Silurian

suites cluster mostly to the left of the "triple point," but the muscovite-biotite association lies partly within the syncollisional granite field, characterized by high Rb contents. A similar pattern is shown by Humber zone examples, on the opposite side of the orogen. Rb:Ba:Sr relationships (Fig. 9, B and C) are less effective in separating the various regions. The highest Rb/Sr ratios (>10) are shown by evolved granites of the Topsails intrusive suite, and some of the muscovite-biotite granites of the Gander zone. However, their absolute Rb contents differ significantly; most Topsails-like granites have Rb < 200 ppm. Ba/Sr ratios display much greater variation in Dunnage zone suites, consistent with their wide compositional variations. However, Silurian suites of the Dunnage zone have distinctly higher Ba/Sr (5–100) than their counterparts in the Humber and Gander zones (Ba/Sr mostly <5), which show better Ba-Sr correlation, a pattern indicating K-feldspar fractionation. Silurian granitoid rocks of the Dunnage zone are enriched in Zr compared to those of the Humber and Gander zones, and many plot within the A-type field in the Zr-(Ga/Al) diagram (Fig. 9D) and below the "arc spectrum" in the Rb/Zr-Nb plot (Fig. 9E). Muscovite-biotite–bearing granites from the Gander zone have the highest Rb/Zr ratios; as for other parameters, Humber zone suites show a closer affinity to those of the Gander zone than to those of the adjacent Dunnage zone.

Devonian plutonic suites. Comparisons are confined to the Gander zone (including the south coast) and the Avalon zone, because only a few data are available from minor Devonian granites of the Humber zone and Notre Dame subzone. As a group, Devonian plutonic suites are characterized more by similarities than by differences. They are compositionally evolved; SiO_2 contents mostly >60%, and CaO mostly <5% (Fig. 10A), and are concentrated in the granite (sensu stricto) and monzogranite fields in the IUGS classification (Fig. 10B). They are metaluminous to weakly peraluminous (Fig. 10D) and overwhelmingly potassic (Fig. 10C). There are no obvious major element contrasts between the Gander and Avalon zones, although Avalon zone suites tend to have higher KN/A values, and are locally of peralkaline affinity. Gander zone examples tend towards more peraluminous compositions. In terms of trace element patterns, both Gander and Avalon zone examples cluster around the triple point in the Rb-(Y+Nb) plot; some Gander zone examples (mostly representing the François granite) fall into the syn-collisional granite field (Fig. 11A, 11B). Gander and Avalon zone examples have broadly similar ranges in Rb/Sr (Fig. 11C), and highly correlated Ba-Sr trends; the Avalon zone examples show a greater range of Ba/Sr ratios. In the Zr-(Ga/Al) plot (Fig. 11D), they are transitional

---

Figure 8. Major-element compositional traits of Silurian plutonic suites across Newfoundland. A: CaO-SiO_2 plot. B: Normative equivalent to International Union of Geological Sciences rock classification (after Streckeisen and LeMaitre, 1979); ANOR = An (An + Or) × 100, Q-value = Q/(Q + Ab + Or + An) (100, rock type abbreviations as in Figure 6. C: Na:K-SiO_2 plot; N/N + K = $Na_2O/(Na_2O + K_2O)$. D: Alkali:alumina plot; A/CNK = molecular Al/(Ca + Na + K), Agpaitic index = molecular (K + Na)/Al.

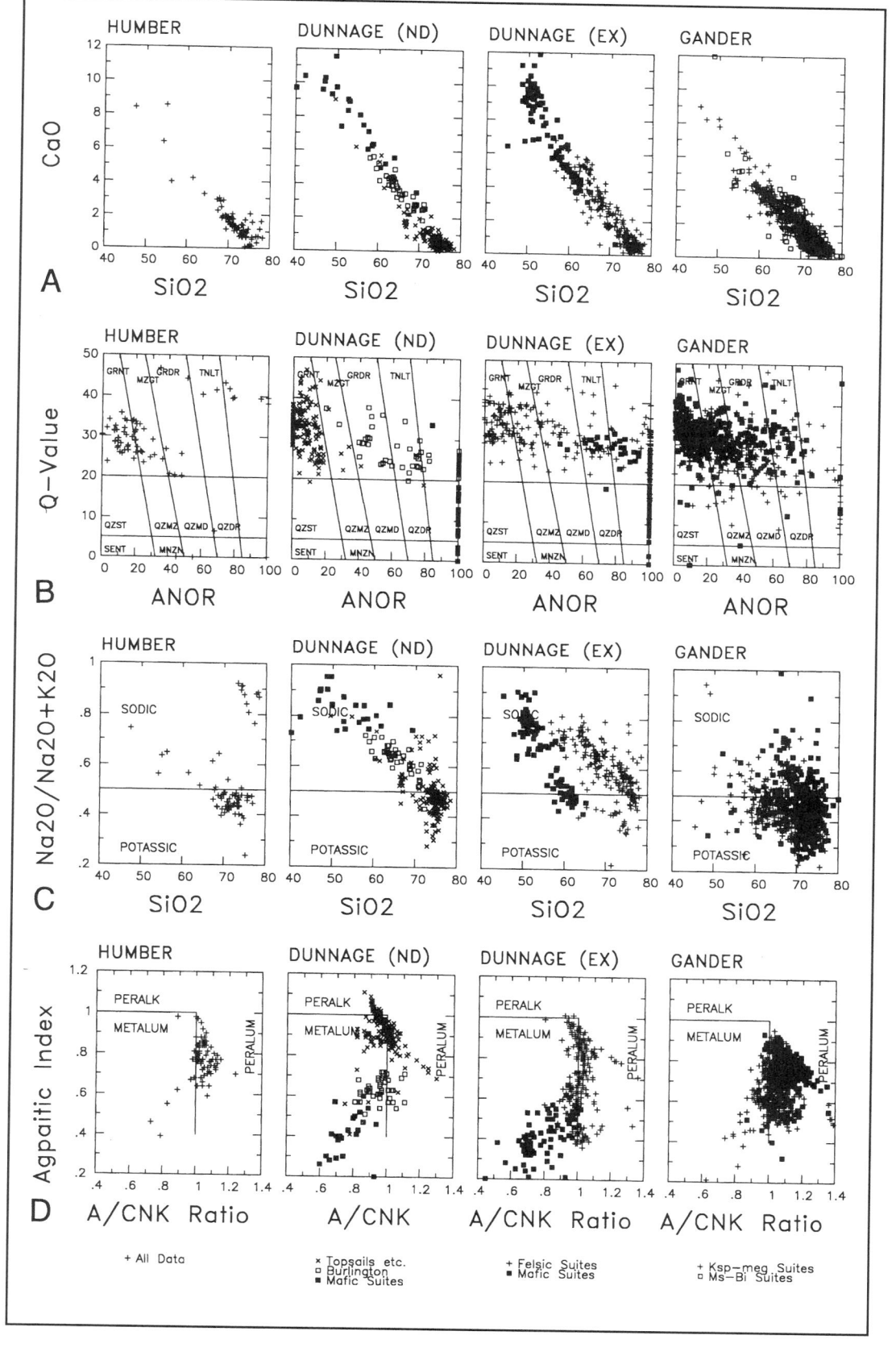

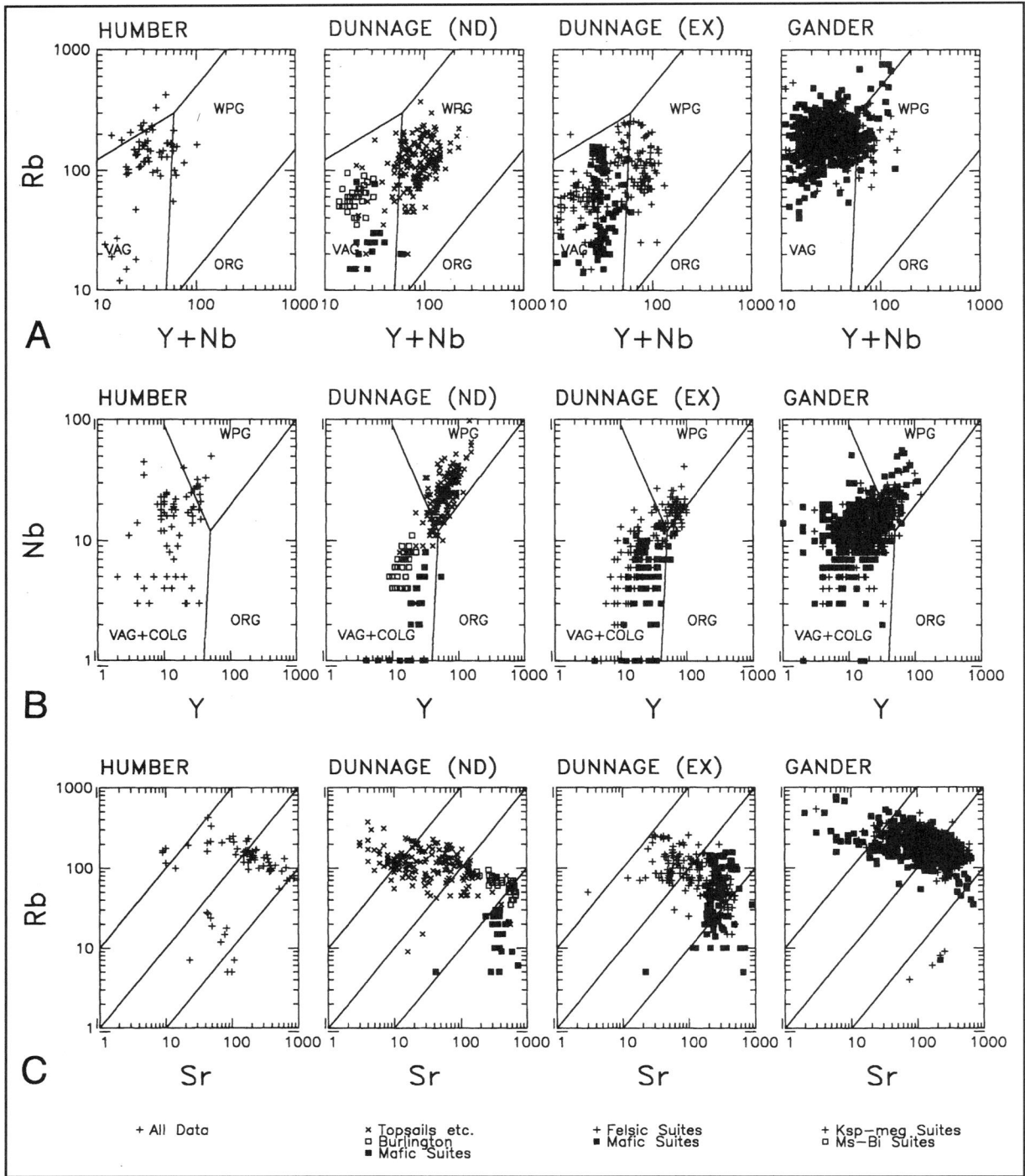

Figure 9 (on this and facing page). Trace-element compositional traits of Silurian plutonic suites across Newfoundland. A: Rb-(Y + Nb) plot, after Pearce et al., 1984. B: Nb-Y plot, after Pearce et al. (1984). C: Rb-Sr plot. D: Ba-Sr plot. E: Rb/Zr-Nb plot, after Brown et al. (1984). F: Zr-(Ga/Al × 10^4) plot, after Whalen et al. (1987b).

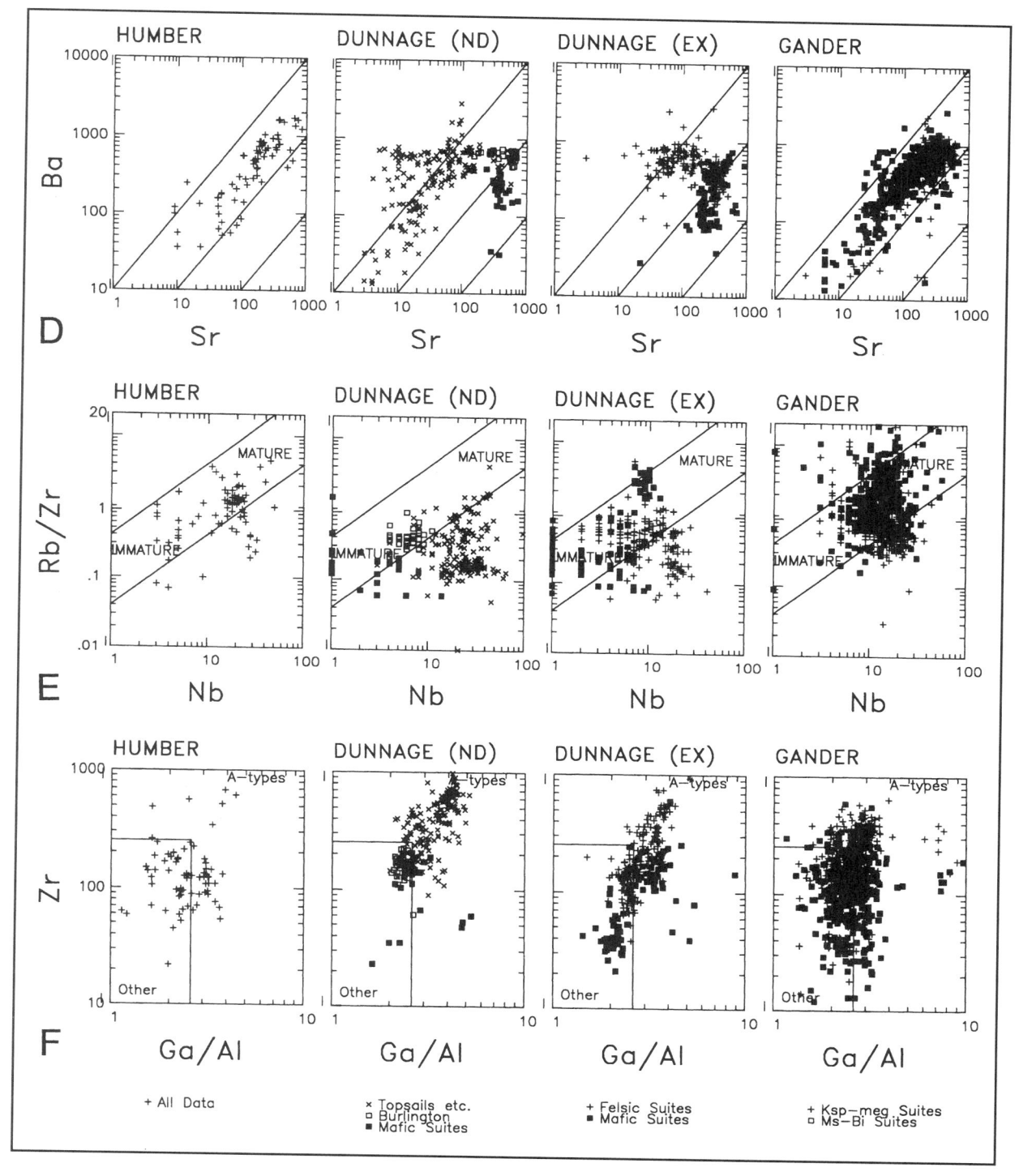

between fractionated I-type granites and A-type granites, but the Avalon zone examples (notably the St. Lawrence granite) have the highest Zr and Ga/Al. Their slightly higher Zr is also apparent in the Rb/Zr-Nb plot (Fig. 11E).

Although subtle differences between Devonian granites of the Gander and Avalon zones are apparent in Figures 10 and 11,

they are outweighed by the strong similarities between these suites. A more detailed analysis of Devonian granites in south-eastern Newfoundland (Kerr et al., 1993a) suggests that contrasts between the northeast Gander zone and the south coast region are more marked than contrasts between the south coast region and the Avalon zone.

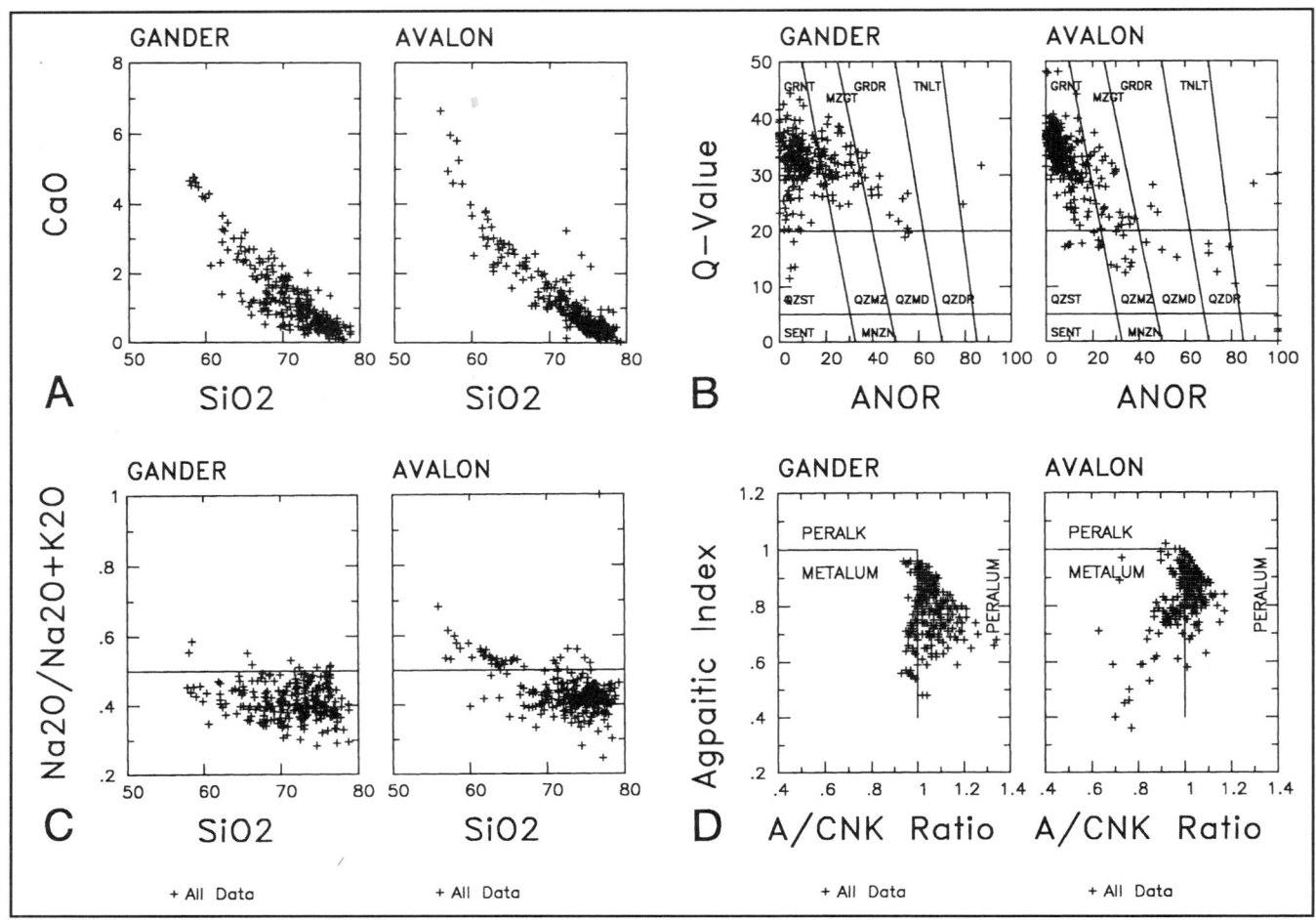

Figure 10. Major-element compositional traits of Devonian plutonic suites in the Gander and Avalon zones of Newfoundland. A: CaO-SiO_2 plot. B: Normative equivalent to International Union of Geological Sciences rock classification (after Streckeisen and LeMaitre, 1979); $ANOR = An (An + Or) \times 100$, Q-value $= Q/(Q + Ab + Or + An) \times 100$, rock type abbreviations as in Figure 6. C: $Na:K$-SiO_2 plot; $N/N + K = Na_2O/(Na_2O + K_2O)$. D: Alkali:alumina plot; $A/CNK = $ molecular $Al/(Ca + Na + K)$, Agpaitic index $=$ molecular $(K + Na)/Al$.

Temporal geochemical trends

Temporal geochemical trends are illustrated using comparisons of compositional evolution, where data are aggregated and averaged across SiO_2 intervals of 5% (Fig. 12 and 13), and by comparative major-element frequency spectra (Fig. 14). Traditional variation diagrams (Figs. 6–11) also illustrate some of the trends discussed in the following.

Humber zone. There is little obvious distinction between Silurian and Devonian suites within the Humber zone. The latter have a more restricted SiO_2 range, and the two can only be compared above 60% SiO_2. The major element frequency spectra (Fig. 14) also show the restricted compositional range of Devonian suites.

Dunnage zone (Notre Dame subzone). There are contrasts between Cambrian-Ordovician and Silurian suites in this region.

Cambrian-Ordovician suites are significantly more calcic, particularly above 60% SiO_2 (Fig. 12A), and remain strongly sodic at high SiO_2 contents, in strong contrast to the steady decrease in $N/N + K$ shown by Silurian suites (Fig. 12B). A/CNK and KN/A ratios show contrasting evolutionary trends, the Silurian suites showing significantly more alkalic and less aluminous compositions at all SiO_2 levels (Fig. 12, C and D). The two groups have broadly similar SiO_2 frequency spectra, but different patterns for most other major element parameters (Fig. 14). Cambrian-Ordovician suites are unevolved, and have lower Rb and higher Sr than their Silurian counterparts (Fig. 13, A, B, and C). Ba trends are similarly arcuate (Fig. 13D), but Cambrian-Ordovician suites are richer in Ba at intermediate SiO_2 contents, and have an inflection point at a lower SiO_2 value. Zr contents are much higher in Silurian suites (Fig. 13E), and zircon fractionation is not evident until around 75% SiO_2, in contrast to early Zr depletion in

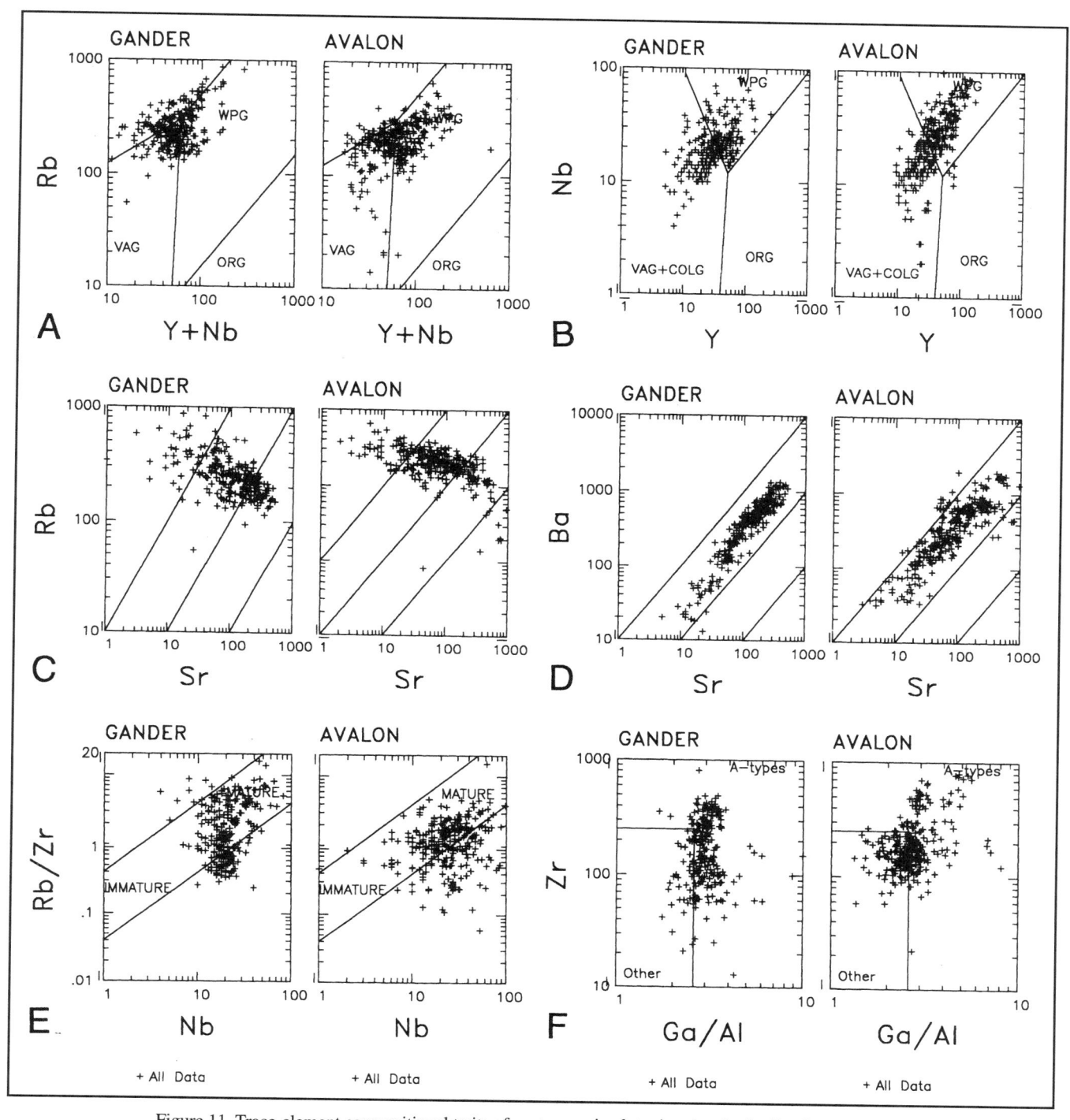

Figure 11. Trace-element compositional traits of postorogenic plutonic suites in the Gander and Avalon zones of Newfoundland. A: Rb-(Y + Nb) plot, after Pearce et al., (1984). B: Nb-Y plot, after Pearce et al., 1984. C: Rb-Sr plot. D Ba-Sr plot. E: Rb/Zr-Nb plot, after Brown et al., 1984. F: Zr-(Ga/Al × 10⁴) plot, after Whalen et al. (1987b).

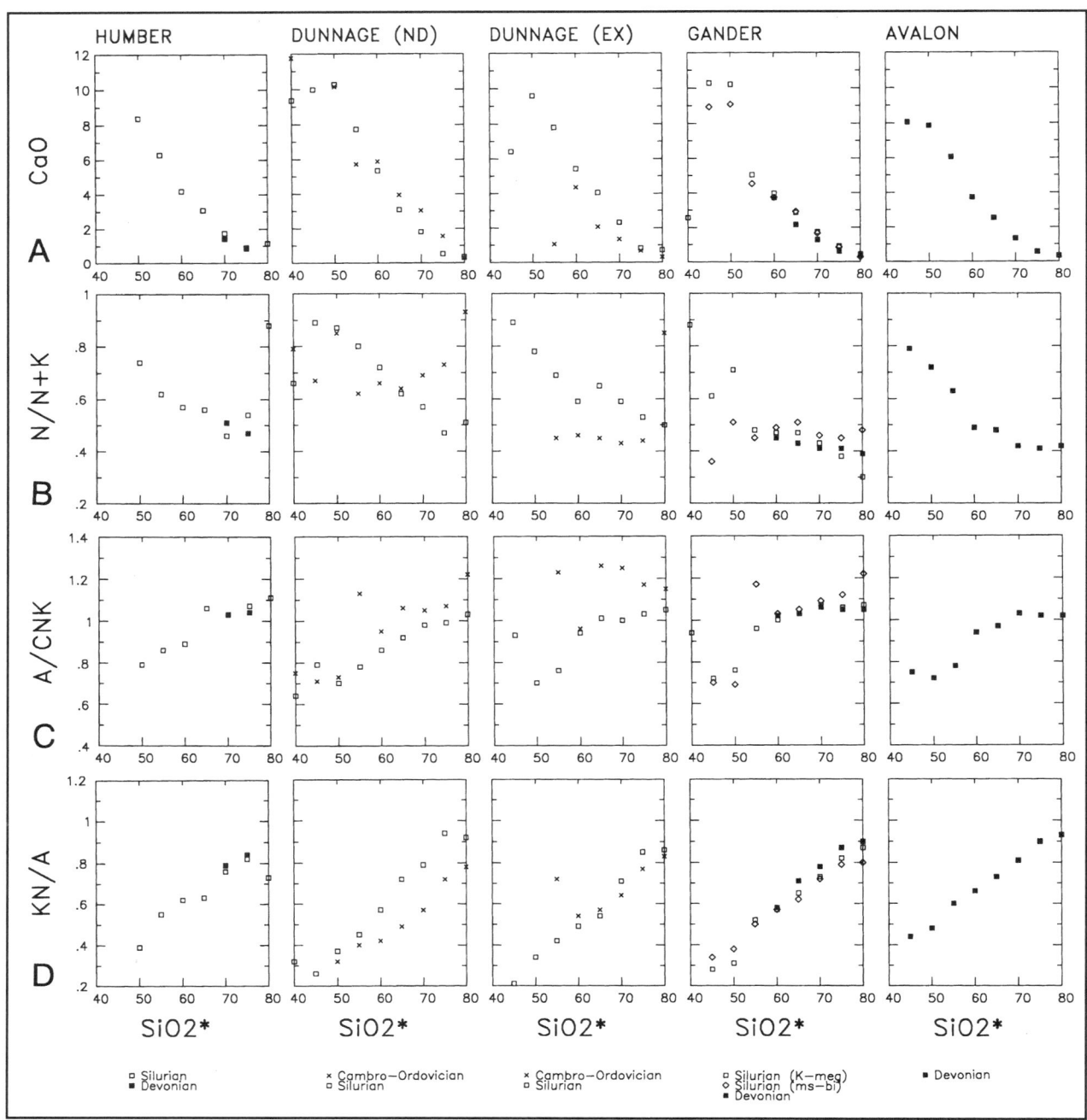

Figure 12. Major-element compositional trends of Appalachian-cycle plutonic suites across Newfoundland, derived by data aggregation to 5% SiO₂ intervals (see text). A: CaO trends. B: N/N + K trends. C: A/CNK trends. D: KN/A (Agpaitic index) trends.

Cambrian-Ordovician suites. Relative enrichment in (U + Th) in Silurian suites above 60% SiO₂ (Fig. 13F) also indicates their greater compositional evolution.

Dunnage zone (Exploits subzone). There are clear compositional shifts between Ordovician and Silurian suites in the Exploits subzone, but these are partly antithetic to those in the Notre Dame subzone. CaO trends are reversed (Fig. 12A) such

that Ordovician suites are more evolved than their Silurian counterparts. Similarly, N/N + K trends show that Ordovician suites are more potassic throughout their evolution (Fig. 12B). Alkali:alumina relationships (Fig. 12, C and D) show that Ordovician suites are more aluminous throughout. Major-element frequency spectra (Fig. 14) illustrate the small range of compositions in the Ordovician suites, and the strongly bimodal pattern of Silurian plutonism. Trace-element patterns, such as Rb and Sr (Fig. 13, A, B, and C) and U + Th (Fig. 13F), also show that Ordovician suites in this area are generally more evolved than the Silurian suites. Patterns for Zr and Ba (Fig. 13, D and E) resemble those of the Notre Dame subzone, and Silurian suites in both areas show Zr enrichment at high SiO_2.

Gander zone and south coast region. Silurian and Devonian plutonic suites of the Gander zone and south coast region show few striking geochemical contrasts. However, subtle distinctions between the three groups of plutonic rocks are visible in alkali:alumina relationships. In the Silurian muscovite-biotite association, A/CNK increases sharply at high SiO_2, but remains stable at just over 1.0 in the other groups. Devonian suites show slightly more alkali-rich compositions throughout evolution (Fig. 12, C and D), and generally have lower CaO (Fig. 12A). Major-element frequency spectra show a consistent pattern, in which Silurian K-feldspar megacrystic suites have the greatest range of compositions, and the Devonian suites the most restricted compositional spectra (Fig. 14). Major element spectra for Silurian muscovite-biotite suites are similar in shape to those for associated K-feldspar megacrystic suites, but are displaced to higher N/N + K and A/CNK, and lower CaO, values. Devonian suites have frequency maxima displaced to higher SiO_2 and KN/A values compared to both of the Silurian associations.

Trace-element patterns indicate that the Devonian suites are slightly more evolved in composition, with higher Rb (Fig. 13A), Rb/Sr (Fig. 13C), U + Th (Fig. 13F), and lower Ba and Sr (Fig. 13, B and D) at most SiO_2 values. It is more difficult to separate the Silurian K-feldspar megacrystic and muscovite-biotite associations by trace-element evolution.

Avalon zone. In the absence of significant Ordovician or Silurian plutonism, no inferences regarding temporal compositional evolution are possible. Major-element trends above 60% SiO_2 are identical to, or closely similar to, those of Devonian suites in the adjacent Gander zone (Fig. 12), and the major-element frequency spectra for both areas are almost identical (Fig. 14). However, Avalon zone suites show a wider compositional range. Trace-element patterns are for the most part similar (Fig. 13), but there may be differences in Zr behavior at high SiO_2 contents.

DISCUSSION AND INTERPRETATION

Orogen-scale patterns in plutonic evolution

The contrasting distributions of early orogenic, late orogenic and postorogenic plutonic assemblages across Newfoundland (Fig. 2) are significant. Ordovician plutonic suites are restricted to the Dunnage zone, excluding minor examples in areas of uncertain zonal affinity (O'Brien et al., 1991), and Exploits subzone plutons that transgress into adjacent Gander zone supracrustal rocks. High-grade metasedimentary rocks in the southwestern Notre Dame subzone have been correlated with the Fleur-de-Lys Supergroup (van Berkel and Currie, 1988), suggesting that some

Ordovician magmas may have locally transgressed Laurentian crust. Overall, Ordovician plutonism appears to be spatially (and presumably genetically) associated with the relics of Iapetus. This contrasts with Silurian plutonism, which is prevalent in all areas except the Avalon zone (Fig. 2). The spatial change, coupled with the Ordovician to Silurian compositional shift within the Dunnage zone, indicates a change in tectonic configuration prior to the onset of Silurian plutonism. Such a change is most simply interpreted to record the closure of Iapetus, or (at the very least) significant terrane accretions on its margin(s).

The strong polarity among Ordovician and Silurian plutonic assemblages is also important. To rephrase Williams (1964), Appalachian plutonism in Newfoundland defines a two-sided, asymmetrical system. Ordovician suites change eastward from calc-alkaline tonalite and granodiorite (Notre Dame subzone) to siliceous peraluminous granites (Exploits subzone). Silurian suites change eastward from locally bimodal plutonism of metaluminous to alkaline character (Dunnage zone) to largely peraluminous, locally S-type granitoid rocks in the Gander zone and on the south coast. However, there are many similarities between Silurian plutons in the Humber zone and those of the Gander zone (see following); with this qualification, the pattern for Silurian suites becomes more symmetrical (Fig. 4, A and B). Such shifts could reflect contrasts in the country rocks, from dominantly metasedimentary at the margins to metavolcanic and igneous in the center, or contrasts in basement terranes. Alternatively, Silurian plutonism may record subtly different processes and/or tectonic settings across the orogen.

The eastward migration of the main locus of plutonism with time is also important. The vast majority of Devonian plutonic suites are associated with the Gander zone, south coast region, and Avalon zone, i.e., the southeastern margin of the orogen (Fig. 2). The Avalon zone (sensu stricto) lacks significant Silurian plutonism. Devonian plutonism has a restricted compositional spectrum, and a subtly more evolved geochemical signature, compared to Silurian plutons of the same region(s). Although such contrasts are muted compared to those between Ordovician and Silurian suites in central and western Newfoundland, the geographic and geochemical shifts may of fundamental tectonic significance. Recent proposals of a Silurian or pre-Silurian linkage of Gander and Avalon zones (e.g., Quinlan et al., 1992) are not entirely consistent with their plutonic histories, as currently known.

Within individual tectonic zones there is a general temporal shift toward more evolved, siliceous plutonic rocks with more restricted compositional spectra (e.g., Fig. 14) and higher abundances of incompatible elements (Figs. 12 and 13). This is particularly evident among Devonian suites along the southeast margin of the orogen. The Exploits subzone is an exception, because Ordovician suites appear more evolved than associated Silurian suites. However, most of these Ordovician granites probably had sources in the underlying Gander zone (see following), whereas bimodal Silurian plutonism must record a mantle input. Overall, Appalachian-cycle plutonism in Newfoundland appears to be a unidirectional process resulting in the stepwise produc-

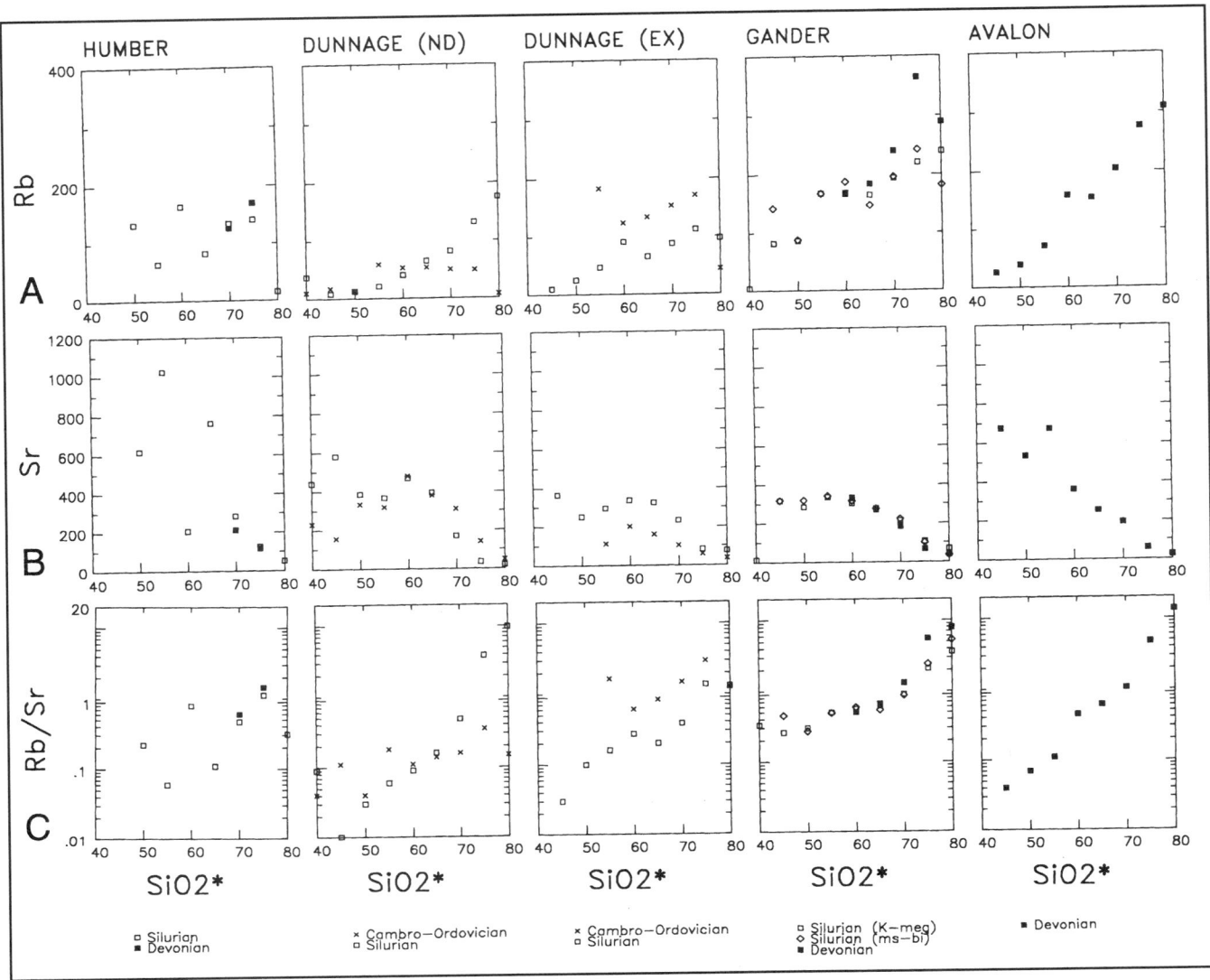

Figure 13 (on this and facing page). Trace-element compositional trends of Appalachian-cycle plutonic suites across Newfoundland, derived by data aggregation to 5% SiO_2 intervals (see text). A: Rb trends. B: Sr trends. C: Rb/Sr trends. D: Ba trends. E: Zr trends. F: (U + Th) trends.

tion of progressively more evolved granitoid magmas, culminating with Devonian high-silica suites along the eastern margin.

Petrogenesis and tectonic settings of individual plutonic associations

Humber zone. Silurian plutonic suites of the Humber zone resemble age equivalents on the opposite side of the orogen, that is, in the Gander zone and on the south coast. High-grade metasedimentary rocks appear to have contributed to granite magmas in both areas. Metasedimentary rocks in the White Bay area have ε_{Nd} (430 Ma) of –11 or so, and associated S-type granites on the Baie Verte Peninsula have ε_{Nd} (430 Ma) of –8, compared to –11 for local metasedimentary rocks, suggesting partial anatexis (Fryer et al., 1992). K-feldspar megacrystic granites have

ε_{Nd}(430) of –4 or so, and must also include a more juvenile (subcrustal?) component. This pattern is directly analogous to that seen in the Gander zone and south coast region (Kerr et al., 1995).

The general absence of Ordovician plutonic suites in the Humber zone argues against any subduction beneath the Laurentian margin prior to the Taconic orogeny. Silurian plutonism in the Humber zone must be postaccretionary (if not postcollisional) in timing, and probably does not reflect subduction of oceanic crust. Much of the metamorphic and structural history along the Humber-Dunnage boundary is Silurian, rather than Ordovician (Cawood et al., 1994), and of similar age to deformational events on the Gondwanan margin, which also argues against any separation of the two at that time.

Notre Dame subzone. This region contains the best candidates for Ordovician subduction-related plutonic suites. Although

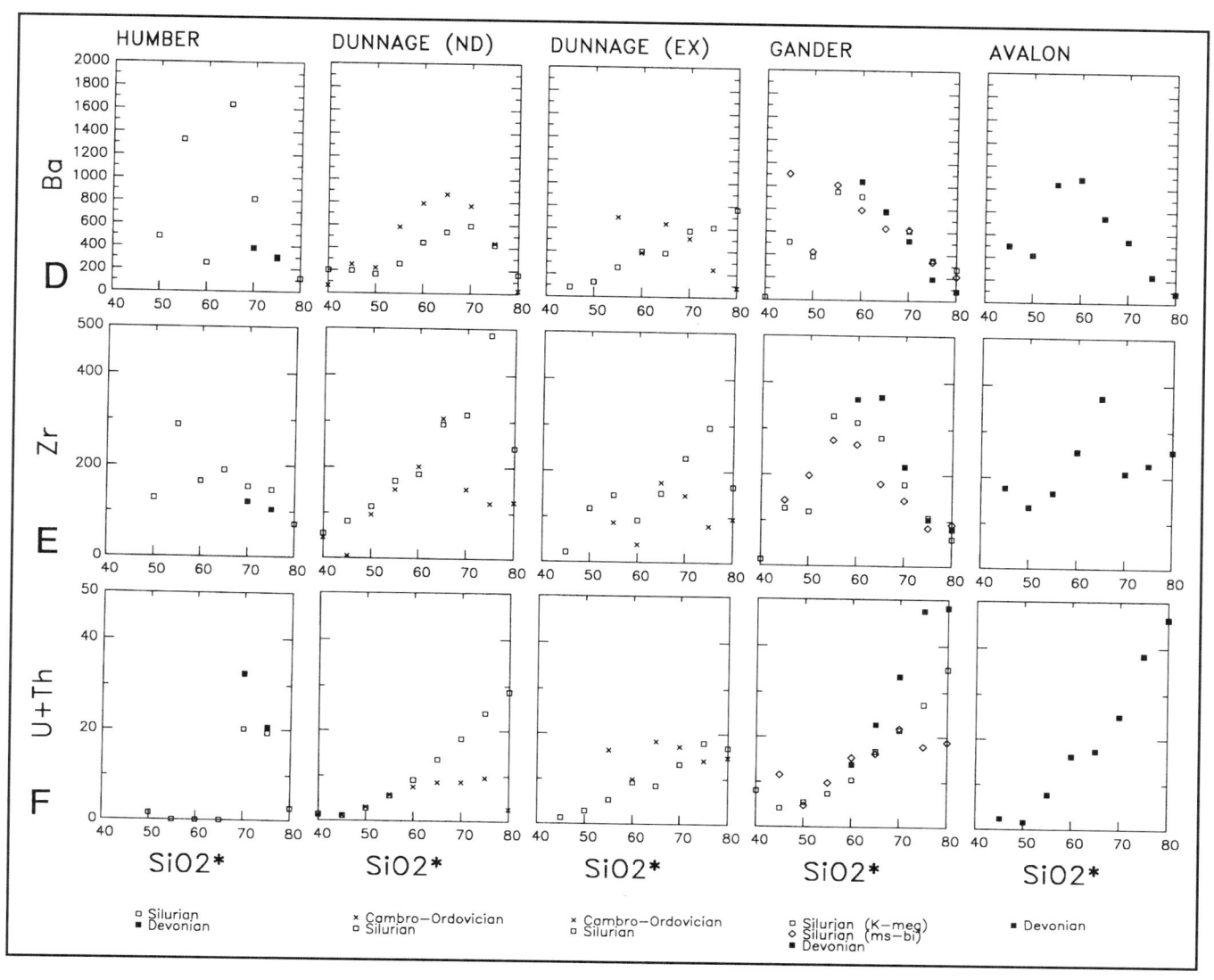

crucial in understanding the evolution of the Newfoundland Appalachians, these arc-like plutonic suites are of minor areal extent. The petrogenesis and evolution of some of these suites are discussed in more detail by Whalen et al. (this volume) and the following comments are of a general, regional nature.

Ordovician plutonic suites cannot represent a single arc system, because they range in age (510–450 Ma), and include suites of both trondjemitic and calcalkaline affinity. A long-held model for the Taconic orogeny in the northern Appalachians is that it records collision of a composite arc system with Laurentia, followed by attempted subduction of the Laurentian margin. Older Ordovician plutonic suites in the Notre Dame subzone may have developed in such an arc or arcs, e.g., the Twillingate trondhjemite, which has a largely juvenile Nd isotopic signature (Fryer et al., 1992). Older volcanic sequences in this region show little

influence from continental crust, but some younger calc-alkaline sequences, and associated plutons, have ε_{Nd} down to –3 (Swinden et al., 1994, this volume). Thus, some younger plutonic rocks of the Notre Dame subzone may represent continental magmatic arc(s) developed at a later stage, e.g., in southwestern Newfoundland, where Ordovician suites intrude metasedimentary rocks correlated with the adjacent Humber zone. Negative ε_{Nd} (460 Ma) values suggest that some incorporate older crustal material (Fryer et al., 1992; Whalen et al., this volume), although a purely anatectic origin is problematic in the light of their primitive elemental geochemistry.

Among Silurian suites, only the ca. 432 Ma Burlington granodiorite clearly resembles Ordovician arc-related suites. Most Silurian granites have the characteristic patterns of so-called A-type granites: the Topsails intrusive suite is cited as a type example of

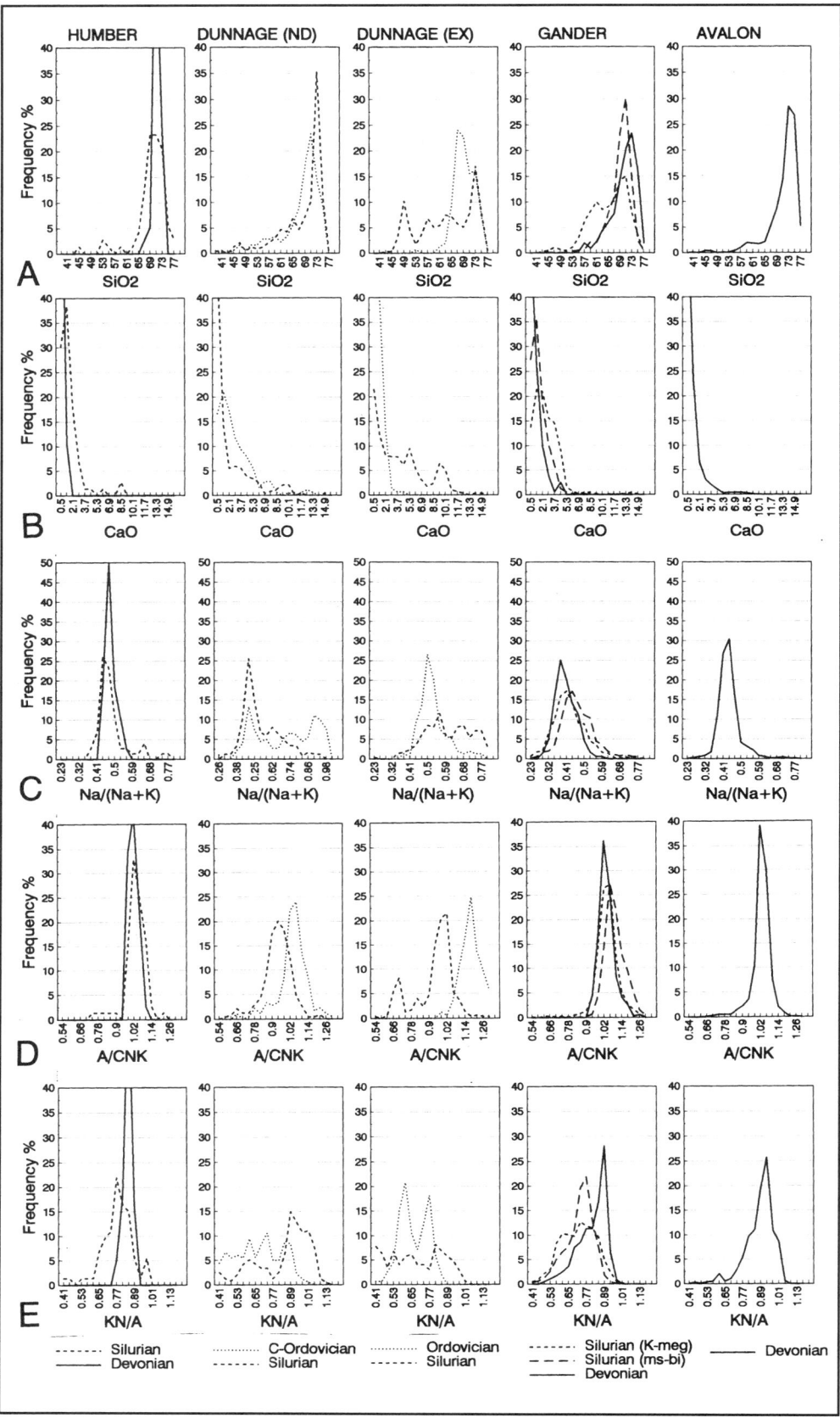

such (Whalen et al., 1987b; Whalen, 1989). Spatially associated mafic suites suggest a tendency toward bimodality, although this is less striking than in the Exploits subzone (see following). A-type granites occur in continental magmatic arcs, postcollisional settings, and anorogenic, rift-related settings (Whalen et al., 1987b; Eby, 1990). In arc settings, they are volumetrically minor, and found in areas distal from the locus of subduction (Brown et al., 1984; Whalen et al., 1987b; Eby, 1990). They are more abundant in postcollisional or rift-related extensional environments, and bimodal magmatism is also commonly linked to extensional tectonics (e.g., Martin and Piwinski, 1972; Petro et al., 1979).

If Silurian plutonism in the Notre Dame subzone was a distal product of a west-dipping subduction zone (cf. Brown et al., 1984), there should be extensive areas of more primitive arc-like plutonic rocks to the east, which are conspicuously absent. Whalen (1989) suggested an arc setting origin for the Topsails intrusive suite, invoking the subduction of small, discontinuous basins following the closure of Iapetus. On the basis of regional patterns, and the strong temporal compositional shift, it is suggested that Silurian suites mostly represent postcollisional or postaccretionary magmatism accompanied (or caused) by crustal thickening and emplacement of mantle-derived magmas. Available Nd isotopic data (Fryer et al., 1992) support the presence of a juvenile component, and argue against the presence of Laurentian (Grenville) basement, in contrast to inferences from seismic models (Marillier et al., 1989; Fig. 1).

Exploits subzone. Most Ordovician plutonic suites in the Exploits subzone cannot be convincingly linked to subduction, although there are arc-type volcanic sequences in this region (e.g., Dunning et al., 1991). Instead, they include compositionally restricted, peraluminous, leucocratic suites with affinities to "S-type" granites. These postdate interaction of the Exploits subzone and underlying Gander zone, and one example (Through Hill granite) is associated with migmatization in the Mount Cormack (Gander zone) window (Colman-Sadd et al., 1992). The ε_{Nd} (460 Ma) of some of these granites overlaps that of nearby Gander zone metasedimentary rocks, implying an anatectic origin, but others have less negative ε_{Nd}, suggesting derivation from a Precambrian basement complex inferred to underlie the supracrustal rocks (Kerr et al., 1995). Ordovician plutonism in the Exploits subzone probably records metamorphism and anatexis in structurally underlying Gander zone rocks related to the accretion of Dunnage zone terranes ca. 475 Ma (cf., Colman-Sadd et al., 1992).

Silurian suites of the Exploits subzone are obviously bimodal and, although they have varied characteristics, they show many major- and trace-element similarities to the Notre Dame subzone. Peralkaline compositions appear to be less abundant than in the Notre Dame subzone, and some granites, notably those around the Bay of Exploits, have sodic and calcic affinities that are transitional toward arc-related plutonism. Nd isotopic data from late orogenic suites in the Exploits subzone argue against a major contribution from older crust, particularly in the northwest (Fryer et al., 1992). Similarities between Silurian plutonic suites in the two portions of the Dunnage zone are consistent with a single tectonic setting at that time. Given the differences in the pre-Silurian geology of these regions (Williams et al., 1988), such commonality supports the idea that they were joined prior to ca. 430 Ma, and that the main Iapetus basin was closed by this time. It is also consistent with the contemporaneity of Silurian deformational and metamorphic events across the Central Mobile Belt (e.g., Dunning et al., 1990; Cawood et al., 1994), and with the waning of faunal provinciality at the end of the Ordovician (e.g., Williams et al., 1992).

Gander zone and south coast region. There is an obvious compositional jump among Silurian plutonic suites at the Dunnage-Gander boundary. Within the Gander zone and south coast region, K-feldspar megacrystic biotite granites and muscovite-biotite granites form a compositional continuum, and are intermixed on varied scales. The K-feldspar megacrystic suites are compositionally expanded, ranging from tonalite to granite (sensu stricto), and their compositions are broadly calc-alkaline. However, they are dominated by monzogranite and granite, and are strongly potassic compared to the Ordovician arc-type suites of the Notre Dame subzone, and to typical Andean arc-type batholiths (e.g., Pitcher, 1983).

Gander zone Silurian magmas appear to have complex, multicomponent sources. Muscovite-biotite granites have ε_{Nd} (430 Ma) similar to, or slightly higher than, the ε_{Nd} of Gander zone metasedimentary rocks (−8), and the closest correspondence is shown by small bodies that probably have local source regions (Fryer et al., 1992; Kerr et al., 1995). K-feldspar megacrystic suites have higher ε_{Nd} of −5 to −2, but must also include older crustal material. In both groups, ε_{Nd} is lowest in the northeast, where metasedimentary rocks are most abundant, but most plutons cannot be derived from these sources alone. Kerr et al. (1995) suggested that they include material derived from supracrustal sources with ancient provenance, and more juvenile infracrustal sources inferred to be a Late Precambrian basement complex. A juvenile magma of mantle derivation is permitted (but not required) by the isotopic data, and is also consistent with the presence of minor amounts of gabbro, diorite, and tonalite (e.g., Dickson et al., 1989).

An arc-type setting cannot be excluded for Silurian suites of the Gander zone and south coast region, but they would have to be distal from the locus of subduction, like the eastern (inland) portions of Cordilleran batholiths, where granites show a greater crustal influence (e.g., Pitcher, 1983). Pre-475 Ma juxtapositon of the Exploits subzone and the Gander zone (Colman-Sadd et al., 1992), and commonality of late orogenic plutonism across the Dunnage zone (see above), rules out southeast-dipping subduction beneath the Gander zone. The only other possibility

Figure 14. Major-element compositional spectra of Appalachian-cycle plutonic suites across Newfoundland, expressed by comparative frequency histograms. A: SiO_2 frequency spectra. B: CaO frequency spectra. C: Na/Na + K frequency spectra. D: A/CNK frequency spectra. E: KN/A (Agpaitic index) frequency spectra.

appears to be northwest-directed subduction of oceanic crust originally located between the Gander and Avalon zones, between which there is (as yet) no clear pre-Devonian linkage. The absence of more primitive, sodic, arc-related plutonic suites, representing the proximal arc magmas, argues against this option. Alternatively, Silurian magmatism on the eastern margin of the orogen may be syncollisional to postcollisional, related to a thermal pulse accompanying and following the complete closure of Iapetus. This is essentially the same model proposed above for Silurian magmatism in the Dunnage zone, and raises an obvious question: If all of these Silurian plutonic suites developed in a similar setting, why do they show such striking compositional polarity?

Devonian granites of the Gander zone are compositionally restricted, more evolved, and more agpaitic compared to spatially associated Silurian suites. They have similar Nd isotopic signatures to the Silurian K-feldspar megacrystic suites, and define a similar northeastward decrease in ε_{Nd}, indicating a contribution from Gander zone supracrustal rocks (Kerr et al., 1993a; 1995). Kerr et al. (1993a; 1995) suggested a three-component origin including mantle-derived magmas, mixed with anatectic melts of both Precambrian basement and Paleozoic cover. These granites postdate juxtaposition of the Gander and Avalon zones, and there are no tenable locations for Devonian subduction zones within the Central mobile belt. Their geochemical features are typical of granites developed in postcollisional environments of uplift and extension (e.g., Pearce et al., 1984; Harris et al., 1984).

Avalon zone. Devonian plutonic suites of the Avalon zone resemble those of the Gander zone and must be interpreted in terms of a single tectonic environment and petrogenetic model (cf., Kerr et al., 1993a). However, they have positive ε_{Nd} (400 Ma) of +1 to +4, unlike the mostly negative ε_{Nd} values of their Gander zone counterparts (Kerr et al., 1993a, 1995). These isotopic contrasts do not necessitate a separate petrogenetic model, but they do suggest that the Avalon zone and Gander zone south coast regions have different basement complexes, and that their boundary is an important crustal-scale structure. It is significant that some Avalon zone Devonian granites have ε_{Nd} values above those expected for Precambrian country rocks at 400 Ma, indicating a juvenile component of subcrustal origin (Kerr et al., 1995). This evidence for distinct basement terranes beneath the Gander and Avalon zones, and the apparent absence of Silurian plutonism in the latter, may support Late Silurian or post-Silurian juxtaposition.

CONCLUDING REMARKS

On an areal basis, 90% of the Appalachian-cycle plutonic suites preserved in Newfoundland are of Silurian-Devonian age, and are broadly late orogenic to postorogenic. Many, if not all, are "ensialic," in the sense that subduction of oceanic crust was not directly involved in their genesis. The Newfoundland Dunnage zone is itself an anomaly within the Appalachians, and deeper erosion would eliminate most ophiolites and arc-related volcanic and plutonic suites. This has implications for more deeply eroded oro-

genic belts (particularly of Precambrian age) where curvilinear plutonic belts are widely interpreted as the roots of magmatic arcs. In Newfoundland, the areally dominant plutonic suites probably record syncollisional to postcollisional magmatism. More deeply eroded Precambrian orogenic belts should not differ in this respect, and some of these older plutonic terranes may be misinterpreted, as suggested elsewhere (Kerr, 1989). Conversely, the absence of arc-like plutonic suites in other Proterozoic orogens does not mean that they were never developed, but simply that they are rarely preserved at the crustal levels typical of such regions.

The wide distribution of late orogenic and postorogenic Silurian-Devonian plutonism across Newfoundland implies a major thermal pulse from Middle Silurian time onward, following closure of the Iapetus. Although these suites were in part derived from older crust, there is evidence that mantle-derived magmas are also involved, particularly within the Dunnage zone. It is suggested that this thermal pulse and mantle melting are connected to postcollisional lithospheric delamination, a process also invoked to satisfy structural and geophysical constraints (e.g., Colman-Sadd, 1982; Quinlan et al., 1992). Such a connection between delamination and magmatism is not a new idea; it was espoused for many years in the context of Proterozoic mobile belts, notably in Africa (e.g., Kröner, 1980). Lithospheric delamination, regardless of details, results in the upwelling of hot, possibly asthenospheric, mantle that is prone to melting via decompression, as at mid-ocean ridges (e.g., Nelson, 1992). These models have been applied to Appalachian magmatism in Newfoundland (Kerr et al., 1992) and New Brunswick (Whalen et al., 1994), but require more thought and development before they can be anything but ad-hoc proposals. In the context of Newfoundland, there are two points that may have a bearing on their refinement. First, there is an eastward shift in the focus of magmatism with time, which may indicate the direction in which delamination propagated or, alternatively, movement of detached crust over a static zone of delamination and upwelling. Second, there is a correlation between compositions and regional geology, with peraluminous tendencies in the Humber and Gander zones, and metaluminous-peralkaline tendencies in the Dunnage and Avalon zones. This may simply indicate that mid-crustal processes and components have the most influence on final compositions, but it could also imply discrete mantle sources, or source depths, below specific tectonic zones. The dynamics of lithospheric delamination in collisional orogens, and the precise links between such processes and late orogenic to postorogenic magmatism, are exciting directions for future research.

ACKNOWLEDGMENTS

The Newfoundland granitoid database project was supported by the Canada-Newfoundland Mineral Development agreement (1989–1994). Many individuals contributed ideas on granites in Newfoundland over the years, and information to the geochemical database used in this chapter. In particular, I thank W. L. Dickson, S. J. O'Brien, S. P. Colman-Sadd, J. P. Hayes, and

J. Tuach (all with the Geological Survey of Newfoundland) and J. B. Whalen (Geological Survey of Canada) for their contributions. At Memorial University, G. A. Jenner and B. J. Fryer contributed greatly through related isotopic work. I also owe a great debt to Hank Williams for long-term contributions, and to David Strong, who first addressed this aspect of Newfoundland geology, and interested me in the origins of granites. K. L. Currie and D. B. Clarke are thanked for exhaustive reviews. This paper is Lithoprobe Contribution Number 707, and is published with the permission of the Executive Director of the Geological Survey of Newfoundland and Labrador.

REFERENCES CITED

Blackwood, R. F., 1977, Geology of the east half of the Gambo (2D/16) map area and the northwest portion of the St. Brendan's (2C/13) map area, Newfoundland: Newfoundland Department of Mines and Energy, Mineral Development Division, Report 77-5, 20 p.

Blackwood, R. F., 1983, Notes on the geology of the Great Gull Lake map area (2D/6), Newfoundland: Department of Mines and Energy, Mineral Development Division, Map 82-71, 10 p., scale 1:50,000.

Brown, G. C., Thorpe, R. S., and Webb, P. C., 1984, The geochemical characteristics of granitoids in contrasting arcs, and comments on magma sources: Geological Society of London Journal, v. 141, p. 413–426.

Brown, P. A., 1977, Geology of the Port-aux-Basques map area, Newfoundland: Newfoundland Department of Mines and Energy, Mineral Development Division, Report 77-2, 11 p.

Cawood, P. A., and Dunning, G. R., 1993, Silurian age for movement on the Baie Verte Line: Implications for accretionary tectonics in the northern Appalachians: Geological Society of America Abstracts with Programs, v. 25, no. 6, p. A422.

Cawood, P. A., Dunning, G. R., Lux, D., and van Gool, J. A., 1994, Timing of peak metamorphism and deformation along the Appalachian margin of Laurentia in Newfoundland: Geology, v. 22, p. 399–402.

Cawthorn, R. G., 1978, The petrology of the Tilting Harbour Igneous Complex, Fogo Island, Newfoundland: Canadian Journal of Earth Sciences, v. 15, p. 526–539.

Chorlton, L., 1978, The geology of the La Poile map area (11O/9), Newfoundland: Newfoundland Department of Mines and Energy, Mineral Development Division, Report 78-5, 14 p.

Collins, C. J., and Strong, D. F., 1988, A fluid inclusion and trace element study of fluorite veins associated with the peralkaline St. Lawrence granite, Newfoundland, *in* Taylor, R. P., and Strong, D. F., eds., Recent advances in the geology of granite-related mineral deposits: Canadian Institute of Mining and Metallurgy, Geology Division, p. 291–302.

Colman-Sadd, S. P., 1982, Two-stage continental collision and plate driving forces: Tectonophysics, v. 90, p. 263–282.

Colman-Sadd, S. P., 1985, Geology of the Burnt Hill map area (2D/5) Newfoundland: Newfoundland Department of Mines and Energy, Mineral Development Division, Report 85-3, 94 p.

Colman-Sadd, S. P., and Swinden, H. S., 1984, A tectonic window in central Newfoundland? Geological evidence that the Appalachian Dunnage zone is allochthonous: Canadian Journal of Earth Sciences, v. 21, p. 1349–1367.

Colman-Sadd, S. P., Greene, B. A., and O'Driscoll, C. F., 1979, Gaultois, Newfoundland: Newfoundland Department of Mines and Energy, Mineral Development Division, Map 79-104, scale 1:50,000.

Colman-Sadd, S. P., Dunning, G. R., and Dec, T., 1992, Dunnage-Gander relationships and Ordovician Orogeny in Central Newfoundland: A sediment provenance and U-Pb age study: American Journal of Science, v. 292, p. 317–355.

Coyle, M. L., and Strong, D. F., 1987, Geology of the Springdale Group: A newly recognized Silurian epicontinental-type caldera in Newfoundland: Cana-

dian Journal of Earth Sciences, v. 24, p. 1135–1148.

Currie, K. L., and Pajari, G. E., 1977, Igneous and metamorphic rocks between Rocky Bay and Ragged Harbour, northeastern Newfoundland, *in* Current research: Geological Survey of Canada, Paper 77-1A, p. 341–346.

Dallmeyer, R. D., Blackwood, R. F., and Odom, A. L., 1981, Age and origin of the Dover Fault: Tectonic boundary between the Gander and Avalon zones of the northeast Newfoundland Appalachians: Canadian Journal of Earth Sciences, v. 18, p. 1431–1432.

DeGrace, J. R., Kean, B. F., Hsu, E., and Green, T., 1976, Geology of the Nippers Harbour map area, Newfoundland: Newfoundland Department of Mines and Energy, Mineral Development Division, Report 76–3, 73 p.

Dickson, W. L., 1983, Geology, geochemistry and mineral potential of the Ackley granite and parts of the Northwest Brook and Eastern Meelpaeg Complexes, southeast Newfoundland: Newfoundland Department of Mines and Energy, Mineral Development Division, Report 83-6, 129 p.

Dickson, W. L., 1990, Geology of the North Bay granite Suite and metasedimentary rocks in southern Newfoundland: Newfoundland Department of Mines and Energy, Geological Survey Branch, Report 90-3, 101 p.

Dickson, W. L., 1992, Ophiolites, sedimentary rocks, post-tectonic intrusions and mineralization in the Eastern Pond map area, central Newfoundland, *in* Pereira, C. P. G., Walsh, D. G., and Blackwood, R. F., eds., Current research: Newfoundland Department Mines and Energy, Geological Survey Branch, Report 92-1, p. 97–118.

Dickson, W. L., 1993, Geology of the Mount Peyton map area (2D/14), Central Newfoundland, *in* Pereira, C. P. G., Walsh, D. G., and Blackwood, R. F., eds., Current research: Newfoundland Department of Mines and Energy, Geological Survey Branch, Report 93-1, p. 1–12.

Dickson, W. L., O'Brien, S. J., and Hayes, J. P., 1989, Aspects of the mid-Paleozoic magmatic history of the south-central Hermitage flexure area, Newfoundland: Newfoundland Department of Mines and Energy, Mineral Development Division, Report 89-1, p. 81–95.

Dubé, B., Dunning, G. R., Lauziere, K., and Roddick, C., 1993, The Gondwanan-Laurentian suture: Timing of deformation on the Cape Ray fault, Newfoundland Appalachians: Geological Society of America Abstracts with Programs, v. 25, no. 6, p. A421.

Dubé, B., Dunning, G. R., Lauziere, K., and Roddick, C., 1994, Deformational events and their timing along the Cape Ray Fault, Newfoundland Appalachians, *in* New perspectives in the Appalachian-Caledonian Orogen (NUNA Conference, Grand Falls, Newfoundland, August 1994): Geological Association of Canada Program with Abstracts, p. 13.

Dunning, G. R., 1987, U-Pb geochronology of the Coney Head Complex, Newfoundland: Canadian Journal of Earth Sciences, v. 24, p. 1072–1075.

Dunning, G. R., and O'Brien, S. J., 1989, Late Proterozoic–Early Paleozoic crust in the Hermitage flexure, Newfoundland Appalachians: U-Pb ages and tectonic significance: Geology, v. 17, p. 548–551.

Dunning, G. R., Kean, B. F., Thurlow, J. G., and Swinden, H. S., 1987, Geochronology of the Buchans, Roberts Arm and Victoria Lake Groups, and the Mansfield Cove Complex, Newfoundland: Canadian Journal of Earth Sciences, v. 24, p. 1175–1184.

Dunning, G. R., Wilton, D. H., and Herd, R. K., 1989, Geology, geochemistry and geochronology of a Taconic calc-alkaline batholith in southwest Newfoundland: Royal Society of Edinburgh Transactions, Earth Sciences, v. 80, p. 159–168.

Dunning, G. R., O'Brien, S. J., Colman-Sadd, S. P., Blackwood, R. F., Dickson, W. L., O'Neill, P., and Krogh, T. E., 1990, Silurian orogeny in the Newfoundland Appalachians: Journal of Geology, v. 98, p. 895–913.

Dunning, G. R., Swinden, H. S., Kean, B., Evans, D., and Jenner, G. A., 1991, A Cambrian island arc in Iapetus: Geochronology and geochemistry of the Lake Ambrose volcanic belt, Newfoundland Appalachians: Geological Magazine, v. 128, p. 1–17.

Dunning, G. R., O'Brien, S. J., O'Brien, B. H., Holdsworth, R. E., and Tucker, R. D., 1993, Chronology of Pan-African, Penobscot and Salinic shear zones on the Gondwanan margin, northern Appalachians: Geological Society of America Abstracts with Programs, v. 25, no. 6, p. A421.

Eby, G. N., 1990, The A-type granitoids: A review of their occurrence and chemical characteristics and speculations on their petrogenesis: Lithos, v. 26, p. 115–134.

Elliot, C. G., Dunning, G. R., and Williams, P. F., 1991, New U-Pb zircon age constraints on the timing of deformation in north-central Newfoundland, and implications for early Paleozoic Appalachian orogenesis: Geological Society of America Bulletin, v. 103, p. 125–135.

Erdmer, P., 1986, Geology of the Long Range Inlier in the Sandy Lake map area, western Newfoundland, in Current research: Geological Survey of Canada Paper 86-1B, p. 19–29.

Fryer, B. J., Kerr, A., Jenner, G. A., and Longstaffe, F. J., 1992, Probing the crust with plutons: regional isotopic geochemistry of granitoid plutonic suites across Newfoundland, in Pereira, C. P. G., Walsh, D. G., and Blackwood, R. F., eds., Current research: Newfoundland Department of Mines and Energy, Geological Survey Branch, Report 92-1, p. 118–139.

Furey, D. J., 1985, Geology of the Belleoram Pluton, southeast Newfoundland, in Current research, 1985: Geological Survey of Canada, Current Research, Paper 85-1A, p. 151–156.

Furey, D. J., and Strong, D. F., 1986, Geology of the Harbour Breton Complex, Newfoundland, in Current research, 1986: Geological Survey of Canada, Current Research, Paper 86-1A, p. 461–464.

Greene, B. A., and O'Driscoll, C. F., 1976, Gaultois Map area: Newfoundland Department of Mines and Energy, Mineral Development Division, Report of Activities for 1975, p. 56–63.

Harris, N. B. W., Pearce, J. A., and Tindle, A. G., 1984, Geochemical characteristics of collision-zone magmatism, in Coward, M. P., and Reis, A. C., eds., Collision tectonics: Geological Society of London Special Publication 19, p. 67–81.

Hayes, J. P., Dickson, W. L., and Tuach, J., 1987, Newfoundland granitoid rocks. Map with marginal notes: Newfoundland Department Mines and Energy, Mineral Development Division, Open File 87-85, scale 1:500,000.

Hibbard, J. P., 1983, Geology of the Baie Verte Peninsula, Newfoundland: Newfoundland Department Mines and Energy, Mineral Development Division, Memoir 2, 279 p.

Hildreth, E. W., 1981, Gradients in silicic magma chambers: Implications for lithospheric magmatism: Journal of Geophysical Research, v. 86, p. 10153–10192.

Holdsworth, R. E., 1991, The geology and structure of the Gander-Avalon boundary zone in northestern Newfoundland, in Pereira, C. P. G., Walsh, D. G., and Blackwood, R. F., eds., Current research: Newfoundland Deptartment of Mines and Energy, Geological Survey Branch, Report 91-1, p. 109–127.

Jayasinghe, N. R., 1978, Geology of the Wesleyville (2F/4) and the Musgrave Harbour east (2F/5) map areas, Newfoundland: Newfoundland Department Mines and Energy, Mineral Development Division, Report 78-8, 11 p.

Jenner, G. A., Malpas, J. G., and Dunning, G. R., 1991, Bay of Islands and the Little Port complexes, revisted: Age, geochemical and isotopic evidence confirm suprasubduction zone origin: Canadian Journal of Earth Sciences, v. 28, p. 1635–1653.

Karlstrom, K. E., 1983, Reinterpretation of Newfoundland gravity data and arguments for an allochthonous Dunnage zone: Geology, v. 11, p. 263–266.

Kean, B. F., and Jayasinghe, N., 1982, Geology of the Badger map area, Newfoundland: Newfoundland Department of Mines and Energy, Mineral Development Division, Report 81-2, 37 p.

Keen, C. E., Keen, M. J., Nichols, B., Reid, I., Stockmal, G. S., Colman-Sadd, S. P., Miller, H., and Quinlan, G., 1986, Deep seismic reflection profile across the northern Appalachians: Geology, v. 14, p. 141–145.

Kerr, A., 1989, Geochemistry of the Trans-Labrador Granitoid Belt, Canada: A quantitative comparative study of a Proterozoic batholith and possible Phanerozoic counterparts: Precambrian Research, v. 45, p. 1–17.

Kerr, A., 1995, The Hodges Hill granite between Grand Falls–Windsor and Badger (NTS 2D/13 and 2E/4): Geology, petrology and dimension-stone potential, in Pereira, C. P. G., Walsh, D. G., and Blackwood, R. F., eds., Current Research: Newfoundland Department of Natural Resources, Geological Survey Branch, Report 95-1, p. 237–256.

Kerr, A., Dickson, W. L., Hayes, J. P., and Fryer, B. J., 1990, Geochemical

overview of late- and post-orogenic granites across Newfoundland: Part of a long-term project to integrate and interpret our large inventory of data, in Hall, J., ed., Lithoprobe East Transect Meeting Report, October, 1990: St. John's, Memorial University of Newfoundland, p. 117–135.

Kerr, A., Hayes, J. P., Dickson, W. L., and Butler, J., 1991, Toward an integrated database for Newfoundland granitoid suites, A project outline and progress report, in Pereira, C. P. G., Walsh, D. G., and Blackwood, R. F., eds., Current research: Newfoundland Department of Mines and Energy, Geological Survey Branch, Report 91-1, p. 127–140.

Kerr, A., Dickson, W. L., Colman-Sadd. S. P., Fryer, B., and Jenner, G. A., 1992, Paleozoic granites and orogenic evolution in the Newfoundland Appalachians: A new type area for Caledonian Magmatism: Geological Association of Canada Program with Abstracts, v. 17, p. A45.

Kerr, A., Dickson, W. L., Hayes, J. P., and Fryer, B. J., 1993a, Devonian postorogenic granites on the southeastern margin of the Newfoundland Appalachians: A review of geology, geochemistry, petrogenesis and mineral potential, in Pereira, C. P. G., Walsh, D. G., and Blackwood, R. F., eds., Current research: Newfoundland Department of Mines and Energy, Geological Survey Branch, Report 93–1, p. 239–279.

Kerr, A., Dunning, G. R., and Tucker, R. D., 1993b, The youngest Paleozoic plutonism of the Newfoundland Appalachians: U-Pb ages from the St. Lawrence and François granites: Canadian Journal of Earth Sciences, v. 30, p. 2328–2333.

Kerr, A., Hayes, J. P., Colman-Sadd, S. P., Dickson, W. L., and Butler, A. J., 1994, An integrated lithogeochemical database for the granitoid plutonic suites of Newfoundland: Newfoundland Department of Mines and Energy, Geological Survey Branch, Open File Report NFLD/2377, 44 p.

Kerr, A., Jenner, G. A., and Fryer, B. J., 1995, Sm-Nd isotopic geochemistry of Precambrian to Paleozoic granites and the deep-crustal structure of the southeast margin of the Newfoundland Appalachians: Canadian Journal of Earth Sciences, v. 32, p. 224–245.

Kontak, D. J., Tuach, J., Strong, D. F., Archibald, D. A., and Farrar, E., 1988, Plutonic and hydrothermal events in the Ackley granite, southeast Newfoundland, as indicated by total-fusion $^{40}Ar/^{39}Ar$ geochronology: Canadian Journal of Earth Sciences, v. 25, p. 1151–1160.

Krogh, T. E., Strong, D. F., O'Brien, S. J., and Papezik, V. S., 1988, Precise U-Pb zircon dates from the Avalon Terrane in Newfoundland: Canadian Journal of Earth Sciences, v. 25, p. 442–453.

Kröner, A., 1980, Pan-African crustal evolution: Episodes, 1980, p. 3–8.

Malpas, J. G., 1979, Two contrasting trondhjemite associations from transported ophiolites in western Newfoundland: Initial report, in Barker F., ed., Trondhjemites, dacites and related rocks: Amsterdam, Elsevier, p. 465–487.

Marillier, F., Keen, C. E., Stockmal, G. S., Quinlan, G., Williams, H., Colman-Sadd, S. P., and O'Brien, S. J., 1989, Crustal structure and surface zonation of the Canadian Appalachians: Implications of deep seismic reflection data: Canadian Journal of Earth Sciences, v. 26, p. 305–321.

Martin, R. F., and Piwinski, A. J., 1972, Magmatism and tectonic settings: Journal of Geophysical Research, v. 77, p. 4966–4975.

McCartney, W. D., 1967, Whitbourne map area, Newfoundland: Geological Survey of Canada Memoir 341, 135 p.

Mercer, B., Strong, D. F., Wilton, D., and Gibbons, D., 1985, The King's Point complex, western Newfoundland, in Current research: Geological Survey of Canada Paper 85-1A, p. 737–741.

Moore, P. V., 1984, The geochemistry and petrogenesis of the Hodges Hill granite–Twin Lakes diorite complex [B.S. thesis]: St. John's, Newfoundland, Memorial University, 36 p.

Neale, E. R. W., Nash, W. A., and Innes, G. M., 1960, King's Point area, Newfoundland: Geological Survey of Canada Map 35-1960, scale 1:63,360.

Nelson, K. D., 1992, Are crustal thickness variations in old mountain belts like the Appalachians a consequence of lithospheric delamination?: Geology, v. 20, p. 498–502.

O'Brien, B. H., 1992, Internal and external relationships of the South Lake Igneous Complex, north-central Newfoundland: Ordovician and later tectonism in the Exploits subzone?, in Pereira, C. P. G., Walsh, D. G., and Blackwood, R. F., eds., Current research: Newfoundland Department of

Mines and Energy, Geological Survey Branch, Report 92-1, p. 159–171.

O'Brien, B. H., O'Brien, S. J., and Dunning, G. R., 1991, Silurian cover, Late Precambrian–Early Ordovician basement, and the chronology of Silurian orogenesis in the Hermitage Flexure (Newfoundland Appalachians): American Journal of Science, v. 291, p. 760–799.

O'Brien, S. J., and Holdsworth, R. E., 1992, Geological development of the Avalon zone, the easternmost Gander zone, and the ductile Dover Fault in the Glovertown area, eastern Newfoundland, *in* Current research: Newfoundland Department of Mines and Energy, Geological Survey Branch, Report 92-1, p. 171–185.

O'Brien, S. J., Nunn, G. A., Dickson, W. L., and Tuach, J., 1984, Geology of the Terrenceville (1M/10) and Gisborne Lake (1M/15) map areas, southeast Newfoundland: Newfoundland Department of Mines and Energy, Mineral Development Division, Report 84-4, 54 p.

O'Brien, S. J., Dickson, W. L., and Blackwood, R. F., 1986, Geology of the central portion of the Hermitage Flexure Area, Newfoundland, *in* Blackwood, R. F., Walsh, D. G., and Gibbons, R. J., eds., Current research: Newfoundland Department of Mines and Energy, Mineral Development Division, Report 86-1, p. 189–209.

O'Driscoll, C. F., and Muggridge, W. W., 1979, Geology of Merasheen (1M/8) and Harbour Buffett (1M/9) areas, Newfoundland: Newfoundland Department of Mines and Energy, Mineral Development Division, Report of Activities for 1979, p. 82–89.

O'Neill, P. P., and Lux, D., 1989, Tectonothermal history and $^{40}Ar/^{39}Ar$ geochronology of the northeastern Gander zone, Weir's Pond area, *in* Pereira, C. P. G., Walsh, D. G., and Blackwood, R. F., eds., Current research: Newfoundland Department of Mines and Energy, Geological Survey Branch, Report 89-1, p. 131–141.

Palmer, A. R., 1984, The Decade of North American Geology 1983 geological time scale: Geology, v. 11, p. 503–504.

Payne, J. G., and Strong, D. F., 1979, Origin of the Twillingate trondhjemite, north-central Newfoundland: Partial melting in the roots of an island arc, *in* Barker, F., ed., Trondhjemites, dacites and related rocks: Amsterdam, Elsevier, p. 489–516.

Pearce, J. A., Harris, N. B. W., and Tindle, A. G., 1984, Trace element discrimination diagrams for the tectonic interpretation of granitic rocks: Journal of Petrology, v. 25, p. 956–974.

Peckham, V. H., 1992, The Iona Islands intrusive suite, Placentia Bay, Newfoundland: Geology, geochronology and geochemistry [B.S. thesis]: St. John's, Newfoundland, Memorial University, 117 p.

Petro, W. L., Vogel, T. A., and Wilbrand, J. T., 1979, Major element chemistry of plutonic rock suites from compressional and extensional plate boundaries: Chemical Geology, v. 26, p. 217–235.

Pitcher, W. S., 1983, granite type and tectonic environment, *in* Hsü, K., ed., Mountain building processes: London, Academic Press, p. 19–44.

Poole, J. C., Delaney, P. W., and Dickson, W. L., 1985, Geology of the François granite, south coast of Newfoundland, *in* Brewer, K., Walsh, D. G., and Gibbons, R. V., Current research: Newfoundland Department Mines and Energy, Mineral Development Division, Report 85-1, p. 145–153.

Quinlan, G. M., Hall, J., Williams, H., Wright, J., Colman-Sadd, S., O'Brien, S. J., Stockmal, G., and Marillier, F., 1992, Onshore seismic reflection transects across the Newfoundland Appalachians: Canadian Journal of Earth Sciences, v. 29, p. 1865–1877.

Sandeman, H. A., and Malpas, J., 1993, Epizonal I-type and A-type granites and associated ash-flow tuffs, Fogo Island, northeast Newfoundland: Geological Association of Canada Program with Abstracts, v. 18, p. A92.

Smyth, W. R., and Schillereff, H. S., 1982, Pre-Carboniferous geology of southwestern White Bay, *in* O'Driscoll, C. F., and Gibbons, R. V., eds., Current research: Newfoundland Department of Mines and Energy, Mineral Development Division, Report 82-1, p. 78–98.

Streckheisen, A. L., and LeMaitre, R. W., 1979, Chemical approximation to modal QAPF classification of the igneous rocks: Neues Jahrbuch für Mineralogie Abhandlungen, v. 136, p. 169–206.

Strong, D. F., 1980, Granitoid rocks and associated mineral deposits of eastern Canada and western Europe, *in* Strangway, D. W., ed., The continental crust and its mineral deposits, Geological Association of Canada Special Paper 20, p. 741–771.

Strong, D. F., and Dickson, W. L., 1978, Geochemistry of Paleozoic granitoid plutons from contrasting zones of northeast Newfoundland: Canadian Journal of Earth Sciences, v. 15, p. 145–156.

Strong, D. F., and Dupuy, C., 1982, Rare earth elements in the bimodal Mount Peyton batholith: Evidence of crustal anatexis by mantle-derived magmas: Canadian Journal of Earth Sciences, v. 19, p. 308–315.

Strong, D. F., Dickson, W. L., O'Driscoll, C. F., and Kean, B. F., 1974, Geochemistry of eastern Newfoundland granitoid rocks: Newfoundland Department of Mines and Energy, Mineral Development Division, Report 74-3, 140 p.

Strong, D. F., O'Brien, S. J., Taylor, S. W., Strong, P. G., and Wilton, D., 1977, Geology of the Marystown (1M/3) and St. Lawrence (1L/14) map areas, Newfoundland: Newfoundland Department of Mines and Energy, Mineral Development Division, Report 77-8, 81 p.

Strong, D. F., Fryer, B. J., and Kerrich, R., 1984, Genesis of the St. Lawrence Fluorspar deposits as indicated by fluid inclusion, rare earth element, and isotope data: Economic Geology, v. 79, p. 1142–1158.

Swinden, H. S., Jenner, G. A., and Szybinski, Z. A., 1994, Geochemical and isotopic signatures of Cambrian-Ordovician volcanism and plutonism in the Notre Dame subzone, Newfoundland Appalachians: Magmatic evolution of the Laurentian margin of Iapetus, *in* Geological Association of Canada, New perspectives in the Appalachian-Caledonian Orogen (NUNA Conference, Grand Falls, Newfoundland, August 1994): Program with Abstracts, p. 27.

Taylor, R. P., Strong, D. F., and Kean, B. F., 1980, The Topsails Igneous Complex: Silurian- Devonian peralkaline magmatism in western Newfoundland: Canadian Journal of Earth Sciences, v. 17, p. 425–439.

Teng, H. C., and Strong, D. F., 1976, Geology and geochemistry of the St. Lawrence peralkaline granite and associated fluorite deposits, southeast Newfoundland: Canadian Journal of Earth Sciences, v. 13, p. 1374–1385.

Tuach, J., Davenport, P. H., Dickson, W. L., and Strong, D. F., 1986, Geochemical trends in the Ackley granite, southeast Newfoundland: Their relevance to magmatic metallogenic processes in high-silica granitoid systems: Canadian Journal of Earth Sciences, v. 23, p. 747–765.

Tucker, R. D., O'Brien, S. J., and O'Brien, B. H., 1994, Age and implications of Early Ordovician (Arenig) plutonism in the type area of the Bay du Nord Group, Dunnage zone, southern Newfoundland Appalachians: Canadian Journal of Earth Sciences, v. 31, p. 351–357.

Van Berkel, J. T., 1987, Geology of the Dashwood's Pond, St. Fintan's and Main Gut map areas, southwest Newfoundland, *in* Current research: Geological Survey of Canada Paper 87-1A, p. 399–408.

Van Berkel, J. T., and Currie, K. L., 1988, Geology of the Puddle Pond and Little Grand Lake Map areas, southwest Newfoundland: Newfoundland Department of Mines and Energy, Mineral Development Division, Report 88-1, p. 99–107.

Van Staal, C. R., Dunning, G. R., Valverde, P., Burgess, J., and Brown, M., 1994, Arenig and younger evolution of the Gander Margin : A comparison of the New Brunswick and Newfoundland segments, *in* New perspectives in the Appalachian-Caledonian Orogen (NUNA Conference, Grand Falls, Newfoundland, August 1994): Geological Association of Canada, Program with Abstracts, p. 28.

Whalen, J. B., 1989, The Topsails Igneous Suite, western Newfoundland: An Early Silurian subduction-related magmatic suite?: Canadian Journal of Earth Sciences, v. 26, p. 2421–2434.

Whalen, J., Currie, K. L., and Van Breemen, O., 1987a, Episodic Ordovician-Silurian plutonism in the Topsails Igneous Terrane, western Newfoundland: Royal Society of Edinburgh Transactions, Earth Sciences, v. 78, p. 17–28.

Whalen, J. B., Currie, K. L., and Chappell, B. W., 1987b, A-type granites: Geochemical characteristics, discrimination and petrogenesis: Contributions to Mineralogy and Petrology, v. 95, p. 407–419.

Whalen, J. B., Jenner, G. A., Currie, K. L., Barr, S. M., Longstaffe, F. J., and Hegner, E., 1994, Geochemical and isotopic characteristics of granitoids of the Avalon zone, southern New Brunswick: Possible evidence for repeated delamination events: Journal of Geology, v. 102, p. 269–282.

Williams, H., 1964, The Appalachians in northeastern Newfoundland—A two-sided symmetrical system: American Journal of Science, v. 262, p. 1137–1158.

Williams, H., 1979, The Appalachian Orogen in Canada: Canadian Journal of Earth Sciences, v. 16, p. 163–174.

Williams, H., and Payne, J. G., 1975, The Twillingate granite and nearby volcanic groups: An island arc complex in northeastern Newfoundland: Canadian Journal of Earth Sciences, v. 12, p. 982–996.

Williams, H., and Smyth, W. R., 1983, Geology of the Hare Bay Allochthon, *in* Geology of the Strait of Belle Isle Area, northwestern insular Newfoundland, southern Labrador and adjacent Quebec, Geological Survey of Canada Memoir 400, p. 109–133.

Williams, H., Colman-Sadd, S. P., and Swinden, H. S., 1988, Tectonic-stratigraphic subdivisions of Central Newfoundland, *in* Current research: Geological Survey of Canada Paper 88-1B, p. 91–98.

Williams, H., Dickson, W. L., Currie, K. L., Hayes, J. P., and Tuach, J., 1989, Preliminary report on classification of Newfoundland granitic rocks and their relations to tectonostratigraphic zones and lower crustal blocks: Geological Survey of Canada, Paper 89–1B, p. 47–53.

Williams, S. H., Boyce, W. D., and Colman-Sadd, S. P., 1992, A new Lower Ordovician (Arenig) faunule from the Coy Pond Complex, central Newfoundland, and a refined understanding of the closure of the Iapetus Ocean: Canadian Journal of Earth Sciences, v. 29, p. 2046–2057.

MANUSCRIPT ACCEPTED BY THE SOCIETY JULY 2, 1996

Geological Society of America
Memoir 191
1997

Concord plutonic suite: Pre-Acadian gabbro-syenite intrusions in the southern Appalachians

Harry Y. McSween, Jr.
Department of Geological Sciences, University of Tennessee, Knoxville, Tennessee 37996-1410
Ralph P. Harvey
Department of Geological Sciences, Case Western Reserve University, Cleveland, Ohio 44106-7216

ABSTRACT

The ca. 400 Ma (Silurian-Devonian) Concord plutonic suite consists of a 500-km-long chain of 20 gabbroic intrusions within the southern Appalachian Piedmont. In the northern part of the outcrop belt, the common occurrence of anorthosite and troctolite with gabbro indicates that plagioclase and olivine were early crystallizing phases, whereas examples of ultramafic rocks within gabbroic plutons in the southern part of the belt suggest that olivine and clinopyroxene crystallized before plagioclase. Most gabbroic rocks fall within the tholeiite field of the normative basalt tetrahedron, but the abundance of olivine and the differentiation of some plutons to syenite suggest parental magma compositions that were somewhat silica deficient and more alkaline than common tholeiites. Limited Fe-enrichment trends in mafic minerals and the general absence of layering in most plutons may be the result of their emplacement as crystal mushes. However, a few plutons have modal layering, and one pluton shows an apparently complete magmatic differentiation sequence to syenite. Radiogenic isotopes suggest that Concord suite magmas formed by melting of mantle materials with minimal crustal contamination. These plutons have been affected to varying degrees by regional metamorphism (presumably Acadian), producing gabbro-metagabbro complexes. Radiometric ages of Concord suite plutons and the related Salisbury suite plutons indicate that they were emplaced just prior to Acadian peak metamorphism. Contrasting tectonic models involving compressional or transtensional regimes have been suggested to account for these magmas. Tectonic discriminants based on trace-element patterns and the compositions of minerals give conflicting results, so it is not yet possible to determine whether these plutons represent anorogenic magmatism or the onset of the Acadian event in the southern Appalachians.

INTRODUCTION

Gabbroic plutons are volumetrically subordinate to granitic plutons in most parts of the Appalachians, and intrusion of mafic magmas was relatively uncommon during most of the orogen's igneous evolution (Misra and McSween, 1984). A notable exception is the Concord plutonic suite (McSween et al., 1991) of Silurian-Devonian age. The emplacement of these plutons immediately preceded the Acadian orogeny, a tectonothermal event that is poorly understood within the southern Appalachians. These gabbroic intrusions and their syenite differentiates have proved difficult to reconcile with current tectonic models.

This distinctive suite of more than 20 plutons forms an arcuate chain extending almost 500 km, predominantly within the Charlotte metamorphic belt of the southern Appalachian Piedmont (Fig. 1). Abbreviations for individual Concord suite plutons in Figure 1 are explained in Table 1, which also includes information on petrology and descriptive references

McSween, H. Y., Jr., and Harvey, R. P., 1997, Concord plutonic suite: Pre-Acadian gabbro-syenite intrusions in the southern Appalachians, *in* Sinha, A. K., Whalen, J. B., and Hogan, J. P., eds., The Nature of Magmatism in the Appalachian Orogen: Boulder, Colorado, Geological Society of America Memoir 191.

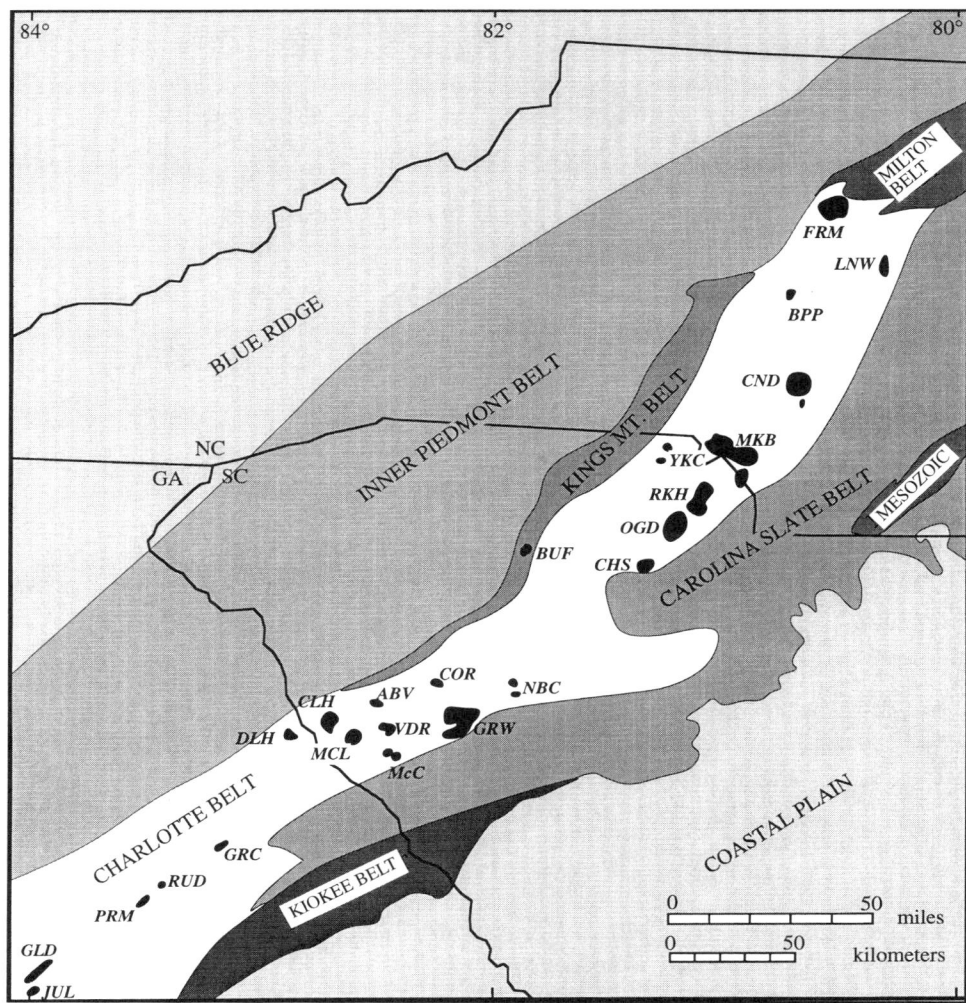

Figure 1. Map showing the distribution of plutons thought to be part of the Concord plutonic suite in the Carolinas and Georgia. Most plutons have no determined emplacement age. The Carolina slate belt, Charlotte belt, and Kings Mountain belt are parts of the exotic Carolina terrane. Pluton abbreviations are explained in Table 1.

(many of which are unpublished theses). This outcrop belt lies within the Carolina terrane, a package of metamorphosed mafic (in the west) and pyroclastic or epiclastic (in the east) rocks that accreted to the North American continent during the early or middle Paleozoic (Secor et al., 1983; Hatcher, 1987; Harris and Glover, 1988).

Despite decades of active research by numerous workers, our understanding of the Concord plutonic suite is limited by poor field exposure and sparse geophysical, geochronological, and isotopic data. In this review we summarize the petrologic and geochemical characteristics of these plutons, and consider the timing and mode of emplacement, magmatic differentiation, and possible relationships to regional metamorphism. We also discuss hypotheses about the tectonic environment in which these magmas were generated and emplaced.

PLUTON FIELD RELATIONS AND EMPLACEMENT

Spatial relationship to metagabbro

The Concord plutonic suite consists mostly of gabbroic rocks, by which we mean igneous rocks composed principally of pyroxenes and plagioclase, with or without olivine. Many, if not most, of these gabbroic plutons are associated with metagabbro, consisting mostly of amphibole, plagioclase, and commonly relict igneous phases. Contacts of the gabbro-metagabbro complexes with surrounding units are sharp and easily delineated in saprolite. Previously, workers (e.g., Hermes, 1968; Chalcraft, 1970; McSween et al., 1984; Hooper and Hatcher, 1989) interpreted the gabbroic plutons to have intruded older metagabbro to form gabbro-metagabbro com-

TABLE 1. PETROLOGY AND BEST DESCRIPTIVE REFERENCES FOR THE CONCORD PLUTONIC SUITE

Pluton (symbol)	Petrology*	Descriptive references
North Carolina:		
Farmington (FRM)†	gb, an, mgb	Taylor, 1982; Harden, 1984; McSween et al., 1984.
Linwood (LNW)		Constantino-Herrera, 1971.
Bear Poplar (BPP)§	gb, mgb, nor	Clark, 1980; McSween et al., 1984.
Concord (CND)	gb, an, syn	Cabaup, 1969; Olsen, 1982; Olsen et al., 1983; McSween et al., 1984.
Mecklenburg (MKB)**	gb, an, mgb	Hermes, 1968; Wilson, 1981.
South Carolina		
York County (YKC)	gb, mgb	Butler, 1966.
Rock Hill (RKH)‡	gb, an, mgb	Chalcraft, 1970; Noble, 1993.
Ogden (OGD)	gb, an, mgb	McSween, 1981; McSween et al., 1984.
Chester (CHS)	gb, um, mgb	Deetz, 1980.
Buffalo (BUF)	gb	Medlin, 1968; Medlin et al., 1972.
Newberry County (NBC)	mgb	
Coronaca (COR)	nor, syn	McSween, 1970.
Greenwood (GRW)	gb, mgb	Chalcraft et al., 1978; Fronabarger, 1984.
Abbeville (ABV)	mgb	Fronabarger, 1984.
Verdery (VDR)	mgb	Fronabarger, 1984.
McCormick (McC)	mgb	Fronabarger, 1984.
Calhoun Falls (CLH)	gb, um	Fronabarger, 1984.
Mt. Carmel (MCL)	gb, syn, mgb	Medlin, 1968; Fronabarger, 1984.
Georgia		
Delhi (DLH)	syn	
Greene County (GRC)		
Rudden (RUD)	um	Libby, 1971.
Presley's Mill (PRM)	gb	Myers, 1968; Libby, 1971.
Gladesville (GLD)§§	gb, um, mgb	Matthews, 1967; Prather, 1971; Hooper, 1986; Hooper and Hatcher, 1989.
Juliette (JUL)§§	gb	Hooper and Hatcher, 1989.

*Rock abbreviations: gb = gabbro; an = plagioclase-rich rocks, including anorthosite and troctolite; nor = quartz norite; um = ultramafic rocks (mostly serpentinized); syn = syenite; mgb = metagabbro.
†Also called Mocksville complex (Butler and Secor, 1991).
§Part of the Barber gabbro-metagabbro complex (Clark, 1980).
**Also called Mecklenburg-Weddington complex (Wilson, 1981).
‡Also called North Rock Hill and South Rock Hill plutons (Chalcraft, 1970).
§§Also called Berner mafic complex (Hooper and Hatcher, 1989).

plexes. However, exposure is generally too poor to allow direct inspection of contact relations between gabbro and metagabbro (both lithologies commonly occur as spheroidally weathered boulders or as small outcrops in stream beds, and they cannot be distinguished in saprolite). Hermes (1968) and McSween (1981) described xenolithic inclusions or roof pendants of metagabbro within several gabbros, attesting to the older age of metagabbro. Distinct (though sometimes overlapping) chemi-

cal compositions for gabbro and associated metagabbro in some complexes (e.g., Hermes, 1968; Strange, 1983) also support the idea that these bodies intruded separately (assuming that metamorphism was isochemical).

McSween et al. (1984) were struck by the observation that composite gabbro-metagabbro intrusions occur repeatedly at approximately regularly spaced intervals in the northern half of this outcrop belt. This association, repeated so consistently, is unlikely to result from random intrusion. McSween et al. (1984) attempted to explain the gabbro-metagabbro association as a result of successive magma pulses utilizing the same channelways. The plutons emplaced earlier would be metamorphosed as multiple magma pulses ascended through them and heated their surroundings (Marsh, 1978). They recognized, however, that this explanation would apply only if the time intervals between metagabbro and gabbro pluton emplacement were small.

In another study, Fronabarger (1984) found that the chemical compositions of metagabbros in the Mt. Carmel pluton helped define a continuous fractionation sequence between gabbro and associated syenite, and argued that gabbro and metagabbro were parts of the same intrusion that had later undergone regional metamorphism. Noble (1993) studied a large quarry within the Rock Hill pluton, which undoubtedly provides the best exposure available within any of the Concord suite plutons. She observed adjacent exposures of gabbro and metagabbro with gradational contacts, and suggested that metagabbro formed locally during metamorphism, wherever fluids could gain access to gabbro through fractures.

We accept this observational evidence for partial metamorphism of Concord suite plutons. Nearby granitoid plutons of comparable age (the Salisbury plutonic suite, discussed below) are foliated and deformed, so the existence of Concord suite gabbro plutons without any metamorphic overprint would require some ad hoc explanation (e.g., gabbroic rocks are less permeable to fluids than granitoids). The pluton shapes illustrated in Figure 1 include some areas mapped as metagabbro by previous workers. We caution, however, that many of these complexes probably represent multiple magmatic pulses and note that there are older metagabbros in the immediate vicinity that are almost certainly not parts of the Concord plutonic suite (e.g., Butler, 1983; Dennis and Shervais, 1991). These older units may constitute the xenoliths that have been previously described in gabbros. Metagabbros that we believe to be parts of Concord suite plutons are nonfoliated, coarse-grained rocks commonly with relict gabbroic textures, distinct from the foliated amphibolites that may compose older mafic units.

Spatial association with syenite

Several plutons contain minor quantities of syenite. In the Concord pluton, syenite forms a horseshoe-shaped ring around the gabbro, open at the southern end (Olsen et al., 1983). The Coronaca pluton is predominantly syenite with a small interior plug of gabbro (McSween, 1970), and the Delhi pluton contains only syenite. An irregular mass of syenite also occurs within the Mt. Carmel pluton (Medlin, 1968). Syenite is apparently a differentiation product of gabbroic magma, as explained in the following.

Timing of emplacement

McSween et al. (1984) reported Sm-Nd internal isochron ages for three unmetamorphosed gabbroic rocks from plutons in the Concord Suite, as follows: Concord, 407 ± 36 Ma; Farmington, 399 ± 27 Ma; Ogden, 406 ± 32 Ma. A Rb-Sr whole-rock isochron for syenite from the Concord pluton (Fullagar, 1971) gives an age of 401 ± 30 Ma (recalculated using a newer decay constant—Olsen et al., 1983), essentially identical to the Sm-Nd age. A $^{40}Ar/^{39}Ar$ plateau age of 406 ± 4 Ma for hornblende from the Farmington gabbro was reported by Sutter et al. (1983); they also reported an age of 408 ± 1 Ma for the Weddington gabbro, which is an alternate name for the Mecklenburg gabbro. Medlin (1968) reported a K-Ar biotite age of 358 Ma for the Mt. Carmel pluton; because of possible argon loss, this age serves only as a minimum estimate for its time of emplacement.

The Sm-Nd age for the Barber pluton is 470 ± 24 Ma (McSween et al., 1984), well outside of the analytical error for the other plutons. This result was reconfirmed by replicate analyses of mineral separates. The analyzed Barber sample was a relatively unmetamorphosed olivine gabbro found within a predominately metagabbro body, and was interpreted to be relict. It is unlikely that emplacement of Concord suite plutons spanned such a long time interval, so this metagabbro may be part of an older Taconic igneous suite (Sinha et al., 1989). A petrologically distinct quartz norite body, called the Bear Poplar pluton (Clark, 1980), apparently intrudes the Barber metagabbro and is tentatively considered to be part of the Concord plutonic suite, although its composition is unique.

The main episode of penetrative deformation and peak metamorphism in the Charlotte belt is thought to have been the Taconic orogeny (Butler, 1991), which ended well before intrusion of the Concord Suite plutons. Hornblende $^{40}Ar/^{39}Ar$ ages for Charlotte belt rocks of 430 to 425 Ma (Sutter et al., 1983) are interpreted to reflect argon closure after peak Taconic metamorphism, so the Taconic event is unlikely to have metamorphosed 400 Ma plutons. However, Butler (1983) recognized a greenschist facies metamorphic overprint in localized areas of the Charlotte belt that probably occurred between 380 and 360 Ma. It is this (presumably Acadian) event that has probably affected the Concord suite plutons. Figure 2 provides a summary of the inferred chronology of pluton emplacement and metamorphism.

Depth of emplacement

The compositions of coexisting clinopyroxene and orthopyroxene in equilibrium with olivine and plagioclase have been used to estimate the pressure during crystallization (from the petrogenetic grid of Herzberg, 1978) at 3.5 to 5.0 kbar for plu-

tons in the northern half of the outcrop belt (McSween et al., 1984). Discrete grains of sodic and potassic feldspars in syenites require pressures of at least 5 kbar if P_{H_2O} equaled lithostatic pressure; because that is unlikely, 5 kbar may be a limiting pressure. These observations suggest depths of emplacement on the order of 12–15 km.

Pluton geometry

In plan form, the plutons are generally ovals or have more irregular shapes. Two-dimensional models of Bouguer gravity data have been used to infer the buried shapes of a number of plutons. These bodies are described as cylindrical plugs (Morgan and Mann, 1964; Hermes, 1968; Chalcraft, 1970; Olsen et al., 1983) or lopoliths (Wilson, 1981; Taylor, 1982) and currently extend to depths of up to 6 km.

Models based on potential field data are always nonunique interpretations but can be better constrained when modeled in three dimensions with multiple datasets. Williams and McSween (1989) formulated a three-dimensional model based on both gravity and aeromagnetic anomaly maps for the Concord pluton. A vertical cylinder extending to several kilometers depth provides a reasonable fit to the gravity data (Olsen et al., 1983) but cannot reproduce the observed magnetic anomaly. Williams and McSween reasoned that a part of the gravity anomaly is due to a mass that does not crop out and thus contributes relatively little to the magnetic anomaly. Their preferred model shows a thin, sheet-like Concord pluton exposed at the surface, perched above a larger, buried pluton at a maximum depth of 5 to 6 km. This geometry may support the suggestion (McSween et al., 1984) that magmas that formed these plutons ascended repeatedly through the same heated conduits. Fractionation within the buried magma chamber presumably produced syenite which intruded to higher levels, providing an explanation for the absence of intermediate rock types between gabbro and syenite in the exposed Concord pluton.

Mesoscopic layering

Although these plutons are petrologically varied, for the most part they are petrographically massive and discernible layering is very scarce. The only pluton in the northern part of the outcrop belt in which layering has been observed is Rock Hill. Chalcraft (1970) mapped wide bands of different lithology and inferred that they represented magmatic layering on a gross scale. Noble (1993) observed centimeter- to meter-scale discontinuous layers of olivine concentrations and anorthosite lenses within troctolite in a Rock Hill quarry; however, these layers showed no systematic variations in modal proportions or grain size with stratigraphic height. In the southern part of the belt, igneous layering is marked by the occurrence of ultramafic lithologies. Fronabarger (1984) described extensive interlayering of now-serpentinized ultramafic rocks, pyroxenite, troctolite, and gabbro in the Calhoun Falls pluton. The Gladesville pluton is reported to have rhythmic layering defined by variations in the

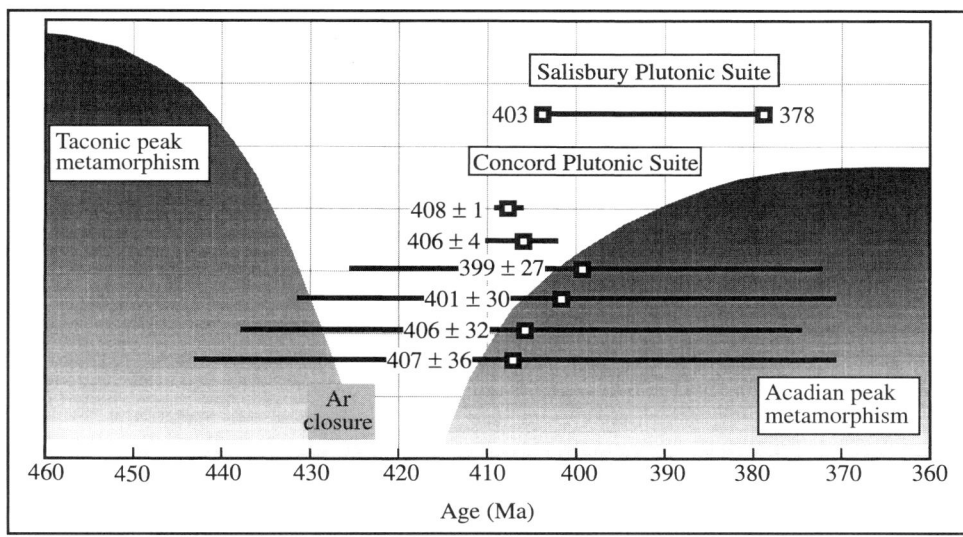

Figure 2. A schematic summary of age relationships between Concord suite plutons and orogenic events. Ages for Concord plutons are from Olsen et al. (1983), Sutter et al. (1983), and McSween et al. (1984).

abundance of olivine (Matthews, 1967); however, Hooper and Hatcher (1989) were unable to confirm this observation because the quarry sites in which layering had previously been described had been filled.

Contact metamorphism

Contact-metamorphic aureoles have been noted around several plutons in the southern half of the pluton outcrop belt: Gladesville (Matthews, 1967; Hooper and Hatcher, 1989), Pressley's Mill (Myers, 1968), Mt. Carmel (Medlin, 1968), and Calhoun Falls (Griffin, 1979). No aureoles have been observed in the northern half of the belt. The presence of ultramafic rocks in the southern part of the belt may indicate that these magmas were emplaced at higher temperatures than in the northern half. It is also possible that contact-metamorphic effects in the northern part of the belt have been obliterated by Acadian metamorphism, known to be discontinuously developed within the Charlotte belt (Butler, 1983).

PETROLOGY

The following discussions will focus only on clearly igneous lithologies, omitting metagabbro (which was described by Hermes, 1968; McSween et al., 1984). Because the relationship between gabbro and metagabbro remains controversial, the origin of the Concord plutons will be explored using rocks that have not been affected by metamorphism.

Petrography

Gabbroic rocks of the Concord plutonic suite are composed predominantly of cumulus olivine, plagioclase, and clinopyroxene, and postcumulus orthopyroxene, hornblende, and biotite. The term cumulus in this sense refers to early crystallizing phases that occur in proportions greater than would obtain if they simply crystallized from their parental liquid without fractionation (Irvine, 1982). True textural cumulates (frameworks of touching cumulus crystals) occur within most plutons, e.g., relatively coarse grained adcumulates and mesocumulates (mostly anorthosites and troctolites) with strong preferred orientations of plagioclase grains. However, most gabbroic rocks are medium grained with no discernible preferred orientations of crystals and with high proportions of postcumulus phases (orthocumulates). Gabbros of the Mt. Carmel pluton have no obvious cumulate textures (Fronabarger, 1984). Minerals interpreted to be postcumulus overgrow cumulus grains, producing poikilitic textures, or fill interstices between cumulus phases. Textural relationships indicate that postcumulus orthopyroxene replaces olivine and brown hornblende replaces clinopyroxene. Hermes (1968) also described clinopyroxene after orthopyroxene and olivine. Biotite is also common, and may be in reaction relationship with opaque Fe-Ti oxides; however, some clinopyroxenes are cumulus. Accessory minerals include apatite, ilmenite, magnetite, hercynitic spinel, hematite, pyrite, and pyrrhotite. Olivine is absent and interstitial quartz is present in a few plutons (e.g., Barber and Coronaca), but quartz-bearing gabbros are uncommon. Photomicrographs of some representative rock textures are shown in Figure 3.

The relative modal proportions of the major minerals in gabbroic rocks are illustrated in Figure 4; nomenclature is from Streckeisen (1976). The inset at the upper left shows how the two diagrams are related. Rock modes are plotted either in the olivine-pyroxene-plagioclase triangle or the pyroxene-plagioclase-hornblende triangle, depending on whether olivine or hornblende predominates. The remaining triangle, which discriminates between orthopyroxene and clinopyroxene, shows

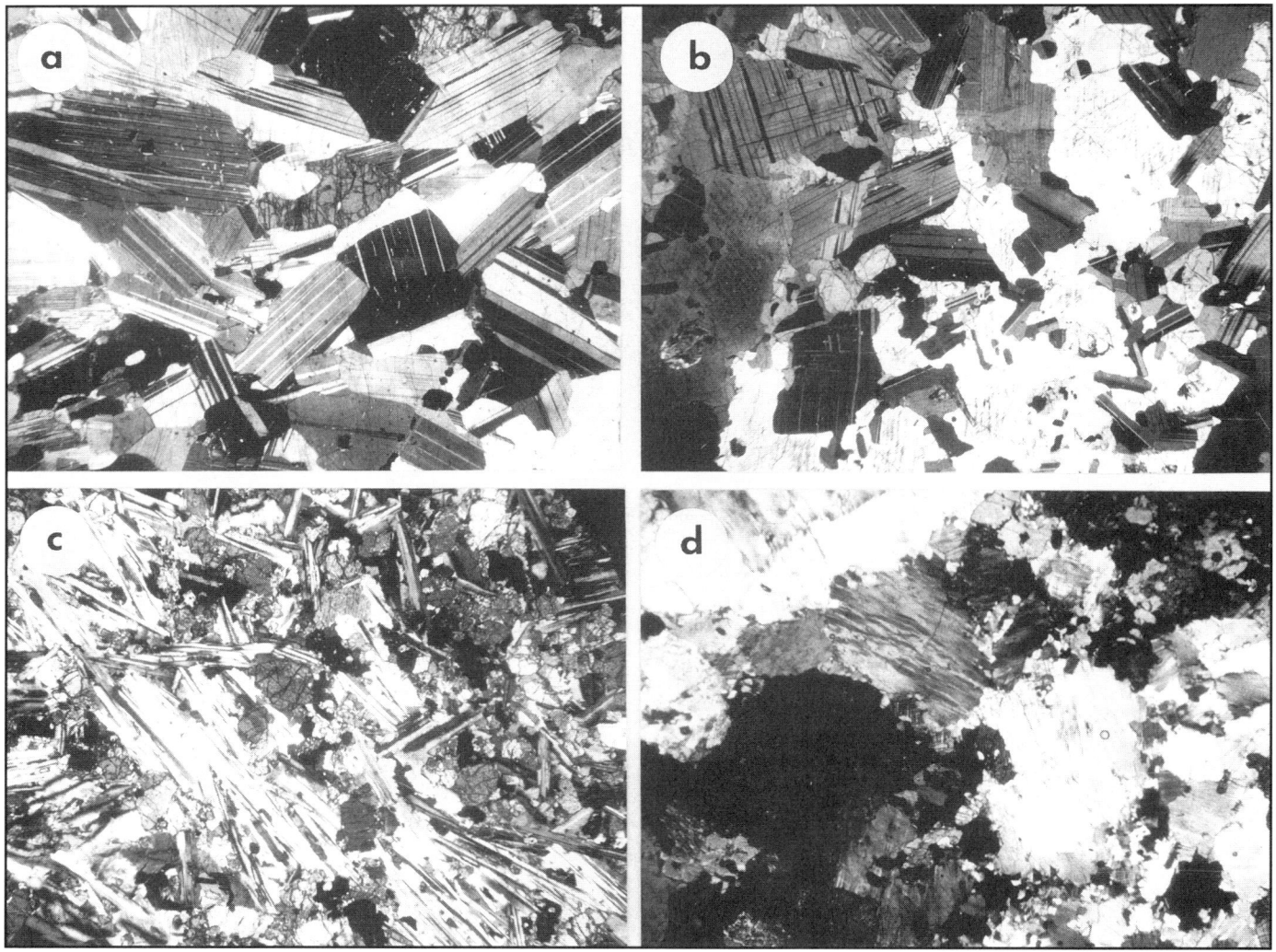

Figure 3. Photomicrographs of representative samples from Concord suite plutons (all under crossed polars, width equals ~1 cm. a: Cumulate troctolite from Mecklenburg. b: Ophitic pyroxene in gabbro from Ogden. c: Relatively fine grained gabbro from Farmington. d: Syenite from Concord.

all of the data. From these figures it is obvious that the gabbroic rocks are rich in plagioclase, forming anorthosites, anorthositic gabbros, and troctolites in some cases. In terms of the abundance of Ca-rich and Ca-poor pyroxenes, gabbros and norites are nearly equally abundant, but clinopyroxene predominates over orthopyroxene in pyroxene-rich rocks. Ultramafic rocks occur in only a few of these plutons; they are not represented in these diagrams because they have been commonly altered to serpentine and other metamorphic minerals.

Syenites are relatively coarse grained seriate porphyries (Fig. 3d), with phenocrysts of perthitic feldspar and groundmass of perthite, albite, microcline, clinopyroxene, hornblende, biotite, magnetite, ilmenite, hematite, pyrite, apatite, zircon, and monazite. Some syenites (e.g., Mt. Carmel and Coronaca) contain quartz, whereas others (e.g., Concord) do not.

Mineral compositions

Most plutons have highly restricted mineral compositional ranges. The compositions of coexisting pyroxenes, hornblende, and olivine for representative rocks from a number of typical plutons are illustrated in Figure 5. The mafic minerals in any one rock are homogeneous in composition and appear to be in equilibrium. Each pluton has its own distinct compositional range of mafic minerals (illustrated in Fig. 5 for two representative plutons), although there is usually some overlap. Noble (1993) analyzed minerals in two layered sequences of troctolite and anorthosite in the Rock Hill pluton to search for cryptic layering, but found no systematic stratigraphic variations. The restricted compositional ranges for mafic minerals in most plutons imply that fractional crystallization was limited. McSween et al. (1984)

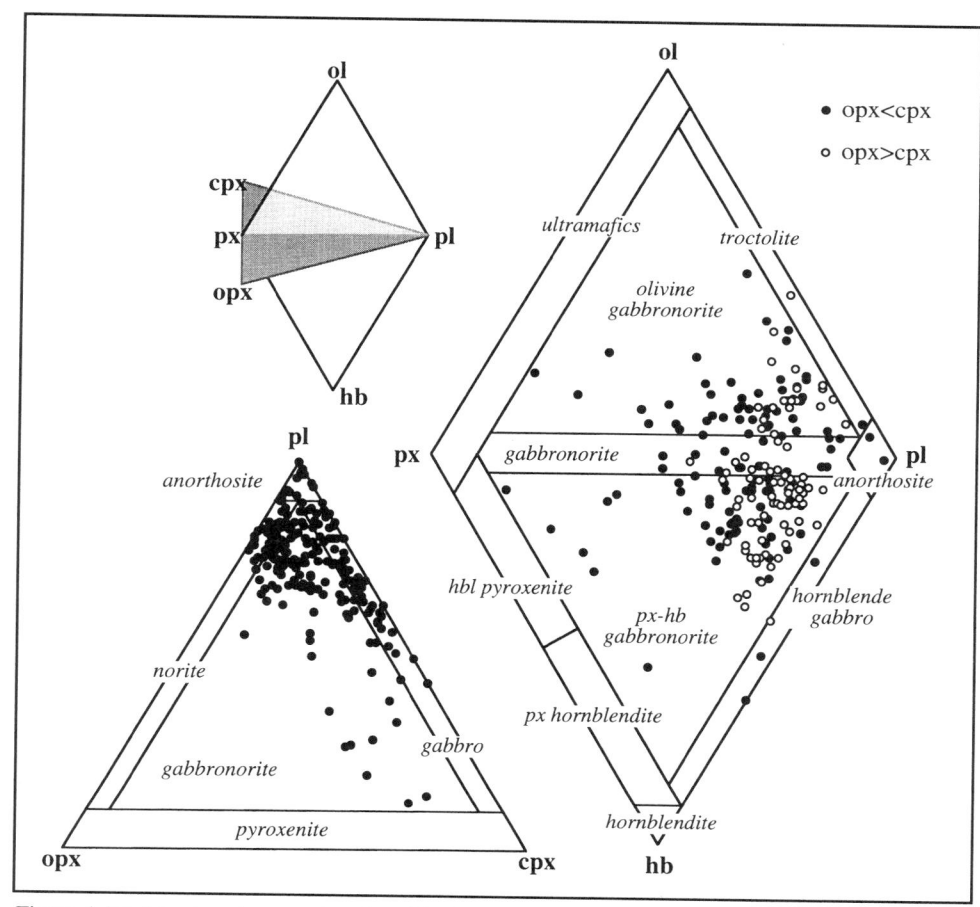

Figure 4. Modal mineral proportions in gabbroic rocks. The inset illustrates how the two figures relate to each other. Rocks are plotted within either the ol-px-pl or px-pl-hb triangles depending on whether olivine or hornblende predominates. All rocks are plotted on the pl-opx-cpx diagram. Gabbro terminology is after Streckeisen (1976). Sources of modal data: Bear Poplar, Clark (1980); Concord, Olsen (1982); Farmington, Harden (1984); Mecklenburg, Hermes (1968); Buffalo, Medlin et al. (1972); Chester, Deetz (1980); Calhoun Falls, Greenwood, and Mt. Carmel, Fronabarger (1984); Ogden, McSween (1981); Rock Hill, Chalcraft (1970); Gladesville, Hooper (1986).

suggested that most of these plutons were emplaced essentially as crystal mushes, to account for the apparent lack of fractionation and general absence of layering. However, the presence of rocks with cumulate textures and the rare occurrence of layers in some plutons suggest at least localized crystal settling.

Postcumulus phases are not noticeably more Fe-rich than cumulus phases (compare hornblende to the clinopyroxene it replaces in Fig. 5). Plagioclase in gabbroic rocks is normally zoned, with cores as calcic as An_{83} and rims as sodic as An_{53}. The zoning may reflect postcumulus overgrowth on cumulus cores.

The Mt. Carmel pluton is unique in that it has an extended range of mafic mineral compositions (Medlin, 1968; Fronabarger, 1984), similar to that found in layered complexes such as the Stillwater (Fig. 6). Plagioclase core compositions also vary sympathetically from An_{78} to An_{42}. Mineral compositions from the Concord pluton, which contains gabbro and syenite but no intermediate rocks, are shown for comparison.

Syenites contain a range of alkali feldspar compositions, from nearly pure albite to nearly pure orthoclase (Olsen et al., 1983). Bulk perthite compositions are commonly near the middle of this range. Clinopyroxene and biotite in syenite are more Fe rich than in associated gabbros, and hornblende is slightly subcalcic (Fig. 6).

Crystallization sequences and late magmatic or subsolidus reactions

On the basis of Fe-enrichment trends in cumulus minerals, Olsen et al. (1983) determined the crystallization sequence for the Concord gabbro to be olivine + plagioclase, followed by olivine + clinopyroxene + plagioclase, and finally clinopyroxene + plagioclase. This allows individual gabbro samples to be classified according to their cumulus phases, into olivine-plagioclase cumulates (OPC), olivine-clinopyroxene-plagioclase cumulates

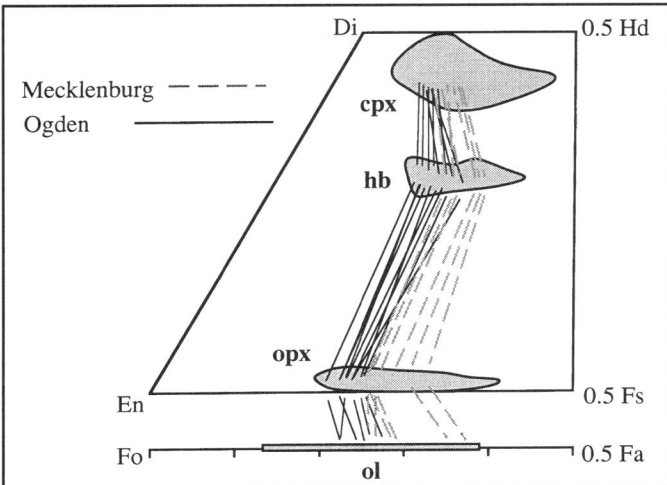

Figure 5. Microprobe molar compositions of mafic minerals in Concord suite plutons. The shaded fields contain analyzed minerals in all plutons, and coexisting phases in two specific plutons are connected by tie lines. Sources of analyses: the Mecklenburg and Ogden pluton data illustrate the limited Fe-enrichment trends for typical plutons, as well as the fact that different plutons have distinct degrees of fractionation. Sources of data: Farmington, Harden (1984); Mecklenburg, Hermes (1970); Calhoun Falls and Greenwood, Fronabarger (1984); Ogden, McSween (1981); Rock Hill, Noble (1993).

(OCPC), and clinopyroxene-plagioclase cumulates (CPC). The distributions of these cumulate types within the unmetamorphosed portions of four plutons show no clear patterns (Fig. 7), although there is perhaps a tendency for CPC rocks to occur near pluton margins. It would be difficult, however, to interpret outcrop patterns as layering phenomena. The crystallization and accumulation of plagioclase before clinopyroxene accounts for the common occurrence of troctolites and anorthosites, at least for plutons in the northern half of the outcrop belt (McSween et al., 1984).

Ultramafic rocks have been described in only a few plutons

(e.g., Calhoun Falls, Rudden, Gladesville) within the southern part of the belt (Matthews, 1967; Fronabarger, 1984). These rocks are heavily metamorphosed, so we can make only guesses about their protoliths. However, the occurrence suggests that crystallization of plagioclase in these plutons may have been delayed, so that olivine + clinopyroxene cumulates formed.

Phases in gabbros that crystallized from, or by reaction with, interstitial melts include orthopyroxene (after olivine), hornblende (after clinopyroxene), and biotite (typically associated with oxide minerals). Late magmatic or subsolidus reaction or exsolution products in gabbros include the following (Dobson, 1987): granules and lamellae of ilmenite and pleonaste within magnetite; hematite lamellae in ilmenite; simplectic intergrowths of orthopyroxene and magnetite or ilmenite replacing olivine; and rods and platelets of magnetite in pyroxenes.

GEOCHEMISTRY

Parental magma compositions

Because almost all of these rocks appear to be cumulates, or at least contain some cumulus phases, it is difficult to determine the compositions of their parental magmas. The plutons for which significant bulk-rock chemistry data have been collected are: Mecklenburg (Hermes, 1968); Concord (Cabaup, 1969); Barber (Strange, 1983); Greenwood (Fronabarger, 1984); Calhoun Falls (Fronabarger, 1984); Mt. Carmel (Medlin, 1968; Fronabarger, 1984), and Gladesville (Hooper, 1986). The compositions of these rocks are generally tholeiitic basalts, as inferred from their locations within the normative basalt tetrahedron (Fig. 8). However, most rocks are richer in normative olivine than typical tholeiites; this either reflects crystal accumulation or lower silica contents than for typical tholeiitic magmas. Fractionation of tholeiitic basalt to form syenite residua (see below) is also unusual and indicates parental magmas that were transitional to alkali basalts.

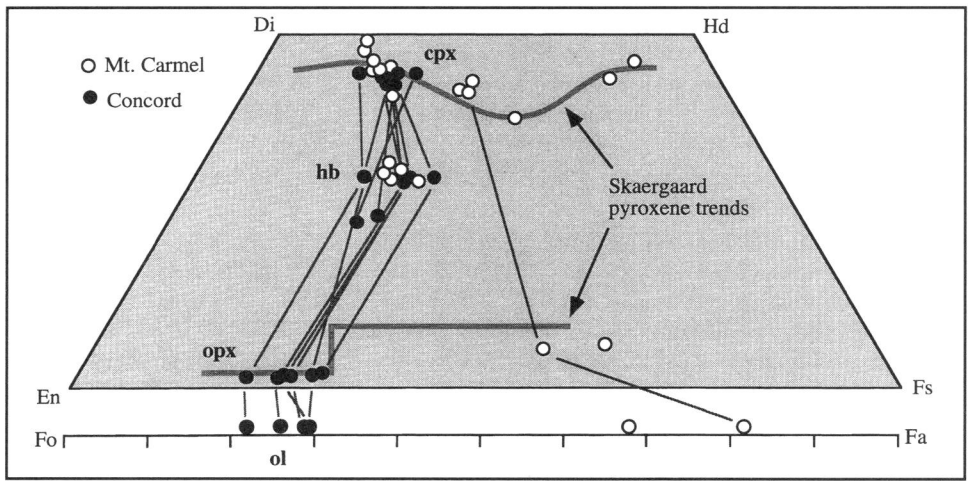

Figure 6. Microprobe molar compositions of mafic minerals in plutons that are differentiated to syenite. Pyroxene compositional trends for the Stillwater complex are shown for reference. Sources of data: Mt. Carmel, Fronabarger (1984); Concord, Olsen (1982).

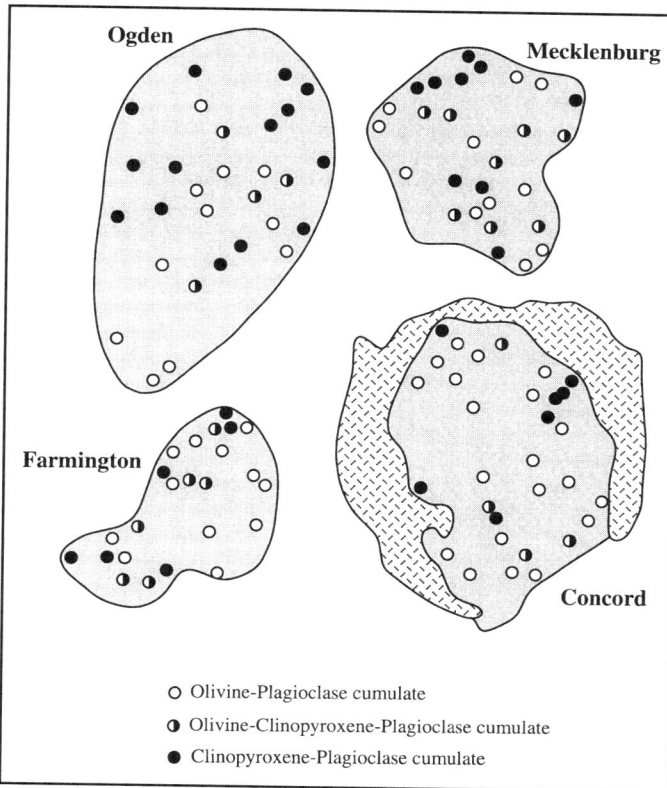

Figure 7. Areal distributions of cumulate types in four representative gabbro bodies. Pluton boundaries define areas of unmetamorphosed gabbro, and may be partly or completely surrounded by metagabbro. The Concord pluton is surrounded on three sides by syenite.

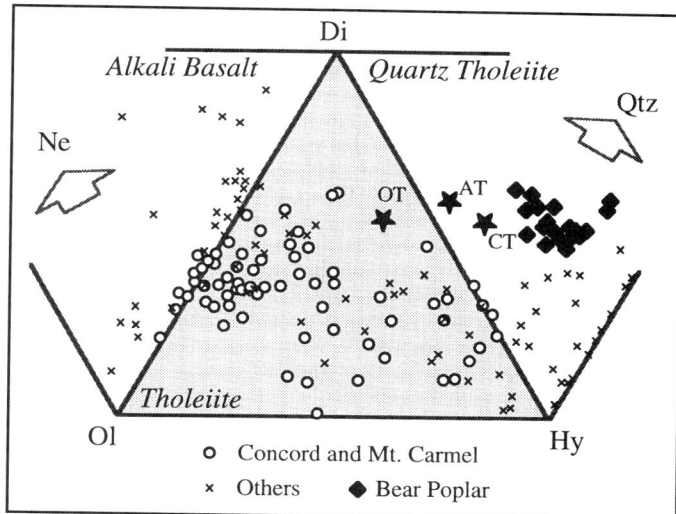

Figure 8. CIPW normative compositions for gabbros, plotted on an expanded basalt tetrahedron. Most of these rocks are more alkaline than typical tholeiites (stars represent the compositions of representative tholeiitic basalts (McSween et al., 1984), as follows: AT = average arc tholeiite, CT = average continental tholeiite, OT = average oceanic tholeiite). The Mt. Carmel and Concord plutons, which contain syenite, are not more noticeably alkaline than other plutons. The Bear Poplar pluton is the only body that is consistently quartz normative. Sources of chemical data: Mecklenburg, Hermes (1968); Concord, Cabaup (1969); Bear Poplar, Strange (1983); Greenwood and Calhoun Falls, Fronabarger (1984); Mt. Carmel, Medlin (1968); Fronabarger (1984); Gladesville, Hooper (1986).

Fractionation sequence

Mt. Carmel is the only pluton of this suite that appears to define a continuous fractionation sequence from gabbro to syenite (Fig. 6). The compositions of its rocks (Medlin, 1968; Fronabarger, 1984) suggest that they may represent magma fractions rather than cumulates, in accord with a general absence of cumulate textures and extended range of mineral compositions. Thus this complex may be particularly important in understanding how these magmas evolved.

The Concord pluton contains gabbro and syenite similar in composition to the least and most fractionated rocks at Mt. Carmel, but without any intervening compositions (Cabaup, 1969). Olsen et al. (1983) demonstrated that 95% fractionation of olivine, clinopyroxene, and plagioclase with compositions of the observed cumulus minerals in roughly cotectic proportions from the bulk gabbro composition would drive residual liquids to syenite. They found that this simple fractionation model also successfully predicted the abundances of trace elements (Rb, Sr, and Zr) in residual syenite. The absence of intervening rock compositions may reflect fractionation within a still-buried magma chamber inferred from geophysical measurements to lie below the currently exposed Concord pluton (Williams and McSween, 1989).

Fractionation of tholeiitic magmas to produce syenite residua, as proposed for the Mt. Carmel and Concord plutons, is unusual. Morse (1980), in a discussion of what he termed the "syenite problem," questioned the ability of a basaltic liquid even slightly deviant from the critical plane of silica saturation (i.e., a liquid containing any normative nepheline or hypersthene; see Fig. 8) to produce syenite. However, Cox et al. (1979) noted that a liquid close to this critical plane (which is also a thermal divide) would become sufficiently enriched in alkalis to form trachyte (the volcanic equivalent of syenite) long before a rhyolitic or phonolitic residue can be reached, as illustrated in Figure 9. The compositions of rocks from Mt. Carmel and Concord are also shown in this diagram. Other plutons in the Concord suite that do not contain syenite either did not undergo sufficient fractionation or had magma compositions that were not close enough to the critical plane. The latter explanation seems less likely, however, because of the absence of granitic residua.

Other workers have assigned a central role to crustal assimilation in the formation of syenites. In the Megantic complex, for example, alkali basaltic magma reacted with crust and evolved by fractional crystallization to produce syenite (Bedard et al., 1987). However, the syenites in such complexes show clear evidence in their radiogenic isotopic compositions of crustal contamination, which the Concord pluton does not (see below).

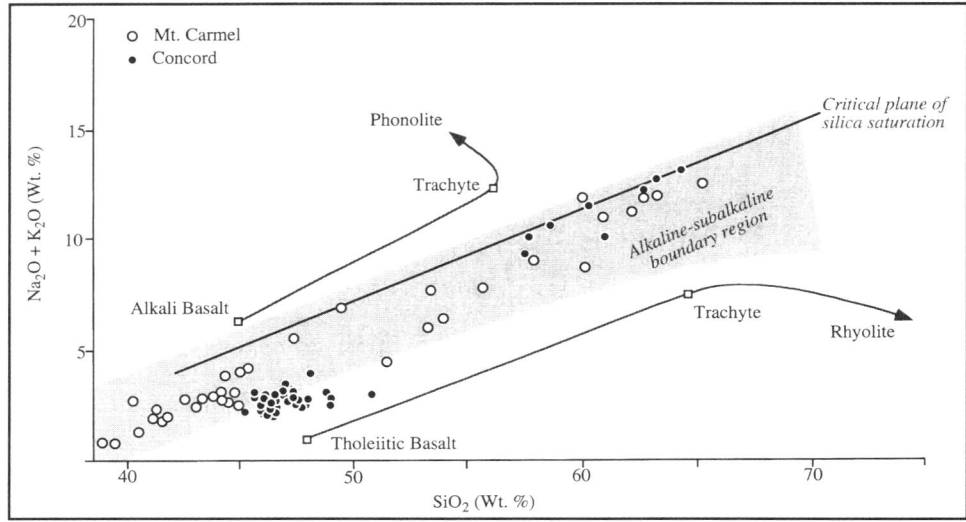

Figure 9. Fractionation sequence to produce syenite in Concord suite plutons. The critical plane of silica saturation is from Cox et al. (1979), and the shaded field is bounded by lines defining the separation of alkaline and subalkaline rocks by Upton (1974) and Irvine and Barager (1971). Sources of chemical data: Mt. Carmel, Medlin (1968); Fronabarger (1984); Concord, Cabaup (1969).

Radiogenic isotopes

Initial Sr and Nd isotopic compositions for three gabbros (Farmington, Concord, and Ogden) were reported by McSween et al. (1984). All the samples plot on the mantle array and show no discernible evidence of interaction with crustal materials. The initial Sr and Nd isotopic composition of Concord syenite is identical to the associated gabbro, indicating little or no crustal contamination (an upper limit of 20% can be inferred when errors in initial isotopic ratios are included) during fractional crystallization (Olsen et al., 1983). However, the latter conclusion has been called into question by Hund (1987), who found that the U-Pb ages of zircons from the Concord syenite appear to have a xenocrystic component with an upper intercept of 1320 Ma, suggesting that a crustal component may have been involved in the formation of syenite. Although these results permit, and perhaps even require, some very limited crustal contamination, we favor a primary role for fractional crystallization because of the continuous fractionation trend observed in the Mt. Carmel pluton and the closed-system chemical and isotopic modeling constraints for the Concord pluton.

Trace element patterns

Trace-element data for gabbros and syenites were obtained by Medlin (1968), Price (1969), and Fronabarger (1984). Nickel, chromium, and cobalt contents decrease with magnesium, indicating fractionation of olivine and pyroxene, and a significant decrease in strontium from gabbro to syenite implies fractionation of plagioclase. Rubidium and zirconium increase in this sequence. Figure 10 illustrates an incompatible trace-element "spiderdia-

gram" for gabbros of the Calhoun Falls and Mt. Carmel plutons; the compositions of several typical basalts are given for comparison. This diagram is interpreted in the following section.

MAGMA GENERATION AND TECTONIC SETTING

Timing in relation to the Acadian event

The almost linear outcrop pattern, along which Concord suite plutons occur at roughly regular intervals (Fig. 1), suggests some kind of tectonic control of magma generation and/or emplacement. However, the ca. 400 Ma intrusion of these plutons did not coincide with a recognized tectonothermal event in the southern Appalachians; rather, it was sandwiched between two well-defined events: the 460 to 440 Ma Taconic orogeny, possibly the time at which the Carolina terrane accreted to Laurentia; and the 330 to 270 Ma Alleghanian orogeny, representing the collision of Laurentia with Gondwana. It is unclear whether this intrusive episode should be defined as an example of anorogenic magmatism, or if it should be considered the beginning of a mid-Paleozoic Acadian event. We favor the latter scenario, and the schematic rendition of the onset of Acadian metamorphism in Figure 2 at about the time of intrusion of the Concord plutonic suite reflects that prejudice.

Unlike the Acadian event in the northern and central Appalachians, where thick clastic sequences in the foreland were deposited synchronously with metamorphism in the hinterland, middle Paleozoic tectonism in the southern Appalachians is poorly understood (Ferrill and Thomas, 1988). Most of the tectonothermal effects of the Acadian orogeny in the southern Appalachians are localized. Peak metamorphism is thought to

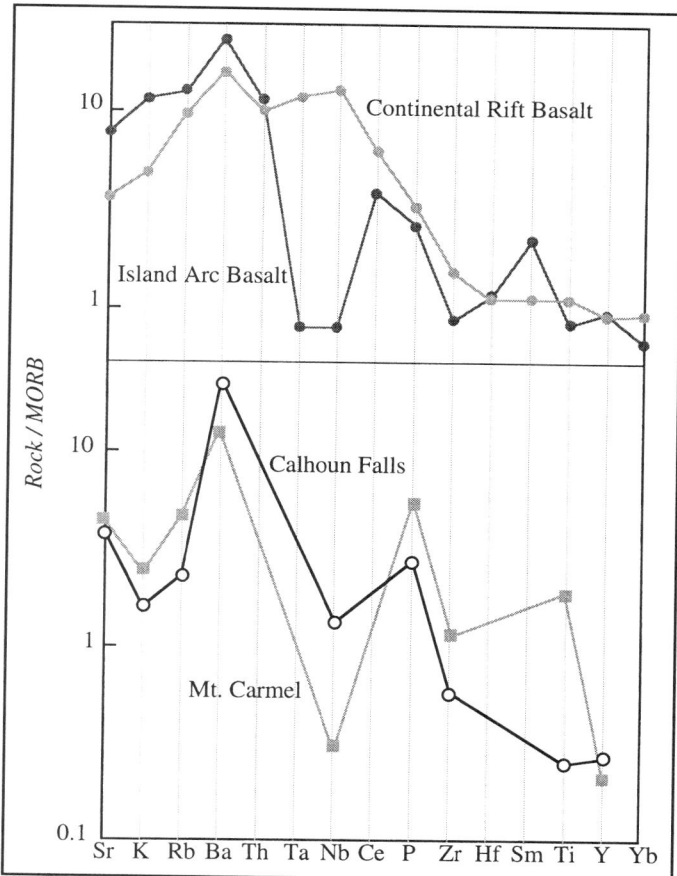

Figure 10. Trace element "spiderdiagram" showing typical patterns for basalts from extensional (continental rift) and compressional (island arc) settings (data from Pearce, 1983). Data for gabbros from the Calhoun Falls (average of 3 samples from Fronabarger, 1984) and Mt. Carmel (average of 12 samples from Medlin, 1968) plutons appear to mimic the spiked appearance of basalts from compressional settings. All element abundances are normalized to mid-ocean ridge basalts (normalizing constants from Pearce, 1983).

ern Appalachians. These alkaline to mildly alkaline plutons are indicative of crustal attenuation following orogenic magmatism that accompanied continental convergence and crustal accretion. Rapid change from calc-alkaline to alkaline plutonism in as little as 10 m.y. also occurred in Pan-African terranes (Sylvester, 1989).

Constraints on tectonic setting

McSween et al. (1984) attempted to use chemical discriminant diagrams to delineate the tectonic setting for Concord suite magmas, but the results were not very informative. Here we examine trace elements in a different way. Incompatible trace-element abundances for basalts from extensional and compressional tectonic settings typically have distinctive patterns, relative to mid-ocean ridge basalts (MORB). MORBs, used for normalization (Pearce, 1983), are the product of high degrees of partial melting, so their trace-element abundances reflect that of their mantle source. Elements are plotted left to right in order of decreasing compatibility; those on the right side should be less enriched during partial melting or fractional crystallization, tilting the curve up to the left. Typical continental rift and island-arc basalt patterns are illustrated in the upper part of Figure 10. Subduction-related basalts are strongly spiked. The positive spikes result from components added to the mantle source by subduction-zone fluids, and the marked depletion in tantalum and niobium may reflect retention of these elements in the mantle source during partial melting.

Average trace-element patterns for gabbros from the Calhoun Falls and Mt. Carmel plutons are illustrated in the bottom part of Figure 10. Although the data are incomplete, the spiked appearance and strong negative niobium anomalies suggest affinities with subduction-zone basalts.

In Figures 11 and 12, we employ other approaches designed to be more useful for cumulate rocks. Figure 11 compares the compositions of coexisting olivine and plagioclase (in the latter case, the most calcic core compositions) with those for cumulate gabbros and xenoliths from island arcs, continental layered intrusions, oceanic islands, and mid-ocean ridges (Beard, 1986). Concord suite plutons have mineral compositions that overlap all of these environments except arcs. For comparison, we show data from the Smartville (Sierra Nevada) gabbro, a cumulate complex formed in the core of a volcanic arc (Beard and Day, 1987). Concord suite gabbros are apparently distinct from plutons found at many compressional settings, and from this diagram it seems difficult to interpret these rocks as representing the eroded core of a continental volcanic arc (as previously advocated by McSween et al., 1984).

Figure 12 compares the Al and Ti contents of clinopyroxenes in Concord suite gabbros with those in plutonic cognate xenoliths from the Mid-Atlantic Ridge, ophiolites, and arcs (Louck, 1990). The slope for arc clinopyroxenes is much steeper than those for fractionating pyroxenes from ocean-floor rocks (indicated by arrows), and the differing slopes are thought to serve as discriminants for plutonic rocks. In this diagram, the

have occurred between 380 and 360 Ma (Connolly and Dallmeyer, 1993), later than that for the Acadian orogeny in the northern Appalachians (Glover et al., 1983; Horton et al., 1989). Peak metamorphism in the southern Blue Ridge at 380 to 360 Ma occurred well inboard of the inferred Carolina terrane suture and Concord plutonic belt in the Piedmont, and might have reached peak metamorphic conditions later. Thus it is conceivable that the emplacement of the Concord plutonic suite ca. 400 Ma might define the beginning of the Acadian orogeny in the Piedmont.

Alternatively, the Concord suite plutons may represent anorogenic magmatism following the Taconic orogeny. Many episodic alkalic igneous events occurred during the middle to late Paleozoic in the New England Avalon zone (e.g., the Coastal Maine magmatic province, Hogan and Sinha, 1989; other plutons in southern New England, Hermes and Zartman, 1992), which is equivalent to the Carolina terrane of the south-

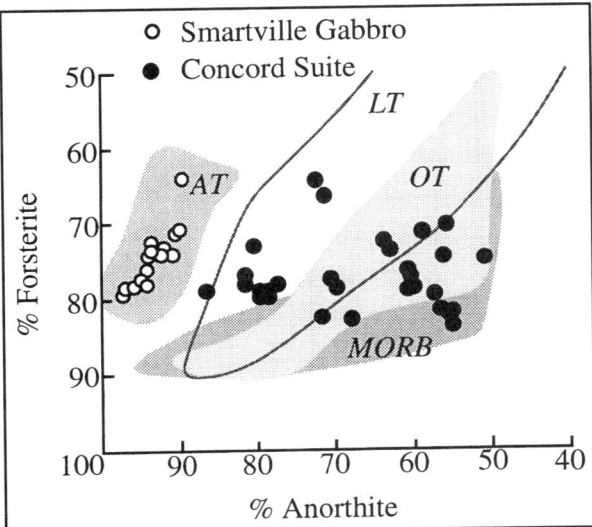

Figure 11. Compositions of coexisting olivine and plagioclase (most calcic core compositions) for Concord suite plutons, compared with cumulate gabbros formed from tholeiitic magmas in island arcs (AT), continental layered intrusions (LT), oceanic islands (OT), and mid-ocean ridge basalts (MORBs). Cumulate gabbros from the Smartville complex, representing plutonic rocks in a conventional compressional tectonic setting (Beard and Day, 1987), are shown for comparison. Sources of data: Ogden, McSween (1981); Concord, Olsen (1982); Farmington, Harden (1984); Calhoun Falls, Fronabarger (1984), Rock Hill, Noble (1993).

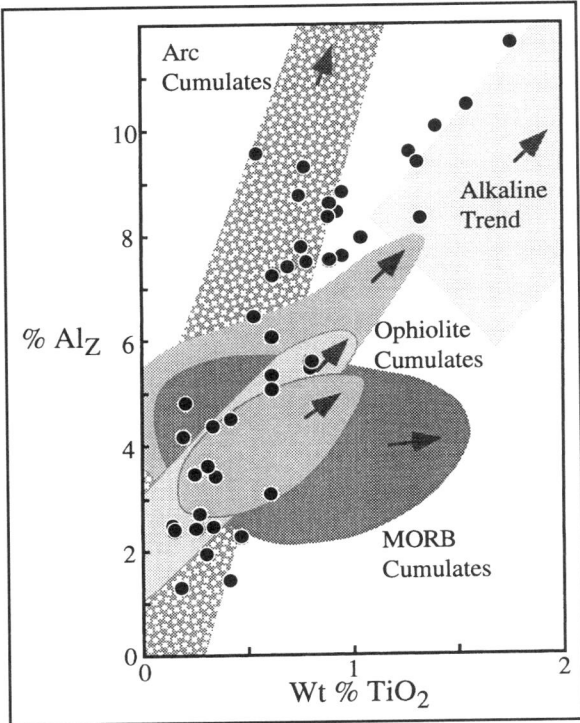

Figure 12. Compositions of clinopyroxenes in Concord suite plutons, compared with plutonic cognate xenoliths from continental and island arcs, ophiolites, and the Mid-Atlantic ridge. Al_z indicates the percentage of octahedral sites occupied by Al. The slopes of these arrays, indicated by arrows, reflect different redox conditions during crystallization, and are thought to serve as discriminants for rocks from these tectonic settings (Louck, 1990). Sources of data: Bear Poplar, Clark (1980); Concord, Olsen (1982); Farmington, Harden (1984); Calhoun Falls, Greenwood, and Mt. Carmel, Fronabarger (1984); Rock Hill, Noble (1993).

slope of the Concord clinopyroxene compositions suggests an arc affinity, although the most evolved clinopyroxenes in syenites display a lesser slope and overlap the alkaline field. The conclusions drawn from Figures 11 and 12 are conflicting and reemphasize the difficulty of assigning these gabbros to a specific tectonic setting on the basis of their mineral and chemical compositions.

Emplacement of the Concord Plutonic Suite was contemporaneous with intrusion of the Salisbury plutonic suite (McSween et al., 1991), a small group of distinctly leucocratic, metaluminous granitoids clustered at one point along the Concord suite outcrop belt (near the Linwood [LNW] gabbro in Fig. 1). The small Salisbury plutons have been dated at 403 to 378 Ma (Fig. 2), and have been affected by Acadian deformation and metamorphism (Fullagar et al., 1971; Butler and Fullagar, 1978). These granitoids possibly formed by anatexis of the lower crust as basaltic magmas of the Concord suite underplated or ascended through this area. Thus, this plutonic outcrop belt can be considered to have a trimodal composition (gabbro-syenite-granite). Such compositional patterns are characteristic of anorogenic magmatism (Sinha et al., 1989).

Tectonic models

Two rather different tectonic models, based on either compressional or extensional environments, have been previously suggested that might explain magma production at 400 Ma.

Rodgers (1987) proposed that Taconic arc collision along an east-dipping subduction zone forced a new west-dipping subduction zone to form, which consumed oceanic crust until the Carolina terrane accreted. Crustal thickening and mantle upwarp resulting from this collision may have caused melting. McSween et al. (1984) previously argued that the Concord suite plutons were emplaced above such a subduction zone. The early crystallization of plagioclase is similar to crystallization patterns of high-alumina basalts found in subduction zones, and the chemical compositions of these rocks fall within the high-alumina basalt field (the position of the shaded alkaline-subalkaline boundary region in Fig. 9 coincides approximately with the high-alumina basalt field defined by Kuno, 1969). However, the observed fractionation to syenite suggests magmas somewhat more alkaline than normally found in such settings. Alkaline rocks (reflecting melting at deeper levels) do occur in secondary magmatic arcs behind primary, tholeiite-andesite arcs in some subduction zones, but they are not the dominant rock types. Concord suite gabbroic rocks fall along the mantle array on an ε_{Nd}-ε_{Sr} diagram (McSween et al., 1984), in a position similar to rocks from some modern subduction zones, although the isotopic data do not provide a conclusive test. Hooper and Hatcher (1989) also interpreted the Gladesville pluton and its surrounding rocks as parts of a developing arc complex.

In contrast, Sinha et al. (1989) argued that the Concord and Salisbury plutonic suites formed in a transtensional environment during strike-slip accretion of the Carolina terrane, where localized zones of extension caused decompression melting. This magmatic belt was one of two contemporaneous, parallel magmatic provinces, the other lying to the west in the Blue Ridge and Inner Piedmont. They suggested that the western belt reflected delayed partial melting of crust that was tectonically overthickened by stacking of nappes during the Taconic orogeny. In their model, the Concord plutonic suite would be characterized as anorogenic magmatism. Petrologic similarities can be found with plutonic suites in rifted continental areas, e.g., subalkaline mafic rocks as part of a trimodal plutonic suite, but such areas also commonly contain peralkaline rocks.

The characteristics of this magmatic belt are difficult to reconcile with either an orogenic or anorogenic setting. We have chosen to call the Concord plutonic suite "pre-Acadian," emphasizing its timing just before that orogenic event. The use of this term hints at our prejudice that there is at least a tenuous, if not direct, link with the Acadian orogeny, but we acknowledge that magmatism may also have been completely unrelated. We cannot rule out an alternative scenario of mildly alkaline plutonism during crustal attenuation following the Taconic event. These igneous rocks may be critical in unraveling the mid-Paleozoic evolution of the terrane they intrude but, as we have shown, the conclusions about tectonic setting drawn from them are ambiguous.

ACKNOWLEDGMENTS

We gratefully acknowledge the many graduate students whose thesis and dissertation research forms the basis for this contribution. Jean Bédard and Don Hermes provided helpful reviews.

REFERENCES CITED

Beard, J. S., 1986, Characteristic mineralogy of arc-related cumulate gabbros: Implications for the tectonic setting of gabbroic plutons and for andesite genesis: Geology, v. 14, p. 848–851.

Beard, J. S., and Day, H. W., 1987, The Smartville intrusive complex, Sierra Nevada, California: The core of a rifted volcanic arc: Geological Society of America Bulletin, v. 99, p. 779–791.

Bédard, J. H. J., Ludden, J. N., and Francis, D. M., 1987, The Megantic Intrusive Complex, Quebec: A study of the derivation of silica-oversaturated anorogenic magmas of alkaline affinity: Journal of Petrology, v. 28, p. 355–388.

Butler, J. R., 1966, Geology and mineral resources of York County, South Carolina: South Carolina State Development Board Bulletin 33, 65 p.

Butler, J. R., 1983, Geological history of the Charlotte belt at the old Pineville quarry, northeastern York County, South Carolina: South Carolina Geology, v. 27, p. 13–24.

Butler, J. R., 1991, Metamorphism, *in* Horton, J.W. Jr., and Zullo, V.A., eds., The geology of the Carolinas: Knoxville, University of Tennessee Press, p. 127–141.

Butler, J. R., and Fullagar, P. D., 1978, Petrochemical and geochronological studies of plutonic rocks in the southern Appalachians: III. Leucocratic adamellites of the Charlotte belt near Salisbury, North Carolina: Geological Society of America Bulletin, v. 89, p. 460–466.

Butler, J. R., and Secor, D. T., Jr., 1991, The central Piedmont, *in* Horton, J. W., Jr., and Zullo, V. A., eds., The geology of the Carolinas: Knoxville, University of Tennessee Press, p. 59–78.

Cabaup, J., 1969, Origin and differentiation of the gabbro in the Concord ring dike, North Carolina Piedmont [M.S. thesis]: Chapel Hill, University of North Carolina, 42 p.

Chalcraft, R. G., 1970, Petrography and geophysics of the Rock Hill gabbro pluton, York County, South Carolina: Southeastern Geology, v. 11, p. 153–171.

Chalcraft, R. G., Lawrence, D. P., and Taylor, C. A., Jr., 1978, The petrology of the Greenwood pluton, Greenwood County, South Carolina: A preliminary report, *in* Snoke, A. W., ed., Carolina Geological Society field trip guidebook: Columbia, South Carolina Geological Survey, p. 40–46.

Clark, S. R., 1980, Petrology of the Bear Poplar and Barber mafic intrusions, North Carolina [M.S. thesis]: Knoxville, University of Tennessee, 77 p.

Connolly, J. B., and Dallmeyer, R. D., 1993, Polymorphic evolution of the western Blue Ridge: Evidence from $^{40}Ar/^{39}Ar$ whole-rock slate/phyllite and muscovite ages: American Journal of Science, v. 293, p. 322–359.

Constantino-Herrera, S. E., 1971, Geology of the Cleveland gabbro, Rowan County, North Carolina [M.S. thesis]: Chapel Hill, University of North Carolina, 88 p.

Cox, K. G., Bell, J. D., and Pankhurst, R. J., 1979, The interpretation of igneous rocks: London, Allen and Unwin, 450 p.

Deetz, S. F., 1980, Mineralogy and petrology of the Chester pluton [M.S. thesis]: Knoxville, University of Tennessee, 55 p.

Dennis, A. J., and Shervais, J. W., 1991, Arc rifting of the Carolina terrane in northwestern South Carolina: Geology, v. 19, p. 226–229.

Dobson, M. L., 1987, Petrography, chemistry, and origin of Fe-Ti oxides in the Concord gabbro/syenite, North Carolina [M.S. thesis]: Knoxville, University of Tennessee, 65 p.

Ferrill, B. A., and Thomas, W. A., 1988, Acadian dextral transpression and synorogenic sedimentary successsions in the Appalachians: Geology, v. 16, p. 604–608.

Fronabarger, A. K., 1984, Petrogenesis of the Calhoun Falls, Mt. Carmel, and Greenwood complexes, South Carolina, and modeling of heat transfer in gabbro [Ph.D. thesis]: Knoxville, University of Tennessee, 200 p.

Fullagar, P. D., 1971, Age and origin of plutonic intrusions in the Piedmont of the southeastern Appalachians: Geological Society of America Bulletin, v. 82, p. 2845–2862.

Fullagar, P. D., Lemmon, R. E., and Ragland, P. C., 1971, Petrochemical and geochronological studies of plutonic rocks in the southern Appalachians: I. The Salisbury pluton: Geological Society of America Bulletin, v. 82, p. 409-416.

Glover, L., III, Speer, J. A., Russell, G. S., and Farrar, S. S., 1983, Ages of regional metamorphism and ductile deformation in the central and southern Appalachians: Lithos, v. 16, p. 223–245.

Griffin, V. S., Jr., 1979, Geology of the Abbeville East, Abbeville West, Latimer, and Lowndesville quadrangles, South Carolina: Columbia, South Carolina Geological Survey, Map Series, MS-24, 58 p., scale 1:24,000.

Harden, J. T., 1984, Petrology of the Farmington gabbro-metagabbro complex, North Carolina [M.S. thesis]: Knoxville, University of Tennessee, 64 p.

Harris, C. W., and Glover, L., III, 1988, The regional extent of the ca. 600 Ma Virgilina deformation: Implications for stratigraphic correlation in the Carolina terrane: Geological Society of America Bulletin, v. 100, p. 200–217.

Hatcher, R. D., Jr., 1987, Tectonics of the southern and central Appalachian internides: Annual Review of Earth and Planetary Sciences, v. 15, p. 337–362.

Hermes, O. D., 1968, Petrology of the Mecklenburg gabbro-metagabbro complex, North Carolina: Contributions to Mineralogy and Petrology, v. 18, p. 270–294.

Hermes, O. D., 1970, Petrochemistry of coexistent mafic silicates from the Mecklenburg gabbro-metagabbro complex, North Carolina: Geological Society of America Bulletin, v. 81, p. 137–164.

Hermes, O. D., and Zartman, R. E., 1992, Late Proterozoic and Silurian alkaline plutons within the southeastern New England Avalone zone: Journal of Geology, v. 100, p. 477–486.

Herzberg, C. T., 1978, Pyroxene geothermometry and geobarometry: Experimental and thermodynamic evaluation of some subsolidus phase relations involving pyroxenes in the system CaO-MgO-Al$_2$O$_3$: Geochimica et Cosmochimica Acta, v. 42, p. 945–957.

Hogan, J. P., and Sinha, A. K., 1989, Compositional variation of plutonism in the Coastal Maine Magmatic Province: Mode of origin and tectonic setting, *in* Tucker, R. D., and Marvinney, R. G., eds., Studies in Maine geology, Volume 4: Orano, Maine Geological Survey, p. 1–33.

Hooper, R. J., 1986, Geologic studies at the east end of the Pine Mountain window and adjacent Piedmont, central Georgia [Ph.D. thesis]: Columbia, University of South Carolina, 322 p.

Hooper, R. J., and Hatcher, R. D., Jr., 1989, The origin of ultramafic rocks from the Berner mafic complex, central Georgia, *in* Mittwede, S. K., and Stoddard, E. F., eds., Ultramafic rocks of the Appalachian Piedmont: Geological Society of America Special Paper 231, p. 87–92.

Horton, J. W., Jr., Drake, A. A., Jr., and Rankin, D. W., 1989, Tectonostratigraphic terranes and their Paleozoic boundaries in the central and southern Appalachians, *in* Dallmeyer, R. D., ed., Terranes in the circum-Atlantic Paleozoic orogens: Geological Society of America Special Paper 230, p. 213–245.

Hund, E., 1987, U-Pb dating of granites from the Charlotte belt of the southern Appalachians [M.S. thesis]: Blacksburg, Viriginia Polytechnic Institute and State University, 82 p.

Irvine, T. N., 1982, Terminology for layered intrusions: Journal of Petrology, v. 23, p. 127–162.

Irvine, T. N., and Baragar, W. R. A., 1971, A guide to the chemical classification of the common volcanic rocks: Canadian Journal of Earth Sciences, v. 8, p. 523–548.

Kuno, H., 1969, Andesite in time and space, *in* McBirney, A. R., ed., Proceedings of the Andesite Conference: Oregon Department of Geology and Mineral Industries Bulletin, v. 65, p. 13–20.

Libby, S. C., 1971, The petrology of the igneous rocks of Putnam County, Georgia [M.S. thesis]: Athens, University of Georgia, 99 p.

Loucks, R. R., 1990, Discrimination of ophiolitic from nonophiolitic ultramafic-mafic allochthons in orogenic belts by the Al/Ti ratio in clinopyroxenes: Geology, v. 18, p. 346–349.

Marsh, B. D., 1978, On the cooling of ascending andesitic magma: Philosophical Transactions of the Royal Society of London, v. 288, p. 611–625.

Matthews, V., III, 1967, Geology and petrology of the pegmatite district in southwestern Jasper County, Georgia [M.S. thesis]: Athens, University of Georgia, 68 p.

McSween, H. Y., Jr., 1970, Petrology of Charlotte and Kings Mountain belt rocks in northern Greenwood County, South Carolina: South Carolina Geologic Notes, v. 14, p. 57–84.

McSween, H. Y., Jr., 1981, Petrology of the Ogden gabbroic intrusion, York County, South Carolina: South Carolina Geology, v. 25, p. 91–100.

McSween, H. Y., Jr., Sando, T. W., Clark, S. R., Harden, J. T., and Strange, E. A., 1984, The gabbro-metagabbro association of the southern Appalachian Piedmont: American Journal of Science, v. 284, p. 437–461.

McSween, H. Y., Jr., Speer, J. A., and Fullagar, P. D., 1991, Plutonic rocks, *in* Horton, J. W., Jr., and Zullo, V. A., eds., The geology of the Carolinas: Knoxville, University of Tennessee Press, p. 109–126.

Medlin, J. H., 1968, Comparative petrology of two igneous complexes in the South Carolina Piedmont [Ph.D. thesis]: State College, Pennsylvania State University, 328 p.

Medlin, J. H., Thornton, C. P., and Gold, D. P., 1972, Petrology of the mafic igneous complexes in the southeastern U.S. Piedmont: II. The Buffalo mafic igneous complex, Union County, South Carolina: Southeastern Geology, v. 14, p. 73–106.

Misra, K. C., and McSween, H. Y., Jr., 1984, Mafic rocks of the southern Appalachians: A review: American Journal of Science, v. 284, p. 294–318.

Morgan, B. A., and Mann, V. I., 1964, Gravity studies in the Concord quadrangle, North Carolina: Southeastern Geology, v. 5, p. 143–155.

Morse, S. A., 1980, Basalts and Phase Diagrams: New York, Springer-Verlag, 493 p.

Myers, C. W., II, 1968, Geology of the Presley's Mill area, northwest Putnam County, Georgia [M.S. thesis]: Athens, University of Georgia, 67 p.

Noble, L. F., 1993, Investigation of layering in the Rock Hill gabbro pluton, South Carolina [M.S. thesis]: Knoxville, University of Tennessee, 110 p.

Olsen, B. A., 1982, Petrogenesis of the Concord gabbro-syenite complex, Cabarras County, North Carolina [M.S. thesis]: Knoxville, University of Tennessee, 72 p.

Olsen, B. A., McSween, H. Y., Jr., and Sando, T. W., 1983, Petrogenesis of the Concord gabbro-syenite complex, North Carolina: American Mineralogist, v. 68, p. 315–333.

Pearce, J. A., 1983, The role of sub-continental lithosphere in magma genesis at destructive plate margins, *in* Hawkesworth, C. J., and Norry, M. J., eds., Continental basalts and mantle xenoliths: Nantwich, Shiva Press, p. 230–249.

Prather, J. P., 1971, The geology of eastern Monroe County, Georgia [M.S. thesis]: Athens, University of Georgia, 82 p.

Price, V., 1969, Distribution of trace elements in plutonic rocks of the southeastern Piedmont [Ph.D. thesis]: Chapel Hill, University of North Carolina, 87 p.

Rodgers, J., 1987, The Appalachian-Ouachita orogenic belt: Episodes, v. 10, p. 259–266.

Secor, D. T., Jr., Samson, S. L., Snoke, A. W., and Palmer, A. R., 1983, Confirmation of the Carolina slate belt as an exotic terrane: Science, v. 221, p. 649–651.

Sinha, A. K., Hund, E. A., and Hogan, J. P., 1989, Paleozoic accretionary history of the North American plate margin (central and southern Appalachians): Constraints from the age, origin, and distribution of granitic rocks: American Geophysical Union Geophysical Monograph, v. 50, p. 219–238.

Strange, E. A., 1983, Geochemistry of the Barber mafic complex, Rowan County, North Carolina [M.S. thesis]: Knoxville, University of Tennessee, 40 p.

Streckeisen, A.L., 1976, To each plutonic rock its proper name: Earth Science Reviews, v. 12, p. 1–33.

Sutter, J. F., Milton, D. J., and Kunk, M. J., 1983, ^{40}Ar/^{39}Ar age spectrum dating of gabbro plutons and surrounding rocks in the Charlotte belt of North Carolina: Geological Society of America Abstracts with Programs, v. 15, p. 110.

Sylvester, P. J., 1989, Post-collisional alkaline granites: Journal of Geology, v. 97, p. 261–280.

Taylor, C. A., Jr., 1982, Geology and gravity of the northern end of the Inner Piedmont and Charlotte belts, Davie County Mesozoic basin, and surrounding areas, central North Carolina Piedmont [M.S. thesis]: Chapel Hill, University of North Carolina, 142 p.

Upton, B. G., 1974, The alkaline province of southeast Greenland, *in* Sorensen, H., ed., The alkaline rocks: London, John Wiley, 622 p.

Williams, R. T., and McSween, H. Y., Jr., 1989, Geometry of the Concord, North Carolina, intrusive complex: A synthesis of potential field modeling and petrologic data: Geology, v. 17, p. 42–45.

Wilson, F. A., 1981, Geologic interpretation of geophysical data from the "Mecklenburg-Weddington" gabbro complex, southern Mecklenburg County, North Carolina, *in* Horton, J. W., Jr., Butler, J. R., and Milton, D. M., eds., Geological investigations of the Kings Mountain belt and adjacent areas in the Carolinas: Carolina Geological Society field trip guidebook, p. 28–38.

MANUSCRIPT ACCEPTED BY THE SOCIETY JULY 2, 1996

Geological Society of America
Memoir 191
1997

Low-potassium, trondhjemitic to granodioritic plutonism in the eastern Blue Ridge, southwestern North Carolina–northeastern Georgia

C. F. Miller
Department of Geology, Vanderbilt University, Nashville, Tennessee 37235
Paul D. Fullagar
Department of Geology, University of North Carolina, Chapel Hill, North Carolina 27599-3315
T. W. Sando
Department of Earth, Atmospheric, and Planetary Science, Massachusetts Institute of Technology, Cambridge, Massachusetts 02139
S. A. Kish
Department of Geology, Florida State University, Tallahassee, Florida 32306
G. C. Solomon
Department of Geology, University of Georgia, Athens, Georgia 30602
G. S. Russell
Department of Geology, University of Southern Mississippi, Hattiesburg, Mississippi 39406-5044
L. F. Wood Steltenpohl
Roy F. Weston, Inc., 1635 Pumphrey Ave., Auburn, Alabama 36830

ABSTRACT

Plutons and dikes of the eastern Blue Ridge, North Carolina and northeastern Georgia, were emplaced syntectonically ca. 400 Ma in the evolving southern Appalachian orogen. These intrusive rocks are uniformly felsic and peraluminous, ranging continuously from trondhjemitic to granodioritic in composition with no associated mafic or intermediate rocks. The trondhjemites are very low in K and in incompatible and high field strength trace elements; are rich in Al, Na, and Sr; and have low $^{87}Sr/^{86}Sr$ and $\delta^{18}O$ and high ε_{Nd}. Granodiorites are less extreme, having elemental and isotopic compositions that are more typical of continent margin granitoids.

Their compositions require that the rocks near the trondhjemitic end of the spectrum had a relatively mafic source that was young and derived from depleted mantle. Trace-element modeling and isotopic constraints suggest that this source had the geochemical characteristics of a primitive arc basalt, and that the residue of melting was garnet amphibolite. The granodiorite end of the compositional continuum was derived in large part from the Proterozoic continental basement of the region. The most plausible genetic model involves development of an early Paleozoic magmatic arc, underthrusting of arc rocks during subsequent orogeny, heating of the deep crust as a consequence of crustal thickening, and anatexis within a heterogeneous lower crust. Magmas generated within this crust ranged from trondhjemite to granodiorite, depending upon the source rock, and coalesced in the source region or during ascent to yield the observed compositional continuum.

Miller, C. F., Fullagar, P. D., Sando, T. W., Kish, S. A., Solomon, G. C., Russell, G. S., and Wood Steltenpohl, L. F., 1997, Low-potassium, trondhjemitic to granodioritic plutonism in the eastern Blue Ridge, southwestern North Carolina–northeastern Georgia, *in* Sinha, A. K., Whalen, J. B., and Hogan, J. P., eds., The Nature of Magmatism in the Appalachian Orogen: Boulder, Colorado, Geological Society of America Memoir 191.

Modern examples of rocks with the geochemical characteristics of the Blue Ridge trondhjemites have been called adakites and have been attributed to melting of subducted warm oceanic crust; it has been further suggested that much of the Archean crust had similar compositions and was generated in the same way. The compositions and tectonic and lithologic associations of the Blue Ridge trondhjemites do not support such an origin here, but instead reinforce the view that such magmas may also be generated by melting of deep (but not subducting) mafic crust.

INTRODUCTION

Felsic plutonic rocks of early to middle Paleozoic age are exposed for 130 km in a northeast-trending belt in the eastern Blue Ridge province of North Carolina and northeasternmost Georgia. Included within this belt are the Pink Beds, Looking Glass, Whiteside, and Rabun plutons, as well as numerous dikes and sills, which total more than 300 km² in outcrop area (Fig. 1). These granitoids show a considerable range in composition, but overall they are nonetheless geochemically coherent and distinctive, being characterized by a low-potassium, geochemically depleted component. They are broadly syntectonic with major continental orogeny; they postdate some regional structures but are ductilely deformed. Understanding the petrogenesis of these rocks bears upon two important problems: the tectonic evolution of the southern Appalachian orogen (e.g., Hatcher, 1978, 1989; Dallmeyer, 1988; Horton et al., 1989; Sinha et al., 1989; Drummond et al., 1994), and the origin of low-K felsic magmas (e.g., Drummond and Defant, 1990; Defant and Drummond, 1990; Rapp et al., 1991; Beard and Lofgren, 1991; Wolf and Wyllie, 1991, 1994; Kay et al., 1993; see summaries by Barker, 1979; Beard et al., 1993).

In this chapter we describe the petrography and elemental and isotope chemistry of the North Carolina–Georgia Blue Ridge granitoids (hereafter referred to as Blue Ridge granitoids). On the basis of these data, we address the following questions. (1) How old are they? Do they represent a single magmatic episode, or several discrete pulses over a protracted period? (2) Are the intrusive units petrogenetically related, either comagmatic or derived from similar sources? (3) What processes led to their compositional diversity? (4) What source materials were involved in their generation? (5) How do they relate in time and space to local tectonism? Although we cannot provide firm answers to all of these questions at this time, we hope to provide sufficient constraints so that we can shed some light on the evolution of the Blue Ridge crust and on the origins of low-K felsic magmas.

METHODS

We collected 1–3 kg samples for whole-rock elemental and isotopic analyses. Two or more very thin slabs, totaling about 100 g, were powdered for analysis of each sample.

Major elements, Rb, Sr, Ba, and Zr were determined by X-ray fluorescence (XRF). Rb and Sr were analyzed for all samples at Vanderbilt University, but we report isotope dilution (ID) values for those samples on which Rb-Sr isotope analyses were made (values by ID and XRF matched closely, generally ±<5%). Major elements, Ba, and Zr data were mostly provided

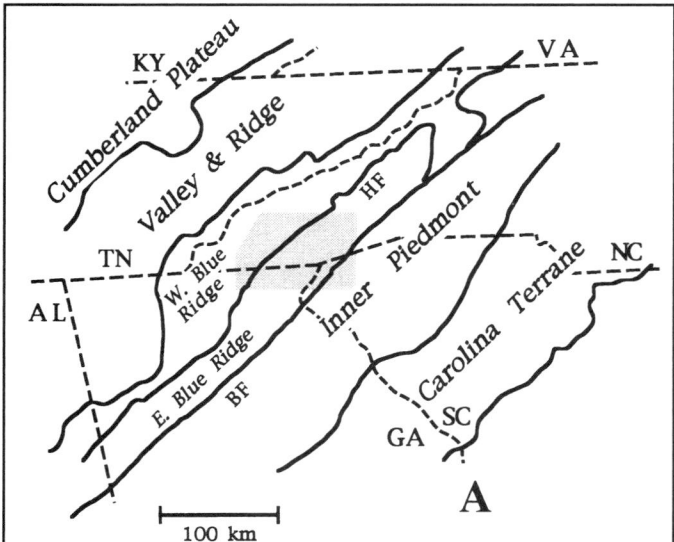

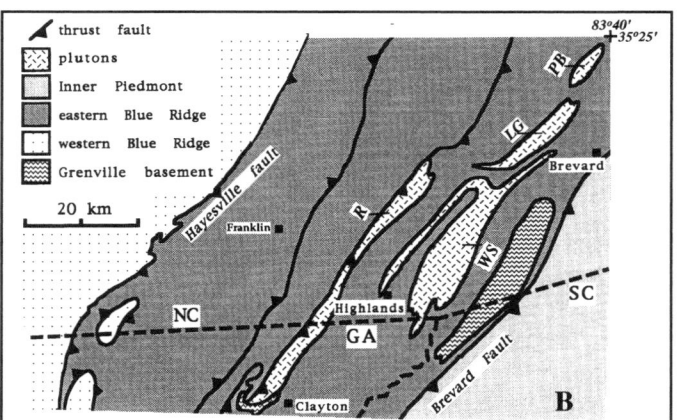

Figure 1. A: Southern Appalachians, with principal tectonic features; HF = Hayesville Fault, BF = Brevard fault; area of B is shaded. B: Sketch map of the eastern Blue Ridge of southwestern North Carolina, northeastern Georgia, and northwestern South Carolina. PB = Pink Beds pluton, LG = Looking Glass pluton, WS = Whiteside pluton, R = Rabun pluton. Trondhjemite dikes (not shown) are mostly located in the western part of the eastern Blue Ridge, west of the plutons, but extend across the Hayesville fault into the western Blue Ridge. (A and B both modified in part from Hopson [1989].)

by X-ray Assay Laboratories, Inc., Ann Arbor, Michigan (XRAL); several samples were analyzed at Vanderbilt University, Nashville, Tennessee.

Rare earth elements were analyzed by instrumental neutron activation analysis (INAA). Most were run at Massachusetts Institute of Technology (MIT), using the procedure described in Rhodes (1983). REE were determined for several other samples, along with U, Th, Ta, and Hf, by INAA at XRAL.

Oxygen isotope ratios were determined at the University of Georgia using methods modified from Taylor and Epstein (1962). In addition to whole rocks, quartz from several samples was analyzed; whole rock-quartz fractionations were ~1‰, consistent with magmatic (or near magmatic temperature [T]) equilibration.

Rb-Sr isotopic analyses were performed at University of North Carolina, Chapel Hill, on a single-collector mass spectrometer. Concentrations of Rb and Sr were determined by isotope dilution. Sr values were fractionation corrected to $^{86}Sr/^{88}Sr$ = 0.1194 and adjusted to $^{87}Sr/^{86}Sr$ for the Eimer and Amend Sr standard = 0.70800.

Nd isotopic compositions were determined at MIT. Powders were dissolved in teflon bombs using a combined HF-HNO_3-HCl digestion procedure over a minimum of three days, and liquids were examined microscopically to ensure complete dissolution of primary mineral phases and absence of insoluble fluoride residues. Sm and Nd concentrations and isotope ratios were then determined on MIT's 9 in mass spectrometer.

Initial Sr and Nd isotope ratios were calculated using $^{87}Rb/^{86}Sr$ and $^{147}Sm/^{144}Nd$ ratios determined by isotope dilution and an assumed age of 400 Ma. Uncertainty introduced by the age approximation is small and does not influence our conclusions.

The isotopic compositions of lead in K-feldspars were determined by Holly Stein at the U.S. Geological Survey isotope lab in Denver, Colorado. Because of the difficulty in separating the sparse, small, interstitial K-feldspars in the trondhjemitic samples, only one trondhjemite was analyzed, along with four granodiorites.

Zircon analyses were performed at the University of Florida using a VG Isomass 354 thermal ionization mass spectrometer. The least magnetic zircons were separated on the basis of size. Splits were handpicked to remove fragments of larger grains. The procedures for zircon dissolution and chemical separation of Pb and U for isotopic analysis were modified from Krogh (1973). Lead isotope ratios were corrected for 400 Ma common lead (Stacey and Kramers, 1975).

REGIONAL SETTING

The Blue Ridge province of southwestern North Carolina and northeastern Georgia is bounded on the east by the Brevard fault and divided into eastern and western portions by the Hayesville fault (Fig. 1). The eastern portion, into which the Blue Ridge granitoids of this study intruded, is a probable accretionary wedge complex that comprises metamorphosed K-feldspar–poor

metasandstones, pelites, and mafic to ultramafic bodies. This structurally complex assemblage of rocks, called the Jefferson terrane by Horton et al. (1989), was thrust along the Hayesville fault over the native North American pelites and K-spar–bearing metasandstones of the western Blue Ridge (e.g., Hatcher, 1989; Quinn and Hatcher, 1990). It includes numerous folded thrust sheets, windows to the underlying western Blue Ridge rocks, and exposures of Grenville-age North American basement (windows, basement, or both? e.g., Hopson et al., 1989; Horton et al., 1989; Quinn and Wright, 1993) The Blue Ridge granitoids are involved to varying degrees in the regional deformation and metamorphism. The eastern Blue Ridge (Jefferson terrane) is of uncertain affinity; it may represent either a distal portion of North America, or an exotic terrane derived from the east side of the Iapetus ocean (Horton et al., 1989).

The tectonic history of the Blue Ridge is dominated by polyphase contraction in response to closure of ocean basins that separated North America from Europe and Africa and intervening island arcs. Contractional events are identified, with varying clarity, as the Penobscotian (ca. 500 Ma), Taconian (ca. 440–480 Ma), Acadian (ca. 350–400 Ma), and Alleghanian (ca. 250–330 Ma) orogenies (e.g., Hatcher, 1989; Drummond et al., 1994). The Hayesville fault is considered to be primarily a Taconian feature, whereas the Brevard fault zone is thought to have accommodated different sorts of displacement at several times from Taconian through Alleghanian time.

Metamorphic grade is variable within the eastern Blue Ridge (mid-amphibolite to granulite facies), but it increases regularly from west to east across the Hayesville fault from upper greenschist facies to lower granulite facies. This suggests that the fault predates the metamorphic peak (e.g., Eckert et al., 1989; Hopson et al., 1989; Eckert and Hatcher, 1992). However, local structures and $^{40}Ar/^{39}Ar$ thermochronology have been interpreted to indicate that at least some of the displacement on the fault was postmetamorphic (Dallmeyer, 1989; Vauchez and Dallmeyer, 1989). Geochronological studies (K-Ar, $^{40}Ar/^{39}Ar$, Rb-Sr, U-Pb) document a protracted and/or polyphase thermal history of the western Blue Ridge, extending at least from ca. 480 to 310 Ma (e.g., Dallmeyer, 1988; Kish, 1989; Goldberg and Dallmeyer, 1992; Quinn and Wright, 1993). Distributions of radiometric ages in the western and eastern Blue Ridge have been interpreted to indicate some combination of diachronous cooling, post-peak metamorphism thrusting, and multiple, discrete thermal events (e.g., Kish, 1989; Dallmeyer, 1989; Connelly and Dallmeyer, 1993).

FIELD AND PETROGRAPHIC ASPECTS OF THE INTRUSIONS

The rocks of the Blue Ridge granitoid assemblage are uniformly felsic. No mafic to intermediate rocks are present within the plutons, and none of probable similar age are known from this region. The only other igneous or metaigneous rocks within this portion of the Blue Ridge are metamorphosed ultramafic to mafic volcanic and plutonic rocks that are probably considerably older than the granitoids.

Abundant quartz and plagioclase (>20 modal% and >40%, respectively) characterize all of the intrusive units; abundance of K-feldspar ranges from near zero to about 25%, and therefore rock type ranges from trondhjemite and felsic tonalite, through granodiorite, and rarely to granite (cf. Fig. 2). All are biotite bearing, and almost all contain muscovite. Epidote is common, occurring in most samples from all plutons. Zircon, apatite, opaque minerals, and monazite are sparse but nearly ubiquitous. Sphene, allanite, and rutile are restricted in occurrence. Garnet occurs in some aplites and pegmatites and rarely in less felsic rocks. Almost all samples have an igneous fabric that has been overprinted, in some cases weakly and in others almost entirely, by metamorphism. The mineral assemblages appear in general to be igneous; on the basis of textural relations, we consider most of the muscovite and perhaps some of the epidote to be magmatic in origin.

Details and distinguishing characteristics of individual intrusive units are described in the following.

Pink Beds pluton

The Pink Beds pluton, the northeasternmost and smallest (20 km^2) of the Blue Ridge plutons (Fig. 1), is uniformly trondhjemitic in composition, with minor K-feldspar accompanying very abundant oligoclase and quartz (Fig. 2). Undeformed aplitic dikes are sparsely distributed in this generally very homogeneous pluton. Well-preserved igneous fabric (coarse, subhedral, oscillatory zoned plagioclase) is overprinted by a moderate temperature ductile fabric. The ductile fabric imparts a rather weak but pervasive foliation, manifested by recrystallized, grain size-reduced quartz lenses and mica trains. Original plagioclase grains are only slightly recrystallized around their margins.

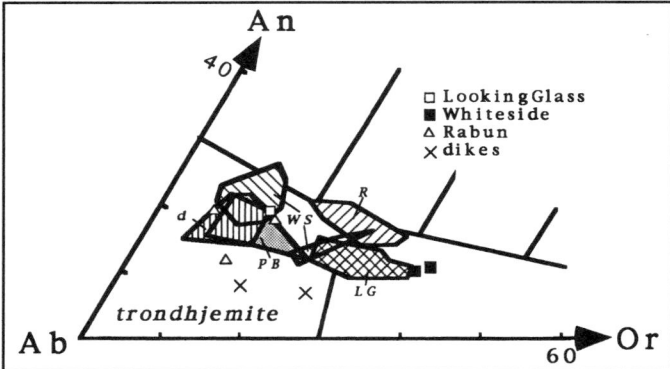

Figure 2. Classification of the Blue Ridge granitoids on the normative Ab-Or-An diagram of Barker (1979). A majority of samples outside the trondhjemite field plot as granites on this diagram, but in the IUGS and other classifications in general use they are granodiorites. All 9 Pink Beds samples, 15 of 16 Looking Glass samples, 19 of 21 Whiteside samples, 11 of 14 Rabun samples, and 14 of 16 dike samples plot within the patterned fields; the remainder are shown by symbols. d = dikes. Other abbreviations as in Figure 1.

Looking Glass pluton

The 35 km^2 Looking Glass pluton is only 2 km southwest of the Pink Beds pluton (Fig. 1), but it is distinctly different in composition and texture. Although the mineral assemblage is the same, K-feldspar is much more abundant, so that the average composition is granodiorite (Fig. 2). Furthermore, the Looking Glass pluton is more strongly metamorphosed than the Pink Beds; only faint vestiges of an igneous fabric are evident in thin section. The fabric is predominantly granoblastic, with largely xenoblastic plagioclase and foliation defined by coarsely recrystallized quartz lenses and discrete mica grains. Small aplite dikes that cut across foliation are sparse but widespread.

Whiteside pluton

The Whiteside pluton, which lies to the southwest, is larger (100 km^2) and more diverse than the Pink Beds and Looking Glass plutons (Fig. 1). Composition ranges continuously from virtually K-feldspar–free trondhjemite to relatively K-feldspar–rich granodiorite; trondhjemite is the most abundant rock type (Fig. 2). Rocks range from extremely weakly to strongly foliated, and fabrics from clearly igneous with a modest metamorphic overprint to thoroughly recrystallized granoblastic. The Whiteside pluton is heterogeneous on outcrop scale, exhibiting considerable small-scale variability in grain size, foliation, and, to a lesser extent, color index. In addition, schistose enclaves and aplite and pegmatite dikes (both deformed and undeformed) are locally abundant, and broad border zones are migmatitic.

Rabun pluton

The batholith-scale Rabun pluton is the southwesternmost and largest (160 km^2) of the intrusions (Hatcher et al., 1995). Granodiorite is by far the most abundant rock type, but trondhjemite is also present. Muscovite is widespread but not ubiquitous, as it is in the other plutons. Foliation is weak and igneous textures are fairly well preserved in many areas, but all samples are at least slightly recrystallized and some are gneissic and strongly modified in texture. Rocks are medium to coarse grained and commonly porphyritic with K-feldspar phenocrysts. Pegmatite and aplite dikes and xenoliths of schist, gneiss, and other country rock-lithologies are common.

Dikes

Trondhjemite dikes and sills are common to the northwest of the plutons described in the preceding sections (Yurkovich and Butkovich, 1982; Wood and Miller, 1984). Our samples are from the eastern Blue Ridge, but similar intrusions are present across the Hayesville fault in the western Blue Ridge. Most dikes range from ca. 0.3 m to a few meters in width; the largest body of which we are aware is a pod roughly 100 m across. The dikes crosscut principal regional fabrics and have very well preserved igneous textures. All dike rocks are porphyritic, and have groundmasses that range from aphanitic to fine-grained phaneritic. Euhedral, oscillatory zoned plagioclase is the dominant phenocryst phase; biotite is also common, and muscovite and quartz occur as phenocrysts in some samples. Although the dikes crosscut foliation in host rocks and generally appear to be unfoliated, the groundmass is commonly recrystallized, and in some cases polycrystalline quartz bands reveal unrecovered strain. This suggests that the deformation that affected the dikes was late compared to the principal regional deformation and that it occurred at relatively low temperature.

Environment of emplacement

The relationships described in the previous section indicate that all of the Blue Ridge granitoids were emplaced syntectonically in a very broad sense (cf. Karlstrom, 1989; Paterson, 1989): they intruded a terrane that had already undergone metamorphism and deformation and then underwent further metamorphism and deformation themselves. The presence of undeformed aplites that cut deformational fabrics in most plutons suggests synchroneity of deformation and intrusion. Given currently available data, it is difficult to assess the spans of time involved or whether all were emplaced during the same deformational episode.

Retention of igneous fabrics and broadly crosscutting relationships with principal metamorphic fabrics indicate that at least most of the granitoids were emplaced after peak metamorphism. Absence of chilled margins or distinct contact aureoles for all plutons as well as the presence of a broad migmatitic zone at the border of the Whiteside pluton and similar but less-well-developed zones at the margins of the other plutons indicate that the host terrane was still hot at the times of intrusion. Peak metamorphic grade in the vicinity of the plutons was probably upper amphibolite facies, although granulite facies rocks are exposed 15–20 km northwest of the Rabun and Whiteside plutons (Absher and McSween, 1985; Eckert et al., 1989). Country-rock temperatures close to 600 °C appear to be consistent with the observed relationships. The quenched textures of the dikes and the absence of recovery of their strained quartz may suggest that the region had cooled more by the time they were emplaced.

Precise estimates of depths of emplacement are not possible at present, because the absence of hornblende eliminates that barometer, and the lack of identified contact assemblages precludes application of metamorphic barometry. Metamorphism in the region is kyanite-sillimanite type and thermobarometry indicates depths during peak metamorphism on the order of 30 km (e.g., Absher and McSween, 1985; Eckert et al., 1989). Appreciable denudation could have occurred between peak metamorphism and pluton emplacement, but, unless it occurred extremely rapidly, the apparently high temperatures in the country rocks at the time of emplacement suggest that the plutons were fairly deep (>10–15 km?). The presence of magmatic(?) epidote, muscovite, and garnet are consistent with this interpretation (e.g., Zen and Hammarstrom, 1984; Hyndman, 1981; Green, 1978),

although absolute depth minima on all of these minerals have been challenged (e.g., Vyhnal et al., 1991; Drummond et al., 1994; Miller et al., 1981; Miller and Stoddard, 1981).

AGE OF PLUTONISM

Relative ages of intrusions

There are no crosscutting relations among the Blue Ridge granitoid intrusions. The only hints at their relative ages lie in the fabrics. The Looking Glass and parts of the Whiteside pluton are the most thoroughly and coarsely recrystallized and therefore could speculatively be considered the oldest. The Rabun pluton is variably deformed and recrystallized, but generally records less overprinting. The Pink Beds pluton and the dikes have undergone little recrystallization and therefore may be the youngest. However, deformation and recrystallization could have been localized and therefore are not very reliable indicators of relative age. Even if these criteria were reliable, we would not know whether all intrusions were emplaced over a brief span of a few million years in a rapidly evolving orogen, or over a much longer span of years (e.g., ≥100 m.y.) in widely separated events.

Radiometric dating

Summary. The precise ages of the intrusions are not yet well established. Exploratory work with Rb-Sr and U-Pb has met with serious difficulties: Rb/Sr ratios are low and initial Sr isotopic ratios variable, and zircon is sparse and indicates complex histories. However, our data indicate that all intrusions were emplaced between about 340 and 440 Ma, and that most and perhaps all probably crystallized during the earlier part of this interval.

Rb-Sr and K/Ar dating. An imprecise, scattered whole-rock Rb-Sr "isochron" suggests an age of about 415 Ma for the Looking Glass pluton (Fig. 3A; Table 1A; cf. Kish, 1983). Whole-rock plus mineral Rb-Sr ages of 335 ± 3 Ma for a trondhjemite dike (Kish et al., 1975; Kish, 1989) and roughly 310–330 Ma for the Pink Beds pluton (Fig. 3B) are clearly minima that are consistent with regional mica K-Ar ages (Kish, 1989).

U-Pb dating. All zircon fractions that have been analyzed to date are discordant, probably reflecting both inheritance and subsequent Pb loss (Table 1B). Four fractions from the Whiteside and Pink Beds plutons have ^{206}Pb/^{238}U ages of 443 to 480 Ma and ^{207}Pb/^{206}Pb ages of 499 to 844 Ma (Fig. 4). A single, small size fraction (<74 μm) from the Rabun pluton has a ^{206}Pb/^{238}U age of 333 and a ^{207}Pb/^{206}Pb age of 438 Ma (Fig. 4). Data for the Whiteside and Pink Beds pluton reveal a significant Proterozoic inherited component, but they do not define a reasonable chord. Either the zircons have undergone a complex Pb loss history, or, more likely, they include more than one age of inheritance (in part Grenville, in part substantially older[?]). The crystallization age remains unknown, but is probably somewhat

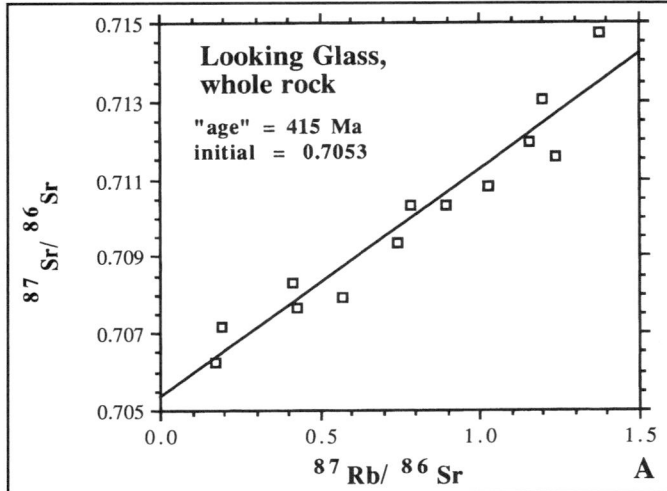

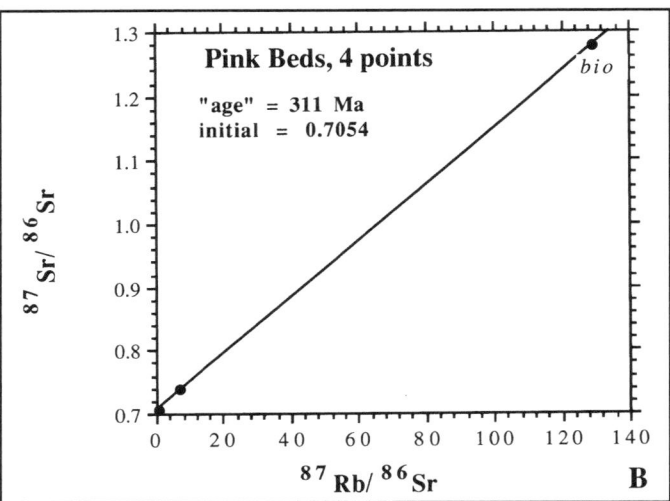

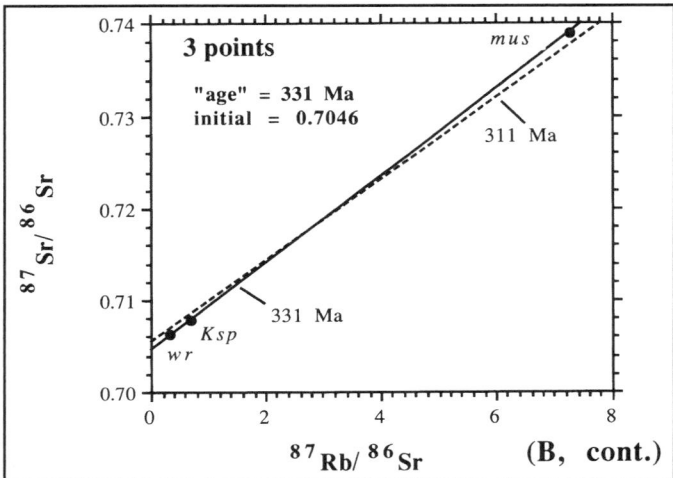

Figure 3. Rb-Sr isotopic diagrams. A: Looking Glass pluton (whole rock); "isochron" is best fit. B: Pink Beds pluton (mineral + whole rock, single sample), with reference isochrons.

older than 400 Ma. The small-size Rabun fraction may represent predominantly magmatic zircons that have undergone relatively recent Pb loss, also suggesting a ca. 400 Ma age. We plan to do further detailed U-Pb work with both zircons and monazites to clarify the ages of all of the intrusions.

GEOCHEMISTRY

Introduction

The chemical compositions of the Blue Ridge granitoids define a crude continuum from trondhjemites and felsic tonalites through potassic granodiorites and granites (cf. Fig. 2). All 76 analyzed samples contain between 65 and 75 wt% SiO_2. Most other chemical variables (major element, trace element, and isotopic) correlate poorly with SiO_2 concentration (e.g., Fig. 5); Na_2O and K_2O contents, however, are fairly well correlated with other significant variables (Fig. 6; see below). These data suggest a simplified compositional model wherein variability is treated in terms of mixing of compositions between hypothetical high Na, low-K trondhjemitic, and moderate Na and K granodioritic series. Rocks that approach the trondhjemitic end of the continuum are distinctly "depleted," with low incompatible element concentrations and isotopic compositions that are depleted relative to bulk Earth, notwithstanding their high silica contents. Samples near the granodiorite end of the spectrum are geochemically typical continent margin granitoids (e.g., >3 wt% K_2O, <5 wt% Na_2O, <500 ppm Sr, >100 ppm Rb). We emphasize that this is by no means a simple continuum and that these rocks cannot be considered to be products of a simple two end-member mix or even a two series mix, but much of the fundamental variability can be evaluated effectively with this model.

The fundamental variability—between trondhjemitic and granodioritic series—does not follow intrusive unit boundaries, although compositions within units tend to be dominantly within one series or the other, as suggested in the section "Nature of the plutonic rocks": the Pink Beds pluton and the dikes are trondhjemitic; the Rabun and Looking Glass plutons are mostly granodioritic; and the Whiteside pluton includes both, with trondhjemite dominating.

Major-element compositions

Major- and trace-element analyses of selected samples are presented in Table 2. As noted above, SiO_2 concentration ranges from 65 to 75 wt% for both the trondhjemite and granodiorite series. K_2O concentrations fall between 0.6 and 4 wt%, and Na_2O between 4 and 7 wt%; the alkalis are negatively correlated (Fig. 6A). Al_2O_3 and CaO are relatively high for such silica-rich rocks, especially among the trondhjemites. FeO, MgO, TiO_2, and P_2O_5 concentrations are normal for granitoids.

All samples are peraluminous. Although most are strongly peraluminous, as indicated by the presence of muscovite (mineralogical definition of Miller, 1985), normative corundum is not especially high, typically near 1 wt%.

TABLE 1. ISOTOPE DATA USED IN GEOCHRONOLOGY FOR BLUE RIDGE PLUTONS

Sample	Rb (ppm)	Sr (ppm)	^{87}Rb/^{86}Sr	^{87}Sr/^{86}Sr	Sample	Rb (ppm)	Sr (ppm)	^{87}Rb/^{86}Sr	^{87}Sr/^{86}Sr
				A. Rb-Sr Data					
————Looking Glass pluton————					————Pink Beds pluton————				
(Whole-rock)					(Mineral + whole-rock, sample PB)				
K-76-11	90.2	332.5	0.786	0.71033	Whole rock	44.2	390.1	0.327	0.70626
K-76-12	96.9	234.9	1.195	0.71307	Muscovite	290.2	115.9	7.269	0.73892
K-76-13	107.9	226.7	1.377	0.71472	K-feldspar	136.6	584.7	0.676	0.70775
K-76-14	42.5	707.2	0.174	0.70626	Biotite	654.7	15.5	128.940	1.27628
K-76-15	77.8	542.2	0.416	0.70829					
K-75-32	92.4	469.1	0.571	0.70794					
K-75-33	114.1	266.2	1.241	0.71157					
K-75-34	101.6	287.9	1.022	0.71083					
K-75-36	102.0	331.2	0.892	0.71032					
K-75-41	83.7	564.2	0.430	0.70764					
LG1	100.0	347.0	0.741	0.70935					
LG7	46.7	711.0	0.190	0.70715					
LG17	121.8	121.8	1.158	0.71193					

Sample	U (ppm)	Pb (ppm)	^{206}Pb*/^{204}Pb	^{206}Pb*/^{238}U	^{207}Pb*/^{235}U	^{207}Pb*/^{206}Pb*	^{206}Pb/^{238}U age	^{207}Pb/^{235}U age	^{207}Pb/^{206}Pb age
				B. U-Pb Data					
			———Rabun pluton (GA 89-10)———						
44-74 μm	816	42.3	3921	0.0530	0.407	0.0556	333	346	438 ± 16
			———Pink Beds pluton (PB)———						
74-149 μm	855	63.3	1779	0.0746	0.629	0.0612	464	496	646 ± 6
>149 μm	699	64.5	224	0.0731	0.614	0.0610	455	486	638 ± 16

*Radiogenic Pb.
All analyses corrected for 100 picogram Pb blank and 400 Ma common Pb.

Trace-element compositions

The distinction between the trondhjemitic and granodioritic series, as well as the continuous range of compositions between them, is emphasized by trace-element concentrations. The trondhjemitic rocks are very poor in incompatible elements such as Rb, light LREEs, Ba, Th, and U, which are commonly abundant in granitoids. In contrast, the granodiorite series rocks have more typical concentrations (cf. Fig. 6). Both series are very poor in heavy REEs and Eu anomalies are small or absent; the trondhjemites are especially poor in heavy REEs and tend to have positive Eu anomalies, whereas some granodiorites have small negative Eu anomalies (Fig. 7). Trondhjemites are mostly very rich in Sr, although the Pink Beds samples do not have especially high concentrations; granodiorites have moderate Sr concentrations (Fig. 6). All samples are rather poor in high field strength elements (HFSE) like Ta, Zr, and Hf; this is particularly pronounced for Ta in the trondhjemites (Fig. 8).

On various element-element discrimination diagrams (e.g., Fig. 8, B and C), the Blue Ridge granitoids show very clear similarities to magmatic arc igneous rocks in general and to arc granitoids in particular (Pearce et al., 1984). The trondhjemitic rocks plot with primitive island and continental arc rocks, whereas the

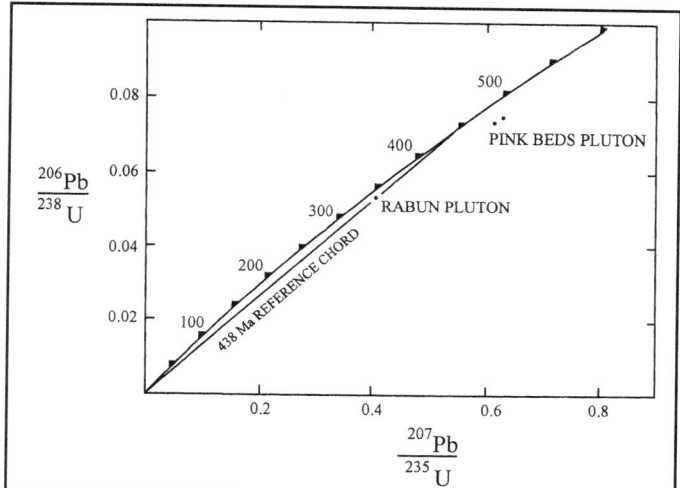

Figure 4. U-Pb concordia, showing composition of single analyzed zircon fraction from Rabun pluton (44–74 μm) and two fractions from Pink Beds pluton (74–149 and >149 μm).

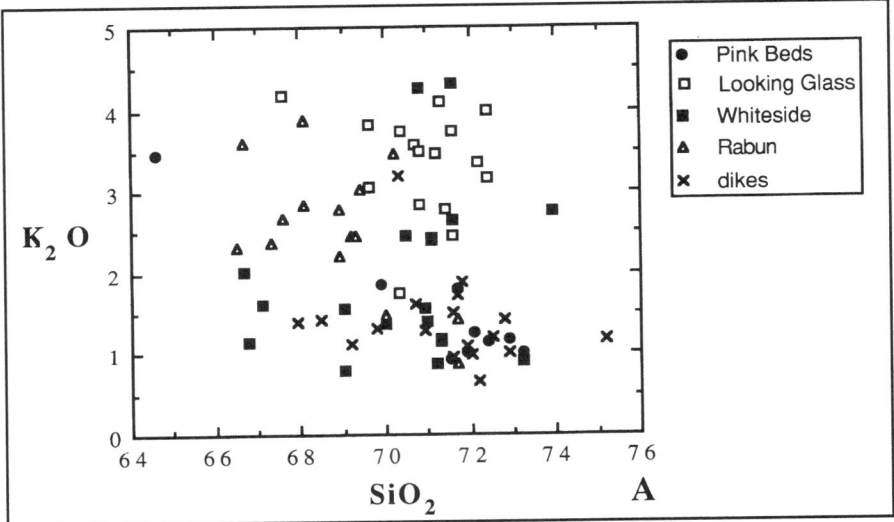

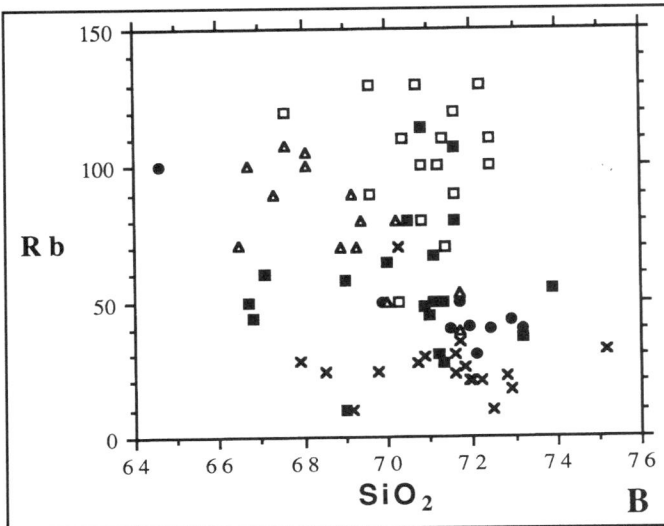

Figure 5. SiO_2 (wt%) plotted versus (A) K_2O (wt%); (B) Rb (ppm); (C) initial $^{87}Sr/^{86}Sr$.

granodiorite series rocks plot within the field of "normal" continental arc rocks (not shown; see Brown et al., 1984).

Isotopic compositions

Sr, Nd, Pb, and O isotopic compositions of analyzed samples are presented in Table 2. There is a pronounced difference between the trondhjemite and granodiorite series. The trondhjemites have a depleted signature: initial $^{87}Sr/^{86}Sr$ ranges from 0.7034 to 0.7050, averaging 0.7042, and initial ε_{Nd} values range from +0.1 to +5.1 (mean +2.6) (all initial ratios are estimated assuming an age of 400 Ma). Their range of Nd and Sr compositions suggests a closer affinity to island arcs than to the mantle or mid-ocean ridge basalts (MORB). The granodiorites, in contrast, have "normal" continent margin granitoid ratios (0.7050 to 0.7089, mean 0.7064; –0.3 to –3.8, mean –1.9) (Fig. 9A).

$\delta^{18}O$ values of 9 of 11 analyzed trondhjemitic samples are in the range +6.2‰ to 7.5‰, averaging 7.0‰; the other two samples have values of 8.2‰ and 8.6‰. Fourteen granodioritic samples range from 7.3‰ to 9.7‰, with an average of 8.6‰; a single sample has a value of 6.7‰.

The feldspar (approximate initial) Pb isotope ratios of the granodioritic rocks are similar to those of typical continental intrusive rocks of Phanerozoic age (cf. Fig. 9, B and C). All three Pb isotope ratios of the single analyzed trondhjemite are distinctly less radiogenic than those of the granodiorites and more radiogenic than those of MORB, falling in the range of island-arc igneous rocks.

PETROGENESIS

We will treat the origins of the Blue Ridge granitoids first from the standpoint of models for generation of magmas representing each of the two hypothetical series, and second from the

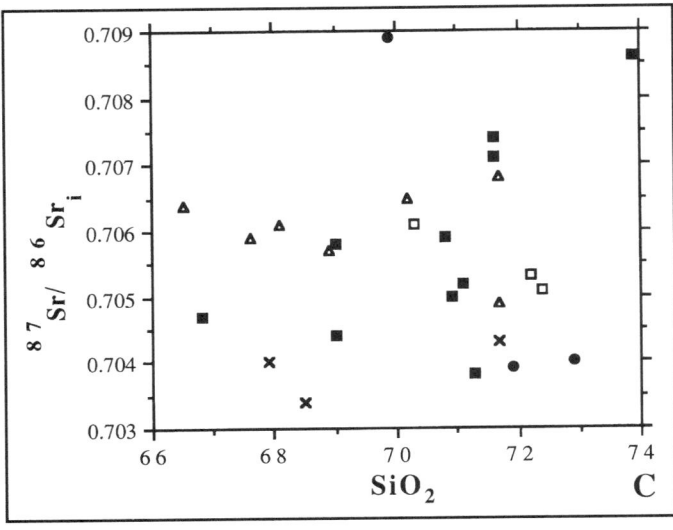

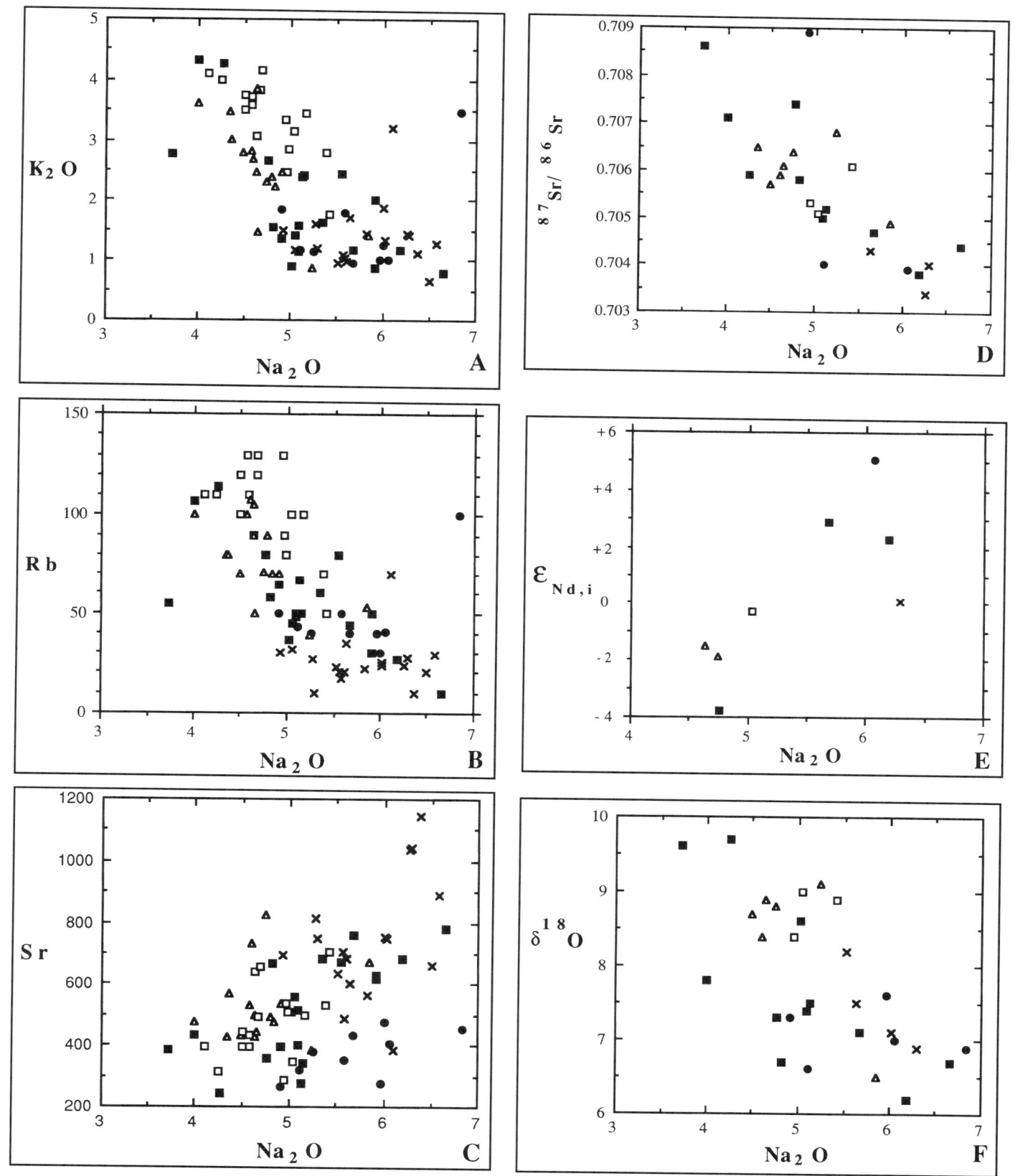

Figure 6. Na_2O (wt%) plotted versus (A) K_2O (wt%); (B) Rb (ppm); (C) Sr (ppm); (D) $^{87}Sr/^{86}Sr$ (at 400 Ma); (E) ϵ_{Nd} (at 400 Ma); (F) $\delta^{18}O$. See Figure 5A for key.

TABLE 2. ELEMENTAL AND ISOTOPIC DATA FOR REPRESENTATIVE SAMPLES FROM BLUE RIDGE PLUTONS

	Pink Beds pluton					Looking Glass pluton			Rabun pluton							Dikes
	PB1	PB3	PB4	PB6B	PB7	LG1	LG7	LG17	R2	R4	R7	R9	R11	R14	R22A	T1
(wt. %)																
SiO$_2$	70.9	73.2	64.6	69.9	72.9	71.5	70.3	72.2	71.7	70.2	67.7	66.8	66.5	71.7	68.9	71.7
TiO$_2$	0.15	0.12	0.09	0.26	0.12	0.20	0.23	0.05	0.20	0.22	0.41	0.33	0.44	0.16	0.37	0.11
Al$_2$O$_3$	15.7	14.9	20.5	15.9	14.4	14.5	16.0	14.8	15.5	14.9	15.6	16.1	16.4	16.1	15.1	15.4
Fe$_2$O$_3$	1.52	1.33	0.61	2.51	1.56	1.81	1.81	1.21	1.65	1.74	2.91	2.61	3.13	1.36	2.73	1.09
MnO	0.01	0.04	......	0.04	0.02	0.02	0.02	0.02	0.02	0.02	0.03	0.03	0.03	0.02	0.03	0.01
MgO	0.45	0.38	0.25	0.89	0.39	0.59	0.52	0.34	0.57	0.55	0.97	0.83	1.05	0.44	0.84	0.42
CaO	2.88	2.00	2.19	2.04	2.11	1.60	2.65	1.29	2.62	1.94	2.65	2.31	3.05	1.64	2.58	2.00
Na$_2$O	5.57	5.97	6.83	4.90	5.11	4.80	5.42	4.94	5.24	4.34	4.60	4.39	4.74	5.85	4.49	5.64
K$_2$O	1.05	1.00	3.48	1.86	1.18	3.28	1.76	3.35	0.87	3.47	2.68	4.03	2.32	1.41	2.79	1.72
P$_2$O$_5$	0.04	0.03	0.08	0.08	0.04	0.06	0.07	0.05	0.12	0.07	0.14	0.13	0.17	0.05	0.12	0.03
LOI	0.54	0.54	0.77	0.77	0.85	0.47	0.54	0.77	1.54	0.62	0.62	0.47	0.54	1.39	0.70	1.00
Total	98.91	99.51	99.40	99.15	98.68	98.83	99.32	99.20	100.03	98.07	98.21	98.03	98.37	100.12	98.65	99.12
(ppm)																
Rb	41	40	100	50	43	100	47	122	39	80	108	105	76	53	77	35
Sr	405	277	454	264	317	347	711	304	385	426	732	497	825	673	431	600
Ba	460	310	540	840	490	1,030	490	550	110	840	940	1,330	850	340	690	590
Th	2.1					5.7						8.1		2.7	7.7	
U	0.6					3.1						0.8		0.8	0.8	
Zr	92	40		40	80	84	120	70	70	100	160	160	180	90	150	50
Hf	2.7					2.9						4.6				
Ta	0.2					0.4						0.4				
La	11	3.95		15.6		11.91	16.80			23.8		35	55	9.2	28	2.65
Ce	19	9.12		30.6		25.71	37.70			47.8		57.8	98.5	18	52	5.96
Nd	7	3.05		11.6		10.67	11.30			15.2		22.7	35	9	19	2.99
Sm	1.30	0.751		2.26		2.10	2.25			2.64		3.92	6.09	2	3.6	0.845
Eu	0.36	0.275		0.926		0.464	0.725			0.714		1.07	1.38	0.69	1.18	0.27
Tb	0.15					0.223								0.27	0.35	
Dy	0.7													1.1	1.4	
Yb	0.31	0.38		0.7		0.633	0.76			0.38		0.7	1.07	0.65	0.64	0.38
Lu	0.05	0.07		0.108		0.087	0.119			0.093		0.108	0.161	0.1	0.1	0.69
^{87}Rb/^{86}Sr	0.294			0.551	0.392	0.741	0.190	1.158	0.295	0.542	0.642	0.613	0.370	0.228	0.518	0.170
^{87}Sr/^{86}Sr$_{meas}$	0.70557			0.71203	0.70625	0.70935	0.70715	0.71193	0.70849	0.70954	0.70956	0.70964	0.70851	0.70615	0.70868	0.70528
^{87}Sr/^{86}Sr$_{400}$	0.7039			0.7089	0.7040	0.7051	0.7061	0.7053	0.7068	0.7065	0.7059	0.7061	0.7064	0.7049	0.7057	0.7043
^{147}Sm/^{144}Nd	0.0983					0.1213						0.0976	0.0937			
^{143}Nd/^{144}Nd$_{meas}$	0.512641					0.512427						0.512303	0.512270			
^{143}Nd/^{144}Nd$_{400}$	0.512384					0.512109						0.512047	0.512025			
$\varepsilon_{Nd.400}$	+5.1					-0.3						-1.5	-1.9			
^{206}Pb/^{204}Pb$_{dwls}$	18.17					18.47									18.49	
^{207}Pb/^{204}Pb$_{feld}$	15.55					15.61									15.63	
^{208}Pb/^{204}Pb$_{feld}$	37.84					38.25									38.35	
δ^{18}O$_{wr}$	+7.0	7.6	6.9	7.3	6.6	9.0	8.9	8.4	+9.1		8.4	8.9	8.8	6.5	8.7	7.5
δ^{18}O$_{qtz}$	+8.2			8.5		10.2										

TABLE 2. ELEMENTAL AND ISOTOPIC DATA FOR REPRESENTATIVE SAMPLES FROM BLUE RIDGE PLUTONS (continued - page 2)

	Dikes (continued)					Whiteside pluton										
	T10A	T10E	T10F	T10X	TRC	WS1	WS9	WS12	WS13	WS14	WS20	WS22	WS23	WS25	WSCGG	WSS
(wt. %)																
SiO_2	70.9	71.8	67.9	68.500	71.6	71.6	70.8	73.2	69.0	73.9	70.6	69.0	71.1	70.9	66.8	71.6
TiO_2	0.16	0.12	0.27	0.270	0.17	0.18	0.28	0.22	0.26	0.06	0.17	0.06	0.13	0.20	0.24	0.11
Al_2O_3	16.5	15.6	17.5	17.400	16.3	14.8	14.6	15.4	16.4	14.8	16.1	18.9	15.1	14.9	17.3	15.6
Fe_2O_{3t}	1.42	1.30	1.60	1.750	1.36	1.63	1.76	1.50	2.71	0.81	1.47	0.37	1.56	2.07	1.68	0.75
MnO	0.02	0.01	0.02	0.020	0.02	0.02				0.01			0.06	0.03	0.02	0.02
MgO	0.61	0.49	0.84	0.570	0.40	0.43	0.42	0.61	0.98		0.38	0.27	0.41	0.54	0.86	0.20
CaO	2.65	2.01	2.99	2.96	2.56	2.02	1.48	2.77	3.32	1.84	2.69	3.77	1.67	2.29	3.65	1.48
Na_2O	6.58	6.01	6.29	6.260	5.52	4.76	4.26	5.01	4.81	3.72	4.99	6.65	5.13	5.10	5.68	4.00
K_2O	1.29	1.88	1.40	1.430	0.95	2.66	4.27	0.90	1.56	2.76	1.02	0.78	2.40	1.57	1.16	4.33
P_2O_5	0.06	0.03	0.08	0.060	0.05	0.07	0.08	0.07	0.10	0.07	0.05	0.05	0.05	0.06	0.13	0.04
LOI	0.62	0.47	0.47			0.47	0.54					0.39	0.70	0.85	0.62	
Total	100.4	99.72	99.36	99.220	98.93	98.64	98.51	99.68	99.14	97.97	97.47	100.24	98.31	98.51	98.14	98.13
(ppm)																
Rb	29	25	28	24	23	80	114	37	58	55	27	10	67	48	44	107
Sr	850	756	1,046	1,035	634	355	243	508	666	387	681	783	277	514	760	432
Ba	420	380	340	310	585	770	1,650	239	380	1,540	271	240	440	350	350	1,098
Th	2.2		1.9	1.6	1.8		21.0	3.0	3.10	6.0	2.4	2.9			1.1	4
U	0.8		1.0	0.8	0.5		1.5	0.6	0.885	1.0	0.1	1.6			0.4	1
Zr	150	90	100			110	190				100	50	40	70		
Hf	3.6				2.4						2.7				2.5	
Ta	0.04				<0.5						0.2					
La	6.8	6.71	8	6.5	5	28.6	56	7.92	24.8		12	13		5.04	4.4	
Ce	19.7	14.2	17	14	14	66.2	94	16.82	47		20	22		12.14	10	
Nd	7.9		10	8	4	17.50	29	7.12	18		9	10		5.12	5	
Sm	1.8	1.61	2.4	2.0	0.64	3.28	4.90	1.37	3.10		2.0	2.1		0.98	1.22	
Eu	0.51	0.484	0.69	0.73	0.28	0.953	1.21	0.492	0.885		0.82	0.95		0.45	0.39	
Tb			0.35	0.3	0.1		0.30	0.163			0.15	0.16			0.2	
Dy	0.6		1.9	1.7	0.7		1.0				0.70	0.80			0.9	
Yb	0.45	0.24	0.99	0.82	0.23	0.62	0.39	0.25	0.53		0.33	0.33		0.33	0.48	
Lu	0.07	0.052	0.15	0.11	0.04	0.111	0.06	0.036	0.086		0.05	0.05	0.059	0.059	0.07	
$^{87}Rb/^{86}Sr$			0.0772	0.0665		0.649	1.355		0.253	0.413	0.11700	0.0354	0.705	0.269	0.168	0.508
$^{87}Sr/^{86}Sr_{meas}$			0.70439	0.70377		0.71109	0.71363		0.70720	0.71098	0.70448	0.70455	0.70921	0.70658	0.70565	0.7100
$^{87}Sr/^{86}Sr_{400}$			0.7040	0.7034		0.7074	0.70590		0.70580	0.70860	0.7038	0.7044	0.7052	0.7050	0.7047	0.7071
$^{147}Sm/^{144}Nd$			0.1481			0.1027					0.1160				0.1658	
$^{143}Nd/^{144}Nd_{meas}$			0.51216			0.512199					0.512543				0.512707	
$^{143}Nd/^{144}Nd_{400}$			0.512128			0.511930					0.512239				0.512273	
εNd_{400}			-0.1			-3.8					+2.3				+2.9	
$^{206}Pb/^{204}Pb_{feld}$						18.43	18.43						18.58		18.42	
$^{207}Pb/^{204}Pb_{feld}$						15.63	15.63						15.63		15.63	
$^{208}Pb/^{204}Pb_{feld}$						38.33	38.33						38.15		38.28	
$\delta^{18}O_{wt}$		7.1	6.9		8.2	+7.3	+9.7	+8.6	+6.7	+9.6	+6.2	+6.7	+7.5	+7.4	+7.1	+7.8
$\delta^{18}O_{qtz}$									+7.5	+10.8					+7.8	+8.6

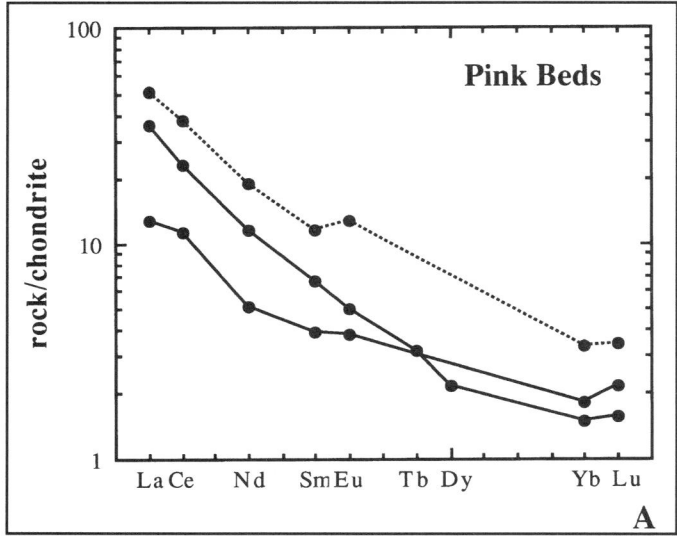

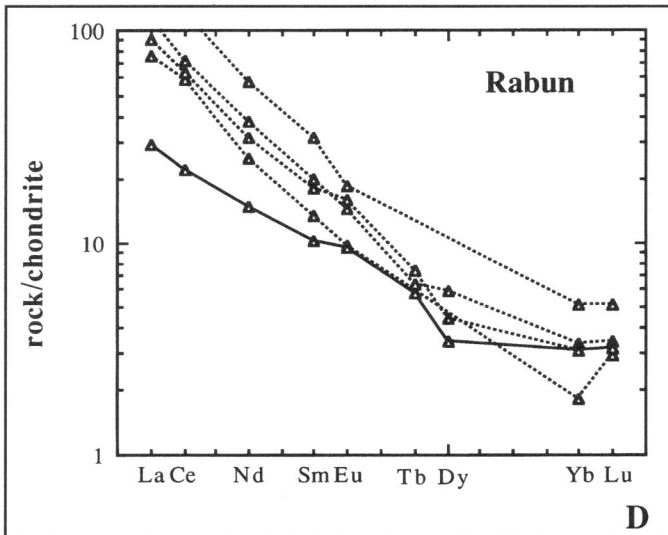

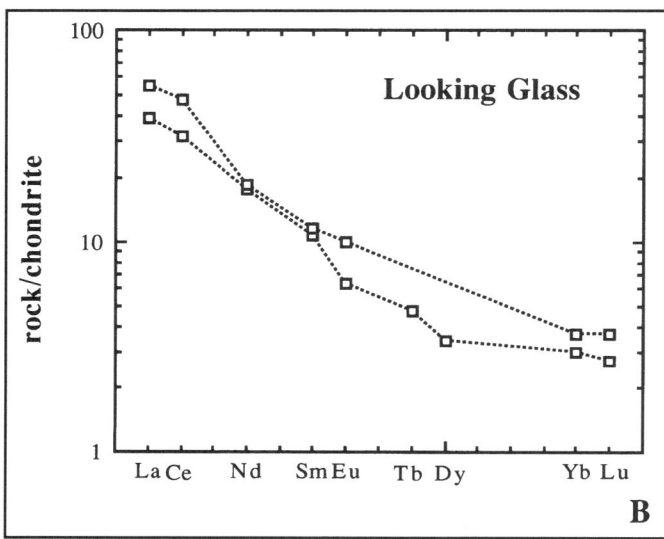

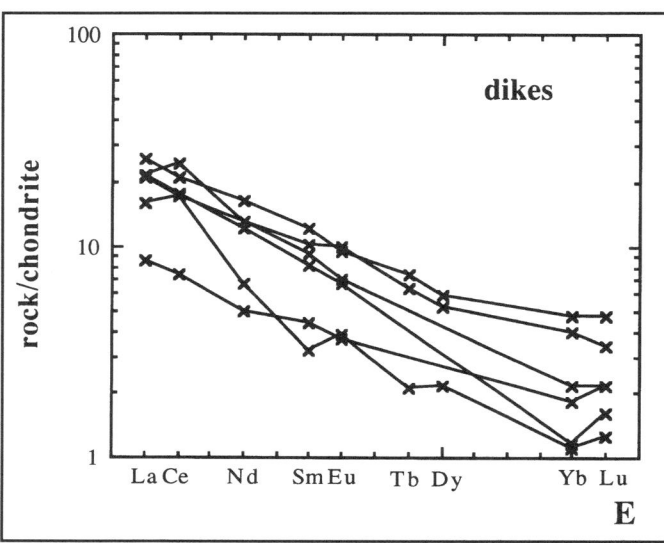

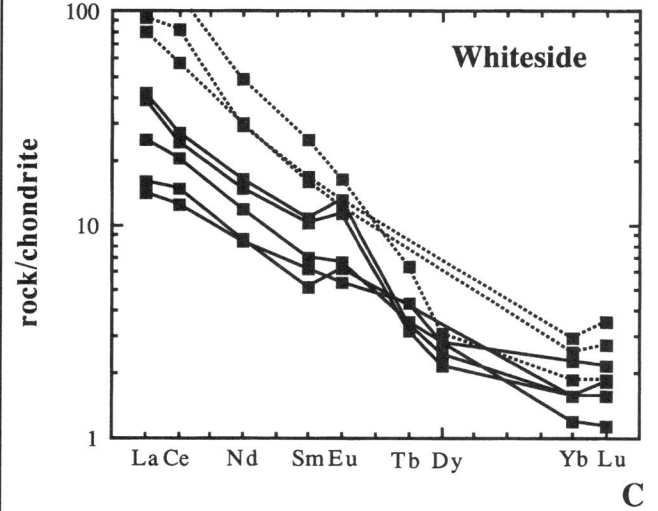

Figure 7. Chondrite-normalized rare earth element patterns of plutons; solid lines represent patterns of samples with >5 wt% SiO$_2$ (approx. trondhjemites), dashed lines those of samples with <5 wt% SiO$_2$ (approx. granodiorites).

standpoint of the development of the observed continuous compositional variation.

Origin of the trondhjemite and granodiorite series

The diversity of the granitoids requires either considerable source heterogeneity or mixing of magmas derived from distinct sources. In either case, at least two types of source material are required. Possible origins of each series are considered below.

Trondhjemite series. Isotope and elemental geochemistry places tight constraints on the nature of the source(s) of the trondhjemites. The isotope data argue strongly against major involvement of typical crustal material in the generation of the trondhjemitic magmas (although zircon inheritance and isotopic

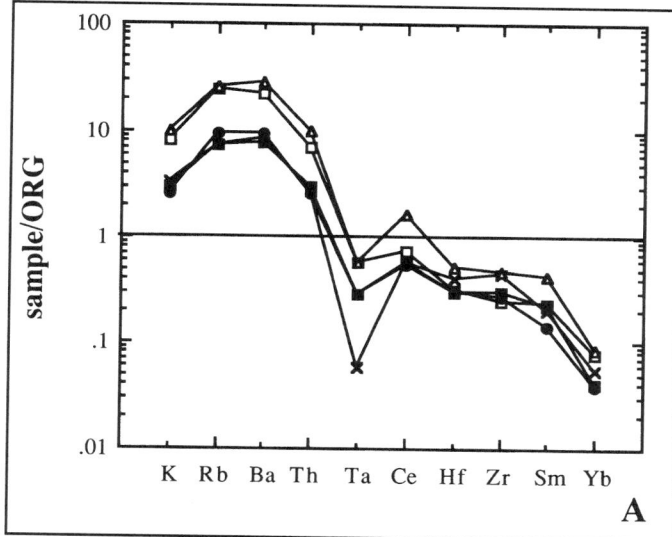

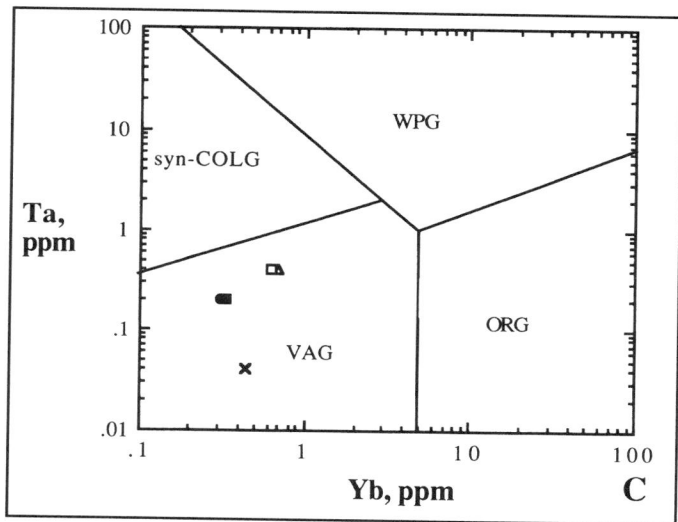

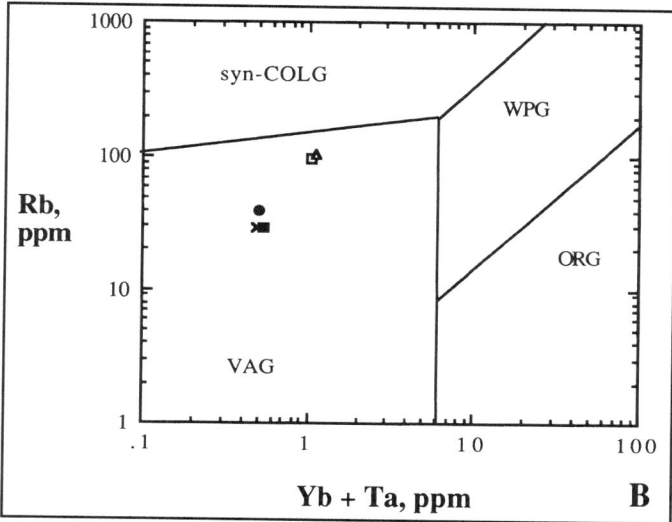

Figure 8. Blue Ridge samples plotted in tectonic discrimination diagrams of Pearce et al. (1984); symbols as in Figure 5 (samples WS20 [Whiteside], PB1 [Pink Beds], and T10A [dike] are trondhjemitic; LG1 [Looking Glass] and R9 [Rabun] are granodioritic). A: Elemental abundances of selected samples normalized to "ocean ridge granite." B: Rb versus Yb + Ta. C: Yb versus Ta.

would tend to nullify the compositional distinctiveness of the trondhjemites (e.g., their high Sr, high light REE/heavy REE, negligible or slightly positive Eu anomalies, low REE, etc., would tend to evolve to more normal values). High-pressure fractionation, which would presumably involve predominantly quartz, pyroxene, and garnet, cannot account for the low concentrations of large ion lithophile elements (LILE: e.g., K, Rb, Ba). The distinctive compositions of the trondhjemites must therefore in large part be inherited from the source. Constraints on the nature of the residues of melting and the original source material are described qualitatively below.

Major element constraints. (1) Very low K_2O eliminates K-feldspar as a possible residual phase because K-feldspar saturation would require higher K concentration in coexisting melt; a mafic to ultramafic residue is suggested.

(2) High SiO_2 and low MgO and Mg# (molecular Mg/[Fe$_t$ + Mg] × 100 = 30–60) eliminate peridotite as source material, because melts in equilibrium with mantle olivine should have an Mg# ≥ ~70 and <50–55 wt% SiO_2 (e.g., Wilson, 1989).

Trace element constraints. (1) High Sr suggests that feldspar, with K_{Sr} >1, was not a major phase in the residue (lower Sr in the Pink Beds trondhjemites permits some residual feldspar); paucity of feldspar is also consistent with absence of or positive Eu anomalies.

(2) Low Rb, Ba, and light REEs require a LILE-poor source, because all of these elements are incompatible under almost all circumstances.

(3) Very low heavy REEs indicate either an anomalously impoverished source or, much more likely, the presence of a mineral in the residue with high partition coefficients for heavy REEs, presumably hornblende or garnet.

compositions require that most or all have a crustal component). Crustal rocks generally have much higher $^{87}Sr/^{86}Sr$ and $^{18}O/^{16}O$ and much lower $^{143}Nd/^{144}Nd$ than the trondhjemites: source rocks with an initially depleted signature and either very short crustal residence time or very low Rb/Sr and high Sm/Nd are required. We conclude that the dominant contributor to these magmas had an isotopic composition closer to that of depleted mantle or derivatives of depleted mantle, such as MORB or primitive island-arc volcanic rocks, than to continental crust.

Textures of the fine-grained porphyritic dikes indicate that they were mostly liquid (>80%–90%) when they were emplaced, so their compositions are reasonable approximations of melt chemistry (Wood and Miller, 1984). The coarse-grained plutonic rocks have similar compositions and therefore apparently reflect similar petrogenetic processes, though some crystal accumulation and melt segregation must have occurred during their formation. Fractionation of the observed early crystallizing assemblages (dominantly plagioclase + minor biotite, muscovite, quartz)

We have modeled residues equilibrated with a melt similar in composition to the Blue Ridge trondhjemites (Fig. 10). We assumed, on the basis of the above reasoning, that the residues must be mafic in composition. Compositions of the source itself were calculated, assuming that the fraction of melting was ≤30%;

higher fractions of melting of mafic rocks would yield liquids less felsic than trondhjemite (e.g., Rapp, 1990; Rapp et al., 1991; Wolf and Wyllie, 1994). In any case, conclusions about the nature of the source would remain the same up to at least 50% melting.

As expected, plagioclase-rich residues (gabbros, granulites) require unrealistically high Sr concentrations in the source, and residues that are free of both hornblende and garnet have extremely low middle and heavy REE contents; no combination of such residues with trondhjemite could yield a plausible source composition. Sources with relatively enriched mafic compositions, such as ocean island basalts, are inappropriate because their incompatible element concentrations are comparable to or higher than those of the trondhjemites. Plausible models involve plagioclase-poor, moderately garnet- and/or amphibole-rich residues of melting of depleted-source mafic rocks, like those found at mid-ocean ridges and in island arcs.

The most successful models specify a residue that contains amphibole modally > garnet > plagioclase, along with minerals with low partition coefficients for the modeled elements (orthopyroxene, quartz, and/or clinopyroxene). Some plagioclase appears to be necessary to counterbalance garnet and amphibole (low Kd for Eu, high Kd for other middle REE) in preventing a large positive Eu anomaly in the melt; high fO_2 could perhaps have the same effect. Plagioclase also serves, along with the other low $K^{s/l}$ minerals mentioned above, to dilute the high partition coefficients for middle to heavy REE of garnet and amphibole, which could otherwise yield unrealistically high middle REE and heavy REE in the residue.

The pronounced relative HFSE and U and Th depletion of both the trondhjemites and their calculated residues, as well as their relative enrichment in Ba, Sr, and light REEs, are more easily reconciled with an arc-like source material than with MORB. The requirement for a strictly arc-like mafic source could be relaxed if the residue contained accessory minerals that would retain appreciable quantities of U, Th, and REEs (sphene, apatite, zircon), Ta (sphene, rutile), P (apatite), and Zr and Hf (zircon). If the trondhjemitic magmas were generated at low temperature (<750–800 °C), their compositions would permit saturation in some of these minerals (e.g., Watson and Harrison, 1983; Harrison and Watson, 1984; Ryerson and Watson, 1987), and the source rock could have had an appreciably different pattern with fewer of the distinctive arc characteristics. Nevertheless, neither normal MORB nor enriched mafic rocks like ocean

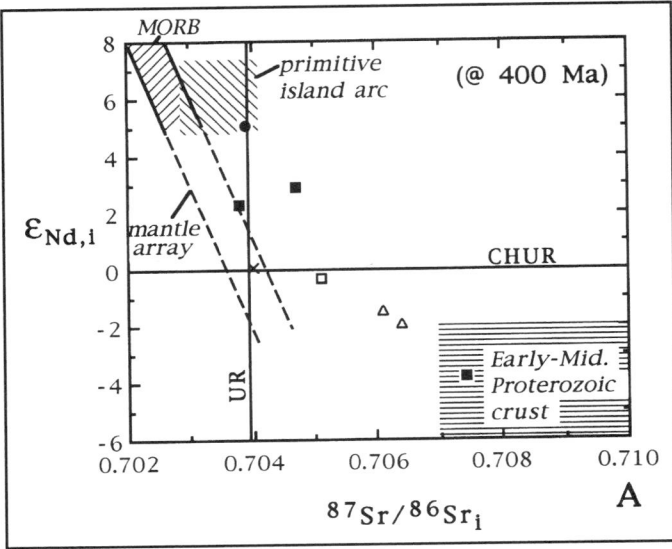

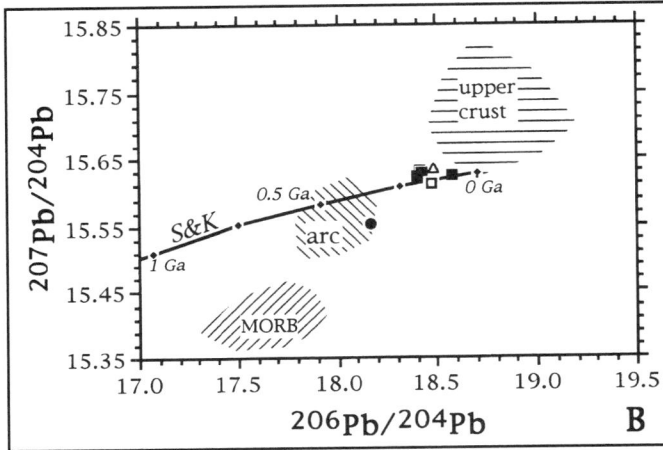

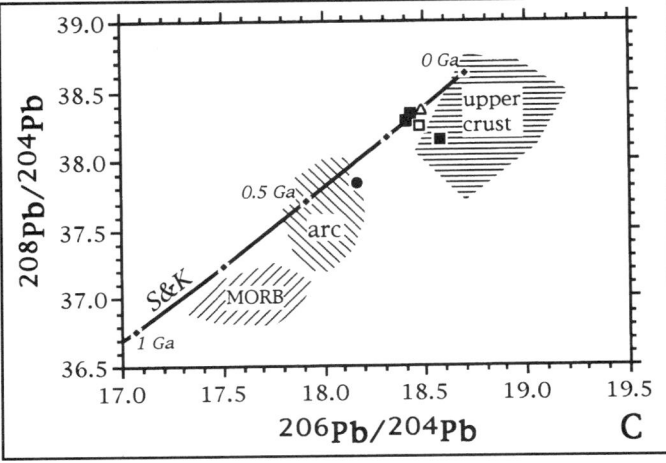

Figure 9. Isotopic compositions compared with those of possible contributing materials at 400 Ma; symbols as in Figure 5. A: $^{87}Sr/^{86}Sr$ vs. ε_{Nd} fields of mid-ocean ridge basalt (MORB), mantle, primitive island arcs, and probable Proterozoic crust of the region are shown for comparison. B: $^{207}Pb/^{204}Pb$ versus $^{206}Pb/^{204}Pb$. Model crustal growth curves of Stacey and Kramers (1975), and fields of upper crust, arcs, and depleted mantle/MORB (modified to 400 Ma; e.g., Zartman and Haines, 1988, Halliday et al., 1992; Kay and Kay, 1994) are shown for comparison here and in C); C: $^{208}Pb/^{204}Pb$ vs. $^{206}Pb/^{204}Pb$. See Figure 5A for key.

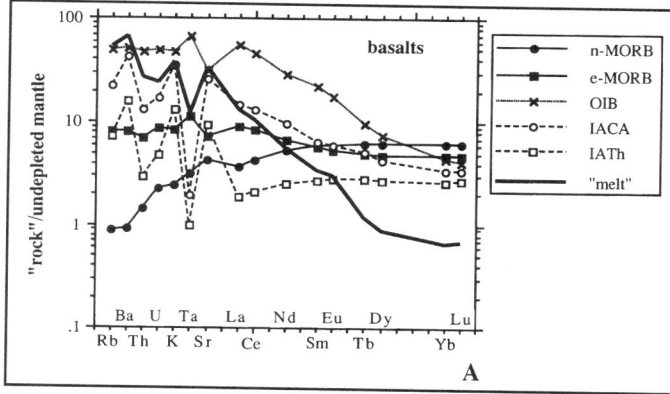

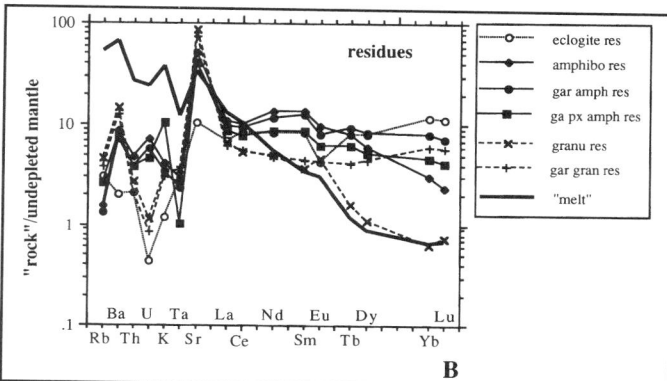

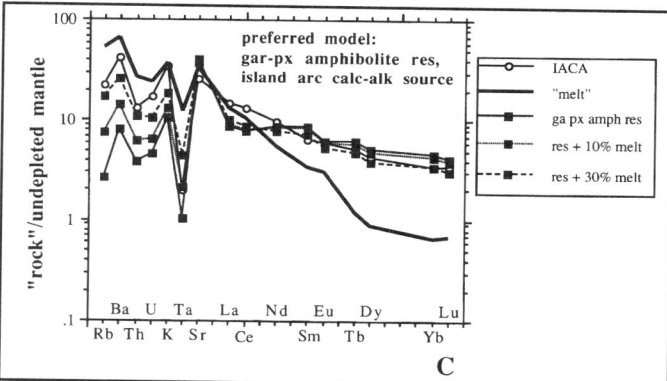

Figure 10. Trace element models for generation of Blue Ridge trondhjemitic magma. Elemental concentrations normalized to undepleted mantle values (Sun and McDonough, 1989); "melt" = mean of four representative samples from Pink Beds and Whiteside plutons and dikes. A: Typical compositions of major basalt types compared with "melt" (normal mid-ocean ridge basalt [n-MORB], enriched MORB [e-MORB], oceanic island basalt [OIB], island-arc calc-alkaline basalt [IACA], island-arc tholeiite [IATh]; from Sun and McDonough, 1989, and Sun, 1980). B: Mafic residues in equilibrium with "melt" (eclogite: 40% garnet, 60% clinopyroxene; amphibolite: 75% hornblende, 25% plagioclase; garnet amphibolite: 20% garnet, 60% hornblende, 20% plagioclase; garnet-pyroxene amphibolite: 10% garnet, 30% orthopyroxene, 40% hornblende, 20% plagioclase; mafic granulite: 30% orthopyroxene, 30% clinopyroxene, 40% plagioclase; garnet granulite: 20% garnet, 20% orthopyroxene, 25% clinopyroxene, 35% plagioclase) (Kds for felsic melts from Henderson, 1982). C: Preferred model: partial melting (roughly 20%–30%) of mafic rock with island-arc calc-alkaline composition, leaving a garnet-pyroxene amphibolite residue.

island or continent interior basalts would be appropriate, because the former are too poor and the latter too rich in LILEs.

We consider the most probable generating process for the trondhjemitic magmas to have been moderate fraction melting (ca. 20%–30%) of a mafic rock with calc-alkaline composition, leaving a garnet-pyroxene amphibolite residue. This is consistent with both elemental (Fig. 10C) and isotopic (Fig. 8) compositions.

Granodiorite series. The granodiorite series has a distinct crustal isotopic signature and much higher concentrations of incompatible elements than the trondhjemite series. Isotopic diversity (Figs. 7 and 8) implies that a variety of materials was involved, which is consistent with crustal anatexis (cf. Miller et al., 1988). Several constraints can be placed on the types of source material.

1. The U-Pb inheritance in zircons indicates involvement of relatively old (Grenville and probably older), variable age crustal material, either in situ or as detrital fragments in sediment. Sr and Nd data support this conclusion, but suggest that most samples also include a more juvenile component (Fig. 8).

2. $\delta^{18}O$ values are typical of the crust—higher than those of mafic rocks, but lower than those of sedimentary rocks. A sedimentary component may have contributed to the melts, but it was probably not dominant.

3. Although not as extreme as the trondhjemites, the granodiorites are poor in heavy REEs, moderately rich in Sr, and have very small negative Eu anomalies. The residue of melting must have contained a heavy REE-concentrating phase, probably garnet or perhaps amphibole, and probably was not dominated by feldspar. The minimal Eu anomalies may be a result of balancing effects of garnet and feldspar.

4. High Ba and moderate K_2O contents suggest that K-feldspar was not abundant in the residue. K-feldspar saturation would require higher potassium concentrations in coexisting melts, and abundant K-spar would result in partitioning of Ba into the residue.

If the granodiorite series did in fact have a source or sources entirely distinct from that of the trondhjemite series, then this source was probably mixed, comprising both Early to Middle Proterozoic and younger rocks, and including both relatively felsic, perhaps sedimentary, crust and more depleted material. However, even the most extreme of the granodiorite series rocks may have been hybrids between trondhjemitic and ancient felsic crust-derived magmas.

Origin of compositional diversity

The continuum of compositions from the "depleted" trondhjemite series to the "normal" granodiorite series suggests a mixing process. However, we see no evidence in the field or in thin sections for magma mixing: potential magmatic enclaves and disequilibrium textures suggesting such mixing are notably absent. Microscopic details could have been obscured in many samples by metamorphism, and the similarity of the magmas in mineralogy and probably in intensive parameters could have facilitated the mixing process and made it less obvious (e.g., Frost and Mahood, 1987). Nonetheless, other mesoscopic igneous features (e.g., dikes, xenoliths, textural variations) are well preserved and presumably some evidence for in situ magma mixing would be retained if it had occurred.

A second possibility is that the compositional continuum reflects crustal contamination of depleted source-derived magma. Interaction between hot, mafic magma and the crust through which it passes is highly plausible and frequently called upon (e.g., DePaolo, 1981; Hildreth and Moorbath, 1988). However, there is no evidence for the involvement of mafic magma, and it is difficult to imagine extensive assimilation of crust by very felsic and probably relatively cool trondhjemitic magmas.

A third possibility is that there was an essentially continuous range in compositions of source materials, and therefore melt increments formed with a continuum of elemental and isotopic compositions. In this case there would be no necessity for magmatism to be coeval, but sharp internal contacts would be likely if the melt fractions within a pluton were separated by much time. A more fundamental problem with this mechanism is that a *continuum* of source compositions, encompassing both elemental abundances and isotope ratios, from basaltic through felsic and perhaps sedimentary, is implausible.

The mechanism that we tentatively favor involves coalescence in the source region of diverse melt increments (Miller et al., 1988). If the lower crust at the time of magma generation included both mafic and more felsic material, the ascending magmas could have been derived from either—or, perhaps more likely, by coalescence of melt increments from each. Source materials could have been either stratified (e.g., mafic underplate beneath older crust) or interleaved by injection or tectonic juxtaposition. Sedimentary material might itself already have been mixed, derived from both Proterozoic and juvenile crust. Fluctuations in conditions brought about by the tectonic evolution of the region could cause the zone of partial melting to migrate, or melting to cease and later to restart at a different location. Tectonism could serve to mix diverse source terranes, at least on a kilometer scale.

In addition to the cryptic mixing process described above, the compositions of the Blue Ridge magmas were clearly affected to some extent by fractional crystallization. Widespread aplitic and pegmatitic dikes represent highly evolved melts, and textures such as plagioclase zonation reflect evolution of coexisting melt. Much of the scatter in the chemical data is probably attributable to overprinting of more or less closed-system fractionation processes upon the products of initial, complex open-system mixing in the source region.

DISCUSSION

Origins of the Blue Ridge magmas and their relationship to southern Appalachian plutonism and orogeny

The Blue Ridge granitoids were derived from diverse sources during early to middle Paleozoic orogeny. The source materials included both depleted mafic rocks and relatively felsic igneous and/or sedimentary rocks with a crustal heritage. The mafic rocks were probably compositionally similar to primitive arc basalts. The broad continuum in compositions of the plutonic rocks is a result of the combination of mixing, probably in the source region, and fractional crystallization. Melting took place at relatively great depth, at least for the mafic rocks, at pressures where hornblende and garnet would dominate over plagioclase in the residue—that is, probably deep within the tectonically thickened crust (>30 km). Dehydration of hornblende was probably a critical reaction in generating the trondhjemite series magmas (dehydration melting; e.g., Rapp, 1990; Rapp et al., 1991; Rushmer, 1991; Beard and Lofgren, 1991; Wolf and Wyllie, 1994); dehydration melting involving biotite (±hornblende) may have been important in producing magma in the more felsic crust.

The Blue Ridge granitoid magmas were generated synctectonically, presumably in a convergent setting. Although both the plutonic rocks and their proposed sources have compositional affinities with arc magmas, there is no evidence for the existence of a typical mafic or compositionally expanded marginal magmatic arc. The exposed mass of igneous rocks is small, and the compositional range narrow, compared with most arcs. We suggest two possible geologic histories that could account for the generation of these magmas.

1. Mafic subduction zone magmas underplated the Blue Ridge crust during the early Paleozoic. These magmas may have interacted with the overlying crust in a MASH (melting-assimilation-storage-homogenization) process (e.g., Hildreth and Moorbath, 1988; Voshage et al., 1990), leading directly to the Blue Ridge felsic magmas. In this scenario, trondhjemites would be little-contaminated fractionates, whereas granodiorites would be highly contaminated subduction-zone magmas or perhaps pure crustal melts. Alternatively, the magmatic underplate may have crystallized as much as 100 m.y. or more prior to the melting event that produced the Blue Ridge granitoids (see discussion following). Neither of these scenarios is entirely satisfying. The lack of coeval mafic intrusives or enclaves argues against direct origin by fractional crystallization. Furthermore, a MASH process would probably not yield uniformly felsic magmas ascending from the ponding zone. Finally, our modeling suggests that the source of the granitoids was hydrous (amphibole bearing), as does the relatively wet nature of the magmas implied by early crystallization of micas; however, basaltic rocks that crystallize and remain in the deep continental crust are not very likely to be sufficiently hydrous to be rich in amphiboles.

2. Fragments of a primitive magmatic arc were emplaced tectonically as a consequence of convergence beneath the Blue Ridge crust. The thermal blanketing resulting from crustal thickening could ultimately have led to temperatures high enough to induce melting in the underaccreted mafic crust, up to 850 °C or more, on a time scale of tens of millions of years to 100 m.y. (e.g., Zen, 1988; Patino Douce et al., 1990). The more ancient, felsic component could have been contributed by overlying crust that may also have exceeded its solidus, or it could have come from North America–derived sedimentary rocks that may have

been part of the near-continent arc assemblage. Mafic and felsic rocks may have been interleaved depositionally, by intrusion of mafic rocks into a sedimentary sequence, or tectonically.

We prefer scenario 2 rather than 1 because shallow mafic rocks are more likely to become hydrated than deep-seated gabbros, because the necessity for coeval, occult mafic magmatism is obviated, and because supracrustal mafic arc rocks of appropriate age (ca. 500 Ma) are present in a number of places in the southern Appalachians (e.g., in the Piedmont [Whitney et al., 1978; Pavlides, 1981] and eastern Blue Ridge [Hopson, 1989; Gillon, 1989]). Drummond et al. (1994) demonstrated the importance of the 500 Ma Penobscotian orogeny and related magmatism in the southeastern United States. Multiple melting episodes at different crustal levels would have been possible 50 to 100 m.y. later (400–450 Ma) as conditions fluctuated in response to continuing tectonism. Under these conditions, the zone of melting could have been largely within mafic crust at one time, largely within felsic crust at another time, and within both at yet another, thus yielding the observed range of rocks and genetic signatures. Sinha et al. (1989) proposed a similar model for plutonism in this region, with peraluminous trondhjemitic magmas forming through "delayed decompressional melting" of mafic rocks within thrust-stacked accretionary sequences.

Candidates for younger analogs of the Blue Ridge granitoids in better understood settings are few. Felsic plutons of Cretaceous to early Tertiary age intrude the accretionary wedge that borders the Gulf of Alaska, far from the coeval volcanic arc (Hudson et al., 1979; Hill et al., 1981; Barker et al., 1992; Pavlis et al., 1988). These plutons have been interpreted to be largely to entirely anatectic in origin, with melting being induced by heating associated with crustal thickening (Hudson et al., 1979), basaltic influx (Barker et al., 1992), or shear heating along deep faults (Barnett et al., 1993). The Alaska case differs from the Blue Ridge in that a well-defined coeval arc is present even if distant, and mafic rocks are associated with the granitoids. Most of the granitoid compositions are more potassic, lower in Sr and Na, and have much higher $\delta^{18}O$ than the Blue Ridge granitoids (early Tertiary plutons; Barker et al., 1992), and thus have a distinctly different petrogenesis. Cretaceous trondhjemites are similar in many respects to the Blue Ridge intrusions, but also have very high $\delta^{18}O$ (Rubenstone et al., 1987). Late Cretaceous trondhjemites of the Patagonian batholith are geochemically similar to those that we have described, but they were emplaced in the middle of a long-lived batholith and are associated with more mafic intrusives (e.g., Bruce et al., 1991).

Relationship to plutonism elsewhere in the Blue Ridge

Plutons are scattered throughout the eastern Blue Ridge from Virginia to Alabama (e.g., Sinha et al., 1989). The largest, the Elkahatchee quartz diorite of Alabama, differs from the intrusions described in this study. It is somewhat more mafic (down to 62 wt% SiO_2, with more mafic hornblende + clinopyroxene-bearing enclaves that are interpreted as cumulates), lacks mus-

covite, and is older (490–500 Ma) (Drummond et al., 1994). Other plutons that have been described (e.g., Rockford, Almond, and Blakes Ferry, Alabama; Spruce Pine, North Carolina) are similar to those described in this chapter in that they are felsic, peraluminous (generally muscovite-bearing), and low in potassium, ranging from trondhjemite to granodiorite in composition; coeval mafic rocks are absent and initial $^{87}Sr/^{86}Sr$ ratios are low (Defant et al., 1988; Drummond et al., 1986, 1988; Russell et al., 1987). Preliminary zircon U-Pb data, although not establishing precise ages, confirm previous interpretations that these plutons are Silurian-Devonian and have some Proterozoic inheritance (Russell et al., 1987).

The Elkahatchee quartz diorite is interpreted to be part of an Ordovician magmatic arc at the eastern edge of Laurentia (North America) (Drummond et al., 1994). The younger plutons of the eastern Blue Ridge do not appear to comprise a typical continent margin arc. Rather, they may share with the intrusions described in this chapter an origin in a mixed, partly young and mafic deep crust, forming in response to collisional thickening and consequent heating (cf. Sinha et al., 1989).

Generation of low-potassium felsic magmas

Low-K felsic igneous rocks have received considerable attention in recent years in connection with two problems: (1) the origin of Earth's early stable crust, which was dominated by trondhjemite, tonalite, and granodiorite (TTG) (e.g., Barker, 1979; Martin, 1986, 1987; Rapp et al., 1991); and (2) recognition of melts derived from subducting slabs, which are also expected to be felsic with low K (e.g., Kay, 1978; Stern et al., 1984; Defant and Drummond, 1993; Kay et al., 1993; Yogodzinski et al., 1995). The two problems have merged with the suggestion that modern subduction of young, hot slabs provides a magmagenic environment similar to that which existed in the Archean, and hence that some arc rocks of today (termed adakites) are TTG analogues (Drummond and Defant, 1990; Beard et al., 1993). Adakites—K-poor, aluminous, Sr-rich, heavy REE-depleted dacites—are relatively uncommon at present, probably both because the conditions for slab melting are not often met and because their distinctive chemistry (the "slab signature") can be modified during ascent through the mantle wedge and crust (e.g., Beard et al., 1993; Kelemen, 1993). Trondhjemites of post-Archean age, although by no means rare, are also far less abundant than they were in the Archean.

The Blue Ridge granitoids possess the adakite or slab-melt geochemical characteristics (Fig. 11). However, this elemental and isotopic signature is distinctive because it reflects high-pressure residue mineralogy (garnet ± amphibole, little feldspar) and isotopic and LILE depletion (depleted mantle-derived source), and not necessarily because it requires a slab origin (e.g., Beard et al., 1993). Melting in deep, young mafic crust would yield similar magmas. The Blue Ridge granitoids lack some of the extreme characteristics of the most convincing slab melts, which have even higher Sr and relatively low La/Nd (because of low La/Nd in MORB sources), and they do not have the elevated Mg

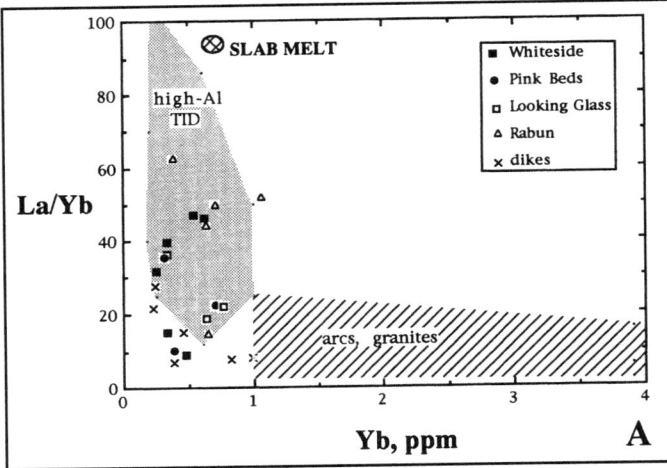

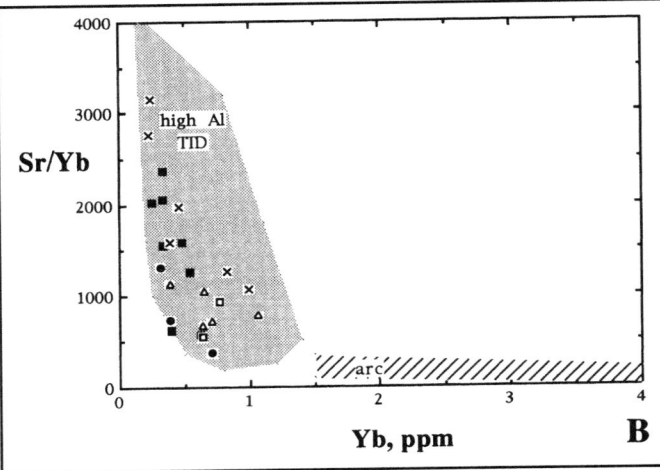

Figure 11. Comparison of Blue Ridge granitoids (symbols as in Fig. 5) with Archean to Cenozoic high Al trondhjemite-tonalite-dacite (TTD) suites and more typical young magmatic arc rocks. A: La/Yb versus Yb (ppm). Field of TTD from Drummond and Defant (1990); "arcs, granites" field from Drummond and Defant (1990; post-Archean granites) and Yogodzinski et al. (1995; central Aleutian arc rocks); "SLAB MELT" is calculated small-fraction melt of subducted, eclogite facies mid-ocean ridge basalts (Yogodzinski et al., 1995). B: Sr/Yb versus Yb (ppm). Field of TTD and "arcs" from Drummond and Defant (1990); "arc" field represents typical lower-Al andesites, dacites, and rhyolites of magmatic arcs. Fields are modified assuming Y = about $10 \times Yb$ (Drummond and Defant fields are based on Y concentration).

that results from passage through the mantle wedge (Kay et al., 1993; Beard et al., 1993; Kelemen, 1993). The suite as a whole and even the most "depleted" trondhjemites show obvious evidence for the influence of ancient, more felsic crust in addition to mafic material, and there is no indication that these granitoids are associated with a directly subduction-related arc. We concur with Kay et al. (1993) that "discrimination of slab melt components is difficult . . . and needs to be justified on the basis of both chemical and tectonic criteria" (see also Beard et al., 1993).

ACKNOWLEDGMENTS

Our research was supported by National Science Foundation grant EAR-8109055, the Vanderbilt University Research Council, the Research Council of the University of North Carolina, and the North Carolina Department of Natural Resources and Community Development. Bob Hatcher, Mark Drummond, Sue Kay, A. K. Sinha, Len Wiener, Steve Yurkovich, Warner Cribb, Miguel Galliski, and participants in the Penrose Conference on low-K silicic magmas all contributed insights that helped us to focus the ideas presented here. The manuscript benefited from thoughtful reviews by Jim Beard, Fred Barker, and John Hogan. Sando thanks Stan Hart and Fred Frey for use of their analytical facilities at the Massachusetts Institute of Technology, and Solomon thanks J. Donahue, C. Morrill, J. Nokes, and J. Whitney at the University of Georgia for their support.

REFERENCES CITED

Absher, S. A., and McSween, H. Y., 1985, Granulites at Winding Stair Gap, North Carolina: The thermal axis of Paleozoic metamorphism in the southern Appalachians: Geological Society of America Bulletin, v. 96, p. 588–599.

Barker, F., 1979, Trondhjemite: Definition, environment and hypotheses of origin, in Barker, F., ed., Trondhjemites, dacites and related rocks: Amsterdam, Elsevier, p. 1–12.

Barker, F., G. L., Ayuso, G. A., Plafker, G., and Lull, J. S., 1992, The 50 Ma granodiorite of the eastern Gulf of Alaska: Melting in an accretionary prism in the forearc: Journal of Geophysical Research, v. 97, p. 6757–6778.

Barnett, D. E., Bowman, J. R., Pavlis, T. S., and Rubenstone, J. R., 1993, Shear heating, metamorphism, and plutonism during subduction initiation, western Chugach Mountains, AK: Geological Society of America Abstracts with Programs, v. 25, no. 6, p. A262–A263.

Beard, J. S., Lofgren, G. E., 1991, Dehydration melting and water-saturated melting of basaltic and andesitic greenstones and amphibolites at 1, 3 and 6.9 kb: Journal of Petrology, v. 32, p. 365–401.

Beard, J. S., Bergantz, G. W., Defant, M. J., and Drummond, M. S., 1993, Penrose Conference report: Origin and emplacement of low-K silicic magmas in subduction settings: GSA Today, v. 3, p. 38.

Brown, G. C., Thorpe, R. S., and Webb, P. C., 1984, The geochemical characteristics of granitoids in contrasting arcs and comments on magma sources: Geological Society of London Journal, v. 141, p. 411–426.

Bruce, R. M., Nelson, E. P., Weaver, S. G., and Lux, D. R., 1991, Temporal and spatial variations in the southern Patagonian batholith; constraints on magmatic arc development, in Harmon, R. S., and Rapela, C. W., eds., Andean magmatism and its tectonic setting: Geological Society of America Special Paper 265, p. 1–12.

Connelly, J. D., and Dallmeyer, R. D., 1993, Polymetamorphic evolution of the western Blue Ridge; evidence from $^{40}Ar/^{39}Ar$ whole rock slate/phyllite and muscovite ages: American Journal of Science, v. 293, p. 322–359.

Dallmeyer, R. D., 1988, Late Paleozoic tectonothermal evolution of the western Blue Ridge, Georgia: Controls on the chronology of terrane accretion and transport in the southern Appalachian orogen: Geological Society of America Bulletin, v. 100, p. 702–713.

Dallmeyer, R. D., 1989, Polymetamorphic evolution of the western Blue Ridge allochthon; evidence from $^{40}Ar/^{39}Ar$ mineral ages: Geological Society of America Abstracts with Programs, v. 21, no. 3, p. 11.

Defant, M. J., and Drummond, M. S., 1990, Derivation of some modern arc magmas by melting of young subducted lithosphere: Nature, v. 347, p. 662–665.

Defant, M. J., and Drummond, M. S., 1993, Mt. St. Helens: Potential example of the partial melting of the subducted lithosphere in a volcanic arc: Geology, v. 21, p. 547–550.

Defant, M. F., Drummond, M. S., Arthur, J. D., and Ragland, P. C., 1988, An example of trondhjemite petrogenesis: The Blakes Ferry pluton, Alabama, U.S.A.: Lithos, v. 21, p. 161–181.

DePaolo, D. J., 1981, Trace element and isotopic effects of combined wallrock assimilation and fractional crystallization: Earth and Planetary Science Letters, v. 53, p. 189–202.

Drummond, M. S., and Defant, M. J., 1990, A model for trondhjemite-tonalite-dacite genesis and crustal growth via slab melting: Archean to modern comparisions: Journal of Geophysical Research, v. 95, p. 21,503–21,521.

Drummond, M. S., Ragland, P. C, and Wesolowski, D. J. 1986, An example of trondhjemite genesis by means of alkali metasomatism: Rockford Granite, Alabama Appalachians: Contributions to Mineralogy and Petrology, v. 93, p. 98–113.

Drummond, M. S., Allison, D. T., and Wesolowski, D. J., 1988, Generaton, diversification, and emplacement of the Rockford granite, Alabama Appalachians: Mineralogic, petrologic, isotopic (C & O), and P-T constraints: Journal of Petrology, v. 29, p. 869–897.

Drummond, M. S., Allison, D. T., and Wesolowski, D. J., 1994, Igneous petrogenesis and tectonic setting of the Elkahatchee Quartz Diorite, Alabama Appalachians: Implications for Penobscotian magmatism in the eastern Blue Ridge: American Journal of Science, v. 294, p. 173–236.

Eckert, J. A., Jr., and Hatcher, R. D., Jr., 1992, Contrasts of prograde, monometamorphic (northwest) and apparently polymetamorphic (southeast) amphibolite-granulite transition to the Wayah granulite core, southwestern North Carolina Blue Ridge; relationships to near-metamophic-peak faults: Geological Society of America Abstracts with Programs, v. 24, no. 2, p. 14.

Eckert, J. A., Jr., Hatcher, R. D., Jr., and Mohr, D. W., 1989, The Wayah granulite facies metamorphic core, southwestern North Carolina: High-grade culmination of Taconic metamorphism in the southern Blue Ridge: Geological Society of America Bulletin, v. 191, p. 1434–1447.

Frost, T. H., and Mahood, G. A., 1987, Field, chemical and physical constraints on mafic-felsic magma interaction in the Lamarck granodiorite, Sierra Nevada, California: Geological Society of America Bulletin, v. 99, p. 272–291.

Gillon, K. A., 1989, The geology of eastern Blue Ridge thrust sheets in the vicinity of Helen, Georgia, *in* Fritz, W. J., Hatcher, R. D., Jr., and Hopson, J. L., eds., Geology of the eastern Blue Ridge of northeast Georgia and the adjacent Carolinas: Georgia Geological Society Guidebook, v. 9, p. 93–110.

Goldberg, S. A., and Dallmeyer, R. D., 1992, Radiometric ages related to the timing of Paleozoic metamorphism in the Blue Ridge of northwestern North Carolina: Geological Society of America Abstracts with Programs, v. 24, no. 7, p. 290.

Green, T. H., 1978, Garnet in silicic liquids and its possible use as a P-T indicator: Contributions to Mineralogy and Petrology, v. 65, p. 59–67.

Halliday, A. N., Davies, G. R., Lee, D.-C., Tommasini, S., Paslick, C. R., Fitton, J. G., and James, D. E., 1992, Lead isotope evidence for young trace element enrichment in the oceanic upper mantle: Nature, v. 359, p. 623–627.

Harrison, T. M., and Watson, E. B., 1984, The behaviour of apatite during crustal anatexis: Equilibrium and kinetic considerations: Geochimica et Cosmochimica Acta, v. 48, p. 1467–1477.

Hatcher, R. D., Jr., 1978, Tectonics of the western Blue Ridge, southern Appalachians: Review and speculation: American Journal of Science, v. 278, p. 276–304.

Hatcher, R. D., Jr., 1989, Tectonic synthesis of the U.S. Appalachians, *in* Hatcher, R. D., Jr., Thomas, W. A., and Viele, G. W., eds., The Appalachian-Ouachita orogen in the United States: Boulder, Colorado, Geological Society of America, The geology of North America, v. F-2, p. 511–535.

Hatcher, R. D., Jr., Miller, C. F., and Lamb, D. D., 1995, Deformation processes related to emplacement of the Rabun granite in the eastern Blue Ridge, Georgia and North Carolina; *in* Driese, S. G., ed., Guidebook for field trip excursions, Southeastern Section, Geological Society of America: Knoxville, University of Tennessee, p. 39–56.

Henderson, P., 1982, Inorganic geochemistry: New York, Pergamon Press, 353 p.

Hildreth, W., and Moorbath, S., 1988, Crustal contributions to arc magmatism in the Andes of central Chile: Contributions to Mineralogy and Petrology, v. 98, p. 455–489.

Hill, M., Morris, J., and Whelan, J., 1981, Hybrid granodiorites intruding the accretionary prism, Kodiak, Shumagin, and Sanak islands, southwest Alaska: Journal of Geophysical Research, v. 86, p. 10569–10590.

Hopson, J. L., 1989, Structure, stratigraphy, and petrogenesis of the Lake Burton mafic-ultramafic complex, *in* Fritz, W. J., Hatcher, R. D., Jr., and Hopson, J. L., eds., Geology of the eastern Blue Ridge of northeast Georgia and the adjacent Carolinas: Georgia Geological Society Guidebook, v. 9, p. 93–110.

Hopson, J. L., Hatcher, R. D., Jr., and Stieve, A. L., 1989, Geology of the eastern Blue Ridge, northeastern Georgia and the adjacent Carolinas, *in* Fritz, W. J., Hatcher, R. D., Jr., and Hopson, J. L, eds., Geology of the eastern Blue Ridge of northeast Georgia and the adjacent Carolinas: Georgia Geological Society Guidebook, v. 9, p. 1–40.

Horton, J. W., Jr., Drake, A. A., Jr., and Rankin, D. W., 1989, Tectonostratigraphic terranes and their Paleozoic boundaries in the central and southern Appalachians, *in* Dallmeyer, R. D., ed., Terranes in the circum-Atlantic Paleozoic orogens: Geological Society of America Special Paper 230, p. 213–245.

Hudson, T., Plafker, G., and Peterman, Z. E., 1979, Paleogene anatexis along the Gulf of Alaska margin: Geology, v. 7, p. 573–577.

Hyndman, D. W., 1981, Controls on source and depth of emplacement of granitic magma: Geology, v. 9, p. 244–249.

Karlstrom, K. E., 1989, Toward a syntectonic paradigm for granites: Eos (Transactions, American Geophysical Union), v. 70, p. 762, 770.

Kay, R. W., 1978, Aleutian magnesian andesites: Melts from subducted Pacific Ocean crust: Journal of Volcanological and Geothothermal Research, v. 4, p. 497–522.

Kay, S. M., and Kay, R. W., 1994, Aleutian magmatism in space and time, *in* Plafker, G., and Berg, H. C., eds., The Geology of Alaska: Boulder, Colorado, Geological Society of America, The geology of North America, v. G-1, p. 687–722.

Kay, S. M., Ramos, V. A., and Marquez, M., 1993, Evidence in Cerro Pampa volcanic rocks for slab melting prior to ridge-trench collision in southern South America: Journal of Geology, v. 101, p. 703–714.

Kelemen, P. B., 1993, Genesis of high Mg andesites and the continental crust: Role of melt/rock reaction in the upper mantle: Eos (Transactions, American Geophysical Union), v. 74, p. 684.

Kish, S. A., 1983, A geochronological study of deformation and metamorphism in the Blue Ridge and Piedmont of the Carolinas [Ph.D. thesis]: Chapel Hill, University of North Carolina, 220 p.

Kish, S. A., 1989, Igneous and metamorphic history of the eastern Blue Ridge, southwestern North Carolina: K-Ar and Rb-Sr studies, *in* Fritz, W. J., Hatcher, R. D., Jr., and Hopson, J. L., eds., Geology of the eastern Blue Ridge of northeast Georgia and the adjacent Carolinas: Georgia Geological Society Guidebook, v. 9, p. 41–55.

Kish, S. A., Merschat, C. E., Mohr, D. W., and Weiner, L. S., 1975, Guide to the geology of the Blue Ridge south of the Great Smoky Mountains: Carolina Geological Society Guidebook, 49 p.

Krogh, T. E., 1973, A low-contamination method for hydrothermal decomposition of zircon and extraction of U and Pb for isotopic age determinations: Geochimica et Cosmochimica Acta, v. 37, p. 485–494.

Martin, H., 1986, Effect of steeper Archean geothermal gradient on geochemistry of subduction-zone magmas: Geology, v. 14, p. 753–756.

Martin, H., 1987, Petrogenesis of Archaean trondhjemites, tonalites, and granodiorites from eastern Finland: major and trace element geochemistry: Journal of Petrology, v. 28, p. 921–953.

Miller, C. F., 1985, Are strongly peraluminous magmas derived from pelitic metasedimentary sources?: Journal of Geology, v. 93, p. 673–689.

Miller, C. F., and Stoddard, E. F., 1981, The role of manganese in the paragenesis of magmatic garnet: an example from the Old Woman-Piute Range, California: Journal of Geology, v. 89, p. 233–246.

Miller, C. F., Stoddard, E. F., Bradfish, L. J., and Dollase, W. A., 1981, Composition of plutonic muscovite: genetic implications: Canadian Mineralogist, v. 19, p. 25–34.

Miller, C. F., Watson, E. B., and Harrison, T. M., 1988, Perspectives on the source, segregation, and transport of granitoid-magmas: Royal Society of Edinburgh Transactions, v. 79, p. 135–156.

Paterson, S. R., 1989, Are syntectonic granites truly syntectonic?: Eos (Transactions, American Geophysical Union), v, 70, p. 763, 770.

Patino Douce, A. E., Humphreys, E. D., and Johnston, A. D., 1990, Anatexis and metamorphism in the tectonically thickened continental crust exemplified by the Sevier hinterland, western North America: Earth and Planetary Science Letters, v. 97, p. 290–315.

Pavlides, L., 1981, The central Virginia volcanic-plutonic belt; an island arc of Cambrian(?) age: United States Geological Survey Professional Paper 1231A, 34 p.

Pavlis, T., Monteverde, D. H., Bowman, J. R., Rubenstone, J. L., and Reason, M. D., 1988, Early Cretaceous near-trench plutonism in southern Alaska: A tonalite-trondhjemite intrusive complex injected during ductile thrusting along the border ranges fault system: Tectonics, v. 7, p. 1179–1199.

Pearce, J. A., Harris, N. B. W., and Tindle, A. G., 1984, Trace element discrimination diagrams for the tectonic interpretation of granitic rocks: Journal of Petrology, v. 25, p. 956–983.

Quinn, M. J., and Hatcher, R. D., Jr., 1990, Structural, stratigraphic and petrologic dissimilarities across the Hayesville fault in western North Carolina: Preliminary report: Geological Society of America Abstracts with Programs, v. 22, no. 4, p. 58.

Quinn, M. J., and Wright, J. E., 1993, Extension of Middle Proterozic (Grenville) basement into the eastern Blue Ridge of southwestern North Carolina: Results from U/Pb geochronology: Geological Society of America Abstracts with Programs, v. 25, no. 6, p. A483.

Rapp, R. P, 1990, Vapor-absent partial melting of amphibolite/eclogite at 8–32 kb: Implications for the origin and growth of the continental crust [Ph.D. thesis]: Troy, New York, Rensselaer Polytechnic Institute, 318 p.

Rapp, R. P, Watson, E. B., and Miller C. F., 1991, Partial melting of amphibolite/eclogite and the origin of Archean trondhjemites and tonalites: Precambrian Research, v. 51, p. 1–25.

Rhodes, J. M., 1983, Homogeneity of lava flows: chemical data for historic Mauna Loa eruptions: Proceedings, 13th Lunar Planetary Science Conference, Part 2: Geophysical Research, v. 88, p. A64.

Rubenstone, J. L., Bowman, J. R., Pavlis, T. L., Reason, M., and Onstott, T. C., 1987, Isotope systematics of a Cretaceous tonalite-trondhjemite complex in southern Alaska: Geological Society of America Abstracts with Programs, v. 19, p. 445.

Rushmer, T., 1991, Partial melting of two amphibolites: contrasting experimental results under fluid-absent conditions: Contributions to Mineralogy and Petrology, v. 107, p. 41–59.

Russell, G. S., Odom, A. L., and Russell, C. W., 1987, Uranium-lead and rubidium-strontium isotopic evidence for the age and origin of granitic rocks in the Northern Alabama Piedmont, *in* Drummond, M. S., and Green, N. L., eds., Granites of Alabama: Tuscaloosa, Geological Survey of Alabama Special Publication, p. 239–249.

Ryerson, F. J., and Watson, E. B., 1987, Rutile saturation in magmas: Implications for Ti-Nb-Ta depletion in island-arc magmas: Earth and Planetary Science Letters, v. 86, p. 225–239.

Sinha, A. K., Hund, E. A., and Hogan, J. P., 1989, Paleozoic accretionary history of the North American plate margin (central and southern Appalachians): Constraints from the age, origin, and distribution of granitic rocks, *in* Hillhouse, J. W., ed., Deep structure and past kinematics of accreted terranes: American Geophysical Union Geophysical Monograph 50, p. 219–238.

Stacey, J. S., and Kramers, J. D., 1975, Approximation of terrestrial lead isotope evolution by a two-stage model: Earth and Planetary Science Letters, v. 26, p. 207–221.

Stern, C. R., Futa, K., and Muehlenbachs, K., 1984, Isotope and trace element data for orogenic andesites from the Austral Andes, *in* Harmon, R. S., and Barreiro, B. A., eds., Andean magmatism: Chemical and isotopic constraints: Cambridge, Massachusetts, Shiva Publishing, p. 31–47.

Sun, S. S., 1980, Lead isotopic study of young volcanic rocks from mid-ocean ridges, ocean islands and island arcs: Royal Society of London Philosophical Transactions, v. A297, p. 409–445.

Sun, S. S., and McDonough, W. F., 1989, Chemical and isotopic systematics of oceanic basalts: Implications for mantle composition and processes, *in* Saunders, A. D., and Norry, M. J., eds., Magmatism in the ocean basins: Geological Society of London Special Publication 42, p. 313–345.

Taylor, H. P., Jr., and Epstein, S., 1962, Relationship between $^{18}O/^{16}O$ ratios in coexisting minerals of igneous and metamorphic rocks; Part 1, Principles and experimental results: Geological Society of America Bulletin, v. 73, p. 461–480.

Vauchez, A. P., and Dallmeyer, R. D., 1989, Polyphase tectonic evolution of the Hayesville Fault, Georgia-North Carolina: Geological Society of America Abstracts with Programs, v. 21, no. 3, p. 63.

Vyhnal, C., McSween, H. Y., Jr., and Speer, J. A., 1991, Hornblende chemistry in southern Appalachian granitoids: Implications for aluminum in hornblende thermobarometry and magmatic epidote stability: American Mineralogist, v. 76, p. 176–188.

Voshage, H., Hofmann, A. W., Mazzuchelli, M., Rivalenti, G., Sinoi, S., Raczek, I., and Demarchi, G., 1990, Isotopic evidence from the Ivrea Zone for a hybrid lower crust formed by magmatic underplating: Nature, v. 347, p. 731–736.

Watson, E. B., and Harrison, T. M., 1983, Zircon saturation revisited: Temperature and composition effects in a variety of crustal magma types: Earth and Planetary Science Letters, v. 64, p. 295–304.

Whitney, J. A., Paris, T. A., Carpenter, R. H., and Hartley, M. E., 1978, Volcanic evolution of the southern slate belt of Georgia and South Carolina: A primitive oceanic island arc: Journal of Geology, v. 86, p. 173–192.

Wilson, M., 1989, Igneous petrogenesis: Boston, Massachussetts, Unwin Hyman, 466 p.

Wolf, M. B., and Wyllie, P. J., 1991, Dehydration-melting of solid amphibolite at 10 kbar: textural development, liquid interconnectivity and applications to the segregation of magmas: Mineralogy and Petrology, v. 44, p. 151–179.

Wolf, M. B., and Wyllie, P. J., 1994, Dehydration-melting of amphibolite at 10 kbar: The effects of temperature and time: Contributions to Mineralogy and Petrology, v. 115, p. 369–383.

Wood, L. F., and Miller, C. F., 1984, Geochemistry and petrogenesis of trondhjemite dikes, Blue Ridge, North Carolina–Georgia: Southeastern Geology, v. 25, p. 13–24.

Yogodzinski, G. M., Kay, R. W., Volynets, O. N., Kay, S. M., and Koloskov, A. V., 1995, Magnesian andesites in the western Aleutian Komandorsky region: Implications for slab melting and processes in the mantle wedge: Geological Society of America Bulletin, v. 107, p. 505–519.

Yurkovich, S. P., and Butkovich, N. J., 1982, Late Paleozoic(?) micro-tonalite intrusives of the North Carolina Blue Ridge: Geological Society of America Abstracts with Programs, v. 14, p. 97–98.

Zartman, R. E., and Haines, S. M., 1988, The plumbotectonic model for Pb isotopic systematics among major crustal reservoirs—A case for bi-directional transport: Geochimica et Cosmochimica Acta, v. 52, p. 1327–1339.

Zen, E-an, 1988, Thermal modelling of stepwise anatexis in a thrust-thickened sicilic crust: Royal Society of Edinburgh Transactions, Earth Science, v. 79, p. 223–235.

Zen, E-An, and Hammarstrom, J. M., 1984, Magmatic epidote and its petrologic significance: Geology, v. 12, p. 515–518.

Manuscript Accepted by the Society July 2, 1996

Geological Society of America
Memoir 191
1997

Tectonic influence on Late Proterozoic Avalonian magmatism: An example from the Greendale complex, Antigonish Highlands, Nova Scotia, Canada

J. Brendan Murphy
Department of Geology, St. Francis Xavier University, P.O. Box 5000, Antigonish, Nova Scotia B2G 2W5, Canada
Andrew J. Hynes
Department of Earth and Planetary Sciences, McGill University, 3450 University, Montreal, Quebec H3A 2A7, Canada
Brian Cousens
Department of Earth Sciences, Carleton University, 1125 Colonel By Drive, Ottawa, Ontario K1S 5B6, Canada

ABSTRACT

The Late Proterozoic tectonothermal history of Avalonia records magmatic activity on the Gondwanan margin prior to its accretion to Laurentia. The Late Proterozoic (ca. 615 Ma) Greendale complex, northern Antigonish Highlands, Nova Scotia, is a localized example of regionally extensive arc-related magmatism that typifies Avalonia in Atlantic Canada. The complex is characterized by intrusive sheets ranging from gabbro to granite, that synkinematically to postkinematically intrude coeval bimodal volcanic rocks and turbidites of the Georgeville Group. Mafic and felsic components of Greendale complex have geochemical characteristics very similar to Georgeville basaltic andesites and rhyolites, respectively, and the Greendale rocks are interpreted as intrusive equivalents of the Georgeville lavas. There is abundant field, geochemical, and isotopic evidence that the compositions of mafic to intermediate Greendale rocks were moderately to extensively affected by mixing and mingling between mafic and felsic magmas and rocks.

Taken together, mafic, intermediate, and felsic compositional variations in the Greendale igneous complex are similar to those of many Late Proterozoic Avalonian complexes, which are commonly regarded as displaying calc-alkalic differentiation trends. However, the Greendale complex has produced similar chemical features by mixing and mingling of mafic and felsic magmas. These characteristics, and their relationships to local structures, may offer an alternative explanation for the apparent calc-alkalic character of Avalonian igneous rocks of this age.

INTRODUCTION

The Late Proterozoic magmatic history of Avalonia is particularly important to Appalachian syntheses because it preserves a Late Proterozoic and early Paleozoic record that is probably exotic to Laurentia (Fig. 1A). Paleogeographic reconstructions (e.g., Bond et al., 1984; Van der Voo, 1988; Murphy and Nance, 1989) imply that Avalonia was situated along the Gondwanan periphery of a supercontinent (known as Vendia) in the Late Proterozoic and early Paleozoic and became attached to Laurentia in the middle Paleozoic (e.g., McKerrow and Scotese, 1990). Recent structural (Keppie, 1989; Currie and Piasecki, 1989; Hibbard, 1994) and isotopic analyses (Dunning et al., 1990; O'Brien et al., 1991; Keppie et al., 1992) suggest that Avalonia was accreted to Laurentia by the latest Ordovician and that this accretion event (generally referred to as the Salinic

Murphy, J. B., Hynes, A. J., and Cousens, B., 1997, Tectonic influence on Late Proterozoic Avalonian magmatism: An example from the Greendale complex, Antigonish Highlands, Nova Scotia, Canada, *in* Sinha, A. K., Whalen, J. B., and Hogan, J. P., eds., The Nature of Magmatism in the Appalachian Orogen: Boulder, Colorado, Geological Society of America Memoir 191.

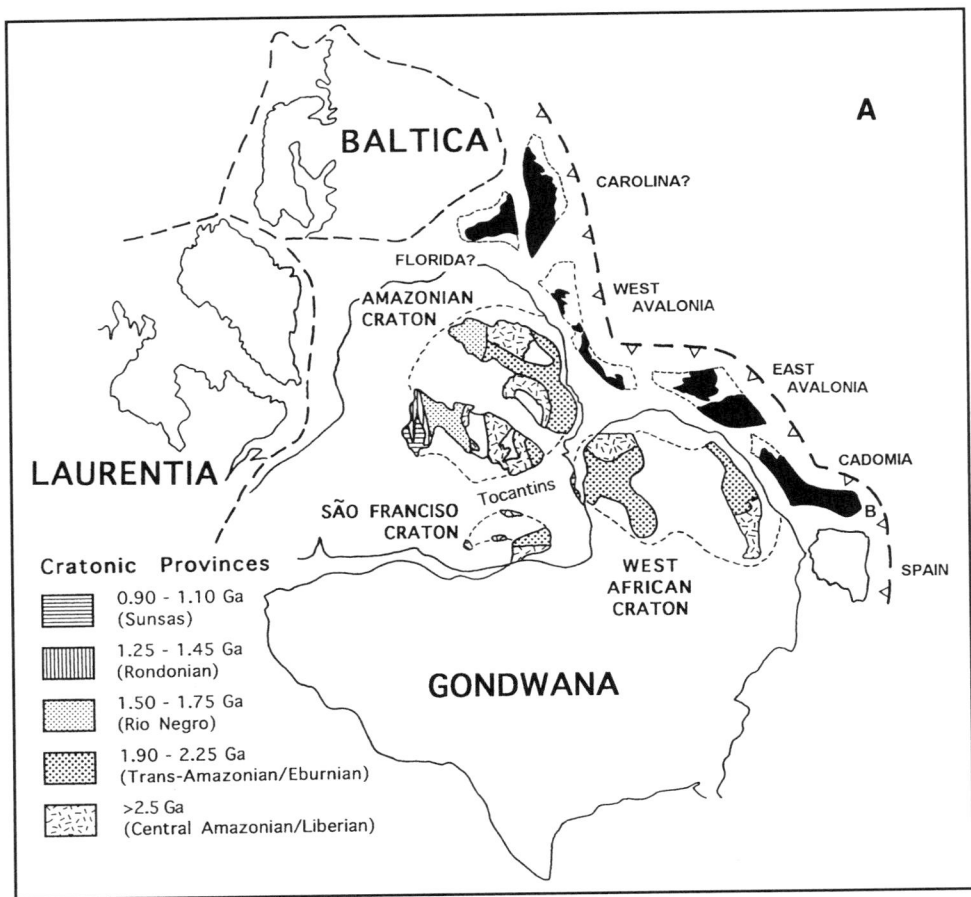

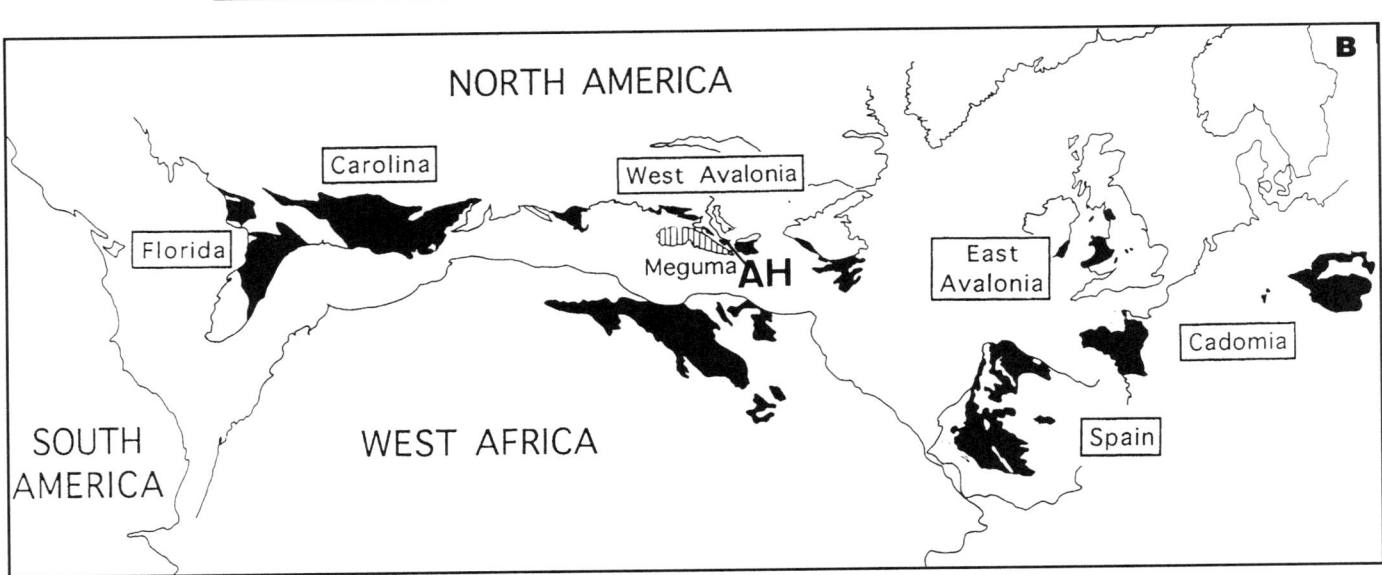

Figure 1. A: Proposed distribution of terranes of the Avalonian-Cadomian orogenic belt (after Nance and Murphy, 1994) on the Late Proterozoic continental reconstruction of Dalziel (1992). Cratonic provinces from Teixeira et al. (1989), Bernasconi (1987), and Rocci et al. (1991). The Antigonish Highlands is in West Avalonia. B: Distribution (black areas) of Late Proterozoic arc-related Peri-Gondwanan terranes that contain early Paleozoic overstep sequences on a predrift reconstruction of the North Atlantic area (after Keppie and Dallmeyer, 1989; Nance and Murphy, 1994). The location of the Antigonish Highlands (AH) in West Avalonia is shown.

orogeny) was one of the most important tectonothermal pulses during the evolution of the Appalachian orogen.

Avalonia has been interpreted a composite terrane (e.g., Keppie, 1993) or a superterrane (Gibbons, 1994) that forms a distinctive tectono-stratigraphic belt and extends discontinuously along much of the southeastern flank of the Appalachian orogen (Fig. 1B). Because Avalonian terrane terminology is controversial, in this chapter we use the term "Avalonia," with no genetic implications for relationships with Gondwana or Laurentia, that is characterized by (1) Late Proterozoic (ca. 630–575 Ma) arc-related tectonothermal activity that produced volcanic and sedimentary rocks and cogenetic intermediate to felsic plutons, (2) latest Proterozoic (ca. 575–550 Ma) intracontinental rift-related bimodal volcanic and continental to shallow-marine rocks overlain by (3) early Paleozoic bimodal volcanic and sedimentary successions that contain Acado-Baltic (Avalonian) fauna (Theokritoff, 1979; Williams, 1979; Keppie, 1985; Barr and White, 1988; Murphy and Nance, 1989). Such usage will facilitate discussion of the tectonic evolution of the region, without getting distracted by terminology.

One of the cornerstones of Avalonian geology is that Late Proterozoic magmatism is related to subduction-related tectonothermal activity (e.g., Barr and White, 1988; Murphy et al., 1990; Keppie and Dostal, 1991) along the Gondwanan margin of a Late Proterozoic supercontinent (Murphy and Nance, 1991) now known as Vendia. This is primarily based on the calc-alkalic differentiation trends exhibited in both volcanic and plutonic complexes. However, there has been little discussion of the role of coeval local tectonic activity in influencing the range of igneous compositions. This chapter presents a study of Late Proterozoic (ca. 618–610 Ma) magmatic activity in the Greendale complex, Antigonish Highlands, Nova Scotia, in which these effects were profound. Spectacular coastal exposures afford an opportunity to examine the processes that influence the range in arc-related magma compositions. Mafic and felsic rocks within the Greendale complex display field and textural evidence of mingling. Chemical evidence suggests that the chemistry of many mafic to intermediate rocks was significantly affected by both mixing and mingling of the mafic and felsic components. The range of compositions evident in the Greendale complex is typical of plutonic rocks in Avalonia and the study offers insights into processes that may have been operative, but were hitherto unidentified, in less-well-exposed regions of Avalonia.

GEOLOGIC SETTING

The Greendale complex occurs in the Antigonish Highlands of northern mainland Nova Scotia. The highlands is one of a number of structurally bound remnants of Avalonia in Atlantic Canada. The highlands are bounded by the Hollow fault to the northwest and the Chedabucto fault to the south, which have been active at various times since the Late Proterozoic (e.g., Keppie, 1983; Keppie and Dostal, 1991). They are underlain predominantly by Late Proterozoic volcanic and sedimentary rocks

of the Georgeville Group and by similar-aged plutonic suites, including the Greendale complex (Murphy et al., 1991). The distribution of the Late Proterozoic rocks is shown in Figure 2. These rocks occur in four fault-bounded blocks: from north to south these are the Georgeville, Maple Ridge, Clydesdale, and Keppoch blocks. The Greendale complex (GC, Fig. 2) occurs between the Hollow and Greendale faults in the northernmost highlands, where it intrudes the Georgeville Group (Murphy et al., 1991). $^{40}Ar/^{39}Ar$ (hornblende) dates from the complex yielded plateau ages of 620 ± 9 Ma and 611 ± 9 Ma (interlaboratory errors), which are interpreted to represent the intrusive age of the complex (Keppie et al., 1990). Taken together, the data constrain the age of intrusion between 620 Ma and 611 Ma.

The Georgeville Group consists of at least 4,000 m of sub-

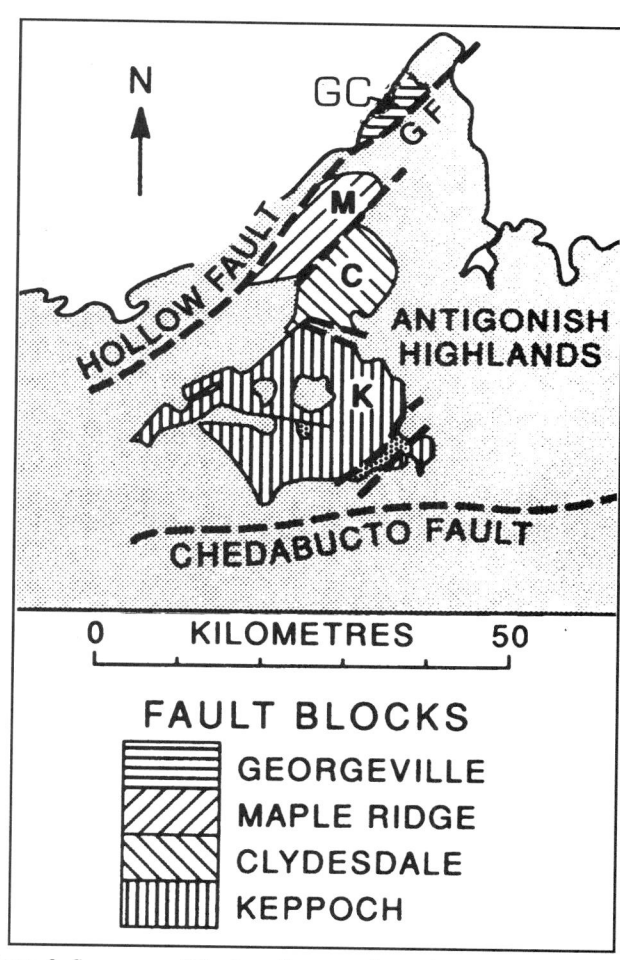

Figure 2. Summary of the Late Proterozoic geology of the Antigonish Highlands (simplified from Murphy et al. 1991). Late Proterozoic rocks (Georgeville Group and coeval plutons) in four fault blocks are shown. From north to south these are the Georgeville, Maple Ridge (M), Clydesdale (C), and Keppoch (K) blocks. Stratigraphic correlations of the Georgeville Group across these blocks are readily made (Murphy and Keppie, 1987). The Greendale complex (GC) occurs on the northern coast between the Hollow fault and the Greendale fault (GF) within the Georgeville block.

aerial to shallow-marine interlayered basalts, basaltic andesites, and felsic volcanic rocks (Keppoch Formation) overlain by thick turbiditic graywackes and mudstones with minor interlayered basalts. The Keppoch volcanic rocks are bimodal with respect to SiO_2 with a gap from about 61 to 67 wt% (on a volatile-free basis), and consist of three chemically distinct contemporaneous magma types: (1) a calc-alkalic basaltic andesite; (2) an intra-continental tholeiitic basalt; and (3) arc-related crustally derived rhyodacite and rhyolite (Murphy et al., 1990). These rocks occur only in the Keppoch block (Fig. 2) in the southernmost highlands. The overlying clastic sedimentary rocks occur in all fault blocks and their stratigraphy can be correlated across the Antigo-nish Highlands. The geochemistry of the volcanic rocks and the stratigraphy in which the subaerial to shallow-marine volcanic rocks give way to marine turbidites are interpreted to reflect the development of an intracontinental rift basin within the volcanic arc (Murphy et al., 1990).

U-Pb (monazite) data from rhyolites near the stratigraphic base of the Georgeville Group in the southern highlands yield a 615 + 5 Ma concordant age (T. E. Krogh, 1992, personal com-mun.). Detrital zircons from turbidites in the stratigraphic middle of group yield a 613 + 5 Ma U-Pb date (single grain, detrital zir-con), which provides a minimum depositional age (Keppie and Krogh, 1990). Taken together, these data constrain the age of deposition of the Georgeville Group to ca. 618–611 Ma and indi-cate a very limited time gap between extrusion of the Keppoch volcanic rocks and intrusion of the Greendale complex.

Structural studies (Murphy et al., 1991) indicate that the Greendale complex was emplaced within a relatively severely deformed portion of the host Georgeville Group. The host rocks to the complex in the northernmost highlands were polyde-formed by large-scale thrusts and recumbent and upright folds (Georgeville block, location in Fig. 2). In contrast, in the south-ern highlands, the style of Late Proterozoic deformation in strati-graphically equivalent rocks is monoclinal and gently dipping (Keppoch block, location in Fig. 2). The heterogeneous style of deformation is attributed to coeval strike-slip motion along major northeast-trending faults (Murphy et al., 1991). The Greendale complex intrudes polydeformed rocks within the zone affected by strike-slip deformation. In contrast, the coeval bimodal vol-canic rocks occur in the southern highlands where they are gen-tly dipping.

Although field relationships indicate that the Greendale com-plex crosscuts the deformation fabrics in the host rock, the above age data indicate a very limited temporal gap between deposition, strike-slip deformation, and intrusion of the Georgeville Group, suggesting that emplacement of the Greendale complex was broadly synchronous with regional strike-slip activity that deformed portions of the Georgeville Group. This interpretation is consistent with field observations within the complex, such as (1) shear zones within the complex that are truncated by intrusive sheets, (2) intrusive sheets that display dextral displacement along fractures and veins that are themselves truncated by intrusive sheets, and (3) shear zones that rotate fresh hornblende and, along

strike, commonly are continuous with felsic veinlets. The orienta-tions of igneous layers within the complex are consistent with penecontemporaneous dextral shear on the bounding Hollow and Greendale faults (Murphy and Hynes, 1990).

DESCRIPTION OF THE GREENDALE COMPLEX

The Greendale complex has a strong magnetic signature (Geological Survey of Canada, 1982) that defines a roughly semicircular or rhomboid shape ~5 km across, and is well exposed along the coastal section. The intrusive rocks are very heterogeneous on both outcrop and hand-specimen scale. They have recognizable mafic and felsic end members consisting pre-dominantly of fine- to coarse-grained hornblende-plagioclase gabbros and diorites, aplitic and pegmatitic felsic rocks, and minor hornblende pegmatites and lamprophyres. All these lith-ologies commonly occur as intrusive sheets that define a steeply dipping layering ranging from 1 cm to 20 m in width. Despite the sheetlike nature of the intrusive phases, there are very few examples of individual sheets cutting the contact of the complex with the Georgeville Group host rocks.

Representative photographs showing typical relationships between the lithologies of the complex are shown in Figure 3. Intrusive sheets consisting of relatively fine grained porphyritic rocks generally have sharp but locally irregular, scalloped contacts that are characterized by a thin zone in which mingling is visible (e.g., Fig. 3A). In many instances, chilling occurs at these contacts (e.g., Fig. 3A). In detail, the intrusive history is complex. Exam-ples of every lithological type being intruded by every other type can be found. For example, fine-grained gabbros contain autoliths of layered porphyritic rock and vice versa (Fig. 3, B and C). Some of the autoliths are dismembered, producing clasts of variable size (Fig. 3C). The smaller clasts are virtually indistiguishable from the matrix of the medium-grained gabbro, and provide evidence of extensive mingling. Felsic veins intrude and are themselves intruded by porphyritic rocks (Fig. 3, D and E), implying that intrusion of felsic magma was coeval with the development of the Greendale complex. Commonly these veins show evidence of both dextral shear (as evidenced by offset of contacts in the mafic host) and dilation (crystals growing inward from walls of the veins) synchronous with intrusion (Fig. 3D). The veins commonly form networks that occur in conjugate sets and terminate in lenses or die out within their mafic porphyritic host, where they form local zones of dioritic hybrid rock (Fig. 3F).

These field relationships indicate that the complex was prob-ably formed by multiple and repeated intrusion of predomantly mafic, but compositionally diverse magma. They also display abundant evidence of mingling between discrete mafic intrusive phases and between mafic and felsic components. For example, irregular contacts between intrusive sheets commonly show evi-dence of assimilation and disintegration producing a local zone of hybrid rock consisting of trains of autoliths and autocrysts, in addi-tion to clouds and ghosts of autolithic material (Fig. 3G). In some instances, texturally homogeneous rock of dioritic composition truncates layering in the porphyritic gabbros, implying that some hybrid rocks existed as liquids (Fig. 3H). If so, mixing may have occurred in subjacent chambers, prior to emplacement into the complex. Irrespective of the relative importance of mingling or mixing, it is clear that the evolution of the complex was profoundly influenced by interaction between coeval mafic and felsic magma.

In general, the complex shows remarkable textural, mineralogical, and lithological similarities to the appinite suite as described by Pitcher and Berger (1972) and Bowes and Mac-Arthur (1976). The most important field characteristics of these rocks, which are typical of appinite suites, are as follows.

1. Amphibole (tschermakitic hornblende) is overwhelmingly the predominant mafic phase. Augite rarely occurs and, where present, is completely enclosed by hornblende.

2. Rapid and irregular textural variations from coarse pegmatitic to relatively fine grained amphibole occur on the scale of an outcrop or a hand specimen.

3. Felsic and mafic magmas are important components of the complex.

COMPARATIVE GEOCHEMISTRY

Detailed accounts of the geochemistry and petrology of the Greendale complex were given in Murphy et al. (1991), and accounts of the Georgeville Group volcanic rocks were given in Murphy et al. (1990). These studies also assessed the effects of postmagmatic alteration on these rocks and concluded that alteration affected the concentrations of typically mobile elements (e.g., Na, K, Rb, Ba, and Sr), but that high-field strength elements (e.g., Ti, Y, Zr, and rare-earth elements [REEs]) were relatively immobile. The discussion that follows assesses the potential genetic relationship between the plutonic and volcanic suites by comparing their geochemical signatures using least mobile elements.

The mineralogy and chemistry of the dominant lithologies of the complex indicate a predominantly mafic to intermediate composition for the Greendale complex (Table 1). In detail, however, the complex is chemically heterogeneous on all scales and a range of compositions from gabbro to granite is present. In order to characterize magma types in the complex, samples were analyzed from fine-grained mafic rocks and adjacent enclaves of felsic composition which have sharp contacts and exhibit little visible evidence of mingling or mixing (Figs. 4A, 5A, 6A). These samples are considered representative of the mafic and felsic compositions of the complex. They are compared with the chemistry of the predominant fine-grained porphyritic rocks of the complex. Some of these porphyritic rocks, although predominantly mafic to intermediate in composition, display visible evidence of variable degrees of interaction between mafic and felsic magma (as shown in Fig. 3, A, B, C, F, G). Others display no obvious visible or geochemical evidence of contamination, and are essentially representative of the mafic intrusive component of the complex. The chemistry of the Greendale complex is also compared with the coeval volcanic host rocks in the Georgeville Group (Keppoch Formation, Figs. 4B, 5B, 6B).

Figures 4 and 5 compare Fe_2O_3/MgO, SiO_2, and Fe_2O_3 contents of the Greendale mafic and felsic components of the complex, the fine-grained porphyries, and the Keppoch lavas. The Greendale mafic rocks (filled squares, Figs. 4A, 5A, 6A) show a pronounced increase in Fe_2O_3/MgO over a limited range of SiO_2, and have moderately high Fe_2O_3, features generally considered typical of tholeiitic mafic suites (e.g., Miyashiro, 1974). Felsic rocks (open squares, Figs. 4A, 5A, 6A), however, display a more gentle increase in Fe_2O_3/MgO relative to SiO_2 and Fe_2O_3, and a positive correlation between TiO_2 and Zr (Fig. 6A). These figures also display the compositional bimodality of the complex, reflecting the contrasting chemistry of the mafic and felsic components of the complex.

The fine-grained porphyritic rocks of the Greendale complex are predominantly mafic to intermediate in composition. Some porphyries compare closely to the mafic rocks, and their chemistry reflects either the mafic component of the complex or mingling between discrete mafic intrusive sheets. Other porphyries (black squares, Figs. 4A, 5A and 6A) are intermediate in composition and have concentrations consistent with the visible evidence of magma mingling and inferred mixing between mafic and felsic compositions. For example, on the Fe_2O_3/MgO versus SiO_2 plot (Fig. 4A), the porphyries with intermediate SiO_2 concentrations have Fe_2O_3/MgO values between that of the mafic and felsic components. The low SiO_2 porphyries have Fe_2O_3/MgO values that are indistinguishable from the mafic component of the complex. As a consequence, the porphyries collectively show a gentle increase in Fe_2O_3/MgO with SiO_2 (Fig. 4A), trends that mimic those generated by typical calc-alkalic differentiation. However, these trends are distinct from those exhibited by the felsic and mafic components, suggesting that intermediate compositions are due to mingling or mixing of the felsic and mafic components rather than crystal fractionation of a more mafic parent.

The volcanic rocks of the Keppoch Formation are bimodal (Figs. 4B, 5B, 6B). The mafic rocks have relatively high Fe_2O_3t concentration (up to 13 wt%), and many samples have Fe_2O_3t, Fe_2O_3t/MgO, SiO_2, TiO_2, and Zr that are similar to the Greendale mafic and porphyritic rocks (Figs. 4, 5, 6). Although the felsic rocks contain wider ranges in Fe_2O_3t/MgO and Zr, there is a considerable degree of overlap with the geochemistry of the Greendale felsic rocks.

The REE distribution of the Greendale mafic and porphyritic rocks (Fig. 7, A and B) displays slight light REE enrichment with La/Sm varying from 1.7 to 4.6 and La/Yb varying from 3.3 to 8.3. These ratios are similar to those of the Keppoch Formation basaltic andesite. The absence of a pronounced Eu anomaly and the generally lower REE when compared with the basaltic andesites (Fig. 7A) are attributed to the enhanced presence of plagioclase in the Greendale rocks and/or more extensive plagioclase fractionation in the Keppoch rocks (Murphy et al., 1990). Mid-ocean ridge basalt (MORB) normalized multielement plots (Fig. 8A) show depletion in high field-strength elements, especially Zr to Yb (inferences from low field-strength elements on the left of the diagram are considered unreliable due

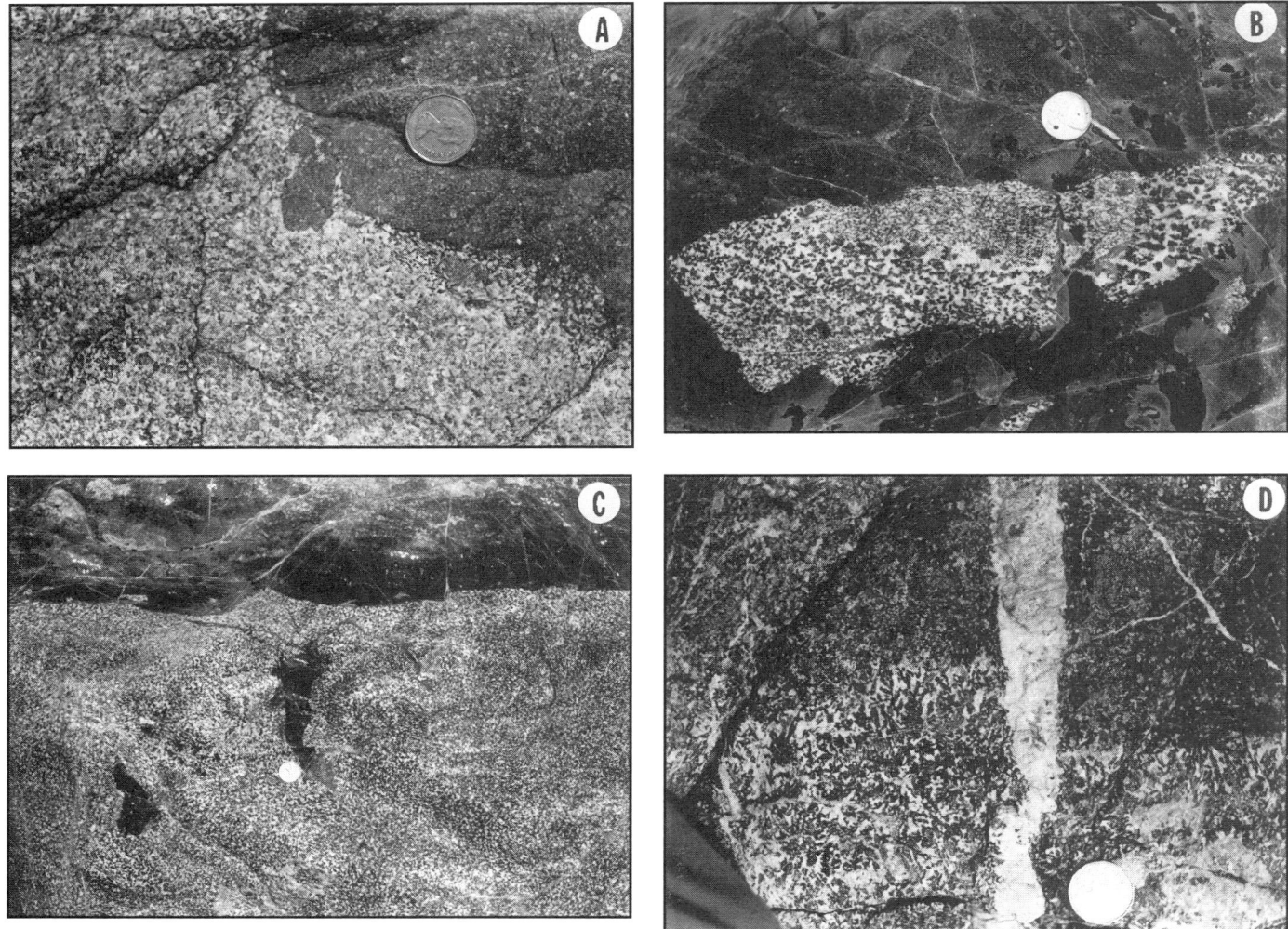

Figure 3 (on this and facing page). Field relationships within the Greendale Complex, with examples illustrating the complex, polycyclic intrusive history and examples of mingling between intrusive phases. A: Intrusion of dark fine-grained mafic phase by medium-grained gabbro. Contact is irregular and scalloped. Mingling along the contact produced rocks of intermediate composition (lower right) consisting of trains of autolith and autocrysts. The fine-grained mafic phase is chilled against the contact. Coin is 27 mm. B: Autoliths of medium-grained layered gabbro within fine-grained gabbro. Coin is 22 mm. C: Autoliths of fine-grained gabbro within medium-grained gabbro. Intrusive contact between these phases is at top of photo. Some of the autoliths are dismembered, producing clasts similar in size to the medium-grained gabbro. Coin is 27 mm. D: Contact between fine-grained equigranular and porphyritic gabbro. Photograph also shows an example of offset of contacts (in a dextral sense) by a felsic vein that intrudes them. The felsic veins also contain crystals aligned perpendicularly to contact, indicating a component of dilation during emplacement. Coin is 27 mm. E: Fine-grained gabbro (top) intruded by felsic veins (top) followed by another phase of fine-grained (bottom) and medium-grained (right) gabbro. Taken together with D, this relationship demonstrates that intrusion of felsic magma, and the dextral shear that commonly accompanied its emplacement, was coeval with the development of the Greendale complex. Coin is 27 mm. F: Example of termination of felsic veins in mafic host that produces a zone of local hybridization. Coin is 27 mm. G: Autolith of mafic rock in felsic host displaying various stages of assimilation and disintegration producing hybrid rock. Coin is 27 mm. H: An example of a dioritic rock (above) of intermediate composition intruding medium-grained layered gabbro. This is an example of intrusive intermediate rocks that suggests that mixing of magmas took place.

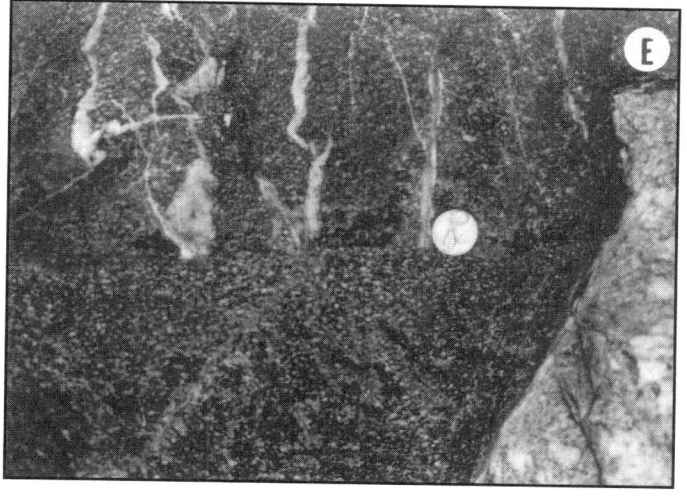

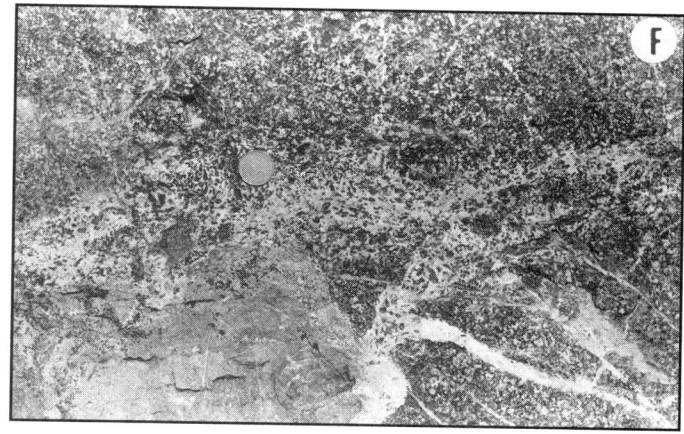

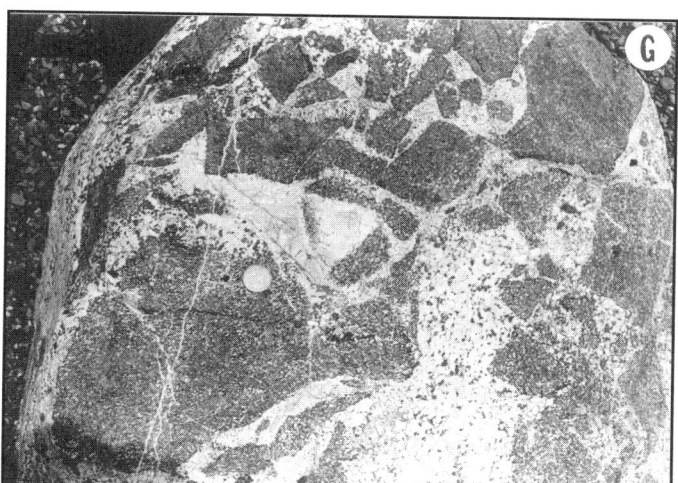

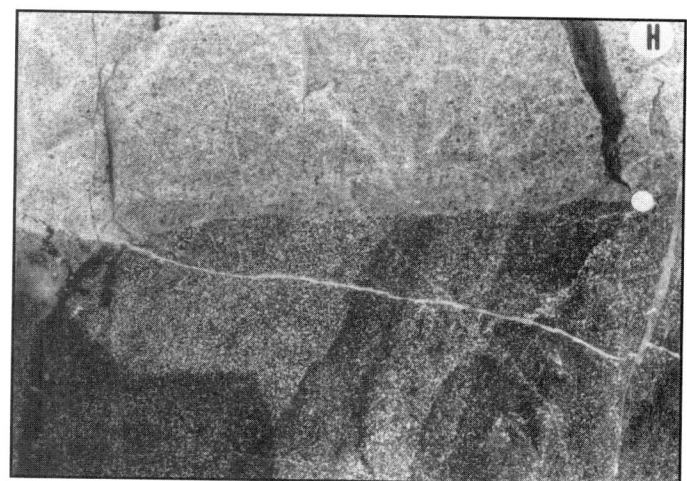

to alteration). Depletion in high field-strength elements is also typical of the basaltic andesites (Fig. 8A). The chemical comparison is strengthened further by some unusual traits both suites share. Although many of the above characteristics are typical of arc-related magmas, concentrations of Fe, Ti, and V in both the Greendale complex and Georgeville Group host rocks are generally slightly higher than normal arc values and both have Ti/V for mafic rocks between 20 and 50, values that are typical of extensional arc settings (Fig. 9; e.g., Shervais, 1982). Although the origin of these unusual traits is unknown, their presence strengthens the geochemical comparison between the two suites.

Multielement plots of the Greendale felsic rocks (normalized to ocean ridge granite, ORG, after Pearce et al., 1984b) show depletion in high field-strength elements such as Ta, Nb, Zr, and Y relative to ocean ridge granitoids in both suites (Fig. 8B), traits that are consistent with the regional arc setting. Inferences from low field-strength elements to the left of this diagram are considered unreliable because of alteration. Chondrite-normalized REE plots show that these rocks are moderately light REE enriched (La/Sm 2.1 to 4.9) with or without a pronounced

europium anomaly (Fig. 7C). In general, the range in REE compositions overlaps significantly with the coeval felsic volcanic rocks in the Georgeville Group (Fig. 7C). However, heavy REE of some Greendale samples are lower than for the Keppoch felsic rocks. The origin of this is unclear. It may be due to the more extensive fractionation of an accessory phase such as zircon, which would lower Sm, gently increase La/Sm, and substantially reduce Lu, and increase Tb/Lu.

Petrogenesis

The geochemical trends exhibited by the felsic rocks of the Greendale complex (e.g., Figs. 4A, 5A, 6A) are distinct from those of the mafic end member, and together with the compositional overlap in magmatophile elements such as Zr and REE (Figs. 4 and 7), indicate that the felsic and mafic magmas are not simply related by liquid-crystal fractionation. These same features have been identified in the volcanic host rocks (see Murphy et al., 1990). Geochemical indicators such as negative Nb and Ti anomalies are consistent with the generation of the Greendale and Keppoch felsic rocks from a crustal source.

TABLE 1. GEOCHEMISTRY OF REPRESENTATIVE SAMPLES OF THE GREENDALE COMPLEX*

Sample	Mafic rocks						Felsic rocks					
	GR-1M	GR-2M	GR-5M	GR-9M	GR-15M	GR-17M	GR-1F	GR-2F	GR-5F	GR-9F	GR-15F	GR-17F
(wt. %)												
SiO_2	48.75	50.65	52.08	48.84	48.23	47.75	67.20	67.28	70.66	66.19	77.71	71.11
Al_2O_3	17.71	17.58	18.54	18.15	17.88	17.78	17.49	18.60	13.01	14.71	12.54	15.56
Fe_2O_3	10.62	10.26	9.95	8.58	11.38	10.46	1.58	0.99	3.44	1.90	0.95	2.15
MgO	4.85	4.88	3.96	6.54	5.97	5.51	0.92	0.63	1.53	1.27	0.59	1.24
CaO	8.85	8.00	6.01	8.63	8.30	9.27	5.24	1.76	4.89	8.63	2.55	3.08
Na_2O	2.78	3.39	3.92	3.02	2.60	2.72	6.36	5.40	3.68	4.24	4.75	5.49
K_2O	0.63	1.09	0.85	1.36	1.45	0.48	0.38	4.99	0.37	0.26	0.38	0.50
TiO_2	1.30	1.25	1.20	1.55	2.08	2.10	0.18	0.08	0.21	0.29	0.07	0.26
MnO	0.25	0.17	0.24	0.15	0.30	0.28	0.04	0.02	0.07	0.04	0.02	0.05
P_2O_5	0.43	0.34	0.40	0.09	0.55	0.48	0.07	0.05	0.08	0.03	0.02	0.05
LOI	3.10	2.60	3.10	2.60	2.00	4.00	1.40	0.80	2.30	3.50	0.70	1.10
Total	99.07	100.21	100.25	99.51	100.74	100.83	100.86	100.6	100.24	101.06	100.28	100.59
(ppm)												
Ba	210	377	319	459	416	147	101	670	120	69	112	194
Rb	11	20	16	33	43	10	5	74	5	<5	<5	10
Sr	330	392	383	371	414	159	251	227	196	234	217	344
Y	29	33	16	25	25	27	9	43	18	7	7	10
Zr	115	105	96	66	58	54	46	107	57	82	52	43
Nb	9	8	7	6	6	9	<5	<5	5	5	<5	5
Th	<10	<10	<10	<10	<10	<10	<10	<10	15	11	<10	10
Pb	<10	<10	<10	11	10	<10	<10	27	11	<10	<10	10
Ga	17	17	18	14	20	19	13	12	13	13	6	11
Zn	725	84	64	68	132	92	31	31	33	24	13	25
Cu	27	83	42	9	10	10	<5	<5	8	42	<5	<5
Ni	<5	11	<5	8	8	<5	<5	17	<5	<5	<5	<5
V	165	206	135	501	276	304	17	5	27	77	10	41
Cr	37	49	37	25	14	14	29	25	37	26	47	35
La	14.07	14.41	12.01	7.8	10.17	10.36	5.92	28.2	21.3	12.39	5.7	11.08
Ce	35.17	37.92	27.97	19.73	27.83	24.69	12.9	61.68	50.82	29.45	11.39	28.29
Nd	20.84	22.74	14.36	14.11	18.23	15.71	5.74	27.7	21.89	10.95	4.93	12.57
Sm	5.49	3.07	3.09	4.46	4.54	4	1.26	8.21	4.69	2.09	0.71	2.47
Eu	1.46	1.51	1.37	1.33	1.45	1.46	0.45	0.52	1.4	0.86	0.62	0.61
Tb	0.81	1.05	0.42	0.83	0.77	0.68	0.24	1.2	0.76	0.33	0.17	0.46
Yb	2.73	3.28	1.46	2.4	2.18	2.2	0.67	5.95	1.65	0.59	0.56	0.94
Lu	0.38	0.46	0.23	0.33	0.33	0.32	0.11	0.94	0.32	0.1	0.09	0.13

Combined melting and fractional crystallization models shown for chondrite-normalized REE abundances (Fig. 10A) for both felsic rocks suites are generally consistent with a crustal anatectic origin. For example, 20% partial melting of lower crust produces profiles that are parallel to each of the felsic suites, with the exception of the Eu anomaly in the rhyolites. Model REE patterns for the 20% partial melt of Figure 10A and residual (or evolved) melts after 50% fractional crystallization of plagioclase and K-feldspar (1:1 ratio) (Fig. 10B) are parallel to the more evolved Greendale compositions and host-rock rhyolites and display a similar Eu anomaly. Differences between the Keppoch and Greendale REE contents in the felsic rocks can be explained in terms of variations in the extent of crystal-liquid fractionation.

REE patterns for the fine-grained porphyritic rocks (Fig. 7B) are also consistent with an origin by mingling or mixing between mafic and felsic magmas, most clearly demon-strated on plots such as La/Sm versus Sm and La/Sm versus Tb/Lu (Fig. 11). On the La/Sm versus Sm plot, both the mafic and felsic rocks show a negative correlation. For a given Sm concentration, the felsic rocks contain higher La/Sm. The porphyritic rocks lie between these two trends and at relatively high Sm, consistent with an origin by contamination of mafic magma with the most evolved (Sm rich) Greendale felsic compositions. The La/Sm versus Tb/Lu plot compares the light REE with the heavy REE. The felsic rocks and mafic rocks of the complex have contrasting trends. The positive felsic trend (note that sample 15F, which contains anomalously low REE, does not lie on the trend) is typical of crustally derived melts and is incompatible with origin by crystal-liquid fractionation of a more mafic parent. The mafic rocks display a negative cor-relation, and the porphyritic rocks occur at the high La/Sm end of the mafic trend, close to the intersection with the felsic trend.

TABLE 1. GEOCHEMISTRY OF REPRESENTATIVE SAMPLES OF THE GREENDALE COMPLEX* (continued - page 2)

Sample	Hybrid rocks				
	E160037	E160079	E160649	E160665	E160685
(wt. %)					
SiO_2	54.9	57.7	59.3	42.7	49.9
Al_2O_3	18.9	20.6	17.6	18.7	21.6
Fe_2O_3	8.9	6.7	7.5	16.7	8.3
MgO	4.3	2.9	4.1	10.3	4.8
CaO	5.9	4.9	6.1	6.5	4.8
Na_2O	3.6	4.7	3.9	2.4	5.9
K_2O	2.8	1.7	1.2	1.5	2.8
TiO_2	1.1	0.9	0.8	2.3	1.5
MnO	0.1	0.1	0.1	0.1	0.1
P_2O_5	0.2	0.2	0.2	0.3	0.2
L.O.I.	0.2	0.4	0.1	0.2	0.4
Total	100.9	100.8	100.9	101.7	100.3
(ppm)					
Ba	n.d.	n.d.	n.d.	n.d.	n.d.
Rb	71	65	57	95	42
Sr	428	461	346	161	179
Y	27	11	67	27	50
Zr	190	349	102	57	175
Nb	<5	<5	<5	<5	<5
Ni	16	7	7	71	23
Cr	92	12	169	148	<5
La	18.8	14.57	19.31	12.42	21.2
Ce	41.73	30.83	45.65	26.06	42.33
Nd	22.26	15.19	26.83	15.84	21.19
Sm	5.69	3.98	6.01	4.04	5.05
Eu	1.34	1.22	1.34	1.8	1.96
Tb	0.82	0.56	0.79	0.58	0.85
Yb	2.96	2.32	3.16	1.81	3.52
Lu	0.42	0.37	0.46	0.28	0.53

*Analytical procedures given in Murphy et al. (1990, 1991). The samples were analyzed for major and selected trace elements by X-ray fluorescence at the Nova Scotia Regional Geochemical Centre at St. Mary's University, Halifax, and at McGill University, Montreal. Rare earth elements (REE) were analyzed by neutron activation at the Nova Scotia Regional Geochemical Centre. The accuracy and precision of analyses are generally more than 10%.

This is consistent with an origin by mingling and/or mixing of the mafic-felsic end members.

ISOTOPIC DATA

In order to test the relationship between the Greendale end-member compositions and coeval host rocks, samples were selected from adjacent mafic and felsic rocks of the Greendale complex (Table 2) for Sm-Nd and Rb-Sr isotopic analyses and were compared to mafic and felsic volcanic host rocks (Fig. 12). In detail, both the mafic and the felsic rocks of the complex exhibit isotopic heterogeneity which is reflected in the wide range in ε_{Nd} and Nd model age (T_{DM}) calculations (after De

Paolo, 1981, 1988) relative to a depleted mantle reservoir. In the mafic rocks, ε_{Nd} ranges from 2.9 to 7.79, T_{DM} from 724 to 1119 Ma and $^{87}Sr/^{86}Sr_i$ from 0.7025 to 0.7044. These values are similar to the range in ε_{Nd} (1.67 to 6.14) and T_{DM} (872 to 1140 Ma) in the host rock and are consistent with the arc-related geochemical signature. In the felsic rocks, $^{87}Sr/^{86}Sr_i$ ranges from 0.7018 to 0.7070, ε_{Nd} ranges from 3.26 to 4.84, and model ages range from 937 to 1057 Ma. Sr isotopes in the felsic host rocks have been affected by alteration associated with subsolidus processes. They cannot be reliably used for comparison purposes and are not discussed further. The Nd isotopic composition of the volcanic host rocks is more homogenous than the felsic component in the Greendale complex with ε_{Nd} ranging from 0.78 to 2.92 and T_{DM} ranging from 955 to 1100 Ma.

Figure 12A presents a plot of ε_{Nd} (t) versus $^{147}Sm/^{144}Nd$ to show the effects of mixing of crustal melts with juvenile basalt magma. Arrows show the trends for pure fractional crystallization and curves indicate assimilation-fractional crystallization (AFC) trajectories using the method of DePaolo (1981). The mafic and felsic components of the Greendale complex plot in distinct fields as arrays oblique to typical fractional crystallization (short arrows) and AFC ("r" curves) trends. This is consistent with the geochemical evidence that the felsic and mafic end-member magmas are not comagmatic and are derived from different sources, each exhibiting a degree of isotopic heterogeneity. The trends are also incompatible with a significant influence of old crust or sedimentary rocks. The felsic rocks of the complex have compositions between that of the felsic host rock (triangles, Fig. 12A) and that of the mafic component of the complex. Given that field evidence suggests that the complex was probably formed by multiple and repeated intrusion of compositionally diverse magma, and the visible evidence of interaction between mafic and felsic components, the felsic signature exhibited in Figure 12A is attributed to injection of small batches of felsic melt with variable assimilation and/or mixing of a mafic component. Thus, it is clear that the compositions of the felsic rocks have also been modified, and that petrogenetic diagrams using Nd-Sm isotopic abundances are more sensitive to these processes than major- and trace-elements diagrams.

The ε_{Nd} of the mafic rocks is generally significantly less than that of depleted mantle ca. 615 Ma. At present, the data cannot effectively distinguish whether this is due to the effects of input of subduction components into the mantle source (fluids, sediments), or to assimilation and/or mixing with felsic components of the complex. The model ages for the both the mafic and felsic rocks of the complex are interpreted to be profoundly influenced by the assimilation and/or mixing of basaltic andesite and felsic magma and source heterogeneities (see Arndt and Goldstein, 1987). However, as indicated by the signature of the felsic volcanic rocks, ultimately the felsic component of the complex is inferred to have been derived from moderately to strongly depleted basement rocks with a mean crustal residence age of ca. 1.0 Ga (Murphy et al., 1996) .

Taken together (Fig. 12B), the range in the Nd isotopic sig-

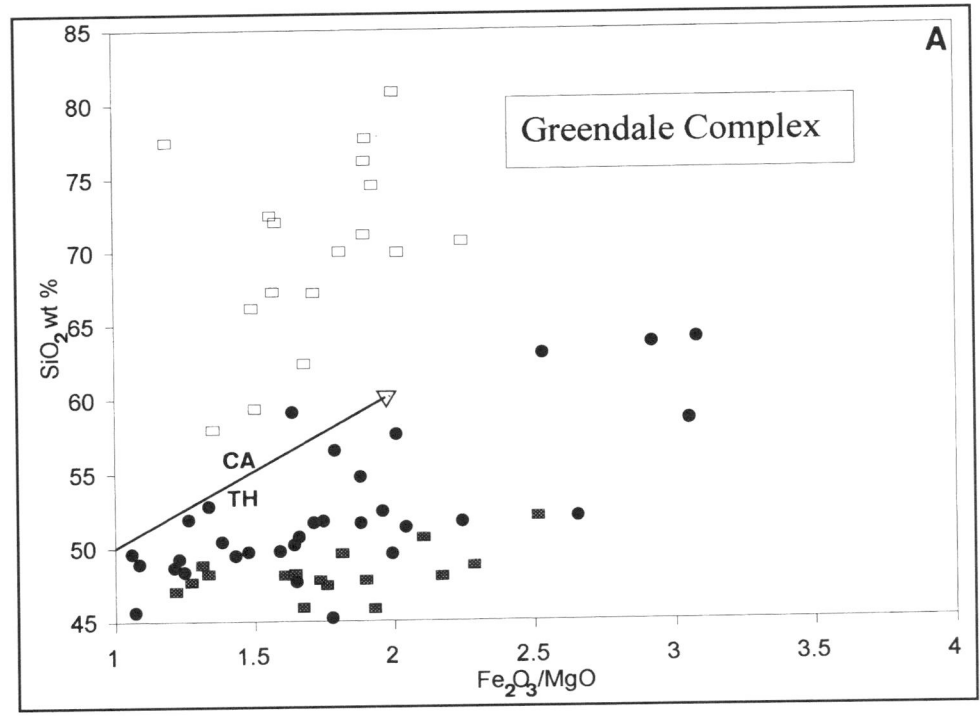

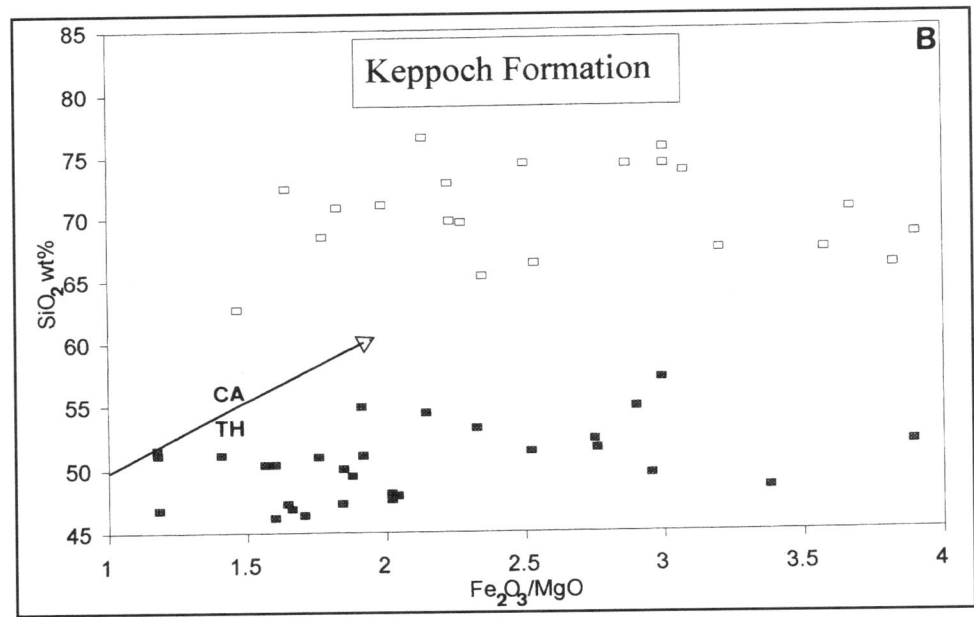

Figure 4. A: SiO$_2$ versus Fe$_2$O$_3$t/MgO for the Greendale complex; mafic rocks are black squares, felsic rocks are white squares, and fine-grained porphyritic rocks are black circles. See text for details of classification. B: SiO$_2$ versus Fe$_2$O$_3$t/MgO for the coeval Keppoch Formation; mafic volcanic rocks are black squares and felsic volcanic rocks are white squares. Dividing slope distinguishes differentiation trends of calc-alkalic (CA) and tholeiitic (TH) mafic suites (after Miyashiro, 1974).

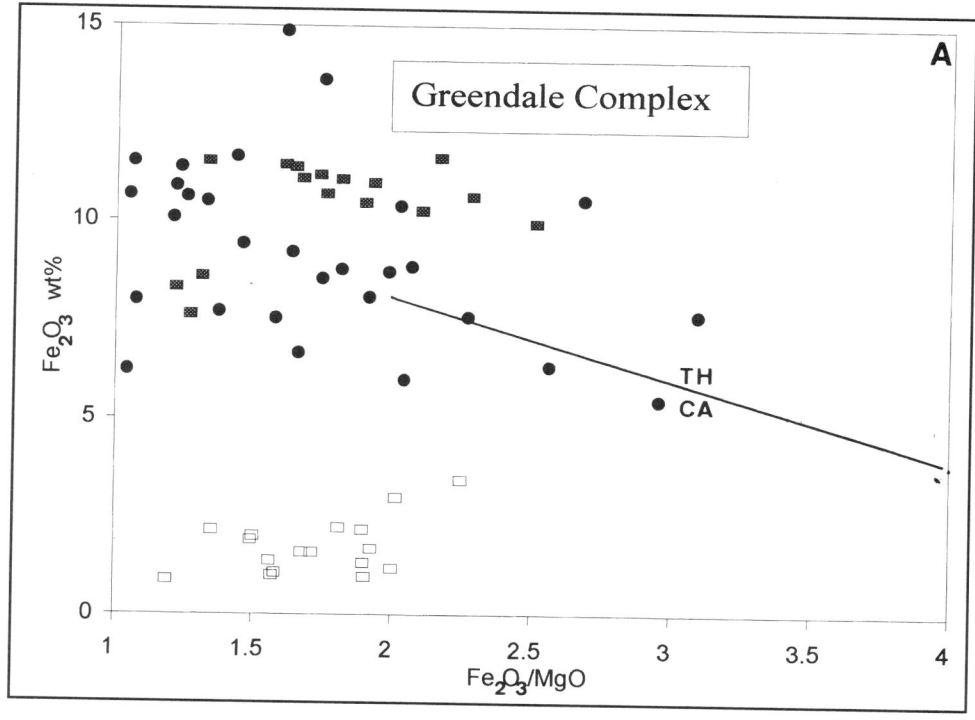

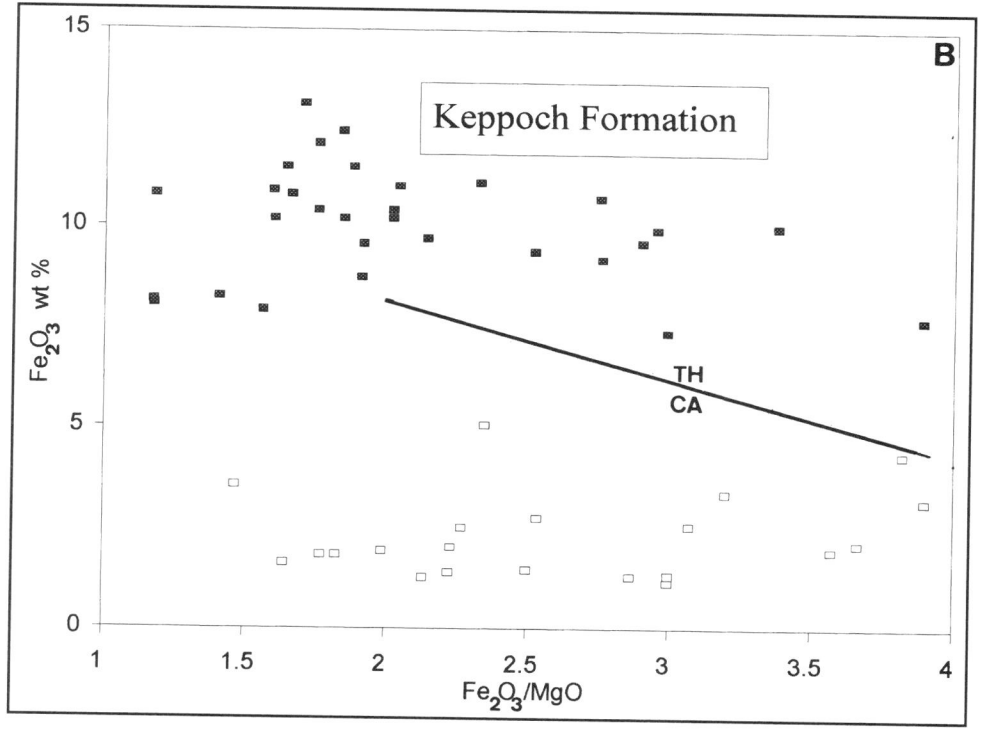

Fig. 5. A: Fe_2O_3t versus Fe_2O_3t/MgO for the Greendale complex; mafic rocks are black squares, felsic rocks are white squares, and fine-grained porphyritic rocks are black circles. See text for details of classification. B: Fe_2O_3t versus Fe_2O_3t/MgO for the coeval Keppoch Formation; mafic volcanic rocks (black squares) and felsic volcanic rocks (white squares). Divide between calc-alkalic (CA) and tholeiitic (TH) mafic suites is after Miyashiro (1974).

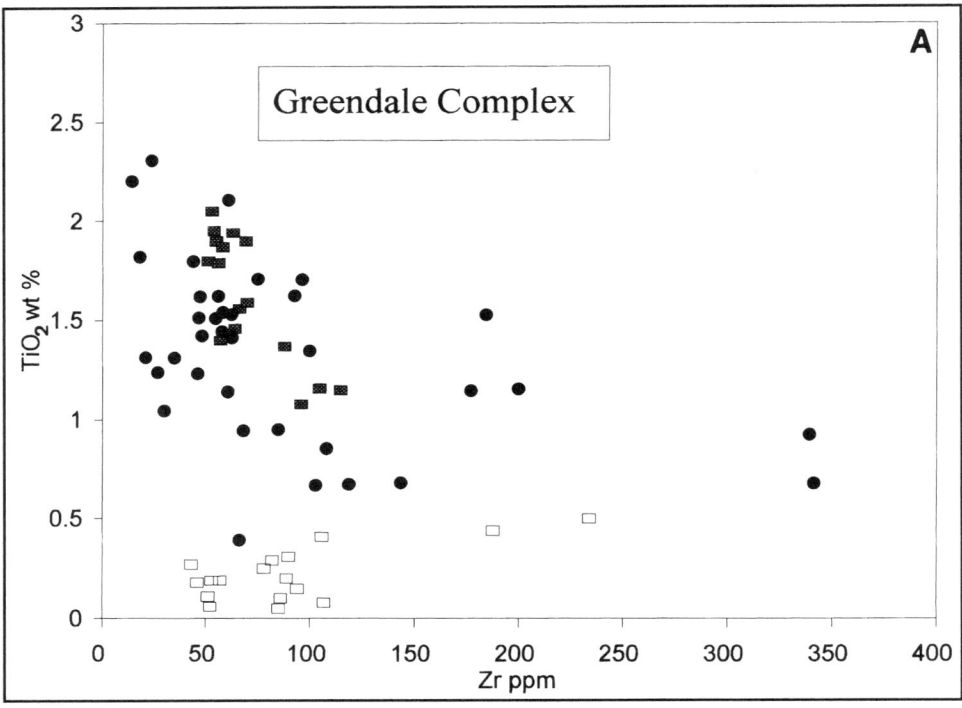

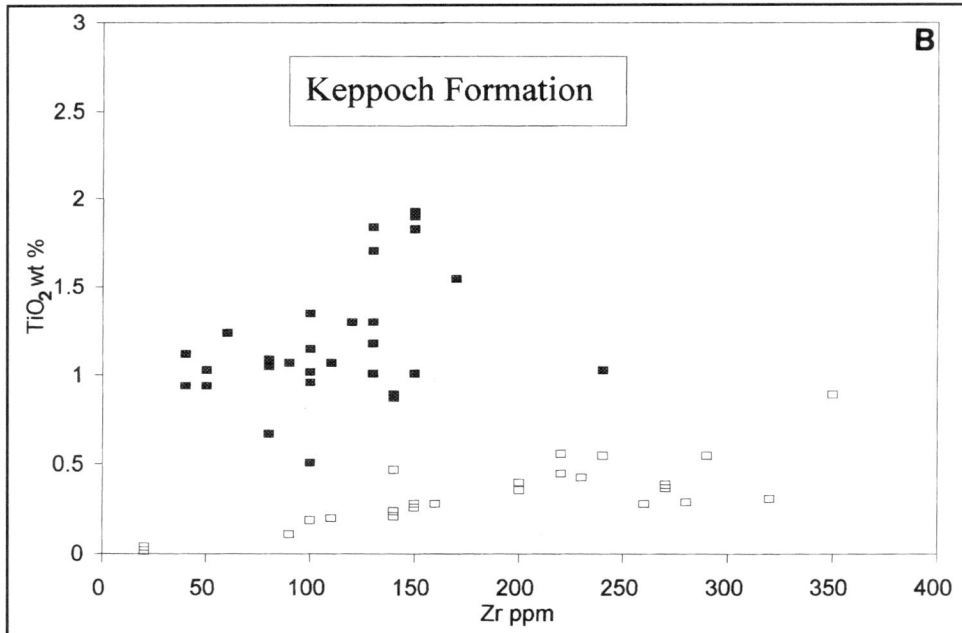

Figure 6. A: TiO$_2$ versus Zr for for the Greendale complex; mafic rocks (black squares), felsic rocks (white squares), and fine-grained porphyritic rocks (black circles). See text for details of classification. B: TiO$_2$ versus Zr for the coeval Keppoch Formation; mafic volcanic rocks (black squares) and felsic volcanic rocks (white squares).

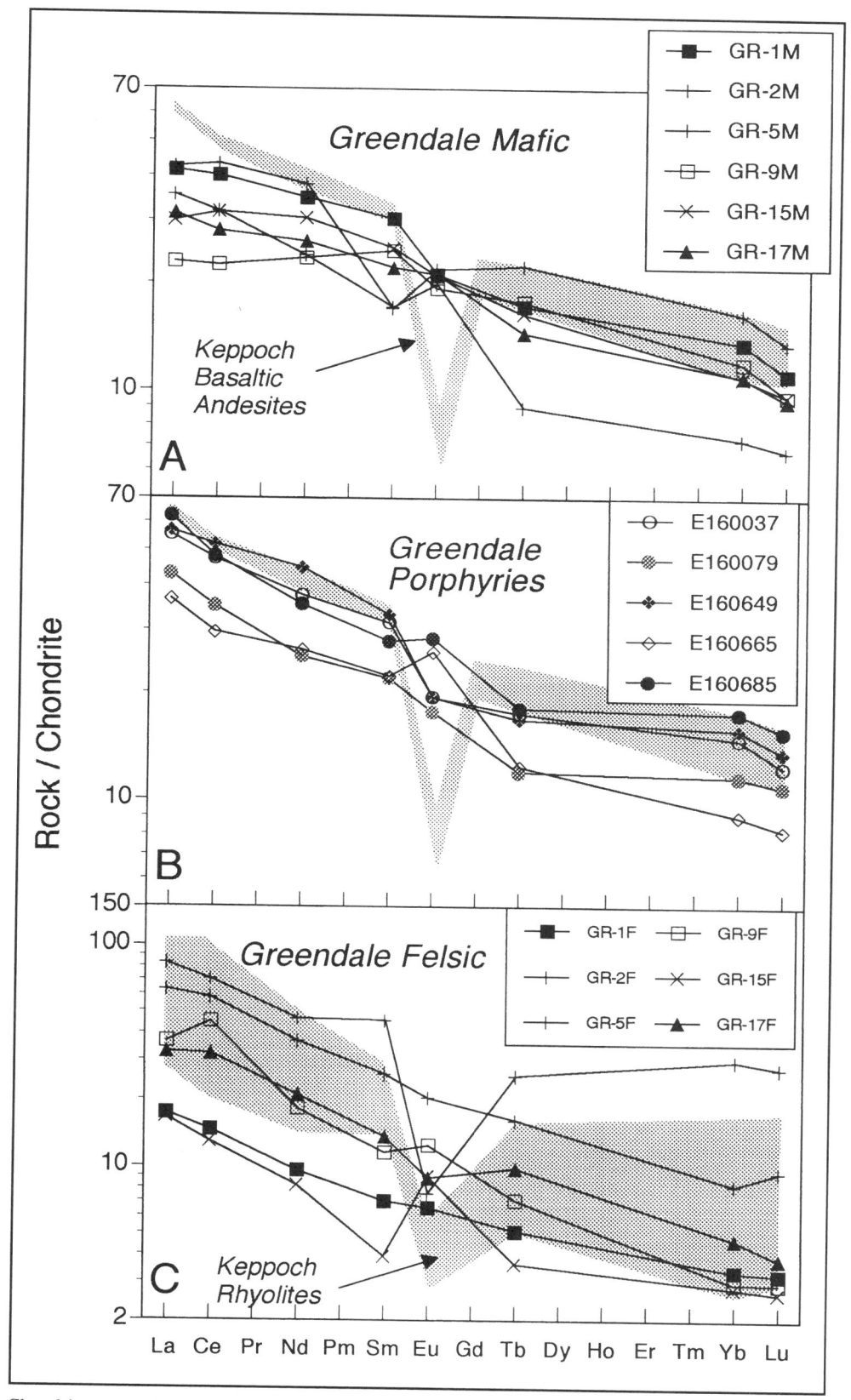

Figure 7. Chondrite-normalized rare earth element (REE) patterns for rocks of the Greendale complex and comparisons with the coeval Keppoch Formation. A: Representative mafic rocks (GR2-M, 5-M, 9-M) and hybrid rocks (73, 649) of the Greendale complex and the range in normalized REE abundances for the Keppoch Formation basaltic andesites (shaded area). B: Porphyritic rocks of the Greendale complex. Keppoch Formation basaltic andesites is shaded area. C: Felsic rocks of the Greendale complex and the range in composition of the Keppoch rhyolites (shaded area).

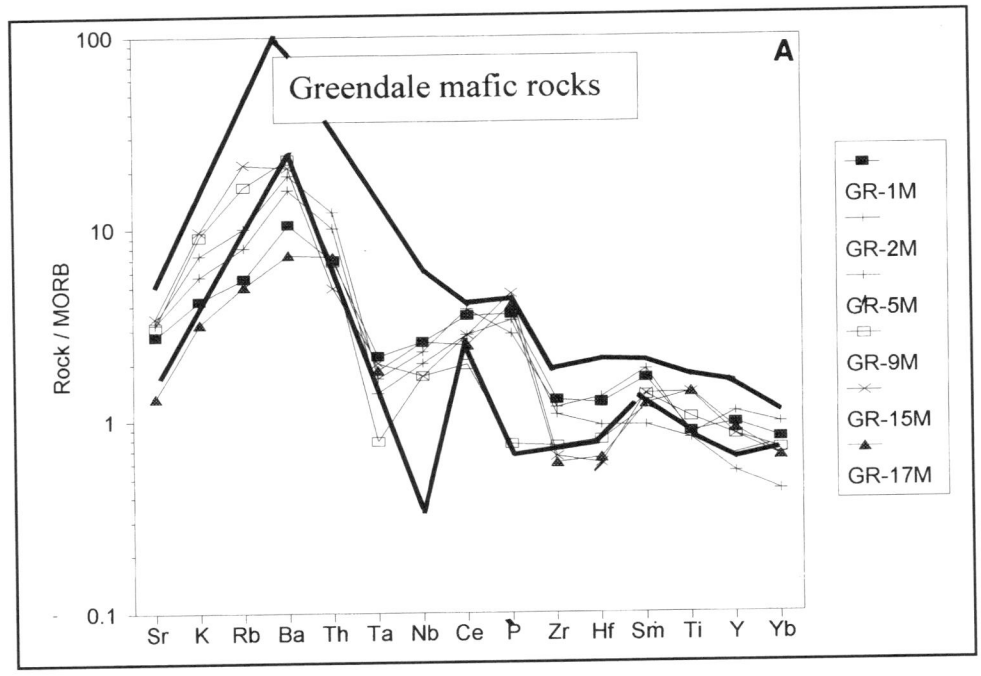

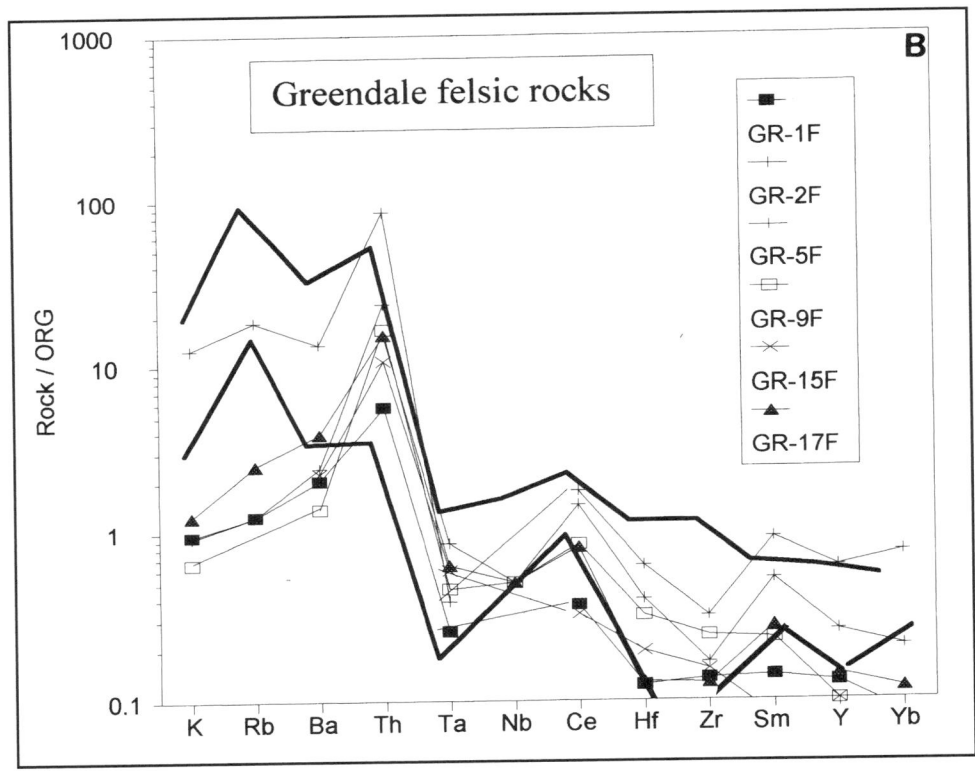

Figure 8. Multielement geochemical characteristics of the Greendale complex. A: Mid-ocean ridge basalt (MORB) normalized mafic rocks of the Greendale complex (values after Pearce et al., 1984b). The thick solid lines show the ranges in composition of the Keppoch Formation basaltic andesites. B: Ocean ridge granite (ORG) normalized plot of the felsic rocks of the Greendale complex (values after Pearce et al., 1984a). The thick solid lines show the range in compositions of the Keppoch Formation felsic volcanic rocks.

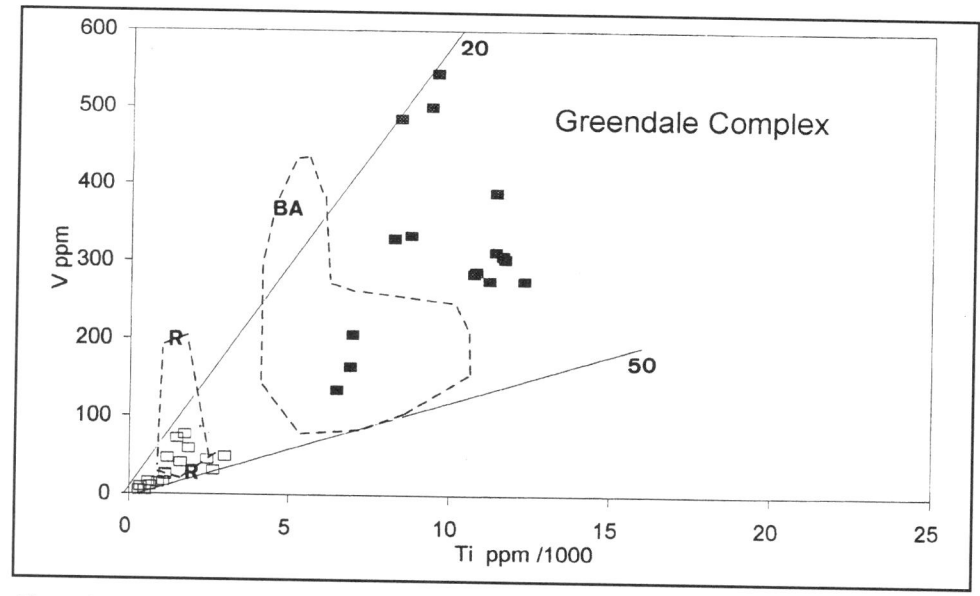

Figure 9. V versus Ti/1000 plot for the mafic (black squares) and felsic (white squares) compositions of the Greendale complex. Diagram modified after Shervais (1982). Compositional ranges of Keppoch Formation basaltic andesites (BA) and rhyolites (R) also shown. Ti/V values between 20 and 50 are typical of extensional arc settings (see text).

nature of the felsic volcanic and intrusive rocks is similar to other areas of Avalonia (e.g., Newfoundland, Fryer et al., 1992; Cape Breton Island, Barr and Hegner, 1992; southern New Brunswick, Currie and Eby, 1990; Whalen et al., 1994). Given that bimodal magmatism is common in Avalonia, the Greendale complex may provide an example of some of the processes responsible for the isotopic heterogeneity of the felsic rocks in these areas.

In conclusion, although it is clear that more isotopic data are required, it is evident that the available data support geochemical evidence that the felsic and mafic end-member magmas are not comagmatic and that interaction between mafic and felsic end-member compositions has occurred. They are also consistent with the interpretation of chemical equivalence between the end members of the complex and the mafic and felsic volcanic host rocks. In addition, because the Greendale isotopic data for felsic rocks span the typical range for Avalonia in Atlantic Canada, they may provide insight into the processes responsible for this range.

SUMMARY AND DISCUSSION

Murphy and Hynes (1990) showed that the Greendale complex was formed by multiple injection of mafic and felsic magmas from subjacent chambers into dilational and conjugate shear fractures, the orientation of which was consistent with the strike-slip setting of the complex. The complex, which displays both field and chemical evidence for extensive interaction between mafic and felsic end members, was emplaced into a fault block in the northern highlands which was undergoing ca. 615 Ma heterogeneous polyphase deformation associated with the strike-slip

activity. This local structural setting facilitated magma interaction by focusing magmas of diverse compositions into zones of local extension within the strike-slip zone. In contrast, in the southern Antigonish Highlands, coeval bimodal mafic and felsic volcanic host rocks are interlayered, and there is relatively limited evidence of mixing between them. These volcanic rocks were emplaced in a structurally homogenous environment; the volcanic rocks are monoclinally dipping and there is no evidence for widespread heterogeneous strain. This suggests that the southern highlands behaved as a coherent rigid block during ca. 615 Ma tectonothermal events.

The petrological evolution of the Greendale complex was profoundly influenced by this tectonic setting. Although the geochemical data cannot distinguish between compositions generated by mingling from those generated by mixing, they indicate clearly that the chemistry of the predominantly mafic fine-grained porphyritic rocks was extensively modified by interaction with coeval felsic magma, and that this interaction produced compositional ranges that mimic calc-alkalic magmatic trends. The mechanism of emplacement, that of multiple injection along fracture systems within a strike-slip setting, may have facilitated interaction between mafic and felsic components of the complex.

It is generally held that extensive Late Proterozoic arc-related tectonothermal activity in Avalonia occurred from ca. 630–570 Ma. Collectively, the Greendale complex and coeval volcanic rocks of the Georgeville Group represent a localized, relatively short lived period of that regionally extensive magmatic event. The presence in the southern highlands of coeval volcanic rocks with similar geochemical characteristics to the

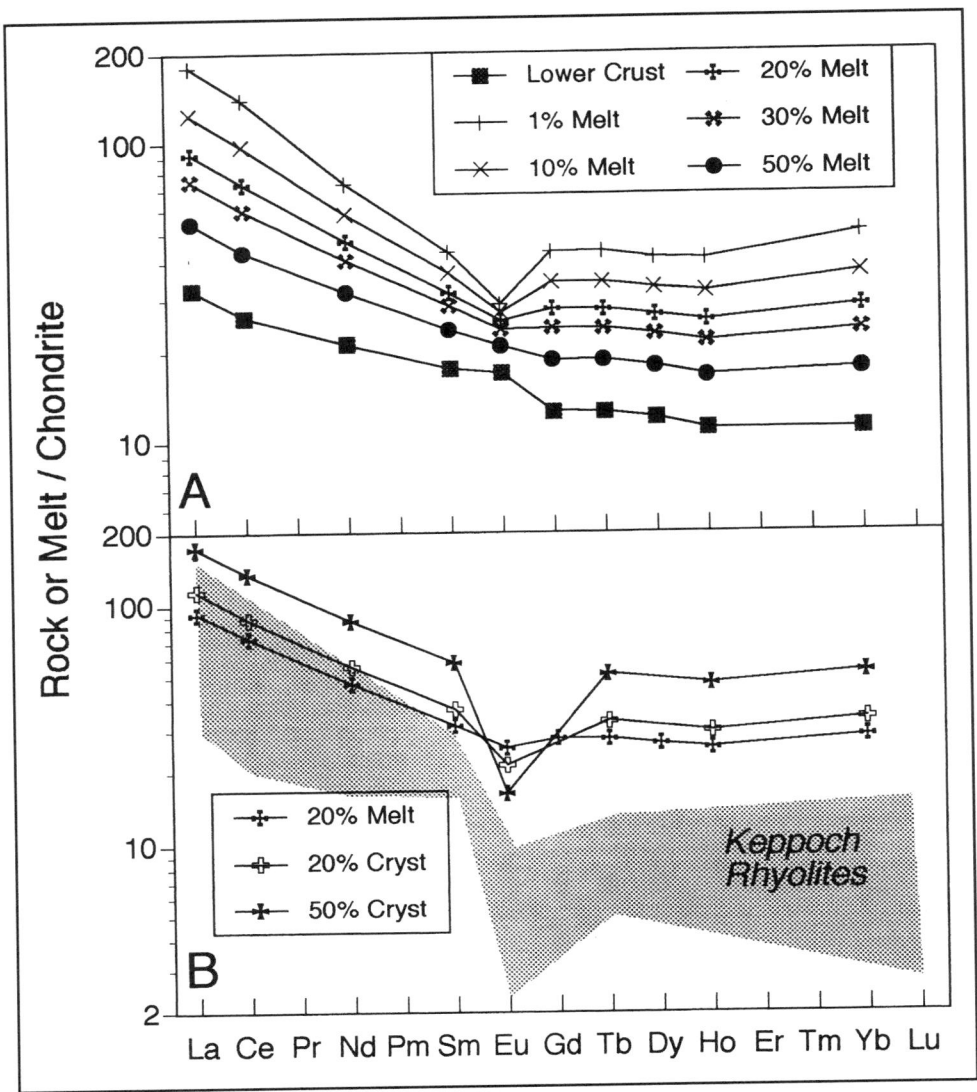

Figure 10. Melting and fractional crystallization model for the generation of chondrite-normalized rare-earth element (REE) patterns for the felsic rocks of the Greendale complex and Keppoch Formation of the Georgeville Group. A: REE patterns in partial melts (1%, 10%, 20%) of average lower crustal (amphibolite facies) composition with an REE content of Taylor and McLennan (1985). Mineral proportions of the source and melting proportions are modified from Stern and Gottfried (1986) and Cleverly et al., (1986). Phases and their values for source and melting proportions, respectively, are amphibole 0.4 and 0.0, plagioclase 0.5 and 0.5, K-feldspar 0.5 and 0.25, and quartz 0.05 and 0.25. B: Calculated REE patterns produced by fractional crystallization of feldspar (20% and 50%, plagioclase: K-feldspar = 1:1) from the 20% partial melt. The field for the Keppoch rhyolites (single hatched) is shown for comparison. The fractional crystallization equation is from Arth (1976) and the partition coefficients are from Pearce and Norry (1979); Arth (1976); Irving and Frey (1984); Baxter et al. (1985).

mafic and felsic components of the complex is strong evidence that the Greendale magmas tapped were similar in composition and genetically related to the basaltic andesites and felsic volcanic rocks of host rocks. Although it is unknown whether the Keppoch and Greendale rocks were directly linked by a common magma chamber or chambers, it is clear that they are both related to the same tectonomagmatic regime and that the respective mafic and felsic rocks were derived from essentially similar sources beneath the Antigonish Highlands.

Unlike the Greendale complex, the Keppoch mafic rocks do not preserve visible evidence of interaction with coeval felsic magma. However, similar geochemical features also occur,

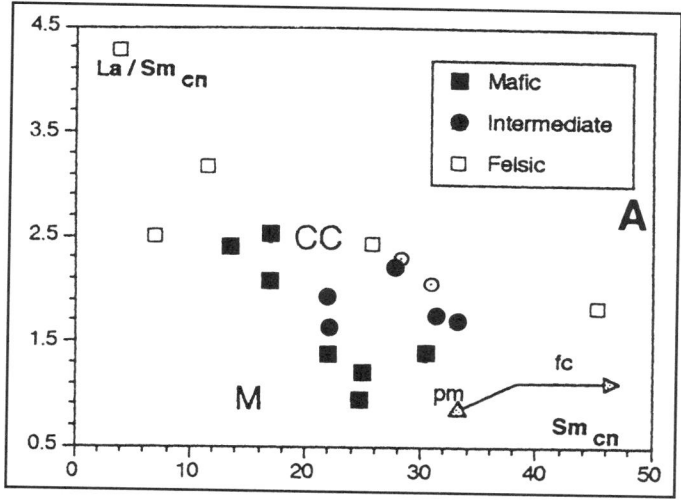
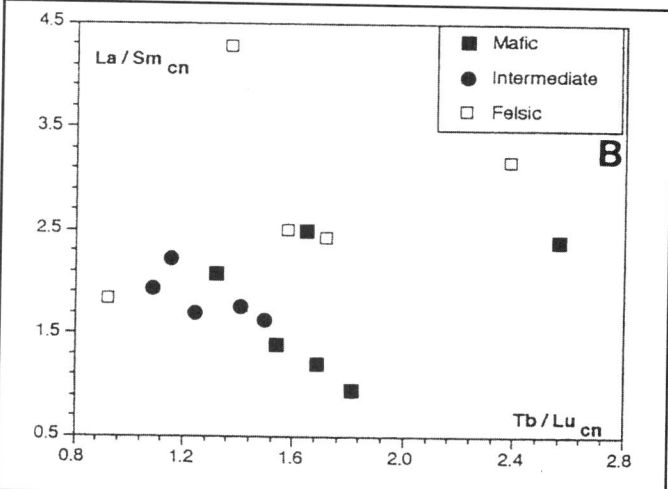

Figure 11. Chondrite-normalized rare-earth element (REE) abundances for the rocks of the Greendale complex. A: La/Sm versus Sm, and (B) La/Sm versus Tb/Lu. Average composition for mantle (M) after Sun and McDonough (1990), for the continental crust (CC) after Hofmann (1988). fc = fractional crystallization; pm = partial melting; cn = chondrite normalized.

TABLE 2. Rb-Sr AND Nd-Sm ISOTOPIC DATA FROM THE GREENDALE COMPLEX, ANTIGONISH HIGHLANDS, NOVA SCOTIA*

Sample	Rb	Sr	$^{87}Sr/^{86}Sr$	Sm	Nd	$^{147}Sm/^{144}Nd$	$^{143}Nd/^{144}Nd$	ε_{Nd}	T_{chur}	T_{DM}
GR-1F	5	251	0.7044	0.92	4.24	0.12176	0.512550 ± 10	4.17	179.7	937
GR-1M	11	330	0.7034	4.71	25.52	0.11002	0.512688 ± 4	7.79	-99.3	724
GR-2F	74	217	0.7070	5.56	21.61	0.15217	0.512626 ± 5	3.26	41.2	1094
GR-2M	20	392	0.7036	5.25	22.38	0.1403	0.512698 ± 5	5.6	-163.1	894
GR-5F	5	196	0.7052	3.22	14.46	0.13192	0.512594 ± 4	4.06	123.4	971
GR-5M	16	383	0.7044	2.79	12.55	0.13295	0.512613 ± 12	4.52	60.1	944
GR-9F	3	234	0.7042	1.68	9.20	0.10803	0.512461 ± 6	4.84	305.3	942
GR-9M	33	371	0.7034	4.10	13.98	0.17456	0.512797 ± 5	3.52	-1107.4	1075
GR-15F	4	217	0.7047	0.56	2.77	0.12018	0.512430 ± 5	1.95	415.7	1057
GR-15M	43	414	0.7032	4.13	16.38	0.15083	0.512695 ± 5	4.72	-190.6	984
GR-17F	10	159	0.7042	3.64	13.94	0.13002	0.512540 ± 8	1.59	-335.7	1214
GR-17M	10	344	0.7050	3.10	14.23	0.15216	0.512608 ± 6	4.65	69.7	928
E16 69M	34	501	0.7025	5.26	20.54	0.152059	0.512730 ± 6	5.3	-316.2	946
E16 660F	58	266	0.7033	2.24	13.51	0.09866	0.512438 ± 5	3.8	311.9	909
E16 661F	52	325	0.7018	2.29	14.14	0.09649	0.512480 ± 5	4.79	241.2	858
E16 192M	22	418	0.7041	5.89	22.61	0.153443	0.512715 ± 5	4.9	-273.1	980

*Chemical separations and isotopic analyses were determined at the Atlantic Universities Regional Isotopic Facility, Memorial University of Newfoundland. Nd and Sm were measured by isotope dilution. The $^{143}Nd/^{144}Nd$ ratios were measured by thermal ionization mass spectrometry, after chemical separation of Nd from Sm and other REE by ion-exchange chemistry. La Jolla Nd standard gave an average value of 0.511862 ± 0.000016. ε_{Nd} values are relative to $^{143}Nd/^{144}Nd = 0.512638$ and $^{147}Sm/^{144}Nd = o.196593$ for present day CHUR (Jacobsen and Wasserburg, 1980) and lambda $^{147}Sm = 6.54 \times 10^{-12}$/year. T_{DM} are calculated using the model of DePaolo (1981, 1988).

albeit in a more limited manner (Figs. 4B, 5B, 6B). The similarity between the geochemistry of the porphyritic rocks and the Keppoch basaltic andesites suggests that their chemistry may also have been influenced by mixing with a felsic component prior to eruption. If so, the calc-alkalic signature of these rocks may also be related to mixing. The available Nd isotopic data show a wide range in composition and may offer insight

into the origin of similar features in other Avalonian areas in Atlantic Canada.

In general, strike-slip settings, such as those in the late Precambrian of the Antigonish Highlands, where faulting accompanies the emplacement of magma of diverse compositions, may facilitate magma mixing and mingling. In the Greendale complex, it is likely that the apparent calc-alkalic trends of the por-

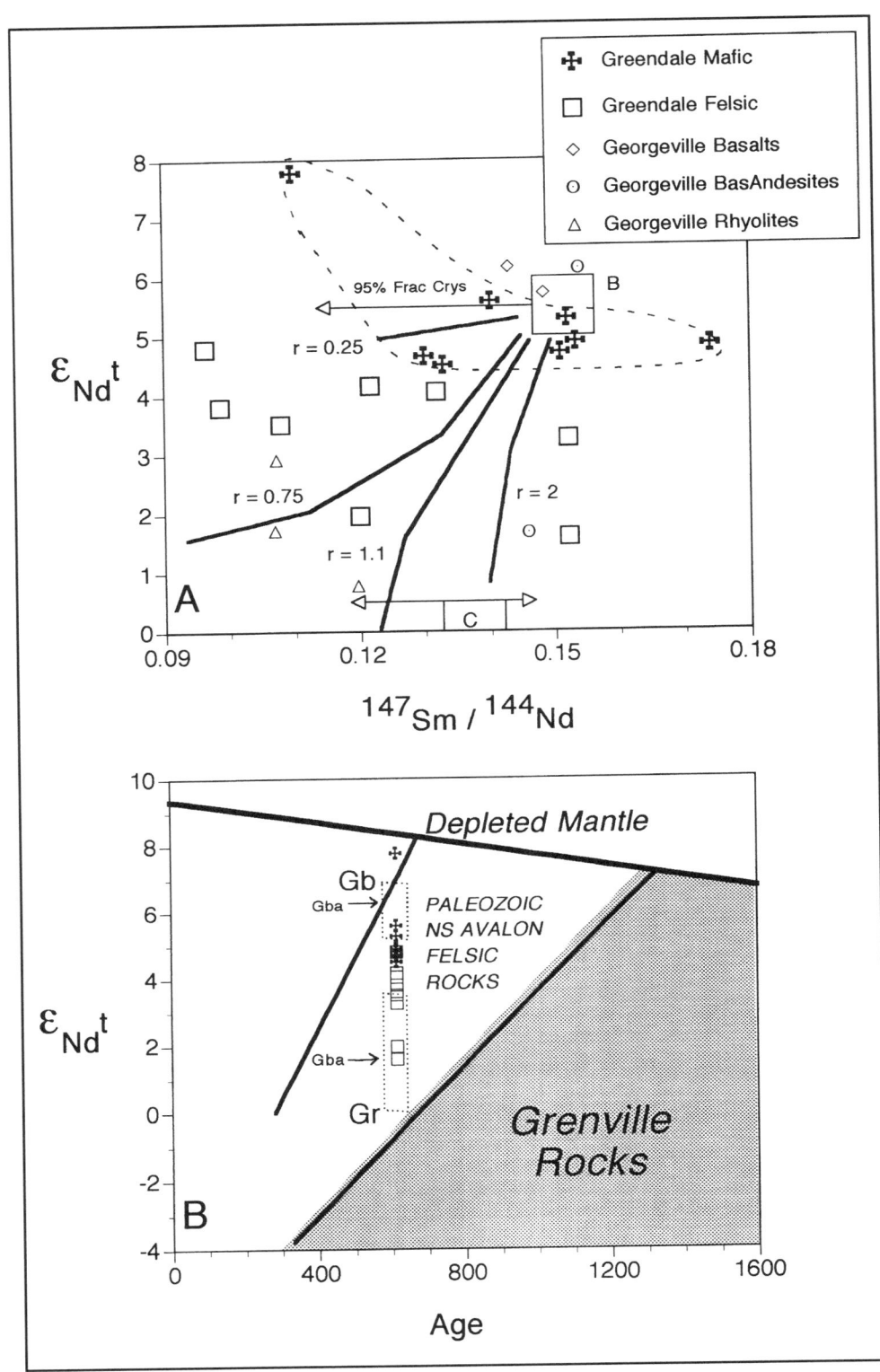

Figure 12. A: $^{147}Sm/^{144}Nd$ for Greendale complex mafic and felsic rocks compared with the volcanic host rocks of the Georgeville Group Keppoch Formation. Curves indicate assimilation-fractional crystallization (AFC; DePaolo, 1981) trends for crust (C) assimilated by basalt magma (B). Values of r (mass assimilated/mass crystallized) indicated adjacent to curves. For curves with r >1, curves extend to values of F (mass magma/mass magma initial) ~4, whereas for curves where r <1, curves end at F ~0.1. Arrows indicate trends for pure fractional crystallization: long arrow shows effect of hornblende, clinopyroxene, apatite, and olivine, short arrow (see C) is for potassium feldspar fractionation. B: Initial ε_{Nd} values plotted against age for the mafic and felsic rocks of the Greendale complex. Solid line outlines the envelope for Nd isotopic composition for Avalonian rocks in mainland Nova Scotia and rectangles labeled Gbas and Grhy show the range in ε_{Nd} of the coeval mafic and felsic volcanic rocks (Murphy et al., 1996). The field for Grenville rocks is compiled from the data of Dickin and McNutt (1989); Dickin et al. (1990); Marcantonio et al. (1990); Daly and McLelland (1991); Patchett and Ruiz (1989).

phyritic rocks were induced by mixing and/or mingling between mafic and felsic components.

The Late Proterozoic geology of the Antigonish Highlands is typical of many areas of Avalonia, and it is conceivable that the processes described here are more widespread than is currently envisaged. If so, the local versus regional influences on compositions of Late Proterozoic magmatism may need to be reevaluated. The geochemical evolution of the Greendale complex raises questions concerning the petrological interpretation, and the tectonic significance of the "calc-alkalic" affinity of other less-well-exposed Avalonian plutonic bodies.

ACKNOWLEDGMENTS

Supported by Natural Sciences and Engineering Research Council (N.S.E.R.C., Canada) research grants, successive Canada–Nova Scotia Mineral Development Agreements and St. Francis Xavier University Council for Research. We thank Ken Currie, Duncan Keppie, and Jarda Dostal for discussions, and John Winchester, Joe Whalen, and an anonymous reviewer for their constructive criticisms.

REFERENCES CITED

Arndt, N. T., and Goldstein, S. L., 1987, Use and abuse of crust formation ages: Geology, v. 15, p. 893–895.
Arth, J., 1976, Behavior of trace elements during magmatic processes and their applications: U.S. Geological Survey Journal of Research, v. 4, p. 41–47.
Barr, S. M., and Hegner, E., 1992, Nd isotopic compositions of felsic igneous rocks in Cape Breton Island, Nova Scotia: Canadian Journal of Earth Sciences, v. 29, p. 650–657.
Barr, S. M., and White, C. E., 1988, Petrochemistry of contrasting Late Precambrian volcanic and plutonic associations, Caledonian Highlands, southern New Brunswick: Maritime Sediments and Atlantic Geology, v. 24, p. 353–372.
Baxter, A. N., Upton, B. G. J., and White, W. M., 1985, Petrology and geochemistry of Rodrigues Island, Indian Ocean: Contributions to Mineralogy and Petrology, v. 89, p. 90–101.
Bernasconi, A., 1987, The major Precambrian terranes of eastern South America: A study of their regional and chronological evolution: Precambrian Research, v. 37, p. 107–124.
Bond, G. C., Nickerson, P. A., and Kominz, M. A., 1984, Breakup of a of supercontinent between 625 Ma and 555 Ma: New evidence and implications for continental histories: Earth and Planetary Science Letters, v. 70, p. 325–345.
Bowes, D. R., and MacArthur, A. C., 1976, Nature and genesis of the appinite suite: Krystalinikum, v. 12, p. 31–46.
Cleverly, R. W., Betton, P. J., and Bristow, J. W., 1986, Geochemistry and petrogenesis of the Lebombo rhyolites, in Erlank, A. J., ed., Petrogenesis of the volcanic rocks of the Karoo Province: Geological Society of South Africa Special Publication 13, p. 171–194.
Currie, K. L., and Eby, G. N., 1990, Geology and geochemistry of the late Precambrian Coldbrook Group near Saint John, New Brunswick: Canadian Journal of Earth Sciences, v. 27, p. 1418–1430.
Currie, K. L., and Piasecki, M. A. J., 1989, Kinematic model for southwestern Newfoundland based on Silurian sinistral shearing: Geology, v. 17, p. 938–941.
Daly, J. S., and McLelland, J. M., 1991, Juvenile Middle Proterozoic crust in the Adirondack Highlands, Grenville Province, northeastern North America: Geology, v. 19, p. 119–122.

Dalziel, I., 1992, On the organization of American plates in the Late Proterozoic and the breakout of Laurentia: GSA Today, v. 2, p. 238–241.
DePaolo, D. J., 1981, Neodymium isotopes in the Colorado Front Range and crust-mantle evolution in the Proterozoic: Nature, v. 291, p. 193–196.
DePaolo, D. J., 1988, Neodymium isotope geochemistry: An introduction: New York, Springer-Verlag, 187 p.
Dickin, A. P., and McNutt, R. H., 1989, Nd model age mapping of the southeast margin of the Archean foreland in the Grenville Province of Ontario: Geology, v. 17, p. 299–302.
Dickin, A. P., McNutt, R. H., and Clifford, P. M., 1990, A neodymium isotope study of plutons near the Grenville Front in Ontario, Canada: Chemical Geology, v. 83, p. 315–324.
Dunning, G. R., O'Brien, S. J., Colman-Sadd, S. P., Blackwood, R. F., Dickson, W. L., O'Neill, P. P., and Krogh, T. E., 1990, Silurian orogeny in the Newfoundland Appalachians: Journal of Geology, v. 98, p. 895–913.
Fryer, B. J., Kerr, A., Jenner, G. A., and Longstaffe, F. J., 1992, Probing the crust with plutons: Regional isotopic geochemistry of granitoid intrusions across insular Newfoundland, in Current research, 1992: Geological Survey of Canada Report 92-4, p. 119–139.
Geological Survey of Canada, 1982, Experimental colour compilation, high resolution aeromagnetic vertical gradient, parts of 11E/8, 11E/9, 11F/5, 11F/12, Nova Scotia: Geological Survey of Canada Map 40 079G, scale 1:50,000.
Gibbons, W., 1994, Suspect terranes, in Hancock, P. L., ed., Continental deformation: Ottawa, Pergamon Press, p. 305–319.
Hibbard, J., 1994, Kinematics of Acadian deformation in the Northern and Newfoundland Appalachians: Journal of Geology, v. 102, p. 215–229.
Hofmann, A. W., 1988, Chemical differentiation of the Earth: The relationship between mantle, continental and oceanic crust: Earth and Planetary Science Letters, v. 90, p. 297–314.
Irving, A. J., and Frey, F. A., 1984, Trace element abundances in megacrysts and their host basalts: Constraints on partition coefficients and megacryst genesis: Geochimica et Cosmochimica Acta, v. 48, p. 1201–1221.
Jacobsen, S. B., and Wasserburg, G. J., 1980, Sm-Nd evolution of chondrites: Earth and Planetary Science Letters, v. 50, p. 139–155.
Keppie, J. D., 1983, The Minas geofracture, in St.-Julien, P., and Beland, J., eds., Major structural zones and faults of the Northern Appalachians: Geological Association of Canada Special Paper 24, p. 263–279.
Keppie, J. D., 1985, The Appalachian College, in Gee, D. G., and Sturt, B., eds., The Caledonide Orogen, Scandinavia, and related areas: New York, John Wiley, p. 1217–1226.
Keppie, J. D., 1989, Northern Appalachian terranes and their accretionary history, in Dallmeyer, R. D., ed., Terranes of the circum-Atlantic Paleozoic orogens: Geological Society of America Special Paper 230, p. 159–192.
Keppie, J. D., 1993, Synthesis of Paleozoic deformational events and terrane accretion in the Canadian Appalachians: Geologische Rundschau, v. 82, p. 381–431.
Keppie, J. D., and Dallmeyer, R. D., compilers, 1989, Tectonic map of Pre-Mesozoic terranes in Circum-Atlantic Phanerozoic orogens: International Geological Correlation Programme, Project 233: Halifax, Nova Scotia Department of Natural Resources, scale 1:5,000,000.
Keppie, J. D., and Dostal, J., 1991, Late Proterozoic tectonic model for the Avalon Terrane in Maritime Canada: Tectonics, v. 10, p. 842–850.
Keppie, J. D., and Krogh, T. E., 1990, Detrital zircon ages from Late Precambrian conglomerates, Avalon Composite Terrane, Antigonish Highlands, Nova Scotia: Geological Society of America Abstracts with Programs, v. 22, no. 2, p. 27–28.
Keppie, J. D., Dallmeyer, R. D., and Murphy, J. B., 1990, $^{40}Ar/^{39}Ar$ geochronology of Late Precambrian plutons in the Avalon Composite Terrane of Nova Scotia: Geological Society of America Bulletin, v. 102, p. 516–528.
Keppie, J. D., Dallmeyer, R. D., and Krogh, T. E., 1992, U-Pb and $^{40}Ar/^{39}Ar$

mineral ages from Cape North area, northern Cape Breton Island: Implications for accretion of the Avalon Composite Terrane: Canadian Journal of Earth Sciences, v. 29, p. 277–295.

Marcantonio, F., Dickin, A. P., McNutt, R. H., and Heaman, L. M., 1990, Isotopic evidence for the crustal evolution of the Frontenac Arch in the Grenville Province of Ontario, Canada: Chemical Geology, v. 83, p. 297–314.

McKerrow, W. S., and Scotese, C. R., 1990, Palaeozoic palaeogeography and biogeography: Geological Society of London Memoir 12, 435 p.

Miyashiro, A., 1974, Volcanic rock series in island arcs and active continental margins: American Journal of Science, v. 274, p. 321–355.

Murphy, J. B., and Hynes, A. J., 1990, Tectonic control on the origin and development of igneous layering: An example from the Greendale Complex Antigonish Highland: Geology, v. 18, p. 403–406.

Murphy, J. B., and Keppie, J. D., 1987, The stratigraphy and depositional environment of the Late Precambrian Georgeville Group, Antigonish Highlands, Nova Scotia: Maritime Sediments and Atlantic Geology, v. 23, p. 49–61.

Murphy, J. B., and Nance, R. D., 1989, A model for the evolution of the Avalonian-Cadomian belt: Geology, v. 17, p. 735–738.

Murphy, J. B., and Nance, R. D., 1991, Contrasting character of Late Proterozoic orogenic belts and the evolution of a Late Proterozoic supercontinent: Geology, v. 19, p. 469–472.

Murphy, J. B., Keppie, J. D., Dostal, J., and Hynes, A. J., 1990, Late Precambrian Georgeville Group: A volcanic arc rift succession in the Avalon Terrane of Nova Scotia, *in* D'Lemos, R. D., Strachan, R. A., and Topley, C. G., eds., The Cadomian orogeny: Geological Society of London Special Publication 51, p. 383–393.

Murphy, J. B., Keppie, J. D., and Hynes, A. J., 1991, Geology of the Antigonish Highlands: Geological Survey of Canada Paper 89–10, 114 p.

Murphy, J. B., Keppie, J. D., Dostal, J., and Cousens, B. L., 1996, Repeated Late Neoproterozoic–Silurian lower crustal melting beneath the Antigonish Highlands, Nova Scotia: Nd isotopic evidence and tectonic interpretations, *in* Nance, R. D., and Thompson, M. D., eds., Avalonian and related peri-Gondwanan terranes of the circum North Atlantic: Geological Society of America Special Paper 304, p. 109–120.

Nance, R. D., and Murphy, J. B., 1994, Contrasting basement signatures and the palinspastic restoration of peripheral orogens: Example from the Late Proterozoic Avalonian-Cadomian belt: Geology, v. 22, p. 617–620.

O'Brien, S. J., O'Brien, B. H., O'Driscoll, C. F., Dunning, G. R., Holdsworth, R. E., and Tucker, R., 1991, Silurian orogenesis and the NW limit of Avalonian rocks in the Hermitage Flexure, Newfoundland Appalachians: Geological Association of Canada Abstract with Programs, v. 16, p. 13A.

Patchett, P. J., and Ruiz, J., 1989, Nd isotopes and the origin of Grenville-age rocks in Texas: Implications for Proterozoic evolution of the United States in the mid-continent region: Journal of Geology, v. 97, p. 685–695.

Pearce, J. A., and Norry, M. J., 1979, Petrogenetic implications of Ti, Zr, Y, and Nb variations in volcanic rocks: Contributions to Mineralogy and Petrology, v. 69, p. 33–47.

Pearce, J. A., Harris, N. B.W., and Tindle, A. G., 1984a, Trace element discrimination diagrams for the tectonic interpretation of granitic rocks: Journal of Petrology, v. 25, p. 956–983.

Pearce, J. A., Lippard, S. J., and Roberts, S., 1984b, Characteristics and tectonic significance of supra-subduction zone ophiolites, *in* Kokelaar, B. P., and Howells, M. F., eds., Marginal basin geology (Geological Society of London Special Publication 16): London, Blackwell Scientific Publications, p. 77–96.

Pitcher, W. S., and Berger, A. R., 1972, The geology of Donegal: London. Wiley Interscience, 435 p.

Rocci, G., Bronner, G., and Deschamps, M., 1991, Crystalline basement of the West African Craton, *in* Dallmeyer, R. D., and Lécorché, J. P., eds., The West African orogens and circum-Atlantic correlatives: Heidelberg, Springer-Verlag, p. 31–61.

Shervais, J. W., 1982, Ti-V plots and the petrogenesis of modern and ophiolitic lavas: Earth and Planetary Science Letters, v. 59, p. 101–118.

Stern, R. J., and Gottfried, D., 1986, Petrogenesis of a Late Precambrian (575–600 Ma) bimodal suite in Northeast Africa: Contributions to Mineralogy and Petrology, v. 92, p. 462–501.

Stewart, B. W., and DePaolo, D. J., 1992, Diffusive isotopic contamination of mafic magma by coexisting silicic liquid in the Muskox Intrusion: Nature, v. 255, p. 708–711.

Sun, S-S., and McDonough, W. F., 1990, Chemical and isotopic systematics of oceanic basalts: Implications for mantle compositions and processes, *in* Saunders, A. D., and Norry, M. J., eds., Magmatism in the ocean basins: Geological Society of London Special Publication 42, p. 313–345.

Taylor, S. R., and McLennan, S. M., 1985, The continental crust: Its composition and evolution: Oxford, Blackwell, 312 p.

Teixeira, W., Tassinari, C. C. G., Cordani, U. G., and Kawashita, K., 1989, A review of the geochronology of the Amazonian Craton: Tectonic implications: Precambrian Research, v. 42, p. 213–227.

Theokritoff, G., 1979, Early Cambrian provincialism and biogeographic boundaries in the North Atlantic region: Lethaia, v. 12, p. 281–295.

Van der Voo, R., 1988, Palaeozoic paleogeography of North America, Gondwana, and intervening displaced terranes: Comparisons of palaeomagnetism within palaeoclimatology and biogeographical patterns: Geological Society of America Bulletin, v. 100, p. 311–324.

Whalen, J. B., Jenner, G. A., Currie, K. L., Barr, S. M., Hegner, E., and Longstaffe, F., 1994, Evolution of the Avalon Terrane in southern New Brunswick-implications of Nd, O, and Pb isotopic data from granitoid rocks: Journal of Geology, v. 102, p. 269–282.

Williams, H., 1979, The Appalachian orogen in Canada: Canadian Journal of Earth Sciences, v. 16, p. 792–807.

MANUSCRIPT ACCEPTED BY THE SOCIETY JULY 2, 1996

Geological Society of America
Memoir 191
1997

Igneous and metamorphic U-Pb zircon ages
from the Baltimore mafic complex, Maryland Piedmont

A. Krishna Sinha
*Department of Geological Sciences, Virginia Polytechnic Institute and State University, Blacksburg,
Virginia 24061–0420*
Barry B. Hanan
*Brooks Institute of Isotope Geology, Department of Geological Sciences, San Diego State University, San Diego,
California 92182–1020*
David M. Wayne
*Chemical Sciences and Technology Division, CST 8, MS G740, Los Alamos National Laboratory, Los Alamos,
New Mexico 87545*

ABSTRACT

The Baltimore mafic complex in the central part of the Appalachian orogen has
been interpreted to have originated as a sub-arc plutonic complex. New U-Pb ages of
zircons separated from four different bulk compositions yield both crystallization
and metamorphic ages. A crystallization age of 489 Ma is obtained on rocks with no
modal pyroxenes, and a metamorphic age of 453 Ma with an inherited zircon age of
~2 Ga is defined by zircons separated from more mafic lithologies with abundant
pyroxenes. Our data suggest that pyroxenes, when involved in the process of amphi-
bolitization, provide sufficient zirconium to form metamorphic zircons. The inherited zircon component cannot be readily identified through chemical mapping of
zircons. Whole-rock Pb isotope data with elevated $^{207}Pb/^{204}Pb$ isotopic ratios support
the model of crustal interaction that probably provided the inherited zircons.

INTRODUCTION

The occurrences of mafic and ultramafic complexes in various parts of the Appalachian orogen have been used as indicators
of the presence of ocean basins or roots of arcs, and their structural location has been used to mark possible sutures and potential terrane boundaries. Although the locations of the mafic
complexes are well known, their stratigraphic positions are dominantly tectonic in nature and provide weak constraints on the
ages and setting of magmatism. The tectonic emplacement also
often precludes the mapping of continuous igneous stratigraphy,
and multiple episodes of metamorphism may partially obscure
the chemical and isotopic signature of the parent magma.

The largest mafic complex in the U.S. Appalachians occurs
in the Maryland-Pennsylvania Piedmont, and is called the Baltimore mafic complex (Crowley, 1976; Hanan and Sinha, 1989;
Southwick, 1970; Hopson, 1964; Morgan, 1977). The eastern

Maryland Piedmont is underlain by the Middle Proterozoic Baltimore Gneiss (Tilton et al., 1970) and is unconformably overlain
by multiply deformed and metamorphosed sedimentary rocks of
the Glenarm Series (Hopson, 1964; Fisher, 1970; Higgins, 1972;
Crowley, 1976). The Baltimore mafic complex (BMC) is tectonically juxtaposed against various lithologies of the Glenarm
Series (Hopson, 1964; Southwick, 1970; Crowley, 1976).

The highly tectonized and metamorphosed rocks of the
BMC occur in four distinct thrust blocks (Fig. 1) and are related
to each other through mineralogical and chemical similarities
(Hanan, 1980; Hanan and Sinha, 1989). Although no one block
has all the elements of an ultramafic-mafic igneous stratigraphy,
a composite stratigraphic column shows a basal serpentinite unit
overlain by metagabbros and quartz gabbros (Hanan and Sinha,
1989). The presence of relict igneous layering accompanied by
an iron-enrichment trend has been used to model the complex as
a dismembered oceanic ophiolite (Morgan, 1977; Crowley,

Sinha, A. K., Hanan, B. B., and Wayne, D. M., 1997, Igneous and metamorphic U-Pb zircon ages from the Baltimore mafic complex, Maryland Piedmont,
in Sinha, A. K., Whalen, J. B., and Hogan, J. P., eds., The Nature of Magmatism in the Appalachian Orogen: Boulder, Colorado, Geological Society of America
Memoir 191.

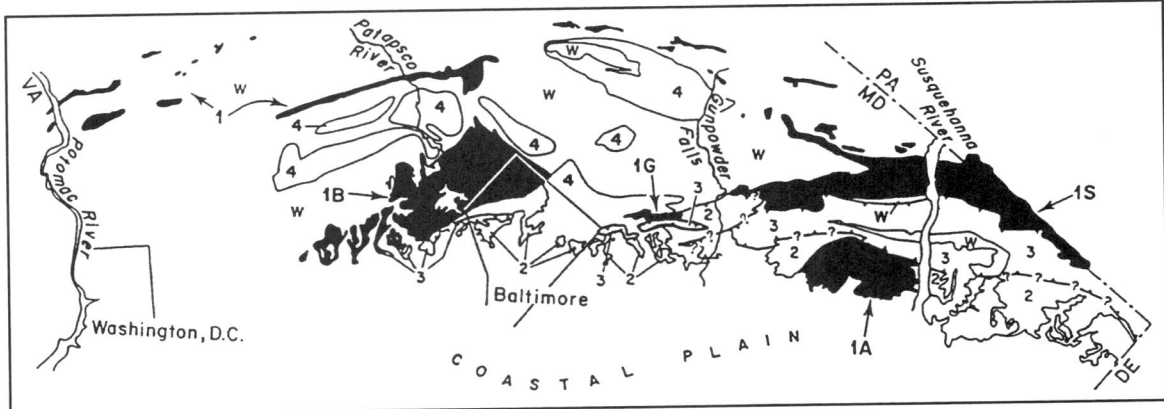

Figure 1. Generalized geologic map of the eastern Maryland Piedmont with plutonic rocks of the Baltimore mafic complex shown in black. 1 = Soldiers Delight; 1B = Baltimore block; 1G = Gunpowder block; 1S = Susquehanna block; 1A = Aberdeen block; 2 = lower volcanic block; 3 = upper volcanic block; 4 = Baltimore Gneiss; W = Glenarm metasedimentary rocks. Adapted from Southwick (1969), Higgins (1972), and Crowley (1976).

1976), an Alpine class stratiform intrusion (Thayer, 1967), the root zone of a continental margin arc or a plutonic sequence within a back arc rift (Sinha et al., 1989; Hanan and Sinha, 1989), and "metamorphosed" remains of differentiated subareal magma reservoirs, perhaps analogous to the reservoirs that must lie below present-day primitive arcs of the Tonga-Kermadec type (D. L. Southwick, 1996, personal commun.). The arc environment is further supported through mineralogical characterization of cumulate rocks (e.g., Beard, 1986), the olivine and plagioclase compositions of which (Hanan and Sinha, 1989) are similar to type I arc cumulate.

PETROGRAPHY AND STRATIGRAPHY OF THE BMC

Although thrusting, folding, and metamorphism have complicated the igneous history of the BMC, field-based reconstruction provides a distinctive magmatic stratigraphy. Of the four major thrust blocks that constitute the BMC, the igneous stratigraphy is best preserved in the Susquehanna block (Fig. 1). A basal ultramafic sequence consisting of serpentinized dunite and chromitite is overlain by a transitional zone metagabbro with basal peridotite and pyroxenite. The main sequence of gabbroic rocks overlies the transitional zone, and has numerous thin peridotite layers. The uppermost quartz gabbro has abundant mafic xenoliths, and is in thrust contact with the overlying metasedimentary rocks of the Wissahickon Formation.

The ultramafic rocks are now represented by an assemblage bearing chrysotile, lizardite, antigorite, and carbonate minerals. Relict igneous mineralogies suggest that early crystallized olivine was followed by orthopyroxene, clinopyroxene, plagioclase, magnetite, and chromite. The gabbroic rocks, though variably metamorphosed, are dominantly hypersthene bearing. Cumulate textures are defined by early crystallizing orthopyroxene, clinopy-

roxene, and plagioclase. Clinopyroxene, plagioclase, and magnetite usually occur as postcumulus minerals. Quartz gabbros consist of minor orthopyroxene and clinopyroxene, and abundant hornblende, plagioclase, and biotite. Late differentiates of the gabbros are also represented by the occurrence of small volumes of plagiogranite that occur as sills and dikes (Hanan, 1980).

Petrographic studies of gabbroic rocks also suggest two major episodes of hydrous recrystallization. Early deuteric alteration produced magnesiohornblende rimming pyroxenes. A later, more pervasive alteration is shown by the actinolite replacing pyroxene, and clinozoisite occurs interstitially between actinolite or magnesiohornblende and plagioclase. Ferroan pargasite, chlorite, epidote, and sphene are usually present along microfractures. Details of mineral compositions (both igneous and metamorphic) were given in Hanan (1980) and Hanan and Sinha (1989).

New U-Pb zircon ages, chemistry of zircons, and whole-rock Pb isotopes in conjunction with both published petrologic and isotopic data (Hanan, 1980) are utilized to construct a more comprehensive temporal and tectonic history of the complex.

ANALYTICAL PROCEDURES

Microprobe

Zircons from norite, pyroxene, gabbro, quartz gabbro, and plagiogranite were analyzed using the electron microprobe. Standards and operating conditions are similar to those specified in Wayne and Sinha (1988). Calculated error estimates and total variation of zircon standard analyses are also within the range of those determined by Wayne and Sinha (1988). However, the microprobe procedures for some of the analyses used in this study differ somewhat from our previous studies. For this study, analysis points were chosen on the basis of relative intensity of cathodoluminescence, in addition to analyses collected as points on straight-line traverses taken parallel to, and perpendicular to, {001}. Furthermore, we modified our analytical scheme to include Ti (standard:synthetic [std:syn.] TiO_2), Th (std: syn. $ThSiO_4$) and Dy (std: syn. Gd-Dy molybdate) and to exclude La and Mn.

Other phases included within zircons were analyzed using the procedure described by Speer and Solberg (1982). Spectral scans of Zr in clinopyroxene, orthopyroxene, Mg-hornblende, actinolite, and ilmenite were conducted at 50 nA sample current for 50 cycles of 40 each, through the Zr L_α peak. The Zr L_α peak was calibrated on synthetic $ZrSiO_4$, a glass ("V") containing 0.79 wt% ZrO_2, and NBS 500 glass.

U/PB ISOTOPIC ANALYSES OF ZIRCON, SPHENE, AND WHOLE ROCK

Zircon and sphene separation was accomplished by using standard techniques of mineral separation. Final analysis-grade material was hand picked for purity prior to dissolution. Column chemistry techniques for zircon are as described by Krogh (1973), and a HBr column procedure (Tilton, 1988, personal commun.) was utilized for sphene. Pb and U blanks during the duration of the project averaged 60 and 10 pg, respectively, for zircon analyses, and 400 pg and 20 pg, respectively, for sphene procedures. Mass-spectrometry analyses were done using a multiple collector VG Sector 54 instrument using Faraday-Daly detector configuration for zircon Pb analyses, and all Faraday detectors for sphene Pb analyses. Replicate analyses of both NBS 983 radiogenic and CIT common Pb standards over the period of the study yielded the following averages.

| CIT | 4/6 = 0.06025 | 7/6 = 0.92993 | 8/6 = 2.17910 |
| NBS 983 | 4/6 = 0.00372 | 7/6 = 0.71196 | 8/6 = 0.01365 |

Linear mass-fractionation correction factors using CIT standard in the Faraday cup detection mode average 0.094% per mass unit and have been applied to sphene analyses. Daly detector measurements for ^{204}Pb coupled with Faraday cup analysis of the other isotopes for NBS 983 yield a fractionation factor of 0.013% per mass unit, and this has been applied to zircon Pb isotope data. U isotope fractionation was monitored by analyzing NBS standard U-500, requiring a mass fractionation adjustment of 0.02%. U/Pb ages and errors are reported as calculated by using PBDAT and ISOPLOT programs of Ludwig (1993).

Whole-rock Pb isotope analyses were done at San Diego State University, where dissolution techniques and Pb extraction methods in a HBr medium are after Tilton (1973). Pb blanks were less than 100 pg, and, as such, the reported analyses have not been corrected for the blank. Pb was loaded on a rhenium filament with silica gel and phosphoric acid and analyzed with a VG Sector 54 multicollector solid source mass spectrometer. The Pb isotope data have been corrected for instrumental mass fractionation and machine bias by applying a discrimination factor determined by multiple analyses of NBS SRM981, using the values of Todt et al. (1985), that averaged 0.916 ± 0.001 (2 standard error [s.e.]) ‰/atomic mass unit (AMU). Standard errors are the 95% confidence level, taking into account within-run precision and the uncertainty in the discrimination factor, and averaged 0.008% for ^{206}Pb/^{204}Pb, 0.008% for ^{207}Pb/^{204}Pb, and 0.011% for ^{208}Pb/^{204}Pb.

MORPHOLOGY AND PHYSICAL CHARACTERIZATION OF ZIRCONS

Zircons from the three mafic lithologies (norite, pyroxene gabbro, quartz gabbro) show similarities as well as marked dissimilarities. Zircons from the quartz gabbro show sharp, well-defined prismatic and pyramidal faces, prismatic habit with length:width ratios in excess of three, development of first- and second-order prism faces, and pronounced pyramidal terminations (Fig. 2a). Zircons from the norite and pyroxene gabbro

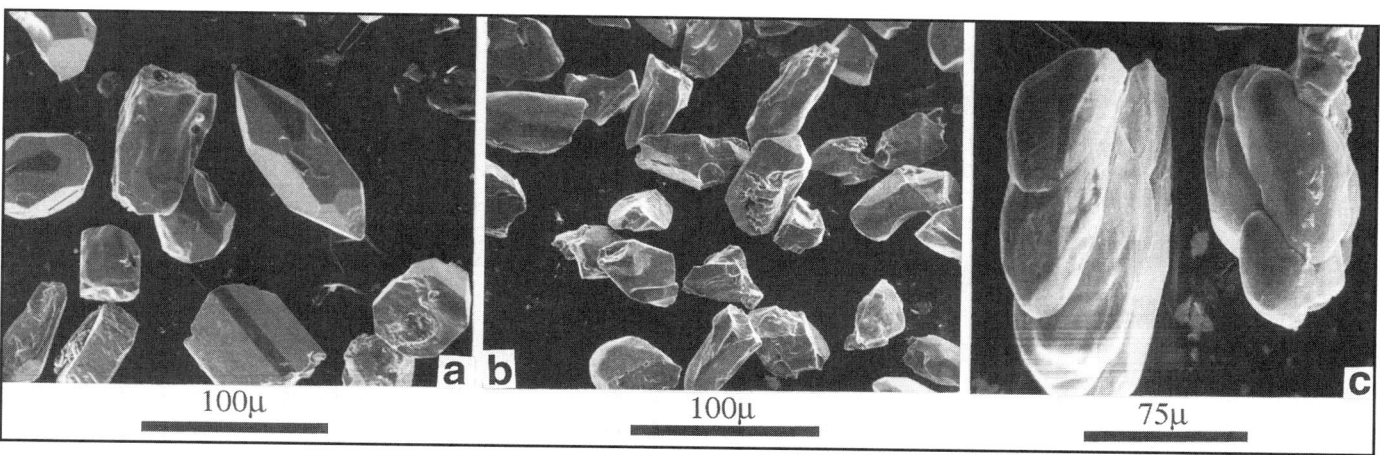

Figure 2. Scanning electron microscope images of grains of zircons from three lithologies. a: Euhedral grains are common in the quartz gabbro, while in (b) grains from a norite are subhedral and show some evidence of surface corrosion. c: Zircons from plagiogranite are ovoid and partially rounded.

show a range in forms, but are typically subhedral and show minor dissolution and surface pitting (Fig. 2b). Some of the zircons (especially those from the norite and olivine gabbro) also contain inclusions that are occasionally large (>50 μm in length), vermiform or acicular, and in some cases, appear to have acted as nuclei. Microprobe analyses of these inclusions (energy dispersive system) from zircons in each separate revealed the dominant presence of clinopyroxene (cpx), orthopyroxene (opx), plagioclase (plag), apatite, and, very rarely, biotite, and quartz. Many of these zircons contained multiphase inclusions, with three or more of the minerals mentioned above (Fig. 3a).

The plagiogranite contains distinctly ovoid, rounded, nearly equant zircons that contrast strongly with the sharp, well-faceted prismatic euhedra found in the mafic rock types. Scanning electron microscope (SEM) images (Fig. 2c) of these zircons suggest that no pitting or corrosion of these zircons has taken place. Inclusions of rock-forming minerals (e.g., feldspars, quartz) were not observed in the plagiogranite zircon separates, although delicate zoning (growth?) is commonly preserved (Fig. 3b). Therefore, we assume that their distinct morphology is the result of the differences in bulk composition, and perhaps differences in cooling history between the plagiogranite and the mafic rocks. Specifically, zircon was probably a very early crystallizing phase in the metaluminous (molar [Na + K]/Al = 0.7) plagiogranite (see Hanan, 1980; Hanan and Sinha, 1989, for geochemical data), whereas the abundance of opx, cpx, and plag inclusions in zircons from the mafic lithologies suggests that zircon crystallization occurred relatively late in the cooling history of the gabbros and norites. Alternatively, the abundance of inclusions within zircons from the metamorphosed mafic rocks indicates that considerable growth of zircon may have occurred during the metamorphism of the rocks, and U/Pb ages may yield metamorphic, rather than igneous, ages of these samples.

ZIRCON CHEMISTRY

In order to better characterize the zircons used for U/Pb ages (e.g., document chemical discontinuities and reversals in search for xenocrystic zircon), selected zircons from each lithology were analyzed for element distribution patterns. Microprobe traverses of zircons (Fig. 4, a, b, c, d and Table 1) from the two of the more mafic rocks (norite and two pyroxene gabbro) show mostly an increase in Zr/Hf ratio from the interior of the crystal to the rim, and P_2O_5, Y_2O_3, and UO_2 show either a flat or uncorrelated trend. In contrast, the Zr/Hf ratio in the quartz gabbro and plagiogranite zircons show a depletion or a flat trend from core to rim. A single crystal of zircon (Fig. 4d) from (<75 μm size) showed very strong enrichment in Zr/Hf ratio (~20 in core region to ~50 at rim) due to a lower measured abundance of Hf. Overall, the plagiogranite zircons contain higher net abundances of HfO_2, P_2O_5, and Y_2O_3.

SEM backscatter images (Fig. 5, a, b, c) show no significant core-rim structures, although in the norite zircon there is a weak gradient from core to rim, especially in the yttrium image. The plagiogranite zircon does show zoning in Hf abundance (Fig. 5c) and is also characterized by "hot spots," i.e., irregular domains of extreme trace-element enrichment as well as zones that are likely to be apatite.

U-PB DATA AND AGES OF ZIRCONS AND SPHENE

U-Pb isotopic analyses of zircons and sphene are given in Table 2 and shown in Figure 6 as a conventional concordia diagram. Analytical data for zircons are easily divisible into two groups corresponding to differences in bulk composition and modal mineralogy described for the rocks (Hanan, 1980), and to

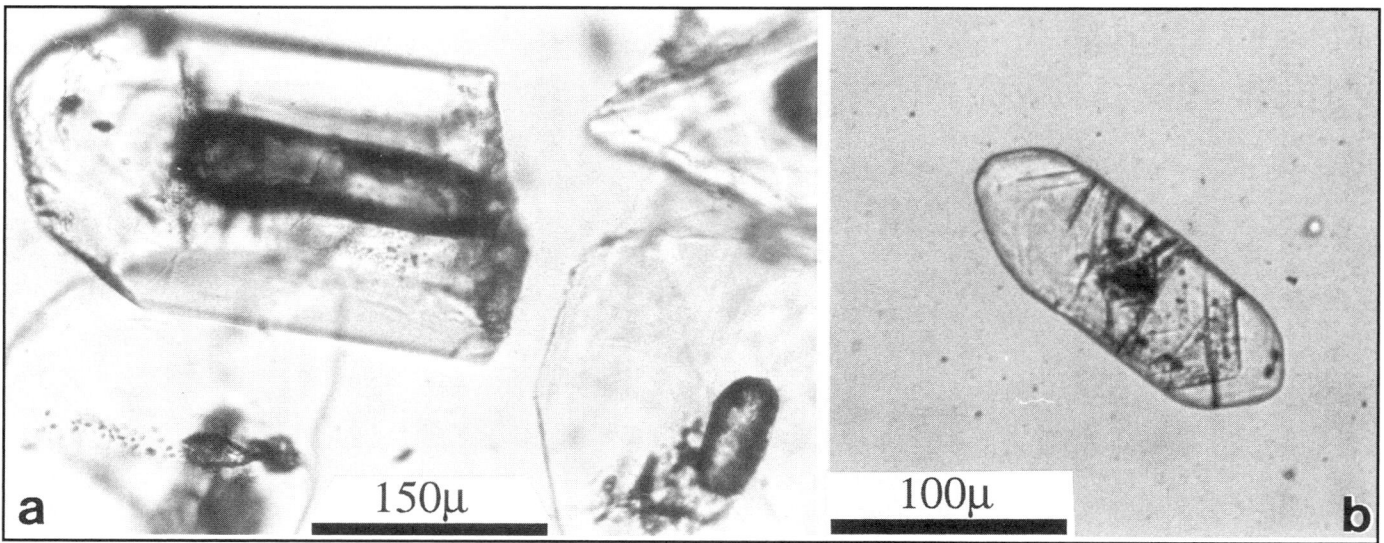

Figure 3. Optical microscope photomicrographs showing (a) abundant inclusions in zircons extracted from norite, and (b) zoning within a crystal from plagiogranite, even though the surface features show ovoid forms.

a limited extent the morphology and chemistry of the zircons. U-Pb data for the zircon fractions from the two mafic rocks (norite and pyroxene gabbro) show limited U enrichment (87 ppm to 126 ppm) and consequently relatively low Pb concentrations (7.3 to 11.0 ppm). The isotopic data from the four analyses define a discordia, with upper and lower intercepts of

2072 ± 617 Ma and 453 ± 11 Ma, respectively. The relatively narrow range of measured U-Pb ratios, coupled with data points plotting much closer to the lower intercept, yields the large statistical error for the upper intercept age.

U-Pb data obtained on two size fractions of sphene separated from the norite yielded very low abundances for U and Pb

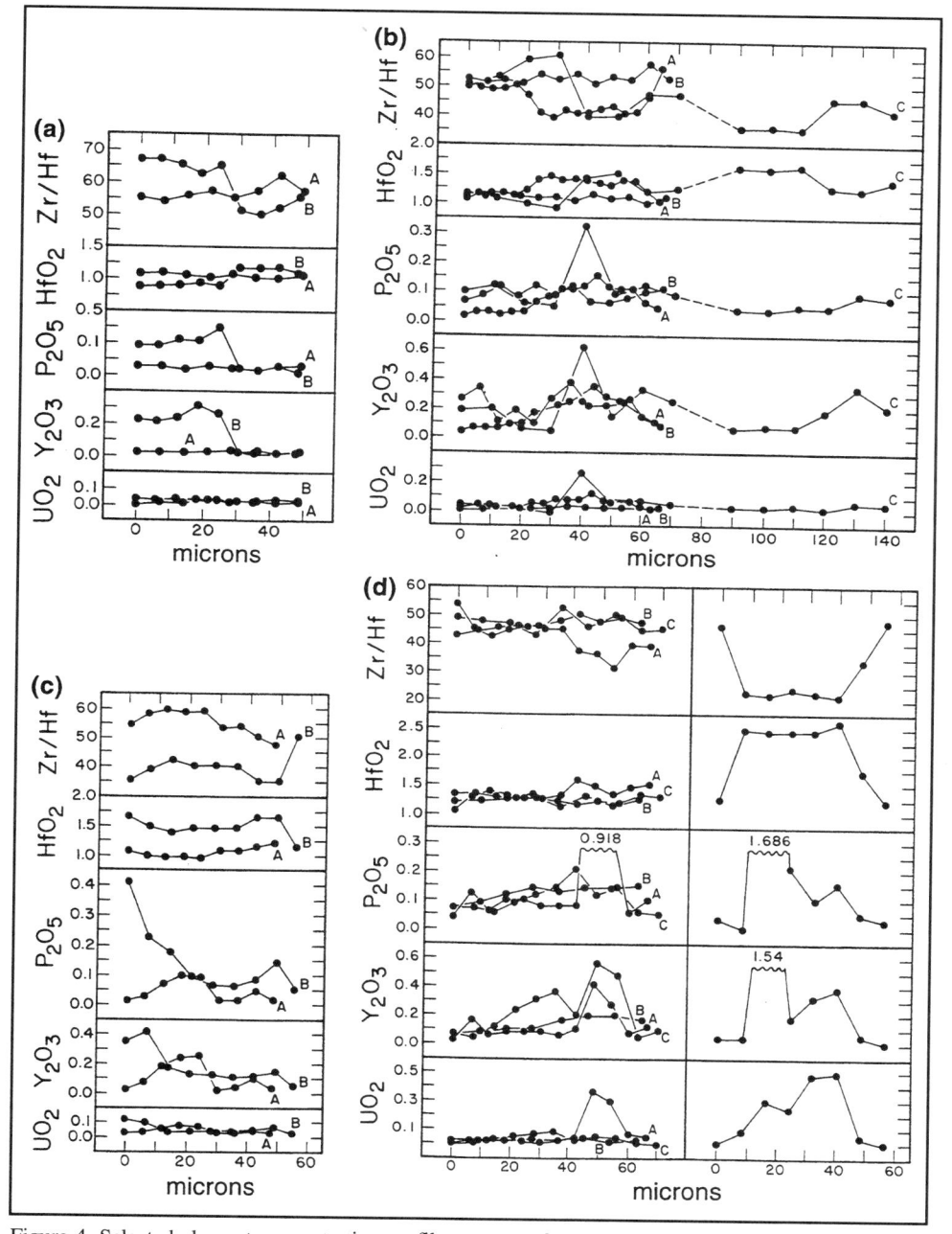

Figure 4. Selected element concentration profiles across a few grains considered representative of the four major lithologies that yielded zircons. Distances in microns (0 at rim) are measured from rim to core. a: Pyroxene gabbro zircons show an increase in Zr/Hf ratio, while changes in Y, P, and Hf appear to be uncorrelated. b: Norite zircons show very complex patterns between three crystals. Crystals A and C show a possible increase in Zr/Hf ratio toward the rim. Zircons from quartz gabbro (c) and plagiogranite (d) show flat trends for most crystals analyzed, although grains from the analyses in (d) labeled A, B, C for >75 μm crystals and a single analysis of a <75 μm grain show evidence of "hot spots."

TABLE 1. ELECTRON MICROPROBE ANALYSES OF ZIRCONS

Analyses	2 Pyroxene Gabbro		Norite		Quartz Gabbro		Plagiogranite (75-150 μ)		Plagiogranite (45-75 μ)	
	Rim (4)	Core (5)	Rim (7)	Core (9)	Rim (5)	Core (4)	Rim (9)	Core (12)	Rim (2)	Core (4)
ZrO_2	67.41 (32)	67.23 (08)	66.49 (54)	65.82 (38)	68.01 (61)	67.22 (26)	67.02 (97)	65.71 (183)	65.80 (20)	62.97 (81)
SiO_2	32.06 (10)	32.02 (01)	32.23 (15)	31.16 (09)	31.81 (19)	31.90 (12)	31.54 (40)	31.36 (85)	31.27 (10)	30.33 (43)
HfO_2	1.12 (05)	0.90 (02)	1.21 (14)	1.39 (04)	1.14 (07)	0.99 (01)	1.29 (02)	1.20 (05)	1.23 (02)	2.46 (11)
P_2O_5	0.02 (00)	0.11 (02)	0.04 (01)	0.11 (02)	0.02 (01)	0.08 (03)	0.07 (02)	0.13 (03)	0.03 (00)	0.12 (09)
Y_2O_3	0.02 (00)	0.25 (04)	0.09 (03)	0.25 (05)	0.05 (03)	0.19 (09)	0.07 (02)	0.41 (12)	tr.	0.23 (16)
UO_2	0.03 (00)	0.04 (00)	tr.	0.07 (02)	0.03 (00)	0.06 (01)	n.d.	0.05 (02)	n.d.	0.33 (20)
FeO	tr.	tr.	n.d.	n.d.	n.d.	tr.	n.d.	tr.	n.d.	0.08 (04)
CaO	n.d.	n.d.	n.d.	n.d.	n.d.	n.d.	n.d.	tr	n.d.	tr.
Total	100.66	100.55	100.07	98.80	101.06	100.44	99.99	98.86	98.33	96.52
Zr/Hf	52.51	65.41	49.75	41.28	52.24	59.18	45.27	48.01	46.72	22.38

and minimally evolved radiogenic Pb. No reliable U/Pb ages could be calculated.

Zircons separated from the plagiogranite and the quartz gabbro show higher U and Pb contents than those from the more mafic rocks, but they do not lie on the same discordia defined by the four zircon fractions described earlier. These four fractions lie on a line with an upper concordia intercept age of 489 ± 7 Ma and a lower intercept age of 9 ± 53 Ma with a MSWD of 0.75. Forcing the regression through 0 Ma does not change the upper intercept age, although the error is predictably reduced to a lower value of ±2 Ma. We adopt the 489 Ma age of crystallization as the best estimate of the age of the Baltimore mafic complex.

DISCUSSION

The three concordia intercept ages defined by the data present a unique opportunity to relate U-Pb ages to igneous and metamorphic events in the Maryland-Pennsylvania Piedmont and extend the tectonic significance of the occurrence of mafic rocks of equivalent age in the Appalachian orogen. The data also permit an evaluation of the process of growth of metamorphic zircons in mafic lithologies.

Of the three concordia intercept ages of 2072, 489, and 453 Ma, the two younger ages are consistent with known geologic events (Sinha et al., 1989; Tilton et al., 1970). The 489 Ma event is clearly associated with an episode of magmatism that has been correlated with the development of a subduction-related volcanism (Sinha and Guy, 1989; Sinha et al., 1989; Higgins and Conant, 1990; Hanan and Sinha, 1989; Pavlides, 1981) and associated low-pressure–high-temperature metamorphism of the Maryland-Pennsylvania Piedmont province (Fisher, 1970; Crawford and Crawford, 1980). The earliest Ordovician age for the zircons from the plagiogranite and quartz gabbro is interpreted as the crystallization age of the Baltimore mafic complex (i.e., 489 Ma). The igneous differentiation process that produced the plagiogranite and quartz gabbro (Hanan and Sinha, 1989) must have been capable of saturating the liquid in zirconium to precipitate igneous zircons. This observation is consistent with the

experimental data on zircon saturation in evolved melts (Watson and Harrison, 1983), which indicates that the saturation level of zircon in metaluminous to peraluminous granitic melts can only be 500–100 ppm Zr at saturation levels. The low (<1) alkali/alumina ratio of the plagiogranite suggests that Zr may have reached saturation at, or below, the 100 ppm level.

In contrast to the U/Pb isotopic behavior of zircons in the plagiogranites and quartz gabbro, the isotopic data from the more mafic gabbro-hosted zircons require an inherited component, but without any significant growth of zircons during crystallization of the mafic magma. We suggest that the solubility of zircon as a function of melt composition is the key relationship for understanding the absence of magmatic zircon associated with crystallization. The data of Dickinson and Hess (1982) indicate that the saturation of zircon in basaltic melts at ~1100 °C can exceed 11,000 ppm, thus resulting in dissolution of xenocrystic zircons, rather than precipitation of new igneous zircons. The presence of a limited inherited component seen clearly on the concordia diagram (Fig. 6) suggests armoring by other silicate minerals or a very short residence time in the melt.

The concordia lower intercept age of 453 Ma is clearly distinguishable from the crystallization age of 498 Ma for the complex. Therefore, it is suggested that the 453–2072 Ma discordia may be related to metamorphic growth of zircon associated with observed retrogression of the mineral assemblages in the mafic lithologies.

Growth of new zircon during amphibolite grade metamorphism of mafic rocks requires a source of zirconium and a medium of transport. We believe that the movement of zirconium was extremely localized due to its relatively immobile nature associated with low solubility (Sinha et al., 1991), despite the

Figure 5. Scanning electron microscope backscatter images of three zircons from three different lithologies. Top: Hf, Y, and Ca distribution in a grain extracted from norite. A weak zonation in Y may be present. Middle row: Zr, Si, Ca distribution in a zircon from quartz gabbro. No measurable zonation is recognized. Bottom row: Hf, Ca, P distribution in a zircon from plagiogranite. Note the measurable zoning in Hf, as well as Ca- and P-rich zones that are likely to be apatite.

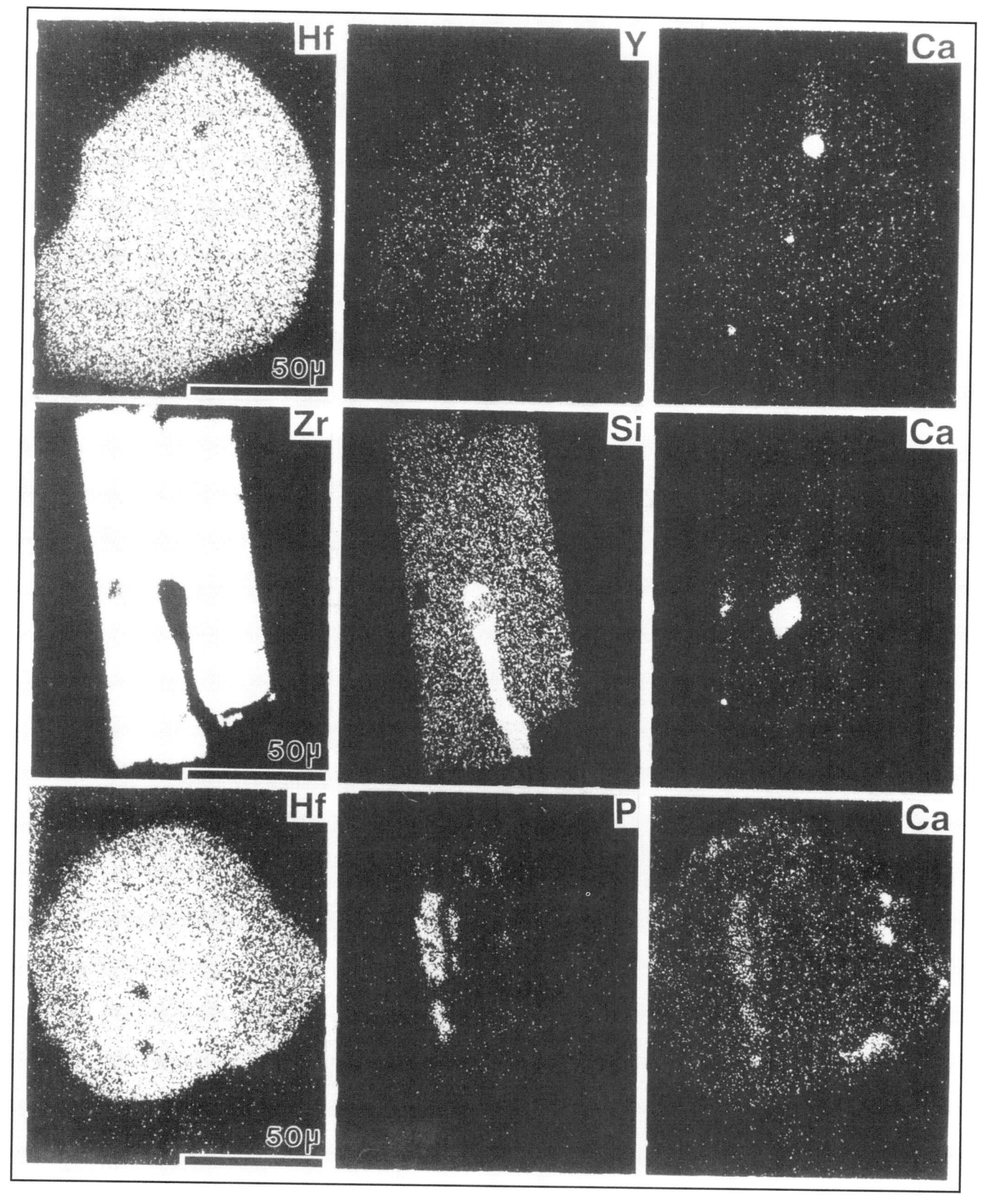

TABLE 2. U-Pb DATA FOR ZIRCONS FROM THE BALTIMORE MAFIC COMPLEX

Sample*	Concentration†		Isotopic composition§			Calculated ages		
	U	Pb	208/206	207/206	204/206	206*/238 (Ma)	207*/235 (Ma)	207*/206* (Ma)
Plagiogranite								
1. 75-150 μ	281.3	20.6	0.1739	0.06675	0.000673	422.9	433.3	489.3
2. 45-75 μ	298.2	21.4	0.1713	0.06899	0.000830	413.6	425.2	488.1
3. Quartz gab-bro	170.2	13.6	0.2176	0.06375	0.000463	447.9	455.1	491.4
4. Quartz gab-bro	171.8	13.7	0.2415	0.06221	0.000364	441.0	448.6	487.9
Pyroxene gabbro								
5. 75-150 μ	116.1	9.4	0.2009	0.06138	0.000178	462.9	479.4	559.3
6. 45-75 μ	118.0	9.4	0.2099	0.06128	0.000332	450.6	453.7	469.6
7. Pyroxene gabbro	125.9	11.0	0.2281	0.07117	0.000670	482.6	514.1	656.6
8 Norite	86.9	7.3	0.2267	0.06546	0.000472	467.1	481.7	552.2
Sphene								
9. >150 μ from norite	3.1	0.1	2.0038	0.80823	0.05146			
10. <150 μ from norite	7.2	0.3	1.9806	0.78610	0.04909			

*Zircon analyses both by size separation and bulk fraction for the four rock types.
†Total U and Pb concentrations in parts per million.
§Observed isotopic compositions corrected for mass fractionation.
**Ages calculated using the program of Ludwig (1993).

presence of a fluid phase during metamorphism, although significant mobility has been documented for fluorine-rich hydrothermal environments (Rubin et al., 1993; Aja et al., 1995). The metamorphic paragenesis (Hanan, 1980) has clearly documented the hydration reactions that converted the igneous assemblage (plagioclase, clinopyroxene, orthopyroxene) to an assemblage dominated by magnesiohornblende, actinolite, ferroan pargasite, chlorite, epidote, and clinozoisite. We suggest that the source of zirconium may be clinopyroxene, which has a relatively high affinity for zirconium (K_D ~0.06 to 1.0, Forsythe et al., 1994) provided it does not co-crystallize with zircon. The latter constraint can be applied to the samples analyzed by us (no igneous zircons in the pyroxene gabbro or norite), and reinforces our suggestion that clinopyroxene may have been the source of zirconium. During breakdown of the clinopyroxene to amphibole or other hydrated ferromagnesian phases, trace zirconium lost from the clinopyroxene may combine with silica (also liberated during hydration reaction) to nucleate a new population of zircon, or form overgrowths on preexisting zircon. Although we attempted to measure zirconium in clinopyroxene, the microprobe data revealed no measurable amounts of zirconium, suggesting abundances below microprobe detection limit. Due to the large modal volume of pyroxene in the mafic rocks (15%–25%) and utilizing an average value of 200 ppm zirconium in clinopyroxene (Forsythe et al., 1994), a sufficient amount of zirconium may be available for zircon growth during metamorphism.

The correlation between U/Pb ages (both igneous and meta-

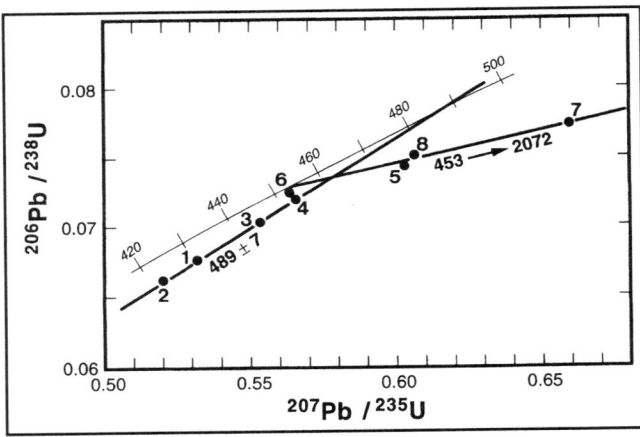

Figure 6. Conventional U-Pb concordia diagram showing the two distinct discordia generated for the zircons analyzed. Numbers correspond to analyses given in Table 2. Samples 1, 2, 3, and 4 yield an upper intercept age of 489 Ma and is interpreted as a crystallization age. Samples 5, 6, 7, and 8 record a xenocrystic component with a dominant metamorphic overgrowth.

morphic) obtained from rocks of varying lithologies is further highlighted by the colinearity of the isotopic data between plagiogranite and quartz gabbro. Our data clearly suggest that the lack of metamorphic zircon in the quartz gabbro can be uniquely related to the absence of modal clinopyroxene in the sample (Hanan, 1980), thus providing no source for zirconium during metamorphism. Therefore, evidence of a metamorphic zircon component in the Baltimore mafic complex is restricted to bulk compositions and modal mineralogies associated with the middle to lower part of the igneous stratigraphy where clinopyroxene is abundant.

ADDITIONAL EVIDENCE FOR CRUSTAL CONTAMINATION

Both petrologic and isotopic studies (Hanan and Sinha, 1989; Shaw and Wasserburg, 1984) have provided data that can be best interpreted through models involving interaction of a mafic liquid with an evolved crust. Isotopic data for Nd (ε_{Nd} of −6) of Shaw and Wasserburg (1984) and Sr (ε_{Sr} of +5) of Hanan and Sinha (1989) provide unequivocal evidence for contamination of the parent liquid. However, the low K content of the Baltimore mafic complex (0.12 wt% K_2O, Hanan, 1980) provides an important constraint that the bulk composition of the contaminant be low in alkalies as well. Experimental work has shown that basaltic liquids are capable of rapid and selective contamination by K_2O if typical crustal rocks are involved in chemical interaction (Watson, 1982). The timing of modification of the parental mafic liquid can be assessed through monitoring the observed correlation between stratigraphic position and initial Sr isotopic composition. Due to the the well-preserved stratigraphic cross section along the Susquehanna River transect, we can show the correlation between mineral chemistry and initial Sr isotopic ratios of samples as a function of igneous stratigraphy (Fig. 7). Because of the cumulate nature of the assemblage, major-element data show large deviations in concentrations, and do not uniquely define the liquid line of descent. However, mineral compositions more adequately reflect the evolving nature of the liquid, i.e., increasing Fe/Mg for pyroxenes and decreasing Ca/Na in plagioclases. The initial Sr isotopic ratios (Hanan and Sinha, 1989) show a positive correlation with stratigraphy, implying that an already contaminated liquid (initial $^{87}Sr/^{86}Sr$ of

~0.709) was progressively capable of assimilating a contaminant during fractional crystallization with the result that the most-evolved magma was the most contaminated ($^{87}Sr/^{86}Sr$ of ~0.712). The U/Pb age measurements of zircons described in the earlier section yield the potential source age of contaminant to be ~2000 Ma, and in the next section on whole-rock Pb isotopes, we further explore the nature of the contaminant.

PB ISOTOPE RESULTS FOR THE BALTIMORE MAFIC COMPLEX

The Pb isotope analytical results for the Baltimore mafic complex and the Wissahickon Group metasedimentary rocks are given in Table 3. The data include analyses of BMC pyroxenites, gabbros, plagiogranite, and amphibolites from the Baltimore, Gunpowder, and Susquehanna blocks, amphibolite from the lower volcanic block, and metasedimentary rock from the Wissahickon Group (Fig. 1). The Pb isotopic results are plotted in the Pb/Pb diagrams in Figure 8, where they are compared with mid-ocean ridge basalts (MORB) and crustal reservoirs from the Grenville superterrane (Sinha et al., 1996). The age of the BMC is considered to be 489 Ma, on the basis of U/Pb studies of zircons from the plagiogranites and quartz gabbro (this chapter) and similar age (490 Ma) Sm-Nd mineral isochrons (Shaw and Wasserburg, 1984). Because rocks ranging from peridotite through plagiogranite would be expected to have different U/Pb ratios and since in situ radioactive decay would produce differences in Pb isotopic ratios, one must use caution in comparing uncorrected ratios with present-day reservoir isotope signatures.

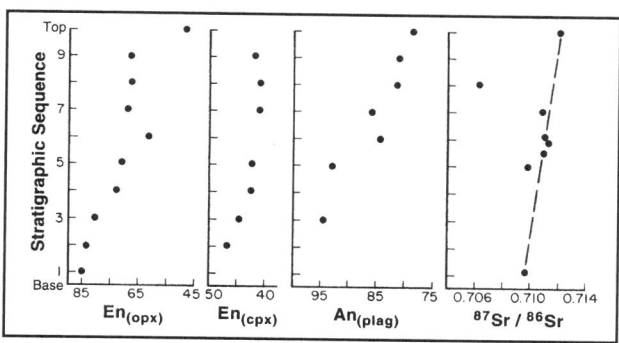

Figure 7. Mineral chemical data (Hanan, 1980) for cumulate rocks that define a progressively fractionating magma. The enstatite component (En) of both orthopyroxenes (opx) and clinopyroxene (cpx) and anorthite content of plagioclase (plag) record a continuous igneous stratigraphy. Note the elevated initial $^{87}Sr/^{86}Sr$ for even the most primitive magma.

TABLE 3. WHOLE-ROCK LEAD ISOTOPE DATA FOR ROCKS OF THE BALTIMORE MAFIC COMPLEX AND ASSOCIATED METASEDIMENTARY ROCKS

Sample	$^{206}Pb/^{204}Pb$	$^{207}Pb/^{204}Pb$	$^{208}Pb/^{204}Pb$
Susquehanna block			
77-77	18.534	15.688	38.366
78-77	18.585	15.652	38.561
91.5-77	18.299	15.689	38.304
14-77	18.254	15.644	38.262
100-77	18.932	15.722	38.811
222-77	18.712	15.698	38.848
25-78	18.899	15.676	38.548
29-79	18.736	15.687	38.484
Gunpowder			
140-77	19.186	15.676	38.520
167-77	18.509	15.618	38.169
Baltimore block			
1758	18.448	15.660	38.234
241066	18.935	15.676	38.521
385-77	18.915	15.670	38.267
395-77	18.345	15.655	38.248
Metasedimentary rocks/Susquehanna block			
51-77	19.439	15.707	39.393
103-77	18.791	15.720	39.497

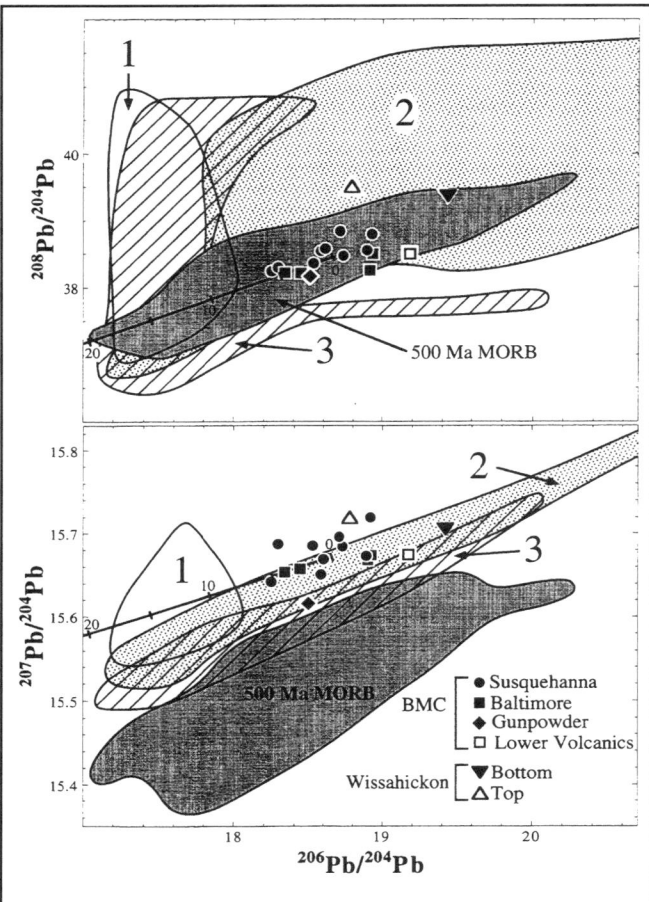

Figure 8. Pb/Pb correlation diagrams showing the Balitmore mafic complex (BMC): black circles are Susquehanna block; black squares are Baltimore block; black triangles are Gunpowder block; white squares are lower volcanic block, and the Wissahickon Formation from above (black inverted trianlges) and below (white triangles) the Susquehanna block. The 500 Ma mid-ocean ridge basalt (MORB) field represents about 900 published MORB analyses for Atlantic, Indian, and Pacific spreading centers corrected to 500 Ma using a μ of 5 and a κ of 2.5. Fields are shown for the Grenville superterrane crustal reservoirs at 500 Ma (Sinha et al., 1996). The solid line with tick marks (0, 10, 20) represents the initial ratio for varying μ at 500 Ma for average BMC.

In general, $^{206}Pb/^{204}Pb$ correlates positively with SiO_2 and Mg# for the BMC rocks. Relationships such as these could be due to varying U/Pb ratios as a result of magmatic processes (fractionation or differentiation). However, previous studies, including Sr and O isotopes, and the identification of an inherited Early Proterozoic age zircon component for the BMC indicate that interaction with an older crust as well as metamorphic reequilibration are also factors that need to be considered. Although we have not yet determined the parent/daughter ratios (i.e., U/Pb and Th/Pb) for the BMC, it is unlikely that very large corrections would occur for mafic rocks because they typically have low $^{238}U/^{204}Pb$ (μ) ratios (<< 10). However, μ values higher than the present-day

ocean crust have been measured in some ophiolite gabbros (Hamelin et al., 1984). To illustrate the possible effect of ingrowth of radiogenic Pb we show a correction trajectory that an average BMC data might follow assuming a 500-Ma crystallization age with varying $^{238}U/^{204}Pb$ (Fig. 8). Although dispersion in the $^{206}Pb/^{204}Pb$ ratio might result from radiogenic ingrowth of Pb, differences in $^{207}Pb/^{204}Pb$ ratio (for a given $^{206}Pb/^{204}Pb$) between the Grenville and MORB fields (corrected to 500 Ma) and the BMC data reflect distinct source evolution histories. This is because the $^{207}Pb/^{204}Pb$ ratio is almost unaffected by recent (<1 Ga) radiogenic growth. The high $^{207}Pb/^{204}Pb$ ratios for the BMC is a characteristic shared by the circum-Mediterranean ophiolites of Troodos, Vourinos, and Antalya. The genesis of these Mediterranean ophiolites is thought to have involved a continental component and an origin in an island-arc setting (Hamelin et al., 1984).

The $^{207}Pb/^{204}Pb$ and $^{208}Pb/^{204}Pb$ ratios for the BMC are significantly higher than 500 Ma MORB. The high $^{207}Pb/^{204}Pb$ and $^{208}Pb/^{204}Pb$ ratios exclude a typical mid-ocean ridge origin for the BMC and require that ancient continental crust material must be involved in its origin. In contrast to previously published $^{87}Sr/^{86}Sr$ initial ratios (Hanan and Sinha, 1989), which are more radiogenic for rocks of the Susquehanna block (>0.710) relative to rocks from the Baltimore block (0.706 to 0.710), the range in $^{206}Pb/^{204}Pb$ is very similar for the two regions (Fig. 8). However, samples from the Susquehanna block show higher $^{207}Pb/^{204}Pb$ and $^{208}Pb/^{204}Pb$ ratios, relative to $^{206}Pb/^{204}Pb$, than the Baltimore data; along with the higher $^{87}Sr/^{86}Sr$ initial ratios, this suggests stronger influence of a crustal component for the rocks in the Susquehanna block. An amphibolite from the lower volcanic unit near Little Gunpowder Falls has the most radiogenic $^{206}Pb/^{204}Pb$ ratio for the BMC rocks. The Pb isotope signature of the amphibolite is more similar to the Baltimore data in terms of $^{207}Pb/^{204}Pb$ and $^{208}Pb/^{204}Pb$ than the Susquehanna data and appears to plot along an extension of Pb/Pb trends defined by the Baltimore data (Fig. 8). Two Wissahickon metasedimentary rocks, one from structurally below (W_B) the mafic stratigraphy along the Susquehanna River and the other from above (W_A), were analyzed. Wissahickon sample W_B plots along the extension of the $^{207/206}Pb$ and $^{208/206}Pb$ trends for the Susquehanna data (Fig. 8). This observation is consistent with the idea that the BMC supplied material to the flysch-like Wissahickon rocks as it was tectonically emplaced (Crowley, 1976). The rock W_B can be modeled as a mixture of Susquehanna BMC and group 2 Grenville component (includes the Baltimore Gneiss). Metasedimentary rock W_A is isotopically distinct with a more radiogenic $^{208}Pb/^{204}Pb$ ratio, relative to $^{206}Pb/^{204}Pb$, than the BMC or W_B data (Fig. 8). In a similar manner to W_A, it could be derived from BMC clastic material and a crustal component, but in this case the crustal component would have to have relatively higher $^{207}Pb/^{204}Pb$ and $^{208}Pb/^{204}Pb$.

The origin of the BMC crustal component cannot be either group 2 (which includes the Baltimore Gneiss) or group 3 Grenville crustal reservoirs, because neither one has the required high $^{207}Pb/^{204}Pb$ ratios. The group 1 type Grenville crustal reservoir, although not exposed at the surface, is a possible high $^{207}Pb/^{204}Pb$ source candidate for the BMC crustal component. The BMC can be modeled as a variable mixture of a depleted 500 Ma Atlantic MORB mantle source and the Grenville group 1–like crustal reservoir (Fig. 8). This model requires that the time-integrated $^{238}U/^{204}Pb$ for the BMC rocks analyzed be about 5–20 because binary mixing in $^{207}Pb/^{204}Pb$ versus $^{206}Pb/^{204}Pb$ and $^{208}Pb/^{204}Pb$ isotope space produces linear arrays (Fig. 8). This is a reasonable range for $^{238}U/^{204}Pb$ in ophiolitic mafic intrusive rocks (Hamelin et al., 1984). However, postcrystallization introduction of radiogenic Pb derived from the Wissahickon Group metasedimentary rocks could have raised the $^{206}Pb/^{204}Pb$ ratios of the BMC, with little or no effect on the $^{207}Pb/^{204}Pb$ ratios.

REGIONAL IMPLICATIONS OF AN EARLY ORDOVICIAN AGE FOR THE BMC

Large mafic complexes of both true oceanic affinities (ophiolites of mid-ocean ridge origin) and ensialic intrusive bodies (associated as sub-arc complexes) are common in the Appalachian orogen (e.g., Williams and Talkington, 1977; Dunning et al., 1991). The distribution of these mafic bodies is presumed to mark ocean-continent boundaries, and this tectonic distinction is used to delineate terranes within the orogen (Williams and Hatcher, 1983). Mafic rocks of Late Cambrian to Early Ordovician age define a distinct belt that extends from Newfoundland to Maryland (Fyffe and Swinden, 1991) and perhaps, through the use of tonalitic complexes, to Alabama (Fig. 2 of Sinha et al., 1989). The extensive linear distribution of mafic complexes of both oceanic and continental affinities provides reasonable evidence for thermal instability along the eastern margin of North America. Therefore, it is likely that during Franconian to Tremadocian time, the Appalachian continental margin had rifted to form ocean basins and island arcs within a period of ~10–15 m.y. The similarity in ages of the larger mafic complexes (e.g., Mattinson, 1975; Dunning and Krogh, 1985a; Jenner et al., 1991) from Newfoundland to Maryland suggests a very rapid and short duration of magmatism over a distance of more than 2,000 km, and perhaps are ancient analogs of the present-day western Pacific Ocean (Dunning and Krogh, 1985b). The ages of obduction of the mafic complexes are much more difficult to evaluate, although ages of approximately 470 Ma have been proposed (Cawood and Suhr, 1992; Pinet and Tremblay, 1995), suggesting very rapid rates of collisional tectonics. The age of metamorphism obtained by us for the Baltimore mafic complex (453 Ma) is measurably younger than those obtained farther north, and may reflect a regional diachroneity of the Taconic collisional process as summarized by Laird (1989). The Late Ordovician age is probably synchronous with the M3 event of Crawford and Crawford (1980) that affected large areas of the central Appalachians.

ACKNOWLEDGMENTS

The research was supported in part by National Science Foundation grant EAR-9303694. We are grateful to Sharon Chiang, Todd Solberg, Hal Pendrak, and Margie Sentelle for technical support. Reviews by J. Beard and D. G. Pyle are acknowledged.

REFERENCES CITED

Aja, S. U., Wood, S. A., and Williams-Jones, A. E., 1995, The aqueous geochemistry of Zr and the solubility of some Zr-bearing mienrals: Applied Geochemistry, v. 10, p. 603–620.

Beard, J. S., 1986, Characteristic mineralogy of arc-related cumulate gabbros: Implications for the tectonic setting of gabbroic plutons and for andesite genesis: Geology, v. 14, p. 848–851.

Cawood, P. A., and Suhr, G., 1992, Generation and obduction of ophiolites: Constraints from the Bay of Island complex, western Newfoundland: Tectonics, v. 11, p. 884–897.

Crawford, M. L., and Crawford, W. A., 1980, Metamorphic and tectonic history of the Pennsylvania Piedmont: Geological Society of London Journal, v. 137, p. 311–320.

Crowley, W. P., 1976, The geology of the crystalline rocks near Baltimore and its bearing on the evolution of the eastern Maryland Piedmont: Maryland Geological Survey Report of Investigations no. 27, 40 p.

Dickinson, J. E., Jr., and Hess, P. C., 1982, Zircon saturation in lunar basalts and granites: Earth and Planetary Science Letters, v. 57, p. 336–344.

Dunning, G. R. and Krogh, T. E., 1985a, Tightly clustered, precise, U/Pb (zircon), ages of ophiolites from the Newfoundland Appalachians: Geological Society of America Abstracts with Programs, v. 15, p. 136.

Dunning, G. R., and Krogh, T. E., 1985b, Geochronology of ophiolites of the Newfoundland Appalachians: Canadian Journal of Earth Sciences, v. 22, p. 1659–1670.

Dunning, G. R., Swinden, H. S., Kean, B. F., Evans, D. T. W., and Jenner, G. A., 1991, A Cambrian island arc in Iapetus: Geochronology and geochemistry of the Lake Ambrose volcanic belt, Newfoundland Appalachians: Geological Magazine, v. 128, p. 1–17.

Fisher, G. W., 1970, The metamorphosed sedimentary rocks along the Potomac River, near Washington, D. C., in Fisher, G. W., et al., eds., Studies of Appalachian geology: central and southern: New York, Wiley Interscience, p. 299–315.

Forsythe, L. M., Nielsen, R. L., and Fisk, M. R., 1994, High-field-strength element partitioning between pyroxene and melt in basalts to dacites: Chemical Geology, v. 117, p. 107–125.

Fyffe, L. R., and Swinden, H. S., 1991, Paleotectonic setting of Cambro-Ordovician volcanic rocks in the Canadian Appalachians: Geoscience Canad, v. 18, p. 145–157.

Hamelin, B., Dupré, B., and Allègre, C. J., 1984, The lead isotope systematics of ophiolite complexes: Earth and Planetary Sciences, v. 67, p. 351–366.

Hanan, B. B., 1980, The petrology and geochemistry of the Baltimore Mafic Complex, Maryland [Ph.D. thesis]: Blacksburg, Virginia Polytechnic Institute and State University, 218 p.

Hanan, B. B., and Sinha, A. K., 1989, Petrology and tectonic affinity of the Baltimore mafic complex, Maryland, in Mittwede, S. K., and Stoddard, E. F., eds., Ultramafic rocks of the Appalachian Piedmont: Geological Society of America Special Paper 231, p. 1–18.

Higgins, M. W., 1972, Age, origin, regional relations, and nomenclature of the Glenarm series, central Appalachian Piedmont: A reinterpretation: Geological Society of America Bulletin, v. 83, p. 989–1026.

Higgins, M. W., and Conant, L. B., 1990, The geology of Cecil County, Maryland: Maryland Geological Survey Bulletin 37, 183 p.

Hopson, C. A., 1964, The crystalline rocks of Howard and Montgomery counties, Maryland: Maryland Geological Survey Report, p. 27–215.

Jenner, G. A., Dunning, G. R., Malpas, J., Brown, M., and Brace, T., 1991, Bay of Islands and Little Port complexes, revisited: Age, geochemical and isotopic evidence confirm suprasubduction-zone origin: Canadian Journal of Earth Sciences, v. 28, p. 1635–1652.

Krogh, T. E., 1973, A low contamination method for hydrothermal decomposition of zircon and extraction of U and Pb for isotopic age determinations: Geochimica et Cosmochimica Acta, v. 37, p. 485–494.

Laird, J., 1989, Metamorphism, *in* Hatcher, R. D., Jr., Thomas, W. A., and Viele, G. W., The Appalachian-Ouachita orogen in the United States: Boulder, Colorado, Geological Society of America, The geology of North America, v. F-2, p. 134–151.

Ludwig, K. R., 1993, Pbdat, a computer program for processing Pb-U-Th isotope data, version 1.24: U. S. Geological Survey Open-File Report 88-542, 32 p.

Mattinson, J. M., 1975, Early Paleozoic ophiolite complexes of Newfoundland: Isotopic ages of zircons: Geology, v. 3, p. 181–183.

Morgan, B. A., 1977, The Baltimore Complex, Maryland, Pennsylvania, and Virginia: Oregon State Department of Geology and Mineral Industries Bulletin 94-95, p. 41–49.

Pavlides, L., 1981, The central Virginia volcanic-plutonic belt: An island arc of Cambrian(?) age: U. S. Geological Survey Professional Paper 1231-A, 34 p.

Pinet, N., and Tremblay, A., 1995, Tectonic evolution of the Quebec-Maine Appalachians: From oceanic spreading to obduction and collision in the northern Appalachians: American Journal of Science, v. 295, p. 173–200.

Rubin, J. N., Henry, D. C., and Price, J. G., 1993, The mobility of zirconium and other "immobile" elements during hydrothermal alteration: Chemical Geology, v. 110, p. 29–47.

Shaw, H. F., and Wasserburg, G. J., 1984, Isotopic constraints on the origin of Appalachian mafic complexes: American Journal of Science, v. 284, p. 319–349.

Sinha, A. K., and Guy, R. E., 1989, Cambro-Ordovician igneous history of the North American margin, *in* Hatcher, R. D., Jr., Thomas, W. A., and Viele, G. W., The Appalachian-Ouachita orogen in the United States: Boulder, Colorado, Geological Society of America, The Geology of North America, v. F-2, p. 117–134.

Sinha, A. K., Hund, E. A., and Hogan, J. P., 1989, Paleozoic accretionary history of the North American plate margin (central and southern Appalachians): Constraints from the age, origin, and distribution of granitic rocks, *in* Hillhouse, J., ed., Deep structure and past kinematics of accreted terranes: American Geophysical Union Monograph 50, p. 219–238.

Sinha, A. K., Student, J., and Essex, R., 1991, Hydrothermal stability of zircons: Experimental and isotopic studies, *in* Sinha, A. K., ed., Zircons and fluids: An experimental investigation with applications for radioactive waste disposal: U.S. Department of Energy Progress Report VPI&SU-13951-4, 70 p.

Sinha, A. K., Hogan, J. P., and Parks, J., 1996, Lead isotope mapping of crustal reservoirs within the Grenville superterrane: I. Central and southern Appalachians, *in* Basu, A., and Hart, S. R., eds., Earth processes: Reading the isotopic code: American Geophysical Union Monograph 95, p. 293–305.

Southwick, D. L., 1969, Structure and petrology of the Harford County port of the Baltimore–State Line gabbro-peridotite complex, *in* Fisher, G. W., et al., eds., Studies of Appalachian geology: Central and southern: New York, Wiley-Interscience, 460 p.

Speer, J. A., and Solberg, T. N., 1982, Rare-earth pyrosilicates ($Re_2Si_2O_7$) as potential microprobe standards, *in* Heinrich, K. F. J., ed., Microbeam analysis: San Francisco, California, San Francisco Press, Inc., p. 445–446.

Thayer, T. P., 1967, Chemical and structural relationships of ultramafic and feldspathic rocks in alpine intrusive complex, *in* Wyllie, P. J., ed., Ultramafic and related rocks: New York, John Wiley and Sons, Inc., p. 222–239.

Tilton, G. R., 1973, Isotopic lead ages of chrondritic meteorites: Earth and Planetary Science Letters, v. 19, p. 321–329.

Tilton, G. R., Doe, B. R., and Hopson, C. A., 1970, Zircon age measurements in the Maryland Piedmont, with special reference to Baltimore Gneiss problems, *in* Fisher, G. W., et al., eds., Studies of Appalachian geology: Central and southern: New York, Wiley Interscience, 460 p.

Todt, W., Cliff, R. A., Hauser, A., and Hofmann, A. W., 1985, [202]Pb + [205]Pb double spike for lead isotope analyses: Tera Cognita, v. 4, p. 209.

Watson, E. B., 1982, Basalt contamination by continental crust: Some experiments and models: Contributions to Mineralogy and Petrology, v. 80, p. 73–87.

Watson, E. B., and Harrison, T. M., 1983, Zircon saturation revisited: Temperature and composition effects in a variety of crustal magma types: Earth and Planetary Science Letters, v. 64, p. 295–304.

Wayne, D. M., and Sinha, A. K., 1988, Physical and chemical response of zircons to deformation: Contributions to Mineralogy and Petrology, v. 98, p. 109–121.

Williams, H. and Hatcher, R. D., Jr., 1983, Appalachian suspect terranes, *in* Hatcher, R. D., Jr., Williams, H., and Zietz, I., eds., Contributions to the tectonics and geophysics of mountain chains: Geological Society of America Memoir 158, p. 33–53.

Williams, H., and Talkington, R. W., 1977, Distribution and tectonic setting of ophiolites and ophiolitic melanges in the Appalachian Orogen, *in* Coleman, R. G., and Irwin, W. P., eds., North American ophiolites: State of Oregon Department of Geology and Mineral Industries Bulletin 95, p. 1–11.

MANUSCRIPT ACCEPTED BY THE SOCIETY JULY 2, 1996

Geological Society of America
Memoir 191
1997

Elemental composition of the Alleghanian granitoid plutons of the southern Appalachians

J. Alexander Speer
Mineralogical Society of America, 1015 Eighteenth Street, N.W., Suite 601, Washington, D.C. 20036-5203
Kevin Hoff
7119 Abbotswood Drive, Charlotte, North Carolina 28226-7516

ABSTRACT

The Alleghanian (Carboniferous-Permian) magmatic rocks in the southern Appalachians are subalkaline and form a compositionally bimodal distribution of abundant granitoids and minor gabbroids with few intermediate composition rocks. The granitoids have a restricted compositional range (mean SiO_2 = 71.26; standard deviation 3.49) that spans the metaluminous-peraluminous boundary and corresponds to leucocratic syenogranites and monzogranites. They exhibit smooth, well-defined negative linear trends with increasing SiO_2 for TiO_2, P_2O_5, total Fe as Fe_2O_3, MgO, CaO, Eu, Br, Al_2O_3, V, Ce, Sm, La, and Zr, with linear correlation coefficients (r) decreasing from 0.87 for Ti to 0.57 for Zr. Tb, Sb, Sn, Cr, Ba, Sc, As, Nd, Sr, and Be have much less defined linear decrease with r from 0.56–0.38. Tl has a well-defined linear increase with increasing silica content (r = 0.87), and Be, U, and Rb have less well-defined increases (r = 0.33–0.43). S, Co, Nb, Pb, Ni, Ga, Th, Er, Gd, Mo, K, Cs, Hg, Zn, Mn, C, Dy, Cu, F, Li, B, Ta, Au, Bi, Y, Lu, Hf, Yb, Na, Cl, Ge, Se, Ag, Cd, Pr, Tm, and W show little systematic compositional variation with r values from 0.34–0.01. Compositional variations result from crystal-melt segregation as well as mixing with disaggregated enclaves and compositional differences of the source rocks. With the possible exception of Sr, no geographic compositional trends are evident. Compositional tectonic discrimination diagrams indicate that the granitoid plutons were produced from source rocks and magmatic processes at a destructive continental plate boundary during or after continental-continental collision. Geologic evidence is ambiguous as to whether two alkaline granitoids are A-type granites or just the differentiated or hydrothermal-enriched roof zones of much larger, normal plutons.

INTRODUCTION

The expression of orogenic magmatism during the late Paleozoic evolution of the southern Appalachians was the emplacement of granitoids and gabbroids mostly between 325 and 285 Ma. About 60 Alleghanian plutons form a northeast-trending band of dispersed, composite bodies covering 10,500 km² (Fig. 1). Of these plutons, 75% are metaluminous biotite or amphibole + biotite granitoids, and 20% are peraluminous biotite + muscovite ± garnet or cordierite + biotite granitoids with more evolved crustal sources. The remaining 5% are

gabbroids, intermediate rocks, and possible alkaline granitoids. The granitoid to gabbroid + intermediate rock area ratio is 180:1. The Alleghanian magmatism occurred in a postcollisional, strike-slip tectonic environment as a result of several possible melting mechanisms (Speer et al., 1994). Field occurrences, petrography, elemental, and isotopic compositions were reviewed by Speer et al. (1980); Fullagar and Butler (1979); and McSween et al. (1991). Melting mechanisms, segregation, ascent, and emplacement of these plutons were discussed by Speer et al. (1994).

The purpose of this chapter is to use available major- and trace-element analyses to (1) characterize the major and trace

Speer, J. A., and Hoff, K., 1997, Elemental composition of the Alleghanian granitoid plutons of the southern Appalachians, *in* Sinha, A. K., Whalen, J. B., and Hogan, J. P., eds., The Nature of Magmatism in the Appalachian Orogen: Boulder, Colorado, Geological Society of America Memoir 191.

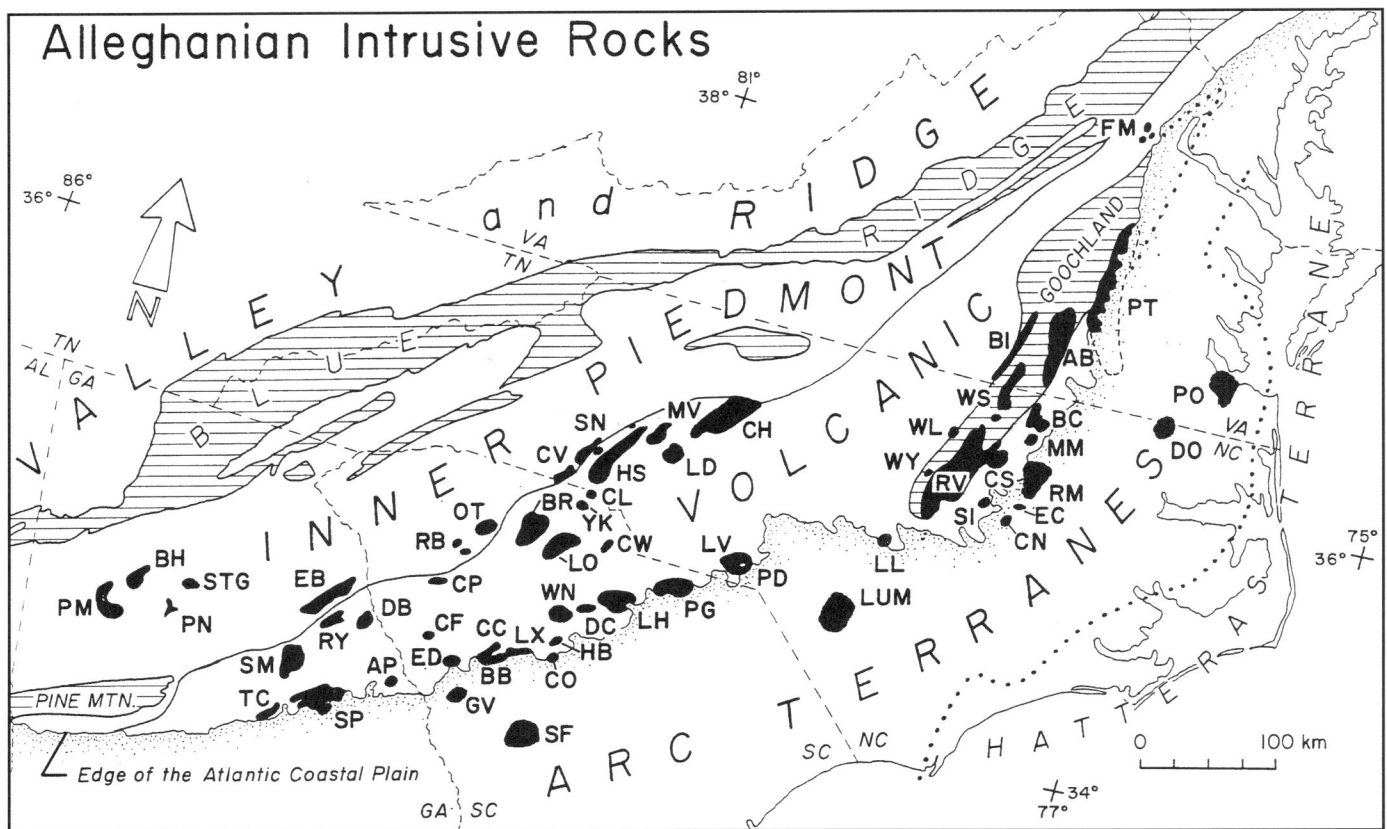

Figure 1. Location map of Alleghanian plutons in the southern Appalachians modified from Speer et al. (1994). Pluton name symbols are given in Appendix 1.

element composition of these magmatic rocks; (2) characterize and determine the origin of any compositional variations; (3) reexamine previously suggested spatial compositional trends; (4) evaluate the formational environment of the granitoids using compositional discriminant diagrams; and (5) examine the evidence for presence of alkaline or A-type granites.

GEOCHEMICAL DATA

Rock analyses reported in the literature and newly analyzed rocks are the two sources of data for this work. There are analyses for 572 rocks reported in the literature from 42 of the 60 plutons considered Alleghanian by Speer et al. (1994). There are both major and trace element analyses for all 42 plutons, although the number of samples and completeness of the analyses vary. Literature sources for the rock analyses are listed by pluton in Appendix 1. Major- and trace-element compositions of 34 newly analyzed rocks are reported in Tables 1 and 2. Analytical procedures are described in Appendix 2. Included with this group of samples in the discussions here, but whose analyses have been previously published elsewhere, are those from the Liberty Hill, South Carolina, and Cuffytown Creek, South Carolina, plutons (Speer et al., 1989; Speer and Becker, 1990).

An attempt was made to include and use all published rock analyses. The data were examined for systematic analytical errors and incongruities with the known petrography. Two literature datasets were omitted: those done by electron microprobe analysis on fused rock powders, and analyses of rocks wherein the samples were too small for the large grain size. In the first case, much of the Na and K were lost during the analysis. In the second excluded dataset, the rock analyses had large compositional variations even though the granitoids in that pluton are modally uniform.

Precision and accuracy of the published trace-element determinations were difficult to interpret. There are scattered outliers for many elements. It was often unknown if a blank entry for an element in a literature table means the element was not determined for the sample or if the result was below the detection limits. Furthermore, detection limits are not always reported. We treated such cases as if the element had not been analyzed. Examination of the remaining data shows apparent problems with Pb, and possibly Y and Ta. Lead determinations for the samples reported here (Table 2) form two populations. Analyses done in 1988 are uniformly greater (24–58 ppm) than those done since 1992 (1–10 ppm). Lead determinations from the literature are limited to the Elberton, Georgia, Sims, North

TABLE 1. MAJOR AND MINOR ELEMENT ANALYSES, ALLEGHANIAN PLUTONS OF THE SOUTHERN APPALACHIANS, U.S.A.

Sample	Castalia, N.C.						Clouds Creek, S.C.	Cuffytown Creek, S.C.					Gastonia N.C.	Landis N.C.	Liberty Hill, S.C.
	RL1-408	CS3-518	CS4-641	CS6-133	CS8-43	CS10-147	CC-4A	S7-50A	S7-53	S7-55	ED1-266	ED1-284	GS-03	LD-6A	F6-24
SiO_2	71.50	76.10	69.60	70.00	75.90	69.60	70.70	75.30	75.80	76.50	75.90	75.20	70.60	73.00	67.20
TiO_2	0.29	0.12	0.50	0.42	0.05	0.42	0.63	0.05	0.03	0.03	0.03	0.03	0.43	0.34	0.78
Al_2O_3	14.91	13.64	16.19	15.09	12.83	15.28	14.05	12.39	12.79	12.85	12.94	12.07	15.72	14.28	14.60
Fe_2O_3	1.37	0.53	1.45	1.13	0.46	1.34	1.05	0.47	0.55	0.48	0.61	0.55	1.21	1.11	1.46
FeO	0.80	0.41	1.77	1.61	0.05	1.43	2.72	0.31	0.24	0.24	0.22	0.20	1.21	0.77	2.38
MnO	0.04	0.05	0.05	0.05	0.04	0.05	0.06	0.14	0.06	0.08	0.10	0.09	0.03	0.03	0.07
MgO	0.74	0.18	1.14	1.21	0.05	0.98	0.96	0.05	0.05	0.05	0.05	0.05	0.81	0.63	0.98
CaO	2.43	1.11	3.26	2.99	0.50	2.88	1.54	0.56	0.49	0.60	0.67	0.59	2.58	1.96	2.66
BaO	0.10	0.03	0.15	0.14	0.01	0.12	0.09	0.00	0.00	0.00	0.00	0.00	0.13	0.10	0.14
Na_2O	4.01	4.48	4.65	4.12	4.43	4.53	3.25	4.42	4.57	4.60	4.68	4.34	3.68	3.20	4.00
K_2O	3.95	4.72	3.31	3.69	4.58	3.39	4.41	4.64	4.89	4.80	4.77	4.48	4.08	4.66	4.78
H_2O^+	0.41	0.01	0.11	0.14	0.06	0.21	0.00	<0.01	0.01	0.05	<0.01	0.02	0.32	0.34	0.04
H_2O^-	0.10	0.08	0.11	0.11	0.08	0.09	0.00	0.07	0.11	0.12	0.04	0.11	0.14	0.19	0.09
P_2O_5	0.09	0.04	0.16	0.13	0.02	0.13	0.15	0.01	0.02	0.01	0.01	0.02	0.10	0.06	0.18
CO_2	<0.20	0.29	0.26	0.26	0.15	0.29	0.22	0.26	0.29	0.22	0.29	0.29	<0.20	<0.20	0.29
F	0.03	0.01	0.02	0.02	0.01	0.02	0.05	0.21	0.21	0.24	0.26	0.23	0.07	0.05	0.08
Cl	<0.01												<0.01	<0.01	
S	<0.001	<0.001	<0.001	<0.001	<0.001	<0.001	<0.001	<0.001	<0.001	<0.001	0.036	<0.001	<0.001	<0.001	0.030
$O=F, Cl, S$	-0.01	-0.01	-0.01	-0.01	0.00	-0.01	-0.02	-0.09	-0.09	-0.10	-0.11	-0.10	-0.03	-0.02	-0.03
Total	100.75	101.75	102.72	101.10	99.21	100.75	99.87	98.79	100.02	100.76	100.51	98.18	101.08	100.70	99.74
Cat. O.R.	0.607	0.538	0.424	0.386	0.892	0.458	0.258	0.577	0.673	0.641	0.715	0.712	0.473	0.566	0.355
Mol. F/(FM)	0.435	0.577	0.430	0.378	0.723	0.431	0.517	0.805	0.805	0.790	0.813	0.797	0.443	0.441	0.514
Cat. F/(FM)	0.607	0.732	0.601	0.549	0.839	0.602	0.681	0.892	0.892	0.883	0.897	0.887	0.614	0.612	0.679
Mol. A/CNK	0.975	0.942	0.943	0.931	0.974	0.934	1.088	0.931	0.933	0.928	0.919	0.924	1.037	1.029	0.880
Date	03-94	02-88	02-88	02-88	02-88	02-88	02-88	02-88	02-88	02-88	02-88	02-88	03-94	03-94	02-88

J. A. Speer and K. Hoff

TABLE 1. MAJOR AND MINOR ELEMENT ANALYSES, ALLEGHANIAN PLUTONS OF THE SOUTHERN APPALACHIANS, U.S.A. (continued - page 2)

Sample	Liberty Hill, S.C.					Palmetto Ga.	Portsmouth, Va.			Rolesville, N.C.					
	K3-1210	S6-47	S6-54	K3-72	K3-924	PM1-205	25A-1866	25A-1880	25A-1964	RVCY-10	RVCY-47	RVKN-1	RVKN-2A	RVKN-2B	RVKN-2C
SiO_2	69.40	68.80	71.90	71.00	73.00	63.84	75.60	74.80	71.80	70.30	71.80	70.00	74.24	70.68	68.40
TiO_2	0.62	0.57	0.47	0.35	0.15	0.92	0.20	0.13	0.18	0.38	0.34	0.42	0.16	0.39	0.47
Al_2O_3	14.92	15.38	13.70	13.58	13.49	16.42	13.92	14.04	12.00	15.28	14.95	15.99	14.39	15.26	16.44
Fe_2O_3	1.36	1.34	0.91	0.76	0.55	1.69	0.80	0.91	0.66	1.40	1.08	1.87	0.87	1.11	1.19
FeO	1.67	1.74	1.65	1.39	0.65	2.71	0.55	0.27	0.55	0.82	0.83	0.61	0.32	1.18	1.47
MnO	0.05	0.05	0.05	0.04	0.04	0.07	0.03	0.02	0.04	0.03	0.04	0.03	0.02	0.02	0.03
MgO	0.73	0.71	0.60	0.38	0.18	1.81	0.41	0.27	0.38	0.72	0.56	0.73	0.37	0.52	1.08
CaO	2.21	2.17	1.73	1.48	1.19	3.79	0.99	0.53	1.11	1.97	1.64	2.05	1.33	1.63	2.86
BaO	0.12	0.10	0.09	0.10	0.08	0.22	0.06	0.06	0.05	0.13	0.08	0.13	0.04	0.15	0.17
Na_2O	3.99	4.00	3.60	3.60	3.77	3.92	4.34	4.23	3.67	4.07	4.09	4.32	4.05	3.74	4.65
K_2O	5.57	5.81	5.37	5.28	5.24	3.70	4.47	5.15	4.07	4.44	4.13	4.09	4.33	4.95	3.21
H_2O^+	0.07	0.04	0.04	0.02	0.12	0.70	0.32	0.14	0.16	0.31	0.28	0.18	0.26	0.25	0.31
H_2O^-	0.12	0.06	0.06	0.07	0.13	0.14	0.23	0.17	0.17	0.03	0.09	0.04	0.07	0.09	0.07
P_2O_5	0.16	0.14	0.09	0.10	0.03	0.41	0.08	0.06	0.08	0.11	0.09	0.14	0.09	0.16	0.19
CO_2	0.18	0.22	0.11	0.18	0.22	0.40	0.26	0.29	0.59	<0.20	<0.20	<0.20	0.50	0.50	0.40
F	0.05	0.08	0.08	0.10	0.03	0.13	0.09	0.09	0.15	0.07	0.10	0.08	0.02	0.06	0.07
Cl	......	......	......	......	......	0.03	......	......	......	<0.01	<0.01	<0.01	0.01	<0.01	<0.01
S	0.014	<0.001	<0.001	<0.001	<0.001	0.109	<0.001	<0.001	<0.001	<0.001	<0.001	<0.001	0.001	0.004	0.038
$O=F, Cl, S$	-0.02	-0.03	-0.03	-0.04	-0.01	0.05	-0.04	-0.04	-0.06	-0.03	-0.04	-0.03	-0.01	-0.02	-0.03
Total	101.22	101.17	100.41	98.39	98.86	100.95	102.31	101.13	95.58	100.03	100.06	100.65	101.07	100.66	101.02
Cat. O.R.	0.423	0.409	0.332	0.329	0.432	0.359	0.568	0.753	0.519	0.605	0.539	0.734	0.711	0.458	0.421
Mol. F/(FM)	0.527	0.537	0.537	0.604	0.638	0.396	0.463	0.536	0.457	0.447	0.474	0.469	0.456	0.540	0.397
Cat. F/(FM)	0.690	0.699	0.699	0.753	0.779	0.567	0.633	0.698	0.627	0.618	0.643	0.638	0.627	0.701	0.569
Mol. A/CNK	0.899	0.914	0.920	0.948	0.960	0.947	1.010	1.040	0.964	1.013	1.054	1.048	1.045	1.054	1.007
Date	02-88	02-88	02-88	02-88	02-88	03-94	02-88	02-88	02-88	03-93	03-93	03-93	03-93	03-93	03-93

TABLE 1. MAJOR AND MINOR ELEMENT ANALYSES, ALLEGHANIAN PLUTONS OF THE SOUTHERN APPALACHIANS, U.S.A. (continued - page 3)

| Sample | Rolesville, N.C. | | | Siloam, Ga. | | Sims, N.C. | | | | | | Rion | Winnsboro, S.C. Winns. | Anderson | York, S.C. |
	RVZB-06	RVZB-10	RVZB-17	AS7-220	SM1-544	SI-3	SI-4	SI-11	SI-14	SI-26	SI-27	WN-2	WN-3	WN-4	YK-03
SiO_2	65.80	62.13	69.82	72.65	69.37	74.97	74.12	74.50	73.95	73.86	73.56	72.60	72.00	70.00	72.80
TiO_2	0.55	1.11	0.57	0.35	0.38	0.26	0.26	0.26	0.30	0.29	0.29	0.21	0.42	0.47	0.29
Al_2O_3	18.13	16.22	15.40	14.10	15.93	13.85	13.57	13.74	14.27	13.82	14.28	14.31	13.57	14.95	14.92
Fe_2O_3	1.01	2.19	1.16	1.42	1.16	0.58	1.12	0.83	1.15	1.11	1.59	0.79	1.78	1.17	1.29
FeO	1.74	2.99	1.56	0.54	0.89	0.99	0.49	0.71	0.80	0.75	0.34	0.80	0.98	1.39	0.49
MnO	0.02	0.09	0.03	0.06	0.05	0.05	0.06	0.06	0.05	0.05	0.05	0.04	0.09	0.04	0.03
MgO	1.03	2.59	0.87	0.50	0.62	0.48	0.43	0.42	0.51	0.50	0.50	0.30	0.52	0.63	0.46
CaO	3.34	4.18	2.35	1.57	1.88	1.33	1.16	1.21	1.57	1.44	1.53	1.43	1.56	1.86	1.98
BaO	0.18	0.18	0.15	0.06	0.10	0.05	0.05	0.05	0.08	0.07	0.07	0.06	0.08	0.11	0.06
Na_2O	5.45	4.02	4.29	3.84	3.95	3.79	3.77	3.91	3.86	3.74	3.96	3.54	3.38	3.27	3.49
K_2O	2.99	3.50	4.15	4.59	5.42	4.49	4.85	4.67	4.53	4.73	4.69	5.16	5.24	5.24	4.66
H_2O+	0.43	0.84	0.38	0.27	0.32	0.45	0.53	0.47	0.47	0.62	0.59	0.28	0.19	0.19	0.27
H_2O-	0.10	0.21	0.16	0.11	0.03	0.13	0.16	0.09	0.08	0.11	0.11	0.03	0.05	0.02	0.12
P_2O_5	0.22	0.48	0.25	0.12	0.17	0.19	0.16	0.17	0.19	0.17	0.18	0.03	0.10	0.11	0.06
CO_2	<0.20	<0.20	<0.20	0.80	0.40	<0.20	0.03	<0.20	<0.20	<0.20	0.30	<0.20	<0.20	<0.20	<0.20
F	0.14	0.18	0.10	0.18	0.09	0.09	0.09	0.09	0.08	0.09	0.09	0.08	0.05	0.15	0.05
Cl	<0.01	<0.01	<0.01	0.01	<0.01	0.02	0.01	<0.01	0.01	<0.01	0.02	<0.01	<0.01	<0.01	<0.01
S	0.008	0.055	0.011	0.004	0.001	0.039	0.072	0.020	<0.001	<0.001	<0.001	0.010	0.017	<0.001	<0.001
$O=F, Cl, S$	-0.06	-0.10	-0.05	-0.08	-0.04	-0.04	-0.04	-0.04	-0.03	-0.04	-0.04	-0.03	-0.02	-0.06	-0.02
Total	101.07	100.86	101.20	101.10	100.73	101.72	100.89	101.16	101.87	101.31	102.11	99.64	100.01	99.53	100.95
Cat. O.R.	0.342	0.397	0.400	0.703	0.540	0.345	0.672	0.513	0.564	0.570	0.808	0.471	0.621	0.430	0.702
Mol. F/(FM)	0.419	0.349	0.456	0.505	0.467	0.469	0.494	0.493	0.502	0.495	0.499	0.586	0.582	0.521	0.501
Cat. F/(FM)	0.590	0.518	0.626	0.671	0.636	0.639	0.661	0.661	0.669	0.662	0.665	0.739	0.736	0.685	0.668
Mol. A/CNK	0.992	0.901	0.973	0.997	1.009	1.025	1.001	1.004	1.012	0.995	0.994	1.022	0.965	1.036	1.037
Date	04-93	04-93	04-93	03-94	03-94	02-92	02-92	02-92	02-92	02-92	02-92	03-94	03-94	03-94	03-94

TABLE 2. TRACE ELEMENT ANALYSES, ALLEGHANIAN PLUTONS OF THE SOUTHERN APPALACHIANS, U.S.A.

Pluton	Castalia, N.C.						Clouds Creek, S.C.	Cuffytown Creek, S.C.				
Sample	RL1-408	CS3-51.8	CS4-641	CS6-133	CS8-43	CS10-147	CC-4A	S7-50A	S7-53	S7-55	ED1-266	ED1-284
Li	27	18	28	24	8	35	32	26	20	40	29	31
Be	1.7	2.2	1.5	1.5	3.7	1.6	3.3	7.4	5.3	4.6	4.9	5
B	10	<10	<10	<10	<10	10	<10	<10	<10	30	<10	<10
F	270	140	240	220	70	220	490	2,100	2,050	2,400	2,600	2,300
Cl	<100	....	....	....	....	....	....	....	....	....	....	....
Sc	4	4	5	7	3	6	9	4	4	5	5	4
V	41	2	42	37	<1	38	37	<1	<1	<1	<1	<1
Cr	10	8	7	16	3	13	28	<1	5	7	5	6
Co	4	....	....	....	....	....	9	....	....	....	....	....
Ni	2	<1	<1	6	<1	4	15	5	<1	<1	<1	<1
Cu	14	<1	13	10	<1	10	22	22	<1	<1	<1	<1
Zn	45	31	67	51	21	56	67	62	33	49	150	93
Ga	10	15	15	13	15	14	18	21	21	23	21	22
Ge	<5	10	10	10	10	10	10	10	10	10	10	10
As	....	2	2	3	1	2	5	1	1	1	3	2
Se	....	0.2	0.2	0.2	0.2	0.2	0.2	0.2	0.2	0.2	0.2	0.2
Br	....	<12	<5	<6	6	<6	<6	5	<6	<7	<6	9
Rb	166	280	120	140	380	150	150	340	250	380	370	350
Sr	220	75	414	305	16	344	185	7	8	7	9	9
Y	23	81	34	42	93	42	59	110	110	110	110	105
Zr	....	69	200	150	48	155	230	110	110	100	100	100
Nb	8	13	6	7	16	7	18	65	51	58	51	57
Mo	<1	1	3	4	5	1	3	3	2	....	5	4
Ag	....	0.5	0.5	0.5	0.5	0.5	0.5	0.5	0.5	0.5	0.5	0.5
Cd	<0.1	0.1	0.1	0.1	0.2	0.1	0.1	0.2	0.2	0.1	0.5	0.3
Sn	<2	1	1	1	1	1	1	1	1	1	1	1
Sb	....	0.2	0.1	0.2	0.2	0.1	0.2	0.1	0.2	0.1	0.1	0.1
Te	....	<0.05	<0.05	<0.05	<0.05	<0.05	<0.05	<0.05	<0.05	<0.05	<0.05	<0.05
Cs	3.5	<2	<2	3	3	<2	2	5	3	4	2	2
Ba	880	230	1,310	1,240	50	1,080	840	30	30	30	20	30
La	....	10	39	34	4	30	40	34	12	12	31	29
Ce	....	41	116	59	47	95	84	66	72	74	40	43
Pr	....	....	....	....	....	....	....	....	....	....	....	....
Nd	....	42	8	6	<5	10	12	12	11	8	24	66
Sm	....	2.2	3.8	3.6	0.6	4	6.8	3.7	5.1	3.5	3.1	6.4
Eu	....	<0.5	<0.5	<0.5	<0.5	<0.5	<0.5	<0.5	<0.5	<0.5	<0.5	<0.5
Gd	....	....	....	....	....	....	....	....	....	....	....	....
Tb	....	<0.1	1	<0.1	0.1	<0.1	<0.1	0.2	<0.1	<0.1	<0.1	<0.1
Dy	....	3	4	3	<2	8	7	12	<10	4	10	7
Ho	....	....	....	....	....	....	....	....	....	....	....	....
Er	....	....	....	....	....	....	....	....	....	....	....	....
Tm	....	....	....	....	....	....	....	....	....	....	....	....
Yb	....	1.7	0.5	<0.1	3.4	0.4	1.3	3.7	3.1	3.7	2.8	2.9
Lu	....	<0.2	<0.2	<0.2	<0.2	<0.2	0.2	0.5	0.4	0.7	0.4	0.2
Hf	10	17	7	7	10	9	6	7	5	8	10	21
Ta	<2.0	2	<2	<2	<2	<3	<2	<2	3	3	<2	<2
W	<2	....	....	....	....	....	1	....	....	....	....	....
Au, ppb	....	5	20	15	15	5	25	10	20	15	20	15
Hg, ppb	....	10	10	10	10	10	30	10	20	10	20	20
Tl	....	0.9	0.3	0.4	1.1	0.3	0.4	1.2	1.2	1.4	1.4	1.4
Pb	4	50	24	28	44	34	32	58	50	46	48	46
Bi	....	0.1	0.1	0.1	0.1	0.3	0.1	0.5	0.1	0.1	0.1	0.3
Th	10	15	15	14	17	19	10	43	30	33	29	33
U	4.6	13	4	3.4	17	3.7	2.2	11	9	11	12	12
Anal. date	03-94	02-88	02-88	02-88	02-88	02-88	02-88	02-88	02-88	02-88	02-88	02-88

TABLE 2. TRACE ELEMENT ANALYSES, ALLEGHANIAN PLUTONS OF THE SOUTHERN APPALACHIANS, U.S.A. (continued - page 2)

Pluton Sample	Gastonia N.C. GS-03	Landis N.C. LD-6A	Liberty Hill, S.C. F6-24	K3-1210	S6-47	S6-54	K3-72	K3-924	Palmetto Ga. PM1-205	Portsmouth, Va. 25A-1866	25A-1880	25A-1964
Li	27	12	16	10	15	18	20	9	11	15	21	25
Be	2	1.5	2	1.6	2.2	2.2	3.6	2.6	2.4	5	4.5	11
B	10	10	<10	<10	<10	<10	<10	<10	20	<10	<10	<10
F	740	500	820	520	780	820	1,000	260	1,250	910	930	1,450
Cl	<100	<100	....	....	....	....	....	....	300	....	....	....
Sc	3	1	10	7	9	6	4	2	7.5	3	3	4
V	56	36	37	24	23	17	14	2	105	9	6	8
Cr	9	8	4	<1	2	13	3	7	20	1	<1	3
Co	3	2	....	....	....	....	....	....	8	....	....	....
Ni	<1	<1	<1	<1	<1	1	<1	<1	5	2	2	1
Cu	26	4	3	<1	<1	<1	<1	<1	10	7	6	25
Zn	78	45	67	52	52	48	56	24	85	35	24	49
Ga	16	15	16	15	15	15	17	17	19	19	21	21
Ge	<5	<5	10	10	10	10	10	10	<5	10	10	10
As	....	....	2	2	3	3	3	2	....	1	2	2
Se	....	....	0.2	0.2	0.2	0.2	0.2	0.2	....	0.2	0.2	0.2
Br	....	....	<6	<7	<6	<5	<4	<5	....	<4	<6	10
Rb	186	130	110	100	160	170	290	180	116	270	320	290
Sr	410	510	304	296	268	209	206	200	750	225	163	174
Y	15	16	55	44	57	51	69	48	28	60	71	59
Zr	....	....	300	260	230	185	265	115	....	115	95	115
Nb	9	9	24	17	20	18	21	14	15	15	15	14
Mo	<1	<1	2	4	5	2	1	4	<1	3	2	1
Ag	....	....	0.5	0.5	0.5	0.5	0.5	0.5	....	0.5	0.5	0.5
Cd	<0.1	<0.1	0.1	0.1	0.1	0.1	0.1	0.1	<0.1	0.1	0.1	0.1
Sn	<2	<2	2	1	2	1	1	1	<2	1	1	1
Sb	....	....	3.4	0.2	2.6	1	0.2	0.2	....	0.2	0.1	0.2
Te	....	....	<0.05	<0.05	<0.05	<0.05	<0.05	<0.05	....	<0.05	<0.05	<0.05
Cs	2	1	2	<2	<2	<2	<2	<2	2	<2	<2	<2
Ba	1,200	860	1,240	1,110	910	780	910	710	1,980	500	540	430
La	....	....	69	111	96	49	101	32	....	26	22	26
Ce	....	....	139	200	181	139	230	62	350	42	50	49
Pr	....	....	....	....	....	....	....	....	....	....	....	....
Nd	....	....	39	25	22	12	32	18	....	54	6	19
Sm	....	....	9.3	7.5	8.4	6.3	8.5	2.9	....	2.9	1.8	2.5
Eu	....	....	0.5	<0.5	<0.5	<0.5	0.5	<0.5	....	<0.5	<0.5	<0.5
Gd	....	....	....	....	....	....	....	....	....	....	....	....
Tb	....	....	0.2	<0.1	<0.1	<0.1	<0.1	0.1	....	<0.1	0.1	<0.1
Dy	....	....	8	<3	4	8	4	5	....	2	<1	<2
Ho	....	....	....	....	....	....	....	....	....	....	....	....
Er	....	....	....	....	....	....	....	....	....	....	....	....
Tm	....	....	....	....	....	....	....	....	....	....	....	....
Yb	....	....	2.6	0.3	1.6	1.3	<0.1	<0.1	....	0.5	<0.1	<0.1
Lu	....	....	0.2	0.2	<0.2	0.3	<0.2	<0.2	....	<0.2	<0.2	<0.2
Hf	12	14	15	5	5	10	6	8	22	24	21	10
Ta	2	2	<3	<2	<2	<3	<2	<2	<2	<2	2	<3
W	<2	<2	....	....	....	....	....	....	<2	....	....	....
Au, ppb	....	....	10	<5	<5	5	10	5	....	15	5	15
Hg, ppb	....	....	10	10	10	10	30	10	....	20	30	20
Tl	....	....	0.4	0.5	0.6	0.6	0.9	0.8	....	1	1.2	1.1
Pb	4	6	42	38	42	44	40	50	1	36	22	32
Bi	....	....	0.1	0.1	0.1	0.1	0.1	0.1	....	0.1	0.1	1.4
Th	21	15	12	16	18	14	36	20	41	21	17	25
U	3.8	2.2	2.4	2.3	3.5	2.8	4.9	12	3.8	5.3	11	9.4
Anal. date	03-94	03-94	02-88	02-88	02-88	02-88	02-88	02-88	03-94	02-88	02-88	02-88

J. A. Speer and K. Hoff

TABLE 2. TRACE ELEMENT ANALYSES, ALLEGHANIAN PLUTONS OF THE SOUTHERN APPALACHIANS, U.S.A. (continued - page 3)

Sample	RVCY-10	RVCY-47	RVKN-1	RVKN-2A	RVKN-2B	RVKN-2C	RVZB-06	RVZB-10	RVZB-17	AS7-220	SM1-544
				Rolesville, N.C.						Siloam, Ga.	
Li	24	44	32	23	29	40	24	17	30	40	31
Be	2.1	2.6	1.8	2.2	1.6	1.6	2.2	2	1.9	5	4.7
B	5	10	10	15	10	15	10	5	5	15	15
F	650	1,040	750	200	580	720	1,390	1,830	1,000	1,800	900
Cl	<100	<100	<100	100	<100	<100	<100	<100	<100	<100	<100
Sc	3.5	3	3.5	3	2.5	3.5	3.5	10.5	3.5	4.5	5
V	46	38	42	24	31	62	60	110	50	35	35
Cr	14	14	11	8	10	13	12	34	12	8	12
Co	<1	<1	<1	2	3	6	6	14	4	....	2
Ni	1	<1	<1	<1	<1	4	2	18	2	<1	1
Cu	19	7	24	<1	1	32	28	25	21	3	2
Zn	54	70	63	27	77	72	65	91	67	49	59
Ga	5	7	6	16	20	19	16	14	13	17	20
Ge	<5	<5	<5	<5	<5	<5	<5	<5	<5	<5	<5
As	....	....	....	....	....	....	....	....	....	....	....
Se	....	....	....	....	....	....	....	....	....	....	....
Br	....	....	....	....	....	....	....	....	....	....	....
Rb	220	270	210	250	240	152	122	90	122	330	380
Sr	330	240	280	120	148	390	390	780	290	162	200
Y	13	25	13	12	13	9	5	15	5	27	40
Zr	....	....	....	....	....	....	....	....	....	....	....
Nb	10	12	9	8	18	5	5	10	5	25	25
Mo	<1	<1	<1	<1	3	1	<1	<1	<1	1	<1
Ag	....	....	....	....	....	....	....	....	....	....	....
Cd	<0.1	<0.1	<0.1	<0.1	<0.1	<0.1	<0.1	<0.1	<0.1	<0.1	<0.1
Sn	<2	<2	<2	<2	<2	<2	<2	<2	2	<2	<2
Sb	....	....	....	....	....	....	....	....	....	....	....
Te	....	....	....	....	....	....	....	....	....	....	....
Cs	1	0.5	2.5	4.5	2.5	4.5	2.5	3	0.5	2	6.5
Ba	1,160	720	1,200	400	1,300	1,560	1,600	1,640	1,380	580	940
La	....	....	....	....	....	....	....	....	....	....	....
Ce	....	....	....	48	250	116	....	....	....	118	136
Pr	....	....	....	....	....	....	....	....	....	....	....
Nd	....	....	....	....	....	....	....	....	....	....	....
Sm	....	....	....	....	....	....	....	....	....	....	....
Eu	....	....	....	....	....	....	....	....	....	....	....
Gd	....	....	....	....	....	....	....	....	....	....	....
Tb	....	....	....	....	....	....	....	....	....	....	....
Dy	....	....	....	....	....	....	....	....	....	....	....
Ho	....	....	....	....	....	....	....	....	....	....	....
Er	....	....	....	....	....	....	....	....	....	....	....
Tm	....	....	....	....	....	....	....	....	....	....	....
Yb	....	....	....	....	....	....	....	....	....	....	....
Lu	....	....	....	....	....	....	....	....	....	....	....
Hf	10	12	10	10	18	14	8	12	12	240	12
Ta	<2	<2	<2	2	<2	4	<2	<2	<2	2	2
W	<2	<2	<2	<2	<2	<2	<2	<2	<2	....	<2
Au, ppb	....	....	....	....	....	....	....	....	....	....	....
Hg, ppb	....	....	....	....	....	....	....	....	....	....	....
Tl	....	....	....	....	....	....	....	....	....	....	....
Pb	<1	1	<1	2	<1	<1	<1	4	<1	7	2
Bi	....	....	....	....	....	....	....	....	....	....	....
Th	31	24	36	22	36	10	12	21	17	36	38
U	2.2	4.2	2.8	8.4	1.6	1.4	4.4	2.6	2.2	7	10.4
Analysis date	03-93	03-93	03-93	03-93	03-93	03-93	04-93	04-93	04-93	03-94	03-94

TABLE 2. TRACE ELEMENT ANALYSES, ALLEGHANIAN PLUTONS OF THE SOUTHERN APPALACHIANS, U.S.A. (continued - page 4)

Sample	Sims, N.C.						Winnsboro, S.C.			York, S.C.
							Rion	Winns.	Anderson	
	SI-3	SI-4	SI-11	SI-14	SI-26	SI-27	WN-2	WN-3	WN-4	YK-03
Li	33	36	35	27	26	29	34	6	14	17
Be	3.7	4	4.2	2.8	3.3	3.3	3	1.4	3	2.2
B	5	5	<5	<5	5	5	10	15	10	<5
F	860	940	860	820	880	910	830	460	1,470	490
Cl	200	100	<100	100	<100	200	<100	<100	<100	<100
Sc	5.5	5.5	5.5	4.5	5	5	3.5	7	4	2
V	30	32	28	33	33	31	20	29	40	31
Cr	14	17	20	16	15	16	10	12	11	5
Co	1	<1	1	1	<1	1	<1	1	<1	2
Ni	1	2	1	1	2	2	<1	<1	1	<1
Cu	8	11	7	5	4	4	2	7	<1	6
Zn	40	38	38	48	47	54	38	55	49	57
Ga	14	14	16	14	14	14	6	5	6	15
Ge	<5	<5	<5	<5	<5	<5	<5	<5	<5	<5
As	....	....	....	....	....	....	....	....	....	....
Se	....	....	....	....	....	....	....	....	....	....
Br	....	....	....	....	....	....	....	....	....	....
Rb	214	220	200	170	161	165	370	158	320	184
Sr	89	98	89	122	106	109	116	134	170	280
Y	20	15	20	15	20	20	34	32	32	16
Zr	....	....	....	....	....	....	....	....	....	....
Nb	40	40	45	20	30	25	19	24	21	12
Mo	<1	1	<1	<1	<1	<1	<1	6	<1	<1
Ag	....	....	....	....	....	....	....	....	....	....
Cd	<0.1	<0.1	<0.1	<0.1	<0.1	<0.1	<0.1	<0.1	<0.1	<0.1
Sn	<2	<2	<2	<2	<2	<2	<2	<2	<2	<2
Sb	....	....	....	....	....	....	....	....	....	....
Te	....	....	....	....	....	....	....	....	....	....
Cs	7	6.5	3.5	1	2	3.5	4.5	0.5	0.5	<0.05
Ba	....	....	....	....	....	....	580	740	980	580
La	42	44	45	46	44	47	....	....	....	....
Ce	100	90	92	94	88	94	....	....	....	....
Pr	10	10	10	10	10	10	....	....	....	....
Nd	15	20	25	30	30	35	....	....	....	....
Sm	4.8	4.7	4.9	4.6	5.4	5.1	....	....	....	....
Eu	<0.5	0.5	<0.5	1	0.5	<0.5	....	....	....	....
Gd	<50	<50	<50	<50	<50	<50	....	....	....	....
Th	0.3	0.4	0.6	0.3	<0.1	<0.1	....	....	....	....
Dy	2	3	2	1	2	2	....	....	....	....
Ho	<1	<1	<1	<1	<1	<1	....	....	....	....
Er	<20	<20	<20	<20	<20	<20	....	....	....	....
Tm	<1	1	<1	<1	1	<1	....	....	....	....
Yb	2.1	1.9	1.3	2	2	1.8	....	....	....	....
La	0.3	0.2	0.3	0.3	0.3	0.3	....	....	....	....
Hf	10	12	12	14	12	14	10	14	12	12
Ta	4	2	4	<2	<2	<2	<2.0	<2.0	<2.0	2
W	<2	<2	<2	<2	<2	<2	<2	<2	<2	<2
Au, ppb	....	....	....	....	....	....	....	....	....	....
Hg, ppb	....	....	....	....	....	....	....	....	....	....
Tl	....	....	....	....	....	....	....	....	....	....
Pb	7	7	7	8	10	10	9	3	3	10
Bi	....	....	....	....	....	....	....	....	....	....
Th	26	22	25	25	24	29	47	20	49	26
U	11	11	12	6	5	6	8	3.4	4	4.6
Analysis date	02-92	02-92	02-92	02-92	02-92	02-92	03.94	03.94	03.94	03.94

Carolina, and Sparta, Georgia, plutons. Each was done by a different analyst, and the values from each pluton form their own distinct cluster. This clustering by different analysts or analysis dates indicates that there may well be systematic errors in the Pb determinations. Ta contents reported here have values less than 5 ppm (Table 2), whereas the only other reported Ta determinations from the Elberton, Georgia pluton are between 10 and 15 ppm. Y values for the Rocky Mount, North Carolina, pluton extend to much greater values (255 ppm) than the values reported by others (<100 ppm). The Elberton rocks may be richer in Ta and Rocky Mount rocks richer in Y than the other granitoids, or there may be systematic analytical errors. At present there are insufficient data to decide.

Table 3 contains summary statistics for the analyzed granitoid samples. Rock (1987, 1988) concluded that the arithmetic mean is the worst estimate of the central compositional value for a number of rock analyses. Three estimates of the central value are included in Table 3: the mean, as well as two of Rock's suggestions for more robust estimates, trimmed means at 10% and 50%. A 10% trimmed mean is formed by removing (trimming) 10% of the values from both ends of the dataset and calculating the arithmetic mean of the remainder. A 50% trimmed mean is the median. We used trimmed means because they are more readily understood than the other estimates Rock suggested. We chose a 10% trimmed mean because estimates of the central value changed slowly at percentages above 10% as compared to values between 1% and 9%. The 50% trimmed mean (median) is included for comparison. The skewness, minimum and maximum values, as well as the number of analytical determinations for each of 66 elements are listed in Table 3. Also included are the linear correlation coefficients (r) between element or oxide concentration and rock silica content. Positive values for r indicate that the element increases with increasing silica; negative values indicate that the element decreases with increasing silica. The correlation coefficients are for descriptive purposes, it is not expected that the relationship between elements is linear.

COMPOSITIONAL FEATURES OF THE ALLEGHANIAN GRANITOIDS

The silica content of all analyzed Alleghanian igneous rocks ranges from 45.15–78.52 wt%; there is a clear compositional separation between the granitoids and gabbroids (Fig. 2). There are few rocks of intermediate composition. The relative difference in the number of granitoid to gabbroid analyses reflects the 180:1 area ratio of the two. The remainder of this chapter concentrates on the granitoids.

The 10% trimmed mean of the silica content of the Alleghanian granitoids is 71.40 (Table 3). The granitoids are subalkaline on the basis of $Na_2O + K_2O$ versus silica (Fig. 2), with $K_2O > Na_2O$ (Table 3). Most rock compositions on this diagram are granites, with lesser amounts of granodiorites (Wilson, 1989). This is consistent with the narrow modal compositional range observable in the field and determined by point counts

(McSween et al., 1991, Fig. 7-6). The granitoids are leucocratic; the average $TiO_2 + Fe_2O_3 + MgO + MnO$ content is less than 3.34 wt%. They are iron rich, and have an average cation Fe/(Fe + Mg) ratio of 0.68 (Table 3). There are generally equal amounts of ferrous and ferric iron, the average cation $Fe^{+3}/(Fe^{+2} + Fe^{+3})$ ratio is 0.49. The granitoids extend into the calc-alkaline field on an AFM plot (not shown), although some gabbroids overlap the tholeiitic field (Irvine and Baragar, 1971). Most of the studied plutons are too felsic, and their compositional range too limited, to make this distinction meaningful.

Data for all plutons show TiO_2, P_2O_5, total Fe as Fe_2O_3, MgO, CaO, Eu, Br, Al_2O_3, V, Ce, Sm, La, and Zr have well-defined, nearly linear negative trends with increasing SiO_2. The correlation coefficients (r) are greater than 0.57 (Table 3). This pattern includes all major elements, except for Na_2O and K_2O. Tl has a well-defined linear increase. The elements Tb, Sb, Sn, Cr, Ba, Sc, As, Nd, Sr, and Be have a much less defined linear decrease and Be, U, and Rb a less well-defined increase with silica with r between 0.56 and 0.38. The remaining elements, including the major oxides of Na and K, have no apparent systematic variation with silica, and r <0.38. A graphical illustration of how the Harker diagrams appear for three correlation coefficients in the observed range (r = 0.84, 0.38, and 0.02) is given in Figure 3.

The granitoids are metaluminous through peraluminous (Shand, 1951) (Fig. 4). The A/CNK (molecular $Al_2O_3/[CaO + Na_2O + K_2O]$) values broadly reflect the mineral assemblages. Amphibole + biotite granitoids have A/CNK < 0.95. Biotite granitoids span the metaluminous-peraluminous boundary with a range of A/CNK values from 0.95 to about 1.05, depending upon the aluminum content of biotite. Biotite + muscovite granitoids have A/CNK from 1.02 to 1.20 or more, depending upon the amount of muscovite present. The few biotite + muscovite + garnet and biotite + cordierite granitoids are >1.08. The relationship between these AFMMn mineral assemblages and the rock composition is also illustrated on an ACFM diagram (Fig. 5).

A lower-crust normalized plot of selected elements is given in Figure 6. The lower crust was chosen for normalization because it is a likely source for the Alleghanian granitoid magmas whereas mid-oceanic ridge basalt, primitive mantle, or chondrites have less clear genetic relationships to the granitoids. The granitoids are enriched over the lower crust in all of the selected elements except for Ti, Sc, and V. Both contain about the same amounts of Sr and Yb. Pb, Ba, Nb, Sr, Ti, Yb, and possibly Sc and V have negative anomalies compared to the trend defined by adjacent elements.

The light rare earth element (LREE) concentrations generally show a well-defined, linear decrease with increasing silica contents, whereas the heavy REEs show no obvious trends (Table 3). This lack of an obvious trend might be accounted for by a lack of precision in determining the less-abundant heavy REEs. Most Alleghanian granitoid chondrite-normalized REE patterns are identical to that of the 10% trimmed mean shown in Figure 7. The REE patterns have gentle slopes, with light

REE enrichment, a small or absent Eu anomaly, and a low abundance of the heavier REEs (Yb < 4× chondrite).

DISCUSSION

Element variations

The linear decrease of most major oxides with increasing silica content results in large part from the increasing silica content itself. The nearly constant amounts of Na_2O and K_2O with increasing silica is an actual enrichment relative to the other oxides. Speer et al. (1989) showed for the Liberty Hill, South Carolina, pluton that the major oxides varied with the modal amounts of quartz, feldspars, and mafic minerals. The modal variations, in turn, were concluded to result from crystal-melt segregation and disaggregation of enclaves during emplacement. This conclusion was based on observed field structures. Identical structures are seen by us in all granitoids listed in Appendix 1 and we conclude that these processes can account for the major element variations in the bivariate plots observed for the entire group (Fig. 3).

The ACFM diagram (Fig. 5) shows the relative variation of the major oxides other than silica. Most points lie between two lines arbitrarily drawn radiating away from (or toward) amphibole. This indicates that differences in much of the relative abundance of the major elements of the granitoids can be explained by the influence of amphibole. For some rocks it could be variations in modal amphibole. More likely, because amphibole-bearing granitoids are uncommon, the compositional trend on the ACFM diagram would result from the fractional crystallization or melting of varying amounts of amphibole during an earlier magmatic stage. The ACFM diagram shows significant metaluminous-peraluminous compositional variation. This is source related. Strongly peraluminous granitoids (Fig. 4), those with cordierite-, garnet-, or abundant muscovite-bearing assemblages, are found in eight plutons and account for less than 10% of the area of the granitoids (Speer et al., 1994). They have initial Sr ratios > 0.7100 and $\delta^{18}O$ > 8.9‰. This indicates a significant continental crustal source component for these rocks. The remaining granitoids, covering 90% of the granitoid exposure, have initial Sr isotope ratios < 0.708 and $\delta^{18}O$ values < 9‰. Of the 30 plutons listed by Speer et al. (1994, Table 1), 20 have initial Sr ratios of 0.7035–0.7052. These features would indicate that most of the late Alleghanian magma was derived from a more primitive source, either in the mantle, crust-mantle boundary, or relatively young continental crust derived from them (Fullagar and Butler, 1979). The few intermediate Sr initial ratio granitoids may reflect varying amounts of mixing or interaction of the magma from primitive sources with radiogenic crust.

The negative Nb, TiO_2, and V anomalies on the lower-crust normalized plot (Fig. 6) indicate fractionation of oxides, whereas the negative Sc anomaly can be explained by fractionation of Fe-Mg silicates. The first row transition elements, starting with V, decrease with increasing silica by increasingly smaller linear correlation coefficients until Cu and Zn are reached (Table 3). This could be explained by fractionation of a changing mix of silicates, oxides, and sulfides across the row, sulfides being more important for Cu and Zn. Negative Ba and Sr anomalies indicate feldspar fractionation. Bivariate Ba-Sr and Rb-Sr log-log plots (Fig. 8) also suggest Sr and Ba variation by fractional melting or crystallizing of the feldspars. The negative correlation coefficient for Eu (r = –0.74) is much more linear than the other REEs (Table 3) and nearly matches that for CaO (r = –0.80). This and the negative Eu anomaly on the chondrite-normalized REE diagram (Fig. 7) implies plagioclase fractionation. Rb content increases slightly with decreasing Sr contents (Fig. 8b). This could be accounted for by fractionation into the alkali feldspar and micas or by incompatible behavior and partitioning of Rb to the fluid phase.

Radiogenic elements

More measurements for radioactive, heat-producing elements (K, Th, and U) have been made on the granitoids of the southern Appalachians than for any other elements (Table 3). In part this is due to the investigation of high-heat–producing granitoids for the Virginia Polytechnic Institute Geothermal Program (Costain et al., 1986), though other specific Th-U studies were done (Davis, 1977). For most of these samples (~400) no other elemental determinations were made. Figure 9 shows histograms with distributions of Th and U values. U shows a lognormal distribution, whereas Th content show several apparent maxima. Examination of the Th data shows that these maxima are formed as a result of the measurements on a large number of samples (up to 90) from single plutons. Many of the Th-rich plutons attracted considerable analytical attention.

Variations in Th-U contents among some granitoids may be a source effect. The composite Liberty Hill pluton is composed of a fine- and a coarse-grained granitoid. Nd-Sm isotopic compositions indicate these are from different sources. The fine-grained granitoid has much more negative $\varepsilon_{Nd}(0)$ value than the coarse-grained granitoid: –10.8 versus –4.3 (Samson and Speer, 1993). The coarse-grained granitoid has a median Th content of 12.7 ppm and 2.4 ppm U, whereas the fine-grained granite has median values of 29.5 ppm Th and 5.0 ppm U.

Spatial compositional trends

Granitoids with values greater than 400 ppm Sr in western North and South Carolina were defined by Price (1969), Fullagar and Butler (1979), and Sando (1979a, b) as the western or high-strontium group of granites. This group includes the Churchland, North Carolina, Clover, South Carolina, Gastonia, North Carolina, Landis, North Carolina, and York, South Carolina, plutons (Fig. 1). The Sr compositional difference is most striking for the

J. A. Speer and K. Hoff

TABLE 3. MAJOR, MINOR, AND TRACE ELEMENT CONCENTRATION DATA
FOR THE ALLEGHANIAN GRANITOID PLUTONS OF THE SOUTHERN APPALACHIANS, U.S.A.

Element	Arith. Mean	Standard Deviation	Trimmed Means 10%	Trimmed Means 50% (median)	Skewness	Minimum	Maximum	r*	Determinations
(wt. %)									
SiO_2	71.26	3.49	71.40	71.47	-0.58	58.68	78.52	....	609
TiO_2	0.36	0.22	0.34	0.33	1.14	0.01	1.65	-0.87	597
Al_2O_3	14.81	1.14	14.82	14.94	-0.05	11.37	20.46	-0.72	609
Fe_3O_3†	2.41	1.23	2.34	2.26	1.12	0.32	8.82	-0.84	609
Fe_2O_3	1.02	0.41	1.01	1.05	0.36	0.15	2.19	-0.66	63
FeO	1.12	0.75	1.07	0.98	1.21	0.05	3.73	-0.78	63
Cat. O.R.§	0.49	0.16	0.48	0.46	0.27	0.11	0.89	0.47	63
MnO	0.06	0.05	0.05	0.05	8.97	0.01	0.83	-0.16	531
MgO	0.63	0.44	0.60	0.56	1.40	0.01	3.52	-0.84	608
CaO	1.66	0.80	1.61	1.56	1.21	0.06	6.78	-0.80	609
Na_2O	3.78	0.56	3.77	3.74	0.45	1.70	6.60	0.02	609
K_2O	4.70	0.86	4.73	4.72	-0.42	1.52	8.82	0.18	609
P_2O_5	0.13	0.09	0.12	0.11	1.56	0.01	0.55	-0.84	400
H_2O^+	0.32	0.24	0.31	0.31	1.25	0.01	1.10	-0.30	56
H_2O^-	0.10	0.05	0.10	0.10	0.56	0.02	0.23	0.05	47
CO_2	0.30	0.15	0.30	0.29	1.40	0.03	0.80	-0.15	29
S	0.028	0.028	0.028	0.017	1.63	0.001	0.109	-0.34	17
Cat. F/(FM)**	0.68	0.10	0.68	0.67	0.64	0.25	1.00	0.51	609
(ppm)									
Li	30	17	28.8	26.5	1.34	2	89	-0.12	96
Be	3.2	1.8	2.9	2.6	2.2	1.4	11	0.43	45
B	10.8	5.8	10.2	10	1.62	5	30	0.09	24
F	915	614	880	820	1.12	70	2,600	0.12	48
Cl	157.1	78.7	157.1	100	1.12	100	300	-0.75	7
Sc	4.7	2.09	4.6	4	1.06	1	10.5	-0.49	45
V	27.9	17.5	26.9	26.5	1.24	1	110	-0.69	170
Cr	12.5	9.4	11.8	10	1.35	1	48	-0.53	132
Co	7	5.1	6.6	7	1.28	1	26	-0.33	46
Ni	5.5	4.5	5.1	4	1.61	1	22	-0.22	114
Cu	20.5	16.1	19.5	15	1.18	1	64	0.12	97
Zn	52.3	16.9	51.8	51.5	1.08	13	150	-0.17	166
Ga	15.2	4.67	15.4	15	-0.71	5	23	0.21	45
Ge	10	10	0	10	....	10	10	....	20
As	2.2	1	2.1	2	1.13	1	5	-0.49	20
Se	0.2	0	0.2	0.2	....	0.2	0.2	....	20
Br	7.5	2.1	7.5	5.5	....	5	10	-0.74	4
Rb	188.5	66.8	186.3	180	0.51	16	382	0.38	459
Sr	237.5	226.5	210.3	185	3.18	1	1,846	-0.43	453
Y	33.1	27.5	29.6	25	3.66	1	266	-0.05	243
Zr	210.5	122.4	200.1	195	2.28	24	943	-0.57	303
Nb	22.4	12.8	21.1	19.2	1.86	5	82	0.24	206
Mo	2.6	3.6	2.2	1.8	4.11	0.03	21	0.18	36
Ag	0.5	0	0.5	0.5	....	0.5	0.5	....	20
Cd	0.15	0.1	0.13	0.1	2.79	0.1	0.5	....	20
Sn	1.1	0.4	1.1	1	2.2	1	2	-0.55	21
Sb	0.5	0.9	0.3	0.2	2.79	0.1	3.4	-0.56	20
Cs	2.7	1.7	2.7	2.4	0.88	0.5	7	0.17	39
Ba	715.9	386.2	702.3	707.9	0.44	20	1,980	-0.52	246
La	72.2	33.09	72.2	77	-0.08	4	144	-0.6	92
Ce	125.9	71.75	121.4	116	1.07	16.4	395	-0.67	74
Pr	10	0	10	10	....	10	10	....	6
Nd	42.4	28.5	40.1	38.5	1.36	6	161	-0.48	60
Sm	7.4	3.8	7.2	7.4	0.61	0.6	20.7	-0.62	68
Eu	1.3	0.8	1.2	1.3	2.34	0.2	5.13	-0.74	47
Gd	6.1	4	6.1	4.1	0.74	1.68	13.04	-0.19	12
Tb	0.9	0.5	0.9	0.9	-0.03	0.1	1.86	-0.56	35

**TABLE 3. MAJOR, MINOR, AND TRACE ELEMENT CONCENTRATION DATA
FOR THE ALLEGHANIAN GRANITOID PLUTONS OF THE SOUTHERN APPALACHIANS, U.S.A.** (continued - page 2)

Element	Arithmetic Mean	Standard Deviation	Trimmed Means 10%	50% (median)	Skew	Minimum	Maximum	r*	Determinations
(ppm)									
Dy	4.7	2.4	4.6	4.6	0.58	0.85	12	-0.15	56
Er	2	1.4	2	1.4	0.58	0.39	4.57	0.2	14
Tm	1	0	1	1	....	1	1	....	2
Yb	2.3	1.2	2.2	2.4	0.22	0.29	5.83	-0.03	61
Lu	0.4	0.2	0.4	0.4	0.93	0.05	0.99	0.04	57
Hf	10.9	4.7	10.7	10	0.86	2.8	24	-0.03	50
Ta	5.1	4.9	5.1	2	1.51	2	15.2	0.06	19
W	1	0	....	1	....	1	1	....	1
Au, ppb	12.8	6.2	12.8	12.5	0.17	5	25	0.05	18
Hg, ppb	15.5	7.6	15	10	1.02	10	30	0.17	20
Tl	0.7	0.4	0.9	0.8	-0.06	0.3	1.4	0.87	20
Pb	33.3	25.6	32.2	27.8	0.72	1	88.2	0.24	84
Bi	0.2	0.2	0.1	0.1	4.75	0.01	1.4	0.05	35
Th	26.9	13.7	26.4	22.2	0.66	0.6	83	0.21	290
Th (all)	24.7	12.2	24.1	22.3	0.61	0.6	83	....	679
U	5.4	3.4	5	4.5	2.13	0.6	24.1	0.39	220
U (all)	5.6	4.8	5.1	4.8	8.24	0.6	84	....	603

*r = linear correlation coefficient with silica variation.
†Fe_2O_3 = total iron as Fe_2O_3.
§Cat. OR = cation $Fe^{+3}/(Fe^{+3} + Fe^{+2})$.
**Cat. F/(FM) = cation Fe/(Fe + Mg).

Churchland pluton (Fig. 10). The reason for the high Sr contents of granitoids in a restricted geographic area is unknown. Fullagar and Butler (1979) suggested contamination by an unknown Sr-rich component, but one that would have low $^{87}Sr/^{86}Sr$ so that the granites could retain low initial ratios. There are only three new Sr analyses from the western group plutons reported in this work (Gastonia, North Carolina, 410 ppm Sr; Landis, North Carolina, 510 ppm; and York, South Carolina, 280 ppm). These Sr values are not unusual for they are in the range expected for the silica content of the rocks (Fig. 10). Sr values for a Rolesville (780 ppm) and a Palmetto (750 ppm) sample are much greater. The Palmetto, Georgia, pluton lies in the "west," but is much farther south than the other high-Sr granitoids, and several intervening plutons lack high Sr contents (Fig. 1). The Rolesville lies well to the east. Thus a widespread and compositionally distinct western group of Alleghanian granitoids that can be singularly defined by high Sr contents cannot be confirmed here.

Evaluation of geochemistry as indicators of tectonic setting

Several of the published approaches to relate the major- and trace-element composition of granitoid rocks to their tectonic setting were applied to the Alleghanian plutons. The major-element–based approach of Batchelor and Bowden (1985) indicates a late orogenic subalkaline magmatism and some overlap with synorogenic anatectic magmatism. The scheme of Maniar and Piccoli (1989) indicates that the granitoid compositions are

consistent with either an island arc, continental arc, or continental collision. The geologic history of the southeast during the Alleghanian magmatism would rule out an island arc, and probably a continental arc as well (Speer et al., 1994).

In the trace element Rb versus Y + Nb scheme of Pearce et al. (1984), the majority of the Alleghanian granitoids span the boundaries between the three fields for volcanic arc granites (VAG) and within plate granites (WPG), and a few analyses of higher Rb values extend into the syncollisional granites (COLG) field (Fig. 11). These analyses also fall within the field of post-collisional granites, which plot in all of the fields. The discriminate trivariate Hf—Rb/30—Tax3 plot of Harris et al. (1986) shows a span of points over the same tectonic environments. Using the Zr versus $(Nb/Zr)_N$ discrimination diagram suggested by Thiéblemont and Tégyey (1994), the Alleghanian granitoid compositions occupy a field that can include rocks from either arc-continent collision, continent-continent collision, or continental tholeiitic provinces.

These results broadly indicate a destructive plate boundary margin, involving continental crust, sometime during or after orogeny. This compares favorably to the postcollisional, strike-slip tectonic environment suggested by Speer et al. (1994) for these granitoids. However, it might be more appropriate to conclude that, rather than the chemical data indicating tectonic environment, the data indicate that Alleghanian magmatism in the southern Appalachians has the same source rocks and magmatic processes commonly found during or after collision of a destructive continental plate boundary.

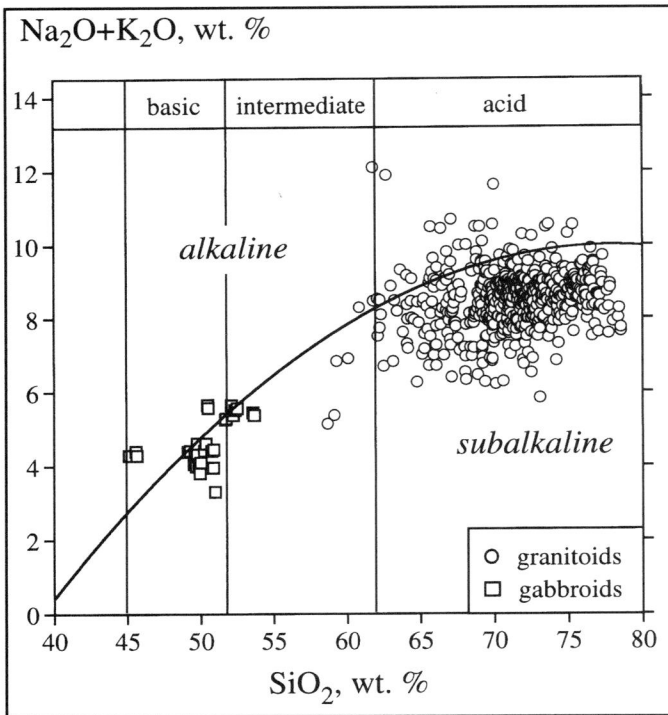

Figure 2. Alleghanian magmatic rocks plotted on a total alkali versus silica (TAS) diagram. Circles are granitoids, Squares are gabbroids. The curved solid line divides alkaline from subalkaline rocks (Irvine and Baragar, 1971).

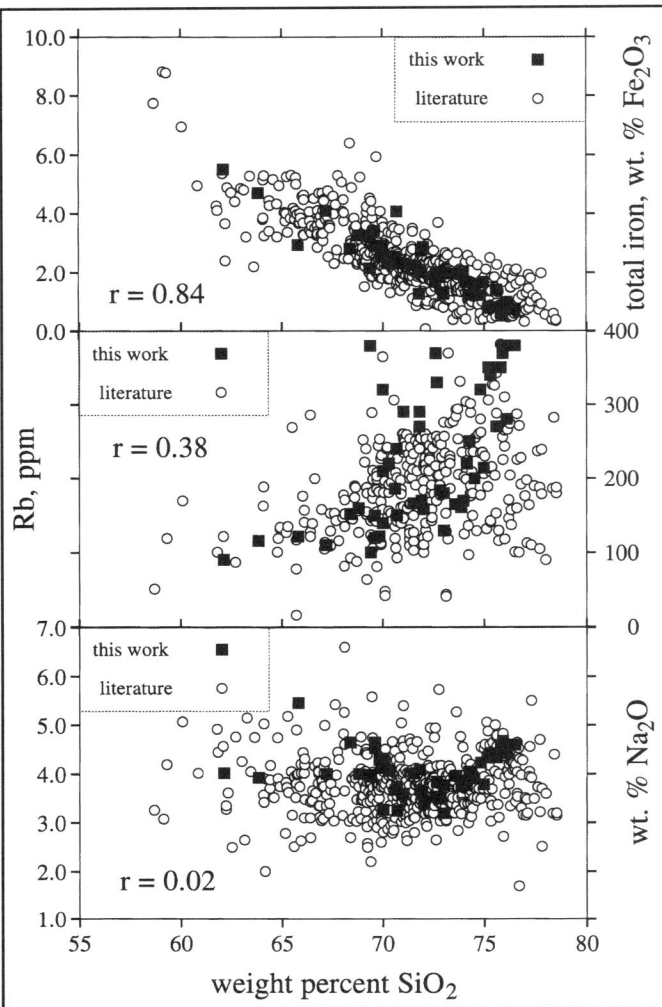

Figure 3. Bivariate plot (Harker diagram) of oxides and elements chosen to illustrate the observed range of correlation coefficients. Data for this work are given in Tables 1 and 2; Speer et al. (1989); Speer and Becker (1990). References for the literature values are given in Appendix 1.

Alkaline granitoids

A few rock analyses tend toward alkaline granitoid compositions, including the leucocratic syenogranites, syenites, and alkali feldspar granites of the Appling, Georgia, Cuffytown Creek, Coronaca, Edgefield, Liberty Hill (all South Carolina), Portsmouth, Virginia, Rocky Mount, North Carolina, and Winnsboro, South Carolina, plutons. Rocks from these plutons are richer in Si, Fe/(Fe + Mg), F, Rb, and Y, and lower in Al, Ti, Fe, Mg, Sr, Zr, Ba, and REEs than the other granitoids, which are compositional characteristics of A-type granitoids (Eby, 1990). Whalen et al. (1987) suggested that the Ga/Al ratio would discriminate between A-type and other granitoids. Only the Cuffytown Creek and Portsmouth plutons meet these criteria for A-type granitoids (Fig. 12). The other alkaline rocks form small segregated portions or dikes in plutons otherwise composed of normal granitoids. This would suggest that these alkaline rocks resulted from fractionation. By contrast, in the Cuffytown Creek and Portsmouth plutons, all samples are alkaline and have high Ga/Al ratios. Both plutons are small bodies with significant negative gravity anomalies and are interpreted as cupolas of much larger bodies (Russell et al., 1985; Speer and Becker, 1990). Thus the evidence for the nature of these plutons is mixed. They have the compositional features of A-type grani-

toids, but geologic evidence allows for the possibility of a fractionated and hydrothermal origin of the alkaline rocks.

CONCLUSIONS

The Alleghanian magmatic event of the southern Appalachians can be summarized as follows.

1. The Alleghanian plutons include both abundant granitoid and minor gabbroid rocks with a compositional hiatus between them. The granitoids are subalkaline and span metaluminous through peraluminous. They are leucocratic syeno- and monzogranites.

2. The event produced rocks that exhibit smooth, well-defined negative linear trends with increasing SiO$_2$ for most major elements, except K and Na, and only a few trace elements. Compositions vary with modal differences in quartz, feldspars,

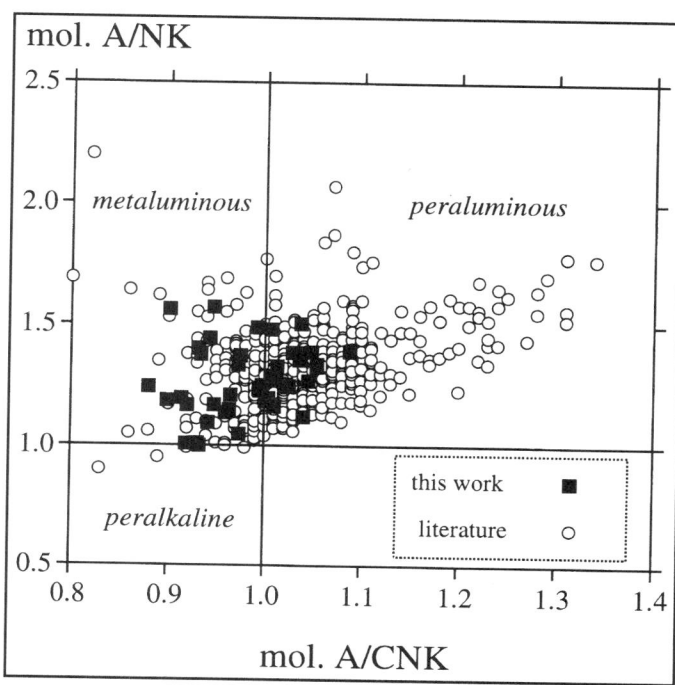

Figure 4. Aluminum saturation index, A/CNK (= molecular Al$_2$O$_3$/[CaO + Na$_2$O + K$_2$O] corrected for apatite) versus A/NK (= molecular Al$_2$O$_3$/[Na$_2$O + K$_2$O]). Data for this work are given in Tables 1 and 2; Speer et al. (1989); Speer and Becker (1990). References for the literature values are given in Appendix 1.

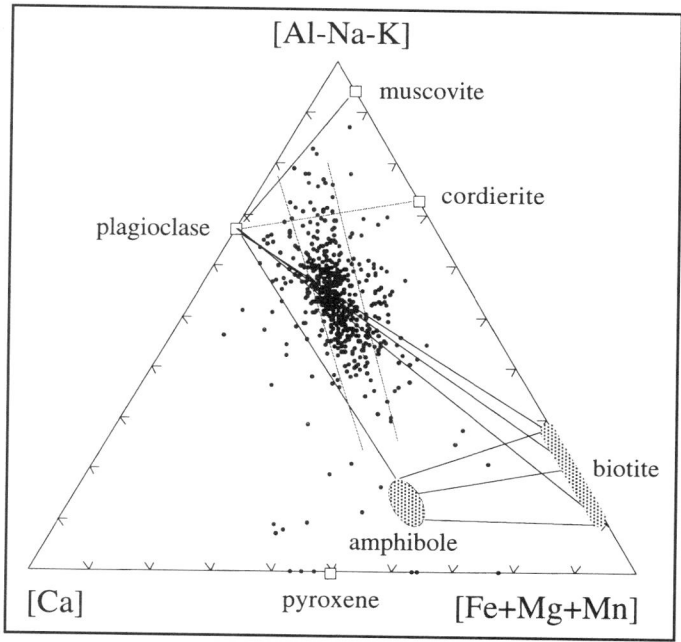

Figure 5. ACFM diagram (A = cation Al − Na − K; C = Ca; F = Fe* + Mg + Mn, where Fe* is total iron) showing the relationship between rock composition and mineral assemblages. Most points lie between two lines arbitrarily drawn radiating away from (or toward) amphibole. Data from Table 1 and Appendix 1.

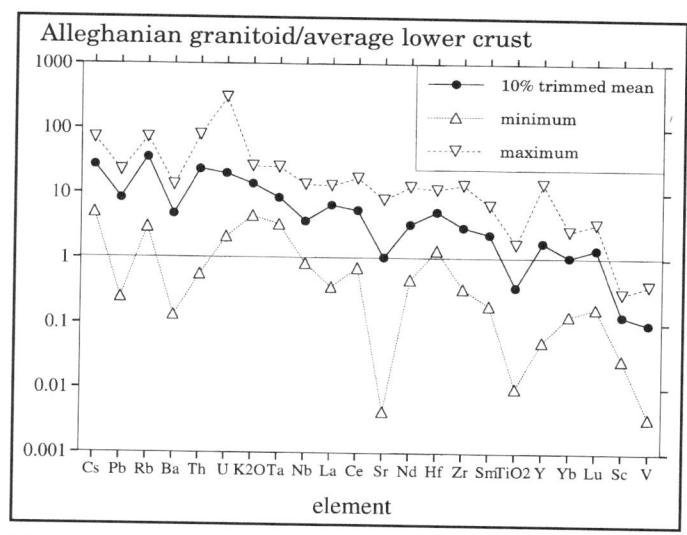

Figure 6. Lower-crust normalized diagram for the 10% trimmed mean, maximum, and minimum values of the Alleghanian granitoids. Data from Table 3, normalizing values from Taylor and McLennan (1985).

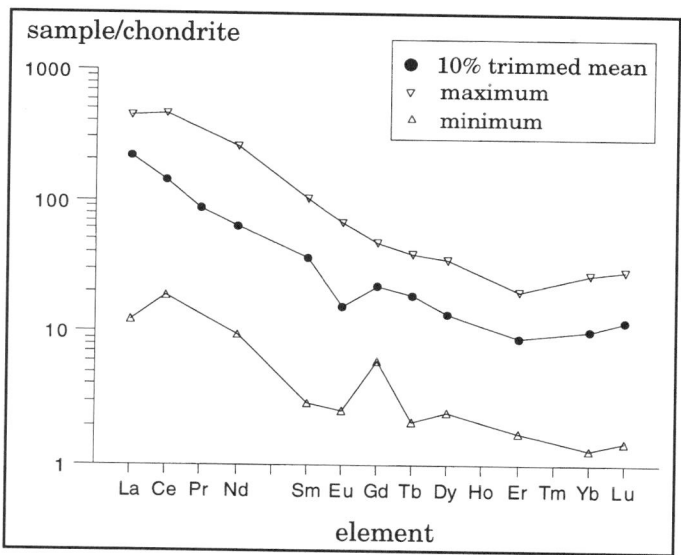

Figure 7. Rare earth element (REE) chondrite normalized diagram for the 10% trimmed mean, maximum, and minimum values for the REE from the Alleghanian granitoids. Data from Table 3, normalizing REE values from Nakamura (1974).

and mafic minerals. The modal variations result, in turn, from crystal-melt segregation and, less commonly, disaggregation of enclaves during emplacement. Compositional variations indicate that the crystal-melt segregation involved fractional crystallization or melting of varying amounts of amphibole, oxides, and feldspar components. High initial Sr ratios and ^{18}O-enrichment of the more peraluminous and Th-rich granitoids indicate compositional control by the source rocks for these few rocks.

3. The magmatic rocks show no geographic compositional

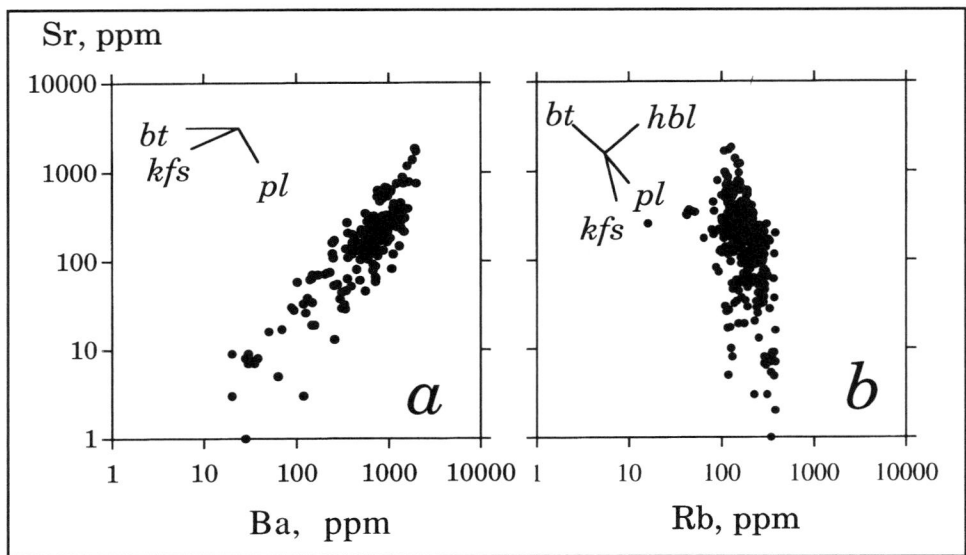

Figure 8. Bivariate diagrams for the large-lithophile elements (ppm): a: Ba-Sr. Decreasing contents of both Ba and Sr are consistent with fractionation primarily of alkali feldspar and lesser amounts of plagioclase. b: Rb-Sr. Significant variation in Sr with smaller variation in Rb is consistent with fractionation primarily of alkali feldspar and lesser amounts of plagioclase. Generalized theoretical vectors produced by Raleigh fractionation of single phases and their effect on melt composition are included for reference: biotite (bt), hornblende (hbl), alkali feldspar (kfs), and plagioclase (pl) (Tindle and Pearce, 1981; Pearce and Norry, 1979; Atherton and Sanderson, 1985).

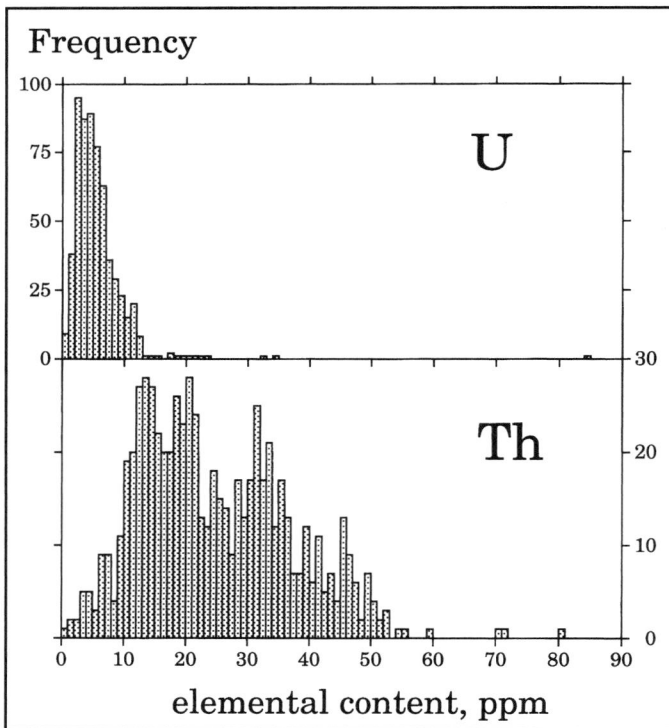

Figure 9. Histograms for U and Th contents of the Alleghanian granitoids. U is log normal whereas Th has several apparent maxima, an artifact of intensive sampling of a few Th-rich plutons.

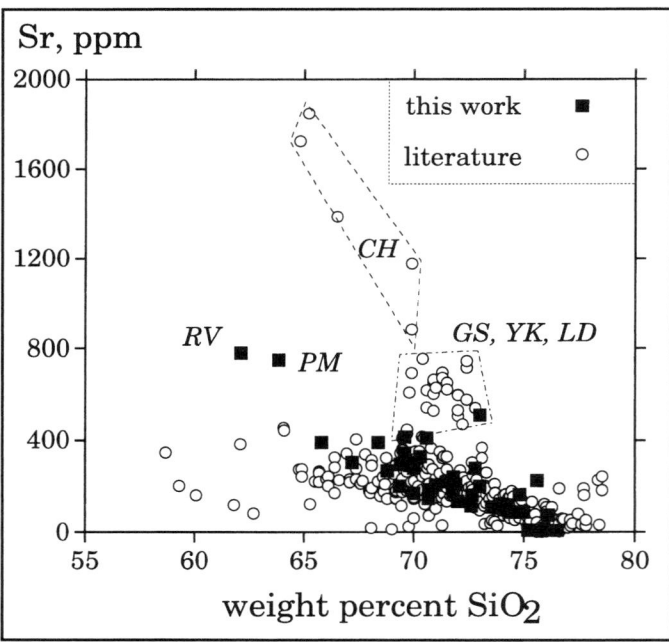

Figure 10. Bivariate diagram of Sr versus silica showing high Sr granitoids of the Churchland (CH), Gastonia (GS), Landis (LD), and York (YK) plutons. The Roleville (RV) and Palmetto (PM) plutons occur well-away from the high Sr granitoids of western Carolinas. Data for this work from Table 2; Speer et al. (1989); Speer and Becker (1990). References for the literature values are given in Appendix 1.

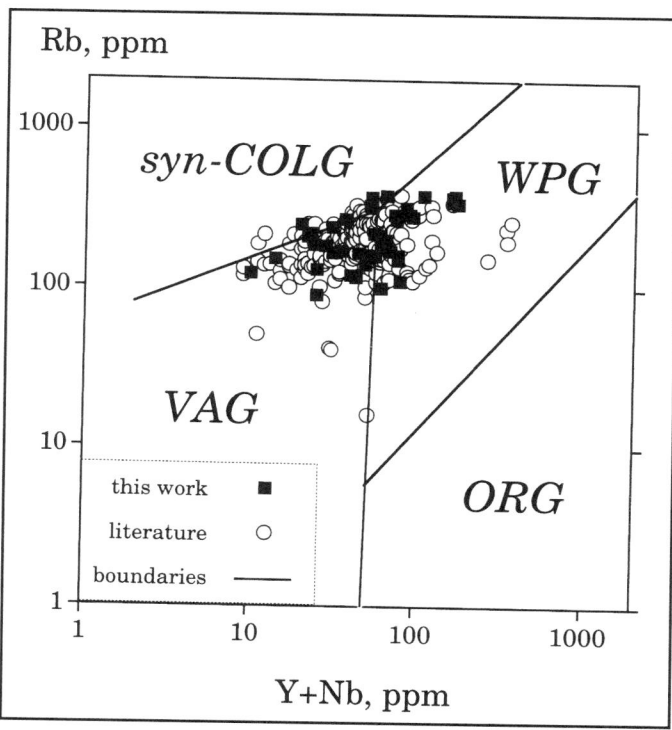

Figure 11. Bivariate Rb versus (Nb + Y) discrimination diagrams for the Alleghanian granitoids of the southern Appalachians. Tectonic classification fields suggested by Pearce et al. (1984) for syncollisional (syn-COLG), volcanic arc (VAG), ocean ridge (ORG), and within-plate (WPG) granites. Data for this work from Table 2; Speer et al. (1989); Speer and Becker (1990). References for the literature values are given in Appendix 1.

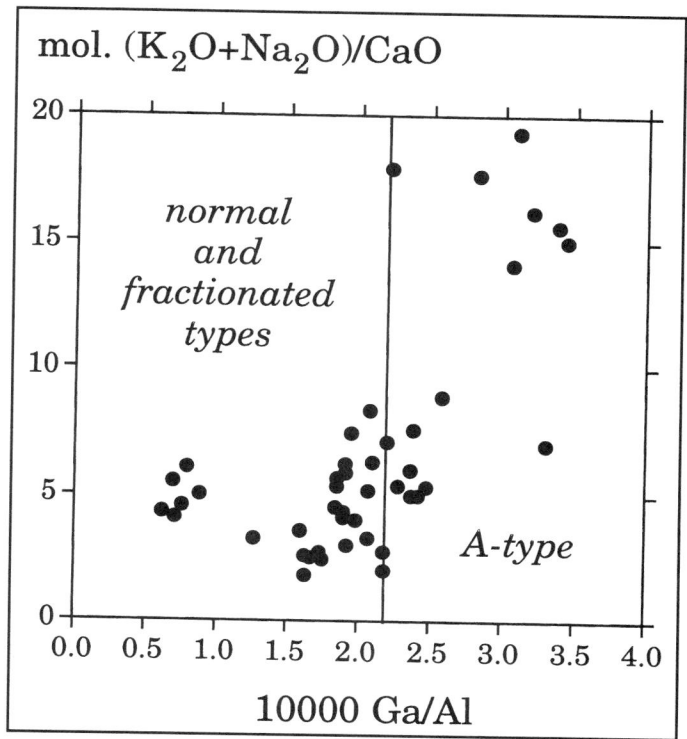

Figure 12. Bivariate molecular (K$_2$O + Na$_2$O)/CaO versus 10,000 Ga/Al discrimination diagrams for the Alleghanian granitoids of the southern Appalachians. Fields for normal or fractionated and A-type granitoids from Whalen et al. (1987). Points within the A-type granitoid field are from the Cuffytown Creek, South Carolina, and Portsmouth, Virginia, plutons. Data for this work from Table 2; Speer et al. (1989); Speer and Becker (1990). References for the literature values are given in Appendix 1.

trends except for possible high-Sr granitoids in western North Carolina.

4. The Alleghanian plutons can best be interpreted on the basis of compositional tectonic discrimination diagrams as having source rocks and magmatic processes found during or after collision at a destructive continental plate boundary.

5. The magmatic rocks may include two alkaline granitoids, the Cuffytown Creek, South Carolina, and Portsmouth, Virginia, plutons. The geologic evidence is ambiguous as to whether these are A-type granites or just the differentiated or hydrothermal-enriched roof zones of much larger, normal plutons.

ACKNOWLEDGMENTS

Financial support for the rock analyses came from the North Carolina Geological Survey contracts C-06005, P-3002, and P-4007, the U.S. Geological Survey through Cooperative Agreement 14-08-0001-A0742, and North Carolina State University. We thank C. Winston Russell for providing his unpublished analytical data and E. S. Stoddard for providing the Rolesville and Castalia analyses. The thorough reviews of Paul D. Fullagar and Gail S. Russell are much appreciated.

APPENDIX 1: LITERATURE DATA SOURCES

The following are the Alleghanian plutons, alphabetically listed by their name, giving their symbol in Figure 1 and literature sources for the chemical data. The type and number of samples are indicated by [type, number] where types are m = major, t = trace, or mt = both major- and trace-elemental data. VA = Virginia, GA = Georgia, SC = South Carolina, NC = North Carolina.

AB—Alberta, VA: no analyzed rocks

AP—Appling, GA: Costain et al. (1986) [t, 3], Fullagar and Butler (1979) *in* Sando (1979a) [m, 2], C. Winston Russell (1981, personal commun.) [m, 3], Sando (1979a) [m, 2; t, 4], Watson (1901) [m, 1]

BR—Bald Rock, SC: Costain et al. (1986) [t, 2]

BB—Batesburg, SC: Costain et al. (1986) [t, 2], Sando (1979a) [m, 4; t, 4]

BH—Ben Hill, GA: Costain et al. (1986) [t, 2], C. Winston Russell (1981, personal commun.) [m, 2]

BI—Buggs Island, VA: no analyzed rocks.

BC—Butterwood Creek, NC: Costain et al. (1986) [t, 3], Grundy (1982) [m, 3; t, 3], C. Winston Russell (1981, personal commun.) [m, 3]

CS—Castalia, NC: Costain et al. (1986) [t, 18], Fullagar (1971) [t, 1], Fullagar and Butler (1978) *in* Sando (1979a) [m, 4], Merz and Sinha (1977a) [m, 2], C. Winston Russell (1981, personal commun.)

[m, 4], Sando (1979a) [t, 3], Sinha and Merz (1977c) [m, 1], E. F. Stoddard (1991, personal commun.) [mt, 1], Tables 1 and 2 [mt, 6]

CW—Catawba, SC: Costain et al. (1986) [t, 1], Fullagar (1971) [t, 4], Fullagar and Butler (1979) [t, 3], Price (1969) [t, 1], Ragland and Butler (1979) [m, 2], *in* Sando (1979a) [m, 1; t, 2]

CV—Cherryville, NC: Price (1969) [t, 3]

CH—Churchland, NC: Costain et al. (1986) [t, 3], Fullagar and Butler (1979) [t, 2], Price (1969) [t, 2], C. Winston Russell (1981, personal commun.) [m, 2], Sando (1979a) [mt, 4]

CC—Clouds Creek, SC: granitoid: Costain et al. (1986) [t, 4], Fullagar and Butler (1979) [t, 7], Price (1969) [t, 3], Ragland and Butler (1969) *in* Sando (1979a) [m, 4], C. Winston Russell (1981, personal commun.) [m, 7], Sando (1979a) [m, 2; t, 4], Shireman (1983) [m, 1], Sloan (1908) [m, 2], Tables 1 and 2 [mt, 1]

CC—Clouds Creek, SC gabbroid: Shireman (1983) [m, 1]

CL—Clover, SC: Costain et al. (1986) [t, 1], Fullagar and Butler (1979) [t, 1], Price (1969) [t, 3], Ragland and Butler (1969) *in* Sando (1979a) [m, 7], C. Winston Russell (1981, personal commun.) [m, 2], Sando (1979a) [t, 4], Sloan (1908) [m, 1]

CP—Cold Point, SC: no analyzed rocks

CO—Columbia, SC: Costain et al. (1986) [t, 2], Fullagar and Butler (1979) [t, 8], Gardner et al. (1978) [m, 7], C. Winston Russell (1981, personal commun.) [m, 2], Sando (1979a) [m, 3; t, 4]

CN—Contentnea Creek, SC: Costain et al. (1986) [t, 2], Price (1969) [t, 1]

CR—Coronaca, SC: Fullagar and Butler (1979) [t, 7], Sando (1979a) [m, 4; t, 4], Costain et al. (1986) [t, 2]

CF—Cuffytown Creek, SC: Becker (1978a) [m, 5], Costain et al. (1986) [t, 22], Fullagar and Butler (1979) [t, 4], C. Winston Russell (1981, personal commun.) [m, 4], Sando (1979a) [m, 3; t, 4], Speer and Becker (1990) [mt, 5]

DB—Danburg, GA: Costain et al. (1986) [t, 3], Cullers (1988) [mt, 1], Davis (1977) [mt, 4], Price (1969) [t, 1], Ragland and Butler (1969) *in* Sando (1979a) [m, 2; t, 1], C. Winston Russell (1981, personal commun.) [m, 2]

DO—Dort, NC: Costain et al. (1986) [t, 1]

DC—Dutchmans Creek, SC: gabbroid, no analyzed rocks.

ED—Edgefield, SC: Costain et al. (1986) [t, 1], C. Winston Russell (1981, personal commun.) [m, 1], Sando (1979a) [mt, 4]

EB—Elberton, GA: Costain et al. (1986) [t, 3], Davis (1977) [mt, 5], Hess (1979) [m, 43; t, 39], Nagel (1981) [mt, 1], C. Winston Russell (1981, personal commun.) [m, 7], Stuckless et al. (1986) [t, 14], Wenner and Spaulding (1982) [t, 43]

EC—Elm City, NC: C. Winston Russell (1981, personal commun.) [m, 1]

FM—Falmouth, VA: no analyzed rocks.

GV—Graniteville, SC: Costain et al. (1986) [t, 1], C. Winston Russell (1981, personal commun.) [m, 1]

HB—Harbison, SC: Costain et al. (1986) [t, 1], C. Winston Russell (1981, personal commun.) [m, 1]

HS—High Shoals and Gastonia, NC: Costain et al. (1986) [t, 2], Fullagar and Butler (1979) [m, 1], Price (1969) [t, 3], C. Winston Russell (1981, personal commun.) [m, 6], Sando (1979a) [mt, 4], Tables 1 and 2 [mt, 1]

LD—Landis, NC: Costain et al. (1986) [t, 2], Fullagar and Butler (1969) *in* Sando (1979a) [m, 4], Fullagar and Butler (1979) [t, 5], Price (1969) [t, 4], C. Winston Russell (1981, personal commun.) [m, 1], Sando (1979a) [t, 4], Tables 1 and 2 [mt, 1]

LX—Lexington, SC: Fullagar and Butler (1979) [t, 4], Sando (1979a) [m, 1; t, 4]

LH—Liberty Hill, SC: J. R. Butler (1978, personal commun.) [m, 2], Costain et al. (1986) [t, 42], Fullagar (1971) [t, 5], Merz and Sinha (1977b) [m, 1], Price (1969) [t, 11], Ragland and Butler (1969) *in* Sando (1979a) [m, 8], C. Winston Russell (1981, personal commun.) [m, 7], Sando (1979a) [t, 8], Sinha and Merz (1977a) [m, 18], Sinha and Merz (1976b) [m, 22], Sloan (1908) [m, 2], Speer et al. (1989) [mt, 6]

LV—Lilesville, NC: Costain et al. (1986) [t, 3], Fullagar (1971) [t, 3], McGinn (1988) [m, 3], Price (1969) [t, 4], Ragland and Butler (1978) *in* Sando (1979a) [m, 5], C. Winston Russell (1981, personal commun.) [m, 1], Sando (1979a) [t, 4]

LL—Lillington, NC: no analyzed rocks

LUM—Lumberton, NC: no analyzed rocks; pluton defined by negative gravity anomaly

MM—Medoc Mountain, NC: no analyzed rocks

MV—Mooresville, NC: Costain et al. (1986) [t, 1], Price (1969) [t, 1], C. Winston Russell (1981, personal commun.)[m, 1]

OT—OTT, SC: no analyzed rocks

PG—Pageland, SC: Costain et al. (1986) [t, 26], Fullagar (1971) [t, 4], Fullagar and Butler (1978) *in* Sando (1979a) [m, 1], Price (1969) [t, 4], Ragland and Butler (1969) in Sando (1979) [m, 3], C. Winston Russell (1981, personal commun.) [m, 3], Sando (1979a) [t, 4]

PM—Palmetto-Tyrone, GA: Costain et al. (1986) [t, 28], C. Winston Russell (1981, personal commun.) [m, 8], Watson (1902) [m, 2], Tables 1 and 2 [mt, 1]

PN—Panola, GA: Costain et al. (1986) [t, 1], Grant et al. (1980) [m, 1]

PD—PeeDee, NC: gabbroid, McGinn (1988)

PT—Petersburg, VA: Costain et al. (1986) [t, 90], Davis (1977) [m, 1], C. Winston Russell (1981, personal commun.) [m, 11], Sinha and Merz (1977b) [m, 1]

PO—Portsmouth, VA: Costain et al. (1986) [t, 8], Russell et al. (1985) [m, 3], Tables 1 and 2 [mt, 3]

RB—Rabun, SC: Costain et al. (1986) [t, 4],

RM—Rocky Mount, NC: Farrar (1980) [t, 4], Fullagar (1988, *in* Moncla, 1990) [t, 8], Moncla (1990) [m, 44; t, 42], Perry et al. (1980) [t, 5], C. Winston Russell (1981, personal commun.) [m, 1], Sinha (1980) [mt, 6]

RV—Rolesville, NC: Costain et al. (1986) [t, 61], Merz and Sinha (1977a) [m, 14], Price (1969) [t, 1], Sinha and Merz (1977c) [m, 3], E. F. Stoddard (1991, personal commun.) [mt, 2], Tables 1 and 2 [mt, 9]

RY—Rayle, GA: no analyzed rocks; pluton defined by negative gravity anomaly

SM—Siloam, GA: Costain et al. (1986) [t, 52], Davis (1977) [mt, 2], Fullagar and Butler (1979) [t, 2], C. Winston Russell (1981, personal commun.) [m, 5], Sando (1979) [mt, 4], Watson (1902) [m, 1], Tables 1 and 2 [mt, 2]

SI—Sims, NC: Costain et al. (1986) [t, 2], Price (1969) [t, 1], Sando (1979) [mt, 4], Tables 1 and 2 [mt, 6]

SP—Sparta, GA: Costain et al. (1986) [t, 1], Davis (1977) [mt, 3], Fullagar (1971) [t, 6], Fullagar and Butler (1976) [m, 29], Price (1969) [t, 3], Roberts-Henry (1983) [mt, 35], C. Winston Russell (personal commun.) [m, 1], Watson (1901) [m, 3]

SF—Springfield, SC: Perry et al. (1980) [t, 7], Sinha (1980) [mt, 6]

STG—Stone Mtn., GA: Costain et al. (1986) [t, 2], Davis (1977) [mt, 5], C. Winston Russell (1981, personal commun.) [m, 3], Washington (1917) [m, 1], Watson (1910) [m, 3], Whitney et al. (1976) [m, 5; t, 4]

SN—Sunnyside, NC: no analyzed rocks

TC—Town Creek, GA: Costain et al. (1986) [t, 3], Watson (1901) [m, 1]

WL—Wilton, NC: Costain et al. (1986) [t, 1], P. D. Fullagar (1981, personal commun.) *in* Sando (1979a) [m, 3], Sando (1979) [m, 1; t, 4]

WS—Wise, NC: Costain et al. (1986) [t, 1]
WN—Winnsboro, SC: Costain et al. (1986) [t, 56], Fullagar (1971) [t, 8], Price (1969) [t, 2], Ragland and Butler (1969) *in* Sando (1979a) [m, 1], C. Winston Russell (1981, personal commun.) [m, 5], Sando (1979) [t, 5], Sinha and Merz (1976a) [m, 27], Sinha and Merz (1977a) [m, 17], Vogel and Wilband (1978) [mt, 1], Wagner (1973) [m, 31; t, 27], Tables 1 and 2 [mt, 3]
WN—Winnsboro mafic dike, SC: Vogel and Wilband (1978)
WY—Wyatt, NC: no analyzed rocks
YK—York, SC: Costain et al. (1986) [t, 2], Fullagar and Butler (1979) [t, 7], Price (1969) [t, 5], Ragland and Butler (1969) *in* Sando (1979a) [m, 4], C. Winston Russell (1981, personal commun.) [m, 7], Sando (1979a) [t, 4], Tables 1 and 2 [mt, 1]

APPENDIX 2: ANALYTICAL TECHNIQUES

Table 1 analyses were done by Chemex Labs, Inc. (Sparks, Nevada) with report dates of 02/88, 02/92, 03–04/93, and 03–04/94. The samples analyzed in 1988 were pulverized in either an alumina or WC grinding apparatus, whereas the 1992–1994 the samples were ground in a zirconia grinding apparatus.

In 1988, Si was determined gravimetrically following a sodium metacarbonate fusion. Al, Ca, Fe(total), Mg, Mn, P, K, Na, and Ti were analyzed by inductively coupled plasma atomic emission spectrometry (ICP-AES) following a perchloric-nitric-hydrofluoric acid digestion. In 1992–1994, Si, Al, Ca, Fe(total), K, Mg, Mn, Na, P, and Ti were analyzed by ICP-AES following a nitric-aqua-regia digestion of a fused meta-borate fusion.

FeO was determined by titration after acid digestion. C and S were determined on a Leco IR detector/induction furnace; C was corrected for WC contamination of the grinding apparatus by using the W value. Crystalline and surface water were determined with a Leco RMC100. F was determined by specific ion electrode after a carbonate-nitrate fusion.

Nb, Y, and Zr were determined by X-ray fluorescence. Br, Ce, Cl, Cs, Hf, La, Sc, Ta, Th, and U were done by neutron activation analysis (NAA). Be, Ga, Ge, Li, Rb, and Tl were done by atomic absorption spectrophotometry (AAS) after a perchloric-nitric-hydrofluoric acid digestion. Ga had an organic extraction and Ga and Tl AAS were corrected for background. In 1988, Cr, Co, Cu, Pb, Mo, Ni, Ag, Na, Sr, V, Zn, and Ba were analyzed by ICP-AES following a perchloric-nitric-hydrofluoric acid digestion. Cd was done by background-corrected AAS. In 1992–1994, Cd, Co, Ni, Cu, Zn, Mo, and Pb were analyzed by AAS following an aqua regia digestion. Cd, Co, Ni, and Pb were corrected for background. Cr, Sr, V, Ge, Ba were analyzed by AAS following a perchloric-nitric-hydrofluoric acid digestion. In 1988 B was done by ICP-AES following digestion of a fused sample, subsequently B was done by prompt-gamma neutron activation.

Bi and Sb were done by background-corrected AAS following an HCl-KClO₃ digestion and organic extraction. As was done by AAS–hydride/EDL following an aqua regia digestion. Sn was determined by AAS after ammonia iodide fusion extraction. Au was determined by fire assay, AAS finish of a 10 g fused sample. Hg was determined by AAS-flameless after a nitric acid-hydrochloric acid digestion. W was determined colorimetrically after a potassium pyrosulfate fusion; samples contaminated by the WC grinding were omitted.

The detection limits and uncertainty of elemental or oxide analyses are reported in Table 4. The equation to calculate the uncertainty is uncertainty = detection limit + precision fact × reported value, where precision fact is 0.05 for geochemical and/or trace analyses, 0.03 for assay analyses, and 0.08 for gold analyses.

REFERENCES CITED

Atherton, M. P., and Sanderson, L. M., 1985, The chemical variation and evolution of the superunits of the segmented Coastal Batholith, *in* Pitcher, W. S., et al., eds., Magmatism at a plate edge: New York, Blackie Halstead, p. 208–227.

Batchelor, R. A., and Bowden, P., 1985, Petrogenetic interpretation of granitoid rock series using multicationic parameters: Chemical Geology, v. 48, p. 43–55.

Becker, S. W., 1978a, Petrology of Drill Core ED-1 from the Cuffytown Creek Pluton, *in* Costain, J. K., Glover, L., III, and Sinha, A. K., eds., Evaluation and targeting of geothermal energy resources in the southeastern United States: U.S. Department of Commerce National Technical Information Service VPI&SU-5648-4, p. A78–A85.

Becker, S. W., 1978b, Petrology of the Cuffytown Creek pluton, *in* Costain, J. K., Glover, L., III, and Sinha, A. K, eds., Evaluation and targeting of geothermal energy resources in the southeastern United States: U.S. Department of Commerce National Technical Information Service VPI&SU-5648-3, p. A4–A30.

Costain, J. K., Speer, J. A., Glover, L., III, Perry, L., Dashevsky, S., and McKinney, M., 1986, Heat flow in the southeastern U.S.: Journal of Geophysical Research, v. 91, p. 2123–2135.

Cullers, R., 1988, Mineralogical and chemical changes of soil and stream sediment formed by intense weathering of the Danburg granite, Georgia, U.S.A.: Lithos, v. 21, p. 301–314.

Davis, M. P., 1977, Investigation of uranium and thorium variation in selected intrusive rocks of the southeastern Piedmont [M.S. thesis]: Gainesville, University of Florida, 107 p.

Eby, G. N., 1990, The A-type granitoids: A review of their occurrence and chemical characteristics and speculations on their petrogenesis: Lithos, v. 26, p. 115–134.

Farrar, S. S., 1980, Petrology of the Rocky Mount granitoid pluton, North Carolina, and comparison to other granitoid plutons of the southern Piedmont, *in* Sinha, A. K., Costain, J. K., and Glover, L., III, eds., Distribution and analysis of 300 m.y. granites as a potential geothermal resource: U.S. Department of Commerce National Technical Information Service Report VPI&SU-LASL-2, p. 1–24.

Fullagar, P. D., 1971, Age and origin of plutonic intrusions in the Piedmont of the southeastern Appalachians: Geological Society of America Bulletin, v. 82, p. 2845–2862.

Fullagar, P. D., and Butler, J. R., 1976, Petrochemical and geochronologic studies of plutonic rocks in the southern Appalachians: II, The Sparta granite complex, Georgia: Geological Society of America Bulletin, v. 87, p. 53–56.

Fullagar, P. D., and Butler, J. R., 1979, 325 to 265 m.y. old granitic plutons in the Piedmont of the southeastern Appalachians: American Journal of Science, v. 279, p. 161–185.

Gardner, L. R., Kheoruenromne, I., and Chen, H. S., 1978, Isovolumetric geochemical investigation of a buried granite saprolite near Columbia, SC, USA: Geochimica et Cosmochimica Acta, v. 42, p. 417–424.

Grant, W. H., Size, W. B., and O'Conner, B. J., 1980, Petrology and structure of the Stone Mountain granite and Mount Arabia migmatite, Lithonia, Georgia, *in* Frey, R. W., ed., Excursions in Southeastern Geology (Geological Society of America 1980 Annual Meeting field trips): American Geological Institute, v. 1, p. 47–57.

Grundy, A .T., 1982, Geology and geochemistry of granitic and diabase rocks in the Littleton and Thelma area, northeastern Piedmont, North Carolina: Geological Society of America Abstracts with Programs, v. 14, p. 22.

Harris, N. B. W., Pearce, J. A., and Tindel, A. G., 1986, Geochemical characteristics of collision-zone magmatism, *in* Coward, M. P., and Reis, A. C., eds., Collision tectonics: Geological Society of London Special Publication 19, p. 67–81.

TABLE 4. UNCERTAINTY IN THE ANALYSES OF TABLE 1

Chemex Codes	Element	Method	Detection Limit (ppm except where noted)	Uncertainty*	Chemex Codes	Element	Method	Detection Limit (ppm except where noted)	Uncertainty*
Geochemical/Trace Analyses					558	Zn	ICP-AES	2	1
2	Cu	AQ/AAS	1	1	559	P	ICP-AES	10	1
3	Mo	AQ/AAS	1	1	560	Pb	ICP-AES	2	1
4	Pb	AQ/AAS	1	1	563	Co	ICP-AES	1	1
5	Zn	AQ/AAS	1	1	564	Ni	ICP-AES	1	1
7	Cd	AQ/AAS	1	1	565	Ba	ICP-AES	10	1
8	Ni	AQ/AAS	1	1	566	Fe	ICP-AES	0.01 wt. %	1
9	Co	AQ/AAS	1	1	568	Mn	ICP-AES	5	1
12	Cr	TOT/AAS	2	1	569	Cr	ICP-AES	1	1
13	As	SP/AAS	1	1	570	Mg	ICP-AES	0.01 wt. %	1
16	Se	EXT/AAS	0.2	1	572	V	ICP-AES	1	1
18	W	Colorimetric	2	1	573	Al	ICP-AES	0.01 wt. %	1
19	Sn	SP/AAS	2	1	576	Ca	ICP-AES	0.01 wt. %	1
20	Hg	AAS-Flameless	0.01	1	577	Cu	ICP-AES	1	1
21	F	Specific Ion	20	1	578	Ag	AQ/AAS	0.2	1
22	Sb	EXT/AAS	0.2	1	579	Ti	ICP-AES	0.01 wt. %	1
23	Bi	EXT/AAS	0.1	1	582	Sr	ICP-AES	1	1
24	Te	EXT/AAS	0.05	1	583	Na	ICP-AES	0.01 wt. %	1
25	Ba	TOT/AAS	10	1	584	K	ICP-AES	0.01 wt. %	1
27	Li	TOT/AAS	1	1	586	Fe_2O_3	ICP-AES	0.01 wt. %	1
30	Rb	TOT/AAS	1	1	588	CaO	ICP-AES	0.01 wt. %	1
31	Ga	SP/AAS	1	1	590	Cr_2O_3	ICP-AES	0.01 wt. %	1
32	Sr	TOT/AAS	1	1	592	SiO_2	ICP-AES	0.01 wt. %	1
33	V	TOT/AAS	5	1	593	MgO	ICP-AES	0.01 wt. %	1
34	Be	TOT/AAS	0.1	1	594	Al_2O_3	ICP-AES	0.01 wt. %	1
39	Tl	SP/AAS	0.1	1	595	TiO_2	ICP-AES	0.01 wt. %	1
40	B	Fusion-ICP	10	1	596	MnO	ICP-AES	0.01 wt. %	1
40	B	NAA	5	1	597	P_2O_5	ICP-AES	0.01 wt. %	1
41	Ge	SP/AAS	5	1	599	Na_2O	ICP-AES	0.01 wt. %	1
103	Sc	NAA	0.5	1	801	Y	XRF	2	1
107	Hf	NAA	2	1	821	K_2O	ICP-AES	0.01 wt. %	1
110	La	NAA	1	1	914	Zr	XRF	3	1
128	Nd	NAA	5	1					
134	Sm	NAA	0.1	1	**Assay Analyses**				
135	Ce	NAA	2	1	367	C	Leco IR Detector	0.01 wt. %	2
136	Lu	NAA	0.1	1	368	CO_2	Leco-gasometric	0.2 wt. %	2
137	Eu	NAA	0.2	1	378	SiO_2	Gravimetric	0.01 wt. %	2
138	Yb	NAA	0.2	1	380	S	Leco-IR Detector	0.001 wt. %	2
140	Dy	NAA	0.5	1	451	FeO	Titration	0.01 wt. %	2
141	Tb	NAA	0.1	1	818	H_2O^+	Leco RMC100	0.01 wt. %	2
150	Th	NAA	1	1	819	H_2O^-	Leco RMC100	0.01 wt. %	2
151	Ta	NAA	2	1					
152	U	NAA	0.2	1	**Gold Analysis**				
154	Br	NAA	0.5	1	100	Au	FA-AAS	5 ppb	3
155	Cl	NAA	100	1					
158	Cs	NAA	0.5	1					
191	Nb	XRF	2	1					
475	LOI	Furnace	0.01 wt. %	1					
554	Mo	ICP-AES	1	1					

*1 = Detection limit + 0.05 x reported result; 2 = Detection limit + 0.03 x reported result; 3 = Detection limit + 0.08 x reported result.

Hess, J. R., 1979, Geochemistry of the Elberton granite and geology of the Elberton West Quadrangle [M.S. thesis]: Athens, University of Georgia, 192 p.

Irvine, T. N., and Baragar, W. R. A., 1971, A guide to the chemical classification of the common volcanic rocks: Canadian Journal of Earth Sciences, v. 8, p. 523–548.

Maniar, P. D., and Piccoli, P. M., 1989. Tectonic discrimination of granitoids: Geological Society of America Bulletin, v. 101, p. 635-643.

McGinn, C. W., 1988, Possible petrogenetic relationships between the Pee Dee gabbro and Lilesville granite, Anson and Richmond counties, North Carolina [M.S. thesis]: Knoxville, University of Tennessee, 83 p.

McSween, H. Y., Jr., Speer, J. A., and Fullagar, P. D., 1991, A survey of the plutonic rocks of the Carolinas, *in* Horton, J. W., Jr., and Zullo, V. A., eds., The geology of the Carolinas: Carolina Geological Society Golden Anniversary Volume, p. 109–126.

Merz, B., and Sinha, A. K., 1977a, Rolesville Batholith, *in* Costain, J. K., Glover, L., III, and Sinha, A. K., eds., Evaluation and targeting of geothermal energy resources in the southeastern United States: U.S. Department of Commerce National Technical Information Service VPI&SU-5103-3, p. B1–B7.

Merz, B., and Sinha, A. K., 1977b, Liberty Hill Bore Holes, *in* Costain, J. K., Glover, L., III, and Sinha, A. K., eds., Evaluation and targeting of geothermal energy resources in the southeastern United States: U.S. Department of Commerce National Technical Information Service VPI&SU-5103-3, p. B8–B18.

Moncla, A. M., III, 1990, Petrography, geochemistry, and geochronology of the Rocky Mount Batholith, northeastern North Carolina Piedmont [M.S. thesis]: Greenville, North Carolina, Eastern Carolina University, 61 p.

Nagel, S. P., 1981, Geochemistry and petrology of xenoliths in the Elberton Batholith [M.S. thesis]: Athens, University of Georgia, 110 p.

Nakamura, N., 1974, Determination of REE, Ba, Mg, Na, and K in carbonaceous and ordinary chondrites: Geochimica et Cosmochimica Acta, v. 38, p. 757–775.

Pearce, J. A., and Norry, M. J., 1979, Petrogenetic implications of Ti, Zr, Y, and Nb variations in volcanic rocks: Contributions to Mineralogy and Petrology, v. 69, p. 33–47.

Pearce, J. A., Harris, N. B. W., and Tindle, A. G., 1984, Trace element discrimination diagrams for the tectonic interpretation of granitic rocks: Journal of Petrology, v. 25, p. 956–983.

Perry, L. D., Higgins, S. P., Costain, J. K., Higgins, S. P., and McKinney, M. M., 1980, Heat flow and heat generation (Rocky Mount and Spring field plutons), *in* Sinha, A. K., Costain, J. K., and Glover, L., III, eds., Distribution and analysis of 300 m.y. old granites as a potential geothermal resource: U.S. Department of Commerce, National Technical Information Service VPI&SU-LASL-2, p. 1–13.

Price, V., Jr., 1969, Distribution of trace elements in plutonic rocks of the southeastern Piedmont [Ph.D. thesis]: Chapel Hill, University of North Carolina, 89 p.

Roberts-Henry, M. A., 1983, A petrographic and geochemical analysis of the Sparta granitic complex, Hancock County, Georgia [M.S. thesis]: Athens, University of Georgia, 343 p.

Rock, N. M. S., 1987, ROBUST: An interactive FORTRAN-77 package for exploratory data analysis using parametric, robust and nonparametric location and scale estimates, data transformations, normality tests, and outlier assessment: Computers & Geosciences, v. 13, p. 463–494.

Rock, N. M. S., 1988, Summary statistics in geochemistry: A study of the performance of robust estimates: Mathematical Geology, v. 20, p. 243–275.

Russell, G. S., Speer, J. A., and Russell, C. W., 1985, The Portsmouth granite, a 263 Ma postmetamorphic biotite granite beneath the Atlantic Coastal Plain, Suffolk, Virginia: Southeastern Geology, v. 26, p. 81–93.

Samson, S. D., and Speer, J. A., 1993, Nd isotope geochemistry of Alleghanian granitoid plutons in the southern Appalachians [abs.]: Eos (Transactions, American Geophysical Union), v. 74, p. 335.

Sando, T. W., 1979a, Trace elements in Hercynian granitic rocks of the southeastern Piedmont, U.S.A. [M.S. thesis]: Chapel Hill, University of North Carolina, 91 p.

Sando, T. W., 1979b, Origin of high-strontium Hercynian granites in the Charlotte belt of the southeastern Piedmont, U.S.A. [abs.]: Eos (Transactions, American Geophysical Union), v. 60, p. 411.

Shand, H. S., 1951, Eruptive rocks (fourth edition): New York, John Wiley and Sons, 488 p.

Shireman, J. W., 1983, Petrology and deformational history of the Clouds Creek igneous complex, central South Carolina Piedmont [M.S. thesis]: Columbia, University of South Carolina, 92 p.

Sinha, A. K., 1980, Geochemistry of Salley and Rocky Mount cores, *in* Sinha, A. K., Costain, J. K., and Glover, L., III, eds., Distribution and analysis of 300 m.y. old granites as a potential geothermal resource: U.S. Department of Commerce National Technical Information Service VPI&SU-LASL-2, p. 12–56.

Sinha, A. K., and Mertz, B. A., 1976a, Winnsboro peraluminous plutonic complex, *in* Costain, J. K., Glover, L., III, and Sinha, A. K., eds., Evaluation and targeting of geothermal energy resources in the southeastern United States: U.S. Department of Commerce National Technical Information Service VPI&SU-5103-2, p. 44–63.

Sinha, A. K., and Mertz, B. A., 1976b, Liberty Hill Pluton, *in* Costain, J. K., Glover, L., III, and Sinha, A. K., eds., Evaluation and targeting of geothermal energy resources in the southeastern United States: U.S. Department of Commerce National Technical Information Service VPI&SU-5103-2, p. B64–B81.

Sinha, A. K., and Mertz, B. A., 1977a, Win 1 core samples, *in* Costain, J. K., Glover, L., III, and Sinha, A. K., eds., Evaluation and targeting of geothermal energy resources in the southeastern United States: U.S. Department of Commerce National Technical Information Service VPI&SU-5103-4, p. B2–B9.

Sinha, A. K., and Mertz, B. A., 1977b, Petersburg Batholith, *in* Costain, J. K., Glover, L., III, and Sinha, A. K., eds., Evaluation and targeting of geothermal energy resources in the southeastern United States: U.S. Department of Commerce National Technical Information Service VPI&SU-5648-1, p. B2–B8.

Sinha, A. K., and Mertz, B. A., 1977c, Rolesville cores, *in* Costain, J. K., Glover, L., III, and Sinha, A. K., eds., Evaluation and targeting of geothermal energy resources in the southeastern United States: U.S. Department of Commerce National Technical Information Service VPI&SU-5648-1, p. B9–B12.

Sloan, E., 1908, Catalogue of the mineral localities of South Carolina: reprinted by the South Carolina Geological Survey, 1979, 505 p.

Speer, J. A., and Becker, S. W., 1990, The Cuffytown Creek pluton, Edgefield and McCormick counties, South Carolina: A highly fractionated alkali-feldspar granite: South Carolina Geology, v. 33, p. 1–17.

Speer, J. A., Becker, S. W., and Farrar, S. S., 1980, Field relations and petrology of the postmetamorphic, coarse-grained granites and associated rocks in the southern Appalachian Piedmont, *in* Wones, D. R., ed., The Caledonides in the USA: Virginia Polytechnic Institute and State University, Department of Geological Sciences Memoir 2, p. 137–148.

Speer, J. A., Naeem, A., and Almohandis, A. A., 1989, Small-scale variations and subtle zoning in granitoid plutons: The Liberty Hill pluton, South Carolina, U.S.A.: Chemical Geology, v. 75, p. 153–181.

Speer, J. A., McSween, H. Y., Jr., and Gates, A. E., 1994, Generation, segregation, ascent, and emplacement of Alleghanian plutons in the southern Appalachians: Journal of Geology, v. 102, p. 249–267.

Stuckless, J. S., Wenner, D. B., and Nkomo, I. T., 1986, Lead-isotope evidence for a pre-Grenville crust under the Piedmont of Georgia: U.S. Geological Survey Bulletin 1622, p. 181–200.

Taylor, S. R., and McLennan, S. M., 1985, The continental crust: Its composition and evolution: Oxford, Blackwell Scientific Publications, 312 p.

Thiéblemont, D., and Tégyey, M., 1994, Une discrimination géochimique des roches différenciées témoin de la diversité d'origine et de situation tectonique des magmas calco-alcalins: Paris, Académie des Sciences, Comptes Rendus, v. 319, série II, p. 87–94.

Tindle, A. G., and Pearce, J. A., 1981, Petrogenetic modeling of in situ fractional crystallization in the zoned Loch Doon pluton, Scotland: Contributions to

Mineralogy and Petrology, v. 78, p. 196–207.

Vogel, T. A., and Wilband, J. T., 1978, Coexisting acidic and basic melts: Geochemistry of a composite dike: Journal of Geology, v. 86, p. 353–371.

Wagener, H. D., 1973, Petrology of the adamellites, granites, and related metamorphic rocks of the Winnsboro quadrangle, South Carolina: The Citadel
   Monograph Series, no. X, 75 p.

Washington, H. S., 1917, Chemical aqnalyses of igneous rocks published from
   1884 to 1913: U.S. Geological Survey Professional Paper 99, 1201 p.

Watson, T. L., 1901, On the origin of the phenocrysts in the porphyritic granites
   of Georgia: Journal of Geology, v. 9, p. 97–122.

Watson, T. L., 1902, Granites and gneisses of Georgia: Geological Survey of
   Georgia Bulletin 9-A, 367 p.

Watson, T. L., 1910, Granites of the southeastern Atlantic states: U.S. Geological Survey Bulletin 426, 275 p.

Wenner, D. B., and Spaulding, J. D., 1982, Uranium and thorium geochemistry
   in the Elberton batholith of the southern Appalachians, USA: Mineralogical
   Magazine, v. 46, p. 227–231.

Whalen, J. B., Currie, K. L., and Chappell, B. W., 1987, A-type granites: Geochemical characteristics, discrimination and petrogenesis: Contributions to
   Mineralogy and Petrology, v. 95, p. 407–419.

Whitney, J. A.; Jones, L. M.; and Walker, R. L., 1976, Age and origin of the
   Stone Mountain granite, Lithonia district, Georgia: Geological Society of
   America Bulletin, v. 87, p. 1067–1077.

Wilson, M., 1989, Igneous petrogenesis: London, Unwin Hyman, 480 p.

Manuscript Accepted by the Society July 2, 1996

Geological Society of America
Memoir 191
1997

Chemical variation in plutonic rocks caused by residual melt migration: Implications for granite petrogenesis

LeeAnn Srogi and Timothy M. Lutz
Department of Geology and Astronomy, West Chester University, West Chester, Pennsylvania 19383

ABSTRACT

We investigate the crystallization history of an early Paleozoic granitic suite within the Arden pluton, Wilmington Complex, Pennsylvania-Delaware Piedmont, and its implications for granite petrogenesis. The pluton intruded into granulite facies gneisses at a depth of 17–25 km, and magmatic textures and mineral and rock compositions are generally well preserved. The granitic suite is characterized geochemically by a wide range of rock compositions (e.g., 54–76 wt% SiO_2; 0.7–5.7 wt% K_2O); strong linear correlation among all elements except Ba, verified by principal components analysis; large apparently random scatter in Ba concentration; limited variation in mineral composition among rocks ranging from 58–73 wt% SiO_2; and no apparent spatial pattern to rock chemical variation within the pluton.

We explain these factors by a model of in situ crystallization within a solidification zone (or boundary layer). We derive equations that integrate both major- and trace-element variations in a quantitative model of the migration and crystallization of residual liquid within a mush of relatively earlier formed crystals. Barium is the key element that traces the history of melt migration, because it changed behavior from incompatible to compatible with the onset of K-feldspar crystallization from the residual granitic liquid. The model explains the large range in rock chemistry as well as the linear correlations among elements in terms of the proportions of earlier formed crystals, and minerals that crystallized from the residual melt. The apparent scatter of Ba concentration in the rocks resulted from the variable depletion of Ba in the residual liquid as it crystallized and migrated through the crystal mush, and requires that trapped liquid did not equilibrate in trace-element composition on a scale of meters or more within the crystal mush.

From our equations, we derive values for parameters that describe the proportion of melt that remained after crystallization of earlier formed minerals, and the proportion of residual melt that ultimately left the rock. Net melt loss for most rocks is ≥50%, suggesting that melt was not only migrating locally, but was being transported from the level of the pluton now exposed. This result may be more compatible with gravity-influenced processes near the base of a growing crystal pile, rather than with sidewall crystallization. Nearly uniform compositions and proportions of the relatively earlier formed crystals could be explained by efficient compositional convection between the granitic magma reservoir and residual melt circulating through the crystal mush. There is a roughly concentric spatial pattern to the model parameters for melt proportions that suggests an outer zone of high initial crystallinity and little melt loss near the present margin of the pluton, an interior zone with large losses of residual melt that is consistent with high melt fluxes and compositional convection,

Srogi, L., and Lutz, T. M., 1997, Chemical variation in plutonic rocks caused by residual melt migration: Implications for granite petrogenesis, *in* Sinha, A. K., Whalen, J. B., and Hogan, J. P., eds., The Nature of Magmatism in the Appalachian Orogen: Boulder, Colorado, Geological Society of America Memoir 191.

and a central zone of low initial crystallinity and melt accumulation in the pluton interior. Our results suggest that plutonic rocks can develop large compositional variations over short (<10² m) distances by melt migration. The portion of the Arden pluton currently exposed probably represents a relatively small section of the magma chamber in which late-stage melt migration controlled rock chemistry more than larger scale processes such as fractionation, and in which detailed sampling revealed the effects of residual melt behavior.

INTRODUCTION

Recent considerations of the thermal histories and dynamics of magma chambers suggest that some chambers crystallize in situ via a migrating solidification zone consisting of a mesh of crystals and a melt. Such a process of in situ or boundary layer crystallization has been proposed for layered mafic complexes (McBirney and Noyes, 1979; McBirney and Hunter, 1995), and is an appealing alternative to the gravitative separation of crystals from liquid for granitic magmas.

There are several examples of granitoid rocks presumed to have formed by boundary layer crystallization. The in situ crystallization of the Cordillera Paine pluton (Michael, 1984) and the sidewall crystallization of the Pallisade Crest intrusive suite (Sawka et al., 1990) are examples at the pluton scale. The compositions of tephra from both calc-alkaline and alkaline volcanoes have been interpreted as erupted crystal mushes; i.e., cumulates with trapped residual melt from the crystallizing boundary layer of the subvolcanic magma chamber (Mount Mazama, Druitt and Bacon, 1989; Laacher See volcano, Tait, 1988; Latera caldera, Turbeville, 1992). Mahood and Cornejo (1992) presented evidence that leucocratic granites in the La Gloria pluton, Chile, represent evolved liquids separated from granitic cumulate rocks and trapped at stepped contacts along the walls and near the roof of the pluton.

In experimental work simulating crystallization in a porous medium, Tait et al. (1984) demonstrated that less-dense residual liquids are released from the crystal mush and presumably are replaced with less-evolved liquid from the main chamber, a process described as compositional convection (equivalent to convective fractionation; Sparks et al., 1984). Clarke (1992, p. 88) cited the importance of "chemically driven convective fractionation" in the formation of granitoid rocks. The extent to which residual liquids are trapped within the crystal mush or are returned to and mix with magma in the chamber depends on such parameters as the relative densities of crystals and residual liquid, and the relative rates of crystallization and melt migration (Tait et al., 1984; Tait and Kerr, 1987). Trapping of residual liquid results in "orthocumulate"-like rocks containing intensely zoned crystals (e.g., Michael, 1984). The magma reservoir remains uniform and unevolved, whereas individual samples show the evolution of magma composition with crystallization (Langmuir, 1989). Circulation of residual liquid with the adjacent portion of the magma reservoir can lead to "adcumulate"-like rocks with nearly uniform mineral compositions. Mineral compositions are not in equilibrium with the magma

as a whole, but reflect "equilibrium" with percolating melt (Lesher and Walker, 1988).

Thus, the migration and crystallization of residual liquid are key aspects of crystallization in solidification zones. In some cases, the effects of melt migration can be recognized. For example, Helz (1987) described the migration of evolved liquids based on evidence from drilling within the lava lake at Kilauea Iki, and Irvine (1980) described metasomatism of cumulate rocks in layered mafic complexes due to infiltration and reaction with interstitial melt.

Numerical models that consider melt-crystal separation have been developed. Building on traditional fractionation theory, DeLong and Chatelain (1989), McCarthy and Robb (1978), and McCarthy and Hasty (1976) modeled plutonic rock compositions in terms of mixtures of cumulus crystals and intercumulus liquids formed during fractional crystallization with perfect or imperfect separation of crystals from liquid. More recent models explicitly consider in situ or boundary layer crystallization assuming equilibrium (Langmuir, 1989) or fractional (Nielsen and DeLong, 1992) crystallization. Lesher and Walker (1988) modeled melt segregation, adcumulus crystal growth, and compaction in a cumulus crystal pile driven by spatial thermal variations between the margin and interior of a magma chamber. These models have been applied mostly to basaltic magmas, and there has been no quantitative treatment of melt migration based on a natural system of granitic composition.

In this chapter, we develop a quantitative model of the chemical effects of residual melt migration and apply it to a suite of granitic rocks that represents a paleosolidification zone. The effects of melt migration can be discerned because fractionation, mixing, assimilation, and unmixing played relatively minor roles. The chemical signature of residual melt migration is produced by a trace element that changes over the course of crystallization from incompatible to compatible behavior. The migration and crystallization of residual melt through an existing crystal mush are then revealed by the variations in abundance of this trace element in the rocks and in the minerals that crystallized from the residual melt. In the granitic suite described in this chapter, Ba is the key element that traces the melt migration process.

GEOLOGIC SETTING AND PREVIOUS WORK

The granitic suite is part of the composite Arden pluton, located in the Wilmington Complex of southeastern Pennsylvania and northern Delaware (Fig. 1). The Wilmington Complex

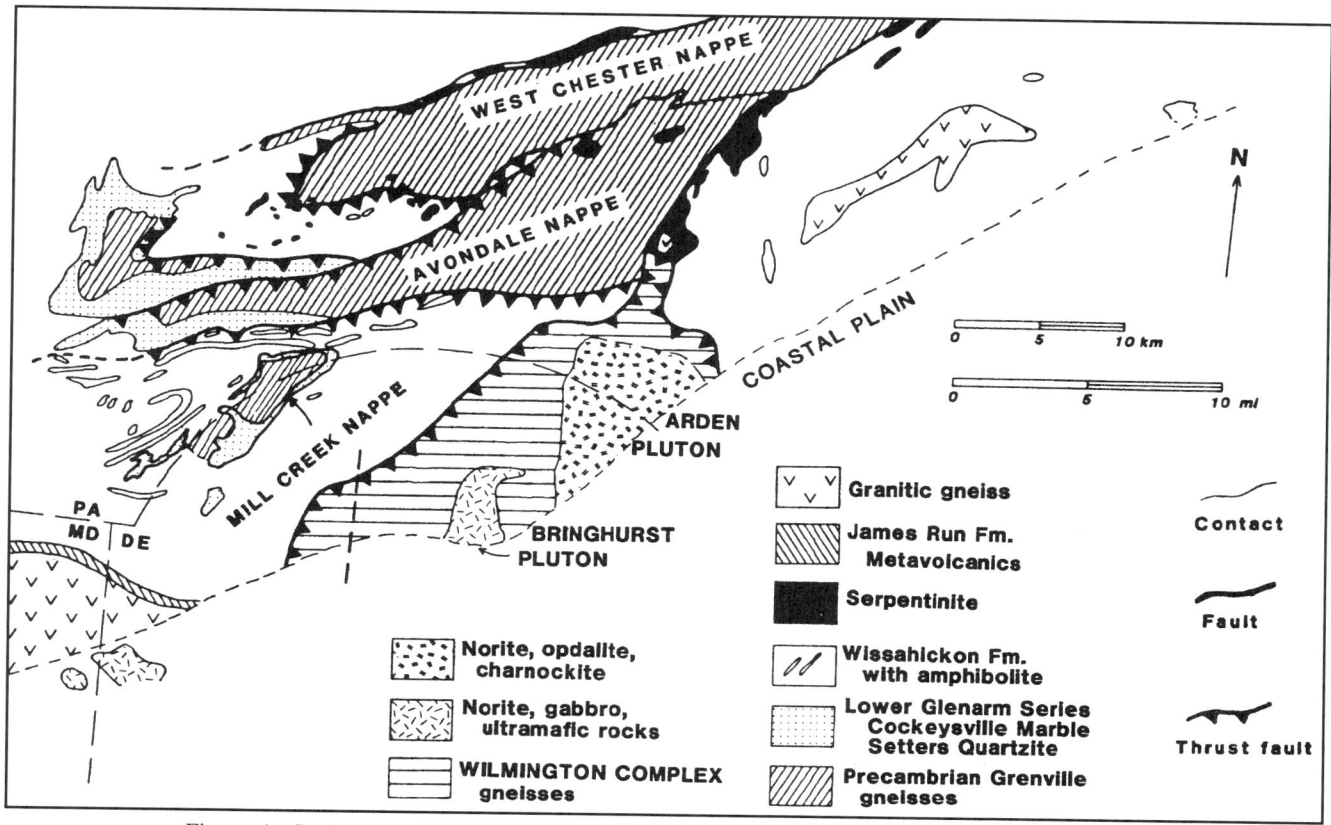

Figure 1. Geologic map of the Arden pluton in the Wilmington Complex, Pennsylvania and Delaware, after Srogi et al., (1993).

was first mapped by Bascom and Miller (1920) and Bascom and Stose (1932). Ward (1959) described the entire Wilmington Complex and was the first to identify the largest plutons, which he named the Arden granite and the Bringhurst gabbro. More recent maps and descriptions include those of Woodruff and Thompson (1975), Wagner and Srogi (1987), Srogi (1988), Wagner et al. (1987, 1991), and Crawford and Crawford (1991).

The Wilmington Complex is important to our understanding of Appalachian magmatism for its information on the nature of the basement to early Paleozoic magmatism and for the study of deep-crustal magmatic and metamorphic processes. The Wilmington Complex is identified in the tectonic models of Crawford and Crawford (1980) and Wagner and Srogi (1987) as a fragment of the deep infrastructure of a magmatic arc, tectonically emplaced onto North America during the Taconic orogeny. This interpretation is in part based on the calc-alkaline chemistry (Wagner and Srogi, 1987), and age (502 ± 20 Ma; Foland and Muessig, 1978) of the granitic rocks in the Arden pluton. In addition, most of the country rocks to the plutons are low-K quartzofeldspathic and mafic gneisses (Ward, 1959; Srogi, 1988) which could be metamorphosed equivalents of arc-related volcanic or volcaniclastic rocks (e.g., compare data in Ward 1959, and Srogi, 1988, with Brouxel et al., 1987). Structures and textures dated or inferred as pre-Taconic are pre-

served in the Wilmington Complex. These include magmatic fabrics and minerals in the plutonic igneous rocks, as well as localized thermal metamorphism associated with igneous intrusions superimposed on regional granulite facies conditions in the country rocks. Plutons were emplaced at depths of ≈17–25 km, based upon pressure estimates of 600 ± 100 MPa in adjacent country-rock gneisses (Wagner and Srogi, 1987; Srogi, 1988; Srogi et al., 1993).

The Arden pluton covers about 20 km², is the largest of the intrusions, and contains distinct suites of both gabbroic and granitic rocks that can be readily recognized and mapped in the field (Figs. 2 and 3). Thompson (1975), Woodruff and Thompson (1975), and Mark (1977) mapped and described the Arden pluton as comagmatic anorthosite, noritic anorthosite, opdalite, and charnockite; however, there is no true anorthosite. Most of the rocks are felsic in composition, and can be recognized by medium to coarse grain sizes, hypidiomorphic-granular textures, and the presence of feldspar phenocrysts and quartz (Fig. 3A). These rocks are assigned to the granitic suite, which comprises pyroxene-bearing quartz diorites, quartz monzodiorites, granodiorites, and granites. The granitic suite has a calc-alkaline chemical signature unlike anorthosites and associated rocks (Wagner and Srogi, 1987; Srogi, 1988). Gabbronorites and olivine gabbronorites, commonly with medium-grained subophitic textures

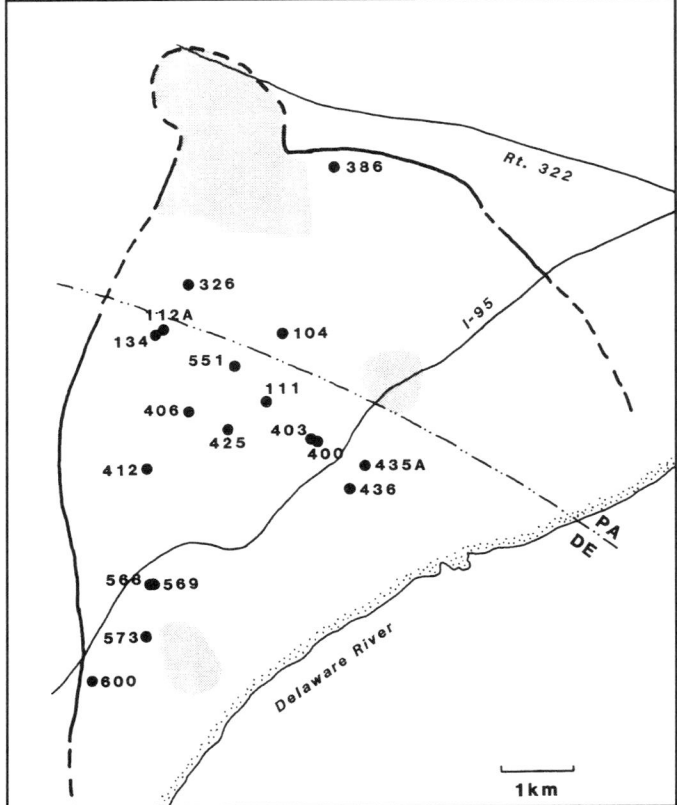

Figure 2. Simplified lithologic map of the Arden pluton showing locations of granitoid samples (black circles). Screened areas indicate gabbroid without granitoid; unpatterned region is primarily granitoid with variable amounts of gabbroid and mafic enclaves. Dotted pattern indicates coastal plain sediments along the Delaware River. The Pennsylvania-Delaware border and major roads (Interstate 95 and Route 322) are shown for reference. The map area is entirely contained within the Marcus Hook 7fi′ topographic quadrangle, Pennsylvania–Delaware–New Jersey.

Figure 3. A: Texture of typical rock from the granitic suite, Arden pluton. White area below and to left of lens cap (~5 cm diameter) is reflection off water on rock surface. B: Subophitic texture of gabbronorite from the Arden pluton. Hammer handle is ~4 cm wide at white stripe.

(Fig. 3B), occur as a mappable unit or units in the northwest, southwest, and eastern portions of the pluton (Fig. 2).

Several features can be used to infer the coexistence of contemporaneous basaltic and silicic magmas within the Arden pluton chamber. For example, the granitic rocks commonly contain mafic enclaves near the gabbroic unit, and the gabbroic rocks show decreasing grain sizes and increasing abundance of hornblende and biotite with proximity to the granitic suite. Away from zones of contact, however, the gabbroic and granitic units show little evidence for extensive interaction in terms of their mineralogies and chemical and isotopic compositions (Srogi, 1988). For example, the strontium and oxygen isotopic compositions of a gabbronorite (0.703997 and $\delta^{18}O$ = +6.3‰, respectively) are significantly different from those of the granitic suite (0.7065 initial Sr ratio, Foland and Muessig, 1978; $\delta^{18}O$ = +7.6‰). For the purposes of this study, granitoid samples were taken as far from contacts with gabbronorite as possible, in order to avoid hybridized or enclave-rich material. Otherwise, gran-

itoid samples were selected in order to obtain a roughly representative distribution of lithologies within the pluton (Fig. 2).

METHODS AND RESULTS

The interpretations of field work in this study are based upon more than 600 localities within the eastern portion of the Wilmington Complex (Fig. 1). More than 100 thin sections and slabs of the igneous rocks were examined for classification, textural interpretation, and for selection of samples for analysis. Modal estimates are approximate because the rocks are porphyritic. Lithologic terms used below and in Table 1 are based on modal estimates and use the terminology of Streckeisen (1976).

Whole-rock chemical analysis

We analyzed 18 samples from the granitic suite for major and selected trace elements; localities are shown in Figure 2.

One large sample (386) was divided roughly in half before crushing and processing in order to evaluate sample homogeneity on a scale of ≤ 1 m; samples are designated 386A and 386B. Samples, typically 10–20 kg, were crushed, split, and then powdered in a Spex tungsten carbide mixer mill. All samples were analyzed at the Directed Coupled Plasma Atomic Emission Spectroscopy (DCP-AES) facility at Rutgers University (Feigenson and Carr, 1985) after preparation according to the procedures of M. J. Carr (1985, personal commun.). AGV-1 was used as an internal standard; additional standards including PCC-1, BHVO-1, BCR-1, GSP-1, QLO-1, G-2, and RGM-1 were analyzed as unknowns along with the samples to provide calibration curves. Data were reduced using the program of M. J. Carr (Feigenson and Carr, 1985). Rb concentrations in the granitic suite were analyzed separately after optimizing the plasma position for Rb to increase sensitivity to low concentrations. The precision of the analyses based on replicate standard analyses is typically 2–3% for major elements, comparable to that described by Feigenson and Carr (1985). The precision of Ba, Sr, and Rb analyses is about 2%. The precision of the remaining trace element analyses is a function of abundance and ranges from <5% for abundances of >100 ppm, to about 10% for abundances <40 ppm.

Ferrous iron was determined by titration for four samples of the Arden granitic suite, ranging in composition from about 64–76 wt% SiO_2, (procedure from S. Mertzman, 1982, personal commun.). Replicate analyses of U.S. Geological Survey (USGS) standard rocks (BHVO-1, W-1, BCR-1, AGV-1, GSP-1, G-2, QLO-1, and RGM-1) consistently gave FeO contents within 0.4 wt% of the values reported by the USGS. For the remaining samples, FeO was estimated from a regression of titrated FeO versus total iron from the DCP analysis, and ferric iron was calculated by difference. The results of whole-rock chemical analysis are presented in Table 1 and discussed in the following section.

Mineral analysis

Mineral compositions were determined by wavelength-dispersive electron probe microanalysis in six samples from the Arden granitic suite spanning the range in whole-rock chemistry from 58–73 wt% SiO_2. Analyses were made using JEOL probes at Lehigh and Rutgers Universities. Operating conditions were 15 kV and sample current of 10 nA at both facilities; a beam current of 20 nA (Lehigh) or 15 nA (Rutgers); and counting times from 5–40 s in order to maximize peak to background ratios for each element. Defocused or rastered beams were used to analyze exsolved portions of pyroxenes and feldspars, and a rastered beam was used for all feldspar analyses at Rutgers. Well-characterized natural and synthetic standards were used for calibration. The analysis was fully automated by an online minicomputer, which standardized counting times and applied the Bence-Albee matrix correction. In most cases, from 3–10 points were analyzed on each mineral grain, and 2 or more grains of each mineral were analyzed in each thin section. The precision of the analyses based on replicate analyses of the standards ranges from $\leq 2\%$ for oxides with abundance greater than 20 wt%, to 5–10% for oxides with abundance ≤ 5 wt%. Results, normalized to oxygens for stoichiometry, are presented in Table 2 (pyroxenes) and Table 3 (feldspars), and are discussed below.

Petrography and mineral chemistry

Both orthopyroxene and clinopyroxene occur in the granitic suite, so these rocks should properly be termed norites and quartz norites (diorites and quartz diorites), quartz monzonorites or quartz jotunites (quartz monzodiorite), opdalites (granodiorites), and charnockites (granites), (Streckeisen, 1976). We refer to all of these rocks as granitoids or the granitic suite. Mineral proportions and textures are correlated with rock composition. The most mafic rocks consist of pyroxenes and plagioclase, with anhedral interstitial quartz and K-feldspar. The most silicic rocks contain abundant K-feldspar phenocrysts and fewer plagioclase phenocrysts set in an equigranular matrix of quartz, plagioclase, and K-feldspar, and only a scant amount of biotite and orthopyroxene. Accessory minerals, such as zircon, apatite, magnetite, and ilmenite, are commonly seen as euhedral grains associated with pyroxenes and plagioclase (Fig. 4A), and are rare in the most felsic rocks.

We infer the textures and mineral associations to indicate primary magmatic crystallization of pyroxenes (Fig. 4) with plagioclase and accessory minerals. Hornblende is absent from all granitic rocks analyzed, an unusual feature for a calc-alkaline granitoid. We do not believe that primary hornblende was replaced by pyroxenes during postmagmatic metamorphism because no relict hornblende is observed, and because this has not happened in the granulite facies country rocks with similar silica contents and even lower alkali contents than the granitoids. If both rock types had been subjected to extensive postintrusive metamorphism, the higher alkali contents of the granitoids would have stabilized hornblende and inhibited pyroxene growth. The absence of hornblende indicates that magmatic water contents were probably below 2–3 wt% (e.g., Naney, 1983; Clemens, 1984, and references therein; Johnson et al., 1994, and references therein). It has been suggested that water is transferred from silicic to basaltic magmas during magma mingling (e.g., Wiebe, 1993; Zorpi et al., 1989), and this might account for the unusually dry conditions of crystallization in the Arden granitic suite. However, this question is beyond the scope of this chapter, particularly because zones of magmatic interaction were not sampled and studied in detail, and is the subject of a separate investigation.

Pyroxenes occur typically as euhedral to subhedral, discrete grains (Fig. 4A) or glomeroporphyritic clusters; in a few instances, they are anhedral and interstitial to plagioclase (Fig. 4B). Orthopyroxene is commonly more abundant than clinopyroxene. Both clinopyroxene and orthopyroxene typically have fine-scale exsolution lamellae, and small grains and rims of

TABLE 1. GRANITOID COMPOSITIONS

Sample	406 Quartz Norite	569 Norite	403 Quartz Norite	436 Quartz Norite	435A Quartz Norite	412 Quartz Norite	600 Quartz Norite	568 Quartz Norite	112A Quartz Norite	425 Quartz Norite
(wt. %)										
SiO_2	56.36	53.65	57.97	61.38	61.87	60.72	63.14	61.01	64.18	64.03
TiO_2	1.51	1.27	1.15	1.00	1.03	0.97	0.92	0.95	0.93	0.90
Al_2O_3	18.47	18.81	18.78	17.86	17.71	18.36	16.59	17.10	16.81	16.84
Fe_2O_3	2.95	2.80	2.51	2.23	2.15	2.15	2.03	2.19	1.98	1.95
FeO	4.87	4.61	4.09	3.58	3.45	3.44	3.22	3.52	3.32	3.09
MnO	0.13	0.12	0.12	0.10	0.10	0.08	0.11	0.09	0.09	0.08
MgO	3.47	3.88	2.69	2.47	2.29	2.32	2.67	2.32	2.01	2.02
CaO	7.60	7.95	6.48	5.89	5.64	5.69	5.29	5.04	4.95	4.93
Na_2O	4.16	4.10	4.40	4.40	4.31	4.32	3.94	4.01	3.84	4.02
K_2O	0.99	0.70	1.07	0.78	1.09	1.51	0.97	2.20	2.47	2.01
P_2O_5	0.44	0.38	0.36	0.31	0.30	0.32	0.27	0.31	0.31	0.30
Total	100.65	97.99	99.37	99.78	99.73	99.66	98.95	98.52	100.69	99.98
(ppm										
Rb	17	15	17	4	10	23	16	62	37	53
Sr	422	391	381	359	351	347	315	293	384	306
Ba	598	515	745	931	1,304	802	235	906	2,155	905
Ni	19	24	14	10	10	18	16	13	13	13
Cr	27	29	20	16	17	26	21	19	22	20
V	147	162	121	92	103	122	103	105	115	109
Sc	18	23	14	11	12	15	12	14	13	14
Cu	154	159	19	19	19	36	23	33	20	45
Zr	281	312	398	317	375	364	232	388	315	318
PC1*	.......†	....	-4.84	-3.40	-3.23	-3.12	-2.28	-2.11	-1.89	-1.46
g*	....	....	0.140	0.234	0.245	0.252	0.307	0.318	0.332	0.360

one pyroxene type on the other are interpreted as granule exsolution during cooling (Fig. 4B). Reaction of pyroxenes with late magmatic or subsolidus fluids to form biotite and Fe-Ti oxides is limited in extent; pyroxene modes range as high as 20%, and biotite is never more than 5% and typically 1–2% of the mode.

Pyroxene grains are slightly zoned, primarily in wollastonite component, as a result of exsolution, and overall show slight iron enrichment from the most mafic to the most silicic sample (Table 2). Maximum temperatures of 850–950 °C (Fig. 5A), estimated from pyroxene thermometry (Lindsley, 1983), are appropriate for relatively dry andesitic-rhyolitic magmas (e.g., Eggler, 1972; Eggler and Burnham, 1973). The pyroxenes have more iron-rich and lower temperature compositions than those analyzed from the gabbroic rocks (Srogi, 1988). Pyroxenes in the Arden granitic suite are most similar in both quadrilateral components (Fig. 5B) and nonquadrilateral components (Fig. 5C) to pyroxenes in dacitic to rhyolitic rocks from convergent tectonic settings (Feeley and Davidson, 1994; Druitt and Bacon, 1989; Cotkin and Medaris, 1993; Weiss and Troll, 1989; Eggins and Hensen, 1987; Czamanske et al., 1981). The somewhat higher aluminum contents in Arden pyroxenes probably result from higher pressure crystallization (600 MPa for the Arden compared with ≤300 MPa for rocks from the other localities).

Plagioclase occurs as large, euhedral to subhedral phenocrysts and as smaller, subhedral matrix grains. Phenocryst shapes, Carlsbad-Albite twinning, and antiperthitic zones with euhedral crystal outlines (Fig. 6) are preserved magmatic features. Analyzed nonantiperthitic plagioclases in all samples, both phenocrysts and matrix grains, span a narrow range of low-temperature compositions; most analyses are around An_{33-37} (Table 3, Fig. 7). Oscillatory zoning in Ab-An content in one sample is in the range An $_{34-40}$. The relative uniformity of plagioclase in the granitoids is in contrast to the extensive zoning in Ab-An contents observed in the more anorthitic plagioclase in the gabbroic rocks (Srogi, 1988). Bulk compositions of the antiperthite zones (Table 3), estimated from point counting back-scattered electron photomicrographs, would indicate temperatures in the range of 900–1000 °C if they formed by crystallization of ternary feldspar from a dry granitic liquid (Fig. 7; Nekvasil, 1992). Alternatively, the antiperthite zones could have resulted from nucleation and growth of orthoclase grains from a K-enriched, Na- and Ca-depleted boundary layer along the margin of a growing plagioclase phenocryst (Fig. 7; Lofgren and Gooley, 1977). Further work to evaluate these hypotheses is beyond the scope of this chapter.

K-feldspar is present in all granitoids, ranging in habit from anhedral interstitial grains to large Carlsbad-twinned phenocrysts, and, more rarely, as poikilitic interstitial grains enclosing euhedral to subhedral plagioclase and pyroxenes. Most of the K-feldspar is microperthitic to cryptoperthitic orthoclase, with a moderate optic axial angle (spindle stage determination;

TABLE 1. GRANITOID COMPOSITIONS (continued - page 2)

Sample	386B Quartz Monzonorite	386A Quartz Monzonorite	573 Opdalite	111 Opdalite	400 Opdalite	134 Opdalite	326 Opdalite	104 Charnockite	551 Charnockite
(wt. %)									
SiO_2	64.10	64.58	63.93	66.01	67.59	72.70	72.99	76.32	75.81
TiO_2	0.75	0.73	0.69	0.72	0.65	0.32	0.42	0.13	0.13
Al_2O_3	17.00	17.27	16.42	16.47	15.94	13.90	13.52	12.09	12.53
Fe_2O_3	1.82	1.80	1.71	1.73	1.53	1.08	1.00	0.33	0.37
FeO	2.86	2.82	2.66	2.56	2.33	1.32	1.38	0.36	0.27
MnO	0.08	0.08	0.07	0.12	0.06	0.07	0.04	0.02	0.02
MgO	1.96	1.93	1.76	1.66	1.55	0.97	0.97	0.22	0.14
CaO	4.87	4.87	4.37	4.03	4.07	2.53	2.54	1.69	1.26
Na_2O	4.06	4.14	4.13	4.31	3.61	3.38	2.61	2.75	2.47
K_2O	1.75	1.87	2.03	1.58	2.91	3.57	4.15	4.18	5.71
P_2O_5	0.25	0.24	0.25	0.09	0.19	0.13	0.11	0.02	0.02
Total	99.33	100.15	97.85	99.11	100.28	99.86	99.63	98.08	98.69
(ppm)									
Rb	43	50	58	51	52	90	77	108	91
Sr	262	264	275	176	264	139	251	178	110
Ba	642	680	709	208	1,111	449	1,317	1,022	981
Ni	21	15	14	12	10	11	9	5	1
Cr	32	23	17	17	15	19	13	6	2
V	113	110	79	86	74	74	57	23	n.d.§
Sc	14	13	11	16	10	11	6	3	n.d.
Cu	27	20	22	11	11	9	3	n.d.	n.d.
Zr	276	284	276	311	245	182	127	42	34
PC1*	-1.03	-0.93	-0.21	....	+1.06	+3.88	+4.42	+7.22	+7.92
g*	0.388	0.394	0.441	....	0.523	0.706	0.742	0.923	0.969

*See text for derviation of PC1 (first principal components score) and g.
†No data, excluded from analysis.
§Not detected or below detection on the instrument.

J. Calem, 1985, personal commun.) and an intermediate structural state (Foland and Muessig, 1978). Polysynthetic twinning typical of low microcline is observed optically in only 2 of more than 50 thin sections examined. Myrmekite is common along K-feldspar grain boundaries. The orthoclase analyses are K-rich, low-temperature compositions, and we have not attempted to reintegrate the bulk perthite compositions. The abundance of barium as celsian component in orthoclase varies from more than 2 wt% to less than 1 wt% BaO (Table 3). Neither plagioclase nor K-feldspars are sericitized or epidotized, but some have chlorite-filled microfractures.

Quartz is typically subhedral to anhedral, equant to elongate, and is interstitial in more mafic rocks and forms larger discrete grains in the more silicic rocks. Biotite is pleochroic in shades of pale yellow to deep reddish-brown. Much of the biotite appears to replace pyroxene by late magmatic and subsolidus reaction, although some grains of possible magmatic origin occur as clusters of flakes with abundant apatite and zircon inclusions. Biotite compositions are variable, probably reflecting a complex origin. In all rocks, however, it is a minor constituent and will not be considered explicitly in the discussions of magmatic processes below.

Mineral composition data are important in the modeling of plutonic rock crystallization. An outstanding feature of the granitic suite is the near uniformity of mineral compositions in rocks ranging from 58–73 wt% SiO_2. Therefore, we consider the extent to which postmagmatic deformation and recrystallization might have created such uniformity. In the field, most granitic rocks appear massive and undeformed or have lineations due to aligned enclaves and phenocrysts that meet the criteria for an origin by magmatic flow (Paterson et al., 1989). Igneous textures are common and none of the rocks analyzed for this study is extensively recrystallized. There is no correlation between mineral compositions and extent of deformation. Sample 568 shows the greatest degree of strain and recovery of the analyzed rocks, including deformation twinning, bent twin lamellae, and kinking in feldspars; sutured grain boundaries in quartz and feldspars; and subgrain development and grain-size reduction in quartz. Nonetheless, this sample has the same pyroxene and plagioclase compositions as the other rocks, and has preserved magmatic oscillatory zoning in plagioclase phenocrysts. Homogenization of pyroxene compositions is possible, but requires significant intercrystalline diffusion of Fe and Mg. Reintegrated pyroxene compositions yield magmatic temperatures and have composi-

TABLE 2. PYROXENE COMPOSITIONS

Sample	403 Core	403 Rest	568 Core	568 Rest	425 Core	425 Int.	425 Rim	386 Core	386 Rest	400 Core	400 Rim	326 Average all
					ORTHOPYROXENES							
(wt. %)												
SiO_2	51.12	51.12	52.00	51.75	50.39	50.23	50.55	51.68	51.30	51.82	52.27	52.37
TiO_2	0.08	0.07	0.08	0.09	0.44	0.07	0.08	0.10	0.11	0.12	0.09	0.08
Al_2O_3	1.12	1.07	1.17	1.11	1.03	1.03	1.00	1.00	1.03	1.19	0.99	1.37
FeO^t	25.96	26.03	26.35	27.04	25.09	26.16	26.05	25.46	26.05	26.02	26.02	26.58
MnO	0.84	0.85	0.83	0.87	1.03	1.02	1.02	0.98	1.01	0.89	0.88	0.65
MgO	20.08	20.76	18.99	19.19	20.35	20.56	20.64	19.84	19.54	19.75	20.22	18.95
CaO	1.00	0.63	1.58	0.59	1.77	1.04	0.77	1.02	0.68	0.87	0.47	0.48
Na_2O	0.09	0.06	0.03	0.01	0.06	0.06	0.04	0.04	0.01	0.05	0.03	0.03
K_2O	n.d.*	n.d.	0.02	0.01	n.d.	n.d.	n.d.	0.04	0.01	n.d.	n.d.	n.d.
Total	100.29	100.59	101.05	100.66	100.16	100.17	100.15	100.16	99.74	100.71	100.97	100.51
Cations†												
Si	1.943	1.939	1.962	1.962	1.921	1.922	1.929	1.960	1.959	1.957	1.965	1.978
Al(IV)	0.050	0.047	0.038	0.038	0.046	0.046	0.045	0.039	0.041	0.043	0.035	0.022
Al(VI)	0	0	0.014	0.012	0	0.013	0	0.006	0.007	0.010	0.009	0.039
Ti	0.002	0.002	0.001	0.003	0.013	0.002	0.002	0.004	0.003	0.003	0.003	0.002
Fe	0.825	0.825	0.832	0.857	0.800	0.837	0.833	0.807	0.832	0.822	0.818	0.839
Mn	0.027	0.027	0.027	0.028	0.033	0.032	0.032	0.032	0.033	0.029	0.028	0.021
Mg	1.138	1.173	1.068	1.085	1.156	1.172	1.175	1.122	1.113	1.112	1.133	1.067
Ca	0.041	0.025	0.064	0.024	0.072	0.044	0.032	0.041	0.028	0.035	0.019	0.019
Na	0.007	0.004	0.002	0.001	0.004	0.004	0.003	0.003	0.001	0.004	0.002	0.002
Wo§	0.021	0.013	0.034	0.013	0.036	0.021	0.016	0.022	0.015	0.018	0.010	0.010**
En	0.575	0.584	0.549	0.557	0.568	0.575	0.579	0.578	0.572	0.565	0.574	0.554**
Fs	0.404	0.403	0.417	0.430	0.396	0.404	0.405	0.401	0.413	0.417	0.417	0.436**

tions similar to those in other plutonic and volcanic igneous rocks. K-feldspar compositions have been more extensively modified by exsolution and myrmekite formation. However, K-feldspars have not recrystallized, and transformation to low structural states has occurred in only a very few rocks. On the basis of these lines of evidence, we interpret the mineral compositions to reflect equilibrium with a granitic magma near the solidus, followed by relatively minor compositional adjustment during subsolidus cooling.

DISCUSSION

Any petrogenetic model for the granitic suite in the Arden pluton must explain the following characteristics: the near-uniformity of mineral compositions (Tables 2 and 3), the wide range of rock compositions (54–76 wt% SiO_2; Table 1), the linear trends on Harker diagrams for all analyzed elements except Ba (Fig. 8), and the behavior of Ba and its decoupling from that of K_2O, Rb, and Sr (Fig. 8). The scatter in Ba is not correlated with biotite abundance, and there is nothing to suggest widespread alkali metasomatism (e.g., Scambos et al., 1986), or another secondary process.

Pyroxene and plagioclase compositions indicate crystallization from a magma of dacitic to rhyolitic composition, even for rocks that currently contain less than 60% SiO_2. The presence of accessory apatite and zircon with pyroxenes and pla-

gioclase, and the compatible behavior of P_2O_5 and Zr, indicate early saturation of the magma with these components and further suggest a melt of granitic composition (Green and Watson, 1982; Watson and Harrison, 1983). This is consistent with the low concentrations of Ni, Cr, and Cu in most of the rocks.

In the following sections, we quantify the extent of linear variation in rock compositions and evaluate petrogenetic models for crystallization of the granitic suite.

Statistical quantification of linear variation in whole-rock compositions

We used principal components analysis to quantify the chemical variation in the granitic suite. This technique, reviewed by Le Maitre (1982), is a purely mathematical transformation and requires no assumptions about the genesis of the variation. The first principal components coordinate, referred to here as PC1, defines the direction in multidimensional space of the greatest variation in the data and is, essentially, the "best-fit straight line" to all the chemical data included in the analysis. All principal components coordinates are uncorrelated with each other statistically.

To define 15-dimensional chemical space for the principal components transformation, 15 elements, including all oxides as well as Rb, Sr, V, and Zr, were used. Cr, Ni, Sc, and Cu were excluded because of their low abundances, and Ba was

TABLE 2. PYROXENE COMPOSITIONS (continued - page 2)

Sample	CLINOPYROXENES								
	403 Average all	568 Core	568 Rest	425 Core	425 Rest	386 Core	386 Int.	386 Rim	400 Average all
(wt. %)									
SiO_2	50.46	51.50	52.28	50.66	50.67	51.54	51.39	51.40	52.00
TiO_2	0.22	0.22	0.16	0.16	0.19	0.16	0.20	0.16	0.22
Al_2O_3	1.91	2.05	1.82	1.82	1.76	1.67	1.73	1.84	2.08
FeO^t	11.05	12.74	11.01	11.54	11.21	12.12	11.16	10.24	11.09
MnO	0.37	0.48	0.29	0.48	0.46	0.45	0.45	0.39	0.41
MgO	13.88	12.82	12.74	13.40	13.18	13.54	13.06	12.93	12.47
CaO	21.25	19.65	21.35	20.40	20.99	19.42	20.52	21.62	21.31
Na_2O	0.55	0.54	0.52	0.57	0.56	0.47	0.50	0.51	0.61
K_2O	n.d.*	0.02	0.02	n.d.	n.d.	0.01	n.d.	n.d.	n.d.
Total	99.69	100.02	100.19	99.03	99.02	99.38	99.01	99.09	100.19
Cations†									
Si	1.914	1.947	1.962	1.933	1.933	1.954	1.954	1.950	1.954
Al(IV)	0.085	0.053	0.038	0.067	0.067	0.046	0.046	0.050	0.046
Al(VI)	0	0.038	0.042	0.016	0.012	0.028	0.032	0.050	0.047
Ti	0.006	0.006	0.005	0.005	0.006	0.005	0.006	0.033	0.006
Fe	0.114	0.403	0.345	0.369	0.358	0.384	0.355	0.004	0.348
Mn	0.249	0.015	0.009	0.016	0.015	0.014	0.015	0.325	0.013
Mg	0.785	0.722	0.713	0.761	0.750	0.766	0.740	0.012	0.699
Ca	0.864	0.796	0.858	0.835	0.858	0.788	0.836	0.731	0.858
Na	0.041	0.039	0.038	0.042	0.042	0.035	0.037	0.879	0.045
								0.038	
Wo§	0.415	0.397	0.426	0.410	0.423	0.393	0.418	0.435	0.428
En	0.444	0.402	0.396	0.423	0.416	0.420	0.408	0.409	0.388
Fs	0.141	0.201	0.178	0.167	0.161	0.186	0.174	0.156	0.184

*Not detected or <0.01 for average of more than one analysis.
†Cations normalized to six oxygens.
§Proportions of Wo, En, Fe end members calculated using the method of Lindsley (1983).
**Porportions of Wo, En, Fe end members calculated from proportions of Ca, Mg, Fe^{2+}; not using method of Lindsley (1983).

excluded because of its large scatter. Three samples with anomalous Cu or P_2O_5 abundances (406, 569, and 111) were eliminated from the dataset. The large variation in the most abundant element, silica, tends to swamp variations in other elements which may in fact be proportionally large. The principal components analysis was performed on the sample correlation matrix so that all elements contribute equally to the variance (Le Maitre, 1982).

PC1 accounts for 92.9% of the total chemical variation in 15 dimensions, substantiating the linearity observed on the two-dimensional Harker diagrams. The values of the granitoid samples on the PC1 coordinate (their principal components scores) are included in Table 1. A score of PC1 = 0 corresponds to the mean of the chemical range of the samples analyzed and is of no genetic significance; PC1 was assigned a negative value for rocks more mafic than the mean, and a positive value for rocks more siliceous than the mean. The linear behavior of elements plotted against PC1 can be seen in Figure 9; the scatter in Ba is not significantly reduced.

Although the PC1 line has no statistically defined end points, several elements go to zero abundance as the PC1 line approaches −7 (K_2O and Rb approach zero) and +8 (TiO_2, iron,

MnO, MgO, CaO, P_2O_5, V, and Zr approach zero). We have selected as end members those compositions along the PC1 line where the first oxide goes to zero at the positive and negative ends. Table 4 summarizes the chemical and CIPW normative compositions of the end members.

The silicic end member (PC1 = +8.4) is essentially a granite in both composition and norm (Table 4). It is remarkably like the composition of leucocratic granite in the La Gloria pluton, Chile (see Table 4), interpreted by Mahood and Cornejo (1992) to represent evolved liquids separated from granitic cumulate rocks. The mafic end member (PC1 = −7.0; Table 4) is not a mafic liquid, but consists of the minerals in the rocks which, on the basis of petrographic evidence, formed relatively earlier during crystallization. The normative mineralogy is largely plagioclase and pyroxenes, and is very similar to the actual minerals in the granitoid suite.

We recast the end members in terms of mineral proportions (Table 4), by finding the intersection (or closest approach) of the first principal components trend with the surface in multi-dimensional chemical space defined by the analyzed compositions of plagioclase and pyroxenes, and pure magnetite, ilmenite, and apatite compositions. We illustrate the variation in rock chemical composition (Fig. 10), expressed in terms of mineral proportions. The line extending from the plagioclase-pyroxene side into the tetrahedron is the PC1 line; the black circles along this line are the compositions of the rocks of the granitic suite, and the dashed line is the projection of PC1 onto the base of the tetrahedron. The silicic end member has a normative Ab/An ratio ≈4 and lies on the plagioclase-quartz-orthoclase plane close to the minimum for a granitic melt of similar composition. For illustrative purposes, we show the eutectic and cotectics for a granite with normative Ab/An ratio = 4.5 at P_{H_2O} = 200 MPa from Winkler (1976). The inset compares the silicic end member with experimentally determined granitic minimum melts compiled by Anderson (1983; his Fig. 5B) on the Ab-Or-Qtz ternary. The silicic end member plots between the curves for normative Ab/An ratios of 2.9 and 5.2 at a P_{H_2O} close to 200 MPa. It could represent a relatively dry granite close to a minimum composition at higher pressure, because lithostatic pressure does not influence the location of the minimum very much.

The granitoid rock samples can be expressed as mixtures of various proportions of the mafic and silicic end members. We define the parameter, g, to indicate the proportion of the silicic end member in any rock along the PC1 line based on the lever rule:

$$g = (PCX - PC1) / (PCX-PCL),   (1)$$

where PCX and PCL refer to the principal components scores of the mafic and silicic end members, respectively. Possible values of g range from 0 to 1; the values of g for each granitoid sample are given in Table 1. The composition of any rock can be calculated as a mixture of end-member compositions in the proportion determined from the value of g. This predicted composition can be compared with the measured rock composition having the same g value, and the sum of squares of the differences (RMS) between predicted and actual compositions can be calculated. In Table 4, the actual composition of sample 386A is compared to the predicted composition of a rock with the same g value (0.39); the RMS of this sample is ~2.7%, about average for the rocks analyzed. Modeling the granitic rock compositions as mixtures of a mafic crystalline assemblage and a granitic minimum melt does a good job of reproducing the chemistry except for Ba.

Crystallization models for the granitoid suite

Fractional crystallization. The granitic suite spans a wide range in chemical composition, which might be attributed to fractional crystallization. A strong argument against fractionation as a dominant process is the uniformity of mineral compositions among samples. We tested the fractionation hypothesis by modeling the behavior of trace elements (Ba, Rb, Sr, and Cr) assuming perfect Rayleigh fractionation of plagioclase, orthopyroxene and clinopyroxene, and Fe-Ti oxides. We selected a starting composition similar to the most mafic rocks analyzed

(Table 1), containing 200 ppm Ba, 420 ppm Sr, 3 ppm Rb, and 35 ppm Cr. Distribution coefficients were estimated from the data in Henderson (1982) for plagioclase, pyroxenes, and magnetite crystallizing from intermediate to silicic liquid. Apatite was ignored because its small abundance does not contribute significantly to the bulk distribution coefficients.

The results (Fig. 11) show that no consistent set of mineral proportions can reproduce the rock compositions. For example, Figure 11A shows that Sr and Cr variations could be explained by fractionation of about 40% minerals (F = 0.6) in proportions similar to those of the mafic end member (plag:opx:cpx:Fe-Ti oxides = 0.747:0.115:0.069:0.047). However, this proportion of minerals does not reproduce rock compositions for Sr versus Rb (Fig. 11B). Moreover, the Rb concentrations require much greater amounts of fractionation (~80%), which would produce significant changes in mineral composition that are not observed. Granitic suite trends also cannot be reproduced by mixtures of cumulate solids and fractionated liquids. Finally, no fractionation model can explain the variation in Ba content of the rocks (Fig. 11C).

Magma mixing. Linear trends in rock composition on Harker or other variation diagrams are commonly used to support a magma mixing origin for igneous rock suites (e.g., Reid et al., 1983), the end points of the trends indicating the end-member magma compositions. However, the mafic end member of the Arden granitic suite is not a silicate liquid; a similar conclusion was reached for the mafic rocks in the Strathbogie granite, cited in Wall et al., (1987). Figure 12 shows that the linear trends in granitoid chemistry are not the result of mixing between analyzed granitic and basaltic end members. For example, mixing evolved granite with the most-evolved hornblende gabbronorites can explain linear trends in some components (Fig. 12A), but not in others (Fig. 12, B and C). Magma mixing, in bulk or combined with fractionation, also cannot explain the near-uniformity of mineral compositions, the scatter in Ba concentration, or the decoupling of Ba behavior from that of K_2O, Rb, and Sr.

Restite unmixing. Linear trends on variation diagrams may also be explained by restite unmixing, the variable separation of liquid from restite components during ascent and emplacement of the magma (Chappell et al., 1987; critically reviewed by Wall et al., 1987). However, there is no compelling evidence that texturally early phases in the Arden granitic suite represent restite components inherited from a high-grade metamorphic source region (White and Chappell, 1977). Plagioclase and pyroxenes have the morphologies and compositions that indicate crystallization from a melt (Figs. 4, 5, 6, and 7). Furthermore, there are no enclaves of restite material within the granitic suite. The observed enclaves are either recrystallized country-rock gneisses (found near the pluton margins), or are modified mafic liquids (now gabbroic to dioritic rocks) containing abundant hydrous minerals absent from the granitoids. The restite unmixing hypothesis is not supported by field, petrographic, or chemical evidence.

TABLE 3. FELDSPAR COMPOSITIONS

Sample	PLAGIOCLASES								
	403 Average all Phenocryst	568 Average all Phenocryst	568 Average all Matrix	425 Average all Phenocryst	425 Average all Matrix	386 Average all Matrix	400 Average all Matrix	326 Average all Phenocryst	326 Average all Blebs in Kspar
(wt. %)									
SiO$_2$	58.33	59.66	59.07	59.60	58.63	58.77	59.70	60.08	59.93
TiO$_2$	0.04	0.02	0.02	0.01	0.02	0.04	0.04	n.d.*	n.d.
Al$_2$O$_3$	25.91	25.07	26.50	25.68	25.19	26.25	26.02	25.95	26.19
FeO^t	0.18	0.11	0.09	0.07	0.16	0.15	0.06	0.09	0.07
MnO	n.d.	0.04	0.01	n.d.	n.d.	0.06	0.04	0.07	0.10
MgO	n.d.	0.02	0.01	0.02	0.04	0.02	n.d.	n.d.	n.d.
CaO	7.55	7.11	7.32	6.98	7.08	7.08	7.08	7.19	7.68
Na$_2$O	7.63	6.56	6.65	7.56	7.33	6.61	7.37	7.55	7.39
K$_2$O	0.46	0.48	0.35	0.56	0.44	0.55	0.11	0.26	0.18
BaO	0.02	0.04	0.02	0.09	0.01	0.06	0.01	0.05	0.04
Total	100.12	100.12	100.04	100.57	98.90	99.59	100.43	101.24	101.58
Cations^t									
Si	2.615	2.655	2.630	2.651	2.650	2.633	2.648	2.650	2.637
Al	1.369	1.367	1.391	1.346	1.342	1.386	1.360	1.349	1.358
Ti	0.001	0.001	0.001	0.000	0.001	0.001	0.001	0	0
Fe	0.007	0.004	0.003	0.003	0.006	0.006	0.002	0.003	0.003
Mn	0	0.001	0.001	0	0	0.002	0.002	0.003	0.004
Mg	0	0.001	0.001	0.001	0.003	0.001	0	0	0
Ca	0.363	0.340	0.350	0.333	0.343	0.340	0.337	0.340	0.362
Na	0.663	0.566	0.574	0.652	0.642	0.574	0.634	0.646	0.630
K	0.026	0.028	0.020	0.032	0.025	0.031	0.006	0.014	0.010
Ba	0.000	0.001	0.000	0.002	0.000	0.001	0.000	0.001	0.001
An	0.345	0.364	0.371	0.327	0.339	0.359	0.345	0.340	0.361
Ab	0.630	0.606	0.608	0.641	0.636	0.607	0.649	0.645	0.628
Or	0.025	0.030	0.021	0.031	0.025	0.033	0.006	0.014	0.010
Cs	0.000	0.001	0.000	0.002	0.000	0.001	0.000	0.001	0.001

Antiperthite§
Inner Zone
An 0.26
Ab 0.49
Or 0.24

Outer Zone
An 0.29
Ab 0.54
Or 0.17

Antiperthite
Inner Zone
An 0.25
Ab 0.51
Or 0.24

Outer Zone
An 0.29
Ab 0.58
Or 0.13

Melt migration. Geochemically, the Arden granitic suite can be modeled as mixtures of earlier formed crystalline phases and a residual granitic melt. Several authors have proposed that some granitoids (Brown, 1991; McCarthy and Robb, 1978; McCarthy and Hasty, 1976; Bacon, 1992) and volcanic ejecta (Druitt and Bacon, 1989; Tait, 1988; Turbeville, 1992) also represent mixtures of cumulus crystals and trapped interstitial liquid. The "mixing process" can be more accurately described as the relative mobility of crystals and liquid leading to an inhomogeneous distribution of crystalline material in the magma chamber (Speer, 1989). For the Arden pluton the scale of melt mobility can be estimated as meters to tens of meters, based on the scale of lithologic variation and sampling. A similar model was proposed for the chemical variation in plutonic rocks from the Meatiq Dome, Egypt (Sultan et al., 1986), although the

range of whole-rock compositions was considerably smaller than that in the Arden pluton.

However, modeling the rocks as mixtures does not account for the apparently anomalous behavior of Ba (Figs. 8 and 9). Ba concentrations cannot simply reflect the proportion of the silicic end member in each rock because there is no systematic variation with g. Ba changes compatibility during crystallization of the granitic suite, and Ba variations must reflect the *history* of the granitic residual melt. Initially, Ba was incompatible in the assemblage of the mafic end member (Table 4), and the melt was progressively enriched in Ba. Once orthoclase began to crystallize, Ba became compatible and the melt was depleted in Ba. Similar changes in Ba behavior have been cited previously as the cause of scatter and changes in slope on trace-element variation diagrams for granitoids (McCarthy and Hasty, 1976; Brown,

TABLE 3. FELDSPAR COMPOSITIONS (continued - page 2)

Sample	403 Average all Matrix	403 Kspar Blebs in Plagioclase	403 Kspar Blebs in Plagioclase	568 Average all Matrix	568 Average all Interstitial	568 Inclusion in Plagioclase	425 Average all Matrix	425 Kspar Blebs in Plagioclase	386 Average all Matrix	386 Average all Interstitial
K-FELDSPARS										
(wt. %)										
SiO_2	61.63	64.19	63.69	64.46	63.95	64.31	64.50	62.65	63.81	63.58
TiO_2	0.04	0.03	0.03	0.02	0.03	0.05	0.02	0.05	0.03	0.03
Al_2O_3	18.84	18.92	18.86	19.26	19.28	19.40	18.82	18.81	19.41	19.20
FeO^t	0.02	0.02	0.02	0.02	0.04	n.d.	0.07	0.03	0.08	0.00
MnO	0.01	n.d.	n.d.	0.05	0.01	n.d.	n.d.	n.d.	0.06	n.d.
MgO	n.d.	n.d.	n.d.	0.01	0.02	0.01	n.d.	n.d.	n.d.	0.01
CaO	0.01	0.15	0.04	0.04	0.05	0.04	0.03	0.05	0.03	0.02
Na_2O	0.65	0.93	0.57	1.29	0.80	0.32	1.22	0.67	1.21	0.83
K_2O	15.25	15.29	15.96	14.56	15.20	16.71	14.70	16.13	14.78	15.37
BaO	2.21	1.05	0.71	0.75	1.11	0.53	0.42	0.42	0.70	1.02
Total	98.66	100.58	99.88	100.46	100.49	101.37	99.78	98.81	100.11	100.06
Cations†										
Si	2.937	2.967	2.965	2.964	2.956	2.953	2.981	2.952	2.951	2.954
Al	1.058	1.030	1.035	1.044	1.050	1.050	1.025	1.044	1.057	1.051
Ti	0.001	0.001	0.001	0.001	0.001	0.002	0.001	0.002	0.001	0.001
Fe	0.007	0.001	0.001	0.001	0.002	0	0.003	0.001	0.003	0.000
Mn	0.000	0	0	0.002	0.000	0	0	0	0.003	0
Mg	0	0	0	0.001	0.001	0.001	0	0	0	0.001
Ca	0.000	0.007	0.002	0.002	0.003	0.002	0.002	0.002	0.001	0.001
Na	0.060	0.083	0.052	0.115	0.072	0.028	0.109	0.062	0.108	0.074
K	0.927	0.902	0.948	0.854	0.896	0.979	0.866	0.969	0.872	0.911
Ba	0.041	0.019	0.013	0.014	0.020	0.010	0.008	0.008	0.013	0.019
An	0.000	0.007	0.002	0.002	0.003	0.002	0.002	0.002	0.001	0.001
Ab	0.059	0.082	0.051	0.117	0.073	0.027	0.111	0.059	0.109	0.074
Or	0.901	0.892	0.934	0.867	0.904	0.961	0.880	0.931	0.877	0.906
Cs	0.040	0.019	0.013	0.014	0.020	0.010	0.008	0.007	0.013	0.019

1991; McCarthy and Robb, 1978), as well as the cause of anomalous enrichments in Ba within a layered mafic complex (Sinigoi et al., 1994). The apparently random scatter in Ba concentration can be explained by the crystallization of a mobile residual melt, variably depleted in Ba, in a crystal mush containing differing proportions of variably Ba enriched orthoclase. Furthermore, the residual melt must have failed to reach equilibrium in Ba concentration on a scale of meters to tens of meters in order to produce the observed variations. In support of this model, we find measured Ba concentrations in orthoclase to vary from 2.2 wt%–0.4 wt% BaO (Table 3). We further test our model with the quantitative analysis developed in the next section.

Derivation of equations describing two-stage crystallization and melt migration

In our model for the Arden granitic suite, the rocks represent samples of crystal mushes comprising both earlier formed crystals and residual granitic melt, in which the melt was mobile at least on a local scale. Such a model is consistent with the hypothesis of in situ (or boundary layer) crystallization in a

solidification zone along the walls and/or floor of the pluton (Tait et al., 1984; Tait and Kerr, 1987). Moreover, the silicic end member is very similar to leucogranite from the La Gloria pluton interpreted to have been a mobile residual liquid derived from boundary layer crystallization (Mahood and Cornejo, 1992; Table 4).

Whereas crystallization in the solidification zone may have been continuous, the change in Ba compatibility provides a geochemical marker that allows us to model crystallization in two stages. During the first stage, the solidification zone contained crystals (X1) with the same compositions and relative proportions as the mafic end member (Table 4), and there were different proportions of crystals and melt in different places. When the melt composition reached a granite minimum the second stage began as orthoclase, plagioclase, and quartz crystallized with the compositions and in the proportions of the silicic end member (Table 4).

We can write the initial mass balance as:

$$M_0 = M_{L1} + M_{X1}, \qquad (2)$$

where M_{X1} refers to the mass of first-stage crystals, and the sub-

TABLE 3. FELDSPAR COMPOSITIONS (continued - page 3)

Sample	K-FELDSPARS			
	400 Average all Phenocryst	325 Interior of Phenocryst	326 Rim of Phenocryst	326 Kspar Blebs in Plagioclase
(wt. %)				
SiO₂	64.10	64.85	64.53	65.86
TiO₂	n.d.	n.d.	n.d.	n.d.
Al₂O₃	19.19	18.71	18.70	19.32
FeOᵗ	0.03	0.04	0.04	0.04
MnO	n.d.	0.07	0.07	0.07
MgO	0.02	n.d.	n.d.	n.d.
CaO	0.12	0.08	0.05	0.07
Na₂O	1.46	1.31	0.72	0.90
K₂O	14.38	14.71	15.45	15.13
BaO	0.74	0.57	0.51	0.73
Total	100.04	100.34	100.07	102.12
Cations†				
Si	2.961	2.985	2.984	2.979
Al	1.045	1.015	1.019	1.030
Ti	0	0	0	0
Fe	0.001	0.002	0.002	0.002
Mn	0	0.003	0.003	0.003
Mg	0.001	0	0	0
Ca	0.006	0.004	0.003	0.004
Na	0.130	0.117	0.065	0.079
K	0.848	0.863	0.911	0.873
Ba	0.013	0.010	0.009	0.013
An	0.006	0.004	0.003	0.004
Ab	0.131	0.117	0.065	0.082
Or	0.850	0.868	0.923	0.901
Cs	0.013	0.010	0.009	0.013

*Not detected or <0.01 for average of more than one analysis.
†Cations normalized to eight oxygens.
§Estimated bulk composition of antiperthitic zones; see text for details of calculation and discussion.

Figure 4. A: Subhedral pyroxene grain in granitoid sample 403 showing enclosed euhedral oxides, apatite, and zircon. Long dimension of photomicrograph is ~3 mm. B: Textural relationships of orthopyroxene (medium gray tone) to plagioclase (lightest gray tone) in granitoid sample 600. Pyroxene is subhedral (almost euhedral; upper right) or anhedral and interstitial to plagioclase (center and left). Thin rims of clinopyroxene on orthopyroxene (enhanced with pen) are interpreted to result from granule exsolution during cooling. Long dimension of photomicrograph is ~10 mm.

scripts 0 and L1 refer to the initial melt before any crystallization, and the melt at the end of the first stage of crystallization, respectively (Fig. 13A). We designate the proportion of residual melt in any rock sample as m, expressed by the mass ratio,

$$m = M_{L1} / M_0. \tag{3}$$

Values of m can range from 0 for a rock consisting of 100% first-stage crystals with no interstitial melt, to 1, for a rock containing 0% first-stage crystals (Fig. 13A).

During the second stage, some of the residual melt crystallized in situ and the rest migrated away from the crystals. At the end of second-stage crystallization the mass-balance constraint is:

$$M_{L1} = M_{L2} + M_{X2}, \tag{4}$$

where X2 refers to the second-stage crystals and L2 designates the melt that leaves the crystals behind (Fig. 13B). Once the melt leaves, the rock, R, remaining to be analyzed is composed of:

$$M_R = M_{X1} + M_{X2}. \tag{5}$$

We designate the proportion of residual melt which leaves the crystals as f (Fig. 13B), expressed by the mass ratio,

$$f = M_{L2} / M_{L1}. \tag{6}$$

The proportion of melt that leaves can have values from 0, in which all the residual melt crystallizes in situ, to 1, in which none of the residual melt crystallizes before migrating. The model involves the net loss of residual melt; flux of melt through the solidification zone is not explicitly considered.

The value of g, defined previously in terms of the PC1 line, also represents the mass fraction of second-stage crystals,

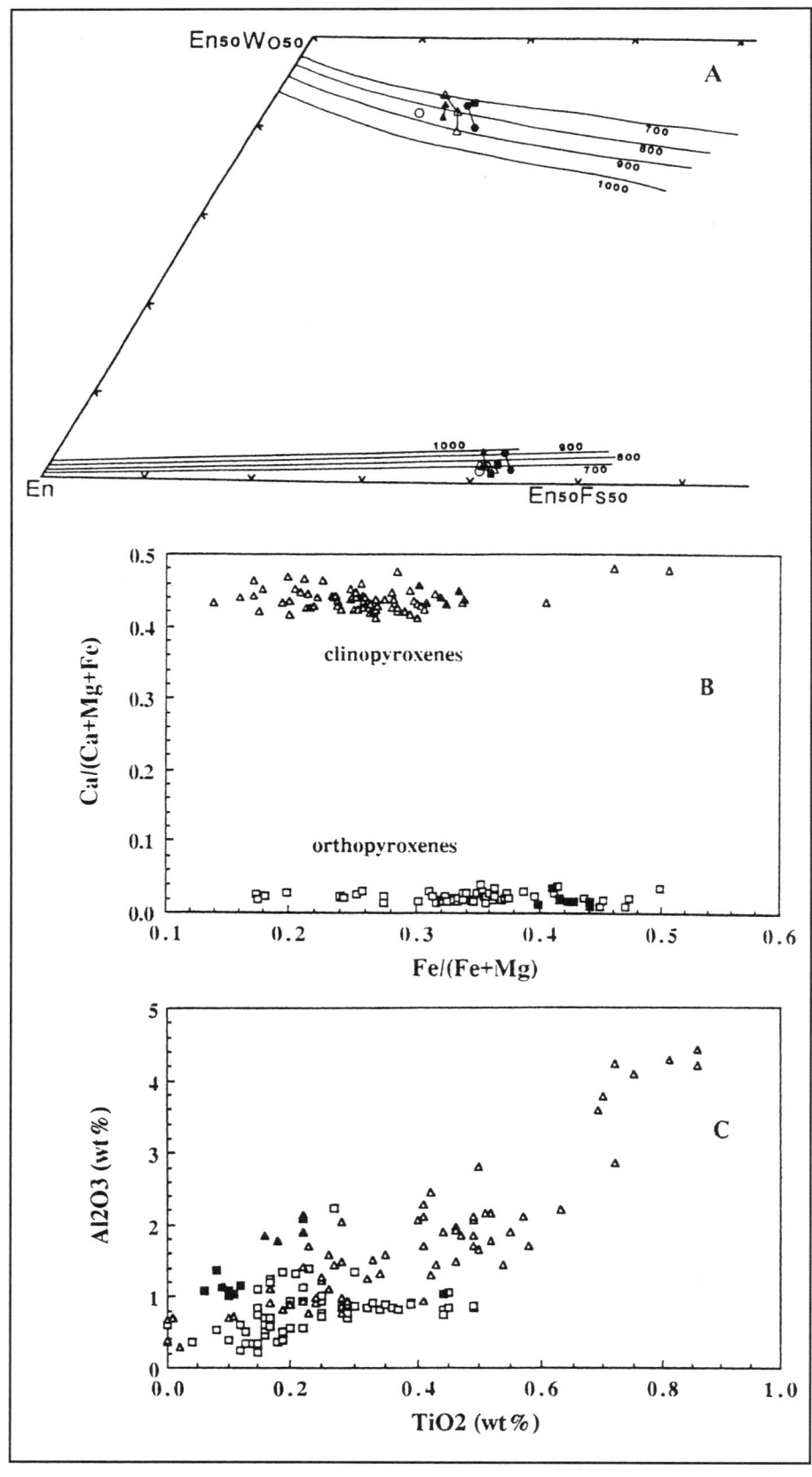

Figure 5. A: Pyroxene compositions from Arden granitoids plotted on graphical pyroxene thermometer for a pressure of 1 atm (Lindsley, 1983). Samples: white circles, 403; black triangles, 386; white triangles, 425; black hexagons, 568; black squares, 400. Tie lines connect core and rim compositions. B and C: Compositions of Arden granitoid pyroxenes (black symbols) compared with pyroxenes from intermediate and silicic volcanic and plutonic rocks from convergent tectonic settings (white symbols). Proportions of quadrilateral components (B: Ca, Mg, Fe) and nonquadrilateral components (C: TiO_2 versus Al_2O_3) for clinopyroxenes (triangles) and orthopyroxenes (squares) are shown. See text for data references and discussion.

◀―――――――

Figure 6. Zoned antiperthitic plagioclase phenocryst in granitoid sample 403 viewed under crossed polars. Carlsbad-Albite twinning parallel to elongate direction of grain is faintly visible. Outlines of inner and outer zones containing orthoclase blebs are euhedral (traced with pen for emphasis). Albite twinning in plagioclase host is continuous, and orthoclase blebs have the same optical orientation in each half of the Carlsbad twin. Long dimension of photomicrograph is ~10 mm.

$$g = M_{X2} / M_R, \qquad (7)$$

and is related to m and f by:

$$g = [m (1 - f)] / (1 - mf). \qquad (8)$$

To relate elemental abundances to m, f, and g, we begin with the mass balance for the rock:

$$C_R M_R = C_{X1} M_{X1} + C_{X2} M_{X2}, \qquad (9)$$

where C refers to the concentration of any trace element. Substituting mass constraints and ratios,

$$(1 - mf)C_R = (1 - m)C_{X1} + m(1 - f)C_{X2}. \qquad (10)$$

Assuming that first-stage crystals equilibrated with interstitial melt, then

$$C_{X1} = EC_{L1}, \qquad (11)$$

where E is the bulk distribution coefficient for the first-stage crystals. We assume equilibrium crystallization of second-stage minerals with a new bulk distribution coefficient, D,

$$C_{X2} = (DC_{L1}) / [D + f(1 - D)]. \qquad (12)$$

Substituting equations for C_{X1} and C_{X2} into equation 10,

$$C_R = C_{L1} \{E(1 - m)[D + f(1 - D)] + \\ m(1 - f)D\} / \{[D + f(1 - D)] (1 - mf)\}. \qquad (13)$$

We substitute g for f using equation 8 because values of g can be estimated directly from the principal components analysis (equation 1). We assume that each rock sample, with index j, has had a different history that can be modeled by parameters g_j and m_j (values of m_j must be estimated from the compositional data and the trace element modeling as described below):

$$C_{R(j)} = C_{L1}(1 - g_j) \{E - [Dm_jg_j / (Dm_jg_j - m_j \\ + g_j - D_{gj})]\}. \qquad (14)$$

For each trace element, with index k, used in the model, three more parameters must be estimated: the melt concentration $C_{L1(k)}$, and the first-stage and second-stage bulk distribution coefficients, E_k and D_k. The result is:

$$C_{R(j,k)} = C_{L1(k)}(1 - g_j) \{E_k - [D_k m_j g_j / \\ (D_k m_j g_j - m_j + g_j - D_k g_j)]\}. \qquad (15)$$

The value of $C_{L1(k)}$ has to be estimated by modeling the data. E_k and D_k could be calculated from the proportions of minerals in the end members (Table 4) and from published values for mineral-melt partition coefficients. However, we estimate E_k and D_k by modeling the data in order to determine whether the values we obtain are consistent with the mineralogy and published partition coefficients.

We estimate the parameters by selecting those that minimize the value of an objective function that measures the difference between the analysis of each sample, $C_{R(j,k)}$, and the model prediction, $C_{R(j,k)}$, based on the sample's g_j. We define the objective function *for each sample*, f_j, to be:

$$f_j = (1/n_e \{\Sigma [(C_{R(j,k)} - C_{R(j,k)}) / (C_{R(k)})']^2\})^{1/2}, \qquad (16)$$

which is the RMS deviation of the data from the model relative to the mean concentration of the element in all samples, $(C_{R(k)})'$, summed over the number of elements, n_e. The complete objective function, F, is the RMS value of f_j summed over the number of samples, n_s.

$$F = \{1/n_s [\Sigma (f_j)^2]\}^{1/2}. \qquad (17)$$

Values of the parameters that are selected so as to minimize F provide the best possible fit of the model to the data in terms of the RMS deviations used in the definition of F.

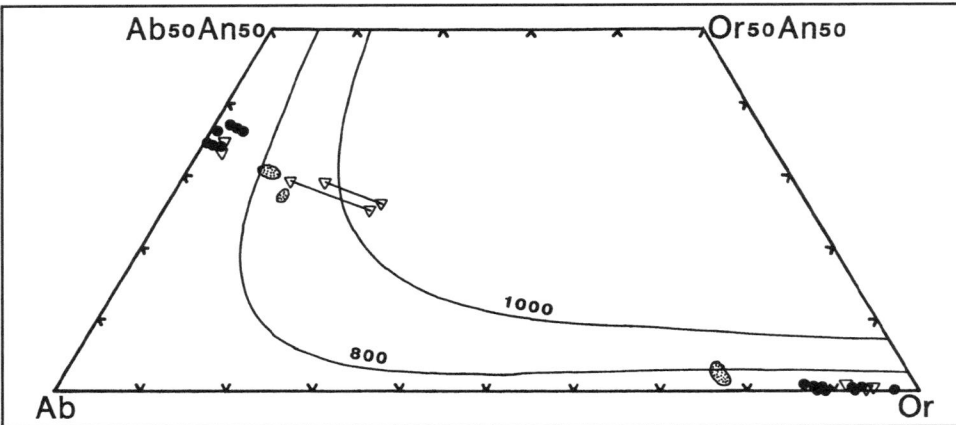

Figure 7. Feldspar compositions (black circles and white inverted triangles) in the Arden granitic suite. Inverted triangles represent recalculated ternary compositions of antiperthitic zones in samples 403 (less Ab rich) and 425 (more Ab rich), and the plagioclase host and orthoclase blebs used in the calculations. Tie lines connect inner (more Or rich) and outer (less Or rich) zones in each sample. Solvus isotherms from Nekvasil (1992; for compositions in wt%). Stippled pattern indicates approximate compositions (in wt%) of feldspar intergrowths from Lofgren and Gooley (1977). Arden feldspars are plotted in mol%, but difference between mol% and wt% is within the size of the symbol at the scale of the figure. See text for discussion.

We use a version of the multidimensional downhill simplex algorithm (Press et al., 1986) to find the parameter values that minimize F. A simplex can be thought of as a polyhedron with N + 1 vertices in an N-dimensional space; a tetrahedron is a simplex in three dimensions. The parameters we minimize using the simplex algorithm are the $C_{L1(k)}$, E_k, and D_k. Therefore, the simplex will have $(3n_e + 1)$ vertices in a $3n_e$-dimensional parameter space. The location of a vertex in this space specifies values for the element parameters, $C_{L1(k)}$, E_k, and D_k, which are subject to the constraints, $C_{L1(k)} \geq 0$, $E_k \geq 0$, and $D_k \geq 0$. For specified values of the element parameters, the values of the m_j that minimize F are estimated by a one-dimensional minimization for each sample on the range $g_j \leq m_j \leq 1$.

Initially, the vertices are placed at arbitrary values of the element parameters, the m_j are estimated, and an F value is calculated for each vertex. The downhill simplex algorithm uses the values of F at the vertices to find the locations of one or more new vertices (i.e., sets of element parameters) for which F is smaller. In successive iterations, the simplex "migrates" through parameter space toward regions that yield smaller values of F. The procedure involves extrapolation toward the minimum of F if it falls outside the simplex, or contraction around the minimum if it lies inside the simplex.

We selected the elements Ba, Sr, and Rb for the modeling: Ba in order to test whether the melt migration model can reproduce the variation in Ba concentration in the rocks; Sr because it is abundant in all rocks and remains compatible over the course of crystallization; Rb because, although it is less abundant, it is the only element that remains incompatible. After several runs, we determined that Rb concentrations do not constrain the values of m_j sufficiently. Therefore, we used Ba and

Sr simultaneously to estimate m_j, $C_{L1(Sr)}$, $C_{L1(Ba)}$, E_{Sr}, E_{Ba}, D_{Sr}, and D_{Ba}. Using these values of m_j, we ran Rb independently to estimate $C_{L1(Rb)}$, E_{Rb}, and D_{Rb}. Whereas the element parameters are based on three trace elements (Ba, Sr, and Rb), the presence of g in equation 15 means that all elements from the principal components analysis are integrated into the model calculations. The results are presented in Table 5.

The results of our model can be understood with reference to the hypothetical solidification zone (Fig. 13). Figure 13 (A, C, and E) shows the layer at the end of stage one consisting of crystals (M_{X1}) and residual melt (M_{L1}). The values of m shown are 0.8 (mostly melt) and 0.4 (mostly crystals). Figure 13 (B, D, and F) shows the same areas after losing residual melt in proportions, f = 0.917, 0.536, and 0.50, respectively. The g values are shown on the right side of Figure 13, calculated from the m and f parameters using equation 8. Rocks that initially contained the same proportion of melt (Fig. 13, A and C) can have very different chemical compositions and g values, depending on how much of the residual melt crystallizes in situ and how much migrates out of the solidification zone (Fig. 13, B and D). However, mafic rocks with similar g values and similar major- and trace-element compositions can result from migration of different amounts of residual melt from rocks initially containing very different proportions of melt (Fig. 13, B and F). Rocks with similar g values have similar Sr concentrations (Fig. 13, B and F), reflecting the linear variation of Sr with g and other elements. The Ba concentrations, however, differ by 600 ppm, reflecting differing values of m and f, and indicating significantly different histories of crystallization and melt migration.

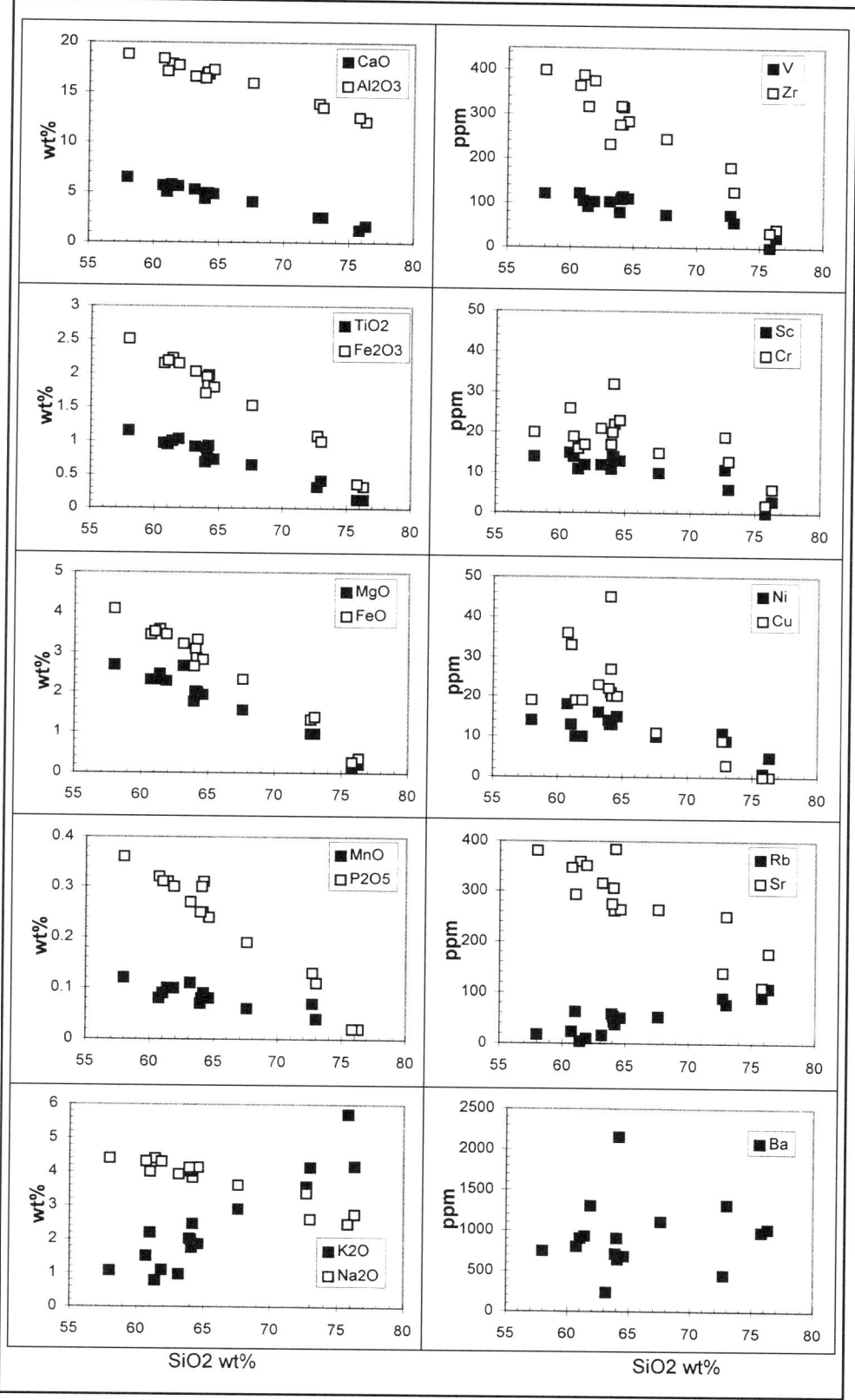

Figure 8. Harker diagrams for all oxides and elements analyzed for the Arden granitoid samples. All oxides and elements except Ba have a strong linear correlation with SiO$_2$.

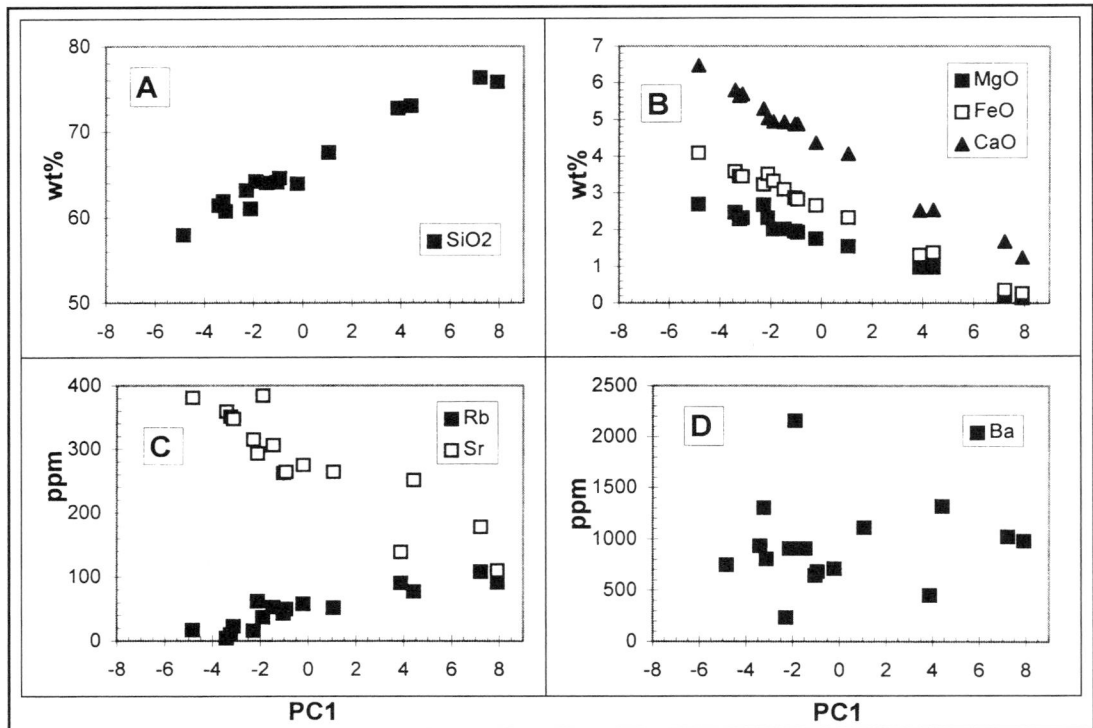

Figure 9. Oxide and element concentrations plotted against the first principal components score (PC1) for the Arden granitic suite. See text for discussion.

Evaluation of model results

We approach the evaluation of the melt migration model by considering how well the model predicts measured concentrations of Ba, Sr, and Rb, and the reasonableness of values predicted for C_{L1}, m, f, D, and E. For example, the concentrations of Rb, Sr, and Ba in the residual liquid (C_{L1}; Table 5) are appropriate for a granitic melt.

Figure 14 tests the fit of the melt migration model for Sr, Rb, and Ba in the granitic suite. The model Ba concentrations fit the data very well (Fig. 14A); the RMS ~2%. Ba tends to control the determination of m, f, and the other parameters in modeling because of its greater abundance and range of concentrations. For Sr and Rb (Fig. 14, B and C, respectively), the melt migration model values are compared with values predicted by mixing of mafic and silicic end members, as well as the actual data. The melt migration model predicts Sr concentrations better than, and Rb concentrations about as well as, modeling the rocks as mixtures. The incompatible behavior of Rb throughout crystallization, and its low abundance in all minerals, probably results in enough inherent scatter that the melt migration model is not a significant improvement on the linear mixing model. Melt migration is the only model, of all those considered in this chapter, that satisfactorily predicts Ba variation.

The parameters D and E (Table 5) can be compared with published mineral-melt partition coefficients. Values of E

depend mostly on $(K_D)^{plag}$ because ~75% of the crystal end member is plagioclase and partition coefficients for Rb, Sr, and Ba are small in pyroxenes. E values suggest plagioclase partition coefficients of ≥6.5 for Sr and ~0.2 for Ba, well within the ranges defined by published partition coefficients (e.g., Gill, 1978; Brown et al., 1981, and references therein; Cullers et al., 1981, and references therein; Henderson, 1982, and references therein; Nash and Crecraft, 1985; Christensen and DePaolo, 1993; Dunn and Sen, 1994; Feeley and Davidson, 1994, and references therein). E_{Rb} is not well constrained, and the value of 0 simply indicates a very small bulk distribution coefficient. D values depend on partition coefficients for both plagioclase and K-feldspar, and in all cases are consistent with K_Ds at the high end of published ranges (e.g., Leeman and Phelps, 1981, and references therein; Nash and Crecraft, 1985, and references therein; Lu et al., 1992; Icenhower and London, 1993).

The melt migration model can explain linear variations of the elements and the decoupling of Ba from geochemically similar elements. For example, the behavior of Rb (incompatible) and Sr (compatible) remained unchanged throughout crystallization, because of the similar bulk distribution coefficients for the first- and second-stage minerals (Table 5). Elements compatible in the early crystallizing assemblage, such as MgO, Zr, and Cr, were depleted to very low values in the residual melt, so that the proportions of second-stage crystals simply had a dilution effect. K and Ba behavior became decoupled

TABLE 4. END MEMBER COMPOSITIONS

	Mafic End Member	Silicic End Member	Leucogranite Mahood and Cornejo (1992)	386A Data	386A Model
(wt. %)					
SiO_2	55.66	77.91	77.5	64.58	64.43
TiO_2	1.30	0.04	0.14	0.73	0.81
Al_2O_3	19.82	11.79	12.3	17.27	16.65
Fe_2O_3	2.99	0.22		1.80	1.90
FeO	4.60	0.11	0.65*	2.82	2.83
MnO	0.13	0.02	0.01	0.08	0.08
MgO	3.20	0.05	0.09	1.93	1.96
CaO	7.19	1.01	0.70	4.87	4.75
Na_2O	4.88	2.45	2.59	4.14	3.92
K_2O	0.00	5.26	5.95	1.87	2.08
P_2O_5	0.42	0.00	0.03	0.24	0.26
(ppm)					
Rb	0	111	155	50	43
Sr	414	119	139	264	298
V	147	16	83	110	95
Zr	457	25		284	287

CIPW Norm	Mafic	Silicic	Mineral Proportions Based on Analyzed Compositions	Mafic	Silicic
Q	6.59	41.29	Quartz	3.0	42.4
C	0.00	0.23			
Or	0.00	31.09	K-feldspar	0.0	34.8
Ab	41.29	20.73			
An	32.18	5.01	Plagioclase†	74.7	21.4
Di	0.61	0.00	Clinopyroxene	6.9	0.0
Hy	11.75	0.12	Orthopyroxene	11.5	1.1
Mt	4.34	0.30	Magnetite	2.3	0.2
Il	2.47	0.08	Ilmenite	2.4	0.0
Ap	0.99	0.00	Apatite	1.0	0.0

*Total iron as FeO.

†Composition An_{34} used for mafic end member; An_{29} used for silicic end member.

because, during crystallization of the residual melt, phase relationships at a granite minimum controlled the major element (e.g., K) composition of the liquid as well as the compositions and proportions of silicate minerals crystallizing, while Ba, as a trace element, was not constrained in the same way.

Figure 15 shows the analyzed Ba contents of the rock samples plotted against g with superimposed curves for m and f calculated from our model equations. Values of m and f can be determined for any rock; e.g., a sample containing roughly 1000 ppm Ba and having a g value of around 0.45 has m = 0.8 and f = 0.8. The wide range in Ba concentrations provides good constraints on the values of both m and f in the modeling. Samples with the highest or lowest Ba concentrations or g values (e.g., 112A, 134, 551) determine the locations of curves for extreme m or f values (0 or 1). If D_{Ba} were constrained to be <10, some samples would fall outside the envelope of m and f curves (Fig. 15). Extreme Ba concentrations in these samples

might be explained by multiple influxes of residual melt rather than a single episode of crystallization and loss.

Values of m and f (Table 5) derived from our modeling are consistent with ideas about melt mobility within granitic crystal mushes. Values of m and f are typically large, as expected for the rheology of relatively viscous granitic magma (e.g., Wickham, 1987; van der Molen and Paterson, 1979). Rocks with the smallest m values also have small f values (Table 5), consistent with the idea that the residual melt is not as mobile and is more likely to crystallize in situ in areas of the magma chamber that contain a high proportion of crystals. In rocks with large m values, the residual melt may crystallize in situ (small f value) to form a silicic rock, or it may migrate away from the crystals (large f value), leaving behind a mafic rock. This is not a result that could be predicted from a model that considers the rocks simply as mixtures of crystals and melt, and illustrates the power of our melt migration model to reveal crystallization history.

Implications of the melt migration model

The equations derived for the Arden granitic suite from whole-rock and mineral chemistry are based on the assumptions that a melt of essentially uniform composition percolated through a mesh of crystals, also of essentially uniform composition and modal proportions. This could be explained by essentially equilibrium crystallization without significant reaction between crystals and residual liquid. This implies that the magma was multiply saturated, crystallizing along a plagioclase-pyroxenes cotectic under conditions in which changes in An-Ab content were minor (e.g., Nekvasil, 1992), and was not far from a granite minimum when first-stage crystallization began. The melt was therefore close to equilibrium with the first-stage minerals (mafic end member) when orthoclase joined the liquidus at or very close to a thermal minimum. Similar conditions have been proposed in studies of volcanic rocks interpreted as crystal mushes erupted from the boundary layers of magma chambers. For example, crystallization of roughly cotectic proportions of plagioclase and pyroxenes under near-equilibrium conditions was suggested to explain the small range of modal mineralogy and nearly uniform, unzoned compositions of ferromagnesian minerals in low-Sr scoriae from Mount Mazama (Druitt and Bacon, 1989). Equilibrium between cumulus crystals and interstitial melt in both mafic and felsic nodules from the Laacher See volcano was inferred from the lack of reaction textures and the systematic, complementary variations in mineral and melt chemistry (Tait, 1988).

In addition, compositional convection with high permeability could help explain the relatively uniform modes and compositions of first-stage minerals in the Arden granitic suite. During compositional convection, residual liquids percolate out of the cumulus crystal mush and are replaced by liquid from the magma reservoir. The extent to which residual liquids participate in compositional convection depends on such parameters as the relative densities of crystals and residual liquid, and the relative rates of crystallization and melt migration (Tait et al.,

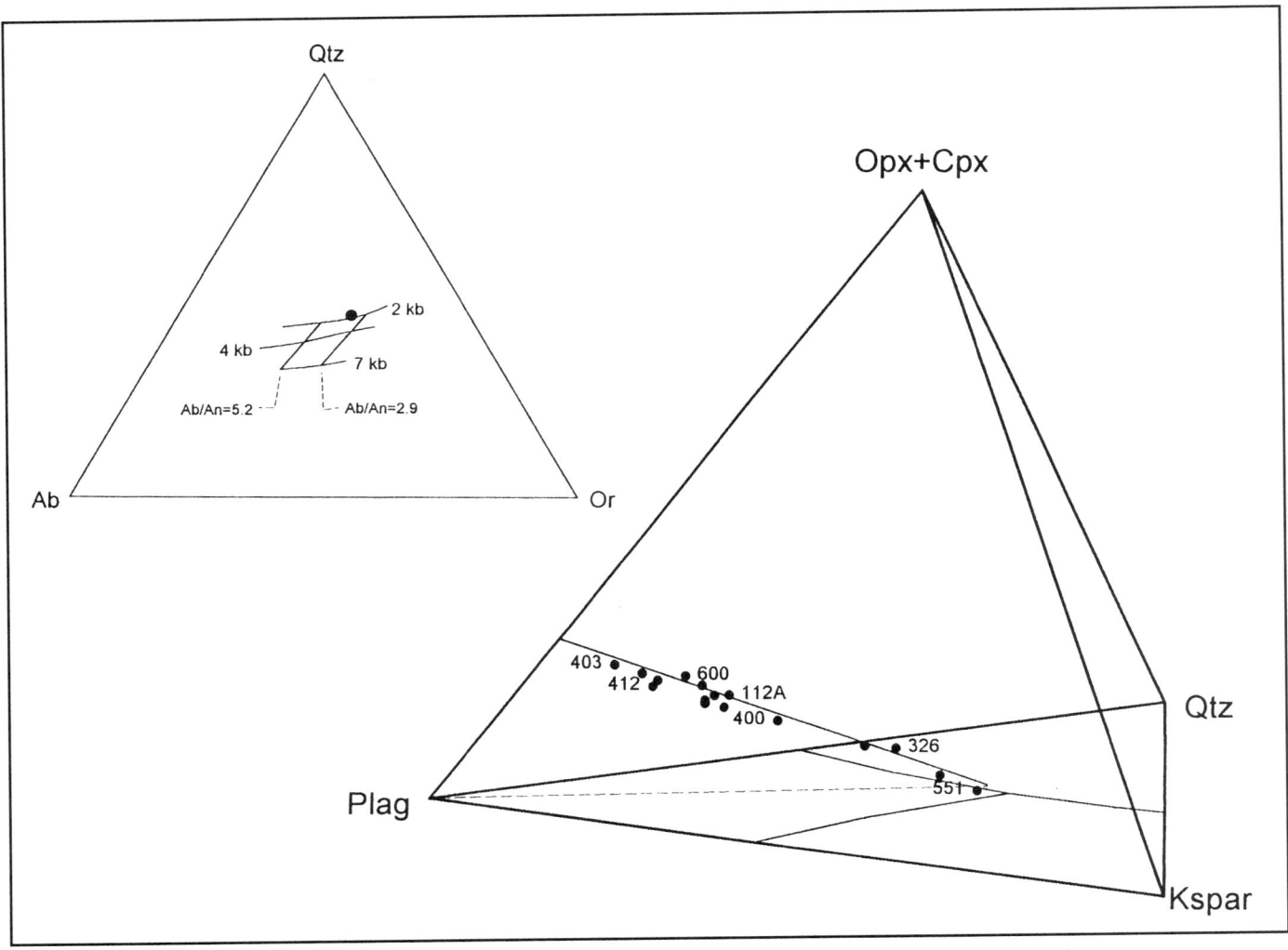

Figure 10. Compositions of Arden granitoids expressed in terms of the proportions of the major minerals in the rocks: plagioclase (Plag), orthopyroxene and clinopyroxene (Opx + Cpx), quartz (Qtz), and orthoclase (Kspar). Rock samples lie along PC1 line (solid line) extending from the plagioclase-pyroxenes edge onto the plagioclase-quartz-orthoclase plane. Dashed line is the trace of the PC1 line on the base of the tetrahedron; solid lines on the base are the cotectics and eutectic for a granite minimum from Winkler (1976). Inset shows the liquid end-member composition (black circle) on a diagram of normative albite-orthoclase-quartz. For comparison, the locations of granite minima at 2, 4, and 7 kbar (200, 400, 700 MPa), for melt compositions with Ab/An ratios of 2.9 and 5.2, are shown (from Anderson, 1983). See text for discussion.

1984; Tait and Kerr, 1987). Cumulates with high permeability or low crystallization rates remain in communication with interstitial liquid of nearly uniform composition, producing adcumulate-like rocks containing unzoned minerals with narrow compositional ranges. The relative isolation of the boundary layer from the magma reservoir as a whole results in apparent "equilibrium" crystallization of minerals that are not in true equilibrium with the evolving liquid in the magma reservoir (Lesher and Walker, 1988). The high m values for most rocks in the Arden granitoid suite (Table 5) suggest the loss of significant volumes of melt and are consistent with high permeabilities in the earlier stage of crystallization. Near-constant

modal proportions of earlier formed minerals are also consistent with the higher viscosities and yield strengths of granitic magmas that prevent gravitative sorting of crystals by density.

There is a spatial pattern to the distribution of m and f values within the pluton (Fig. 16) that is also consistent with magma chamber models. Lower m values (or larger M_{X1}) are found in samples close to the margins of the pluton, and the highest m values (smallest M_{X1}) are located near the center. Values of f [$M_{L2} / (M_{L2} + M_{X2})$] have a more complex distribution; low values are near the pluton margins *and* in the center, and high f values are in between. The pattern is consistent with the more rapid crystallization of magma near the margins,

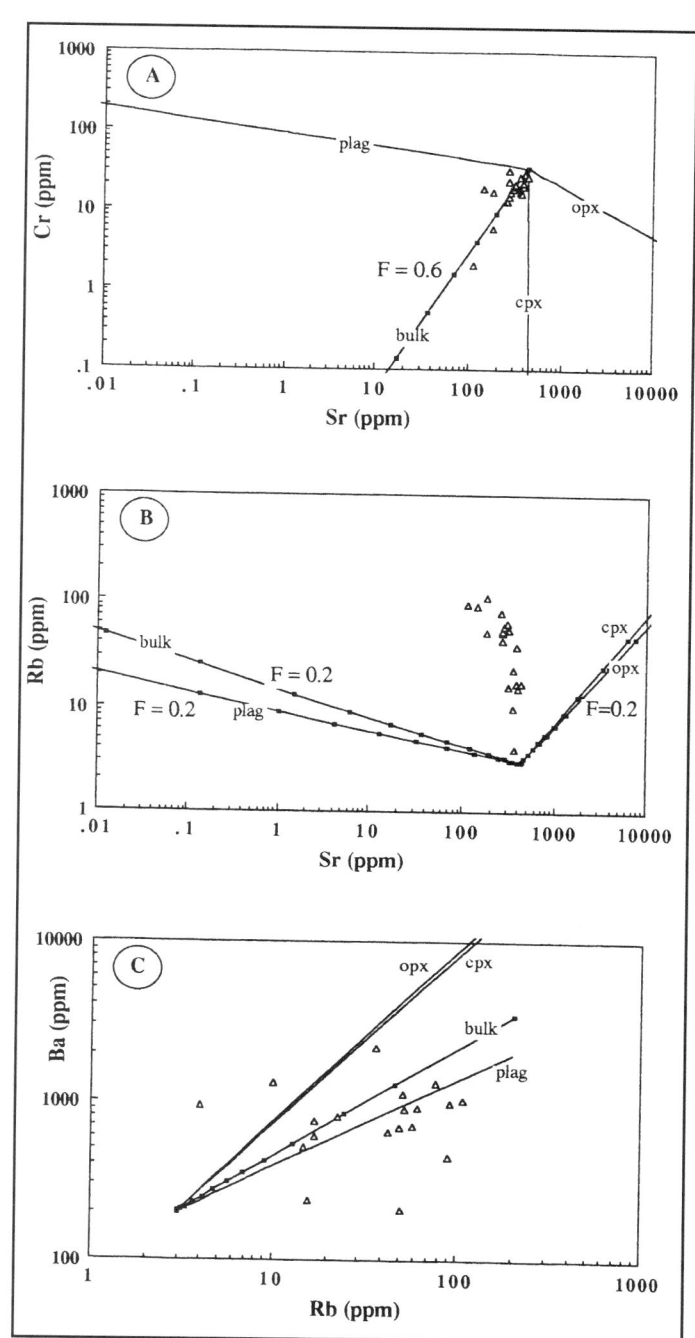

Figure 11. Results of fractionation modeling using parameters described in the text. Solid lines represent trends for fractionation of only plagioclase (plag); only orthopyroxene (opx); only clinopyroxene (cpx); or the assemblage plagioclase-orthopyroxene-clinopyroxene-oxides (bulk) in proportions defined in the text. Black squares along lines indicate values of liquid remaining (F); values illustrated in these figures are 0.99, 0.95, 0.90, 0.80, 0.70, 0.60, 0.50, 0.40, 0.30, 0.20, 0.10, and 0.05. White triangles are the analyzed compositions of Arden granitoids. A: Variation of Cr with Sr. B: Variation of Rb with Sr. C: Variation of Ba with Rb. See text for discussion.

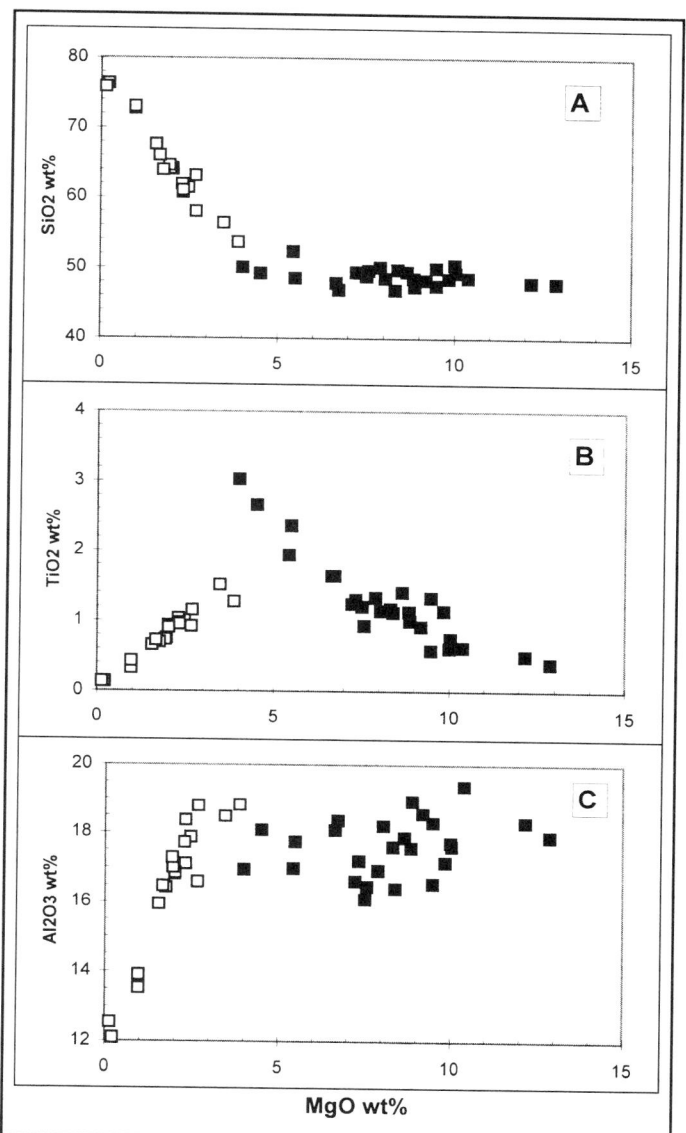

Figure 12. Variation of elements with MgO (wt%) to evaluate possible mixing relationships between granitoids (white squares) and gabbroids (black squares) from the Arden pluton. A: Some components (SiO_2; also CaO, Fe, Cr, Ni, Cu, K_2O, and P_2O_5), form a continuous trend from granitoid to gabbroids that could be explained by mixing evolved granite with the most-evolved hornblende gabbronorites. B: Other components (TiO_2; also Sc and V) would require a mafic end member closer to the mid-range of the gabbroids. C: Apparently discontinuous trend between rock types that cannot be explained by bulk mixing, illustrated by the variation of Al_2O_3 with MgO (also Sr, Na_2O, Zr, and Ba). See text for discussion.

which trapped interstitial liquid (low m and f). The increase in f to very high values toward the pluton interior could be interpreted to indicate a zone of high permeability and compositional convection. The central samples with low f values could indicate an interior zone in which residual liquid accumulated and crystallized in situ. The pattern makes petrogenetic sense

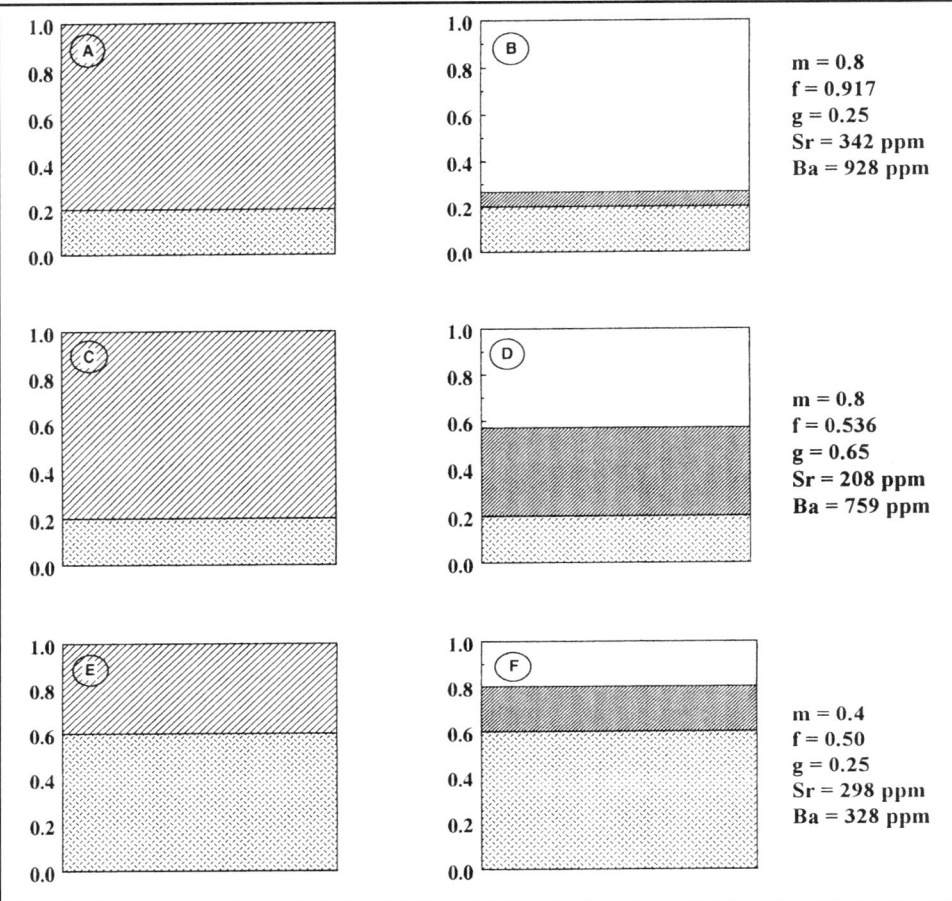

Figure 13. Boxes representing crystallization of hypothetical solidification zone according to our model of two-stage crystallization and melt migration. Cross-hatched pattern represents mass of stage-one crystals, M(X1). Less closely spaced diagonal line pattern represents mass of melt at end of stage one, M(L1). M(0), mass of original portion of solidification zone, = M(X1) + M(L1) = 1.0. More closely spaced diagonal line pattern represents mass of second-stage crystals formed from residual liquid, M(X2). Unpatterned area represents mass of residual melt that leaves rock, M(L2). The final rock, M(R) = M(X1) + M(X2). A and B: Magma chamber with low initial crystallinity (m = 0.8) and large f (0.917), producing a relatively mafic rock (g = 0.25) with high Sr and Ba concentrations. C and D: Magma chamber with low initial crystallinity (m = 0.8) but intermediate f (0.536), producing a relatively felsic rock (g = 0.65), with low Sr and intermediate Ba concentrations. E and F: Magma chamber with higher initial crystallinity (m = 0.4) and intermediate f (0.50), producing a relatively mafic rock (g = 0.25) with low Sr and Ba concentrations. See text for discussion and derivation of elemental concentrations.

of the chemical variations in the samples, in contrast to the spatial distribution of g values, which shows no apparent pattern. This further demonstrates the predictive power of the melt migration model.

The spatial pattern of m and f values is also helpful because the geometry of the Arden pluton is not well constrained. While contacts can be mapped or estimated along most of the margin, the orientation of the pluton in space is not known. Srogi et al. (1993) argued that there are no significant differences in pressure across the eastern portion of the Wilmington complex. This suggests that it is unlikely that the pluton is tilted on its side and revealed in cross section. Some gab-

bronorites in the eastern portion contain blue-green hornblende and actinolitic amphibole, which may indicate the presence of a fluid phase, initially trapped along the walls or closer to the roof of the pluton. We consider it most likely, on the basis of the field and petrographic evidence as well as the pattern of m and f values, that the exposed rocks of the Arden pluton represent a subhorizontal section through a larger chamber.

CONCLUSIONS

Our conclusions concerning the crystallization of the granitic suite in the Arden pluton and its significance are as follows.

1. Compositions of the Arden granitic suite can be explained

TABLE 5. RESULTS OF MELT MIGRATION MODEL

Sample	m	f	Element	C_{LI}	E	D
403	0.845	0.970	Ba	575.3	0.15	11
436	0.816	0.931	Sr	71.3	5.0	5.9
435A	0.924	0.974	Rb	114.0	0.0	0.93
412	0.746	0.885				
600	0.362	0.221				
568	0.768	0.859				
425	0.769	0.832				
112A	1.000	1.000				
386B	0.657	0.669				
386A	0.673	0.684				
573	0.709	0.677				
400	0.838	0.788				
134	0.706	0.000				
326	0.917	0.741				
104	0.963	0.540				
551	0.983	0.468				

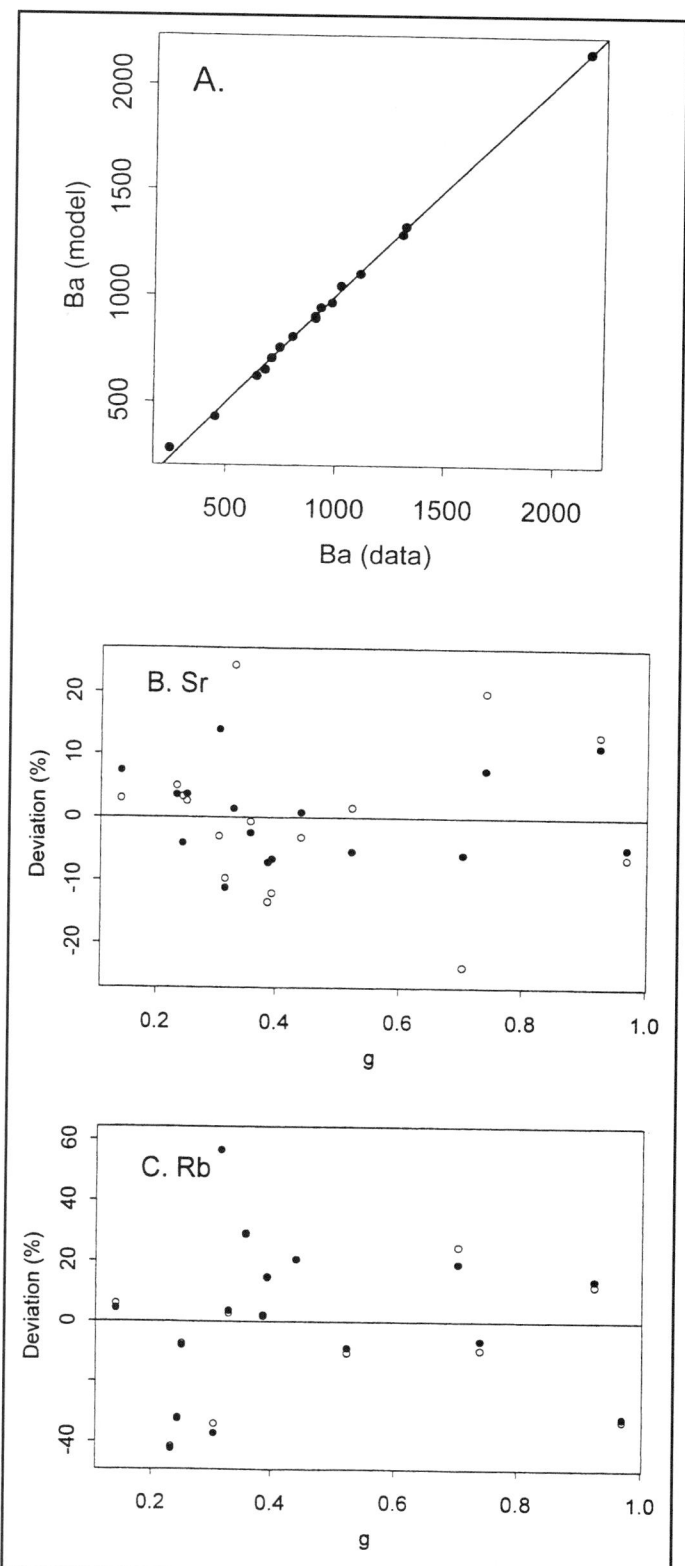

by a model that includes crystallization in a migrating solidification zone, possibly under near-equilibrium conditions, and residual melt migration. Ba concentration in the rocks is a significant geochemical marker, sensitive to the crystallinity at the time of melt migration and to the amount of melt lost. This results from the change in compatibility of Ba from <1 to >>1 with the onset of K-feldspar crystallization.

2. The proportion of melt lost relative to the initial melt varied, but in many cases was >50%, suggesting that melt was not only migrating locally but was being transported from the rocks now exposed. This result may be more compatible with gravity-influenced processes that occurred near the base of a growing crystal pile, rather than with side-wall crystallization processes.

3. The compositions of the rocks, for major elements and most trace elements, depend on both the initial crystallinity and the proportion of residual melt lost. As a result, there is no simple concentric compositional zoning within the pluton. However, parameters describing melt loss calculated from our melt migration model show a systematic spatial pattern roughly concentric in form. The pattern is interpreted to reflect an outer zone of lesser melt loss, an interior zone of high melt mobility

Figure 14. A. Concentrations of Ba predicted from melt migration model compared with Ba concentration data from analyzed samples. 1:1 line shown for comparision; root mean square of (data – model) values is ~2%. B and C: Comparison of deviations of two models of rock compositions from analyzed data plotted against g. Black circles are values for each sample ([data – melt migration model] / mean concentration of all sample data). White circles are calculated in the same way except that model values for each rock are calculated from g assuming bulk mixing of mafic and silicic end members. Solid line at 0 is for 0% deviation of model from data. B: Results for Sr concentrations; value of r^2 (multiple correlation coefficient) for melt migration model is 0.936, compared with $r^2 = 0.823$ for the mixing model. C: Results for Rb concentrations; value of r^2 for melt migration model is 0.820, compared with $r^2 = 0.819$ for the mixing model. See text for further discussion.

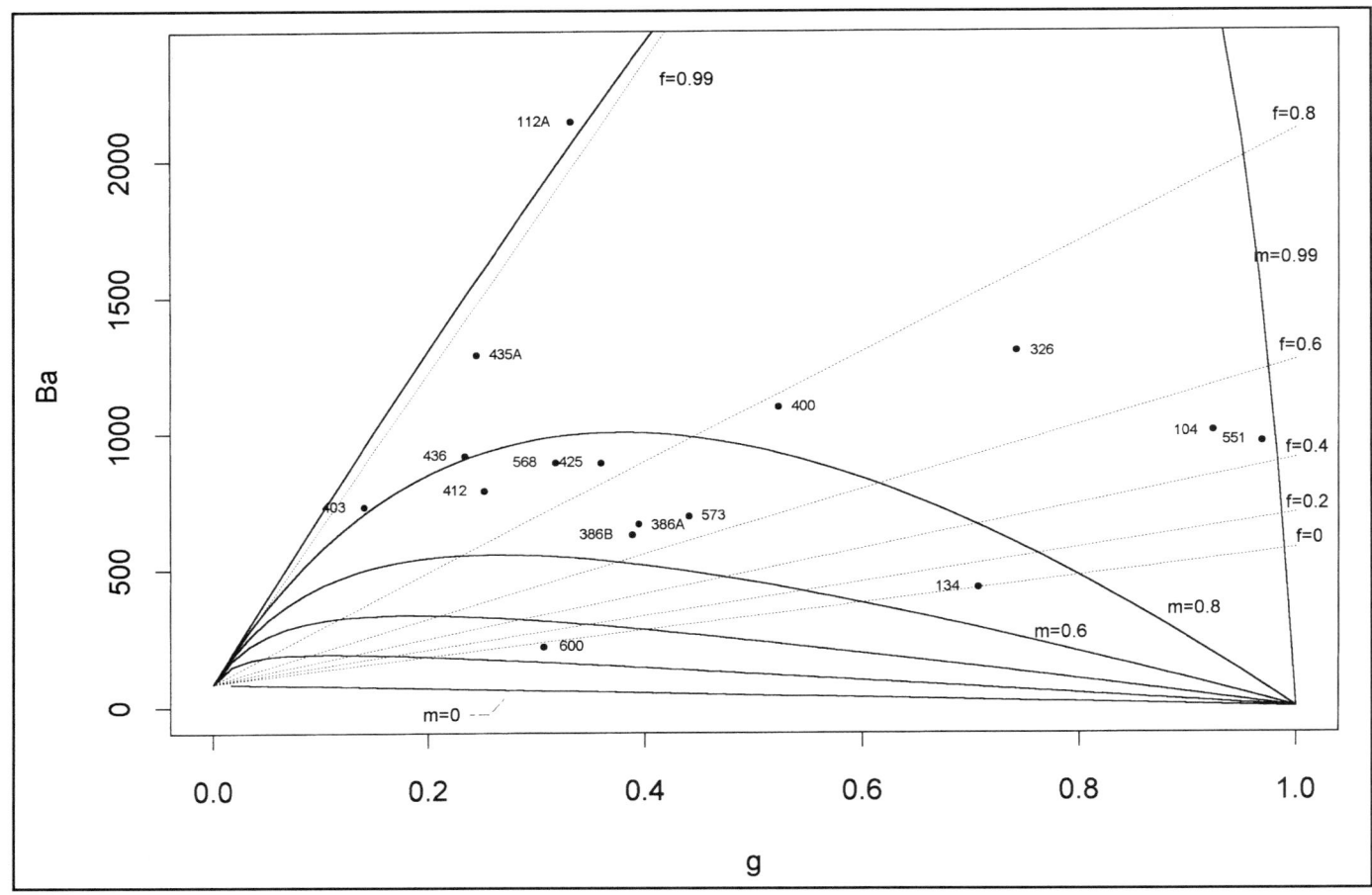

Figure 15. Analyzed concentrations of Ba (ppm) versus g in granitoid samples (black circles) with superimposed curves for m (solid lines) and f (dotted lines) calculated from our melt migration model equations. See text for discussion.

and compositional convection, and an innermost zone of melt retention and accumulation. The spatial pattern may also indicate that gravity-driven processes were affected to some extent by differences in cooling rate, crystal growth rate, or permeability related to proximity to the floor or walls of the intrusion.

4. The Arden granitic suite and the Cordillera Paine pluton (Michael, 1984) may represent extreme cases of in situ crystallization in granites. In the latter case, in situ crystallization of a shallow-level intrusion under conditions of low permeability or rapid crystallization rate produced rocks with strongly zoned minerals that reflect extreme differentiation within individual samples. In the deeper Arden pluton, conditions of high permeability or slow crystallization rate produced rocks with nearly uniform mineral compositions over a wide range of rock compositions.

5. Our results suggest that plutonic rocks can develop large compositional variations over short (<10^2 m) distances by melt migration. This is probably a common process that could be masked by other larger scale magmatic processes. Compositional variations caused by local melt migration within large plutons could easily be interpreted to result from larger scale

processes if sampling is sparse and if apparently random variations in trace elements (e.g., Ba) cannot be accounted for by fractional crystallization or other standard petrogenetic models.

ACKNOWLEDGMENTS

This study was begun as part of Srogi's Ph.D. dissertation at the University of Pennsylvania. The work was partially supported by Geological Society of America and Sigma Xi Grants-in-aid-of-research to Srogi; a University of Pennsylvania Research Fund grant to R. I. Harker; a Smith College Faculty Development Award to Srogi; an IBM Threshold grant to Lutz; and by a West Chester University Faculty Development Committee Award to Srogi. Srogi thanks the following for use of analytical facilities: W. L. Griffen and E.-R. Neumann for Sr and Nd isotopic work at the Geological Museum of Oslo; S. R. Hart for preliminary isotopic work at the Massachusetts Institute of Technology; J. R. Delaney for probe work at Rutgers University; J. Kerner for probe work at Lehigh University; M. J. Carr for DCP-AES analyses at Rutgers University; and S. Mertzman for x-ray fluorescence analyses at Franklin and Marshall Col-

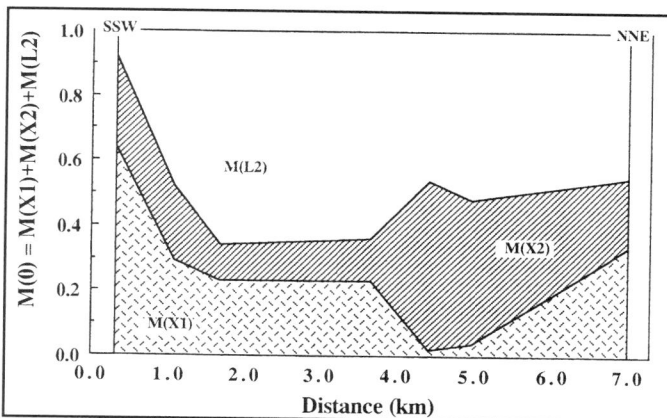

Figure 16. Proportions of earlier formed crystals (M[X1]; cross-hatched pattern), later formed crystals from residual liquid (M[X2]; diagonal line pattern), and residual melt that migrated away from rock (M[L2]; unpatterned) in seven samples of Arden granitoids along a south-south-west–north-northeast traverse across the pluton. Samples used are 600, 573, 568, 425, 551, 104, and 386 (average of 386A and 386B); sample 600 is actually closer to the contact than shown because traverse line is not orthogonal to pluton margin. Pattern is of high initial crystallinity and melt retention at margin (sample 600), increasing melt loss toward interior (samples 573, 568, 425, 386), and innermost zone of low initial crystallinity and melt accumulation (samples 551 and 104). For M(0) = 1, m = (1 – M[X1]), so m is low at the margin and increases toward the interior. f can be written as the proportion M(L2) / (M[L2] + M[X2]), and is low at the margin, reaches a maximum, and then declines to lower values in the interior. See text for further discussion.

lege. Oxygen isotope analyses were performed by I. Richards and K. Ferguson in R. T. Gregory's lab at Southern Methodist University. Srogi acknowledges the guidance, support, and stimulating ideas of her graduate adviser, Mary Emma Wagner. Srogi and Lutz acknowledge thoughtful reviews by J. A. Speer and M. B. Wolf that significantly improved the manuscript.

REFERENCES CITED

Anderson, J. L., 1983, Proterozoic anorogenic granite plutonism of North America, *in* Medaris, L. G., Jr., Byers, C. W., Mickelson, D. M., and Shanks, W. C., eds., Proterozoic geology: Selected papers from an international Proterozoic symposium: Geological Society of America Memoir 161, p. 133–154.

Bacon, C. R., 1992, Partially melted granodiorite and related rocks ejected from Crater Lake caldera, Oregon, *in* Brown, P. E., and Chappell, B. W., eds., The second Hutton symposium on the origin of granites and related rocks: Geological Society of America Special Paper 272, p. 27–47.

Bascom, F., and Miller, B. L., 1920, Elkton-Wilmington folio: U.S. Geological Survey Atlas, Folio 211, 22 p.

Bascom, F., and Stose, G. W., 1932, Description of the Coatesville and Westchester quadrangles: U.S. Geological Survey Atlas, Folio 223, 15 p.

Brouxel, M., Lapierre, H., Michard, A., and Albarède, F., 1987, The deep layers of a Paleozoic arc: Geochemistry of the Copley-Balaklala Series, northern California: Earth and Planetary Science Letters, v. 85, p. 386–400.

Brown, M., 1991, Comparative geochemical interpretation of Permian-Triassic plutonic complexes of the Coastal Range and Altiplano (25°30′ to 26°30′S), northern Chile, *in* Harmon, R. S., and Rapela, C. W., eds.,

Andean magmatism and its tectonic setting: Geological Society of America Special Paper 265, p. 157–177.

Brown, M., Friend, C. R. L., McGregor, V. R., and Perkins, W. T., 1981, The late Archaean Qôrqut granite complex of southern West Greenland: Journal of Geophysical Research (Solid Earth), v. 86, no. B11, p. 10617–10632.

Chappell, B. W., White, A. J. R., and Wyborn, D., 1987, The importance of residual source material (restite) in granite petrogenesis: Journal of Petrology, v. 28, p. 1111–1138.

Christensen, J. N., and DePaolo, D. J., 1993, Time scales of large volume silicic magma systems: Sr isotopic systematics of phenocrysts and glass from the Bishop Tuff, Long Valley, California: Contributions to Mineralogy and Petrology, v. 113, p. 100–114.

Clarke, D. B., 1992, Granitoid rocks: New York, Chapman and Hall, 283 p.

Clemens, J. D., 1984, Water contents of silicic to intermediate magmas: Lithos, v. 17, p. 273–287.

Cotkin, S. J., and Medaris, L. G., Jr., 1993, Evaluation of the crystallization conditions for the calcalkaline Russian Peak Intrusive Complex, Klamath Mountains, northern California: Journal of Petrology, v. 34, p. 543–571.

Crawford, M. L., and Crawford, W. A., 1980, Metamorphic and tectonic history of the Pennsylvania Piedmont: Geological Society of London Journal, v. 137, p. 311–320.

Crawford, M. L., and Crawford, W. A., eds., 1991, Evolution and assembly of the Pennsylvania-Delaware Piedmont: Geological Association of New Jersey, Eighth Annual Meeting, Field Guidebook and Proceedings, 126 p.

Cullers, R. L., Koch, R. J., and Bickford, M. E., 1981, Chemical evolution of magmas in the Proterozoic terrane of the St. Francois Mountains, southeastern Missouri, 2. Trace element data: Journal of Geophysical Research (Solid Earth), v. 86, no. B11, p. 10388–10401.

Czamanske, G. K., Ishihara, S., and Atkin, S. A., 1981, Chemistry of rock-forming minerals of the Cretaceous-Paleocene batholith in southwestern Japan and implications for magma genesis: Journal of Geophysical Research (Solid Earth), v. 86, no. B11, p. 10431–10469.

DeLong, S. E., and Chatelain, C., 1989, Complementary trace-element fractionation in volcanic and plutonic rocks: Imperfect examples from ocean-floor basalts and gabbros: Contributions to Mineralogy and Petrology, v. 102, p. 154–162.

Druitt, T. H., and Bacon, C. R., 1989, Petrology of the zoned calcalkaline magma chamber of Mount Mazama, Crater Lake, Oregon: Contributions to Mineralogy and Petrology, v. 101, p. 245–259.

Dunn, T., and Sen, C., 1994, Mineral/matrix partition coefficients for orthopyroxene, plagioclase, and olivine in basaltic to andesitic systems: A combined analytical and experimental study: Geochimica et Cosmochimica Acta, v. 58, p. 717–733.

Eggins, S., and Hensen, B. J., 1987, Evolution of mantle-derived, augite-hypersthene granodiorites by crystal-liquid fractionation: Barrington Tops Batholith, eastern Australia: Lithos, v. 20, p. 295–310.

Eggler, D. H., 1972, Water-saturated and undersaturated melting relations in a Paricutín andesite and an estimate of water content in the natural magma: Contributions to Mineralogy and Petrology, v. 34, p. 261–271.

Eggler, D. H., and Burnham, C. W., 1973, Crystallization and fractionation trends in the system andesite-H_2O-CO_2-O_2 at pressures to 10 kb: Geological Society of America Bulletin, v. 84, p. 2517–2532.

Feeley, T. C., and Davidson, J. P., 1994, Petrology of calc-alkaline lavas at Volcán Ollagüe and the origin of compositional diversity at central Andean stratovolcanoes: Journal of Petrology, v. 35, p. 1295–1340.

Feigenson, M. D., and Carr, M. J., 1985, Determination of major, trace, and rare-earth elements in rocks by DCP-AES: Chemical Geology, v. 51, p. 19–27.

Foland, K. A., and Muessig, K. W., 1978, A Paleozoic age for some charnockitic-anorthositic rocks: Geology, v. 6, p. 143–146.

Gill, J. B., 1978, Role of trace element partition coefficients in models of andesite genesis: Geochimica et Cosmochimica Acta, v. 42, p. 709–724.

Green, T. H., and Watson, E. B., 1982, Crystallization of apatite in natural magmas under high pressure, hydrous conditions, with particular reference to "orogenic" rock series: Contributions to Mineralogy and Petrology, v. 79, p. 96–105.

Helz, R. T., 1987, Differentiation behavior of Kilaeua Iki lava lake, Kilaeua Volcano, Hawaii: An overview of past and current work, *in* Mysen, B. O., ed., Magmatic processes: Physicochemical principles: The Geochemical Society Special Publication 1, p. 241–258.

Henderson, P., 1982, Inorganic geochemistry: Amsterdam, Pergamon Press, 353 p.

Icenhower, J. P., and London, D., 1993, Experimentally determined partitioning of Ba and Rb between alkali feldspar, biotite, muscovite, and peraluminous silicic melt [abs.]: Eos (Transactions, American Geophysical Union), v. 74, p. 342.

Irvine, T. N., 1980, Magmatic infiltration metasomatism, double-diffusive fractional crystallization, and adcumulus growth in the Muskox intrusion and other layered intrusions, *in* Hargraves, R. B., ed., Physics of magmatic processes: Princeton, New Jersey, Princeton University Press, p. 325–383.

Johnson, M. C., Anderson, A. T., Jr., and Rutherford, M. J., 1994, Pre-eruptive volatile contents of magmas, *in* Carroll, M. R., and Holloway, J. R., eds., Volatiles in magmas: Reviews in Mineralogy, v. 30, p. 281–330.

Langmuir, C. H., 1989, Geochemical consequences of in situ crystallization: Nature, v. 340, p. 199–205.

Leeman, W. P., and Phelps, D. W., 1981, Partitioning of rare earths and other trace elements between sanidine and coexisting volcanic glass: Journal of Geophysical Research (Solid Earth), v. 86, no. B11, p. 10193–10199.

Le Maitre, R. W., 1982, Numerical petrology: Amsterdam, Elsevier Scientific Publishing Co., 291 p.

Lesher, C. E., and Walker, D., 1988, Cumulate maturation and melt migration in a temperature gradient: Journal of Geophysical Research (Solid Earth), v. 93, no. B9, p. 10295–10311.

Lindsley, D. H., 1983, Pyroxene thermometry: American Mineralogist, v. 68, p. 477–493.

Lofgren, G. E., and Gooley, R., 1977, Simultaneous crystallization of feldspar intergrowths from the melt: American Mineralogist, v. 62, p. 217–228.

Lu, F., Anderson, A. T., Jr., and Davis, A. M., 1992, New and larger sanidine/melt partition coefficients for Ba and Sr as determined by ion microprobe analyses of melt inclusions and their sanidine host crystals: Geological Society of America Abstracts with Programs, v. 24, no. 7, p. A44.

Mahood, G. A., and Cornejo, P. C., 1992, Evidence for ascent of differentiated liquids in a silicic magma chamber found in a granitic pluton, *in* Brown, P. E., and Chappell, B. W., eds., The second Hutton symposium on the origin of granites and related rocks: Geological Society of America Special Paper 272, p. 63–69.

Mark, L. E., 1977, Petrology and metamorphism in the Marcus Hook quadrangle, southeastern Pennsylvania [M.A. thesis]: Bryn Mawr, Pennsylvania, Bryn Mawr College, 57 p.

McBirney, A. R., and Hunter, R. H., 1995, The cumulate paradigm reconsidered: Journal of Geology, v. 103, p. 114–122.

McBirney, A. R., and Noyes, R. M., 1979, Crystallization and layering of the Skaergaard intrusion: Journal of Petrology, v. 20, p. 487–554.

McCarthy, T. S., and Hasty, R. A., 1976, Trace element distribution patterns and their relationship to the crystallization of granitic melts: Geochimica et Cosmochimica Acta, v. 40, p. 1351–1358.

McCarthy, T. S., and Robb, L. J., 1978, On the relationship between cumulus mineralogy and trace and alkali element chemistry in an Archean granite from the Barberton region, South Africa: Geochimica et Cosmochimica Acta, v. 42, p. 21–26.

Michael, P. J., 1984, Chemical differentiation of the Cordillera Paine granite (southern Chile) by in situ fractional crystallization: Contributions to Mineralogy and Petrology, v. 87, p. 179–195.

Naney, M. T., 1983, Phase equilibria of rock-forming ferromagnesian silicates in granitic systems: American Journal of Science, v. 283, p. 993–1033.

Nash, W. P., and Crecraft, H. R., 1985, Partition coefficients for trace elements in silicic magmas: Geochimica et Cosmochimica Acta, v. 49, p. 2309–2322.

Nekvasil, H., 1992, Ternary feldspar crystallization in high-temperature felsic magmas: American Mineralogist, v. 77, p. 592–604.

Nielsen, R. L., and DeLong, S. E., 1992, A numerical approach to boundary layer fractionation: Application to differentiation in natural magma systems: Contributions to Mineralogy and Petrology, v. 110, p. 355–369.

Paterson, S. R., Vernon, R. H., and Tobisch, O. T., 1989, A review of criteria for the identification of magmatic and tectonic foliations in granitoids: Journal of Structural Geology, v. 11, p. 349–363.

Press, W. H., Flannery, B. P., Teukolsky, S. A., and Vetterling, W. T., 1986, Numerical Recipes: Cambridge, Cambridge University Press, 818 p.

Reid, J. B., Evans, O. C., and Fates, D. G., 1983, Magma mixing in grantic rocks of the central Sierra Nevada, California: Earth and Planetary Science Letters, v. 66, p. 243–261.

Sawka, W. N., Chappell, B. W., and Kistler, R. W., 1990, Granitoid compositional zoning by side-wall boundary layer differentiation: Evidence from the Pallisade Crest intrusive suite, central Sierra Nevada, California: Journal of Petrology, v. 31, p. 519–553.

Scambos, T. A., Loiselle, M. C., and Wones, D. R., 1986, The Center Pond pluton: The restite of the story (phase separation and melt evolution in granitoid genesis): American Journal of Science, v. 286, p. 241–280.

Sinigoi, S., and seven others, 1994, Chemical evolution of a large mafic intrusion in the lower crust, Ivrea-Verbano Zone, northern Italy: Journal of Geophysical Research (Solid Earth), v. 99, no. B11, p. 21575–21590.

Sparks, R. S. J., Huppert, H. E., and Turner, J. S., 1984, The fluid dynamics of evolving magma chambers: Royal Society of London, Philosophical Transactions, ser. A, v. 310, p. 511–534.

Speer, J. A., 1989, Small-scale variations and subtle zoning in granitoid plutons; the Liberty Hill pluton, South Carolina, U.S.A.: Chemical Geology, v. 75, p. 153–181.

Srogi, E. L., 1988, The petrogenesis of the igneous and metamorphic rocks in the Wilmington Complex, Pennsylvania-Delaware Piedmont [Ph.D. thesis]: Philadelphia, University of Pennsylvania, 613 p.

Srogi, L., Wagner, M. E., and Lutz, T. M., 1993, Dehydration partial melting and disequilibrium in the granulite facies Wilmington Complex, Pennsylvania-Delaware Piedmont: American Journal of Science, v. 293, p. 405–462.

Streckeisen, A., 1976, To each plutonic rock its proper name: Earth Science Reviews, v. 12, p. 1–33.

Sultan, M., Batiza, R., and Sturchio, N. C., 1986, The origin of small-scale geochemical and mineralogic variations in a granitic intrusion, a crystallization and mixing model: Contributions to Mineralogy and Petrology, v. 93, p. 513–523.

Tait, S. R., 1988, Samples from the crystallising boundary layer of a zoned magma chamber: Contributions to Mineralogy and Petrology, v. 100, p. 470–483.

Tait, S. R., and Kerr, R. C., 1987, Experimental modelling of interstitial melt convection in cumulus piles, *in* Parsons, I., ed., Origins of igneous layering: Dordrecht, D. Reidel Publishing Co., p. 569–587.

Tait, S. R., Huppert, H. E., and Sparks, R. S. J., 1984, The role of compositional convection in the formation of adcumulate rocks: Lithos, v. 17, p. 139–146.

Thompson, A. M., 1975, Anorthosite in the Piedmont of northern Delaware: Geological Society of America Abstracts with Programs, v. 7, p. 124–125.

Turbeville, B. N., 1992, Relationships between chamber margin accumulates and pore liquids: Evidence from arrested in situ processes in ejecta, Latera caldera, Italy: Contributions to Mineralogy and Petrology, v. 110, p. 429–441.

van der Molen, I., and Paterson, M. S., 1979, Experimental deformation of partially-melted granite: Contributions to Mineralogy and Petrology, v. 70, p. 299–318.

Wagner, M. E., and Srogi, L., 1987, Early Paleozoic metamorphism at two crustal levels and a tectonic model for the Pennsylvania-Delaware Piedmont: Geological Society of America Bulletin, v. 99, p. 113–126.

Wagner, M. E., Srogi, L., and Brick, E., 1987, Bringhurst gabbro and banded gneiss of the Wilmington Complex, Bringhurst Woods Park, northern Delaware: Geological Society of America Centennial Field Guide, Northeastern Section, p. 25–28.

Wagner, M. E., Srogi, L., Wiswall, C. G., and Alcock, J., 1991, Taconic collision in the Delaware-Pennsylvania Piedmont and implications for subsequent geologic history, *in* Schultz, A., and Compton-Gooding, E., eds., Geologic evolution of the eastern United States (Field trip guidebook, Northeastern-Southeastern Geological Society of America): Virginia Museum of Natural History, Guidebook 2, p. 91–119.

Wall, V. J., Clemens, J. D., and Clarke, B. D., 1987, Models for granitoid evolution and source composition: The Journal of Geology, v. 95, p. 731–750.

Ward, R. F., 1959, Petrology and metamorphism of the Wilmington Complex, Delaware, Pennsylvania, and Maryland: Geological Society of America Bulletin, v. 70, p. 1425–1458.

Watson, E. B., and Harrison, T. M., 1983, Zircon saturation revisited: Temperature and composition effects in a variety of crustal magma types: Earth and Planetary Science Letters, v. 64, p. 295–304.

Weiss, S., and Troll, G., 1989, The Ballachulish igneous complex, Scotland: Petrography, mineral chemistry, and order of crystallization in the monzodiorite-quartz diorite suite and in the granite: Journal of Petrology, v. 30, p. 1069–1115.

White, A. J. R., and Chappell, B. W., 1977, Ultrametamorphism and granitoid genesis: Tectonophysics, v. 43, p. 7–22.

Wickham, S. M., 1987, The segregation and emplacement of granitic magmas: Geological Society of London Journal, v. 144, p. 281–297.

Wiebe, R. A., 1993, Basaltic injections into floored silicic magma chambers: Eos (Transactions, American Geophysical Union), v. 74, p. 1 and 3.

Winkler, H. G. F., 1976, Petrogenesis of the metamorphic rocks (fourth edition): New York, Springer-Verlag, 334 p.

Woodruff, K. D., and Thompson, A. M., 1975, Geology of the Wilmington area, Delaware: Delaware Geological Survey, Geologic Map Series, no. 4, scale 1:24,000.

Zorpi, M. J., Coulon, C., Orsini, J. B., and Cocirta, C., 1989, Magma mingling, zoning, and emplacement in calc-alkaline granitoid plutons: Tectonophysics, v. 157, p. 315–329.

MANUSCRIPT ACCEPTED BY THE SOCIETY JULY 2, 1996

Geological Society of America
Memoir 191
1997

Magmatic and tectonic evolution of the Cambrian-Ordovician Laurentian margin of Iapetus: Geochemical and isotopic constraints from the Notre Dame subzone, Newfoundland

H. Scott Swinden*
Geological Survey of Newfoundland and Labrador, Department of Natural Resources, P.O. Box 8700,
St. John's, Newfoundland A1B 4J6, Canada
G. A. Jenner and Z. A. Szybinski
Department of Earth Sciences, Memorial University of Newfoundland, St. John's, Newfoundland A1B 3X5, Canada

ABSTRACT

Late Cambrian to Early Ordovician volcanic and hypabyssal rocks in the Notre Dame subzone, Newfoundland Appalachians, are generally considered to have formed in a series of island arcs and back arc basins on the Laurentian side of Iapetus. Our compilation of new geochemical and Nd isotopic data provides a more detailed look at the nature of magmatism in these environments than has heretofore been possible. Nd isotopic data constrain the nature of the magma sources for the various volcanic episodes and, in particular, allow us to track the early Paleozoic interaction of mantle and continental lithosphere at the Laurentian margin. New and published geochronological data permit us to assign a time sequence to the various events that we recognize.

Geochemical data show that volcanic rocks in the Notre Dame subzone can be divided into several groups, most of which have well-documented analogs in modern plate environments. In nonarc environments, tholeiitic rocks with characteristics of N-MORB (normal mid-ocean basalt ridge) and E-MORB (enriched-MORB) are present, as are tholeiitic and alkalic basalts with characteristics of oceanic island basalts. The geochemical and isotopic data indicate derivation from time-integrated depleted mantle sources. We interpret these to have formed in ensimatic back arc basins.

Arc volcanic rocks include island arc tholeiites, transitional island arc tholeiites, calc-alkalic basalt and/or andesite, boninites, and felsic volcanics. Geochemical and Nd isotopic data indicate that the tholeiitic rocks were derived from time integrated LREE- (light rare earth element-) depleted mantle sources contaminated by subducted, hydrous oceanic lithospheric and continentally derived sediments. Calc-alkalic rocks and associated felsic volcanic rocks have Nd isotopic compositions that indicate the direct involvement of continental lithosphere in their petrogenesis.

Integration of geochemical, geological, and geochronological evidence suggests the following sequence of events: (1) formation of a Late Cambrian subduction com-

---

*Present address: Mineral and Energy Resources Division, Department of Natural Resources, P.O. Box 698, Halifax, Nova Scotia B3J 2T9, Canada.

Swinden, H. S., Jenner, G. A., and Szybinski, Z. A., 1997, Magmatic and tectonic evolution of the Cambrian-Ordovician Laurentian margin of Iapetus: Geochemical and isotopic constraints from the Notre Dame subzone, Newfoundland, *in* Sinha, A. K., Whalen, J. B., and Hogan, J. P., eds., The Nature of Magmatism in the Appalachian Orogen: Boulder, Colorado, Geological Society of America Memoir 191.

plex prior to 506 Ma; (2) emplacement of these rocks on the Laurentian margin and initiation (or continuation) of westward-dipping subduction under the composite margin, resulting in intrusion of a distinctive suite of high-Mg andesitic dikes ca. 501–498 Ma.; (3) formation of an ensimatic back arc basin(s) by about 488 Ma (recorded by Early Ordovician ophiolites), accompanied from about 484 Ma by eruption of a calc-alkalic arc complex on continental lithosphere (recorded by calc-alkalic mafic and felsic volcanic rocks in the eastern part of the subzone). Tonalitic plutonism at the Laurentian margin throughout the Early Ordovician was approximately coeval with the arc–back arc complex(es) (and petrogenetically similar to the felsic volcanism) and continued following the end of active volcanism. Spatial relationships of the various volcanic assemblages in the Early Ordovician ocean are not well constrained and at least three general tectonic models can account for the observed temporal and geochemical relationships. These models variously invoke Early Ordovician subduction under: (1) an irregular Laurentian margin, in which subduction ocurs simultaneously beneath continental and oceanic lithosphere; (2) a partially rifted continental margin; and (3) an outboard continental fragment.

INTRODUCTION

The Appalachian Dunnage zone is characterized by Cambrian to Silurian oceanic volcanic, hypabyssal, and epiclastic rocks, widely interpreted to comprise vestiges of the Iapetus ocean, which separated the Laurentian and Gondwanan continents during the early Paleozoic (Wilson, 1966; Bird and Dewey, 1970; Harland and Gayer, 1972; Williams et al., 1974; Williams, 1979). Early models for the plate tectonic evolution of the Dunnage zone involved Cambrian to Early Ordovician opening of Iapetus, recorded by ophiolites, followed by Early to Middle Ordovician closing of the ocean, recorded by thick volcanic and/or epiclastic sequences. Orogeny was envisaged to have occurred in two stages (Colman-Sadd, 1982), an Early to Middle Ordovician Taconian event in which oceanic terranes were accreted to Laurentia, and a Silurian-Devonian event, the Acadian orogeny, marked by widespread granitoid plutonism. An eastward dip for the subduction zone was favored by most workers because this provided a mechanically easy way of emplacing the ophiolites on the continental margin during collision (Strong et al., 1974; Searle and Stevens, 1984).

However, more recent work has shown that this simple interpretation is untenable. First, geochemical and geochronological evidence indicates that most if not all ophiolites actually formed in suprasubduction environments, that some of the volcanic and/or epiclastic rocks in other sequences apparently did not form in arc environments (e.g., Coish et al., 1982; Dunning and Chorlton, 1985; Jenner and Fryer, 1980) and that some of the island arc sequences are considerably older than the oldest ophiolitic sequences (Dunning and Krogh, 1985; Dunning et al., 1991; Evans et al., 1990). Second, a regional tectonic synthesis by Williams et al. (1988) showed that the Dunnage zone in Newfoundland is bipartite. They recognized two subzones based on contrasts in pre-Silurian stratigraphic, geochemical, and geophysical relationships, which they termed the Notre Dame and Exploits, to the west and east, respectively, of a structural boundary termed the Red Indian line. Colman-Sadd et al. (1992a) sug-

gested that the two subzones record events in widely disparate parts of Iapetus, the Notre Dame subzone having formed near the Laurentian margin and the Exploits subzone having formed closer to the Gondwanan margin. Third, recent models of the structural relationships between the allochthonous oceanic terranes and their respective basements indicate that there was significant Silurian deformation and/or movement of the allochthonous rocks (Cawood 1989, 1991). Simple piggyback models for Ordovician allochthon assembly and emplacement (e.g., Williams, 1971) are no longer adequate to account for the observed relationships.

Rocks in the Notre Dame subzone (Fig. 1) are now widely interpreted as representing a series of Cambrian to Early Ordovician intraoceanic island arcs and back arc basins that were accreted to the Laurentian margin during the Taconian orogeny (Jenner and Fryer, 1980; Coish et al., 1982; Williams and Hatcher, 1983; Jenner et al., 1991; Swinden, 1991). However, the detailed tectonic history of, and the relationships among, the various geologic elements in the Notre Dame subzone are relatively poorly understood. For example, the age of emplacement of the Humber Arm allochthon (ca. 479 Ma, Dallmeyer and Williams, 1975) is widely considered to represent the age of accretion of outboard elements to the Laurentian margin. However, Dallmeyer (1977) and Jamieson (1988) have shown that the Hare Bay allochthon to the north was emplaced on the Laurentian margin as early as 495 Ma. This geologic evidence for diachronous accretion of outboard elements or for interaction of continental and oceanic lithosphere very early in the history of the orogen has not been widely integrated in tectonic models for the development of the Laurentian margin.

In this chapter, we investigate the tectonic development of the Notre Dame subzone using our extensive geochemical, geochronological, and Nd isotopic database for the Cambrian and Ordovician magmatic rocks. Our objectives are to provide a comprehensive review of the tectonic setting of the magmatism and to track the nature of the magma sources for these rocks, in particular the timing of interaction with continental lithosphere. Our interpretation of these data is that they demonstrate a com-

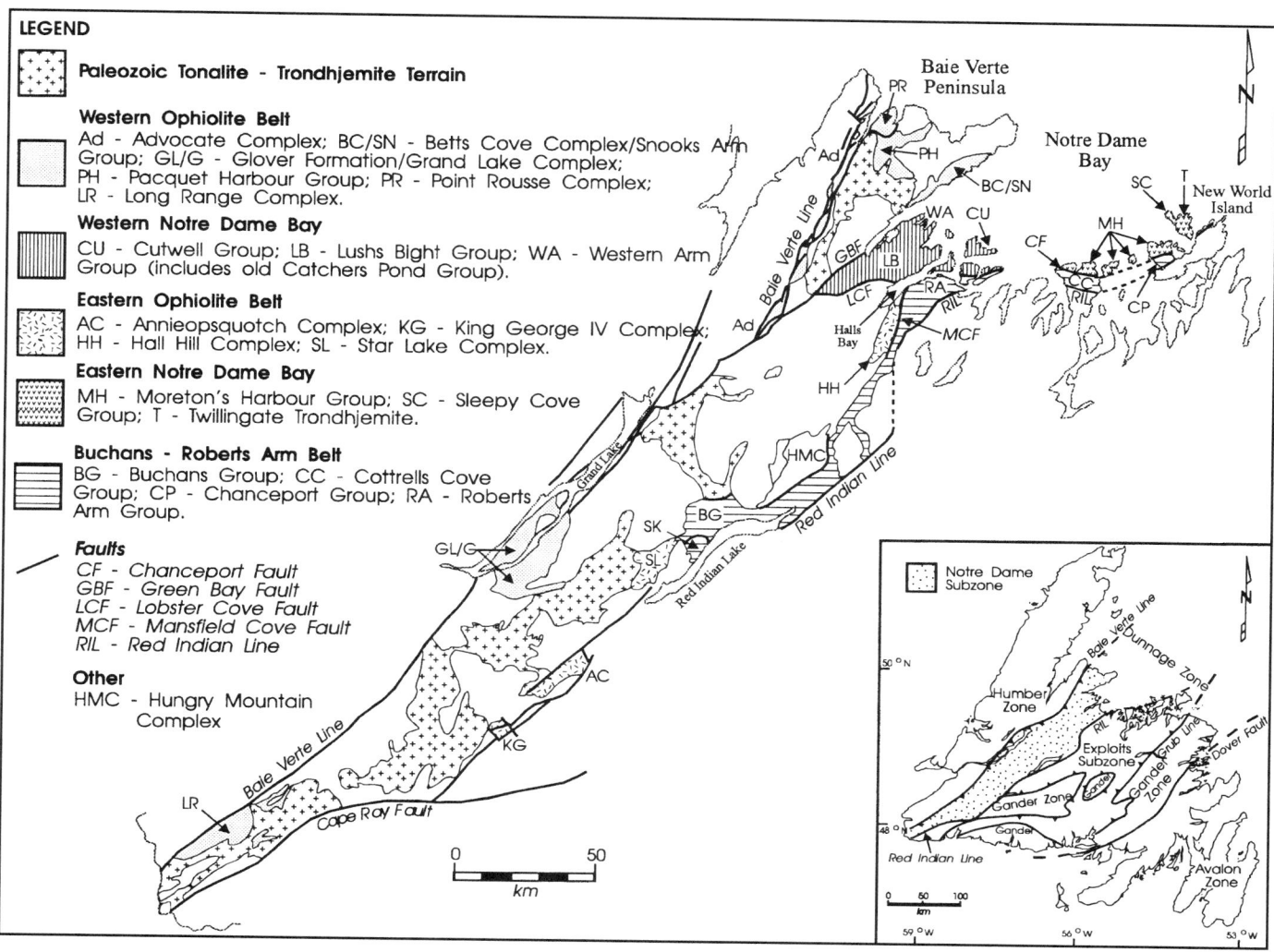

Figure 1. General geologic map of the Notre Dame subzone in Newfoundland showing the areas described in the text, lithostratigraphic units, and major structural boundaries.

plex tectonic history spanning more than 60 m.y. and a history of interaction between mantle and continental lithosphere that is more widespread and long lived than has previously been appreciated. These results require a substantial rethinking of extant models for the magmatic and tectonic development of the Laurentian margin during the Cambrian and Early Ordovician.

METHODOLOGY

Introduction

Our approach in this chapter is to integrate a large volume of high-quality geochemical and isotopic data to interpret, in as much detail as possible, the petrogenesis and tectonic history of early Paleozoic magmatic rocks in the Notre Dame subzone. All of the trace-element data in this chapter represent more than 400 whole-rock samples, and were analyzed by inductively coupled plasma-mass spectrometry (ICP-MS) at Memorial University; analytical methods, accuracy, and precision were given by Jenner et al. (1990). Representative analyses are given in Table 1. Nd isotopic data represent more than 70 whole rock analyses. Ion exchange chemistry was carried out at the Memorial University of Newfoundland and analysis by thermal ionization mass spectrometry was done at the Geological Survey of Canada and the Max Planck Institut für Chemie. Analytical methods were described by Swinden et al. (1990). Representative analyses are given in Table 2.

The following summary is provided to help the reader understand the context in which we use and interpret these diagrams. In the first instance we use geochemistry to discriminate between arc and nonarc environments. Within these environments, we recognize a number of distinct petrochemical types that permit refining of our understanding of finer structure of the tectonic settings. Nd isotopes are used in conjunction with the geochemistry to inter-

TABLE 1. REPRESENTATIVE GEOCHEMICAL ANALYSES OF VOLCANIC AND SUBVOLCANIC INTRUSIVE ROCKS IN THE NOTRE DAME SUBZONE

Sample	86SS-0241	SK3088	AC-11	B982-07	85-SS-0501	85-SS-0486	RA-1120B	RA-0049B
Area	END	EOP	EOP	BRAB	BRAB	BRAB	BRAB	BRAB
Type	TIAT	IAT	N-MORB	CAB	IAT	N-MORB	E-MORB	OIB
(wt. %)								
SiO_2	52.58	54.03	51.60	58.19	52.77	52.98	51.22	47.41
TiO_2	0.77	1.14	1.15	0.84	1.34	2.45	0.95	1.98
Al_2O_3	14.69	15.92	15.62	17.07	14.35	13.63	16.33	18.22
FeO^t	8.62	9.33	9.63	9.01	10.83	15.79	6.79	9.75
MnO	0.17	0.11	0.23	0.11	0.21	0.24	0.17	0.23
MgO	6.93	9.47	8.45	5.27	7.91	5.71	10.03	9.32
CaO	11.75	4.20	8.78	4.05	8.23	5.99	9.92	8.72
Na_2O	4.36	5.50	4.35	4.80	4.05	2.87	1.71	2.30
K_2O	0.06	0.18	0.12	0.47	0.19	0.11	2.80	2.30
P_2O_5	0.07	0.13	0.07	0.19	0.12	0.23	0.10	0.36
(ppm)								
Cr	411	137	212	b.d.*	248	b.d.	212	419
Ni	181	27	57	8	59	10	101	181
Sc	36	53	44	32	37	44	44	34
V	250	279	310	376	444	658	262	325
Rb	b.d.	2	6	8	1	b.d.	49	41
Ba	14	b.d.	4	255	b.d.	197	167	408
Sr	177	76	140	305	187	112	99	336
Nb	0.4	2.9	0.8	2.8	1.0	4.0	2.8	41.4
Zr	42	58	51	77	70	153	48	144
Y	19	25	28	18	29	58	19	27
Th	0.12	0.52	0.08	4.29	0.43	0.36	0.42	2.53
La	1.57	4.20	1.44	15.75	3.13	5.30	3.14	20.62
Ce	4.69	10.73	4.71	33.71	9.10	17.12	7.94	44.03
Pr	0.91	1.67	0.94	4.07	1.53	2.96	1.23	5.01
Nd	4.77	8.43	5.51	16.36	8.58	17.31	6.10	19.83
Sm	1.79	2.77	2.06	3.61	2.95	6.05	1.98	4.52
Eu	0.76	0.97	0.93	0.97	1.10	2.21	0.87	1.59
Gd	2.56	3.52	3.43	3.62	4.09	8.46	2.86	5.33
Tb	0.52	0.69	0.65	0.55	0.79	1.63	0.51	0.79
Dy	3.44	4.65	4.46	3.51	5.28	11.05	3.51	4.79
Ho	0.82	0.98	0.96	0.75	1.22	2.43	0.75	1.03
Er	2.13	2.74	2.70	1.94	3.28	6.36	1.93	2.58
Tm	0.30	n.d.†	n.d.	0.27	0.46	0.85	0.26	0.35
Yb	2.00	2.54	2.54	1.88	3.07	5.40	1.72	2.34
Lu	0.30	0.35	0.37	0.28	0.45	0.65	0.25	0.34

pret the nature of the sources and, particularly in the context of this study, as evidence of the influence or lack thereof of continental lithosphere in the petrogenesis of the magmatic rocks.

Petrology and geochemistry

Arc and nonarc geochemical signatures. The literature provides a large number of geochemical discriminants to distinguish rocks formed in different tectonic environments (e.g., Pearce, 1975; Pearce and Cann, 1971; Pearce and Norry, 1979; Wood et al., 1979; Shervais, 1982; Meschede, 1986). For altered volcanic rocks, the principal elements used in these diagrams are Zr, Nb, Hf, Ta, Ti, and Y, i.e., predominantly the high field strength elements (HFSE) (Winchester and Floyd, 1975; Swinden et al.,

1990). Used alone, these elements provide a preliminary guide to both the petrologic and tectonic affinity of mafic and intermediate volcanic rocks. Additional alteration-resistant trace elements, i.e., the rare earth elements (REE) and Th, must also be used for detailed petrologic and tectonic analysis (Jenner et al., 1991; Swinden et al., 1990). Th is a low field strength element (LFSE, i.e., Rb, Ba, Sr, Cs, U, Pb, Th), which, unlike the other elements in this group, is resistant to alteration and/or metamorphic effects, and thus provides the only opportunity to compare the primary behavior of these two fundamentally different groups of elements (LFSE versus HFSE) in altered volcanic rocks. This is important because the behavior of these groups of elements is known to reflect processes operative in specific tectonic environments. To facilitate comparison of the behavior of these different elements, it

TABLE 1. REPRESENTATIVE GEOCHEMICAL ANALYSES OF VOLCANIC AND SUBVOLCANIC INTRUSIVE ROCKS IN THE NOTRE DAME SUBZONE (continued - page 2)

Sample Area Type	88BC-17 WOP BON	BC-1 WOP IAT	BC-10 WOP N-MORB	PH-4 WOP E-MORB	1543328 WND BON	1542237 WND IAT	WA-3344 WND N-MORB	CL-24-17a WND CAB	WB-1 WND HIMAG
(wt. %)									
SiO_2	57.10	54.14	48.38	47.62	57.53	55.38	50.88	49.98	61.48
TiO_2	0.13	0.50	1.41	1.38	0.11	0.87	1.48	0.83	0.75
Al_2O_3	11.13	16.50	16.30	17.34	8.51	15.21	15.44	20.56	15.76
FeO^t	7.40	7.43	10.07	10.97	8.11	9.12	10.21	9.94	5.65
MnO	0.16	0.12	0.18	0.16	0.18	0.16	0.21	0.14	0.11
MgO	14.28	10.88	7.60	7.94	15.59	8.05	6.62	4.19	5.88
CaO	5.75	4.20	12.83	12.03	7.94	7.72	11.28	8.05	5.75
Na_2O	4.03	5.27	2.90	2.29	0.45	3.29	3.59	4.76	4.19
K_2O	0.02	0.93	0.24	0.11	1.56	0.13	0.15	1.33	0.11
P_2O_5	0.01	0.03	0.10	0.17	0.01	0.06	0.14	0.22	0.32
(ppm)									
Cr	640	404	307	290	988	81	96	b.d.	317
Ni	131	71	66	49	205	37	30	b.d.	160
Sc	64	57	52	56	n.d.	n.d.	n.d.	n.d.	20
V	280	276	289	340	208	344	311	345	143
Rb	n.d.	12	5	3	28	1	3	27	59
Ba	n.d.	44	18	n.d.	48	31	n.d.	n.d.	487
Sr	63	85	172	330	73	158	232	320	270
Nb	0.7	0.6	2.0	6.3	0.9	1.0	3.2	1.2	6.2
Zr	10	25	88	93	18	37	114	61	139
Y	3	9	31	22	4	21	36	19	18
Th	0.24	0.34	0.18	0.81	0.44	0.28	0.35	3.43	4.99
La	1.47	1.71	3.22	6.56	1.91	1.91	4.22	11.31	26.03
Ce	2.29	4.13	10.45	16.96	3.51	5.60	12.52	23.99	57.09
Pr	0.33	0.59	1.72	2.41	0.41	0.88	2.08	3.01	6.64
Nd	1.03	3.16	9.58	12.48	1.40	4.75	10.82	12.77	24.73
Sm	0.22	1.06	3.20	3.56	0.44	1.84	3.72	3.28	4.42
Eu	0.05	0.39	1.43	1.51	0.13	0.76	1.44	1.18	1.07
Gd	0.26	1.55	4.51	4.19	0.34	2.57	4.78	3.99	2.59
Tb	0.06	0.29	0.80	0.75	0.07	0.52	0.95	0.56	0.38
Dy	0.52	1.98	5.27	4.79	0.53	3.82	6.18	3.48	2.85
Ho	0.15	0.46	1.15	1.01	0.13	0.87	1.38	0.74	0.57
Er	0.56	1.23	3.06	2.61	0.48	2.46	3.87	1.95	1.59
Tm	0.07	n.d.	n.d.	n.d.	0.08	0.35	0.56	0.31	0.23
Yb	0.91	1.26	2.81	2.36	0.59	2.43	3.53	1.96	1.46
Lu	0.16	0.17	0.39	0.31	0.12	0.36	0.56	0.28	0.22

Note: For abbreviations, see text.
*b.d. = below detection limit.
†n.d. = not determined.

is common to plot them normalized relative to the abundances in the hypothetical primitive mantle (Hofmann, 1988; Sun and McDonough, 1989) in increasing order (left to right) of compatibility in a basaltic melt. In this chapter, we use a customized primitive mantle normalized plot, in which only those elements that are resistant to alteration have been plotted. We also illustrate the geochemical systematics on three tectonic discrimination diagrams, all of which utilize different trace element ratios to discriminate between various arc and nonarc environments.

There is substantial variation in the geochemical and iso-topic signatures of magmatic rocks in oceanic and continental environments, signatures that reflect variations in source characteristics and magmatic differentiation processes (i.e., partial melting, fractional crystallization, contamination). Nonetheless, it is possible to recognize a limited number of magmatic types within the Notre Dame subzone that have analogs in modern environments. The geochemical signatures in the modern analogs are illustrated in Figure 2 and the framework for interpretation of Nd isotopic data in Figure 3.

Nonarc volcanic rocks. Nonarc oceanic volcanic rocks are

TABLE 2. Nd ISOTOPIC DATA FOR REPRESENTATIVE VOLCANIC AND SUBVOLCANIC INTRU- SIVE ROCKS FROM THE NOTRE DAME SUBZONE*

Sample	Unit	Type	$^{143}Nd/^{144}Nd$ (m)	$^{147}Sm/^{144}Nd$ (m)	$^{143}Nd/^{144}Nd$ (i)	$\varepsilon_{Nd(t)}$
Western Ophiolite Belt						
Ph-4	Pacquet Hbr.	E-MORB	0.512846	0.1720	0.512305	5.5
VB-3	Snooks Arm	E-MORB	0.512902	0.1736	0.512356	6.5
BC-5	Betts Cove	N-MORB	0.512951	0.1898	0.512354	6.5
BC-10	Betts Cove	N-MORB	0.513081	0.2063	0.512432	8.0
BC-1	Betts Cove	IAT	0.512938	0.2064	0.512289	5.2
BC-3	Betts Cove	IAT	0.513135	0.2364	0.512392	7.2
88BC-17	Betts Cove	BON	0.512534	0.1512	0.512059	0.7
88bc-23	Betts Cove	BON	0.512713	0.1566	0.512221	3.9
Western Notre Dame Bay						
Wh-1	Lushs Bight	HIMAG	0.512277	0.1401	0.511836	-3.6
Cl16-02b	Lushs Bight	HIMAG	0.512723	0.1791	0.512160	2.7
1542206	Lushs Bight	BON	0.512433	0.1381	0.511999	-0.4
1542118	Lushs Bight	BON	0.512704	0.1722	0.512163	2.8
WA-13	Western Arm	IAT	0.512774	0.1829	0.512199	3.5
1542024	Lushs Bight	IAT	0.513140	0.2357	0.512399	7.4
CP 32-11	Catchers Pd.	CAB	0.512654	0.1802	0.512087	1.3
CP 29-6A	Catchers Pd.	CAB	0.512670	0.1707	0.512133	2.2
Br-7	Brighton	Hornblendite	0.512288	0.1159	0.511924	-1.9
CP 5-5	Catchers Pd.	Felsic	0.512599	0.1583	0.512101	1.6
CP 20-71	Catchers Pd.	Felsic	0.512638	0.1499	0.512167	2.8
WA-16	Western Arm	OIB	0.512822	0.1741	0.512275	4.9
CP 1-8A	Catchers Pd.	OIB	0.512886	0.1796	0.512321	5.9
Eastern Ophiolite Belt						
Ac-11	Annieopsquotch	N-MORB	0.513162	0.2384	0.512410	7.6
Ac-14	Annieopsquotch	N-MORB	0.513263	0.2511	0.512470	8.4
Sk3088	Skidder	IAT	0.512890	0.1924	0.512285	5.1
Ac-7	Annieopsquotch	IAT	0.513293	0.2683	0.512450	8.3
Buchans-Robert's Arm Belt						
Ra0044b	Robert's Arm	OIB	0.512743	0.1246	0.512351	6.4
85ss395	Robert's Arm	N-MORB	0.513110	0.2232	0.512408	7.6
85ss383	Robert's Arm	N-MORB	0.513252	0.2611	0.512431	8.0
85ss052	Robert's Arm	IAT	0.512899	0.1842	0.512320	5.8
85ss0529	Robert's Arm	IAT	0.513178	0.2445	0.512409	7.6
85ss571b	Robert's Arm	Felsic	0.512241	0.1231	0.511854	-3.3
TD93-176	Cottrells Cove	Felsic	0.511857	0.1144	0.511494	-10.2
Ra-0075c	Robert's Arm	CAB	0.512525	0.1548	0.512038	0.3
B2681-04	Robert's Arm	CAB	0.512533	0.1466	0.512072	1.0
Ra1108b	Robert's Arm	CAB	0.512869	0.1879	0.512278	5.0

Note: For abbreviations, see text.
*$^{143}Nd/^{144}Nd$(m) and $^{147}Sm/^{144}Nd$(m) are measured values. Analytical uncertainty in $^{143}Nd/^{144}Nd$(m) is ± 0.000015 or better. $^{143}Nd/^{144}Nd$(i) is initial ratio at t = 480 Ma. Data are fractionation corrected to $^{146}Nd/^{144}Nd$ = 0.7219. $^{143}Nd/^{144}Nd$(CHUR) today is 0.512638 and $^{147}Sm/^{144}Nd$(CHUR) today is 0.1967. Analytical uncertainty in $^{143}Nd/^{144}Nd$ is ± 15.

derived from heterogeneous mantle sources, which give rise to mantle-normalized patterns ranging from positive to negative in slope, but in which there are no anomalous enrichments or depletions in elements of similar geochemical character; i.e., the patterns are generally smooth. Primarily on the basis of the behavior of the most incompatible elements, we recognize three principal magmatic types in the Notre Dame subzone that are of nonarc origin. All are recognized in modern environments and widely described in the literature, and examples are given in Figure 2.

N-MORB (normal mid-ocean ridge basalts) represent tholeiitic, mafic volcanism from segments of spreading ridges in major ocean basins or back arc basins. They are characterized by depletion in the most incompatible elements (i.e., Th, Nb, and the light REEs) (see Fig. 2). They represent a depleted mantle source unaffected by hotspot and/or plume influences or subduction.

OIB (ocean island or oceanic intra-plate basalts) represent tholeiitic to alkalic volcanism generally related to hotspot or

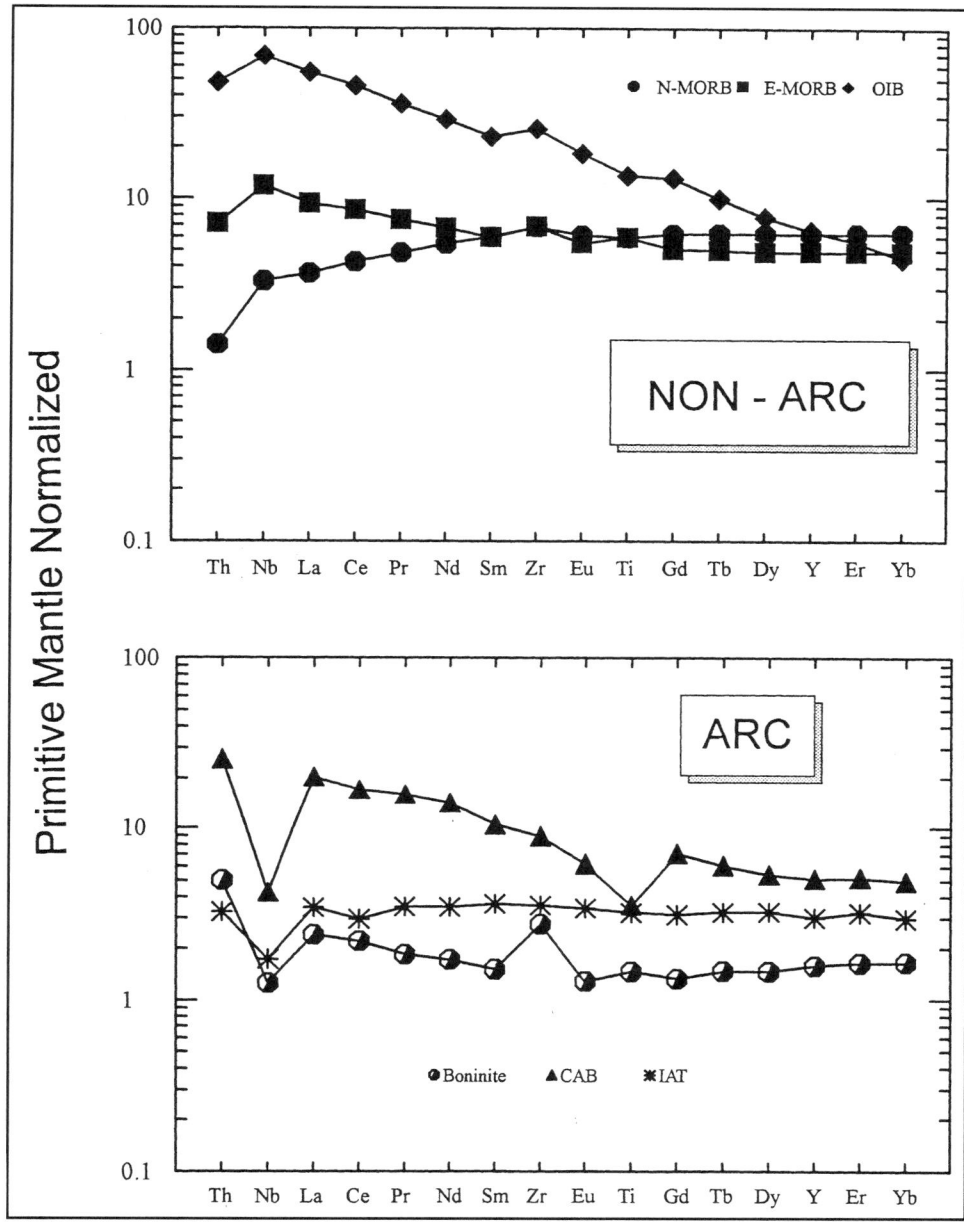

Figure 2. Representative mantle-normalized geochemical patterns for recent volcanic rocks used as modern analogs for the principal volcanic rock types in the Notre Dame subzone. Patterns for representative nonarc rocks are from Sun and McDonough (1989). Boninite is from Cape Vogel (Jenner, 1981), calc-alkalic basalt and island arc tholeiites (CAB, IAT) are our unpublished data. OIB is oceanic island basalt; MORB is mid-ocean ridge basalt (N is normal, E is enriched).

mantle plume activity. They are characterized by enrichment in the most incompatible elements. Note that this enrichment peaks at Nb, so that normalized Nb concentrations may be greater than those of Th and La (i.e., they may exhibit a positive Nb anomaly on mantle-normalized diagrams). They represent enriched mantle sources.

E-MORB (enriched mid-ocean ridge basalts) represent

tholeiitic volcanism from segments of spreading ridges affected by hotspot or plume activity. They may also occur in back arc basins. They are characterized by mantle-normalized incompatible element patterns having slopes intermediate between those of N-MORB and OIB (see Fig. 2).

Arc volcanic rocks. Rocks from arc environments are characterized by an enrichment of the LFSE (represented in altered

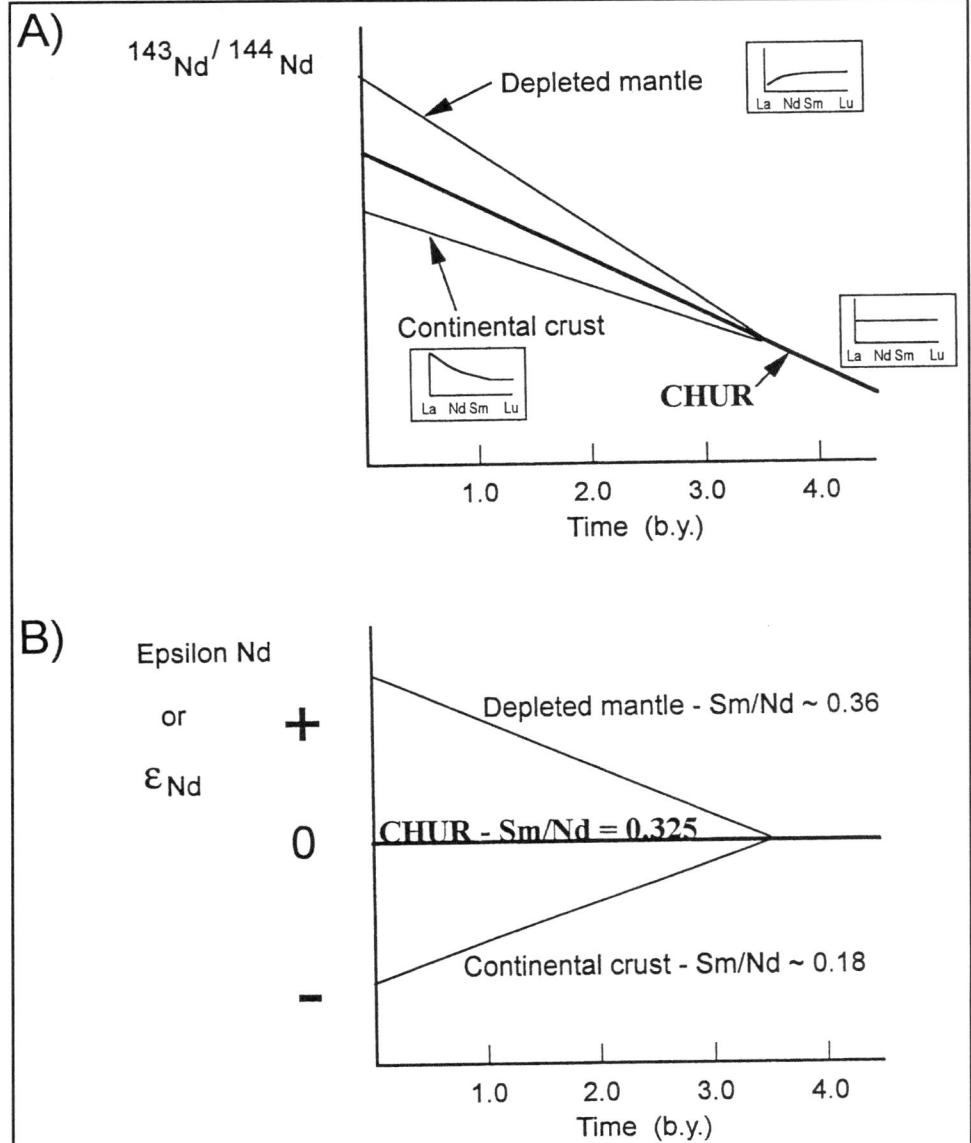

Figure 3. Nd isotope systematics for crustal reservoirs. In A, time integrated light rare earth element-(LREE-) depleted sources produce $^{143}Nd/^{144}Nd$ that are greater than CHUR (chrondritic uniform reservoir) and time-integrated LREE-enriched sources (i.e., continental crust) produce $^{143}Nd/^{144}Nd$ that is less than CHUR. In B, this results in ε_{Nd} values that are increasingly positive with time for LREE-depleted sources and increasingly negative with time for LREE-enriched sources.

rocks by Th) relative to the most incompatible HFSE (i.e., Nb and Ta), and a depletion in Nb relative to La. This results in negative Nb anomalies relative to Th and La on mantle-normalized plots (Wood et al., 1979). In intraoceanic environments, these anomalies are our primary indicator of magmas sourced in subduction-contaminated mantle. In continental settings, this anomaly may be reinforced by crustal contamination, in which case Nd isotopic data are needed to fully interpret the patterns.

BON (boninites) are intraoceanic suprasubduction zone volcanics, showing an overall strong depletion in incompatible elements and a distinctive concave-upward pattern on mantle normalized plots (Fig. 2). They represent high-temperature, hydrous partial melting of refractory mantle sources and are interpreted to form during initiation of subduction zones or in arc rifting events (Beccaluva and Serri, 1988).

HIMAG (high-Mg andesites, sanukitoids, bajaites) are andesites characterized by high MgO, Cr, Ni, and have abundances of HFSEs, LFSEs, and REEs that are more typical of calc-alkalic basalts and/or andesites (see below) than BON. They appear to represent hydrous partial melting of subduction contaminated mantle sources and are found in island arc settings that are characterized by an input of hot asthenospheric material associated with subduction of a spreading ridge (Saunders et al., 1987; Tatsumi and Maruyama, 1989) and/or formation of a slab window (Rogers and Saunders, 1989; Hole et al., 1991), active continental rifting (Luhr et al., 1989), and possibly with the initiation of normal back arc spreading (Tatsumi and Maruyama, 1989).

IAT (island arc tholeiites) represent partial melting of a mantle source similar to that of N-MORB, but which has been contaminated by mass transfer from the subducting slab. They are found in intraoceanic island arcs and are characterized by a tholeiitic differentiation trend. A representative mantle normalized diagram, shown in Figure 2, is characterized by depletion of the most incompatible elements and a negative Nb anomaly.

TIAT (transitional island arc tholeiites) have geochemical characteristics transitional between N-MORB and IAT, with depletion of the most incompatible elements and a weakly developed arc signature. Although not widely represented in modern environments, they are relatively common in the Notre Dame subzone. We interpret these rocks to form in back arc basin settings.

CAB (calc-alkalic basalts and/or andesites) display enrichment of the highly incompatible elements, strong negative Nb and positive Th anomalies, and commonly negative Ti anomalies on mantle-normalized diagrams. They represent partial melting of subduction-contaminated mantle sources and, in continental arcs, may also be affected by contamination by continental crust.

Felsic volcanic rocks of dacitic to rhyolitic composition are associated with CAB throughout the Notre Dame subzone. They are commonly enriched in the highly incompatible elements and exhibit prominent negative Nb and Ti (and locally Eu) and positive Th anomalies. In modern arc environments, they are generally considered to represent either the end result of fractional crystallization of mafic magmas or partial melting of crust, either oceanic arc or continental, at the base of the arc.

Nd isotope systematics

Epsilon Nd notation (ε_{Nd}) describes the time-integrated variation in the radiogenic Nd ratio ($^{143}Nd/^{144}Nd$) compared to the chondritic uniform reservoir (CHUR) (see Fig. 3). CHUR represents the evolution of an undifferentiated primitive mantle that began with the chondritic radiogenic $^{143}Nd/^{144}Nd$ ratio and Sm/Nd composition found in meteorites. The mantle reservoirs from which normal-MORB are derived are depleted in the light REEs relative to the primitive mantle (or CHUR), whereas the continental crust is the complementary reservoir, enriched in light REEs. Because Sm/Nd ratios in these reservoirs are nonchondritic, there are time-integrated differences in their respective radiogenic Nd isotopic signatures. The present day ε_{Nd} composition of the N-MORB reservoir ranges from about +8 to +14, and the present-day continental crust has negative values (generally < −3). It is crucial to calculate the ε_{Nd} of rocks at the

time of their formation, and to compare source materials of the same age. For the Notre Dame subzone, we have used an average age of 480 Ma for calculating ε_{Nd} and we have corrected the Nd isotopic signature of present-day reservoirs (compiled from the literature) to this time (Fig. 3).

Combining Nd and geochemical signatures

The basis of recognition of tectonic environments of ancient rocks is comparison of their geochemical and isotopic signatures with modern analogs. However, it is possible to acquire similar geochemical signatures by different processes. For example, the island arc signature (negative Nb anomaly) can result from subduction of continentally derived sediment and subsequent incorporation in the mantle wedge above the subducting plate before partial melting, or by contamination of a mafic magma with continental crust during ascent. Integration of geochemical and Nd isotopic data allows us to more precisely constrain the tectonic environment in which the geochemical signature was acquired. In the modern environment, arc volcanic rocks are erupted in both oceanic and continental settings. Arc CAB from these different settings may have very similar geochemical signatures, but ε_{Nd} in the continental setting ranges to much lower values. In intraoceanic island arcs remote from continental sources, sediment subduction does not typically produce negative ε_{Nd} values in arc volcanics. Lower ε_{Nd} values are prevalent in arcs built upon, or in close proximity to, continental lithosphere; these probably reflect either enhanced delivery of continentally derived sediment to the subduction zone, assimilation of time-integrated old continental crust by the ascending magmas, or some combination of the two.

GEOLOGIC SETTING OF THE NOTRE DAME SUBZONE

The Notre Dame subzone comprises the western half of the Dunnage zone in Newfoundland. It is bounded to the east and west by major structural zones, the Red Indian line (Williams et al., 1988; Fig. 1) and the Baie Verte line (Williams and St. Julien, 1978), respectively. Seismic reflection studies show that the entire Notre Dame subzone is allochthonous, underlain by the eastward-dipping extension of the ancient Laurentian continental margin (Marillier et al., 1989; Quinlan et al., 1992). Geologic data provide no evidence of the spatial relationships between the oceanic terranes and continental lithosphere during the Cambrian and Early Ordovician. For example, there are no geologic contacts exposed at the base of the sequence, no clasts of older predeformed or metamorphosed rocks in conglomerates or breccias, and no indications in sedimentary provenance of derivation from continental sources.

The Cambrian and Early Ordovician geologic record in the Notre Dame subzone is dominantly magmatic. The tectonic history of the Laurentian margin began about 615 ± 2 Ma (Kamo et al., 1989) with rifting of the supercontinent. The rift-drift transition occurred in the Early Cambrian (ca 545 Ma; Williams and Hiscott, 1987), and presumably oceanic crust was generated after this time, although none of this early crust was preserved (Dunning et al., 1991). Geochronological and geochemical evidence show that volcanic activity occurred for at least 40 m.y., from before 507 Ma to about 468 Ma (Elliot et al., 1991; Jenner et al., 1991; Dunning and Krogh, 1991) in a variety of stratigraphic and tectonic settings. Ordovician tonalitic plutonic rocks were intruded into the oceanic sequences between about 490 and 455 Ma (Whalen et al., this volume). Early Ordovician rocks in the Notre Dame subzone are unconformably overlain by Lower Silurian terrigenous volcanic rocks and related red clastic sedimentary rocks (Williams et al., 1988).

Accretion of outboard terranes to the Laurentian margin is generally considered to have begun during the Taconian orogeny, on the basis of ophiolite emplacement ages now preserved in the Humber zone. The timing of emplacement of oceanic rocks of the Notre Dame subzone upon the Laurentian margin is not constrained by direct data. However, they are generally considered to have been in place prior to the arrival of the Exploits subzone, considered on sedimentological grounds to have occurred in the Middle Ordovician (Williams et al., 1988; Colman-Sadd et al., 1992a).

In the following sections, a geographic framework has been adopted for description and discussion of the chemostratigraphy and isotopic characteristics of the various volcanic sequences in the Notre Dame subzone (Fig. 1). The areas are described from west to east in present coordinates. Details of the various lithostratigraphic units in each area are given in Table 3.

WESTERN OPHIOLITE BELT

Lithostratigraphy and geochemistry

Dominantly ophiolitic rocks in and immediately east of the Baie Verte line are best preserved in the Baie Verte Peninsula

TABLE 3. SUMMARY OF LITHOSTRATIGRAPHIC UNITS IN THE NOTRE DAME SUBZONE

Area	Group Name	Lithologies	Age	References
WOP	Grand Lake Complex/ Glover Group	Ophiolite overlain by volcanic/epiclastic sequences	Arenig	Knapp, 1983; Cawood and van Gool, 1993
	Betts Cv. Complex	Complete ophiolite from petrological Moho to extrusives	Ca. 489	Upadhyay et al., 1971; Coish and Church, 1979
	Snooks Arm Group	Volcanic/epiclastic (~50:50) sequence	Arenig	Jenner and Fryer, 1980
	Pacquet Harbour Group	Pillow lava	N/c	Gale, 1973; Hibbard, 1984
	Pt. Rousse Complex	Complete ophiolite, structurally disrupted	N/c	Norman and Strong, 1975; Hibbard, 1984
	Advocate Complex	Ophiolite, dismembered	N/c	Hibbard, 1984
WND	Lushs Bight Group/ lower Western Arm Group	Sheeted diabase dykes, pillow lava, pyroclastics at top	>Ca. 495 Ma.	Szybinski, 1995; Kean et al., 1995
	Cutwell/upper Western Arm Group	Pillow lava, felsic, volcanics, epiclastic rocks	Ca. 478-465 Ma.	Kean and Strong, 1975; Szybinski, 1995
EOP	Annieopsquotch/Star Lake/King George IV Complex	Mafic cumulate, sheeted dykes, pillow lava	Ca. 480 Ma.	Dunning, 1987; Dunning and Chorlton, 1985
	Skidder basalt	Pillow lava, trondhjemite	N/c	Pickett, 1987
	Hall Hill Complex	Mafic plutonic/volcanic rocks, minor trondhjemite	>Ca. 479 Ma.	Bostock et al., 1979; Dunning et al., 1987
END	Moreton's Harbour Group	Pillow lava, mafic dykes, felsic volcanics, epiclastic rocks	N/c	Strong and Payne, 1973
	Sleepy Cove Group	Pillow lava	>560 Ma.	Williams and Payne, 1975; Williams, 1994
BRA	Buchans, Robert's Arm, Cottrell's Cove, Chanceport Group	Mafic pillow lava, felsic volcanics lesser epiclastic rocks	CAB-475-484 Ma.	Thurlow and Swanson, 1987; Dec and Swinden, 1994

N/c = not constrained.

(Hibbard, 1984) and the Grand Lake area (Knapp, 1983). This belt of ophiolitic rocks is bounded to the west by the Baie Verte line and to the east by the Green Bay fault in the north, and by tonalitic intrusive rocks farther south. The most complete stratigraphic sequence is preserved in the western part of the Baie Verte Peninsula, where the Betts Cove Complex (an ophiolitic sequence lacking only the ultramafic tectonite) is stratigraphically overlain by a sequence of mafic volcanic and epiclastic rocks assigned to the Snooks Arm Group (Fig. 1). The more deformed Pacquet Harbour Group to the west consists mainly of mafic pillow lavas with lesser tuffaceous and silicic volcanic rocks. The Point Rousse Complex is composed of cumulate gabbro, diabase, and pillow lavas and highly altered ultramafic rocks disposed in a complex thrust stack. The Advocate Complex comprises disconnected slices of ophiolitic rocks (ultramafic rocks, gabbro, pillow lava) in a structural melange within the Baie Verte line. Farther south along the Baie Verte line, similar ophiolitic rocks are preserved in the Grand Lake Complex and the overlying Glover Group (Fig. 1).

Geochemical data show that the volcanic rocks are dominated by tholeiitic rocks of MORB, OIB, and IAT affinity (Fig. 4). Also present are BON, which locally form a significant component (e.g., Pacquet Harbour Group). Stratigraphic relationships among the various rock types are complex, but mutual crosscutting and other field relationships suggest that all are approximately coeval. The age of volcanism in this belt is constrained by a U-Pb date of 489+3/–2 on gabbro in the Betts Cove Complex (Dunning and Krogh, 1985), and lower-middle Arenig graptolites in the overlying Snooks Arm Group and in the Glover Formation east of Grand Lake (Williams, 1989).

Nd isotopes

As illustrated in Figure 5, the Nd isotopic composition of N-MORB and E-MORB rocks in the western ophiolite belt ranges from about +5.5 to +8.0. Coupled with the geochemical data, which show no negative Nb anomalies, this suggests that these rocks were derived from intraoceanic mantle sources. Primitive IAT and BON have ε_{Nd} ranging from about +5.2 to 7.2 and 0 to +4.2, respectively; the IAT overlap the MORB rocks, but BON rocks extend to lower ε_{Nd} values. The IAT, with ε_{Nd} values as high as +7.2, could have been derived from a source similar to that of the N-MORB rocks. However, their negative Nb anomalies as well as the lower ε_{Nd} in BON require a subducted sedimentary component derived from older crustal material.

WESTERN NOTRE DAME BAY

Lithostratigraphy and geochemistry

The western Notre Dame Bay area is bounded to the northwest by the Green Bay fault and to the southeast and south by the Lobster Cove fault (Fig. 1). The oldest rocks in this area are assigned to the Lushs Bight Group and part of the overlying Western Arm Group (Szybinski, 1995). The stratigraphic sequence recorded in these rocks comprises sheeted dikes and pillow lavas in the Lushs Bight Group (generally interpreted as a fragmented ophiolite; Kean et al., 1995) and pillow lavas, tuffs, and minor epiclastic rocks in the Western Arm Group. Magmatic rocks are dominantly mafic, tholeiitic, and have arc geochemical signatures (IAT, TIAT, lesser BON) (Fig. 6). Minor amounts of N-MORB occur in the Western Arm Group. In contrast to the western ophiolite belt, BONs in the Lushs Bight Group appear to be the oldest rocks observed, and are associated with tholeiitic rocks of clear arc affinity.

This sequence is cut by a series of high Mg andesitic dikes that postdate the first deformation of the stratified rocks. These dikes have strongly LREE–enriched patterns and negative Nb anomalies (Fig. 7), and show geochemical affinities with sanukitoids and bajaiites (Saunders et al., 1987; Rogers and Saunders, 1989; Tatsumi and Ishizaka, 1982). These rocks play a crucial role in establishing the age and tectonic history of the older stratified rocks, because they postdate the first deformation but do not cut the overlying Early Ordovician sequences (see below). The $^{40}Ar/^{39}Ar$ age of these dikes ranges within quoted errors from 488 to 501 Ma (Szybinski, 1995). The Lushs Bight Group and the older part of the Western Arm Group must be older than the oldest dikes that intrude them, i.e., Late Cambrian or older, rendering previously proposed correlations with the Ordovician Betts Cove Complex untenable.

The older stratified rocks are in fault contact with a younger sequence assigned to the upper Western Arm (including part of the former Catchers Pond Group) and Cutwell groups (Szybinski, 1995). These rocks are essentially bimodal mafic-felsic flow sequences punctuated by significant volumes of felsic pyroclastic and associated epiclastic rocks. The mafic volcanic rocks are dominantly CAB with strong arc signatures (Fig. 6). The age of volcanic rocks in this younger sequence is constrained by radiometric ages of 469+5/–3 (U-Pb, Dunning and Krogh, 1991), 479 ± 4 Ma (U-Pb, Szybinski, 1995), 462 ± 3 and 465 ± 1 Ma ($^{40}Ar/^{39}Ar$, Szybinski, 1995) and by Upper Arenig to Llandeilo conodonts in associated limestones in the Cutwell Group (O'Brien and Szybinski, 1989).

Nd isotopes

Nd isotopes in the western Notre Dame Bay area are variable, reflecting the geologic and geochemical diversity of the rocks. Rocks of IAT and MORB affinity in both the older and younger sequences have ε_{Nd} signatures indicating derivation from Ordovician depleted mantle (Fig. 8). BON exhibit ε_{Nd} values ranging from about 0 to +2.8. To satisfy both geochemical and isotopic constraints, both BON and IAT must have been derived from mantle sources contaminated by sediment from a subducting slab.

The ε_{Nd} of the HIMAG dikes that intrude the older sequence ranges from +2.8 to –3.5. The petrology and geochemistry of similar rocks in modern environments require a

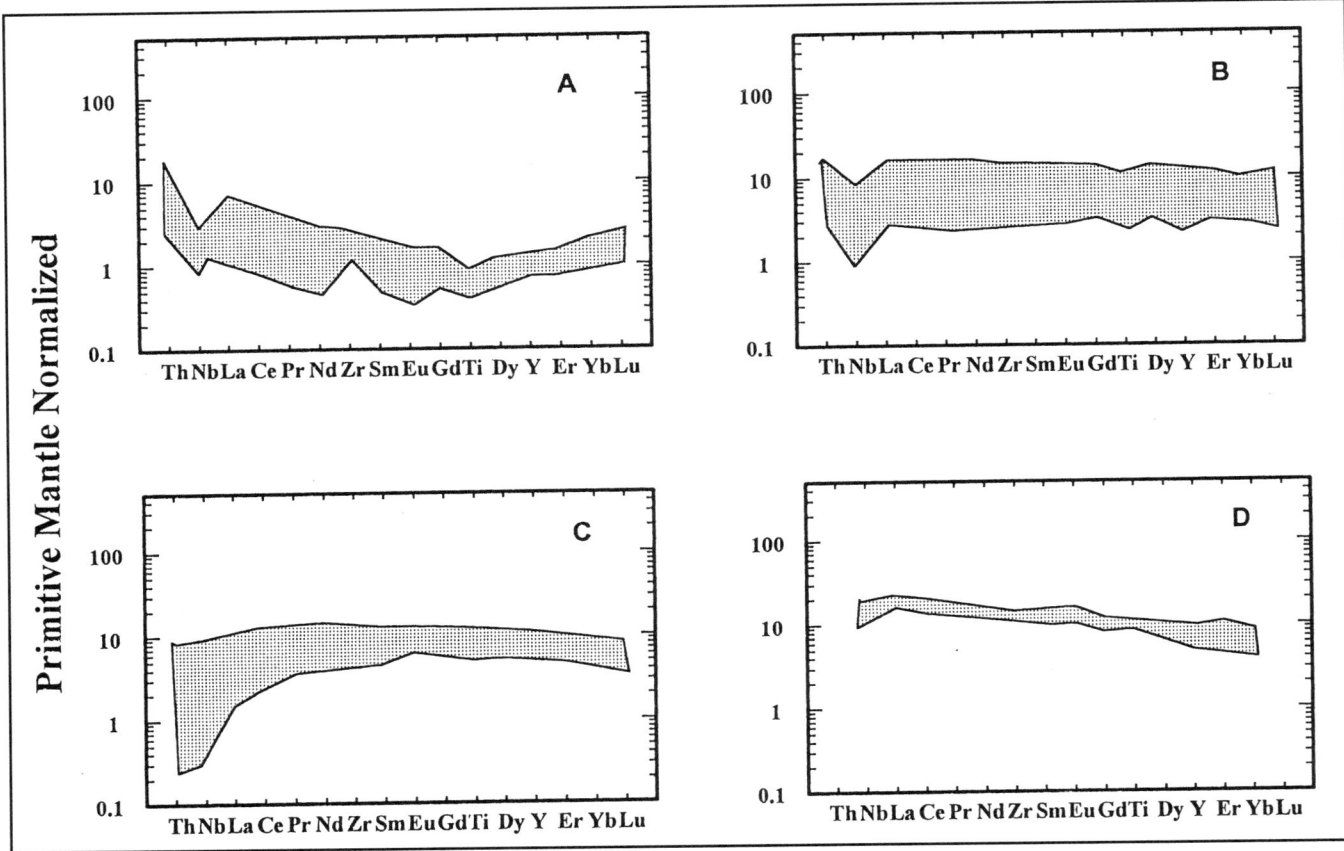

Figure 4 (on this and facing page). Geochemical characteristics of volcanic rocks in the western ophiolite belt. A: BON (boninite); B: IAT (island arc tholeiite); C: N-MORB (normal mid-ocean ridge
basalt); D: E-MORB (enriched-MORB). Tectonic discrimination diagrams in E, F, and G are from
Pearce and Cann (1971), Shervais (1982), and Jenner et al. (1991), respectively. Symbols for all geochemical and isotopic diagrams: nonarc rocks are black; normal-MORB is inverted triangle;
enriched-MORB is square; OIB (ocean island basalt) is diamond; arc rocks are white; IAT (island arc
tholeiites) is large upright triangle, BON (boninites) is small upright triangle, CAB (calc-alkalic
basalt) is circle.

substantial contribution from continental lithosphere (e.g.,
Saunders et al., 1987; Rogers and Saunders, 1989; Tatsumi
and Ishizaka, 1982). Geochemical and isotopic characteristics
of these rocks in the western Notre Dame Bay area also suggest that their petrogenesis involves mixing of mantle and
continental lithospheric sources (Fig. 8). More specifically,
Szybinski (1995) interpreted these rocks to have formed by
assimilation of continental lithosphere by a primitive, mantle-
derived magma.

The younger CAB rocks have low ε_{Nd} values, ranging from
+1.3 to +2.2. Although not as variable, nor as widely ranging, as
the HIMAG dikes, ε_{Nd} in these rocks is clearly less positive than
is typical of all modern intraoceanic environments, but is within
the range of values typical of continentally based island arcs
(Fig. 8). A continental influence in their petrogenesis is postulated. The Brighton gabbro, interpreted on geochemical and
geochronological evidence to be part of this calc-alkalic mag-

matic episode, has ε_{Nd} of −1.9, likewise apparently influenced by
continental lithosphere.

EASTERN OPHIOLITE BELT

Lithostratigraphy and geochemistry

The eastern ophiolite belt comprises disrupted ophiolitic
sequences that crop out in a northeast-trending linear belt from
east of Halls Bay to southwest of Red Indian Lake. The belt is
bounded to the west by Ordovician tonalitic intrusive rocks and
to the east by a series of faults that juxtapose the ophiolitic rocks
with the Buchans and Robert's Arm groups in the north and with
the Victoria Lake Group south of Red Indian Lake. The eastern
ophiolite belt is excised in Halls Bay between the Mansfield
Cove and Lobster Cove faults.

The southernmost lithostratigraphic units in this belt are

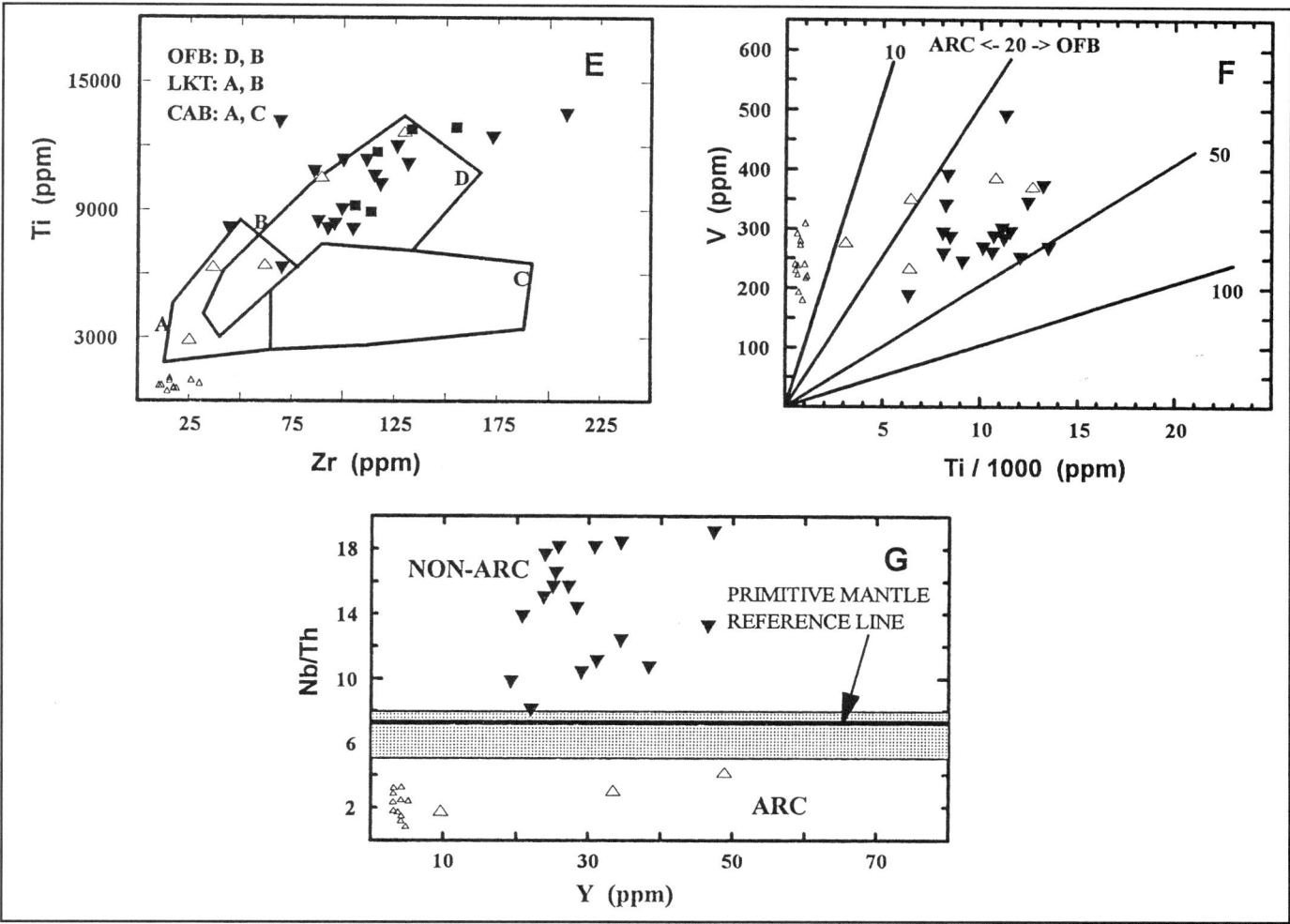

assigned to the Annieopsquotch, Star Lake, and King George IV complexes and the Skidder basalt. The Annieopsquotch Complex, most complete of these, comprises mafic cumulates, sheeted dikes, and pillow lavas with dominantly MORB geochemical signatures, and the Skidder basalt comprises mainly transitional IAT (Fig. 9). The Annieopsquotch Complex has yielded U-Pb ages of 478+3/–2 and 481+4/–2 (Dunning and Krogh, 1985).

Slivers of ophiolitic rocks are believed to be present in the Hungry Mountain Complex west of Red Indian Lake (some aspects of their chemistry are discussed by Whalen et al., this volume). The Hall Hill Complex immediately east and south of Halls Bay comprises dominantly mafic intrusive rocks (pyroxenite, gabbro, diabase), minor pillow lava, and trondhjemite, and is intruded by trondhjemite of the Mansfield Cove Complex, which has been dated as 479 ± 3; (Dunning et al., 1987).

The three radiometric ages in the eastern ophiolite belt are younger within the quoted errors than the radiometric age of the Betts Cove Complex (489+3/–2). This indicates that ophiolites in the eastern belt are probably younger than those in the western belt.

Nd isotopes

The only Nd isotopic data from the eastern ophiolite belt come from the Annieopsquotch Complex and the Skidder basalt. N-MORB and IAT lavas have ε_{Nd} ranging from +7.6 to +8.3 and +5.2 to +8.4, respectively (Fig. 10). These data indicate that rocks in the eastern ophiolite belt were sourced mainly in depleted mantle. A minor component of slab-derived contamination is indicated by the transitional arc signatures in some of the lavas.

EASTERN NOTRE DAME BAY

Lithostratigraphy and geochemistry

The eastern Notre Dame Bay area includes volcanic, subvolcanic, and intrusive rocks assigned to the Moreton's Harbour

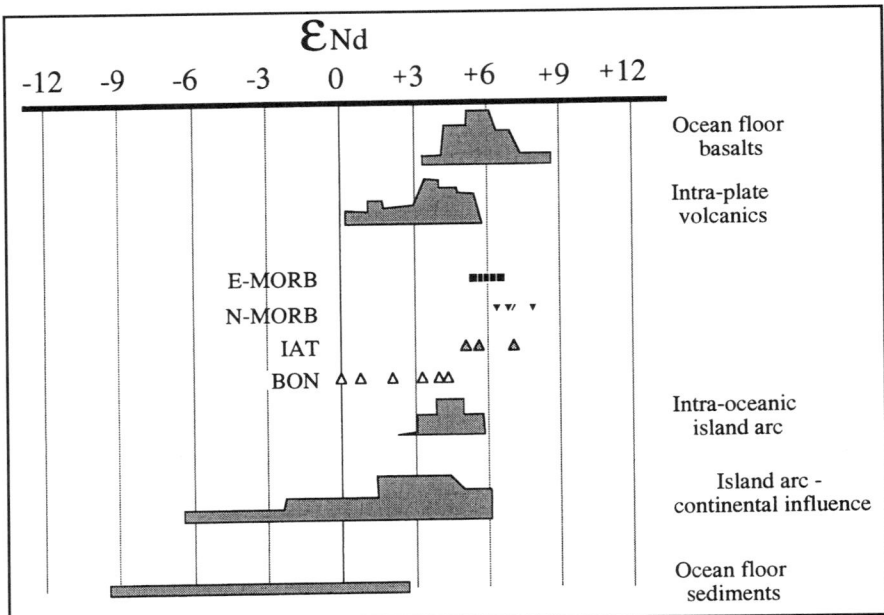

Figure 5. Summary of Nd isotopic data for the western ophiolite belt. Compilations of Nd isotopic data from various modern environments, described in the methodology section, are recalculated to 480 Ma. MORB = mid-ocean ridge basalt; IAT = island-arc tholeiite; BON = boninite.

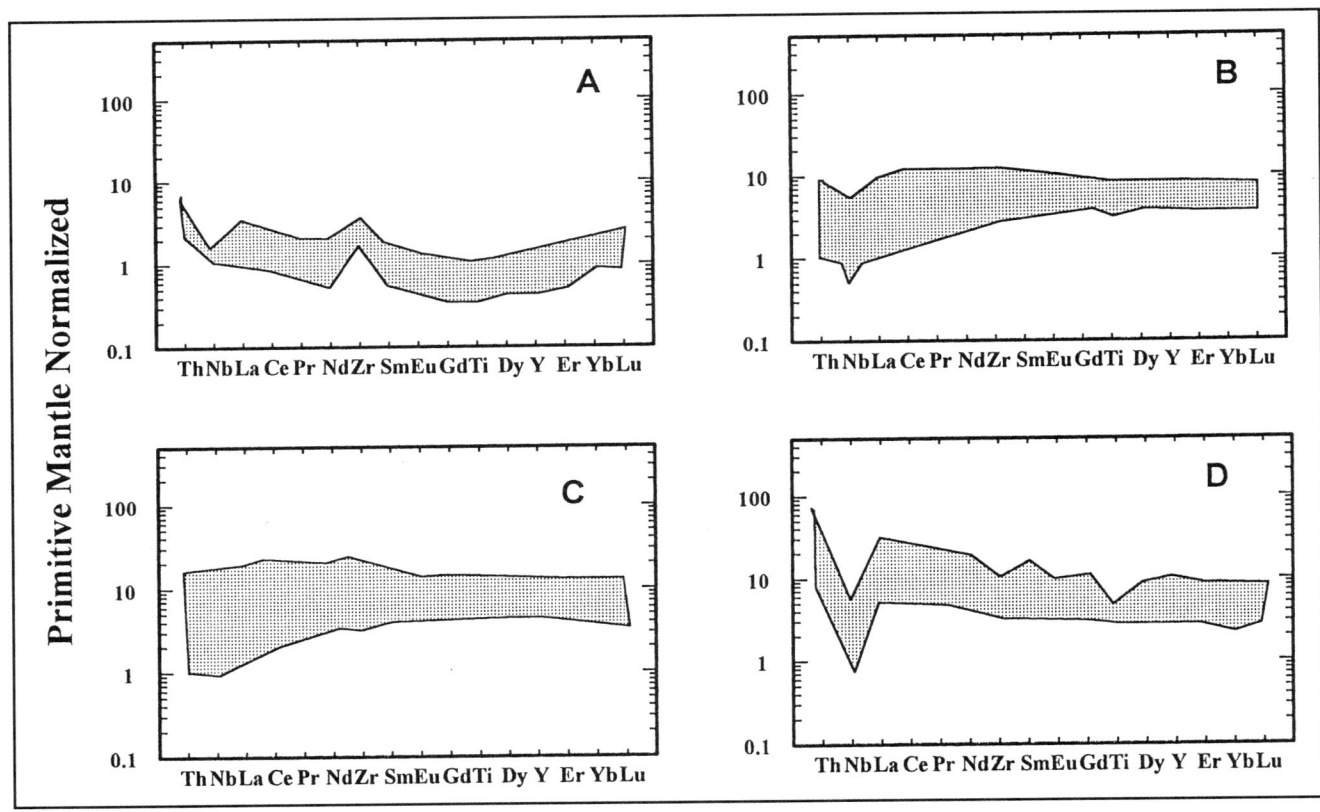

Figure 6 (on this and facing page). Geochemical characteristics of volcanic rocks in the Western Notre Dame Bay area. A: BON; B: IAT; C: N-MORB and E-MORB; D: CAB. Tectonic discrimination diagrams, symbols, and abbreviations as in Figure 4.

(Strong and Payne, 1973; Kay and Strong, 1983) and the Sleepy Cove (Williams and Payne, 1975) groups (Fig. 1). It is bounded to the south by the Chanceport fault. The Moreton's Harbour Group comprises mainly pillow lavas and sheeted dikes as well as significant volumes of epiclastic rocks and rhyolite. We have no geochemical data from this group and there is no direct control on its age.

The Sleepy Cove Group comprises mafic pillow lava and lesser massive mafic flows, subvolcanic intrusions, and local felsic volcanic rocks (Williams and Payne, 1975; Williams, 1994). It is intruded by the Twillingate trondhjemite, which has been dated (U-Pb, zircon) as 507+3/–2 (Elliot et al., 1991). Pillow lavas in the Sleepy Cove Group are of TIAT affinity (Fig. 11).

Nd isotopes

There are no Nd isotopic data from volcanic rocks in this area. However, two published analyses from the Twillingate trondhjemite yielded ε_{Nd} of about +3 and +6 (Fryer et al., 1992). This, coupled with the REE systematics of the trondhjemite (flat REE patterns with pronounced negative Nb anomalies), suggests that it was formed through partial melting of mafic rocks in the roots of an older island arc (cf. Payne and Strong, 1979). Following Strong and Payne (1973), we consider the Sleepy Cove Group to comprise the extrusive products of this arc complex.

BUCHANS–ROBERT'S ARM BELT

Lithostratigraphy and geochemistry

The Buchans–Robert's Arm volcanic belt (Dean, 1978) comprises a linear belt of mafic and felsic and lesser epiclastic rocks that can be traced from Red Indian Lake northward to Halls Bay and then eastward across Notre Dame Bay to New World Island. South of Halls Bay, it is bounded to the west by the faults that juxtapose it with the eastern ophiolite belt. Across

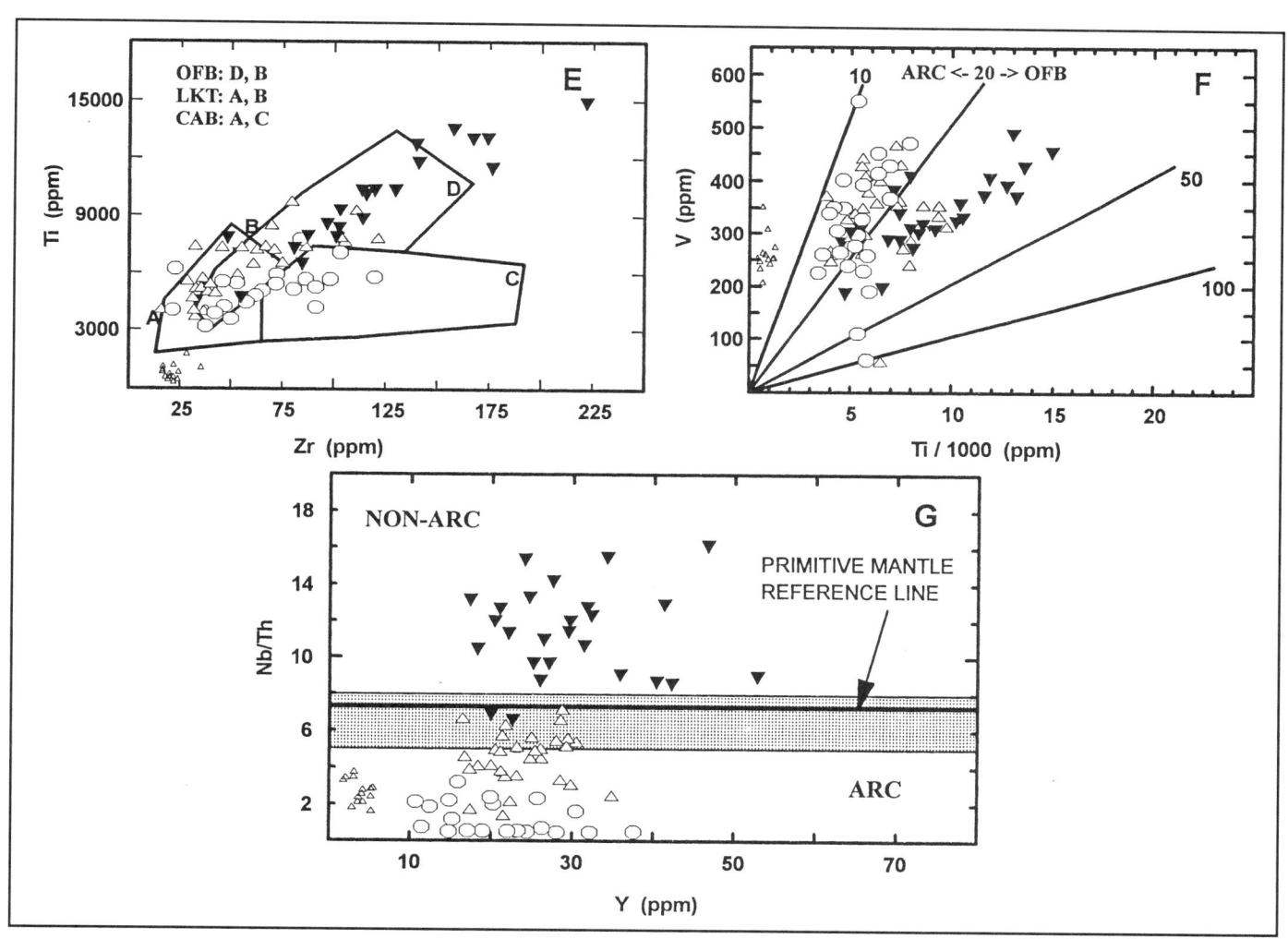

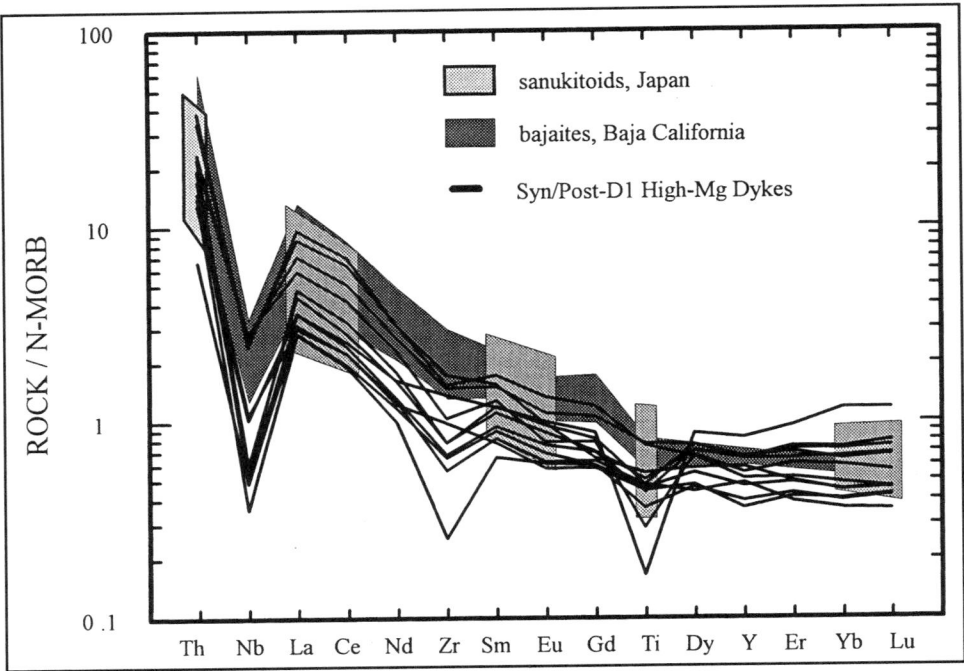

Figure 7. Geochemistry of HIMAG dikes in the western Notre Dame Bay area. Shown for comparison are compositions of sanukitoids from the Sentouchi belt, Japan (Tatsumi and Ishizaka, 1982) and bajaites from Baja California (Saunders et al., 1987; Rogers and Saunders, 1989).

Notre Dame Bay, it is bounded to the north by the Lobster Cove and Chanceport faults. The Buchans–Robert's Arm belt comprises four lithostratigraphic units, the Buchans, Robert's Arm, Cottrell's Cove, and Chanceport groups. Geochemical data indicate that throughout the strike extent of the belt, both calc-alkalic and tholeiitic rocks are present (Fig. 12).

The CAB rocks are dominated by amygdaloidal pillow lavas, locally reddened by oxidation, with lesser high-silica rhyolites and relatively minor amounts of volcanically derived sedimentary rocks. The most detailed lithostratigraphy for these rocks has been recognized in the Buchans area, where five formations have been identified, disposed in a southeast-verging fold and thrust belt (Thurlow and Swanson, 1987; Thurlow et al., 1993). The mafic rocks are dominantly andesitic with a lesser basaltic component and are uniformly LREE enriched with very strong negative Nb and positive Th anomalies and prominent negative Ti anomalies. In terms of Gill's (1981) classification, most of these rocks could be termed high-K andesites. Minor variations in the slope of the patterns and the relative size of the Nb, Th, and Ti anomalies along the belt can be recognized and used to aid in lithostratigraphic correlation (Dec and Swinden, 1994). Felsic volcanic rocks likewise tend to be strongly LREE enriched, with geochemical signatures typical of silicic rocks derived from continental crust.

Rhyolites, the only rocks in the calc-alkalic successions from which radiometric dates have been obtained, have yielded two U-Pb (zircon) ages of 474 (+3/–2) (the Buchans and Robert's

Arm groups, respectively; Dunning et al., 1987) and one U-Pb age of 484 ± 2 (the Cottrell's Cove Group; Dec et al., in press). The younger radiometric age is consistent with the presence of Llanvirnian conodonts in carbonate breccia in the Buchans Group (Nowlan and Thurlow, 1984).

The tholeiitic rocks are most abundant on the eastern side of the belt, adjacent to the Red Indian line. The tholeiitic sequence includes a substantially larger component of epiclastic sedimentary rocks than does the calc-alkalic sequence.

The tholeiitic rocks exhibit a wide range of geochemical signatures, including MORB, E-MORB, TIAT, IAT, and OIB (Fig. 12). There are few good stratigraphic relationships preserved among these rocks, and most are structurally interleaved. The OIB lavas are geochemically distinct, have steep REE patterns and pronounced positive Nb anomalies, and are restricted to a single area in the Robert's Arm Group.

The tholeiitic rocks do not lend themselves to radiometric age determinations and no fauna have been discovered within them. Tholeiitic lavas in this belt and those in the adjacent eastern ophiolite belt have similar geochemical signatures, and this, coupled with their close proximity and similar structural setting, suggests that they may be coeval (i.e., ca. 486 to 476). This is consistent with the only direct evidence for the age of these rocks; Dec and Swinden (1994) described epiclastic debris flows in the Cottrell's Cove Group containing clasts of CAB lava (ca. 484 Ma) that stratigraphically overlie a tholeiitic flow with E-MORB characteristics.

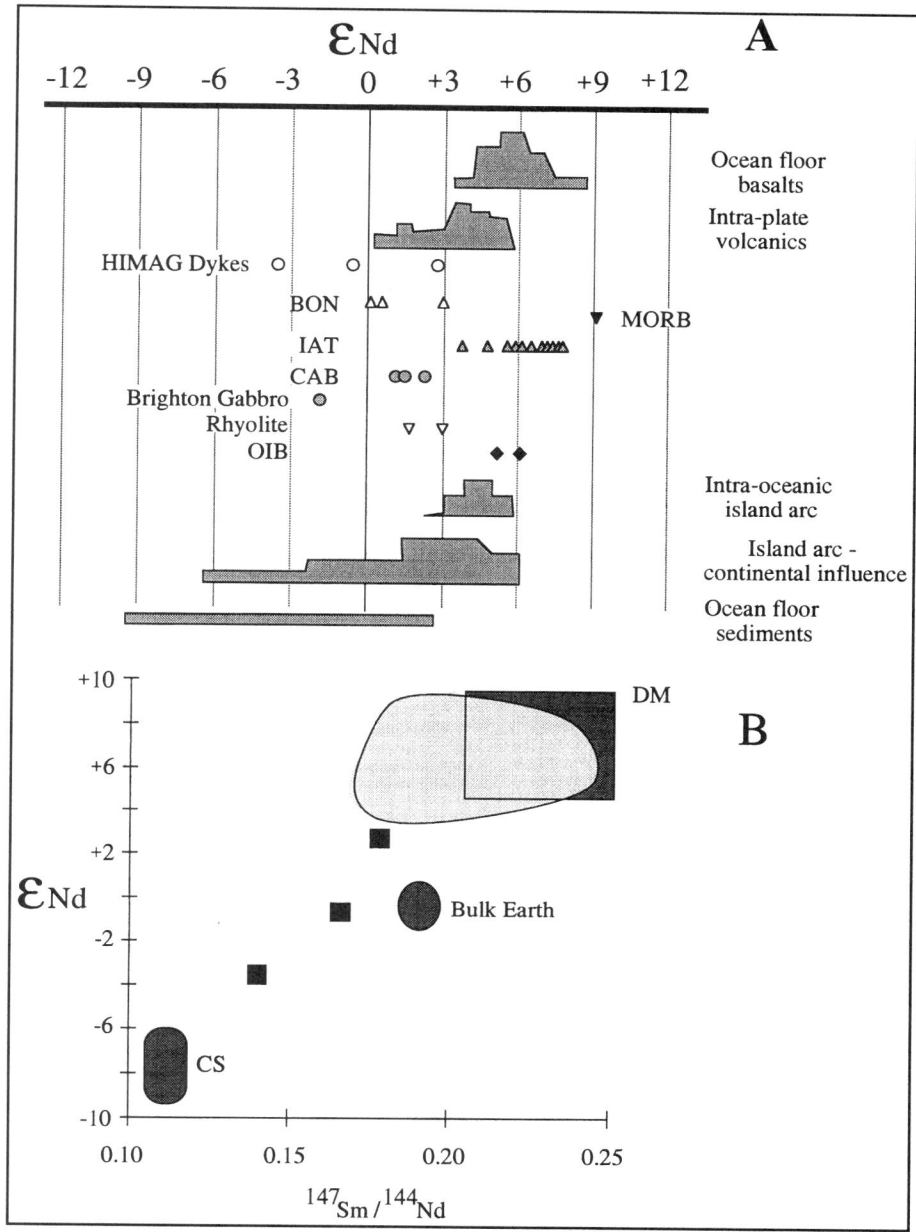

Figure 8. Summary of Nd isotopic data for the western Notre Dame Bay area. In A, compilations of Nd isotopic data from various modern environments are described in the methodology section. In B, HIMAG dikes (black squares) are shown on a Nd isochron diagram, illustrating the mixing relationship between depleted mantle (DM) and continental crust (CS) (fields from Swinden et al., 1990). The light screened field is the field of Lushs Bight Group, lower Western Arm Group tholeiites.

Nd isotopes

Tholeiitic rocks in the Buchans–Robert's Arm belt are similar isotopically to tholeiitic rocks in the ophiolite belts to the west. The ε_{Nd} in IAT ranges from +5 to +8, and in OIBs ranges from +4.9 to +6.3 (Fig. 13). None of these rocks require a con-

tinental crustal influence in their petrogenesis, although rocks with negative Nb anomalies require a component of subducted sediment.

The CAB mafic rocks, in contrast, have ε_{Nd} ranging from +4.2 to –2.7 and isotopically overlap the upper Western Arm–Cutwell groups CAB rocks in the western Notre Dame Bay area.

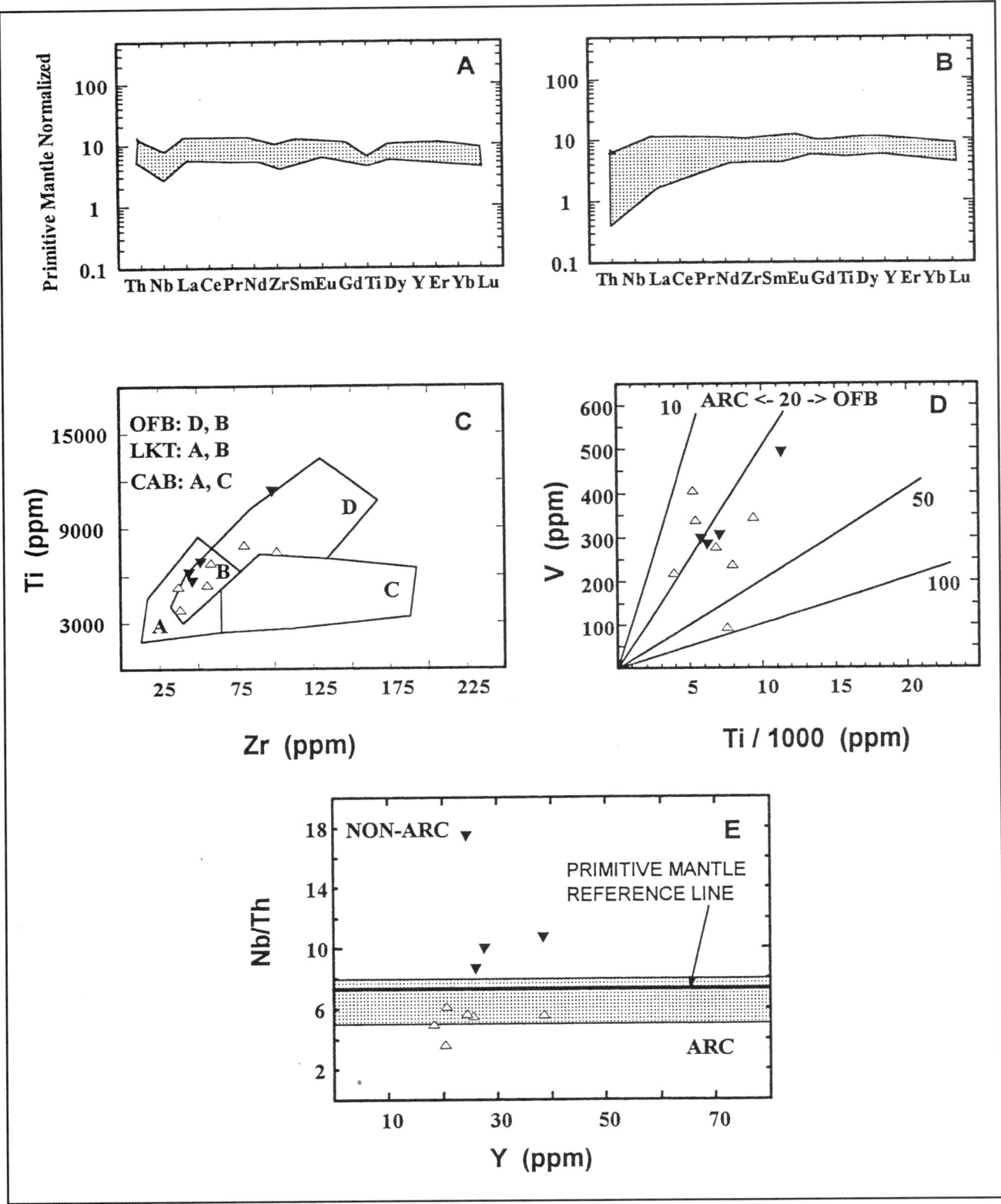

Figure 9. Geochemical characteristics of volcanic rocks in the eastern ophiolite belt. A—IAT; B—N-MORB. Tectonic discrimination diagrams, symbols, and abbreviations as in Figure 4.

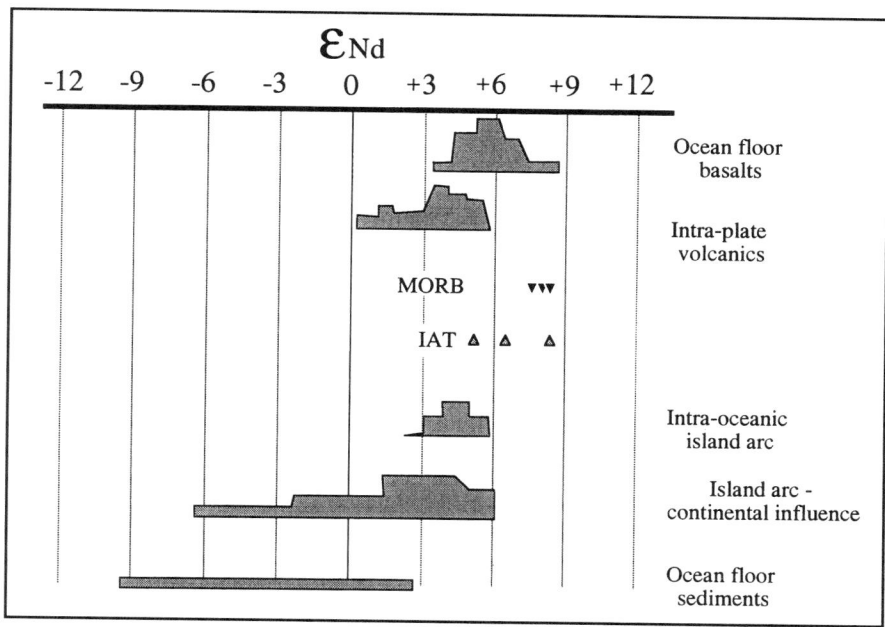

Figure 10. Summary of Nd isotopic data for the eastern ophiolite belt. Compilations of Nd isotopic data from various modern environments are described in the methodology section.

A role for continental lithosphere in their petrogenesis is clearly indicated. A role for continental lithosphere is also clearly indicated for the rhyolitic rocks in this sequence, which have ε_{Nd} ranging from +2.2 to –10.

VOLCANIC HISTORY OF THE LAURENTIAN MARGIN OF IAPETUS

General statement

Our data indicate that Cambrian and Ordovician magmatism in the Notre Dame subzone in Newfoundland can be conveniently considered in terms of a minimum of four broad events defined on the basis of temporal and paleotectonic constraints. The sequence of events and their broad spatial relationships with respect to the Laurentian margin are illustrated in Figure 14. Geochemical and isotopic evidence allows us to interpret the tectonic settings of these rocks and to track the magmatic evolution and the history of interaction of mantle and continental sources on a regional scale.

Event 1: Pre-ca. 500 Ma Cambrian back arc(s)

The oldest magmatic rocks in the Notre Dame subzone are found in the western and eastern Notre Dame Bay areas. Minimum ages are provided by crosscutting intrusions; on the basis of similar lithological and geochemical character and structural position (north of the Lobster Cove–Chanceport faults), our favoured interpretation is that the +500 Ma magmatic rocks in the two areas are correlative. This being the case, their minimum age is defined by the Twillingate trondhjemite (507+3/–2 Ma) and an E-MORB

dike in the lower Western Arm Group (506 ± 5 Ma; Szybinski, 1995). Detailed field relationships and the geochemical and isotopic signatures suggest that the Twillingate trondhjemite and the dated E-MORB dike are approximately coeval with the dominantly tholeiitic arc and nonarc volcanic successions (e.g., see Szybinski, 1995). This being the case, ophiolite generation in this portion of the Notre Dame subzone was initiated substantially earlier than has previously been supposed.

These rocks apparently record the earliest postdrift magmatism preserved on the Laurentian margin, an episode of submarine volcanism and plutonism that initially comprised BON and IAT and TIAT with generally weak arc signatures evolving into an environment in which some magmas were derived from mantle unaffected by subduction. Geochemical and Nd isotopic data indicate that the boninitic and tholeiitic magmatism can be reasonably modeled as resulting from partial melting of refractory and normal depleted mantle sources, variably contaminated by mass transfer from a subducting slab. At about 506 Ma trondhjemite with juvenile geochemical characteristics, inherited either through partial melting of primitive arc crust, or through fractionation of arc magmas, invaded the arc sequences. The magmatic succession from arc to nonarc volcanism intruded by tonalitic plutons derived from similar source materials is similar to the record of magmatism in modern arc–back arc systems. For example, in Fiji, tonalitic plutonism similar in character to the Twillingate trondhjemite (Gill and Stork, 1979) intruded as little as 2–3 m.y. after eruption of the host lavas.

The stratigraphic, geochemical, and isotopic data suggest a tectonic environment in which magmatism representing both normal and refractory arc and nonarc mantle sources as well as

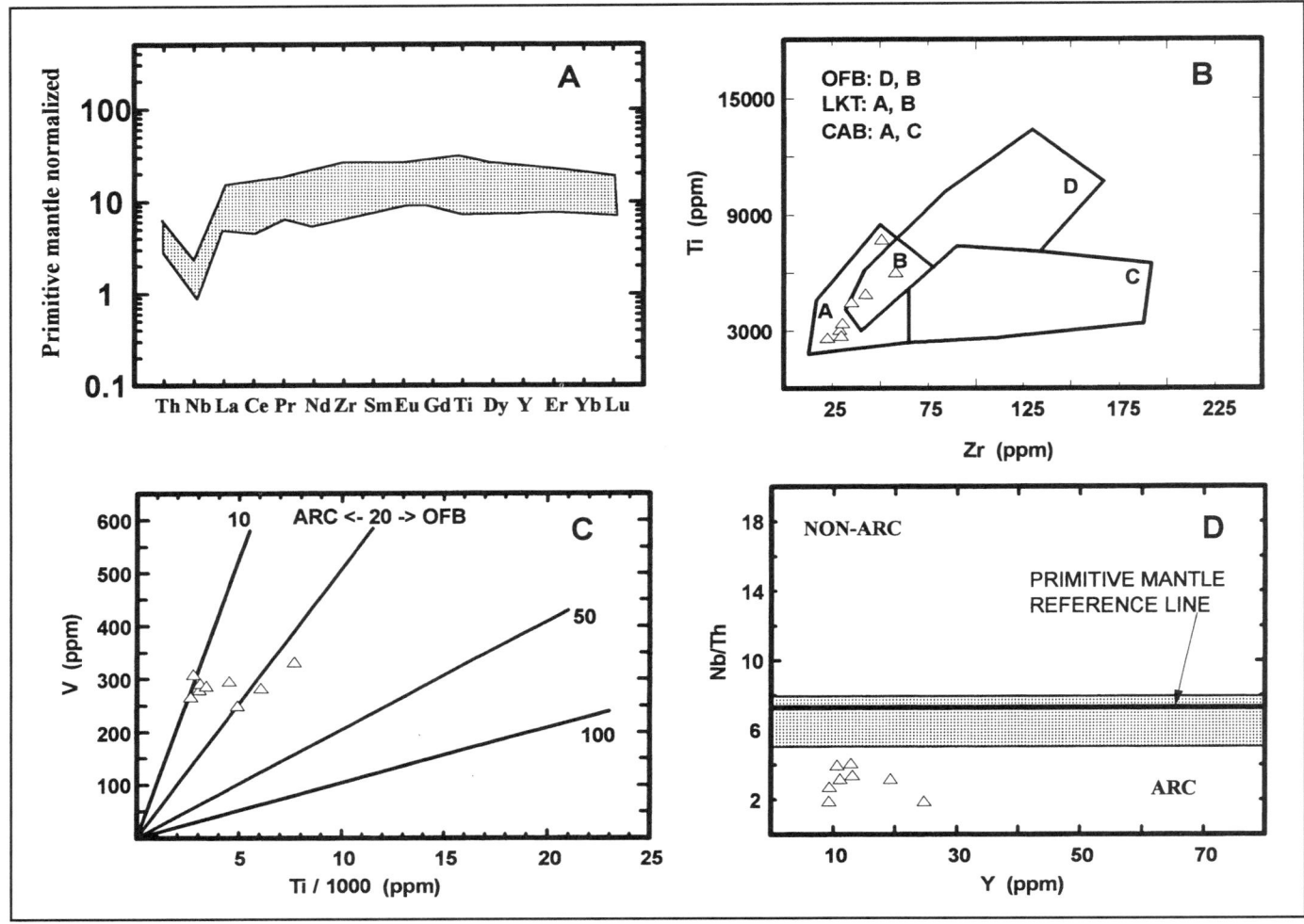

Figure 11. Geochemical characteristics of volcanic rocks in the eastern Notre Dame Bay area. A—
Primitive mantle normalized diagram for Sleepy Cove Group basalts. Tectonic discrimination diagrams, symbols, and abbreviations as in Figure 4.

basal arc sources (mafic volcanics, trondhjemites, respectively) were closely associated in time and space. Our favored interpretation is that these rocks collectively record a Late Cambrian back arc basin. The fact that nonarc rocks only occur in the topmost part of the sequence may indicate that input of new, uncontaminated asthenosphere occurred in the late stages of arc development. MORB-like rocks in the lower Western Arm Group may therefore signal the beginning of a mature stage of back arc volcanism, in which arc-related rocks had migrated away from the subduction zone and magmatism was relatively less influenced by slab-contaminated mantle.

Event 2: ca. 495 Ma early rift intrusions

The intrusion of HIMAG mafic dikes between about 501 and 488 Ma in the western Notre Dame Bay area provides two critical constraints on our interpretation of the magmatic and tec-

tonic history of the early Paleozoic Laurentian margin. First, field relations show that the Lushs Bight Group was deformed prior to intrusion of these dikes. This deformation (D_1) must, therefore, be at least Late Cambrian in age. Second, the geochemical and isotopic data show that the petrogenesis of these dikes involves a substantial component of old continental lithosphere. This suggests that the Lushs Bight and lower Western Arm groups were deformed and emplaced upon continental lithosphere as early as the latest Cambrian. This being the case, D_1 in these rocks may be related to emplacement.

Coupled with the earlier date on the emplacement of the Hare Bay allochthon (Dallmeyer, 1977), which has not been widely integrated in tectonic models for the Laurentian margin, the age and character of HIMAG dikes provide substantive evidence that oceanic rocks were emplaced upon Laurentia at a very early stage of its history. It is clear that some old ophiolitic rocks were transported onto the Laurentian margin well before ca.

476 Ma, the age of the metamorphic aureole at the base of the allochthonous Bay of Island complex (Dallmeyer and Williams, 1975), which is widely cited as marking the initiation of the Taconian orogeny.

The intrusion of these HIMAG dikes, by analogy with other areas where similar rocks have been recognized (e.g., Japan, Baja California), probably records a period of crustal rifting and anomalous heat injection at the Laurentian margin, allowing elevation of geotherms and promoting hydrous partial melting and easy access of the resulting melts to upper crustal levels.

Event 3: ca. 490–475 back arc basin(s)

Immediately following (or perhaps temporally overlapping) intrusion of the HIMAG dikes on the already composite Laurentian margin, a long-lived episode of tholeiitic basaltic volcanism was initiated. The oldest representatives of this event are preserved in the western ophiolite belt, where early MORB and/or BON and IAT volcanic activity is preserved. Subsequent volcanism with E-MORB character (Snooks Arm, Glover groups) is interbedded with thick sequences of volcanically derived turbidites. Previous studies have suggested that the Betts Cove and/or Snooks Arm sequence, the best preserved of the early ophiolitic sequences, represents rifting of an island arc and the subsequent establishment of a back arc basin (Coish and Church, 1979; Jenner and Fryer, 1980; Coish et al., 1982).

Extrusive rocks in the eastern ophiolite belt are dominantly N-MORB-like, have significant volumes of IAT, and contain no BON. Considering that these rocks are slightly younger than those in the western ophiolite belt, it is possible that they represent a relatively more mature stage of back arc development, characterized by magmatic activity further removed from the influence of the subducting slab.

Tholeiitic rocks in the Buchans–Robert's Arm belt are also tentatively interpreted to have formed during this magmatic event. Although rocks that are geochemically very similar to the Annieopsquotch Complex lavas are represented in these sequences, they display a much wider range of geochemical types than the eastern ophiolite belt, including OIB, transitional IAT, and true IAT. All rocks, regardless of their geochemical signatures, have Nd isotopic characteristics indicating derivation from depleted mantle sources. Because evidence for their age is sparse, we are unable to say whether all tholeiitic rocks in the Buchans–Robert's Arm belt are coeval.

Collectively, tholeiitic rocks of the western and eastern ophiolite belts and the Buchans–Robert's Arm belt record a protracted time period in the Early Ordovician when oceanic island arcs and back arc basins were active outboard of the Laurentian margin. There is no indication that any of the resultant magmatism was petrogenetically influenced by continental lithosphere. Evidence is inconclusive as to whether these various oceanic tholeiitic rocks represent different stages of development of a single back arc basin.

Event 4: ca. 484–475 Ma calc-alkalic island arc

Bimodal mafic-felsic volcanism, preserved throughout the Buchans–Robert's Arm belt and in the Cutwell–upper Western Arm groups in the western Notre Dame Bay area, is characterized by calc-alkalic basalt and/or andesite and high-silica rhyolite. Early Ordovician hornblende-rich intrusions in the western Notre Dame Bay area (e.g., Brighton Gabbro) are part of the same magmatic episode.

The geochemistry and Nd isotopic data suggest that magmatism was generally similar in all areas, minor local variations in petrogenesis being reflected in relatively minor contrasts in geochemical signatures. The very strong positive Th and negative Nb anomalies are a feature of almost all mafic rocks in the belt. Detailed geochemical interpretation of the Cutwell Group rocks (Szybinski, 1995) as well as ε_{Nd} signatures of the Robert's Arm, Buchans, upper Western Arm, and Cottrell's Cove groups, suggest a substantial contribution by continental lithosphere to the magma. Mafic rocks with ε_{Nd} as low as −3 are not found in any modern ensimatic arcs; in fact, these values are more negative than most mafic volcanic rocks in modern ensialic arcs (e.g., Japan). The ε_{Nd} values in the silicic rocks are locally even more negative, up to −10, strongly indicating that these rocks in some instances formed through the melting of dominantly continental lithosphere. Taken together, the geochemistry and Nd isotope data for these rocks strongly suggest that the island arc they represent was built upon a basement of continental lithosphere.

The age data show that calc-alkalic volcanism occurred over a longer time span than has been previously supposed. A substantial part of the calc-alkalic volcanic episode overlaps in time with at least some of the mantle-derived Early Ordovician tholeiitic volcanism in the ophiolite belts, although this style of volcanism continued for some time following production of the back arc ophiolitic rocks. That tholeiitic volcanic rocks can be shown to lie stratigraphically above CAB rocks in the Bay of Exploits provides evidence of the (at least local) proximity of calc-alkalic and tholeiitic volcanic eruption.

RELATIONSHIPS TO COEVAL TONALITE-TRONDHJEMITE PLUTONISM

Felsic volcanic rocks are commonly associated with CAB in the Lower Ordovician arc sequences of the Buchans–Robert's Arm and western Notre Dame Bay areas. Radiometric dates of rocks in the Western Arm, Cutwell, Robert's Arm, Buchans, and Cottrell's Cove groups, already cited, show that rhyolitic volcanism occurred from at least ca. 484 to 468 Ma. Geochemical analyses of felsic volcanic rocks from these groups are illustrated in Figure 15. These rocks range from low-Si to high-Si rhyolites ($SiO_2 = 65\%$ to 74%), are LREE enriched, and have prominent negative Nb and positive Th anomalies and a pronounced negative Ti anomaly on primitive mantle normalized plots. Nd isotopic analyses of four of these rocks have yielded ε_{Nd} ranging from +2 to −4 and a single analysis from the Cottrell's Cove Group has

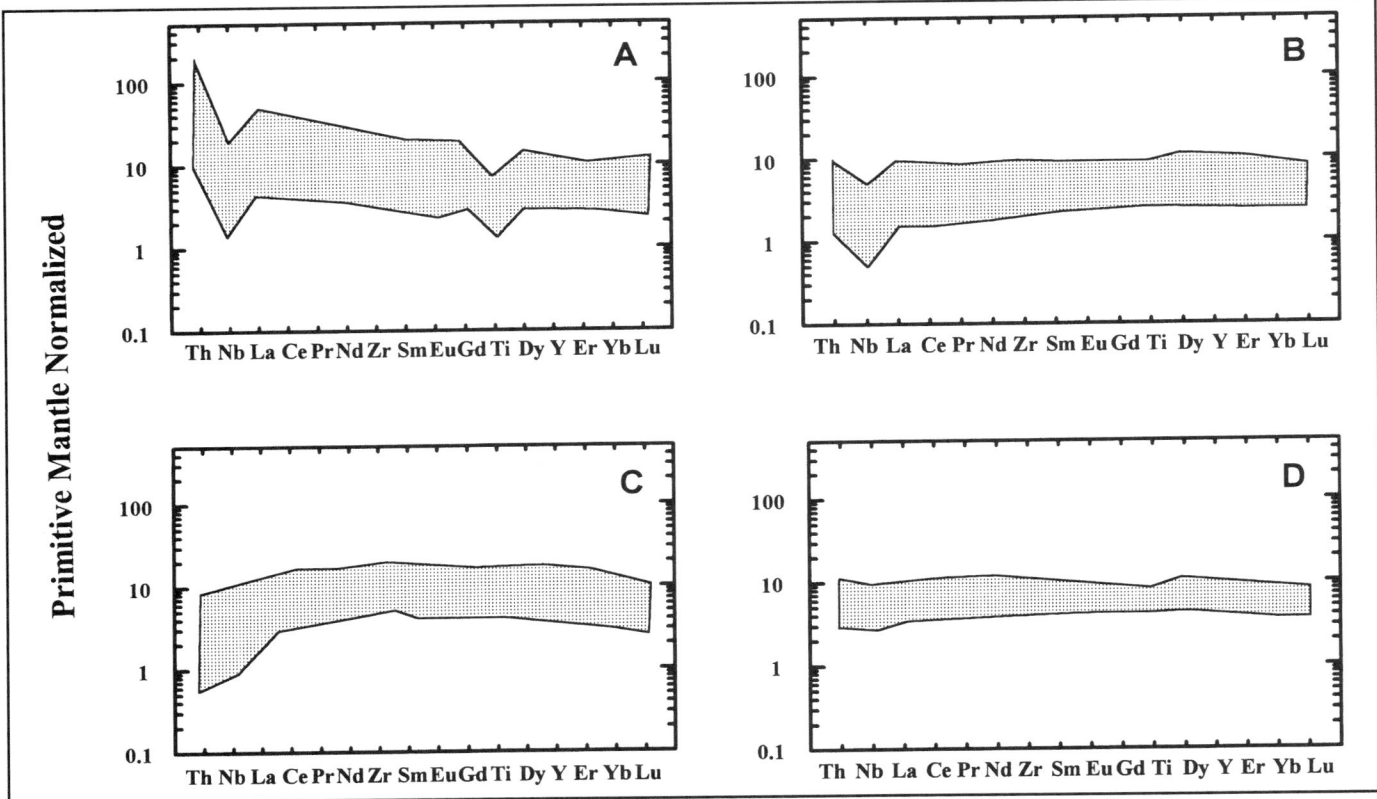

Figure 12 (on this and facing page). Geochemical characteristics of volcanic rocks in the Buchans–Robert's Arm area. A: CAB; B: IAT; C: N-MORB; D: E-MORB; E: OIB. Tectonic discrimination diagrams, symbols, and abbreviations as in Figure 4.

yielded ε_{Nd} of −10 (Figs. 8 and 13). The isotopic data require a significant component of continental lithosphere in the petrogenesis of these rhyolites.

The geochemical signatures of rhyolites in the Early Ordovician arc sequences substantially overlap in time with tonalitic plutonism at the Laurentian margin (Whalen et al., this volume) and exhibit similar geochemical and isotopic signatures (ε_{Nd} of the tonalitic rocks range from ~ +2 to ~ −13; Whalen et al., this volume). In particular, the Robert's Arm Group rhyolites are very similar geochemically and isotopically to the arc-type tonalites and diorites with (La/Yb)n <12 from areas immediately west of the Buchans–Robert's Arm belt (areas 2 and 3 of Whalen et al., this volume). It would appear that felsic volcanic rocks and tonalitic plutonic rocks intruded into the Early Ordovician Laurentian margin represent similar magma sources and petrogenetic processes.

RELATIONSHIPS TO THE WESTERN NEWFOUNDLAND ALLOCHTHONOUS OPHIOLITIC ROCKS

Ophiolitic rocks in the western Newfoundland allochthons are widely considered to have been derived from the Notre Dame subzone of the Dunnage zone during Taconian tectonism (e.g.,

Church and Stevens, 1971; Williams, 1979; Williams and Hatcher, 1983). Disparate ages yielded by the metamorphic aureoles of the St. Anthony and Bay of Islands complexes (ca. 495 Ma and ca. 476 Ma, respectively) have generally been interpreted as reflecting diachronous convergence during oblique collision of oceanic tectonic elements with the continental margin (Dallmeyer, 1977; Williams and Hatcher, 1983; Colman-Sadd et al., 1992b). In the context of our synthesis, some brief comments on the correlation of the allochthons with tectonic environments represented by the Notre Dame subzone are appropriate.

Ophiolitic rocks in the St. Anthony complex were apparently emplaced upon the Laurentian margin ca. 495 Ma, the age of metamorphic zircons in the thermal aureole (Jamieson, 1988). This ophiolite is, therefore, substantially older than the Early Ordovician ophiolites in the Notre Dame subzone and is potentially a temporal correlative of the volcanic sequences in the western and eastern Notre Dame Bay areas. Available age data are consistent with, although they do not demand, the St. Anthony Complex and the Lushs Bight and Sleepy Cove sequences having been emplaced on the Laurentian margin during the same Late Cambrian event.

The Bay of Islands Complex (ca. 486 Ma; MORB, IAT lavas; Jenner et al., 1991) can be correlated in terms of age and

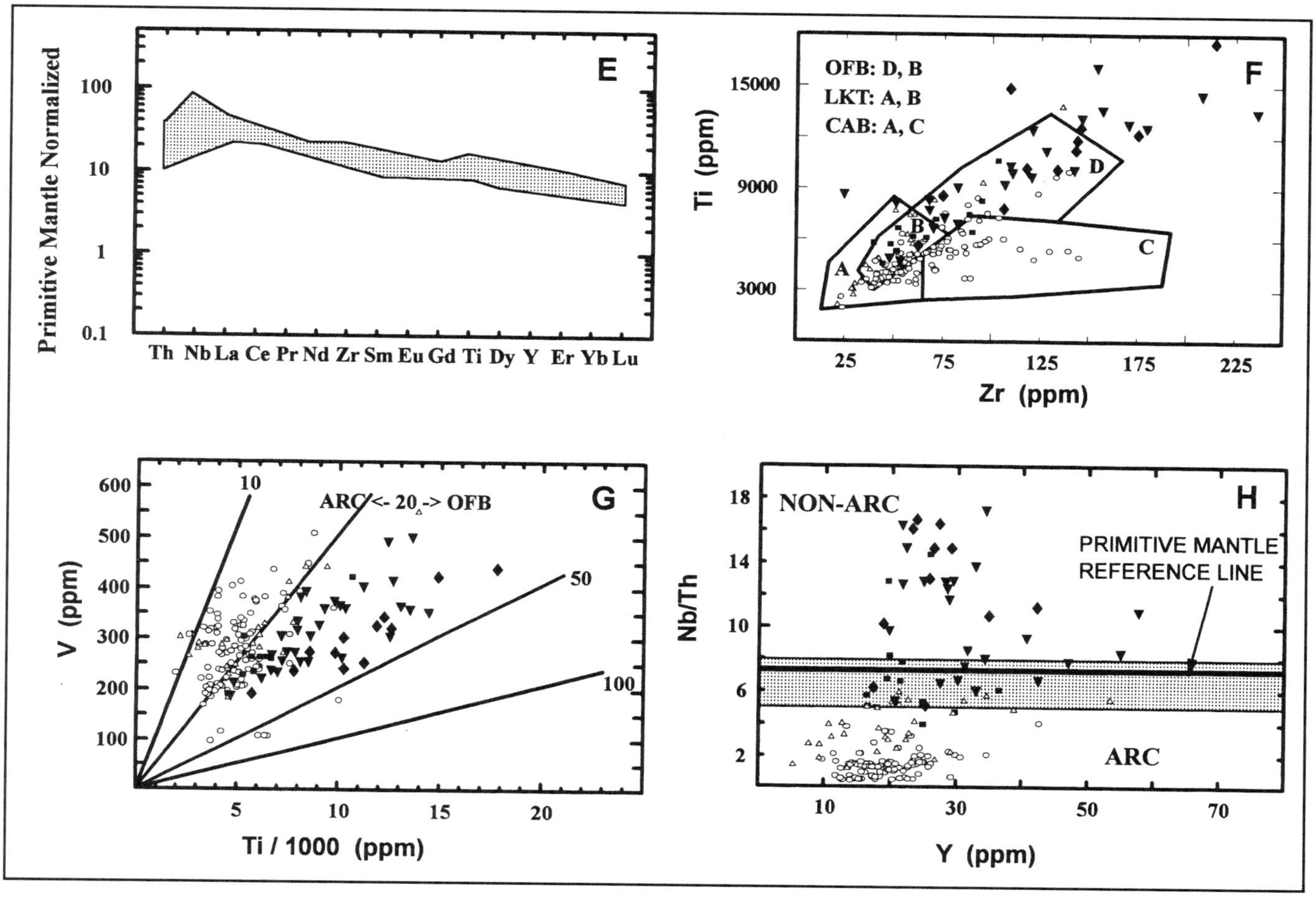

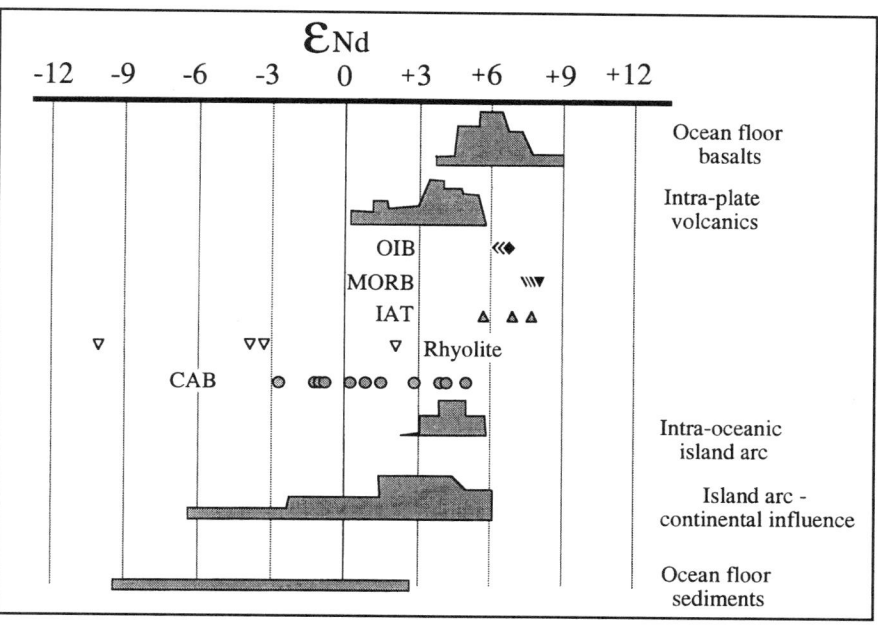

Figure 13. Summary of Nd isotopic data for the Buchans–Robert's Arm belt. Compilations of Nd isotopic data from various modern environments are described in the methodology section. Abbreviations as in Figure 4.

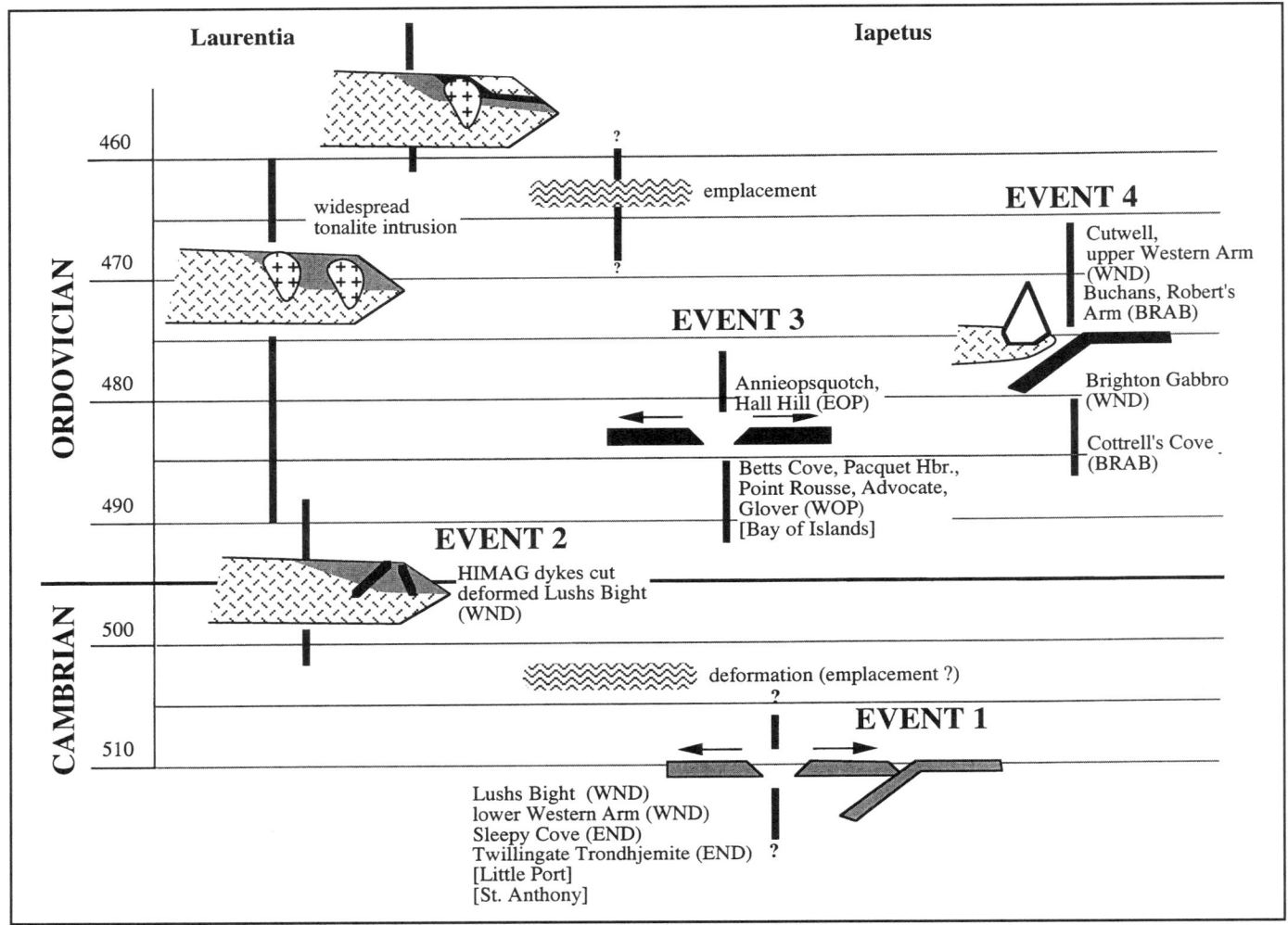

Figure 14. Time and space relationships of Cambrian and Ordovician magmatism in the Notre Dame subzone. Lithostratigraphic units are indicated; the area in which they occur is indicated in parentheses (WND—western Notre Dame Bay area; END—eastern Notre Dame Bay area; WOP—western ophiolite belt; EOP—eastern ophiolite belt; BRAB—Buchans–Robert's Arm belt). Magmatic sequences in the Humber zone taconic allochthons are in square brackets. Time scale after Tucker and MacKerrow (1995). Vertical bars represent age ranges of events permitted by geochronological evidence. Events are described in the text. Polarity of subduction in event 1 is not constrained. Emplacement of oceanic rocks upon the Laurentian margin occurred between events 1 and 2 and after events 3 and/or 4. Tonalite was intruded into the composite (i.e., with emplaced Cambrian ophiolites) Laurentian margin from about 490 Ma. However, the first evidence of tonalite intruding the Laurentian margin after emplacement of Early Ordovician rocks is ca. 460 Ma.

geochemical character with the Early Ordovician back arc basin in the Notre Dame subzone. Its age and the presence of a MORB-IAT volcanic assemblage show a petrological affinity with the western ophiolite belt. The Little Port Complex, which is immediately to the west of, and structurally above, the Bay of Islands Complex, includes pillow lavas with arc signatures and related diabase dikes, but their age is equivocal; it is only known that dikes related to the volcanic rocks intrude trondhjemite with an age of ca. 505 Ma. and εNd of -1 to $+1$ (Jenner

et al., 1991). The Little Port Complex lavas are geochemically similar to lavas in the Early Ordovician back arc sequences of the Notre Dame subzone and potentially correlative, although definitive evidence is lacking. Initial emplacement of the Bay of Islands Complex, in contrast to the St. Anthony Complex, apparently occurred ca. 476 Ma, substantially later than, and probably representing an entirely separate collisional event than, the +500 Ma event during which the Event 1 volcanic and plutonic rocks were emplaced.

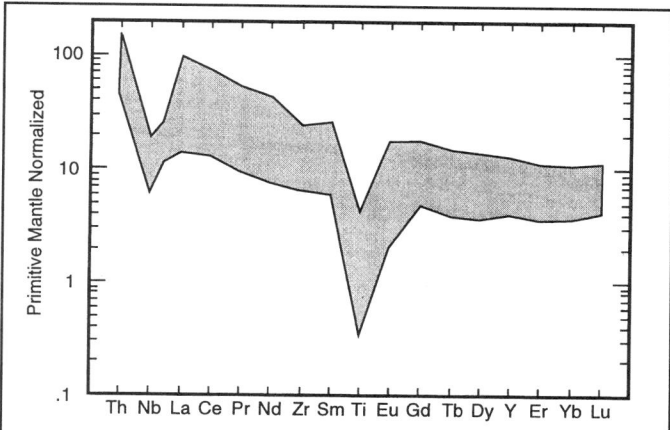

Figure 15. Geochemical characteristics of felsic volcanic rocks in the Buchans–Robert's Arm belt.

TECTONIC DEVELOPMENT OF THE LAURENTIAN MARGIN

General statement

Our data require substantial revision of extant tectonic models for the development of the Laurentian margin in Newfoundland during the Cambrian and Early Ordovician. Considerations that must form part of any actualistic model for the tectonic history of the Laurentian margin include the following.

1. The presence of a Late Cambrian subduction complex has previously been proposed on the basis of the Twillingate Trondhjemite–Sleepy Cove relationships. Our data show that elements of this arc–back arc system are more widespread than previously supposed and, more significant, that they must have been emplaced upon the Laurentian margin by the latest Cambrian.

2. The presence of HIMAG dikes in the Lushs Bight Group is a new discovery that appears to require extensional tectonics and a substantial heat source under the Laurentian margin immediately following emplacement of rocks derived from the Late Cambrian subduction complex. By analogy with modern examples (see methodology section), this would appear to be best accommodated by some form of westward subduction under this margin (see models below). The apparent temporal overlap between intrusion of the HIMAG dikes on the Laurentian margin and the initiation of oceanic arc–back arc volcanism preserved in the western ophiolitic belt raises the possibility that these events may represent the same geodynamic regime, although manifested in contrasting tectonostratigraphic settings (continental margin versus oceanic).

3. The protracted episode of oceanic back arc volcanism in the Early Ordovician has previously been widely interpreted as representing one or more back arc basins. It has not previously been recognized that calc-alkalic volcanism outboard (in present coordinates) of most of these rocks floored by continental lithosphere apparently began relatively soon

(i.e., possibly within as few as 5 m.y.) after formation of the earliest ophiolites.

4. Tonalitic plutonism at the composite Laurentian margin, which we interpret to reflect a similar petrogenesis to felsic volcanics in the calc-alkalic sequences (i.e., partial melting of continental lithosphere), began almost simultaneously with formation of the western belt ophiolites and continued long after cessation of calc-alkalic arc volcanism. The maximum age at which such plutons cut Early Ordovician rocks is ca. 460 Ma, and this provides a minimum age by which at least some of these rocks must have been accreted to the Laurentian margin.

Discussion

On the basis of our new data, and taking into consideration the timing and nature of the interaction of oceanic and continental tectonic elements, we propose a revised Cambrian and Early Ordovician tectonic history of the Laurentian margin in Newfoundland. There are still insufficient data to constrain many of the fundamental features of Laurentian margin tectonic development, particularly in the Early Ordovician, and there are many aspects that remain equivocal.

The best estimate of the rift-drift transition is still ca. 545 Ma, based upon sedimentological evidence (Williams and Hiscott, 1987). No oceanic crust from this early spreading episode has been identified, and it seems unlikely that any is preserved in the Notre Dame subzone. The earliest magmatism apparently records a Cambrian subduction complex. We have few data that could constrain the polarity or location of subduction zones that were responsible for this magmatism. Consistent with current models for the obduction of the Taconic allochthons (Searle and Stevens, 1984; Cawood, 1991), eastward (present coordinates) subduction might be invoked as the best way of facilitating emplacement of the ophiolites on the Laurentian margin. A consequence of this process is that following collision of outboard arcs with the continental margin, a reversal of subduction polarity could result (e.g., Cooper and Taylor, 1987). However, as in the case of the Taconic allochthons, this requires obduction of a substantial part of an arc complex, for which there is little evidence. More complex models can be envisaged in which westward or oblique subduction might result in the observed relationships.

Closely following emplacement, HIMAG dikes were intruded through Laurentian lithosphere into the deformed oceanic rocks. The extensional tectonics and anomalous heat suggested by this event could have resulted from a variety of tectonic events, including subduction of a back arc spreading center; alternatively, it may reflect rifting at the continental margin during the early stages of subduction under the continental margin. It is important that almost any scenario that is envisaged to provide the heat and extensional tectonics necessary to form these rocks would appear to require westward (in present coordinates) subduction under the Laurentian margin. If this event is a continuation of westward-directed subduction, then all that is required

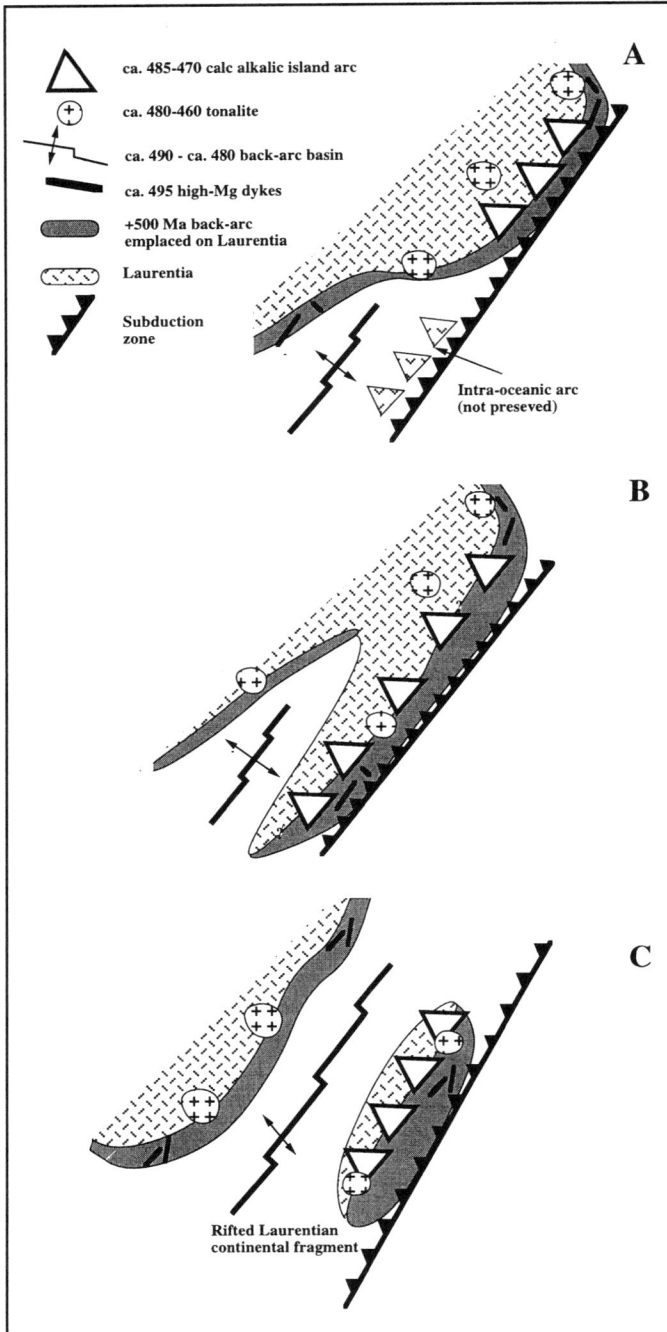

Figure 16. Schematic illustrations of possible tectonic models for the development of the Notre Dame subzone. Detailed descriptions are in the text. The models illustrate a time slice broadly in the Lower Ordovician during events 3 and 4 (Fig. 14). Cambrian ophiolitic rocks are already emplaced upon the Laurentian margin and intruded by HIMAG dikes. In any of these models, subsequent closing of the back basin eventually results in emplacement of the Lower Ordovician successions upon Laurentia. Subduction associated with this closing may be responsible for some of the younger tonalitic plutonic rocks.

tectonically is an oceanward migration of the locus of active magmatism (i.e., a stepping back of the subduction zone) and no change in the polarity of subduction is required.

Geochronological data from the western ophiolite belt shows that an arc–back arc complex was established outboard of the Laurentian margin soon after intrusion of the HIMAG dikes. Within a 5 to 10 m.y. span, tonalitic plutonism, probably related to subduction, is recorded on the Laurentian margin (Whalen et al., this volume) and bimodal felsic and/or calc-alkalic mafic volcanism contaminated by continental lithosphere is recorded in the Buchans–Robert's Arm belt. If one is prepared to accept that the Early Ordovician volcanic history of the Notre Dame subzone can be explained by a single long-lived subduction complex, then there are at least three scenarios that can accommodate this data. These are illustrated in Figure 16.

In the first model (Fig. 16A), Early Ordovician westward-directed subduction under a highly irregular Laurentian margin occurs soon after emplacement of rocks derived from the Late Cambrian subduction complex. From a very early stage, subduction occurs simultaneously under continental crust on promontories and under oceanic crust in reentrants. HIMAG dike intrusion occurs in response to either initiation of subduction or perhaps as a result of subduction of some other tectonic element from the old back arc (i.e., a spreading center). Tonalitic plutonism, manifesting subduction under the Laurentian margin, is closely followed by eruption of CAB arc volcanics through and upon the Laurentian margin. In the adjacent reentrant, a protracted history of back arc rifting is recorded in ophiolitic rocks. That different sequences have different relative abundances of rocks with arc geochemical signatures reflects their varying proximity to the subduction zone. Closing of this back arc basin ca. 476 Ma results in emplacement of the Bay of Islands Complex on the Laurentian margin; this subduction is reflected magmatically by the continued intrusion of tonalite into the Laurentian margin. This scenario implies the existence of an Early Ordovician intra-oceanic island arc, which has not to date been identified. It also requires a substantial amount of strike-slip and thrust faulting to move the various tectonic and magmatic elements into their present relative positions in the Notre Dame subzone.

In the second model (Fig. 16B), Early Ordovician subduction under the Laurentian margin results in extension, rifting, and eventually formation of an ensialic back arc basin in which mantle-derived magmatism generates new oceanic crust. This model presents a scenario somewhat similar to that observed in the present-day Gulf of California. Tonalitic plutonism and CAB volcanism are the magmatic response to continued subduction under the continental margin. Eventual closing of the back arc basin (with continued tonalitic intrusion) results in the emplacement of the Bay of Islands Complex. This model implies that the initiation of subduction-related volcanism at the Laurentian margin probably would have predated eruption of the earliest oceanic tholeiites. This is not confirmed by the available data, but the model has the advantage that an intraoceanic island arc for which there is no observational evidence need not be invoked. It also requires a substantial redistribution of the rock units during orogeny to account for their present relative positions.

The third model (Fig. 16C), invokes an outboard continental fragment, under which westward-directed subduction occurred during the Early Ordovician. It is arguable whether this continental fragment was rifted from the Laurentian margin by this subduction, in which case this model is an extension of model 2. Alternatively, the continental fragment may have resulted from an earlier rifting event at the margin, and was brought into position by strike-slip faulting. The main attraction of this model is that it accounts for the present spatial distribution of magmatic elements in the Notre Dame subzone without the necessity to invoke substantial redistribution by strike-slip tectonics.

CONCLUSIONS

Integration of a large body of new geochemical, geochronological, and Nd isotopic data for magmatic rocks in the Notre Dame subzone of Newfoundland permits a more detailed interpretation of the magmatic and tectonic history of the early Paleozoic Laurentian margin of Iapetus than has previously been possible. In particular, it allows us to track the interactions of mantle and continental lithosphere through the Cambrian and Ordovician history of the Notre Dame subzone, and to show that there was an extended history of mantle-crust interaction at the Laurentian margin, beginning in the Late Cambrian and continuing through the Ordovician. These data may have significant implications for our interpretation of the Taconian orogeny. If one accepts that the Taconian orogeny records the entire span of accretion of Iapetan oceanic terranes to Laurentia, then our data require that the maximum age of initiation of this event be substantially older than the generally accepted ca. 476 Ma age. Alternatively, if the Taconian orogeny is considered to record only Early Ordovician accretionary events, then our data identify a separate, Cambrian orogenic event that has not previously been accounted for in tectonic models of the Laurentian margin.

Our data for the Notre Dame subzone magmatic rocks require revision of current tectonic models for the early Paleozoic Laurentian margin. A principal new result of this work is recognition of a well-developed subduction complex, elements of which were emplaced on the Laurentian margin prior to the end of the Cambrian. We believe that the Laurentian margin was tectonically composite well before the Early Ordovician emplacement of the Taconic allochthons. Furthermore, we now recognize that generation of oceanic crust in Early Ordovician back arc basins (now preserved in ophiolitic successions), uninfluenced by continental lithosphere, substantially overlapped in time the generation of a calc-alkalic magmatic arc that was apparently rooted in continental lithosphere. Both of these magmatic events overlap the extended time period during the Ordovician, when voluminous tonalitic plutons, apparently related to subduction, intruded the Laurentian margin.

We propose three alternative tectonic models to explain the magmatic relationships in the Notre Dame subzone; the models differ depending on how the original spatial relationships of the various elements of the Early Ordovician arc–back arc complexes are interpreted. Common elements of these models include Cambrian emplacement of an old subduction complex, westward subduction under the Laurentian margin as early as the Early Ordovician, and the emplacement of the Taconic allochthons during closure of the lower Ordovician back arc basin(s?) upon an already composite Laurentian margin.

ACKNOWLEDGMENTS

Funding for the research was provided by a National Science and Engineering Research Council operating grant and Lithoprobe grant to Jenner, by the Geological Survey of Canada under the Canada-Newfoundland Mineral Development Agreement (1984–1989), and by the Geological Survey, Newfoundland Department of Natural Resources. Swinden publishes with the permission of the Executive Director of the Geological Survey, Newfoundland Department of Natural Resources. We thank R. A. Coish and Richard Stern for constructive and helpful reviews of the manuscript. All of the $^{40}Ar/^{39}Ar$ analyses, which contribute substantially to the conclusions in this chapter, were carried out by C. R. Roddick of the Geological Survey of Canada, tragically killed in February 1995. We dedicate this chapter to his memory.

REFERENCES CITED

Beccaluva, L., and Serri, G., 1988, Boninitic and low-Ti subduction-related lavas from intraoceanic arc–back arc systems and low-Ti ophiolites: A reappraisal of their petrogenesis and original tectonic setting: Tectonophysics, v. 146, p. 291–315.

Bird, J. M., and Dewey, J. F., 1970, Lithosphere plate–continental marginal tectonics and the evolution of the Appalachian orogen: Geological Society of America Bulletin, v. 81, p. 1031–1060.

Bostock, H. H., Currie, K. L., and Wanless, R. K., 1979, The age of the Robert's Arm Group, north-central Newfoundland: Canadian Journal of Earth Sciences, v. 16, p. 599–606.

Cawood, P. A., 1989, Acadian remobilization of a Taconian ophiolite, western Newfoundland: Geology, v. 17, p. 257–260.

Cawood, P. A., 1991, Acadian Orogeny in west Newfoundland: Definition, character and significance, *in* Roy, D. C., and Skehan, J. W., eds., The Acadian orogeny: Recent studies in New England, Maritime Canada, and the autochthonous foreland: Geological Society of America Special Paper 275, p. 135–152.

Cawood, P. A., and van Gool, J. A.M., 1993, Stratigraphic and structural relations within the western Dunnage zone, Glover Island region, western Newfoundland, *in* Current research, Part D: Geological Survey of Canada Paper 93-1D, p. 29–37.

Church, W. R., and Stevens, R. K., 1971, Early Paleozoic ophiolite complexes of the Newfoundland Appalachians as mantle-oceanic crust sequences: Journal of Geophysical Research, v. 76, p. 1460–1466.

Coish, R. A., and Church, W. R., 1979, Igneous geochemistry of the Betts Cove ophiolite, Newfoundland: Contributions to Mineralogy and Petrology, v. 20, p. 29–39.

Coish, R. A., Hickey, R., and Frey, F. A., 1982, Rare earth element geochemistry of the Betts Cove ophiolite, Newfoundland: Complexities in ophiolite formation: Geochimica et Cosmochimica Acta, v. 46, p. 2117–2134.

Colman-Sadd, S. P., 1982, Two stage continental collision and plate driving forces: Tectonophysics, v. 90, p. 263–282.

Colman-Sadd, S. P., Dunning, G. R., and Dec, T., 1992a, Dunnage-Gander relationships and Ordovician orogeny in central Newfoundland: A sediment provenance and U/Pb age study: American Journal of Science, v. 292, p. 317–355.

Colman-Sadd, S. P., Stone, P., Swinden, H. S., and Barnes, R. P., 1992b, Parallel geological development in the Dunnage zone of Newfoundland and the Lower Paleozoic terranes of southern Scotland: An assessment: Royal Society of Edinburgh Transactions, Earth Sciences, v. 83, p. 571–594.

Cooper, P., and Taylor, B., 1987, Seismotectonics of New Guinea: A model for arc reversal following arc-continent collision: Tectonics, v. 6, p. 53–67.

Dallmeyer, R. D., 1977, Diachronous ophiolite obduction in western Newfoundland: Evidence from $^{40}Ar/^{39}Ar$ ages of the Hare Bay metamorphic aureole: American Journal of Science, v. 277, p. 61–72.

Dallmeyer, R. D., and Williams, H., 1975, $^{40}Ar/^{39}Ar$ release spectra of hornblende from Bay of Islands metamorphic aureole, western Newfoundland: Their bearing on the timing of ophiolite obduction at the Ordovician continental margin of eastern North America: Canadian Journal of Earth Sciences, v. 12, p. 1685–1690.

Dean, P. L., 1978, The volcanic stratigraphy and metallogeny of Notre Dame Bay: St. John's, Memorial University of Newfoundland, Geological Report 7, 204 p.

Dec, T., and Swinden, H. S., 1994, Lithostratigraphic model, geochemistry and sedimentology of the Cottrells Cove Group, Buchans–Robert's Arm volcanic belt, Notre Dame Bay, in Current Research: Newfoundland Department of Mines and Energy, Geological Survey Branch, Paper 94-1, p. 77–100.

Dec, T., Swinden, H. S., and Dunning, G. R., 1996, Sedimentology, geochemistry and stratigraphy of the Cottrells Cove Group (Buchans–Robert's Arm belt), eastern Notre Dame Bay, Newfoundland Appalachians: Canadian Journal of Earth Sciences (in press).

Dunning, G. R., 1987, Geology of the Annieopsquotch Complex, southwest Newfoundland: Canadian Journal of Earth Sciences, v. 24, p. 1162–1174.

Dunning, G. R., and Chorlton, L. B., 1985, The Annieopsquotch ophiolite belt of southwest Newfoundland: Geology and tectonic significance: Geological Society of America Bulletin, v. 96, p. 1466–1476.

Dunning, G. R., and Krogh, T. E., 1985, Geochronology of ophiolites of the Newfoundland Appalachians: Canadian Journal of Earth Sciences, v. 22, p. 1659–1670.

Dunning, G. R., and Krogh, T. E., 1991, Stratigraphic correlation of the Appalachian Ordovician using advanced U-Pb zircon geochronology techniques, in Barnes, C. R., and Williams, S. H., eds., Advances in Ordovician geology: Geological Survey of Canada Paper 90-9, p. 85–92.

Dunning, G. R., Kean, B. F., Thurlow, J. G., and Swinden, H. S., 1987, Geochronology of the Buchans, Robert's Arm and Victoria Lake Groups and the Mansfield Cove Complex, Newfoundland: Canadian Journal of Earth Sciences, v. 24, p. 1175–1184.

Dunning, G. R., Swinden, H. S., Kean, B. F., Evans, D. T. W., and Jenner, G. A., 1991, A Cambrian island arc in Iapetus: Geochronology and geochemistry of the Lake Ambrose volcanic belt, Newfoundland Appalachians: Geological Magazine, v. 128, p. 1–17.

Elliott, C. G., Dunning, G. R., and Williams, P., 1991, New U/Pb zircon age constraints on the timing of deformation in north-central Newfoundland and implications for early Paleozoic Appalachian orogenesis: Geological Society of America Bulletin, v. 103, p. 125–135.

Evans, D. T. W., Kean, B. F., and Dunning, G. R., 1990, Geological studies, Victoria Lake Group, central Newfoundland, in Current Research: Newfoundland Department of Mines and Energy, Geological Survey Branch, Report 90-1, p. 131–144.

Fryer, B. J., Kerr, A., Jenner, G. A., and Longstaffe, F. J., 1992, Probing the crust with plutons: Regional isotopic geochemistry of granitoid intrusions across insular Newfoundland, in Current research: Newfoundland Department of Mines and Energy, Geological Survey Branch, Report 92-1, p. 119–139.

Gale, G. H., 1973, Paleozoic basaltic komatiite and ocean-floor type basalts from northeastern Newfoundland: Earth and Planetary Science Letters, v. 18, p. 22–28.

Gill, J. B., 1981, Orogenic andesites and plate tectonics: Heidelberg, Springer-Verlag, 390 p.

Gill, J. B., and Stork, A. L., 1979, Miocene low-K dacites and trondhjemites of Fiji, in Barker, F., ed., Trondhjemites, dacites and related rocks: New York, Elsevier, p. 629–649.

Harland, W. B., and Gayer, R. A., 1972, The Arctic Caledonides and earlier oceans: Geological Magazine, v. 109, p. 289–314.

Hibbard, J. P., 1984, Geology of the Baie Verte Peninsula, Newfoundland: Newfoundland Department of Mines and Energy, Mineral Development Division, Memoir 2, 279 p.

Hofmann, A. W., 1988, Chemical differentiation of the Earth: The relationship between mantle, continental crust and oceanic crust: Earth and Planetary Science Letters, v. 90, p. 297–314.

Hole, M. J., Rogers, G., Saunders, A. D., and Storey, M., 1991, Relation between alkalic volcanism and slab-window formation: Geology, v. 19, p. 657–660.

Jamieson, R. A., 1988, Metamorphic P-T-t data from western Newfoundland and Cape Breton—Implications for Taconian and Acadian tectonics [abs.]: Geological Association of Canada Program with Abstracts, v. 13, p. A60.

Jenner, G. A., 1981, Geochemistry of high-Mg andesites from Cape Vogel, Papua New Guinea: Chemical Geology, v. 33, p. 307–332.

Jenner, G. A., and Fryer, B. J., 1980, Geochemistry of the upper Snooks Arm Group basalts, Burlington Peninsula, Newfoundland: Evidence against formation in an island arc: Canadian Journal of Earth Sciences, v. 17, p. 888–900.

Jenner, G. A., Longerich, H. P., Jackson, S. E., and Fryer, B. J., 1990, ICP-MS—A powerful tool for high precision trace element analysis in earth sciences: Evidence from analysis of selected USGS reference samples: Chemical Geology, v. 83, p. 133–148.

Jenner, G. A., Dunning, G. R., Malpas, J., Brown, M., and Brace, T., 1991, Bay of Islands and Little Port Complexes revisited: Age, geochemical and isotopic evidence confirm supra-subduction zone origin: Canadian Journal of Earth Sciences, v. 28, p. 1635–1652.

Kamo, S. L., Gower, C. F., and Krogh, T. E., 1989, Birthdate for the Iapetus ocean? A precise U-Pb zircon and baddeleyite age for the Long Range dikes, southeast Labrador: Geology, v. 17, p. 602–605.

Kay, A., and Strong, D. F., 1983, Geologic and fluid controls in As-Sb-Au mineralization in the Moreton's Harbour area, Newfoundland: Economic Geology, v. 78, p. 1590–1604.

Kean, B. F., and Strong, D. F., 1975, Geochemical evolution of an Ordovician island arc of the Central Newfoundland Appalachians: American Journal of Science, v. 275, p. 97–118.

Kean, B. F., Evans, D. T.W., and Jenner, G. A., 1995, Geology and mineralization of the Lushs Bight Group: Newfoundland Department of Natural Resources, Geological Survey, Report 95-2, 204 p.

Knapp, D. A., 1983, Ophiolite emplacement along the Baie Verte–Bromton Line at Glover Island, western Newfoundland [Ph.D. thesis]: St. John's, Memorial University of Newfoundland, 338 p.

Luhr, J. F., Allan, J. F., Carmicheal, I. S.E., Nelson, S. A., and Hasenaka, T., 1989, Primitive calc-alkaline and alkaline rock types from the western Mexican volcanic belt: Journal of Geophysical Research, v. 94, p. 4515–4530.

Marillier, F., Keen, C. E., Stockmal, G. S., Quinlan, G., Williams, H., Colman-Sadd, S. P., and O'Brien, S. J., 1989, Crustal structure and surface zonation of the Canadian Appalachians: Implications of deep seismic reflection data: Canadian Journal of Earth Sciences, v. 26, p. 305–321.

Meschede, M., 1986, A method of discriminating between different types of mid-ocean ridge basalts and continental tholeiites with the Nb-Zr-Y diagram: Chemical Geology, v. 56, p. 207–218.

Norman, R. E., and Strong, D. F., 1975, The geology and geochemistry of ophiolitic rocks exposed at Ming's Bight, Newfoundland: Canadian Journal of Earth Sciences, v. 12, p. 777–797.

Nowlan, G. S., and Thurlow, J. G., 1984, Middle Ordovician conodonts from the Buchans Group, central Newfoundland, and their significance for regional stratigraphy of the Central Volcanic Belt: Canadian Journal of Earth Sciences, v. 21, p. 284–296.

O'Brien, F. H. C., and Szybinski, Z. A., 1989, Conodont faunas from the Catchers Pond and Cutwell Groups, central Newfoundland, *in* Current Research: Newfoundland Department of Mines, Geological Survey of Newfoundland, Report 89-1, p. 121–125.

Payne, J. G., and Strong, D. F., 1979, Origin of the Twillingate trondhjemite, north-central Newfoundland: Partial melting in the roots of an island arc, *in* Barker, F., ed., Trondhjemites, dacites and related rocks: Amsterdam, Elsevier, p. 489–516.

Pearce, J. A., 1975, Basalt geochemistry used to investigate past tectonic environments on Cyprus: Tectonophysics, v. 25, p. 41–67.

Pearce, J. A., and Cann, J. R., 1971, Ophiolite origin investigated by a discriminant analysis using Ti, Zr, and Y: Earth and Planetary Science Letters, v. 15, p. 271–285.

Pearce, J. A., and Norry, M. J., 1979, Petrogenetic implications of Ti, Zr, Y, and Nb variations in volcanic rocks: Contributions to Mineralogy and Petrology, v. 69, p. 33–47.

Pickett, J. W., 1987, Geology and geochemistry of the Skidder basalt, *in* Kirkham, R. V., ed., Buchans geology, Newfoundland: Geological Survey of Canada Paper 86-24, p. 195–218.

Quinlan, G. M., Hall, J., Williams, H., Wright, J. A., Colman-Sadd, S. P., O'Brien, S. J., Stockmal, G. S., and Marillier, F., 1992, Lithoprobe onshore seismic reflection transects across the Newfoundland Appalachians: Canadian Journal of Earth Sciences, v. 29, p. 1865–1877.

Rogers, G., and Saunders, A. D., 1989, Magnesian andesites from Mexico, Chile and the Aleutian Islands: Implications for magmatism associated with ridge-trench collision, *in* Crawford, A. J., ed., Boninites: London, Unwin Hyman, p. 416–445.

Saunders, A. D., Rogers, G., Marriner, G. F., Terrell, D. J., and Verma, S. P., 1987, Geochemistry of Cenozoic volcanic rocks, Baja California, Mexico: Implications for the petrogenesis of post-subduction magmas: Journal of Volcanology and Geothermal Research, v. 32, p. 223–245.

Searle, M. P., and Stevens, R. K., 1984, Obduction in ancient, modern and future ophiolites, *in* Gass, I. G., Lippard, S. J., and Shelton, A. W., eds., Ophiolites and oceanic lithosphere, Geological Society of London Special Publication 13, p. 303–319.

Shervais, J. W., 1982, Ti-V plots and the petrogenesis of modern and ophiolitic lavas: Earth and Planetary Science Letters, v. 59, p. 101–118.

Strong, D. F., and Payne, J. G., 1973, Early Paleozoic volcanism and metamorphism of the Moreton's Harbour–Twillingate area, Newfoundland: Canadian Journal of Earth Sciences, v. 10, p. 1363–1379.

Strong, D. F., Dickson, W. L., O'Driscoll, C. F., Kean B. F., and Stevens, R. K., 1974, Geochemical evidence for an east-dipping Appalachian subduction zone in Newfoundland: Nature, v. 248, p. 37–39.

Sun, S.-S., and McDonough, W. F., 1989, Chemical and isotopic systematics of oceanic basalts: Implications for mantle composition and processes, *in* Saunders, A. D., and Norry, M. J., eds., Magmatism in the ocean basins, Geological Society of London Special Publication 42, p. 313–345.

Swinden, H. S., 1991, Paleotectonic settings of volcanogenic massive sulphide deposits in the Dunnage zone, Newfoundland Appalachians: CIM Bulletin, v. 84, no. 946, p. 59–69.

Swinden, H. S., Jenner, G. A., Fryer, B. J., Hertogen, J., and Roddick, J. C., 1990, Petrogenesis and paleotectonic history of the Wild Bight Group, an Ordovician rifted island arc in central Newfoundland: Contributions to Mineralogy and Petrology, v. 105, p. 219–241.

Szybinski, Z. A., 1995, Paleotectonic and structural setting of the western Notre Dame Bay area, Newfoundland Appalachians [Ph.D. thesis]: St. John's, Memorial University of Newfoundland, 690 p.

Tatsumi, Y., and Ishizaka, K., 1982, Origin of high-magnesian andesites in the Setouchi volcanic belt, southwest Japan, I. Petrographical and chemical characteristics: Earth and Planetary Science Letters, v. 60, p. 293–304.

Tatsumi, Y., and Maruyama, S., 1989, Boninites and high-Mg andesites: Tectonics and petrogenesis, *in* Crawford, A. J., ed., Boninites: London, Unwin Hyman, p. 50–71.

Thurlow, J. G., and Swanson, E. A., 1987, Stratigraphy and structure of the Buchans Group, *in* Kirkham, R. V., ed., Buchans geology: Geological Survey of Canada Paper 86-24, p. 35–46.

Thurlow, J. G., Spencer, C. P., Boerner, D. E., Reed, L. E., and Wright, J. A., 1993, Geological interpretation of a high resolution reflection seismic survey at the Buchans mine, Newfoundland: Canadian Journal of Earth Sciences, v. 29, p. 2022–2037.

Tucker, R. D., and MacKerrow, W. S., 1995, Early Paleozoic chronology: A review in light of new U-Pb zircon ages from Newfoundland and Britain: Canadian Journal of Earth Sciences, v. 32, p. 368–379.

Upadhyay, H. D., Dewey, J. F., and Neale, E. R. W., 1971, The Betts Cove Ophiolite complex, Newfoundland: Appalachian oceanic crust and mantle: Geological Association of Canada Proceedings, v. 24, p. 27–34.

Williams, H., 1971, Mafic-ultramafic complexes in western Newfoundland Appalachians and the evidence for their transport: A review and interim report: Geological Association of Canada Proceedings, v. 24, p. 9–25.

Williams, H., 1979, Appalachian orogen in Canada: Canadian Journal of Earth Sciences, v. 16, p. 792–807.

Williams, H., 1994, Dunnage Mélange and Ordovician-Silurian rocks of New World Island, *in* Williams, H., and O'Brien, B. H., eds., New perspectives in the Appalachian-Caledonian orogen: Geological Association of Canada Field Trip Guidebook, p. 48–65.

Williams, H., and Hatcher, R. D., Jr., 1983, Appalachian suspect terranes, *in* Hatcher, R. D., Williams, H., and Zeitz, I., eds., Contributions to the tectonics and geophysics of mountain chains: Geological Society of America Memoir 158, p. 33–53.

Williams, H., and Hiscott, R. N., 1987, Definition of the Iapetus rift-drift transition in western Newfoundland: Geology, v. 15, p. 1044–1047.

Williams, H., and Payne, J. G., 1975, The Twillingate Granite and nearby volcanic groups: An island arc complex in northeastern Newfoundland: Canadian Journal of Earth Sciences, v. 12, p. 982–995.

Williams, H., and St. Julien, P., 1978, The Baie Verte–Brompton Line in Newfoundland and regional correlations in the Canadian Appalachians, *in* Current research: Geological Survey of Canada Paper 78-1A, p. 225–229.

Williams, H., Kennedy, M. J., and Neale, E. R. W., 1974, The northeastern termination of the Appalachian orogen, *in* Nairn, A. E., and Stehli, F. G., eds., The ocean basins and margins, Volume 2: New York, Plenum Press, p. 79–123.

Williams, H., Colman-Sadd, S. P., and Swinden, H. S., 1988, Tectonostratigraphic subdivisions of central Newfoundland, *in* Current research, Part B: Geological Survey of Canada Paper 88-1B, p. 91–98.

Williams, S. H., 1989, New graptolite discoveries from the Ordovician of western Newfoundland, *in* Current research: Newfoundland Department of Mines and Energy, Geological Survey Branch, Report 89-1, p. 149–158.

Wilson, J. T., 1966, Did the Atlantic close and then re-open?: Nature, v. 211, p. 676–681.

Winchester, J. A., and Floyd, P. A., 1975, Geochemical magma type discrimination: Application to altered and metamorphosed basic igneous rocks: Earth and Planetary Science Letters, v. 28, p. 459–469.

Wood, D. A., Joron, J.-L., and Treuil, M., 1979, A re-appraisal of the use of trace elements to classify and discriminate between magma series erupted in different tectonic settings: Earth and Planetary Science Letters, v. 45, p. 326–336.

MANUSCRIPT ACCEPTED BY THE SOCIETY JULY 2, 1996

Geological Society of America
Memoir 191
1997

Implications of granitoid geochemical and isotopic (Nd, O, Pb) data from the Cambrian-Ordovician Notre Dame arc for the evolution of the Central Mobile belt, Newfoundland Appalachians

Joseph B. Whalen
Geological Survey of Canada, 601 Booth Street, Ottawa, Ontario K1A 0E8, Canada
George A. Jenner
Department of Earth Sciences, Memorial University of Newfoundland, St. John's, Newfoundland A1B 3X5, Canada
Frederick J. Longstaffe
Department of Earth Sciences, University of Western Ontario, London, Ontario N6A 5B7, Canada
Clément Gariépy
Departement des Sciences de la Terre and GEOTOP, Université du Québec à Montréal, P. O. Box 8888, Station Centre-Ville, Montréal, Québec H3C 3P8, Canada
Brian J. Fryer
Department of Earth Sciences, University of Windsor, 401 Sunset Avenue, Windsor, Ontario N9B 3P4, Canada

ABSTRACT

Iapetus closure involved multiple independent collisions, including that of the Notre Dame arc (NDA) with Laurentia during Early to Middle Ordovician time. The NDA contains significant volumes of well-preserved but disrupted Ordovician plutonic rocks. A predominance of intermediate compositions, calc-alkaline character, and primordial mantle normalized patterns with marked negative Nb and Ti anomalies over the full silica range (46 to 76 wt%) indicate formation in an arc-type setting. Their low- to medium-K contents, associated gabbros and diorites, and low large ion lithophile element contents suggest that the NDA was relatively immature or primitive.

Derivation of NDA plutons from infracrustal sources is suggested by their amphibole-bearing mineralogy, metaluminous compositions, igneous microgranitoid enclaves and $\delta^{18}O$ values of +6 to +8‰. Associated gabbros and geochemical evidence for slab-derived granitoids indicate they received contributions from a mantle-derived component. However, ε_{Nd} (t) values of +2.6 to –13.5 require significant input from old continental crust. Pb isotopic data are compatible with a lower crustal origin for this old crustal component. These plutons are interpreted as containing contributions from mantle and slab-derived magmas modified through assimilation-fractional-crystallization processes in the lower crust and/or mantle wedge, and also partial melts of solidified, previously hybridized, lower crustal rocks.

The NDA was a continental arc formed on older crust than that exposed in adjacent Grenvillian inliers of the Humber zone (Laurentian margin). The granitoid data are consistent with current models for the NDA in which oceanic crust formation, subaqueous arc-type volcanism, and plutonism occurred contemporaneously in a suprasubduction zone setting.

Whalen, J. B., Jenner, G. A., Longstaffe, F. J., Gariépy, C., and Fryer, B. J., 1997, Implications of granitoid geochemical and isotopic (Nd, O, Pb) data from the Cambrian-Ordovician Notre Dame arc for the evolution of the Central Mobile belt, Newfoundland Appalachians, *in* Sinha, A. K., Whalen, J. B., and Hogan, J. P., eds., The Nature of Magmatism in the Appalachian Orogen: Boulder, Colorado, Geological Society of America Memoir 191.

INTRODUCTION

Closure of Iapetus in the Canadian Appalachians was complex, involving a number of independent collisions (Colman-Sadd et al., 1992a; van Staal, 1994), including that of the Cambrian-Ordovician Notre Dame arc (NDA) with Laurentia. Although plutonic rocks constitute a major proportion of the preserved magmatic record of the NDA in western Newfoundland (Fig. 1), they have hitherto received little attention. We present and summarize herein some of the general features of a large new geochemical and isotopic data set collected from these rocks. The presence of xenocrystic zircons in some of the

plutonic rocks indicated they received contributions from Proterozoic crust or sediments derived from such crust (Whalen et al., 1987a; Dunning et al., 1989). Our data indicate derivation of NDA plutons from old (>1.5 Ga) but isotopically (Pb, O) mantle-like and relatively geochemically unevolved sources. On the basis of these results, we pose some questions, and offer tentative answers, concerning the nature and evolution of the NDA. (1) Was the arc continental or oceanic? (2) What was the source of the old crustal component in NDA plutons? (3) Were "slab-derived" granitoid rocks (Drummond and Defant, 1990) generated by subduction of the contemporaneous, to only slightly older (<5 to 15 Ma), back arc basins in

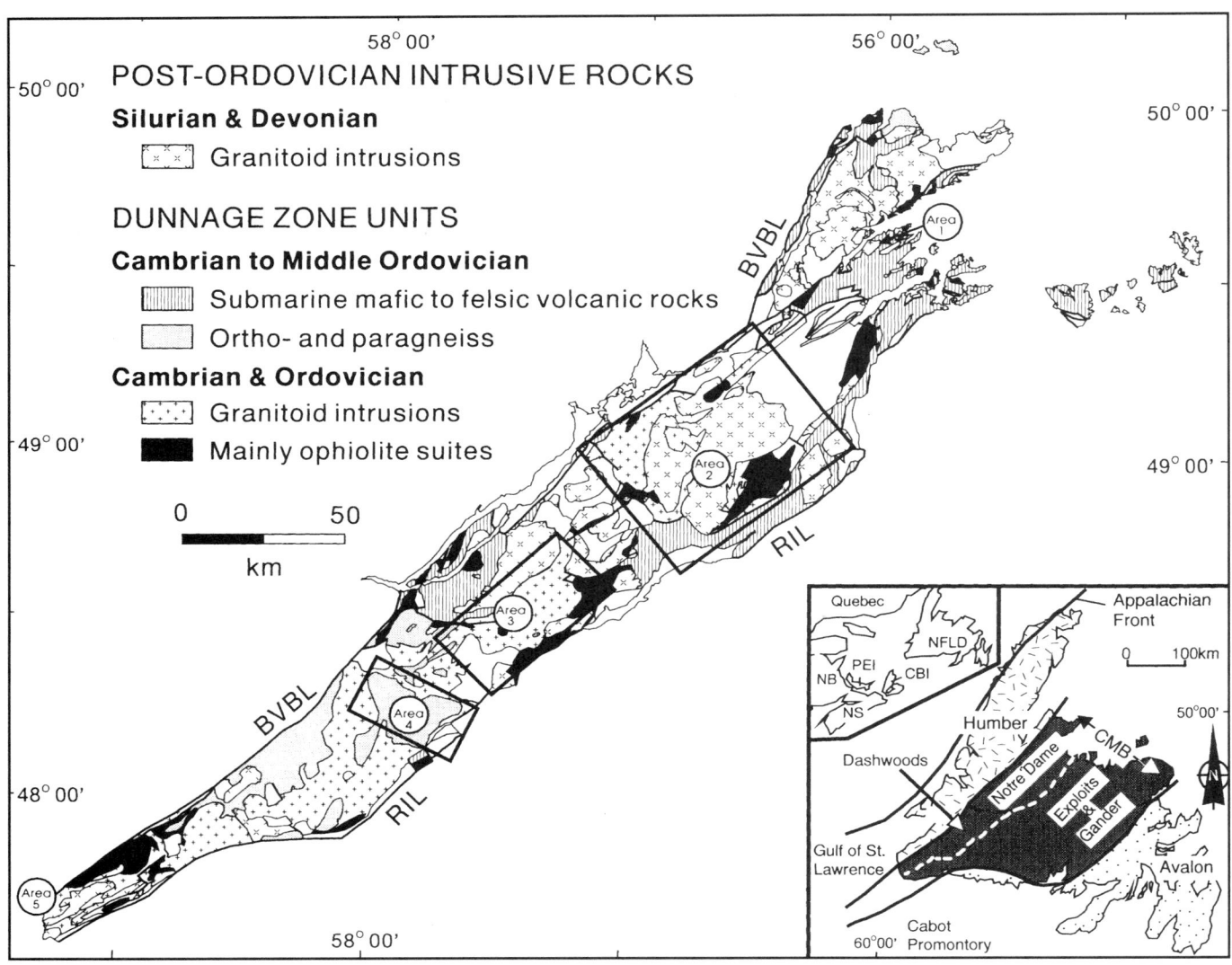

Figure 1. Generalized geologic map of the Notre Dame arc showing the distribution of Early to Middle Ordovician plutonic and volcanic rocks; areas 1 to 5 where granitoid rock samples were collected are indicated (see text for discussion). Lower right inset shows tectonostratigraphic subdivision of Newfoundland (modified after Williams et al. [1988] and Piasecki et al., 1990). Abbreviations are as follows: RIL—Red Indian line; BVBL—Baie Verte–Brompton Line.

which the ophiolite allochthons were rooted (Cawood and Suhr, 1992)?

TECTONIC AND GEOLOGICAL CONTEXT

The Canadian Appalachians contain the vestiges of the early Paleozoic Iapetus ocean, which formerly separated the Laurentian and Gondwanan continents. The western margin (Humber zone [HZ]), a late Late Proterozoic to Early Ordovician passive margin sequence deposited on Grenville crust, collided and amalgamated with a Cambrian-Ordovician magmatic arc, the NDA, during Early to Middle Ordovician time (Cawood and Suhr, 1992). The NDA is bounded to the west by the Baie Verte– Brompton line (BVBL) and to the east by the Red Indian Line (RIL) (Fig. 1). The Exploits subzone, to the east of the RIL, is dominated by oceanic and arc-type remnants of a second, unrelated, Cambrian-Ordovician arc system (Exploits arc) (Williams et al., 1988). Final Iapetus closure in the Late Ordovician to Early Silurian, by westward-directed subduction (e.g., van Staal, 1994), resulted in collision of the eastern margin (Gander zone), a continentally derived sedimentary wedge deposited on Precambrian basement (Gondwanan plate) (van Staal et al., 1996; Whalen et al., 1996), plus the previously accreted Exploits arc, with the composite Laurentian margin (i.e., HZ plus NDA). Voluminous Late Ordovician to Early Silurian magmatism within the NDA (e.g., Whalen, 1989) was a product of this closure and collisional event.

The northern NDA or Notre Dame subzone (Fig. 1) contains significant volumes of well-preserved but disrupted Early to Middle Ordovician, arc-type plutonic and volcanic rocks (Williams et al., 1988). In contrast, the southern NDA (Dashwoods subzone) is underlain mainly by a mixture of high-grade equivalents of the arc-type plutonic rocks with abundant rafts and lenses of dismembered ophiolitic remnants and screens of paragneisses (Dunning and Chorlton, 1985; Piasecki et al., 1990). NDA plutonic rocks and volcanic sequences range in age from about 502 to 456 Ma (Dube et al., 1994; Dunning et al., 1989; Whalen et al., 1987b) and from 500 to 462 Ma (Dunning et al., 1987; Szybinski, 1995), respectively. Volcanic sequences are exclusively subaqueous and include stratigraphically and structurally juxtaposed rocks of oceanic-, arc-, and non–arc-type (see Swinden et al., 1994; Swinden et al., this volume and references therein). Ophiolitic fragments preserved within the NDA range in age from about 490 to 478 Ma (Dunning and Krogh, 1985; Jenner et al., 1991). In the model of Cawood and Suhr (1992), these ophiolites were generated in a suprasubduction zone setting by extension within the NDA during its collision with an irregular Laurentian margin. Oceanic crust formation and subaqueous arc-type volcanism and plutonism were contemporaneous, and were probably also generated in close spatial proximity. More modern analogues probably exist in arc to back arc regions in the southwest Pacific (e.g., Sarewitz and Lewis, 1991; Florendo, 1994).

GENERAL GEOLOGY OF NOTRE DAME ARC PLUTONS

Five general areas of NDA plutonic rocks were sampled (see Fig. 1); each of these areas, plus sampled Grenville basement inliers in the Humber zone, are briefly described in Appendix 1. Areas 2 and 3, which were mapped by J. B. Whalen (Whalen and Currie, 1988; Whalen, 1993a, 1993b), were sampled in the most detail; unit letter abbreviations (e.g., OHM for Hungry Mountain complex) used below and in Appendices 1 and 2 are those employed on these geologic maps. In general, outcrop abundance and quality is poor, and original pluton morphology is rarely preserved because of tectonic dismemberment, making unit correlation and determination of relative age relationships difficult. NDA plutonic rocks are both lithologically and compositionally variable, even at the outcrop scale. They range in texture from fine grained to coarse grained and equigranular to porphyritic, and in composition from gabbroic and dioritic to tonalitic and granodioritic. Blue quartz-eye, porphyritic tonalite is the predominant lithology; granites (sensu stricto) are rare. Ordovician units in which K-feldspar was an early liquidus phase are rare and relatively late. Most plutons are slightly to moderately foliated; some, especially in the Dashwoods subzone, are metamorphosed and recrystallized. In plutonic rocks preserving primary igneous mineralogy, amphibole normally is the main mafic mineral, even at high silica levels. Fine- to medium-grained, angular to ovoid, hornblende-rich gabbro and diorite inclusions, which probably represent quenched samples of coexisting mafic magmas, are common and locally abundant. In contrast, metasedimentary inclusions are rare or absent in NDA plutons, except in area 4, where they are locally abundant.

An U-Pb upper intercept age of 2090 ± 75 Ma obtained from Hungry Mountain complex sample WXHM-1 (area 2) demonstrated the presence of a significant xenocrystic zircon component of Aphebian age (Whalen et al., 1987b). Middle Proterozoic U-Pb inheritance ages were obtained from plutons in area 4 (1430 ± 18 Ma) and area 5 (1541 ± 173 Ma) (Dunning et al., 1989). Inherited zircons were interpreted as indicating that NDA plutons formed in part by partial melting of Proterozoic crust, or sediments derived from such crust.

To evaluate potential wall-rock contaminants or basement source rocks, older Notre Dame subzone orthogneisses and paragneisses and Grenvillian basement inliers in the Humber zone were sampled. On the basis of field relationships, rocks in both the Cariboo Lakes (area 3) and the Cormacks Lake (area 4) complexes predate Middle Ordovician plutonic rocks in these areas. Preliminary U-Pb results from area 3 suggest that these rocks are Early Ordovician in age, i.e., they represent earlier pulses of NDA magmatism. Both retrograded granulitic orthogneisses and a late (460 ± 10 Ma; Currie et al., 1992) charnockite pluton were sampled from the Cormacks Lake complex. Similar orthogneisses and charnockite, plus younger granitoid rocks, all of Late Proterozoic age, were sampled from Grenvillian basement inliers.

GEOCHEMISTRY

Introduction

Table 1 contains major- and trace-element analyses from 80 Early to Middle Ordovician plutonic rock samples and 15 gneissic rocks; locations and descriptions of samples are tabulated in Appendix 2. Table 2 contains isotopic analyses for a subset of samples that includes those that were isotopically dated (see Appendix 1). Analytical techniques are described in Appendix 3.

Analyzed Ordovician plutonic rocks from areas 2, 3, and 4 cover a large silica range (46.5 to 76.0 wt%) and exhibit significant variation in major- and trace-element characteristics. As an aid to data presentation and interpretation, samples were subdivided, mainly on the basis of rare earth element (REE) patterns and presence or absence of Nb anomalies, into mid-ocean ridge basalt (MORB)-, arc-, and non–arc-like groups (see below). The arc-like group was further subdivided, on the basis of chondrite normalized REE patterns, into $(La/Yb)_N$ >12 (La-rich arc) and <12 (La-poor arc) groups. The tectonic and petrogenetic relevance of these relatively arbitrary geochemical subdivisions is evaluated in a subsequent section. In general, they appear to have geologic significance; for example, multiple samples from individual map units consistently are within one or other of these geochemical groups, rather than being split between groups. Discussion herein is restricted to the arc- and non–arc-like plutonic rock groups. MORB-like diabases and gabbros from the Hungry Mountain complex (unit OHMa) and the Star Lake ophiolite complex (Whalen, 1993a) will be presented elsewhere. Limited crosscutting relationships in areas 2 and 3 suggest that the MORB-like group predates the arc- and non–arc-like groups and that the La-rich arc-like units (e.g., Oib, OLc, and OPc) postdate the La-poor arc units.

Although the freshest available material was collected for geochemical analyses, alteration associated with penetrative deformation and metamorphism is present. Consistent major- and trace-element results obtained from both relatively undeformed and well-foliated portions of particular lithological units (such as late K-feldspar porphyritic units Oib, OLc, and OPc) suggest that potentially mobile elements, such as Rb and Sr, were relatively unaffected by fabric formation.

The oxygen-isotope data for minerals (Table 3) exhibit the pattern of ^{18}O-enrichment expected for granitoid rocks (quartz > K-feldspar > hornblende > biotite > magnetite; Taylor, 1968, 1978). However, most isotopic "temperatures" calculated using these data are subsolidus (e.g., quartz-magnetite, 510 to 620 °C; quartz-biotite, 460 to 490 °C; Bottinga and Javoy, 1975), and indicate that retrograde isotopic exchange has affected some minerals more than others. Such behavior is typical of most granitoid rocks (Taylor, 1978; Longstaffe, 1982). Of most importance here is that significant modification of rock or mineral $\delta^{18}O$ values during hydrothermal or lower temperature alteration is not a general or

widespread feature of NDA plutonic rocks. However, petrographic evidence, such as extensive sericite alteration of plagioclase and epidote plus chlorite alteration of mafic minerals, indicates that most NDA samples with $\delta^{18}O$ values >+8‰ (e.g., WXNF-25, WXNF-26, WXNF-32 and WXNF-57) have undergone low-temperature syndeformation and postdeformation alteration. On the basis of results obtained from other studies (e.g., Wenner and Taylor, 1976; Harper et al., 1992), their somewhat elevated $\delta^{18}O$ values probably reflect this alteration (see below).

Major- and trace-element data

Most NDA plutonic rocks are tonalitic to granodioritic in composition (Fig. 2A) and have silica contents between 60 and 72 wt% (Fig. 2B). However, significant volumes of gabbro, diorite, quartz diorite, and lesser quartz monzonite and granite are also present. They plot almost exclusively in the calc-alkaline field on an AFM diagram (Fig. 2C) and include low-, medium-, and high-K compositions (Fig. 3A). In keeping with their generally amphibole bearing mineralogy, almost all samples are metaluminous to only slightly peraluminous (Al index <1.1) (Fig. 3B). The trace element characteristics of each geochemical group are illustrated by means of primitive mantle normalized plots (Figs. 4 to 8). Within these groups, individual mapped lithological units plus samples with similar silica content exhibit very similar and regular patterns.

La-poor arc-like group. This, the largest group (N = 45), covers a silica range of 46 to 76 wt% and consists mainly of low- to medium-K rocks (Figs. 2 and 3A). Although a few mafic samples from the Hungry Mountain complex (unit OHMa) have low REE abundances, average REE content does not correlate with silica. Heavy REEs are slightly depleted, relative to light REEs ($[La/Yb]_N$ = 2 to 8), and Eu anomalies are mainly absent. Except for negative Nb anomalies, which are pronounced at all silica levels, primitive mantle-normalized patterns of low silica samples are relatively smooth (Fig. 4A). Higher silica content unit OHMb exhibits more positive anomalies for Ba and Zr, and negative anomalies for P and Ti become more pronounced (Fig. 4, B and C).

Area 3 samples (n = 18) are about twice as enriched in Rb, Ba, K, Th, and Nb and in light REEs relative to heavy REEs ($[La/Yb]_N$ = 6 to 11) (Fig. 5, A to D) as area 2 samples (Fig. 4, A and B) of similar silica content. Multiple, widely separated samples from distinctive lithological map units, such as quartz-eye porphyritic tonalite unit OLa, have almost identical normalized patterns (Fig. 5D), whereas less lithologically homogeneous units, such as tonalite unit OPa, are geochemically variable (Fig. 5B). Patterns of dioritic to tonalitic samples from areas 1 and 4 (n = 7) (Fig. 5, A and E) closely resemble those of samples from area 3 at similar silica contents.

La-rich arc-like group. This, the second-largest group (n = 24), spans a silica range similar to that of the other arc-like group (49 to 76 wt%), but is characterized by mainly medium to high K contents (Figs. 2A, 3A). It includes relatively late, K-feldspar porphyritic granodioritic to granitic units in area 2

TABLE 1. MAJOR- AND TRACE-ELEMENT DATA FOR NOTRE DAME ARC PLUTONIC AND VARIOUS GNEISSIC ROCKS*

	Arc-Like with $(La/Yb)_N < 12$ (La-Poor Arc-Like Group)												
WXNF#	126	138	109	107	85	115	111	106	122	26	25	93	43
Area	3	3	4	4	3	4	4	4	4	1	1	2	2
Unit	Om	Opb	Odi	Odi	Om	Odi	Odi	Ogd	Otn	Ogd	Og	OHMa	OHMa
(wt. %)													
SiO_2	47.07	48.99	50.51	51.80	53.36	57.41	63.00	64.65	70.60	71.40	73.82	46.38	47.90
TiO_2	0.53	0.28	1.49	1.53	0.90	0.87	0.75	0.82	0.45	0.28	0.21	0.34	1.06
Al_2O_3	16.01	19.55	17.15	17.95	16.00	15.90	17.80	16.10	14.25	14.31	14.18	17.01	19.35
Fe_2O_3	4.25	2.90	3.27	2.98	3.20	2.77	1.92	1.94	1.61	1.27	0.64	3.90	5.90
FeO	6.95	5.00	5.75	5.40	5.35	5.00	2.30	2.30	1.50	1.63	0.20	5.90	5.45
MnO	0.23	0.17	0.16	0.18	0.16	0.15	0.08	0.11	0.10	0.09	0.03	0.18	0.17
MgO	8.52	6.70	6.14	4.17	4.96	3.63	1.89	1.48	1.11	0.85	0.61	9.70	4.07
CaO	12.75	12.10	10.60	7.77	7.76	6.89	4.96	3.69	3.46	3.12	1.36	12.11	9.00
Na_2O	1.42	1.40	2.94	3.87	2.27	2.36	4.84	5.17	3.81	4.34	2.76	1.38	2.81
K_2O	0.34	1.02	0.41	1.65	1.71	2.44	1.42	1.96	1.92	1.50	2.59	0.48	1.24
P_2O_5	0.06	0.03	0.24	0.35	0.33	0.31	0.22	0.22	0.14	0.06	0.05	0.03	0.27
LOI	1.08	1.48	0.55	1.13	1.05	0.93	0.58	0.53	0.43	0.85	3.13	2.27	1.43
TTE	0.34	0.15	0.24	0.40	0.34	0.33	0.28	0.27	0.31	0.09	0.31	0.14	0.26
Total	99.51	99.75	99.44	99.16	99.39	98.99	100.03	99.23	99.68	99.79	99.89	99.79	98.89
Mg#	58.5	61.1	55.7	47.9	51.8	46.3	45.5	39.4	40.1	35.2	58.4	64.8	40.3
(ppm)													
Cr	263	98	50	<7	118	34	21	<7	<7	7	12	65	18
Ni	26	55	71	<4	43	19	25	<4	<4	<4	<4	68	6
Sc	61	53	45	29	29	24	14	19	15	8	<6	46	33
V	356	207	232	172	239	192	73	61	45	38	12	230	245
Cu	97	32	48	23	25	43	9	5	<3	<3	<3	84	19
Pb	6	6	6	14	7	17	7	13	14	<4	10	<4	8
Zn	71	47	65	111	81	68	48	42	23	20	3	48	79
S	1,085	161	479	705	63	351	236	125	37	44	1,432	71	72
F	281	97	349	919	753	747	459	555	512	115	295	73	442
Cl	710	257	178	194	168	402	168	112	152	66	75	278	215
Rb	5	33	9	54	47	86	30	41	51	31	63	17	43
Ba	138	226	127	646	1,029	647	749	870	1,697	267	611	138	477
Sr	203	191	427	661	459	331	670	377	286	139	219	207	530
Ga	15	14	19	24	18	18	20	18	14	....	....	12	25
Ta	1.4	1.4	1.7	1.6	1.9	2.2	3.4	3.5	3.1	1.9	1.6	0.7	1.3
Nb	2.6	1.2	6.4	12.2	6.5	11.8	5.3	11.9	5.7	3.9	7.7	1.1	5.4
Hf	0.9	0.5	4.2	6.0	6.4	5.4	5.3	7.5	3.6	2.0	3.0	0.4	5.4
Zr	21	14	194	235	156	203	192	268	137	86	160	12	219
Y	17	10	27	43	18	22	14	31	11	12	20	3	14
Th	0.6	0.8	1.4	3.4	1.3	1.6	3.4	5.0	1.3	2.5	14.9	0.6	3.2
U	<3	<3	<3	<3	<3	<3	<3	<3	<3	<3	5.3	<3	<3
La	5.4	3.2	12.1	27.5	20.5	16.8	18.8	35.8	13.5	8.2	30.9	1.7	17.6
Ce	15.8	6.2	30.2	66.8	53.9	45.8	36.1	75.7	27.2	17.6	53.9	3.1	37.9
Pr	2.4	0.8	4.1	8.9	7.5	6.7	4.3	8.6	3.7	2.0	6.0	0.4	4.7
Nd	10.6	3.6	18.5	38.0	32.4	28.7	18.1	31.6	16.9	7.3	20.1	1.8	19.0
Sm	2.4	1.1	4.7	8.4	6.6	6.6	3.6	6.3	3.7	1.6	3.6	0.5	3.4
Eu	0.60	0.36	1.42	2.46	1.61	1.64	1.40	1.57	1.55	0.46	0.60	0.20	1.01
Gd	2.33	1.58	5.02	8.46	5.04	6.02	3.58	5.90	3.51	1.56	2.85	0.58	2.90
Tb	0.37	0.29	0.75	1.19	0.64	0.76	0.47	0.85	0.45	0.25	0.42	0.09	0.41
Dy	2.44	1.99	5.12	8.10	3.74	4.67	3.20	5.62	2.56	1.64	2.71	0.64	2.38
Ho	0.55	0.40	1.02	1.61	0.68	0.89	0.60	1.14	0.49	0.35	0.59	0.14	0.59
Er	1.72	1.19	2.93	4.68	1.86	2.41	1.74	3.32	1.26	1.11	1.77	0.43	1.69
Tm	0.28	0.17	0.42	0.70	0.25	0.35	0.24	0.50	0.17	0.18	0.30	0.07	0.24
Yb	2.10	1.10	2.55	4.46	1.59	2.17	1.54	3.14	1.12	1.22	2.05	0.42	1.63
Lu	0.32	0.17	0.39	0.71	0.26	0.31	0.23	0.48	0.17	0.20	0.37	0.06	0.21
$(La/Yb)_N$	1.7	2.0	3.2	4.1	8.6	5.2	8.2	7.6	8.1	4.5	10.1	2.8	7.2

TABLE 1. MAJOR- AND TRACE-ELEMENT DATA FOR NOTRE DAME ARC PLUTONIC AND VARIOUS GNEISSIC ROCKS*
(continued - page 2)

	Arc-Like with $(La/Yb)_N$<12 (La-Poor Arc-Like Group)												
WXNF#	44	94	89	42	45	HM-1	48	41	49	96	101	132	87
Area	2	2	2	2	2	2	2	2	2	2	2	2	2
Unit	OHMa	OHMa	OHMa	OHMa	OHMa	OHMb	OHMb	OHMb	OHMb	OHMb	OHMb	OHMb	OHMb
(wt. %)													
SiO_2	48.46	48.65	50.55	53.05	56.08	63.00	65.80	67.34	68.15	68.21	69.01	69.15	69.20
TiO_2	1.21	0.61	0.85	0.81	0.80	0.68	0.66	0.59	0.54	0.46	0.46	0.75	0.46
Al_2O_3	15.53	18.25	17.55	18.24	16.74	15.70	14.55	14.52	14.80	15.17	14.30	13.72	14.50
Fe_2O_3	3.66	4.99	5.58	4.38	3.84	3.24	2.72	2.80	2.15	2.43	1.68	2.83	2.14
FeO	6.45	5.05	5.55	4.45	3.80	3.40	2.45	2.60	1.75	1.70	2.30	1.85	1.90
MnO	0.21	0.17	0.20	0.14	0.15	0.15	0.11	0.13	0.10	0.11	0.15	0.06	0.10
MgO	8.03	5.45	4.38	4.06	4.00	2.30	1.71	1.90	1.20	1.39	0.74	1.36	1.31
CaO	10.06	11.40	8.27	8.40	7.24	7.36	5.60	4.92	5.08	4.98	3.54	5.36	4.81
Na_2O	2.57	2.08	2.83	3.17	3.47	2.47	3.75	3.14	3.53	3.96	5.01	3.50	3.53
K_2O	1.36	0.61	1.49	1.71	2.31	0.34	0.71	0.86	1.02	0.87	0.73	0.57	0.93
P_2O_5	0.39	0.07	0.21	0.36	0.31	0.15	0.14	0.12	0.13	0.11	0.13	0.19	0.12
LOI	1.85	1.20	1.55	1.08	1.27	0.00	0.43	1.16	0.65	1.04	0.75	0.77	0.70
TTE	0.37	0.18	0.47	0.29	0.30	0.17	0.17	0.16	0.18	0.16	0.14	0.18	0.15
Total	100.13	98.70	99.46	100.13	100.32	98.95	98.78	100.24	99.26	100.60	98.92	100.28	99.85
Mg#	59.5	50.5	42.4	46.3	49.6	39.4	38.3	39.8	36.6	39.0	25.6	35.6	37.9
(ppm)													
Cr	377	18	<7	20	42	<7	13	12	<7	<7	<7	14	<7
Ni	117	8	<4	12	16	13	5	<4	<4	<4	<4	<4	<4
Sc	35	39	44	23	24	18	18	18	14	14	19	22	16
V	294	323	291	213	206	137	104	116	57	78	6	57	56
Cu	82	93	87	7	29	11	3	13	10	15	<3	4	6
Pb	8	8	8	10	10	4	6	7	8	6	8	5	4
Zn	80	59	82	62	56	37	22	43	17	35	45	0	14
S	165	111	2,522	61	54	<11	46	99	31	45	26	17	48
F	875	207	489	560	525	760	342	245	227	240	336	330	220
Cl	275	277	277	276	225	<23	215	138	202	125	249	339	76
Rb	43	20	66	44	57	10	15	24	24	24	18	19	26
Ba	486	216	358	623	824	109	306	430	537	534	198	300	518
Sr	592	268	325	725	673	271	254	220	280	311	177	272	253
Ga	19	17	19	20	19	16	15	14	14	14	17	13	15
Ta	1.6	1.1	1.4	1.8	2.1	1.3	2.1	1.9	3.7	2.7	3.2	3.1	4.0
Nb	11.0	2.8	3.4	5.8	4.9	5.2	7.1	4.4	6.6	4.5	7.2	4.3	4.6
Hf	2.8	1.1	1.6	3.2	3.4	5.7	3.8	4.7	5.9	3.3	3.7	7.9	3.8
Zr	67	40	37	114	86	201	142	183	223	119	153	302	140
Y	23	13	23	18	15	11	31	12	15	15	38	19	13
Th	2.0	1.6	1.8	3.9	4.0	1.6	2.1	1.2	3.1	1.7	1.2	2.6	2.2
U	<3	2.6	<3	<3	<3	0.4	1.8	<3	<3	0.2	<3	<3	<3
La	19.8	5.9	11.4	19.5	20.8	9.1	16.1	9.4	15.4	10.5	11.2	11.2	13.1
Ce	46.9	13.6	25.9	43.6	43.5	19.9	36.3	19.3	30.3	20.6	27.7	22.5	25.3
Pr	6.1	1.8	3.5	5.7	5.3	2.5	4.7	2.5	3.5	2.4	3.8	2.7	3.0
Nd	26.1	8.0	15.4	24.0	21.6	10.0	20.0	10.5	13.7	9.9	17.2	11.4	11.7
Sm	5.7	2.0	4.1	5.0	4.0	2.2	4.7	2.5	2.9	2.3	4.8	2.9	2.6
Eu	1.61	0.55	1.13	1.36	1.20	0.60	0.94	0.75	1.07	0.79	1.34	1.01	0.82
Gd	4.97	1.98	4.10	4.37	3.54	2.18	4.79	2.44	2.65	2.43	5.41	3.35	2.39
Tb	0.71	0.31	0.62	0.61	0.47	0.29	0.76	0.37	0.40	0.38	0.89	0.49	0.35
Dy	4.30	2.02	4.42	3.42	2.83	2.12	5.00	2.33	2.71	2.59	6.48	3.37	2.42
Ho	0.84	0.44	0.91	0.74	0.61	0.42	1.06	0.50	0.53	0.56	1.34	0.74	0.50
Er	2.50	1.37	2.60	2.10	1.74	1.28	3.26	1.50	1.65	1.64	4.00	2.27	1.45
Tm	0.37	0.20	0.37	0.29	0.27	0.18	0.48	0.21	0.24	0.23	0.60	0.33	0.22
Yb	2.36	1.41	2.46	1.92	1.73	1.09	3.11	1.49	1.56	1.60	3.88	2.26	1.45
Lu	0.36	0.21	0.37	0.27	0.25	0.18	0.47	0.22	0.26	0.23	0.58	0.38	0.23
$(La/Yb)_N$	5.6	2.8	3.1	6.8	8.0	5.5	3.5	4.2	6.6	4.4	1.9	3.3	6.1

TABLE 1. MAJOR- AND TRACE-ELEMENT DATA FOR NOTRE DAME ARC PLUTONIC AND VARIOUS GNEISSIC ROCKS*
(continued - page 3)

	Arc-Like with $(La/Yb)_N$<12 (La-Poor Arc-Like Group)												
WXNF#	34	47	33	68	69	21	70	71	22	72	63	50	61
Area	2	2	2	3	3	3	3	3	3	3	3	3	3
Unit	OHMb	OHMb	OHMb	OLa	OLa	OLa	OLa	OLa	OLb	OLb	OLb	OPa	OPa
(wt. %)													
SiO_2	69.55	69.60	70.78	64.45	65.40	67.97	68.11	69.86	56.69	63.10	61.05	61.85	62.10
TiO_2	0.42	0.50	0.37	1.13	0.78	0.58	0.63	0.58	0.80	0.95	0.63	0.67	0.69
Al_2O_3	14.22	14.15	13.68	14.95	14.30	14.02	14.00	13.45	16.63	16.20	15.80	15.85	15.80
Fe_2O_3	2.16	2.16	1.89	3.18	2.95	2.50	2.23	2.59	3.44	4.08	2.48	2.91	2.92
FeO	1.50	1.60	1.53	3.75	3.20	2.25	2.55	1.70	4.30	2.40	3.30	3.25	3.35
MnO	0.10	0.07	0.09	0.13	0.14	0.11	0.10	0.10	0.14	0.13	0.12	0.14	0.14
MgO	1.23	1.26	1.04	2.15	2.04	1.50	1.60	1.61	3.66	1.06	2.79	2.42	2.49
CaO	4.26	4.89	2.72	3.37	5.19	3.76	3.40	2.16	7.38	4.03	5.96	6.32	5.15
Na_2O	3.62	3.39	4.83	1.92	2.26	2.62	2.41	2.46	2.52	4.09	2.50	3.09	3.23
K_2O	1.16	0.52	0.71	2.64	1.76	2.68	2.91	3.01	2.54	2.16	3.00	1.30	1.93
P_2O_5	0.10	0.09	0.07	0.17	0.16	0.10	0.10	0.09	0.31	0.20	0.23	0.19	0.18
LOI	1.39	0.80	1.75	1.60	1.78	1.70	1.40	1.95	1.08	0.65	1.20	0.78	0.95
TTE	0.17	0.14	0.12	0.27	0.20	0.20	0.19	0.19	0.39	0.45	0.38	0.24	0.28
Total	99.87	99.17	99.57	99.71	100.14	99.99	99.62	99.74	99.86	99.48	99.45	98.98	99.22
Mg#	38.9	38.8	36.6	36.7	38.3	37.3	38.5	41.5	46.9	23.6	47.3	42.3	42.6
(ppm)													
Cr	13	<7	15	82	14	13	11	11	48	12	34	21	<7
Ni	<4	<4	<4	58	4	8	7	11	12	34	12	34	<4
Sc	19	10	12	20	32	18	16	16	22	12	20	18	18
V	56	60	40	138	124	92	94	87	217	25	144	149	155
Cu	<3	15	38	38	22	7	14	14	50	11	17	11	14
Pb	9	7	<4	13	14	19	16	15	16	14	19	6	9
Zn	18	11	8	74	56	45	36	48	60	86	49	48	65
S	32	248	46	225	128	31	34	29	201	86	81	409	357
F	175	140	245	544	366	295	313	386	850	389	561	26	590
Cl	108	140	103	73	126	169	122	84	358	117	417	166	103
Rb	24	15	13	102	62	85	92	95	92	71	87	50	75
Ba	770	216	229	640	467	689	635	642	1,053	1,463	1,519	756	826
Sr	265	333	195	202	193	153	163	148	514	584	485	383	316
Ga	....	13	....	20	16	14	16	15	9	22	15	16	16
Ta	2.0	4.4	1.9	2.9	2.6	0.8	3.7	3.4	1.5	3.7	2.4	2.5	2.5
Nb	5.9	3.1	4.5	17.1	10.5	9.1	11.4	11.0	8.7	17.9	8.9	6.0	5.4
Hf	3.3	4.0	3.5	8.1	5.7	5.1	5.1	5.0	5.8	26.4	3.9	4.8	4.5
Zr	140	172	142	322	201	179	169	149	193	1,176	141	159	143
Y	18	6	21	13	21	16	19	18	17	26	16	18	19
Th	2.6	1.9	2.5	6.2	4.2	7.8	10.1	10.7	3.5	6.2	5.8	3.1	1.7
U	2.4	<3	2.1	<3	<3	1.5	<3	<3	3.7	<3	2.7	<3	<3
La	15.6	9.0	9.3	27.1	18.9	25.7	31.0	29.7	21.4	58.0	19.3	22.0	25.1
Ce	32.1	15.9	19.9	54.6	43.0	51.4	63.3	61.5	52.3	118.4	46.6	45.0	50.4
Pr	3.8	1.8	2.4	6.4	5.3	5.8	7.2	7.2	6.8	13.4	6.2	5.5	6.1
Nd	15.0	6.5	9.6	24.6	21.5	21.2	27.0	27.0	26.6	47.9	25.0	22.6	24.3
Sm	3.1	1.4	2.4	4.4	4.5	3.8	4.9	5.1	5.3	8.0	4.9	4.8	4.9
Eu	0.85	0.61	0.69	1.21	1.09	0.89	1.00	0.96	1.28	4.46	1.12	1.27	1.07
Gd	2.93	1.16	2.53	3.52	4.10	3.19	4.04	4.12	3.70	6.70	3.72	4.22	4.17
Tb	0.44	0.15	0.42	0.51	0.62	0.46	0.58	0.63	0.51	0.85	0.49	0.60	0.59
Dy	2.92	1.14	3.01	3.38	3.96	3.08	3.82	3.93	2.91	5.42	2.92	3.90	3.58
Ho	0.61	0.27	0.66	0.59	0.77	0.56	0.73	0.76	0.57	1.07	0.56	0.71	0.70
Er	1.81	0.88	2.12	1.65	2.36	1.66	2.12	2.19	1.59	3.27	1.60	2.03	1.99
Tm	0.26	0.14	0.34	0.26	0.35	0.25	0.32	0.31	0.24	0.53	0.23	0.29	0.27
Yb	1.66	1.00	2.38	1.70	2.20	1.61	2.10	2.16	1.46	3.87	1.52	1.75	1.68
Lu	0.25	0.16	0.37	0.25	0.34	0.26	0.31	0.32	0.24	0.67	0.23	0.32	0.25
$(La/Yb)_N$	6.3	6.0	2.6	10.7	5.8	10.7	9.9	9.2	9.8	10.0	8.5	8.4	10.0

TABLE 1. MAJOR- AND TRACE-ELEMENT DATA FOR NOTRE DAME ARC PLUTONIC AND VARIOUS GNEISSIC ROCKS*
(continued - page 4)

	Arc-Like with (La/Yb)$_N$<12 (La-Poor Arc-Like Group)						Arc-Like with (La/Yb)$_N$>12 (La-Rich Arc-Like Group)						
WXNF#	56	62	55	135	36	73	5	108	90	117	144	116	32
Area	3	3	3	3	3	3	4	4	2	4	3	4	5
Unit	OPa	OPa	OPa	OPd	OPd	OLd	Odi	Ogb	OHMa	Odi	OLb	Odi	Ogd
(wt. %)													
SiO$_2$	62.64	63.74	68.75	71.48	68.85	58.06	47.88	49.06	51.57	53.46	54.11	55.61	57.43
TiO$_2$	0.64	0.63	0.52	0.27	0.42	0.43	1.12	0.80	0.69	0.64	0.97	1.00	0.67
Al$_2$O$_3$	15.97	15.30	15.26	14.95	15.45	13.40	17.77	16.50	14.31	16.70	16.65	16.40	16.29
Fe$_2$O$_3$	3.51	3.80	2.16	1.09	1.40	3.56	3.77	3.43	3.17	3.62	4.14	2.53	3.10
FeO	2.95	2.40	1.40	1.20	1.70	4.50	6.20	5.55	5.75	3.80	4.45	5.05	2.43
MnO	0.15	0.15	0.08	0.06	0.09	0.22	0.15	0.17	0.18	0.17	0.13	0.12	0.13
MgO	2.25	2.37	1.10	0.58	1.09	5.80	6.07	5.49	7.01	4.11	4.40	4.28	2.87
CaO	5.72	4.94	5.70	2.79	3.36	8.31	9.28	9.28	10.70	7.77	7.36	7.06	4.87
Na$_2$O	5.04	2.90	2.82	4.77	4.27	2.32	2.58	2.08	2.02	2.40	2.09	2.46	3.25
K$_2$O	0.39	1.87	1.06	1.89	2.09	1.11	2.17	3.70	1.24	4.49	2.25	3.26	3.91
P$_2$O$_5$	0.22	0.17	0.11	0.09	0.14	0.07	0.52	0.72	0.28	0.53	0.35	0.48	0.43
LOI	0.66	1.13	0.83	0.40	0.68	1.45	1.52	0.90	1.20	1.10	2.48	0.43	3.63
TTE	0.23	0.44	0.22	0.16	0.19	0.21	0.55	0.58	0.30	0.50	0.34	0.60	0.61
Total	100.37	99.82	100.01	99.73	99.71	99.44	99.59	98.25	98.40	99.26	99.69	99.26	99.60
Mg#	39.7	42.0	37.0	32.2	39.7	57.3	53.0	53.1	59.2	50.9	48.9	51.0	49.5
(ppm)													
Cr	18	22	20	14	<7	123	120	103	280	61	73	100	43
Ni	4	34	29	32	<4	30	57	33	51	22	59	42	12
Sc	30	19	8	8	11	52	41	37	49	25	25	22	14
V	113	151	75	20	44	188	279	295	306	224	247	198	135
Cu	8	33	21	3	11	11	6	76	17	59	19	52	<3
Pb	7	7	<4	20	18	4	10	14	4	20	13	20	24
Zn	47	86	16	21	43	61	105	63	56	59	85	75	63
S	214	1,938	212	50	45	156	276	116	166	231	86	151	34
F	505	50	113	250	319	270	1,250	1,390	680	940	311	1,150	995
Cl	177	144	33	36	77	302	356	207	510	256	295	928	63
Rb	4	83	32	55	85	32	71	121	43	164	80	118	118
Ba	302	1,182	1,154	587	677	512	1,106	2,092	294	1,720	1,002	1,595	2,660
Sr	355	332	351	319	276	156	1,072	829	359	710	663	856	1,168
Ga	19	16	11	19	16	13	17	13	13	14	18	20	10
Ta	1.8	2.4	2.7	5.8	3.8	2.2	1.3	1.7	1.2	1.9	1.8	2.1	1.3
Nb	4.9	7.4	1.6	6.2	8.8	5.2	19.6	11.4	4.9	8.1	9.2	15.4	14.2
Hf	5.8	4.9	1.3	2.3	3.5	2.0	7.2	3.1	1.7	4.5	5.0	8.4	7.3
Zr	179	159	64	94	130	51	286	86	54	137	193	283	278
Y	91	21	1	10	17	27	38	23	14	21	14	17	17
Th	1.1	2.0	0.5	4.1	5.5	9.5	3.6	9.6	4.3	10.4	10.0	10.6	21.2
U	<3	<3	<3	<3	<3	<3	3.0	<3	<3	<3	<3	<3	8.1
La	24.0	20.0	2.3	12.3	25.4	18.0	68.8	62.7	22.6	58.4	39.8	61.6	92.9
Ce	58.0	43.5	4.2	23.1	49.1	41.7	173.6	127.0	48.0	120.0	83.7	134.3	184.4
Pr	8.6	5.6	0.5	2.5	5.6	5.2	23.2	15.6	5.9	14.1	9.5	15.6	20.2
Nd	41.4	23.0	2.0	9.5	20.4	20.3	91.8	59.9	23.8	56.9	36.4	57.6	68.5
Sm	11.6	5.1	0.4	2.0	4.0	4.4	16.9	10.8	4.9	10.2	6.6	9.1	9.7
Eu	1.74	1.19	0.80	0.57	0.81	0.98	3.16	2.62	1.16	2.40	1.61	2.07	2.02
Gd	13.53	4.66	0.56	2.05	3.63	4.18	10.63	8.37	3.72	7.56	4.49	6.13	5.50
Tb	2.35	0.66	0.07	0.31	0.52	0.66	1.33	0.99	0.46	0.93	0.58	0.72	0.63
Dy	15.65	4.49	0.43	1.99	3.45	4.71	7.15	5.29	2.64	5.12	3.24	3.88	3.26
Ho	3.54	0.80	0.08	0.37	0.71	0.97	1.29	0.88	0.50	0.96	0.55	0.68	0.56
Er	10.64	2.35	0.21	1.08	2.12	2.92	3.44	2.34	1.40	2.50	1.46	1.85	1.45
Tm	1.55	0.34	0.04	0.17	0.33	0.47	0.47	0.30	0.19	0.35	0.21	0.26	0.19
Yb	9.79	2.19	0.23	1.08	2.34	3.16	2.76	1.86	1.19	2.06	1.33	1.70	1.19
Lu	1.37	0.32	0.04	0.17	0.37	0.50	0.41	0.27	0.19	0.31	0.21	0.27	0.18
(La/Yb)$_N$	1.6	6.1	6.7	7.6	7.3	3.8	16.7	22.5	12.7	18.9	20.0	24.2	52.3

TABLE 1. MAJOR- AND TRACE-ELEMENT DATA FOR NOTRE DAME ARC PLUTONIC AND VARIOUS GNEISSIC ROCKS*
(continued - page 5)

	Arc-Like with $(La/Yb)_N$>12 (La-Rich Arc-Like Group)												
WXNF#	6	119	1	10	31	112	74	123	98	105	TB119	TB121	102
Area	4	4	3	4	5	4	3	4	2	2	2	2	2
Unit	Odi	Ogd	OPa	Ogd	Og	Ota	OLd	Ogd	OHMb	Oib	Oib	Oib	Oib
(wt. %)													
SiO_2	64.26	65.35	66.52	69.62	70.02	70.98	72.70	73.40	75.75	70.45	70.10	69.32	66.99
TiO_2	1.61	0.51	0.65	0.33	0.36	0.46	0.30	0.24	0.25	0.24	0.30	0.43	0.37
Al_2O_3	14.06	15.90	15.76	15.86	13.51	14.20	13.70	14.20	12.80	15.15	15.05	14.44	16.10
Fe_2O_3	2.77	1.82	1.82	1.26	1.83	1.55	1.48	0.89	1.20	0.79	0.88	1.41	1.25
FeO	5.20	3.20	3.07	1.60	1.43	1.85	0.60	0.70	0.70	0.50	1.35	2.23	1.10
MnO	0.10	0.12	0.21	0.04	0.07	0.08	0.07	0.07	0.05	0.06	0.04	0.09	0.05
MgO	2.33	1.90	0.46	0.97	1.08	1.01	0.72	0.47	0.65	0.56	1.07	1.28	1.48
CaO	2.99	4.15	2.42	4.61	3.39	3.41	2.89	1.87	1.91	2.19	2.92	3.90	3.60
Na_2O	2.47	3.39	7.05	3.91	3.19	3.52	3.55	3.96	5.31	4.42	3.35	2.58	4.20
K_2O	2.28	2.03	1.07	1.14	1.65	2.36	2.29	3.39	0.95	3.40	3.52	3.32	2.78
P_2O_5	0.06	0.15	0.14	0.14	0.06	0.10	0.08	0.08	0.03	0.08	0.12	0.08	0.15
LOI	0.78	0.75	0.68	0.58	3.47	0.43	0.90	0.63	0.50	1.00	1.15	1.19	0.73
TTE	0.41	0.21	0.25	0.23	0.13	0.29	0.33	0.26	0.13	0.40	0.27	0.21	0.44
Total	99.32	99.48	100.09	100.28	100.18	100.24	99.61	100.14	100.22	99.23	100.12	100.48	99.22
Mg#	35.1	41.2	14.9	38.7	38.4	35.7	39.9	35.5	39.4	44.9	47.1	39.5	54.2
(ppm)													
Cr	104	<7	43	21	20	37	<7	<7	<7	<7	12	10	32
Ni	45	<4	17	<4	<4	<4	<4	<4	<4	<4	5	<4	38
Sc	18	21	9	8	14	<6	<6	<6	<6	<6	<6	12	7
V	114	91	43	36	61	54	27	12	10	15	39	66	42
Cu	52	25	<3	<3	9	4	6	<3	5	3	<3	4	<3
Pb	10	20	20	13	10	12	8	30	10	25	19	10	19
Zn	88	48	20	16	21	21	7	16	0	10	29	34	24
S	1,051	83	52	49	124	43	80	22	36	37	100	100	66
F	370	639	315	225	210	275	247	145	222	438	400	300	407
Cl	67	235	30	111	35	86	67	28	112	142	200	200	142
Rb	58	119	72	31	50	61	58	134	24	95	122	99	74
Ba	1,120	275	861	601	475	1,829	2,328	1,505	488	1,801	900	765	2,123
Sr	307	197	705	866	155	265	253	286	158	1,038	580	194	1,059
Ga	7	20	10	9	....	13	9	15	13	20	18	14	20
Ta	1.8	3.6	1.6	1.8	1.3	1.9	3.6	0.2	5.3	4.9	0.7	0.8	4.1
Nb	17.2	15.5	9.1	5.1	5.4	4.8	4.8	11.1	5.1	22.0	6.0	10.0	9.7
Hf	10.5	4.4	3.5	4.5	1.7	3.9	3.5	3.8	3.1	5.1	5.3	4.9	5.5
Zr	386	150	124	176	63	139	111	173	115	135	124	141	178
Y	11	13	8	6	5	8	8	15	6	8	4	13	4
Th	12.3	8.3	10.8	3.1	1.4	2.7	3.7	21.7	3.5	14.7	17.5	9.0	10.8
U	<3	<3	4.0	1.5	<3	<3	<3	5.6	<3	4.7	3.5	1.5	<3
La	46.5	43.7	22.5	16.8	9.1	21.7	17.5	53.3	13.0	36.2	20.3	26.6	33.5
Ce	96.4	79.4	43.5	31.7	16.2	37.5	31.0	88.6	23.6	73.1	40.4	50.6	63.9
Pr	11.5	8.6	5.0	3.5	1.7	4.0	3.4	8.5	2.5	8.3	4.5	5.3	7.2
Nd	42.9	31.1	17.8	12.9	5.6	14.9	11.8	27.4	8.6	29.1	15.5	17.9	25.6
Sm	7.3	4.8	2.9	2.0	1.0	2.6	2.2	4.0	1.5	4.8	2.4	3.1	4.0
Eu	1.67	1.01	0.82	1.13	0.63	1.14	0.87	0.82	0.56	0.95	0.48	0.83	1.05
Gd	4.99	3.32	2.06	1.41	0.81	2.30	1.78	3.15	1.26	2.92	1.65	3.20	2.18
Tb	0.53	0.45	0.24	0.16	0.10	0.30	0.25	0.46	0.17	0.33	0.18	0.41	0.28
Dy	2.50	2.74	1.35	0.96	0.68	1.75	1.63	3.00	1.03	1.88	0.90	2.48	1.40
Ho	0.38	0.53	0.24	0.19	0.14	0.35	0.33	0.61	0.20	0.35	0.16	0.52	0.23
Er	0.82	1.55	0.66	0.52	0.39	0.99	0.90	1.96	0.62	0.92	0.41	1.41	0.55
Tm	0.10	0.21	0.09	0.07	0.06	0.16	0.14	0.29	0.10	0.13	0.05	0.20	0.07
Yb	0.51	1.33	0.59	0.45	0.33	0.93	0.87	2.01	0.71	0.81	0.37	1.40	0.45
Lu	0.11	0.18	0.10	0.08	0.06	0.14	0.15	0.32	0.11	0.10	0.06	0.21	0.07
$(La/Yb)_N$	60.4	22.1	25.7	25.1	18.2	15.6	13.5	17.7	12.3	29.9	36.3	12.7	50.1

TABLE 1. MAJOR- AND TRACE-ELEMENT DATA FOR NOTRE DAME ARC PLUTONIC AND VARIOUS GNEISSIC ROCKS*

(continued - page 6)

						Non-Arc-Like Group									
WXNF#	64	51	137	52	57	113	114	75	77	76	53	86	125	136	95
Area	3	3	3	3	3	4	4	3	3	3	3	3	3	3	2
Unit	OLc	OPc	OPc	OPc	OPc	Odie	Otn	OPa	OPa	OPa	OPa	OPa	OPa	OPd	OHMb
(wt. %)															
SiO_2	67.31	74.99	74.59	72.10	69.60	64.77	65.06	67.45	72.35	72.35	67.25	67.05	69.10	67.12	65.81
TiO_2	0.45	0.20	0.18	0.24	0.29	1.08	0.86	0.54	0.41	0.22	0.40	0.45	0.50	0.43	0.72
Al_2O_3	15.31	12.90	13.47	13.45	14.35	15.81	14.15	14.90	13.50	13.55	14.45	14.90	14.55	16.59	15.33
Fe_2O_3	1.83	0.91	1.03	0.94	1.33	2.08	3.58	2.34	1.36	1.14	2.87	2.28	2.40	1.29	2.76
FeO	1.90	0.40	0.45	0.65	1.00	3.60	3.75	2.05	1.60	0.90	2.70	2.05	1.90	2.05	2.60
MnO	0.08	0.04	0.04	0.04	0.06	0.06	0.08	0.09	0.05	0.05	0.12	0.09	0.11	0.09	0.13
MgO	1.51	0.44	0.40	0.48	0.74	2.46	2.52	1.56	1.09	0.72	1.66	1.58	1.24	1.29	1.67
CaO	4.28	1.78	1.23	1.85	2.31	4.37	5.43	4.66	3.88	2.91	6.23	6.20	5.65	3.96	5.77
Na_2O	2.70	2.99	3.12	2.52	2.79	2.54	1.80	3.28	3.42	2.78	3.07	3.29	3.46	4.47	3.31
K_2O	3.43	3.94	4.67	5.31	4.62	1.86	1.58	1.28	1.12	3.15	0.18	0.36	0.19	1.62	0.73
P_2O_5	0.16	0.06	0.05	0.07	0.10	0.03	0.12	0.17	0.09	0.08	0.10	0.12	0.12	0.15	0.17
LOI	0.78	0.73	0.73	0.73	0.93	0.85	0.75	0.93	0.65	0.75	0.48	0.90	0.33	0.85	1.23
TTE	0.38	0.35	0.25	0.27	0.48	0.38	0.27	0.31	0.24	0.43	0.06	0.16	0.11	0.18	0.18
Total	100.11	99.71	100.20	98.64	98.59	99.88	99.94	99.54	99.75	99.02	99.55	99.43	99.64	100.10	100.40
Mg#	43.1	39.0	34.1	36.1	37.5	44.4	39.2	40.0	40.6	39.8	35.8	40.7	35.2	41.7	37.0
(ppm)															
Cr	9	12	12	<7	<7	89	45	<7	8	<7	15	<7	<7	17	13
Ni	<4	30	28	6	<4	60	21	<4	<4	<4	<4	<4	<4	32	<4
Sc	17	<6	<6	<6	<6	15	18	11	<6	<6	16	16	18	8	15
V	69	18	13	24	36	96	175	81	55	40	93	90	51	53	94
Cu	5	9	3	9	6	56	52	<3	<3	3	14	25	5	10	16
Pb	23	11	13	22	16	11	10	6	7	8	<4	4	4	12	5
Zn	26	0	0	0	13	41	51	35	23	6	31	28	13	43	40
S	50	972	70	67	80	676	433	32	39	24	81	115	40	85	166
F	450	443	303	111	209	420	509	388	266	139	-20	209	110	208	230
Cl	195	42	107	132	63	107	154	57	39	52	137	111	166	103	136
Rb	86	89	104	97	83	54	53	29	22	51	4	6	2	63	21
Ba	1,960	1,396	1,358	1,703	3,574	1,281	469	1,758	1,443	3,478	21	355	166	584	355
Sr	505	204	182	234	369	374	347	398	369	344	154	474	336	398	310
Ga	15	8	10	9	8	19	18	15	10	8	14	12	13	18	16
Ta	3.7	2.8	4.3	4.6	3.4	3.1	3.2	2.8	1.0	2.9	3.1	3.0	4.1	3.7	3.1
Nb	6.5	4.0	2.8	4.8	2.4	14.5	8.5	3.5	2.6	2.1	1.4	2.3	2.0	4.7	9.4
Hf	4.6	3.4	2.6	2.7	3.7	10.1	5.5	4.7	2.9	2.8	0.0	3.1	2.9	3.0	7.1
Zr	141	106	99	100	114	339	210	161	124	75	6	108	115	137	249
Y	13	6	2	12	5	2	7	8	1	2	4	12	15	6	15
Th	7.5	24.2	18.8	26.4	11.2	1.5	0.7	0.4	0.3	0.5	0.2	0.3	0.3	0.4	1.3
U	1.6	<3	<3	<3	<3	<3	<3	<3	<3	<3	<3	<3	<3	<3	0.6
La	41.3	50.5	52.2	49.1	59.1	22.2	13.9	16.1	7.7	12.1	1.6	9.2	5.2	3.3	10.8
Ce	80.9	71.9	69.1	77.8	91.5	37.6	28.2	30.8	12.7	19.9	3.7	20.4	10.6	6.3	23.3
Pr	9.4	7.0	7.1	7.6	8.4	3.9	3.4	3.8	1.3	2.1	0.5	2.8	1.5	0.8	3.1
Nd	34.5	22.0	20.7	24.9	25.8	12.8	13.6	15.0	5.0	7.8	2.4	12.8	7.6	3.5	13.5
Sm	5.6	3.2	2.4	3.9	3.3	1.6	2.7	2.9	0.8	1.3	0.6	3.0	2.2	1.0	3.0
Eu	1.24	0.83	0.71	0.83	0.99	1.60	0.95	1.26	0.72	0.90	0.48	1.00	0.93	0.66	1.08
Gd	4.13	2.23	1.22	2.96	2.10	1.12	2.18	2.52	0.56	0.93	0.69	2.73	2.58	1.19	2.98
Tb	0.55	0.27	0.14	0.41	0.25	0.12	0.25	0.31	0.06	0.11	0.09	0.38	0.38	0.21	0.48
Dy	3.00	1.64	0.83	2.63	1.37	0.56	1.55	1.83	0.33	0.63	0.66	2.45	2.72	1.48	2.83
Ho	0.61	0.28	0.12	0.49	0.25	0.12	0.28	0.34	0.07	0.12	0.17	0.47	0.59	0.26	0.62
Er	1.69	0.73	0.36	1.42	0.63	0.33	0.78	0.89	0.19	0.34	0.51	1.34	1.82	0.75	1.80
Tm	0.24	0.10	0.06	0.20	0.09	0.06	0.11	0.11	0.03	0.05	0.07	0.18	0.25	0.12	0.26
Yb	1.65	0.66	0.36	1.26	0.63	0.43	0.61	0.67	0.17	0.34	0.52	1.10	0.51	0.87	1.78
Lu	0.23	0.12	0.07	0.19	0.10	0.09	0.10	0.10	0.04	0.05	0.07	0.17	0.24	0.15	0.27
$(La/Yb)_N$	16.8	50.9	97.1	26.0	63.1	34.3	15.4	16.0	29.7	24.0	2.1	5.6	2.3	2.5	4.1

TABLE 1. MAJOR- AND TRACE-ELEMENT DATA FOR NOTRE DAME ARC PLUTONIC AND VARIOUS GNEISSIC ROCKS*

(continued - page 7)

							Gneiss Samples								
WXNF#	67	141	65	66	143	175	24	121	124	79	81	2	11	27	13
Area	3	3	3	3	3	3	4	4	4	3	3	HZ	HZ	HZ	HZ
Unit	OECa	OECa	OECb	OECb	OECc	OECc	Ochr	Ogn	Ogn	EOgn	EOgn	PEgn	PEgn	PEgn	PEg
(wt. %)															
SiO_2	53.61	80.73	62.31	65.41	69.72	71.40	67.30	67.31	71.30	69.56	58.36	68.88	67.81	68.75	63.49
TiO_2	1.65	1.09	0.93	1.52	0.45	0.33	0.29	0.43	0.30	1.25	1.51	0.41	0.79	0.57	1.00
Al_2O_3	21.15	7.51	16.45	13.10	14.30	13.85	15.57	14.09	13.75	12.45	18.45	15.36	13.91	14.32	15.04
Fe_2O_3	3.96	2.90	2.84	3.39	2.01	1.69	1.66	1.66	1.80	2.49	4.38	1.22	2.42	2.39	2.31
FeO	7.10	1.35	3.70	4.35	1.80	1.40	1.63	2.17	2.20	3.40	5.00	1.10	2.87	1.53	2.87
MnO	0.13	0.07	0.11	0.12	0.08	0.07	0.11	0.10	0.10	0.10	0.20	0.06	0.08	0.08	0.08
MgO	2.23	1.01	2.33	2.36	1.33	1.04	0.09	1.19	1.48	1.73	2.33	1.46	0.71	0.16	1.15
CaO	1.11	1.49	3.45	2.40	3.74	3.62	0.85	3.58	3.05	1.99	1.73	2.59	2.21	0.87	3.58
Na_2O	0.91	1.49	2.22	2.46	2.89	2.95	5.70	3.45	4.15	2.31	2.19	4.28	3.07	3.53	3.83
K_2O	4.67	1.23	3.01	2.10	2.51	2.48	5.21	2.77	1.11	2.66	3.15	3.33	4.75	6.45	3.66
P_2O_5	0.19	0.07	0.15	0.13	0.11	0.08	0.03	0.13	0.07	0.09	0.10	0.15	0.27	0.05	0.39
LOI	2.18	0.73	1.85	1.33	0.80	0.53	0.40	0.32	0.55	0.73	1.80	0.91	0.63	0.29	1.27
TTE	0.41	0.19	0.33	0.25	0.28	0.23	0.37	0.18	0.12	0.26	0.32	0.36	0.32	0.26	0.47
Total	99.27	99.84	99.66	98.89	100.03	99.65	99.20	97.38	99.97	99.00	99.51	100.10	99.83	99.25	99.13
Mg#	27.3	31.3	39.9	36.2	39.5	38.7	4.9	36.7	40.8	35.3	31.7	54.2	20.1	7.31	29.3
(ppm)															
Cr	65	46	61	95	23	13	<7	<7	8	72	55	8	10	<7	18
Ni	45	11	56	40	31	<4	<4	<4	<4	26	43	<4	<4	<4	<4
Sc	24	<6	19	15	10	8	<6	10	17	15	9	10	9	<6	10
V	138	83	145	141	69	51	<6	57	67	92	97	7	9	<6	40
Cu	7	7	52	30	8	<3	<3	4	57	8	11	162	<3	12	<3
Pb	17	6	22	15	14	13	<4	7	15	11	20	10	23	88	26
Zn	133	14	73	88	24	25	121	22	22	54	115	78	113	20	171
S	91	45	300	217	57	94	18	43	77	75	126	1,349	238	125	289
F	435	237	896	328	125	186	705	350	272	590	40	375	210	45	1,015
Cl	32	25	103	96	232	180	41	184	29	123	158	33	92	66	96
Rb	144	41	124	74	67	77	74	68	19	93	60	32	129	0	94
Ba	1,806	763	695	532	1,531	1,195	891	565	197	677	1,536	220	1,259	192	1,600
Sr	184	138	255	275	262	178	62	248	224	246	261	159	294	29	459
Ga	23	9	21	20	13	12	38	13	13	17	25	27	18	26	16
Ta	2.0	2.9	2.6	2.9	2.7	0.4	4.4	2.1	1.2	3.1	2.2	5.2	1.4	2.6	1.9
Nb	21.6	10.3	13.5	19.3	9.1	7.8	126.8	6.2	6.9	16.4	22.9	74.7	11.4	47.3	23.0
Hf	11.3	8.8	7.7	9.5	4.1	2.2	13.9	3.0	2.9	6.6	7.7	15.4	14.4	20.1	12.9
Zr	416	392	251	335	137	115	783	86	86	248	307	669	487	1,112	458
Y	39	13	14	18	11	6	74	16	26	17	27	63	31	50	47
Th	20.6	1.9	9.0	7.4	10.1	5.9	9.6	1.3	5.4	7.8	14.7	9.6	1.0	10.6	3.9
U	3.8	<3	<3	3.8	<3	<3	<3	<3	2.0	<3	<3	5.3	<3	<3	<3
La	86.4	14.8	32.4	35.9	28.9	21.5	171.3	19.1	16.3	31.1	63.6	62.6	40.2	175.0	66.4
Ce	174.1	27.7	68.3	67.0	54.3	38.0	308.9	35.2	31.4	64.3	122.6	133.4	87.2	340.4	141.8
Pr	20.5	3.2	8.2	8.3	6.1	4.1	34.3	4.0	3.6	7.4	15.3	16.3	11.2	39.8	17.7
Nd	77.1	12.2	31.2	31.1	22.7	13.6	124.0	14.9	13.5	28.5	57.7	62.9	46.5	146.9	68.5
Sm	12.2	2.2	6.1	5.2	3.8	2.1	20.6	3.2	3.1	5.1	9.5	12.8	9.4	21.8	12.5
Eu	2.57	0.61	1.31	1.38	1.10	0.59	2.23	0.82	0.53	1.20	1.88	3.61	2.67	1.63	3.25
Gd	9.22	2.05	4.61	4.06	3.01	1.38	15.10	2.92	3.22	4.04	7.30	11.56	8.03	14.19	9.42
Tb	1.30	0.28	0.60	0.54	0.39	0.21	2.07	0.46	0.56	0.60	0.99	1.83	1.07	1.80	1.35
Dy	7.95	1.92	3.51	3.44	2.55	1.28	11.34	2.79	3.94	3.94	6.35	11.26	5.89	9.00	7.63
Ho	1.41	0.39	0.61	0.67	0.45	0.28	2.14	0.62	0.91	0.80	1.21	2.25	1.08	1.59	1.42
Er	3.94	1.16	1.64	2.05	1.35	0.89	5.62	1.85	3.02	2.44	3.60	6.59	2.73	4.14	3.83
Tm	0.54	0.18	0.24	0.32	0.20	0.14	0.78	0.29	0.48	0.39	0.52	0.97	0.38	0.55	0.53
Yb	3.62	1.18	1.52	2.35	1.15	0.96	4.98	1.85	3.40	2.81	3.30	6.27	1.99	3.51	3.16
Lu	0.54	0.19	0.24	0.34	0.21	0.16	0.80	0.30	0.54	0.45	0.52	1.01	0.31	0.62	0.48
(La/Yb)$_N$	16.0	8.4	14.3	10.2	16.9	15.0	23.0	6.9	3.2	7.4	12.9	6.7	13.5	32.9	14.0

For locations of different areas aee Figure 1,; for map units, see Appendices 1 and 2 plus published geological maps (Whalen and Currie, 1988; Whalen, 1993a, 1993b). Abbreviations: TTE = total of trace elements; LOI = loss on ignition; Mg# = 100(MgO/FeO total + MgO).

TABLE 2. ISOTOPIC ANALYSES AND ADDITIONAL INFORMATION FOR NOTRE DAME ARC PLUTONIC AND VARIOUS GNEISSIC ROCKS*

Sample	Area	Pluton, Complex, or Suite	Unit	Mg#	$(La/Yb)_N$	SiO_2	Age (Ma)	Al Index
Arc-Like with $(La/Yb)_N$<12 (La-Poor Arc-Like Group)								
WXNF-126	3	Early mafic	Om	58.5	1.7	47.1	....	0.62
WXFN-26	1	Mansfield Cove	Ogd	35.2	4.5	71.4	....	0.99
WXNF-25	1	Shoal Arm	Og	58.4	10.1	73.8	....	1.45
WXNF-94	2	Hungry Mountain	OHMa	50.5	2.8	48.7	469	0.74
WXHM-1	2	Hungry Mountain	OHMa	39.4	5.4	63.0	467	0.88
WXNF-48	2	Hungry Mountain	OHMa	38.3	3.5	65.8	480	0.85
WXNF-41	2	Hungry Mountain	OHMb	39.8	4.2	67.3	....	0.97
WXNF-96	2	Hungry Mountain	OHMb	39.0	4.4	68.2	....	0.92
WXNF-87	2	Hungry Mountain	OHMb	37.9	6.1	69.2	....	0.93
WXNF-34	2	Hungry Mountain	OHMb	38.9	6.3	69.5	....	0.95
WXNF-33	2	Hungry Mountain	OHMb	36.6	2.6	70.8	....	1.00
WXNF-69	3	Lewaseechjeech Brook	OLa	38.3	5.8	65.4	....	0.95
WXNF-21	3	Lewaseechjeech Brook	OLa	37.3	10.7	68.0	....	1.00
WXNF-22	3	Lewaseechjeech Brook	OLb	46.9	9.8	56.7	....	0.82
WXNF-63	3	Lewaseechjeech Brook	OLb	47.3	8.5	61.1	466	0.87
WXNF-56	3	Pierre's Pond	OPa	39.7	1.6	62.6	....	0.84
WXNF-73	3	Lewaseechjeech Brook	OLd	57.3	3.8	58.1	....	0.67
Arc-Like with $(La/Yb)_N$>12 (La-Rich Arc-Like Group)								
WXNF-5	4	Southwest Brook	Odi	53.0	16.7	47.9	....	0.76
WXNF-90	2	Hungry Mountain	OHMa	59.2	12.7	51.6	....	0.59
WXNF-32	5	Cape Ray	Ogd	49.5	52.3	57.4	488	0.88
WXNF-6	4	Southwest Brook	Odi	35.1	60.4	64.3	....	1.18
WXNF-1	3	Pierre's Pool	OPa	14.9	25.7	66.5	....	0.92
WXNF-10	4	Southwest Brook	Ogde	38.7	25.1	69.6	....	0.99
WXNF-31	5	Cape Ray	Og	38.4	18.2	70.0	....	1.02
WXTB-119	2	Hinds Brook	Oib	47.1	36.3	70.1	460	1.03
WXTB-121	2	Hinds Brook	Oib	39.5	12.7	69.3	460	0.97
WXNF-102	2	Hinds Brook	Oib	54.2	50.1	67.0	460	0.98
WXNF-64	3	Lewaseechjeech Brook	OLc	43.1	16.8	67.3	....	0.96
WXNF-57	3	Pierre's Pond	OPc	37.5	63.1	69.6	....	1.04
Non-Arc-Like Group								
WXNF-76	3	Pierre's Pond	OPa	39.8	24.0	72.4	....	1.02
WXNF-53	3	Pierre's Pond	OPa	35.8	2.1	67.3	....	0.87
WXNF-86	3	Pierre's Pond	OPa	40.7	5.6	67.1	....	0.87
WXNF-125	3	Pierre's Pond	OPa	35.2	2.3	69.1	....	0.90
WXNF-136	3	Pierre's Pond	OPd	41.7	2.5	67.1	....	1.02
WXNF-95	2	Hungry Mountain	OHMb	37.0	4.1	65.8	....	0.92
Gneiss Samples								
WXNF-67	3	Cariboo Lakes gneiss	OECa	27.1	16.0	53.6	>480	2.47
WXNF-141	3	Cariboo Lakes gneiss	OECa	31.3	8.4	80.7	>480	1.16
WXNF-65	3	Cariboo Lakes gneiss	OECb	39.9	14.3	62.3	>480	1.25
WXNF-24	4	Cormacks Lake	Ochr	4.9	23.0	67.3	460	0.94
WXNF-121	4	Cormacks Lake	Ogn	36.7	6.9	67.3	>480	0.93
WXNF-124	4	Cormacks Lake	Ogn	40.8	3.2	71.3	>480	1.01
WXNF-81	3	Fleur de Lys?	EOga	31.7	12.9	58.4	>480	1.82
WXNF-2	HZ	Disappointment Hill	PEgn	54.2	6.7	68.9	1,100	1.00
WXNF-11	HZ	Long Range Gneiss	PEgn	20.1	13.5	67.8	1,550	0.98
WXNF-27	HZ	Disappointment Hill	PEgn	7.3	32.9	68.7	1,000	1.00
WXNF-13	HZ	Lake Michel	PEg	29.3	14.0	63.5	1,000	0.90

**TABLE 2. ISOTOPIC ANALYSES AND ADDITIONAL INFORMATION FOR
NOTRE DAME ARC PLUTONIC AND VARIOUS GNEISSIC ROCKS*** (continued - page 2)

Sample	$\delta^{18}O$ (%)	$\frac{^{206}Pb}{^{204}Pb}$	$\frac{^{207}Pb}{^{204}Pb}$	$\frac{^{206}Pb}{^{204}Pb}$	$\left(\frac{^{143}Nd}{^{144}Nd}\right)_m$	$\left(\frac{^{147}Sm}{^{144}Nd}\right)_m$	$\left(\frac{^{143}Nd}{^{44}Nd}\right)_i$	$\varepsilon_{Nd}(t)$	ε_{Nd} (0.47 Ga)	T_{DM} (Ga)
Arc-Like with $(La/Yb)_N<12$ (La-Poor Arc-Like Group)										
WXNF-126	+5.8	....	....	....	....	....	....	....	....	....
WXNF-26	+8.8	17.669	15.453	37.622	0.512559	0.1289	0.512162	....	2.5	1.06
WXNF-25	+9.9	....	....	....	0.512282	0.1056	0.511972	....	-1.5	1.22
WXNF-94	+5.3	17.629	15.537	37.457	0.512088	0.1482	0.511632	-7.8	-7.8	2.46
WXHM-1	+7.7	....	....	....	0.511955	0.0517	0.511797	-4.7	-4.6	1.12
WXNF-48	+6.2	17.529	15.447	37.261	0.512172	0.1461	0.511722	-0.6	-6.1	2.20
WXNF-41	+8.0	....	....	....	....	....	....	....	....	....
WXNF-96	+4.6	....	....	....	0.512229	0.1421	0.511792	....	-4.7	1.95
WXNF-87	+6.7	....	....	....	....	....	....	....	....	....
WXNF-34	+6.6	17.807	15.458	37.509	0.512046	0.1261	0.511666	....	-7.3	1.91
WXNF-33	+7.8	17.404	15.329	37.390	0.512515	0.1484	0.512058	....	0.5	1.48
WXNF-69	+7.6	....	....	....	....	....	....	....	....	....
WXNF-21	+7.2	17.128	15.366	37.242	0.511685	0.1111	0.511343	....	-13.5	2.17
WXNF-22	+7.1	17.915	15.516	37.602	0.512042	0.1158	0.511685	....	-6.8	1.72
WXNF-63	+7.3	17.905	15.530	37.636	0.512054	0.1200	0.511687	-6.8	-6.8	1.78
WXNF-56	+6.5	18.372	15.714	38.111	0.512523	0.1813	0.511965	....	-1.3	2.93
WXNF-73	+6.7	....	....	....	....	....	....	....	....	....
Arc-Like with $(La/Yb)_N>12$ (La-Rich Arc-Like Group)										
WXNF-5	+7.9	19.326	15.625	38.416	0.512049	0.1101	0.511710	....	-6.3	1.62
WXNF-90	+5.2	....	....	....	....	....	....	....	....	....
WXNF-32	+8.7	18.506	15.586	37.942	0.512056	0.0867	0.511789	-4.5	-4.8	1.31
WXNF-6	+9.2	18.009	15.478	37.548	0.511874	0.1023	0.511559	....	-9.2	1.74
WXNF-1	+7.7	18.665	15.491	37.379	0.512192	0.1024	0.511877	....	-3.0	1.31
WXNF-10	+8.3	....	....	....	0.511874	0.0951	0.511581	....	-8.8	1.64
WXNF-31	+6.8	....	....	....	0.511864	0.0984	0.511561	....	-9.2	1.70
WXTB-119	+7.9	....	....	....	0.512074	0.0891	0.511805	-4.7	-4.5	1.32
WXTB-121	+8.8	18.340	15.667	38.275	0.511887	0.1024	0.511579	-9.1	-9.0	1.73
WXNF-102	+7.1	....	....	....	....	....	....	....	....	....
WXNF-64	≠7.6	17.873	15.502	37.551	0.511964	0.1051	0.511643	....	-7.7	1.66
WXNF-57	+8.3	....	....	....	....	....	....	....	....	....
Non-Arc-Like Group										
WXNF-76	+7.7	....	....	....	....	....	....	....	....	....
WXNF-53	+6.5	....	....	....	....	....	....	....	....	....
WXNF-86	+7.0	....	....	....	....	....	....	....	....	....
WXNF-125	+7.1	....	....	....	....	....	....	....	....	....
WXNF-136	+7.3	....	....	....	0.512700	0.1747	0.512162	....	2.5	0.00
WXNF-95	+5.9	....	....	....	0.511935	0.1297	0.511536	....	-9.7	2.20
Gneiss Samples										
WXNF-67	+5.7	....	....	....	0.511812	0.1023	0.511497	....	-10.5	1.83
WXNF-141	+10.1	....	....	....	0.511469	0.1059	0.511143	....	-17.4	0.00
WXNF-65	+6.9	....	....	....	....	....	....	....	....	....
WXNF-24	+7.6	18.803	15.549	38.513	0.512658	0.1005	0.512348	6.0	6.2	0.66
WXNF-121	+6.1	18.377	15.590	38.136	0.512451	0.1251	0.512066	....	0.7	1.20
WXNF-124	+8.1	....	....	....	0.512521	0.1350	0.512105	....	1.4	1.22
WXNF-81	+9.7	....	....	....	....	....	....	....	....	....
WXNF-2	+7.3	19.344	15.587	37.923	0.512386	0.1253	0.511482	5.2	-0.6	1.32
WXNF-11	+8.7	17.428	15.477	36.604	0.512110	0.1206	0.511240	4.8	-5.7	1.70
WXNF-27	+7.2	19.273	15.701	38.339	0.512194	0.0882	0.511326	5.0	-2.1	1.16
WXNF-13	+9.1	17.782	15.487	37.306	0.512015	0.1093	0.511226	-1.0	-6.9	1.65

For locations of different areas see Figure 1; for map units, see Appendices 1 and 2 plus published geological maps (Whalen and Currie, 1988; Whalen, 1993a, 1993b). Abbreviations: Mg# = 100(MgO/FeO total + MgO); Al index = mol. $(Al_2O_3/(K_2O+Na_2O+CaO))$; N = chondrite normalized; m = measurement; i = initial.

**TABLE 3. OXYGEN ISOTOPIC COMPOSITIONS FOR GRANITOID MINERALS
IN NOTRE DAME ARC PLUTONS**

Group	WX#	Whole Rock	Quartz	K-feldspar	Hornblende	Biotite	Magnetite
Gneiss	NF24	+7.6	+8.4	....	....	....	....
La-poor Arc	NF34	+6.6	+8.2	....	....	....	-0.9
La-poor Arc	NF48	+6.2	+7.9	+7.1	+4.6	....	....
La-poor Arc	NF63	+7.3	+9.3	+8.2	+5.5	+3.5	....
La-rich Arc	TS121	+8.8	+10.2	+9.7	....	+3.9	+3.2

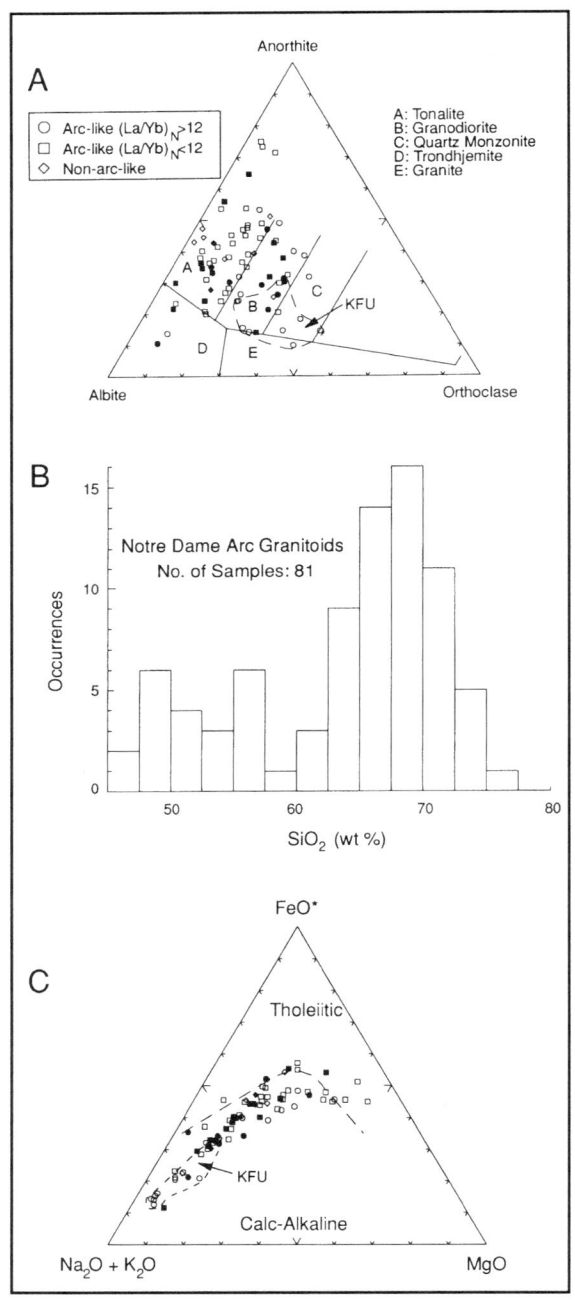

(Hinds Brook granite, unit Oib) and area 3 (units OPc and OLc) and mafic through felsic units from areas 2, 3, 4, and 5. In general, negative Nb and Ti anomalies (Fig. 6, A to C) are more pronounced than the La-poor arc-like group (Figs. 4 and 5), Ba and Sr anomalies vary from positive to negative, and some slightly negative Eu anomalies are present. Negative P anomalies occur in some felsic samples. $(La/Yb)_N$ values are variable, ranging from 17 to 97, even within relatively lithologically homogeneous units Oib and OPc (Fig. 6, D and E).

Non-arc-like group. The non-arc group was subdivided on the basis of $(La/Yb)_N$ into samples with values <12 (n = 6) and >12 (n = 5) (Fig. 7). Non-arc samples have silica contents >65 wt% and are tonalites (Fig. 2A) with low to medium K contents (Fig. 3A). In general, non-arc samples with $(La/Yb)_N$ >12 are more consistently enriched in Rb, Ba, and K, relative to Th, Nb, and light REE, than samples with $(La/Yb)_N$ <12; all samples have slight to pronounced positive Sr and Eu anomalies, most have positive Ba and Zr anomalies, and some have negative Ti anomalies (Fig. 7, A and B). Relative to arc-like samples with similar silica contents (Figs. 4, 5, and 6), most non-arc samples are depleted in the elements from Th to Eu.

Gneissic group. Silica content of these samples ranges from 55 to >80 wt% and K content from low to high (Fig. 3A); as would be expected, many paragneiss samples are peraluminous (Fig. 3B). Included are gneisses with non–arc-like (WXNF-2, WXNF-11, WXNF-24, WXNF-141) and arc-like (all others) Nb anomalies (Fig. 8). Although there is considerable dispersion, in general, normalized patterns for most samples from areas 3 and 4 (Fig. 7, A and B) are very similar to, or even indistinguishable from, Ordovician plutonic rocks of the same silica content from these areas (Fig. 5, B to E). The Cormacks Lake complex charnockite (WXNF-24), which yielded a 460 ± 10 Ma age (Currie et al., 1992), has high K and is remarkably enriched in high field strength elements (Th, Nb, REE, Zr and Y) with very pronounced negative Sr, P, Eu, and Ti anomalies (Fig. 7A). Grenville base-

Figure 2. Notre Dame arc plutonic rocks plotted on: (A) the CIPW normative Ab-An-Or ternary granite rock classification diagram of Barker (1979); (B) a silica histogram; and (C) an AFM diagram (after Irvine and Baragar, 1971). Fields labeled KFU in A and C outline K-feldspar porphyritic units Oib, OPc, and OLc.

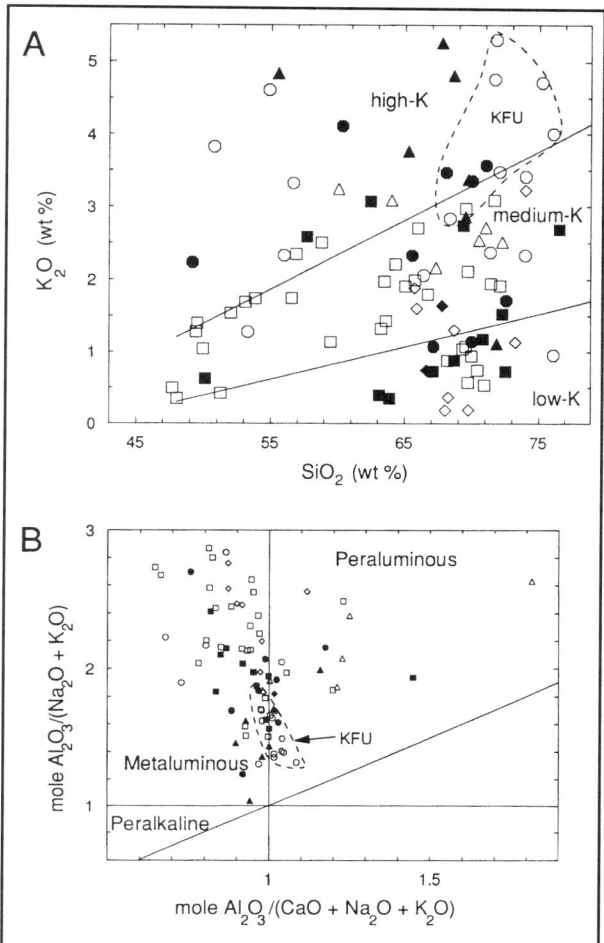

Figure 3. Notre Dame arc plutonic rocks and older gneissic rocks plotted on: (A) SiO$_2$-K$_2$O classification diagram after LeMaitre (1989); and (B) molecular Al/(Ca + Na + K) versus Al/(Na + K) plot after Maniar and Piccoli (1989). Fields labeled KFU in A and B outline K-feldspar porphyritic units Oib, OPc, and OLc.

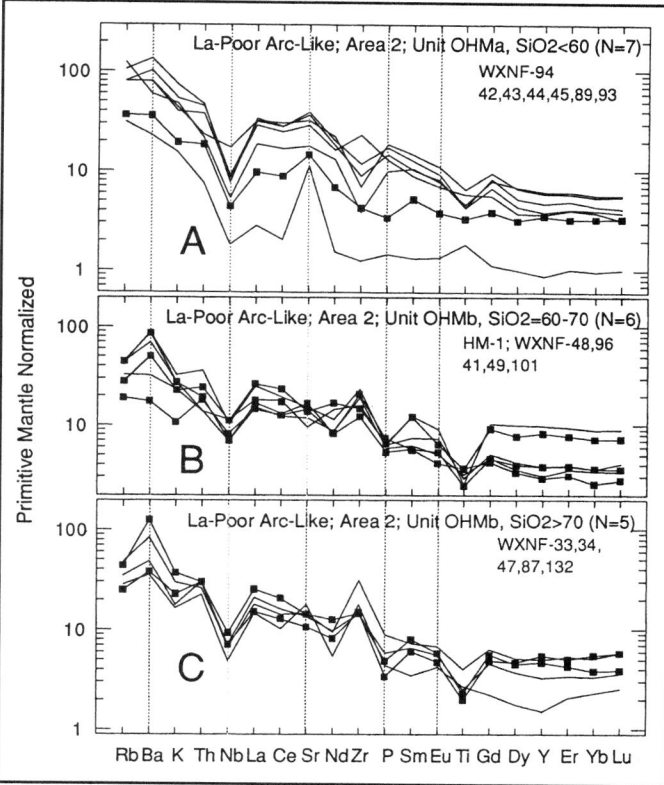

Figure 4. Primordial mantle normalized plots for La-poor arc-like plutonic rocks from the Hungry Mountain complex in area 2; samples are subdivided according to map units of Whalen and Currie (1988) and silica content into three groups, wt% SiO$_2$ <60 (A), 60–70 (B), and >70 (C). Filled symbols are used for Nd isotopic samples; normalizing values from Taylor and McLennan (1985).

ment samples are less heavy REE-depleted and more enriched in all elements to the right of Th (Fig. 8C) than comparable Ordovician rocks. A Disappointment Hill complex charnockite (WXNF-27) is geochemically nearly identical to the Cormacks Lake charnockite.

The relatively consistent and similar normalized geochemical patterns exhibited by NDA plutonic rocks over a large silica range (see above; Figs. 4 to 7) suggest that similar source materials and/or processes were involved in their petrogenesis. However, elemental variations relative to silica (Figs. 3A and 9) range from relatively linear (e.g., Al$_2$O$_3$, MgO, CaO) to nonlinear or scattered (e.g., K$_2$O and Nb). Such large scatter on Harker diagrams suggests that these rocks do not belong to a comagmatic suite; this is hardly surprising because they cover a large area (see Fig. 1) and span a considerable age range (~488 to 456 Ma; see Appendix 2).

Isotopic data

The Nd isotopic data, expressed as epsilon Nd (ε_{Nd}), are plotted against $\delta^{18}O\%_o$ (SMOW) in Figure 10; comparison fields for potential source materials are also plotted. ε_{Nd} values were calculated at time (t) = 470 Ma because U-Pb ages have been determined on only a small portion of the samples. The uncertainty introduced by assuming an age of 470 Ma for all samples is judged to be minimal: the greatest difference between ε_{Nd} at the time of formation (ε_{Nd} [t]) and ε_{Nd} (470 Ma) values in Table 2 is 0.3 for sample WXNF-32. The range in ε_{Nd} (t) values of the La-rich arc group (n = 9) is exclusively negative (–3.0 to –9.2), whereas those of the La-poor arc (n = 12; range = +2.5 to –13.5) and non–arc-like groups (n = 2; range = +2.5 to –9.7) include positive values. The ranges in ε_{Nd} of gneisses from Grenville inliers (–0.6 to –6.9) and the Cariboo Lakes (–10.5 to –17.4) and Cormacks Lake (+6.0 to +0.6) complexes at 470 Ma are each distinct. Generally negative ε_{Nd} (t) values of NDA plutons indicate derivation mainly from a reservoir with a long term history of light REE enrichment; the dispersion to positive values suggests involvement of light REE depleted sources.

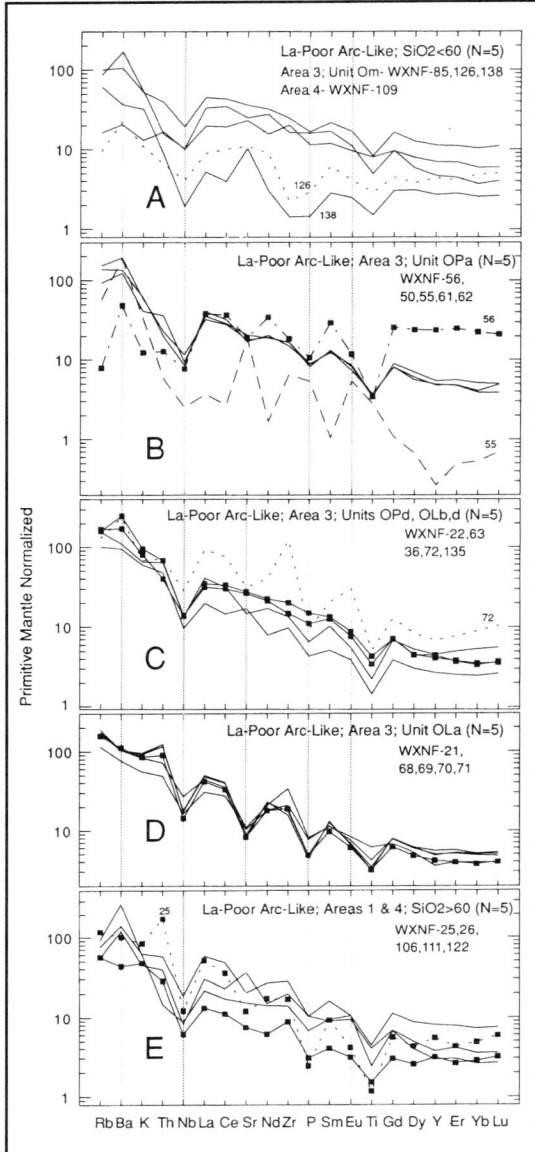

Figure 5. Primordial mantle normalized plots for La-poor arc-like plutonic rocks from area 3 (A, B, C, and D) and areas 1 and 4 (A and E); area 3 samples are grouped according to map units of Whalen (1993a, 1993b). Black symbols are used for Nd isotopic samples; normalizing values from Taylor and McLennan (1985).

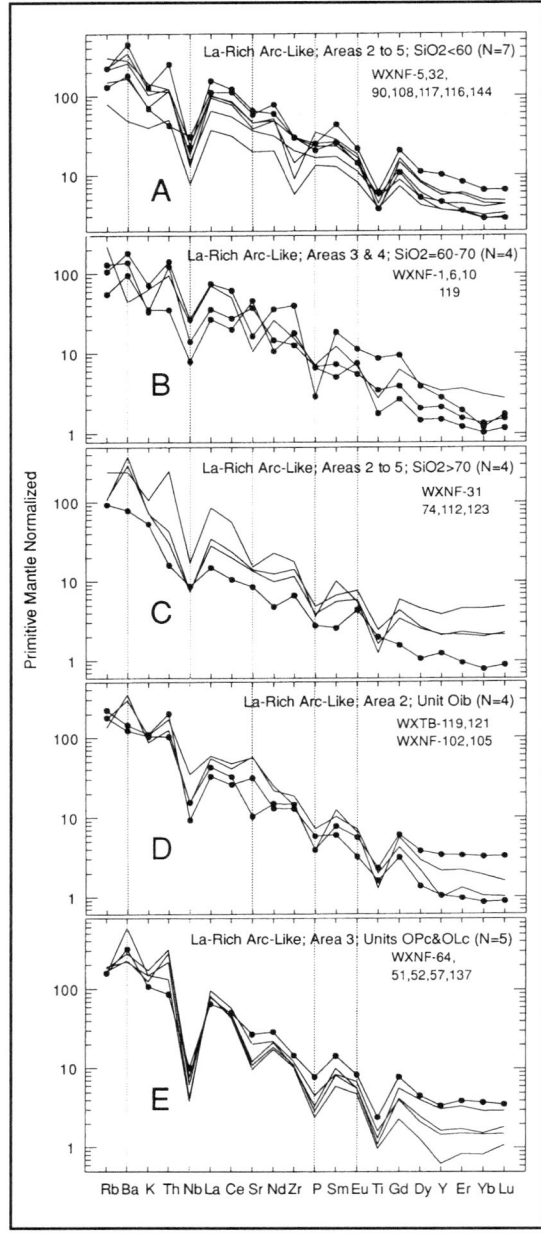

Figure 6. Primordial mantle normalized plots for La-rich arc-like plutonic rocks from areas 2 to 5 grouped according to silica content (A, B, and C) or by map unit (D and E). Black symbols are used for Nd isotopic samples; normalizing values from Taylor and McLennan (1985).

Although the ranges in $\delta^{18}O$ values of the La-rich arc group (+5.2 to +9.2‰) and the La-poor arc group (+4.6 to +9.9‰) are similar, the average $\delta^{18}O$ value of the former group (+7.8‰) is higher than the latter group (+7.0‰) (Fig. 10). The range and average for the non-arc group is less positive (+5.9 to +7.7‰; +6.9‰). These values are in the range expected of granitoid rocks derived from mantle-like sources (+6 to +8‰; Taylor, 1968, 1978) (see Fig. 10). The ranges in $\delta^{18}O$ values of Grenville basement (+7.3 to +9.1‰), Cariboo Lakes gneisses (+5.7 to +10.1‰), and areas 3 and 4

gneisses (+6.1 to +9.7‰) include more positive values than NDA plutons.

K-feldspar Pb isotopic data are shown in Figure 11 on conventional Pb-Pb diagrams with single-stage reference growth curves. The La-poor arc group has, with the exception of a single sample (WXNF-56), the least radiogenic compositions ($^{206}Pb/^{204}Pb$= 17.13–17.92) and plots generally close to the reference 0.47 Ga geochron (Fig. 11A). Significant variations in $^{207}Pb/^{204}Pb$ ratios, not complemented by similar $^{206}Pb/^{204}Pb$ varia-

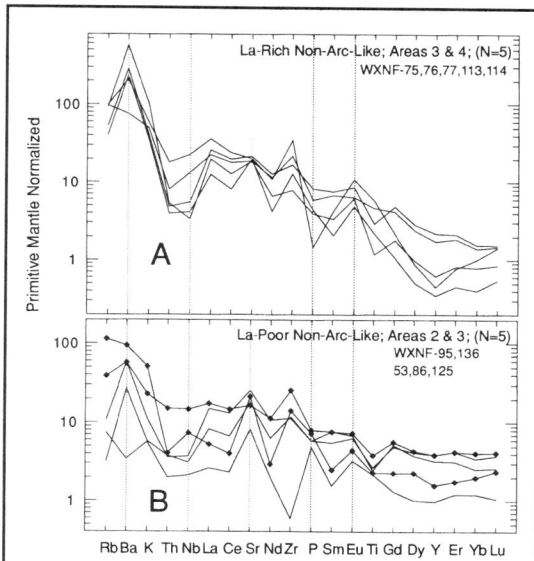

Figure 7. Primordial mantle normalized plots for non-arc-like plutonic rocks from areas 2, 3, and 4 subdivided into groups with $(La/Yb)_N$ >12 (A), and <12 (B). Black symbols are used for Nd isotopic samples; normalizing values from Taylor and McLennan (1985).

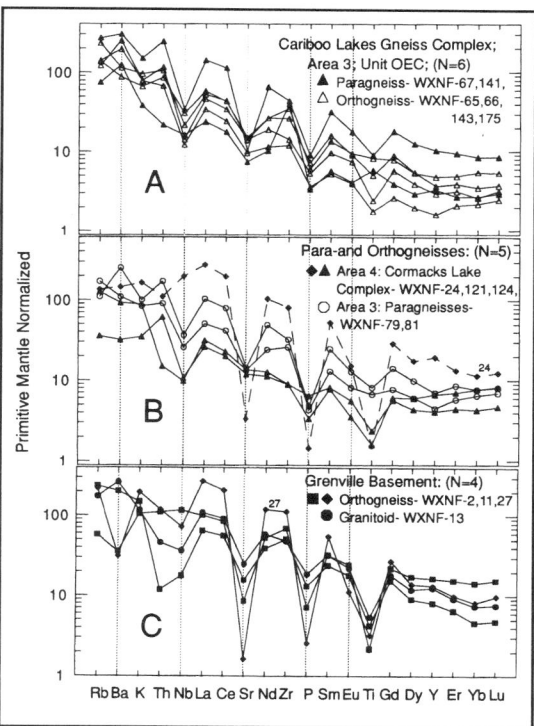

Figure 8. Primordial mantle normalized plots for older paragneisses and orthogneisses from: (A) the Cariboo Lake gneiss complex; (B) area 3 paragneisses and Cormacks Lakes complex; and (C) Grenville basement in the Humber zone of western Newfoundland. Black symbols are used for Nd isotopic samples; normalizing values from Taylor and McLennan (1985).

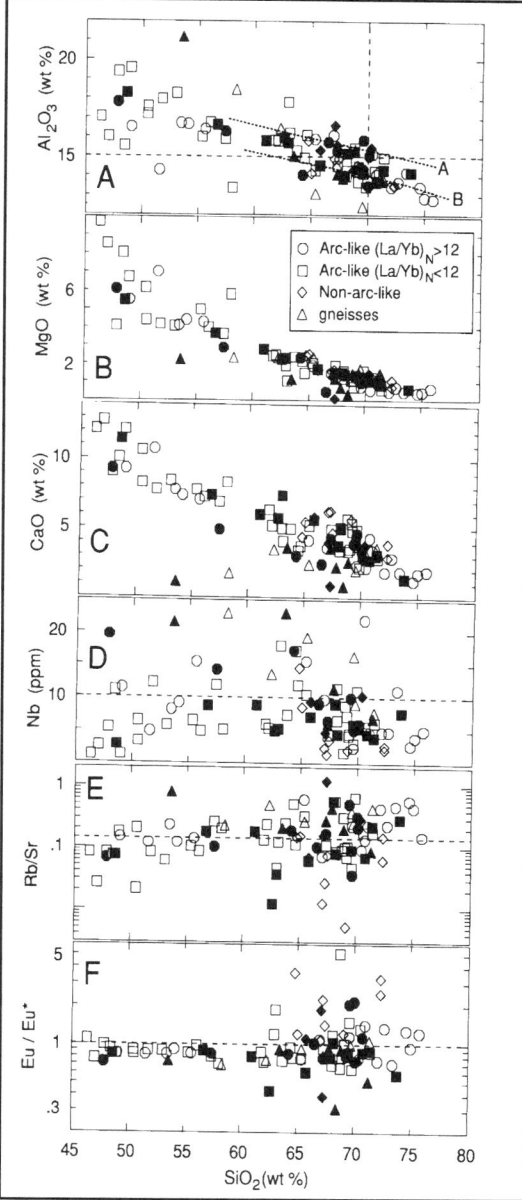

Figure 9. Harker variation diagrams for various major and trace elements plus elemental ratios for Notre Dame arc (NDA) plutons and older gneisses. Various reference lines correspond to lower (A) or upper (D, E) compositional criterion for "slab-derived melts" from Drummond and Defant (1990); in (A) apparent high-Al (trend A) and low-Al (trend B) trends within NDA samples are illustrated; see text for explanation.

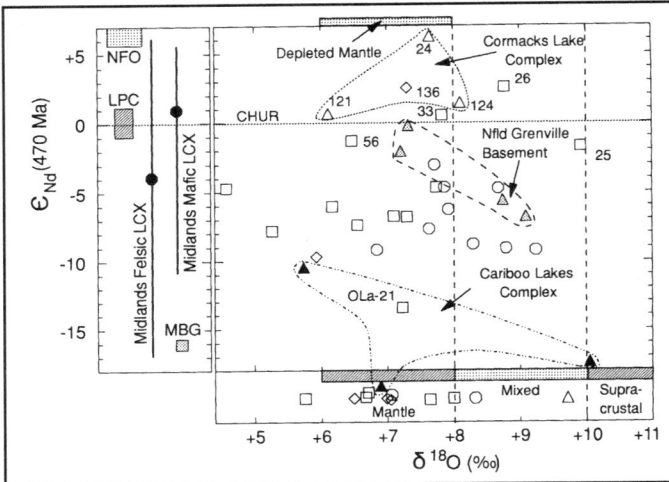

Figure 10. ε_{Nd} (470 Ma) versus $\delta^{18}O$‰ (SMOW) plot for Notre Dame arc plutonic rocks and older gneisses; additional $\delta^{18}O$ data for samples not analyzed for Nd are shown at the bottom of the diagram along with the ranges in $\delta^{18}O$‰ (SMOW) for granitoids derived from mantle, mixed mantle-supracrustal, and supracrustal sources (from Taylor, 1968, 1988). ε_{Nd} for Grenville basement from western Newfoundand and the depleted mantle (DePaolo, 1988) were calculated for 470 Ma. Shown for comparison are ε_{Nd} (470 Ma) ranges for the Little Port complex (LPC) and western. Newfoundland ophiolites (NFO) (Jenner et al., 1991), Mings Bight Group sediments (MBG) (Fryer et al., 1992), and both the range and average for mafic and felsic lower crustal xenoliths (LCX) from beneath the Midland Valley arc, Scotland (Halliday et al., 1993).

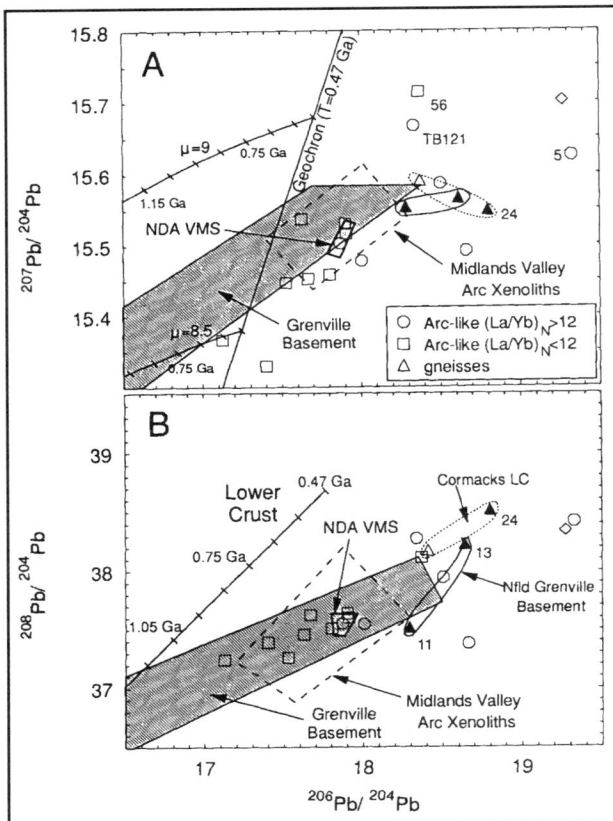

Figure 11. $^{206}Pb/^{204}Pb$ versus: (A) $^{207}Pb/^{204}Pb$, and; (B) $^{208}Pb/^{204}Pb$ for K-feldspars from Notre Dame arc (NDA) plutonic rocks and older gneissic rocks. Single-stage reference growth curves for $^{238}U/^{204}Pb$ ratios (μ) of 8.5 and 9, a $^{232}Th/^{204}Pb$ ratio of 40.5, and the geochron were calculated using 4.5 Ga for the age of the Earth and Canyon Diablo troilite (Tatsumoto et al., 1973) for initial values. The curve labeled lower crust is comparable to that of the plumbotectonics model of Zartman and Doe (1988); tick marks on growth curves represent time increments of 0.1 b.y. Also shown for comparison purposes are the fields for Grenville basement from Ayuso and Bevier (1991), galenas from NDA volcanic massive sulfide deposits (VMS) from Swinden and Thorpe (1984), and mafic lower crustal xenoliths from the Midland Valley arc of Scotland (Halliday et al., 1993), all at 470 Ma. Fields for Midland Valley xenoliths were recalculated back to 470 Ma using the published whole rock μ values from Halliday et al. (1993) and assuming a $^{232}Th/^{238}U$ ratio of four. Hawk's Nib locality xenoliths were excluded.

tions, can only be ascribed to very ancient geological events. The La-rich arc group is generally more radiogenic ($^{206}Pb/^{204}Pb$ = 17.87 to 19.33) than the former group, and also displays large variations in $^{207}Pb/^{204}Pb$ ratios (Fig. 11A). Although these two arc-like groups generally have distinct Pb isotopic signatures, their Nd isotopic characteristics are not as distinct. The Cormacks Lake charnockite has a relatively radiogenic Pb isotopic signature, comparable to the La-rich arc group. K-feldspars from the four analyzed Grenville basement samples (Table 2) display either very unradiogenic ($^{206}Pb/^{204}Pb$ = 17.4 to 17.8) or very radiogenic ($^{206}Pb/^{204}Pb$ = 19.3) signatures. The least radiogenic K-feldspars, which might represent initial Pb isotopic compositions, overlap the radiogenic end of the Grenville basement field (Fig. 11). The very radiogenic K-feldspars (not plotted in Fig. 11), which must have reequilibrated with their host rocks during tectono-thermal event(s) postdating their initial formation, cannot be used in a straightforward way to constrain the Pb isotopic composition of the Grenville basement reservoir at the time of NDA pluton formation.

No obvious correlations were found between isotopic and geochemical compositions of NDA plutons or gneisses. This may reflect the large area (Fig. 1) and age range (about 488 to 456 Ma) (see Appendix 2) of plutons included in our dataset. In addition, the lack of coherent or linear trends on Harker diagrams (Figs. 3A and 9) is most compatible with our data set including multiple comagmatic suites. The isotopic sample subset (Table 2) may not include enough samples from an individ-

ual comagmatic suite to enable resolution of isotopic and geochemical interrelationships.

Discussion

Major- and trace-element characteristics are consistent with NDA plutonic rocks forming in a volcanic-arc type setting. These features include the volumetric predominance of intermediate (silica of 60 to 70 wt%) compositions (Fig. 2, A and B), calc-alkaline character (Fig. 2C), and primordial mantle normalized patterns with marked negative Nb and Ti anomalies over the full silica range (Figs. 4 to 6). The prominence of low- to medium-K tonalitic and granodioritic rocks with significant volumes of associated gabbros and diorites (Figs. 2A, 3A) and low large ion lithophile (LIL) element concentrations (Figs. 4 to 7) suggest that the arc was relatively immature. Contemporaneous plutonic rocks lacking Nb and Ti anomalies (i.e., non-arc rocks) imply derivation either from a mantle source without crustal assimilation, or from a mafic precursor lacking this anomaly.

Mainly metaluminous compositions (Fig. 3B), generally amphibole-bearing mineralogy, and common igneous microgranitoid enclaves indicate derivation of NDA plutons from infracrustal (I-type) sources (Chappell and Stephens, 1988). Little or no involvement of weathered or altered sources is also indicated by $\delta^{18}O$ values lying mainly within the range of mantle-derived granitoid rocks (i.e., +6 to +8‰; Taylor, 1968, 1978) (see Fig. 10). Although limited values between +8 to +10‰ could reflect some minor involvement of supracrustal sources, petrographic evidence suggests that these somewhat elevated $\delta^{18}O$ values reflect low-temperature alteration. Granitoid rocks with average $\delta^{18}O$ values as low as +6.9 to +7.8‰ are not particularly common in the Phanerozoic, although significant volumes of such material are known in some localities (e.g., Central Andes; Longstaffe et al., 1983). Such values are more common among Archean granitoid assemblages, where it is thought that relatively direct derivation of granitoids from mantle sources was common (e.g., Longstaffe and Schwarcz, 1977; Longstaffe, 1979; Longstaffe et al., 1981; Longstaffe and Gower, 1983) (Fig. 10).

The relatively nonradiogenic Pb isotopic compositions of the La-poor arc group indicate derivation from source regions with relatively low time-integrated U/Pb ratios, similar to both Early Ordovician mantle, as represented by NDA volcanic massive sulfide (VMS) deposits (Swinden and Thorpe, 1984), and Grenville basement (Ayuso and Bevier, 1991) (Fig. 11). Because the least radiogenic sample (WXNF-21) in this group also has the most negative ε_{Nd} (*t*) value, direct derivation from a depleted, MORB-like mantle reservoir is precluded. Significant variations in $^{207}Pb/^{204}Pb$ ratios, without complementary $^{206}Pb/^{204}Pb$ variations, are also more compatible with input from an older basement rather than a juvenile mantle component. The generally more radiogenic signatures of the La-rich arc group and the Cormacks Lake charnockite imply involvement of either a larger proportion of infracrustal or supracrustal rocks, with high time-integrated U/Pb and Th/Pb ratios, or a lower proportion of mafic precursors.

Input from old (>1.5 Ga) crustal sources to NDA plutons was previously recognized based on inherited zircon data (Whalen et al., 1987b; Dunning et al., 1989). The large range in ε_{Nd} (*t*) values (+2.6 to −13.5) exhibited by NDA plutons (most values are between −2 and −10), indicates major involvement of either old crustal or subcontinental lithospheric material in their petrogenesis. Trace-element plus O and Pb isotopic characteristics suggest that this old source component was otherwise quite primitive or mantle-like.

SLAB-DERIVED, HIGH BaSr GRANITOIDS: IMPLICATIONS FOR NDA PLUTONS

There has been considerable literature attention devoted recently to granitoid rocks that exhibit geochemical characteristics considered indicative of derivation from mafic protoliths under relatively high pressure-temperature (*P-T*) conditions, both with respect to residual minerals during melting and to their implications for tectonic and crustal evolution processes. Phanerozoic volcanic rocks, termed adakites (Defant and Drummond, 1990), and high-Al trondhjemite-tonalite-dacite (TTD) plutonic suites (Drummond and Defant, 1990; Drummond et al., 1994) with geochemical features similar to Archean tonalite-trondhjemite-granodiorite (TTG) suites (see Martin, 1986, 1993) have been recognized. They are interpreted as reflecting tectonothermal conditions that duplicate those thought to have prevailed during the Archean, in particular slab melting at sites of young (<20 Ma), hot oceanic plate subduction. Compositional differences between adakites and melts generated under experimental conditions approximating those for slab melting suggest that the high Mg and Ca of adakites may be achieved through reaction within the mantle wedge between ascending slab melts and mantle peridotite (Sen and Dunn, 1994; Kelemen, 1995). Tarney and Jones (1994) defined a more general group of high-BaSr granitoid rocks, the characteristics of which, like high-Al TTD suites, are in part attributed to melting of a mafic source with residual garnet and hornblende, plus a titanate phase, but no residual plagioclase. High-BaSr granitoids are interpreted as reflecting tectonic regimes with elevated geotherms, such as ridge subduction, mantle plume activity, or rifting or subduction of young hot oceanic crust. Kelemen (1995) defined a group of high Mg# andesites characterized by Mg# >30 and MgO <10 wt%, interpreted as either depleted-mantle-melts or as reaction products between mantle melts and mantle peridotite.

Some NDA samples have heavy REE-depleted patterns that resemble those of Archean TTG suites (i.e., low Yb [$0.3 < Yb_N < 8.5$] and [$5 < [La/Yb]_N < 150$]; Martin, 1986) rather than post-Archean granitoid rocks. Most NDA plutonic rocks exhibit the features described by Tarney and Jones (1994) for their high-BaSr granitoid group, including high relative (to Rb) and absolute Ba and Sr abundances (Fig. 12), low Y (Fig. 13), and positive (Ba, Sr, Eu, P) and negative (Th, Nb, Ti, Y) anomalies on primordial mantle normalized plots that are relatively insensitive to silica abundance (see Figs. 4 to 7, 9F). In addition, on the basis of their Mg#s (almost all >30) and MgO contents, all intermediate-composition NDA samples are of high Mg# andesitic composition. Drummond and Defant (1990) and Defant and Drummond (1990) proposed detailed criteria to identify slab-derived magmas. It appears, on the basis of the spread in sample Al_2O_3 values between 60 and 75 wt% SiO_2 (see Fig. 9A), that both high-Al (trend A) and low-Al (trend B) trends are present in the NDA data; more than 50% of the samples probably belong to a trend with $Al_2O_3 \geq 15$ wt% at 70% SiO_2. About two-thirds of the samples have Yb <1.9 ppm (Table 2), Y <15 ppm (Fig. 13), Nb <10 ppm (Fig. 9D), and K/Rb <550; more than half have Rb/Sr <0.15 (Fig. 9E), Sr >300 ppm (Fig. 12), and (La/Yb)N >20 (Table 1); about one-quarter have Sr/Y >40 (Fig. 13). Although about one-eighth have somewhat negative Eu anomalies, the remainder have either little or no, or significantly positive, Eu

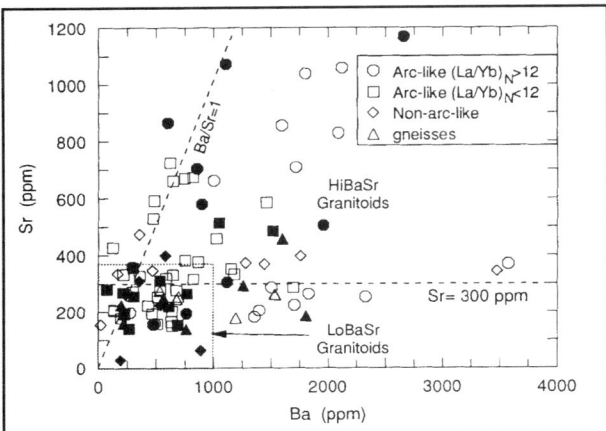

Figure 12. Sr versus Ba plot for Notre Dame arc plutonic rocks and older gneissic rocks; high-BaSr granitoids, as defined by Tarney and Jones (1994), are relatively (to Rb) and absolutely enriched in Ba and Sr. Also shown for reference is the lower compositional limit (Sr = 300 ppm) for "slab-derived melts" from Drummond and Defant (1990).

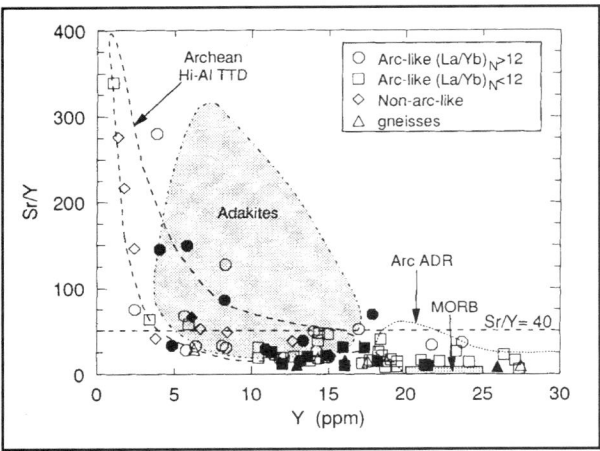

Figure 13. Y versus Y/Sr plot for Notre Dame arc plutonic rocks and older gneisses; also shown for comparison are fields for Archean high-Al trondhjemite-tonalite-dacite (TTD) suites, adakites, arc andesite-dacite-rhyolite (ADR) suites and mid-ocean ridge basalt (MORB) (fields derived from Fig. 10B of Defant et al., 1991).

anomalies (Fig. 9F). Although about one-third of NDA samples exhibit many "slab-derived melt" geochemical characteristics, only one-tenth fulfill all criteria. Normalized REE and extended element patterns for these eight samples and those of proposed "slab-derived melt" examples are remarkably similar (Fig. 14). The NDA non–arc-like samples have strong positive Eu anomalies and most closely resemble El Valle dacites (Defant and Drummond, 1991), one of which is "non-arc-type" (i.e., no negative Nb anomaly). The NDA La-rich arc samples most closely resemble the Early Ordovician Elkahatchee quartz diorite (EQD) in Alabama (Drummond et al., 1994), except that the EQD lacks the markedly positive Ba and Sr anomalies exhibited by all NDA and El Valle samples. On the basis of extensive petrochemical

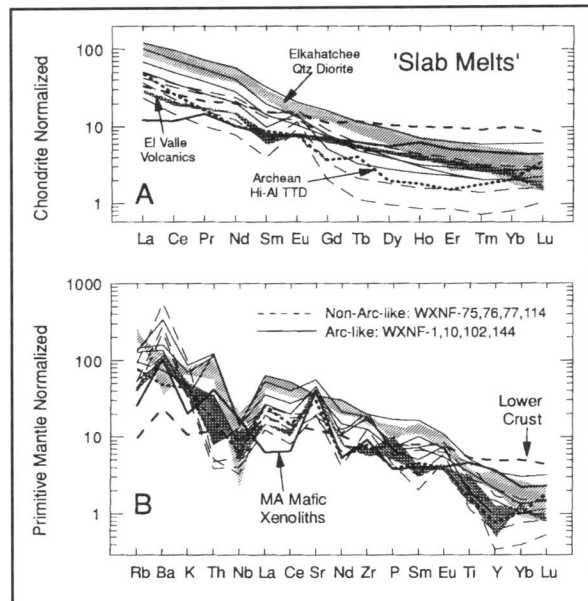

Figure 14. Chondrite normalized rare earth element (A) and primordial mantle normalized extended element (B) plots for Notre Dame arc plutonic rocks that fulfill the compositional criterion for slab-derived melts (see text). Also shown for comparison are patterns or fields for the El Valle Volcano, Panama (Defant et al., 1991), average Archean high-Al trondhjemite-tonalite-dacite (TTD) (Drummond and Defant, 1990), the Early Ordovician Elkahatchee quartz diorite (EQD), Alabama (Drummond et al., 1994), model lower continental crust of Taylor and McLennan (1985), and average mafic lower crustal xenoliths from beneath the Midland Valley arc, Scotland (data of Halliday et al., 1993).

modeling and discussions in the papers from which these examples were obtained and in Drummond and Defant (1990), it can be inferred that some NDA plutons may represent partial melts of MORB-like rocks (i.e., the slab) with residual garnet and amphibole but no residual plagioclase. P-T conditions of 1.5 to 2.0 Pa (50 to 60 km) and 850 to 1150 °C would be required to generate such melts (Sen and Dunn, 1994). However, most NDA samples display only some "slab-derived melt" geochemical features. Similar variations in "slab-derived" geochemical characteristics of high Mg# andesites within the Aleutian arc have been interpreted as reflecting mixed input from depleted mantle wedge, slab melt, and sediment components (Yogodzinski et al., 1995). In contrast to the Aleutian arc, almost all NDA plutons have non-MORB-like Nd isotopic signatures (Fig. 11), a characteristic that dictates a more complex petrogenesis than "simple" slab melting (see below).

ORIGIN OF THE OLD CRUSTAL COMPONENT WITHIN NDA PLUTONS

On the basis of their generally amphibole bearing mineralogy and metaluminous compositions, along with their mainly mantle-like $\delta^{18}O$ values, significant contributions to NDA plutons from metasedimentary sources can be ruled out. The NDA plutonic assemblage contains major volumes of contemporaneous gabbroic to dioritic phases, and mafic microgranitoid enclaves are common. These basaltic materials, which must have been mainly mantle derived, undoubtedly played a significant role in the petrogenesis of NDA plutons. Furthermore, as discussed earlier, geochemical evidence suggests that some NDA plutons either represent or received input from high-P-T melts of MORB-like source rocks. For these reasons, petrogenesis of NDA plutonic rocks by simple anatexis of old but isotopically variable infracrustal sources can be ruled out. The large range in ε_{Nd} (470 Ma) values (+2.6 to −13.5) exhibited by NDA plutons must result from mixing of mantle- and old infracrustal-derived components, either as magmas or by assimilation–fractional crystallization (AFC) processes.

The mantle-derived or positive end member involved in the mixing process can be constrained by ε_{Nd} (t = 470 Ma) values for western Newfoundland ophiolites (Jenner et al., 1991); these values (+5.6 to +8.3) approximate the depleted mantle at this time (Fig. 10). The Pb isotopic composition of Early Ordovician mantle may be given by NDA volcanogenic massive sulfide (VMS) deposits, which include the ophiolitic York Harbour deposit (Swinden and Thorpe, 1984). The NDA VMS Pb field falls within the range exhibited by the La-poor arc-like group (see Fig. 11). However, contributions from Ordovician mantle versus Grenvillian basement type sources cannot be easily distinguished on the basis of Pb alone (Whalen et al., 1994).

Constraining the possible crustal or negative ε_{Nd} end member(s) involved in the hypothetical mixing process is more difficult. For a two-component mixing model, the crustal component must have an ε_{Nd} (470 Ma) <−13.5, the most negative NDA sample. Sources that require evaluation as the negative crustal end member are gneissic rocks in western Newfoundland and lower crustal compositions inferred from xenoliths.

1. Exposures of gneissic rocks in the Notre Dame and Humber zone Grenvillian basement inliers are each distinct in their ε_{Nd} (t = 470 Ma) signatures (Fig. 10). The positive signatures of Cormacks Lake complex orthogneisses make them inappropriate as the negative end member for a mixing model. Although the Pb isotopic ratios of most NDA plutons overlap that of Grenville basement (Fig. 11), their Nd isotopic compositions are too negative for Grenville basement, as exposed in inliers in Newfoundland, to be an appropriate protolith. In general, gneisses of the Cariboo Lakes complex, which range to −17.4, might be a suitable negative end-member. For example, the most negative value (−13.5) for NDA plutons was obtained from tonalite unit OLa (WXNF-21; see Fig. 10), which fringes the west side of the Cariboo Lakes complex. Available field and U-Pb isotopic data suggest that the Cariboo Lakes complex represents a group of somewhat older (i.e., 480 to 490 Ma) orthogneisses and paragneisses which are more enriched in this old crustal component. It has already been noted that primitive mantle normalized patterns of many of the gneisses from the NDA are, in general, remarkably similar to NDA plutonic rocks (see Fig. 8, A and B). Such rocks as a contaminant of NDA granitoid magmas would not be easily distinguishable.

2. An extensive study of lower crustal xenoliths in Carboniferous and Tertiary basalts from Scotland provides many important insights into the nature and composition of the lower crust beneath both the Precambrian craton and the accreted Paleozoic Midland Valley arc and forearc (Halliday et al., 1993). This Midland Valley arc has been correlated, on the basis of tectonostratigraphic evidence, with the NDA (see Colman-Sadd et al., 1992b). ε_{Nd} (t = 470 Ma) values of mafic and felsic granulite xenoliths from beneath the Midland Valley arc range from −10.8 to +5.4 (average = +0.9) and from −16.9 to +6.2 (average = −3.8), respectively. Data for xenoliths from the Hawk's Nib locality, interpreted by Halliday et al. (1993) to be from a layered mafic-ultramafic intrusion, have been excluded. In contrast, mafic granulite lower crustal xenoliths from beneath the Scottish Highlands and the northwestern Hebrides portions of the craton range from +1.8 to −16.5 (average = −10.3), and −8.7 to −24.9 (average = −17.5), respectively. There is little evidence of U-depletion and the Pb isotopic compositions of both mafic and felsic xenoliths are similar and relatively uniform, despite large variations in Sr and Nd isotopic compositions. This implies that the xenoliths have been metamorphosed and/or underwent isotopic reequilibration during the early to middle Paleozoic (Halliday et al., 1993). Nd, Sr, and Pb isotopic characteristics of these xenoliths are interpreted as indicating crustal assimilation by underplated mantle-derived magmas, a process that produced a hybrid mafic lower crust with old crustal Nd isotopic signatures. The more negative ε_{Nd} (t = 470 Ma) values of xenoliths from beneath the craton reflect the older age of the crust beneath these areas (e.g., the Lewisian complex). The xenoliths, which were derived from precursors formed in the Late Proterozoic and early Paleozoic, provide evidence of widespread deep crustal magma reservoirs, underplating, crustal assimilation and arc accretion.

The ε_{Nd} (t = 470 Ma) ranges of both mafic and felsic xenoliths from beneath the Midland Valley arc almost exactly match that in NDA plutons (+2.5 to −9.7; Table 3 and Fig. 10). K-feldspar Pb isotopic data from the La-poor arc-like group (and some of the La-rich arc-like group) also show remarkable similarity with these xenoliths (Fig. 11) and could represent magmas that interacted with such deep crustal rocks. However, because their age is poorly constrained, it is unclear whether the xenoliths should be evaluated as samples from a lower crust hybridized during NDA magmatism (i.e., products of that event), or as actual NDA source materials.

An extensive literature has been generated on the composition of the lower crust, lower crustal processes, and the lower crust as a potential granitoid protolith (see reviews by Taylor and McLennan, 1985; Farmer, 1979; Kay et al., 1992). Model lower crustal compositions (e.g., Taylor and McLennan, 1985; see Fig. 14) resemble, in major elements, a high-alumina basalt which has low K (0.28%), K/Rb (530), and Rb/Sr (0.023), slightly fractionated REEs ([La/Yb]$_N$ = 3.8), positive Eu and no negative Nb anomalies, and high Cr and Ni. Although lower crustal rocks obtained from xenoliths are compositionally variable, mafic xenoliths with these general compositional features are the most common lithology (Taylor and McLennan, 1985).

For example, average compositional features of the Midland Valley mafic xenoliths include high Al_2O_3 (18.8 wt%), Sr and Ba (758 and 441 ppm), and low Rb (12 ppm) (Halliday et al., 1993). Their mean primitive mantle normalized pattern (Fig. 14B) has the same distinctive positive Ba, Th, and Sr anomalies as NDA plutons. Due to these bulk compositional similarities, even significant interaction of slab-derived melts with such mafic lower crust would likely be difficult to detect in either the major- or trace-element compositions of the resultant hybridized magma. One obvious distinction is that the lower crust generally lacks a negative Nb anomaly. Although differences in Pb and O isotopic compositions between these two potential end members likely would not have been great, Nd would have differed by at least 20 ε units, making it very sensitive to even the slightest lower crustal interaction.

Compositionally diverse suites of Mesozoic (170 to 70 Ma) plutonic rocks in the Old Woman Mountains of California, studied in detail by Miller and Wooden (1994), exhibit a similar very large contrast (>18 ε_{Nd} units) between crustal- and mantle-derived components. Even the most mafic plutonic rocks, with SiO_2 <55 wt%, have ε_{Nd} (t) values <–9. The model proposed for their petrogenesis involved multievent lower crustal modification and hybridization by mantle-derived mafic magmas. The plutonic suites include mantle-derived magmas which were modified through AFC processes in the lower crust, partial melts of solidified, previously hybridized lower crustal rocks, and all combinations in between. If NDA plutonic magmatism was similarly multistage, the hybridized lower crustal–lithospheric mantle source region would probably have remained hot and at least partially molten due to its shorter time span.

INFERENCES FROM PLUTONIC ROCKS FOR NOTRE DAME ARC EVOLUTION

The Nd isotopic data presented herein indicates significant contributions from old infracrustal sources to NDA plutonism from about 488 to 456 Ma. The arc-related 505 Ma Little Port Complex, one of the structural slices associated with the Bay of Islands ophiolite complex, is interpreted as an obducted early remnant of the NDA (Jenner et al., 1991; Cawood and Suhr, 1992). ε_{Nd} (t) values from Little Port Complex trondhjemites of –0.9 to +1.2 (Jenner et al., 1991) also reflect input from old crustal sources. Strongly negative ε_{Nd} values of –10 to –16 obtained from the Cariboo Lakes complex and the Mings Bight Group (Fryer et al., 1992) indicate that time-correlative NDA sediments were receiving contributions from probable Archean detritus during Late Cambrian to Early Ordovician time. Thus, the combined Nd isotopic evidence indicates that old continental crustal material was present from the earliest stage of NDA development. This old crustal component was not, therefore, derived from Grenvillian basement when it was underthrust beneath the NDA as it impinged on Laurentia after 490 to 485 Ma (Cawood and Suhr, 1992). Evidence summarized herein suggests that the NDA, as preserved in the plutonic suite,

was a continental arc that formed on Early Proterozoic or older basement, not on Middle Proterozoic Grenvillian basement as exposed in Humber zone inliers.

Evidence from ophiolite allochthons (Jenner et al., 1991; Cawood and Suhr, 1992) and NDA volcanic sequences (Swinden et al., this volume) indicates that analogues for the NDA are to be found in the southwestern Pacific area. Like NDA volcanic rocks, the arc-, non-arc, and transitional geochemical characteristics exhibited by NDA plutonic rocks can be interpreted as consistent with their formation in a suprasubduction-zone environment (e.g., Jenner et al., 1987; Miller et al., 1994). Alternatively, these variations may reflect tapping of different sources or source components, such as the slab versus the mantle wedge. For example, a close association between Early Cretaceous high- and low-Sr arc-type plutonic suites in NE Japan is interpreted as resulting from slab-melting and mantle-wedge melting, respectively (Tsuchiya and Kanisawa, 1994). Generation of these two granitoid suites in the same forearc region, where they intrude an accretionary complex and a microcontinental block, is attributed to high thermal flux in the mantle wedge resulting from ridge subduction. The Bay of Islands complex, which formed within a back arc basin (Jenner et al., 1991), is interpreted to have formed within the NDA synchronous with its oblique impingement and collision with an irregular Laurentian margin. Most NDA intermediate to felsic volcanic rocks geochemically resemble the La-poor arc-like pluton group; equivalents of the La-rich arc-like group have not been identified (see Swinden et al., this volume). Somewhat similar geochemical differences between arc plutonic and volcanic components have been interpreted as reflecting andesitic magmas being dominantly emplaced as plutons in the lower to middle crust of arcs, rather than as lavas at the surface, plus the selective preservation of these plutons during later erosion and tectonic processes (Kelemen, 1995).

There is good geochemical evidence that NDA plutonic rocks received significant input from slab-derived melts. Models for the formation of such magmas suggest that, in post-Archean time, generation of such melts is only possible in tectonic environments where young (<20 Ma), hot oceanic crust is subducted (Defant and Drummond, 1990; Drummond and Defant, 1990). Geochronological data summarized herein, and in Cawood and Suhr (1992), indicate that NDA plutonism is either contemporaneous with, or only somewhat younger (<5 to 15 Ma) than ophiolite formation. Most of the ocean-floor within the back arc basin(s) would have to have been subducted, prior to or during ophiolite obduction. Therefore, the presence within the NDA of plutonic rocks displaying "slab-derived melt" geochemical characteristics represents corroborating evidence for the Cawood and Suhr (1992) model of ophiolite generation and obduction. That similar "slab-derived" arc plutonic rocks have been documented from the extension of the NDA in Alabama (Drummond et al., 1994) suggests that this model may be applicable along the length of the Appalachian orogen.

Although space did not permit discussion of this subject, our NDA plutonic rock data have significant implications for arc magmatic and crustal evolution processes. If not for their distinctively negative range in ε_{Nd} signatures, these plutonic rocks would have been interpreted as consisting of mainly new crustal additions formed by a combination of slab melting and melting of the overlying mantle wedge. The presence together in these arc plutonic rocks of a compositionally distinctive slab-derived component and a very old crustal component provide readily identifiable crustal and slab fingerprints. Further detailed evaluation of this dataset, plus a similar unpublished dataset from subsequent Middle Ordovician to Early Silurian plutonism in the NDA, is required. In general, our data substantiate the arc magmatic and crustal evolution processes discussed and modeled by Miller and Wooden (1994); these include mafic magma influx, hybridization, and remelting of hyridized lower crust.

ACKNOWLEDGMENTS

This project was funded under the Canada-Newfoundland Cooperation Agreement (1990–1994). Partial support for O and Pb isotopic analyses was provided by National Science and Engineering Research Council (NSERC) grants to Longstaffe and Gariépy. Additional funding for some analyses was provided by NSERC and LITHOPROBE grants to Jenner and Fryer. The manuscript was significantly improved by constructive reviews by W. Davis, C. A. Miller, and an anonymous reader. J. Whalen also benefited from discussions with W. Davis, K. L. Currie, and C. van Staal. We thank P. Middlestead and D. Harper for assistance in the stable isotope laboratory, F. Robert for help in the Pb measurements, and C. Collins for help in trace-element and Nd isotopic analyses.

APPENDIX 1. GEOLOGY AND PETROGRAPHY OF NOTRE DAME ARC PLUTONIC AND "BASEMENT" ROCKS

Five general areas were sampled (see Fig. 1); each of these is briefly described separately below, from northeast to southwest. Subsequently, samples collected from Grenville basement inliers in the Humber zone of western Newfoundland are described. Unit letter abbreviations used below (e.g., OHM for Hungry Mountain complex) are those employed on geologic maps of these areas (Whalen and Currie, 1988; Whalen, 1993a, 1993b).

1. Area 1 is located near Robert's Arm on Notre Dame Bay, at the northeastern end of the Notre Dame subzone (Fig. 1). The geology of this area was described by Bostock (1988). The Mansfield Cove complex, which is in fault contact with pillow basalts of the Robert's Arm Group, has given a U-Pb zircon age of 479 ± 3 Ma (Dunning et al., 1987). The sampled lithology (WXNF-26) from this complex is a coarse-grained, quartz-eye porphyritic hornblende-biotite tonalite. A Robert's Arm Group rhyolite gave a U-Pb zircon age of 473 ± 2 Ma. On the basis of field relationships, common felsic intrusions in the area, one of which was sampled from Shoal Arm (WXNF-25), are somewhat younger in age.

2. Area 2 lies north of Red Indian Lake and east of the north end of Grand Lake, within the central Notre Dame subzone (Fig. 1). In general, except for limited stream and lake shore areas, exposures of Ordovician plutonic rocks are small and widely separated. The main unit, the Hungry Mountain complex (unit OHM), was originally defined by Thurlow (1981) as a suite of mafic to felsic and rare ultramafic plutonic rocks that

are thrust southeastward over the Buchans Group, northwest of Buchans. Whalen and Currie (1988) extended this unit to include similar intrusive rocks that occur throughout the central portion of the Notre Dame subzone. Unit OHM varies from massive to strongly foliated, but epidote veins and patches are ubiquitous and characteristic. Foliation is variable in intensity, dips steeply, and varies in trend from northeast to northwest. This fabric is crosscut by unfoliated Early Silurian intrusions (Whalen et al., 1987b).

The complex has been subdivided into mafic (unit OHMa) and felsic (unit OHMb) subunits. Subunit OHMa consists principally of hornblende gabbro or diorite with numerous mafic to ultramafic inclusions. Significant amounts of various types of younger quartz diorite to tonalite (subunit OHMb) intrude subunit OHMa. Sampled areas, such as exposures in Sheffield Brook or the upper portion of Mary March Brook, are heterogeneous on a small scale; contact relationships are often suggestive of coexisting mafic to felsic magmas. Fine-grained basaltic and medium-grained amphibolitic rocks are intruded by coarse-grained, prominent clotty blue quartz, amphibole-biotite tonalite, which in turn is cut by both deformed and undeformed diabase dikes. Another extensively sampled area, the southwest shoreline of Hinds Lake, consists of abundant (~50% by volume) flattened and elongated basaltic and amphibolitic inclusions in a texturally diverse hornblende-biotite, quartz dioritic to tonalitic matrix.

A unit OHMa pegmatitic hornblende gabbro (WXNF-94) from a quarry southeast of Hinds Lake gave a U-Pb zircon age of 469 ± 1 Ma (Whalen and van Breeman, unpublished data). Older portions of unit OHMa, which have been geochemically characterized in this study as of MORB affinity, are interpreted as being the same age (481.4 +4.0–1.9 Ma; Dunning and Krogh, 1985) as the Annieopsquotch ophiolite complex. Unit OHMb tonalites from near Hinds Lake (WXHM-1) and in Kings Brook (WXNF-48) gave U-Pb zircon ages of 467 ± 8 Ma (Whalen et al., 1987b) and 480 ± 3 Ma (Whalen and van Breeman, unpublished data), respectively.

The Hinds Brook pluton (unit Oib), which intrudes the Hungry Mountain complex, is located northwest and adjacent to Hinds Lake. It is a massive to slightly foliated, white to pink, K-feldspar porphyritic, biotite-amphibole granodiorite to granite. Unit Oib is cut by epidote-lined fractures that are fringed by chlorite alteration of mafic silicates and dark pink alteration of feldspars. A unit Oib granodiorite sample (WXTB-121) gave a U-Pb zircon age of 460 ± 10 Ma (Whalen et al., 1987b).

3. Area 3, which lies west of Red Indian Lake and east of the south end of Grand Lake, straddles the Notre Dame–Dashwoods subzone boundary, a zone of imbrication containing juxtaposed, contrasting plutonic rocks (Whalen et al., 1987b) (Fig. 1). Ordovician plutonic rocks, which include a diverse suite of gabbro, diorite, quartz diorite, tonalite, granodiorite, and granite, underlie extensive low-lying areas of poor exposure. Whalen and Currie (1988) and Whalen (1993a, 1993b) subdivided these intrusive rocks; radiometric studies (Whalen and van Breeman, unpublished data) have substantiated their Ordovician age. Numbers of the units described below (e.g., OLa, OLb, OPa, and OPc) are elongated west to east to southwest to northeast, with width to length ratios of 1 to 3 km by 11 to 34 km, probably due to a combination of original intrusive geometry and latter faulting plus flattening. Pre-Middle Ordovician units will be described from oldest to youngest.

The Cariboo Lake gneiss complex (unit OEC) exhibits steep north-trending compositional banding overprinted by a steep east-west tectonic foliation. It includes a medium-grained, gray, biotite-muscovite granodiorite, which contains large inclusions of massive quartz, derived from older veins. This granodiorite grades to migmatitic paragneiss cut by numerous large, sinuously folded quartz veins and coarse-grained muscovite-bearing pegmatite veins. Both the granodiorite and the migmatite contain pseudomorphs of yellow chlorite and sericite after cordierite and rare relict sillimanite. Another major component of unit OEC is a coarse-grained, white, compositionally banded, biotite-hornblende tonalite. Preliminary U-Pb zircon results from a sample (WXNF-

175) of this unit suggest an age in excess of 484 Ma (Whalen and van Breeman, unpublished data).

Northeast of Star Lake, a well-preserved body of layered pyroxene gabbro, sheeted dikes, and pillow lavas is interpreted as remnants of an ophiolite suite (Star Lake ophiolite suite; unit OES) (Whalen, 1993b). These mafic rocks are generally undeformed, but they are cut by veins and dikes of younger granitoid suites. Preliminary U-Pb zircon data from a pegmatitic diorite dike indicate that it overlaps the age (481.4 +4.0/–1.9 Ma; Dunning and Krogh, 1985) of the Annieopsquotch ophiolite complex, which is ~15 km to the southeast of area 3. Rocks of similar mafic to ultramafic composition (unit Om) occur in area 3 as small (<10 cm) to large (>0.5 by 2 km) inclusions in units OPa and OPb. These fragments were, like the Star Lake ophiolite, interpreted by Dunning and Chorlton (1985) as being of ophiolitic affinity and the same age as the Annieopsquotch ophiolite complex. These basaltic and fine-grained to coarse-grained (2 to 3 cm) amphibolitic and gabbroic rocks commonly exhibit metamorphic rather than igneous textures, and have epidote plus chlorite alteration patches and fracture fillings. In many cases, it is apparent that amphibole is a replacement of primary pyroxene.

The Pierre's Pond plutonic suite (unit OP), located at the northern edge of the Dashwoods subzone, includes moderately to strongly foliated, blue quartz-eye porphyritic hornblende-biotite tonalite (OPa) and hornblende gabbro to diorite (OPb), which bear a close resemblance to portions of the Hungry Mountain complex. These rocks intrude, and are host to, mafic to ultramafic inclusions (unit Om). Foliation in unit OPa is mainly east-northeast, but locally strikes northeast, and is generally steeply dipping. Unit OPa generally exhibits metamorphic rather than igneous textures and contains evidence of brittle deformation followed by recrystallization with formation of ragged biotite aggregates and coarse-grained euhedral epidote. Quartz is generally highly strained and flattened, and amphibole may be completly replaced by biotite. Some samples contain relics of clinopyroxene in amphibole. Unit OPc, a white to pink, potash feldspar porphyritic to megacrystic, biotite-amphibole granodiorite to granite, intrudes rocks belonging to unit OPa. It varies from slightly foliated to feldspar augen gneiss and contains large strongly zoned plagioclase, inclusion-rich (plagioclase and mafics) K-feldspar, euhedral biotite, and rare amphibole phenocrysts. Unit OPd, a foliated, white, equigranular, hornblende-biotite tonalite to granodiorite is only exposed east of Star Lake. It has not been seen in contact with other units of the Pierre's Pond plutonic suite.

Massive to moderately foliated, tonalitic to granodioritic rocks belonging to the Lewaseechjeech Brook plutonic suite (units OLa, OLb, OLc, OLd) occur at the southern edge of the Notre Dame subzone. Contact relations between units OL and OP are very poorly exposed, but rocks of unit OL appear to be younger because of their largely preserving igneous textures and exhibiting a lesser degree of penetrative deformation. Foliation in unit OL, where developed, varies from weak to moderate, is steeply dipping, and varies in strike from east-southeast in the southwest to north-south in the southeast part of its exposure area. Subunit OLa consists of generally massive, coarse-grained, white to medium green, amphibole-biotite tonalite to granodiorite. Abundant, large, composite-grained blue quartz aggregates are its most distinctive feature. In places, massive quartz xenoliths (2 to 5 cm) are common. It is only rarely unaltered; alteration consists of pervasive chlorite plus epidote alteration of mafics and feldspar. At its northeastern end, subunit OLa abuts quartz-vein–rich gneisses of unit OEC, a potential source for its quartz inclusions. Subunit OLb consists of coarse-grained, equigranular, white to pale yellow, acicular amphibole-biotite granodiorite to tonalite. It varies from quite fresh and igneous-textured, to brittlely sheared with extensive epidote plus chlorite alteration of biotite and amphibole, and sericite alteration of plagioclase. A granodiorite from unit OLb (WXNF-63) gave a preliminary U-Pb zircon age of 466 ± 2 Ma. Unit OLc, a slightly foliated K-feldspar porphyritic hornblende-biotite granodiorite, lithologically resembles the Hinds Brook granodi-

orite (unit Oib) in area 2. This unit, and also the late K-feldspar porphyritic unit OPc, are interpreted as being the same age (460 ± 10 Ma; Whalen et al., 1987b) as the Hinds Brook pluton (unit Oib). Subunit OLd consists of medium-grained, white to pink, biotite and biotite-amphibole tonalite, but also includes some granodiorite. Unit OLd plutonic rocks, which are in fault contact with unit OPa, contain metamorphic biotite and associated coarse-grained, euhedral epidote pseudomorphs of amphibole.

4. Area 4 is located along or close to the Burgeo road (Route 480) within the Southwest Brook complex (Dunning et al., 1989) in the northern Dashwoods Subzone (Fig. 1). Rocks in this area consist of (1) granulite-grade paragneisses and orthogneisses and migmatitic rocks (Cormacks Lake complex [CLC]); (2) younger, voluminous, generally foliated, dioritic to tonalitic and granodioritic plutonic phases (Southwest Brook complex [SBC]); and (3) post-tectonic basic intrusions (Dunning et al., 1989; van Berkel and Currie, 1988; Currie and van Berkel, 1992). A U-Pb zircon age of 460 ± 10 Ma obtained from a leucocratic, igneous-textured charnockite from the CLC (sample WXNF-24) established a Middle Ordovician age for granulite facies metamorphism in the CLC (Currie et al., 1992). Additional samples (WXNF-121, WXNF-124) were collected from retrograded orthogneisses of the CLC. The CLC was interpreted by Currie et al. (1992) as high-grade equivalents of Cambrian-Ordovician Dunnage zone supracrustal sequences. Plutonic rocks of the SBC characteristically have elongated blue quartz eyes and are amphibole-biotite bearing; blocks of probably cognate hornblende gabbro to diorite are locally abundant. Metasedimentary inclusions, which locally predominate in SBC tonalites, were not observed in areas 1, 2, or 3. An U-Pb age of 456 ± 3 Ma, with an upper intercept of 1430 +18/–17 Ma, was obtained from a SBC tonalite (Dunning et al., 1989); xenocrystic zircon was attributed to partial melting of Grenville crust or sediments derived from such crust. Samples of the SBC for this study (n = 17) were collected from excellent road cuts on Route 480, and include the geochronological sample sites of Dunning et al. (1989).

5. Area 5, located west of Port aux Basques, at the southwest end of the Dashwoods subzone (Fig. 1), is underlain by the Long Range complex (LRC). The LRC is bounded to the east by the Cape Ray fault zone and to the west by the Long Range fault. The general geology of this area was described by van Staal et al. (1992), Dubé et al. (1994), and Dunning et al. (1989). It consists of older ultramafic to mafic rocks and local sillimanite-bearing paragneisses, intruded by felsic plutonic rocks belonging to the Cape Ray igneous complex (CRIC). The CRIC includes both Ordovician and Silurian plutons; Ordovician rocks exhibit many of the features described above from areas 2 to 4. Rocks within the CRIC were correlated with tonalitic rocks in the Southwest Brook complex (Dunning et al., 1989). The Cape Ray "granite," which forms part of the CRIC, includes a distinctive plagioclase megacrystic phase at Cape Ray and a more extensive equigranular quartz-eye tonalite. The porphyritic phase, from the same site as sample WXNF-32, gave a U-Pb age of 488 ± 2 Ma, whereas an equigranular Cape Ray tonalite, similar to sample WXNF-31, gave a U-Pb zircon age of 464 ± 2 Ma (Dubé et al., in 1994).

6. Grenville basement samples were collected from K-feldspar megacrystic granodiorite of the ca. 1023 to 970 Ma Lake Michel intrusive suite (WXNF-13) and adjacent orthogneiss of the ca. 1550 Ma, Long Range gneiss complex (WXNF-11) (Owen, 1991) northwest of Sops Arm in the Long Range inlier. West of the Long Range fault and area 3 is another Grenvillian inlier that includes the Steel Mountain anorthosite complex and granulite facies gneisses of the Disappointment Hill complex (Currie et al., 1992). A charnockite from the Disappointment Hill complex (WXNF-27), which yielded a U-Pb zircon age of 1498 +9/–8 Ma, was interpreted to represent a pluton metamorphosed with the intermediate to mafic gneisses of the complex (Currie et al., 1992). An additional retrograded orthogneiss (WXNF-2) was also collected from this complex.

APPENDIX 2. LOCATIONS AND DESCRIPTIONS OF NOTRE DAME PLUTONIC ROCKS AND VARIOUS GNEISSIC SAMPLES

Sample	Area	NTS	UTM Coordinates			Pluton, Complex, or Suite	Unit	Description
			Zone	Easting	Northing			

Arc-Like with (La/Yb)$_N$<12 (La-Poor Arc-Like Group)

Sample	Area	NTS	Zone	Easting	Northing	Pluton, Complex, or Suite	Unit	Description
WXNF-126	3	12A/12	21	4589	53739	Early mafic	Om	Fol cg eq hbl qtz gabbro, included in WXNF-125
WXNF-138	3	12A/11	21	4677	53785	Pierre's Pond	OPb	mg eq gray hbl-bf quartz diorite, cut by shear bands
WXNF-109	4	12A/5	21	4549	53523	Southwest Brook	Odi	mg-cg eq hbl-bt diorite or gabbro
WXNF-107	4	12A/5	21	4625	53651	Southwest Brook	Odi	mg-cg hbl-bt diorite, cut by ep veins
WXNF-85	3	12A/12	21	4406	53724	Early mafic	Orn	fol cg eq hbl-bt diorite or gabbro
WXNF-115	4	12A/5	21	4366	53681	Southwest Brook	Odi	fol cg bt-hbl qtz diorite
WXNF-111	4	12A/5	21	4503	53527	Southwest Brook	Odi	mass white cg eq bt-hbl qtz diorite
WXNF-106	4	12A/5	21	4486	53585	Southwest Brook	Ogd	fol cg bt-hbl granodiorite
WXNF-122	4	12A/5	21	4362	53643	Southwest Brook	Otn	fol cg bt tonalite
WXNF-26	1	12H/8	21	5691	54758	Mansfield Cove	Ogd	fol gray cg qtz-eye (4-10 mm) hbl-bt tonalite
WXNF-25	1	2E/12	21	5804	54857	Shoal Arm	Og	vfg dk pink musc felsite
WXNF-93	2	12A15	21	5046	54153	Hungry Mountain	OHMa	mg hbl gabbro
WXNF-43	2	12A/14	21	4965	54241	Hungry Mountain	OHMa	vcg eq hbl-bt qtz diorite
WXNF-44	2	12A/14	21	4965	54241	Hungry Mountain	OHMa	mg eq hbl diorite
WXNF-94	2	12A/15	21	5046	54153	Hungry Mountain	OHMa	cg eq hbl diorite, water-rich variant of WXNF-93
WXNF-89	2	12A/15	21	5328	54262	Hungry Mountain	OHMa	mg eq hbl-bt qtz diorite
WXNF-42	2	12A/14	21	4965	54241	Hungry Mountain	OHMa	mg eq hbl-bt diorite to qtz diorite
WXNF-45	2	12A/14	21	4969	54246	Hungry Mountain	OHMa	mg eq hbl diorite
WXHM-1	2	12A/14	21	4972	54230	Hungry Mountain	OHMb	cg eq fol hbl-bt qtz-eye porph tonalite
WXNF-48	2	12H/1	21	5404	54347	Hungry Mountain	OHMb	gray mg-cg qtz-eye porph hbl-bt tonalite
WXNF-41	2	12A/15	21	5013	54203	Hungry Mountain	OHMb	cg eq fol hbl-bt qtz-eye porph tonalite
WXNF-49	2	12H/1	21	5404	54347	Hungry Mountain	OHMb	cg-vcg qtz-eye porph hbl-bt tonalite
WXNF-96	2	12H/2	21	5290	54538	Hungry Mountain	OHMb	cg gray qtz-eye porph hbl-bt tonalite
WXNF-101	2	12H/7	21	5270	54562	Hungry Mountain	Ol-Mb	gray mg eq hbl-bt qtz diorite
WXNF-132	2	12A/14	21	4935	54038	Hungry Mountain	OHMb	fol cg eq hbl tonalite, bt alt hbl
WXNF-87	2	12H/2	21	5322	54306	Hungry Mountain	OHMb	fol mg-cg eq hbl-bt tonalite
/WXNF-34	2	12H/7	21	5279	54584	Hungry Mountain	OHMb	mass cg gray qtz-eye (5–15 mm) hbl tonalite
WXNF-47	2	12A/15	21	5240	54107	Hungry Mountain	OHMb	strongly fol vcg gabbro or diorite, silicified with hamatite alt
WXNF-33	2	12H/7	21	5362	54651	Hungry Mountain	OHMb	mass mg-cg dk pink qtz-eye (4–10 mm) hbl-bt tonalite
WXNF-68	3	12A/11	21	4699	53938	Lewaseechjeech Brook	OLa	fol mg-cg bt granodiorite or tonalite, 2–5 cm qtz lumps
WXNF-69	3	12A/11	21	4683	53915	Lewaseechjeech Brook	OLa	mass cg qtz-eye porph hbl-bt tonalite or granodiorite
WXNF-21	3	12A/12	21	4612	53827	Lewaseechjeech Brook	OLa	cg gray qtz-eye (4–8 mm) hbl tonalite
WXNF-70	3	12A/11	21	4658	53878	Lewaseechjeech Brook	OLa	mass beige cg qtz-eye porph bt tonalite or granodiorite
WXNF-71	3	12A/11	21	4637	53835	Lewaseechjeech Brook	OLa	cg qtz-eye porph bt-hbl tonalite, ep veins and chl alt mafics
WXNF-22	3	12A/12	21	4588	53795	Lewaseechjeech Brook	OLb	fol cg eq white hbl-bt granodiorite
WXNF-72	3	12A/11	21	4642	53819	Lewaseechjeech Brook	OLb	white fol fg-mg bt granodiorite
WXNF-63	3	12A/11	21	4757	53889	Lewaseechjeech Brook	OLb	fol cg eq hbl granodiorite
WXNF-50	3	12A/11	21	4721	53779	Pierre's Pond	OPa	fol cg qtz-eye porph bt-hbl tonalite
WXNF-61	3	12A/11	21	4709	53763	Pierre's Pond	OPa	fol cg hbl-bt qtz diorite or tonalite
WXNF-56	3	12A/11	21	4673	53754	Pierre's Pond	OPa	cg eq fol hbl qtz diorite
WXNF-62	3	12A/11	21	4716	53780	Pierre's Pond	OPa	strongly fol cg eq bt-hbl qtz diorite or tonalite, ep veins
WXNF-55	3	12A/11	21	4652	53764	Pierre's Pond	OPa	white fg-mg eq bt tonalite
WXNF-135	3	12A/11	21	4784	53764	Pierre's Pond	OPd	fg fol white bt porph granodiorite
WXNF-36	3	12A/11	21	4809	53779	Pierre's Pond	OPd	slightly fol pink fg-mg eq bt granodiorite
WXNF-73	2	12A/11	21	4638	53784	Lewaseechjeech Brook	OLd	mg-cg hbl-bt diorite

APPENDIX 2. LOCATIONS AND DESCRIPTIONS OF NOTRE DAME PLUTONIC ROCKS AND VARIOUS GNEISSIC SAMPLES (page 2)

Sample	Area	NTS	UTM Coordinates Zone	Easting	Northing	Pluton, Complex, or Suite	Unit	Description
Arc-Like with (La/Yb)$_N$>12 (La-Rich Arc-Like Group)								
WXNF-5	4	12A/5	21	4304	53691	Southwest Brook	Odi	mass mg-cg eq hbl diorite cut by pegmatitic veins
WXNF-108	4	12A/5	21	4625	53651	Southwest Brook	Ogb	mg plag porph (2–5 cm) hbl gabbro
WXNF-90	2	12A/15	21	5328	54262	Hungry Mountain	OHMa	black fg hbl-bt diorite
WXNF-117	4	12A/5	21	4560	53615	Southwest Brook	Odi	well fol Kfd porph (2–5 cm) hbl-bt monzo-diorite
WXNF-144	3	12A/11	21	4767	53856	Lewaseechjeech Brook	OLb	mg eq fol hbl qtz diorite, bt alt hbl, common fg mafic incl
WXNF-116	4	12A/5	21	4330	53682	Southwest Brook	Odi	white mg-cg eq hbl-bt qtz diorite
WXNF-32	5	11O/11	21	3268	52766	Cape Ray	Ogd	fol mg-cg pink fld porph (1–3 cm) hbl-bt qtz monzonite
WXNF-6	4	12A/5	21	4397	53681	Southwest Brook	Odi	strongly fol fg-mg hbl diorite
WXNF-119	4	12A/5	21	4308	53674	Southwest Brook	Ogd	fol white cg bt granodiorite
WXNF-1	3	12A/12	21	4373	53842	Pierre's Pond	OPa	mass mg eq bt-hbl tonalite, cut by ep and pegmatitic veins
WXNF-10	4	12A/5	21	4273	53686	Southwest Brook	Ogd	fol mg eq hbl qtz diorite
WXNF-31	5	11O/11	21	3323	52791	Cape Ray	Og	fol greenish cg qtz-eye (2–10 mm) hbl tonalite, chl alt hbl
WXNF-112	4	12A/5	21	4443	53650	Southwest Brook	Otn	strongly fol cg bt tonalite, associated diorite and gabbro
WXNF-74	3	12A/12	21	4612	53780	Lewaseechjeech Brook	OLd	white fol mg bt granodiorite, chl alt mafics, ep veins
WXNF-123	4	12A/5	21	4373	53651	Southwest Brook	Ogd	slightly fol fg eq bt granodiorite
WXNF-98	2	12H/2	21	5294	54534	Hungry Mountain	OHMb	gray cg eq bt tonalite
WXNF-105	2	12H/2	21	5068	54494	Hinds Brook	Oib	white and pink mg Kfd porph bt granite
WXTB-119	2	12H/3	21	4992	54435	Hinds Brook	Oib	pink Kfd porph bt-hbl granite
WXTB-121	2	12H/3	21	4901	54328	Hinds Brook	Oib	vcg pink and white hbl-bt granodiorite
WXNF-102	2	12H/2	21	5096	54464	Hinds Brook	Oib	gray and pink Kfd porph (0.3–2.5 cm) mg bt granite
WXNF-64	3	12A/11	21	4746	53897	Lewaseechjeech Brook	OLc	slightly fol cg Kfd porph (1–2.5 cm) hbl-bt granite
WXNF-51	3	12A/11	21	4720	53778	Pierre's Pond	OPc	fol cg-vcg eq bt granite
WXNF-137	3	12A/11	21	4679	53735	Pierre's Pond	OPc	cg-vcg eq strongly fol dark pink hbl granite
WXNF-52	3	12A/11	21	4734	53777	Pierre's Pond	OPc	fol gray cg bt granite
WXNF-57	3	12A/11	21	4708	53762	Pierre's Pond	OPc	pink fol vcg bt granite
Non-Arc-Like Group								
WXNF-113	4	12A/5	21	4399	53680	Southwest Brook	Odie	well fol black mg eq bt-hbl diorite
WXNF-114	4	12A/5	21	4382	53677	Southwest Brook	Otn	fol banded cg bt-hbl tonalite or qtz diorite
WXNF-75	3	12A/12	21	4482	53757	Pierre's Pond	OPa	white strongly fol cg bt tonalite
WXNF-77	3	12A/12	21	4450	53753	Pierre's Pond	OPa	white fol cg bt tonalite
WXNF-76	3	12A/12	21	4458	53751	Pierre's Pond	OPa	white fol cg bt tonalite
WXNF-53	3	12A/11	21	4707	53803	Pierre's Pond	OPa	fol cg qtz-eye porph hbl-bt tonalite
WXNF-86	3	12A/12	21	4436	53728	Pierre's Pond	OPa	well fol cg-vcg hbl-bt tonalite
WXNF-125	3	12A/12	21	4589	53739	Pierre's Pond	OPa	gray cg eq hbl-bt tonalite
WXNF-136	3	12A/11	21	4842	53791	Pierre's Pond	OPd	mg well fol white bt granodiorite
WXNF-95	2	12H/2	21	5122	54526	Hungry Mountain	OHMb	cg gray qtz-eye porph hbl-bt tonalite
Gneiss Samples								
WXNF-67	3	12A/11	21	4706	53934	Cariboo Lakes gneiss	OECa	black fg bt-musc paragneiss, qtz veined
WXNF-141	3	12N/11	21	4746	53943	Cariboo Lakes gneiss	OECa	fg strongly banded gray bt tonalitic gneiss
WXNF-65	3	12A/11	21	4724	53928	Cariboo Lakes gneiss	OECb	gray fol fg-mg bt qtz monzonite, part migmatite complex
WCNF-66	3	12A/11	21	4706	53934	Cariboo Lakes gneiss	OECb	gray fol fg-mg bt qtz monzonite, bt-rich incl and qtz lumps
WXNF-143	3	12A/11	21	4728	53890	Cariboo Lakes gneiss	OECc	mg-cg fol white bt-hbl granodiorite, banded and kfd veins
WXNF-175	3	12A/11	21	4751	53884	Cariboo Lakes gneiss	OECc	mg-cg gneissic white qtz-porph hbl granodiorite

Implications of geochemical and isotopic data, Notre Dame arc

APPENDIX 2. LOCATIONS AND DESCRIPTIONS OF NOTRE DAME PLUTONIC ROCKS AND VARIOUS GNEISSIC SAMPLES (page 3)

Sample	Area	NTS	UTM Coordinates Zone Easting Northing			Pluton, Complex, or Suite	Unit	Description
Gneiss Samples (continued)								
WXNF-24	4	12A/5	21	4000	53000	Cormacks Lake	Ochr	fol mg-cg eq brown charnockite
WXNF-121	4	12A/5	21	4273	53590	Cormacks Lake	Ogn	strongly fol gray bt granitic orthogneiss
WXNF-124	4	12A/5	21	4418	53514	Cormacks Lake	Ogn	comp-banded bt orthogneiss, qtz lumps or eyes (1–2 cm)
WXNF-79	3	12A/12	21	4359	53729	Fleur de Lys Group??	EOgn	banded mg bt-musc paragneiss
WXNF-81	3	12A/12	21	4348	53727	Fleur de Lys Group??	EOgn	banded mg eq bt-musc paragneiss
WXNF-2	HZ	12B/9	21	4221	53888	Disappointment Hill	PEgn	cg gray comp-banded granodioritic bt orthogneiss
WXNF-11	HZ	12H/15	21	5032	55144	Long Range Gneiss	PEgn	very strongly fol dk pk bt granodioritic orthogneiss
WXNF-27	HZ	12B/9	21	4159	53846	Disappointment Hill	PEgn	mass beige cg eq charnockite
WXNF-13	HZ	12H/15	21	4120	55268	Lake Michel	PEg	vcg well fol pk Kfd porph (1–3 cm) hbl-bt granodiorite

Note: Abbreviations are as follows: vfg = very fine grained, fg = fine grained, mg = medium grained, cg = coarse grained, vcg = very coarse grained, eq = equigranular, porph = porphyritic, mass = massive, fol = foliated, incl = inclusions, alt = alteration, comp = compositionally, dk = dark, hbl = amphibole, bt = biotite, chl = chlorite, ep = epidote, fld = feldspar, Kfd = K-feldspar, musc = muscovite, plag = plagioclase, qtz = quartz.

APPENDIX 3. ANALYTICAL TECHNIQUES

Major elements were determined in duplicate on fused glass discs by X-ray fluorescence spectrometry (XRF) by X-ray Assay Laboratories (XRAL), Toronto. FeO was determined in duplicate by dichromate titration and F contents by ion electrode by XRAL. Pressed powder pellets were used for trace element (Rb, Ba, Sr, Ga, Nb, Zr, Y, Cr, Ni, Cu, Zn, V, and Sc) determinations by XRF at Memorial University of Newfoundland (MUN). The rare earth elements (REE) and selected trace elements (U, Pb, Th, Li, Cs, Ta, and Hf) were determined by inductively coupled plasma–mass spectrometry (ICP-MS) at MUN using the methods and with the precision and accuracy described by Jenner et al. (1990). ICP-MS and XRF data on the same elements (Rb, Sr, Ba, Y, Zr, and Nb) allowed checks on dissolution procedures and intertechnique calibrations. Supplementary data on some elements were available from instrumental neutron activation analyses.

Sm/Nd isotopic separations were carried out at MUN, using the techniques described in Swinden et al. (1990). Isotopic measurements ($^{143}Nd/^{144}Nd$ and $^{147}Sm/^{144}Nd$) were made at MUN, using a Finnigan-Mat 261 multicollector mass spectrometer. Data are reported relative to a value of 0.511850 for $^{143}Nd/^{144}Nd$ in the La Jolla standard. The maximum error on the $^{143}Nd/^{144}Nd(m)$, calculated as twice the standard error of the mean (2SE), is ±0.000015, the maximum error on the $^{147}Sm/^{144}Nd(m)$, calculated as the two-sigma error, is ±0.2% and the estimated error on an individual epsilon Nd calculation is ±0.5 units. In addition to reporting measured $^{143}Nd/^{144}Nd$ ratios in Table 2, Nd isotopic data are reported as epsilon values (ε_{Nd}) that measure the deviation in $^{143}Nd/^{144}Nd$ between a given sample and the chondritic uniform reservoir (CHUR) at the time chosen (see DePaolo, 1988, for a complete review). Depleted-mantle Nd model ages (t_{DM}) are based on the model of DePaolo (1988).

Pb isotope measurements were done at the Universite du Québec à Montréal on carefully hand-picked populations (5 to 10 mg) of K-feldspar, a mineral almost devoid of uranium, in order to obtain the best estimate of the initial isotopic composition. The K-feldspar populations were acid leached to remove, as much as possible of any radiogenic Pb component present in the minerals (e.g., Carignan et al., 1993), and the supernatants and residues were analyzed separately. When the supernatant was significantly more radiogenic than the residue, which may indicate the presence of uranium and/or impurities in the K-feldspar populations, the results were discarded and new material analyzed. Procedures for Pb separation and isotopic analysis were identical to those described by Carignan et al. (1993).

Mineral separations were performed at the University of Western Ontario using standard magnetic and heavy liquid separation methods. The purity of all separates was greater than 98%, as determined by high brilliance X-ray diffraction and optical microscopy. Oxygen isotopic analyses were performed at the University of Western Ontario using a Fisons-Optima dual-inlet mass spectrometer (Tables 2 and 3). Oxygen was extracted from silicate and oxide minerals or rocks using the BrF_5 method of Clayton and Mayeda (1963), and quantitatively converted to CO_2 over red-hot graphite. The oxygen-isotope data are presented in the normal δ-notation relative to SMOW (standard mean ocean water) (Craig, 1961). An oxygen-isotope CO_2-H_2O fractionation factor of 1.0412 at 25 °C has been employed in these calculations to calibrate the mass spectrometric reference gas. An average $\delta^{18}O$ value of +9.66‰ ± 0.18‰ was obtained for more than 50 samples of silicate standard NBS-28 analyzed during the period of this study.

REFERENCES CITED

Ayuso, R. A., and Bevier, M. L., 1991, Regional differences in lead isotopic compositions of feldspars from plutonic rocks of the northern Appalachian mountains, U.S.A. and Canada: A geochemical method of terrane correlation: Tectonics, v. 10, p. 191–212.

Barker, F., 1979, Trondhjemite: definition, environment and hypotheses of origin, *in* Barker, F., ed., Trondhjemites, dacites, and related rocks: New York, Elsevier, p. 1–12.

Bostock, H. H., 1988, Geology and petrochemistry of the Ordovician volcano-plutonic Robert's Arm Group, Notre Dame Bay, Newfoundland: Geological Survey of Canada, Bulletin 369, 84 p.

Bottinga, Y., and Javoy, M., 1975, Oxygen isotope partitioning among the minerals in igneous and metamorphic rocks: Review of Geophysics and Space Physics, v. 13, p. 401–418.

Carignan, J., Gariépy, C., Machado, N., and Rive, M., 1993, Pb isotopic geochemistry of granitoids and gneisses from the late Archean Pontiac and Abitibi Subprovinces of Canada: Chemical Geology, v. 106, p. 299–316.

Cawood, P. A., and Suhr, G., 1992, Generation and obduction of opiolites: Constraints from the Bay of Islands complex, western Newfoundland: Tectonics, v. 11, p. 884–897.

Chappell, B. W., and Stephens, W. E., 1988, Origin of infracrustal (I-type) granite magmas: Royal Society of Edinburgh Trasnactions, Earth Sciences, v. 79, p. 71–86.

Clayton, R. N., and Mayeda, T. K., 1963, The use of bromine pentafluoride in the extraction of oxygen from oxides and silicates for isotopic analysis: Geochimica et Cosmochimica Acta, v. 27, p. 43–45.

Colman-Sadd, S. P., Dunning, G. R., and Dec, T., 1992a, Dunnage-Gander relationships and Ordovician orogeny in central Newfoundland: A sediment provenance and U-Pb study: American Journal of Science, v. 292, p. 317–355.

Colman-Sadd, S. P., Stone, P., Swinden, H. S., and Barnes, R. P., 1992b, Parallel geological development in the Dunnage Zone of Newfoundland and the lower Palaeozoic terranes of southern Scotland: An assessment: Royal Society of Edinburgh Transactions, Earth Sciences, v. 83, p. 571–594.

Craig, H., 1961, Standard for reporting concentrations of deuterium and oxygen-18 in natural waters: Science, v. 133, p. 1833–1834.

Currie, K. L., and van Berkel, J. T., 1992, Notes to accompany a geological map of the southern Long Range, southwestern Newfoundland: Geological Survey of Canada Paper 91-10, 10 p.

Currie, K. L., van Breeman, O., Hunt, P. A., and van Berkel, J. T., 1992, The age of granulitic gneisses south of Grand Lake, Newfoundland: Atlantic Geology, v. 28, p. 172–181.

Defant, M. J., and Drummond, M., 1990, Derivation of some modern arc magmas by melting of young subducted lithosphere: Nature, v. 347, p. 662–665.

Defant, M. J., and 8 others, 1991, Andesite and dacite genesis via contrasting processes: The geology and geochemistry of El Valle Volcano, Panama: Contributions to Mineralogy and Petrology, v. 106, p. 309–324.

DePaolo, D. J., 1988, Neodymium isotope geochemistry: An introduction: New York, Springer-Verlag, 187 p.

Drummond, M. S., and Defant, M. J., 1990, A model for trondhjemite-tonalite-dacite genesis and crustal growth via slab melting: Archean to modern comparisons: Journal of Geophysical Research, v. 95, p. 21503–21521.

Drummond, M. S., Allison, D. T., and Wesolowski, D. J., 1994, Igneous petrogenesis and tectonic setting of the Elkahatchee Quartz Diorite, Alabama Appalachians: Implications for Penobscotian magmatism in the eastern Blue Ridge: American Journal of Science, v. 294, p. 173–236.

Dubé, B., Dunning, G. R., Lauzière, K., and Roddick, J. C., 1994, Deformational events and their timing along the Cape Ray fault, Newfoundland Appalachians, in Cawood, P. A., and Hibbard, J., eds., New perspectives in the Appalachian-Caledonian orogen, Program and Abstracts, Geological Association of Canada NUNA Conference: St. John's, Newfoundland, Geological Association of Canada, p. 13.

Dunning, G. R., and Chorlton, L. B., 1985, The Annieopsquotch ophiolite belt of southwest Newfoundland: Geology and tectonic significance: Geological Society of America Bulletin, v. 96, p. 1466–1476.

Dunning, G. R., and Krogh, T. E., 1985, Geochronology of ophiolites of the Newfoundland Appalachians: Canadian Journal of Earth Sciences, v. 22, p. 1659–1670.

Dunning, G. R., Kean, B. F., Thurlow, J. G., and Swinden, H. S., 1987, Geochronology of the Buchans, Roberts Arm, and Victoria Lake groups and Mansfield Cove Complex, Newfoundland: Canadian Journal of Earth Sciences, v. 24, p. 1175–1184.

Dunning, G. R., Wilton, D. H., and Herd, R. K., 1989, Geology, geochemistry and geochronology of a Taconic calc-alkaline batholith in southwest Newfoundland: Royal Society of Edinburgh Transactions, Earth Sciences, v. 80, p. 159–168.

Farmer, G. L., 1979, Magmas as tracers of lower crustal composition: An isotopic approach, in Fountain, D. M., Arculus, R., and Kay, R. W., eds., Continental lower crust: Amsterdam, Elsevier, Developments in Geotectonics, v. 23, p. 363–390.

Florendo, F. F., 1994, Tertiary arc rifting in northern Luzon, Philippines: Tectonics, v. 13, p. 623–640.

Fryer, B. J., Kerr, A., Jenner, G. A., and Longstaffe, F. J., 1992, Probing the crust with plutons: Regional isotopic geochemistry of granitoid intrusions across insular Newfoundland: Newfoundland Geological Surveys Branch, Report 92–1, p. 119–140.

Halliday, A. N., Dickin, A. P., Hunter, R. N., Davies, G. R., Dempster, T. J., Hamilton, P. J., and Upton, B. G., 1993, Formation and composition of the lower continental crust: Evidence from Scottish xenolith suites: Journal of Geophysical Research, v. 98, p. 581–607.

Harper, D. A., Longstaffe, F. J., and Wadleigh, M. A., 1992, Secondary K-feldspar at the Precambrian-Paleozoic boundary, Ontario, Canada, in Kharaka, Y. K., and Maest, A. A., eds., Proceedings of the 7th International Symposium on Water-Rock Interaction: Rotterdam, The Netherlands, Balkema Publishers, p. 1169–1172.

Irvine, T. N., and Baragar, W. R.A., 1971, A guide to the chemical classification of the common volcanic rocks: Canadian Journal of Earth Sciences, v. 8, p. 523–548.

Jenner, G. A., Cawood, P. A., Rautenschlein, M., and White, W. M., 1987, Composition of back-arc basin volcanics, Valu Fa Ridge, Lau Basin: Evidence for a slab-derived component in their mantle source: Journal of Volcanology and Geothermal Research, v. 32, p. 209–222.

Jenner, G. A., Longerich, H. P., Jackson, S. E., and Fryer, B. J., 1990, ICP-MS—A powerful new tool for high precision trace element analysis in earth sciences: Evidence from analysis of selected USGS standards: Chemical Geology, v. 83, p. 133–148

Jenner, G. A., Dunning, G. R., Malpas, J., Brown, M., and Brace, T., 1991, Bay of Islands and Little Port complexes, revisited: Age, geochemical and isotopic evidence confirm supra-subduction zone origin: Canadian Journal of Earth Sciences, v. 28, p. 1635–1652.

Kay, R. W., Kay, S. M., and Arculus, R. J., 1992, Magma genesis and crustal processing, in Fountain, D. M., Arculus, R., and Kay, R. W., eds., Continental lower crust: Amsterdam, Elsevier, Developments in Geotectonics, v. 23, p. 423–445.

Kelemen, P. B., 1995, Genesis of high Mg# andesites and the continental crust: Contributions to Mineralogy and Petrology, v. 120, p. 1–19.

Le Maitre, R. W., 1989, A classification of igneous rocks and glossary of terms: Oxford, United Kingdom, Blackwell, 193 p.

Longstaffe, F. J., 1979, The oxygen isotope geochemistry of Archean granitoids, in Barker, F., ed., Trondhjemites and related rocks: Amsterdam, Elsevier, p. 363–399.

Longstaffe, F. J., 1982, Stable-isotopes in the study of granitic pegmatites and related rocks, in Cerny, P., ed., Granitic pegmatites in science and industry: Mineralogical Association of Canada Short Course, v. 8, p. 373–404.

Longstaffe, F. J., and Gower, C. F., 1983, Oxygen-isotope geochemistry of Archean granitoid gneisses and related rocks in the English River Subprovince, Northwesten Ontario: Precambrian Research, v. 22, p. 203–218.

Longstaffe, F. J., and Schwarcz, H. P., 1977, $^{18}O/^{16}O$ of Archean clastic metasedimentary rocks: A petrogenetic indicator for Archean gneisses?: Geochimica et Cosmochimica Acta, v. 41, p. 1303–1312.

Longstaffe, F. J., Cerny, P., and Muehlenbachs, K., 1981, Oxygen-isotope geochemistry of the granitoid rocks in the Winnipeg River pegmatite district, southeastern Manitoba: Canadian Mineralogist, v. 19, p. 195–204.

Longstaffe, F. J., Clark, A. H., McNutt, R. H., and Zentilli, M., 1983, Oxygen isotopic compositions of Central Andean plutonic and volcanic rocks, latitudes 26°–29° south: Earth and Planetary Science Letters, v. 64, p. 9–18.

Maniar, P. D., and Piccoli, P. M., 1989, Tectonic discrimination of granitoids: Geological Society of America Bulletin, v. 101, p. 635–643.

Martin, H., 1986, Effects of steeper Archean geothermal gradient on geochemistry of subduction-zone magmas: Geology, v. 14, p. 753–756.

Martin, H., 1993, The mechanisms of petrogenesis of the Archean continental crust—Comparison with modern processes: Lithos, v. 30, p. 373–388.

Miller, C. A., Barton, M., Hanson, R. E., and Fleming, T. H., 1994, An Early Cretaceous volcanic arc/marginal basin transition zone, Peninsula Harding, southernmost Chile: Journal of Volcanology and Geothermal Research, v. 63, p. 33–58.

Miller, C. F., and Wooden, J. L., 1994, Anatexis, hybridization and the modification of ancient crust: Mesozoic plutonism in the Old Woman Mountains area, California: Lithos, v. 32, p. 111–133.

Owen, J. V., 1991, Geology of the Long Range Inlier, Newfoundland: Geological Survey of Canada, Bulletin 395, 89 p.

Piasecki, M. A.J., Williams, H., and Colman-Sadd, S. P., 1990, Tectonic relationships along the Meelpaeg, Burgeo and Burlington LITHOPROBE transects in Newfoundland, *in* Current research: Newfoundland Department of Mines and Energy, Geological Survey Branch, Report 90-1, p. 327–339.

Sarewitz, D. R., and Lewis, S. D., 1991, The Marinduque intra-arc basin, Philippines: Basin genesis and in situ ophiolite development in strike-slip setting: Geological Society of America Bulletin, v. 103, p. 597–614.

Sen, C., and Dunn, T., 1994, Dehydration melting of a basaltic composition amphibolite at 1.5 and 2.0 Gpa: Implications for the origin of adakites: Contributions to Mineralogy and Petrology, v. 117, p. 394–409.

Swinden, H. S., and Thorpe, R. I., 1984, Variations in style of volcanism and massive sulfide deposition in Early to Middle Ordovician island-arc sequences of the Newfoundland Central Mobile Belt: Economic Geology, v. 79, p. 1596–1619.

Swinden, H. S., Jenner, G. A., Fryer, B. J., Hertogen, J., and Roddick, J. C., 1990, Petrogenesis and paleotectonic history of the Wild Bight Group, an Ordovician rifted island arc in Central Newfoundland: Contributions to Mineralogy and Petrology, v. 105, p. 219–241.

Swinden, H. S., Jenner, G. A., and Szybinski, A. Z., 1994, Geochemical and isotopic signatures of Cambrian-Ordovician volcanism and plutonism in the Notre Dame subzone, Newfoundland Appalachians: Magmatic evolution of the Laurentian margin of Iapetus, *in* Cawood, P. A., and Hibbard, J., eds., New perspectives in the Appalachian-Caledonian orogen, Program and Abstracts, Geological Association of Canada NUNA Conference: St. John's, Newfoundland, Geological Association of Canada, p. 28.

Szybinski, A., 1995, Paleotectonic and structural setting of the western Notre Dame Bay area, Newfoundland Appalachians [Ph.D. thesis]: St. John's Memorial University of Newfoundland, 382 p.

Tarney, J., and Jones, C. E., 1994, Trace element geochemistry of orogenic igneous rocks and crustal growth models: Geological Society of London Journal, v. 151, p. 855–868.

Tatsumoto, M., Knight, R. J., and Allegre, C. J., 1973, Time difference in the formation of meteorites as determined from the ratio of lead 207 to lead 206: Science, v. 180, p. 1279–1283.

Taylor, H. P., Jr., 1968, The oxygen isotope geochemistry of igneous rocks: Contributions to Mineralogy and Petrology, v. 19, p. 1–71.

Taylor, H. P., Jr., 1978, Oxygen- and hydrogen-isotope studies of plutonic rocks: Earth and Planetary Science Letters, v. 38, p. 177–210.

Taylor, H. P., Jr., 1988, Oxygen, hydrogen, and strontium isotope constraints on the origin of granites: Royal Society of Edinburgh Transactions Earth Sciences, v. 79, p. 317–338.

Taylor, S. R., and McLennan, S. M., 1985, The continental crust: Its composition and evolution: Oxford, United Kingdom, Blackwell, 312 p.

Thurlow, J. G., 1981, The Buchans Group: Its stratigraphic and structural setting, in Swanson, E. A., Strong, D. F., and Thurlow, J. G., eds., The Buchans orebodies: Fifty years of geology and mining: Geological Association of Canada Special Paper 22, p. 79–91.

Tsuchiya, N., and Kanisawa, S., 1994, Early Cretaceous Sr-rich silicic magmatism by slab melting in the Kitakami Mountains, northeast Japan: Journal of Geophysical Research, v. 99, p. 22205–22220.

van Berkel, J. T., and Currie, K. L., 1988, Geology of the Puddle Pond (12A/5) and Little Grand Lake (12A/12) map-areas, southwestern Newfoundland: Newfoundland Department of Mines, Mineral Development Division, Report 88–1, p. 97–107.

van Staal, C. R., 1994, Brunswick subduction complex in the Canadian Appalachians: Record of the Late Ordovician to Late Silurian collision between Laurentia and the Gander margin of Avalon: Tectonics, v. 13, p. 946–962.

van Staal, C. R., Burgess, J. L., Hall, L., Lee, C., Lin, S., and Schofield, D. I., 1992, Geology of the Port aux Basques-Rose Blanche area (NTS 11-O/10 & 11-O/11), *in* Report of activities 1992: Newfoundland Department of Mines and Energy, Geological Survey Branch, p. 41–43.

Wenner, D. B., and Taylor, H. P., 1976, Oxygen- and hydrogen-isotope studies of a Precambrian granite-rhyolite terrane, St. Francois Mountains, southeastern Missouri: Geological Society of America Bulletin, v. 87, p. 1587–1598.

Whalen, J. B., 1989, The Topsails igneous suite, western Newfoundland: An Early Silurian subduction-related magmatic suite?: Canadian Journal of Earth Sciences, v. 26, p. 2421–2434.

Whalen, J. B., 1993a, Geology of the Star Lake Sheet, Newfoundland (NTS 12A/11)—1:50 000 colour map with descriptive notes: Geological Survey of Canada Open File 2735.

Whalen, J. B., 1993b, Geology of the Little Grand Lake sheet, Newfoundland (NTS 12A/12)—1:50 000 colour map with descriptive notes: Geological Survey of Canada Open File 2736.

Whalen, J. B., and Currie, K. L., 1988, Geology of the Topsails igneous terrane of western Newfoundland: Geological Survey of Canada Map 1680A, scale 1:200 000.

Whalen, J. B., Currie, K. L., and Chappell, B. W., 1987a, A-type granites: Geochemical characteristics, discrimination and petrogenesis: Contributions to Mineralogy and Petrology, v. 95, p. 407–419.

Whalen, J. B., Currie, K. L., and van Breemen, O., 1987b, Episodic Ordovician-Silurian plutonism in the Topsails Igneous Terrane, western Newfoundland: Royal Society of Edinburgh Transactions, v. 78, p. 17–28.

Whalen, J. B., Jenner, G. A., Hegner, E., Gariépy, C., and Longstaffe, F. J., 1994, Geochemical and isotopic (Nd, O, and Pb) constraints on granite sources in the Humber and Dunnage zones, Gaspésie, Quebec, and New Brunswick: Implications for tectonics and crustal structure: Canadian Journal of Earth Sciences, v. 31, p. 323–340.

Whalen, J. B., Jenner, G. A., Longstaffe, F. J., and Hegner, E., 1996, Nature and evolution of the eastern margin of Iapetus: Geochemical and isotopic constraints from Siluro-Devonian granitoid plutons in the New Brunswick Appalachians: Canadian Journal of Earth Sciences, v. 33, p. 140–155.

Williams, H., Colman-Sadd, S. P., and Swinden, H. S., 1988, Tectonic-stratigraphic subdivision of central Newfoundland, *in* Current research, Part B: Geological Survey of Canada Paper 88-1B, p. 91–98.

Yogodzinski, G. M., Kay, R. W., Volynets, O. N., Koloskov, A. V., and Kay, S. M., 1995, Magnesian andesite in the western Aleutian Komandorsky region: Implications for slab melting and processes in the mantle wedge: Geological Society of America Bulletin, v. 107, p. 505–519.

Zartman, R. E., and Doe, B. R., 1988, Plumbotectonics—The model: Tectonophysics, v. 75, p. 135-162.

MANUSCRIPT ACCEPTED BY THE SOCIETY JULY 2, 1996
GEOLOGICAL SURVEY OF CANADA CONTRIBUTION NO. 54994

Geological Society of America
Memoir 191
1997

The Cadillac Mountain intrusive complex, Maine:
The role of shallow-level magma chamber processes in
the generation of A-type granites

Robert A. Wiebe and Jonathan B. Holden*
Department of Geological Sciences, Franklin and Marshall College, Lancaster, Pennsylvania 17604
Michelle L. Coombs* and Reinhard A. Wobus
Department of Geology, Williams College, Williamstown, Massachusetts 01267
Kathleen J. Schuh*
Department of Geology, College of Wooster, Wooster, Ohio 44691
Benjamin P. Plummer*
Department of Geology, Washington and Lee University, Lexington, Virginia 24450

ABSTRACT

The Silurian Cadillac Mountain intrusive complex occurs along the coast of Maine and consists of the Cadillac Mountain granite (CMG), a gabbro-diorite unit, and three smaller granitic units that were emplaced at a shallow depth into coeval volcanic rocks. Multiple infusions of basaltic magma were injected into and ponded on the floor of the CMG magma chamber, producing the gabbro-diorite unit. Fractionation and mixing of these infusions generated layers of mafic to intermediate magma enriched in incompatible elements that were trapped beneath silicic magma. Granitic rocks that crystallized before the basaltic infusions (lower CMG) are relatively hydrous with two feldspars, and early hornblende and biotite (I-type). Granitic rocks that crystallized after the basaltic infusions (upper CMG) are hypersolvus with late interstitial hornblende, greatly enriched in high-field-strength elements, and have higher Ga/Al (A-type). Mafic enclaves in the upper CMG originated from the incompatible-rich intermediate magma that developed at the base of the chamber. The CMG provides a record of the thermal and chemical transformation of resident granitic magma from I-type to A-type due to interactions between resident silicic magma and basaltic infusions. It demonstrates that A-type characteristics can be produced by processes in high-level magma chambers and need not reflect the original conditions of melting or the chemical character of the source rocks for the granitic magma. The processes that operated in the CMG may be important in the generation of other A-type granites that occur in areas of bimodal magmatism.

*Present addresses: Holden, Department of Earth Sciences, University of New Hampshire, Durham, New Hampshire 03824; Coombs, 412 8th Street, N.W., Albuquerque, New Mexico 87102; Schuh, Department of Geology, University of North Carolina, Chapel Hill, North Carolina 27599-3315; Plummer, 663 Carriage Way, N.W., Atlanta, Georgia 30339.

Wiebe, R. A., Holden, J. B., Coombs, M. L., Wobus, R. A., Schuh, K. J., and Plummer, B. P., 1997, The Cadillac Mountain intrusive complex, Maine: The role of shallow-level magma chamber processes in the generation of A-type granites, *in* Sinha, A. K., Whalen, J. B., and Hogan, J. P., eds., The Nature of Magmatism in the Appalachian Orogen: Boulder, Colorado, Geological Society of America Memoir 191.

INTRODUCTION

Granitic rocks classified as A-type (Loiselle and Wones, 1979; Collins et al., 1982) are characterized by relatively high temperatures of crystallization and low H$_2$O contents. The majority appear to have been emplaced in anorogenic settings and are commonly closely associated with basaltic magma in bimodal, extensional terranes. Concurrent basaltic magmatism provides an efficient means of heating the crust to produce high-temperature crustal melts. A-type granites typically have low CaO, and high Fe/Mg and Ga/Al ratios (Whalen et al., 1987), and are enriched in high-field-strength elements (HFSE), rare earth elements (REEs) (except Eu), F, and Cl. Individual complexes may be alkaline, subaluminous, or, less commonly, peraluminous. Models for their origin focus mainly on different possible crustal sources (Anderson, 1983; Collins et al., 1982; Whalen et al., 1987; Bedard, 1990; Eby, 1990, 1992; Creaser et al., 1991). However, the close association with basalts has led some workers to suggest, as an alternative, that some A-type granites have developed by extended fractionation of basaltic magmas (Eby, 1990, 1992; Turner et al., 1992). The relatively high temperature and anhydrous character of A-type granites has led several workers to suggest that they represent second melts from the crust (e.g., Whalen et al., 1987). Creaser et al. (1991) reviewed the "residual source" model and concluded that the thermal and chemical characteristics of A-type granites (especially the high Fe/Mg) can be better explained by initial partial melting of tonalitic to granodioritic rocks, in agreement with Anderson (1983). It has been suggested that the enrichment of HFSEs and high Ga/Al could be caused by differential complexing of these elements with F during melting (Collins et al., 1982), but this process has not been demonstrated experimentally. The high Ga/Al of A-type granites has also been explained by retention of An-rich plagioclase in the source (Whalen et al., 1987). However, because plagioclase is likely to be retained in the source of nearly all crustal granitic melts, it is not clear why the high Ga/Al should be characteristic only of A-type granites.

This brief literature review suggests that there remains considerable disagreement over the significance of A-type characteristics. This is in contrast with the more widely accepted view that the mineralogical and geochemical characteristics of I- and S-type granites convey information about genetically different sources. Because A-type granites range in composition from peralkaline to peraluminous, it is highly unlikely that their distinctive mineralogical and chemical characteristics relate to any single source. It is more likely that these characteristics have been acquired by the granitic magma at some time between its initial formation and final crystallization at higher crustal levels.

The purpose of this chapter is to describe a Silurian plutonic complex in coastal Maine that suggests that A-type characteristics can be acquired by a silicic magma after its emplacement into a high-level magma chamber. The Cadillac Mountain intrusive complex (CMIC) provides evidence for the initial emplacement of silicic magma, continuing activity within the chamber due to

periodic infusions of basaltic magma, and final consolidation after late injections of new silicic magma. The many injections of basaltic magma underwent fractional crystallization beneath a cap of silicic magma. This recharge and fractional crystallization generated a layer of mafic to intermediate magma with high concentrations of HFSEs and other incompatible elements that was trapped beneath silicic magma that filled the top of the chamber. A double-diffusive boundary was commonly active between this enriched intermediate magma and overlying silicic magma. Thermal and selective chemical exchange, as well as some turbulent mixing, occurred along this boundary. Mafic enclaves in the upper Cadillac Mountain granite are variably contaminated samples of the enriched magma that were stirred into overlying silicic magma (Wiebe et al., 1997). Roughly equal volumes of basaltic and granitic magmas would be needed to produce the chemical changes shown by the upper CMG compared with the lower CMG. Gravity data for the CMIC suggest that there may be a sufficient volume of mafic rock beneath the upper CMG.

REGIONAL GEOLOGIC SETTING

The Silurian Cadillac Mountain intrusive complex (CMIC), located on Mount Desert Island, Maine (Fig. 1), belongs to the Coastal Maine magmatic province and is emplaced into the Ellsworth–Coastal volcanic terrane (Hogan and Sinha, 1989). The bimodal character of this province is well established (Chapman, 1962), and there is widespread evidence for commingling between mafic and felsic magmas (Taylor et al., 1980; Stewart et al., 1988; Chapman and Rhodes, 1992; Wiebe, 1993, 1994). Gravity studies (Hodge et al., 1982) indicate that many of the granitic plutons in this province are less than a few kilometers thick, with gently dipping floors, and probably rest on mafic rocks similar to the interlayered diorite and gabbro that partly surround and dip beneath several of them. The plutons of the Coastal Maine magmatic province intrude a variety of metasedimentary and metavolcanic rocks in several fault-bounded, northeast-trending terranes featuring different stratigraphies and different structural and metamorphic histories (Williams and Hatcher, 1982). The age and field relations of these plutons suggest that they postdate the main assembly of these lithotectonic terranes (Ludman, 1986), but predate the accretion of the province to North America (West et al., 1992). Hogan and Sinha (1989) suggested that some of the magmatism was related to rifting in a region of transtension along a transcurrent fault system.

FIELD RELATIONS

Introduction

The CMIC occurs in an irregular, roughly oval area about 14 by 20 km (Fig. 1). It consists of three major units: the Cadillac Mountain granite (CMG), a hybrid unit of gabbroic to granitic rocks (G-D), and the Somesville granite (SG). There are, in addition, two small units: (1) a small, sheet-like mass of granite, the

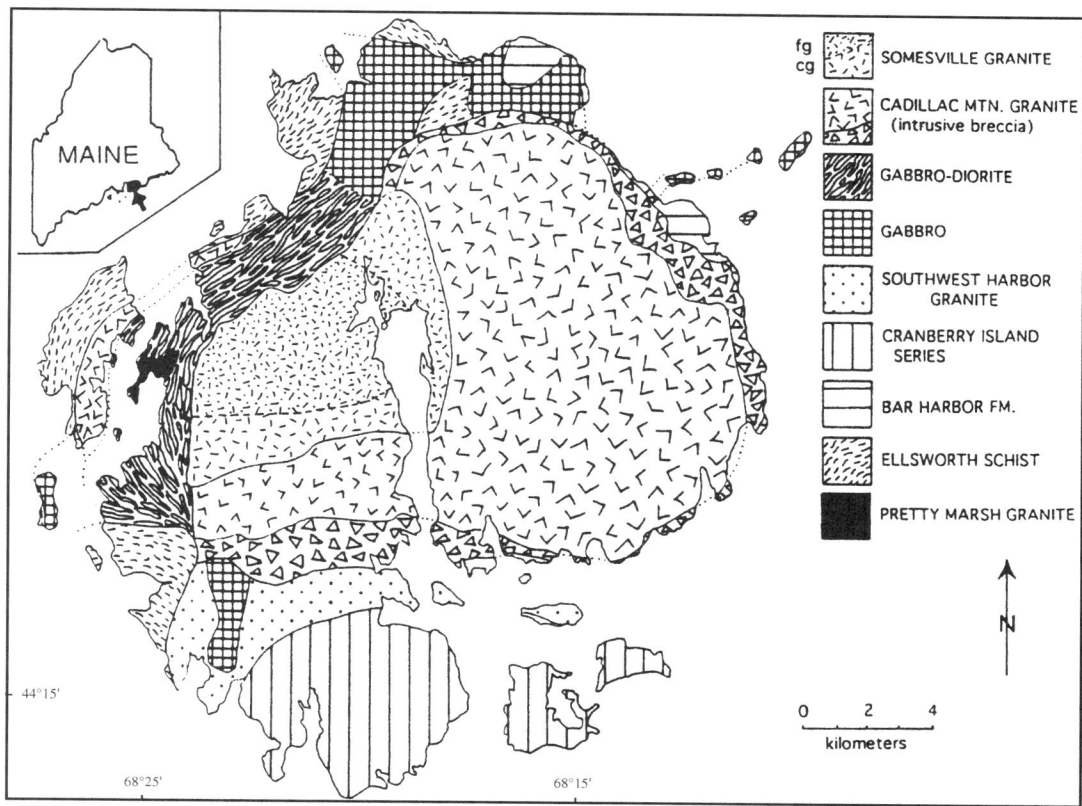

Figure 1. Geologic map of Mount Desert Island, Maine (modified from Wiebe, 1994).

Southwest Harbor granite, and (2) small, irregular masses and dikes of the Pretty Marsh granite that cut the G-D unit. The relationships between the major units can be seen more clearly in a schematic east-west cross section (Fig. 2).

Emplacement of the CMIC appears to have been largely controlled by the unconformity between the Ellsworth schist and the gently dipping Bar Harbor Formation. The areal distribution of these country rock units indicates that the unconformity now dips moderately to the southeast, so that the base of the CMIC is exposed along its western and northwestern contacts with the Ellsworth schist (Fig. 1). The Cranberry Island series (CIS), a sequence of mainly silicic pyroclastic and flow material with subordinate mafic volcanic rocks, lies immediately above the Bar Harbor Formation and south of the CMIC (Fig. 1). Silicic rocks in this unit have compositions that are most similar to the Southwest Harbor granite. Preliminary zircon ages from the CMIC and these volcanic rocks (CIS = 424 ± 1 Ma: CMG = 419 ± 2 Ma; SG = 424 ± 2 Ma) are overlapping in age (Seaman et al., 1995). Although the SG age is older than the CMG age, field relations clearly indicate that the CMG is older than the SG, so there must be some problems with the accuracy of these ages. Brief descriptions of the Ellsworth schist, Bar Harbor Formation, and the Cranberry Island series are provided in Gilman et al. (1988). To the north, east, and south of the CMG, dikes and sills of gabbro and diabase occur in the Bar Harbor Formation. The Southwest

Harbor granite was emplaced into the lower part of the Bar Harbor Formation and immediately beneath a sill of gabbro. All of these rocks are truncated by an intrusive breccia along the southern margin of the CMG. Steeply bounded masses of gabbro in the Ellsworth schist appear to have been feeders for gabbroic rocks both within and outside the CMIC.

Cadillac Mountain granite

There are two areas of CMG separated by the hybrid G-D unit (Fig. 1); field relations indicate that the smaller western area of CMG lies below the G-D unit, and the larger eastern area lies above it. On the basis of gravity data, Hodge et al. (1982) suggested that the upper CMG is a saucer-shaped mass of granite that is less than 3 km thick at its center and that the G-D unit forms a saucer-shaped body, 2 to 3 km thick, beneath it. The thickness of the lower CMG at depth is not well constrained. The upper CMG is rimmed (except on its western margin against the SG and the G-D unit) by an intrusive breccia (termed a "shatter zone" by Gilman et al. 1988). This intrusive breccia varies in character from intensely veined country rock to closely packed, rotated blocks of the Bar Harbor Formation, gabbroic sills, and the Cranberry Island series—units that probably provided a roof to the CMG chamber.

Just south of the SG, the upper CMG is in contact with the

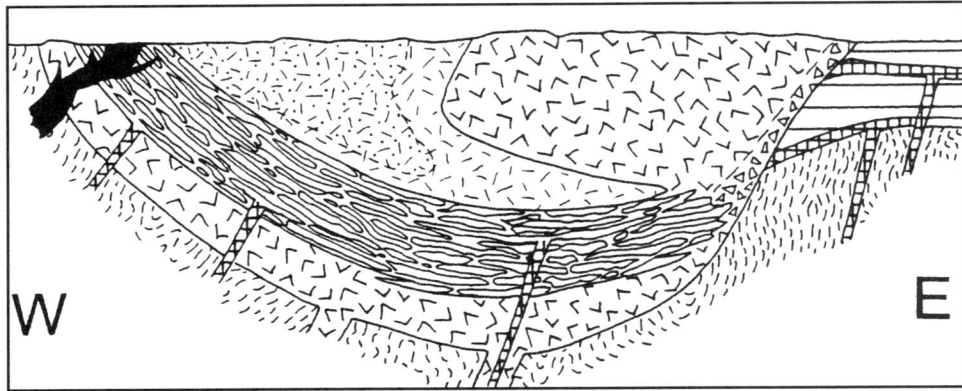

Figure 2. East-west cross section through the Cadillac Mountain intrusive complex (modified from Wiebe, 1994). Patterns as in Figure 1.

gabbro-diorite unit. Gravity data, the attitudes of layering in the gabbro-diorite, the occurrence of CMG as layers within the G-D, and the lack of crosscutting relations between the CMG and the gabbro-diorite unit suggest that the CMG rests "conformably" on the gabbro-diorite.

The upper CMG is cut by some narrow arcuate zones of variably porphyritic granophyre that Chapman (1970) originally interpreted as recrystallized zones. Boundaries between granophyre and granite range from sharp to gradational. A small body immediately south of the SG has a sharp southern contact against coarse-grained CMG and grades northward over a distance of several meters from chilled, aphyric microgranophyre back to coarse-grained granite. Scarce aplite veins (1–5 cm thick) occur in the CMG within about 100 m of the contact with the SG. These veins trend roughly parallel with the contacts and dip about 65° toward the SG, with some cutting across north-south–trending basaltic dikes in the CMG (see below). En eche-lon sets of veins suggest that the inner block of granite (toward the SG) moved up relative to the outer (marginal) block. At high elevations, scarce aplite veins occur as subhorizontal to gently dipping sheets.

Quartz veins are locally common in the CMG. These veins probably formed from hydrothermal solutions that were expelled from depth along fractures in the solid granite. The CMG is also cut in one locality by two lensoid en echelon zones (each about 2 to 4 cm thick and several meters long) of desilication. These zones occur within 200 m of the contact with the SG and are par-allel both to the contact and to nearby aplitic veins. Strong corro-sion of quartz and feldspar is apparent in thin section. An intensely corroded central zone grades outward to normal granite over a distance of a few centimeters. Cordierite, minor garnet, and scarce spinel occur within this central zone, which retains relicts of the granitic texture.

The lower CMG contains several sheet-like masses (layers and lenses) of variably chilled and pillowed gabbroic to dioritic rocks that closely resemble mafic material in the G-D unit (Wiebe, 1994). These layers all dip steeply to the east. Silicic

pipes that are approximately perpendicular to one gabbro layer extend upward from the underlying granite through the chilled base of the gabbro. Because the pipes were probably vertical when they formed, their present orientations indicate that the gabbroic layers were initially deposited roughly horizontally and subsequently tilted. The formation of silicic pipes implies that the granitic material beneath the gabbro was incompletely solidified with up to 40% to 50% interstitial liquid (Wiebe, 1993). Other basally chilled gabbroic layers in the lower CMG clearly grade upward (to the east) to granite through hybrid diorite. These mafic layers represent early, relatively small infusions of basaltic magma into the CMG magma chamber prior to the voluminous influx that generated the G-D unit (Wiebe, 1994).

Mafic enclaves occur widely but sparsely throughout the CMG (Chapman, 1969; Seaman and Ramsay, 1992; Wiebe et al., 1997). They appear to be much less abundant in the lower CMG. Most common and widespread are mafic enclaves with sub-equant to irregular shapes that range in size from about 0.5 to 2 cm in diameter. Many of these inclusions are sufficiently small that they appear in outcrop to be mafic interstitial areas between the coarse-grained feldspar and quartz. They typically have inter-granular to subophitic textures and consist mainly of hornblende and plagioclase. Lensoid, intermediate to silicic enclaves (about 30 cm in maximum diameter) occur very sparsely in the outer portions of the upper CMG, and their attitudes appear to define a basinform shape (Chapman, 1969; Gilman et al., 1988) that is consistent with the shape of the floor suggested by gravity data. Some of the larger silicic enclaves contain small fine-grained mafic inclusions. Inclusions of country rock units are essentially absent except within and very near the shatter zone.

Gabbro-diorite unit

The gabbro-diorite unit displays all of the characteristic field relations of mafic-silicic layered intrusions (Wiebe, 1994). Much of the G-D unit consists of layers of gabbro to diorite (typically 2 to 50 m thick) in macrorhythmic units that grade upward from basally chilled gabbro to coarser-grained gabbroic, dioritic, or granitic rocks. Compared with the Pleasant Bay mafic-silicic layered intrusion (Wiebe, 1993), silicic tops of macrorhythmic layers in the G-D unit more commonly approach granitic compositions, and the upward transitions from gabbro to granite are generally more abrupt. Layers dip moderately (20°–50°) to the east in an arcuate pattern roughly conformable with the basinal shape indicated by gravity for both the granite and the mafic rocks. The orientations of silicic pipes in mafic layers suggest that the layers were originally deposited close to the horizontal and subsequently bowed downward as the chamber evolved.

Southwest Harbor granite

The Southwest Harbor granite (SHG) is a generally fine grained hornblende, biotite granite that sharply intrudes the Ellsworth schist and the Bar Harbor Formation; its contacts with the Cranberry Island (CI) volcanic rocks are enigmatic. The map distribution suggests that the SHG is a sheet-like mass emplaced near the unconformity between the Ellsworth schist and the Bar Harbor Formation and overlain by a sheet of diabasic gabbro. Although that contact is not exposed, granitic veins in the gabbro close to the contact suggest that the SHG is younger. The granite contains rare enclaves of two types: irregularly shaped, very fine grained, commonly banded silicic bodies up to several tens of centimeters in long dimension, and smaller mafic enclaves. The former may be inclusions of CI volcanic rocks; the latter probably represent partly digested mafic material that mixed with the SHG.

Somesville granite

The Somesville granite (SG) lies between the layered gabbro-diorites and the upper CMG (Fig. 1). A medium- to coarse-grained variety occurs mainly in an arcuate area, 1–2 km in width, along the contact with the CMG. An inner, fine-grained variety is in contact with the underlying G-D unit. The SG varieties grade into each other over distances of several tens of meters. Transitional rocks are commonly porphyritic with phenocrysts comparable in size to crystals in the coarse-grained variety. The Somesville granite sharply cuts the upper CMG along steep contacts that appear to dip about 60° to 70° inward. Locally, dikes of the SG can be seen to extend a few meters into the CMG.

Both gravity data (Hodge et al., 1982) and field relations suggest that the G-D unit dips moderately beneath the SG. Within about 100 m of its contact with the G-D unit, the Somesville granite has abundant (up to 50%), small (1–5 cm), variably chilled and assimilated inclusions of gabbro-diorite. Partly resorbed xenocrysts of quartz and feldspar from the SG occur with hornblende and pyroxene reaction rims in the mafic inclusions. Near the top of the G-D unit some layers of granite (both sharply bounded against and gradational to gabbroic layers) resemble the SG. These relations indicate that the Somesville magma was contemporaneous and partially mixed with rapidly

cooling basaltic magma at the top of the gabbro-diorite unit. A small area of variably chilled gabbro that occurs at the base of the SG may represent a late pulse of basaltic magma into the SG magma chamber.

Away from the contact with the G-D unit, small (1–3 cm) mafic enclaves occur very sparsely, mainly in the fine-grained SG. Larger (5–20 cm) enclaves of fine-grained and porphyritic silicic material occur within the coarser variety of the SG; some of these are double enclaves with inclusions of more mafic material.

Pretty Marsh granite and related dikes

The Pretty Marsh granite (PMG) is a fine-grained biotite granite that occurs as irregular masses and dikes that sharply cut the G-D unit. There is abundant evidence for contemporaneous mafic magmatism: (1) PMG occurs as the matrix to chilled gabbroic pillows in many composite dikes (Chapman, 1962) that cut the G-D unit, and (2) some areas of the PMG grade to hybrid rocks that contain abundant, irregularly distributed, partly digested mafic inclusions that suggest mechanical mixing with rapidly cooling basaltic magma.

Basaltic Dikes

Basaltic dikes trend roughly north-south to N20°W in all units of the CMIC; they are much more abundant in the CMG than in the younger Somesville and Pretty Marsh granites. Dikes in the CMG locally contain concentrations of partly resorbed quartz and alkali-feldspar xenocrysts that probably were derived from the CMG. Where several dikes in the upper CMG approach the Somesville granite, they trail off into linear zones of basaltic pillows before reaching the SG contact. These relations indicate that basaltic dikes were emplaced into the CMG magma chamber while it was incompletely crystallized in its interior. Pulses of basaltic magma that fed these dikes probably also ponded at the base of the remaining chamber of silicic magma in the center of the CMIC where the SG now resides.

PETROGRAPHY AND MINERAL CHEMISTRY

Cadillac Mountain granite

Most of the Cadillac Mountain granite (the upper CMG) consists of homogeneous, massive, medium- to coarse-grained, hypersolvus granite with a color index (CI) of less than 10. Quartz and mesoperthitic alkali-feldspar are equant and range from 2 to 7 mm in diameter. Larger quartz crystals commonly show evidence of resorption channels partly filled with feldspar. Although some alkali feldspars are unexsolved, most are typically coarsely exsolved. Relative proportions of plagioclase and alkali-feldspar lamellae suggest that, in different rocks, the original compositions ranged between $An_{10}Ab_{85}Or_5$ and $An_2Ab_{30}Or_{68}$ (Fig. 3). (All mineral compositions were obtained using a Cameca SX 50 microprobe at Princeton University.) Hornblende is the dominant mafic

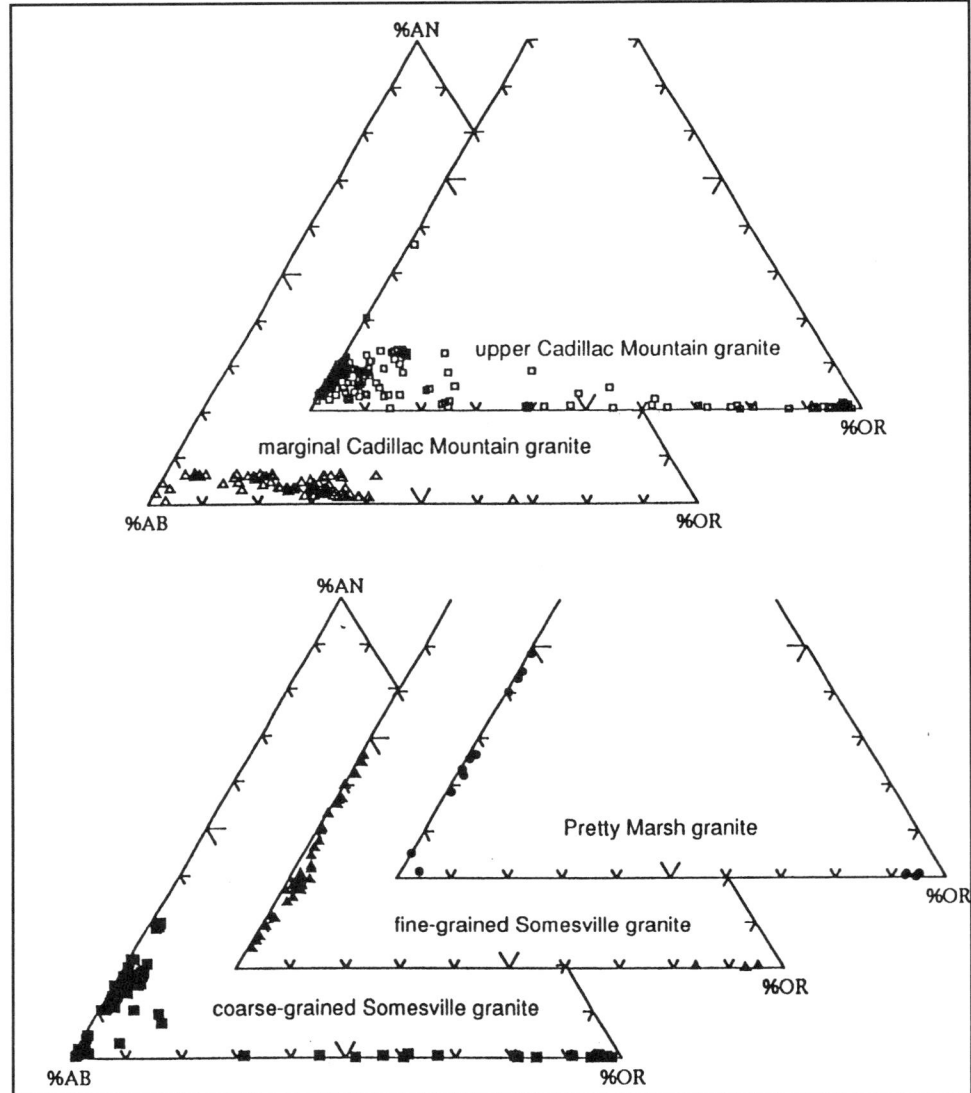

Figure 3. Ternary plots of feldspar compositions in the Cadillac Mountain, Somesville, and Pretty Marsh granites. Feldspars vary widely in the degree of exsolution. Analyses were obtained using a focused beam so that analyses from exsolved feldspars are of homogeneous exsolution lamellae. Unexsolved feldspars commonly preserve hypersolvus compositions.

mineral; scarce biotite occurs locally. Both mafic minerals are typically interstitial. Accessory phases include ubiquitous opaque minerals, zircon and apatite, common allanite, titanite, and fluorite, and scarce ferrohedenbergite. The last phase occurs as subhedral to corroded cores in hornblende or as euhedral inclusions in feldspar. Epidote, chlorite, stilpnomelane, carbonate, and sericite occur sparsely as alteration products and, in some rocks, as subsolidus fillings of interstitial primary cavities. Representative compositions of hornblende (ferroedenite) in the CMG are given in Table 1.

Near the base of the upper CMG (against the G-D unit), the granite commonly has subhedral hornblende crystals that enclose corroded biotite crystals. This granite also contains scarce grains of intermediate plagioclase (An_{40-30}) The more silicic layers in the G-D unit have comparable petrographic features.

Granitic rocks within and near the shatter zone (marginal CMG) are more variable in mineralogy and texture, and some have cumulate textures. These latter rocks contain variable proportions of euhedral, sodic alkali-feldspar ($An_5Ab_{70}Or_{25}$) (Fig. 3), minor euhedral to subhedral ferrohedenbergite, and rare fayalite in a touching framework that resembles a cumulate texture as defined by Irvine (1982). These cumulate varieties grade inward within meters to tens of meters to typical CMG. In some transitional rocks unexsolved alkali-feldspars have sodic plagioclase cores and show thin, but strong oscillations of the Na/K ratio in a transition from core to rim (Fig. 4). Most rocks from

TABLE 1. REPRESENTATIVE MICROPROBE ANALYSES OF AMPHIBOLES FROM THE CADILLAC MOUNTAIN GRANITE*

	Marginal CMG (Shatter Zone)				Upper CMG (Main Phase)				Lower CMG	
	CM-33		GH-1B		MDI-148		MDI-118		MDI-67X	
SiO$_2$	41.74	41.43	44.56	42.93	44.59	41.00	42.29	43.07	44.26	44.77
Al$_2$O$_3$	7.02	7.55	4.28	5.54	5.13	9.38	6.63	6.63	7.14	6.94
TiO$_2$	1.69	1.55	0.71	0.44	1.18	0.23	1.44	1.73	1.80	1.63
FeO$^{(t)}$	31.99	30.63	35.51	35.30	27.22	30.83	29.34	27.66	23.12	22.99
MnO	0.65	0.63	0.65	0.97	0.62	0.68	0.94	0.62	0.93	1.00
MgO	2.05	3.04	0.92	0.74	6.20	2.45	3.84	5.30	7.45	7.65
CaO	10.24	10.13	10.31	10.06	9.15	11.40	9.83	10.00	10.46	10.38
Na$_2$O	1.96	2.12	1.06	1.26	1.99	0.89	1.94	2.16	1.86	1.81
K$_2$O	1.18	1.13	0.83	1.11	0.61	0.87	0.95	0.89	1.09	0.98
Total	98.52	98.21	98.83	98.35	96.70	97.73	97.21	98.06	98.11	98.15
				NUMMBER OF CATIONS BASED ON 23 OXYGENS						
Si	6.741	6.670	7.218	7.029	7.089	6.615	6.823	6.813	6.842	6.899
Al	1.336	1.433	0.817	1.069	0.961	1.783	1.261	1.236	1.301	1.261
Ti	0.205	0.188	0.086	0.054	0.142	0.027	0.175	0.206	0.209	0.189
Fe	4.321	4.124	4.811	4.834	3.619	4.160	3.959	3.660	2.989	2.963
Mn	0.089	0.086	0.089	0.135	0.083	0.092	0.129	0.084	0.122	0.131
Mg	0.494	0.730	0.222	0.181	1.470	0.590	0.923	1.249	1.717	1.758
Ca	1.772	1.748	1.790	1.765	1.558	1.971	1.700	1.694	1.732	1.714
Na	0.614	0.662	0.333	0.400	0.612	0.278	0.608	0.662	0.556	0.541
K	0.243	0.232	0.172	0.232	0.124	0.180	0.196	0.179	0.215	0.193
Fe/(Fe+Mg)	0.90	0.85	0.96	0.96	0.71	0.88	0.81	0.75	0.64	0.63

*All Fe calculated as ferrous iron.

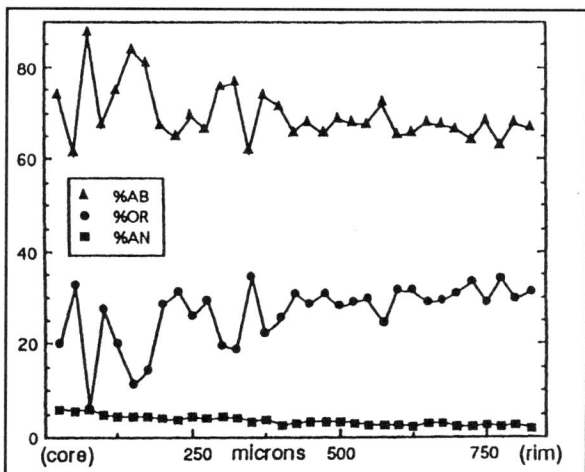

Figure 4. Profile of typical oscillatory zoning in ternary feldspars from the marginal Cadillac Mountain granite.

the marginal zone contain both hornblende and biotite, and some rocks have early subhedral biotite partly enclosed by later hornblende. Fluorite, zircon, and allanite appear to be more abundant in the cumulates than in CMG from the interior.

Granitic rocks of the lower CMG commonly have two feldspars—a normally zoned plagioclase (An$_{30-20}$) and a K-rich alkali-feldspar. Scarce, more-calcic plagioclase (An$_{50-30}$) occurs sporadically along with small concentrations of hornblende. Although hornblende is the dominant mafic mineral, biotite is common in many rocks, and both minerals are commonly subhedral. These features are even more common in granitic layers within the G-D unit.

Rocks from the granophyric zones commonly contain euhedral phenocrysts of equant quartz and alkali-feldspar with scarce subhedral hornblende and biotite. Clinopyroxene and fayalite occur in a few samples. The matrix is typically dominated by microgranophyre. Accessory phases (opaque minerals, apatite, zircon, allanite, and fluorite) are comparable to those in the coarser grained CMG.

Widespread, small, mafic enclaves are dominated by fine-grained, subhedral, tabular, normally zoned plagioclase and hornblende with subordinate opaque minerals and apatite. Zircon occurs as an accessory phase in many enclaves. In some enclaves hornblende encloses scarce anhedral clinopyroxene. The scattered occurrences of small plagioclase and local concentrations of small hornblende crystals in the CMG may be explained by disaggregation of these enclaves.

Gabbro-diorite unit

Rocks in this unit vary in composition from gabbroic to granitic and in texture from chilled mafic rocks to gabbroic, dioritic, and granitic cumulates (Wiebe, 1994). All varieties are closely associated within macrorhythmic layers that grade upward from chilled gabbro to diorite and, less commonly, to granite. Chilled margins of gabbroic layers typically have basaltic textures with radiating thin lathes of strongly zoned plagioclase (An_{70-30}). Mafic minerals in chilled gabbroic layers are dominated by hornblende with subordinate augite, orthopyroxene, opaque minerals, and biotite. Coarser grained gabbroic layers are typically massive with randomly arranged, normally zoned plagioclase lathes (An_{70-30}). Augite and/or hornblende are typically ophitic to subophitic; equant olivine occurs in many layers. Accessory Fe-Ti oxides and apatite are ubiquitous. In rocks of intermediate composition there is abundant evidence for hybridization between mafic and silicic magmas.

The most silicic portions of the G-D unit occur at the tops of macrorhythmic units or as layers and lenses between chilled gabbroic layers; they closely resemble the Cadillac Mountain granite in terms of grain size, texture, and mineralogy. Biotite is, however, more common than in the upper CMG. Within macrorhythmic units, the upward transition from leucocratic, quartz-poor, plagioclase-rich rock to granite typically occurs over distances of several centimeters.

Southwest Harbor granite

The Southwest Harbor granite is a fine- to medium-grained, two-feldspar granite with a CI of less than 10 and highly variable proportions of biotite and hornblende. Many rocks have a matrix of microgranophyre with 10% to 30% of subhedral plagioclase up to 5 mm in diameter. These plagioclase crystals typically show complex oscillatory and normal zoning in the range An_{25-15}; plagioclase with patchy zoning is common in many rocks. Subordinate subhedral quartz occurs in many rocks and typically displays prominent irregular resorption channels. Perthitic alkali-feldspar is generally interstitial or a major constituent with quartz in microgranophyre; a very few samples contain larger, subhedral perthitic alkali-feldspar crystals. Biotite and hornblende vary from subhedral to interstitial. Accessory minerals include opaque minerals (mainly Fe-Ti oxides and pyrite), allanite, apatite, zircon, and titanite. Alteration products include sericite, epidote, chlorite, titanite, and scapolite.

Somesville granite

There are two varieties of the Somesville granite. A medium- to coarse-grained, two-feldspar granite with a CI of less than 10 occurs mainly in an outer arc adjacent to the CMG (Fig. 1). It is dominated by large (up to 10 mm) equant, perthitic alkali-feldspar with smaller (1–4 mm) equant quartz and subordinate complexly zoned plagioclase (An_{30-15}) with patchy and oscillatory zoning that records multiple episodes of resorption. Some of the alkali-feldspar is hypersolvus and unexsolved (Fig. 3). Biotite is the dominant mafic mineral; hornblende is scarce and commonly absent. Accessory phases include opaque minerals, apatite, titanite, zircon, allanite, and fluorite.

A finer grained variety of the SG occurs within a large central area and adjacent to the G-D unit. It contains varying proportions of quartz and alkali-feldspar phenocrysts comparable in size to those in the coarser grained SG. It also contains two distinct varieties of plagioclase: (1) scarce phenocrysts that resemble crystals found in the coarse-grained SG, and (2) abundant, small (0.1–0.3 mm), tabular plagioclase crystals with strong normal and oscillatory zoning (An_{45-15}). Representative feldspar compositions are plotted in Figure 3.

Several textural features, more common in the fine-grained variety, suggest that the SG has been affected by hybridization with mafic material. Partly disaggregated mafic clots rich in hornblende and plagioclase occur sparsely. Hornblende appears to be more abundant where small zoned plagioclase is also more abundant. In many rocks, some plagioclase crystals have rounded, more sodic cores inside more calcic zones. Rarely, plagioclase rims occur on irregular cores of alkali-feldspar. Both types of feldspar zoning record corrosional events that may be related to magma mixing. The mafic enclaves and irregular concentrations of hornblende and plagioclase that are sparsely but widely distributed throughout the SG are petrographically similar to the abundant mafic inclusions that occur in a narrow zone adjacent to the gabbro-diorite unit.

Pretty Marsh granite and related dikes

The Pretty Marsh granite and most of the dikes that cut the G-D unit are two-feldspar, biotite granites. Hornblende occurs sporadically and may be derived by disaggregation of scarce mafic enclaves. Accessory minerals include apatite, allanite, zircon, titanite, and opaque minerals. Perthitic alkali-feldspar is commonly equant and up to several millimeters in diameter; plagioclase is much smaller, tabular, and typically zoned from small cores of about An_{40} to broad rims of An_{15}. This zoning closely resembles that of the smaller, strongly zoned plagioclase crystals in the SG (Fig. 3).

GEOCHEMISTRY

Analytical methods

Whole-rock major- and trace-element compositions for about 200 samples from the CMIC were determined at Franklin and Marshall College. Major elements and some trace elements (Rb, Sr, Ni, Nb, Ga, Cu, Zn, U, and Th) were determined by X-ray fluorescence using a Phillips PW2400 spectometer with a Rh tube. For major element analysis 3.6 g of $Li_2B_4O_7$ was mixed with 0.4 g of rock powder and fused into a homogeneous glass disc. Working curves were determined by analyzing 51 geochemical rocks standards; data for each were compiled by Govindaraju (1989). Trace elements were analyzed using a pressed powder briquette consisting of 1.4 g of microcrystalline cellulose and 7.0 g of sample. Other trace elements (Ba, Y, Zr, Cr, Be, Co, Sc, Ce, and Yb) were determined using a Thermo Jarrel Ash Corp. inductively-coupled atomic plasma spectrometer (ICP). Sample (0.2 g) and $LiBO_2$ (0.7 g) were mixed, fused, and dissolved in a 6% HNO_3 solution containing 2 ppm Cd as an internal standard. Rock standards prepared similarly (n=16) were used to construct working curves. Repetitive analyses of standards suggest that errors for SiO_2 and MgO are ±1%; all other major elements were ±2% except Na_2O, which was ±5%. Analyses of standards suggest that the accuracy of most trace elements analyses is largely between ± 5% and ± 10%. REE analyses were done by INAA at two commercial laboratories (XRAL Activation Services, Inc. and Activation Laboratories Ltd.) and at the U.S. Geological Survey in Reston, Virginia.

Cadillac Mountain granite (CMG)

Analyzed samples from the CMG have been placed into four different groups on the basis of field relations: (1) samples from the interior of the upper CMG; (2) samples near and within the shatter zone (marginal CMG); (3) samples from the lower CMG and from conformable layers within the G-D unit (lower CMG); and (4) granophyric bodies in the upper CMG. Representative analyses are given in Table 2. Plots of several major and trace elements versus SiO_2 show clear distinctions between these four groups (Fig. 5). Most upper CMG granites have between 72% and 75% SiO_2 and, relative to the other groups, are noticeably enriched in Y, Zr, and Ga (Fig. 5) as well as Ce, Yb, Nb, and Zn. Granites from the marginal and lower CMG trend to significantly lower SiO_2. The greater scatter shown by the lower CMG may be attributed to contamination from closely associated contemporaneous gabbro and/or diorite. Granitic rocks from near the shatter zone are anomalously low in MgO and, with decreasing SiO_2, show well-defined trends away from the upper CMG to higher Na_2O, MnO, and Ga (Fig. 5) as well as FeO_T, Al_2O_3, and Sr. These marginal rocks are also relatively enriched in Ba, Zr, and Zn, and depleted in K_2O, Rb, Y, Ce, Yb, and Nb. Compared with these marginal granites at similar SiO_2 contents, the lower granites are relatively depleted in Y and Zr, and enriched in MgO, TiO_2, and CaO. They are also distinct in terms of Na_2O, MnO, V,

TABLE 2. REPRESENTATIVE CHEMICAL ANALYSES OF WHOLE-ROCK SAMPLES FROM THE CADILLAC MOUNTAIN GRANITE

Subunit	Upper GMG (Main Phase)				Lower CMG (Below and in the G-D unit)				Marginal CMG (Near the Shatter Zone)				Granophyres	
Sample	89	90	91A-3	GH-22	68X	111	114	115	GH-1B	GH-1C	GH-4	122B	124B	KS-30
(wt. %)														
SiO_2	74.25	72.80	71.06	71.40	72.54	73.02	69.14	66.71	67.83	68.32	67.35	72.80	78.19	77.79
TiO_2	0.32	0.40	0.42	0.04	0.38	0.34	0.62	1.05	0.41	0.37	0.42	0.31	0.09	0.07
Al_2O_3	12.30	12.55	12.90	13.07	13.66	13.74	14.09	14.74	14.41	14.33	14.68	12.82	12.38	12.30
$Fe_2O_3^{(t)}$	3.44	4.14	4.66	4.48	3.36	2.56	4.89	5.68	6.00	5.70	6.00	4.29	0.93	1.02
MnO	0.07	0.10	0.11	0.12	0.07	0.05	0.11	0.12	0.18	0.16	0.19	0.12	0.02	0.01
MgO	0.24	0.27	0.28	0.21	0.43	0.42	0.68	1.14	0.11	0.09	0.11	0.09	0.00	0.03
CaO	1.10	1.17	1.20	1.19	1.26	0.84	1.78	3.16	1.19	1.69	1.73	1.12	0.50	0.47
Na_2O	4.21	4.40	4.52	4.73	3.54	3.86	4.39	3.75	5.42	5.41	5.40	4.65	3.38	3.72
K_2O	3.82	3.61	3.60	3.73	4.82	4.33	3.59	3.53	3.12	3.20	3.21	3.88	4.81	4.80
P_2O_5	0.06	0.06	0.06	0.06	0.07	0.07	0.11	0.23	0.05	0.04	0.05	0.02	0.00	0.01
LOI	0.52	0.65	0.71	0.33	0.31	1.15	0.89	0.62	0.19	0.46	0.60	0.83	0.41	0.36
Total	100.33	100.15	99.52	99.72	100.44	100.38	100.29	100.73	99.63	99.77	99.74	100.93	100.71	100.58
(ppm)														
Rb	117	103	101	107	111	155	100	115	92	84	71	87	215	236
Sr	60	62	70	54	65	80	100	153	116	117	122	50	19	10
Ba	610	780	858	970	641	562	794	628	1,102	1,373	1,202	1,073	181	59
Y	82	84	72	87	66	67	76	47	70	68	54	55	44	29
Zr	461	592	601	806	348	311	501	257	732	815	721	645	116	107
V	7	10	10	12	20	19	34	84	6	6	7	7	1	3
Ni	2	2	4	4	4	5	4	4	4	4	3	2	0	1
Be	2.9	2.6	2.3	2.7	2.7	3.8	2.3	2.1	2.3	2.2	1.5	1.3	3.5	2.8
Sc	6	7	7	8	6	6	10	11	16	12	16	9	3	3
Ce	153	144	153	103	111	95	107	73	76	85	78	115	72	22
Yb	9	8	8	9	7	7	8	4	8	8	7	6	6	3
Nb	20	16	17	19	15	15	17	10	15	12	14	10	11	12
Ga	22	21	23	22	20	18	22	18	25	24	24	23	15	16
Cu	3	5	3	5	7	6	5	9	4	6	8	6	3	1
Zn	59	96	116	119	40	41	94	54	126	125	152	109	30	14
U	3	4	2	4	1	5	3	3	2	2	3	2	7	5
Th	12	9	7	13	10	19	8	6	8	10	6	4	23	28

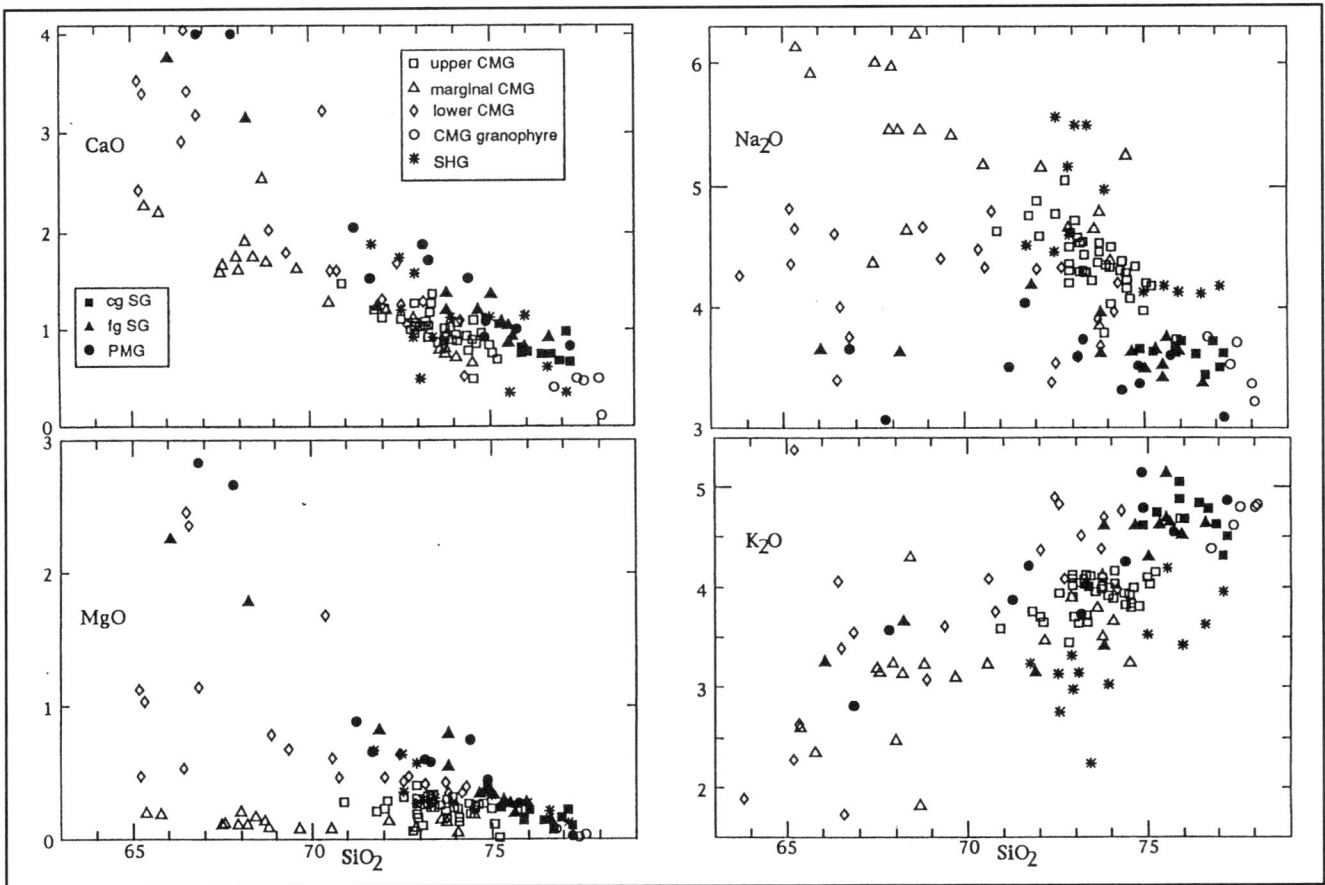

Figure 5 (on this and following two pages). Harker variation diagrams for all granitic units of the Cadillac Mountain intrusive complex. Concentrations of oxides are in weight percent and elements in parts per million (ppm). CMG is Cadillac Mountain granite; SHG is Southwest Harbor granite; PMG is Pretty Marsh granite.

Ga, and Zn. Granophyric rocks range from about 76% to 78% SiO$_2$. Relative to the upper CMG, they have higher abundances in SiO$_2$, K$_2$O, Rb, Be, U, and Th and are depleted in all other elements. They are strongly depleted in CaO, MgO, and Sr. In a plot of normative Ab-Or-SiO$_2$, rocks from the upper CMG fall in a tight group that trends from the center roughly toward Ab; transgressive granophyres in the CMG appear to extend that trend to the 500 bar minimum (Fig. 6). Rocks from near the shatter zone and from the lower CMG show considerable scatter and many samples extend the trend of the main CMG toward the Ab corner.

Representative REE analyses of rocks from the CMG are given in Table 3, and the ranges of chondrite-normalized REEs in all analyzed rocks are plotted in Figure 7. The upper CMG is characterized by moderate enrichment in light REEs with La between 90 and 300 times chondrites and flat heavy REEs with a small negative Eu anomaly. Samples from near the shatter zone have similar slopes for REE patterns, substantial positive Eu anomalies, and lower REE abundances. These patterns are consistent with the petrographic evidence for feldspar accumulation. Three samples from the lower CMG have patterns and abun-

dances comparable to the marginal CMG with the exception of prominant negative Eu anomalies.

Most rocks from the CMG plot close to the boundary between metaluminous and peraluminous granites; granophyres are weakly peraluminous (Fig. 8A). Except for some samples from the lower CMG and some granophyres, they are relatively high in Ga/Al (Fig. 9A) and consistently plot as A-type granites in discrimination diagrams. In tectonic discrimination diagrams the upper CMG plots in the field of within-plate granites (Fig. 10A). Granitic rocks from the lower CMG define trends that cross boundaries in Figures 9A and 10A.

Somesville granite (SG) and the Pretty Marsh granite (PMG)

The Somesville and Pretty Marsh granites have similar compositions that are generally in the range of 73% to 77% SiO$_2$ (Table 4). Relative to the CMG, these granites are characterized by higher SiO$_2$, K$_2$O, and Rb, and lower Ga, Ba, Zr, and Y (Fig. 5). The SG is also characterized by lower abundances of

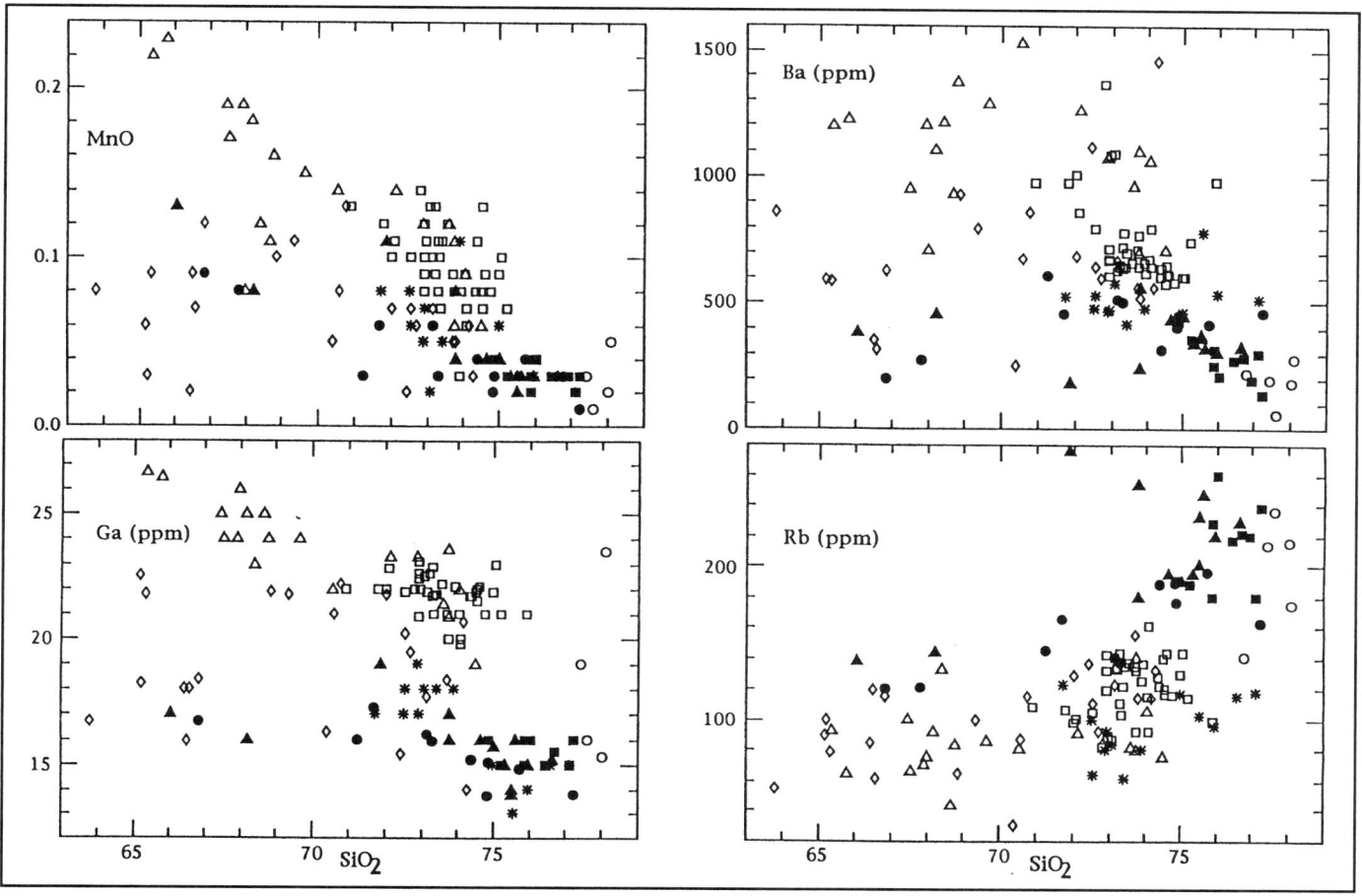

REEs and prominent negative Eu anomalies (Table 5, Fig. 11). The fine-grained variety of the SG is similar in composition to the coarse-grained variety, but extends along with the PMG to lower SiO_2 on trends that generally merge with the less-silicic rocks of the lower CMG. In a plot of normative Ab-Or-SiO_2, the most silicic rocks plot close to the 500 bar minimum (Fig. 12). Except for lower-SiO_2 rocks that show contamination with mafic material, both the SG and the PMG are peraluminous (Fig. 8B). On discrimination diagrams these granites plot within the field of I and S granites rather than in the A-type field (Fig. 9B). In tectonic discrimination diagrams they straddle the boundary between the fields of within-plate granites and volcanic arc or syncollision granites (Fig. 10B).

Southwest Harbor granite (SHG)

Analyses of the Southwest Harbor granites fall into two groups: a more evolved one with SiO_2 between 75% and 78%, and a more tightly clustered one with SiO_2 between 72% and 74% (Table 4; Fig. 5). On plots of SiO_2 versus most major and trace elements (including Zr, Y, Nb, and Ga), the more evolved SHG group generally plots with more evolved rocks of the SG

and PMG (Fig. 5). The major exceptions are the alkalies and Ba, which have concentrations comparable to those in the CMG. The lower-SiO_2 group of SHG has abundances of nearly all elements that most closely resemble those in the lower CMG (at similar SiO_2 contents). In terms of many distinctive incompatible trace elements (Nb, Ga, Zr, Y, and Zn) (Tables 2 and 4) this group is typically intermediate between the widely separated trends shown by the CMG, the SG, and the PMG (Fig. 5). REEs in the SHG have similar slopes to other granites in the CMIC and abundances that are on average lower than the CMG (Figs. 7 and 11). They show a negative Eu anomaly that is less pronounced than that of the SG. The lower-SiO_2 group plots near the boundary between metaluminous and peraluminous granites; the more evolved rocks are peraluminous (Fig. 8). The Southwest Harbor granites plot close to the boundary but largely within the field of I- and S-type granites (Fig. 9) and in the field of within-plate granites (Fig. 10A). High-SiO_2 rocks of the SHG plot close to the 500 bar minimum in the system Ab-Or-SiO_2; the low-SiO_2 group defines a trend toward the Ab corner that terminates at about the 5 kbar cotectic (Fig. 12). This trend is parallel to that shown by the CMG rocks, but shifted slightly toward lower Or. In terms of all elements reported in this chapter, the Southwest Harbor gran-

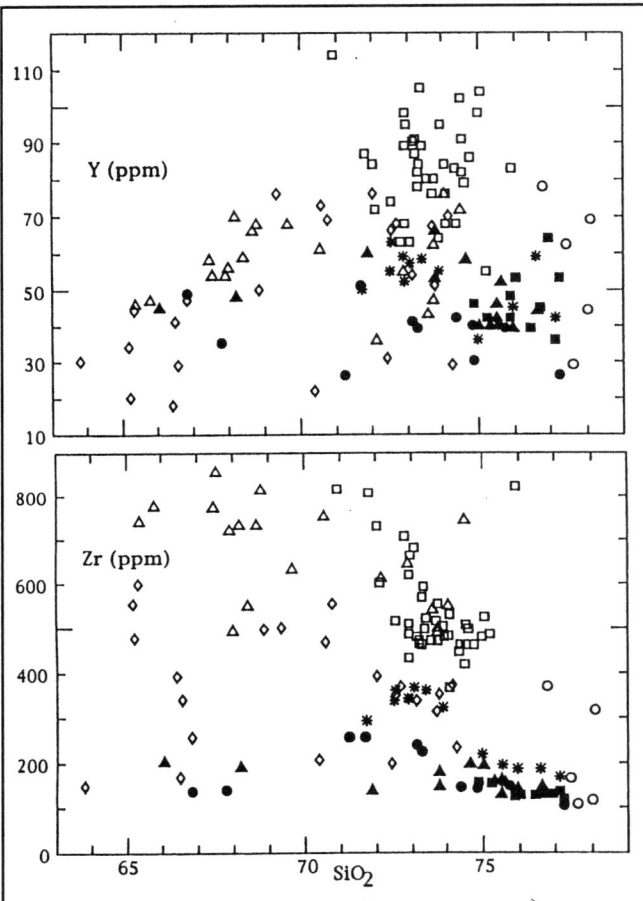

ites have major- and trace-element compositions that closely resemble felsites and tuffs of the Cranberry Island volcanics (Seaman et al., 1995).

CONDITIONS OF CRYSTALLIZATION IN THE CMIC

Depth of emplacement in the CMIC

Several lines of evidence indicate that the CMIC was emplaced at shallow crustal levels. Qualitative evidence includes: (1) emplacement of the plutonic complex into volcanic rocks of similar composition and age, (2) miarolitic cavities at high elevations in the CMG, and (3) the relatively low pressure mineral assemblage cordierite-hypersthene-alkali feldspar and widespread occurrence of andalusite in pelitic rocks of the Ellsworth schist near the base of the complex. Although the granitic rocks lack the appropriate equilibrium mineral assemblage needed for hornblende geobarometry (e.g., Hammarstrom and Zen, 1986), magmatic hornblende compositions are edenitic and nearly devoid of Al_{VI} (Table 2), which suggests a crystallization pressure of less than 2 kbar. In terms of normative Ab-Or-SiO_2, the most evolved rocks related to the Cadillac Mountain, Somesville, Pretty Marsh, and Southwest Harbor granites all lie close to the minimum compositions at pressures between 0.5 and 1 kbar (Figs. 6 and 12).

The narrow zones of desilication provide some information on the depth at the time of subsolidus cooling. Because the alteration zones have replaced solid granite along fractures that are parallel to nearby aplite dikes, it is likely that the desilication formed by vapor ascent along the fractures. Under most conditions, cooling and rising vapor would result in the deposition of

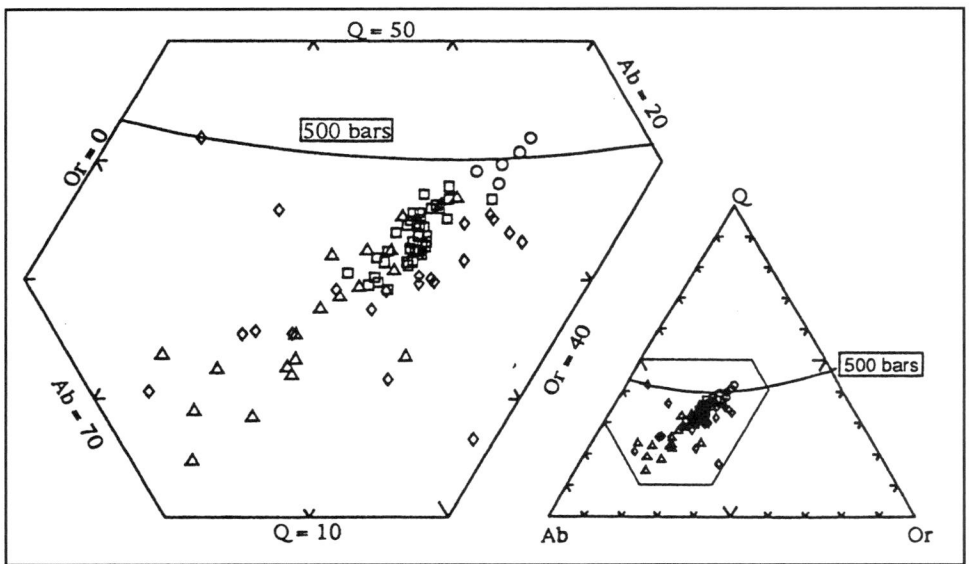

Figure 6. Weight normative (CIPW) compositions of all phases of the Cadillac Mountain granite in terms of quartz, albite, and orthoclase. 500 bar boundary after Tuttle and Bowen (1958). Symbols as in Figure 5.

TABLE 3. REPRESENTATIVE ANALYSES OF REES IN THE CADILLAC MOUNTAIN GRANITE

Sample	Upper GMG (Main Phase)			Lower CMG		Marginal CMB (Shatter Zone)		
	90	91A3	GH-22	68X	111	GH-1B	GH-1C	GH-4
La	53.0	35.7	47.1	27.2	41.3	31.1	35.7	35.7
Ce	103.0	83.0	99.0	91.2	83.6	72.0	80.0	78.0
Nd	60.0	44.2	50.0	33.4	38.5	40.0	41.0	40.0
Sm	14.8	12.3	11.3	9.9	10.1	9.3	9.2	9.3
Eu	3.0	3.1	3.0	1.7	1.3	5.5	6.2	5.9
Tb	2.5	2.1	1.8	1.8	1.8	1.6	1.6	1.6
Yb	8.3	7.65	7.90	6.99	6.97	6.8	6.8	5.9
Lu	1.2	1.09	1.28	0.96	0.97	1.18	1.07	1.01

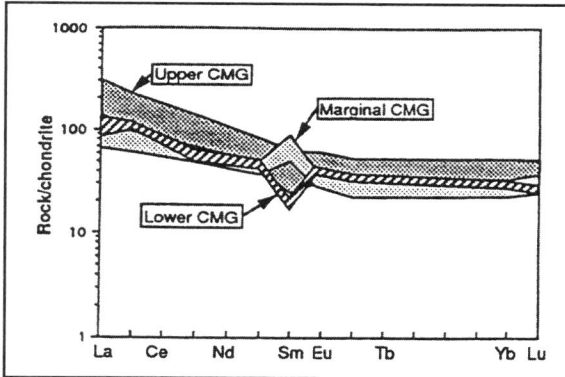

Figure 7. Ranges of chondrite-normalized rare earth elements in the Cadillac Mountain granite (CMG). Average chondrite values of Haskin et al. (1968) were used for normalization.

quartz veins; however, at pressures (P) of less than about 700 bar and temperatures (T) between about 500 °C and 400 °C, the solubility of SiO_2 increases with decreasing (P) (Kennedy, 1950). The occurrence of these desilication veins implies a pressure of less than 700 bar. However, if the fractures opened to the surface and the effective pressure were hydrostatic rather than lithostatic, the pressure gradient would be about 100 bar/km rather than 300 bar/km (Holland and Malinin, 1979). Under these circumstances, a hydrostatic pressure of 500 bar would correspond to a depth of 5 km and a geothermal gradient of about 100 °C/km.

Crystallization of the Cadillac Mountain granite

The mineralogy of the upper and marginal CMG (that portion above the gabbro-diorite unit) is distinct from all other granites in the CMIC in that it is dominated by hypersolvus ternary feldspar. Granite samples with a single coarsely exsolved alkalifeldspar typically have normative compositions that average about $An_5Ab_{60}Or_{35}$. This composition is also well preserved in oscillatory-zoned cores of feldspars (Fig. 4), particularly in marginal rocks where cooling was apparently more rapid. At pressures of about 1 kbar these feldspars imply crystallization temperatures above at least 825 °C (Fuhrman and Lindsley, 1988).

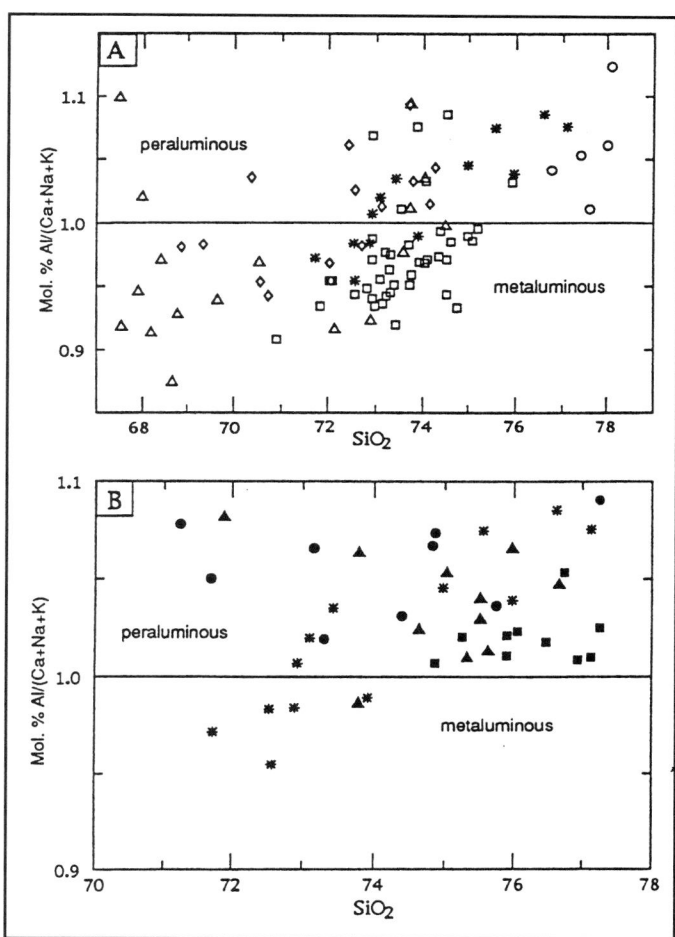

Figure 8. Mole percent $Al_2O_3/(CaO + Na_2O + K_2O)$ versus SiO_2. A: Cadillac Mountain and Southwest Harbor granites. B: Somesville, Pretty Marsh, and Southwest Harbor granites. Symbols as in Figure 5.

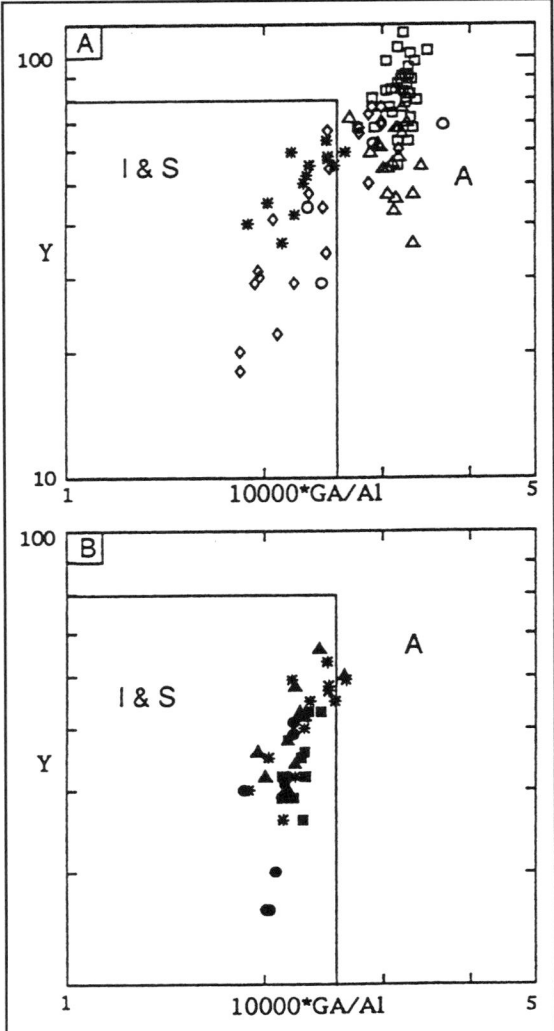

Figure 9. 10000 Ga/Al versus Y (in ppm). A: Cadillac Mountain and Southwest Harbor granites. B: Somesville, Pretty Marsh, and Southwest Harbor granites. Symbols as in Figure 5. Field boundaries after Whalen et al. (1987).

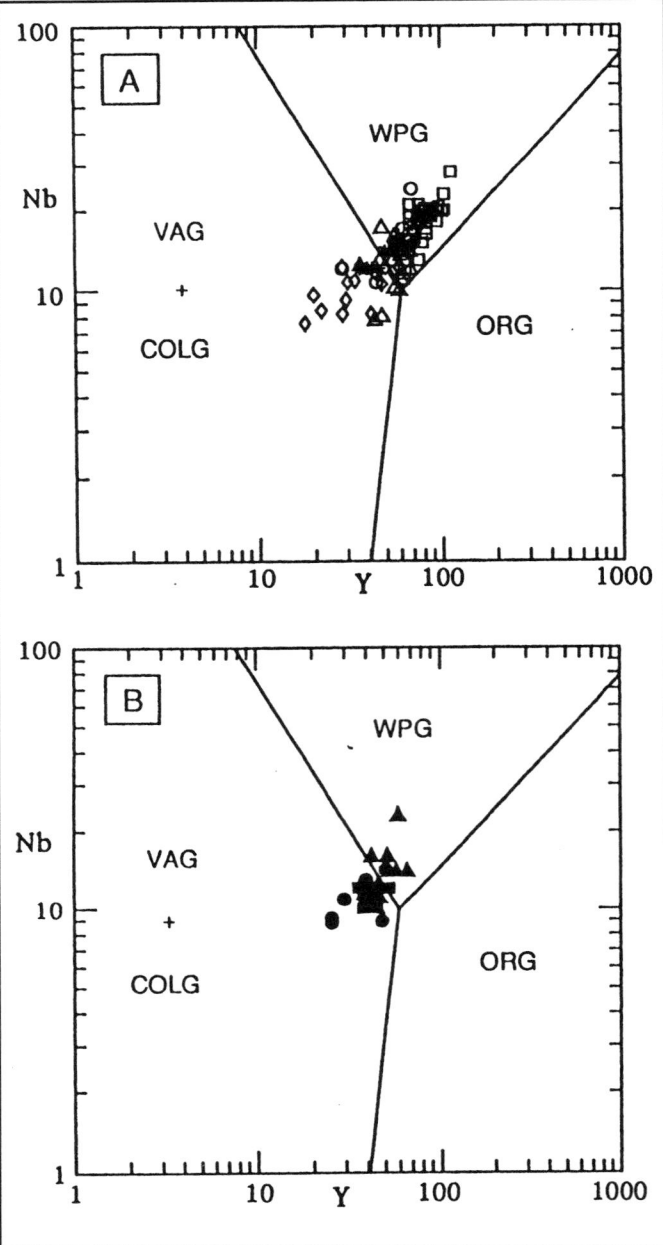

Figure 10. Distribution of Cadillac Mountain intrusive complex granites on the Nb-Y discrimination diagram of Pearce et al. (1984). A: Cadillac Mountain and Southwest Harbor granites. B: Somesville and Pretty Marsh granites. Symbols as in Figure 5. VAG is volcanic arc granites; COLG is collision granites; ORG is ocean ridge granites; WPG is within plate granites.

The mineralogy and textures also indicate low a_{H2O} (a = activity) during crystallization of the CMG. Cotectic crystallization of ternary feldpar and quartz at a pressure of about 1 kbar and temperatures above 825 °C clearly implies H_2O-undersaturated conditions (Tuttle and Bowen, 1958; Holtz et al., 1992). Widespread evidence for quartz resorption can be explained by loss of pressure in an H_2O-undersaturated magma (Whitney, 1988). Low H_2O content of the granitic magma is also supported by the absence of early crystallizing hydrous minerals within the upper CMG (Naney, 1983).

Mineralogical variation inward from the intrusive breccia suggests major and rapid changes in the conditions of crystallization. Many granitic rocks from within the shatter zone and along chilled

contacts against country rock blocks are two-feldspar granites with early biotite, and, less commonly, hornblende. These rocks appear to have crystallized at relatively low temperatures and higher a_{H2O}. This hydrous mineralogy grades rapidly inward to rocks with cumulus ternary-feldspar, ferrohedenbergite, fayalite, zircon, and

**TABLE 4. REPRESENTATIVE CHEMICAL ANALYSES OF WHOLE-ROCK SAMPLES
FROM THE CADILLAC MOUNTAIN INTRUSIVE COMPLEX**

Unit	Southwest Harbor Granite				Somesville Granite				Pretty Marsh Granite			
	Low SiO$_2$		Evolved		Coarse-grained		Fine-grained					
	30	34	17A	38B	152	KS7	151	150	116A	177	179	180
(wt. %)												
SiO$_2$	72.60	73.92	74.22	76.98	76.24	77.37	76.56	74.04	73.08	73.02	71.54	75.70
TiO$_2$	0.29	0.26	0.18	0.19	0.15	0.12	0.17	0.26	0.31	0.29	0.34	0.17
Al$_2$O$_3$	13.60	13.30	12.70	13.19	12.76	12.39	12.83	13.40	14.20	13.81	14.63	13.11
Fe$_2$O$_3$$^{(t)}$	3.59	2.99	2.24	1.85	1.27	2.18	1.30	1.62	2.54	2.38	2.71	1.47
MnO	0.06	0.11	0.03	0.03	0.03	0.03	0.03	0.04	0.06	0.03	0.06	0.04
MgO	0.35	0.27	0.26	0.26	0.07	0.10	0.14	0.33	0.60	0.58	0.66	0.26
CaO	1.20	1.12	0.34	1.15	0.75	0.67	0.93	1.35	1.98	1.71	1.53	1.00
Na$_2$O	5.54	4.96	4.11	4.17	3.42	3.64	3.38	3.45	3.59	3.72	4.03	3.60
K$_2$O	2.74	3.01	4.11	3.45	4.75	4.52	4.63	4.24	3.72	3.99	4.19	4.55
P$_2$O$_5$	0.06	0.05	0.03	0.04	0.00	0.02	0.00	0.03	0.07	0.08	0.08	0.04
LOI	0.52	0.65	0.63	0.54	0.21	0.45	0.37	0.53	1.22	0.56	0.84	0.54
Total	100.55	100.64	98.85	101.85	99.65	101.49	100.34	99.29	101.27	100.17	100.61	100.48
(ppm)												
Rb	64	80	102	96	221	238	229	190	141	137	165	196
Sr	84	78	44	92	36	22	46	86	130	115	106	58
Ba	530	474	778	532	284	138	324	444	514	502	456	414
Y	63	55	40	45	45	53	44	40	41	39	51	39
Zr	360	320	194	186	129	118	146	195	239	223	257	146
V	14	10	9	11	5	6	9	15	28	21	29	11
Ni	4	4	2	3	1	2	1	1	5	4	5	1
Be	2	2	1.9	1.9	3.1	3.1	2.9	2.9	2.5	2.5	3.1	2.5
Sc	10	8	6	6	3	4	4	5	6	5	6	4
Ce	80	68	45	63	62	62	66	83	93	72	90	52
Yb	7	6	4	5	5	6	7	5	4	5	6	4
Nb	14	14	12	12	11	12	12	12	12	12	14	10
Ga	18	18	13	14	16	16	15	16	16	16	17	15
Cu	5	5	5	3	9	2	1	7	2	5	5	1
Zn	43	51	23	34	18	17	18	23	34	29	38	23
U	3	3	2	4	4	9	6	4	3	3	5	3
Th	11	13	14	14	20	31	20	21	18	14	32	12

magnetite, a mineral assemblage that implies high T and low a_{H_2O} conditions similar to those of granites within the interior of the upper CMG. The relative lack of exsolution and preservation of delicate oscillatory zoning in low-Ca ternary feldspars implies rapid cooling and low H$_2$O content. Mineral assemblages and textures in granophyric bodies indicate that they crystallized at lower temperatures and higher a_{H_2O} than the main CMG. Even in these rocks, quartz phenocrysts exhibit resorption channels, indicating H$_2$O-undersaturated conditions (Whitney, 1988).

The lower CMG differs mineralogically from the upper CMG in several ways. In the most silicic rocks with insignificant contamination by mafic material, two feldspars, plagioclase (An$_{30-15}$) and Or-rich perthitic alkali-feldspar, are generally present. Early biotite is the dominant mafic mineral, and early subhedral hornblende is common in many rocks. These differences in mineralogy and sequence of crystallization imply that the early magma that produced the lower CMG was more hydrous and cooler than the later magma that produced the upper CMG.

Crystallization of the Southwest Harbor, Somesville, and Pretty Marsh granites

The SHG is a two-feldspar granite with early crystallizing biotite. Evolved SHG samples approach the minimum melt composition for pressures between 0.5 and 1 kbar (Fig. 12). Partial resorption of equant quartz and crystallization of biotite before hornblende in the less-evolved portions of the SHG suggest that it was undersaturated in H$_2$O. In the Ab-Or-SiO$_2$ system, the SHG trend is parallel to that of the upper CMG but shifted slightly toward the Ab-SiO$_2$ join (Fig. 12). This shift may reflect relatively higher a_{H_2O} in the SHG (Holtz et al., 1992). An/(An + Ab) ratios are slightly higher in the SHG (0.10) than in the CMG (0.08), indicating that their Ab-Or-SiO$_2$ relations are independent of An differences (Anderson and Cullers, 1978).

The Somesville and Pretty Marsh granites are two-feldspar granites with early crystallizing biotite and subordinate hornblende. In the system Ab-Or-SiO$_2$, these granites plot close to the 1 kbar minimum and most are shifted, relative to the CMG,

**TABLE 5. REPRESENTATIVE ANALYSES OF REES
IN THE SOUTHWEST HARBOR AND SOMESVILLE GRANITES**

| | Southwest Harbor Granite | | | | Somesville Granite | | | |
| | Low SiO$_2$ | | Evolved | | Coarse-Grained | | Fine-Grained | |
Sample	30	34	17A	38B	KS-7	KS-9A	KS-8A	KS-13
La	48.8	39.8	23.1	35.3	29.6	28.9	31.0	38.8
Ce	95	78	47	69	64	61	64	82
Nd	44	38	16	28	29	25	28	35
Sm	9.2	8.1	4.3	5.9	6.4	5.3	5.7	7.9
Eu	1.6	1.8	0.8	0.9	0.7	0.8	0.6	0.4
Tb	1.2	1.2	0.7	0.8	1.0	0.8	0.8	1.7
Yb	5.9	5.4	4.4	4.5	5.4	4.2	5.0	5.4
Lu	0.92	0.83	0.73	0.71	0.90	0.70	0.85	0.80

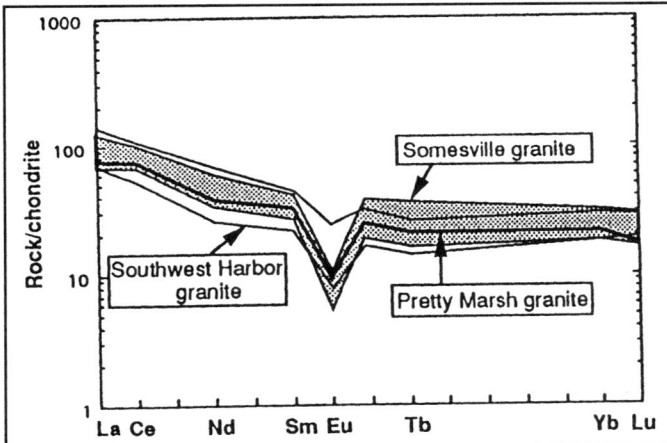

Figure 11. Ranges of chondrite-normalized rare earth elements in the Somesville and Southwest Harbor granites. Also included is a single analysis of the Pretty Marsh granite.

toward the join Or-SiO$_2$ (Fig. 12), consistent with their slightly higher An/(An + Ab). These rocks presumably crystallized at lower temperatures and higher a_{H2O} than the CMG.

ORIGIN OF COMPOSITIONAL VARIATION IN THE CMIC

Field relations and petrography provide an important framework for considering the origin of compositional variation within the CMIC. On the basis of precise zircon ages (Seaman et al., 1995) for two of the granitic units and for the Cranberry Island volcanic rocks, it is likely that all of these igneous rocks were emplaced and crystallized within a period of 1 to 2 m.y. This small range in ages is strongly supported by gradational contacts between some units and by evidence for commingling and hybridization between others. On the basis of field relations, the granitic rocks can be placed into three age groups that also have distinctive geochemical characteristics: (1) the earliest Southwest Harbor granite, (2) the Cadillac Mountain granite, and (3) the

younger Somesville and Pretty Marsh granites. There is significant compositional variation in all of these units that needs to be understood before it is possible to develop a model that explains relations between them.

Southwest Harbor granite

There is no evidence for sharp boundaries between the high- and low-SiO$_2$ varieties discussed above. Both compositional types occur apparently randomly throughout the pluton. The variability of textures and general abundance of granophyric textures suggests that the SHG was built up of many small, compositionally similar pulses of silicic magma that cooled rapidly. Most compositional differences between these two groups (Fig. 5) can be explained by fractional crystallization of early-forming sodic plagioclase and minor hornblende and biotite. The decreases in Zr and Y at higher SiO$_2$ may reflect early crystallization of zircon, hornblende, apatite, and allanite. The tight compositional group of samples between 72% and 74% SiO$_2$ may approximate the composition of the injected magma. The high-SiO$_2$ group probably represents liquid that evolved within the chamber. Because the compositions of the high-SiO$_2$ group closely resemble the compositions of aphyric felsites and lapilli from tuffs in the Cranberry Island volcanic rocks (Seaman et al., 1995), these rocks probably represent liquid compositions. The low-SiO$_2$ group plots near the 5 kbar quartz-feldspar cotectic in the system Ab-Or-SiO$_2$ (Fig. 12). This pressure may approximate the depth of magma generation or the highest crustal level of cotectic crystallization.

Cadillac Mountain granite

Although compositions of rocks from the lower and upper CMG overlap, rocks from the lower CMG are much more scattered and trend to lower SiO$_2$ with increasing CaO, MgO (Fig. 5), Al$_2$O$_3$, TiO$_2$, Sr, and V (not shown). This variation may be attributed to a combination of crystal accumulation (plagioclase, hornblende or pyroxene, and Fe-Ti oxides) and contamination by mafic material. There is abundant petrographic evidence for both of these processes in rocks with lower abun-

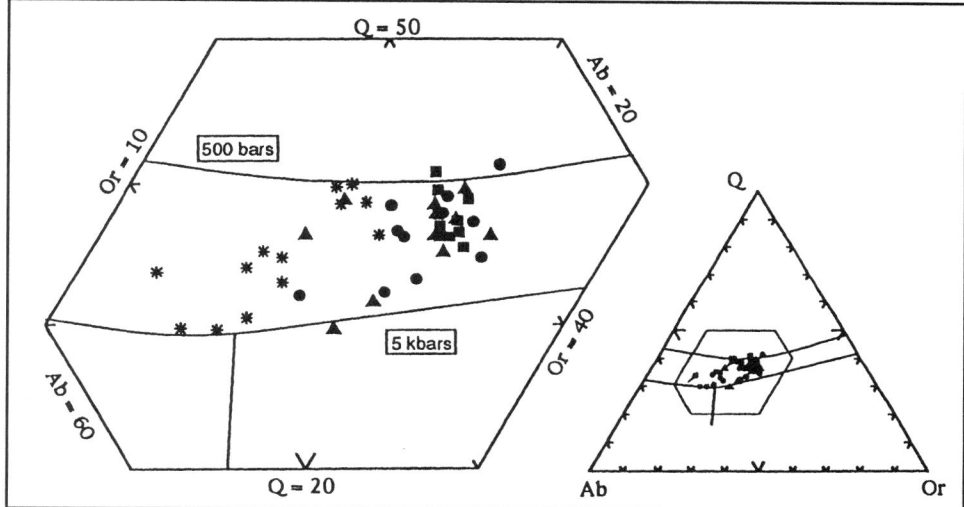

Figure 12. Weight normative (CIPW) compositions of the Somesville, Pretty Marsh, and Southwest Harbor granites in terms of quartz, albite, and orthoclase. The 500 bar boundary is after Tuttle and Bowen (1958). The 5 kbar boundaries (H_2O saturated) are after Holtz et al. (1992). Symbols as in Figure 5.

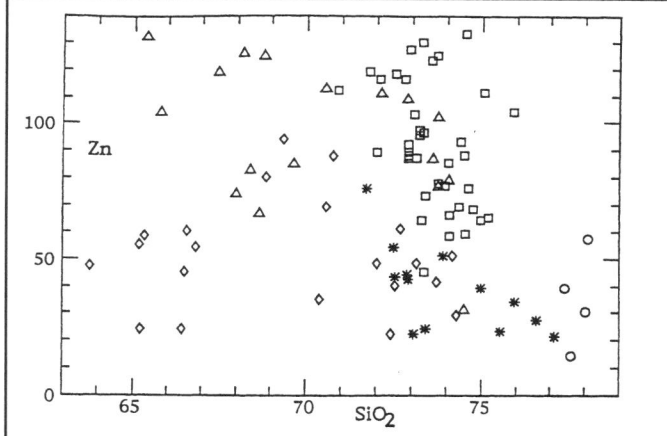

Figure 13. SiO_2 versus Zn for the Cadillac Mountain and Southwest Harbor granites. Symbols as in Figure 5.

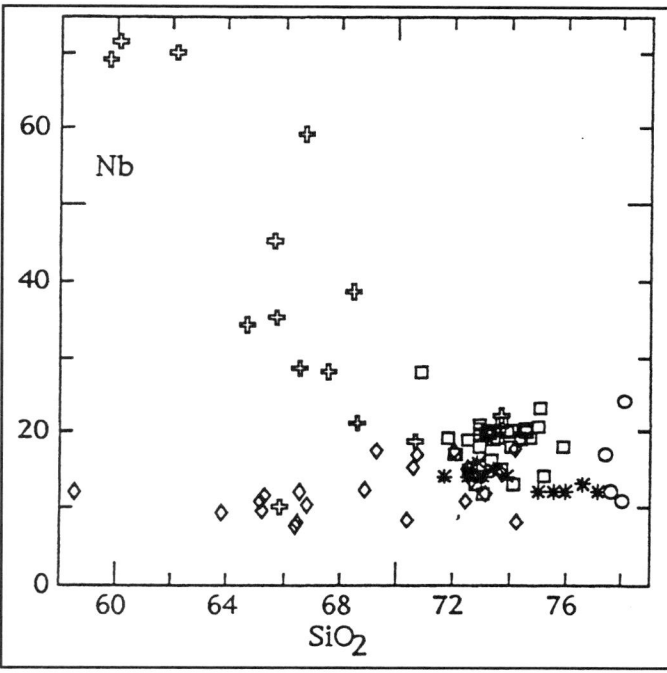

Figure 14. SiO_2 versus Nb for the Cadillac Mountain (CMG) and Southwest Harbor granites (symbols as in Fig. 5) and mafic enclaves within the CMG (open crosses)

dances of SiO_2. At constant SiO_2 content, the lower CMG tends to have lower Ga, Zr, and Y (Fig. 5) as well as Zn (Fig. 13) and Nb (Fig. 14). Because SiO_2 content is identical, it is not likely that these chemical differences were brought about by fractional crystallization or simple mixing with mafic material. Instead it is most likely that the magma that produced the lower CMG was less enriched in these trace elements than later CMG magma.

Granitic rocks that occur along the margin of the shatter zone overlap with the upper CMG and define compositional trends at lower SiO_2 that are consistent with fractional crystallization. With decreasing SiO_2, these rocks trend to higher Ga, Zr, Ba, CaO, Na_2O, MnO (Fig. 5), FeO_T, Al_2O_3, and Sr (not shown). As SiO_2 decreases they also trend to lower K_2O, Rb, and Y (Fig. 5) and have lower REE concentrations with positive Eu

anomalies (Fig. 7). These chemical characteristics strongly support petrographic evidence that these marginal rocks contain cumulus feldspar, ferrohedenbergite, fayalite, and zircon. The extremely low concentrations of MgO (Fig. 5) in these marginal rocks compared with the upper CMG suggest that the magma at the margins was distinct from that which produced CMG inward from the chamber walls.

Although both the lower and marginal CMG appear to have been influenced by crystal accumulation, at similar SiO$_2$ contents the marginal CMG has substantially higher abundances of Na$_2$O, MnO, Ga, Zr, Y, Ba (Fig. 5), Zn (Fig. 13), Yb, and Nb. Magma that produced cumulates along the higher level margin of the CMG chamber must have been more depleted in MgO and enriched in these incompatible elements, probably due to extensive fractional crystallization at depth within the chamber. These compositional differences, therefore, probably reflect compositional variation at different levels of the magma chamber. That CMG inward from the shatter zone has substantially higher Mg/(Mg + Fe$_T$) than cumulates at the margin suggests either that less-evolved silicic magma at depth continued to move upward after the formation of the shatter zone or that the magma in the interior was affected by mixing with and/or contamination by less-evolved, perhaps mafic magma. Both upward movement and contamination could have been caused by the multiple infusions of basaltic magma recorded in the gabbro-diorite unit.

Relative to the upper CMG, the granophyres are enriched only in SiO$_2$, K$_2$O, and Rb (Fig. 5). On the basis of compositional trends and locally gradational contacts between granophyre and the upper CMG, it is likely that these granophyric bodies represent interstitial liquid that collected in fractures which formed at a late stage in the crystallization of the CMG—after the beginning of crystallization of accessory phases including zircon and allanite.

Somesville and Pretty Marsh granites

On plots of most elements against SiO$_2$ these granites define a single trend from about 65% to 77% SiO$_2$ (Fig. 5) The coarse-grained SG is restricted to the SiO$_2$-rich end of this trend and both the PMG and the fine-grained SG span the entire range. The compositional trends to low SiO$_2$ (Fig. 5) are consistent with petrographic evidence for minor contamination with basaltic material. This can be seen particularly in the steeper trends of CaO and MgO with decreasing SiO$_2$ (Fig. 5).

The coarse-grained Somesville granites are compositionally similar to the CMG granophyres (Fig. 5). These similarities, in conjunction with their comparable structural setting and age, make it likely that the granophyres and the coarse-grained SG represent late residual liquids in the CMG magma chamber. This is supported by the occurrence of some hypersolvus alkali-feldspar in the coarse-grained SG (Fig. 3). Fractional crystallization of feldspar, hornblende, zircon, and allanite from a CMG magma could produce magma comparable to the coarse-grained SG.

The occurrence of two different types of plagioclase in the fine-grained SG (see above) argues for generating this unit by mixing of PMG with coarse-grained SG. Both the field relations and the compositional trends seen in Figure 5 strongly support this interpretation.

PARENTAL MAGMA OF THE CMIC

Most rocks in the CMIC that plot far from the 500 bar minimum in the system Ab-Or-SiO$_2$ (Figs. 6 and 12) display petrographic evidence for either crystal accumulation or contamination by mafic material. Most of the SG and PMG samples plot between the 500 bar and 2 kbar minima, and those that plot farther into the feldspar field typically show petrographic evidence for contamination by basaltic material. All of the fine-grained or chilled rocks within the shatter zone are highly evolved and relatively hydrous with early biotite. No samples with the petrographic or chemical characteristics of the upper CMG have been identified that could be interpreted as liquids (e.g., chilled margins, dikes).

The granitic unit that most likely approaches the composition of a parental liquid is the Southwest Harbor granite. The SHG also matches closely the range of compositions of aphyric material in the lower units of the Cranberry Island volcanics (Seaman et al., 1995). Petrographic evidence in the SHG for rapid cooling and a lack of crystal accumulation provides further support. In the system Ab-Or-SiO$_2$, a group of fine-grained, aphyric samples from the SHG with 72% to 74% SiO$_2$ plot close to the 5 kbar cotectic between quartz and feldspar. These SHG samples may have compositions equivalent to magma that equilibrated at that depth. Samples from this group of SHG plot consistently close in composition to the lower CMG (Fig. 5). The main difference is in the alkalies where, at comparable SiO$_2$, the SHG has slightly higher abundances of Na$_2$O and lower abundances of K$_2$O and Rb (Fig. 5). These differences in alkalies may reflect the higher a_{H_2O} in the SHG magma.

ORIGIN OF THE UPPER CADILLAC MOUNTAIN GRANITE

Although the most likely parental magma for the CMIC has the composition of the Southwest Harbor granite with 72% to 74% SiO$_2$, the SHG is relatively hydrous with early biotite and hornblende and two feldspars, in contrast to the upper CMG, which is hypersolvus with late-crystallizing hornblende. The SHG also lacks the chemical characteristics of A-type granites shown by the upper CMG. Although fractional crystallization of feldspar and quartz from a SHG liquid might explain the increased concentrations of many incompatible elements in the CMG (Fig. 5), it cannot explain the relatively anhydrous character and higher crystallization temperature of the CMG. Furthermore, if fractional crystallization were important, then a great deal of cumulate granite (cumulus quartz plus feldspar) would have been produced to cause the enrichment of incompatible trace elements (two to four times that of the original SHG magma). Such efficient fractional crystallization of granitic magma is highly unlikely. In any event, rocks of the lower CMG have concentrations of incompatible trace elements similar to those of the SHG (e.g., Fig. 13). The marginal CMG (with cumulus feldspar and clinopyroxene) cannot have been produced by either the SHG magma or any magma that crystallized the lower CMG because, among many other petrographic and chemical characteristics, it is much too low in MgO and normative An.

The compositional range of the lower CMG provides strong evidence for the link between the SHG and the upper CMG. In Figures 5 and 13, it is apparent that many samples from the lower CMG and the SHG have nearly identical compositions and that there is a compositional continuum between the lower and upper CMG. If fractional crystallization cannot explain this continuum, then it is worth considering how the intervening gabbro-diorite unit might have affected the evolution from lower to upper CMG.

The gabbro-diorite unit is a typical mafic-silicic layered intrusion and is comparable to the nearby Pleasant Bay layered gabbro-diorite (Wiebe, 1993). The intermediate to silicic tops of many macrorhythmic units in both of these intrusions commonly show rapid increases in some incompatible elements. For example, in the G-D unit of the CMIC, Ba rises from about 150 ppm to over 5000 ppm in the upper portions of some macrorhythmic units. Very high Ba concentrations occur even if sodic plagioclase remains the only feldspar. The incompatible element increases are gradational, rather than abrupt, and there is no petrographic evidence for the incoming of a new "cumulus" phase. These rapid increases in incompatible elements probably reflect strong concentration gradients within the liquids that produced the macrorhythmic layers, rather than simple accumulation of crystals.

Multiple basaltic infusions, mixing and fractional crystallization make mafic-silicic layered intrusions ideal settings in which to generate extremely high concentrations of incompatible elements and establish strong vertical compositional gradients in a magma chamber. The macrorhythmic layers indicate that mafic magma emplaced into a silicic magma chamber is trapped at the base of the chamber and undergoes fractional crystallization. After Fe-Ti oxides begin to crystallize, residual liquid tends to collect upward (Sparks and Huppert, 1984) and remain trapped beneath much lighter, overlying silicic melt. The stratigraphy of the gabbro-diorite unit records hundreds of mafic replenishments that occurred at varying stages of fractionation of the preceeding mafic infusion. Multiple replenishments, mixing, and fractional crystallization (RFC) should lead to a decoupling of major and incompatible trace elements—in a manner similar to that proposed by O'Hara and Mathews (1981) for mid-ocean ridge magma chambers. The process of decoupling here can lead to extreme enrichments of incompatible trace elements in the mafic-silicic layered intrusions because the evolving mafic and intermediate magmas are trapped beneath the overlying silicic magma (i.e., there are many replenishments and little or no tapping of the evolving mafic to intermediate magma).

Many studies of silicic volcanic rocks have proposed that multiple infusions of mafic magma were emplaced into silicic magma chambers, and that mixing and fractional crystallization of these underlying mafic magmas played a major role in establishing strong compositional zonation of the source magma chambers (e.g., Ferriz and Mahood, 1987; Druitt and Bacon,

1988). Grunder (1994) suggested that this RFC process was responsible for generating intermediate liquids (basaltic andesite) with extreme enrichments of incompatible trace elements within otherwise bimodal magmatic systems.

Mafic enclaves in the upper CMG provide direct evidence for the existence of these enriched intermediate liquids. Concentrations of many incompatible trace elements in these enclaves far exceed concentrations in either the basaltic infusions or any granitic rock, and increase with decreasing SiO_2 (Fig. 14). Their compositions are analogous to the highly-enriched enclaves described by Grunder (1994), and provide strong support for the RFC process in the trapped mafic magmas (Wiebe et al., 1997). The vast majority of these enclaves are texturally and chemically homogeneous and lack chilled margins. If, as seems likely, they represent variably contaminated, quenched magma from the boundary layer, the original chilled margins must have been eroded during convection and contaminated the granite at the microscopic scale. Enclave material may have been introduced into the upper CMG by several convective mechanisms, including disruption of the intermediate layer by diapiric upwelling of silicic cumulate mush trapped beneath the ponded, crystallizing, basaltic infusions (Wiebe et al., 1997).

The multiple infusions of basaltic magma also provide the means to convert a hydrous subsolvus granitic magma like the SHG into a higher temperature and drier hypersolvus magma capable of producing the upper CMG. Heat from these ponded and crystallizing basaltic magmas is readily transferred upward by double-diffusive convection across a boundary layer into the overlying silicic magma (Wiebe, 1993). Interaction between repeated infusions of basaltic magma and resident silicic magma can also affect the activity of H_2O in the overlying silicic magma because hornblende and biotite commonly nucleate and grow within mafic magma in the boundary layer, and this hydrous crystalline mush is convected downward to form hydrous mafic cumulates at the floor of the chamber. Evidence for this process is shown by macrorhythmic layers in the Pleasant Bay intrusion that commonly grade upward from hornblende-rich gabbro to nearly anhydrous silicic cumulates (Wiebe, 1993). Basaltic infusions will therefore tend to dehydrate the overlying silicic magma.

Other processes operating at the boundary between mafic and silicic magmas may also have been important. For example, selective exchange of isotopes (Lesher, 1990) and alkalies (Watson and Jurewicz, 1984) probably occurred across this double-diffusive boundary. Growth of biotite in the boundary layer (Johnston and Wyllie, 1988) probably also promoted exchange of alkalies between the basaltic and granitic magmas. As a result, neither the alkali ratios nor the isotopic compositions of mafic rocks in the gabbro-diorite unit and the overlying granitic rocks can be assumed to represent compositions of parental magmas.

EVOLUTION OF THE CADILLAC MOUNTAIN INTRUSIVE COMPLEX

The Cadillac Mountain intrusive complex (CMIC) provides a record of the beginning, development, and solidification of a shallow-level silicic magma chamber that existed in a bimodal extensional terrane during more or less continuous basaltic magmatism. Available radiometric ages suggest that the active life of the system was at most a few million years and possibly less than one million years. Initial silicic magmatism is represented by the hypabyssal Southwest Harbor granite (SHG), which was emplaced as sheet-like masses at and above the unconformity between the Ellsworth schist and the Bar Harbor Formation. Next, the base of the CMG magma chamber was established immediately to the north of the SHG at the same unconformity. Before more than a few hundred meters of granitic material had accumulated on the floor, injections of basaltic magma began to enter and pond on the base of the chamber, forming isolated sheets of basally chilled gabbroic material that graded upward into hybrids with CMG silicic magma. The early granitic rocks that formed in the SHG and the lower CMG closely resemble the lower, silicic portions of the Cranberry Island series (Seaman et al., 1995), and are interpreted to represent the subvolcanic magma chambers that produced these silicic volcanic rocks.

An extended episode of more intense basaltic magmatism was responsible for the voluminous ponding of basaltic magma within the CMG chamber and produced the 1–2 km-thick gabbro-diorite unit that separates the lower from the upper CMG. This episode of magmatism may be equivalent to that recorded in the upper Cranberry Island series, which is dominated by basaltic volcanic rocks with compositions that closely resemble those of chilled layers in the gabbro-diorite unit.

During the development of the gabbro-diorite unit, hundreds of basaltic infusions ponded on the chamber floor. A variety of processes operating during these infusions (see above) converted the hydrous lower CMG magma into the relatively anhydrous, hypersolvus magma that produced the upper CMG. Compositional stratification probably developed in the overlying silicic magma with hotter and drier silicic magma beneath cooler, more hydrous, and more evolved silicic magma. During the development of the gabbro-diorite unit it is likely that substantial volumes of cooler and more hydrous silicic magma erupted from the top of the CMG chamber. The character of granitic dikes and chilled margins within the shatter zone suggests that one or more of these eruptions may have been responsible for establishing the shatter zone.

While basaltic magma continued to enter the chamber, little or no silicic magma could solidify on the floor. Instead, solidification proceeded mainly inward from the roof and walls. As basaltic magmatism waned, the volume of the remaining magma was greatly reduced and located immediately above the central area of the gabbro-diorite unit beneath a roof of upper CMG. The decrease in basaltic infusions permitted cooling of the magma, and crystallization increased a_{H2O} so that the remaining magma approached the composition of the cooler, more hydrous, coarse-grained Somesville granite. The waning silicic chamber was disrupted by new injections of the Pretty Marsh granite which mixed with the resident Somesville magma. The emplacement of new granitic magma appears to be responsible for inflating the chamber and displacing upward a central block of the CMG roof. This event may correspond to late resurgent doming, which commonly occurs in silicic systems with a central caldera. There is, however, no evidence that a caldera had been established at higher levels in the CMG. Small amounts of basaltic magma continued to enter the magma chamber after the mixing between the Somesville and Pretty Marsh magmas, and basaltic dikes of similar composition cut through these bodies after they were solidified.

A NEW MODEL FOR THE ORIGIN OF A-TYPE GRANITES

The evolution of the CMIC and the occurrence of the A-type upper CMG within this complex suggest that many of the geochemical and thermal characteristics of A-type granites may relate not to source, but rather to processes that operate within high-level magma chambers. Many of the geochemical characteristics of A-type granites (e.g., high Fe/Mg and Ga/Al, and relatively high abundances of Zn, Zr, Nb, Ga, Y, and REEs) are difficult to explain solely on the basis of second melts (Creaser et al., 1991), and the occurrence of these characteristics in granites that range from peralkaline to peraluminous is particularly difficult to reconcile with the concept of any single source for all A-type granites (Whalen et al., 1987).

The great enrichment of many incompatible trace elements in the upper CMG appears to have originated through gradual contamination of silicic magma by ponded basaltic magmas that have undergone replenishment, mixing, and fractional crystallization (RFC). Multiple infusions of basaltic magmas also led to heating and dehydration of the silicic magma. Replenishment, mixing, and fractional crystallization of basaltic magma can lead to extreme enrichments in incompatible trace elements if that "processed" magma cannot erupt out of the chamber (O'Hara and Mathews, 1981). The main cumulus phases within the gabbro-diorite unit are olivine, calcic plagioclase, and augite. Fractionation of these phases should lead to great enrichments in Nb, Zn, Zr, Y, REEs, Be, and Ba—all elements that are typically enriched in A-type granites and in the upper CMG.

Recharge and fractional crystallization should also lead to enrichment in Ga and increased Ga/Al in the evolving mafic liquids (Goodman, 1972). The partition coefficient of Ga in plagioclase relative to basaltic magma is close to one, while that for Al is close to two. Because these elements mainly go into plagioclase rather than cocrystallizing mafic phases, the Ga concentration and the Ga/Al should increase in the evolving liquid. Mafic enclaves in the upper CMG, which appear to have originated from such "processed" mafic magma, are even more greatly enriched in Ga and in Ga/Al than the CMG (Wiebe et al., 1997). The enclaves are probably representative of material that contaminated the original lower CMG magma and converted it into the high-temperature, anhydrous A-type upper CMG.

In this setting, interactions between mafic and silicic magmas may also result in selective diffusion of alkalies (Watson and Jurewicz, 1984) and isotopes (Lesher, 1990), so that neither the alkali ratios nor isotopic compositions of A-type granites need closely reflect their sources. As a result mantle-type isotopic signatures in A-type granites may not reliably demonstrate a mantle source or fractional crystallization from basalt, as Turner et al. (1992) suggested.

Ponding of basaltic magmas could, presumably, occur within any silicic magma chamber, regardless of the source of the silicic magma. In different areas, different crustal sources for the original granitic magmas may help explain the wide compositional range (e.g., peralkaline to peraluminous) shown by A-type granites. In evaluating the chemical character of an A-type granite, it should also be important to take into account the chemical character (e.g., tholeiitic versus alkaline) of the basaltic infusions.

CONCLUSIONS

The CMIC provides a record of the magmatic evolution of a high-level, subvolcanic magma chamber. It documents the influence of basaltic infusions on the evolution of a silicic magma and demonstrates that the chemical and mineralogical characteristics of an A-type granite can be produced within a high-level magma chamber. The geochemical and thermal characteristics of A-type granites need not be fundamentally related to the source rock from which they melted, but may rather be related to the subsequent history of the silicic magma within a chamber invaded by contemporaneous basaltic magma. If magma chamber processes are fundamentally responsible for the generation of A-type granites, it becomes clear why they commonly appear to grade to the I- and S-types (Whalen et al., 1987), and why they range in composition from peralkaline to peraluminous. This model for the generation of A-type granites is consistent with their occurrence in anorogenic or extensional terranes with bimodal magmatism.

ACKNOWLEDGMENTS

This research was supported by National Science Foundation grants EAR-9003712 and 9204475 to Wiebe. In addition, during the summer of 1993, funds from The Keck Foundation, through the Keck Twelve-College Geology Consortium, provided additional support for several undergraduates and faculty from a total of seven different colleges. We profited greatly from interactions in the field with the other Keck participants (Sam Kozak, Naomi Lubick, Mike Seckler, Marnie Sturm, Elizabeth Symchych, and Fred vanden Bergh), as well as visitors to our project (Marshall Chapman, Dan Lux, Sheila Seaman, Diane Smith, and Dave West). We are grateful to Steve Sylvester for much assistance with analytical work at Franklin and Marshall College, to Ed Vicenci for help with microprobe analysis at Princeton, and to Robert Ayuso (U.S. Geological Survey) for analyses of several samples. The staff at Acadia National Park were helpful in many ways, and we are grateful to innumerable landowners who allowed us to tromp over their land. Helpful reviews were provided by M. S. Drummond, G. N. Eby, S. J. Seaman, and J. B. Whalen.

REFERENCES CITED

Anderson, J. L., 1983, Proterozoic anorogenic granite plutonism of North America, *in* Medaris, L. G., Jr., Byers, C. W., Mickelson, D. M., and Shanks, W. C., eds., Proterozoic geology: Selected papers from an international Proterozoic symposium: Geological Society of America Memoir 161, p. 133–154.

Anderson, J. L., and Cullers, R. L., 1978, Geochemistry and evolution of the Wolf River Batholith, a Late Precambrian rapakivi massif in north Wisconsin, U.S.A.: Precambrian Research, v. 7, p. 287–324.

Bedard, J., 1990, Enclaves from the A-type granite of the Megantic complex, White Mountain Magma Series: Clues to granite magmagenesis: Journal of Geophysical Research, v. 95, p. 17797–17819.

Chapman, C. A., 1962, Diabase-granite composite dikes, with pillow-like structure, Mount Desert Island, Maine: Journal of Geology, v. 70, p. 539–564.

Chapman, C. A., 1969, Oriented inclusions in granite—Further evidence for floored magma chambers: American Journal of Science, v. 267, p. 988–998.

Chapman, C. A., 1970, The geology of Acadia National Park: Old Greenwich, Connecticut, The Chatham Press, 127 p.

Chapman, M., and Rhodes, J. M., 1992, Composite layering in the Isle au Haut Igneous Complex, Maine: Evidence for periodic invasion of a mafic magma into an evolving magma reservoir: Journal of Volcanology and Geothermal Research, v. 51, p. 41–60.

Collins, W. J., Beams, S. D., White, A. J. R., and Chappell, B. W., 1982, Nature and origin of A-type granites with particular reference to southeastern Australia: Contributions to Mineralogy and Petrology, v. 80, p. 189–200.

Creaser, R. A., Price, R. C., and Wormald, R. J., 1991, A-type granites revisited: Assessment of a residual-source model: Geology, v. 19, p. 163–166.

Druitt, T. H., and Bacon, C. R., 1988, Compositional zonation and cumulus processes in the Mount Mazama magma chamber, Crater Lake, Oregon: Royal Society of Edinburgh Transactions, Earth Sciences, v. 79, p. 289–297.

Eby, G. N., 1990, The A-type granitoids: A review of their occurrence and chemical characteristics and speculations on their petrogenesis: Lithos, v. 26, p. 115–134.

Eby, G. N., 1992, Chemical subdivision of the A-type granitoids: Petrogenetic and tectonic implications: Geology, v. 20, p. 641–644.

Ferriz, H., and Mahood, G. A., 1987, Strong compositional zonation in a silicic magmatic system: Los Humeros, Mexican Neovolcanic Belt: Journal of Petrology, v. 28, p. 171–209.

Fuhrman, M. L., and Lindsley, D. H, 1988, Ternary-feldspar modeling and thermometry: American Mineralogist, v. 73, p. 201–215.

Gilman, R. A., Chapman, C. A., Lowell, T. V., and Borns, H. W., Jr., 1988, The geology of Mount Desert Island: Maine Geological Survey Bulletin 38, 50 p.

Goodman, R. J., 1972, The distribution of Ga and Rb in coexisting groundmass and phenocryst phases of some basic volcanic rocks: Geochimica et Cosmochimica Acta, v. 36, p. 303–317.

Govindaraju, K., 1989, 1989 compilation of working values and sample description for 272 geostandards: Geostandards Newsletter, v. 13, special issue, 113 p.

Grunder, A. L., 1994, Interaction of basalt and rhyolite in a bimodal suite: Geological Society of America Abstracts with Programs, v. 26, no. 7, p. A476–A477.

Hammarstrom, J. M., and Zen, E-an, 1986, Aluminum in hornblende: An empirical igneous geobarometer: American Mineralogist, v. 71, p. 1297–1313.

Haslkin, L. A., Haskin, M. A., Frey, F. A., and Wildeman, T. R., 1968, Relative and absolute terrestrial abundances of the rare earths, *in* Ahrens, L. H., ed., Origin and distribution of the elements, 1: Oxford, Pergamon, p. 889–911.

Hodge, D. S., Abbey, D. A., Harbin, M. A., Patterson, J. L., Ring, M. J., and Sweeney, J. F., 1982, Gravity studies of subsurface mass distributions of granitic rocks in Maine and New Hampshire: American Journal of Science, v. 282, p. 1289–1324.

Hogan, J. P., and Sinha, A. K., 1989, Compositional variation of plutonism in the coastal Maine magmatic province: Mode of origin and tectonic setting, *in* Tucker, R. D., and Marvinney, R. G., eds., Studies of Maine geology, Volume 4: Igneous and metamorphic geology. Maine Geological Survey, Department of Conservation, p. 1–33.

Holland, H. D., and Malinin, S. D., 1979, The solubility and occurrence of non-ore minerals, *in* Barnes, H. L., ed., Geochemistry of hydrothermal ore deposits (second edition): New York, Wiley and Sons, p. 461–508.

Holtz, F., Pichavant, M., Barbey, P., and Johannes, W., 1992, Effects of H_2O on liquidus phase relations in the haplogranite system at 2 and 5 kbar: American Mineralogist, v. 77, p. 1223–1241.

Irvine, T. N., 1982, Terminology for layered intrusions: Journal of Petrology, v. 23, p. 127–162.

Johnston, A. D., and Wyllie, P. J., 1988, Interaction of granitic and basic magmas: Experimental observations on contamination processes at 10 kbar with H_2O: Contributions to Mineralogy and Petrology, v. 98, p. 352–362.

Kennedy, G. C., 1950, A portion of the system silica-water: Economic Geology, v. 45, p. 629–653.

Lesher, C. E., 1990, Decoupling of chemical and isotopic exchange during magma mixing: Nature, v. 344, p. 235–237.

Loiselle, M. C., and Wones, D. R., 1979, Characteristics and origin of anorogenic granites: Geological Society of America Abstracts with Programs, v. 11, p. 468.

Ludman, A., 1986, Timing of terrane accretion in eastern and east-central Maine: Geology, v. 14, p. 411–414.

Naney, M. T., 1983, Phase equilibria of rock-forming ferromagnesian silicates in granitic systems: American Journal of Science, v. 283, p. 993–1033.

O'Hara, M. J., and Mathews, R. E., 1981, Geochemical evolution in an advancing, periodically replenished, periodically tapped, continuously fractionating magma chamber: Geological Society of London Journal, v. 138, p. 237–277.

Pearce, J. A., Harris, N. B. W., and Tindle, A. G., 1984, Trace element discrimination diagrams for the tectonic interpretation of granitic rocks: Journal of Petrology, v. 25, p. 956–983.

Seaman, S. J., and Ramsey, P. C., 1992, Effects of magma mingling in the granites of Mount Desert Island, Maine: Journal of Geology, v. 100, p. 395–409.

Seaman, S. J., Wobus, R. A., Wiebe, R. A., Lubick, N., and Bowring, S. A., 1995, Volcanic expression of bimodal magmatism: The Cranberry Island-Cadillac Mountain Complex, coastal Maine: Journal of Geology, v. 103, p. 301–311.

Sparks, R. S. J., and Huppert, H. E., 1984, Density changes during fractional crystallization of basaltic magmas: Fluid dynamic implications: Contributions to Mineralogy and Petrology, v. 85, p. 300–309.

Stewart, D. B., Arth, J. A., and Flohr, M. J. K., 1988, Petrogenesis of the South Penobscot Intrusive Suite, Maine: American Journal of Science, v. 288-A, p. 75–114.

Taylor, T. R., Vogel, T. A., and Wilband, J. T., 1980, The composite dikes of Mount Desert Island, Maine: An example of coexisting acidic and basic magmas: Journal of Geology, v. 88, p. 433–444.

Turner, S. P., Foden, J. D., and Morrison, R. S., 1992, Derivation of some A-type magmas by fractionation of basaltic magma: An example from the Padthaway Ridge, South Australia: Lithos, v. 28, p. 151–179.

Tuttle, O. F., and Bowen, N. L., 1958, Origin of granite in light of experimental studies in the system $NaAlSi_3O_8$-$KAlSi_3O_8$-SiO_2-H_2O: Geological Society of America Memoir 74, 153 p.

Watson, E. B., and Jurewicz, S. R., 1984, Behavior of alkalies during diffusive interaction of granitic xenoliths with basaltic magma: Journal of Geology, v. 92, p. 121–131.

West, D. P., Jr., Ludman, A., and Lux, D. R., 1992, Silurian age for the Pocomoonshine gabbro-diorite, southeastern Maine, and its regional tectonic implications: American Journal of Science, v. 292, p. 253–273.

Whalen, J. B., Currie, K. L., and Chappell, B. W., 1987, A-type granites: Geochemical characteristics, discrimination, and petrogenesis: Contributions to Mineralogy and Petrology, v. 95, p. 407–419.

Whitney, J. A., 1988, The origin of granite: The role and source of water in the evolution of granitic magmas: Geological Society of America Bulletin, v. 100, p. 1886–1897.

Wiebe, R. A., 1993, The Pleasant Bay layered gabbro-diorite, coastal Maine: Ponding and crystallization of basaltic injections into a silicic magma chamber: Journal of Petrology, v. 34, p. 461–489.

Wiebe, R. A., 1994, Silicic magma chambers as traps for basaltic magmas: the Cadillac Mountain intrusive complex, Mount Desert Island, Maine: Journal of Geology, v. 102, p. 423–437.

Wiebe, R. A., Smith, D., Sturm, M., King, E. M., and Seckler, M. S., 1997, Origin of magmatic enclaves in the Cadillac Mountain granite, coastal Maine: Journal of Petrology (in press).

Williams, H., and Hatcher, R. D., 1982, Suspect terranes and accretionary history of the Appalachian orogen: Geology, v. 10, p. 530–536.

MANUSCRIPT ACCEPTED BY THE SOCIETY JULY 2, 1996

Index

[Italic page numbers indicate major references]

Typeset in U.S.A. by Johnson Printing, Boulder, Colorado
Printed in U.S.A. by Malloy Lithographing, Inc., Ann Arbor, Michigan